America's
TEST KITCHEN

Also by the Editors of *Cook's Illustrated*

The Best Recipe Series:
The New Best Recipe
Cover & Bake
Steaks, Chops, Roasts, and Ribs
Baking Illustrated
Restaurant Favorites at Home
Perfect Vegetables
The Quick Recipe
Italian Classics
American Classics
Soups & Stews
Grilling & Barbecue

Inside America's Test Kitchen
Here in America's Test Kitchen
The America's Test Kitchen Cookbook

The Best Kitchen Quick Tips

The Complete Book of Pasta and Noodles
The Cook's Illustrated Complete Book of Poultry

How to Barbecue and Roast on the Grill
How to Cook Chicken Breasts
How to Cook Chinese Favorites
How to Cook Garden Vegetables
How to Cook Shrimp and Other Shellfish
How to Grill
How to Make an American Layer Cake
How to Make Cookie Jar Favorites
How to Make Ice Cream
How to Make Muffins, Biscuits, and Scones
How to Make Pasta Sauces
How to Make Pot Pies and Casseroles
How to Make Salad
How to Make Sauces and Gravies
How to Make Simple Fruit Desserts
How to Make Soup
How to Make Stew
How to Sauté

To order any of our books, visit us at
www.cooksillustrated.com
www.americastestkitchen.com
or call us at 800-611-0759

What Viewers Are Saying About
America's Test Kitchen

"I have watched a lot of cooking shows, and many of them were a waste of time. America's Test Kitchen is by far the best I have ever seen. You understand the everyday cook. Most of us don't grocery shop at places that sell the most exotic and expensive products. I enjoy your recipes because I know they will be good. I also appreciate your product testing. By following your suggestions, I have saved a lot of money."

Frances Williamson
via e-mail

"It just doesn't get any better than your flourless chocolate cake! In fact, if you can only bake one chocolate cake, this should be it."

Mindy Keys
Pittsburg, California

"I watched your show for the first time today on NJ Public Television. Bravo!!!! A cooking show that had a brain! I am so tired of the glitz that is featured nowadays on many cooking shows. I enjoyed your show because it reflected science rather than cute quips."

Bruce
via e-mail

"You have the best cooking show on TV. Not only the recipes, but all of the other interesting cooking and equipment information."

Tom and Annie
West Bend, Wisconsin

"Thank you for your show . . . it is the best cooking show on television! Every recipe of yours that I have made has been fabulous. My favorites are the raspberry-oat squares and the country-style Greek salad. I tell my friends that you are the Consumer Reports of the kitchen. I appreciate all the testing you do to make your viewers' lives easier. Please don't ever quit!"

Victoria Siegel
St. Louis, Missouri

"I just LOOOOOOVE the show. Finally, a cooking show that uses 'regular' ingredients we can find at the grocery store. I access your Web site all the time to find recipes and also tips about equipment if I want to make a purchase. I have to say that all the tips and recipes I have tried from your show have been 'phenomenal.'"

Patti Butz
Chicago, Illinois

"I am 61 years young, with a passion for cooking and baking, and have been doing it 'with love' for the past 50 years, or so. Just when I think that I have perfected something, I see a new tip or suggestion on your show to make it even better. It never ceases to amaze me that I always learn something new, every time I see your show. How great is that?"

Nancy Awwe
Milwaukee, Wisconsin

"I just wanted to send a note to let you know that this show is the very best cooking show EVER!!! I have learned so very, very much and have improved my cooking substantially purely due to tips and things I learned from the show. DON'T CHANGE A THING!! I have watched cooking shows for as long as I can remember, but this is the only show that has provided truly useful and practical information. PLEASE, PLEASE continue to produce the show exactly the way you have been doing . . . it is OUTSTANDING."

Becky
Ritzville, Washington

"I love America's Test Kitchen. I watch it regularly on WTTW from Chicago. It is the most informative and truly applicable show of its type. I think of it as The Joy of Cooking televised. Love the information, recipes, hosts . . . it's all great, don't change a thing."

Amy Tollas
Sawyer, Michigan

"So far, every single thing we've tried from watching your show on PBS has been a complete success. While we love the show, I have to admit that we are sorry to see that everything you show works as well as or better than you say it will. We really didn't need MORE great things to eat."

Robert and Lori Fore
Surprise, Arizona

"Just a quick note of thanks for your WONDERFUL show on PBS! My daughter and I stumbled across your show one afternoon, and now we are hooked. Finally, a cooking show for regular people that features food we would actually eat! I did not grow up in a house where people cooked, and I am totally enjoying the process of learning to cook."

Alisa Rawlins
Vancouver, Washington

AMERICA'S TEST KITCHEN LIVE!

AMERICA'S TEST KITCHEN LIVE!

BY THE EDITORS OF
COOK'S ILLUSTRATED

ILLUSTRATIONS
John Burgoyne

PHOTOGRAPHY
Daniel J. van Ackere
Carl Tremblay

AMERICA'S TEST KITCHEN
BROOKLINE, MASSACHUSETTS

America's Test Kitchen
17 Station Street
Brookline, MA 02445

ISBN 0-936184-82-5
Library of Congress Cataloging-in-Publication Data
The Editors of *Cook's Illustrated*

America's Test Kitchen Live!: The All-New Companion to America's Favorite Public Television Cooking Series
1st Edition

ISBN 0-936184-82-5 (hardback): $29.95
I. Cooking. I. Title
2004

Manufactured in the United States of America

Distributed by America's Test Kitchen
17 Station Street, Brookline, MA 02445

Editor: Jack Bishop
Series Designer: Amy Klee
Jacket Designer: Beth Tondreau
Book Production Specialist: Ron Bilodeau
Photographers: Carl Tremblay (color and selected black-and-white food photography);
Daniel J. van Ackere (documentary and silhouette photography and color photograph on page 86);
Keller + Keller (color photograph on page 200)
Illustrator: John Burgoyne
Production Manager: Jessica Lindheimer Quirk
Copyeditor: Cheryl Redmond
Proofreader: Jean Rogers
Indexer: Cathy Dorsey

CONTENTS

PREFACE

AS I WRITE THIS, MY WIFE, ADRIENNE, AND I ARE organizing an end-of-summer pig roast for our small Vermont town. Much like putting on a TV show, it involves a lot of planning: We have to order the pig and have it butterflied, get more than 50 pounds of charcoal for the cooker, draw up a guest list, hire an old-time band (fiddler, frail banjo, and guitar), put together a list of desserts (we do the pig and desserts; neighbors bring the other covered dishes), make sure there is wood for the late-night sauna after the roast, and then go over the guest list one more time to make sure that nobody has been left out.

All of this reminds me a great deal of the filming of *America's Test Kitchen*. Sure, it involves a lot of hard work and planning, but it is also a party of sorts, and you, the audience, are invited. If you are new to *America's Test Kitchen,* you should know that everyone on the show actually works there. It is a real place just outside of Boston and is also the home of *Cook's Illustrated* magazine. I am happy to say that much of the original cast from the first season (2001) is still together: test cooks Julia Collin Davison and Bridget Lancaster, tasting expert Jack Bishop, equipment guru Adam Ried, and me, Christopher Kimball, the host. This season (2005), we will also be introducing you to a few new faces from our kitchen, including test cooks Erika Bruce, Rebecca Hays, and Jeremy Sauer.

Of course, this is just the tip of the iceberg. Our kitchen has almost two dozen test cooks, 40 burners, 20 ovens, and more cookware than we can keep track of. We test a recipe 10, 20, 30, even up to 100 times to get it right. After a recipe is done, we make it with the wrong cookware and bad ingredients to see what will happen. We send it out to *Cook's Illustrated* readers who have volunteered to make the recipes at home and then give us their no-nonsense feedback. But on the show, what we want to do above all is to take you behind the scenes to show you why recipes so often fail and how to make them a success. And, please, this is real home cooking. We will never tell you that you can cook a gala dinner for 12 in just 20 minutes; we all know about promises made and promises not kept, especially in the kitchen.

Like our pig roast, *America's Test Kitchen* is mostly about the people we invite to join us. Cooking is not about perfect food; it is about the process of bringing folks together around the table and sharing a meal. As I often say, "Happy Meals Are Made at Home," and that is the higher purpose of our show. We want to give you the recipes and the confidence to get back into the kitchen and do good work. There is nothing wrong with meatloaf and mashed potatoes when made well. (Most "gourmet" cooking, at least in my opinion, is best left to restaurant chefs.) Home cooking ought to be straightforward, dependable, and satisfying. That is what we are all about.

One last thing you might notice about our show: We look like we're having fun. There are no scripts and no speechwriters. Everything is filmed "live" in that we never really know what is going to happen—and neither do you. Julia and I may disagree about technique. I may not choose the same winner that our panel chose in an earlier blind tasting. (In the bottled water tasting, I chose Boston tap water!) Or Adam may have me demonstrate a particularly useless kitchen gadget in an effort to show you what not to buy. The show is very much like our everyday test kitchen: unpredictable, surprising, practical, and, on occasion, inspiring.

My family just attended our local Fireman's Parade last weekend. My daughter Caroline and I baked a chocolate cake for the "Win a Cake" booth and dropped it off just before the parade started. (To win a cake, you bet 25 cents on a number, the wheel of fortune is spun, and you hope for the best.) I noticed that there were more than 50 cakes in that booth, all donated by local bakers. Some were works of art, but most were simple enough: Bundt cakes, sheet cakes, cupcakes, and layer cakes covered with everything from sprinkles to a whipped chocolate fudge frosting. In a moment, I understood why we do the show. We want to bring folks back into the kitchen, where they belong. For our part, we are happy to share our recipes, our food, and our time. For your part, we hope to see you each week in our kitchen, *America's Test Kitchen*.

Christopher Kimball
Founder and editor, *Cook's Illustrated* magazine
Host, *America's Test Kitchen*
Brookline, Massachusetts, 2004

WELCOME TO AMERICA'S TEST KITCHEN

AMERICA'S TEST KITCHEN IS A VERY REAL 2,500-SQUARE-foot kitchen located just outside of Boston. It is the home of *Cook's Illustrated* magazine and is the Monday through Friday destination of more than two dozen test cooks, editors, food scientists, tasters, photographers, and cookware specialists. Our mission is to test recipes over and over again until we understand how and why they work and until we arrive at the "best" version.

Our television show highlights the best recipes developed in the test kitchen during the past year—those recipes that our test kitchen staff makes at home time and time again. These recipes are accompanied by our most exhaustive equipment tests and our most interesting food tastings.

Christopher Kimball, the founder and editor of *Cook's Illustrated* magazine, is host of the show and asks the questions you might ask. It's the job of our two chefs, Julia Collin Davison and Bridget Lancaster, to demonstrate our recipes. They show Chris what works, what doesn't, and explain why. In the process, they discuss (and show us) the best and worst examples from our development process—the bread that burned, the cake that collapsed, and the pork chops that were tough.

Adam Ried, our equipment guru, shares the highlights from our detailed testing process in Equipment Corner segments. He brings with him our favorite (and least favorite) gadgets and tools. He tells you which knives performed best in a dozen kitchen tests and shows why most stain removers are nearly worthless.

Jack Bishop is our ingredient expert. He has Chris taste our favorite (and least favorite) brands of common food products—everything from bacon and chocolate ice cream to bottled water and chicken. Chris may not always enjoy these exercises (fish sauce is not much fun to taste), but he usually learns something as Jack explains what makes one brand superior to another.

Although there are just five cooks and editors who appear on the television show, another 50 people worked to make the show a reality. Executive chefs Erin McMurrer and Dawn Yanagihara ran the "back kitchen," where all the food that appeared on camera originated. Along with the on-air crew, Erin and Dawn also planned and organized the 26 television episodes shot in May 2004. Melissa Baldino researched the Q & A segments, and Garth Clingingsmith organized the tasting and equipment segments.

During the actual filming, chefs Stephanie Alleyne, Erika Bruce, Keith Dresser, Sean Lawler, Jeremy Sauer, and Diane Unger-Mahoney were in the kitchen from early in the morning to late at night helping Erin and Dawn cook all the food needed on set. Nadia Domeq and Nina West were charged with the herculean task of making sure all the ingredients we needed were on hand. Kitchen assistants

Katie Archimbault, Barbara Akins, Maria Elena Delgado, Ena Guidel, Rebecca King, and Cali Todd also worked long hours. Garth Clingingsmith, Becky Hays, Charles Kelsey, and Nina West helped coordinate the efforts of the kitchen with the television set by readying props, equipment, and food.

The staff of A La Carte Communications turned our recipes, tastings, testing, and science experiments into a lively television show. Special thanks to executive producers Geoffrey Drummond and Nat Katzman; director Herb Sevush; coordinating producer Richard Dooley; production manager Anne-Sophie Brieger; director of photography Dean Gaskill; and editor Hugh Elliot. We also appreciate the hard work of the video production team, including Stephen Hussar, Michael McEachern, Peter Dingle, Eliat B. Goldman, Gilles Morin, Brenda Coffey, Tommy Hamilton, Patrick Ruth, Jack McPhee, Aaron Frutman, Kaliel Roberts, Mark Romanelli, and Paul Swensen.

We also would like to thank Hope Reed, who handles station relations, and the team at American Public Television that presents the show: Cynthia Fenniman, Chris Funkhauser, Judy Barlow, and Tom Davison. Thanks also for production support from DGA Productions, Boston; Paul Swensen Productions, Santa Rosa, California; and Zebra Productions, New York.

Sub-Zero, Wolf, Vendange Wines, and Viva Towels helped underwrite the show, and we thank them for their support. Equipment for the show was supplied by Olgo Russo at A. Russo & Sons, Mahoney's Garden Center of Cambridge, Massachusetts, and DuPont Corian.

We hope this book gives you an inside look at America's Test Kitchen. We are passionate about our work, and we hope you enjoy our recipes as well as reading about the process by which they were created. Our mission is pretty simple. We want to help make you a better cook. We hope that our television show and this book will do just that. If you have comments or questions about the show or the book, contact us at www.americastestkitchen.com. Visit www.cooksillustrated.com for information about *Cook's Illustrated* magazine.

AMERICA'S TEST KITCHEN LIVE!

Bridget and Chris taste an array of easy appetizers—
beef satay, spinach dip with pita chips, and spiced nuts.

APPETIZERS

CHAPTER I

When preparing and serving appetizers, you're also answering the front door, pouring drinks, and catching up with old friends who know their way to the kitchen. Appetizers are, after all, party food. If you're the host, you can bet that having lots of time alone in the kitchen is an unlikely proposition.

The challenge, then, when choosing appetizers is to find recipes that won't keep you away from guests for very long. But a quick appetizer that doesn't taste very good isn't worth the bother. If the only choice is some bland dip and tired crudités, we'd rather go hungry and wait for dinner.

We've chosen recipes for this chapter that deliver big flavor without much work. This means spiced nuts that are not overly sweet (the most common flaw in other recipes), spinach dip that is bold and creamy (not watery and insipid), and beef satay that is tender and vibrant (rather than the usual cold shoe leather with sticky, sweet sauce). These recipes will start any meal on the right note.

SPICED NUTS

WHAT WE WANTED: Party nuts that are packed with flavor but not overly sticky or sweet.

At parties, spiced nuts usually disappear faster than the host can replenish the bowl. But most spiced nuts are made with a heavy sugar syrup, which can leave your hands sticky and cause the nuts to clump together in unappealing, indelicate clusters.

Finding the right coating method required a good deal of testing. The most common technique, boiling the nuts in a thick, sweet syrup, was not even an option because it made the nuts sticky. Another popular method, toasting or sautéing the nuts in butter or oil before tossing them with spices, dulled the finish of the nuts and made them taste bland or oily. A third possibility, coating the nuts with a spiced egg white mixture, created such a chunky, candy-like coating that the nuts themselves were barely visible.

Our answer came when we made a light glaze for the nuts from very small amounts of liquid, sugar, and butter. It worked like a charm. This treatment left the nuts shiny and just tacky enough for a dry spice coating to stick perfectly, giving the nuts both a consistent, beautiful appearance and plenty of flavor.

Kosher salt is important here because it adds crunch and has a clean flavor. If you can, make the nuts ahead of time; as they sit, they will better absorb the flavorings.

Toasting the nuts (before they are coated) is also key to developing their flavor. We like the even heat of the oven for this task. Make sure the oven isn't too hot (350 degrees is ideal) and shake the pan once or twice to turn the nuts so they toast evenly. Finally, stick close by the oven. Nuts can go from perfectly toasted to burnt in a few minutes.

WHAT WE LEARNED: Glaze toasted nuts with butter, sugar, and a little liquid (we like either rum or water) and then toss them with the spices for an even, light coating.

SPICED PECANS WITH RUM GLAZE

Makes about 2 cups

The spiced nuts can be stored in an airtight container for up to 5 days.

   2   cups (8 ounces) raw pecan halves

spice mix
   2   tablespoons sugar
   ¾   teaspoon kosher salt
   ½   teaspoon ground cinnamon
   ⅛   teaspoon ground cloves
   ⅛   teaspoon ground allspice

rum glaze
   1   tablespoon rum, preferably dark
   2   teaspoons vanilla extract
   1   teaspoon light or dark brown sugar
   1   tablespoon unsalted butter

1. Adjust an oven rack to the middle position and heat the oven to 350 degrees. Line a rimmed baking sheet with parchment paper and spread the pecans on it in an even layer; toast for 4 minutes, rotate the pan, and continue to toast until fragrant and the color deepens slightly, about 4 minutes longer. Transfer the baking sheet with the nuts to a wire rack.

2. FOR THE SPICE MIX: While the nuts are toasting, stir the sugar, salt, cinnamon, cloves, and allspice together in a medium bowl; set aside.

3. FOR THE GLAZE: Bring the rum, vanilla, brown sugar, and butter to a boil in a medium saucepan over medium-high heat, whisking constantly. Stir in the toasted pecans and cook, stirring constantly with a wooden spoon, until almost all the liquid has evaporated, about 1½ minutes.

4. Transfer the glazed pecans to the bowl with the spice mix; toss well to coat. Return the glazed spiced pecans to the parchment-lined baking sheet to cool.

MEXICAN-SPICED ALMONDS, PEANUTS, AND PUMPKIN SEEDS

Makes about 2 cups

The spiced nuts can be stored in an airtight container for up to 5 days.

  1¼ cups (4½ ounces) sliced almonds
  ⅔   cup (3 ounces) roasted unsalted shelled peanuts
  ¼   cup (1 ounce) raw pumpkin seeds

mexican spice mix
  1   tablespoon sugar
  1   teaspoon kosher salt
  ¼   teaspoon ground cinnamon
  ¼   teaspoon ground cumin
  ¼   teaspoon ground coriander
  ⅛   teaspoon cayenne
  ⅛   teaspoon garlic powder

simple glaze
  2   tablespoons water
  1   teaspoon light or dark brown sugar
  1   tablespoon unsalted butter

1. Adjust an oven rack to the middle position and heat the oven to 350 degrees. Line a rimmed baking sheet with parchment paper and spread the almonds on it in an even layer. Toast for 4 minutes and rotate the pan; add the peanuts and pumpkin seeds, spreading them in an even layer. Continue to toast until fragrant and the color deepens slightly, about 4 minutes longer. Transfer the baking sheet with the nuts and seeds to a wire rack.

2. FOR THE SPICE MIX: While the nuts and seeds are toasting, stir the sugar, salt, cinnamon, cumin, coriander, cayenne, and garlic powder together in a medium bowl; set aside.

3. FOR THE GLAZE: Bring the water, brown sugar, and butter to a boil in a medium saucepan over medium-high heat, whisking constantly. Stir in the toasted nuts and seeds and cook, stirring constantly with a wooden spoon, until the nuts are shiny and almost all the liquid has evaporated, about 1½ minutes.

4. Transfer the glazed nuts and seeds to the bowl with the spice mix; toss well to coat. Return the glazed and spiced nuts and seeds to the parchment-lined baking sheet to cool.

INDIAN-SPICED CASHEWS AND PISTACHIOS WITH CURRANTS

Makes about 2 cups

The spiced nuts can be stored in an airtight container for up to 5 days.

1¼   cups (6 ounces) raw cashews
½   cup (2 ounces) raw unsalted shelled pistachios
2   tablespoons currants

indian spice mix
1   tablespoon sugar
1   teaspoon kosher salt
1   teaspoon curry powder
¼   teaspoon ground cumin
¼   teaspoon ground coriander

simple glaze
2   tablespoons water
1   teaspoon light or dark brown sugar
1   tablespoon unsalted butter

1. Adjust an oven rack to the middle position and heat the oven to 350 degrees. Line a rimmed baking sheet with parchment paper and spread the cashews on it in an even layer; toast for 4 minutes, rotate the pan, and toast for 4 minutes more. Add the pistachios, spreading them in an even layer; continue to toast until fragrant and the color deepens slightly, about 2 minutes. Transfer the baking sheet with the nuts to a wire rack; add the currants.

2. FOR THE SPICE MIX: While the nuts are toasting, stir the sugar, salt, curry powder, cumin, and coriander together in a medium bowl; set aside.

3. FOR THE GLAZE: Bring the water, brown sugar, and butter to a boil in a medium saucepan over medium-high heat, whisking constantly. Stir in the nut mix and cook, stirring constantly with a wooden spoon, until the nuts are shiny and almost all the liquid has evaporated, about 1½ minutes.

4. Transfer the glazed nuts and currants to the bowl with the spice mix; toss well to coat. Return the glazed and spiced nuts and currants to the parchment-lined baking sheet to cool.

Q&A

What's the best way to store nuts?

Improper storage and a harsh kitchen environment (think hot, bright, or humid) are enough to make a good nut go bad. Nuts are filled with oils that can spoil rather quickly, even when stored in a cool, dark, dry cabinet. When this happens, the nuts taste rancid and must be discarded. To avoid such a costly mistake, the test kitchen stores all shelled nuts in the freezer. Sealed in a freezer-safe, zipper-lock storage bag, nuts will stay fresh tasting for months, if not a year. And there's no need to defrost them. Frozen nuts chop up just as easily as (if not more so than) fresh. You can toast nuts straight from the freezer, but you might need to add a minute or two to the oven time.

SPINACH DIP

WHAT WE WANTED: Spinach dip—a quick, simple concoction made with vegetable soup mix, sour cream, and frozen spinach—often tastes simply awful. We wanted a rich, thick, and creamy spinach dip brimming with big, bold flavors. Could we bring this old-fashioned recipe into the twenty-first century?

In 1954, America was introduced to what would become our most popular party fare: Lipton's onion soup mix combined with sour cream. Spinach dip—made with vegetable soup mix, sour cream, and frozen spinach—was hot on its heels.

Fifty years later, most spinach dips are still based on soup mixes, and the flavors are still flat, exorbitantly salty, and nowhere near fresh. Yet a good spinach dip can be made easily enough with just a few fresh ingredients, a couple of kitchen tools, and no more than 30 minutes of preparation. (A good onion dip takes much longer because the onions must be caramelized in a skillet for at least 45 minutes.) We set out to rejuvenate spinach dip, without compromising its quick and easy appeal.

To begin, we gathered five varieties of spinach: curly (or crinkly), flat (or smooth), semi-savoy (a hybrid of the two), baby, and, for the sake of comparison, frozen spinach. We then trimmed, washed, chopped, and wilted the fresh spinaches in hot pots (we simply thawed the frozen spinach), made the dips, chilled them until thickened, and let tasters dig in. The results were so surprising we had to tally them twice. Frozen spinach was the victor. Tasters liked its "familiar," "intense" flavor and even used the word "fresh" to describe it. The fresh varieties were too "meek," their flavor lost among the other ingredients. After a few more tests to determine the best consistency, we found that 20 to 30 seconds in the food processor chopped the thawed frozen spinach into small, manageable bits and made the dip smooth and creamy.

The '50s were creeping their way back into our recipe—frozen spinach, no cooking (so far), and speedy preparation—but we weren't about to backtrack on flavor. Armed with a host of fresh herbs and other pungent ingredients, we began developing the flavor components for the dip sans soup mix. Among the herbs, parsley and dill were by and large the standards, and they worked appealingly well when combined. Onions and shallots were problematic, however, as they required cooking to mellow their astringency and soften their crunch. We weren't cooking the spinach and thought it would be a waste of time and effort to start pulling out pots and pans now. In the end, a combination of raw scallion whites and a single small clove of garlic added the perfect amount of bite and pungency. With a dash of hot pepper sauce for a kick and some salt and pepper, the dip came out of the processor light, fresh, and full of bold flavors—far better than the soup mix recipe and not much more work.

The only problem remaining was that the dip, which took only about 15 minutes to make, took almost two hours to chill. Wanting to skip this polar timeout, we found the solution was simple enough. Instead of thawing the spinach completely, we simply thawed it only partially. Before processing, we microwaved the frozen block for three minutes on low, broke it into icy chunks, and squeezed each to extract a surprising amount of liquid. The chunks were still ice cold and thoroughly cooled the dip as they broke down in the processor. Although our hands were slightly numb, the dip was quick to make, thick, creamy, and cool enough for immediate service.

WHAT WE LEARNED: Frozen spinach actually makes a better-tasting dip than fresh spinach. Use the food processor to chop partially thawed spinach and then enrich it with sour cream, mayonnaise, and a mixture of fresh herbs and seasonings.

CREAMY HERBED SPINACH DIP

Makes about 1½ cups, serving 8 to 10

Partial thawing of the spinach produces a cold dip that can be served without further chilling. If you don't own a microwave, the frozen spinach can be thawed at room temperature for 1½ hours, then squeezed of excess liquid. The garlic must be minced or pressed before going into the food processor; otherwise, the dip will contain large chunks of garlic.

1	(10-ounce) box frozen chopped spinach
½	cup sour cream
½	cup mayonnaise
3	medium scallions, white parts only, sliced thin (about 2 tablespoons)
1	tablespoon chopped fresh dill leaves
½	cup packed fresh parsley leaves
1	small garlic clove, minced or pressed through a garlic press (about 1 teaspoon)
¼	teaspoon hot pepper sauce, such as Tabasco
½	teaspoon salt
¼	teaspoon ground black pepper
½	medium red bell pepper, diced fine

1. Thaw the spinach in a microwave for 3 minutes at 40 percent power. (The edges should be thawed but not warm; the center should be soft enough to be broken into icy chunks.) Squeeze the partially frozen spinach to remove excess water.

2. In a food processor, process the spinach, sour cream, mayonnaise, scallions, dill, parsley, garlic, hot pepper sauce, salt, and pepper until smooth and creamy, about 30 seconds. Transfer the mixture to a serving bowl and stir in the bell pepper; serve. (The dip can be covered with plastic wrap and refrigerated for up to 2 days.)

VARIATIONS

SPINACH DIP WITH BLUE CHEESE AND BACON

If making this dip in advance, hold off sprinkling the bacon over the top until just before serving.

Cut 3 ounces (about 3 slices) bacon into ¼-inch pieces and fry them in a small skillet over medium-high heat until crisp and browned, about 5 minutes; using a slotted spoon, transfer the bacon to a paper towel–lined plate and set aside. Follow the recipe for Creamy Herbed Spinach Dip, omitting the dill, hot pepper sauce, salt, and red bell pepper, and processing 1½ ounces crumbled blue cheese (about ⅓ cup) along with the spinach. Season with salt; before serving, sprinkle the bacon over the dip.

SPINACH DIP WITH FETA, LEMON, AND OREGANO

Do not substitute dried oregano for the fresh oregano in this recipe.

Follow the recipe for Creamy Herbed Spinach Dip, omitting the hot pepper sauce, salt, and red bell pepper, and processing 2 tablespoons fresh oregano leaves, 2 ounces crumbled feta cheese (about ½ cup), and 1 tablespoon lemon juice plus 1 teaspoon grated lemon zest along with the spinach. Season with salt.

CILANTRO-LIME SPINACH DIP WITH CHIPOTLE CHILES

This dip is particularly good served with tortilla chips.

Follow the recipe for Creamy Herbed Spinach Dip, omitting the hot pepper sauce and red bell pepper, and processing ¼ cup packed fresh cilantro leaves, 1 tablespoon seeded and minced chipotle chiles in adobo (about 2 medium chiles), 1 tablespoon lime juice plus ½ teaspoon grated lime zest, ½ teaspoon light brown sugar, and ⅛ teaspoon ground cumin along with the spinach.

PITA CHIPS

WHAT WE WANTED: An accompaniment to dips that would taste better than the store-bought alternatives.

Because pita chips are essentially pieces of toast made from pita bread, we figured that developing this recipe was going to be a breeze. Surprisingly, it took more than a few tests to get the results we were after.

We took advantage of the pocket in the middle of each pita by first cutting the pitas into two thin, round layers. Thin one-layer chips not only baked more evenly than double-layered chips but also were easier to dip and eat. Next, we tried baking two batches—one plain, the other brushed with a little olive oil. Hands down, we preferred the crisp, flavorful chips made with a little oil. The oil made all the difference between authentic pita chips and boring pita toast. Not only did the oil matter but, surprisingly, which side of the pita was oiled made a difference as well. After the pita is cut into layers, each chip has two distinct sides—one smooth (the exterior of the original pita bread), the other rough (the inside of the original bread). When the oil was brushed onto the smooth side, tasters claimed the chips felt greasy. Not so when the oil was brushed onto the rough side, which seemed to absorb it.

We also noted that it made a difference which side was facing up or down during baking. When baked rough-side down, the chips stuck to the cookie sheet, requiring a fair amount of prying to remove. But when they were baked smooth-side down, no such problem developed. Finding it necessary to flip the chips during baking for an even toasting, we decided to begin with the smooth side down, giving the rough side a chance to toast so it wouldn't stick.

WHAT WE LEARNED: Cut each pita into two thin rounds and then into chips so they will bake more evenly. Brush the chips with oil and then make sure to start the chips smooth-side down on the baking sheet so they won't stick.

PITA CHIPS
Makes 48 chips, enough to accompany 2 cups dip

- 4 (8-inch) pita breads, split and cut into 6 wedges
- ¼ cup olive oil
- 1 teaspoon salt

1. Adjust the oven racks to the upper- and lower-middle positions and heat the oven to 350 degrees. Spread the pita wedges, smooth-side down, over 2 rimmed baking sheets. Brush each chip lightly with oil and sprinkle with salt.

2. Bake the chips until lightly browned, about 6 minutes. Flip the chips so their smooth side is up. Continue to bake until the chips are fully toasted, about 6 minutes longer. Cool the chips before serving.

TECHNIQUE: Cutting Pita Chips

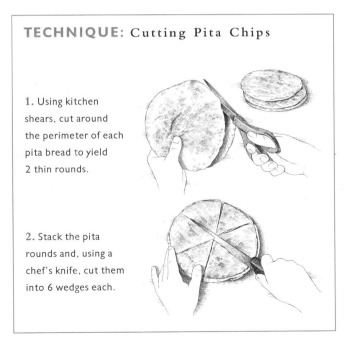

1. Using kitchen shears, cut around the perimeter of each pita bread to yield 2 thin rounds.

2. Stack the pita rounds and, using a chef's knife, cut them into 6 wedges each.

BEEF SATAY

WHAT WE WANTED: Tender meat that is easily pulled apart into small bites right off the skewer. The accompanying peanut sauce should be potent and spicy, with just a hint of sweetness.

Slender slices of marinated beef weaved onto bamboo skewers and thrown briefly on the grill are a traditional Indonesian favorite, known as satay (or saté). The meat has a sweet yet salty flavor, and the skewers are served as an appetizer, snack, or light main course alongside a spicy peanut sauce. All too often, however, the beef is tough and sliced so thick it doesn't pull apart, leaving you with an ungainly mouthful of meat. The peanut sauce can be graceless, with a glue-like consistency and muddy peanut flavor. Not only would finding the right cut of beef and slicing it correctly be key for a tender satay, but we wondered how to make the exotic-tasting marinade and accompanying peanut sauce.

Starting with the beef, we surveyed the local meat counter for possibilities. Skipping over the expensive cuts such as top loin, rib eye, and tenderloin, we focused on the cheaper cuts more appropriate for marinating and skewering—sirloin, sirloin flap, round, skirt, flank, and blade steaks. Bringing these cheaper cuts back to the test kitchen, we immediately noted that slicing the raw beef into thin strips is a difficult task. To make it easier, we found it best to firm the meat in the freezer for about 30 minutes. Sliced, skewered, and cooked, these various cheaper cuts of meat produced substantially different textures. Steaks from the round were the worst, with a tough, dry texture, followed closely by chewy sirloin, and stringy sirloin flap (a cut from the bottom sirloin). The blade steaks tasted great and were fairly tender, but their small size made it difficult to slice them into long, elegant strips. Both the skirt and flank steaks were easy to slice and tasted best. Since skirt steak can be difficult to find and is a bit more expensive, flank steak is the best option.

We found the key to tenderness hinges on slicing the meat perpendicular to its large, obvious grain. Using a small, 1½-pound flank steak, we could make about 24 skewers, enough for 12 people as an appetizer. Although satay is classically grilled, we found the broiler to be a simpler and more party-friendly cooking method. Thin wooden skewers worked better than metal skewers, which tend to be thicker and tore up the small pieces of meat. Protecting the bamboo skewers with foil, however, is necessary to prevent them from burning or catching on fire. Cooked roughly six inches from the broiler element, these thinly sliced pieces of meat are done in only six to seven minutes.

Having found a tender cut of meat, we focused next on adding flavor with the marinade. Researching a variety of traditional Indonesian recipes, we noted that most were

based on a combination of fish sauce and oil. Using vegetable oil, we tested various amounts of fish sauce, but tasters simply did not like its fermented fish flavor in combination with the beef. Replacing it with soy sauce, although not traditional, worked well; the soy sauce lent its salty, fermented flavor without any "fishiness."

We then tried adding other flavors such as coconut milk, lime juice, Tabasco, Asian chili sauce, sugar, and an array of fresh herbs. Coconut milk dulled the beef's natural flavor, while the tart, acidic flavor of lime juice tasted out of place. Asian chili sauce added a pleasant, spicy heat without the sour, vinegary flavor that Tabasco contributed. The sweet, molasses flavor of the brown sugar added a welcome balance to the hot chili sauce and salty soy, while enhancing the beef's ability to brown under the broiler. Garlic and cilantro rounded out all of these flavors nicely. Marinating the beef for more than one hour turned the texture of the thin sliced beef mushy, while less time didn't give the meat long enough to pick up the marinade flavors. One hour of marinating was perfect.

Lastly, we focused on the peanut sauce. Using creamy peanut butter, we tried spicing it up using a variety of flavorings. In the end, the same ingredients used in the marinade also tasted good in the peanut sauce—soy sauce, Asian chili sauce, dark brown sugar, garlic, cilantro, and scallion. This time, however, lime juice added a welcome burst of tart acidity. We then stumbled on the obvious way to keep the sauce from being too thick or pasty: Thin it with hot water. Pairing perfectly with the flavor of the marinated beef, the peanut sauce turns these exotic-tasting skewers into an authentic satay.

WHAT WE LEARNED: Choose flank steak and use thin wooden skewers so the meat won't tear. Marinating the beef for an hour in a potent mixture of soy sauce, chili sauce, brown sugar, cilantro, garlic, and scallions adds flavor. The same ingredients work well in the peanut sauce, which should be thinned with hot water and sparked with fresh lime juice.

BEEF SATAY

Serves 12

Meat that is partially frozen is easier to slice into thin strips. Asian chili sauce is available in most supermarkets under the name Sriracha. A chili-garlic sauce, known as sambal, could also be used; however, it is much spicier. Use 6-inch-long skewers for this recipe; you'll need about 24.

1½	pounds flank steak
¼	cup soy sauce
¼	cup vegetable oil
2	tablespoons Asian chili sauce, or more to taste
¼	cup packed dark brown sugar
¼	cup minced fresh cilantro leaves
2	medium garlic cloves, minced or pressed through a garlic press (about 2 teaspoons)
4	scallions, white and green parts, sliced thin
1	recipe Spicy Peanut Dipping Sauce (recipe follows)

1. Cut the flank steak in half lengthwise and freeze it for 30 minutes.

2. Combine the soy sauce, oil, chili sauce, brown sugar, cilantro, garlic, and scallions in a measuring cup; set aside. Remove the flank steak from the freezer and slice each piece across the grain into ¼-inch-thick strips. Weave the meat onto individual bamboo skewers. Dunk the meat end of each skewer in the marinade to coat; lay the skewers in a shallow dish, propping up the exposed ends of the skewers to keep them clean. Pour the remaining marinade over the meat. Refrigerate for exactly 1 hour.

3. Adjust an oven rack to the top position and heat the broiler. Following the illustration on page 12, lay the skewers on a wire rack set over a rimmed baking sheet and cover the skewer ends with foil. Broil for 6 to 7 minutes, flipping the skewers over halfway through, until the meat is browned. Serve immediately with the peanut sauce.

SPICY PEANUT DIPPING SAUCE

Makes about 1 ½ cups

This sauce can be made a day in advance and refrigerated. Bring the sauce to room temperature before serving.

½ cup creamy peanut butter
¼ cup hot water
1 tablespoon soy sauce
2 tablespoons juice from 1 lime
2 tablespoons Asian chili sauce
1 tablespoon dark brown sugar
1 medium garlic clove, minced or pressed through a garlic press (about 1 teaspoon)
1 tablespoon chopped fresh cilantro leaves
2 scallions, white and green parts, sliced thin

Whisk the peanut butter and hot water together in a medium bowl. Stir in the remaining ingredients. Transfer to a small serving bowl.

TECHNIQUE: Arranging the Skewers

Using a narrow strip of aluminum foil, cover the exposed portion of each skewer to prevent burning. Secure the foil by crimping it tightly at the edges.

TASTING LAB: Salsa

THE MEXICAN WORD FOR "SAUCE," SALSA GENERICALLY refers to a chilled tomato relish that is seasoned with garlic, onions, cilantro, and/or chiles. It sounds simple enough, but if you've ever tried supermarket salsas, you know that simple doesn't always translate into good. In fact, after tasting nine brands of jarred and refrigerated salsas, we can tell you that simple can taste downright awful.

There are two types of supermarket salsa: refrigerated, which only last a month or two, thanks to added preservatives; and bottled salsas, which will stay "fresh" for over a year (thanks to vacuum sealing and, yes, preservatives). The two types vary texturally: refrigerated salsas are raw and have a texture that most resembles homemade, while bottled salsas are cooked, with a more saucy consistency. Refrigerated salsas are often store or regional brands; we found one that was widely distributed. We tasted this brand alongside eight popular bottled brands, all in the basic version (no roasted garlic or chipotle) at a medium level of spiciness.

While none of the salsas measured up to homemade (few supermarket products do), we did find three that we can recommend. The refrigerated salsa topped the ratings, with a flavor and texture that compared most favorably with homemade. Two jarred salsas, Old El Paso and Tostitos, were also recommended for their clean, bright flavors and chunky textures. Conversely, our lowest rated salsas, Herdez and Embasa, were downgraded for muddy flavors and soupy textures.

So if you don't have time to make salsa to go with those chips, head for the refrigerator case for the best store-bought salsa. Jars of Old El Paso and Tostitos are decent options, too.

Rating Salsas

FIFTEEN MEMBERS OF THE *COOK'S ILLUSTRATED* STAFF TASTED ALL OF THE SALSAS PLAIN, WITH CHIPS offered for dipping. The salsas are listed in order of preference based on their scores in this tasting. Look for these salsas in supermarkets nationwide.

RECOMMENDED
Santa Barbara Medium Salsa (refrigerated) $3.49 for 16 ounces
Tasters liked this "fresh-tasting" refrigerated salsa, praising its "good herbal flavors."

RECOMMENDED
Old El Paso Thick 'n Chunky Medium Salsa $2.79 for 16 ounces
Our favorite bottled salsa was called "spicy" and "bright."

RECOMMENDED
Tostitos Restaurant Style Medium Salsa $3.29 for 16 ounces
Although this salsa received decent scores, tasters were not overly enthusiastic about this sample, calling it "not bad" and "very mild."

NOT RECOMMENDED
Muir Glen Organic Medium Salsa $3.99 for 16 ounces
Tasters complained about the "mushy" texture and "ketchup-y" flavor.

NOT RECOMMENDED
Taco Bell Home Thick 'n Chunky Medium Salsa $2.69 for 16 ounces
One taster quipped, "Is this salsa or tomato sauce?"

NOT RECOMMENDED
Newman's Own Medium Salsa $2.69 for 16 ounces
This salsa was deemed "bland" and "sweet."

NOT RECOMMENDED
Green Mountain Gringo Medium Salsa $3.99 for 16 ounces
There were several complaints about the "cooked flavor" in this "too sweet" salsa.

NOT RECOMMENDED
Herdez Medium Salsa Casera $2.99 for 16 ounces
"Tastes like unseasoned canned tomatoes" was the general consensus about this bland offering imported from Mexico.

NOT RECOMMENDED
Embasa Medium Salsa Mexicana $2.95 for 16 ounces
A "gluey" texture and "bitter" aftertaste sank this salsa to the bottom of the ratings.

Canned beans can be the basis of a great soup if you follow our simple method for infusing them with flavor.

SIMPLE soups

CHAPTER 2

Not surprisingly, the differences in flavor between soup from a can and homemade soup are immeasurable. The former is usually too salty, mushy, and altogether unappealing. But most cooks are under the impression that good soup takes all day to prepare. Maybe that's what our mothers wanted us to think, but the truth is that homemade soup need not be a complicated affair.

Rich chicken stock is the basis for many soups, including our favorite, chicken noodle soup. Simply put, there's no way to make this kind of brothy soup without homemade stock. We found an unusual technique and a remarkably simple recipe (just four ingredients, plus salt and water) that yields great stock in less than an hour.

Pasta e fagioli (pasta and beans) is well known to Italian-Americans. This hearty peasant soup deserves a wider audience. It's a meal in a bowl and can be made from pantry ingredients most cooks will have on hand.

CHICKEN STOCK

WHAT WE WANTED: A stock potent enough to use in a simple chicken noodle soup that doesn't take all day to cook. Was there a way to make great stock quickly?

Most standard chicken stocks are not flavorful enough for a robust chicken soup. They are fine if ladled into risotto, but we wanted a stock that really tastes like chicken. We knew that the conventional method—simmering chicken parts and aromatics, such as onions, carrots, and celery, in water for hours—was part of the problem. This method takes too long (at least three hours) to extract flavor from the chicken. We wanted to see if we could do better, and in less time.

We tried blanching a whole chicken on the theory that blanching keeps the chicken from releasing foam during cooking. The blanched chicken was then partially covered with water and placed in a heatproof bowl over a pan of simmering water. Cooked this way, the chicken never simmered, and the resulting stock was remarkably clear, refined, and full-flavored. The only problem: It took four hours for the stock to take on sufficient flavor. We also noted that our 4-pound chicken was good for nothing but the garbage bin after being cooked for so long.

A number of recipes promote roasting chicken bones or parts and then using them to make stock. The theory, at least, is that roasted parts will flavor stock in minutes, not hours. We gave it a try several times, roasting chicken backs, necks, and bones—with and without vegetables. We preferred the stock made with roasted chicken parts and vegetables, but the actual chicken flavor was too tame.

Finally, we tried a method described by Edna Lewis in her book *In Pursuit of Flavor* (Knopf, 1988). She chops a chicken into small pieces and then sautés it with an onion until the chicken loses its raw color. The pot is then covered, and the chicken and onion cook over low heat until they release their rich, flavorful juices, which takes about

20 minutes. Only at that point is the water added, and the stock is simmered for just 20 minutes longer.

We knew we were onto something as we smelled the chicken and onion sautéing, and the finished stock confirmed what our noses had detected. The stock tasted pleasantly sautéed, not boiled. We had some refining to do, though. For once, we had made too strong a brew.

First, we tried using more water. The stock was less intense, but just the right strength to make a base for some of the best chicken soup we've ever tasted. We made the stock twice more, once without the onion and once with onion, celery, and carrot. The onion added a flavor dimension we liked; the extra vegetables neither added nor detracted from the final soup, so we left them out.

After much trial and error, we had a recipe that delivered liquid gold in just 40 minutes. While this recipe requires more hands-on work (hacking up a chicken, browning an onion, then the chicken parts), it is ready in a fraction of the time required to make stock by traditional methods.

If you are making a soup that needs some chicken

meat, use a whole chicken. The breast is removed in two pieces and reserved. The rest of the bird—the legs, back, and wings—is hacked into small pieces, browned, and then sweated with the onions. The water is added to the pot along with the reserved breast pieces. After 20 minutes of simmering time, the breast meat is perfectly cooked, ready to be skinned and shredded when cool. The hacked-up chicken pieces are strained and discarded. We particularly liked the tidiness of this method: One chicken yields one pot of soup.

If you are making a soup that doesn't require chicken meat, use four whole legs that have been cut into 2-inch pieces. Don't try to salvage the meat from the legs. After five minutes of sautéing, 20 minutes of sweating, and another 20 minutes of simmering, the meat is void of flavor.

One note about this method. We found it necessary to cut the chicken into pieces small enough to release their flavorful juices in a short period of time. A meat cleaver, a heavy-duty chef's knife, or a pair of heavy-duty kitchen shears makes the task fairly simple. Cutting up the chicken for stock doesn't require precision.

To cut up a whole chicken, start by removing the whole legs and wings from the body; set them aside. Separate the back from the breast, then split the breast and set the halves aside. Hack the back crosswise into three or four pieces, then halve each of these pieces. Cut the wing at each joint to yield three pieces. Leave the wing tip whole, then halve each of the remaining joints. Because of their larger bones, the legs and thighs are the most difficult to cut. Start by splitting the leg and thigh at the joint, then hack each to yield three to four pieces.

WHAT WE LEARNED: An unusual method—one that calls for browning small pieces of chicken, sweating them in a covered pot with an onion, and then simmering them for just 20 minutes—yields rich stock that's perfect for soup.

TECHNIQUE:
Using a Cleaver to Cut Up Chicken

Chicken hacked into small pieces with a meat cleaver will give up its flavor in record time. To cut through bone, place your hand near the far end of the cleaver handle, curling your fingers securely around it in a fist. Handle the cleaver the way you would a hammer, holding your wrist stiff and straight and letting the weight of the blade's front tip lead the force of the chop.

QUICK CHICKEN STOCK FOR SOUP
Makes about 2 quarts

This soup yields plenty of perfectly cooked white meat that can be used in soups. Make sure to reserve the breast pieces in the refrigerator until step 2—they should not be browned. To make stock without meat for soup, use 4 pounds of cut-up legs, wings, or back. If you use a cleaver, you will be able to cut up the chicken parts quickly. A chef's knife or kitchen shears will also work, albeit more slowly. See the illustration above for tips on using a cleaver.

1   tablespoon vegetable oil
1   whole chicken (about 4 pounds), breast removed, split, and reserved; remaining chicken cut into 2-inch pieces
1   medium onion, cut into medium dice
2   quarts boiling water
2   teaspoons salt
2   bay leaves

1. Heat the oil in a large stockpot or Dutch oven over medium-high heat. Add half of the chopped chicken pieces and cook until no longer pink and the skin is lightly browned, 4 to 5 minutes. Transfer the cooked chicken to a bowl. Brown the remaining chicken pieces and transfer them to the bowl with the first batch. Add the onion and cook until colored and softened slightly, 2 to 3 minutes. Return the chicken pieces to the pot. Reduce the heat to low, cover, and cook until the chicken releases its juices, about 20 minutes.

2. Increase the heat to high; add the boiling water, reserved chicken breast pieces, salt, and bay leaves. Return to a simmer, then cover and barely simmer until the stock is rich and flavorful, about 20 minutes.

3. Remove the breast pieces from the pot and set aside. When cool, discard the skin and bones from the breast pieces and shred the meat into bite-size pieces. Strain the stock into a container and discard the solids. Skim the fat from the stock and reserve for later use in the soup. (The shredded chicken, strained stock, and fat can be covered and refrigerated separately up to 2 days.)

TECHNIQUE:
Freezing Small Portions of Stock

In the test kitchen, we ladle the cooled stock into nonstick muffin tins and freeze. When the stock is frozen, twist the muffin tin just as you would twist an ice tray. Place the frozen blocks in a zipper-lock plastic bag and seal it tightly.

1. An alternative is to pour stock into a coffee mug lined with a quart-size plastic zipper-lock bag.

2. Place the filled bags in a large, shallow roasting pan and freeze. Once the stock is frozen solid, the bags can be removed from the pan and stored in the freezer.

EQUIPMENT CORNER: Fat Separators

IS THERE ANYTHING AS FRUSTRATING AS SKIMMING THE fat from the top of a homemade soup, sauce, or stock? Endlessly blotting with messy paper towels, flaccid lettuce leaves, or, worst of all, ladling ounces of delicious liquid down the drain just to remove a few droplets of oil, defatting is probably the most thankless task in the kitchen. Luckily, separating liquid fat is easy to do with a specially designed fat separator, aka gravy strainer or soup strainer. Anticipation was high as we recently lined up eight widely available fat separators and put them to the test. In addition to their individual performance, the separators would also be judged on their price, material, capacity, handle comfort, and ease of use. Faced with a wide range of designs and price tags, we were out to find the fat separator that would finally liberate us from our skimming woes.

Fat separators typically come in three formats: pitcher-type measuring cups with sharply angled spouts opening out from the base of the cup; ladles with slots around the perimeter; and "fat mops," brushes with long, soft bristles made from plastic fibers. Such extreme design differences raise the obvious question—which kind works best? Fat-separating ladles offer a series of slot-shaped holes along one side of the ladle that allow fat to drain into the bowl of the ladle so it can be discarded. Our testers found this to be a tedious process requiring fine control of the ladle, which, when dipped too low, let in the broth along with the fat. Although we tested only one, fat mops are designed to wick away fat from stews, gravies, soups, chilis, and fried foods—items for which it would be impossible to use another kind of fat separator. This clever design proved successful in smaller capacities but was unable to effectively defat large amounts of liquid. The pitcher-type separators offered convenience, reliable performance, and, owing to the large capacity, a level of efficiency that the other styles could not provide.

Because of its oblong shape, the Trudeau Gravy Separator ($9.99) had the widest mouth of all, a point in its favor. The Trudeau also had an integrated strainer, which is helpful when you're defatting pan drippings that are still mixed with chunks of aromatic vegetables, herb sprigs, or other flavorings. The "As Seen on TV" OMI Original Fat Mop ($4.99) turned out to be pretty interesting. In our tests, it did in fact prove effective with chunky tomato sauce and pot-au-feu. Strictly speaking, however, the Fat Mop is not intended for use with large amounts of liquid. If we could have just one fat separator in the kitchen, Trudeau's version of the common pitcher type would be our choice. For another five bucks, though, the Fat Mop makes a useful supplement, especially if you have to remove fat from chunky stews and chilis. Between the two, neither the fat nor the process of removing it should be cause for anxiety.

Rating Fat Separators

WE TESTED EIGHT FAT SEPARATORS BY SIMMERING I GALLON OF CANNED LOW-SODIUM CHICKEN BROTH WITH 10 ounces of rendered chicken fat for 30 minutes. The stock was allowed to cool for 15 minutes prior to testing. Each of the fat separators was evaluated on its price, material, capacity, performance, handle comfort, and ease of use. The fat separators are listed in order of preference. See www.americastestkitchen.com for up-to-date prices and mail-order sources for top-rated products.

HIGHLY RECOMMENDED
Trudeau Gravy Separator with Integrated Strainer, Model 099-1105 $9.99
The clear-cut winner. Its wide, oblong shape makes it easy to pour into, the integrated strainer is a great feature, and an angled shield near the spout prevents spillovers. Reasonably priced, too.

RECOMMENDED
Pedrini Gravy Separator $14.95
This model has the largest capacity of all the contestants at 5 cups. Its very ergonomic handle was also praised by the testers.

RECOMMENDED
East Hampton Industries Souper Strain, No. 824 $5.69
The basic design of this separator is certainly function over form, but its performance was strong. Because the handle is not attached to the bottom of the cup, this separator was slightly unstable at full capacity.

RECOMMENDED
OMI (Oil Mop, Inc.) The Original Fat Mop $4.99
This tool was inefficient when defatting large quantities of liquid, but it worked like a champ on stews, sauces, and other chunky dishes. Does not clean easily, but at $4.99 a pop, it is inexpensive enough to replace periodically.

RECOMMENDED
East Hampton Industries Gravy Strain, No. 823 $2.49
Works as well as its big brother but lost some points because of its small capacity.

RECOMMENDED
Catamount Glass 2-Cup Fat Separator/Strainer $16.95
This model won points for its measurement lines that are printed in dark ink and are therefore very easy to read. Unfortunately, difficulty pouring and a lofty price tag hurt this separator in our rankings.

NOT RECOMMENDED
WMF Profi Plus I I-inch Stainless Steel Fat Skimming Ladle $19.99
Although it performed decently as a ladle-style skimmer, it required considerable steadiness and patience to defat the stock.

NOT RECOMMENDED
East Hampton Industries Skim It Fat Separator, No. 826B $4.99
Even considering its reasonable price, this separator performed poorly in most of the tests. It was difficult to dip into the liquid with enough precision to control the flow of fat, and the design only works with large volumes of liquid.

CHICKEN NOODLE SOUP

WHAT WE WANTED: A great chicken noodle soup with tender, flavorful vegetables and perfectly cooked noodles.

With homemade chicken stock on hand, making chicken noodle soup is a relatively easy proposition. Add some vegetables, herbs, and noodles and you've got a great bowl of soup. We did have several questions, though. Which vegetables are best added to this soup? Should the vegetables be sautéed first, or can diced vegetables simply be simmered in chicken stock? As for the pasta, which kind of noodles work best, and should they be cooked in the soup or in a separate pot of boiling water?

We tackled the vegetable issue first. We tested a wide range of vegetables, including onions, carrots, celery, leeks, potatoes, zucchini, tomatoes, and mushrooms. We concluded that the classic mirepoix ingredients (onions, carrots, and celery) should be part of a basic chicken noodle soup. Other vegetables are fine choices, but we concluded that they are more appropriate for variations. For instance, tomatoes and zucchini give chicken noodle soup an Italian character, and spring vegetables are a natural choice with delicate orzo.

To settle the issue of how to cook the vegetables, we prepared two batches of soup. For the first batch, we sautéed the onions, carrots, and celery in a little vegetable oil until softened and then added the chicken stock. For the second batch, we simply simmered the sliced vegetables in stock. We found that sautéing brought out flavors in the vegetables and made a big difference in the finished soup.

We saw a few recipes that suggested saving chicken fat skimmed from homemade stock and using this fat as a cooking medium for the vegetables. We tested this method and found that chicken fat does in fact add another level of chicken flavor to the soup. Although not essential, it makes sense to use chicken fat if you have planned ahead and saved the congealed fat skimmed from the surface of your stock.

In addition to the vegetables, we found the use of thyme and parsley brightened flavors. We added dried thyme along with the chicken stock so it would have time to soften and permeate the stock. To preserve its freshness, the parsley is best added just before serving.

The noodles were the last (and the most important) element that we needed to investigate. Although dried egg noodles are the most common choice, we ran across several recipes that suggest fresh or dried pasta. Before testing various noodles, we decided to clarify the issue of how to cook them. We simmered egg noodles in the soup as well as in a separate pot of salted water. The noodles cooked in the soup pot shed some starch that clouded the soup slightly but not horribly so. In contrast, noodles cooked in a separate pot and added to the finished soup left it completely clear.

The effect on the soup, however, paled in comparison to the effect on the noodles. Noodles cooked separately tasted bland and did not meld with the soup. The noodles cooked in the soup absorbed some of the chicken stock, giving them a rich, well-rounded flavor. We concluded that you must cook the noodles in the soup.

We identified five possible noodle choices—Pennsylvania Dutch dried egg noodles, dried linguine, dried spaghetti, fresh fettuccine, and fresh linguine. We cooked 2 ounces of each in a pot of chicken soup. Tasters preferred the egg noodles to either the fresh or dried pasta. These noodles cooked up very soft and yielding. They were tender to the bite and nearly melted in the mouth. In addition to their texture, tasters liked the ridged edges on these noodles, which provide nooks and crannies that can trap pieces of vegetable. (See the Tasting Lab on page 22 for brand recommendations.)

WHAT WE LEARNED: Sauté the onion, carrot, and celery in chicken fat (reserved from the stock) for maximum flavor. Cook the egg noodles right in the soup pot so they can absorb some chicken flavor.

CHICKEN NOODLE SOUP

Serves 6 to 8

Three components from the stock—chicken fat, strained stock, and shredded breast meat—are all used to make this soup, but each goes into the pot at a different point in the process.

2 tablespoons chicken fat (reserved from making stock) or vegetable oil
1 medium onion, cut into medium dice
1 large carrot, peeled and sliced ¼ inch thick
1 celery rib, sliced ¼ inch thick
½ teaspoon dried thyme
1 recipe Quick Chicken Stock for Soup (page 17), stock and meat separated
2 cups (3 ounces) wide egg noodles
¼ cup minced fresh parsley leaves
   Ground black pepper

1. Heat the chicken fat in a large stockpot or Dutch oven over medium-high heat. Add the onion, carrot, and celery and cook until softened, about 5 minutes. Add the thyme and stock and simmer until the vegetables are tender and the flavors meld, 10 to 15 minutes.

2. Add the noodles and shredded chicken and cook until just tender, 5 to 8 minutes. Stir in the parsley and pepper to taste, adjust the seasonings, and serve.

VARIATIONS

CHICKEN SOUP WITH ORZO AND SPRING VEGETABLES

Follow the recipe for Chicken Noodle Soup, replacing the onion with 1 medium leek, rinsed thoroughly, quartered lengthwise, then sliced thin crosswise. Substitute ½ cup orzo for the egg noodles. Along with the orzo, add ¼ pound asparagus, trimmed and cut into 1-inch lengths, and ¼ cup fresh or frozen peas. Substitute 2 tablespoons minced fresh tarragon leaves for the parsley.

CHICKEN SOUP WITH SHELLS, TOMATOES, AND ZUCCHINI

Follow the recipe for Chicken Noodle Soup, adding 1 medium zucchini, cut into medium dice, with the onion, carrot, and celery and increase the sautéing time to 7 minutes. Add ½ cup chopped tomatoes (fresh or canned) with the stock. Substitute 1 cup small shells or elbow macaroni for the egg noodles and simmer until the noodles are cooked, about 10 minutes. Substitute an equal portion of fresh basil for the parsley. Serve with grated Parmesan, if desired.

TASTING LAB: Egg Noodles

EGG NOODLES ARE NOT THE STARS OF THE PASTA WORLD. They lack the panache of penne, the sultriness of spaghetti, the rotundity of rotini. Yet they are essential in chicken noodle soup. Noodles that are mealy or pasty have no place in your cupboard.

Classic egg noodles are thick, wide ribbons of pasta that have a slightly higher fat content than other kinds of pasta because of their high percentage (up to 20 percent) of eggs. Their firm, sturdy texture is what makes them so appealing.

We chose eight widely available brands and tasted them plain (tossed in a small amount of canola oil to prevent clumping). We were looking for a clean, slightly buttery flavor and a firm yet yielding texture. The top two finishers were clearly superior to the rest of the pack. Problems with the rest of the field included excessive thickness, gumminess, off flavors, or no flavors (the only no-yolk brand in the testing fell victim to the last problem). In two cases, the flaws were serious enough to sink the noodles to the "not recommended" category.

The top choice, Light 'n Fluffy, was praised for its "clean, neutral" flavor and superior texture. Close behind was Black Forest Girl, a German brand found in the international aisle of some supermarkets (or by mail order from www.germandeli.com), and described by fans as "yummy" with a "wheaty" flavor and "firm" texture.

Rating Egg Noodles

FIFTEEN MEMBERS OF THE *COOK'S ILLUSTRATED* STAFF TASTED ALL OF THE EGG NOODLES, WHICH WERE BOILED, drained, and tossed with a tiny amount of canola oil to prevent clumping. The noodles are listed in order of preference based on their scores in this tasting. Brands are available in supermarkets.

HIGHLY RECOMMENDED
Light 'n Fluffy Wide Egg Noodles $1.95 for 12 ounces
This brand won fans with its "buttery" flavor and "firm, delicate" texture.

HIGHLY RECOMMENDED
Black Forest Girl Extra Broad Noodles $3.29 for 8.8 ounces
"Has bite, but is tender," wrote one fan of these expensive German noodles. Tasters were split on flavor; some praised its "clean, neutral" flavor, while others found it "bland."

RECOMMENDED
Streit's Wide Egg Noodles $1.59 for 12 ounces
This brand was praised for "good pasta flavor," though many found the texture "too thick and gummy."

RECOMMENDED
Manischewitz Wide Egg Noodles $1.49 for 12 ounces
"Your everyday noodle," wrote one taster. Both fans and detractors noted the "substantial egg flavor."

RECOMMENDED
Pennsylvania Dutch Homestyle Egg Noodles $1.39 for 16 ounces
Fans praised the "wheaty" flavor, though many found these noodles "slightly gummy."

RECOMMENDED
Mueller's Hearty Wide Egg Noodles $1.79 for 16 ounces
"Very neutral," wrote one taster of this popular supermarket brand, which many tasters found "familiar."

NOT RECOMMENDED
No Yolks Cholesterol Free Egg Noodle Substitute $2.05 for 12 ounces
Not surprisingly, there were few fans of this "substitute," which was deemed "too firm" by most tasters, who also lamented that there was "no egg flavor."

NOT RECOMMENDED
Goodman's Wide Egg Noodles $2.79 for 16 ounces
Tasters were put off by the texture of these "thick, gummy" noodles and their "stale" flavor.

PASTA E FAGIOLI

WHAT WE WANTED: A rich broth with perfectly cooked pasta and beans.

Pasta fazool, the Italian-American version of Italy's pasta e fagioli (pasta and bean soup) is hearty, thick, almost stew-like, and always orange-red in color from the presence of tomatoes. Each spoonful is laden with pasta and beans, and the soup is full of harmonious flavors, with no one taste standing out. The vegetables are cut small and used as accents to the pasta. Typically, in mediocre pasta fazool, the beans have no flavor, the pasta is mushy, the broth is too tomatoey, and the soup is bland. We wanted to make a pasta fazool that would make any Italian-American family proud.

We began by preparing a half dozen recipes, most of which followed a similar procedure. First the aromatics (vegetables and often some pork product) were sautéed in olive oil. Then the tomatoes and broth went into the pot, followed by the beans and, finally, the pasta. Almost all of these recipes produced bland soups with mushy pasta. The soup with the best flavor took more than four hours to prepare and used dried beans. Although the long hours at the stove paid off, the speed with which some other recipes came together was certainly appealing. So the challenge became clear. Could we make a really good soup using canned beans, a shortcut that would save hours of cooking time?

Many recipes for pasta e fagioli contain pancetta (unsmoked Italian bacon), while completely Americanized recipes call for regular bacon. The simplest recipes avoid the pork and use only olive oil. Our first test showed that even a small amount of a pork product added much flavor to the soup, so we sautéed 3 ounces of finely diced pancetta in 1 tablespoon olive oil. We served this batch to tasters alongside a version made with the same amount of bacon and oil. The pancetta gave the soup a subtler pork flavor, but tasters did not mind the stronger, smokier flavor of regular bacon. (Pancetta is preferred, but you can use either.)

Most Italian recipes use the same quartet of aromatic vegetables: onions, celery, carrots, and garlic. Tasters liked the onions, celery, and garlic but were divided over the sweetness of the carrots. We decided to omit carrots from the recipe.

In most recipes, the aromatics are sautéed, and then the pan is deglazed with either tomatoes or broth. For the tomatoes, we tried crushed, diced, and sauce. The crushed tomatoes and tomato sauce were overpowering, but the diced tomatoes worked well, helping to intensify the flavors of the aromatics. We also tested chicken broth, a close second to the tomatoes (we would add the broth later), and white wine, the latter simply turning the soup sour.

Cranberry beans, a beautiful pink-and-white-mottled variety, are popular in Italy but hard to find in this country. We tested two common substitutes, pinto beans and red kidney beans. Neither had the sweet, delicate flavor of a cranberry bean, so we tried cannellini beans, also known as white kidney beans. Tasters found these oval-shaped beans to be sweet and creamy and most like cranberry beans. Smaller white beans (navies and great Northerns) did not have quite enough heft for this soup but are certainly fine if that's what you have on hand.

Although a taste test (see page 27) revealed some good choices among canned beans, we wanted to find a way to boost their flavor. Our first thought was to add the beans to the tomato mixture, a step that might infuse them with the flavors of the pancetta, oil, and vegetables. We prepared two batches of soup—one with beans and broth added simultaneously and one with beans added to the tomatoes and cooked for 10 minutes prior to adding the broth. The results were black and white. The beans added to the tomato mixture adopted its flavors readily, easily beating out the bland beans added later in the recipe.

The makeup of the broth was also critical. Although chicken broth is standard in many recipes, tasters felt that the resulting pasta fazool tasted like chicken soup. We tried water instead of chicken stock, adding some Parmesan rind to boost flavor. This test was a success, but we went on to try a 60/40 combination of broth and water, retaining the cheese rind. This soup was the winner: good body, good flavor, and not too "chickeny."

For additional flavorings, we added oregano and red pepper flakes to the pot with the aromatic vegetables; tasters approved. Parsley is typically added at the end of cooking, and it took just one test to show that it brightened the flavor and color of the soup. The last flavor-enhancing idea—a long shot, perhaps—was a teaspoon of minced anchovy fillet. Tasters could not identify what was different about the batch with anchovy, but everyone agreed that it was more complex and fuller in flavor.

Our tests showed that pasta with relatively small shapes is best in this soup. Larger shapes, like elbows and shells, crowded out the other ingredients and soaked up too much broth. Tiny pasta, such as stars and pastina, was lost next to the more sizable beans and tomatoes.

WHAT WE LEARNED: Construct a flavorful base with pancetta, sautéed aromatic vegetables, oregano, pepper flakes, anchovies, and tomatoes. Cook canned beans directly in this mixture before adding chicken broth and water. Finish by cooking a small pasta shape right in the soup pot.

ITALIAN PASTA AND BEAN SOUP (PASTA E FAGIOLI)

Serves 8 to 10

This soup does not hold well because the pasta absorbs the liquid, becomes mushy, and leaves the soup dry. You can, however, make the soup in two stages. Once the beans are simmered with the tomatoes, before the broth and water are added, the mixture can be cooled and refrigerated for up to 3 days. When ready to complete the soup, discard the Parmesan rind (otherwise it will become stringy), add the liquid, bring the soup to a boil, and proceed with the recipe.

1	tablespoon extra-virgin olive oil, plus more for drizzling
3	ounces pancetta or bacon, chopped fine
1	medium onion, chopped fine
1	celery rib, chopped fine
4	medium garlic cloves, minced or pressed through a garlic press (about 1 heaping tablespoon)
1	teaspoon dried oregano
¼	teaspoon red pepper flakes
3	anchovy fillets, minced to a paste
1	(28-ounce) can diced tomatoes
1	piece Parmesan cheese rind, about 5 inches by 2 inches
2	(15.5-ounce) cans cannellini beans, drained and rinsed
3½	cups low-sodium chicken broth
2½	cups water
	Salt
8	ounces small pasta shape (see page 26)
¼	cup chopped fresh parsley leaves
	Ground black pepper
	Grated Parmesan cheese for the table

1. Heat the oil in a large heavy-bottomed stockpot or Dutch oven over medium-high heat until shimmering. Add the pancetta and cook, stirring occasionally, until it begins to brown, 3 to 5 minutes. Add the onion and celery and cook, stirring occasionally, until the vegetables are softened, 5 to 7 minutes. Add the garlic, oregano, red pepper flakes, and anchovies and cook, stirring constantly, until fragrant, about 1 minute. Add the tomatoes with their liquid, scraping up any browned bits from the pan bottom. Add the cheese rind and beans; bring to a boil, then reduce the heat to low and simmer to blend the flavors, 10 minutes. Add the chicken broth, water, and 1 teaspoon salt; increase the heat to high and bring to a boil. Add the pasta and cook until tender, about 10 minutes (refer to the package instructions to better estimate pasta cooking time).

2. Discard the cheese rind. Off the heat, stir in 3 tablespoons of the parsley; adjust the seasonings with salt and pepper to taste. Ladle the soup into individual bowls; drizzle each serving with olive oil and sprinkle with a portion of the remaining parsley. Serve immediately, passing the grated Parmesan separately.

VARIATION

ITALIAN PASTA AND BEAN SOUP WITH ORANGE AND FENNEL

Ditalini and orzo are especially good pasta shapes for this variation.

Trim 1 medium fennel bulb of its stalks and fronds; trim the bottom ½ inch. Halve the bulb lengthwise and, using a paring knife, remove the core. Slice the bulb lengthwise into ¼-inch-thick strips, then chop fine. Follow the recipe for Italian Pasta and Bean Soup, cooking the fennel along with the onion and celery and adding 2 teaspoons grated orange zest and ½ teaspoon fennel seeds along with the garlic, oregano, pepper flakes, and anchovies. Proceed as directed.

GETTING IT RIGHT: The Four Best Shapes for Pasta e Fagioli

Ditalini
These "little thimbles" are ½ inch square when cooked, about the same size as the beans and tomatoes. They create the chunkiest soup.

Tubetini
These "tiny tubes" are similar in shape to ditalini but not even half the size when cooked. The soup will have a more brothy appearance.

Conchigliette
These "small shells," the largest of the recommended pasta shapes, are close to ¾ inch square when cooked.

Orzo
This rice-shaped pasta cooks up thinner than the beans but has a similar shape and length, making the soup look a bit more refined.

TECHNIQUE: Freezing Small Portions of Soup

1. Set out a number of 10- to 12-ounce paper cups for hot beverages and fill each with a portion of cooled soup (but not all the way to the top). Label, wrap, and freeze each cup.

2. Whenever you want a quick cup of soup, remove as many servings as necessary from the freezer and microwave them until they're hot and ready to serve.

TASTING LAB: Canned White Beans

WE SAMPLED FOUR CANNED WHITE BEANS IN OUR SEARCH for the best beans for this soup. Because so few brands of canned cannellini beans (our favorite for this soup) are distributed nationwide, we broadened our taste test to include other white beans with widespread distribution. We tasted each contender twice: straight from the can (after being drained and rinsed) and prepared in our recipe for pasta e fagioli made without the pasta.

The tasting had two clear winners, one clear loser, and one brand with mixed comments from tasters. Westbrae great Northern beans had the best flavor and texture—described as "earthy" and "creamy" by our tasters—but they were a bit small for our soup recipe. Progresso cannellini beans were "plump" and "sweet" and were the perfect size for soup. Eden navy beans were small and broken and rejected by our tasters. Goya cannellini beans received mixed scores. Their flavor received high marks, but tasters were put off by their "weird" gray color and "tough" skins.

BEST CANNED WHITE BEANS
Westbrae organic great Northern beans (left) had great flavor but are a bit small for soup. Progresso cannellini beans (right) are excellent in soup (although their flavor is a bit less complex).

Chris watches Julia demonstrate the secrets to a quick cheese bread—the perfect accompaniment to our hearty lentil soup.

A SOUP supper

CHAPTER 3

Soup for supper is an appealing concept, especially on a cold, snowy night. But for soup to work as a main course, it better be hearty. A light, clear broth simply won't do.

Lentil soup fits the bill, but more often than not this soup is starchy, thick, and stodgy. It may be hearty, but who wants to eat more than a few spoonfuls let alone a big bowl? Our goal when developing this recipe was clear: create a vibrant lentil soup around which we could build a meal. It would be substantial and satisfying but not leaden.

We cannot live by soup alone. A salad might round out the meal, but we usually want some bread, and preferably something homemade. Since our lentil soup is a relatively straightforward affair, a complex yeast bread that takes all day to prepare doesn't feel like the right choice. Instead, we turned to a quick cheese bread, ready for the oven after just 15 minutes of work. This full-flavored bread is so good, you might want to skip the soup and have bread for dinner. Certainly not a balanced meal, but delicious nonetheless.

LENTIL SOUP

WHAT WE WANTED: Lentil soup is cheap to make, quick to make, and when properly prepared, tastes great—maybe even better—the next day. We wanted a hearty lentil soup worthy of a second bowl, not the tasteless variety we have so often encountered.

We started our testing process for lentil soup by preparing five representative recipes, and two discoveries came quickly to light. First, garlic, herbs, onions, and tomatoes are common denominators. Second, texture is a big issue. None of our tasters liked the soup that was brothy or, at the other extreme, the one that was as thick as porridge. They also gave a big thumbs down to those that looked like brown split pea soup. Consequently, recipes that included carrots, tomatoes, and herbs were lauded for their brighter colors (and flavors). There was also a clear preference for the subtle, smoky depth that meat provides. The next step was to determine which lentils to buy and how to cook them.

Brown, green, and red lentils are the most common choices on supermarket shelves. At specialty markets and natural food stores, you can also find black lentils and French green lentils (lentils du Puy), the latter being the darling of chefs everywhere. In addition to color differences, lentils can be divided according to their size—large or small—and to whether they are split, like peas, or not. Ordinary brown and green lentils are large, while red, black, and lentils du Puy are small. Red lentils are often sold split and are used most frequently in Indian dishes such as dal.

To make some sense of all of this, we made five pots of lentil soup, each one using a different color lentil. Red lentils were out; they disintegrated when simmered. All four of the remaining choices produced an acceptable texture, but tasters preferred, as expected, the earthy flavor and firm texture of the lentils du Puy. To our surprise, however, the larger green and brown lentils fared reasonably well,

exceeding the low expectations of the test kitchen.

Next, we set out to test cooking methods. Some lentils, especially the large brown and green varieties, have a greater tendency to fall apart if overcooked, even for just a few minutes. Searching for a way to avoid this problem, we employed a common Indian culinary trick: sweating the lentils in a covered pan with aromatic vegetables prior to adding the liquid. Using brown lentils, we cooked up two batches and, bingo, we had solved the problem! The sweated lentils remained intact, while the unsweated lentils had broken down.

To better understand this phenomenon, we set up a series of tests. We sweated one batch of lentils with just onions and carrots. In the second batch we added salt, and in the third batch we added vinegar to test the role of acids. The results were clear. The first batch—without any salt or acid—was the worst, with a very mushy texture. The lentils sweated with salt were the most intact, while the vinegar helped keep the lentils firm but it was not as effective as the salt (at least in amounts that would taste good). So why did we get these results? When legumes are cooked, their pectin breaks down into a gelatinous goo, similar to jam. Salt and acids (such as those found in canned tomatoes or vinegar) reinforce the original insoluble pectin and retard its conversion to gel. Sweating the lentils with bacon, canned tomatoes, and salt (as well as aromatic vegetables and herbs) not only ensured an ideal texture but boosted the flavor of the legumes as well.

One issue concerning texture remained. Tasters wanted a chunkier soup and did not like the brothy base. We tried pureeing a few cups of the soup and then adding it back to the pot. Tasters praised the contrast of the now creamy base with the whole lentils and found the entire soup more interesting.

Pork was the meat of choice in all of the recipes we examined. We found that the lentils cooked too quickly to absorb the smoky flavor that a ham bone or hock can impart. Prosciutto and pancetta were too mild. Tasters preferred the smoky flavor of bacon and liked the textural addition of the bacon bits. Another advantage bacon offered was rendered fat. We used it to sauté the vegetables and aromatics, which further infused the soup with smoky flavor. Bay leaves, thyme, and parsley rounded out the other flavors and added a touch of bright green to the pot.

Last, but not least, was the question of liquids. We prepared two batches, one with water and one with chicken broth. Neither was ideal. Water produced a soup that was not as rich in flavor as desired, while the broth-only version tasted too much like chicken soup. After several more tests, we concluded that a mix of 3 parts broth to 1 part water produced a hearty depth of flavor without being overpowering.

Many recipes call for the addition of vinegar or lemon juice just before the soup is served. We stirred a touch of balsamic vinegar into the pot at completion, and tasters gave this soup a perfect 10.

With our recipe complete, we developed a few variations. Stirring a hefty amount of spinach into the pot at the end of cooking created a popular version: lentil soup with greens. For a spicier and more exotic rendition, we added some of the aromatic spices used in North African cooking—cumin, coriander, cinnamon, and cayenne—and substituted cilantro for the parsley and lemon juice for the vinegar.

WHAT WE LEARNED: Almost any lentil (other than red lentils) can be used to make soup. To keep the lentils from losing their shape as they cook, sweat them with the sautéed aromatic vegetables, bacon, and tomatoes before adding the liquid to the soup pot. Lentil soup needs plenty of acidity, so use white wine as part of the broth and finish the soup with balsamic vinegar.

HEARTY LENTIL SOUP

Serves 4 to 6

Lentils du Puy, sometimes called French green lentils, are our first choice for this recipe, but brown, black, or regular green lentils are fine, too. Note that cooking times will vary depending on the type of lentils used. Lentils lose flavor with age, and because most packaged lentils do not have expiration dates, try to buy them from a store that specializes in natural foods and grains. Before use, rinse and then carefully sort through the lentils to remove any small stones.

3   ounces (3 slices) bacon, cut into ¼-inch pieces
1   large onion, chopped fine
2   medium carrots, peeled and chopped medium
3   medium garlic cloves, minced or pressed
    through a garlic press (about 1 tablespoon)
1   (14.5-ounce) can diced tomatoes, drained
1   bay leaf
1   teaspoon minced fresh thyme leaves
1   cup (7 ounces) lentils, rinsed and picked over
1   teaspoon salt
    Ground black pepper
½   cup dry white wine
4½ cups low-sodium chicken broth
1½ cups water
1½ teaspoons balsamic vinegar
3   tablespoons minced fresh parsley leaves

1. Fry the bacon in a large stockpot or Dutch oven over medium-high heat, stirring occasionally, until the fat is rendered and the bacon is crisp, 3 to 4 minutes. Add the onion and carrots; cook, stirring occasionally, until the vegetables begin to soften, about 2 minutes. Add the garlic and cook until fragrant, about 30 seconds. Stir in the tomatoes, bay leaf, and thyme; cook until fragrant, about 30 seconds. Stir in the lentils, salt, and pepper to taste; cover, reduce the heat to medium-low, and cook until the vegetables are softened and the lentils have darkened, 8 to 10 minutes.

2. Uncover, increase the heat to high, add the wine, and bring to a simmer. Add the chicken broth and water; bring to a boil, cover partially, and reduce the heat to low. Simmer until the lentils are tender but still hold their shape, 30 to 35 minutes; discard the bay leaf.

3. Puree 3 cups of the soup in a blender until smooth, then return to the pot. Stir in the vinegar and heat the soup over medium-low until hot, about 5 minutes. Stir in 2 tablespoons of the parsley and serve, garnishing each bowl with some of the remaining parsley. (The soup can be made up to 2 days in advance. After adding the vinegar in step 3, cool the soup to room temperature and refrigerate it in an airtight container. To serve, heat it over medium-low until hot, then stir in the parsley.)

VARIATIONS

HEARTY LENTIL SOUP WITH SPINACH

Follow the recipe for Hearty Lentil Soup, replacing the parsley with 5 ounces baby spinach. Continue to heat the soup, stirring frequently, until the spinach is wilted, about 3 minutes; serve.

GETTING IT RIGHT:
A Good Sweat Makes a Difference

Firm Lentils   Mushy Lentils

Sweating the lentils with salt and an acidic component (from the canned tomatoes) retards the conversion of pectin-like compounds to a gel. Once sweated, these lentils easily remain intact during a long simmer in broth (left) while becoming tender on the inside. Lentils simmered without first being sweated fall apart (right) if overcooked.

HEARTY LENTIL SOUP WITH FRAGRANT SPICES

Follow the recipe for Hearty Lentil Soup, adding 1 teaspoon ground cumin, 1 teaspoon ground coriander, 1 teaspoon ground cinnamon, and ¼ teaspoon cayenne along with the garlic; substitute lemon juice for the balsamic vinegar and minced fresh cilantro leaves for the parsley.

TASTING LAB: Lentils

LENTILS COME IN VARIOUS SIZES AND COLORS, AND the differences in flavor and texture are surprisingly distinct. Tasters evaluated five kinds of lentils in our soup, rating them in terms of taste, texture, and appearance. Here's what we found, with the lentils listed in order of preference.

Lentils du Puy

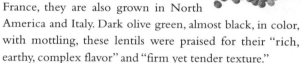

These green lentils are smaller in size than the more common brown and green varieties. While they take their name from the city of Puy in central France, they are also grown in North America and Italy. Dark olive green, almost black, in color, with mottling, these lentils were praised for their "rich, earthy, complex flavor" and "firm yet tender texture."

Black Lentils

Like lentils du Puy, black lentils are slightly smaller than the standard brown lentils. They have a deep black hue that tasters likened to the color of caviar. In fact, some markets refer to them as beluga lentils. Tasters liked their "robust, earthy flavor" and "ability to hold their shape while remaining tender." A few tasters found the color of the soup made with them "too dark and muddy."

Brown Lentils

These larger lentils are the most common choice in the marketplace and are a uniform drab brown. Tasters commented on their "mild yet light and earthy flavor." Some found their texture was "creamy," while others complained that they were "chalky." But everyone agreed that they held their shape and were tender inside.

Green Lentils

Another larger lentil, this variety is the same size as the brown lentil and is greenish-brown in color. Although tasters accepted the "mild flavor" of these lentils and liked the way they "retain their shape while being tender," most complained that the soup made from them looked unappealing.

Red Lentils

These small orange-red lentils "completely disintegrate when cooked." They made a soup that looked "anemic."

EQUIPMENT CORNER:
Vegetable Peelers

THE OXO GOOD GRIPS PEELER HAS BEEN A STANDARD IN our test kitchen since our 1998 rating of vegetable peelers. But two new peelers—the Oxo I-Series and Messermeister serrated—recently led us back into the kitchen for another look. We tested these peelers on thin-skinned fruits and vegetables, tough-skinned squash, and craggy root vegetables. They were evaluated on sharpness, maneuverability, comfort, and the downward pressure required to peel.

Oxo's new I-Series line offers a completely redesigned vegetable peeler that we found to be exceptionally sharp. In addition to its new feature—replaceable blades—the I-Series peeler (which costs about $10) also dons a sleek, more slender handle—something the Good Grips model lacks. And tipping the scale at nearly a quarter pound (3.75 ounces), we liked the heft of the I-series, compared with the lighter Good Grips (which weighs only 2.25 ounces). It may sound like a picky difference, but testers felt that the balance of extra weight on the I-Series falls to the blade end, making it seem like the peeler does some of the work for you. After extensive use, we recognized the likelihood that the I-Series might cause some hand strain; however, you would have to peel a lot of potatoes to notice.

The Messermeister serrated blade peeler ($5.50) looks a bit like the Oxo Good Grip peeler, except for the zigzag blades. We were surprised that this peeler—which we took for a novelty—could rival and even replace a Good Grips at the usual peeling tasks. And what makes this peeler exceptional is its ability to peel ripe peaches and tomatoes—a difficult task, even for the noticeably sharper I-Series peeler. The only problem with the Messermeister is its narrow 2¾-inch diameter black rubber handle. Testers complained of difficulties getting a good grip. For most peeling chores, including potatoes and apples, we prefer the Oxo I-Series, but we recommend keeping the Messermeister on hand just to deal with peaches and tomatoes.

In addition to these basic peelers, we've noticed that several companies are now making julienne peelers. A skilled chef with a sharp knife can turn a carrot into a pile of perfect julienne (pieces that measure ⅛-inch square by 2 to 3 inches in length) in minutes. The rest of us, however, might need a little assistance. Julienne peelers promise to help you "julienne your way to restaurant-style presentations" and "add authenticity to Asian dishes."

Shaped like a Y-peeler, julienne peelers have one flat blade and one blade set with a row of tiny metal teeth. When you run the blades over the surface of the food, the flat blade removes a strip of food and the teeth cut it into perfectly squared strips—in theory.

Unfortunately, most of the peelers we tested shredded rather than julienned, and the resulting shreds were nowhere near the elongated square shape of a proper julienne. Also, the jagged blades were often bent out of alignment, making the tool little more than a crude, hand-held juicer. The one exception was the Oxo Good Grips Julienne Peeler ($6.99). This peeler could produce perfectly squared slices of carrot and zucchini with no trouble and could even julienne blocks of firm cheddar. This model also offers a cover for the nasty little protruding blades. Should the small blades come out of alignment, they can be bent back into shape rather easily. If your knife skills are not up to julienning vegetables, this peeler is a good addition to your kitchen.

BEST PEELERS
The sleek-handled Oxo I-Series peeler (left) is our favorite all-purpose peeler. The Messermeister peeler (center) works great on delicate fruit, but the handle is less than ideal. Save this model for tomatoes and peaches. And for julienning vegetables, we recommend the Oxo Good Grips Julienne Peeler (right). See www.americastestkitchen.com for up-to-date prices and mail-order sources for these top-rated products.

TASTING LAB: Mail-Order Bacon

TO FIND OUT IF PREMIUM BACON REALLY TASTES BETTER than our supermarket favorite, Farmland, we cooked up six popular smokehouse brands and summoned our tasters.

First a little on how bacon is made. All bacon starts with a pork belly. The spare ribs are removed from the belly's interior, the skin is taken off the exterior, and the remaining slab is trimmed.

The next step is curing, which is generally done in one of two ways. Many small producers of artisan (aka smokehouse or premium) bacon choose to dry-cure by rubbing the slab with a dry mixture of seasonings (which always includes salt and sugar). Large producers usually inject the slabs with a liquid brine containing salt, sugar, and sometimes liquid smoke for flavor; sodium phosphate for moisture retention during processing and cooking; ascorbate or sodium erythorbate to accelerate the curing process and promote color retention; and a curing salt that includes sodium nitrite to stave off bacteria and set flavor and color characteristics. (Are you still hungry for supermarket bacon?) Once the cure has been applied or injected, the slabs are hung. If a dry cure has been applied, this process could stretch up to one week. Curing with an injected brine can be completed in a mere one to three hours and so is quite cost-efficient.

The final step is thermal processing—which can take as few as four to five hours or as many as 24, depending on the processor. During thermal processing, the cured pork bellies are smoked and partially cooked to an internal temperature of roughly 130 degrees, after which they finally merit the term bacon. The bacon is chilled to approximately 24 degrees, pressed to square it off for uniform slicing, sliced to the processor's specifications, and packaged. A package of regular-cut bacon usually contains between 18 and 22 slices, 1/16 inch thick, per pound, whereas a package of thick-cut bacon, sometimes called country style, contains 12 to 16 slices, 1/8 inch thick, per pound.

So how did our six expensive mail-order brands do against Farmland, our favorite supermarket bacon? Although every one of these premium bacons outscored Farmland, in some cases the differences in scores were minimal. Several premium bacons had strong flavor characteristics, erring on the side of salty or smoky or sweet, which overwhelmed tasters who were looking for meaty flavor and balance, just as they had with the supermarket brands. That said, the top finisher, Niman Ranch, was a hands-down winner over Farmland. So premium bacons are better than the best supermarket bacon. But they're also much more expensive. Be prepared to pay up to 250 percent more for the experience and shop carefully to make sure that extra money is well spent.

Rating Mail-Order Bacons

TWENTY-FOUR MEMBERS OF THE *COOK'S ILLUSTRATED* STAFF TASTED ALL OF THE BACONS, WHICH WERE COOKED TO the same degree of doneness. The bacons are listed in order of preference based on their scores in this tasting. For up-to-date prices and mail-order information on these products, see www.americastestkitchen.com.

HIGHLY RECOMMENDED
Niman Ranch Dry Cured Center Cut Bacon
Oakland, California
$8 for 12 ounces
Tasters found this bacon hearty, rich, balanced, and smoky. One taster said, "Yum . . . what bacon should be."

RECOMMENDED
New Braunfels Smokehouse Comal County Smoked Sliced Bacon
New Braunfels, Texas
$8.25 for 1 pound
This was deemed overly smoky by many tasters, though one said, "Has all the right elements. I could eat a lot of this one."

RECOMMENDED
Burgers' Smokehouse Sliced Country Bacon, Sugar Cured and Hickory Smoked
California, Missouri
$18.95 for 2 pounds
This bacon was characterized by many as too salty and lacking in deep meaty flavor.

RECOMMENDED
Nodine's Smokehouse Apple Bacon
Torrington, Connecticut
$5.50 for 1 pound
Over and over, tasters commented on the sweetness of this bacon, using adjectives such as "caramelized," "candy-sweet," and "mapley."

RECOMMENDED
Nueske's Smoked Bacon
Wittenberg, Wisconsin
$19.95 for 2 pounds
Nearly every taster zeroed in on this bacon's strong smoky character, with comments such as "whoa, smoky!," "crazy-smoky," "carbon-like," and "tastes like a campfire."

RECOMMENDED
Edwards Virginia Bacon, Hickory-Smoked, Country Style, Dry Cured
Surry, Virginia
$4 for 12 ounces
"Too salty," "way salty," "very salty," "overpowering salt," "salty like Ruffles potato chips." Get the picture?

QUICK CHEESE BREAD

WHAT WE WANTED: A moist, hearty quick bread with bits of cheese tossed throughout, plus a cheesy crust.

Cheese bread sounds like a great idea, a pairing of two of America's favorite foods. Unlike pizza, wherein bread dough is merely topped with cheese, a true cheese bread involves a more intimate relationship, going well beyond the quick blind date in which the two ingredients are merely thrown together and then heated. Good cheese bread displays a subtle balance of flavor and texture, neither party getting the upper hand. But most of the recipes we tested offered the worst of both worlds: dry bread and no cheese flavor.

Our first step was to create a working recipe that consisted of 3 cups flour, 1 tablespoon baking powder, 6 tablespoons melted butter, 2 cups milk, and 1 egg. For the cheese, we chose shredded cheddar, the most frequently used type in our stack of research recipes. Our working recipe had lots of problems, but we could now test every variable.

First, we tinkered with the amount of butter. Starting with 6 tablespoons, we worked our way down to a mere 3, putting an end to the slick hands and lips we'd been

experiencing after eating a piece of the bread. Less fat also pushed the bread away from the texture of a delicate cake and toward that of a hearty muffin. The single egg we'd been using turned out to be just right.

Because we wanted a rich loaf, similar to a good banana bread, we replaced a portion of the milk in each of two breads with scoops of yogurt and sour cream, respectively. Given that this was cheese bread, it also seemed logical to try cottage cheese, cream cheese, goat cheese, and ricotta. In the end, most tasters chose the sour cream–based bread. It was rich and moist without being greasy. The sour cream also added a nip of tartness to the bread, offsetting the richness of the cheese without overpowering it.

Test results showed that small chunks of cheese, not shreds, were best, as they melted into luscious, cheesy pockets. In terms of the cheese itself, we tested five readily available types: extra-sharp cheddar, Muenster, Asiago, Gruyère, and Monterey Jack. Cheddar and Asiago were the leaders of the pack, with Muenster and Monterey Jack being too mild and Gruyère too pungent (although we liked this last cheese in a variation that also included bacon). We quickly determined that excess cheese weighed down the bread, causing it to collapse into itself. With a modest 4 ounces of cheese, the bread had plenty of flavor but still rose to its full potential.

We had arrived at the top crust. We wanted rich flavor and color. The solution was a topping of shredded Parmesan. We then decided to coat the bottom of the pan with cheese as well, thus doubling the cheesy exterior. Nutty and salty, every bite was packed with flavor. The Parmesan also turned the crust a deep bronze color.

WHAT WE LEARNED: Sour cream adds richness and flavor to this bread, and whole milk is the best choice for the liquid ingredient. Small chunks of cheese melt into luscious cheesy pockets. For a crust with great flavor and crunch, sprinkle the loaf pan as well as the batter with Parmesan.

QUICK CHEESE BREAD

Makes one 9 by 5-inch loaf

If using Asiago, choose a mild supermarket cheese that yields to pressure when pressed. Aged Asiago that is as firm as Parmesan is too sharp and piquant for this bread. If, when testing the bread for doneness, the toothpick comes out with what looks like uncooked batter clinging to it, try again in a different—but still central—spot; if the toothpick hits a pocket of cheese, it may give a false indication.

3	ounces Parmesan cheese, shredded on the large holes of box grater (about 1 cup)
3	cups (15 ounces) unbleached all-purpose flour
1	tablespoon baking powder
¼	teaspoon cayenne
1	teaspoon salt
⅛	teaspoon ground black pepper
4	ounces extra-sharp cheddar cheese, cut into ½-inch cubes, or mild Asiago, crumbled into ¼- to ½-inch pieces (about 1 cup)
1¼	cups whole milk
3	tablespoons unsalted butter, melted
1	large egg, beaten lightly
¾	cup sour cream

1. Adjust an oven rack to the middle position and heat the oven to 350 degrees. Spray a 9 by 5-inch loaf pan with non-stick cooking spray, then sprinkle ½ cup of the Parmesan evenly over the bottom of the pan.

2. In a large bowl, whisk the flour, baking powder, cayenne, salt, and pepper to combine. Using a rubber spatula, mix in the cheddar, breaking up clumps. In a medium bowl, whisk together the milk, melted butter, egg, and sour cream. Using a rubber spatula, gently fold the wet ingredients into the dry ingredients until just combined (the batter will be heavy and thick). Do not overmix. Scrape the batter into the prepared loaf pan; level the surface with a rubber spatula. Sprinkle the remaining ½ cup Parmesan evenly over the surface.

3. Bake until deep golden brown and a toothpick inserted into the center of the loaf comes out clean, 45 to 50 minutes. Cool in the pan on a wire rack 5 minutes; invert the loaf onto the rack, turn right-side up, and continue to cool until warm, about 45 minutes. Cut into slices and serve.

VARIATION

QUICK CHEESE BREAD WITH BACON, ONION, AND GRUYÈRE

1. Cut 5 ounces (5 slices) bacon into ½-inch pieces and fry in a medium nonstick skillet over medium heat, stirring occasionally, until crisp, about 8 minutes. Using a slotted spoon, transfer the bacon to a paper towel–lined plate and pour off all but 3 tablespoons fat from the skillet. Add ½ cup minced onion to the skillet and cook, stirring frequently, until softened, about 3 minutes; set skillet with onion aside.

2. Follow recipe for Quick Cheese Bread, substituting Gruyère for cheddar, adding the bacon and onion to the flour mixture along with the cheese, and omitting the butter.

Q & A

What's the best way to wrap quick breads before freezing them?

Wrap the cooled loaf tightly with a double layer of aluminum foil and then place it in a large, plastic zipper-lock bag. When protected this way, the loaf will keep for several months in the freezer. When you're ready to serve the bread, remove it from the freezer, slip the foil-wrapped bread out of the bag, place it on the center rack of a 375-degree oven, and bake until the loaf yields under gentle pressure, 10 to 15 minutes. Remove the foil (watch out for steam) and return the loaf to the oven for a few minutes to crisp the crust. Cool the bread on a rack for 15 minutes to make slicing easier.

Bridget serves up a taste of Louisiana in a big bowl.

REGIONAL *classics*

On occasion local dishes become so popular that they transcend their region. Gumbo is a taste of Louisiana in a big old bowl. Its distinct aroma and flavor are like a quick trip to the bayous outside of New Orleans. Gumbo is Louisiana and Louisiana is gumbo.

The history of Cincinnati chili dates back almost a century to an Ohio diner. This dish combines Middle Eastern spices with homespun Midwestern cooking to create an American original, served with buttered spaghetti, kidney beans, cheddar cheese, and chopped onions.

Our goal when developing our versions of these dishes was to remain faithful to originals while making the recipes approachable for cooks who may not have grown up with them. Regional classics must remain authentic, or they lose their distinct personality. But if the dishes require hard-to-find ingredients or difficult techniques, no one will make them. We've balanced authenticity with practicality in our renditions of these regional classics.

GUMBO

WHAT WE WANTED: A true Louisiana gumbo with a rich, thick sauce studded with shrimp and sausage.

Gumbo usually includes some combination of seafood, poultry, or small game along with sausage or some other highly seasoned, cured smoked pork. Also present is the Creole and Cajun "holy trinity" of onion, bell pepper, and celery. Quite often, gumbos are thickened with okra or ground dried sassafras leaves, known as filé (pronounced fee-LAY) powder. Last, but very important, most gumbos are flavored with a dark brown roux. For us, this roux is the heart of a good gumbo.

In classic French cooking, a roux is nothing more than flour cooked gently in some type of fat to form a paste that is used to thicken sauces. If the flour is just barely cooked, you have a white roux; if cooked to a light beige, you have a blond roux. When it reaches the color of light brown sugar, you have brown roux. Creole and Cajun cooks push this process to the outer limit. When they make roux, they keep cooking until the flour reaches a shade of very dark brown, sometimes just short of black. This breaks down the starches in the flour to the point where the roux offers relatively little thickening power. Instead, it imbues gumbo with a complex, toasty, smoky flavor and a deep, rich brown color that define the dish. The problem is that the flour can burn very easily, and the only safeguards against that are relatively low heat and constant stirring.

Most of the recipes we saw called for cooking the roux over low heat while stirring constantly for anywhere from 40 to 60 minutes. Since the roux truly does need to be stirred constantly as it cooks to avoid burning the flour, which will give the mixture a noticeable bitter taste, time was the first issue we had to tackle. We decided on 20 minutes as our limit for stirring. Any longer than that, we reasoned, and most cooks would probably skip over this dish.

To hit that 20-minute mark, we knew we'd have to increase the heat and probably preheat the oil before adding the flour. We also thought we'd try a microwave roux, instructions for which we'd seen along the way. For our testing, we began with the widely used 1:1 ratio of all-purpose flour to vegetable oil, using ½ cup of each.

Some cooks recommend heating the oil until it smokes and then cooking the roux over high heat. Though this method produced a very dark roux, about the color of bittersweet chocolate, in less than 10 minutes there was too much sizzle and smoke. The process felt out of control, and the specter of burnt roux loomed large.

We slowed things down a bit, preheating the oil over medium-high heat for two minutes (to well below the smoke point) before adding the flour, then lowering the heat to medium to cook the roux. At the 20-minute stopping point, the roux had cooked to a deep reddish brown, about the color of a shelled pecan or a dirty penny. It had started to smoke once or twice, but it cooled fairly quickly when we removed it from the heat, stirred it for a minute, then returned it to the burner. In all, the process was much less nerve-wracking than the high-heat methods we had tried, and it yielded absolutely acceptable results. Unfortunately, though, another problem popped up. We began to have trouble incorporating the simmering stock into the roux. The roux and stock generally would mix smoothly, but sometimes they wouldn't, and the result was little globs of brown flour floating in a layer of oil at the surface. Nonetheless, we pressed on with our testing of the roux.

We tried different ratios of fat to flour, varying them by as much as 6 tablespoons up and down from the ½-cup starting point, but none improved on the original 1:1 ratio in terms of either taste or performance. Switching the all-purpose flour from a high-protein, unbleached Northern brand to a slightly lower-protein, bleached national brand improved the texture of the gumbo slightly, making it a little smoother and more satiny. The gumbo's consistency also benefited from a thorough skimming of the foam from the surface of the liquid, both just after it had come to a boil and throughout the simmering time.

The microwave roux had seemed vaguely promising until the day we turned the test kitchen into a scene from a *Lethal Weapon* movie by putting a superheated, microwave-safe bowl with its smoking hot contents down on a damp counter. The bowl did not merely shatter; it exploded, literally raining glass shards and globs of fiery hot roux into every corner of the room. We were very lucky that no one was hurt and, sure enough, a quick call to the test kitchens at Corning Consumer Products confirmed that they do not recommend heating oil in any Pyrex product for 10 minutes on high in the microwave.

Throughout the roux testing, the occasional separation of the flour and oil upon the addition of simmering liquid continued to perplex us. All along, we had followed the instructions in most of the recipes we'd studied to add simmering stock, which is about 200 degrees, to a hot roux-vegetable mixture, also about 200 degrees.

But there is another, if less popular, school of thought. Legendary New Orleans restaurateur Leah Chase advises cooling either the roux or the stock before combining them. Sure enough, cooling the stock (which took less time than cooling the roux) did the trick. Room-temperature stock, at about 75 degrees, mixed into the hot roux beautifully; stock at about 150 degrees also mixed in very well and was only slightly less smooth than its cooler counterpart. In terms of the timing in the recipe, then, we decided to make a concentrated shrimp stock and cool it rapidly by adding ice water rather than making the full amount and allowing it to cool at its own slow pace. This quick-cooling technique brought the stock to about 110 degrees within minutes, and the gumbo made with this concentrated, then diluted, stock easily passed muster with tasters.

The rest of the recipe development process focused on testing the wide range of ingredients and flavorings we encountered on our trip and in our research. First, we experimented with the liquid. Our testing thus far had been done with a simple shrimp stock made by simmering the shells in water. We tried boiling the shells in chicken stock instead of water, combining equal parts shrimp and chicken stock, adding bottled clam juice to the shrimp stock, and adding small amounts of white wine and beer to the gumbo. The clam juice did the trick, adding a depth of flavor that supplemented the 20-minute roux.

Two big flavoring questions concerned tomatoes—some say that gumbo just isn't gumbo without them—and garlic. Well, our tasters said that gumbo was just fine without tomatoes, but they gave the thumbs up to garlic, six cloves of it, in fact. We tried what seemed like a hundred seasoning variations and finally settled on a simple combination of dried thyme and bay leaves. Our experiments with different proportions of onion, bell pepper, and celery in the holy trinity notwithstanding, the classic ratio of 1 part celery to 2 parts pepper to 4 parts onion tasted best. We did, however, switch from the traditional green bell pepper to red peppers, preferring their sweeter, fuller flavor.

The gumbos we tasted in Louisiana were only subtly spicy, with the pepper heat very much in the background. You want to feel a slight heat in the back of your throat after you've swallowed a couple of spoonfuls. A mere ½ teaspoon of cayenne did the trick for our tasters, all of whom favored the powder over the vinegary taste of bottled hot sauce.

Last, we considered whether to thicken the gumbo with okra or filé powder. We think both are probably acquired tastes. Thus far, everyone had been satisfied without either, and because both added distinct—and to some, unwelcome—flavors, we decided to reserve them for the variations on our master recipe.

WHAT WE LEARNED: Make the roux over medium-high heat with an equal mixture of vegetable oil and flour. Cook the roux, stirring constantly, for about 20 minutes or until the color is dark reddish brown. To keep the gumbo silky smooth, add lukewarm stock (made with bottled clam juice and shrimp shells) to the hot roux. Finally, okra and filé powder are traditional but optional ingredients.

CREOLE-STYLE SHRIMP AND SAUSAGE GUMBO

Serves 6 to 8

Making a dark roux can be dangerous. The mixture reaches temperatures in excess of 400 degrees. Therefore, use a deep pot for cooking the roux and long-handled utensils for stirring it and be careful not to splash it on yourself. One secret to smooth gumbo is adding shrimp stock that is neither too hot nor too cold to the roux. For a stock that is at the right temperature when the roux is done, start preparing it before you tend to the vegetables and other ingredients, strain it, and then give it a head start on cooling by immediately adding ice water and clam juice. So that your constant stirring of the roux will not be interrupted, start the roux only after you've made the stock. Alternatively, you can make the stock well ahead of time and bring it back to room temperature before using it. Spicy andouille sausage is a Louisiana specialty that may not be available everywhere; kielbasa or any fully cooked smoked sausage makes a fine substitute. Gumbo is traditionally served over white rice.

1½	pounds small shrimp (51 to 60 per pound), shells removed and reserved
1	cup clam juice
3½	cups ice water
½	cup vegetable oil
½	cup all-purpose flour, preferably bleached
2	medium onions, chopped fine
1	medium red bell pepper, stemmed, seeded, and chopped fine
1	medium celery rib, chopped fine
6	medium garlic cloves, minced or pressed through a garlic press (about 2 tablespoons)
1	teaspoon dried thyme
	Salt
¼	teaspoon cayenne
2	bay leaves
1	pound smoked sausage, such as andouille or kielbasa, sliced ¼ inch thick
½	cup minced fresh parsley leaves
4	medium scallions, white and green parts, sliced thin
	Ground black pepper

1. Bring the reserved shrimp shells and 4½ cups water to a boil in a stockpot or large saucepan over medium-high heat. Reduce the heat to medium-low and simmer for 20 minutes. Strain the stock and add the clam juice and ice water (you should have about 2 quarts of tepid stock, 100 to 110 degrees); discard the shells. Set the stock aside.

2. Heat the oil in a Dutch oven or large, heavy-bottomed saucepan over medium-high heat until it registers 200 degrees on an instant-read thermometer, 1½ to 2 minutes. Reduce the heat to medium and gradually stir in the flour with a wooden spatula or spoon, making sure to work out any lumps that may form. Continue stirring constantly, reaching into the corners of the pan, until the mixture has a toasty aroma and is deep reddish brown, about the color of an old copper penny or between the colors of milk chocolate and dark chocolate, about 20 minutes. (The roux will thin as it cooks; if it begins to smoke, remove the pan from the heat and stir the roux constantly to cool slightly.)

3. Add the onions, bell pepper, celery, garlic, thyme, 1 teaspoon salt, and cayenne to the roux and cook, stirring frequently, until the vegetables soften, 8 to 10 minutes. Add 1 quart of the reserved stock in a slow, steady stream while stirring vigorously. Stir in the remaining quart of stock. Increase the heat to high and bring to a boil. Reduce the heat to medium-low, skim the foam from the surface, add the bay leaves, and simmer, uncovered, skimming the foam as it rises to the surface, about 30 minutes. (The mixture can be covered and set aside for several hours. Reheat when ready to proceed.)

4. Stir in the sausage and continue simmering to blend the flavors, about 30 minutes. Stir in the shrimp and simmer until cooked through, about 5 minutes. Off the heat, stir in the parsley and scallions and season with salt, ground black pepper, and cayenne to taste. Serve immediately.

VARIATIONS

SHRIMP AND SAUSAGE GUMBO WITH OKRA

Fresh okra may be used in place of frozen, though it tends to be more slippery, a quality that diminishes with increased cooking. Substitute an equal amount of fresh okra for frozen; trim the caps, slice the pods ¼ inch thick, and increase the sautéing time with the onion, bell pepper, and celery to 10 to 15 minutes.

Follow the recipe for Creole-Style Shrimp and Sausage Gumbo, adding 10 ounces thawed frozen cut okra to the roux along with the onions, bell pepper, and celery. Proceed as directed.

SHRIMP AND SAUSAGE GUMBO WITH FILÉ

Follow the recipe for Creole-Style Shrimp and Sausage Gumbo, adding 1½ teaspoons filé powder along with the parsley and scallions after the gumbo has been removed from the heat. Let rest until slightly thickened, about 5 minutes. Adjust the seasonings and serve.

Q&A

What's the best way to buy shrimp?

Even the most basic market now sells several kinds of shrimp. We cooked more than 100 pounds to find out just what to look for (and avoid) at the supermarket.

Should you buy fresh or frozen? Because nearly all shrimp are frozen at sea, you have no way of knowing when those "fresh" shrimp in the fish case were thawed (unless you are on very personal terms with your fishmonger). We found that the flavor and texture of thawed shrimp deteriorate after a few days, so you're better off buying frozen.

Should you buy peeled or unpeeled? If you think you can dodge some work by buying frozen shrimp that have been peeled, think again. Someone had to thaw those shrimp in order to remove their peel, and the shrimp can get pretty banged up (compare the left and center photos).

Should you buy treated shrimp? Make sure to check the ingredient list. Frozen shrimp are often treated or enhanced with additives such as sodium bisulfate, STP (sodium tri-polyphosphate), or salt to prevent darkening (which occurs as the shrimp age) or to counter "drip loss," the industry term referring to the amount of water in the shrimp that is lost as they thaw. We have found that treated shrimp have a strange translucency and an unpleasant texture and suggest that you avoid them (see right photo). Look for the bags of frozen shrimp that list "shrimp" as the only ingredient.

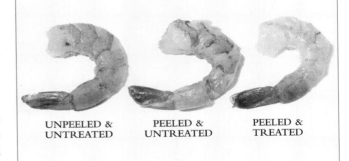

UNPEELED & UNTREATED   PEELED & UNTREATED   PEELED & TREATED

SCIENCE DESK:
How to Thicken Gumbo

IN A CREOLE OR CAJUN DARK ROUX, MOST OF THE STARCH
in the flour breaks down in the cooking, so the roux does
more to flavor the stew than thicken it. That leaves the task to
one of two other traditional Southern ingredients, okra and
filé powder. (It's also possible, as we do in our master recipe,
to go without either one for a slightly thinner stew.)

Okra pods, said to have been brought to the southern
United States from Africa by the slave trade, are slender,
green, usually about 3 inches in length, ridged in texture,
tapered in shape, and often slightly fuzzy. The interior of
the pods is sticky and mucilaginous, so once they are cut
open, they thicken any liquid in which they are cooked.
Okra's flavor is subtle, with hints of eggplant, green bean,
and chestnut. In our gumbo testing, we could detect no taste
difference between fresh and frozen okra.

The other possible thickener, filé powder, is made of
ground dried sassafras leaves. It is said to have been introduced to the settlers of southern Louisiana by the native
Choctaw Indians. Filé, also referred to in Louisiana as
gumbo filé, adds both a gelatinous thickness and a subtle,
singular flavor to gumbo. Though difficult to describe
precisely, the flavor is distinctly earthy, with notes of straw,

bay, marjoram, and oregano. Filé is as much a hallmark of
authentic Louisiana cooking as dark roux and the holy trinity of onion, bell pepper, and celery. Filé is used in one of
two ways. Diners can sprinkle a little bit onto their portion
of gumbo right at the table, or the cook can stir some into
the pot at the very last moment of cooking or even once the
pot has come off the heat. In our recipe variation, we prefer
to add it to the pot, which mellows the flavor somewhat. In
stores that carry it, pale green filé powder is generally sold
in tall, slender, 1-ounce jars.

One thing on which most Creole and Cajun cooks
agree is that you should never use okra and filé together
because the gumbo will get too thick, even gummy.

GETTING IT RIGHT:
The Temperature Matters

Lukewarm stock and constant stirring
are the keys to gumbo with the right
consistency. The roux in the spoonful of
gumbo on top is dispersed smoothly
in the liquid. The roux in the second
spoonful of gumbo (below) has broken,
with globs of browned flour floating in oil.

GETTING IT RIGHT: Making a Roux

With flour just added to the oil, the roux at left is very light in color. After about 10 minutes of cooking, the mixture browns to
about the color of peanut butter (center). The completed dark roux (right) is a deep reddish brown, almost the color of dark
chocolate. A long-handled, straight-edged wooden spatula is best for stirring the roux. Be sure to scrape the pan bottom and
reach into the corners to prevent burning. The cooking roux will have a distinctive toasty, nutty aroma. If it smells scorched or
acrid, or if there are black flecks in the roux, it has burned.

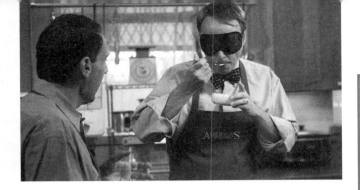

TASTING LAB: Long-Grain White Rice

THE BEAUTY OF WHITE RICE RESIDES IN ITS NEUTRAL flavor, which makes it good at carrying other flavors. But is all long-grain white rice created equal? We set up a few taste tests to find out.

We rounded up a converted rice, three standard super-market options, and an organic white rice available in bulk from a natural foods market. These samples were tasted plain and in our Mexican Rice recipe (page 168). All five brands rated well in the Mexican Rice. Flavor differences were minuscule. With so many potent ingredients in this recipe (tomatoes, chiles, lime juice), these results are not terribly surprising. The most noticeable difference was an unpredict-able variance in cooking time. According to the U.S. Rice Producers Association, the age of the rice, its moisture con-tent, and the variety used can affect the rate of water uptake. Inconsistent cooking times are barely noticeable in plain rice, but they can become more apparent when other ingre-dients—such as the tomatoes and aromatics in our Mexican rice—are added to the pot. When making Mexican Rice, we suggest checking for doneness after 30 minutes and be prepared to keep the rice in the oven a bit longer.

When tasted plain, all of the rices were noted for being "clean" and "like rice should be," with the excep-tion of Uncle Ben's. This converted rice failed to meet our standards on all fronts. Converted rice is processed in a way that ensures separate grains, a firm texture, and more pronounced flavor. Those "round," "rubbery" grains and the telltale yellowish tint immediately brought back not-so-fond memories of "dining hall rice." Tasters agreed that some "stickiness" and minor "clumping" make for more natural-looking and better-tasting rice. So when choosing long-grain rice, you really can't go wrong, as long as you avoid converted rice.

CINCINNATI CHILI

WHAT WE WANTED: An authentic version of this Midwestern classic flavored with Middle Eastern spices and served over spaghetti.

Redolent of cinnamon and warm spices, Cincinnati chili is unlike any chili served in Texas or the rest of the country, for that matter. On sight alone, its sauciness makes it look more like a Sloppy Joe filling or some strange sauce for pasta. One taste reveals layers of spices you expect from Middle Eastern or North African cuisine, not food from the American heartland.

Legend has it that Cincinnati chili was created in the 1920s by a Macedonian immigrant named Athanas Kiradjieff. He ran a hot dog stand called the Empress, where he served his chili over hot dogs. This deluxe hot dog eventually morphed into the "five-way" concoction beloved by locals.

Cincinnati chili is as much about the garnishes, or "ways," as the chili itself. On its own, it is merely one-way Cincinnati chili. Served over buttered spaghetti, it is two-way. Add shredded cheddar cheese and it becomes three-way. Chopped onions make it four-way, and the final garnish, for five-way chili, is with warmed kidney beans.

To get a handle on this unusual chili, we tested a number of recipes. We noticed two problems. First, most of the versions tested were much too greasy. Second, the myriad spices used in many recipes were overwhelming. Our goals were clear—cut the fat and figure out which spices were essential and which were not.

In most chili recipes, the meat is browned to build flavor and render some fat, which can be spooned off. Cincinnati chili is unique because it calls for boiling ground beef instead of browning it. The boiled meat had a texture described as "wormy" by most tasters, which, as odd as it sounds, pairs well with the pasta and the other accompaniments. But boiling the meat can make it difficult to rid the meat of excess fat, particularly since traditional recipes use the blanching liquid as the base for the chili.

We decided to try replacing the ground chuck (80 to 85 percent lean), which is the usual choice for chili, with ground round (90 percent lean). This idea sounded great, but tasters felt that the flavor of the chili made with ground round suffered. Ground chuck has a beefier flavor, so we would have to figure out some way to eliminate the excess grease from the final dish.

For our next batch of chili, we added the beef to salted, boiling water and blanched it for three minutes, or until an unappetizing raft of oily meat foam had risen to the surface. We then drained the beef and discarded the water—along with the fat. The resulting chili was grease-free but lacked the body and flavor that fat provides. We had gone too far. Next, we cut the blanching time back to only 30 seconds, and the results were much better. The chili was rich and fully flavored, without being slick or greasy.

Like curries in India, the spice mixture in Cincinnati chili varies from recipe to recipe (and house to house). Some mixes contain just two or three spices, while others embrace the entire spice cabinet and are more evocative of a Moroccan souk than an Ohio hot dog stand. We hoped to isolate the key flavors and create a streamlined spice mixture.

We had uncovered all kinds of incongruous combinations in our research, including one recipe that called for coriander, cardamom, turmeric, and nutmeg—a simply dreadful mixture. Tasters also objected to cloves and mace, both of which were deemed too overpowering. Chili powder, cinnamon, and cayenne pepper were essential, although the latter had to be used sparingly.

Cumin, in addition to the small amount of cumin already blended into the chili powder, proved too much, so it was pulled. The cinnamon was not strong enough in early batches and was almost doubled in the final recipe. We were almost content with the basic spice mixture, but it needed a little more depth. After trying several ideas, a combination of black pepper and allspice proved winning.

Many recipes call for unsweetened chocolate, but we figured that cocoa powder would achieve much the same thing and would be easier to add along with the spices. (Further testing bore out the hypothesis.) Dried oregano rounded out our list of "spices." To further boost the flavors of our spice mixture, we toasted it in the oil before adding the liquid ingredients.

While the spices vary from recipe to recipe, the aromatics are consistently onion and garlic. Most recipes add them to the water with the meat. We decided to draw out a little more flavor and sweetness by sautéing them.

As far as the liquids go, most recipes call for tomato sauce and water. We tried to replace the generic canned tomato sauce suggested in most recipes with canned whole peeled tomatoes that we pureed in the blender. While the canned tomatoes made the chili taste a bit brighter, the chili made with canned tomato sauce was favored by most tasters.

Tasters felt that the water did little to improve the chili and wondered if it should be replaced. To add body, we tried using red wine as part of the liquid. We decided it was superfluous due to the strength of the rest of the flavors. In the end, we went with canned chicken broth for the sake of convenience. To keep the chicken flavor from dominating, we used half chicken broth and half water. A small amount of cider vinegar (very traditional) brightened the broth. Some brown sugar added the necessary sweetness to balance the vinegar and spices.

We turned our attention to the garnishes. After several tests, we realized it was best to leave tradition alone. Sure you could do without the beans or onions, but why compromise? Five-way Cincinnati chili is almost sacrosanct.

WHAT WE LEARNED: Use ground chuck for the best flavor and blanch it for 30 seconds to give the meat its characteristic texture. Add a mix of spices and cocoa powder to create depth of flavor. A combination of chicken broth, water, and tomato sauce becomes a rich base for the chili, while some vinegar and brown sugar enliven all the other flavors.

CINCINNATI CHILI
Serves 6 to 8

Choose a relatively plain tomato sauce—nothing too spicy or herbaceous. To warm the kidney beans, simmer them in water to cover for several minutes and then drain.

chili

2	teaspoons salt, plus more to taste
1½	pounds ground chuck
2	tablespoons vegetable oil
2	medium onions, chopped fine (about 2 cups)
2	medium garlic cloves, minced or pressed through a garlic press (about 2 teaspoons)
2	tablespoons chili powder
2	teaspoons dried oregano
2	teaspoons cocoa
1½	teaspoons ground cinnamon
½	teaspoon cayenne
½	teaspoon ground allspice
¼	teaspoon ground black pepper
2	cups low-sodium chicken broth
2	cups water
2	tablespoons cider vinegar
2	teaspoons dark brown sugar
2	cups tomato sauce
	Tabasco sauce

accompaniments

1	pound spaghetti, cooked, drained, and tossed with 2 tablespoons unsalted butter
12	ounces sharp cheddar cheese, shredded
1	(15-ounce) can red kidney beans, drained, rinsed, and warmed
1	medium onion, chopped fine (about 1 cup)

1. FOR THE CHILI: Bring 2 quarts of water and 1 teaspoon of the salt to a boil in a large saucepan. Add the ground chuck, stirring vigorously to separate the meat into individual strands. As soon as the foam from the meat rises to the top

(this takes about 30 seconds) and before the water returns to a boil, drain the meat into a strainer and set it aside.

2. Rinse and dry the empty saucepan. Set the pan over medium heat and add the oil. When the oil is warm, add the onions and cook, stirring frequently, until the onions are soft and browned around the edges, about 8 minutes. Add the garlic and cook until fragrant, about 1 minute. Stir in the chili powder, oregano, cocoa, cinnamon, cayenne, allspice, black pepper, and the remaining 1 teaspoon salt. Cook, stirring constantly, until the spices are fragrant, about 30 seconds. Stir in the broth, water, vinegar, sugar, and tomato sauce, scraping the pan bottom to remove any browned bits.

3. Add the blanched ground beef and increase the heat to high. As soon as the liquid boils, reduce the heat to medium-low and simmer, stirring occasionally, until the chili is deep red and has thickened slightly, about 1 hour. Adjust the seasonings, adding salt and Tabasco sauce to taste. (The chili can be refrigerated in an airtight container for up to 3 days. Bring to a simmer over medium-low heat before serving.)

4. TO SERVE: Divide the buttered spaghetti among individual bowls. Spoon the chili over the spaghetti and top with the cheese, beans, and onion. Serve immediately.

EQUIPMENT CORNER:
Useful Kitchen Gadgets

THERE ARE HUNDREDS OF KITCHEN GADGETS ON THE market today. Over the years, we've pretty much tested them all. Sure, we've come across some real duds, but we've also uncovered some true gems. The following is a list of gadgets that we couldn't live without in the test kitchen, or at home. See www.americastestkitchen.com for up-to-date prices and mail-order sources.

Taylor Classic Oven Guide Thermometer
$14.95
Temperature readings are spot on with our favorite thermometer—it even passed our knock-over test with flying colors! Not only is it the most accurate thermometer we've tested, it's also the most stable, in part because of its 4-inch length—and it hangs.

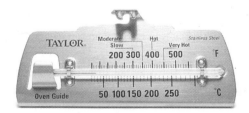

Polder Electronic Clock/Stopwatch/Timer
$12.99

A well-deserved honorable mention in our useful gadget lineup, the Polder times up to 10 hours and can be worn around your neck (so it goes where you go).

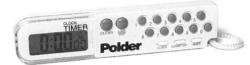

Polder Cooking Thermometer/Timer
$24.99

With its easy, intuitive design, this gadget is the secret weapon for properly cooked meat. It has a 4-foot-long thermometer probe cord and a loud alarm (great for outside grilling), and it's magnetized (sticks right to the side of the oven).

Oxo Oven Thermometer
$11.99

We like the Oxo, a superb newcomer to the market, for its large, bold-print numbers, glass back panel (that allows light from the oven to illuminate the numbers), and adjustable clip (that attaches the thermometer to the oven rack).

Microplane Zester/Grater
$12.95

The combination of very sharp teeth and a solid handle makes grating cheese a breeze. It also makes quick work of ginger and citrus zest.

Oxo Good Grips Locking 12-Inch Tongs
$9.99

These stainless steel tongs with rubber handles earned high marks in our battery of tests. We use them for everything, from retrieving corn on the cob from boiling water to turning large roasts in the oven.

Oxo Good Grips Stainless Steel Multi-Purpose Scraper & Chopper
$7.99

It's perfect for scraping sticky dough off the counter or cutting board. The wide metal blade makes it easy—and safer than a sharp chef's knife blade—to transfer chopped ingredients from the cutting board to a sauté pan.

KitchenArt Adjust-A-Cup
$9.95

It effortlessly measures and releases hard-to-measure ingredients such as molasses, shortening, and peanut butter. Every bit of the ingredient is removed from the cup with ease.

Egg Slicer
$5–$8

In addition to slicing hard-boiled eggs, we use the model with smooth wire blades to cut mushrooms and strawberries.

Keith checks the progress of his simple gravy recipe that uses basic pantry items—and no meat.

PORK CHOPS and gravy

CHAPTER 5

It sometimes seems like the simplest recipes suffer the worst fate in modern cookbooks. Maybe it's because no one really cares enough about these dishes to get them right. Most of these recipes are not terribly sexy. But when done right, this kind of food can be incredibly satisfying and comforting.

Stuffed pork chops, gravy, and glazed carrots almost always fall into this disappointing category. The pork chops are dry and bland. In theory, the gravy should help mitigate these problems, but all too often the gravy has odd chemical flavors (caused by the use of "gravy enhancers"), and the texture is either lumpy or too thick. And the carrots are so sweet they might as well be dessert.

The test kitchen was committed to breathing new life into these old-fashioned American recipes. Taste the results of our labor—we hope you'll think we succeeded.

STUFFED PORK CHOPS

WHAT WE WANTED: Most stuffed pork chops are extremely dry and bland. We wanted the stuffing to be especially flavorful to offset the mildness of the pork, and we wanted the chops to be moist and juicy.

A simple garlic and herb bread stuffing seems an easy way to load flavor and richness into today's leaner pork chops. Whenever stuffing occurs, however, a host of challenges enters the kitchen. Chief among them is bringing the stuffing (often bound with raw eggs) up to a safe internal temperature without overcooking the surrounding meat. Many of the recipes we consulted employ a crude strategy to tackle this problem—surround the chops in liquid and cook them for an hour or more. This old-fashioned technique (essentially a braise) may have worked with fattier chops, but modern-day pork is lean

and tender—much better suited to searing in a hot skillet, which can then be used to make a quick pan sauce.

Determining which type of chop to stuff was fairly simple. Rib chops were the obvious choice for their higher fat content (making them less likely to dry out) and wide, unbroken eye of meat. Center-cut or loin chops, on the other hand, are divided down the middle like a T-bone steak, making them tough to stuff. Thick-cut rib chops (about 1½ inches) are widely available and big enough to handle a hearty amount of filling.

Our favorite recipe for sautéing thick-cut pork chops pointed the way. We knew from our testing that the best results came from brining the chops beforehand and then finishing them in a hot oven instead of in the pan. As stuffed chops require more time in the oven than unstuffed ones, the brining step was crucial for retaining moisture. By first cutting a pocket in each chop, we allowed the brine to penetrate to the center of the meat.

No amount of brining could save a pork chop from 30 minutes in a 450-degree oven, however. That's about how long it took for the stuffing inside of the seared chops to reach a temperature of 160 degrees, the minimum temperature for the safe consumption of raw eggs. By that time, temperature of the meat near the edges of the chop had topped 180 degrees, and the meat was dry and tough. Using eggs to bind the stuffing was evidently out—but did we, in fact, need them?

It seemed so at first. Without the eggs, the stuffing had been loose and crumbly, spilling out all over the plate when the chops were served. Our working method for stuffing the chops had been part of the problem. We slit the pork chops open from the side and spooned loose stuffing into the middle, then tried using toothpicks to keep the chops closed. But the toothpicks interfered with the searing of the meat and did a poor job of keeping the chop closed in the heat of the oven as the pork contracted and curled open.

When it came time to plate the chops, we had to dig the toothpicks out of the meat (we missed one once), which only encouraged the stuffing to come tumbling out.

Some careful knife work solved the problem. Instead of butterflying the meat, we made an inch-long cut in the side of the chop with a thin boning knife, then used the blade to clear a cavity in the center of the meat without any further cuts at the edge. We stuffed the meat through this smaller opening, and the natural shape of the chop held the stuffing in place. No eggs, no toothpicks. Furthermore, the natural juice from the brined pork moistened the stuffing while the chop cooked.

Next we experimented with adding bacon and sausage to our basic bread stuffing. The flavors were overbearing, tasters said, and the extra meat made the stuffing too salty. (Thanks to the brine, the juice from the pork was enough to season the stuffing without adding extra salt.) Tasters preferred the simpler version made with garlic and fresh herbs. A few tablespoons of cream added richness and enough moisture to bring the stuffing together.

The meat near the edges of the chops still tended to dry out when left in the oven until the stuffing reached 145 degrees, the temperature that recipes with non-egg stuffings recommend. Our standard operating procedure is to tent resting meat loosely with aluminum foil to allow the juices to redistribute while the residual heat gently brings the internal temperature to the desired doneness. In this case, we were able to pull the meat from the oven when the temperature at the center of the stuffing was just 130 degrees. After 5 to 10 minutes of resting, the temperature of the pork and the stuffing had evened out around 145 degrees.

WHAT WE LEARNED: Use cream rather than eggs to bind a stuffing made with fresh bread, garlic, herbs, and aromatic vegetables. Because the stuffing doesn't contain eggs, the chops can be cooked to a lower (and more palatable) internal temperature. Start the chops in a skillet to develop a nice brown crust but finish cooking them through on a sheet pan in a hot oven.

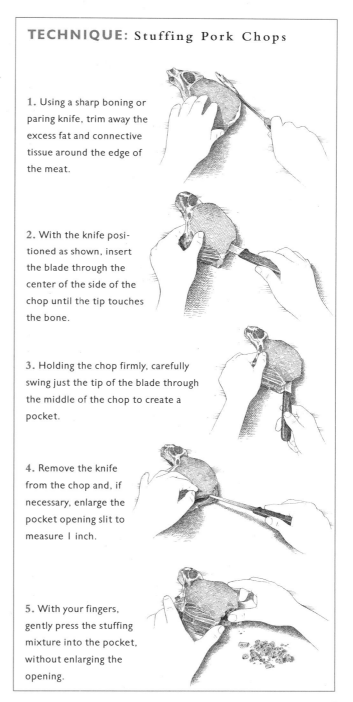

TECHNIQUE: Stuffing Pork Chops

1. Using a sharp boning or paring knife, trim away the excess fat and connective tissue around the edge of the meat.

2. With the knife positioned as shown, insert the blade through the center of the side of the chop until the tip touches the bone.

3. Holding the chop firmly, carefully swing just the tip of the blade through the middle of the chop to create a pocket.

4. Remove the knife from the chop and, if necessary, enlarge the pocket opening slit to measure 1 inch.

5. With your fingers, gently press the stuffing mixture into the pocket, without enlarging the opening.

STUFFED PORK CHOPS

Serves 4

These stuffed pork chops may be served with All-Purpose Gravy (page 57), applesauce, or Quick Ginger-Apple Chutney (recipe follows). The gravy is best made before you start the chops and then reheated as needed. If you choose to serve the chops with the chutney instead, prepare it in the skillet used to cook the chops while the chops are in the oven.

chops

- 4 bone-in rib loin pork chops, 1½ inches thick (about 12 ounces each)
- ¾ cup packed light brown sugar
- ½ cup Diamond Crystal Kosher Salt, 6 tablespoons Morton Kosher Salt, or ¼ cup table salt
  Ground black pepper
- 1 tablespoon vegetable oil

GETTING IT RIGHT:
Buying the Right Chop

CENTER-CUT CHOP   RIB CHOP

When shopping, make sure to buy the right kind of pork chops. A center-cut chop (left) has a bone running through the middle and will be very hard to stuff. The bone runs along the outside of rib chop (right), making it much easier to cut a large pocket in the side of the chop. We find that rib chops are also juicier and more flavorful than center-cut chops, and they are our top choice for cooking, even when stuffing is not part of the equation.

---

stuffing

- 3 tablespoons unsalted butter
- 1 small onion, diced small
- 1 medium celery rib, diced small
- ½ teaspoon salt
- 2 medium garlic cloves, minced or pressed through a garlic press (about 2 teaspoons)
- 2 teaspoons minced fresh thyme leaves
- 1 tablespoon minced fresh parsley leaves
- 2 cups ¼-inch bread cubes from 1 baguette
- 2 tablespoons heavy cream
- ⅛ teaspoon ground black pepper

1. FOR THE CHOPS: Following the illustrations on page 53, cut a small pocket through the side of each chop. Dissolve the sugar and salt in 6 cups of cold water in a gallon-size, zipper-lock plastic bag. Add the pork chops and seal the bag, pressing out as much air as possible. Refrigerate until fully seasoned, about 1 hour.

2. FOR THE STUFFING: Melt the butter in a 12-inch skillet over medium heat until the foaming subsides. Add the onion, celery, and salt and cook until the vegetables are softened and beginning to brown, about 10 minutes. Add the garlic and herbs and cook until fragrant, about 1 minute. Transfer to a medium bowl, add the bread cubes, cream, and pepper, and toss well to combine. Using a rubber spatula, press the stuffing lightly against the sides of the bowl until it comes together.

3. TO STUFF, SEASON, AND COOK THE CHOPS: Adjust an oven rack to the lower-middle position, place a shallow roasting pan or rimmed baking sheet on the rack, and heat the oven to 450 degrees. Remove the chops from the brine, rinse, and pat dry with paper towels. Place one quarter of the stuffing (about ⅓ cup) in the pocket of each pork chop. Season the chops with pepper.

4. Heat the oil in a heavy-bottomed 12-inch skillet over high heat until shimmering. Lay the chops in the skillet and cook until well browned and a nice crust has formed, about 3 minutes. Turn the chops over with tongs and cook until well browned and a nice crust has formed on the second side, 2 to 3 minutes longer.

5. Using the tongs, transfer the chops to the preheated pan in the oven. Roast until an instant-read thermometer inserted into the center of the stuffing registers 130 degrees, about 15 minutes, turning the chops over once halfway through the cooking time. Transfer the chops to a platter, tent loosely with foil, and let rest at least 5 minutes. Check the internal temperature; it should register 145 degrees.

QUICK GINGER-APPLE CHUTNEY

Makes enough for 4 pork chops
This chutney works well with pork chops or roast pork.

1	tablespoon vegetable oil
1	small onion, cut into ½-inch dice
2	Granny Smith apples, peeled, cored, and cut into ½-inch dice
1	tablespoon minced ginger
¼	teaspoon ground allspice
⅛	teaspoon cayenne
¼	cup packed light brown sugar
1	cup apple cider
	Salt and ground black pepper

While the chops are in the oven, pour off any fat in the skillet used to sear the chops. Add the oil and heat over medium-high heat until shimmering. Add the onion and apples and cook, stirring occasionally, until softened and browned, about 10 minutes. Stir in the ginger, allspice, and cayenne and cook until fragrant, about 1 minute. Add the sugar and cider and bring to a boil, scraping the browned bits off the pan bottom, until the cider is slightly thickened, about 4 minutes. Season with salt and pepper to taste.

Q & A

Should pork be cooked until well done, and why do recipes often mention different temperatures?

The reason you will see different recommended finished temperatures for pork is simple: Some sources are concerned with safety first, while other sources put a premium on palatability. Guidelines for cooking pork to temperatures as high as 190 degrees originated decades ago when pork quality was inconsistent and fears of trichinosis ran high. Today the risk of trichinosis is nearly nonexistent in the United States. What's more, even when the trichina parasite is present, it is killed when the temperature of the meat rises to 137 degrees.

Both the U.S. Department of Agriculture and the National Pork Board recommend cooking pork to a final internal temperature of 160 degrees. If you are concerned about contamination from salmonella (which is possible in any type of meat, including beef), you must cook the pork to 160 degrees to be certain that all potential pathogens are eliminated. Unfortunately, given the leanness of today's pork, these recommendations result in dry, tough meat.

In the test kitchen, we have found cooking modern pork beyond 150 degrees to be a waste of time and money. We cook pork chops to a final internal temperature of 145 degrees—the meat will still be slightly rosy in the center and juicy. Depending on the size of the chops and the cooking method, the chops will probably need to be removed from the heat source before they reach this temperature. As the chops rest and the juices are redistributed throughout the meat, the internal temperature will continue to climb. Follow recipes as to when to take the chops off the heat and then check the temperature again just before serving to make sure it has reached 145 degrees. Of course, if safety is your top concern, cook all meat (including pork) until it is well done; that is, when the internal temperature reaches 160 degrees.

ALL-PURPOSE GRAVY

WHAT WE WANTED: We wanted to make really good gravy without a roast, using only canned broth and a few vegetables. Was this even possible?

Gravy, by definition, is a thickened sauce made of meat juices and pan drippings, usually left over from a roast. But what if you don't have a roast on hand and want gravy for some mashed potatoes or pork chops? What if you are limited to just some canned broth and a few vegetables? The problem is that a roast provides concentrated flavor through the fond, the browned bits at the bottom of the roasting pan. Without these small flavor jewels, a professional chef would say that any gravy is a lost cause. However, being fond (no pun intended) of lost causes, we set out to create a top-notch all-purpose gravy that could be made quickly, without one special ingredient, including a roast.

Our first thought was to turn to the supermarket short-cuts for making gravy, including products such as Kitchen Bouquet and Gravy Master. The results were unacceptable (see page 58 for details). Next, we researched gravy recipes that can be made without a roast and without homemade stock. They ran the gamut from a six-minute gravy prepared in the microwave to one that had more than 20 ingredients and took 1½ hours to make. The flavors were, to say the least, disappointing. Most were thick and bland with no meat flavor; others were just downright frightening with odd, out-of-place Asian overtones.

What we did learn from all this testing was that some combination of supermarket broth and sautéed vegetables thickened with flour was the likely solution, given the fact that this approach seemed to deliver the most authentic, richest flavor. We began our recipe development with the liquid base. We quickly ruled out both water and vegetable broth because they made flavorless gravies. This left us with three options: chicken broth, beef broth, or a combination of both. Using a base recipe (some sautéed vegetables and

flour), we prepared two batches of gravy, one using beef broth, the other using chicken. Tasters agreed that the beef broth gravy was acidic and contained a metallic aftertaste. On the other hand, the chicken broth was well liked, although the strong poultry flavor was inappropriate for all-purpose gravy. Finally, we tried equal amounts of chicken and beef broth and found that combination to be a winner.

We had started with a standard mirepoix (a mixture of onions, carrots, and celery) that was lightly sautéed in oil. While this combination of vegetables lent the gravy a balanced sweetness and body, it failed to accent the gravy's meatiness or impart any roasted flavor. We replaced the mirepoix in our basic recipe with 1 cup of mushrooms in one test and 2 cups of onions, lightly caramelized, in a second test. The gravy made with the mushrooms was a complete miss. Both the color and the appearance became muddy, and the overall flavor was bland and vegetal. The caramelized onions didn't perform much better. One taster thought that the gravy tasted like French onion soup.

However, we did learn an important lesson from these tests. The process of caramelizing onions creates a fond on the bottom of the pan—not unlike the fond created after roasting meat—which gave the gravy an appealing nutty-brown color; we could also detect the hint of a pleasant roasted essence. It occurred to us that the development of a vegetable fond might be the key to increasing the gravy's flavor. We went back to the original mirepoix and merely extended the cooking time until the vegetables were well browned. This meant cooking the vegetables in butter (for more flavor) over medium-high heat for about seven minutes. As we had hoped, the gravy had a more pronounced roasted, meaty flavor. Much to our delight, we also found that if we chopped the vegetables in the food processor, we not only saved time but also created a better-tasting fond in less time due to the smaller pieces.

The last step in gravy making involves thickening. Our

basic recipe called for browning the vegetables in butter and then sprinkling flour over them to create a roux, the classic combination of fat and flour that thickens liquids. We then whisked in the broth and simmered the gravy until thickened, after which time the raw flour taste had dissipated. We also tested other thickeners (cornstarch and arrowroot) and thickening techniques (making a paste of butter and flour that is added to the gravy at the end of the cooking time). Believe it or not, we also tried gingersnaps, as suggested in one of the initial test recipes. Each of these options (even the gingersnaps) thickened the gravy to a similar consistency, but they created other problems. The cornstarch and arrowroot variations tasted fine but had an unappealing, translucent quality; the gingersnaps, meanwhile, produced a gravy that tasted like cake batter. All in all, the butter-based roux produced a superior gravy.

Still short in terms of depth of flavor, we thought to employ a technique used by Creole cooks in making gumbo and cooked the roux until it was the color of milk chocolate, far beyond the pale blond color of previous tests. Much to our amazement, this simple technique substantially boosted the flavor of the gravy, helping to develop complex flavor elements in our simple recipe. In conjunction with the caramelized vegetable fond, the toasted flour provided an unexpectedly rich roasted flavor as well as a bold meaty flavor—exactly what we had been looking for. And the gravy's color was now a rich, deep brown as well.

We were close, but we still wanted to test some of the more unusual flavor-building ingredients, including miso (which made the gravy taste like a stir-fry sauce), coffee (which colored the gravy but added no flavor), and molasses (which thickened the gravy but made it sweet and bitter). In the end, we opted for a more classic combination of dried thyme, bay leaf, and peppercorns.

WHAT WE LEARNED: To make good gravy without a roast, you must eke out as much flavor as possible from every ingredient. Brown the vegetables and the flour thoroughly, and add both beef and chicken broth.

ALL-PURPOSE GRAVY

Makes 2 cups

This gravy can be served with almost any type of meat and with mashed potatoes as well. The recipe can be doubled. If doubling it, use a Dutch oven so that the vegetables brown properly and increase the cooking times by roughly 50 percent. The finished gravy can be frozen. To thaw it, place the gravy and a tablespoon of water in a saucepan over low heat and slowly bring it to a simmer. It may appear broken or curdled as it thaws, but a vigorous whisking will recombine it.

1	small carrot, peeled and chopped into rough ½-inch pieces (about ½ cup)
1	small celery rib, chopped into rough ½-inch pieces (about ½ cup)
1	small onion, chopped into rough ½-inch pieces (about ¾ cup)
3	tablespoons unsalted butter
¼	cup unbleached all-purpose flour
2	cups low-sodium chicken broth
2	cups low-sodium beef broth
1	bay leaf
¼	teaspoon dried thyme
5	whole black peppercorns
	Salt and ground black pepper

GETTING IT RIGHT:
Process the Vegetables

In addition to saving time, chopping the carrot, celery, and onion in a food processor breaks down the vegetables' cell walls and speeds the release of their flavors when cooked. Because the vegetables are strained out of the finished gravy, the fact that the food processor makes them mushy is not a big deal.

1. Process the carrot in a food processor until broken into rough ¼-inch pieces, about five 1-second pulses. Add the celery and onion; pulse until all the vegetables are broken into ⅛-inch pieces, about five 1-second pulses.

2. Heat the butter in a large heavy-bottomed saucepan over medium-high heat. When the foaming subsides, add the vegetables and cook, stirring frequently, until softened and well browned, about 7 minutes. Reduce the heat to medium; stir in the flour and cook, stirring constantly, until thoroughly browned and fragrant, about 5 minutes. Whisking constantly, gradually add the broths; bring to a boil, skimming off any foam that forms on the surface. Reduce the heat to medium-low and add the bay leaf, thyme, and peppercorns. Simmer, stirring occasionally, until thickened and reduced to 3 cups, 20 to 25 minutes.

3. Strain the gravy through a fine-mesh strainer into a clean saucepan, pressing on the solids to extract as much liquid as possible; discard the solids. Adjust the seasonings with salt and pepper to taste. Serve hot.

TASTING LAB: Gravy Additives

IN OUR RESEARCH, WE FOUND SEVERAL RECIPES THAT called for Kitchen Bouquet or Gravy Master. Although we had heard of these ingredients, we had never before cooked with them. A trip to the supermarket revealed that these were not the only gravy "additives" that are available.

These products, which primarily consist of caramel or caramel coloring, vegetable extracts, salt, and preservatives, are made to impersonate fond, the little flavor-packed bits left in the pan after roasting meat. Since fond was exactly what we were trying to replicate in our all-purpose pantry gravy, we thought these items might be the key to the best recipe.

We choose four gravy additives, two powders and two liquids, and prepared four gravies following the instructions on each of the packages. Overall results were dismal and tasters all complained that the gravies tasted artificial. While the theory behind the supermarket additives—a store-bought replacement for the time-consuming fond—was right on, the results were off base. Our suggestion: Build your own fond with fresh vegetables and leave these items on the shelf.

GETTING IT RIGHT: Building Great Flavor from Ordinary Ingredients

BROWNING VEGETABLES

ADDING BROTH AND HERBS

PRESSING VEGETABLES

In the absence of pan drippings, making a good-tasting gravy requires several crucial flavor-building steps. To start, the vegetables must be well browned (left). Caramelizing the sugars in the vegetables gives the gravy a complex roasted flavor. Browning the flour also heightens the roasted flavor of the gravy and gives it a distinctive chestnut color. A combination of beef and chicken broth contributes a rich, well-rounded, meaty flavor. Whisking the broths in slowly (center) releases the vegetable fond from the bottom of the pan and ensures a lump-free gravy. When straining the finished gravy, it is important to press on the vegetables (right) to extract as much flavor as possible. Straining also guarantees a velvety smooth gravy.

GLAZED CARROTS

WHAT WE WANTED: Fully tender, well-seasoned carrots with a glossy, clingy, yet modest glaze.

Glazing is probably the most popular way to prepare carrots. However, glazed carrots are often saccharine and ill-suited as a side dish on a dinner plate. These defamed vegetables, adrift in a sea of syrup, often lie limp and soggy from overcooking or retain a raw, fibrous resistance from undercooking.

To rescue glazed carrots from such poor treatment, we began with how to prepare the carrots for cooking. Matchsticks were out from the get-go—we were looking for simplicity, not to improve our knife skills. A bag of "baby" carrots unceremoniously emptied into a pan for cooking revealed pieces of wildly different girth, with some more than twice as big around as others. Surely these would cook unevenly, so we halved the large pieces lengthwise. Gone was the convenience of this product. Once these baby carrots were cooked, tasters remarked that they were shy on both carrot flavor and good looks. We peeled regular bagged carrots and cut them on the bias into handsome oblong shapes. Once cooked, these comely carrots earned much praise for their good flavor. Slender bunch carrots (sold with their tops on and at a higher price), also cut on the bias, were no more flavorful, and their diminutive size lacked presence. Regular bagged carrots it was.

Most recipes suggest that the carrots need to be steamed, parboiled, or blanched prior to glazing, resulting in a battery of dirtied utensils. Instead, we put the carrots with a bit of liquid in a skillet (nonstick, for the sake of easy cleanup), along with some salt and sugar for flavor, covered the skillet, and simmered. Mission accomplished: The carrots were cooked through without much ado. Chicken broth as a cooking liquid lent the carrots savory backbone and a full, round flavor, whereas water left them hollow and wine turned them sour and astringent. We tried swapping the sugar for more compelling sweeteners but found brown sugar too muddy flavored, maple syrup too assertive, and honey too floral (but good for a variation, we noted). We stood by clean, pure, easy-to-measure granulated sugar.

We moved on to finessing the glaze. After the carrots simmered for a few minutes, when just on the verge of tender (they would see more heat during glazing, so we simmered them shy of done), we lifted the lid from the skillet, stepped up the heat, and let the liquid reduce to 2 tablespoons. (If the liquid is not reduced, it is thin and watery.) Finally, we added butter, cut into small pieces for quick melting, and a bit more sugar to encourage glaze formation and to favorably increase sweetness. All of this resulted in a light, clingy glaze that with a few more minutes of high-heat cooking took on a pale amber hue and a light caramel flavor. A sprinkle of fresh lemon juice gave the dish sparkle, and a twist or two of freshly ground black pepper provided depth. We were surprised, as were our tasters, that glazed carrots could be this good and this easy.

WHAT WE LEARNED: Avoid bags of "baby" carrots (often filled with carrots of varying sizes) and choose more flavorful bagged, full-size carrots that can be sliced to yield ovals that will cook more evenly. Cooking and glazing the carrots is one single operation. Start by cooking the sliced carrots in a covered skillet with chicken broth, salt, and sugar. Remove the lid and glaze with a little butter and a bit more sugar.

GLAZED CARROTS

Serves 4

A nonstick skillet is easier to clean, but this recipe can be pre-pared in any 12-inch skillet with a cover.

1	pound carrots (about 6 medium), peeled and sliced ¼ inch thick on the bias (see the illustration below)
½	teaspoon salt
3	tablespoons sugar
½	cup low-sodium chicken broth
1	tablespoon unsalted butter, cut into 4 pieces
2	teaspoons juice from 1 lemon
	Ground black pepper

1. Bring the carrots, salt, 1 tablespoon of the sugar, and the chicken broth to a boil in a 12-inch nonstick skillet, cov-ered, over medium–high heat. Reduce the heat to medium and simmer, stirring occasionally, until the carrots are almost tender when poked with the tip of a paring knife, about 5 minutes. Uncover, increase the heat to high, and simmer rapidly, stirring occasionally, until the liquid is reduced to about 2 tablespoons, 1 to 2 minutes.

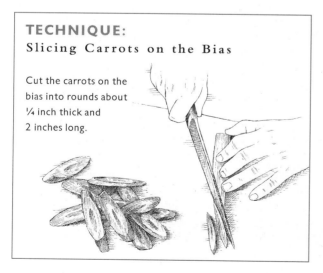

TECHNIQUE:
Slicing Carrots on the Bias

Cut the carrots on the bias into rounds about ¼ inch thick and 2 inches long.

2. Add the butter and remaining 2 tablespoons sugar to the skillet. Toss the carrots to coat and cook, stirring frequently, until the carrots are completely tender and the glaze is light gold, about 3 minutes. Off the heat, add the lemon juice and toss to coat. Transfer the carrots to a serving dish, scraping the glaze from the pan into the dish. Season to taste with pepper and serve immediately.

VARIATIONS

GLAZED CARROTS WITH GINGER AND ROSEMARY

Cut a 1-inch piece of fresh ginger crosswise into ¼-inch coins. Follow the recipe for Glazed Carrots, adding the gin-ger to the skillet along with the carrots and adding 1 tea-spoon minced fresh rosemary along with the butter. Discard the ginger pieces before serving.

HONEY-GLAZED CARROTS WITH LEMON AND THYME

Follow the recipe for Glazed Carrots, substituting an equal amount of honey for the sugar and adding ½ teaspoon minced fresh thyme leaves and ½ teaspoon grated lemon zest along with the butter.

GLAZED CURRIED CARROTS WITH CURRANTS AND ALMONDS

Lightly toasting the curry powder in the warm, dry skillet brings forth its full flavor.

Toast ¼ cup sliced almonds in a 12-inch nonstick skillet over medium heat until fragrant and lightly browned, about 5 minutes; transfer to a small bowl and set aside. Off the heat, sprinkle 1½ teaspoons curry powder in the skillet; stir until fragrant, about 2 seconds. Follow the recipe for Glazed Carrots, adding the carrots, salt, sugar, and chicken broth to the skillet with the curry powder. Add ¼ cup currants along with the butter; add the toasted almonds along with the lemon juice.

GLAZED CARROTS WITH ORANGE AND CRANBERRIES

Dried cherries can be used in place of the cranberries if you prefer.

Follow the recipe for Glazed Carrots, adding ¼ cup dried cranberries with the carrots in step 1 and replacing ¼ cup of the chicken broth with ¼ cup orange juice and ½ teaspoon grated orange zest. Reduce the amount of sugar in step 2 to 1 tablespoon and omit the lemon juice.

GLAZED CARROTS WITH BACON AND PECANS

The rich caramel flavor of brown sugar goes well with the bacon and pecans.

3	ounces (about 3 slices) bacon, cut into ½-inch pieces
⅓	cup chopped pecans
1	pound carrots (about 6 medium), peeled and sliced ¼ inch thick on the bias (see the illustration on page 60)
½	teaspoon salt
3	tablespoons light brown sugar
½	cup low-sodium chicken broth
½	teaspoon minced fresh thyme leaves
1	tablespoon unsalted butter, cut into 4 pieces
2	teaspoons juice from 1 lemon
	Ground black pepper

1. Cook the bacon in a 12-inch nonstick skillet over medium-high heat until crisp. Transfer the cooked bacon to a paper towel–lined plate to drain. Remove all but 1 tablespoon of the bacon drippings from the pan. Add the pecans and cook until fragrant and slightly browned, about 3 minutes. Transfer the pecans to the plate with the bacon.

2. Add the carrots, salt, 1 tablespoon of the brown sugar, the chicken broth, and thyme to the skillet. Bring to a boil, covered, over medium-high heat. Reduce the heat to medium and simmer, stirring occasionally, until the carrots are almost tender when poked with the tip of a paring knife, about 5 minutes. Uncover, increase the heat to high, and simmer rapidly, stirring occasionally, until the liquid is reduced to about 2 tablespoons, 1 to 2 minutes.

3. Add the butter and remaining 2 tablespoons brown sugar to the skillet. Toss the carrots to coat and cook, stirring frequently, until the carrots are completely tender, about 3 minutes. Off heat, add the lemon juice and toss to coat. Transfer the carrots to a serving dish, scraping the glaze from the pan into the dish. Season to taste with pepper and serve immediately.

TECHNIQUE: Impromptu Salt Cellars

Measuring from the pouring spout on a cardboard container of salt can be frustrating when the salt flows out in an uncontrollable rush. Here are two ways around this problem.

A. Use a lidded sugar shaker or covered sugar bowl as a salt cellar. The lid keeps out any grease or dust but can be easily removed to grab a quick pinch.

B. Turn the salt container itself into a salt cellar by cutting off the top of the partially empty salt container with a serrated knife. Cover the container with a sheet of plastic wrap and secure it with a rubber band. When you want to measure salt, remove the plastic cover and stick the measuring spoon right into the box.

Julia is willing to try almost any idea—
even cooking a whole chicken in a skillet.

TWO ROAST chickens

Despite its apparent simplicity, roast chicken is a hard recipe to get right. First, you've got to deal with the skin, which never seems to crisp up properly. Then there's the odd structure of the bird, with legs and wings tucked close against the body (and thus slow to cook through), while the delicate breast is exposed directly to the oven heat. The fact that dark meat tastes better when cooked to a higher temperature makes it nearly impossible to get the entire bird properly cooked. And even if you do everything right, roast chicken can be a bit plain.

This chapter looks at two inspired takes on roast chicken. Our roast lemon chicken starts by following a conventional path but ends with a twist. And there's nothing conventional about cooking a butterflied chicken under a brick. But these two recipes do have some things in common. Both deliver crisp skin and lots of flavor. Best of all, these two roast chicken recipes are fairly easy to execute.

ROAST LEMON CHICKEN

WHAT WE WANTED: Moist, evenly roasted chicken, with crisp skin, and a bright, pure lemon flavor without a trace of bitterness.

From the simplest incarnation (throw a whole lemon into the cavity of a chicken) to the most ridiculous (smother a chicken with homemade candied lemon peel), there are as many ways to make roast lemon chicken as there are cooks ready to try it. But while this familiar dish suffers from an identity crisis, one thing is sure: Roast lemon chicken can be disappointing. The chicken itself can be dry and uninteresting, tasting nothing like lemon or, even worse, bursting with bitter citric acidity. The accompanying pan sauce (if any) usually suffers a similar fate—bland, with no lemon flavor, or pucker-up harsh.

Our goal was simple: Find a way to bring out the full potential of the two main ingredients. Although such a quest seemed simple and straightforward, we soon discovered that the path to success would be a long and winding one.

We used our favorite basic roast chicken as a starting point, including no lemons in the initial testing. We brushed a chicken with melted butter, placed it wing-side up in an oiled V-rack, and roasted it in a moderate oven set to 375 degrees. After 20 minutes, we flipped the chicken, other wing-side up, and roasted it for 20 more minutes. Finally, we rotated the chicken breast-side up and roasted it for a final 25 minutes. This chicken was exceptionally good. Rotating the bird while it roasted kept the breast meat from drying out before the thigh meat was done, yielding an evenly roasted bird. The only downside was the lack of a crackling crisp skin. To solve this problem, we raised the oven temperature to 450 degrees while the chicken was breast-side up. Now the chicken skin was nicely browned and reasonably crisp. Satisfied with our results, we decided to introduce a little lemon into the game.

We threw a whole lemon, cut in half, into the cavity of the chicken and roasted it according to our method. While this did not produce lemon-flavored chicken, the meat was perfumed with a light lemon essence. Cutting the lemon into smaller pieces helped to develop the lemon flavor, although it was still a bit muted. We also tossed in several cloves of garlic and a handful of fresh thyme, but while the garlic flavor was pleasantly evident, the thyme lent little of its flavor to the meat. At this point, lemon testing was interrupted by one annoying occurrence. Invariably, the small pieces of lemon and garlic would tumble out of the chicken each time it was turned. This problem was readily solved by stitching the skin of the cavity closed using a long wooden skewer. We also wondered if we could simplify the recipe by turning the bird only once instead of three times, so we started the chicken breast-side down (rather than wing-side down) at 375 degrees and then flipped it breast-side up just before raising the temperature to 450. We had the perfect roasting method—or at least we thought so.

Our next step was to heighten the lemon flavor. Our first test involved making a compound butter to which we added finely grated lemon zest. We spread the butter under the skin of the chicken and proceeded to roast it. While the lemon flavor was notable, it came with an unpleasant bitter flavor. Next we marinated the chicken in a mixture of lemon juice, lemon zest, and herbs. But no matter how long we let the chicken soak in the marinade (even overnight), the lemon flavor failed to travel much beyond the skin. Next we tried soaking the chicken in a brine (a saltwater solution) flavored with lemon juice and lemon peel, but this gave the chicken a weird, lemonade-like flavor that tasted artificial. Still, the test wasn't a complete wash because the brining without the lemon flavorings turned out a superior chicken—moist, juicy, and well seasoned.

But at what cost? Now, owing to the moisture added by the brine, the chicken skin had lost its crispy texture. We

thought that a blast from the broiler might do the trick, but because the chicken was still in whole form, it browned unevenly. A colleague then suggested a method that she had picked up working in a restaurant. After cutting the roast chicken into parts, we put them back, skin-side up, in the roasting pan and broiled them, producing a deep brown skin that was crackling crisp. An added benefit of the brine/roast/broil method is that the meat, which is face-down in the pan drippings, becomes extremely moist and succulent.

Now we had a perfectly good, evenly roasted, well-seasoned chicken with very crisp skin and ultra-moist meat. But we couldn't yet sell this dish as roast lemon chicken—we needed a lemon-infused pan sauce to really make this chicken shine. Working with the pan drippings as the basis for a lemony sauce, we added a squirt of lemon juice to the pan drippings. This was exactly what we were looking for—a sauce with bright, pure lemon flavor. Now all that was necessary was a little butter to thicken the sauce and some fresh parsley and thyme to lend an herbal note. Served with the sauce on the side, this roast lemon chicken—perfectly cooked, crisp-skinned, and lemon-scented—was one we could be proud of.

WHAT WE LEARNED: Place a quartered lemon in the cavity to perfume the chicken as it roasts. For crisp skin, quarter the roast chicken and then run the pieces under the broiler. And for a final hit of lemon flavor, make a quick lemon pan sauce to accompany the chicken.

CRISPY ROAST LEMON CHICKEN

Serves 3 to 4

If using a kosher chicken, skip the brining and begin with step 2. Broiling the fully roasted and quartered chicken skin-side up as it sits in a shallow pool of sauce crisps and browns the skin while keeping the meat succulent. If you decide to skip the broiling step, go directly from quartering the chicken to finishing the sauce with lemon juice, butter, and herbs.

1	cup Diamond Crystal Kosher Salt, ¾ cup Morton Kosher Salt, or ½ cup table salt
1	whole chicken (3½ to 4 pounds), trimmed of excess fat, giblets removed and discarded, chicken rinsed and patted dry
	Vegetable cooking spray
2	medium lemons
6	medium garlic cloves, crushed and peeled
4	tablespoons (½ stick) unsalted butter, 2 tablespoons melted and the remaining 2 tablespoons chilled and cut into 2 pieces
	Ground black pepper
1¾	cups low-sodium chicken broth
1	tablespoon minced fresh parsley leaves
1	teaspoon minced fresh thyme leaves

1. Dissolve the salt in 2 quarts cold water in a large bowl, stockpot, or Dutch oven. Immerse the chicken in the brine and refrigerate 1 hour. Remove the chicken from the brine and pat dry with paper towels.

2. Adjust an oven rack to the lower-middle position; heat the oven to 375 degrees. Spray a V-rack with cooking spray and set in a flameproof roasting pan.

3. Cut 1 of the lemons lengthwise into quarters. Place the lemon quarters and garlic in the cavity of the chicken. Following the illustration on page 66, thread a long wooden skewer through the flaps of skin on either side of the cavity. Turn the skewer and rethread back through the skin flaps.

TECHNIQUE:
Sealing the Chicken Cavity

Lemon, garlic, and herbs placed inside a chicken as it roasts can fall out when the bird is turned. In the test kitchen, we use a wooden skewer to sew the cavity shut. Holding the two flaps of skin together over the cavity with one hand, thread a long wooden skewer through both flaps about 1 inch down from the top of the cavity. Turn the skewer and rethread back through the flaps about ½ inch below the first stitch. Turn the skewer one last time and make the third stitch. Cut off the excess skewer with shears.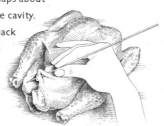

Repeat stitching as necessary to shut the cavity. Brush the breast side of the chicken with 1 tablespoon of the melted butter and season generously with pepper. Place the chicken breast-side down in the V-rack, then brush the back with the remaining 1 tablespoon melted butter and season generously with pepper.

4. Roast the chicken 40 minutes. Remove the roasting pan from the oven; increase the oven temperature to 450 degrees. Using 2 large wads of paper towels, rotate the chicken breast-side up; add 1 cup of the chicken broth to the roasting pan. Return the roasting pan to the oven and continue roasting until the thickest part of a thigh registers 165 to 170 degrees on an instant-read thermometer, about 35 to 40 minutes longer. Remove the roasting pan from the oven; tip the V-rack to let the juices from the chicken cavity run into the roasting pan. Transfer the chicken to a cutting board and let rest, uncovered, while making the sauce. Remove the V-rack from the roasting pan.

5. Adjust the oven rack to the upper-middle position; heat the broiler. Skim the fat from the drippings in the roasting pan, add the remaining ¾ cup chicken broth, and set the roasting pan over high heat on a burner. Simmer the liquid, scraping the pan bottom with a wooden spoon to loosen the browned bits, until reduced to ½ cup, about 4 minutes; set aside off heat.

6. Discard the lemons and garlic from the chicken cavity. Following the illustrations on page 68, cut the chicken into quarters. Pour the accumulated chicken juices into the roasting pan, then place the chicken quarters, skin-side up, into the sauce in the roasting pan; broil the chicken until the skin is crisp and deep golden brown, 3 to 5 minutes. Transfer the chicken to a serving platter.

7. Halve the remaining lemon lengthwise; squeeze the juice of one half into the roasting pan; cut the remaining half into 4 wedges and set aside. Whisk the remaining 2 tablespoons butter into the sauce until combined; stir in the parsley and thyme. Adjust the seasoning with salt and pepper to taste. Serve the chicken with the pan sauce and lemon wedges.

EQUIPMENT CORNER:
Countertop Rotisserie Ovens

IS THERE ANYTHING AS HUNGER-INDUCING AS A ROTIS-serie oven? Just thinking about a deliciously greasy lamb souvlaki, a Chinatown window jam-packed with Peking ducks, or the mesmerizing merry-go-round of chicken at the local Boston Market can send us on a half-hour trek toward the nearest rotisserie joint. Well, according to a recent infomercial and a slew of imitators, any cook with a wealth of counter space can now have that authentic rotisserie flavor at home. Too good to be true, you say? We picked up five of the most popular and easily accessible countertop rotisserie ovens to see if our dream could become a reality.

To evaluate the ovens, we decided to roast a whole chicken, a 4-pound beef rib roast, and a pork tenderloin in

each one. We also selected one recipe from each machine's instruction manual and cooked it in its respective oven.

Countertop rotisserie ovens come in two distinct styles—horizontal roasters and vertical roasters. The two horizontal roasters were the George Jr. Rotisserie ($100) and the Ronco Showtime Jr. ($74.98). The chickens cooked in these ovens were decent, but the lurid, ashen pork tenderloins were entirely unappetizing and utterly bland. The beef rib roasts browned beautifully but, when sliced, revealed egregiously uneven cooking—the perimeter of the roasts was well done, while the very core was medium. The George Jr. oven also had its share of flaws. The instruction manual suggested securing our 4-pound beef roast in an 8-inch-square by 2¼-inch-deep basket—an utterly impossible feat. (The roast had to go directly on the spit.) In addition, this rotisserie oven was difficult to clean, and the recipe we tested for Dijon Mustard Steaks was lousy. Since the Ronco Showtime Jr. did a slightly better job at roasting the chicken and was easier to load, unload, and clean, we thought it the best of its kind.

The others, all vertical roasters, were the Betty Crocker Vertisserie Plus ($100), the Farberware Vertical Rotisserie ($75), and the Sunbeam Carousel Rotisserie ($80). The first two looked surprisingly similar and were, hands down, the most simple to use. The Sunbeam was the most awkward to use, and it managed to perform just as poorly as its vertical roasting cousins. On a positive note, this model was entertaining to watch. Several spectators were captivated by the pirouetting "spit-roasted cobra"—baby back ribs threaded on the center skewer in a serpentine "S" shape.

As our tests indicated, rotisserie nirvana will continue to be accessible only by automobile. Although we had high hopes that our rotisserie cravings would be satiated by these countertop counterfeits, it seems as if we will have to keep an eye out for the next generation of infomercials.

Rating Countertop Rotisserie Ovens

IN EACH OVEN, WE ROASTED A WHOLE BRINED CHICKEN, a 4-pound beef rib roast, and a pork tenderloin. Then, we selected one recipe from each recipe booklet/instruction manual and cooked it in its respective oven. In general, we found that the two horizontal ovens produced a more moist and flavorful chicken than the vertical roasters, but overall we could find little to recommend a countertop rotisserie oven of any type. The ovens are listed below in order of preference.

RECOMMENDED WITH RESERVATIONS
Ronco Showtime Jr. **$74.98**
The top performer won points for ease of use and for including a surprisingly tasty recipe, Ron's Spicy Lemon Pepper Chicken Wings.

RECOMMENDED WITH RESERVATIONS
George Jr. Rotisserie **$100**
This model performed nearly as well as the Ronco oven but was more difficult to operate. It lost points because of difficulty fitting the rib roast in the suggested roasting basket.

NOT RECOMMENDED
Betty Crocker BCF6000 Vertisserie Plus **$100**
Although we found this model to be the easiest to operate, the vertical spit cooked the meats poorly in most of our tests.

NOT RECOMMENDED
Farberware Vertical Rotisserie **$75**
Similar to the Betty Crocker model but with a smaller capacity, this oven was comparatively lightweight and fragile.

NOT RECOMMENDED
Sunbeam Carousel Rotisserie **$80**
This oven performed poorly in almost all the tests and seemed very flimsy. It did win style points with those who enjoyed watching meats pirouette just beyond the clear oven door.

TECHNIQUE:
Quartering the Chicken after Roasting

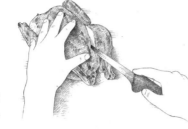

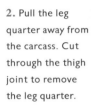
1. Cut into the chicken where the leg skin meets the breast.

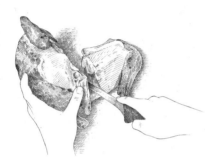

2. Pull the leg quarter away from the carcass. Cut through the thigh joint to remove the leg quarter.

3. Cut down along one side of the breastbone, pulling the breast meat away as you cut.

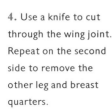
4. Use a knife to cut through the wing joint. Repeat on the second side to remove the other leg and breast quarters.

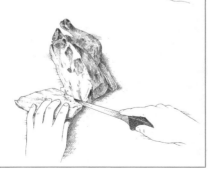

Q&A

Is there a way to get the benefits of brining (that is, moister meat) without so much salt?

We often hear from readers who like the moisture that brining gives to chicken and turkey but find that the meat sometimes tastes too salty. To see if salt-sensitive cooks could brine with less salt, we tested reducing the salt in our standard brine. Unfortunately, we found there was no marked difference between birds brined in a half-strength solution and non-brined samples. The brined birds were a bit saltier than the unbrined birds, but they were not substantially moister, which, after all, is the most important reason to brine a chicken or turkey.

Although brining offers great benefits in terms of flavor and texture, it may not be right for all cooks. But before eliminating this technique from your repertoire, make sure that you are using the right salt at the right strength for brining. Remember that 1 cup table salt equals 1½ cups Morton Kosher Salt but 2 cups Diamond Crystal Kosher Salt.

CHICKEN UNDER A BRICK

WHAT WE WANTED: A perfectly cooked butterflied chicken with super-skin crisp that could be on the table—with some roasted potatoes—in less than one hour.

Cooking a butterflied chicken under a brick in a skillet not only looks cool but also shaves half an hour off the cooking time of a regular roast chicken and produces an amazingly crisp skin. The brick helps keep the chicken flat as it cooks, forcing all of the skin to make contact with the pan. Yet, after trying a few recipes, we noted two big problems. First, the beautiful, crisp skin often turns soggy or greasy as the chicken finishes cooking. Second, the chicken is often marinated, but we found the marinade scorches in the hot pan.

We also noted a few problems that could be immediately rectified. Not only did we find that a single brick on top of the chicken didn't offer an even distribution of weight but that very few people actually have bricks hanging about in the kitchen. Also, we found that chickens much larger than three pounds were difficult to fit into a 12-inch skillet.

To start, we set the idea of a marinade aside for the moment and focused on the cooking method. Using two unmarinated, butterflied chickens, we tested the difference between pounding the chicken to an even thickness with a mallet and simply pressing it flat by hand. When pounded with a mallet, the super-flat chicken cooked very evenly, and more of the skin made contact with the pan, thus turning crisp. By comparison, only portions of skin on the thicker sections of the chicken flattened by hand were nicely browned.

We cooked these chickens according to the method cited in most of the recipes we researched—skin-side down first with bricks on top, then flipped to cook the underside, replacing the bricks to help keep the chicken flat. This, however, didn't work. After the chickens were flipped and the weight placed back on top, the skin (which was now crisp and delicate) was torn to pieces and steamed itself flaccid.

We then tried not replacing the bricks after the chicken was flipped, but the skin still turned rubbery from the steam and splattering oil. Next, we tried cooking the underside of the chicken first, finishing breast-side down, but this didn't work either. By flipping time, the pan was so loaded with grease and burned bits that the skin had no chance of looking pretty. It was greasy, spotty, and slightly bitter.

We then decided to try a different approach altogether. We cooked the chicken skin-side down underneath the bricks until it had a beautiful color. We then removed the bricks, flipped the bird over, and finished it, still in the skillet, in a 450-degree oven. The hot, dry air of the oven ensured that the skin remained crisp and intact as the meat finished cooking through. As for the bricks, we found that heavy cans and a cast-iron pot worked just as well (see the recipe headnote for further ideas).

Why is dark meat dark?

Leg muscles are exercised much more than breast muscles. As a result, leg muscles contain more myoglobin, a compound that helps store oxygen in muscle cells. Muscles with a high concentration of myoglobin are darker than muscles with little myoglobin. Increased exercise also makes muscle tissue tougher, which is why most recipes suggest cooking dark meat to a higher internal temperature than white meat. While breast meat is done at 160 degrees, we find that dark meat should be cooked to an internal temperature of 165 to 170 degrees for maximum palatability.

Based on our oven-finish method, we quickly figured out an easy way to include a flavorful marinade as well as some accompanying potatoes. Brushing the marinade onto the crisp chicken before finishing it in the oven was the obvious answer to our initial scorching problem. The heat of the oven fused the marinade to the skin without ruining its crisp texture, and the brief cooking time made it easy to retain the fresh, potent flavors in the marinade. Tasters preferred a simple oil-based marinade made with garlic, lemon, thyme, and a kick of red pepper flakes.

We found an easy method for roasting potatoes, too. We simply threw them into the pan underneath the chicken before it went into the oven. Emerging from the oven fragrant and gorgeous, the chicken must rest for 10 minutes, during which time the potatoes are returned to the oven to finish cooking and pick up some color.

WHAT WE LEARNED: With the help of both the stovetop and the oven, a complete meal can be made in a skillet. Start by browning the weighted chicken skin-side down in the skillet, remove the chicken from the pan, add some potatoes, and place the chicken back in the pan on top of the potatoes. Finish cooking the chicken and potatoes in the oven.

CHICKEN UNDER A BRICK WITH HERB-ROASTED POTATOES

Serves 4

Instead of two bricks and a rimmed baking sheet, you may use a heavy cast-iron skillet loaded with several cans or a large stockpot partially filled with water. Be careful when removing the pan from the oven, as the handle will be hot.

1   small whole chicken (about 3 pounds), trimmed of excess fat, giblets removed and discarded, chicken rinsed and patted dry
Salt and ground black pepper
2   tablespoons plus 1 teaspoon vegetable oil
3   medium garlic cloves, minced or pressed through a garlic press (about 1 tablespoon)
1   tablespoon minced fresh thyme
⅛   teaspoon red pepper flakes
2   tablespoons juice from 1 lemon, plus 1 lemon, cut into wedges
1½ pounds small Red Bliss potatoes, scrubbed, dried, and cut into ¾-inch wedges
1   tablespoon minced fresh parsley leaves

1. Following the illustrations on page 71, remove the backbone from the chicken and pound flat with a rubber mallet. Season the chicken with salt and pepper to taste.

2. Adjust an oven rack to the lowest position and heat the oven to 450 degrees. Heat 1 teaspoon of the oil in a heavy-bottomed 12-inch ovenproof nonstick skillet over medium-high heat until it begins to smoke. Swirl the skillet to coat evenly with oil. Place the chicken, skin-side down, in the hot pan and reduce the heat to medium. Place the weight (see the note above) on the chicken and cook, checking every 5 minutes or so, until evenly browned, about 25 minutes. (After 20 minutes, the chicken should be fairly crisp and golden; if not, turn the heat up to medium-high and continue to cook until well browned.)

3. Meanwhile, mix the remaining 2 tablespoons oil, garlic, 1½ teaspoons of the thyme, the pepper flakes, lemon juice, ½ teaspoon salt, and ¼ teaspoon black pepper in a small bowl and set aside.

4. Using tongs, carefully transfer the chicken, skin-side up, to a clean plate. Pour off any accumulated fat in the pan and add the potatoes, sprinkling them with ¼ teaspoon salt, ⅛ teaspoon black pepper, and the remaining 1½ teaspoons thyme. Place the chicken, skin-side up, on the potatoes and brush the skin with the reserved thyme–lemon juice mixture.

5. Transfer the pan to the oven and roast until the thickest part of the breast registers 160 degrees on an instant-read thermometer, 10 to 15 minutes longer. Transfer the chicken to a cutting board and let rest 10 to 15 minutes.

6. Return the skillet with the potatoes to the oven and roast until browned and cooked through, about 10 minutes. Using a slotted spoon, transfer the potatoes to a large bowl, leaving the fat behind. Toss the potatoes with the parsley. Cut the chicken into pieces. Serve the chicken and potatoes immediately with the lemon wedges.

TECHNIQUE: Butterflying a Chicken

1. With the breast side down and the tail of the chicken facing you, use poultry shears to cut along the length of one side of the backbone.

2. With the breast side still down, turn the neck end to face you, cut along the other side of the backbone and remove it.

3. Turn the chicken breast-side up. Open the chicken on the work surface. Use the palm of your hand to flatten the chicken, then pound it with the flat side of a mallet to a fairly even thickness.

A four-ingredient compound butter flavor[ed] with garlic and lemon gives a big flavor boo[st] to pan-seared shrimp.

FLASH in a pan

Dinner in less than 20 minutes is the holy grail of weeknight cooking. Many recipes make good on this promise, but most ultimately reflect the minimal effort exerted on the part of the cook. They are fine in a pinch but rarely worth making again. But it doesn't have to be this way.

For this chapter, we started with two quick-cooking classics— sautéed chicken cutlets and pan-seared shrimp—and worked to elevate them from the everyday. We refused to employ lengthy ingredient lists or difficult techniques, and the total preparation and cooking time had to remain under the 20-minute mark. We've figured out the secrets to these dishes and what separates the merely serviceable from the truly memorable. So heat up your skillets and get ready to cook.

SAUTÉED CHICKEN CUTLETS

WHAT WE WANTED: Sautéed super-thin cutlets are satisfying midweek fare, except when they are tough and dry. We set out to improve chicken paillards.

The ultra-thin sautéed chicken cutlets known as paillards owe their invention to Monsieur Paillard, a Parisian restaurateur of the late nineteenth century. Although his namesake juicy cutlets are now legendary, the test kitchen quickly came to the conclusion that he took the secret of chicken paillards to his grave, given the bland, dry, shoe-leather-tough chicken cutlets we prepared from a wide variety of recipes.

Classically defined, a paillard is a cutlet trimmed or pounded to a wafer-thin thickness of ¼ inch. Technically speaking, a paillard can be any variety of meat, although it is most often associated with poultry. Any thicker than ¼ inch and it's a workaday cutlet; any thinner and it overcooks at the mere sight of a skillet. The recipes we found offered little or conflicting advice about preparation and loaded the cutlets with sauces ranging from basic to baroque (demi-glace, truffles, and cockscombs). We decided to tackle the cutlets first and deal with a sauce in due time.

The first step, of course, was to flatten the chicken into cutlets. We sandwiched whole boneless, skinless breasts between plastic wrap and went at them with a heavy meat pounder. By the time the meat was ¼ inch thick, our hands were throbbing—it took a long time to get a cutlet that was more than an inch thick this thin. Even worse, the cutlet looked as if it had gone a few hard-fought rounds with a heavyweight (the edges were frayed and the interior was mottled with peek-a-boo holes). More important, the cutlets were not even in thickness, so there was no way they could cook properly. Following the lead of another paillard recipe, we halved the breasts horizontally before pounding. Roughly ½ to ¾ inch thick, these cut breasts required less pounding, were consistently even, and also ended up being

a reasonable size for skillet cooking. (The first round of cutlets ended up the size of dinner plates.) A sharp chef's knife proved essential for this task, something not everyone has at home. We solved this problem by chilling the chicken breasts in the freezer for about 15 minutes, which firmed the chicken sufficiently to slice with just about any knife.

We also learned a bit about using a meat pounder. Brute force is out. The chicken breaks apart when hit too hard. We had better luck with a firm yet gentle stroke—methodical, not murderous. Moistening the plastic wrap with a little water—a common technique when pounding cutlets—appeared to help by allowing the cutlet to slide under the mallet's assault. Seasoned generously with salt and pepper, the cutlets were ready for cooking.

A 12-inch skillet was the obvious choice for a pan as it could fit a recipe's worth of cutlets into just two batches. But the eternal question loomed: nonstick or traditional? Nonstick made for goof-proof cooking and easy cleanup, but the coating prevented the buildup of fond—the bits of meat that stick to the pan during cooking and lend depth and body to pan sauces. Not willing to sacrifice flavor for the sake of convenience, we chose a traditional skillet.

For our first attempt at cooking the cutlets, we heated a scant 2 teaspoons vegetable oil in the skillet until shimmering and then cooked each side of the cutlets until golden brown. The attractive coloring masked a leathery, desiccated texture. Increasing the heat to medium-high yielded slightly moister cutlets, but the texture was still too dry.

Thinking that a hotter initial temperature (which would get the cutlets in and out of the pan as quickly as possible) might be the key, we heated the skillet over medium-high until the oil was smoking. The resulting cutlets were promising, though the edges were very tough and the meat just shy of appealing. On a whim, we tried partially freezing the cutlets before cooking, but the cutlets browned less and the meat was just as dry. Weighting the cutlets with a heavy lid and pressing forcefully with a spatula also accomplished little.

Confident that high heat was the right direction, we revisited our method. Did both sides of the cutlet have to be browned for the best flavor? Or was it necessary to brown just one side, as is the case with fish fillets? We thoroughly browned the first side, about two minutes, and cooked the second side until just opaque—mere seconds. While the cutlet was just shy of fully cooked, it heated through within a few minutes' repose in a warm oven (long enough to make a pan sauce), and the results were the best yet: juicy, tender, and flavorful. Those pesky tough edges, however, persisted.

We thought more oil in the skillet might protect the edges, which it did, but the excess oil also splattered wildly and coated both the stovetop and the cook in a shower of grease. Rubbing the cutlet with oil before seasoning was a better approach, as it kept splattering to a minimum. But then it occurred to us: Why not replace the water used to lubricate the cutlets during pounding with oil? A scant ½ teaspoon per cutlet was all that was necessary to thinly coat each cutlet. Once cooked, the cutlets were—in their entirety—ideal. Shielded by a veneer of oil, both the edges and the interior were moist, tender, and juicy.

Now ready to prepare a couple of pan sauces, we searched through classic French cookbooks for inspiration, first settling on an apple and mustard sauce. We sautéed shallots in the "dirty" skillet and reduced some apple cider to concentrate it (and deglaze the fond), then finished with whole-grain French-style mustard, parsley, and butter. A shot of apple cider vinegar cut the sweetness and sharpened the apple flavor. We made a second sauce with chicken broth, white wine vinegar, tomato paste, and a large pinch of brown sugar that was finished with butter. Shallots, thyme, and white wine were the basis for a third sauce.

WHAT WE LEARNED: The cutlets must be halved horizontally before they are pounded. Coating the cutlets with oil as they are pounded keeps their edges from drying out when cooked. To keep the cutlets juicy, they should be browned on only one side.

SAUTÉED CHICKEN CUTLETS WITH MUSTARD-CIDER SAUCE
Serves 4

To make slicing the cutlets in half even easier, pop the chicken into the freezer until firm, about 15 minutes.

chicken cutlets

4   boneless, skinless chicken breasts (6 to 8 ounces each), prepared according to the illustrations on page 76
    Salt and ground black pepper
    Vegetable oil

mustard-cider sauce

2   teaspoons vegetable oil
1   medium shallot, minced (about 3 tablespoons)
1¼   cups apple cider
2   tablespoons cider vinegar
2   teaspoons whole-grain mustard
2   teaspoons minced fresh parsley leaves
2   tablespoons unsalted butter
    Salt and ground black pepper

1. FOR THE CHICKEN: Adjust an oven rack to the middle position and heat the oven to 200 degrees. Season both sides of each cutlet with salt and pepper. Heat 2 teaspoons of oil in a 12-inch skillet over medium-high heat until smoking. Place 4 cutlets in the skillet and cook without moving them until browned, about 2 minutes. Using a spatula, flip the cutlets and continue to cook until the second sides are opaque, 15 to 20 seconds. Transfer to a large heatproof plate. Add 2 teaspoons of oil to the now-empty skillet and repeat to cook the remaining cutlets. Cover the plate loosely with foil and transfer it to the oven to keep warm while making the sauce.

2. FOR THE SAUCE: Off the heat, add the oil and shallots to the hot skillet. Using residual heat, cook, stirring constantly, until softened, about 30 seconds. Set the skillet over medium-high heat and add the cider and vinegar. Bring to a simmer, scraping the pan bottom with a wooden spoon to loosen any browned bits. Simmer until reduced to ½ cup, 6 to 7 minutes. Off the heat, stir in the mustard and parsley; whisk in the butter 1 tablespoon at a time. Season with salt and pepper and serve immediately with the cutlets.

VARIATIONS

SAUTÉED CHICKEN CUTLETS WITH TOMATO, THYME, AND WHITE WINE VINEGAR SAUCE

Follow the recipe for Sautéed Chicken Cutlets with Mustard-Cider Sauce, adding 2 teaspoons tomato paste along with the shallot, substituting 1 cup low-sodium chicken broth for the cider and 3 tablespoons white wine vinegar for the cider vinegar, and adding 1½ teaspoons light brown sugar and 6 sprigs fresh thyme along with the liquids. Omit the mustard and parsley.

SAUTÉED CHICKEN CUTLETS WITH SHALLOT AND WHITE WINE SAUCE

Follow the recipe for Sautéed Chicken Cutlets with Mustard-Cider Sauce, substituting ½ cup dry white wine and ¾ cup low-sodium chicken broth for the cider, omitting the vinegar and mustard, replacing the parsley with 1 teaspoon minced fresh thyme, and increasing the butter to 3 tablespoons.

GETTING IT RIGHT:
How Pounding Can Fail

If you try to pound a whole breast (most are more than an inch thick) without first splitting it in half, the end result is ragged. We found that halving the breast horizontally and then pounding it yielded neat, even paillards.

TECHNIQUE:
Preparing Chicken Paillards

1. Lay each cutlet tenderloin-side down (the floppy, thin piece of meat attached to the breast) and smooth the top with your fingers. Any yellow fat will slide to the periphery, where it can be trimmed with a knife.

2. Tenderloins tend to fall off or disintegrate during pounding, so they are best removed and reserved for another use, such as a stir-fry.

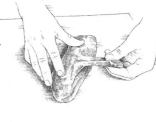

3. Holding the knife parallel to the cutting board, halve each breast horizontally to form two cutlets of even thickness.

4. Pour ½ teaspoon vegetable oil in the center of a sheet of plastic wrap. Turn one cutlet in the oil to coat. Top with a second sheet of plastic wrap and pound gently to an even ¼-inch thickness. Repeat with the remaining cutlets, adding additional oil as needed.

Q&A

Is there a non-alcoholic substitute for white wine in pan sauces?

Our first impulse was to replace wine or vermouth with an equal amount of broth, but upon testing we found that sauces prepared this way lacked acidity and balance. After several rounds of tests, we found four ingredients—dealcoholized white wine (Sutter Home Fre, for example), verjus (the unfermented juice of unripe wine grapes), lemon juice, and white wine vinegar—that could make up for the lack of acidity. Formulas are summarized below. For ingredients added when the sauce is ready to serve, use the lower amount, taste, and add more if greater acidity is desired.

ALCOHOL-FREE PAN SAUCES
To replace ½ cup wine or vermouth, try:

Ingredient	When to Add
¼ cup each DEALCOHOLIZED WINE and CHICKEN BROTH	Use to deglaze the pan
2–4 tablespoons VERJUS	Just before serving
½–1 teaspoon LEMON JUICE	Just before serving
½–1 teaspoon WHITE WINE VINEGAR	Just before serving

TASTING LAB: Chicken Cutlets

IN A WORLD OF LOW-FAT FANATICISM AND A SOCIETY obsessed with weight, it is not surprising that boneless, skinless chicken breasts are a standard in many home kitchens. No fat, no fuss, and unfortunately, no flavor. We've come up with countless recipes to add zip to these otherwise boring birds, but we never stopped to look at the chicken itself. Was there a difference in flavor among the popular brands? Do terms like "organic," "free range," "natural," or "kosher" have any real bearing on the quality of the meat?

To find out, we gathered six brands of boneless, skinless chicken breasts, broiled them without seasoning, and had 20 tasters sample the chickens side by side. Among the contenders were one kosher bird, two "natural," and one "free-range." The remaining two were just "chicken."

The U.S. Department of Agriculture defines "natural" as "a product containing no artificial ingredients or added color and is only minimally processed (a process which does not fundamentally alter the raw product)…" In the case of the chicken, it means there are no antibiotics or hormones, and the birds are fed a vegetarian diet. "Free-range" means exactly what it says: The birds are not confined to small cages but allowed to roam freely. Some people find that this excess motion yields tougher meat, but our tasters did not find this to be the case.

As in our last tasting of whole chickens, Empire Kosher topped the charts, this time tying for first place with all-natural Bell & Evans. The only kosher bird, Empire won points with tasters for its superior flavor: namely, salt. The koshering process involves coating the chicken with salt to draw out any impurities; this process, similar to brining, results in moist, salty meat (for this reason, we do not recommend brining kosher birds). Springer Farms All-Natural and Eberly's Free Range chickens also scored well.

Last place finishers (and lowest priced) Perdue and White Gem (our local store brand) were downgraded for poor texture and unnatural flavor. Tasters were also put off by the brash yellow color of the birds.

In the end, it seems that more money can buy you a better bird and, many would argue, a better-for-you bird. (Kosher birds are also all-natural and contain no hormones or antibiotics.) As for lower-priced supermarket staples and store brands, a cheaper price does indicate a cheaper product.

Rating Chicken Cutlets

TWENTY MEMBERS OF THE *COOK'S ILLUSTRATED* STAFF TASTED ALL OF THE CHICKEN CUTLETS, WHICH WERE cooked to the same degree of doneness under a broiler and without seasoning. The chicken cutlets are listed in order of preference based on their scores in this tasting. All brands are available in supermarkets, although distribution for poultry products is generally not nationwide.

RECOMMENDED

Empire Kosher Chicken Breast Boneless and Skinless

$6.69 per pound

This top finisher was deemed "nicely seasoned" and "buttery." Others praised its "great texture—no dryness." Almost all tasters noted the "salty" flavor.

RECOMMENDED

Bell & Evans Naturally Raised Boneless Skinless Breast

$5.99 per pound

Tied for first place, this all-natural chicken was praised for its "good texture" and "clean flavor." Though a minority of tasters found it "bland," most favored its "clean," "rich" flavor.

RECOMMENDED

Springer Mountain Farms Boneless Skinless Breasts

$5.99 per pound

"Tastes like chicken," wrote one taster of this boutique brand from Georgia. Many found this chicken to have a "natural flavor," though others found it "bland."

RECOMMENDED

Eberly's Free Range Young Organic Chicken Boneless Skinless Breast

$7.99 per pound

"Nondescript," wrote one taster of the only free-range chicken in the tasting, "though very tender." Others found the taste "slightly sour."

NOT RECOMMENDED

Perdue Fit 'N Easy Skinless and Boneless Fresh Chicken Breasts

$4.99 per pound

This supermarket staple lost points for its "unnatural" flavor, "mustard color," and "chalky" texture. Some tasters complained of an unpleasant aftertaste.

NOT RECOMMENDED

White Gem Boneless Skinless Chicken Breast

$4.29 per pound

There were no fans of this store brand from Stop & Shop supermarkets, which tasters found "chewy," "mushy," "stringy," and "bland." One taster wrote simply, "awful."

PAN-SEARED SHRIMP

WHAT WE WANTED: Nicely browned shrimp that were still juicy, moist, and tender.

Having prepared literally tons of shrimp in the test kitchen and in our own home kitchens, we have found that pan-searing produces the ultimate combination of a well-caramelized exterior and a moist, tender interior. If executed properly, this cooking method also preserves the shrimp's plumpness and trademark briny sweetness.

That being said, a good recipe for pan-seared shrimp is hard to find. Of the handful of recipes we uncovered, the majority resulted in shrimp that were variously dry, flavorless, pale, tough, or gummy—hardly appetizing. It was time to start some serious testing.

We quickly uncovered a few basic rules. First, tasters unanimously favored shrimp that were peeled before being cooked. Peeled shrimp are easier to eat, and unpeeled shrimp fail to pick up the delicious caramelized flavor that pan-searing provides. Second, the shrimp were best cooked in a 12-inch skillet; its large surface area kept the shrimp from overcrowding the pan and steaming—a surefire way to prevent caramelization. Third, oil was the ideal cooking medium, favored over both a dry pan (which made the shrimp leathery and metallic tasting) and butter (which tended to burn).

Next, in pan-searing the shrimp, we found that in the time it took to get the shrimp to brown, they turned out tough and overcooked. Looking for another way to promote browning in a shorter time frame, we thought to add a pinch of sugar to the shrimp. Not only did the sugar caramelize into a nice brown crust, it also accentuated the natural sweetness of the shrimp, nicely setting off their inherent sea-saltiness.

Even in a 12-inch skillet, 1½ pounds of shrimp must be cooked in two batches or they will steam instead of sear. The trick was to develop a technique that neither overcooked

the shrimp nor let half of them turn cold while the other half finished cooking. To prevent overcooking, we tried searing the shrimp on one side, removing the pan from the flame, and then allowing the residual heat to finish cooking the other side of the shrimp. This worked like a charm. Better yet, the residual heat from the pan also solved the cold shrimp problem. As soon as the second batch finished cooking (the first batch was now near room temperature), we tossed the first batch back into the pan, covered it, and let residual heat work its magic once again. After about a minute, all of the shrimp were perfectly cooked and piping hot. Now all we needed were a few ideas for some quick sauces.

We tested sauces made from assertive ingredients such as garlic, ginger, and chipotle chile mixed with plenty of acidity as a foil for the shrimp's richness. The most successful of these sauces were those that clung to the shrimp like a glaze. All of them could easily be made ahead of time and quickly tossed with the shrimp during the last stage of cooking, once the pan was removed from the heat.

WHAT WE LEARNED: Season peeled shrimp with salt, pepper, and sugar (to promote browning) before cooking them in a very hot pan. Cook just ¾ pound of shrimp at a time, searing on just one side, and then use residual heat to cook the second side. Finish the shrimp with a potent flavored butter or glaze.

PAN-SEARED SHRIMP

Serves 4

The cooking times below are for extra-large shrimp (there are 21 to 25 in 1 pound). If this size is not available in your market, buy large shrimp—the next size down—and adjust the cooking time slightly. Either a nonstick or a traditional skillet will work for this recipe, but a nonstick simplifies cleanup. See page 43 for tips on buying shrimp.

   2   tablespoons vegetable oil
   1½   pounds extra-large shrimp (21 to 25 per
        pound), peeled and deveined
   ¼   teaspoon salt
   ¼   teaspoon ground black pepper
   ⅛   teaspoon sugar

Heat 1 tablespoon of the oil in a 12-inch skillet over high heat until smoking. Meanwhile, toss the shrimp, salt, pepper, and sugar in a medium bowl. Add half of the shrimp to the pan in a single layer and cook until spotty brown and the edges turn pink, about 1 minute. Remove the pan from the heat. Using tongs, flip each shrimp and let stand until all but the very center is opaque, about 30 seconds. Transfer the shrimp to a large plate. Repeat with the remaining tablespoon of oil and the remaining shrimp. After the second batch has stood off the heat, return the first batch to the skillet and toss to combine. Cover the skillet and let stand until the shrimp are cooked through, 1 to 2 minutes. Serve immediately.

VARIATIONS

PAN-SEARED SHRIMP WITH GARLIC-LEMON BUTTER

Beat 3 tablespoons softened unsalted butter with a fork in a small bowl until light and fluffy. Stir in 1 medium garlic clove, minced, 1 tablespoon lemon juice, 2 tablespoons chopped parsley, and ⅛ teaspoon salt until combined. Follow the recipe for Pan-Seared Shrimp, adding the flavored butter when returning the first batch of shrimp to the skillet. Serve with lemon wedges, if desired.

PAN-SEARED SHRIMP WITH GINGER-HOISIN GLAZE

Stir 2 tablespoons hoisin sauce, 1 tablespoon rice vinegar, 1½ teaspoons soy sauce, 2 teaspoons grated fresh ginger, 2 teaspoons water, and 2 scallions, sliced thin, together in a small bowl. Follow the recipe for Pan-Seared Shrimp, substituting an equal amount of red pepper flakes for the black pepper and adding the hoisin mixture when returning the first batch of shrimp to the skillet.

PAN-SEARED SHRIMP WITH CHIPOTLE-LIME GLAZE

Stir 1 chipotle chile in adobo, minced, 2 teaspoons adobo sauce, 4 teaspoons brown sugar, 2 tablespoons lime juice, and 2 tablespoons chopped fresh cilantro leaves together in a small bowl. Follow the recipe for Pan-Seared Shrimp, adding the chipotle mixture when returning the first batch of shrimp to the skillet.

EQUIPMENT CORNER:
Cookware Cleaning Products

IF YOU COOK A LOT (LIKE WE DO), YOU CLEAN A LOT. In the test kitchen, we've long debated the merits of various cleaning methods and cleansers. We decided to end the debate and apply the same exhaustive methods we use to develop recipes to figure out the best, most efficient ways to clean cookware. We dirtied pots and pans by burning food onto surfaces. We also rounded up the worst-looking cookware in the test kitchen (and in our kitchens at home) to test methods for bringing a new shine to old pans.

Along the way, we tested a dozen cleansers on pots and pans made from a variety of materials. After weeks of work, our testers' hands were rough and chapped, but we did find some winners and losers among these cleansers. And by the end of this marathon cleaning session, the cookware in the test kitchen was looking much brighter.

Cast iron

Old, well-seasoned cast-iron pans have become heirlooms, making it hard to find even dirty, rusty, perfectly cruddy pans for a bargain at yard sales and flea markets. If you are lucky enough to find one, it deserves a place on the stovetop. After scraping up a couple of dirty pans with several grades of sandpaper and emery cloth—both being too harsh for even these badly rusted pans—we settled on the following method to restore pans that have been subject to such neglect.

First, rub the pan with fine steel wool and wipe out loose dirt and rust with a cloth (repeat until the pan is largely cleared of rust). Then place the pan on the burner over medium-low heat and add enough vegetable oil to coat the pan bottom heavily. Heat it for five minutes, or until the handle is too hot to touch; turn off the burner. Add enough salt to form a liquid-like paste and, wearing a work or gardening glove, scrub with a thick wad of paper towels, steadying the pan with a potholder. Repeat the heating and scrubbing steps until the pan is slick and black.

And to maintain a clean pan, we recommend the following after each use of the pan: Rinse the pan thoroughly in hot water, wipe it dry, and then coat it with a thin film of vegetable oil, wiping off any excess oil with paper towels. If hot water does not work to rid the pan of stuck-on food, try a washcloth to scrub the pan with salt.

Copper

We came across a number of ways for removing tarnish: a salted lemon half, Worcestershire sauce, tomato sauce, ketchup, vinegar, cream of tartar and water, yogurt, even boiling milk. Enterprising and interesting as they all are, these home remedies were not as effective as the traditional commercial polishes we tried, which not only removed tarnish but added shine. Among the home remedies, ketchup was the only one that effectively removed tarnish. Unfortunately, it did not add shine.

But if you're desperate to clean up a tarnished copper pan and have no commercial polish on hand, we recommend spreading an even layer of ketchup over the surface of a pan with a paper towel or dishcloth. After five minutes, wipe off the ketchup with a damp towel or sponge. Wash the pan with warm water and dishwashing liquid, and dry.

Stainless steel, nonstick, and hard-anodized aluminum

We found that these pans, which see the most action in the kitchen, present similar cleaning challenges. We identified three types of cleaning tasks: everyday messes on just-used cookware, stubborn messes that have built up over time, and burnt, blackened messes that make the cookware almost unusable.

When testing ways to handle these three types of jobs, we continually ran into stern warnings about mixing cleaning chemicals—bleach and ammonia in particular, as well as commercially prepared cleansers (which may contain bleach, ammonia, or any other harmful chemicals). When combined, bleach and ammonia create chloramine gases that are highly irritating to the lungs and can cause coughing and choking. With these warnings in mind, we forged ahead with testing.

For cleaning everyday messes, you can soak the pan overnight in sudsy water, but is there an alternative if you don't want to be greeted with greasy dishwater in the morning? Yes. Boil water in it. And you don't need to add either vinegar or baking soda to the water, as some sources recommend. We tried these formulas and they were no more effective than plain water. (The boiling water method is especially kind to nonstick cookware, as it allows you to clean the sensitive surface without any rough scrubbing.)

Fill the pan halfway with tap water and put it on the stovetop, uncovered. Bring the water to a boil and continue to boil briskly for about three minutes, and then turn off the burner. Next, using a wooden spatula, scrape the pan and then pour off the water. Let the pan sit for a few minutes and the residue will flake off as the pan dries. Wash the pan with hot water and dishwashing liquid, and dry.

Unfortunately, we found that our neat trick of boiling water in a pan doesn't clean up the stubborn, brown, sometimes tacky residue seared into a pan from many past meals. Neither does boiling water work on two forms of discoloration a pan may suffer: rainbows and brown tints likely caused by prolonged exposure to heat in excess of 500 degrees.

After tests with dishwashing liquid, SOS pads, and various home remedies, such as baking soda, we found two powdered cleansers—Bar Keepers Friend and Cameo—to be superior for these tasks. Stainless steel responded especially well to this technique, but it is also safe for nonstick surfaces. For anodized aluminum surfaces, do not use Bar Keepers Friend; Cameo can be used, although some manufacturers recommend Soft Scrub, which we found to be less effective.

Start by moistening the pan with water, then shake a film of cleanser over it to cover. Using a copper scrubber for stainless steel or a nylon scrubber for nonstick or anodized aluminum, scrub the pan; we found that circular motions work best. Finish cleaning the pan by washing it out with hot water and dishwashing liquid, and dry.

For pans with a stainless steel exterior that has been deeply, darkly blackened and seems immune to any amount of scrubbing with powdered cleanser, we did find a cleanser of last resort: oven cleaner. We recommend its use only on the exterior of pans (so this method is fine on pans with steel exteriors and nonstick interior finishes) and in extreme cases; ideally, you'll treat a pan with oven cleaner only once, to get it back up to snuff. Oven cleaner should not be used on hard-anodized aluminum pans. If possible, bring the pan to a shady spot outdoors; otherwise, clean the pan in a well-ventilated room, with the windows wide open.

Place the pan upside down on newspapers and, wearing rubber gloves, apply an even layer of cleaner. Let it sit for 20 minutes (or the time recommended on the can). With the gloves still on and using an old damp cloth or sponge, wipe off the oven cleaner. Discard the newspapers and thoroughly rinse or discard the cloth or sponge. Thoroughly rinse the pan in the sink under warm running water, then wash it with dishwashing liquid; thoroughly rinse again and dry.

BEST CLEANSERS FOR CAST IRON

We found that a thick paste of warm vegetable oil and salt does the best job of bringing rusty cast-iron pots and pans back to life.

BEST CLEANSERS FOR COPPER

Among widely available polishes, Weiman Metal Polish did the best job of removing tarnish and adding shine to copper pots and pans. Ketchup does a great job of removing tarnish but won't add a brilliant luster to copper cookware.

BEST CLEANSERS FOR STAINLESS STEEL, NONSTICK, AND ANODIZED ALUMINUM

We found Bar Keepers Friend and Cameo to be the most effective in removing stubborn messes from most of the cookware in the test kitchen. Cameo can be used on stainless steel, anodized aluminum, or nonstick surfaces; Bar Keepers Friend is too harsh for anodized aluminum but works well on stainless steel or nonstick surfaces.

Pan-Seared Shrimp **page 80**

Salad with Apples, Walnuts, Dried Cherries, and Herb Baked Goat Cheese **page 259**

French Onion Soup **page 263**

Sweet and Tangy Oven-Barbecued Chicken **page 102**

Campanelli with Asparagus, Basil, and Balsamic Glaze **page 175**

Hearty Lentil Soup **page 31**

Quick Cheese Bread **page 37**

Mexican Rice **page 168**

Chicken Enchiladas with Red Chili Sauce **page 162**

Mushroom Risotto **page 235**

Polenta with Gorgonzola **page 255**

93

Salsa Verde **page 141**

Crispy Roast Lemon Chicken **page 69**

Creole-Style Shrimp and Sausage Gumbo **page 42**

Pasta all'Amatriciana **page 239**

Classic Macaroni and Cheese **page 107**

FAMILY favorites

Cooking for a family isn't as easy as it was once. In Norman Rockwell pictures, the entire clan (with aunts, uncles, cousins, and grandparents) is gathered around the table with a dozen different dishes in front of them. No one has soccer practice or is working late. No one is on a weird diet, and the kids seem to eat the same thing as the adults.

Times have certainly changed, and meals are much more rushed. But we think it's important for families to spend an hour every evening gathered around the table. The challenge for the modern cook is figuring out what to make. Dishes that require all-day attention won't work, and kids today are much more likely to express their own opinions about what they want to eat. (As for dieters, well, you can't please everyone.)

The recipes in this chapter represent the best of modern home cooking. They are delicious, relatively straightforward fare that will appeal to young and old. What kid—or adult—won't look forward to macaroni and cheese or barbecued chicken?

OVEN-BARBECUED CHICKEN

WHAT WE WANTED: The idea—barbecued chicken straight from your oven—is a great one. Unfortunately, the real thing is often dry and tough, with a tasteless, baked-on sauce. Could we save this recipe and create an oven-barbecued chicken with a rich and tangy sauce?

When you hear the phrase "hospital food," what do you see in your mind's eye? That's right—plain baked chicken, the very portrait of bland institutional fare, a culinary yawn. The need to dress up this dull, workaday recipe probably inspired the idea of oven-barbecued chicken, which should, in theory at least, add sweet, tangy, spicy flavors to tender chicken by way of a rich, tomatoey sauce in the classic Kansas City style. In our experience, though, the idea remains just that—a theory. As expected, the five initial recipes we tried in the test kitchen delivered tough, rubbery, or unevenly cooked chicken in sauces ranging from pasty and candy-sweet to greasy, stale, thin, or commercial tasting.

Monumental as these problems seemed, we were inspired by the challenge. Surely this dish would be worthwhile if the chicken was juicy, tender, and evenly cooked and the sauce tasted fresh and multidimensional, clinging to the chicken in a thick, lightly caramelized coat.

The recipes we scoured indicated that our chicken options were wide open, as they called for, variously, half chickens, quarter chickens, whole chickens cut into serving pieces, bone-in breasts, thighs, drumsticks, and wings, and even meat that was cooked, boned, shredded, and mixed with barbecue sauce, à la pulled pork. To methodically test each option, we cobbled together a basic baking procedure: Bake the chicken at 350 degrees until partially done, coat with barbecue sauce—a bottled brand from the supermarket for now—and continue baking until the chicken is cooked through, basting with the sauce several times along the way.

Success was elusive. The halved and quartered chickens cooked unevenly and were awkward to eat. Butchering a whole chicken was more work than we saw fit to do for an easy Tuesday-night supper. Of course, purchasing cut-up serving pieces eliminated the work, but time and time again we found them to be sloppily butchered or even mismatched. Using a single cut of chicken, such as all breasts or thighs, helped with the evenness of cooking, at least, and we confirmed that tasters preferred the mild white meat of the breasts as a backdrop for the sauce. Shredding the cooked chicken to mix with the sauce was a messy, tedious process, so we settled on breasts as our best option.

One of the first problems to solve was the skin, which was consistently flabby, rubbery, and fatty. Any fat that rendered from the skin during cooking left the sauce not thick and clingy but greasy and loose, so it slid right off the chicken. To cover our bases, we tried cooking the chicken skin-side down in a preheated pan, slashing the skin lightly to expose extra surface area and expedite rendering, and air-drying the chicken prior to cooking. In the end, we rejected all of these methods as either not successful enough or too fussy for a quick weeknight dinner.

The solution, we hoped, would be to jettison the skin entirely. We gave skinless, boneless breasts a whirl and were delighted to find that they made for a dramatic improvement. The chewy skin became a nonissue, and we discovered an extra benefit in that both sides of the chicken breasts were now coated with sauce.

We were next determined to achieve our goal of a fresh, lively sauce with a properly thick and sticky texture. Could we find it in a bottled sauce? Hoping for an easy out, we tried several types, from supermarket standards to fancy mail-order products. We had the best luck with Bull's-Eye, a sauce that won a blind tasting here in the test kitchen, but we still felt that a homemade sauce could lift this recipe from pretty good to great.

That certainly didn't mean that the sauce had to be complicated. We began with our own Simple Sweet and Tangy Barbecue Sauce, a quick-cooked number developed several years ago. Although this sauce took about half an hour to prepare and required the use of a food processor and strainer, it did offer both fresh, balanced flavors and a thick, clingy texture.

Rather than building a new recipe from the ground up, we tried stripping this one down to make it even faster and simpler. After dozens of tests, we learned that ketchup, Worcestershire, mustard, molasses, chili powder, and cayenne were absolutely necessary, as were maple syrup and the tang of cider vinegar. We substituted grated onion for the onion juice in the original recipe and eliminated the hot pepper sauce, garlic, and liquid smoke. Only four minutes over medium heat were needed to blend the flavors, which became further concentrated when the sauce cooked again on the chicken.

We tried a few other flavoring tricks, including rubbing the chicken with a dry spice rub and marinating it overnight in the sauce before cooking it, but none was worth the effort. Brining was also a bust. The extra seasoning was superfluous in the face of the assertively flavored barbecue sauce, and the extra moisture in the meat from the brine tended to thin the sauce.

In terms of cooking temperature and method, we tried dousing the chicken with sauce and then baking it as well as dredging the chicken in seasoned flour and pan-frying it before undertaking an intricate dance of baking and basting. Both approaches failed.

From there, we focused on oven mechanics, testing various oven rack positions, various combinations of low and high temperatures (from 325 to 500 degrees), and additions of sauce at various points during cooking. Alas, despite the moniker "oven-barbecued," none of these oven-based methods worked, although we did learn that lower oven temperatures cooked the irregularly shaped chicken breasts evenly and that higher temperatures helped to concentrate the sauce.

Standing in the kitchen, scratching our heads after the umpteenth test, we looked at the skillet of waiting barbecue sauce and an idea flashed. We remembered a method we had used to make maple-glazed pork roast. It involved searing the roast in a skillet, reducing the glaze in the same skillet, and then finishing the roast in that already hot skillet in the oven. Would a similar technique help us to master our current challenge?

The first attempt showed promise, but it wasn't perfect because the exteriors of the breasts were dry from aggressive pan-searing. The solution was to sear the chicken breasts very lightly, just until they began to color and develop a slightly rough surface to which the sauce could adhere. The chicken was then removed from the pan, the sauce made, the chicken added back and coated with sauce, and the pan slipped under the broiler. The results were good, but the heat of the broiler had dried out the chicken a bit. The solution was to start the skillet in a 325-degree oven and then finish it under the broiler. The chicken was now juicy and thickly coated with a perfectly concentrated sauce.

WHAT WE LEARNED: Boneless, skinless breasts are the best choice for this recipe. Lightly brown the breasts in a hot skillet, build a quick sauce in the empty pan, return the chicken to the pan, and bake until the chicken is nearly cooked. Finish the recipe by turning the oven to broil to caramelize the sauce.

SWEET AND TANGY OVEN-BARBECUED CHICKEN

Serves 4

Real maple syrup is preferable to imitation syrup, and "mild" or "original" molasses is preferable to darker, more bitter types. If you are content to use bottled sauce, we had the best luck with Bull's-Eye Original, winner of a blind tasting held last year. Use 1¾ cups of sauce and, in step 3, reduce the sauce cooking time from 4 minutes to 2 minutes.

Some notes on equipment: First, to grate the onion, use a Microplane grater or the fine holes of a box grater. Second, resist the temptation to use a nonstick skillet; most nonstick skillets are not broiler-safe. Third, and most important, you should make this recipe only in an in-oven broiler; do not use a drawer-type broiler. Finally, be aware that broiling times may differ from one oven to another. For instance, in one editor's powerful professional-style oven, the chicken took just 4 minutes to reach 160 degrees, so we urge you to check the chicken for doneness after only 3 minutes of broiling. You may also have to lower the oven rack if your broiler runs very hot.

1 cup ketchup
2 tablespoons finely grated onion
2 tablespoons Worcestershire sauce
2 tablespoons Dijon mustard
3 tablespoons molasses
2 tablespoons maple syrup
3 tablespoons cider vinegar
1 teaspoon chili powder
¼ teaspoon cayenne
4 boneless, skinless chicken breasts, 6–7 ounces each (with tenderloins), patted dry with paper towels
Salt and ground black pepper
1 tablespoon vegetable oil

1. Adjust an oven rack to the upper-middle position, about 5 inches from the upper heating element; heat the oven to 325 degrees. Whisk the ketchup, onion, Worcestershire, mustard, molasses, maple syrup, vinegar, chili powder, and cayenne together in a small bowl; set aside. Season the chicken with salt and pepper.

2. Heat the oil in a heavy-bottomed, nonreactive 12-inch ovenproof skillet over high heat until beginning to smoke. Brown the chicken skinned-side down until very light golden, 1 to 2 minutes; using tongs, turn the chicken and brown until very light golden on the second side, 1 to 2 minutes longer. Transfer the chicken to a plate and set aside.

GETTING IT RIGHT: Oven-Barbecued Chicken, Reinvented in a Skillet

1. Lightly brown the chicken, transfer the pieces to a plate, and pour off the fat from the skillet.

2. Add the sauce ingredients to the empty pan and cook until a heatproof spatula leaves a clear trail.

3. Return the chicken to the skillet, turn to coat with sauce, then spoon more sauce over each piece.

4. Bake the chicken and sauce in the skillet, broil to caramelize the sauce, and then serve.

3. Discard the fat in the skillet; off the heat, add the sauce mixture and, using a wooden spoon, scrape up the browned bits on the bottom of the skillet. Simmer the sauce over medium heat, stirring frequently with a heatproof spatula, until the sauce is thick and glossy and a spatula leaves a clear trail in the sauce, about 4 minutes. Off the heat, return the chicken to the skillet and turn to coat thickly with the sauce; set the chicken pieces skinned-side up and spoon extra sauce over each piece to create a thick coating.

4. Place the skillet in the oven and cook until the thickest parts of the chicken breasts register 130 degrees on an instant-read thermometer, 10 to 14 minutes. Set the oven to broil and continue to cook until the thickest parts of the chicken breasts register 160 degrees, 5 to 10 minutes longer. Transfer the chicken to a platter and let rest 5 minutes. Meanwhile, whisk to combine the sauce in the skillet and transfer to a small bowl. Serve the chicken, passing the extra sauce separately.

GETTING IT RIGHT: The Problem with Packaged Chicken Breasts

Uniformly sized chicken breasts will cook more evenly than breasts of varying sizes. Unfortunately, it's difficult to discern the size of individual breasts when they're squished into a supermarket package (left). Once we removed the breasts from this package (right) and weighed them, we discovered that one breast weighed 9 ounces, two weighed 6 ounces, and one weighed just 4½ ounces. To prepare oven-barbecued chicken, we recommend buying a family pack with at least six breasts and then freezing the largest and smallest breasts for future use in a stir-fry, where size won't matter.

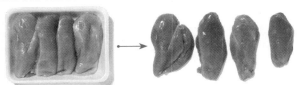

THESE BREASTS LOOK THE SAME . . . BUT OUT OF THE PACKAGE, THEY ARE QUITE DIFFERENT.

EQUIPMENT CORNER: Stain Removal Products

FOOD-STAINED CLOTHING IS A SAD REALITY IN OUR test kitchen. Tired of throwing out otherwise perfectly good shirts, we decided to get serious about laundry and put 16 supermarket stain removers to the test. These products fell into four categories: pretreaters, laundry additives, spot removers, and oxygen-based powders.

Pretreaters
These products are applied to the stained garment, which is then thrown into the wash. This group included Spray 'n Wash, Shout, Zout, Shout Ultra Gel, Shout Action Gel, Extra-Strength Spray 'n Wash, and Spray 'n Wash Stain Stick.

Laundry additives
These products go right into the machine with the wash to boost the stain-removing power of the detergent used. Both products in this group were made by Spray 'n Wash, one a liquid additive and one a concentrated tablet referred to as Actionball.

Spot removers
These products are applied to clothes, rubbed to remove the stains, and finally washed. Those tested included Gonzo Stain Remover, Amodex Premium Spot Remover, and Didi Seven Ultra Super Concentrated Cleaner.

Oxygen-based powders
These products are diluted with water to make a soaking solution for garments. Once the stains are gone, the clothes can be washed. This group included All Oxi-Active, Shout Oxy Power, Clorox Oxygen Action, and Oxi-Clean.

For our tests, we took plain 100 percent cotton T-shirts and dirtied them with the foods most infamous for leaving

unrelenting stains: pureed blueberries, pureed beets, black coffee, red wine, ketchup and yellow mustard (to simulate a hot dog mishap), melted bittersweet chocolate, and chili (which also covered grease stains). Each cleaning product was applied according to the manufacturer's instructions for maximum stain removal.

All of the products removed the coffee, wine, ketchup, and beet stains, but only the spot removers and oxygen-based powders managed to completely remove the tougher stains left by chili, blueberries, chocolate, and mustard. T-shirts tested with the pretreaters and laundry additives came out of the wash with several distinct, if muted, stains.

Spot removers call for brushing or blotting the stain until it is gone, and although this method is the most labor-intensive (in some cases up to seven applications were necessary), even the toughest stains were gone before the garment went into the washing machine. If time is a luxury you can afford and scrubbing and blotting are not your thing, then the oxygen-based powders are the way to go. T-shirts treated with these cleaners—used as concentrated soaking solutions, as per the manufacturers' instructions—needed only a light rubbing to remove the toughest stains. Although the T-shirts did need to soak for up to three hours (with Oxi-Clean working in the shortest amount of time), the process was mostly hands-off.

So if you can't part with that favorite blouse or pair of pants and you don't mind an investment of time but little elbow grease, use an oxygen-based powder.

Rating Stain Removers

WE PURCHASED 16 STAIN REMOVERS AND DIRTIED plain 100 percent cotton T-shirts with the foods most infamous for leaving unrelenting stains: pureed blueberries, pureed beets, black coffee, red wine, ketchup and yellow mustard, melted bittersweet chocolate, and greasy chili. Each cleaning product was applied according to the manufacturer's instructions for maximum stain removal. The 16 products we tested can be divided into four basic categories, which are listed below in order of preference.

RECOMMENDED
Oxygen-Based Powders
With very little work but considerable soaking time, these products removed the toughest food stains. Among the four products tested, Oxi-Clean worked best.

RECOMMENDED WITH RESERVATIONS
Spot Removers
Although labor-intensive—it took up to seven applications in some cases—these products worked well to remove the stains before the shirts were washed.

NOT RECOMMENDED
Pretreaters
These apply-and-wash products couldn't cut through the toughest stains, leaving muted shadows behind on the washed shirts.

NOT RECOMMENDED
Laundry Additives
Not enough boosting power to remove chili, blueberry, chocolate, and mustard stains.

MACARONI AND CHEESE

WHAT WE WANTED: A classic mac 'n cheese recipe that would appeal to everyone, from the finickiest kid to the snobbiest adult.

With the possible exception of meatloaf and fried chicken, few dishes are as personal as macaroni and cheese. Baked or stovetop, custard-based or little more than white sauce and pasta, with or without toasted bread crumbs, there must be a million recipes out there—surely enough to satisfy nearly everyone. Unfortunately, no one of these recipes can satisfy everyone at the same time. Sure, the kids would be fine with the contents of the blue box brand, but for most adults this ready-mix mac and cheese lost its appeal soon after we learned how to boil water. Conversely, decadent recipes replete with cream, eggs, and a who's-who list of pungent cheeses are decidedly adults-only; just try to serve them to the kids and you'll get upturned noses and pushed-back plates.

To get our bearings, we scoured the aforementioned million recipes (or at least 40), starting with our own recipe, published in *Cook's Illustrated* almost 10 years ago. A custard-style macaroni and cheese, this recipe uses eggs and evaporated milk (as opposed to the more traditional whole milk) to prevent the custard from curdling (a common occurrence in recipes with eggs). Although a long-standing test kitchen favorite, this dish is incredibly rich. We wanted something simpler but, as our next test revealed, not too simple. When we layered cooked pasta and cheese into a casserole dish, poured milk over the lot, and put the dish in the oven, the fat from the cheese separated and the result was a greasy mess. We concluded that the cheese needs some sort of binder—either eggs or flour.

We were now left with the path chosen by the vast majority of recipe writers: béchamel sauce. Béchamel is a white sauce made by cooking flour and butter to form a light roux. Milk is gradually whisked in, and the béchamel is cooked until it thickens. Combined with cheese and partially cooked noodles, the mix is then poured into a casserole dish and baked.

Traditional recipes incorporate the cheese into the béchamel before stirring in parcooked pasta and then baking until the sauce is bubbling hot and thick. It sure sounds easy. But no matter how much attention we paid, we just couldn't pull a great baked macaroni and cheese out of the oven. Sometimes the pasta was overcooked—a result of just one minute too many of boiling on the stovetop. Even worse were the batches made with undercooked noodles. We tried to remedy these by keeping the dishes in the oven longer (anywhere from 20 to 30 minutes), but after a while the bubbling cheese began to separate and the dishes took on an oily, grainy feel.

Frustrated, we pushed the idea of using the oven aside (to heck with tradition) and started working solely on the stovetop. Maybe we could better prevent the overcooking (and undercooking) of the pasta.

We made the next batch of sauce and boiled the pasta on the side. We cooked the pasta until it was a few minutes shy of being done, tossed it in with the sauce and cheese, and simmered it until the pasta was tender, which took a good 10 minutes. To our dismay, this batch had begun to separate, just like our oven-baked experiments, and the parcooked pasta released its starch to the sauce, giving it a gritty feel. Next we cooked the pasta until very tender and quickly mixed it with the cheese and sauce. This time tasters thought that the noodles needed more time to absorb the sauce. We needed to cook the pasta less at the outset. Boiled until just past al dente, the noodles still had enough structure to stand up to the heat of the sauce for a few minutes without turning mushy, and the cheese sauce filled every nook and cranny.

We now decided to work on the correct proportions of butter to flour to milk, reasoning that the winning combination would provide the desired silky sauce. Béchamel recipes that used more butter than flour lacked cohesion. Those using equal parts butter and flour seemed heavy and dull. We had much better luck using slightly more flour than butter (6 tablespoons to 5 tablespoons, respectively). Just this little change cut enough of the richness that we were trying to avoid, and, when we added 5 cups of whole milk, there was a plenitude of sauce with which to smother the noodles.

Technically speaking, as soon as we added cheese to the white sauce, it turned from béchamel to Mornay. We knew that choosing the right cheese (and using the right amount) would affect not only the flavor of the dish but also its texture. Indeed, an unpleasant grainy feel was introduced by hard cheeses such as Parmesan, Gruyère, and some aged cheddars, to say nothing of their overly distinct flavor. On the other hand, incredibly mild, soft cheeses such as mascarpone and ricotta contributed no flavor, and their creamy texture pushed the macaroni and cheese right back into sickly territory. In the end, what worked best was two cheeses—sharp cheddar for flavor and Monterey Jack for creaminess.

How much cheese to use? Many recipes call for twice as much cheese as pasta (we were using 1 pound of pasta). The result was a sticky, stringy macaroni and cheese that was off the charts in terms of richness. More frugal recipes seem designed around an impending cheese shortage, using merely ½ pound of cheese for 1 pound of pasta. The result was more macaroni and milk than macaroni and cheese. We found that 1 pound of cheese was the perfect amount for 1 pound of pasta. Just the right texture and flavor, and easy to remember, too.

We were done, right? Wrong. Many of the tasters wanted at least the option of adding a toasty, golden topping of bread crumbs—a flashback to the baked versions. To keep to our stovetop commitment, we tossed homemade bread crumbs with melted butter and toasted them on the stovetop, then portioned them out over individual servings in generous amounts. But these crumbs seemed more like

an afterthought than part of the dish. We weren't about to go back to baking the macaroni and cheese but wondered if using the broiler instead for a quick blast of heat would work. We placed fresh buttered bread crumbs on top of the next batch of macaroni and cheese and placed it under the broiler. This was it. The broiler concentrated the heat right on the bread crumbs, turning them a deep, golden brown. Better still, the process took only a few minutes—yet it was just enough time to let the bottom of the crumbs sink into the cheese sauce and seem baked right in.

WHAT WE LEARNED: To prevent curdling, keep the macaroni and cheese on the stovetop for as long as possible—and out of the oven. Cook the macaroni just past al dente, then simmer it with a flour-thickened cheese sauce for several minutes so the noodles can absorb some of the sauce. A combination of cheddar and Jack cheese gives the sauce optimal flavor and texture. Finally, don't forget the bread-crumb topping, which should be crisped under the broiler.

CLASSIC MACARONI AND CHEESE

Serves 6 to 8 as a main course or 10 to 12 as a side dish

It's crucial to cook the pasta until tender—that is, just past the al dente stage. Whole, low-fat, and skim milk all work well in this recipe. The recipe may be halved and baked in an 8-inch square, broiler-safe baking dish. If desired, offer celery salt or hot sauce (such as Tabasco) for sprinkling at the table.

bread crumb topping
- 6 slices (about 6 ounces) good-quality white sandwich bread, torn into rough pieces
- 3 tablespoons cold unsalted butter, cut into 6 pieces

pasta and cheese
- 1 tablespoon plus 1 teaspoon salt
- 1 pound elbow macaroni
- 5 tablespoons unsalted butter
- 6 tablespoons all-purpose flour
- 1½ teaspoons powdered mustard
- ¼ teaspoon cayenne (optional)
- 5 cups milk (see note)
- 8 ounces Monterey Jack cheese, shredded (2 cups)
- 8 ounces sharp cheddar cheese, shredded (2 cups)

1. FOR THE BREAD CRUMBS: Pulse the bread and butter in a food processor until the crumbs are no larger than ⅛ inch, ten to fifteen 1-second pulses. Set aside.

2. FOR THE PASTA AND CHEESE: Adjust an oven rack to the lower-middle position and heat the broiler. Bring 4 quarts water to a rolling boil in a stockpot. Add 1 tablespoon of the salt and the macaroni and stir to separate the noodles. Cook until tender, drain, and set aside.

3. In the now-empty stockpot, heat the butter over medium-high heat until foaming. Add the flour, mustard, cayenne (if using), and remaining 1 teaspoon salt and whisk well to combine. Continue whisking until the mixture becomes fragrant and deepens in color, about 1 minute.

Whisking constantly, gradually add the milk; bring the mixture to a boil, whisking constantly (the mixture must reach a full boil to fully thicken), then reduce the heat to medium and simmer, whisking occasionally, until thickened to the consistency of heavy cream, about 5 minutes. Off the heat, whisk in the cheeses until fully melted. Add the pasta and cook over medium-low heat, stirring constantly, until the mixture is steaming and heated through, about 6 minutes.

4. Transfer the mixture to a broiler-safe 13 by 9-inch baking dish and sprinkle with the bread crumbs. Broil until deep golden brown, 3 to 5 minutes. Cool 5 minutes, then serve.

VARIATION

MACARONI AND CHEESE WITH PEAS AND HAM

Cut 8 ounces baked deli ham, sliced ¼ inch thick, into 1-inch squares. Follow the recipe for Classic Macaroni and Cheese, adding the chopped ham and 1 cup frozen peas to the cheese sauce along with the pasta. Proceed as directed.

GETTING IT RIGHT:
Some Failed Experiments

OILY AND SEPARATED   CURDLED AND CLUMPY

RICH AND CLOYING

Some early tests revealed common problems with this recipe. When we layered the noodles, milk, and cheese (without first cooking them together) in the pan, the fat separated from the cheese and the macaroni and cheese was oily (top left). When we added eggs to the recipe, they curdled and produced a lumpy sauce (top right). Too much cheese made the macaroni so rich you could eat only two or three spoonfuls (bottom).

SCIENCE DESK:
Two Cheeses Are Better Than One

IN TESTING VARIOUS CHEESES FOR OUR RECIPE, WE came upon a dichotomy: Monterey Jack could provide appealing texture but only modest flavor, while cheddar brought the best flavor but rough texture. Curious about this, we started digging for answers.

A major distinction between Monterey Jack and cheddar is moisture content. Government regulations allow Jack cheese to have 5 percent more total moisture than cheddar, and more moisture makes a cheese easier to blend into a liquid. Moreover, cheddar cheese has more fat than Jack cheese. Aside from fat and water content, age also has a profound effect on how a cheese behaves when melted. Monterey Jack is never aged for more than a few months, but cheddar can be aged for years. As cheddar ages, casein, the primary protein in cheese, breaks down, and the strong flavor compounds we associate with good cheddar develop.

What does this difference in age mean for cheese sauce? Cheddar, particularly older cheddar, is gritty because the casein structure has been broken down. In contrast, Monterey Jack is creamy because the casein structure is more intact and better able to retain fat and moisture.

GETTING IT RIGHT: How Cheese Melts

When cheddar is melted (right), the fat separates from the cheese. Monterey Jack (left) has a higher moisture content and looks creamier when melted, with less separation.

TASTING LAB: Microwave Popcorn

CHOOSING A MICROWAVE CAN BE EASIER THAN choosing a brand of microwave popcorn. We narrowed the field to nine popular brands. We selected the most basic butter flavor each brand offered; no "butter light" or "butter bonanza." We also threw in some "homemade" microwave popcorn, popping kernels in a paper bag in the microwave and then dousing them with fresh melted butter.

Tasters were asked to give each sample an overall score, as well as to score the popcorns on the following characteristics: buttery, artificial, and corn-y. We discovered what tasters looked for in popcorn: good corn flavor, nothing artificial, and a moderate amount of butter flavor—not too much and not too little. Our top two overall finishers, homemade and Newman's Own, were ranked among the lowest for artificiality and the highest for corniness, and they were right in the middle of the pack when it came to butteriness. Ironically, the two brands deemed the most buttery, Orville Redenbacher and Pop Secret, were also deemed the most artificial and ranked at the bottom of the tasting.

The real surprise of the tasting was the showing of the "homemade" popcorn, which barely squeaked a victory over Newman's Own. Though many tasters praised the real butter flavor of our fresh popped, several described that popcorn as soggy or greasy. Most of the commercial popcorns were flavored with a dry butter powder, which lent a buttery flavor (sometimes) but not a buttery texture. That real butter texture was more appealing when the homemade popcorn was warm, but when the popcorn cooled, it became soft and greasy.

The benefit of popping your own, other than the monetary savings (kernels cost about half as much as packaged microwave popcorn), is that you control the flavor and can add as much butter, salt, or any other seasoning you wish. However, for true convenience and a taste that's almost as good as homemade, choose Newman's Own Butter.

Rating Microwave Popcorns

EIGHTEEN MEMBERS OF THE *COOK'S ILLUSTRATED* STAFF TASTED ALL OF THE POPCORNS AT ROOM TEMPERATURE—IT wasn't possible to taste them hot, so we decided to cool all samples to the same temperature. The popcorns are listed in order of preference based on their scores in this tasting. All brands are available in supermarkets nationwide.

RECOMMENDED
Kernels and Butter **$3.69 for 30 ounces**
We popped our corn in a paper bag and added melted butter. Tasters praised the flavor—"nice toastiness" and "tastes like real butter, yum!"—but weren't wild about the soft texture.

RECOMMENDED
Newman's Own Oldstyle Picture Show Butter Popcorn **$2.49 for 10.5 ounces**
We liked the "good corn flavor" of this popular brand, and most panelists agreed that it was "real tasting."

RECOMMENDED
Shaw's Theater Style Extra Butter Popcorn **$1.59 for 9 ounces**
This inexpensive supermarket brand was described as "quite buttery" and "pretty good, really."

RECOMMENDED
Guiltless Gourmet Butter Popcorn **$3.29 for 10.5 ounces**
Tasters liked the "good corn flavor" but complained that there was "no discernible butter."

RECOMMENDED
Act II Butter Popcorn **$1.99 for 10.5 ounces**
"Average" and "salty" were the best comments this sample could muster.

NOT RECOMMENDED
Healthy Choice Butter Popcorn **$2.49 for 8.55 ounces**
"Dry" and "artificial" was the consensus about this low-fat brand.

NOT RECOMMENDED
Orville Redenbacher's Butter Popcorn **$2.49 for 10.5 ounces**
One taster summed up: "can't taste the corn for all that fake butter."

NOT RECOMMENDED
Pop Secret Butter Popcorn **$2.29 for 10.5 ounces**
"Greasy" and "off tasting" were common complaints.

NOT RECOMMENDED
Newman's Own Pop's Corn (Organic) Butter Popcorn **$2.69 for 10.5 ounces**
The organic version of our winner was deemed "dry and dusty," with one taster complaining that it "tastes like dried shrimp."

NOT RECOMMENDED
Black Jewell Butter Popcorn **$2.99 for 10.5 ounces**
This low-fat sample was "hard and chewy" and tasted "kinda burnt."

Julia demonstrates the classic restauran method for cutting up a lobster and the pan-roasting and flambéing it.

RESTAURANT COOKING
comes home

CHAPTER 9

Have you ever been tempted to prepare a restaurant recipe only to be disappointed with the results? The recipe sounded great, but once you got to work you realized it was never tested in a home kitchen. Many restaurant recipes require a professional stove, hard-to-find ingredients, and skills that most home cooks simply don't possess.

But there is something awe-inspiring about good restaurant cooking. The combinations of flavors and textures are exciting, and the presentation usually exceeds anything you might ordinarily attempt at home.

Our test kitchen staff eats in a lot of restaurants, and we decided to take some of our favorite chefs' recipes and make them work in a home kitchen. This meant improvising with equipment, ingredients, and techniques, but the results in this chapter will put restaurant creations within reach for the ambitious home cook.

CRAB TOWERS WITH AVOCADO AND GAZPACHO SALSAS

WHAT WE WANTED: To take a stunning appetizer with 35 ingredients and three separate components, plus garnishes, and re-create it at home.

Developing a menu for a large hotel restaurant allows you abundant freedom that you won't find in a standard restaurant, thanks to access to endless ingredients and many able hands to prepare them. A hotel kitchen staff wouldn't break a sweat preparing multi-component appetizers using more than 35 ingredients. The Crab Tower at the Mayflower Park Hotel in Seattle is a prime example of such hotel kitchen exuberance. It is a tidy, striated tower composed of three salads—an avocado–hearts of palm salsa, a crab salad, and a gazpacho salsa—garnished with frisée lightly dressed in a champagne vinaigrette, pea tendrils, grapefruit segments, and minced chives. Although replicating this dish sounds like a huge undertaking, we found a few ways to simplify the recipe without losing either its flavor or its impressive appearance.

Breaking the plate down into its various components, we focused on each component separately before combining them on the plate. All in all, the focus of this dish is on the crab, so we began with the crab salad. In the test kitchen, we prefer Atlantic blue crabmeat. Sold in both lump and backfin forms, the lump offers tender pieces of crab, while the backfin has a more shredded texture. Both types work in this recipe, although tasters preferred the bite-size pieces of lump to the shredded backfin. The cost, however, may make the decision between the two for you—lump can cost up to twice as much as backfin.

To make the crab salad, the Mayflower mixes the crabmeat with a little mayonnaise and a champagne vinaigrette. When preparing the crabmeat, do not rinse it, but rather spread it out on a plate and check for small pieces of shell. Finding that 12 ounces of crabmeat was plenty for six plates, we tossed it with 2 tablespoons of mayonnaise and 3 tablespoons of vinaigrette to produce a flavorful, well-bound salad that highlights crabmeat's naturally sweet flavor.

Next, we focused our attention on the champagne vinaigrette. Because they prepare it in bulk at the hotel, it makes sense that the chefs use it as a flavoring in the crab salad, as well as to dress the frisée garnish. Figuring that we needed a total of 4 tablespoons of vinaigrette, we pared down the Mayflower's 8-cup recipe, which called for two types of oil; we simplified the ingredients to include only olive oil. Other ingredients we included were champagne vinegar, lemon zest, Dijon mustard, salt, and pepper.

Moving on to the avocado–hearts of palm salsa, we figured that our six plates would require a total of 3 cups of salsa. Because we had a hard time finding decent-tasting hearts of palm with any regularity, we decided to omit them, using three avocados and an appropriate amount of the recipe's original seasonings—lime and coriander. Tasters liked the clean, streamlined avocado flavor in combination with the array of other ingredients.

We next turned our attention to the gazpacho salsa, which contained 16 ingredients (eight of which are time-consumingly cut into small dice). We simplified the recipe, which yielded three times more than we needed, by cutting both ingredients and amounts. Although it called for both yellow and red bell peppers, we decided to use just yellow, which contrasts nicely with the red tomato and green cucumber. We also omitted the 1/8-inch dice of lime and orange segments. Not only were they difficult to cut in a tidy fashion, but their juice turned the gazpacho unnecessarily wet. Keeping the sherry vinegar and olive oil, we omitted the other seasonings, including lemon juice, celery salt, and sugar. The result was a crisp, clean flavor and colorful presentation that the tasters liked just as well as the original.

Addressing the last few ingredients used to garnish the plate—dressed frisée, grapefruit segments, pea tendrils, and chives—we omitted both the chives and the hard-to-find,

sweet-tasting pea tendrils. On their own, the grapefruit segments tasted a bit too tart, so we substituted orange segments, a flavor that we had omitted from the gazpacho salsa.

At the hotel, tall, open-ended metal rings, called timbale rings, are used to build the tall towers of crab and avocado and gazpacho salsas. However, we found that a round biscuit cutter worked just as well after accommodating for its lack of depth (see the illustrations on page 115). Although it sounds a bit fussy, layering the salad into a tall-towered presentation is a simple way to bring the hotel dining experience to the kitchen table.

WHAT WE LEARNED: It's possible to eliminate about a third of the ingredients in the original recipe and still keep the contrasting flavors and textures that make this dish special. And to assemble the towers, biscuit cutters (which most home cooks have on hand) can double for the more traditional timbale rings used in a restaurant.

CRAB TOWERS WITH AVOCADO AND GAZPACHO SALSAS

Serves 6

You can prepare the crabmeat salad and gazpacho salsa several hours ahead of serving, but the avocado salsa should be prepared just before assembly.

crabmeat salad

3	tablespoons extra-virgin olive oil
1	tablespoon champagne vinegar
1	teaspoon minced or grated lemon zest
½	teaspoon Dijon mustard
½	teaspoon salt
⅛	teaspoon ground black pepper
2	tablespoons mayonnaise
12	ounces lump or backfin Atlantic blue crabmeat, carefully picked over for shell fragments

gazpacho salsa

1	small yellow bell pepper, cored, seeded, and cut into ⅛-inch pieces (about ½ cup)
½	small cucumber, peeled if desired, seeded, and cut into ⅛-inch pieces (about ½ cup)
1	medium plum tomato, cored, seeded, and cut into ⅛-inch pieces (about ½ cup)
1	small celery rib, cut into ⅛-inch pieces (about ½ cup)
½	small red onion, minced (about ¼ cup)
½	small jalapeño chile, stemmed, seeded, and minced
1	tablespoon minced fresh cilantro leaves
¾	teaspoon salt
¼	teaspoon ground black pepper
2	tablespoons extra-virgin olive oil
1	tablespoon sherry vinegar

avocado salsa

3	ripe avocados, cut into ¼-inch dice (see the illustrations on page 115)

¼ teaspoon ground coriander
½ teaspoon salt
⅛ teaspoon ground black pepper
2 tablespoons juice from 1 lime

1 cup frisée
2 oranges, peeled using a paring knife and segmented (see the illustrations below), optional

1. FOR THE CRABMEAT SALAD: Whisk the olive oil, champagne vinegar, lemon zest, mustard, salt, and pepper together in a small bowl. Measure 3 tablespoons of the vinaigrette into a medium bowl and mix with the mayonnaise. Add the crabmeat to the mayonnaise mixture and toss to coat. Cover with plastic wrap and refrigerate until needed. Set the remaining vinaigrette aside.

2. FOR THE GAZPACHO SALSA: Toss the yellow bell pepper, cucumber, tomato, celery, red onion, jalapeño, cilantro, salt, pepper, olive oil, and sherry vinegar in a medium bowl and set aside.

3. FOR THE AVOCADO SALSA: Toss the avocado, coriander, salt, pepper, and lime juice in a medium bowl and set aside.

4. TO ASSEMBLE: Place a 3-inch-wide round biscuit cutter in the center of an individual plate. Following the illustrations on page 115, use a slotted spoon to press ⅓ cup of the Avocado Salsa into the bottom of the cutter using the back of a soup spoon. Lift the cutter off the plate slightly to reveal some but not all of the avocado. Holding the cutter aloft, press ⅓ cup of the Crabmeat Salad evenly into the cutter on top of the avocado. Lift the cutter farther to reveal some but not all of the crab salad. Holding the cutter aloft, use a slotted spoon to press ⅓ cup of the Gazpacho Salsa evenly into the cutter on top of the crab. Gently lift the cutter up and away from the plate to reveal the crab tower. Repeat the procedure five more times with the remaining ingredients.

5. Dress the frisée with the remaining champagne vinaigrette. Place a few sprigs of the dressed frisée on top of each crab tower and arrange the orange segments, if using, around the towers. Serve immediately.

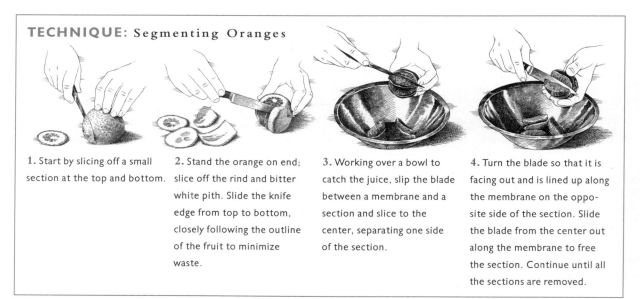

TECHNIQUE: Segmenting Oranges

1. Start by slicing off a small section at the top and bottom.

2. Stand the orange on end; slice off the rind and bitter white pith. Slide the knife edge from top to bottom, closely following the outline of the fruit to minimize waste.

3. Working over a bowl to catch the juice, slip the blade between a membrane and a section and slice to the center, separating one side of the section.

4. Turn the blade so that it is facing out and is lined up along the membrane on the opposite side of the section. Slide the blade from the center out along the membrane to free the section. Continue until all the sections are removed.

TECHNIQUE: Assembling Crab Towers

1. Place the biscuit cutter in the center of the plate and, using the back of a soup spoon, press ⅓ cup of the Avocado Salsa evenly into the cutter.

2. Lift the cutter off the plate slightly to reveal some but not all of the avocado.

3. Holding the cutter aloft, press ⅓ cup of the Crabmeat Salad evenly into the cutter, on top of the avocado.

4. Lift the cutter farther off the plate to reveal some but not all of the crab mixture and press ⅓ cup of the Gazpacho Salsa evenly into the cutter, on top of the crab.

5. Gently lift the cutter up and away from the plate to reveal the crab tower.

TECHNIQUE: Dicing Avocado

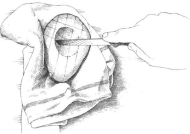

1. Halve and pit the avocado. Hold one half steady in a dish towel. Make ¼-inch crosshatch incisions in the flesh with a dinner knife, cutting down to but not through the skin.

2. Separate the diced flesh from the skin by inserting a soup spoon or rubber spatula between the skin and the flesh, gently scooping out the diced avocado.

FLAMBÉED PAN-ROASTED LOBSTER

WHAT WE WANTED: An alternative to the usual boiled or steamed lobster that would not take much longer to prepare but would deliver tastier results.

When it comes to lobster, most people follow the tried-and-true method and boil it, serving the whole crustacean with a side of drawn butter and a bib. Not that there's anything wrong with tradition, but Jasper White, the renowned New England–based chef and owner of the Summer Shack in Cambridge, Massachusetts, has long applied another practice that we think—at the risk of sounding heretical—produces tastier results. White "pan-roasts" his lobster, employing a combination of high-heat stovetop cooking, broiling, and flambéing. The intense heat yields very rich-flavored, succulent lobster meat—nothing rubbery or bland here. And to replace the side of butter, White whips up a quick pan sauce from the lobster drippings, shallots, bourbon, and tomalley, the lobster's liver. Everything's feasible for the home cook, and we highly recommend that

lobster lovers give this dish a whirl, though be forewarned: the bravura cooking method takes some steely nerves and kitchen confidence.

Progress no further if you are unwilling to cut up a live lobster. Some people—even a few pacifists in the test kitchen—are unwilling to commit the deed, so we fully understand any reticence. The first step in preparing the dish is halving the lobster lengthwise and then crosswise, separating the head from the tail and the claws from the body. The head doesn't contain much meat, but it does lend flavor to the dish, so we include it. The best tool for the job is a large heavy-duty chef's knife or cleaver, which can easily puncture the hard shell without damage to the blade. Center the blade on the lobster's upper portion (that is, the head) and give it a sturdy whack with a mallet. The blade should cleanly cleave the lobster in two. If the knife's blade is short, you may need to finish splitting the tail. The halved lobster may twitch a bit, but it's strictly reflexive—by no means is it alive at this point. The claws can be easily cut at their narrow junction with the body. The legs should be left attached; they don't have much meat inside, but they're great to nibble on.

The lobsters are now ready for cooking. The original recipe specifies heating the skillet on the stovetop over high heat for upward of five minutes before adding the peanut oil and segmented lobsters, but we found this a little dangerous for the home kitchen. Instead, we preferred to heat the oil in the skillet over high heat until smoking. The lobsters are added to the pan shell-side down; otherwise the meat overcooks. The high heat effectively roasts the shells, which imbues the meat with an intense, almost nutty flavor. When the shells are flame red and lightly speckled with browned or blackened spots, the pan is transferred to the broiler to cook the exposed meat.

Now the recipe starts getting really interesting. The skillet is removed from the broiler and returned to the

stovetop, and the lobster is flambéed with a shot of bourbon or cognac. For those who have never flambéed before, it's a little intimidating, but fun, too. And it's for more than just show: In a side-by-side taste test using shrimp and bourbon, we found the flambéed shrimp more fully flavored than those in which the bourbon had simply been reduced. In a restaurant kitchen, there's little worry about setting things alight, but the home kitchen presents a different story. White specifies ¼ cup of bourbon, enough to send a two-foot curtain of flames skyward when ignited—way too dangerous for the home kitchen. For a safer method, we allow the bourbon to reduce for 10 seconds prior to ignition. The flames are lower and the flavor the same. A long fireplace or grill match is the safest bet for lighting the alcohol.

After the lobster is flambéed, it is removed from the pan, and what is essentially a classic pan sauce is quickly "built" in the skillet. Shallots are sautéed and the reserved tomalley and a splash of white wine are added. Despite its unappetizing hue, the tomalley packs an intense flavor and is important to the end result. But if tomalley leaves you cold, exclude it; the sauce will still taste fine. Drizzled with the sauce, the lobster makes for messy eating (and still requires a bib), but it's well worth it.

WHAT WE LEARNED: Pan-roast quartered lobsters in a hot skillet with the shells facing down. Transfer the pan to the broiler to cook the exposed meat. Return the pan to the stovetop to flambé the lobster. Finally, set the lobster aside on a plate while you make a quick pan sauce with shallots, white wine, and herbs.

FLAMBÉED PAN-ROASTED LOBSTER
Serves 2

If you want to prepare more than two lobsters, we suggest that you engage some help. This dish requires close attention, and managing multiple extremely hot pans can be tricky. Before flambéing, make sure to roll up long shirtsleeves, tie back long hair, turn off the exhaust fan (otherwise the fan may pull up the flames), and turn off any lit burners (this is critical if you have a gas stove). For equipment, you will need a large ovensafe skillet, oven mitts, a pair of tongs, and long fireplace or grill matches.

2   live lobsters (1½ to 2 pounds each)
2   tablespoons peanut or canola oil
¼   cup bourbon or cognac
6   tablespoons (¾ stick) unsalted butter, cut into
     6 pieces
2   medium shallots (6 tablespoons), minced
3   tablespoons dry white wine
1   teaspoon minced fresh tarragon leaves
1   tablespoon minced fresh chives
     Salt and ground black pepper
1   lemon, cut into wedges (optional)

1. TO QUARTER THE LOBSTERS: Using a large, heavy-duty chef's knife or cleaver, which can easily puncture the hard shell without damage to the blade, center the blade lengthwise on the lobster's upper portion (its head) and give it a sturdy whack with a mallet. Place the blade crosswise behind the lobster's head and split again. Break the claws free from the head and, using a spoon, remove and reserve the green tomalley, if desired. Keep the split lobsters shell-side down. (Don't be put off if the lobsters continue to twitch a little after quartering; it's a reflexive movement.)

2. TO COOK THE LOBSTERS: Adjust an oven rack so it is 6 inches from the broiler element and heat the broiler. Heat the peanut oil in a large ovensafe skillet over high heat until smoking. Add the lobster pieces shell-side down in a single layer and cook, without disturbing, until the shells are bright red and lightly browned, 2 to 3 minutes. Transfer the skillet to the broiler and cook until the tail meat is just opaque, about 2 minutes.

3. Carefully remove the pan from the oven and return it to the stovetop. Off the heat, pour the bourbon over the lobsters. Wait for 10 seconds, then light a long match and wave it over the skillet until the bourbon ignites. Return the pan to medium-high heat and shake it until the flames subside. Transfer the lobster pieces to a warmed serving bowl and tent with foil to keep warm.

4. TO FINISH THE SAUCE: Using tongs, remove any congealed albumen (white substance) from the skillet and add 2 tablespoons of the butter and the shallots. Cook, stirring constantly, until the shallots are softened and lightly browned, 1 to 2 minutes. Add the tomalley and white wine and stir until completely combined. Remove the skillet from the heat and add the tarragon and chives. Stirring constantly, add the remaining 4 tablespoons butter, 1 piece at a time, until fully emulsified. Season with salt and pepper to taste. Pour the sauce over the lobster pieces. Serve immediately, accompanied by the lemon wedges, if desired.

SCIENCE DESK: How a Flambé Works

A FLAMBÉ LOOKS IMPRESSIVE AND IS EASY ENOUGH TO execute, but how does it actually work? Is it just for show or does flambéing make a flavor difference? In tests we have noticed that sauces made with flambéed alcohol usually taste richer and sweeter than sauces made with alcohol that has been simmered. But we wondered why.

A flambé is the ignition of the alcohol vapor that lies above the pan, a reaction that generates significant amounts of heat. To measure this heat, we used an infrared thermometer and discovered that the temperature at the surface of the alcohol quickly climbed past 500 degrees; this

heat would indeed change the chemistry of the bourbon or cognac below. Curious to know whether the high heat served to remove all of the alcohol from the pan, we sent a sample of the completed sauce to the lab for alcohol analysis. The flambé removed most of the alcohol, but what was the high heat doing to the flavor?

Many of the great, flavor-boosting chemical reactions of cooking require high heat. Reactions involving sugar, such as caramelization and browning, occur at temperatures higher than 300 degrees. Because the surface of the sauce had reached above 500 degrees, we noticed some of this type of flavor development. Simmered alcohol, in contrast, maintains a steady heat of about 180 degrees. Another benefit of the flambé is that at very high heat many molecules absorb enough energy to isomerize, or change shape. The consequences of this reconfiguration might include improved solubility and changed flavor perception.

The mystery was solved. A flambéed sauce burns off most of its alcohol but gains flavor from several high-heat cooking reactions. The final result is a sauce with a hint of alcohol and great depth of flavor.

EQUIPMENT CORNER: Meat Cleavers

EVERY GOOD COOK HAS A FAVORITE KNIFE. FOR SOME, it is an impeccably honed chef's knife that can reduce an onion to confetti in a matter of seconds. For others, it is a paring knife so beloved that they do not even own a vegetable peeler. For many of us in the test kitchen, it is a perfectly balanced meat cleaver possessing a blade as sharp as a Lady Bic and as strong as a woodman's axe. But does it matter which brand? We asked five test cooks to evaluate the performance of five brands of meat cleavers based on their comfort, balance, and performance.

A cleaver comes in especially handy when chopping up meat and bones for a stock. It's also great when dealing with lobster. Capitalizing on the opportunity to release some stress, the testers chopped chicken wings, breasts, legs,

and thighs with each cleaver and recorded their conclusions. The best of the lot was the Global 6-Inch Meat Cleaver ($110), which featured a razor-sharp blade and perfectly balanced design that easily finished hacking jobs none of the other cleavers could tackle. For a more reasonable price of $40, the LamsonSharp 7-Inch Meat Cleaver offered a comfortable handle, a sharp blade, and a comparatively light weight, which made it popular among testers with less arm strength.

Of the other models tested, both the J.A. Henckels Professional S 6-Inch Cleaver ($50) and the Wüsthof Trident 6-inch Cleaver ($70) provided good control, though some testers felt the squared-off handles did not provide a secure grip. Other testers, however, praised the Henckels for being substantial without being too heavy.

Bringing up the rear was the Forschner (Victorinox) Fibrox 6-inch Household Cleaver ($71), which had two major strikes against it: It featured a wooden handle whose porous construction could cause cross-contamination, and its thick blade was not sharp enough for many testers, requiring the use of a sawing motion rather than a quick chop.

Although the meat cleaver may not be the go-to knife for carving a turkey or peeling an apple, it is certainly an invaluable tool in the kitchen. Its formidable size and weight make it a formidable adversary to even the toughest bone or shell.

Rating Meat Cleavers

WE TESTED FIVE MEAT CLEAVERS FOR THEIR COM- fort, balance, and performance while cutting through meat and bone. The tests were conducted with chicken parts and were per- formed by five different members of our test kitchen, possessing various hand sizes and arm strengths. The meat cleavers are listed in order of preference. See www.americastestkitchen.com for up- to-date prices and mail-order sources for top-rated products.

HIGHLY RECOMMENDED
Global 6-Inch Meat Cleaver $110
Perfectly balanced, with a razor-sharp blade and a very handsome appearance. Easily handled tasks that stymied other meat cleavers, but this type of performance doesn't come cheap.

RECOMMENDED
LamsonSharp 7-Inch Meat Cleaver $40
This model was lightweight, with a comfortable handle and a thin, sharp blade. It was praised for both performance and value.

RECOMMENDED WITH RESERVATIONS
J.A. Henckels Professional S 6-Inch Cleaver $50
Some testers thought that the small handle on this model was difficult to grip. Did not always chop cleanly through the chicken.

RECOMMENDED WITH RESERVATIONS
Wüsthof Trident 6-Inch Cleaver $70
This cleaver was unbalanced because the handle was heavier than the blade. Additionally, this cleaver tended to shatter the chicken bones.

NOT RECOMMENDED
Forschner (Victorinox) Fibrox 6-inch Household Cleaver $71
Criticized for being too heavy and unwieldy, the blade of this cleaver was also described as thick and dull.

We turned the alley behind the test kitchen into a little bit of Texas as we barbecued beef ribs.

TEXAS rib house

In Texas, good beef ribs are the secret handshake between experienced grillers. With a price tag of roughly $2 a pound and availability at nearly every butcher counter (they are the scrap bones from trimming rib-eye steaks), beef ribs manage to maintain a cool, cult-like obscurity only because their more popular porky brethren hog all the attention. Cost and anonymity aside, it is their huge meaty flavor—combined with spice, smoke, and fire—that epitomizes beef barbecue for many serious Texans.

Could we figure out how to make authentic Texas beef ribs in the alley behind our Boston test kitchen? Could we learn the secret handshake? We knew this recipe would be a challenge to produce, but we think we've succeeded.

And, to our mind, you can't serve ribs without some cornbread. And it better not be the fluffy, cakey, sweet stuff you might see up North. No, we wanted the crusty, baked-in-a-skillet cornbread served throughout the South.

TEXAS BEEF RIBS

WHAT WE WANTED: To re-create authentic Texas barbecued ribs—with their intense beef flavor—at home.

Reckoning that we'd better get a sense of what authentic Texas beef ribs taste like before we fired up the grill, we flew to Texas and spent a hot day driving around Austin and neighboring towns to check out some of the country's best rib joints and road-side stands. Sampling plates of beef ribs throughout the day, we were repeatedly surprised by how much they weren't like what we thought of as barbecued ribs. The meat was not fall-off-the-bone tender but actually required a small toothy tug, and the immense, meaty flavor of the ribs was relatively unadorned by spice rubs and sticky sauces. In fact, if we hadn't been looking for evidence of a spice rub, we might have missed it all together. Served dry with a vinegary dipping sauce on the side, the ribs did not boast a lot of smoke flavor, either; instead, the smoke served as a backdrop for the incredible beefy flavor.

How were these surprisingly flavorful ribs—basically bones lined with juicy steak trimmings—produced? That became our problem. The various barbecue chefs we talked to at each stop simply set dials and pushed buttons on gargantuan, electric smokers outfitted with automated temperature controls. We flew home having learned nothing of value in terms of backyard cooking in a simple kettle-style grill, but at least we knew exactly what we were looking for: potent meat flavor with a bit of honest Texas chew.

Back in Boston, our first task was to track down beef ribs at the local supermarket. Known to butchers as beef back ribs (not to be confused with beef short ribs), they were in fact widely available; we probably had been reaching over them for years. Because these ribs are often considered scrap bones (especially by Yankee butchers), the real challenge is finding any with a decent amount of meat (see "Where's the Beef?" on page 124), and we learned the hard

way that skimpy ribs are simply not worth cooking.

There is a membrane with a fair amount of fat that runs along the backside of the bones, and we tested the effects of removing it, scoring it, and leaving it alone. A number of the recipes we had looked at provided detailed instructions on how to remove the membrane using a screwdriver (no joke), but we found this step to be wholly unnecessary, as it resulted in drier meat. Scoring the membrane with a sharp knife also failed to wow tasters; now the ribs presented relatively dry meat as well as a shaggy appearance. The best results—the juiciest meat with the most flavor—were had by means of the easiest route: simply leaving the membrane in place. The fat not only bastes the ribs as they cook but also renders to a crisp, bacon-like texture, which one old local told us is called candy—and a real Texan never trims away the candy.

Moving on to the rub, we remembered the comments of one Austin cook, who said, "It's not about what you put on beef ribs that makes the difference, it's what you leave off." Using a simple mixture of salt, pepper, cayenne, and chili powder, we found that a mere 2 teaspoons rubbed into each rack were all that it took to bring out the flavor of the meat. We then tested the effects of rubbing the slabs and refrigerating them, both wrapped in plastic and unwrapped, on wire racks for two days, one day, and one hour versus the effects of rubbing a slab and cooking it straight away. Surprisingly, we found that the differences in flavor were not the result of the rub's having infiltrated the meat but rather the result of the aging of the beef. Here in the test kitchen, we have generally found that aged beef roasts take on a pleasant hearty flavor. In this case, however, the aged ribs were a bust. They tasted sour and smelled tallowy. We did make one useful discovery, though: Ribs left at room temperature for an hour cooked through more evenly.

The next question was how to turn a kettle grill into a backyard smoker. The first step was choosing the correct

fuel. Hardwood charcoal was out; briquettes burn cooler and longer, making them perfect for barbecue. We had already discovered that cooking the ribs directly over the briquettes didn't work—the ribs burned long before they had cooked through and turned tender. We needed indirect heat, and there were two ways to get it. We could bank all of the coals on one side of the grill, or we could create two piles on opposite sides. A single pile on one side of the grill proved best, providing a slow, even fire that was easy to stoke with fresh coals and left more room for the ribs.

In Texas, barbecue fanatics can be particular about the kind of wood they use to create smoke, so we tested the three most popular varieties: hickory, mesquite, and green oak. The green oak had a clean, gentle smoke that was mild and pleasant, but this wood was hard to find. Dried hickory chunks offered a similar flavor profile and were easy to locate at a hardware store. Mesquite, on the other hand, had a fake, pungent flavor that tasters universally hated. We then wondered if chips (rather than chunks) wrapped in a foil packet were as good. No, they reduced the heat of the charcoal (the aluminum foil acted as a shield), whereas the chunks extended its burning power, acting as a fuel source.

Not wanting the meat to taste too smoky, we then tested the difference among using one, two, and three medium-size (about 2 ounces each) chunks (all soaked in water, as dry chunks burn rather than smoke). One chunk was too little, three were too many, but two were just right. We tried adding both chunks to the fire right at the beginning versus adding just one and letting it burn out before adding the second. Tasters favored the ribs smoked steadily during the entire cooking time, which is how an electric smoker works. These ribs had a more complex flavor than those that were bombarded with lots of smoke at the beginning.

Inspired by the temperature-controlled smokers we saw in Texas, we decided to use an indoor oven to test various cooking temperatures. We would then go back outside to the grill to apply what we'd learned. We tested more than 15 combinations of time and temperature until we got it right. The first thing we learned was that the cooking temperature should never exceed 300 degrees. Higher temperatures render too much fat and turn the meat dry and stringy. Yet the temperature should not dip below 250 degrees. At that temperature the fat won't render, the meat stays tough, and the ribs never achieve that signature roasted beefy flavor. The ideal temperature, then, was a range of 250 to 300 degrees, and the ideal time was about 2½ hours, which causes some, but not all, of the fat to render and makes the ribs juicy, tender, and slightly toothy. When cooked any longer, as is the case with pork ribs, the meat disintegrates into messy shreds, taking on a sticky, pot-roasted sort of texture that any real Texan would immediately reject.

Now we were ready to go back to the grill and add the finishing touches. The first problem was maintaining a constant temperature. The solution was to count out exactly 30 briquettes (and one wood chunk) to start, which brought the grill up to 300 degrees. Over the next hour, the grill cooled to 250 degrees, and it became necessary to add another 20 briquettes along with the second wood chunk. We also found that the top vents should be open two thirds of the way and positioned at the side of the grill opposite from the wood chunk, so that the smoke is drawn across the grill, not straight up and out.

So, yes, you can make authentic Texas ribs at home, with big beef flavor, great chew, and just a hint of smoke and spice. The secret handshake? Confidence. Let the wood and smoke do their work without constant peeking and checking. Don't mess with Texas ribs.

WHAT WE LEARNED: Buy the meatiest ribs you can find, keep the spice rub simple, and barbecue them over a 250- to 300-degree fire with a couple of wood chunks until the ribs are tender but still have some chew.

TEXAS-STYLE BARBECUED BEEF RIBS

Serves 4

It is important to use beef ribs with a decent amount of meat, not bony scraps; otherwise, the rewards of making this recipe are few. For more information about what to look for when buying ribs, see the photos on this page. Because the ribs cook slowly and for an extended period of time, charcoal briquettes, not hardwood charcoal (which burns hot and fast), make a better fuel. That said, do not use Match Light charcoal, which contains lighter fluid for easy ignition. For the wood chunks, use any type of wood but mesquite, which can have an overpowering smokiness. It's a good idea to monitor the grill heat; if you don't own a reliable grill thermometer, insert an instant-read thermometer into the lid vent to spot-check the temperature. Except when adding coals, do not lift the grill lid, which will allow both smoke and heat to escape. When barbecuing, we prefer to use a Weber 22-inch kettle grill.

- 4 teaspoons chili powder
- ½ teaspoon cayenne
- 2 teaspoons salt
- 1½ teaspoons ground black pepper
- 3–4 beef rib slabs (3 to 4 ribs per slab, about 5 pounds total)
- 1 recipe Barbecue Sauce for Texas-Style Beef Ribs (see page 126)

1. Mix the chili powder, cayenne, salt, and pepper in a small bowl; rub the ribs evenly with the spice mixture. Let the ribs stand at room temperature for 1 hour.

2. Meanwhile, cover 2 large wood chunks (see the note above) with water and soak 1 hour; drain. About 20 minutes before grilling, open the bottom grill vents. Using a chimney starter, ignite 30 briquettes (about one third of a large chimney, or 2 quarts) and burn until covered with a thin coating of light gray ash, about 10 minutes. Empty the coals into the grill, then bank the coals against one side of the grill, stacking them 2 to 3 coals high; place 1 soaked wood chunk on top of the coals. Position the grill grate over the coals, cover the grill, and adjust the lid vents two-thirds open. Heat the grate until hot, about 5 minutes (you can hold your hand 5 inches above the grill grate for 2 seconds); scrape the grill grate clean with a grill brush.

3. Position the ribs, meat-side down, on the cool side of the grill (they may overlap slightly); cover, positioning the lid so that the vents are directly above the ribs. (The temperature on a thermometer inserted through the vents should register about 300 degrees.) Cook until the grill temperature

---

GETTING IT RIGHT:
Where's the Beef?

Be careful when shopping for beef ribs—some ribs will yield poor results when barbecued. We prefer partial slabs (with three or four bones) that are very meaty.

TOO SKIMPY
The butcher trimmed too much meat from this slab; you can see the bones.

TOO SMALL
"Shorties" are cut in half and don't offer much meat.

TOO BIG
A whole slab (with seven ribs) is hard to maneuver on the grill.

JUST RIGHT
This partial slab has a thick layer of meat that covers the bones.

drops to about 250 degrees, about 1 hour. (On cold, windy days, the temperature may drop more quickly, so spot-check the temperature. If necessary, add 5 additional briquettes to maintain the temperature above 250 degrees during the first hour of cooking.)

4. After 1 hour, add 20 more briquettes and the remaining wood chunk to the coals. Using tongs, flip the ribs meat-side up and rotate so that the edges once closest to the coals are now farthest away. Cover the grill, positioning the lid so that the vents are opposite the wood chunk. Continue to cook until a dinner fork can be inserted into and removed from the meat with little resistance, the meat pulls away from the bones when the rack is gently twisted, and the meat shrinks ½ to 1 inch up the rib bones, 1¼ to 1¾ hours longer. Transfer the ribs to a cutting board and let rest 5 minutes. Using a chef's knife, slice between the bones to separate into individual ribs. Serve, passing the sauce separately.

VARIATION

TEXAS-STYLE BARBECUED BEEF RIBS ON A GAS GRILL

On a gas grill, leaving one burner on and turning the other(s) off simulates the indirect heat method on a charcoal grill. Use wood chips instead of wood chunks and a disposable aluminum pan to hold them. On a gas grill, it is important to monitor the temperature closely; use an oven thermometer set on the grate next to the ribs and check the temperature every 15 minutes. Try to maintain a 250- to 300-degree grill temperature by adjusting the setting of the lit burner.

1. Follow the recipe for Texas-Style Barbecued Beef Ribs through step 1.

2. Cover 3 cups wood chips with water; soak 30 minutes, then drain. Place the wood chips in a small disposable aluminum pan; set the pan on the gas grill burner that will remain on. Turn all the burners to high, close the lid, and heat the grill until the chips smoke heavily, about 20 minutes (if the chips ignite, extinguish the flames with a water-filled squirt bottle). Scrape the grill grate clean with a grill brush; turn off the burner(s) without wood chips. Position an oven thermometer and the ribs, meat-side down, on the cool side of the grill. Cover and cook 1¼ hours, checking the grill temperature every 15 minutes and adjusting the lit burner as needed to maintain a temperature of 250 to 300 degrees.

TECHNIQUE:
Soak-Ahead Wood Chunks

Wood chunks are essential when barbecuing, and soaking the chunks ensures that they will smoke slowly, giving food great flavor. If you can never remember to soak the wood in advance (it should stay in cold water for 1 hour), try this tip.

1. Soak as many chunks as you like at the same time. Drain the chunks, seal them in a zipper-lock plastic bag, and store them in the freezer.

2. When ready to barbecue, place the frozen chunks on the grill. They defrost quickly and impart as much flavor as freshly soaked chunks.

3. Using tongs, flip the ribs meat-side up and rotate so that the edges once closest to the lit burner are now farthest away. Cover and continue to cook and check/adjust grill temperature until a dinner fork can be inserted into and removed from the meat with a little resistance, the meat pulls away from the bones when the rack is gently twisted, and the meat shrinks ½ to 1 inch up the rib bones, 1 to 1½ hours longer. Transfer the ribs to a cutting board and let rest 5 minutes. Using a chef's knife, slice between the bones to separate into individual ribs. Serve, passing the sauce separately.

BARBECUE SAUCE FOR TEXAS-STYLE BEEF RIBS

Makes 1¾ cups

Every plate of beef ribs we tasted in Texas was accompanied by a simple, vinegary dipping sauce quite unlike the sweet, thick barbecue sauces found in the supermarket. After more than 30 tries, we figured out that the light flavor of tomato juice was the key.

2   tablespoons unsalted butter
¼   cup minced onion
1   medium garlic clove, minced or pressed through a garlic press (about 1 teaspoon)
1½   teaspoons chili powder
2   cups tomato juice
¾   cup distilled white vinegar
2   tablespoons Worcestershire sauce
½   teaspoon powdered mustard mixed with 1 tablespoon water
1   teaspoon minced chipotle chile in adobo
2   tablespoons mild or dark (not blackstrap) molasses
1½   teaspoons salt
¼   teaspoon ground black pepper

Heat the butter in a small nonreactive saucepan over medium heat until foaming. Add the onion and cook, stirring occasionally, until softened, 2 to 3 minutes. Add the garlic and chili powder and cook, stirring constantly, until fragrant, about 20 seconds. Add the tomato juice, ½ cup of the vinegar, the Worcestershire sauce, mustard, chipotle, molasses, and salt. Increase the heat to high and bring to a simmer, then reduce the heat to medium and continue to simmer, stirring occasionally, until the sauce is slightly thickened and reduced to 1½ cups, 30 to 40 minutes. Off the heat, stir in the pepper and remaining ¼ cup vinegar. Cool to room temperature before serving. (The sauce can be refrigerated in an airtight container for up to 4 days; bring to room temperature before serving.)

SCIENCE DESK:
Best Fire for a Barbecue

BARBECUE EXPERTS HAVE PLENTY OF THEORIES AS TO exactly what goes on inside a covered grill, but agreement is hard to come by. In search of wisdom rather than witchcraft, we wanted to see if we could scientifically determine the best way to lay a fire. What, once and for all, really is the best way to arrange the coals to secure evenly, thoroughly, deeply barbecued meat?

To answer this question, we outfitted a Weber kettle grill with five temperature probes, four around the edges of the grill and one in the center. Through holes drilled in the lid, we attached these probes—or thermocouples—to a computer data recorder that would measure the temperature inside the grill every minute for up to two hours. After running more than a dozen tests over a six-week period, we arrived at some answers.

Because barbecue is by definition slow cooking over low heat, the high temperatures produced by so-called direct heat (cooking directly over a pile of coals) are unacceptable. What's wanted is indirect heat, and, in a kettle grill, you can produce indirect heat in one of two ways: by banking two piles of coals on opposite sides of the grill or by banking one pile on one side.

The computer data showed that splitting the coals between two sides produced worrisome temperature spikes. This was unacceptable if the goal was to maintain a near-constant temperature. Moreover, the temperature at different sites in the grill showed significant variation.

If anything, we expected the variation in heat distribution with the single-banked coals to be even worse. With the exception of the probe placed directly over the fire, however, the probes in this case produced temperature readings that were within a few degrees of each other. This was surprising considering that one probe was about twice the distance from the fire as the other three. This was also good news, as it meant that a large part of the cooking area was being held at a pretty constant temperature. The single-banked method also showed almost no heat spikes and held the temperature between the ideal (for barbecue) 250 and 300 degrees for the longest period of time.

The results of these tests, then, seemed clear: It's best to have a single pile of coals rather than two piles, because one source of heat produced steady, evenly distributed heat, while two sources produced greater temperature variation.

But this wasn't the only thing we learned. Barbecue experts often recommend placing the lid vent (or vents) away from the fire, so this is what we'd been doing during testing. Was it really part of the reason why the pile of banked coals was providing even, steady heat? Sure enough, when we placed the open vent directly over the fire, the fire burned hotter and faster. With the vent in this position, a direct convection current was formed inside the egg-shaped

Weber kettle. When the vent was placed away from the fire, a more diffuse convection current ensured a more even distribution of heat. Also important was the degree to which we opened the lid vent. When the vent was opened up completely, the fire burned much hotter, and the heat was less even throughout the grill. The vent is best kept partially cracked. (Close the vent completely, of course, and you risk snuffing out the fire.)

The final, and most important, thing we learned was also probably the most obvious: When you open the lid to check on the progress of your barbecue, you lose all of the even heat distribution that you have worked so hard to establish. Above all, resist the temptation to peek.

SOUTHERN CORNBREAD

WHAT WE WANTED: A crusty, savory Southern-style cornbread baked in a cast-iron skillet.

Although the two ingredient lists may look similar, the cornbreads of the North and South are as different as Boston and Birmingham. White, not yellow, is the cornmeal of choice for Southern-style cornbread. Unlike Northerners, Southerners use only trace amounts of flour, if any, and if sugar is included it is treated like salt, to be measured out in teaspoons rather than by the cup. Buttermilk moistens, bacon drippings enrich, and a combination of baking powder and soda provides lift.

Classic Southern cornbread batter is poured into a scorching hot, greased cast-iron skillet, which causes it to develop a thin, shattery-crisp crust as the bread bakes. At its best, this bread is moist and tender, with the warm fragrance of the cornfield and the subtle flavor of the dairy in every bite. It is the best possible accompaniment to soups, salads, chilis, stews, and, of course, ribs. So we set out to create a recipe for it that would be foolproof.

We began by testing 11 different cornmeals in one simple Southern cornbread recipe. Before the cornmeal tests, we would have bet that color was a regional idiosyncrasy that had little to do with flavor. But tasting proved otherwise. Cornbreads made with yellow cornmeal consistently had a more potent corn flavor than those made with white cornmeal. Although we didn't want Southern cornbread to taste like dessert, we wondered whether a little sugar might enhance the corn flavor. So we made three batches—one with no sugar, one with 2 teaspoons, and one with a heaping tablespoon. The higher-sugar bread was really too sweet for Southern cornbread, but 2 teaspoons of sugar seemed to enhance the natural sweetness of the corn without calling attention to itself.

Most Southern-style cornbread batters are made with just buttermilk, but we found recipes calling for the full range of acidic and sweet dairy products—buttermilk, sour cream, yogurt, milk, and cream—and made batches with each of them. We still loved the pure, straightforward flavor of the buttermilk-based cornbread, but the batch made with sour cream was actually more tasty and baked into a more attractive shape.

At this point we began to feel a little uneasy about where we were taking this bread. A couple of teaspoons of sugar might be overlooked; yellow cornmeal was a big blow; but the sour cream felt like we were crossing the border, giving up our claim to a recipe for Southern cornbread.

So far all of our testing had been done with a composite recipe under which most Southern cornbread recipes seemed to fall. There were two recipes, however, that didn't quite fit the mold—one very rich and one very lean—and now seemed like the right time to give them a try.

After rejecting the rich version as closer to spoonbread, a soufflé-like dish, than cornbread, we went to the other extreme. In this simple version, boiling water is stirred into the cornmeal, then modest amounts of milk, egg, oil, salt, and baking powder are stirred into the resulting cornmeal mush, and the whole thing is baked. So simple, so lean, so humble, so backwater, this recipe would have been easy to pass over. But given our options at this point, we decided to give it a quick test. Just one bite completely changed the direction of our pursuit. Unlike anything we had tasted so far, the crumb of this cornbread was incredibly moist and fine and bursting with corn flavor, all with no flour and virtually no fat.

We were pleased, but since the foundation of this bread was cornmeal mush, the crumb was actually more mushy than moist. In addition, the baking powder, the only dry ingredient left, got stirred into the wet batter at the end. This just didn't feel right.

After a few unsuccessful attempts to make this cornbread less mushy, we started thinking that this great idea was a bust.

In a last attempt to salvage it, we decided to make mush out of only half the cornmeal and mix the remaining cornmeal with the leavener. To our relief, the bread made this way was much improved. Decreasing the mush even further, from a half to a third of the cornmeal, gave us exactly what we were looking for. We made the new, improved cornbread with buttermilk and mixed a bit of baking soda with the baking powder, and it tasted even better. Finally our recipe was starting to feel Southern again. Although we still preferred yellow cornmeal and a sprinkle of sugar, we had achieved a moist, tender, rather fine-crumbed bread without flour, and a

nicely shaped one at that, without sour cream, thus avoiding two ingredients that would have interfered with the strong corn flavor we wanted.

With this new recipe in hand, we performed a few final tests. Our recipe called for 1 tablespoon of oil, but many Southern cornbreads call for no more fat than is needed to grease the pan. We tried vegetable oil, butter, and bacon drippings, as well as a batch with no fat at all. The cornbread with no added fat was a bit less rich than the other batches—good but not great. The butter burned in the oven, so it was out. Oil was fine, but tasters loved the flavor imparted by bacon drippings. Vegetable oil adds no flavor but is the best substitute if you don't have bacon drippings on hand.

Before conducting these cornbread tests, we didn't think it was possible to bake cornbread in too hot an oven, but after tasting breads baked on the bottom rack of a 475-degree oven, we found that a dark brown crust makes bitter bread. We moved the rack up a notch, reduced the oven temperature to 450 degrees, and were thus able to cook many loaves of bread to golden brown perfection.

One final question: Do you need to heat up the skillet before adding the batter? If you're not a Southerner, the answer is no. Although the bread will not be as crisp in an unheated pan, it will ultimately brown up with a longer baking time. If you are a Southerner, of course, the answer is yes. More than the color of the meal or the presence of sugar or flour, cornbread becomes Southern when the batter hits the hot fat in a cast-iron skillet.

WHAT WE LEARNED: An odd recipe actually makes the best cornbread. Combine part of the cornmeal with boiling water, and then stir the buttermilk and egg into this cornmeal mush before adding it to the remaining cornmeal and other dry ingredients. Pour the batter into a hot, greased cast-iron skillet and bake until crusty.

SOUTHERN CORNBREAD

Serves 8

Though some styles of Southern cornbread are dry and crumbly, we favor this dense, moist, tender version. Cornmeal mush of just the right texture is essential to this bread. Make sure that the water is at a rapid boil when it is added to the cornmeal. Though we prefer to make cornbread in a preheated cast-iron skillet, a 9-inch round cake pan or 9-inch square baking pan, greased lightly with butter and not preheated, will also produce acceptable results if you double the recipe and bake the bread for 25 minutes. For information on the use and care of cast-iron skillets, see page 81.

4	teaspoons bacon drippings or vegetable oil
1	cup (about 5 ounces) yellow cornmeal, preferably stone-ground
2	teaspoons sugar
½	teaspoon salt
1	teaspoon baking powder
¼	teaspoon baking soda
⅓	cup rapidly boiling water
¾	cup buttermilk
1	large egg, beaten lightly

1. Adjust an oven rack to the lower-middle position and heat the oven to 450 degrees. Set an 8-inch cast-iron skillet with the bacon drippings in the heating oven.

2. Measure ⅓ cup of the cornmeal into a medium bowl. Whisk the remaining cornmeal, sugar, salt, baking powder, and baking soda together in a small bowl; set aside.

3. Pour the boiling water all at once into the ⅓ cup cornmeal; stir to make a stiff mush. Whisk in the buttermilk gradually, breaking up lumps until smooth, then whisk in the egg. When the oven is preheated and the skillet is very hot, stir the dry ingredients into the mush mixture until just moistened. Carefully remove the skillet from the oven.

Pour the hot bacon fat from the pan into the batter and stir to incorporate, then quickly pour the batter into the heated skillet. Bake until golden brown, about 20 minutes. Remove from the oven and instantly turn the cornbread onto a wire rack. Cool for 5 minutes, then serve immediately.

TASTING LAB: Cornbread Mixes

MAKING CORNBREAD FROM SCRATCH IS NOT DIFFI-cult, but with all the mixes on the market we wondered if we could get from-scratch quality out of a box. We gathered seven brands of cornbread mix, including Southern favorites White Lily and Martha White, supermarket staples Jiffy and Betty Crocker, as well as Washington, Krusteaz, and Hodgson Mills, prepared them in the test kitchen, and held a blind tasting.

As easy as our Southern Cornbread is, nothing can beat the convenience of these mixes—just pour into a bowl, add milk (and sometimes egg), mix, and bake. Within 30 minutes, you can have a hot, steaming cornbread on the table. But can the taste come close to homemade? Not remotely.

All seven of the cornbreads were dismissed by tasters as tremendously inferior to homemade. All received scores that hovered just above or below the "Not Recommended" cutoff; three are barely recommended and four are not recommended.

The problem with all of the cornbreads was summed up by one taster who wrote, "Overall, there is no corn flavor; all have an inexplicable savory flavor." Breads were overwhelmingly dry and bland; none tasted like the corn for which they are named. The better-rated cornbreads rated high for sweetness and moistness.

So what to do if you're looking for easy cornbread with great corn flavor and moist texture? Unfortunately, there just isn't any shortcut; you have to make it yourself.

Rating Cornbread Mixes

FIFTEEN MEMBERS OF THE *COOK'S ILLUSTRATED* STAFF TASTED ALL OF THE PRODUCTS PREPARED ACCORDING to the package instructions. The mixes are listed in order of preference based on their scores in this tasting. All of these mixes are available in supermarkets, although several are regional brands.

RECOMMENDED WITH RESERVATIONS
Betty Crocker Golden Corn Muffin and Bread Mix
$.55 for 6.5 ounces, yielding an 8-inch pan of cornbread

Though one vocal fan called it "pretty darn good," most agreed that it was too "coarse," "crumbly," and "dry." The best of a pretty bad bunch.

RECOMMENDED WITH RESERVATIONS
Jiffy Corn Muffin Mix
$.55 for 8.5 ounces, yielding an 8-inch pan of cornbread

Despite its "buttery" flavor and "rustic" texture, this brand was downgraded for being "sandy" (one taster compared it to "a day at the beach") and "way too dry."

RECOMMENDED WITH RESERVATIONS
Washington Corn Muffin Mix
$.45 for 8 ounces, yielding an 8-inch pan of cornbread

Though there was "not much corn flavor," this brand was "moister than most."

NOT RECOMMENDED
Hodgson Mill Cornbread and Muffin Mix
$1.55 for 7.5 ounces, yielding an 8-inch pan of cornbread

Its "dry" texture and "wheaty" flavor had one taster asking, "Is it made with tree bark?"

NOT RECOMMENDED
Krusteaz Honey Cornbread and Muffin Mix
$1.69 for 15 ounces, yielding an 8-inch pan of cornbread

Most tasters compared this brand unfavorably to dry yellow cake. One taster wrote, "like a sponge—not a sponge cake, a sponge."

NOT RECOMMENDED
Martha White Yellow Cornbread Mix
$1.25 for 6.5 ounces, yielding an 8-inch pan of cornbread

Despite one taster detecting "some corn flavor," most tasters agreed that the flavor of this Southern favorite was "flat" and "salty, salty, salty!"

NOT RECOMMENDED
White Lily White Cornbread Mix
$.67 for 6.5 ounces, yielding an 8-inch pan of cornbread

The "bland, very salty" flavor and "lingering chemical aftertaste" led one taster to remark that this Southern favorite "tastes like the box it came from," though it actually came in a bag.

Television requires an army of charcoal grills ready to cook tenderloin and more.

GRILL-ROASTED
CHAPTER 11
beef tenderloin

We don't part easily with money, but we will on occasion break the bank and buy a beef tenderloin. The tender, buttery interior is the big draw, and the combination of a healthy dose of seasoning and the flavor from the charcoal grill is a perfect solution to a rather mild-tasting (boring) piece of meat. Recently, we ordered a whole beef tenderloin from a local supermarket. Six pounds of perfectly trimmed tenderloin later, we had shelled out a jaw-dropping $167.94 (that's $27.99 per pound).

We heated up the grill and gingerly placed our new, most valuable possession over the hot coals. Even though we watched it like a hawk, we couldn't get the tenderloin to cook evenly. The exterior was charred and tough; the interior of the fat butt end was pink, and the thinner tail end was beyond well-done. Worst of all, because we were able to season only the exterior of the tenderloin, the interior was bland.

We wondered if there was a way to take this mammoth and insanely expensive cut of beef and grill it to absolute perfection. And, after having spent nearly $170 on a complete flop, we were determined to find a cheaper alternative to supermarket shopping.

GRILL-ROASTED BEEF TENDERLOIN

WHAT WE WANTED: With a whole tenderloin going for as much as $180, uneven cooking, bland flavor, and a tough outer crust just don't cut it. We wanted it cheaper and better.

Great tenderloin begins at the market. At local supermarkets, we learned, whole beef tenderloin isn't a meat case–ready item. Most butchers we talked to said they keep the tenderloins in the back to be cut for filets, so if you want one, you've got to ask for it. When you do ask for whole tenderloin, it will usually come "peeled," which means the outer membrane of fat and sinew has been removed. These peeled tenderloins run anywhere from $13.99 per pound for Choice grade meat to an even more astounding $32.99 per pound for Prime grade at a high-end butcher—that's $200 dollars for a 6-pound roast. At that price, we expect the butcher to come to our house, grill the meat for us, wash the dishes, and throw in a back rub as well.

A few days later, we found ourselves in a wholesale club. No longer just a place to buy giant cans of beans, most wholesale clubs sell meat as well. We soon found ourselves eye-to-eye with a case full of vacuum-sealed, Choice grade, whole tenderloins. If the mountain of meat hadn't caught our attention, the price sure would have. Weighing in at about $9 per pound, these tenderloins were one third the cost of the roast we had bought from our butcher. We grabbed as many as we could stuff into the giant shopping cart and headed back to the kitchen.

We soon discovered the one downside of using the wholesale club tenderloins. They came "unpeeled," so a fair amount of trimming, tugging, and prying was necessary to rid the meat of its fat, sinew, and silver skin. But we had to be judicious, as we found the trimmings could weigh more than 1½ pounds, including the loss of some valuable meat. The best way to trim one of these tenderloins was to first

peel off as much fat as possible with our hands; the fat came away clean and took very little of the pricey meat with it (see illustrations on page 136). Next, we used a flexible boning knife (a sharp paring knife works well in a pinch) to remove the silver skin, the muscle sheath that would otherwise cause the tenderloin to curl up on the grill. Last, we took the advice of many cookbooks and tucked the narrow tip end of the tenderloin under and tied it securely. This tuck-and-tie step gave the tenderloin a more consistent thickness that would allow it to grill more evenly.

Was this extra 20 minutes of preparatory work worth the effort? We got out our calculators and crunched the numbers. Let's see . . . with a loss of about a pound of trimmings, our $48 roast was now divided by the 5 pounds of remaining meat . . . and that came to around $9.60 per pound. You better believe it was worth it! It still was by no means a "cheap" piece of meat, but it didn't empty our wallet.

While some love beef tenderloin for its "mild" beef flavor, others scoff at it for exactly the same reason. We found ourselves in the latter camp and felt that the tenderloin could use a flavor boost. Many recipes suggested marinades, spice rubs, or herb crusts. Tasters rejected the marinated tenderloins for their weird, spongy texture. Spice rubs made the beef taste too much like barbecue (if we wanted barbecue, we'd buy a cheap rack of ribs), while herb rubs were too powerful for such a tame cut of meat. We were looking for a way to enhance the beef flavor, not to mask it.

Then a colleague suggested a recently heralded technique in which the tenderloin is salted and left to sit overnight in the fridge. The theory goes that the salt penetrates the meat all the way to the center, seasoning the tenderloin throughout. Sure enough, the salted-overnight beef was seasoned through and through, but at quite a cost. The meat had turned a sickly brown-gray (even when the center was cooked to medium-rare), and the texture was webby, like that of an undercooked pot roast (see the photo on page 138). We played around a bit with amounts of salt, going up to ¼ cup of kosher salt and down to 1 tablespoon. But it seemed that time was the villain here—an overnight salting was just too much.

For the next round, we went back to the original 1½ tablespoons of kosher salt and rubbed a couple of tenderloins. We wrapped both in plastic and refrigerated one for four hours, the other for one hour. Although both were markedly better than the overnight-salted tenderloin, the winner was the beef that was salted for only one hour. With just enough time for the salt to season the meat without compromising the texture, the salt brought out a decidedly beefier flavor, one that we greatly appreciated. Even better was letting the salted tenderloin sit on the countertop rather than refrigerating it. The big tenderloin lost some of its chill, and it grilled at a more even rate. After scaling the salt back to 1½ tablespoons, we took our well-seasoned tenderloin in hand and headed for the nearest grill.

Up to this point, we had been grilling the tenderloin directly over the hot fire, an approach that burned the outer crust before the interior had a chance to cook properly. We tried a more moderate heat. Now the exterior was no longer scorched, but the outer inch-thick perimeter of the meat was approaching the well-done mark before the interior was cooked.

In a forehead-slapping moment, it struck us that we were treating (and grilling) the tenderloin as a steak and not as what it was—a roast. For our next test, we set up the grill for grill-roasting, in which indirect heat is used to cook the meat. We piled the coals up on one side of the grill, leaving the other side empty, then placed the tenderloin over the empty side (opposite the coals), covered the grill, and left it alone. About 45 minutes later, we knew that we were onto something. The indirect heat had cooked the tenderloin evenly from tip to tip (OK, so the very ends were more well-done), and the meat had taken on a mild, smoky flavor from spending so much time exposed to the hot coals. But we missed the crust that came with searing the meat. The

solution was to first sear the tenderloin over the hot coals on all sides before switching to the cooler (coal-free) side to finish grilling. This was it: a remarkable, well-browned crust and a rosy pink interior. We tried adding a couple of soaked wood chunks to the pile of hot coals, in hopes of imparting even more smoky flavor to the meat. And smoky was just what we got; there was no denying that this cut of meat had been cooked on the grill. (Some in the test kitchen thought the smoke flavor was too strong for the mild beef. For those in this camp, just omit the wood chunks.)

When we cut into a tenderloin right off the grill, it gave off a lot of juice—not a good idea with such a lean piece of meat. The easy solution was to let the meat rest for 10 to 15 minutes before cutting, but during this rest period the meat rose from medium-rare (about 135 degrees) to medium-well (over 150 degrees). We next removed the tenderloin from the grill when the meat was still rare. After resting, the roast was incredibly juicy, with a rosy pink interior, a beautiful dark brown crust, and a smoky, seasoned flavor—all of which was worth every cent we had paid for it.

WHAT WE LEARNED: Buy an unpeeled tenderloin at a warehouse club, take the 20 minutes to trim the fat yourself, and save $100. Tie the roast up (so it cooks evenly) and then salt the meat an hour before it goes onto the grill. Cook the roast over a two-level fire to achieve a nicely browned crust and perfectly even, rosy interior.

GRILL-ROASTED BEEF TENDERLOIN

Serves 10 to 12

Beef tenderloins purchased from wholesale clubs require a good amount of trimming before cooking. At the grocery store, however, you may have the option of having the butcher trim it for you. Once trimmed, and with the butt tenderloin still attached (the butt tenderloin is the lobe attached to the large end of the roast), the roast should weigh 4½ to 5 pounds. If you purchase an already-trimmed tenderloin without the butt tenderloin attached, begin checking for doneness about 5 minutes early. If you prefer your tenderloin without a smoky flavor, you may opt not to use wood chips or chunks. Serve as is or with Salsa Verde (page 141).

1   beef tenderloin (about 6 pounds), trimmed of fat and silver skin (according to the illustrations below), tail end tucked and tied at 2-inch intervals

1½   tablespoons kosher salt
2   tablespoons olive oil
1   tablespoon ground black pepper

1. About 1 hour before grilling, set the tenderloin on a cutting board or rimmed baking sheet and rub with the salt. Cover loosely with plastic wrap and let stand at room temperature. Cover two 2-inch wood chunks with cold water and soak 1 hour; drain.

2. About 25 minutes before grilling, open the bottom grill vents. Using a chimney starter, ignite about 2½ pounds charcoal briquettes (1 large chimney, or 6 quarts) and burn until covered with a layer of light gray ash, about 15 minutes. Empty the coals into the grill and build a two-level fire by arranging the coals to cover one half of the grill, piling them about 3 briquettes high. Set the wood chunks on the coals. Position the grill grate over the coals, cover the grill,

---

TECHNIQUE: Trimming and Tying a Tenderloin

Although wholesale clubs offer whole beef tenderloins at an affordable price, most come unpeeled, with the fat and silver skin (a tough membrane) intact. Here's how to trim and tie a tenderloin for the grill. Expect to lose between 1 and 1½ pounds during the trimming process. A boning knife is the best tool for this job.

1. Pull away the outer layer of fat to expose the fatty chain of meat.

2. Pull the chain of fat away from the roast, cut it off, and discard the chain.

3. Scrape the silver skin at the creases in the thick end to expose the lobes.

4. Trim the silver skin by slicing under it and cutting upward.

5. Remove the remaining silver skin in the creases at the thick end.

6. Turn the tenderloin over and remove the fat from the underside.

and heat the grate until hot, about 10 minutes (the grill should be medium-hot; you can hold your hand 5 inches above the grill grate for 4 seconds). Scrape the grill grate clean with a grill brush.

3. Uncover the tenderloin, coat with the olive oil, and sprinkle all sides with the pepper. Place the tenderloin on the hot side of the grill directly over the coals. Cook until well browned, about 2 minutes, then rotate one quarter turn and repeat until all sides are well browned, a total of 8 minutes. Move the tenderloin to the cooler side of the grill and cover, positioning the lid vents over the tenderloin. Cook until an instant-read thermometer inserted into the thickest part of the tenderloin registers 120 degrees for rare, 16 to 20 minutes, or 125 degrees for medium-rare, 20 to 25 minutes.

4. Transfer the tenderloin to a cutting board, tent loosely with foil, and let rest 10 to 15 minutes. Cut into ½-inch-thick slices and serve.

VARIATION

GRILL-ROASTED BEEF TENDERLOIN ON A GAS GRILL

If you're using a gas grill, wood chips are a better option than wood chunks.

1. Follow step 1 of the recipe for Grill-Roasted Beef Tenderloin, substituting 2 cups wood chips for the wood chunks and soaking the chips 20 minutes. Drain the chips, place in a small disposable foil pan, and cover with heavy-duty foil; poke 6 holes in the foil and set aside.

2. About 20 minutes before grilling, place the wood chip tray on the primary burner (the burner that will remain on during grilling); position the cooking grates. Turn all the burners to high, close the lid, and heat the grill until the chips smoke heavily, about 20 minutes (if the chips ignite, extinguish the flames with a water-filled squirt bottle). Scrape the grill grate clean with a grill brush.

3. Uncover the tenderloin, coat with the olive oil, and sprinkle all sides with the pepper. Place the tenderloin on the side of the grate opposite the primary burner. Grill the tenderloin over the burner(s) without wood chips until well browned, 2 to 3 minutes, then rotate one quarter turn and repeat until all sides are well browned, for a total of 8 to 12 minutes. Turn off all burners except the primary burner (the tenderloin should be positioned over the extinguished burner[s]). Cover and cook until an instant-read thermometer inserted in the thickest part of the tenderloin registers 120 degrees for rare, 16 to 20 minutes, or 125 degrees for medium-rare, 20 to 25 minutes.

4. Transfer the tenderloin to a cutting board, tent loosely with foil, and let rest 10 to 15 minutes. Cut into ½-inch-thick slices and serve.

SCIENCE DESK:
When Should You Salt Meat?

SALTING MEAT IS NOTHING NEW; IT WAS USED CENTURIES before refrigeration as a method of preservation. Recently, though, there has been a renewed chorus of voices singing the praises of the simple salt rub, sometimes applied the night before. One might understand why salt could make a tough cut more palatable, but would this technique improve pricey tenderloin?

We found that salting the meat an hour before cooking gave the roast a beefier flavor. A four-hour salt produced much the same results, but salting the roast the night before cooking was a disaster. The roast turned brown. But why?

Anyone who lives in a cold climate knows that the salting of roadways causes cars to rust. This is due to salt's ability to promote oxidation in iron. Salt can also help to oxidize myoglobin, an iron-containing protein that gives meat its red color. The brown-as-pot-roast color of the tenderloin that had been salted overnight indicated that much of the myoglobin had been oxidized and most of its red color lost.

Perhaps the poor color could be excused if the procedure had produced phenomenal flavor. In fact, the opposite was true; the meat was stringy and the flavor was tired. In addition to oxidizing the myoglobin, the salt had drawn water from the meat, causing it to look thready, as if it had been overcooked. Moreover, little of the mild but juicy beef flavor normally associated with tenderloin was present; instead it tasted dull. In the case of tenderloin, which is beautifully textured and delicately flavored out of the package, there is really no good reason to salt for extended periods—unless, of course, you want to pay $9 a pound for pot roast.

OVERNIGHT SALTING
Looks like overcooked
pot roast.

ONE-HOUR SALTING
A tender, juicy, and
flavorful roast.

TASTING LAB: Beef Tenderloin

WHEN IT COMES TO BUYING A SPECIAL CUT OF BEEF like tenderloin, more and more cooks are bypassing the supermarket and either seeking bargain prices at wholesale clubs or paying a premium for the "specialty" beef available through mail-order sources. Is there a difference between roasts that cost $9 and $55 per pound?

In a blind tasting, we evaluated a broad selection of tenderloins—one from a local supermarket, three from warehouse clubs, and three from well-known mail-order sources. This last group included several Prime roasts; the roasts from the supermarket and warehouse clubs were either Choice or Select, the next two grades down the quality chain and those commonly found in supermarkets. Given the price differential as well as the various grades of beef in the tasting, we were shocked by the results.

As a whole, our panel found only subtle differences in flavor and texture among the seven tenderloins. None of the mail-order tenderloins managed to stand out from the crowd. The top choice came from the supermarket. And our panel's second choice was a Select roast from a warehouse club. Only the previously frozen Omaha Steaks tenderloin failed to please tasters and is not recommended. So when it comes to tenderloin, you don't have to pay a king's ransom for a princely roast.

SO WHAT DO YOU REALLY GET?

The chart on page 139 indicates the price we paid per pound for our tenderloin. But some tenderloins required much more trimming than others. The figures below indicate the edible portion (as a percentage of the initial weight) we obtained once trimming was complete. We then recalculated the prices to indicate what each pound of edible meat really cost us.

So what did we learn? All of the tenderloins purchased at the supermarket and warehouse clubs required more trimming than the mail-order samples but not enough to really affect overall prices. Even taking into account the extra waste on the tenderloins we purchased at warehouse clubs, they averaged just $13 per pound, compared with $23 per pound for our supermarket sample, and from $41 to $57 per pound for the mail-order samples. Note that the tenderloin from Lobel's required no trimming at all, making this expensive mail-order sample the best choice for lazy cooks with money to burn.

	EDIBLE PORTION (after trimming)	ACTUAL COST (per pound)
Stop & Shop	64%	$23.34
BJ's	67%	$13.24
Lobel's	100%	$54.84
Niman Ranch	76%	$57.50
Costco	70%	$12.60
Sam's Club	64%	$13.87
Omaha	80%	$40.94

Rating Beef Tenderloin

NINETEEN MEMBERS OF THE *COOK'S ILLUSTRATED* STAFF TASTED ALL OF THE TENDERLOINS, WHICH HAD BEEN RUBBED lightly with oil, sprinkled with salt and pepper, and roasted in the oven. The tenderloins are listed in order of preference based on their scores in this tasting. Note that prices for mail-order brands have been adjusted to include shipping and handling. The tenderloins varied significantly in the amount of fat that needed to be trimmed. See the chart on page 138 to see how this affected the actual cost.

RECOMMENDED
Stop & Shop Beef Tenderloin
$14.99 per pound

This roast purchased at our local supermarket won the tasting. "The truest, most pure flavor" raved one taster. The "silky," "almost falling apart" meat was especially tender. One panelist summed up, "best texture, nice flavor."

RECOMMENDED
BJ's Beef Tenderloin
$8.89 per pound

This warehouse club tenderloin finished in a strong second place, with comments such as "rich," "tender," and "beefy." Several tasters thought this roast had more fat than the rest of the pack. A few naysayers complained about a "too soft" texture.

RECOMMENDED
Lobel's Beef Tenderloin Roast
$54.84 per pound

This mail-order sample from a famed New York butcher was the only one to arrive in the test kitchen perfectly trimmed and ready to cook. "Great marbling" with "rich," "meaty" flavor. "Like a good steak," wrote one taster, but look at that price.

RECOMMENDED
Niman Ranch Whole Beef Tenderloin
$43.55 per pound

This mail-order brand is a favorite with chefs. There were several complaints about the "chalky" or "dusty" texture. Panelists were divided about the flavor of this roast, calling it "beefy" and "deep" as well as "too strong" and "strange."

RECOMMENDED
Costco Beef Tenderloin
$8.79 per pound

This warehouse club roast earned decent scores, although it didn't really elicit much strong support. Several tasters objected to the "cottony," "mealy" texture. The flavor was described as either "bland" or "mild."

RECOMMENDED
Sam's Club Beef Tenderloin
$8.87 per pound

This warehouse club tenderloin has a lot of personality. Tasters used adjectives such as "gamey" to "metallic" to describe the flavor. The texture was both "chewy on the outside" and "a bit mushy" in the middle.

NOT RECOMMENDED
Omaha Steaks Chateaubriand Roast
$32.60 per pound

This mail-order sample was the only one deemed unacceptable by tasters. It was shipped frozen, and there were many complaints about the texture of the meat, ranging from "powdery" and "gritty" to "wet cardboard" and "gummy."

SALSA VERDE

WHAT WE WANTED: This all-purpose green sauce made from parsley, olive oil, garlic, and vinegar can be overwhelming and harsh, and it easily separates to boot. We wanted a smooth sauce to accompany grilled tenderloin.

The promise of a brilliant green salsa verde is clear enough. It suggests the possibility of culinary wizardry, transforming a host of bland, forgettable dishes into something memorable. The ingredients are simple enough: parsley, olive oil, lemon juice or vinegar, something pickled or brined (capers, cornichons, and/or green olives), garlic, and sometimes anchovies. Despite its innate simplicity, salsa verde can easily go wrong. In fact, many of the recipes we tested were overly potent and harsh, leaving tasters with puckered lips and raging garlic breath. The texture was problematic, too; all of our initial salsas separated into pools of oil and clumps of parsley. Our intent was to create a balanced yet still bold sauce with a thick, uniform texture.

We started with the parsley. Previous analysis in our test kitchen revealed that Italian, or flat-leaf, parsley is preferable to curly parsley for its fresh, tender flavor, when parsley is a dominant ingredient. Extra-virgin olive oil, red wine vinegar, green olives, a couple of anchovy fillets, and a large clove of garlic completed our starting recipe. The resulting sauce was too tangy and sharp, even in small bites, and the solids collected on the bottom of the bowl, while the oil rested on top. When we reduced the quantity of vinegar, the sauce became dull and flat-tasting. Decreasing the amount of anchovies, garlic, and olives had the same effect. We were at a standstill.

Additional research turned up two possibilities. One recipe called for the addition of hard-cooked egg yolks, while others suggested bread. We assumed that these bland ingredients were included to temper the assertive ones; it was a theory worth testing. The egg yolks did soften the blow of the other flavors, but the sauce tasted fatty and had a mealy texture. (The sauce did not separate, however, which was a major improvement.) Next, we processed chunks of bread with oil and vinegar to create a smooth base, added the remaining ingredients, and crossed our fingers. This sauce was top-notch. The flavors were bright but not aggressive, and the texture was lush and well blended. Further testing proved that airy, moist bread produced gummy sauce. Firm, dry bread with a tight crumb was much better. However, we wanted the option to use whatever bread was on hand. We found that 15 seconds in the toaster dried out even the squishiest bread so that it could be used in this sauce.

We wondered if the parsley should be chopped by hand for maximum flavor. A side-by-side taste test of salsa verde made in the food processor versus finely hand-chopped salsa verde (tasters rejected very roughly chopped sauces) revealed minimal differences; the two were nearly indistinguishable. (Yes, the food processor method won.)

Among olives, capers, cornichons, and combinations thereof, capers alone were the top choice for their salty, pungent bite. As for the acidic component, fresh lemon juice narrowly won out over an array of vinegars. The lemon juice nicely accented the fresh, clean flavor of the parsley. Lemon juice is also less acidic (and less harsh) than most vinegars, which tasters appreciated. When we varied the amount of garlic, tasters favored only one medium clove, preferring to let the flavor of the parsley take center stage. Four anchovy fillets, on the other hand, seemed mandatory, adding a welcome complexity (but not fishiness) to the sauce. A pinch of salt performed its usual work and further improved the sauce.

WHAT WE LEARNED: Start with Italian parsley leaves and add some lightly toasted bread to give the sauce a smooth, well-blended texture. Use lemon juice (rather than vinegar) to keep the sauce from tasting harsh and add garlic sparingly. Finally, capers and anchovies give salsa verde its characteristic piquant flavor.

SALSA VERDE

Makes a generous 1½ cups

Two slices of sandwich bread pureed with the sauce keeps the flavors balanced and gives the sauce texture. Toasting the bread rids it of excess moisture that might otherwise make a gummy sauce. Salsa verde is excellent with grilled or roasted meats, fish, or poultry; poached fish; boiled or steamed potatoes; sliced tomatoes; or as a condiment on sandwiches. It is best served immediately after it is made but can be refrigerated in an airtight container for up to 2 days. If it's refrigerated, bring the sauce to room temperature and stir it to recombine before serving.

2	large slices white sandwich bread
1	cup extra-virgin olive oil
¼	cup juice from 2 lemons
4	cups lightly packed fresh Italian parsley leaves, washed and dried thoroughly
4	medium anchovy fillets
¼	cup capers, drained
1	medium garlic clove, minced or pressed through a garlic press (about 1 teaspoon)
¼	teaspoon salt

1. Toast the bread in a toaster at the low setting until the surface is dry but not browned, about 15 seconds. Cut the bread into rough ½-inch pieces (you should have about 1½ cups).

2. Process the bread pieces, oil, and lemon juice in a food processor until smooth, about 10 seconds. Add the parsley, anchovies, capers, garlic, and salt. Pulse until the mixture is finely chopped (the mixture should not be smooth), about five 1-second pulses, scraping down the bowl with a rubber spatula after 3 pulses. Transfer the mixture to a small bowl and serve.

Q&A

What's the difference between flat-leaf and curly parsley?

Most food professionals use flat-leaf parsley (also called Italian parsley) rather than curly parsley, regarding the latter as pretty but flavorless. To find out if this is true, we chopped up bunches of each and held a taste test. When tossed with hot pasta and garlic, there was little flavor distinction between the two types of parsley. It wasn't until the chopped parsley was tasted alone that we noted differences. On its own, the flat-leaf parsley was preferred for its "fresh," "grassy" flavor and "tender" texture, while some tasters found the curly-leaf parsley to be "bitter" and "tough." The moral of the story? If you're making a dish in which parsley gets star billing, go for flat-leaf. However, if you're sprinkling a little parsley into stew or onto pasta, don't worry if your local supermarket only carries the curly stuff.

VARIATIONS

LEMON-BASIL SALSA VERDE

This variation pairs especially well with fish.

Follow the recipe for Salsa Verde, substituting 2 cups lightly packed roughly chopped fresh basil leaves for 2 cups of the parsley, and adding 1 teaspoon grated lemon zest to the food processor along with the herbs.

SALSA VERDE WITH ARUGULA

Arugula gives this variation a peppery kick that's a nice match for grilled foods.

Follow the recipe for Salsa Verde, substituting 2 cups lightly packed roughly chopped arugula for 2 cups of the parsley.

BROILED ASPARAGUS

WHAT WE WANTED: With tenderloin on the grill, we wanted a simple recipe for cooking asparagus under the broiler that would yield nicely browned, tender spears.

Asparagus presents one main preparation issue—should the spears be peeled, or is it better to discard the tough, fibrous ends entirely? In our tests, we found that peeled asparagus have a silkier texture, but we preferred the contrast between the crisp peel and tender inner flesh. Peeling also requires a lot of work. We prefer to simply snap off the tough ends and proceed with cooking.

The intense dry heat of the broiler concentrates the flavor of the asparagus, and the exterior caramelization makes the spears especially sweet. The result is asparagus with a heightened and, we think, delicious flavor.

The two primary questions related to broiling concerned the thickness of the stalks and the distance they should be kept from the heat sources as they cook. In our tests with thicker asparagus, anywhere from ¾ to 1 inch in diameter, the peels began to char before the interior of the spears became fully tender. When we used thinner spears (no thicker than ⅝ inch), the interior was tender by the time the exterior was browned.

We then focused on how far to keep the spears from the heating element. At 3 inches, the asparagus charred a bit. At 5 inches, the asparagus took a little too long to cook, and they failed to caramelize properly. The middle ground, 4 inches, proved perfect for cooking speed and browning. To encourage browning, toss the asparagus spears with olive oil before cooking them.

WHAT WE LEARNED: Choose medium-thick green asparagus, snap off the tough ends, and then cook the spears under the broiler until lightly browned. Make sure to shake the pan with the asparagus as it cooks so that the spears are turned and cook evenly.

BROILED ASPARAGUS
Serves 6

Broilers vary significantly in intensity, thus the wide range of cooking times in this recipe. Choose asparagus no thicker than ⅝ inch for this recipe.

> 2 pounds thin asparagus spears, tough ends snapped off (see the illustration on page 177)
> 1 tablespoon olive oil
> Salt and ground black pepper

Adjust an oven rack to the uppermost position (about 4 inches from the heating element) and heat the broiler. Toss the asparagus with the oil and salt and pepper to taste, then lay the spears in a single layer on a heavy, rimmed baking sheet. Broil, shaking the pan halfway through to turn the spears, until the asparagus are tender and lightly browned, 6 to 10 minutes. Serve hot or warm.

VARIATIONS
BROILED ASPARAGUS WITH REDUCED BALSAMIC VINAIGRETTE AND PARMESAN
The balsamic glaze will keep in the refrigerator for a week.

> ¾ cup balsamic vinegar
> 1 recipe Broiled Asparagus
> ¼ cup extra-virgin olive oil
> ¼ cup shaved Parmesan cheese (see the illustration on page 173)

Bring the vinegar to a boil in an 8-inch skillet over medium-high heat. Reduce the heat to medium and simmer slowly until the vinegar is syrupy and reduced to ¼ cup, 15 to 20 minutes. Arrange the broiled asparagus on a serving platter. Drizzle the balsamic glaze and olive oil over the asparagus. Sprinkle with the Parmesan and serve immediately.

BROILED ASPARAGUS WITH SOY-GINGER VINAIGRETTE

Putting the garlic through a press ensures that the pieces are very fine. If you don't own a press, mince the garlic to a paste with a knife.

2   medium scallions, white and green parts, minced
1   piece (about 1 inch) fresh ginger, minced (about 1 tablespoon)
2   small garlic cloves, minced or pressed through a garlic press (about 2 teaspoons)
3   tablespoons toasted sesame oil
3   tablespoons soy sauce
¼   cup juice from 2 large limes
1   tablespoon honey
1   recipe Broiled Asparagus

Whisk the scallions, ginger, garlic, sesame oil, soy sauce, lime juice, and honey together in a small bowl. Arrange the asparagus on a serving platter. Drizzle the vinaigrette over the asparagus and serve immediately.

BROILED PROSCIUTTO-WRAPPED ASPARAGUS WITH MASCARPONE

Serves 8 as an appetizer

Mascarpone is an Italian cheese with a consistency similar to cream cheese. It can be found in the specialty cheese section of most large grocery stores. The asparagus will have to be broiled in two batches so the prosciutto can brown properly. Keep the uncooked prosciutto-wrapped asparagus in the refrigerator until they are ready to be broiled.

½   cup mascarpone cheese
12 ounces prosciutto, cut into 4 by 1-inch strips
2   pounds thin asparagus spears, tough ends snapped off (see the illustration on page 177)
    Ground black pepper

1. Adjust an oven rack to the uppermost position (about 4 inches from the heating element) and heat the broiler. Smear a scant teaspoon of mascarpone onto each strip of prosciutto. Tightly wrap each asparagus spear in a strip of prosciutto (starting with the tip of the asparagus), securing the end with a toothpick. Place half the spears in a single layer on a heavy, rimmed baking sheet, leaving about ½ inch space between the spears.

2. Broil, turning the spears with tongs halfway through the cooking time, until the asparagus is tender and the prosciutto is lightly browned, 8 to 10 minutes. Transfer the broiled asparagus to a serving platter. Broil the remaining asparagus on the empty baking sheet. Transfer the second batch of broiled asparagus to the platter, season with pepper to taste, and serve warm.

Diane prepares our favorite new chicken recipe with Thai spices.

NEW FLAVORS
CHAPTER 12
from the grill

Even expert grillers can get in a rut. They make the same four or five recipes over and over again. Sure, the steaks are great, but isn't there something a bit more exciting? This chapter looks at two dishes with plenty of sex appeal.

Thai grilled chicken takes boring old chicken parts and adds the potent flavors of Southeast Asia. There's nothing boring about a dish that depends on fish sauce, cilantro, lime juice, hot pepper flakes, and garlic. Our goal for this recipe was simple—develop authentic flavor with ordinary ingredients.

Glazed salmon is a restaurant classic. The fish is coated with a sweet, sticky glaze that turns to a crisp crust over hot coals. The glazes makes basic salmon something special. Although recipes for this dish look simple enough, everyone knows that sticking and burning are constant threats. Sure, a professional can glaze salmon in a restaurant, but will your average Joe and Jane be able to pull this dish off without losing the fish to the grill grate? With a thick marinade, a two-level fire, and a well-oiled grill, the answer is yes.

THAI GRILLED CHICKEN

WHAT WE WANTED: Could we capture the complex flavors and aromas that make this chicken recipe special while keeping the dish practical for the American kitchen?

Thai grilled chicken, or *gai yang,* is classic street food. This herb- and spice-rubbed chicken is served in small pieces and eaten as finger food, along with a sweet and spicy dipping sauce. Thai flavors are wonderfully aromatic and complex, making this dish a refreshing change of pace from typical barbecue fare. But is it possible to bring the flavors of Thailand into the American kitchen (or backyard) without using an ingredient list as long as your arm and making several trips to Asian specialty stores?

An initial sampling of recipes made us wonder if this dish ought to remain as indigenous street food. Among the hard-to-find ingredients were cilantro root and lemon grass, and there was a profusion of odd mixtures, including an unlikely marriage of peanut butter and brown sugar. In the end, the simplest version won out: a rub made only with cilantro, black pepper, lime juice, and garlic. We would use this as our working recipe.

Because tasters preferred white meat, we decided to go with bone-in breasts. Brined chicken was vastly preferred to unbrined, and tasters liked the addition of sugar along with salt, which complemented the sweetness of the sauce. We settled on ½ cup of each in 2 quarts of water.

Tasters liked the working rub recipe, but they wanted more complexity of flavor. Our first step was to reduce the amount of cilantro, as it had been overpowering the other ingredients. Curry powder made the chicken taste too much like Indian food, and coconut milk turned the chicken milky and soggy, with flabby skin. The earthy flavor of coriander was welcome, and fresh ginger worked well in balance with the garlic. Tasters praised this blend as more complex but still lacking bite, so we added more garlic.

The skin on the chicken was now crisp and flavorful, but not much rub was getting through to the meat. Test cooks offered suggestions ranging from slicing pockets in the meat and stuffing them with the rub to butterflying the breasts and placing the rub inside. In the end, the best alternative proved to be the easiest: We took some of the rub and placed it in a thick layer under the skin as well as on top of it. Now it was not only the crisp skin that was flavorful but the moist flesh beneath as well.

Most recipes call for grilling the chicken over a single-level fire, but this resulted in a charred exterior and an uncooked interior. We tried a two-level fire (one side of the grill holds all of the coals; the other side is empty) and, voilà, partial success! We first browned the chicken directly

over the coals and then moved it to the cool side of the grill to finish cooking. This was a big improvement, but the chicken still wasn't cooking through to the middle. Covering the grill—to make it more like an oven—was an obvious solution, but better yet was using a disposable foil pan, which creates a "mini oven." (Charcoal grill covers are home to deposits of smoke, ash, and debris that lend "off" flavors to foods.)

The true Thai flavors of this dish come through in the sauce, a classic combination of sweet and spicy. Most recipes suffered from one extreme or the other. In our working recipe, we had tried to create a balance of flavors: 2 teaspoons of hot red pepper flakes, ⅓ cup of sugar, ¼ cup of lime juice, ¼ cup of white vinegar, and 3 tablespoons of fish sauce. But tasters found even this sauce to be overwhelmingly sweet and spicy.

Reducing the red pepper flakes was a step in the right direction, as it allowed the other flavors to come through. Everyone liked garlic, but not too much; there was already a lot of garlic on the chicken. A decrease in the amount of fish sauce was welcomed, reducing the fishy flavor of the sauce but not its salty complexity. We found it best to mix the sauce right after the chicken goes into the brine, which gives the flavors time to meld.

Traditionally, gai yang is cut into small pieces and eaten as finger food. But our version is just as good (and a whole lot neater) when served whole with a knife and fork. Is this an Americanized dish? Yes. But its flavors are true to its Thai roots, and its ingredients can be found in most supermarkets.

WHAT WE LEARNED: Brine the chicken to keep it juicy, then coat it with a mixture of garlic, fresh ginger, black pepper, ground coriander, fresh cilantro, and lime juice. Grill the chicken over a two-level fire to prevent scorching and serve it with a dipping sauce that is salty, spicy, and tart.

THAI GRILLED CHICKEN WITH SPICY, SWEET, AND SOUR DIPPING SAUCE
Serves 4

For even cooking, the chicken breasts should be of comparable size. The best way to ensure this is to buy whole breasts and split them yourself (see the instructions on page 148). If you prefer to skip this step, try to purchase split bone-in, skin-on breasts that weigh about 12 ounces each. If using a charcoal grill, you will need a disposable aluminum roasting pan to cover the chicken (the lid on a charcoal grill can give the chicken resinous "off" flavors). Some of the rub is inevitably lost to the grill, but the chicken will still be flavorful.

chicken and brine
½ cup sugar
1 cup Diamond Crystal Salt, ¾ cup Morton Kosher Salt, or ½ cup table salt
4 split bone-in, skin-on chicken breasts, about 12 ounces each (see note)

dipping sauce
1 teaspoon red pepper flakes
3 small garlic cloves, minced or pressed through a garlic press (about 1½ teaspoons)
¼ cup distilled white vinegar
¼ cup juice from 2 to 3 limes
2 tablespoons fish sauce
⅓ cup sugar

rub
12 medium garlic cloves, minced or pressed through a garlic press (about ¼ cup)
1 piece (about 2 inches) fresh ginger, minced (about 2 tablespoons)
2 tablespoons ground black pepper
2 tablespoons ground coriander

⅔ cup chopped fresh cilantro leaves

¼ cup juice from 2 to 3 limes

2 tablespoons vegetable oil, plus more for the grill grate

1. TO BRINE THE CHICKEN: Dissolve the sugar and salt in 2 quarts cold water in a large container or bowl. Submerge the chicken in the brine and refrigerate at least 30 minutes but not longer than 1 hour. Rinse the chicken under cool running water and pat dry with paper towels.

2. FOR THE DIPPING SAUCE: Whisk the ingredients in a small bowl until the sugar dissolves. Let stand 1 hour at room temperature to allow the flavors to meld.

3. TO MAKE AND APPLY THE RUB: Combine all rub ingredients in a small bowl; work the mixture with your fingers to thoroughly combine. Slide your fingers between the skin and meat of one chicken piece to loosen the skin, taking care not to detach the skin. Rub about 2 tablespoons of the mixture under the skin. Thoroughly rub an even layer of the mixture onto all exterior surfaces, including the bottom and sides. Repeat with the remaining chicken pieces. Place the chicken in a medium bowl, cover with plastic wrap, and refrigerate while preparing the grill.

4. TO GRILL THE CHICKEN: Using a chimney starter, ignite about 2½ pounds charcoal briquettes (1 large chimney, or 6 quarts) and burn until covered with a layer of light gray ash, about 15 minutes. Empty the coals into the grill and build a two-level fire by arranging the coals to cover one half of the grill, piling them about 3 briquettes high. Position the grill grate over the coals, cover the grill, and heat until the grate is hot, about 5 minutes (the grill should

---

GETTING IT RIGHT: Splitting a Chicken Breast

Store-bought split chicken breasts are highly problematic, and we do not recommend that you buy them. Some are so sloppily cut that the tenderloins are often missing, some retain only tattered shreds of skin, and some packages contain wildly divergent sizes. You're better off buying whole breasts and splitting them yourself.

The basic method for splitting a chicken breast is to simply push a chef's knife through the skin, flesh, and bone. While this method is straightforward, sometimes the split breasts are lopsided or both lobes are marred by unruly bits of bone and cartilage around which the knife and fork must eventually navigate. Enter a classic technique to split a chicken breast. It involves the removal of the keel bone and cartilage that divides the breast, thereby making the chicken easier to eat. This method takes a few extra minutes, but we think it's time well spent.

Begin by trimming the rib sections off the split breast (kitchen shears work particularly well for this task). Then, with the breast turned skin-side down on a cutting board, use a chef's knife to score the membrane down the center along the length of the breast. Pick up the breast and, using both hands and some force, bend back the breast lobes, forcing the keel bone to pop free. Put the chicken back on the board, grasp the keel bone, and pull it free. (On occasion, the cartilage breaks—if it does, just dig in with your fingers, grip the remaining piece, and pull it out.) Finally, use the chef's knife to halve the breast down the center at the seam, applying force near the top to cut through the wishbone.

   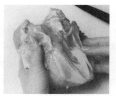 

1. Trim rib sections.　　2. Score membrane.　　3. Pop out keel bone.　　4. Pull out keel bone.　　5. Halve breast.

be medium-hot; you can hold your hand 5 inches above the grill grate for 4 seconds). Scrape the grill grate clean with a grill brush. Using long-handled grill tongs, dip a wad of paper towels in vegetable oil and wipe the grill grate.

5. Place the chicken, skin-side down, on the hotter side of the grill and cook until browned, about 3 minutes. Using tongs, flip the chicken breasts and cook until browned on the second side, about 3 minutes longer. Move the chicken, skin-side up, to the cool side of the grill and cover with a disposable aluminum roasting pan; continue to cook until an instant-read thermometer inserted into the thickest part of the breast (not touching the bone) registers 160 degrees, 10 to 15 minutes longer. Transfer the chicken to a platter and let rest 10 minutes. Serve, passing the sauce separately.

VARIATION

THAI GRILLED CHICKEN ON A GAS GRILL

1. Follow the recipe for Thai Grilled Chicken with Spicy, Sweet, and Sour Dipping Sauce through step 3.

2. Turn all the burners to high, close the lid, and heat until the grill is very hot, about 15 minutes. Scrape the grill grate clean with a grill brush. Using long-handled grill tongs, lightly dip a wad of paper towels in vegetable oil and wipe the grill grate. Turn all but one burner to low. Place the chicken, skin-side down, on the hotter side of the grill and cook until browned, 4 to 5 minutes. Using tongs, flip the chicken breasts and cook until browned on the second side, 4 to 5 minutes longer. Move the chicken, skin-side up, to the cool side of the grill and close the lid; cook until an instant-read thermometer inserted into the thickest part of the breast (not touching bone) registers 160 degrees, 12 to 15 minutes. Transfer the chicken to a platter and let rest 10 minutes. Serve, passing the sauce separately.

SCIENCE DESK:
Cutting Boards and Bacteria

IN 1994, A RESEARCH REPORT WAS PUBLISHED THAT proved to be the opening salvo in a long battle over which material was more sanitary for cutting boards, wood or plastic. The researchers found that fewer bacteria could be recovered from wooden boards infected with live cultures than from plastic boards treated the same way. These results caused the researchers to question the prevailing view that plastic was more sanitary than wood; some have further interpreted the data to mean that wood is, in fact, a safer material for cutting boards. In a report that followed, researchers at a U.S. Department of Agriculture lab concluded that beef bacteria on polyethylene and wooden cutting boards had statistically similar patterns of attachment and removal. Even so, the idea that wood is more sanitary than plastic persists and was recently reaffirmed in the food section of the *New York Times*.

We wanted to get our own perspective on the problem and so asked four staff members to donate their used boards, two wooden and two plastic. We found very little bacteria growing on these boards when we sampled them, so we took the boards to a local lab to have them artificially inoculated with bacteria. The procedure worked as follows: A drop of the medium was placed on the boards, the boards were left to sit for 40 minutes to allow for absorption of the bacteria, and an attempt was then made to remove the bacteria. In repeated tests, between 6.0 percent and 8.1 percent of the bacteria were recovered from the plastic and between 1.3 percent and 6.2 percent from the wood. Given that the number of bacteria recovered from each type of board was well into the hundreds of thousands, there was little to assure us that one material was much safer than the other.

Scrubbing the boards with hot soapy water was a different story. Once the contaminated boards were cleaned, we recovered an average of 0.00015 percent from the plastic and 0.00037 percent from the wood—or fewer than 100 bacteria from each board. In a related test, we were also able to transfer bacteria from contaminated, unwashed boards made from both wood and plastic to a Petri dish using potatoes and onions. But our most surprising discovery by far was that the bacteria could persist on unwashed boards of both types for up to 60 hours!

What, then, is the truth about cutting boards? Both plastic and wooden boards can hold on to bacteria for long periods of time. Both plastic and wooden boards allow for easy transference of bacteria to other foods. Luckily, we found that scrubbing with hot soapy water was quite an effective (though not perfect) way of cleaning both kinds of boards; the USDA also recommends the regular application of a solution of 1 teaspoon bleach per quart of water and then allowing the board to dry. Simply put, maintenance, not material, provides the greatest margin of safety.

Q&A

What are the small green shoots that are sometimes found in garlic cloves?

These green shoots mean that the garlic is old enough to have sprouted. Most experts say these sprouts will give garlic a bitter flavor. To find out if this is true, we used raw garlic in aioli and cooked garlic in pasta with olive oil and tried each recipe with the shoots removed before mincing the garlic as well as with the shoots left in. With the aioli, tasters could clearly identify a more bitter, unpleasant taste in the batch made with the shoots left in. The same thing held true in the pasta test.

When shopping, we suggest that you avoid heads of garlic with green shoots. At home, store garlic in a cool, dark, well-ventilated spot to prolong its freshness. If your garlic does sprout, cut out the green shoots before mincing the cloves.

TASTING LAB: Fish Sauce

AS SOON AS WE OPENED THE FIRST BOTTLE OF FISH sauce, coworkers were off, scattering to the far corners of the office. Why the histrionics? Fish sauce is a very potent Asian condiment based on the liquid from salted, fermented fish—and smells as such. Fish sauce has a very concentrated flavor and, like anchovy paste, when used in appropriately small amounts, lends foods a salty complexity that is impossible to replicate.

We gathered six brands of fish sauce—one from Vietnam (known as *nuoc mam*), one from the Philippines (*patis*), and the rest from Thailand (*nam pla*) from our local supermarket, natural food store, and Asian market. Tasters had the option of tasting the fish sauce straight up (which few could stomach) or in a modified version of the Thai grilled chicken dipping sauce.

There were differences noted immediately among the sauces. Color correlated with flavor; the lighter the sauce, the lighter the flavor. Tasters had preferences among the sauces, but those preferences varied greatly from taster to taster. In the end, all of the sauces were recommended. In fact, there was only one point (out of 10) separating all six sauces.

With such a limited ingredient list—most of the brands contained some combination of fish extract, water, salt, and sugar—the differences among sauces were minimal. And because fish sauce is used in such small amounts, minute flavor differences get lost among the other flavors of a dish.

If you are a fan of fish sauce and use it often, you might want to make a special trip to an Asian market to buy a rich, dark sauce that is suitably pungent. But for most applications, we found that the differences were negligible. Because most supermarkets don't carry a wide selection of fish sauce, we recommend buying whatever is available. That will most likely be Thai Kitchen, an Americanized brand found in most supermarkets, which was the lightest colored (and flavored) brand we tasted.

Rating Fish Sauce

TEN MEMBERS OF THE *COOK'S ILLUSTRATED* STAFF TASTED ALL OF THE FISH SAUCES, EITHER STRAIGHT UP OR IN A modified version of our dipping sauce for Thai grilled chicken. The sauces are listed in order of preference based on their scores in this tasting. Brands are available in supermarkets, natural food stores, and Asian markets.

RECOMMENDED

Tiparos Fish Sauce

Thailand

$2.39 for 23 ounces

This top-rated sauce was described as "really aggressive" as well as "dark and pungent." A favorite among fish sauce aficionados.

RECOMMENDED

Thai Kitchen Fish Sauce

Thailand

$3.25 for 7 ounces

This widely available brand has a "very light flavor" and is "easy to take." The best bet for fish sauce novices.

RECOMMENDED

Golden Boy Brand Fish Sauce

Thailand

$1.09 for 24 ounces

The sauce is intense, with tasters remarking on a "slight smokiness" and saying that it "smells cheesy."

RECOMMENDED

Rufina Fish Sauce

Philippines

$2.09 for 25 ounces

Tasters thought this "very fermented" sauce "tastes like soy." Overall, it was deemed "plain."

RECOMMENDED

Squid Brand Fish Sauce

Thailand

$.95 for 25 ounces

Most panelists thought this sauce was "nicely balanced," and a few called it "a bit sweet."

RECOMMENDED

Three Crabs Brand Fish Sauce

Vietnam

$2.99 for 24 ounces

This sauce provoked strong reactions, with comments such as "musty," "salty," and "acidic."

GRILLED GLAZED SALMON

WHAT WE WANTED: To avoid the burnt, stuck-to-the-grill crust and flavorless interior that plague most glazed salmon. We also hoped to create sweet, crisp, and flavorful salmon.

We have always felt confident in our ability to produce great grilled salmon. With its firm, meaty texture and rich, buttery interior, the salmon on our grill had at least a chance of coming off that hot grate moist and in one piece. Then one day we tried grilled glazed salmon and watched as our dinner (as well as our bravado) went up in smoke. "Sticky" was the operative word here as the glazed salmon gripped the grill grate for dear life and could only be torn off in many tiny pieces. Not that it was actually worth getting off the grill, mind you, because each of those tiny pieces was charred beyond recognition. When it comes to grilled glazed salmon, you can call us chicken.

So why glaze (and inevitably ruin) an otherwise perfect piece of fish? Well, because truly great glazed salmon off the grill is a thing of beauty, both inside and out. Working double duty, the sweet glaze not only forms a glossy, deeply caramelized crust but also permeates the flesh, making the last bite of fish every bit as good as the first. This was the salmon that we wanted to re-create—sweet, crisp, moist, and oh-so-flavorful—and we were willing to ruin a few more fish to get there.

We knew we needed all the help we could get, and we went straight to cookbooks in hopes of direction. The first choice was easy. When confronted with fillets, steaks, and whole sides, we were going with the fillets for ease of grilling (ever try flipping a whole side?) and ease of eating (who wants to eat around all those salmon steak bones, anyway?). The next choice was glazing method, and here things were less clear. We could try using a marinade to flavor the fish. We could try brushing the fish with a thick glaze before throwing it on the grill. Finally, we could simply grill the fish plain and apply the glaze afterward. We fired up the grill and got to work.

After testing, there was no doubt that marinating gave the salmon flavor. Soy sauce was chosen for its ability to season the fish through and through, while vinegar (another standard marinade ingredient) was omitted, as it broke down the salmon until it was too fragile to hold its shape on the grill. In a perfect world, the marinade would also work as a glaze of sorts, with the sugars caramelizing once they hit the hot grill. In fact, tests demonstrated that the marinated salmon failed to produce any kind of crust. Increasing the amount of sugar only served to make the salmon too sweet. Taking a cue from some brush-on glaze recipes, we tested more viscous sweeteners, such as maple syrup, honey, and molasses. While the molasses was rejected for its bitter flavor, the maple syrup and honey worked like a dream. With a thicker marinade, the sweet flavors clung to the salmon rather than dripping through the bars of the grate, and a crust (however thin) was beginning to form.

Using a marinade alone wasn't going to produce the thick crust we wanted, however. The next step was to brush the marinated salmon with a much thicker glaze—a winning combination of soy sauce and maple syrup—very similar to the marinade. Yep, here was a crust—a burnt, stuck-to-the-grill crust; not what we were after. Instead, we basted the salmon with this glaze a few moments after it hit the hot grill. Better. Not as charred, not as sticky, but still not acceptable. Not sure where else to turn at this point, we thought it might be time to examine the fire.

Up to this point, we had been cooking the salmon in a pretty traditional way. We were searing the fish skin-side down, then skin-side up over a hot fire; the superhot grill grate helped to keep the fish from sticking. The problem now was that the hot fire was causing the sweet glazed salmon to burn.

After trying more temperate medium and low fires (both of which failed), we tried a two-level fire. Piling the hot briquettes one-high on one side and two-high on the other, we seared the marinated salmon over the high heat. We then brushed the salmon with some of the glaze and pulled it to the cooler side of the grill to cook through. This was a big improvement, with a decent crust.

But we were still having a problem. When started skin-side down, the fillet buckled, causing the other side to cook unevenly. The solution was to start the salmon skin-side up, flip it to sear the skin side, brush on some glaze, and then flip it again to finish cooking on the cool side of the grill. The downside of this approach was that the grill had to be well oiled to prevent sticking, a step that is not optional. The good news was that we had an incredible crust, built in two layers, that was both sweet and substantial. All that was left to do was to brush the grilled salmon with more glaze before serving. Gilding the lily, perhaps, but with a high-gloss shine and potent flavor within, this fish never looked (or tasted) so good.

WHAT WE LEARNED: Marinate the flesh side of the fish in a mixture of soy sauce and maple syrup. Grill the fish, flesh-side down, then flip, glaze twice, and flip again. When the fish comes off the grill, glaze it again. Needless to say, a well-oiled grill is a must, as is a two-level fire with hotter and cooler cooking areas.

GRILLED GLAZED SALMON

Serves 4

Scraping the grill grate clean will help prevent the salmon from sticking. Also, be sure to oil the grate just before placing the fillets on the grill.

- 1 recipe glaze (recipes follow)
- ⅓ cup soy sauce
- ⅓ cup maple syrup
- 4 salmon fillets (about 8 ounces each), each about 1½ inches at the thickest part
  Ground black pepper
  Vegetable oil for grill grate
  Lemon wedges for serving

1. Measure 2 tablespoons of the glaze into a small bowl and set aside.

2. Whisk the soy sauce and maple syrup in a 13 by 9-inch baking dish until combined. Carefully place the fillets flesh-side down in a single layer in the marinade (do not coat the salmon skin with the marinade). Refrigerate while preparing the grill.

3. Using a chimney starter, ignite about 2½ pounds charcoal briquettes (1 large chimney, or 6 quarts) and burn until covered with a layer of light gray ash, about 15 minutes. Empty the coals into the grill and build a two-level fire by stacking two-thirds of the coals in one half of the grill and arranging the remaining coals in a single layer in the other half. Position the grill grate over the coals, cover the grill, and heat until the grate is hot, about 5 minutes (the grill should be medium-hot; you can hold your hand 5 inches above the grill grate for 4 seconds). Scrape the grill grate clean with a grill brush.

4. Remove the salmon from the marinade and sprinkle the flesh liberally with pepper. Using long-handled grill tongs, dip a wad of paper towels in vegetable oil and wipe the hot side of the grill grate. Place the fillets flesh-side down on the hot side of the grill (at a 45-degree angle to the grate) and cook until grill-marked, about 1 minute. Using tongs, flip the fillets skin-side down, still on the hot side of the grill. Brush the flesh with the glaze and cook until the salmon is opaque about halfway up the thickness of the fillets, 3 to 4 minutes.

5. Using long-handled grill tongs, dip a wad of paper towels in vegetable oil and wipe the cooler side of the grill grate. Brush the flesh again with the glaze, then turn the fillets flesh-side down onto the cooler side of the grill. Cook until a deeply browned crust has formed and the center of the fillet is still translucent when cut into with a paring knife, about 1½ minutes. Transfer the fillets to a platter, brush with reserved 2 tablespoons glaze, and serve with the lemon wedges.

CATCH AND RELEASE

Few things are more frustrating than trying to pull the daily catch off the grill in one piece. But there's no shortage of equipment, gadgets, or plain old advice intended to help you get around this problem. After testing them all, using both sturdy salmon fillets and more fragile flounder, we found that the best method requires equipment that you probably own already. The methods are listed in order of effectiveness.

Tool	Method	Results
Oiled wad of paper towels	Using long-handled tongs, dip the towels in vegetable oil and brush over the heated grill grate.	The most failsafe way to keep fish from sticking to the grill.
Cooking spray	Spray the cold grate before heating.	Worked well, although part of one fillet needed some prodding.
Oil on the fish	Oil the fish before placing on the hot grill.	Mixed reviews. Although the fish released well, flare-ups were a problem.
Lemon slices	Place lemon slices on the grate, then place the fish on top.	Mixed reviews. Although the fish did not stick to the grill, the lemon slices kept the fish from developing exterior color. Works well for fragile fish, though, when browning is not important.
Stainless steel screen material	Place the screen on the grate, then place the fish on top.	Not bad. Worked well when sprayed with vegetable oil spray. The fish must be rapidly removed from the screen after being grilled, as it will begin to stick as it cools.
Fish basket	Place fish in an oiled fish basket.	Not recommended. Salmon stuck to basket. Doesn't work with glazing because one can't get at the caged salmon to brush it.
Grill grate	Tested enameled steel, cast-iron, and stainless steel grates.	When it comes to types of grill grates, fish is nondiscriminatory. It will stick to any surface. It's best to use the oiled grate method with any of these grill grate materials.

GRILLED GLAZED SALMON ON A GAS GRILL

1. Follow the recipe for Grilled Glazed Salmon through step 2.

2. Turn all the burners to high, cover, and heat until very hot, about 15 minutes. Scrape the grill grate clean with a grill brush. Turn all but one burner to medium-low. Remove the salmon from the marinade and sprinkle the flesh liberally with pepper. Using long-handled grill tongs, dip a wad of paper towels in vegetable oil and wipe the hot side of the grill grate. Place the fillets flesh-side down on the hot side of the grill and cook until grill-marked, 1 to 2 minutes. Using tongs, flip the fillets skin-side down, still on the hot side of the grill. Brush the flesh with the glaze, cover the grill, and cook until the salmon is opaque about halfway up the thickness of the fillets, 3 to 4 minutes.

3. Again using long-handled grill tongs, dip a wad of paper towels in vegetable oil and wipe the cooler side of the grill grate. Brush the flesh again with the glaze, then turn the fillets flesh-side down onto the cooler side of the grill. Cook until a deeply browned crust has formed and the center of the thickest part of the fillet is still translucent when cut into with a paring knife, about 2 minutes. Transfer the fillets to a platter, brush with the reserved 2 tablespoons glaze, and serve immediately with the lemon wedges.

MAPLE-CHIPOTLE GLAZE

Offer lime wedges instead of lemon when serving.

Stir together 2 tablespoons soy sauce, ¼ cup maple syrup, and 1 teaspoon minced chipotle chile in adobo sauce in a small saucepan. Bring to a simmer over medium-high heat and cook until slightly thickened, 3 to 4 minutes. Off the heat, whisk in 2 tablespoons lime juice.

MAPLE-SOY GLAZE

Stir together 2 tablespoons soy sauce and ¼ cup maple syrup in a small saucepan. Bring to a simmer over medium-high heat and cook until slightly thickened, 3 to 4 minutes.

HONEY-MUSTARD GLAZE

Stir together 2 tablespoons soy sauce and ¼ cup honey in a small saucepan. Bring to a simmer over medium-high heat and cook until slightly thickened, 3 to 4 minutes. Off the heat, whisk in 3 tablespoons Dijon mustard.

GETTING IT RIGHT: The Soft, the Sticky, and the Good

Here's how we solved two common problems that came up during recipe testing.

Too Soft
Salmon that was marinated for more than 30 minutes became mushy and fell apart on the grill.

Too Sticky
When we skipped the step of oiling the grill grate, the salmon stuck terribly.

Just Right
With a short marinating time and a thorough oiling of the grill, our salmon came off the fire intact.

EQUIPMENT CORNER:
Portable Gas Grills

THE GREAT OUTDOORS AND GRILLED MEATS ARE AN indisputable match. Unfortunately, owing to the immense bulk of today's grills, our grilling efforts are almost always confined to the back patio. Many companies are addressing this issue with a new line of portable, propane-powered grills.

There are dozens of portable gas grills on the market, ranging from the inexpensive (about $50) to the truly outrageous ($1,000 or more). We set our ceiling at $200 and gathered five prominent models to test. Our selection included two models that are truly portable and three whose size makes it difficult to venture very far from the back of the SUV. We quickly learned that the smaller models, though very convenient, offered little else of value. The Weber Gas Go Anywhere ($59.99) was extremely easy to carry, but its measly heat output caused us to question whether this model was meant to be a grill or a hand warmer. The Tool Box Gas ($50) grill, as the name implies, is a spitting image of your grandfather's toolbox, but its flimsy grates and inconsistent heat garnered poor marks from the testers. Overall, the portability of these two smaller grills could not make up for their lack of performance.

The three largest models were, predictably, stronger players. The Coleman Road Trip Sport ($170), Weber Q Portable Propane Gas Grill ($159.99), and Thermos Grill-2-Go ($150) all featured large, cast-iron grilling surfaces, high heat outputs, and sturdy designs. These characteristics not only increased the cooking ability of the grills but also added to their heft, and even the strongest among us found it difficult to carry these grills. Although their portability came into question, all three of these grills performed well. The Thermos Grill-2-Go came out on top during testing because of its consistent performance and low price. The Weber Q Portable Propane Gas Grill, a close second, was applauded for its even heating and sturdy construction.

Rating Portable Gas Grills

WE TESTED FIVE PORTABLE GRILLS, GRILLING STEAKS (TO judge searing ability and heat output) and hamburgers (to judge evenness of heating and ability to handle grease). The portable grills were rated for performance as well as design and ease of use. The portable grills are listed below in order of preference. See www.americastestkitchen.com for up-to-date prices and mail-order sources for top-rated products.

RECOMMENDED
Thermos Grill-2-Go #4656110
$150
With an even heating surface and a reasonable price, this model took top honors. Also praised for its handy flat griddle that is perfect for pancakes.

RECOMMENDED
Weber Q Portable Propane Gas Grill #396001
$159.99
The largest and heaviest of the bunch, but also has the most even heating.

RECOMMENDED
Coleman Road Trip Sport
$170
Gets very hot very fast, but the ceramic grill grate is a bit delicate for heavy grilling.

NOT RECOMMENDED
Weber Gas Go Anywhere #1520
$59.99
Very easy to carry, but where's the heat?

NOT RECOMMENDED
Tool Box Gas #112000
$50
Cute concept but weak output.

Julia takes the assembly line approach to fill and roll chicken enchiladas.

MEXICAN favorites

There's a significant disconnect between real Mexican food (as prepared in Mexico) and the food served in "Mexican" restaurants in the United States. The real deal is noted for its bright, intense flavors, rather than the mounds of cheese and sour cream that cover most Americanized dishes served in nacho and salsa joints. Unfortunately, many authentic Mexican dishes require ingredients that can still be hard to find.

For this chapter, we decided to look at two long-time favorites with Americans—enchiladas and Mexican rice. We wanted to make these dishes fresher and livelier—more like the Mexican originals than the bastardized versions most Americans know. Although we didn't want to be slaves to tradition, we wanted dishes that any Mexican cook could proudly serve. We think we've succeeded.

CHICKEN ENCHILADAS

WHAT WE WANTED: Mexican cooking is notoriously time-consuming but delivers rich, deep flavors. We wanted to produce a reasonably authentic chicken enchilada with far less work.

Take a softened tortilla, stuff it with a savory chicken filling, roll it, encase it in a spicy chili sauce, and serve it with an assortment of creamy and crunchy toppings, and you have quite possibly the most popular Mexican dish in the world. And for good reason. Chicken enchiladas are a complete meal that offers a rich and complex combination of flavors, textures, and ingredients. The problem with preparing enchiladas at home is that traditional cooking methods require a whole day of preparation. Could we simplify the process, yet retain the authentic flavor of the real thing?

We began by preparing five simplified recipes, hoping to uncover valuable tips and techniques. All of them produced disappointing results. Mushy tortillas, bland or bitter sauces, uninspired fillings, too much cheese, and lackluster flavor left tasters yearning for something tastier and more authentic.

A side-by-side tasting of corn and wheat flour tortillas came out clearly in favor of the corn, with its more substantial texture. Tasters also preferred the small 6-inch tortillas, with 8-inch tortillas a close second. These sizes provided the best proportion of tortilla to filling and sauce, and both sizes fit neatly into a 9-inch-wide baking pan. Although ingredients and size mattered, we were happy to discover that brand didn't. Given the big flavors from the sauce and filling, flavor differences among various brands of tortillas (which are rather bland-tasting anyway) were not important in the final dish.

Our next task was to figure out how to treat the tortillas so that they would be soft and pliable to roll and toothsome to eat. The traditional approach is to dip each tortilla in hot oil (to create a moisture barrier) and then in the sauce (to add flavor) prior to assembly. Although this technique works well, it is time-consuming, tedious, and messy. We tried rolling chilled corn tortillas straight from the package, but they were tough and cracked easily. Heating a stack of tortillas in the microwave also proved disappointing. The tortillas were soft, but the resulting enchiladas were mushy. Next we tried wrapping the tortillas in foil and steaming them on a plate over boiling water. These tortillas were also easy to roll but were wet and soggy when baked.

Thinking back to the traditional first step of dipping the tortillas in oil gave us an idea. Using the modern-day convenience of oil in an aerosol can, we placed the tortillas in a single layer on a baking sheet, lightly sprayed both sides of the tortillas with vegetable oil, and warmed them in a moderate oven. This proved to be the shortcut we were hoping to find. The oil-sprayed, oven-warmed tortillas were pliable, and their texture after being filled, rolled, and baked was nearly perfect.

Because red chili sauce is the most common sauce used in enchiladas, we decided to prepare a half dozen traditional recipes. The flavors were spicy and complex, the textures smooth and somewhat thick, the colors deep orange-red. The problem was that whole dried chiles played a central role in all of these sauces. Not only are whole chiles difficult to find in some areas, but they require substantial preparation time, including toasting, seeding, stemming, rehydrating, and processing in a blender. Store-bought chili powder would have to be part of the solution.

The obvious question was how to augment the flavor of the usually bland chili powder available in the supermarket. Our first thought was to heat the chili powder in oil, a process that intensifies flavors. We began by sautéing onion and garlic and then added the chili powder to the pan. This indeed produced a fuller, deeper flavor. We enhanced the flavor by adding ground cumin and coriander—ingredients often found in authentic red chili sauce. Tasters gave this combo a thumbs-up.

Many traditional recipes incorporate tomatoes for substance and flavor. With a nod toward convenience, we explored canned tomato products first. We tried adding diced tomatoes and then pureeing the mixture. The texture was too thick and too tomatoey. Canned tomato sauce turned out to be a better option. Focusing on flavor next, we prepared a batch with 2 teaspoons of sugar, which succeeded in expanding and enriching the flavor of the spices.

Next, we were on to the filling and started with how to cook the chicken. We tried the common method of poaching, but tasters said this chicken was dry and bland. We tried roasting both white and dark meat, which was extremely time-consuming, although tasters really liked the dark meat. Obsessed with speed and flavor, we had an idea. Why not use boneless, skinless thighs and cook them right in the sauce? Cutting the thighs into thin strips across the grain, we added them to the pan after the spices were fragrant. The chicken cooked in less than 10 minutes, and it was nicely seasoned. Cooking the chicken in the sauce also lent the sauce a wonderful richness. To separate the chicken from the sauce, we poured the contents of the pot through a medium-mesh strainer.

With the chicken cooked and ready for the filling, we needed to add just a few complementary ingredients. Cheese topped our list. Queso fresco, the traditional choice, is a young, unripened cheese with a creamy color, mild flavor, and crumbly texture. Because it is not readily available in the United States, we tried farmer's cheese. Tasters liked this cheese for its creamy texture and mellow flavor. But it was Monterey Jack and sharp white cheddar that made the top of the list. The Jack is mellow, while the cheddar adds a sharp, distinctive flavor. Our first choice was the cheddar, though certainly the Jack is just fine as well. (Cheese, we discovered, also helps to bind the filling ingredients.) Looking for more heat, we taste-tested the addition of fresh jalapeños, chipotles in adobo sauce, and canned jalapeños. The fresh jalapeños were too mild. Chipotles (smoked

jalapeños stewed in a seasoned liquid) added a distinctive, warm heat and smoky flavor that some tasters enjoyed but that most found too spicy and smoky. Everyone was surprised to find that the very convenient canned jalapeños were the favorite. (Because the peppers are pickled in a vinegar solution before being canned, they added spicy, bright, and sour notes.)

Some recipes suggest filling and rolling one enchilada at a time, but we much preferred the efficiency offered by the assembly-line approach. We spread the oil-sprayed, oven-warmed tortillas on the countertop and spread ⅓ cup of filling down the center of each. We rolled them tightly and placed them seam-side down, side by side, along the length of a 13 by 9-inch baking pan that had a little sauce in it. We then poured the rest of the sauce over the enchiladas and sprinkled them with a bit of extra cheese. We experimented with oven temperatures and times before settling on 400 degrees for 20 minutes, at which point the enchiladas were hot and ready to be served.

Enchiladas are traditionally eaten with an array of raw, salad-like garnishes. Tasters passed on chopped tomatoes, saying they did not add much flavor or texture. Raw onions were considered too harsh. Sour cream and avocado were chosen for their cooling qualities, and romaine lettuce was favored for its fresh, crispy crunch. Finally, there were the lime wedges, which gave a nice brightness to the finished dish. Start to finish, our chicken enchiladas now took less than an hour and a half to make: 20 minutes for the sauce, 15 for the filling, 30 to assemble and bake, and 10 to prepare the toppings.

WHAT WE LEARNED: Create a quick red sauce with onions, garlic, spices, and tomato sauce. Cook the chicken right in the sauce (to save time and mess) and then strain it out. For tortillas that will roll without cracking, spray them with oil and bake for several minutes until pliable. Use cilantro, pickled jalapeños, and cheddar cheese to round out the filling and then serve with more cheese, sour cream, avocado, lettuce, and limes.

CHICKEN ENCHILADAS WITH RED CHILI SAUCE

Makes 10 enchiladas, serving 4 or 5 as a main dish

Monterey Jack can be used instead of cheddar, or for a mellower flavor and creamier texture, try farmer's cheese. Be sure to cool the chicken before filling the tortillas, otherwise the hot filling will make the enchiladas soggy.

sauce and filling

1½	tablespoons vegetable or corn oil
1	medium onion, chopped fine (about 1 cup)
3	medium garlic cloves, minced or pressed through a garlic press (about 1 tablespoon)
3	tablespoons chili powder
2	teaspoons ground coriander
2	teaspoons ground cumin
½	teaspoon salt
2	teaspoons sugar
12	ounces boneless, skinless chicken thighs (about 4 thighs), trimmed of excess fat and cut into ¼-inch-wide strips
2	(8-ounce) cans tomato sauce
¾	cup water
½	cup coarsely chopped fresh cilantro leaves
1	(4-ounce) can pickled jalapeño chiles, drained and chopped (about ¼ cup)
8	ounces sharp cheddar cheese, shredded (about 2 cups)

tortillas and toppings

10	(6-inch) corn tortillas
	Vegetable oil cooking spray
3	ounces sharp cheddar cheese, shredded (about ¾ cup)
¾	cup sour cream
1	ripe avocado, diced medium
5	romaine lettuce leaves, shredded
2	limes, quartered

1. FOR THE SAUCE AND FILLING: Heat the oil in a medium saucepan over medium-high heat until hot and shimmering but not smoking. Add the onion and cook, stirring occasionally, until softened and beginning to brown, about 5 minutes. Add the garlic, chili powder, coriander, cumin, salt, and sugar and cook, stirring constantly, until fragrant, about 30 seconds. Add the chicken and cook, stirring constantly, until coated with the spices, about 30 seconds. Add the tomato sauce and water, stir to separate the chicken pieces, and bring to a simmer. Reduce the heat to medium-low and simmer, uncovered, stirring occasionally, until the chicken is cooked through and the flavors have melded, about 8 minutes. Pour the mixture through a medium-mesh strainer into a medium bowl, pressing on the chicken and onions to extract as much sauce as possible; set the sauce aside. Transfer the chicken mixture to a large plate; place in the freezer for 10 minutes to cool, then combine with the cilantro, jalapeños, and cheese in a medium bowl.

2. Adjust the oven racks to the upper- and lower-middle positions and heat the oven to 300 degrees.

3. TO ASSEMBLE: Following the illustrations on page 163, smear the entire bottom of a 13 by 9-inch baking dish with ¾ cup of the chili sauce. Place the tortillas in a single layer on two baking sheets. Spray both sides lightly with cooking spray. Bake until the tortillas are soft and pliable, about 4 minutes. Transfer the warm tortillas to a work surface. Increase the oven temperature to 400 degrees. Spread ⅓ cup of the filling down the center of each tortilla. Roll each tortilla tightly by hand and place, seam-side down, side by side on the sauce in the baking dish. Pour the remaining chili sauce over the top of the enchiladas. Use the back of a spoon to spread the sauce so it coats the top of each tortilla. Sprinkle ¾ cup grated cheese down the center of the enchiladas.

4. TO BAKE: Cover the baking dish with foil. Bake the enchiladas on the lower-middle rack until heated through and the cheese is melted, 20 to 25 minutes. Uncover and serve immediately, passing the sour cream, avocado, lettuce, and lime wedges separately.

CHICKEN ENCHILADAS WITH GREEN CHILI SAUCE

In Mexico, sauce is so central to enchiladas that it often defines them. While the red sauce used in enchiladas rojas is made with dried chiles and is robust and fiery, the green sauce used in enchiladas verdes is prepared with fresh chiles and is more tart and vibrant tasting. Green sauces typically include tomatillos, onions, garlic, and cilantro in addition to fresh chiles. Washing the tomatillos in a bowl of cold water will quickly remove their papery husks.

sauce

2	teaspoons vegetable or corn oil
1	medium onion, chopped (about 1 cup)
3	medium garlic cloves, minced or pressed through a garlic press (about 1 tablespoon)
¾	pound tomatillos, husks and stems removed, each tomatillo quartered (about 1½ cups)
3	large jalapeños, seeded and chopped large (about 1 cup)
1	teaspoon sugar
½	teaspoon salt
⅓	cup water

TECHNIQUE: Assembling Enchiladas

1. Smear the entire bottom of a 13 by 9-inch baking dish with ¾ cup of the chili sauce.

2. Place the tortillas in a single layer on two baking sheets. Spray both sides lightly with cooking spray. Bake until the tortillas are soft and pliable, about 4 minutes.

3. Place the warm tortillas on a work surface. Increase the oven temperature to 400 degrees. Place ⅓ cup of the filling down the center of each tortilla.

4. Roll each tortilla tightly by hand and place, seam-side down, side by side on the sauce in the baking dish.

5. Pour the remaining chili sauce over the top of the enchiladas. Use the back of a spoon to spread the sauce so it coats the top of each tortilla.

6. Sprinkle ¾ cup shredded cheese down the center of the enchiladas.

filling

- 2 teaspoons vegetable or corn oil
- 1 medium onion, chopped (about 1 cup)
- 1 tablespoon ground cumin
- 12 ounces boneless, skinless chicken thighs (about 4 thighs), trimmed of excess fat and cut into ¼-inch-wide strips
- ½ cup coarsely chopped fresh cilantro leaves
- 8 ounces sharp cheddar cheese, shredded (about 2 cups)

tortillas and toppings

- 10 (6-inch) corn tortillas
  Vegetable oil cooking spray
- 3 ounces sharp cheddar cheese, shredded (about ¾ cup)
- ¾ cup sour cream
- 1 ripe avocado, diced medium
- 5 romaine lettuce leaves, shredded
- 2 limes, quartered

1. FOR THE SAUCE: Heat the oil in a medium saucepan over medium-high heat until hot and shimmering but not smoking. Add the onion and cook, stirring occasionally, until softened and beginning to brown, about 5 minutes. Add the garlic, tomatillos, jalapeños, sugar, and salt and cook, stirring constantly, until fragrant, about 30 seconds. Add the water and bring to a simmer. Reduce the heat to medium-low and simmer, uncovered, until the tomatillos are softened, about 8 minutes. Transfer the mixture to a blender and puree until smooth, about 30 seconds; set aside. Rinse out the saucepan.

2. FOR THE FILLING: Heat the oil in the saucepan over medium-high heat until hot and shimmering but not smoking. Add the onion and cook, stirring occasionally, until beginning to soften and brown, about 3 minutes, then reduce the heat to medium and continue to cook until browned, about 3 minutes longer. Add the cumin and cook, stirring constantly, until fragrant, about 15 seconds. Add the chicken and cook, stirring frequently, until the chicken is cooked through, about 5 minutes. Transfer the chicken mixture to a large plate; place in the freezer for 10 minutes to cool, then combine with the cilantro and cheese in a medium bowl and set aside.

3. Follow the recipe for Chicken Enchiladas with Red Chili Sauce from step 2, using the green sauce in place of the red chili sauce.

GETTING IT RIGHT:
Rolling Tortillas Made Easy

Cool and Stiff　　　　**Warm and Pliable**

Straight from the fridge, a corn tortilla is too stiff to roll and will tear at the edges (left). Spraying the tortilla with oil and heating it for 4 minutes in a 300-degree oven makes the tortilla pliable and easy to work with (right).

EQUIPMENT CORNER: Spice Grinders

EVERY ONE OF US IS ACQUAINTED WITH A SPICE SNOB. You know, the neighbor who is constantly bragging about her spice rack that is graced only by whole nutmeg, white peppercorns, and dried chiles. That's right, the bake sale braggart who always hand grinds whole cinnamon for that blue-ribbon Bundt cake. Is all this whole spice hoopla reasonable, or do preground spices measure up to their intact brethren? Well, we are sorry to tell you, but the spice snobs are right—freshly ground spices are far superior to their preground relatives.

To illustrate this fact, we set up a blind tasting of a cardamom pound cake and a savory chutney, both of which pitted preground spices against freshly ground spices. In a unanimous victory, the freshly ground spices were lauded for their superior aroma, vibrancy, and roundness of flavor. With their dominance established, the next question was obvious: How can we enjoy freshly ground spices without driving out to the McCormick's processing plant every morning before work? To find the answer, we set out to identify a spice grinder that is as easy on the arms as it is on the wallet.

The test kitchen standard for grinding spices is an inexpensive blade-type electric coffee grinder (which we use for spices only, reserving a separate unit to grind coffee), but we had never put it up against other devices designed specifically for the task. Could we be missing out on something? To determine the answer to that question, we gathered 13 devices in three basic designs—dedicated spice grinders that are similar to pepper mills, old-fashioned mortars and pestles (and variations), and electric coffee grinders—and used them to reduce mountains of cardamom seeds, toasted whole cumin and coriander seeds, and chipotle chiles to fine powders. We chose these spices because of their varying hardnesses, densities, shapes, and oil content. We were looking for a grinder that would produce the most delicate, uniform powder and that was easy to both use and clean.

First up were the dedicated spice grinders. Like pepper mills, they are torsion-operated, meaning that you twist one part of the device while holding a second part steady. As the device is twisted, internal grooves grind the spices. Because the moving parts on this grinder are largely internal, cleaning the unit was difficult. Additionally, the relentless twisting of these models made testing six of them consecutively seem like an act of masochism.

The next tests revolved around three versions of the age-old mortar and pestle, including a Japanese suribachi with a textured grinding surface to help break down the contents. As a group, these were no more effective than the torsion-operated grinders. To us, using the mortar and pestle was less stressful than the repetitive motion required to work the torsion-operated grinders, but it was still too much effort considering the disappointing piles of bruised, mangled seeds that it produced.

Last up were the electric coffee grinders, which were, in short, like breaths of fresh air. The only physical exertion required to use them was pressing a button. No stress, strain, or sore forearms, and they produced consistently strong results on all of the test spices. And it only got better: The coffee grinders were easy to brush or wipe clean (just mind the blade!), easy to control for texture of grind, and no more expensive than the manual grinders and mortars and pestles. All four blade grinders tested did an equally good job with small and large amounts of all spices tested.

So check your preground spices at the door and join the rest of the spice snobs—freshly ground spices are more flavorful and, thanks to the electric coffee grinder, just as accessible as preground spices. The bright aroma and earthiness of fresh spices can breathe life into your food. From complex dishes to everyday meals, from savory to sweet preparations, a cabinet full of whole spices and an electric coffee grinder are invaluable assets in the kitchen.

Rating Spice Grinders

WE TESTED 13 DEVICES, INCLUDING DEDICATED SPICE GRINDERS, MORTARS AND PESTLES, AND BLADE-TYPE coffee grinders. Grinders are grouped by type and listed in order of preference within their type. See www.americastestkitchen.com for up-to-date prices and mail-order sources for top-rated products.

RECOMMENDED: ELECTRIC COFFEE GRINDERS

Krups Fast-Touch Coffee Mill, Model 203 $19.95
Our top choice produced an exceptionally fine and consistent grind regardless of the amount of spice in the chamber.

Braun Aromatic Coffee Grinder, Model KSM 2B $14.99
This model produced a fine and even grind in small and medium amounts. Also did an impressive job grinding a large amount of each spice.

Mr. Coffee Coffee Grinder, Model IDS55 $14.99
An all-around strong performer that required a bit of extra grinding to break down a small amount of chipotle.

Capresso Cool Grind $19.99
The Capresso required a bit of extra grinding time to fully process large amounts of cumin and coriander but still performed well.

NOT RECOMMENDED: MORTARS AND PESTLES

Mortar & Pestle, Marble $8.99
Did a good job on cardamom and chiles but did not produce a satisfactory grind of cumin or coriander, even after working them for 30 minutes.

Suribachi $16
The chiles broke down completely in this mortar, but not before showering the kitchen floor with partially ground spices.

Creative Home Marble Spice Grinder $11.99
Holy hand strain! The stubby pestle was uncomfortable, especially since you must bear down with considerable pressure to grind anything.

NOT RECOMMENDED: TORSION-OPERATED

Genius Spice Grinder Set $24.99
Did a better job than all other grinders of its kind, but the output was slow compared with that of electric grinders. The grip was relatively comfortable for this type of grinder.

Emsa Würzmühle Spice Mill with Ceramic Grinders $15.95
This model processed chiles very well, albeit slowly. One of our large-handed testers found this narrow model uncomfortable.

WMF Gewürzmühle Ceramill Glass Spice Mill $20
Relatively easy to open, fill, and twist. Did a good job on cardamom but choked on chiles.

Oxo Grind It Spice Grinder $14.99
Good grind quality, but too easy to accidentally pop the grinder housing off the jar while grinding, which sent seeds flying in every direction.

Spice Essentials Grinder with Ceramic Mechanism $27.95
Chiles brought it to a grinding halt. Though not difficult to dismantle, cleaning was a chore.

William Bounds Spice Mill $14.95
The crank was so hard to turn that testers feared onset of carpal tunnel syndrome and tennis elbow! The output was meager as well.

MEXICAN RICE

WHAT WE WANTED : Mexican rice promises bright flavor and a pilaf-style texture, but it rarely delivers. We wanted a rich-tasting side dish—without the usual pools of oil.

A cursory look at Mexican rice reveals a simple pilaf prepared by sautéing raw white rice in oil, then slowly cooking the grains in chicken broth flavored with pureed tomatoes, onion, and garlic. Some cooks finish the dish with a sprinkle of fresh chiles and cilantro. In Mexico, this pilaf is frequently presented as a separate course, in the manner that Italians serve pasta, but on the American table it makes a unique side dish.

Yet for a basic dish with a remarkably short ingredient list, we found it vexing. Variable ingredient quantities and cooking techniques produced disparate results when we put a selection of recipes from respected Mexican cookbook authors to the test. Two of these recipes turned out soupy and greasy, spurring tasters to crack jokes about "Risotto à la Mexicana" and "Mexican Porridge." These descriptions, along with our own taste buds, told us that these super-soggy, oily versions were off-track. Other recipes seemed misguided in terms of ingredient amounts. Some had just a hint of garlic, others tasted of tomato and nothing else, and one was overtaken by pungent cilantro.

To our way of thinking, the perfect version of this dish would exhibit clean, balanced flavors and tender, perfectly cooked rice. It would be rich but not oily, moist but not watery. We returned to the test kitchen with some basic questions in mind: What is the proper ratio of liquid to rice for a moist but not brothy dish? Would canned tomatoes provide for more balanced flavor than fresh? Could we skip the sautéing step and still end up with an agreeable texture?

The liquid traditionally used in this dish is a mixture of chicken broth and pureed fresh tomatoes (plus a little salt); experiments with a variety of ratios helped us to settle on equal parts of each. With too much tomato puree, the rice

tasted like warm gazpacho; with too little, its flavor waned. Though past *Cook's* recipes for pilaf have called for less liquid, we found that when pulpy tomatoes make up a portion of the fluid, a 2:1 ratio of liquid to rice produces just the right texture.

Each and every recipe we consulted called for fresh tomatoes, and when we pitted rice made with canned tomatoes against rice made with fresh, the reason for using the latter became clear. Batches made with fresh tomatoes tasted, well, fresh. Those made with canned tomatoes, however eye-catching, tasted overcooked and too tomatoey; the rice should be scented with tomatoes, not overtaken by them. To capture the one benefit of canned tomatoes—an intense, tomato-red color—we stirred in an untraditional ingredient: tomato paste. Mexican rice often appears washed out, and the tomato paste gave it an appealing hue while adding a little flavor to boot.

To further enhance the flavor of the tomatoes, we investigated charring. The technique of blackening fresh tomatoes on a comal (a flat griddle) is often employed for this dish and other Mexican preparations such as salsa. Because it is a rare American cook who owns a comal, we instead charred some tomatoes in a cast-iron skillet. This deeply flavored, complex rice was a hit, but given that the process was time-consuming and we wanted a dish that could serve as a midweek side dish, we relegated charring to a recipe variation.

The usual method for making Mexican rice is to sauté rinsed, long-grain white rice in oil before adding the cooking liquid. Rice that was rinsed indeed produced more distinct, separate grains when compared with unrinsed rice. While some recipes call for only a quick sauté, cooking the rice until it was golden brown proved crucial in providing a mild, toasted flavor and satisfying texture. As for the amount of oil, we experimented with a wide range, spanning from 3 tablespoons to 1¼ cups. When we essentially deep-fried the rice in copious amounts of oil, as more than one recipe suggested, the rice was much too oily; even straining off excess oil from the rice, as directed, didn't help, and it was a messy process. Insubstantial amounts of oil made rice that was dry and lacking richness, while ⅓ cup seemed just right—this rice was rich but not greasy.

We had questions about whether to sauté other components of the recipe, such as the aromatics and the tomato pulp. We tried multiple permutations and landed on a compromise technique of sautéing a generous amount of garlic and jalapeños, then mixing in a puree of raw tomato and onion. This technique produced the balanced yet fresh flavor we were after and allowed us to process the onion in the food processor along with the tomatoes.

We were having trouble achieving properly cooked rice on the stovetop. The grains inevitably scorched and then turned soupy when we attempted a rescue with extra broth. In the past, we've converted rice recipes from finicky to infallible by simply baking the rice, and testing proved that this recipe was no exception. Still, as we baked batch after batch of rice, we were frustrated by cooking times that were inconsistent. Most batches contained a smattering of crunchy grains mixed in with the tender ones. Prolonged cooking didn't solve the problem; what did was stirring the rice partway through cooking to reincorporate the tomato mixture, which had been settling on top of the pilaf. With this practice in place, every last grain cooked evenly.

While many traditional recipes consider cilantro and jalapeño optional, in our book they are mandatory. The raw herbs and pungent chiles complement the richer tones of the cooked tomatoes, garlic, and onions. When a little something still seemed missing from the rice, we thought to offer wedges of lime. A squirt of acidity illuminated the flavor even further.

WHAT WE LEARNED: Rinse the rice to remove excess starch and then fry it in a modest ⅓ cup of oil for a rich but not greasy flavor. Use fresh tomatoes for the best flavor, but add a little tomato paste for color. Bake the rice to ensure even cooking and finish with chiles, cilantro, and lime juice.

MEXICAN RICE

Serves 6 to 8 as side dish

Because the spiciness of jalapeños varies from chile to chile, we try to control the heat by removing the ribs and seeds (the source of most of the heat) from those chiles that are cooked into the rice. It is important to use an ovensafe pot about 12 inches in diameter so that the rice cooks evenly and in the time indicated. The pot's depth is less important than its diameter; we've successfully used both a straight-sided sauté pan and a Dutch oven. Whichever type of pot you use, it should have a tight-fitting, ovensafe lid. Vegetable broth can be substituted for the chicken broth.

2	medium ripe tomatoes (about 12 ounces), cored and quartered
1	medium onion, preferably white, peeled, trimmed of root end, and quartered
3	medium jalapeño chiles
2	cups long-grain white rice
⅓	cup canola oil
4	medium garlic cloves, minced or pressed through a garlic press (about 4 teaspoons)
2	cups low-sodium chicken broth
1	tablespoon tomato paste
1½	teaspoons salt
½	cup minced fresh cilantro leaves
1	lime, cut into wedges for serving

1. Adjust an oven rack to the middle position and heat the oven to 350 degrees. Process the tomatoes and onion in a food processor until smooth and thoroughly pureed, about 15 seconds, scraping down the bowl if necessary. Transfer the mixture to a liquid measuring cup; you should have 2 cups (if necessary, spoon off excess so that the volume equals 2 cups). Remove the ribs and seeds from 2 jalapeños and discard; mince the flesh and set aside. Mince the remaining jalapeño, including the ribs and seeds; set aside.

2. Place the rice in a large fine-mesh strainer and rinse under cold running water until the water runs clear, about 1½ minutes. Shake the rice vigorously in the strainer to remove all excess water.

3. Heat the oil in a heavy-bottomed straight-sided 12-inch ovenproof sauté pan or Dutch oven with a tight-fitting lid over medium-high heat for 1 to 2 minutes. Drop 3 or 4 grains of rice into the oil; if the grains sizzle, the oil is ready. Add the rice and fry, stirring frequently, until the rice is light golden and translucent, 6 to 8 minutes. Reduce the heat to medium, add the garlic and seeded minced jalapeños, and cook, stirring constantly, until fragrant, about 1½ minutes. Stir in the pureed tomato mixture, chicken broth, tomato paste, and salt. Increase the heat to medium-high and bring to a boil. Cover the pan and transfer to the oven. Bake until the liquid is absorbed and the rice is tender, 30 to 35 minutes, stirring well after 15 minutes.

4. Stir in the cilantro and reserved minced jalapeño with seeds to taste. Serve immediately, passing the lime wedges separately.

VARIATION

MEXICAN RICE WITH CHARRED TOMATOES, CHILES, AND ONION

In this variation, the vegetables are charred in a cast-iron skillet, which gives the finished dish a deeper color and a slightly toasty, smoky flavor. A cast-iron skillet works best for toasting the vegetables; a traditional or even a nonstick skillet will be left with burnt spots that are difficult to remove, even with vigorous scrubbing.

- 2 medium ripe tomatoes (about 12 ounces), cored
- 1 medium onion, preferably white, peeled and halved
- 6 medium garlic cloves, unpeeled
- 3 medium jalapeño chiles, 2 halved with ribs and seeds removed, 1 minced with ribs and seeds

- 2 cups long-grain white rice
- ⅓ cup canola oil
- 2 cups low-sodium chicken broth
- 1 tablespoon tomato paste
- 1½ teaspoons salt
- ½ cup minced fresh cilantro leaves
- 1 lime, cut into wedges for serving

1. Heat a large cast-iron skillet over medium-high heat for about 2 minutes. Add the tomatoes, onion, garlic, and halved chiles and toast the vegetables, using tongs to turn them frequently, until softened and almost completely blackened, about 10 minutes for the tomatoes and 15 to 20 minutes for the other vegetables. When cool enough to handle, trim the root ends from the onion and halve each piece. Remove the skins from the garlic and mince. Mince the jalapeños.

2. Adjust an oven rack to the middle position and heat the oven to 350 degrees. Process the toasted tomato and onion in a food processor until smooth and thoroughly pureed, about 15 seconds, scraping down the bowl if necessary. Transfer the mixture to a liquid measuring cup; you should have 2 cups (if necessary, spoon off any excess so that the volume equals 2 cups).

3. Follow the recipe for Mexican Rice from step 2, adding the toasted minced jalapeños and garlic in step 3 along with the pureed tomato mixture.

Basil and onions get ready for their starring role in a quick pasta sauce.

QUICK pasta

Pasta is usually quick, but all too often quick pasta dishes taste like little time or effort was expended during their preparation. But that doesn't mean the only good pasta dishes take forever to prepare. Many Italian recipes are ready in the time it takes to bring a large pot of water to a boil and cook the pasta. The difference between a good quick pasta dish and a mediocre one is details, details, details.

Nothing is faster than a raw tomato sauce for pasta, but if the sauce is watery and bland, who cares if it's fast? Likewise, asparagus can be easily turned into a pasta sauce, but all too often it's bland and boring. And nontraditional pestos can be a hodgepodge of flavors that don't belong together.

Our goal when developing the recipes in this chapter was to keep things simple while avoiding these common problems. Take 20 minutes to make one of these recipes and see if you agree.

PASTA WITH RAW TOMATO SAUCE

WHAT WE WANTED: An easy, not too watery sauce with rich flavor.

Our favorite way to enjoy summer-ripe tomatoes is tossed with pasta, as a fresh and easy summer dinner. In focusing on summer's beefsteak tomatoes, however, we found that they contain excess liquid that results in a watery, bland sauce. One obvious solution was to seed the tomatoes; it is also customary to peel tomatoes intended for sauce, so we thought we'd try that as well. With an armful of tomatoes, we set out to determine the best, most efficient preparation for a light yet satisfying pasta supper.

The process of both peeling and seeding is time-consuming, and the results were only mediocre. Because many of the tomatoes we bought at the farmers market had thin skins, peeling them was particularly difficult. Also, once peeled and added to the pasta, the tomatoes fell apart, the peel having provided structure that was now gone.

Merely seeding the tomatoes produced the better sauce. We cut the tomatoes along their equator, gave the halves a gentle squeeze, and shook them, easily ridding them of their seeds. Moreover, with the skin left on, the tomatoes held their shape and maintained a rich presence; the tomato flavor stayed in the foreground rather than disappearing into the pasta.

While the rich sun-ripened tomatoes were certainly the focus of these sauces, a few more assertive flavors were needed to take them out of the realm of the ordinary. Olive oil is a classic choice. And because these sauces are raw, the robust and complex flavor of a high-quality extra-virgin olive oil was preferred by tasters. In addition to flavor, the oil also provided moisture and helped to coat the pasta, binding the pasta and sauce together.

But we wanted more flavor, so we developed a variety of taste combinations, including the pungent pairing of garlic and scallions, the briny pairing of feta cheese and black olives, and the fragrant crunchiness of fennel with Parmesan. None of these combinations required any cooking—just a quick chop and toss with the tomatoes. All of these combinations brought the acidity and sweetness of the tomatoes into an ideal balance. A word to the wise: Making these tomato sauces in mid-January with supermarket tomatoes will be disappointing. Only the freshest summer-ripe tomatoes are good enough for these sauces.

WHAT WE LEARNED: Seed the tomatoes to rid them of excess moisture but leave the skins on so the chopped tomatoes have some structural integrity. Add extra-virgin olive oil for flavor and moisture and finish with potent ingredients like olives, garlic, and cheese.

FARFALLE WITH TOMATOES, OLIVES, AND FETA

Serves 4

To prevent the feta from melting into the pasta, add it only after the tomatoes have been tossed with the pasta, which gives the mixture the opportunity to cool slightly.

    Salt
1   pound farfalle
1½ pounds ripe tomatoes, cored, seeded, and cut into ½-inch dice
¼   cup extra-virgin olive oil
1   tablespoon chopped fresh mint leaves
½   cup kalamata olives, pitted and chopped coarse
    Ground black pepper
6   ounces feta cheese, crumbled (about 1½ cups)

1. Bring 4 quarts of water to a rolling boil in a stockpot. Add 1 tablespoon salt and the pasta, stir to separate, and cook until al dente. Drain and return the pasta to the stockpot.

2. Meanwhile, combine the tomatoes, oil, mint, olives, ½ teaspoon salt, and ¼ teaspoon pepper in a medium bowl. Add the tomato mixture to the pasta in the stockpot and toss to combine. Add the feta and toss again. Season with salt and pepper to taste and serve immediately.

FUSILLI WITH TOMATOES AND FRESH MOZZARELLA

Serves 4

For maximum creaminess, use fresh mozzarella packed in water rather than the shrink-wrapped cheese sold in supermarkets.

    Salt
1   pound fusilli
1½ pounds ripe tomatoes, cored, seeded, and cut into ½-inch dice
¼   cup extra-virgin olive oil

1   medium garlic clove, minced or pressed through a garlic press (about 1 teaspoon)
3   medium scallions, sliced thin
    Ground black pepper
8   ounces fresh mozzarella, cut into ½-inch cubes

1. Bring 4 quarts of water to a rolling boil in a stockpot. Add 1 tablespoon salt and the pasta, stir to separate, and cook until al dente. Drain and return the pasta to the stockpot.

2. Meanwhile, combine the tomatoes, oil, garlic, scallions, ½ teaspoon salt, and ¼ teaspoon pepper in a medium bowl. Add the tomato mixture and mozzarella to the pasta in the stockpot and toss to combine. Season with salt and pepper to taste and serve immediately.

ORECCHIETTE WITH TOMATOES, FENNEL, AND PARMESAN

Serves 4

See the illustration below for tips on using a vegetable peeler to cut shavings from a wedge of Parmesan.

    Salt
1   pound orecchiette
1½ pounds ripe tomatoes, cored, seeded, and cut into ½-inch dice

---

TECHNIQUE:
Making Parmesan Shavings

Thin shavings of Parmesan can be used to garnish pasta dishes as well as salad. Simply run a sharp vegetable peeler along the length of a piece of cheese to remove paper-thin curls.

1 small fennel bulb, trimmed of stalks and
   fronds, bulb halved, cored, and sliced thin
   (about 1½ cups)
¼ cup extra-virgin olive oil
¼ cup chopped fresh basil leaves
   Ground black pepper
2 ounces Parmesan cheese, shaved with a
   vegetable peeler

1. Bring 4 quarts of water to a rolling boil in a stockpot.
Add 1 tablespoon salt and the pasta, stir to separate, and cook
until al dente. Drain and return the pasta to the stockpot.

2. Meanwhile, combine the tomatoes, fennel, oil, basil, ½
teaspoon salt, and ¼ teaspoon pepper in a medium bowl.
Add the tomato mixture to the pasta in the stockpot and
toss to combine. Season with salt and pepper to taste and
serve immediately, garnishing individual bowls with the
shaved Parmesan.

GETTING IT RIGHT:
The Effects of Seeding

The tomatoes on the left were not seeded and exuded ¼ cup of
liquid, which would make the pasta sauce watery. The tomatoes
on the right were seeded and exuded just 1 tablespoon of liquid—
not enough to have an adverse effect on the sauce.

Q&A

What is light olive oil?

Light olive oil has been stripped of its characteristic
flavor. It was invented by marketers to appeal to
Americans interested in the heart-healthy properties
of this oil but not its flavor. Light olive oil contains
just as many calories and fat grams as other kinds of
olive oil.

We don't use light olive oil in the test kitchen.
When we want a flavorless oil, we reach for vegetable
or canola oil. When we want the flavor of olive oil in
a salad dressing or pesto, we use extra-virgin olive oil.
When cooking, we choose pure olive oil, which doesn't
have the subtlety of more expensive extra-virgin oils
but is fine for pan-frying or sautéing Italian dishes.

PASTA WITH ASPARAGUS

WHAT WE WANTED: Asparagus sauces for pasta are often bland and boring. We wanted to keep it simple but make this dish livelier.

Asparagus is a natural starting point when trying to make a vegetarian pasta sauce. But more often than not, this dish sounds better than it tastes. Could we create big, intense flavors?

First, we focused on how to cook the asparagus. We ruled out boiling or steaming because the residual water diluted the flavor of the asparagus and made the pasta sauce bland. Grilling added bold and smoky characteristics and broiling also concentrated flavors, but we wanted a simpler method, one that would also allow for the easy introduction of other flavors. We also wanted a cooking method that could be used year-round. The answer, it turned out, was a quick sauté.

We cut the asparagus into 1-inch pieces and sautéed them with other ingredients over high heat. The asparagus caramelized just a bit, and the heat also brought out the flavors of the other ingredients, such as onions, walnuts, garlic, and shallots. To finish off each dish, we tried a variety of additions, including balsamic vinegar, basil leaves, lemon juice, blue cheese, and arugula. The key, we discovered, is not to overpower the asparagus with too much of one bold ingredient. What's wanted instead is a good balance of salty, sweet, and sour ingredients that allow the asparagus flavor to come through.

The bold recipes that follow should forever dispel the myth than pasta and asparagus will be boring.

WHAT WE LEARNED: Cut the asparagus spears into 1-inch pieces and brown them in a hot skillet for a sauce that's both quick and flavorful. And be sure to pair the asparagus with ingredients, like cheese and herbs, that won't overwhelm its delicate, woodsy flavor.

CAMPANELLI WITH ASPARAGUS, BASIL, AND BALSAMIC GLAZE
Serves 4 to 6 as a main dish

Campanelli is a frilly trumpet-shaped pasta that pairs nicely with this sauce. If you cannot find it, fusilli works well, too.

1	tablespoon plus ½ teaspoon salt
1	pound campanelli
¾	cup balsamic vinegar
5	tablespoons extra-virgin olive oil
1	pound asparagus, tough ends snapped off (see the illustration on page 177), spears halved lengthwise if larger than ½ inch in diameter and cut into 1-inch lengths
1	medium-large red onion, halved and sliced thin (about 1½ cups)
½	teaspoon ground black pepper
¼	teaspoon hot red pepper flakes
1	cup chopped fresh basil leaves
1	tablespoon juice from 1 lemon
2	ounces Pecorino Romano cheese, shaved (about 1 cup) (see the illustration on page 173)

1. Bring 4 quarts of water to a rolling boil in a stockpot. Add 1 tablespoon salt and the pasta, stir to separate, and cook until al dente. Drain and return the pasta to the stockpot.

2. Immediately after putting the pasta in the boiling water, bring the balsamic vinegar to a boil in an 8-inch skillet over medium-high heat; reduce the heat to medium and simmer slowly until reduced to ¼ cup, 15 to 20 minutes.

3. While the pasta is cooking and the balsamic vinegar is reducing, heat 2 tablespoons of the oil in a 12-inch non-stick skillet over high heat until it begins to smoke. Add the asparagus, onion, black pepper, pepper flakes, and remaining

½ teaspoon salt and stir to combine. Cook, without stirring, until the asparagus begins to brown, about 1 minute, then stir and continue to cook, stirring occasionally, until the asparagus is crisp-tender, about 4 minutes longer.

4. Add the asparagus mixture, basil, lemon juice, ½ cup of the Pecorino, and remaining 3 tablespoons oil to the pasta in the stockpot and toss to combine. Serve immediately, drizzling 1 to 2 teaspoons balsamic glaze over individual servings and passing the remaining Pecorino separately.

CAVATAPPI WITH ASPARAGUS, ARUGULA, WALNUTS, AND BLUE CHEESE

Serves 4 to 6 as a main dish

Cavatappi is a short, tubular corkscrew-shaped pasta. Penne is a fine substitute. The grated apple balances the other flavors in this dish.

1	tablespoon plus ½ teaspoon salt
1	pound cavatappi
5	tablespoons extra-virgin olive oil
1	pound asparagus, tough ends snapped off (see the illustration on page 177), spears halved lengthwise if larger than ½ inch in diameter and cut into 1-inch lengths
½	teaspoon ground black pepper
1	cup walnuts, chopped
4	cups lightly packed arugula leaves from 1 large bunch, washed and dried thoroughly
6	ounces strong blue cheese, preferably Roquefort, crumbled (about 1½ cups)
2	tablespoons cider vinegar
1	Granny Smith apple, peeled, for garnish

1. Bring 4 quarts of water to a rolling boil in a stockpot. Add 1 tablespoon salt and the pasta, stir to separate, and cook until al dente. Drain and return the pasta to the stockpot.

2. While the pasta is cooking, heat 2 tablespoons oil in a 12-inch nonstick skillet over high heat until it begins to smoke.

Add the asparagus, pepper, and remaining ½ teaspoon salt and cook, without stirring, until the asparagus is beginning to brown, about 1 minute. Add the walnuts and continue to cook, stirring frequently, until the asparagus is crisp-tender and the nuts are toasted, about 4 minutes longer. Toss in the arugula until wilted.

3. Add the asparagus mixture, blue cheese, vinegar, and the remaining 3 tablespoons oil to the pasta in the stockpot and toss to combine. Serve immediately, grating the apple over individual servings.

FARFALLE WITH ASPARAGUS, TOASTED ALMONDS, AND BROWNED BUTTER

Serves 4 to 6 as a main dish

Watch the butter carefully to make sure it does not burn.

1	tablespoon plus ½ teaspoon salt
1	pound farfalle
2	tablespoons vegetable oil
1	pound asparagus, tough ends snapped off (see the illustration on page 177), spears halved lengthwise if larger than ½ inch in diameter and cut into 1-inch lengths
3	large garlic cloves, sliced thin
2	medium shallots, sliced into thin rings
½	teaspoon ground black pepper
6	tablespoons unsalted butter, cut into 6 pieces
1	cup sliced almonds
¼	cup sherry vinegar
1	teaspoon chopped fresh thyme leaves
2	ounces Parmesan cheese, grated (about 1 cup)

1. Bring 4 quarts of water to a rolling boil in a stockpot. Add 1 tablespoon salt and the pasta, stir to separate, and cook until al dente. Drain and return the pasta to the stockpot.

2. While the pasta is cooking, heat the oil in a 12-inch nonstick skillet over high heat until it begins to smoke. Add the asparagus and cook, without stirring, until beginning to brown, about 1 minute. Add the garlic, shallots, remaining ½ teaspoon salt, and pepper and cook, stirring frequently, until the asparagus is crisp-tender, about 4 minutes. Transfer the asparagus mixture to a large plate and set aside.

3. Return the skillet to high heat and add the butter. When the foaming subsides, add the almonds and cook, stirring constantly, until the almonds are browned and the butter is fragrant, 1 to 2 minutes. Off heat, add the vinegar and thyme. Return the asparagus to the skillet and toss to coat.

4. Add the asparagus mixture and ½ cup of the Parmesan to the pasta in the stockpot and toss to combine. Serve immediately, passing the remaining ½ cup Parmesan separately.

EQUIPMENT CORNER: Pasta Pots

THE NIGHT OWLS KNOW THAT LATE-NIGHT TV OFFERS a plethora of kitchen gadgets. Well, curiosity got the best of us when we saw the pasta pot. We decided to order from TV, as well as round up others from local stores and mail-order sources. In all, we tested five different pasta cooking pots—ranging in price from $7 to $100 (OK . . . the $100 one didn't come from late-night TV) to see if we could retire our trusty stockpot and colander.

These devices come in two basic designs: pots with locking, perforated lids that allow you to drain out the water while keeping the food in the pot in place and pots with fitted perforated inserts that you lift right out of the pot, with the food in it. To test each pot, we cooked a pound each of spaghetti, orzo (small, rice-shaped pasta), potatoes, and frozen corn.

The inserts were a real pain to use. We found that they were sloppy, often drenching the counter or stovetop with water when we pulled them out of the pot. The remedy was to move them into the sink, which is really no easier than transferring a regular pot to the sink with a waiting colander. Worse was the boil-over problem with inserts. Surface tension between the insert and the wall of the pot often caused the water to climb up and boil over where the pot and insert meet at the top, sometimes even extinguishing the gas flame on our test kitchen burners.

By and large, we prefer the locking lids with perforations, but design flaws prevent each model tested from performing perfectly. The lid on the Pasta Pro ($9.95) locks into place and stays put even when we turned the pot fully upside down, but at 6 quarts, the pot itself is too small to comfortably accommodate a gallon of boiling water and one pound of pasta without the danger of overflow. The Ontel Better Pasta Pot ($6.98) was larger, but the locking mechanism for the lid was tricky because it was held in place by the user's hands. You really have to watch how you handle this lid—one adjustment of the hands and the lid can come loose and your pasta will land in the sink.

If you are compelled to purchase a pasta cooking pot, we recommend one with a perforated lid rather than an insert. We didn't find any model with an ideal design though. For now, we'll stick to the trusty stockpot and colander combo.

TECHNIQUE:
Trimming Tough Ends from Asparagus

In our tests, we found that the tough, woody part of the stem will break off in just the right place if you hold the spear the right way. With one hand, hold the asparagus about halfway down the stalk; with the thumb and index fingers of the other hand, hold the spear about an inch up from the bottom. Bend the stalk until it snaps.

Rating Pasta Pots

WE TESTED FIVE DIFFERENT PASTA COOKING POTS BY EVALUATING HOW WELL THEY COOKED AND DRAINED A POUND EACH OF spaghetti, orzo, potatoes, and frozen corn. The results are listed in order of preference. See www.americastestkitchen.com for up-to-date prices and mail-order sources for top-rated products.

HIGHLY RECOMMENDED
Endurance Stainless Steel Footed Colander/Strainer
$25
A colander is still the best way to drain pasta. Our favorite model has a mesh-like perforated bowl that traps even the smallest bits of food.

RECOMMENDED WITH RESERVATIONS
Ontel Better Pasta Pot 5-Piece Set
$6.98
The price is right, but this 8-quart model requires sure hands to secure the lid and a steamy wait for the water to drain.

NOT RECOMMENDED
Pasta Pro Pasta Pot Set
$9.95
The locking lid is secure, but 4 quarts of water and a pound of pasta won't fit in this small 6-quart pot.

NOT RECOMMENDED
Krona Pasta Pot with Strainer Lid
$44.95
A decent 7.5-quart pot, but the perforations in the lid's lip are too few for a pound of pasta to drain in less than 30 seconds.

NOT RECOMMENDED
All-Clad Stainless Steel Multi-Cooker
$99.99
Large space between the bottom of the insert and the 12-quart pot necessitates using the full 12 quarts to boil a pound of pasta. A good pot, but lose the messy insert.

NOT RECOMMENDED
Columbian Home Graniteware Insert
$21.99
Spaghetti gets stuck in the perforations, and orzo falls to the bottom of this 12-quart pot.

PASTA WITH NONTRADITIONAL PESTOS

WHAT WE WANTED: Pesto doesn't have to be made with just basil. We wanted to make quick pestos with a variety of other potent ingredients.

I n the United States, the concept of pesto has moved way beyond basil. Any pureed, highly flavorful oil-based sauce for pasta—including those made from herbs, sun-dried tomatoes, arugula, nuts, or olives—is given the name pesto. Although Italians generally reserve the term pesto for sauces made with basil, they do traditionally use purees of olives and herbs or, perhaps, sun-dried tomatoes and arugula to sauce pasta, especially when fresh basil is out of season.

We found the food processor to be the fastest way to produce a consistently good basil pesto. We found that it's important to use extra-virgin olive oil and a high-quality cheese. When using garlic, we prefer to use it toasted rather than raw. The mellowed and slightly sweetened flavor of toasted garlic allows other flavors to really shine. Unpeeled cloves can be easily toasted in a skillet in less than 10 minutes.

When adding any pesto to cooked pasta, it is important to include some of the cooked pasta water for proper consistency and even distribution. We reserve a portion of the cooking water and stir some of this hot water into the pesto to loosen its consistency and let its flavor bloom. We use more reserved cooking water to moisten the pasta, as necessary, once it has been tossed with the pesto.

Although these pestos will come together very quickly, they can be made in advance. Just store the pestos in an airtight container in the refrigerator for up to 3 days. Press some plastic wrap directly onto the surface of the pesto to prevent discoloration or loss of freshness.

WHAT WE LEARNED: When making pesto, tame the garlic by toasting unpeeled cloves in a hot skillet. And to keep the pasta moist, make sure to reserve some of the pasta cooking water to thin the pesto.

PASTA WITH ARUGULA, GOAT CHEESE, AND SUN-DRIED TOMATO PESTO

Serves 4 to 6

Make sure to rinse the herbs and seasonings from the sun-dried tomatoes. See page 181 for information about buying sun-dried tomatoes.

1	cup drained oil-packed sun-dried tomatoes (one 8½-ounce jar), rinsed, patted dry, and chopped very coarse
6	tablespoons extra-virgin olive oil
¼	cup walnuts, toasted in a small dry skillet over medium heat until browned and fragrant, about 6 minutes
1	small garlic clove, minced or pressed through a garlic press (about ½ teaspoon)
1	ounce Parmesan cheese, grated (about ½ cup) Salt and ground black pepper
1	pound campanelli or farfalle
1	medium bunch arugula (about 10 ounces), washed, dried, stemmed, and cut into 1-inch lengths (about 6 cups)
3	ounces goat cheese

1. In a food processor, pulse the sun-dried tomatoes, oil, walnuts, garlic, Parmesan, ½ teaspoon salt, and ⅛ teaspoon pepper until smooth, stopping as necessary to scrape down the sides of the workbowl. Transfer the mixture to a small bowl and set aside.

2. Bring 4 quarts of water to a rolling boil in a stockpot. Add 1 tablespoon salt and the pasta, stir to separate, and cook until al dente. Drain, reserving ¾ cup cooking water, and return the pasta to the stockpot. Immediately stir in the arugula until wilted. Stir ½ cup of the pasta cooking water into the pesto and then stir the pesto into the pasta.

Toss, adding more pasta cooking water as necessary. Serve immediately, dotting individual bowls with ½-inch pieces of the goat cheese.

PENNE WITH TOASTED NUT AND PARSLEY PESTO

Serves 4 to 6

Toasting the unpeeled garlic in a skillet reduces its harshness and gives it a mellow flavor that works well in pesto.

    3   medium garlic cloves, unpeeled
    1   cup pecans, walnuts, whole blanched almonds,
        skinned hazelnuts, unsalted pistachios, or pine
        nuts, or any combination thereof
    ½   cup packed fresh parsley leaves
    7   tablespoons extra-virgin olive oil
    1   ounce Parmesan cheese, grated (about ½ cup)
        Salt and ground black pepper
    1   pound penne

1. Toast the garlic in a small, dry skillet over medium heat, shaking the pan occasionally, until softened and spotty brown, about 8 minutes; when cool, remove and discard the skins.

2. Toast the nuts in a medium, dry skillet over medium heat, stirring frequently, until golden and fragrant, 4 to 5 minutes. Cool the nuts.

3. In a food processor, process the garlic, nuts, parsley, and oil until smooth, stopping as necessary to scrape down the sides of the workbowl. Transfer the mixture to a small bowl and stir in the Parmesan; season to taste with salt and pepper.

4. Bring 4 quarts of water to a rolling boil in a stockpot. Add 1 tablespoon salt and the pasta, stir to separate, and cook until al dente. Drain, reserving ½ cup cooking water, and return the pasta to the stockpot. Stir ¼ cup of the pasta cooking water into the pesto and then stir the pesto into the pasta. Toss, adding more pasta cooking water as needed. Serve immediately.

SPAGHETTI WITH OLIVE PESTO

Serves 4 to 6

This black pesto is called olivada in Italy. Make sure to use high-quality olives in this recipe. The anchovy adds flavor but not fishiness to the pesto and we recommend its inclusion.

    3   medium garlic cloves, unpeeled
    1½   cups kalamata olives, pitted
    1   medium shallot, chopped coarse
    8   large basil leaves
    ¼   cup packed fresh parsley leaves
    1   anchovy fillet, rinsed (optional)
    1   ounce Parmesan cheese, grated (about ½ cup),
         plus extra for serving
    6   tablespoons extra-virgin olive oil
    1   tablespoon juice from 1 lemon
         Salt and ground black pepper
    1   pound spaghetti
    1   lemon, cut into wedges

1. Toast the garlic in a small, dry skillet over medium heat, shaking the pan occasionally, until the garlic is softened and

spotty brown, about 8 minutes; when cool, remove and discard the skins.

2. In a food processor, pulse the toasted garlic, olives, shallot, basil, parsley, anchovy, Parmesan, olive oil, and lemon juice, stopping as necessary to scrape down the sides of the workbowl. Transfer the mixture to a small bowl and add salt and pepper to taste.

3. Bring 4 quarts of water to a rolling boil in a stockpot. Add 1 tablespoon salt and the pasta, stir to separate, and cook until al dente. Drain, reserving ½ cup cooking water, and return the pasta to the stockpot. Stir ¼ cup of the pasta cooking water into the pesto and then stir the pesto into the pasta. Toss, adding more pasta cooking water as needed. Serve immediately, passing the lemon wedges and extra Parmesan at the table.

TASTING LAB: Sun-Dried Tomatoes

WHEN SHOPPING FOR SUN-DRIED TOMATOES, YOU HAVE two basic choices. You can buy dried, shelf-stable tomatoes that you reconstitute yourself by soaking them in boiling water, or you can buy ready-to-use tomatoes packed in oil. Is one style of sun-dried tomatoes better than the other? To answer this question, we tested several brands of each style. Tasters were very clear in their preferences. When reconstituted, the dried tomatoes were either mushy or tough. It was very hard to get them just right. The dried tomatoes were also very salty, bitter, or musty. In contrast, the ready-to-use samples packed in oil were pleasantly chewy. However, their flavors were not necessarily good.

We tasted seven samples straight from the jar—Harry's Bazaar, Pastene, Mezzetta, Bella San Luci, Mediterranean Organic, L'Esprit De Campagne, and Trader Joe's. Tasters thought that only the Trader Joe's tomatoes ($3.29 for an 8.5-ounce jar), which are packed in olive oil, garlic, herbs, spices, and sulfur dioxide (to retain color), had the right balance of flavor and sweetness. They were the clear favorite of our tasters. All other brands were thought to have an overpowering musty, herbal flavor, and these tomatoes were indeed noticeably covered in herbs.

Two brands, Mediterranean Organic and L'Esprit De Campagne, were packed in extra-virgin olive oil, which many tasters thought too strong in flavor. Tasters weren't wild about Harry's Bazaar, packed in sunflower oil, or Pastene, packed in a blend of olive and canola oils. We concluded that pure olive oil is the best packing medium for sun-dried tomatoes—it adds just the right amount of flavor without overwhelming the tomatoes. Tasters also noted that brands with brightly colored tomatoes tasted best; darker tomatoes were dull tasting.

Although Trader Joe's tomatoes taste best straight from the jar, we found that we could improve the flavor of the other brands by rinsing away excess herbs and spices. The rinsed tomatoes won't taste as good as our favorite brand, but they won't taste musty, either.

BEST SUN-DRIED TOMATOES
After tasting seven brands, our panel of tasters proclaimed Trader Joe's sun-dried tomatoes the best choice.

Erin is making a list, and checking it twice, before we start shooting our show on Indian cooking.

A PASSAGE to india

Indian food has a reputation for being spicy (most of it is not) and hard to prepare at home (tell that to one billion Indians). However, it is true that many recipes require a long list of spices and other ingredients. Although these ingredients are widely available in most supermarkets, these authentic recipes can be daunting, especially because many of the cooking techniques are unfamiliar to American cooks. Our goal when developing recipes for this chapter was to create dishes with authentic flavors but approachable techniques and ingredient lists.

Mulligatawny is a hearty pureed vegetable soup flavored with coconut, curry powder, ginger, and garlic. It can be thick and gluey or watery and bland. We wanted a rich, aromatic soup that would be hearty but not stodgy. It should also be silky smooth with a good balance of sweet, salty, spicy, and acidic flavors.

Chicken biryani is chicken and rice, Indian style, with saffron-flavored rice, spicy chicken, and a cooling yogurt sauce. Many recipes require a lot of prep time, and the results can be greasy. Our objective was to make this dish lighter, quicker, and better.

MULLIGATAWNY SOUP

WHAT WE WANTED: A mildly spicy and rich soup with a balance of spices and flavors.

Mulligatawny is a pureed vegetable soup that originated in India during the British Raj. The soup is mildly spicy but not hot. There should be some faint sweetness as well, usually from the coconut. The finished soup should be silky and elegant with potent yet balanced spices and aromatics.

We decided to start with the question of the liquid base. Research indicated that chicken stock, lamb stock, beef stock, vegetable stock, and water were possible choices. Tasters found vegetable stock too sweet and vegetal, and beef stock was too strong, even a bit sour. Lamb stock was overpowering, and we ruled it out because of the work involved in making it. In the end, we decided that chicken stock was the ideal base for the competing spices and vegetables. We found that canned broth was fine in this soup. Water made a tasty vegetarian soup that was not quite as rich as the version made with chicken stock.

Curry powder, which is a blend of spices, is a central ingredient in mulligatawny soup. We wondered whether to use a prepackaged blend or to make our own. After experimenting with several homemade curries, we found that the end product was not worth the effort of toasting and grinding our own spices. If we had homemade curry powder on hand, we would use it, but commercial curry powder is just fine with some modifications. We found it best to start with a good-quality curry powder and then boost the flavor with a little additional ground cumin and some cayenne for a bit of heat.

We decided to focus next on the aromatics (garlic and ginger) and coconut. After testing various strategies for adding garlic and ginger flavor to this soup, we found that tasters preferred versions with a small amount of raw garlic and ginger added just before serving and most of the garlic

and ginger sautéed in fat at the outset. To keep tasters from biting into a piece of raw garlic, we adopted a technique common in Indian cooking. We pureed the raw garlic and ginger with water so they could be fully incorporated into the soup for a fresh hit of garlic and ginger.

Coconut gives mulligatawny its distinctive sweet flavor and is authentically Indian along with the curry and ginger. Some recipes call for coconut milk, others for fresh coconut meat, and still others add dried coconut, either sweetened or not. The coconut milk gave the soup a silky consistency but not much coconut flavor. Fresh coconut was not flavorful enough, either, and in any case is much too troublesome to prepare. Dried coconut was the best option, adding enough flavor to the soup without taking over. Sweetened shredded coconut struck many tasters as odd, but unsweetened shredded coconut was delicious.

With our aromatics and spices under control, it was time to test the vegetables, which would give the soup flavor, bulk, and color when pureed. We tested onions, carrots, celery, cauliflower, spinach, peas, potatoes, and bananas. Not surprisingly, we found that onions are a must in the soup. Carrots added color and sweetness, and the celery provided a cool flavor that contrasted nicely with the hot spices. Cauliflower was rejected for the cabbage-like flavor it gave to the soup. Spinach and peas did little to enhance the soup's flavor. In addition, they imparted an undesirable color when pureed.

Potato, which was originally added for flavor, also improved the soup's texture. When pureed, the potato added body to the soup, thickening it slightly. Upon recommendation from several sources, we tried using a banana instead of a potato. The banana produced soup with the same rich body as that made with the potato, but this soup had a richer, slightly sweet flavor that offset the heat from the ginger. Afraid that the banana flavor might be too strong, we held a blind taste test between the banana and the potato.

The tasters unanimously preferred the soup made with the banana, although all were unable to identify the source of the flavor.

A single banana or potato gave the soup some body but did not thicken it quite enough. Adding more banana or potato was the most obvious solution, but more bananas made the soup sweet and the potatoes became gritty in larger amounts. Several recipes suggest using pureed rice or lentils to thicken the soup, but we did not like the thick, porridge-like results. We finally settled on sprinkling flour over the sautéed aromatics to make a roux. One-quarter cup of flour gave the soup the perfect consistency—silky and substantial but not heavy.

Although a few sources say that pureeing is optional, we think that mulligatawny must be smooth. Chunks of meat can float in the finished soup (we developed one variation with chicken, another with lamb), but the soup itself is meant to be refined and smooth. A dollop of yogurt and a shower of cilantro finish the soup. Traditionally, mulligatawny is served over basmati rice or red lentils, although it can stand on its own.

WHAT WE LEARNED: Chicken broth is the best base for this pureed vegetable-laden soup. Shredded unsweetened coconut is the best source for this distinct ingredient. Banana or potato, along with a roux, will give the soup proper body when pureed.

MULLIGATAWNY SOUP

Serves 6 to 8

For freshness, puree some of the garlic and ginger with water in a blender, then leave this mixture in the blender while making the soup. The finished soup is pureed in the same blender, where it will pick up a hit of spicy raw garlic and ginger flavor.

4	medium garlic cloves, 2 peeled and 2 finely minced
1	piece (about 1½ inches) fresh ginger, peeled and grated (about 1½ tablespoons)
¼	cup water
3	tablespoons unsalted butter
2	medium onions, chopped medium
1	teaspoon tomato paste
½	cup shredded unsweetened coconut
1½	tablespoons curry powder
1	teaspoon ground cumin
¼	teaspoon cayenne
¼	cup all-purpose flour
7	cups low-sodium chicken broth
2	medium carrots, peeled and chopped coarse
1	medium celery rib, chopped coarse
1	medium very ripe banana (about 5 ounces), peeled, or 1 small boiling potato (about 5 ounces), peeled and cut into 1-inch pieces
	Salt and ground black pepper
	Plain yogurt
2	tablespoons minced fresh cilantro leaves

1. Place the 2 peeled whole garlic cloves, 2 teaspoons of the grated ginger, and the water in a blender. Blend until smooth, about 25 seconds; leave the mixture in the blender jar and set aside. (You will be pureeing the soup right in the blender with the garlic and ginger.)

2. Heat the butter in a large stockpot or Dutch oven over medium heat until foaming. Add the onions and tomato paste and cook, stirring frequently, until the onions are softened and beginning to brown, about 3 minutes. Stir in the coconut and cook until fragrant, about 1 minute. Add the minced garlic, remaining 2½ teaspoons ginger, curry powder, cumin, cayenne, and flour; stir until evenly combined, about 1 minute. Whisking constantly and vigorously, gradually add the chicken broth.

3. Add the carrots, celery, and whole banana to the pot. Increase the heat to medium-high and bring to a boil. Cover, reduce the heat to low, and simmer until the vegetables are tender, about 20 minutes.

4. Puree the soup in batches in the blender with the garlic and ginger until very smooth. Wash and dry the pot. Return the pureed soup to the clean pot and season to taste with salt and pepper. Warm the soup over medium heat until hot, about 1 minute. (The soup can be refrigerated in an airtight container for up to 3 days. Warm over low heat until hot; do not boil.) Ladle the soup into individual bowls, spoon a dollop of the yogurt over each bowl, sprinkle with the cilantro, and serve immediately.

TECHNIQUE: Grating Ginger

Most cooks who use fresh ginger have scraped their fingers on the grater when the piece of ginger gets down to a tiny nub. Instead of cutting a small chunk of ginger off a larger piece and then grating, try this method: Peel a small section of the large piece of ginger. Grate the peeled portion, using the rest of the ginger as a handle to keep fingers safely away from the grater.

VARIATIONS

MULLIGATAWNY SOUP WITH CHICKEN
Serves 8
Basmati rice makes a good accompaniment to this soup.

Follow the recipe for Mulligatawny Soup, adding 4 medium (about 1½ pounds) boneless, skinless chicken breasts to the simmering stock in step 3 just before covering the pot. Simmer until cooked through, about 20 minutes. With tongs, transfer the cooked chicken to a cutting board, cool slightly, and cut crosswise into slices ¼ inch wide. Continue with the recipe, adding the reserved chicken to the pureed soup in the pot in step 4. Warm over medium heat until the chicken is hot, about 5 minutes. Garnish as directed.

MULLIGATAWNY SOUP WITH LAMB
Serves 8 to 10
This hearty, stew-like variation is especially good served with red lentils. It's also quite nice with basmati rice.

4	medium garlic cloves, 2 peeled and 2 finely minced
1	piece (about 1½ inches) fresh ginger, peeled and grated (about 1½ tablespoons)
¼	cup water
2	tablespoons olive oil
5	pounds lamb shoulder chops, bone, fat, and gristle discarded; meat cut into 1½-inch pieces
7	cups low-sodium chicken broth
3	tablespoons unsalted butter
2	medium onions, chopped medium
1	teaspoon tomato paste
½	cup shredded unsweetened coconut
1½	tablespoons curry powder
1	teaspoon ground cumin
¼	teaspoon cayenne
¼	cup all-purpose flour
2	medium carrots, peeled and chopped coarse
1	medium celery rib, chopped coarse

1 medium very ripe banana (about 5 ounces), peeled, or 1 boiling potato (about 5 ounces), peeled and cut into 1-inch pieces
Salt and ground black pepper
Plain yogurt
2 tablespoons minced fresh cilantro leaves

1. Place the 2 peeled whole garlic cloves, 2 teaspoons of the ginger, and the water in a blender. Blend until smooth, about 25 seconds; leave the mixture in the blender jar and set aside. (You will be pureeing the soup right in the blender with the garlic and ginger.)

2. Heat a large stockpot or Dutch oven over medium-high heat until very hot. Add 1 tablespoon of the olive oil, swirl to coat the pan bottom, and add half of the lamb pieces. Cook until the lamb is well browned, about 2 to 3 minutes. Transfer the browned lamb to a medium bowl with a slotted spoon. Add the remaining tablespoon of oil to the pot, swirl to coat the pan bottom, add the remaining lamb, and cook until the lamb is well browned on all sides. Return all the lamb to the pot and add the chicken broth, scraping up the browned bits from the pan bottom with a wooden spoon. Bring to a simmer, cover, reduce the heat to medium-low, and simmer until the lamb is tender, about 20 minutes. With a slotted spoon, transfer the lamb to a medium bowl, cover, and reserve. Pour the broth into another bowl and reserve.

3. Heat the butter in a large stockpot or Dutch oven over medium heat until foaming. Add the onions and tomato paste and cook, stirring frequently, until the onions are softened and beginning to brown, about 3 minutes. Stir in the coconut and cook until fragrant, about 1 minute. Add the minced garlic, remaining 2½ teaspoons ginger, curry powder, cumin, cayenne, and flour; stir well until evenly combined, about 1 minute. Whisking constantly and vigorously, gradually add the reserved broth used to cook the lamb.

4. Add the carrots, celery, and whole banana to the stock. Increase the heat to medium-high and bring to a boil. Cover, reduce the heat to low, and simmer until the vegetables are tender, about 20 minutes.

5. Puree the soup in batches in the blender with the garlic and ginger until very smooth. Wash and dry the pot. Return the pureed soup to the clean pot and season to taste with salt and pepper. Add the lamb pieces and warm the soup over medium heat until the lamb is hot, about 5 minutes. Ladle the soup into individual bowls, spoon a dollop of the yogurt over each bowl, sprinkle with the cilantro, and serve immediately.

TASTING LAB: Curry Powder

LIKE CHILI POWDER, CURRY POWDER IS NOT A SINGLE spice but rather a blend of spices. Unlike chili powder, which contains about 80 percent chile pepper, there is no such dominant spice in curry powder. Because of this, flavors vary greatly depending on the blend. Among the spices most commonly used are cardamom, cumin, fenugreek, turmeric (which gives curry its characteristically yellow color), fennel, nutmeg, and chiles. We chose seven mild curry powders (hot curry powder, which contains more red pepper and other hot spices, is also available) and tasted them all in a simple rice pilaf, cooking the curry powder in oil briefly to allow the flavors to bloom.

Overall, tasters leaned toward big, bolder, brighter blends that delivered a lot of color and flavor. First place finisher, Tone's, a darling of the discount club stores, was praised for its "good, heavy spice mix." Distant second place finisher Durkee was also noted for its "shocking color" and "round" flavor. On the other hand, last-place finisher Sun Brand, though praised by some as "nutty and rich," ultimately lost points for its "pale, boring" appearance (in contrast to the bright yellow of the other brands, Sun Brand was very light and almost beige in color).

Unfortunately, some manufacturers consider their exact spice blends to be proprietary information, and they would not share that information with us. Therefore, we cannot speculate on why Tone's dominated over such specialty brands as Penzeys and Kalustyan's.

Rating Curry Powders

FIFTEEN MEMBERS OF THE *COOK'S ILLUSTRATED* STAFF TASTED ALL OF THE CURRY POWDERS IN A SIMPLE RICE PILAF. We briefly cooked the curry powder in oil to allow the flavors to bloom. The curry powders are listed in order of preference based on their scores in this tasting. Brands are available in supermarkets or by mail-order as indicated. When possible, we've listed ingredients as printed on labels. Note that manufacturers list ingredients according to the amount used, starting with the most and ending with the least.

HIGHLY RECOMMENDED
Tone's Curry Powder   **$7.39 for 16 ounces**
Proprietary Blend

Though there was "nothing exotic" about this brand sold in many warehouse clubs, tasters did praise its "strong" curry flavor.

RECOMMENDED
Durkee Curry Powder   **$6.70 for 17 ounces**
Proprietary Blend

Tasters praised this supermarket brand for its "good balance" and deep color. Look for extra-large containers of this brand in warehouse clubs.

RECOMMENDED
Penzeys Sweet Curry Powder   **$4.19 for 2.2 ounces**
Contains turmeric, Moroccan coriander, cumin, ginger, fenugreek, nutmeg, fennel, cinnamon, white pepper, cardamom, cloves, Tellicherry black pepper, cayenne red pepper

"Extremely mild" wrote one taster about this mail-order favorite. Seemed "typical" to others.

RECOMMENDED
Spice Islands Curry Powder   **$4.75 for 2.1 ounces**
Proprietary Blend

Fans praised this blend's "warmth," but others dismissed it as "flat." Available in supermarkets, especially in the West.

NOT RECOMMENDED
Kalustyan's Imperial Mild Curry Powder   **$4.49 for 4 ounces**
Cumin, coriander, black pepper, cinnamon, cloves, cardamom, ginger, nutmeg, turmeric, chili powder

Tasters picked up on the heavy cardamom and clove flavors in this mail-order brand and were not impressed. "No depth or complexity," wrote one taster. "Bland and uninteresting."

NOT RECOMMENDED
McCormick Curry Powder   **$5.15 for 1.75 ounces**
Proprietary Blend

Several tasters noted the "strangely vegetal" flavor of this supermarket staple, which many compared unfavorably to celery salt.

NOT RECOMMENDED
Sun Brand Madras Curry Powder   **$2.79 for 4 ounces**
Coriander, turmeric, chilies, salt, cumin, fennel, black pepper, garlic, ginger, fenugreek, cinnamon, cloves, anise, mustard

Most tasters were put off by the "pale and brown" color of this curry. They were not impressed by the "burnt," "bland" flavor either.

CHICKEN AND RICE, INDIAN-STYLE

WHAT WE WANTED: Chicken biryani is a complicated (and often greasy) classic Indian dish. Could we make this dish simpler and lighter?

Chicken biryani has about as much in common with American-style chicken and rice as naan does with Wonder bread. They both share the same major ingredients but diverge widely from there. In biryani, long-grain basmati rice takes center stage, enriched with butter, saffron, and a variety of fresh herbs and pungent spices. Pieces of tender chicken and browned onions are layered with the rice and baked until the flavors have mingled. This is India in a pot.

But it comes at a stiff price. Traditional biryani recipes are long in both ingredients and labor. The chicken is rubbed with spices and marinated before being browned; the rice is soaked, blanched, and mixed with a complex masala, or blend, of innumerable spices; the onions are deep-fried. Finally everything is layered (rice, onions, chicken, repeat) into a cooking vessel and baked or steamed until the flavors have blended. In addition, most biryani recipes we tested were made greasy by the deep-fried onions, and the rice had overcooked by the time the chicken was done. We set out to find a middle path between the extremes of dull simplicity and epicurean complexity.

We prepared a few classic biryani recipes to better acquaint ourselves with the dish, a task that required a full day in the test kitchen and produced a huge pile of dirty dishes. We made three time-saving discoveries. First, we learned that we could skip the step of marinating the chicken (too much time, too little flavor enhancement). Second, we could prepare the whole recipe on the stovetop, eliminating the need for an oven. Third, it was possible to cook the onions and the chicken in the same large skillet, saving a pan. The streamlined recipe, although still not a 30-minute supper, now consisted of cooking the onions, browning the chicken, parboiling the rice, and then simmering/steaming the layered biryani until done.

The best-tasting biryani from our recipe tests was made with two abundant layers of deep-fried onions, but they inevitably turned the dish greasy. Onions sautéed in a tablespoon of fat (oil or butter) failed to brown properly. More fat was clearly necessary, but how much could we add without turning the dish greasy? We started with ½ cup of fat for two sliced onions and reduced it 1 tablespoon at a time. In the end, 3 tablespoons proved sufficient. Butter prevailed over oil, adding more flavor and color.

Tasters preferred dark meat chicken—it was more flavorful and juicy than white meat, which ended up dry. Bone-in thighs are the test kitchen favorite because they are so meaty. Having already eliminated marinating, we followed test kitchen protocol for braising chicken pieces. (Biryani is, in essence, a braise because it uses moist, low heat for cooking.) To eke out as much flavor as we could, we browned the chicken deeply, with the skin on for protection. Before layering the pieces with the rice, we stripped off the skin. With this last step, the greasiness issue was finally put to rest.

Biryani's subtle, delicate flavor and aroma are largely derived from the masala of whole spices blended into the rice. (Ground spices—we tested these as well—tasted raw.) Cardamom and cinnamon are essential, but too much of

either easily overwhelmed other flavors. Tasters quickly ruled out nutmeg and cloves as overpowering. Coriander, too, was excluded, because it was too mild. In the end, tasters approved of cardamom, cinnamon, cumin seed, and fresh ginger sliced into coins. Sweet, earthy, sharp, and musky, the spices paired well together. Lightly smashing the cardamom and ginger with a chef's knife intensified their flavor.

Before serving, we diligently fished out the spices from the rice as tasters strongly objected to unexpectedly biting down on whole cardamom pods, but this nitpicky task grew tiresome. We began thinking of ways to isolate the spices. In French cooking, herbs and spices are often bundled together in cheesecloth and added to soups. The liquid flows through the permeable bundle, and the soup is flavored. We decided to try a little fusion cooking and give the bundle idea a whirl. We tied the spices together and added the bundle to the layered biryani before steaming, but that accomplished little. In the end, an even easier solution delivered big flavor. We simply simmered the bundle in the water used to parboil the rice. We also found that adding a portion of this flavored liquid to the layered biryani—sort of like adding pasta cooking water to a pasta dish—further intensified the spice flavor. Now we had included both French and Italian technique in streamlining a classic Indian dish.

Saffron is mixed with the rice as both a coloring and a flavoring agent. Any more than a pinch turned the rice Day-Glo orange and made it taste medicinal. Tasters demanded a fair amount of garlic and jalapeño, as well as some seeds from the chiles for additional fire. A little sweetness from currants (or raisins, in a pinch) helped to temper the heat and accent the warm spices. Cilantro and mint, both standard biryani ingredients, found favor with tasters.

WHAT WE LEARNED: Sauté the onions in just 3 tablespoons of butter for extra flavor without greasiness. Brown the chicken and then remove the skin, again to keep greasiness under control. Use a spice-flavored broth to cook the rice and perfume the dish with the flavors of cardamom, cinnamon, ginger, and cumin.

CHICKEN BIRYANI

Serves 4

This recipe requires a 3½- to 4-quart saucepan about 8 inches in diameter. Do not use a large, wide Dutch oven, as it will adversely affect both the layering of the dish and the final cooking times. Begin simmering the spices in the water prior to preparing the remaining ingredients; the more time the spices have to infuse the water (up to half an hour), the more flavor they will give to the rice. Biryani is traditionally served with a cooling yogurt sauce; ideally, you should make it before starting the biryani to allow the flavors in the sauce to meld, but no longer than a day ahead, otherwise the garlic flavor will become overpowering.

yogurt sauce

1	cup whole milk or low-fat plain yogurt
1	medium garlic clove, minced or pressed through a garlic press (about 1 teaspoon)
2	tablespoons minced fresh cilantro leaves
2	tablespoons minced fresh mint leaves
	Salt and ground black pepper

chicken and rice

10	cardamom pods, preferably green, smashed with a chef's knife
1	cinnamon stick
1	piece (about 2 inches) fresh ginger, cut into ½-inch-thick coins and smashed with a chef's knife
½	teaspoon cumin seed
3	quarts water
	Salt
4	bone-in, skin-on chicken thighs (about 1½ pounds), trimmed of excess skin and fat and patted dry with paper towels
	Ground black pepper
3	tablespoons unsalted butter
2	medium onions, sliced thin (about 4 cups)
2	medium jalapeño chiles, one seeded and chopped fine, the other chopped fine with seeds

4   medium garlic cloves, minced or pressed
    through a garlic press (about 1 generous
    tablespoon)
1¼ cups basmati rice
½   teaspoon saffron threads, lightly crumbled
¼   cup dried currants or raisins
2   tablespoons chopped fresh cilantro leaves
2   tablespoons chopped fresh mint leaves

1. FOR THE YOGURT SAUCE: Combine the yogurt, garlic, cilantro, and mint in a small bowl; season to taste with salt and pepper. Let stand at least 30 minutes to blend flavors or cover and refrigerate up to 1 day before serving.

GETTING IT RIGHT: The Layered Look

Layering the ingredients into a saucepan is the secret to the min-gling of flavors in chicken biryani. Here's the assembly method that works best: Return half of the parboiled rice to the sauce-pan, top with half the onions, followed by the chicken pieces, the rest of the onions, and then the rest of the rice. Moisten everything with the spice-infused cooking liquid from the rice, cover, and steam over medium-low heat until the chicken is done and the rice is tender.

---

2. FOR THE CHICKEN AND RICE: Wrap the carda-mom pods, cinnamon stick, ginger, and cumin seed in a small piece of cheesecloth and secure with kitchen twine. In a 3½- to 4-quart heavy-bottomed saucepan about 8 inches in diameter, bring the water, spice bundle, and 1½ teaspoons salt to a boil over medium-high heat. Reduce the heat to medium and simmer, partially covered, until the spices have infused the water, at least 15 minutes (but no longer than 30 minutes).

3. Meanwhile, season both sides of the chicken thighs with salt and pepper and set aside. Heat the butter in a 12-inch nonstick skillet over medium-high heat until the foaming subsides; add the onions and cook, stirring frequently, until soft and dark brown about the edges, 10 to 12 minutes. Add the jalapeños and garlic and cook, stirring frequently, until fragrant, about 2 minutes. Transfer the onion mixture to a bowl, season lightly with salt, and set aside. Wipe out the skil-let with paper towels, return the heat to medium-high, and place the chicken thighs skin-side down in the skillet; cook, without moving the chicken, until well browned, about 5 minutes. Flip the chicken and brown the second side, 4 to 5 minutes longer; transfer the chicken to a plate and remove and discard the skin. Tent with foil to keep warm.

4. If necessary, return the spice-infused water to a boil over high heat; stir in the rice and cook 5 minutes, stirring occa-sionally. Drain the rice through a fine-mesh strainer, reserv-ing ¾ cup of the cooking liquid; discard the spice bundle. Transfer the rice to a medium bowl; stir in the saffron and currants (the rice will turn splotchy yellow). Spread half of the rice evenly in the bottom of the now-empty saucepan using a rubber spatula. Scatter half of the onion mixture over the rice, then place the chicken thighs, skinned-side up, on top of the onions; add any accumulated chicken juices. Sprinkle evenly with the cilantro and mint, scatter the remaining onions over the herbs, then cover with the remaining rice; pour the reserved cooking liquid evenly over the rice.

Several American rice growers now sell their own basmati. Unfortunately, the two products we tasted couldn't compare with the real thing. Their flavor was not nearly as aromatic as Indian-grown basmati, and the cooked grains were soft and stubby. We later learned that American-grown basmati is not aged and hence doesn't expand as much as Indian-grown rice. Luckily, Indian rice is available in most supermarkets and costs about the same as domestic basmati. Make sure that the label indicates that the rice has been aged; otherwise your biryani might be uncharacteristically mushy.

5. Cover the saucepan and cook over medium-low heat until the rice is tender and the chicken is cooked through, about 30 minutes (if a large amount of steam is escaping from the pot, reduce the heat to low). Run a heatproof rubber spatula around the inside rim of the saucepan to loosen any affixed rice; using a large serving spoon, spoon the biryani into individual bowls, scooping from the bottom of the pot and serving 1 chicken thigh per person.

CALIFORNIA DREAMIN'
This California rice lacked the aroma and flavor of the Indian original, and tasters found the cooked grains "mushy" and broken.

TASTING LAB: Basmati Rice

BASMATI IS A VARIETY OF VERY LONG-GRAIN RICE most commonly grown in northern India and Pakistan. It is aged for a minimum of a year, though often much longer, before being packaged. Aging dehydrates the rice, which translates into grains that, once cooked, expand greatly—more so than any other long-grain rice.

TROUBLE IN TEXAS
Comments on this rice were nearly identical to those about the California rice, including "gummy," "soft," and "chewed-up looking."

THE ORIGINAL AND THE BEST
Tasters' comments on Indian-grown, aged rice included "great texture," "great grain separation," "something to chew on," and "toasty."

SCIENCE DESK:
Where's the Chile Heat?

Chiles get their "heat"—or "pungency," as the experts like to say—from a group of chemical compounds called capsaicinoids, the best known of which is capsaicin. To figure out where most of these compounds reside, we donned rubber gloves and separated the colored green flesh, whitish pith (also called membranes or ribs), and seeds from 40 jalapeños. We then sent the lot to our food lab. It turned out there were just 5 milligrams of capsaicin per kilogram of green jalapeño flesh (not enough to really make much impact on the human tongue), 73 mg per kg of seeds, and an impressive 512 mg per kg of pith.

According to the Chile Pepper Institute, a research and education center housed at New Mexico State University, capsaicin is produced in the pith, not by the seeds. The reason why the seeds registered more heat than the flesh is simply because they are embedded in the pith; they are essentially guilty—or hot—by reason of association. From now on, then, when we want to carefully mete out the fire in our salsa or biryani, we'll do it by means of the pith. The seeds will just be along for the ride.

TASTING LAB: Saffron

While most cooks know that saffron is the world's most expensive spice, few are aware that it is grown in many locations and that price and quality can vary considerably. Though the bulk of commercially produced saffron comes from Spain and Iran, it is also harvested on a small scale in India, Greece, France, and, closer to home, in Lancaster County, Pennsylvania.

We decided to toss saffron from different places purchased at different prices into a few pots and set up a test. We prepared three batches of risotto alla Milanese and flavored one with Spanish saffron, one with Indian, and one with American. (Chicken biryani is so complex that we worried it would not provide a neutral background against which to taste the delicate flavor of the saffron.)

The finished risottos were similar in hue, though the Indian Kashmir saffron threads were darkest prior to cooking. Surprisingly, no one cared for the Indian saffron, although it was almost twice as costly as the other two and is generally regarded as one of the best in the world. Despite its heady aroma, floral tones, and earthy scent, many tasters found it "tinny" and "bland" when cooked. The risotto made with the Spanish saffron was better, but we overwhelmingly favored the risotto made with the Pennsylvania-grown saffron, judging it the "most potent" and "perfumed" of the three samples.

Our conclusion: Just because saffron has an expensive pedigree doesn't mean it will taste good. Shop carefully, buying only saffron threads, not ground saffron. And, if you find domestic saffron, it can be an excellent—and relatively inexpensive—alternative.

TECHNIQUE:
Crumbling Saffron Threads

To extract as much flavor as possible from saffron, crumble the threads between your fingers just before adding them to recipes. Crumbling the threads releases flavorful oils and helps the saffron dissolve quickly in liquid.

Chicken Biryani **page 191**

Thai Grilled Chicken with Spicy, Sweet, and Sour Dipping Sauce **page 147**

196

Glazed Carrots **page 60**

Eggplant Parmesan **page 225**

198

Pasta e Fagioli **page 25**

Crab Towers with Avocado and Gazpacho Salsas **page 113**

Grilled Glazed Salmon **page 153**

Grill-Roasted Beef Tenderloin **page 136**

202

Southern Cornbread **page 130**

Sticky Buns with Pecans **page 272**

Nut Crescent Cookies **page 301**

Classic Brownies **page 283**

Chocolate Sour Cream Bundt Cake **page 307**

Spiced Pumpkin Cheesecake **page 320**

Glazed Butter Cookies, Jam Sandwiches, Lime-Glazed Coconut Snowballs, and Chocolate-Cherry Bar Cookies with Hazelnuts **page 295**

209

Pissaladière page 214

PISSALADIÈRE

CHAPTER 16

Pissaladière is Provençal street food, a fragrant, pizza-like tart prized for its contrast of salty black olives and anchovies against a backdrop of sweet caramelized onions and thyme. Supporting this rough and rustic flavor combination is a wheaty crust with a texture that is part chewy pizza and part crisp cracker. Commonly eaten as an appetizer or even a light supper alongside a salad, this classic French favorite is still something of a foreigner to most Americans—darkly handsome but a bit difficult to understand.

But the ingredients are simple enough. The crust is basically pizza dough, and the toppings are caramelized onions, herbs, anchovies, and olives. The key is to balance all of these strong flavors so that they work together. We knew we could figure out how to make a great version of this French classic.

PISSALADIÈRE

WHAT WE WANTED: The classic olive, anchovy, and onion pizza from Provence is easy enough to prepare, but each ingredient must be handled just so. We wanted a recipe worthy of the finest bakery in Nice.

When coming up with our version of pissaladière, we had to start with a series of "get acquainted" tests to fully comprehend the range of possibilities. Most recipes produced a crust in the style of a pizza, others called for savory pie dough fit into a fluted tart pan, and we even found a few that used squares of store-bought puff pastry. All of them called for caramelized onions, black olives, thyme, and anchovies, but additional sources of flavor, such as Parmesan, sun-dried tomatoes, basil, and oregano, were not uncommon. As for the basic flavor ingredients, almost all of the caramelized onions were underdone, while the bullish flavor of anchovies overran the olives and thyme. Anchovies, we thought, should not rule but rather act as a counterpoint to the sweet onions, briny olives, and fragrant thyme.

As for the crust, the test kitchen quickly eliminated puff pastry and pie dough. Unfortunately, the more authentic pizza-like crusts weren't very good, either. Textures were too short (think shortbread) and crackery or overly soft and doughy. Tasters thought that good pissaladière should have a dual-textured crust that is crisp on the outside (like a cracker) and chewy on the inside.

Although they are not exactly right for pissaladière, we whipped up three different pizza crusts to see if any could be used as a jumping-off point. The thin crust wasn't sturdy enough and the deep-dish crust was too doughy, but the traditional crust was the right thickness (about half an inch) and had the right flavor. Knowing that we wanted it to be chewier, with a more cracker-like exterior, we took a closer look at each of its four major ingredients—bread flour, oil, water, and yeast—to see where we could make adjustments.

We replaced various amounts of bread flour with all-purpose flour but made zero headway. Bread flour has more protein than all-purpose, and that translates into a more substantial chew. Testing amounts of olive oil ranging from none at all up to 6 tablespoons, we again found that the original recipe (which called for 1 tablespoon) produced the best balance of crisp to tender without causing the dough to be brittle (a problem when the amount of oil dropped below 1 tablespoon) or greasy (a problem when the amount of oil exceeded 1 tablespoon).

Next on the list of ingredients to tinker with was water. The original recipe called for ¾ cup of water to 2 cups of flour. Less water made the crust drier (no surprise) and tougher. More water made the dough chewier, but we soon learned that there was such a thing as too chewy. When we increased the water to 1¼ cups, the crust baked up with huge holes and was as chewy as bubble gum. The crust made with 1 cup of water proved to be a happy medium—chewier than the original pizza crust but not over the top.

When we varied the amount of yeast, the flavor changed (as did the rising time), but not the texture. Less yeast and an overnight rise—a common flavor-enhancing technique—did produce a crust with a slightly more complex flavor, but it was awfully hard to detect once it came up against the onions, olives, and anchovies. One teaspoon of yeast pumped the dough through the first rise in a convenient 75 minutes (give or take 15 minutes, depending on the humidity and the kitchen temperature), during which there was ample time to prepare and caramelize the onions.

Doughs made in a standing mixer, a food processor, and by hand showed substantial differences and, surprisingly, tasters preferred the method most professional bakers would scoff at. Doughs made by hand and in the mixer were tough and snappy after being baked, requiring a full set of well-rooted molars. To achieve the best texture, this dough apparently would accept only minimal handling. We knew

that bread dough could be kneaded in a food processor in a two-step process. Step 1 is to whiz the ingredients for a mere 15 seconds until they come together; step 2 is to wait for two minutes and then knead the dough in the food processor an additional 30 seconds. It turned out that the secret to perfect pissaladière dough was to complete step 1 and simply ignore step 2! This crust was a winner, unanimously favored for its cracker-like exterior and decently chewy crumb. (We eventually figured out how to make the dough by hand and in a standing mixer, but the process for both was more time-consuming and difficult, and the timing and results were never as consistent.) The best part of the food processor technique is that it's foolproof. You know that the dough has been processed properly when it comes together in a ball. Nothing could be simpler.

Dough pressed onto a rimmed baking sheet didn't brown nearly as well as a free-form oval baked directly on a preheated baking stone at 500 degrees. Pressing the dough out on parchment paper made for an easy transfer to the oven. Tasters also preferred the rustic texture of dough that was pressed out by hand as opposed to the uniform consistency of dough flattened by a rolling pin.

A key problem with this recipe is the stickiness of the dough. We had been using plenty of flour when shaping the dough, until, on a whim, we tried oil instead. Good idea. Not only was it a snap to shape the dough on the parchment, but the extra oil pressed into the bottom of the crust made it even crisper. Brushing the dough with yet more olive oil before adding the toppings further ensured a cracker-like exterior, officially turning this crust from pizza to pissaladière.

Most recipes for caramelized onions subscribe to one of two methods—low and slow or fast and furious—yet neither works. Low and slow dries out the onions before they have a chance to get dark, while fast and furious leaves the onions crunchy and burnt tasting. Taking a cue from our caramelized onion recipe, we used a combination of high and low heat, starting the onions on high to release their juices and soften them, then turning the heat to medium-low to let the juices caramelize.

A nonstick skillet works best for caramelizing onions. The low sides of a skillet (as opposed to the high sides of a Dutch oven) allow the steam to evaporate rather than interfere with browning, while the nonstick surface ensures that the caramelization sticks to the onions, not the pan. Once the onions were cooked, though, we had problems sprinkling them over the pizza, as they tended to clump. The solution? We stirred in just a bit of water once we removed the onions from the heat.

Whereas most recipes call for whole black olives, we found that they roll around and occasionally fall off the crust. In addition, the intense heat of the oven dries them to a leathery texture. A better method is to chop the olives coarsely and layer them underneath the onions, where they are protected from overcooking. This same trick also works with the leaves of fresh thyme.

It's traditional to arrange anchovies across the top of a pissaladière in a crosshatch pattern. This was too much anchovy for the test kitchen staff, so we focused on how to incorporate their strong flavor without offending anyone. As with the olives, we found it best to chop and spread them underneath the onions. Just four anchovies per tart was perfect, and rinsing them first made sure they weren't too salty or fishy. (Still, several fish lovers missed the crosshatching, so we included it as an option.) The only untraditional flavors that passed our relatively strict code of authenticity were fennel seeds and freshly minced parsley, and both are optional.

WHAT WE LEARNED: Make the dough in a food processor and knead it as little as possible to create a crust with a crisp exterior and chewy crumb. Bury the anchovies and olives under the caramelized onions to protect them from burning in the oven.

PISSALADIÈRE

Makes 2 tarts, serving 8 to 10 as a first course

If your food processor includes a plastic dough blade attachment, use it; its short blades and dull edges make kneading easier on the motor. If not, the regular metal blade works almost as well. For best flavor, use high-quality oil-packed anchovies; in a recent tasting, Ortiz was our favorite brand. The dough in this recipe rises for 1 to 1½ hours. If a longer or overnight rise is more convenient, make the dough with ½ teaspoon of instant yeast and let it rise in the refrigerator for 16 to 24 hours. The caramelized onions can also be made a day ahead and refrigerated.

dough

- 2 cups (11 ounces) bread flour, plus more for dusting the work surface
- 1 teaspoon instant yeast
- 1 teaspoon salt
- 1 tablespoon olive oil, plus more for brushing the dough and greasing hands
- 1 cup warm water (about 110 degrees)

caramelized onions

- 2 tablespoons olive oil
- 2 pounds yellow onions, sliced ¼ inch thick
- ½ teaspoon salt
- 1 teaspoon brown sugar
- 1 tablespoon water

olives, anchovies, and garnishes

- Olive oil
- ½ teaspoon ground black pepper
- ½ cup niçoise olives, pitted and chopped coarse
- 8 anchovy fillets, rinsed, patted dry, and chopped coarse (about 2 tablespoons), plus 12 fillets, rinsed and patted dry for garnish (optional)
- 2 teaspoons minced fresh thyme leaves
- 1 teaspoon fennel seeds (optional)
- 1 tablespoon minced fresh parsley (optional)

1. FOR THE DOUGH: In the workbowl of a food processor fitted with the plastic dough blade (see note), pulse the flour, yeast, and salt to combine, about five 1-second pulses. With the machine running, slowly add the oil, then the water, through the feed tube; continue to process until the dough forms a ball, about 15 seconds. Generously dust the work surface with flour. Using floured hands, transfer the dough to the work surface and knead lightly, shaping the dough into a ball. Lightly oil a 1-quart measuring cup or small bowl, place the dough in the measuring cup (see the photo below), cover tightly with plastic wrap, and set aside in a draft-free spot until doubled in volume, 1 to 1½ hours.

2. FOR THE CARAMELIZED ONIONS: While the dough is rising, heat the oil in a 12-inch nonstick skillet over high heat until shimmering but not smoking. Stir in the onions, salt, and brown sugar and cook, stirring frequently, until the moisture released by the onions has evaporated and the onions begin to brown, about 10 minutes. Reduce the heat to medium-low and cook, stirring frequently, until the onions have softened and are medium golden brown, about 20 minutes longer. Off the heat, stir in the water; transfer to a bowl and set aside. Adjust the oven rack to the lowest position, set a baking stone on the rack, and heat the oven to 500 degrees.

GETTING IT RIGHT: Rising the Dough

Just Mixed   Fully Risen

A quart-size liquid measuring cup is good for more than just holding liquid. We let the pissaladière dough rise in a measuring cup covered with plastic wrap. The lines on the measuring cup make it easy to tell when the dough has doubled in size.

3. TO SHAPE, TOP, AND BAKE THE DOUGH: When the dough has doubled, remove it from the measuring cup and divide into two equal pieces using a dough scraper. Working with one piece at a time, form each piece into a rough ball by gently pulling the edges of the dough together and pinching to seal (see illustration 1, at right). With floured hands, turn the dough ball seam-side down. Cupping the dough with both hands, gently push the dough in a circular motion to form a taut ball (illustration 2). Repeat with the second piece. Brush each piece lightly with oil, cover with plastic wrap, and let rest 10 minutes. Meanwhile, cut two 20-inch lengths of parchment paper and set aside.

4. Coat your fingers and the palms of your hands generously with oil. Using a dough scraper, loosen one piece of dough from the work surface. With well-oiled hands, hold the dough aloft and gently stretch it to a 12-inch length (illustration 3). Place the dough on a parchment sheet and gently dimple the surface of the dough with your fingertips (illustration 4). Using oiled palms, push and flatten the dough into a 14 by 8-inch oval (illustration 5). Brush the dough with oil and sprinkle with ¼ teaspoon pepper. Leaving a ½-inch border around the edge, sprinkle ¼ cup of the olives, 1 tablespoon of the chopped anchovies, and 1 teaspoon of the thyme evenly over the dough, then evenly scatter with half of the onions (illustration 6). Arrange 6 whole anchovy fillets, if using, on the tart and sprinkle with half of the fennel seeds, if using. Slip the parchment with the tart onto a pizza peel (or inverted rimless baking sheet), then slide it onto the hot baking stone. Bake until deep golden brown, 13 to 15 minutes. While the first tart bakes, shape and top the second tart.

5. Remove the first tart from the oven with a peel or pull the parchment onto a baking sheet. Transfer the tart to a cutting board and slide the parchment out from under the tart. Cool 5 minutes; sprinkle with 1½ teaspoons of the parsley, if using. Cut the tart into 8 pieces; serve immediately. While the first tart cools, bake the second tart.

TECHNIQUE: Shaping Pissaladière

1. Pull the dough edges together.

2. Roll the dough into a taut ball.

3. Hold the dough aloft and stretch it.

4. Dimple the dough with your fingers.

5. Push the dough into an oval.

6. Add the toppings.

GETTING IT RIGHT:
Understanding the Dough

We found that the same basic ingredients—flour, water, yeast, salt, and oil—can yield doughs that bake up quite differently, depending on the ratio of ingredients as well as the shaping technique and baking temperature. Here are the characteristics and differences of four of our dough recipes.

Focaccia Dough

Focaccia is made with a lot of olive oil and is baked in a pan in a moderate oven. As a result, it bakes up thick, chewy, and very soft.

Thin-Crust Pizza Dough

This dough is rolled with a rolling pin until very thin and baked directly on a heated stone in a superhot oven. It bakes up crisp and brittle.

Deep-Dish Pizza Dough

This dough is baked in a pan set on a preheated stone. Adding olive oil to the pan ensures a crisp bottom. However, because the dough is so thick, the top and interior are fairly soft.

Pissaladière Dough

This recipe combines attributes of all the other doughs. A moderate amount of olive oil is rubbed into the exterior to crisp the crust, and, because the dough is not stretched thin, the interior remains chewy.

EQUIPMENT CORNER: Baking Stones

BAKING STONES (ALSO CALLED PIZZA STONES) ARE prized for their ability to retain heat and lessen the effects of hot spots and temperature fluctuations in home ovens. Usually made of clay or ceramics (although soapstone and composite cement stones are also available), baking stones, when coupled with extreme heat, absorb moisture, thus producing crispier, drier pizzas and breads.

We tested seven stones in different shapes, sizes, and materials, ranging in price from $20 to $80. We judged the stones on two main criteria: design (including ease of use, installation, and storage) and performance (including heat conductivity, evenness of browning, and crispness of baked goods). There was little issue with heat conductivity. We took the surface temperature of each stone, and each one exceeded 500 degrees after 60 minutes of preheating. Also, with little variance, all seven stones produced evenly colored and crisp crusts on pizzas.

Although performance was similar in all the models we tested, some designs were much easier to work with. Lipped edges inhibited easy placement and removal of food from a peel, and stones with this feature were downgraded, as were stones that were extremely heavy (one weighed a whopping 19 pounds). We did not like clay tiles (they seemed easy to lose and were hard to install), and stones that were either too big to fit in most home ovens or too small to handle a large pizza received low marks. Our recommendation is to choose a good-size stone (14 by 16 inches is ideal) with smooth edges.

Rating Baking Stones

WE TESTED SEVEN STONES IN DIFFERENT SHAPES, SIZES, AND MATERIALS. STONES WERE EVALUATED ON DESIGN (including ease of use, installation, and storage) and performance (including evenness of browning, crispness of baked goods, and heat conductivity). The stones are listed in order of preference. See www.americastestkitchen.com for up-to-date prices and mail-order sources for top-rated products.

HIGHLY RECOMMENDED
The Baker's Catalog Baking Stone (Manufactured by Old Stone Oven)
$34.95
We like this ceramic stone for its moderate weight and good size (14½ inches by 16½ inches).

RECOMMENDED
Handmade Pizza/Bread Stone
$38.50
This 15¼-inch round clay stone is just a tad smaller than our winner. Very light and easy to maneuver.

RECOMMENDED
Exeter Round Pizza Stone
$19.99
This 16-inch ceramic stone is another good choice, and the price is right.

RECOMMENDED WITH RESERVATIONS
Sur la Table Pizza Stone with Copper Handles
$79.95
The appearance of this 14-inch soapstone stone was intriguing, but its steep price tag and lipped edge were not. The handles are convenient for this very heavy stone, but they get extremely hot in the oven.

RECOMMENDED WITH RESERVATIONS
FibraMent Rectangular Oven Stone
$59.99
This cement stone lost points for its incredible heft (19 pounds) and large size (20 by 15 inches), which won't work in many ovens. A slight cement odor was also detected each time the stone was heated, though it did not transfer to the food.

RECOMMENDED WITH RESERVATIONS
Old Stone Oven Baking Tiles
$29.99
When these ceramic tiles are installed correctly (which takes some work), they approximate the size of a baking stone. The pieces might be easy to lose if you don't store them in your oven.

RECOMMENDED WITH RESERVATIONS
Sassafras Baking and Pizza Stone
$23.95
The small size (12 by 15 inches) and lipped edge on this clay stone landed it at the bottom of our ratings.

TASTING LAB: Black Olives

PRIZED IN PROVENCE FOR THEIR NUTTY, SMOKY FLAVOR, tiny niçoise olives are a staple of the region's cuisine and the traditional olive of choice for topping a pissaladière. These brine-cured olives are generally sold loose or packed in deli containers, and they cost a pretty penny—usually $11 per pound or more (and most of that weight is pit!). On a pizza already packed with the powerful flavors of caramelized onions and anchovies, would other types of readily available black olives make acceptable substitutes? After ruling out canned black "California" olives (which are really green olives colored black with a chemical additive), we gathered eight varieties of jarred and fresh black olives.

Sampled plain, most other black olives, with the exception of kalamatas, made poor substitutes for the niçoise. Buried beneath a layer of onions and anchovies, however, most of the olives were hard to distinguish from the niçoise, although there were two exceptions. Salt-cured black olives (often erroneously labeled "oil-cured" and known for their wrinkled exterior) were far too salty and bitter in combination with the anchovies. The other loser was the oversized cerignola, which was so mild that the pissaladière was left with almost no olive flavor at all.

BEST OLIVES FOR PISSALADIÈRE
Niçoise olives (left) are our first choice for this recipe. They have a smoky, nutty flavor that works well with the onions. Kalamatas (right) are the best substitute. They are fruitier and brinier than niçoise olives.

Q&A

In yeasted breads, can whole-wheat flour be substituted for all-purpose flour or bread flour?

We generally do not recommend a wholesale substitution because the whole wheat will compromise the structure and texture of the original recipe. But a partial substitution is often possible. In general, you can replace one quarter to one third of the white flour with whole-wheat flour. The texture will be slightly heartier but still good. However, if you use more whole-wheat flour, many loaves will be dense and tough.

Q&A

Can I make pizza crust, freeze it, and then add toppings at a later date?

We found that pizza crusts, including pissaladière, can be parbaked and then frozen. Here's what to do. Make and shape the dough as directed. Brush the crust liberally with oil and then bake as directed, just until the crust has set, about 2 to 3 minutes if making our pissaladière. Remove the crust from the oven, cool, wrap in plastic, and freeze for up to two months. When ready to serve, preheat the oven and baking stone and defrost the crust for about one hour. Add the toppings and bake, shaving a couple of minutes off the baking time in the original recipe.

EQUIPMENT CORNER: Pizza Cutters

HOMEMADE PIZZA CAN BE THE MOST REWARDING OF comfort foods, but all too often you end up with uneven, half-cut slices because you don't have a knife big enough to cut through the thick crust and extra cheese. Purchasing a pizza cutter is a natural solution, but our local kitchen store offered more pizza cutter models than Domino's has toppings. A shoddy pizza cutter drags melted cheese and toppings out of place, sprays hot grease, and fails to cut through crispy crust cleanly, leaving you to finish the job by tearing loose a slice by hand. A good pizza cutter gets the job done quickly, cleanly, and safely (and also makes an excellent tool for trimming the edges of rolled-out pastry dough). But with so many different options, how do you know which brand to choose? We decided to line up 10 different models ranging from double-wheeled pizza cutters to straight-edged pizza choppers to see which model would stand supreme.

The basic wheel cutter is the most common variety with dozens of models to choose from, priced from $3 to $25. Pre-testing eliminated the flimsiest models from further consideration, leaving eight sturdy wheels to test on thin- and thick-crust pizzas, evaluating them on price, cutting ability, ease of use, and safety. All of the pizza wheels cut through crisp thin-crust pies without a problem, but thick-crust, deep-dish pizzas overloaded with gooey cheese and toppings quickly thinned the pack. Cutters with large, 4-inch diameter wheels were able to plow through the pies without a problem, while those with smaller wheels were quickly mired in the mess and left us with greasy knuckles. Of the large-wheel cutters, the clear winner was the Oxo Good Grips 4-inch ($10). Testers liked its rubberized, non-slip handle, protective thumb guard, and angled neck, which made cutting easier on the wrist. The large KitchenAid cutter ($15) also performed well and was the only cutter to come with a protective sheath, but it was heavy (almost 1 pound) and testers with smaller hands found it hard to grip the oversized handle, which was made from hard plastic and tended to get slippery.

Instead of a wheel cutter, professional pizzerias often employ a large rocking knife to cut clean through the pie in one stroke without dragging any hot cheese out of place. A few home versions of these knives are available, though usually by mail order. VillaWare's 14-inch Stainless Pizza Chopper ($14) cuts cleanly through crusts both thick and thin, but its size makes it doubly awkward: It's a bit too short to cut through a larger diameter pizza, but still too large for easy storage. LamsonSharp makes a similar size rocker ($25), but its wooden handles are trouble in the dishwasher, and its ultra-sharp edge curves up toward the grips, posing a serious hazard to exposed pinkies. Although these models managed to cleave the pizzas with relative ease, their over-sized, machete-like blades seemed a bit over the top—not only difficult to store but just flat-out dangerous.

As the tests concluded, the superior performance of the pizza wheel means that we can finally have handsome homemade pizza. So save your money (and your fingers) and go with our champion—the Oxo Good Grips.

Rating Pizza Cutters

WE TESTED 10 WIDELY AVAILABLE MODELS AND RAN THEM THROUGH THIN-CRUST AND DEEP-DISH PIZZAS. THE PIZZA CUTTERS were rated for their cutting ability, ease of use, price, and safety and are listed in order of preference. See www.americastestkitchen.com for up-to-date prices and mail-order sources for top-rated products.

RECOMMENDED
Oxo Good Grips 4-inch Pizza Wheel
$10

The large wheel and comfortable handle on this cutter took home the trophy. It plowed through thin-crust and deep-dish pies alike.

RECOMMENDED WITH RESERVATIONS
Farberware Nonstick Pizza Wheel
$6

This model's large wheel rolled over even the deepest-dish pies with ease, but the straight handle made for an uncomfortable arm angle while cutting. The nonstick wheel is a nice touch, but testers thought it was extraneous.

RECOMMENDED WITH RESERVATIONS
VillaWare 14-inch Pizza Chopper
$14

This model was very effective, particularly on personal size pizzas. It lost some points for being heavy, awkward, and dangerous—there is a lot of sharp metal on this model.

RECOMMENDED WITH RESERVATIONS
KitchenAid Pizza Wheel
$15

Both powerful and substantial, this model made quick work of the pizzas, but its hard plastic handle got greasy during testing. Some testers also considered this model too heavy.

NOT RECOMMENDED
Henckels Twin Select Pizza Wheel
$15

With a small wheel, straight grip, and uncomfortable handle, this model seemed to be designed for form not function. The wheel guard made for tough cleanup and was considered unnecessary.

NOT RECOMMENDED
Oxo Good Grips Pizza Wheel
$8

Even though this model's big brother took the blue ribbon, we found the small wheel and slightly canted, small handle to be unsatisfactory. It performed especially poorly with deep-dish pizza.

NOT RECOMMENDED
WMF Double Wheel
$29.99

This model was flashy for sure, but its small wheels and flimsy construction prove that aesthetics aren't everything.

NOT RECOMMENDED
Zyliss Pizza Wheel
$10

The lack of a handle made it very difficult to control, particularly on straight cuts. Cleaning was also a pain.

NOT RECOMMENDED
LamsonSharp Pizza Rocker
$25

Bulky and sharp, and deemed unsafe due to its unprotected, curved blade. The wooden handles are not dishwasher safe.

NOT RECOMMENDED
Stelton Pizza Knife
$48

Possessing a design similar to a pie wedge, this model was the clear loser in the group. Testers blasted this model for its cost (which was by far the highest), its uncomfortable handle, its poor design, and its inexcusably dull serrated cutting edge.

Our eggplant Parmesan uses oven-fried slices of breaded eggplant for a less greasy take on this perennial favorite.

IN AN ITALIAN-

CHAPTER 17

american
kitchen

THE RECIPES

Eggplant Parmesan

Pasta with Chicken and Broccoli

In the test kitchen, we enjoy authentic Italian dishes such as pasta all'amatriciana (chapter 18) and osso buco and polenta (chapter 19). But we also like to prepare Italian-American dishes. These recipes may have their inspiration in Italy, but they are decidedly American in their execution. This is the kind of food you are more likely to encounter at a chain "Italian" restaurant, such as Olive Garden, than at a traditional Italian restaurant run by a Roman, Tuscan, or Sicilian chef.

So what kind of food are we talking about? Eggplant Parmesan, with its layers of breaded eggplant, tomato sauce, and cheese, is a classic example of this exuberant cooking. It's hearty (some might say heavy) and tasty. Pasta with chicken and broccoli in a creamy sauce is another Italian-American creation. This pasta is a one-dish meal, with carbohydrates, protein, and vegetables all in one bowl.

While this food is great when done correctly, more often than not eggplant Parmesan is a soggy, oily mess and pasta with chicken and broccoli is heavy and bland. But after many tests in the kitchen, we feel we've come up with recipes that give these simple, honest dishes the respect they deserve.

EGGPLANT PARMESAN

WHAT WE WANTED: A fresher, lighter take on this classic but often greasy Italian dish. Could we eliminate the frying, streamline the dish, and make it taste better than the original?

The main objection we have to most eggplant Parmesan recipes is their requirement to fry the eggplant in four or five batches. It takes an attentive eye to keep the oil at just the right temperature, making the risk of greasy eggplant great. And even if things go right with the breading, frying, and sauce-making steps, most versions are oily and dense. We decided to reinvent this dish by baking the eggplant rather than frying it.

Most recipes for eggplant Parmesan begin by purging (salting) the eggplant to expel bitter juices and prevent the porous flesh from soaking up excess oil. To double-check this theory, we baked some unsalted eggplant. Oil absorption wasn't a problem, but the eggplant did taste bitter, and it had a raw, mealy texture. Thirty minutes of salting remedied the problem. For efficiency's sake, we chose good-size globe eggplants; we didn't want to multiply the number of slices we'd have to prepare. For the best appearance, taste, and texture, we settled on unpeeled ¼-inch-thick crosswise slices, not lengthwise planks.

In our first effort to sidestep deep-frying, we dispensed with the breading altogether, baking naked, salted eggplant slices on a baking sheet coated with cooking spray. (This method is often employed in low-calorie recipes for eggplant Parmesan.) The resulting eggplant earned negative comments from tasters. We concluded that breading was essential and ticked off a list of possibilities. Flour alone wasn't substantial enough. Eggplant swathed in mayonnaise and then bread crumbs turned slimy. Eggplant coated in a flour and egg batter and then bread crumbs was thick and tough. A standard single breading (dipping the eggplant first in egg, then bread crumbs) was too messy—the egg slid right off the eggplant, leaving the crumbs with nothing to adhere to.

A double, or bound, breading proved superior. Dipping the eggplant first in seasoned flour, then egg, then bread crumbs created a substantial (but not heavy) and crisp coating that brought the mild flavor and tender, creamy texture of the eggplant to the fore. The initial coating of flour in a bound breading creates a dry, smooth base to which the egg can cling. We seasoned the bread crumbs with generous amounts of Parmesan, salt, and pepper.

We'd been using fresh bread crumbs and wondered whether we could get away with using store-bought crumbs. The answer was no. Store-bought crumbs were so fine that they disappeared under the blankets of tomato sauce and cheese.

After considerable experimentation, we found that the best way to achieve a crisp coating is to bake the breaded slices on two preheated baking sheets, each coated with a modest 3 tablespoons of vegetable oil (olive oil tasted sour), rotating the pans and flipping the slices partway through. At 425 degrees, the slices sizzled during cooking and became fully tender in 30 minutes. Using this technique, we turned out crisp, golden brown disks of eggplant, expending a minimum of effort (and using very little oil). And now, seeing that we weren't busy frying up four batches of eggplant in hot oil, we had time to grate cheese and whip up a quick tomato sauce while the eggplant baked.

Eggplant Parmesan couldn't be called such without Parmesan cheese, so that was a given. We'd already used some for breading the eggplant, and a little extra browned nicely on top of the casserole. Mozzarella is another standard addition. A modest amount (8 ounces) kept the casserole from becoming stringy.

A few cloves of minced garlic, a sprinkling of red pepper flakes, and some olive oil started off a quick tomato sauce, followed by three cans of diced tomatoes, with just

two of them pureed in the food processor to preserve a chunky texture. A handful of fresh basil leaves (we reserved some basil for garnish, too) plus salt and pepper were the final flourishes.

Because breading softens beneath smothering layers of sauce and cheese, we left most of the top layer of eggplant exposed. This left us with about one cup of extra sauce, just enough to pass at the table. Another benefit of this technique was that without excess moisture, the casserole was easy to cut into tidy pieces. With the eggplant fully cooked, the dish needed only a brief stay in a hot oven to melt the cheese.

In the end, we had drastically reduced the amount of oil and attention required to make this dish, and we had done it without compromising flavor.

WHAT WE LEARNED: Salt the eggplant to remove some bitterness and improve its texture. The best coating is a double breading of flour, eggs, and fresh bread crumbs. Baking the breaded eggplant on a preheated, oiled baking sheet yields crisp, golden brown disks. Finally, leaving the top layer of eggplant unsauced keeps it crisp in the oven.

EGGPLANT PARMESAN

Serves 6 to 8

Use kosher salt when salting the eggplant. The coarse grains don't dissolve as readily as the fine grains of regular table salt, so any excess can be easily wiped away. It's necessary to divide the eggplant into two batches when tossing it with the salt. To be time-efficient, use the 30 to 45 minutes during which the salted eggplant sits to prepare the breading.

eggplant

- 2 pounds globe eggplant (2 medium eggplants), cut crosswise into ¼-inch-thick rounds
- 1 tablespoon kosher salt
- 8 slices high-quality white sandwich bread (about 8 ounces), torn into quarters
- 2 ounces Parmesan cheese, grated (about 1 cup)
  Salt and ground black pepper
- 1 cup all-purpose flour
- 4 large eggs
- 6 tablespoons vegetable oil

tomato sauce

- 3 (14.5-ounce) cans diced tomatoes
- 2 tablespoons extra-virgin olive oil
- 4 medium garlic cloves, minced or pressed through a garlic press (about 1 generous tablespoon)
- ¼ teaspoon red pepper flakes
- ½ cup coarsely chopped fresh basil leaves
  Salt and ground black pepper

- 8 ounces whole-milk or part-skim mozzarella, shredded (about 2 cups)
- 1 ounce Parmesan cheese, grated (about ½ cup)
- 10 fresh basil leaves, torn, for garnish

1. FOR THE EGGPLANT: Toss half of the eggplant slices and 1½ teaspoons of the kosher salt in a large bowl until combined; transfer the salted eggplant to a large colander set over a bowl. Repeat with the remaining eggplant and kosher salt, placing the second batch on top of the first. Let stand until the eggplant releases about 2 tablespoons liquid, 30 to 45 minutes. Spread the eggplant slices on a triple thickness of paper towels; cover with another triple thickness of paper towels. Press firmly on each slice to remove as much liquid as possible, then wipe off the excess salt.

2. While the eggplant is draining, adjust the oven racks to the upper- and lower-middle positions, place a rimmed baking sheet on each rack, and heat the oven to 425 degrees. Pulse the bread in a food processor to fine, even crumbs, about fifteen 1-second pulses (you should have about 4 cups). Transfer the crumbs to a pie plate and stir in the Parmesan, ¼ teaspoon salt, and ½ teaspoon pepper; set aside. Wipe out the workbowl (do not wash) and set aside.

3. Combine the flour and 1 teaspoon pepper in a large zipper-lock bag; shake to combine. Beat the eggs in a second pie plate. Place 8 to 10 eggplant slices in the bag with the flour; seal the bag and shake to coat the slices. Remove the slices, shaking off the excess flour, dip into the eggs, let the excess egg run off, then coat evenly with the bread crumb mixture; set the breaded slices on a wire rack set over a baking sheet. Repeat with the remaining eggplant.

4. Remove the preheated baking sheets from the oven; add 3 tablespoons oil to each sheet, tilting to coat evenly with the oil. Place half of the breaded eggplant slices on each sheet in a single layer; bake until the eggplant is well browned and crisp, about 30 minutes, switching and rotating the baking sheets after 10 minutes, and flipping the eggplant slices with a wide spatula after 20 minutes. Do not turn off the oven.

GETTING IT RIGHT: The Crumbs

We prepared eggplant in nearly a dozen ways. Here are some failed samples, with tasters' harsh comments.

Baked Naked
"Nasty"

Flour Alone
"Insubstantial"

Mayo & Crumbs
"Slimy"

Batter & Crumbs
"Thick and tough"

Eggs & Crumbs
"Too messy"

A WINNING COMBINATION

Flour, Eggs, & Crumbs
Dipping the eggplant into flour, then egg, then bread crumbs created a substantial (but not heavy) and crisp coating.

5. FOR THE SAUCE: While the eggplant bakes, process 2 cans of the diced tomatoes in the food processor until almost smooth, about 5 seconds. Heat the olive oil, garlic, and red pepper flakes in a large heavy-bottomed saucepan over medium-high heat, stirring occasionally, until fragrant and the garlic is light golden, about 3 minutes; stir in the processed and remaining can of diced tomatoes. Bring the sauce to a boil, then reduce the heat to medium-low and simmer, stirring occasionally, until slightly thickened and reduced, about 15 minutes (you should have about 4 cups). Stir in the basil and season with salt and pepper to taste.

6. TO ASSEMBLE: Spread 1 cup of the tomato sauce in the bottom of a 13 by 9-inch baking dish. Layer in half of the eggplant slices, overlapping the slices to fit; distribute 1 more cup of the sauce over the eggplant; sprinkle with half of the mozzarella. Layer in the remaining eggplant and dot with 1 more cup of the sauce, leaving the majority of eggplant exposed so it will remain crisp; sprinkle with the Parmesan and the remaining mozzarella. Bake until bubbling and the cheese is browned, 13 to 15 minutes. Cool 10 minutes, scatter the basil over the top, and serve, passing the remaining tomato sauce separately.

Q&A

When is it appropriate to use kosher versus table salt?

Kosher salt is used in the koshering process, which involves blanketing raw meat or poultry with salt to purify it. The salt crystals must be coarse and irregular, so that they will cling to the surface of the meat during koshering.

At home, some cooks prefer kosher salt for its clean flavor, as it lacks iodine and other additives found in table salt. However, in our taste tests we've found these flavor differences are very subtle and hard to detect.

More significant is the difference in texture. Table salt is quite fine, while kosher salt is coarse. When sprinkled over meat or vegetables at the table, kosher salt adds a pleasing crunch. The large crystals make it easier to pick up kosher salt with your fingers and sprinkle some over foods as they cook. For this reason, many cooks keep a ramekin of kosher salt near the stovetop. We also use kosher salt to draw moisture out of vegetables such as eggplant and zucchini. It's easier to wipe away large crystals of excess kosher salt once the vegetables have shed moisture. Table salt tends to dissolve when used this way.

Kosher salt may not dissolve when used in baked goods, so fine table salt is usually preferred.

Because of its fluffy texture, a teaspoon of kosher salt contains less salt than a teaspoon of table salt. A single teaspoon of table salt is roughly equivalent to two teaspoons of Diamond Crystal Kosher Salt or 1½ teaspoons of Morton Coarse Kosher Salt.

PASTA WITH CHICKEN AND BROCCOLI

WHAT WE WANTED: This Italian-American favorite makes a complete meal but is often bland and heavy. Could we take this appealing concept and turn it into a light yet flavorful one-dish meal with tender chicken, crisp broccoli, and toothsome pasta?

Italian chain restaurants known for cheap wine and doughy breadsticks almost always list pasta with chicken and broccoli on the menu. Unfortunately, the broccoli is mushy and drab, the pasta has no bite, and the chicken tastes tough and generic. The whole mess is drowned in a fatty cream sauce whose only flavor is garlic. Our goal was obvious: We wanted to reclaim this dish with fresh, crisp broccoli, tender chicken, and a flavorful sauce. We also wanted a recipe that was easy and healthy enough to appear as a regular on the supper table at home.

A quick sampling of existing recipes turned up the obvious issues of overcooking and blandness as well as a few others. Many recipes called for very small amounts of chicken and broccoli, treating them more as garnishes to the pasta rather than as major elements of the dish. Most of the recipes also required far too many pots and pans for a simple, midweek meal. Lastly, a few casseroles cropped up, but they took a long time to put together and didn't solve any of the overcooking problems. In order to figure this dish out, we needed to tear it apart into its four components—chicken, sauce, broccoli, and pasta—and tackle each individually.

Right off the bat, we decided that boneless, skinless chicken breasts were the best choice for this recipe and tested various cooking methods, including broiling, sautéing, microwaving, and poaching (simmering in a liquid). Microwaving produced bland chicken, and the timing was tricky—one minute too long and the chicken was completely dry. Broiling and sautéing produced meat with the most flavor; however, the nicely seared edges of the chicken seemed tough and stringy after being tossed with the pasta

and sauce. Poaching the chicken, either in the pasta water or simmering sauce, produced meat that was tender and juicy; however, the flavor was badly washed out.

Wanting the flavor of the sautéed chicken yet the tenderness of the poached chicken, we wondered if we could combine the two methods. First we lightly cooked the chicken with a little butter in a skillet until it just began to turn golden, then we removed it from the pan while still partly raw. Building a sauce using the residual drippings left in the skillet, we then returned the chicken to the sauce and let it simmer until fully cooked. Bingo—the chicken was perfectly cooked, tender, and flavorful. Throughout all this testing, we realized that cutting the chicken into bite-size pieces before cooking was best because it eliminated the last-minute rush of having to slice or shred it into fork-friendly pieces. We also noted that a nonstick skillet made cleanup a breeze, and that 1 pound of chicken and half a pound of pasta was an ample amount for four people for dinner.

With the chicken cooked properly, it was time to focus on the broccoli. We tried multiple ways to cook the florets, including simmering them in the sauce, steaming, blanching (a quick dunk in boiling water), and microwaving. Simmering them in the sauce was a disaster—the broccoli gave the sauce both an off flavor and a dirty color. Steaming on the stovetop and in the microwave both worked OK, but neither was as easy as blanching, especially since there was already a pot of boiling water going for the pasta. Cooking the broccoli florets in the pasta water first, we simply scooped them from the water using a slotted spoon, then returned the water to a boil before adding the pasta.

We ran into the problem of broccoli with an army green color and slightly mushy texture when we simply let the florets sit in a bowl after being blanched—they continued to steam as they sat in a big pile. Dunking them in a bowl of ice water prevented this, but then we had a hard time warming them up again before tossing them with the

pasta and sauce (they always remained a bit chilled). Finally, we tried spreading the blanched florets out over a large plate as the pasta cooked. This allowed them to cool off enough so as not to turn an ugly color, yet they were easily warmed through by the hot pasta and sauce. The key, then, was to slightly undercook the florets in the boiling water and let them continue to cook a little as they waited for everything to be done.

Finally, we turned our attention to the sauce. Using a classic base of cream thickened with a roux (a flour and butter combination), we determined that garlic, pepper flakes, fresh herbs, and white wine were all critical components. Tasters were still unimpressed, commenting that the sauce tasted lifeless. We then tried omitting the roux and simply letting the cream simmer and thicken on its own, but this produced a very fatty sauce. Using milk or half-and-half instead of cream didn't work either—the sauces tasted watery and dull.

Having exhausted all our cream sauce options, we wondered how tasters would react to a broth-based sauce that was finished with butter. We simmered store-bought chicken broth with the aromatics before whisking in some butter and were relieved to see the tasters nod their heads with approval. The flavor of the aromatics now jumped out, and there was a significant boost in chicken flavor. The sauce still needed a final kick of flavor, and tasters cheered over the addition of sun-dried tomatoes along with a handful of Asiago cheese. The sauce now had serious flavor and when it was tossed with the perfectly cooked broccoli and tender chicken, we had a dish that is worth staying home for.

WHAT WE LEARNED: Partially cook the chicken in a hot pan with butter, build a quick broth-based sauce from the drippings, and then finish the sauce with a bit more butter and the chicken. The broccoli should be blanched in the pasta pot and then removed so the pasta can be cooked.

PASTA WITH CHICKEN AND BROCCOLI

Serves 4

Use low-sodium chicken broth in this recipe; regular chicken broth will make the dish unpalatably salty. The broccoli is ready to be removed from the boiling water when it's tender at the edges but still crisp at the core; it will continue to cook with residual heat.

4 tablespoons (½ stick) unsalted butter
1 pound boneless, skinless chicken breasts, trimmed of excess fat and prepared according to the illustrations on page 230
   Salt and ground black pepper
1 small onion, chopped fine (about ⅔ cup)
6 medium garlic cloves, minced or pressed through a garlic press (about 2 tablespoons)
¼ teaspoon red pepper flakes
1 tablespoon chopped fresh thyme leaves
2 teaspoons unbleached all-purpose flour
1 cup dry white wine
2 cups low-sodium chicken broth
1 large bunch broccoli (about 1½ pounds), florets cut into 1-inch pieces, stems discarded
½ pound penne, ziti, campanelli, or cavatappi
2 ounces Asiago cheese, grated fine (about 1 cup), plus extra for serving
2 tablespoons minced fresh parsley leaves or chives
1 (8½-ounce) jar oil-packed sun-dried tomatoes, drained, rinsed, patted dry, and sliced into ¼-inch strips (about 1 cup)
1 lemon, cut into wedges (optional)

1. Bring 4 quarts of water to a rolling boil in a stockpot.

2. Meanwhile, melt 1 tablespoon of the butter in a 12-inch nonstick skillet over high heat until just beginning to brown, about 1 minute. Add the chicken in a single layer and sprinkle with salt and pepper to taste. Cook for 1 minute without stirring, then stir the chicken and continue to cook until most, but not all, of the pink color has disappeared and the chicken is lightly browned around the edges, about 2 minutes longer. Transfer the chicken to a clean bowl; set aside.

3. Return the skillet to high heat and melt 1 more tablespoon of the butter. Add the onion and ¼ teaspoon salt and cook, stirring occasionally, until browned around the edges, 2 to 3 minutes. Stir in the garlic, red pepper flakes, thyme, and flour; cook, stirring constantly, until fragrant, about 30 seconds. Add the wine and chicken broth. Bring to a simmer, then reduce the heat to medium and continue to simmer, stirring occasionally, until the sauce has thickened slightly and is reduced to 1¼ cups, about 15 minutes.

4. While the sauce simmers, add 1 tablespoon salt and the broccoli florets to the boiling water. Cook until the broccoli is bright green and tender but still crisp at the center, about 2 minutes. Using a slotted spoon, transfer the broccoli to a large paper towel–lined plate and set aside. Return the water to a boil, stir in the pasta, and cook until al dente. Drain, reserving ½ cup pasta cooking water, and return the pasta to the stockpot.

5. A minute or so before draining the pasta, stir the remaining 2 tablespoons butter, the Asiago, parsley, sun-dried tomatoes, and chicken into the sauce in the skillet. Cook until the chicken is hot and cooked through, about 1 minute. Off the heat, season the sauce with pepper to taste. Pour the chicken-and-sauce mixture over the pasta and add the broccoli. Toss gently to combine, adding the reserved pasta cooking water as needed to adjust the sauce consistency. Serve immediately, passing additional Asiago and the lemon wedges (if using) separately.

TECHNIQUE:
Preparing the Chicken

1. Separate the tenderloin from the breast. Starting at the thick end, cut into ¼-inch slices. Stop slicing when you reach the tapered triangle end.

2. With the flat side of the knife, press each slice to an even ¼ inch thickness and then cut the slices into 1-inch squares.

3. Use the same technique for the tenderloin, flattening it with the side of the knife and then cutting it into 1-inch pieces.

Sautéing mushrooms in a skillet and folding them into the rice at the last minute is the key to great mushroom risotto.

ITALIAN classics

There seems to be an endless supply of "classic" Italian dishes. Just when we think we've mastered the canon, we realize there are more seminal Italian dishes to learn—recipes as important as pesto, steak fiorentina, or pasta with garlic and oil. The depth of classic recipes is testament to the genius of the Italian cook. There are dozens of core recipes, known by almost every Italian cook, and almost all of these recipes are appropriate and appealing for American cooks.

Risotto is a basic Italian recipe, and with mushrooms this dish becomes hearty enough to serve as a main course. Besides cooking the rice right, the key challenge here is getting intense mushroom flavor. Spending a fortune on fancy mushrooms is one route. Instead, we wanted to coax great flavor from everyday mushrooms.

Pasta all'amatriciana is perhaps Rome's most famous dish. Despite the fancy name, it's nothing more than long-strand pasta sauced with tomatoes, onion, bacon, and hot pepper flakes and dusted with cheese. This simple dish is about the details, and we knew they could be mastered.

MUSHROOM RISOTTO

WHAT WE WANTED: To make risotto with potent mushroom flavor without turning to pricey foraged fungi.

A favorite main-course risotto dish of ours is one packed with earthy robust flavor courtesy of myriad wild mushrooms—the puffball, hen-of-the-woods, trompette de la mort. These are mushrooms with fanciful names to match their exotic flavor. The trouble is, these exotically flavored wild mushrooms are both elusive and expensive. We wondered if we could approximate (even surpass) that paragon of risottos with supermarket mushrooms and a bit of test-kitchen determination.

Simply put, risotto is medium-grain, Italian-grown rice cooked in such a manner that some of the grains' starch renders into a creamy sauce, the mechanics of which we have previously tested. Our technique eschews what most recipes consider sacrosanct: feverish stirring and small, frequent additions of broth. We found that half the liquid can be added at the beginning and the rice stirred infrequently until the liquid is absorbed (about halfway through the cooking process). At that point, we return to standard protocol and add the remaining broth in modest amounts and stir often until the rice is both creamy and al dente. While our method doesn't expedite matters, it does allow some freedom from the tedium of constant attention. With our tested method in hand, then, we could focus our attention on flavor.

Most of the mushroom risotto recipes we found were divided into two camps: authentic recipes using wild mushrooms and workaday ones using cultivated mushrooms. But there was a small third group of recipes that relied largely on dried porcini mushrooms for flavor. Sold by the ounce and packing a punch, dried porcini are both robustly flavored and aromatic—just the thing for that earthy edge we craved. We prepared several of these recipes to mixed reviews. Tasters appreciated the porcini flavor but missed the firm texture and visual presence of fresh mushrooms. Some combination

of the two, then, looked to be the best tack to take.

We knew that corralling the bullish flavor of the porcini was our first order of business. Using our basic Parmesan risotto as a baseline (flavored with onion, garlic, white wine, chicken broth, and Parmesan cheese), we made batches laced with dried porcini, each varying in content by ¼ ounce. We prepared the mushrooms according to standard procedure: reconstituted in hot water and chopped fine (if left large, they're rubbery). We also added the porcini-infused soaking liquid to the chicken broth, after straining it to filter out any debris. A scant ¼ ounce lent little flavor, as did ½ ounce. But 1 ounce suffused the rice with a forceful flavor and aroma.

As far as fresh mushrooms go, experience has taught us that they are at their best when cooked in the dry, intense heat of a smoking skillet or a fiery oven. Moist cooking, such as simmering in risotto, renders them rubbery and bland. A preliminary test of roasted mushrooms versus sautéed showed little difference, so we opted for the skillet to keep things on the stovetop. We sautéed the three most common supermarket mushrooms—the standard button, the brown-capped, meaty cremini, and the cremini's larger though similarly flavored sibling, the portobello—and added them to separate batches of the porcini-flavored risotto.

Tasters found the button mushrooms mild and better appreciated the fuller flavor and meatier texture of the cremini and portobellos. Cremini were easier to prepare than portobellos, as the latter's feathery gills must be trimmed before cooking lest they stain the risotto inky black. Over medium-high heat and lightly sprinkled with salt, the mushrooms first shed their liquid, then browned deeply. To preserve their texture and flavor, we didn't add the mushrooms to the risotto until the rice was fully cooked.

The hot skillet and a knob of butter (which tasters preferred to olive oil) did wonders for the mushrooms' flavor, but we wanted more. With onions prepped for the rice, we purloined a portion to sauté with the mushrooms.

This step proved successful, as the onions lent both sweetness and piquancy. On a roll, we added a couple of cloves of minced garlic and scored again: These mushrooms were good enough to eat on their own.

The risotto's flavor was emphatically mushroomy but one-dimensional and in need of refinement. We added ½ cup more wine to bring some much-needed acidity to the fore. As for herbs, thyme pairs well with mushrooms, so we added a minced teaspoon and then, heeding tasters' demands, minced parsley as well. We kept the Parmesan cheese to 1 cup.

Even with these changes, though, the risotto still fell short of our expectations, being milder and less dynamic than we wanted. We wondered if we were missing obvious flavor enhancements, hemmed in by the confines of Italian cooking. Throwing tradition out the window, we turned to a cuisine known for its deft touch with mushrooms: Chinese. A quick thumbing through several Chinese cookbooks inspired us to try replacing the chicken broth with mushroom broth. We combined the dried porcini with bundled herbs and chicken broth cut with water and simmered the mixture until the mushrooms were tender, about 15 minutes (time enough to prepare the other ingredients). We then strained the fungi from the broth and finely minced them before returning them to the rice. The results were promising: The risotto was much fuller-flavored than before and we had cut preparation time.

Borrowing again from the Chinese palette, we added soy sauce to the broth. Sweet, salty, and earthy, soy sauce has a galvanizing effect on the flavor of mushrooms that we sensed might pay off in the risotto. The scantest splash rounded out the broth's flavor and gave it indescribable depth. Tasters couldn't detect the soy sauce in the finished risotto, but everyone commented on the dish's fuller, earthier flavor.

WHAT WE LEARNED: Combine dried porcini with fresh cremini mushrooms for an inexpensive but potent flavor base. Brown the mushrooms in a separate skillet and then fold them into the finished risotto to maintain their texture. Add soy sauce for meaty intensity.

MUSHROOM RISOTTO

Serves 6 as a main course, 8 as a first course

Cremini mushrooms are sometimes sold as baby bella mushrooms. If they're not available, button mushrooms make a fine though somewhat less flavorful substitute. Toward the end of cooking, judge the doneness of the rice by tasting it.

- 2 bay leaves
- 6 sprigs fresh thyme
- 4 sprigs fresh parsley, plus 2 tablespoons minced parsley leaves
- 1 ounce dried porcini mushrooms, rinsed in a mesh strainer under running water
- 3½ cups low-sodium chicken broth
- 2 teaspoons soy sauce
- 6 tablespoons (¾ stick) unsalted butter
- 1¼ pounds cremini mushrooms, wiped clean with a paper towel, stems discarded, and caps cut into fourths if small or sixths if medium or large
- 2 medium onions, chopped fine (about 2 cups)
  Salt
- 3 medium garlic cloves, minced or pressed through a garlic press (about 1 tablespoon)
- 1 pound (2⅛ cups) Arborio rice

GETTING IT RIGHT:
An Unusual Broth for Risotto

Soy Sauce   Dried Porcini

Our search for a better cooking medium for the rice led us to an unusual culinary pairing: soy sauce and dried porcini mushrooms.

1 cup dry white wine or dry vermouth
2 ounces Parmesan cheese, grated fine
(about 1 cup)
Ground black pepper

1. Tie the bay leaves, thyme sprigs, and parsley sprigs together with kitchen twine. Bring the bundled herbs, porcini mushrooms, broth, soy sauce, and 3½ cups water to a boil in a medium saucepan over medium-high heat; reduce the heat to medium-low and simmer until the dried mushrooms are softened and fully hydrated, about 15 minutes. Remove and discard the herb bundle and strain the broth through a fine-mesh strainer set over a medium bowl (you should have about 6½ cups strained liquid); return the liquid to the saucepan and keep warm over low heat. Finely mince the porcini and set aside.

2. Adjust an oven rack to the middle position and heat the oven to 200 degrees. Heat 2 tablespoons of the butter in a 12-inch nonstick skillet over medium-high heat. When the foaming subsides, add the cremini mushrooms, 1 cup of the onions, and ½ teaspoon salt; cook, stirring occasionally, until the moisture released by the mushrooms evaporates and the mushrooms are well browned, about 7 minutes. Stir

in the garlic until fragrant, about 1 minute, then transfer the mushrooms to an oven-safe bowl and keep warm in the oven. Off the heat, add ¼ cup water to the now-empty skillet and scrape with a wooden spoon to loosen any browned bits on the pan bottom; pour the liquid from the skillet into the saucepan with the broth.

3. Heat 3 more tablespoons of the butter in a large saucepan over medium heat. When the foaming subsides, add the remaining 1 cup onions and ¼ teaspoon salt; cook, stirring occasionally, until the onions are softened and translucent, about 9 minutes. Add the rice and cook, stirring frequently, until the edges of the grains are transparent, about 4 minutes. Add the wine and cook, stirring frequently, until the rice absorbs the wine. Add the minced porcini and 3½ cups of the broth and cook, stirring every 2 to 3 minutes, until the liquid is absorbed, 9 to 11 minutes. Stir in an additional ½ cup broth every 2 to 3 minutes until the rice is cooked through but the grains are still somewhat firm at the center, 10 to 12 minutes (the rice may not require all of the broth). Stir in the remaining 1 tablespoon butter, then stir in the mushrooms (and any accumulated juices), the cheese, and reserved chopped parsley. Season with salt and pepper to taste; serve immediately in warmed bowls.

MUSHROOM RISOTTO WITH PANCETTA AND SAGE

Follow the recipe for Mushroom Risotto through step 2, omitting the thyme from the broth. Cook 2 ounces finely chopped pancetta and 1 tablespoon butter in a large sauce-pan over medium heat, stirring frequently, until the pancetta has rendered some fat, about 5 minutes. Add the remaining 1 cup onions, cooking the onions until softened and trans-lucent, about 7 minutes; continue with the recipe, adding and cooking the rice as in step 3 and adding 1 tablespoon minced fresh sage leaves along with the chopped parsley.

TASTING LAB: Rice for Risotto

VARIETIES OF RICE ARE ROUGHLY GROUPED AS LONG grain, medium grain, or short grain according to their cooked length and width. Long-grain rice is about four times as long as it is wide, medium grain is twice as long, and short grain is almost round. The manner in which they cook is largely defined by the ratio of two starches that (in part) constitute rice: amylose and amylopectin. The former does not break down (gelatinize) when heated; the latter does. Rice with a high percentage of amylose, then, is long, firm, and discrete when cooked; rice with a lower percentage (and thus more amylopectin) is shorter and starchy, or "sticky." For comparison's sake, long-grain rice contains between 23 and 26 percent amylose, and medium-grain rice contains between 18 and 26 percent amylose. Italian Arborio rice, the classic choice for risotto, contains roughly 19 to 21 percent amylose.

But say a hankering for risotto hits and you can't find Italian rice. Will any other type of rice do? We made Parmesan risotto with four types of rice: standard long grain, converted par-cooked long grain, regular medium grain (we chose Goya brand from the supermarket), and short grain (sushi-style rice). The two long-grained varieties bombed, turning mushy and lacking the creaminess essential to risotto. The par-boiled rice—Uncle Ben's, in this case—also had the jarring, unmistakable flavor of pre-cooked rice. Medium- and short-grain rice fared much better, earning passing grades from most tasters, who agreed that these batches possessed all the creaminess of risotto made with Arborio, though not its al dente bite.

That desirable "bite" is due to a defect in Arborio and other Italian-grown superfino-grade rices called chalk. During maturation, the starch structures at the grain's core deform, making for a firm, toothy center when cooked. An aberration in other varieties of rice, chalk is a sought-after attribute in Italian medium-grain rices, a category that includes Arborio as well as Carnaroli and Vialone Nano.

So the long and short of it? If you're in a pinch and can't find Arborio, look for medium- or short-grain rice for an acceptable—but not perfect—batch of risotto.

LONG-GRAIN RICE
Discrete, firm grains and no creaminess.
Good for pilaf; bad for risotto.

MEDIUM-GRAIN RICE
Creamy sauce, but rice is a bit soft.
Acceptable for risotto in a pinch.

SHORT-GRAIN RICE
Very creamy, but rice is a bit mushy.
Acceptable for risotto in a pinch.

PASTA ALL'AMATRICIANA

WHAT WE WANTED: An easy version of this Roman pasta dish with tomatoes, bacon, and onion.

Pasta all'amatriciana is arguably Rome's most famous dish. This lusty pasta dish starts with bucatini, an extralong tube pasta that looks like a drinking straw. The sauce contains tomato, bacon, onion, dried chile, and pecorino cheese. Like most Roman cooking, this dish is bold and brash.

What makes Amatriciana so popular? First, most cooks have all the ingredients on hand. Second, the sauce can be made in the time it takes to boil the water and cook the pasta. Third, although the recipe is simple, the flavors are complex and perfectly balanced—acidity from the tomatoes, sweetness from the sautéed onions, heat from the dried chile, meatiness and salt from the bacon, and tangy dairy from the cheese. Our goals in developing our version were to stay faithful to the traditional recipes but to use ingredients available to Americans. The biggest challenge was the bacon. Romans use guanciale, which is bacon made from pork jowls. In the rest of Italy, pancetta (bacon made from pork belly) is used.

We tested pancetta, American bacon, Canadian bacon, Irish bacon (the latter two are cured pork loin), and salt pork (unsmoked pork belly). Tasters preferred the pancetta, which was the meatiest. The pure pork and salt flavors of the pancetta worked best with the sauce.

All three bacons were good, but most tasters felt that the smoke flavor and sweetness were distracting. The Canadian bacon and the Irish bacon (also called Irish back bacon) were meatier than the American bacon, although both were deemed a bit "ham-like." Regular American bacon was excessively fatty. If using it, you will need to drain off the rendered fat (up to ⅓ cup), an unnecessary step when using pancetta, Canadian bacon, or Irish bacon.

The only product we don't recommend is the salt pork. Although it comes from the belly and is not smoked, it is much too fatty to use in a pasta sauce.

Whatever kind of bacon you use, make sure it is sliced thick. When we used thinly sliced pancetta or regular American bacon, the meat nearly disappeared in the sauce.

About half of the recipes we consulted called for sautéing the bacon and onion together, then building the tomato sauce on top of them. In the remaining recipes, the bacon was fried until crisp and removed from the pan, and then the onion was cooked in the bacon fat. Once the onion softened, it was time to make the tomato sauce. The crisped bacon was added back just before tossing the sauce with the pasta.

When we simmered the bacon with the tomatoes, the bacon was leathery and lacking in flavor. We much preferred bacon that was fried and then removed from the pan. It was crisp, flavorful, and chewy when tossed with the pasta.

The next issue was the tomato. Crushed tomatoes made the worst sauce—the tomato flavor was weak, and the consistency of the sauce was too thin. We missed the chunks of tomato, which give this sauce some character. Fresh tomatoes were good, but tasters liked canned diced tomatoes even better. They were a tad juicier, and the preparation was certainly easier—no peeling, seeding, or chopping.

We tried simmering a small dried red chile in the sauce as an alternative to hot red pepper flakes. The red pepper flakes won out, as they provide a more consistent heat level and are more likely to be on hand.

Some Amatriciana recipes call for Parmesan cheese, although pecorino is traditional. We found the taste of Parmesan too subtle to stand up to the chile's heat. Sharp, robust pecorino works better.

WHAT WE LEARNED: The pork flavor of thickly sliced pancetta (unsmoked Italian bacon) is the best choice for this recipe. Once the pancetta is crisp, remove it from the pan and build the sauce in the remaining fat. Toss the crisp pancetta with the tomato sauce and pasta.

PASTA WITH TOMATO, BACON, AND ONION (PASTA ALL'AMATRICIANA)

Serves 4

This dish is traditionally made with bucatini, also called perciatelli, which appear to be thick, round strands but are actually thin, extralong tubes. Linguine works fine, too. When buying pancetta, ask the butcher to slice it ¼ inch thick; if using bacon, buy slab bacon and cut it into ¼-inch-thick slices yourself. If the pancetta that you're using is very lean, it's unlikely that you will need to drain off any fat before adding the onion. Use 1½ small (14½-ounce) cans of diced tomatoes, or dice a single large (28-ounce) can of whole tomatoes packed in juice.

2	tablespoons extra-virgin olive oil
6	ounces ¼-inch-thick sliced pancetta or bacon, cut into strips about 1 inch long and ¼ inch wide
1	medium onion, chopped fine
½	teaspoon red pepper flakes, or to taste
2½	cups canned diced tomatoes
	Salt
1	pound bucatini, perciatelli, or linguine
⅓	cup grated pecorino cheese

1. Bring 4 quarts of water to a rolling boil in a stockpot.

2. Meanwhile, heat the oil in a large skillet over medium heat until shimmering but not smoking. Add the pancetta and cook, stirring occasionally, until lightly browned and crisp, about 8 minutes. Transfer the pancetta with a slotted spoon to a paper towel–lined plate; set aside. If necessary, drain all but 2 tablespoons of fat from the skillet. Add the onion to the skillet; sauté over medium heat until softened, about 5 minutes. Add the pepper flakes and cook to release their flavor, about 30 seconds. Stir in the tomatoes and salt to taste; simmer until slightly thickened, about 10 minutes.

3. While the sauce is simmering, add 1 tablespoon salt and the pasta to the boiling water. Stir to separate and cook until the pasta is al dente; drain and return the pasta to the stockpot.

4. Add the pancetta to the tomato sauce and adjust the seasonings with salt. Add the sauce to the pot with the pasta and toss over low heat to combine, about 30 seconds. Add the pecorino and toss again; serve immediately.

TASTING LAB: Jarred Pasta Sauces

JARRED PASTA SAUCES CONSTITUTE A BOOMING $1.4 billion market. They are certainly popular, but are they any good? In a past tasting, held back in 1999, we were not very impressed. Even the winner of that tasting, Barilla, didn't exactly sweep tasters off their feet. It won for being the freshest tasting of a not-very-fresh-tasting lot. Fast forward five years and we wanted to find out if any of the new players could do better.

Because there are just too many nationally available brands to include in a blind tasting, we narrowed the lineup to the following: the winner of the last jarred pasta sauce tasting (Barilla), the nation's three top-selling brands (Prego, Classico, and Ragú, respectively), and five of the most widely available newcomers since the 1999 tasting. All of the sauces were either marinaras or the brand's most basic tomato and herb–style sauce.

From our perspective, the challenge of making a good-tasting jarred pasta sauce is to preserve a fresh tomato flavor. In the 1999 tasting, we learned that the pervasive lack of freshness among jarred sauces can be credited to the common practice of using tomato paste, reconstituted with water, as the primary tomato ingredient instead of a fresher product, such as canned diced tomatoes. Made from tomatoes that are cooked for several hours until reduced to a thick, spreadable consistency, tomato paste is a highly concentrated product. In the test kitchen, we typically buy tomato paste in toothpaste-sized tubes because it's the kind of ingredient we use just a tablespoon or two at a time, typically to add depth of flavor or body to a sauce or stew.

Why do most jarred pasta sauce manufacturers prefer to use tomato paste—and in relatively large quantities? Robert Graf, president of the California League of Food Processors, helped to clear this up. (He ought to know; California grows 11 million tons of tomatoes in a typical year, supplying 35 percent of the world's processed tomatoes.) His explanation was simple enough: Most jarred pasta sauces are manufactured east of the Rockies, and fresher-tasting products, such as diced or crushed tomatoes, contain a lot of water. "Water," he said, "is very expensive to ship." It is therefore much cheaper to ship tomato paste and reconstitute the paste with water at the manufacturing plant as a first step in making the jarred sauce.

The good news is that some manufacturers, such as Patsy's, Bertolli, and Barilla, do use fresher tomato products. Each of them uses some fresher form of canned tomatoes, such as diced or freshly pureed, as their main tomato ingredient (although some tomato paste may be used as a secondary ingredient). This difference delivered not only winning flavor but a pleasant chunky consistency instead of the smooth, ketchup-like texture of most other sauces.

To get a better handle on the differences between a "tomato paste" sauce and one made with less processed tomatoes, we ran a small experiment in the test kitchen. We took a portion of each sauce and rinsed it with water in a fine-meshed sieve until all of the soluble ingredients were rinsed away. A reputable portion of tomato chunks remained in the sieves with the favored sauces (see photo at near right). But the tomato paste sauces displayed only meager bits of tomato flesh (see photo at far right). With one sauce, we could see little besides flecks of herbs, tomato skin, and dehydrated onion.

Another key to a good jarred pasta sauce turned out to be balanced flavor. Many sauces couldn't get it right, over-dosing on the dried herbs or loading up on sweetener (sugar or corn syrup) and salt. When comparing the amount of sodium and sugar in the sauces, it was readily apparent that the top three contained only moderate amounts of both. Colavita was the perfect example of a potentially good sauce that missed its mark by way of unbalanced flavor. It was the

only other sauce in the tasting that wasn't made primarily of tomato paste—containing whole and crushed canned tomatoes—but it also contained absolutely no added salt or sugar. Tasters felt that it tasted incomplete, more like canned tomatoes than pasta sauce.

There has not, then, been a revolution underway in the making of jarred sauces. What has happened is that the options for a half-decent jarred sauce have broadened, albeit slightly. Given this finding, we continue to plead the case—as we did in 1999—that a quick homemade marinara remains a far better option.

Finally, we wondered if kids would agree with the assessment made by the adults in our tasting panel. To find out, we brought in a group of 19 fifth and sixth graders from the Atrium School in Watertown, Mass., who were happy to take the job seriously. Their favorite, as predicted, was the sauce with nearly twice as much sugar (from corn syrup) as the others, Prego, which had 13 grams per serving versus an average 7 grams among the other sauces. But there is good news for parents who prefer not to buy such sugary tomato sauces. The kids' second choice (third place for the adults) was Barilla, which they appreciated for its "tomatoey" chunky texture.

GETTING IT RIGHT: Where Are the Tomatoes?

| Sauce made with diced tomatoes | Sauce made with tomato paste |

We spooned equal amounts of each sauce into a strainer and then rinsed the sauce under running water to see what would be left. Our top-rated sauces, including Bertolli (left), showed off nice chunks of tomatoes, even after rinsing for about 45 seconds. In contrast, the low-rated sauces washed away to almost nothing. After rinsing the Ragú (right), we were left with nothing but tomato skin, herbs, and bits of diced vegetables.

Rating Jarred Pasta Sauces

TWENTY-FOUR MEMBERS OF THE *COOK'S ILLUSTRATED* STAFF TASTED ALL OF THE SAUCES, WHICH WERE SERVED warm with cooked ziti on the side. The sauces are listed in order of preference based on their scores in this tasting. All brands are available in supermarkets.

RECOMMENDED
Patsy's Marinara
$8.49 for 24 ounces

Garlic lovers rallied around this marinara, said to be the very same sauce served at the popular Patsy's Italian Restaurant in New York City. In addition to the garlic, which is added fresh (not in a powder), the sauce had an equally strong herbal punch and an "OK balance of acid, sweetness, and salt." The chunky tomato texture was deemed appealing. But talk about sticker shock: Patsy's was more than three times the price of most other sauces.

RECOMMENDED
Bertolli Tomato & Basil Pasta Sauce
$2.49 for 26 ounces

Tasters thought that this sauce had the freshest flavor. As one taster summed it up, "bright, zesty, tomatoes, with some depth of flavor." The texture was "meaty," with an agreeable balance of tomato chunks and puree. Herbs and spices were evident but not assertive.

RECOMMENDED
Barilla Marinara Tomato & Onion
$2.79 for 26 ounces

The top jarred sauce in our 1999 tasting, Barilla held its own among sauces new to the market for being one of the freshest in flavor. Many tasters indicated that they would like the sauce more if it wasn't so heavily seasoned with oregano. The oregano notwithstanding, it had good balance and a pleasant chunky texture.

RECOMMENDED WITH RESERVATIONS
Emeril's Home Style Marinara
$4.29 for 25 ounces

More than one taster likened this famed chef's marinara to pizza sauce. There was no "Bam!" This was instead a balanced, "plain and simple" sauce that some found "not very interesting" and even "kinda boring." The texture was that of a smooth puree.

RECOMMENDED WITH RESERVATIONS
Prego Traditional Pasta Sauce
$2.19 for 26 ounces

As America's top-selling jarred pasta sauce, Prego was the favorite in our kids' tasting. Its heavy oregano taste was popular with many tasters but a "dried-herb nightmare" for others.

RECOMMENDED WITH RESERVATIONS
Classico Sweet Basil Marinara
$2.50 for 26 ounces

This familiar-tasting national top seller wasn't a favorite but was ranked among those considered decent enough. A cooked tomato paste flavor contributed to a noted sweetness and thick, paste-like texture. It "tastes like nondescript pasta sauce from a jar," noted one taster.

RECOMMENDED WITH RESERVATIONS
Buitoni Marinara Pasta Sauce
$2.99 for 26 ounces

Another sauce that was strong on oregano and likened to pizza sauce. It did have a relatively good balance of flavors, but the flavorless, crunchy bits of something unidentifiable were troubling to munch on.

NOT RECOMMENDED
Ragú Traditional Old World Style Pasta Sauce
$2.19 for 26 ounces

More than one taster said that this sauce tasted as if it came from a tin can. The absence of favorable comments was striking: "might as well be tomato paste," "extremely salty," and tastes "heavily cooked/cooked for days," "like V-8," and "more like tomato soup." It had a texture like ketchup.

NOT RECOMMENDED
Colavita Marinara Sauce
$4.69 for 26 ounces

A little doctoring with salt and sugar (neither of which is listed in the ingredients) might have saved this ultrabland sauce that tasted "like a can of crushed tomatoes." The herbs were also too understated.

EQUIPMENT CORNER:
Rotary Cheese Graters

"SOME CHEESE, SIR?" AS UBIQUITOUS AS A SALTSHAKER in many Italian restaurants, the rotary cheese grater is the waiter's sidearm. Tirelessly descending upon table after table and showering pastas, risottos, and salads with wonderfully earthy wisps of Parmesan cheese, the grater-laden waiter will not take "no" for an answer. It is almost impossible to refuse the touch of class (and flavor) that the rotary grater brings to the restaurant table. But do these graters have a place at home? To find out, we tested eight models by grating Parmesan, cheddar, mozzarella, and even chocolate. To ensure the validity of the results, these tests were performed by a variety of test cooks with different hand sizes and strengths.

As we began testing, one point was immediately obvious—this was deceptively difficult work! Most of the handles were tiny and slippery, and even the most comfortable of the lot became painful after extended use. All but the Pedrini ($14.99) and KitchenAid ($19.99) struggled with the mozzarella and cheddar cheeses; these two were more successful because of their larger grating drums, which kept the cheese from sticking. Additionally, none of the grater hoppers could accommodate more than 1 or 2 ounces of cheese at a time, and each grater gave us hand fatigue after just a few moments of use. The rotary grater is adept at providing a light dusting of cheese, but it is much too slow for use in the kitchen. If you are making a recipe that calls for more than a few tablespoons of grated cheese, get out a box or rasp grater; your arm will thank you.

On the positive side, having an internal grating plate, the rotary grater eliminates the risk of raking your knuckles—a common occurrence with a box or rasp grater. (Do use caution when cleaning the grater, however, as the internal blades are very sharp.) A rotary grater also produces a much finer grind of cheese than traditional graters. This provides a more subtle texture to the grated cheese that is particularly appropriate for dusting bowls of pasta. Lastly, a rotary grater offers a taste of the restaurant experience at home. Guests have the option of grating their own cheese at the table.

Overall, the rotary grater is a fairly inexpensive and reasonably useful tool for the table. Half showpiece and half functional equipment, a rotary grater will, at the very least, bring some excitement to your dining room. So while rotary graters are not a kitchen necessity, they certainly do offer a sprinkle of charm to your everyday meals.

Q&A

How can I prevent pasta from sticking to the pot and boiling over?

First of all, don't skimp on water. You need a lot of water so the pasta has room to swell. Also, there must be enough water to dilute the starches released by the pasta. We found that 1 pound of pasta should be cooked in 4 quarts of water. Waiting to add the pasta until the water is at a rolling boil will also reduce the likelihood of pasta sticking together or to the pot. Finally, make sure to stir the pasta often, especially during the first few minutes of the cooking time, when the noodles are most likely to fuse to each other and the pot.

Given what we just said about using a lot of water to prevent sticky pasta, you should not use less water thinking you will reduce the likelihood of boil-overs. Pasta must be cooked in a big pot. You might be able to get away with a 6-quart Dutch oven or stockpot, but we prefer to use an 8-quart pot.

Rating Rotary Graters

WE RATED EIGHT MODELS BASED ON DESIGN, EASE OF USE, AND PERFORMANCE. TESTERS WITH DIFFERENT HAND SIZES and strengths rated each model for its ability to grate Parmesan cheese, cheddar cheese, mozzarella cheese, and chocolate. The rotary graters are listed in order of preference. See www.americastestkitchen.com for up-to-date prices and mail-order sources for top-rated products.

RECOMMENDED
Pedrini Rotary Grater
$14.99

An Italian-made grater with a large hopper, sharp grating teeth, and well-designed handle, the Pedrini took top honors.

RECOMMENDED
KitchenAid Rotary Grater
$19.99

Similar to the Pedrini, this model also had a large hopper, sharp grating teeth, and a fairly comfortable grip. One issue—this model was not designed for the left-handed.

NOT RECOMMENDED
Cuisipro Rotary Cheese Grater
$20

This stainless steel grater was very sturdy and made quick work of the cheese and chocolate. However, testers repeatedly noted that this model was uncomfortable in their hands.

NOT RECOMMENDED
Microplane Revolutionary Rotary Grater
$16.95

Turns out the fluffiest, finest shreds, but it was the slowest model tested.

NOT RECOMMENDED
Oxo Good Grips Seal & Store Rotary Grater
$14.99

Likable rubberized handle, but the hopper is rather small. Not designed for lefties.

NOT RECOMMENDED
Hoffritz Stainless Steel Rotary Grater
$15.99

Awkward design hurt testers' hands. Not designed for lefties.

NOT RECOMMENDED
Norpro Stainless Steel Commercial Drum Grater
$15.99

This heavy-duty stainless steel grater quickly caused hand fatigue.

NOT RECOMMENDED
Zyliss Transparent Cheese Grater
$14.99

Downgraded for its small handle, which becomes slippery with use.

A heavy, enameled cast-iron Dutch oven is the perfect vessel for a slow-simmering braise.

WINTER supper

Stew and starch is a familiar and comforting winter combination. Stew-and-starch pairings include everything from beef stew and mashed potatoes to chicken paprikash and egg noodles. Our favorite Italian stew-and-starch combo is osso buco and polenta.

Osso buco, literally "bone with a hole," is the Italian term for veal shanks. This meaty cut, akin to beef shanks or lamb shanks, becomes meltingly tender when stewed for several hours in a covered pot. Because veal is so delicate, the stewing liquid usually starts with white wine, rather than the red wine used with most beef stews, and also includes tomatoes. Our goal was to create a recipe that guaranteed perfectly tender meat with rich flavor.

Polenta is Italian for cornmeal mush. Nothing more than cornmeal cooked in salted water, good polenta should burst with corn flavor. It is the perfect base for many stews, including osso buco. But getting the texture just right is a challenge. Not-so-tiny lumps often mar the polenta. To avoid this problem, most recipes suggest constant stirring for a half hour or more. We found a way to get good results with a lot less work.

OSSO BUCO

WHAT WE WANTED: Meltingly tender veal shanks cooked in a rich broth for spooning over polenta, potatoes, or noodles.

Osso buco, or Italian braised veal shanks, is too venerable a recipe to fiddle with. With humility, we headed into the kitchen. We decided the best way to approach the dish was to perfect (and simplify, if possible) the cooking technique and to extract the most flavor from the simple ingredients: veal shanks (which are browned), aromatics (onions, carrots, and celery, all sautéed), and liquids (a blend of wine, stock, and tomatoes).

To start, we gathered three classic recipes and prepared each in the test kitchen. At the tasting, there was little consensus about the recipes, although white wine was clearly preferred to red wine. Tasters did, however, offer similar ideas as to what constitutes the perfect osso buco; it should be rich in flavor and color and somewhat brothy but not stewy. This first goal is the reason why we prefer osso buco to veal stews made with boneless shoulder meat. While shoulder meat can be a bit wan, the shank is robust, and the bone adds tremendous flavor to the stewing liquid. With these traits in mind, we created a rough working recipe and set out to explore the two main components in this dish—the veal shanks and the braising liquid.

Most recipes we reviewed call for shanks from the upper portion of the hind leg, cut into pieces between 1 and 1½ inches thick. We found that purchasing shanks is tricky, even when we special-ordered them. From one market, we received stunning shanks with a lovely pinkish blush, which were ideal except for the weight. Each shank weighed between 12 and 16 ounces—too large for individual servings. Part of the charm of osso buco is receiving an individual shank as a portion. We concluded that shanks should weigh 8 to 10 ounces (with the bone) and no more. At another market, the shanks were generally in the ideal weight range,

but the butchering job was less than perfect. In the same package, shank widths varied from 1 to 2½ inches and were occasionally cut on an extreme bias, making it difficult to tie them (see the explanation below) and sear them evenly.

The first step, then, is to shop carefully. We found a thickness of 1½ inches and a weight of 8 ounces ideal. Make sure all the shanks you buy are close to these specifications. Each shank should have two nicely cut, flat sides to facilitate browning.

Preparing the meat for braising was the next step. Most recipes call for tying the shanks and dredging them in flour before searing. We found that tying a piece of butcher's twine around the equator of each shank does prevent the meat from falling apart and makes for a more attractive presentation. When we skipped this step, the meat fell off the bone and floated about in the pot.

Although we do not generally dredge meat in flour before browning, we felt we should at least try it, considering that the majority of osso buco recipes include this step. Tasters felt that the meat floured before searing was gummy and lacked depth. The flour on the meat browns rather than the meat itself, and the flour coating may peel off during the long braising time.

To develop the best flavor in the shanks, we seasoned them heavily with salt and pepper and seared them until a thick, golden brown crust formed. We seared the shanks in two batches (even if they could all fit in the pan at the same time) so that we could deglaze the pan twice with wine, thereby enriching the braising liquid doubly.

The most difficult part of developing this recipe was attaining an ideal braising liquid and sauce. Braising, by design, is a relatively inexact cooking method because the rate at which the liquid reduces can vary greatly. Some of the initial recipes we tried yielded far too much liquid, which was thin in flavor and texture. In other cases, the liquid nearly evaporated by the time the meat was tender. We needed to create a foolproof, flavorful braising liquid and cooking technique that produced a suitable volume of rich sauce and did not need a lot of last-minute fussing.

We experimented with numerous techniques to attain our ideal liquid, including reductions before braising and after braising (with the aromatics and without) and a reduction of the wine to a syrup during the deglazing process. In the end, we settled on the easiest method: natural reduction in the oven. The seal on most Dutch ovens is not perfectly tight, so the liquid reduces as the osso buco cooks. We found further simmering on the stovetop unnecessary as long as we started with the right amount of liquid in the pot.

The braising liquid traditionally begins with meat stock and adds white wine and tomatoes. As few cooks have homemade meat stock on hand and canned versions are often unappealing, we knew that canned chicken broth would be our likely starting point. Two cups (or one can) seemed the right amount, and tests confirmed this. To enrich the flavor of the broth, we used a hefty amount of diced onions, carrots, and celery. Tasters liked the large amount of garlic in one recipe, so we finely minced about five cloves and added them to the pot prior to the broth. We rounded out the flavors with two bay leaves.

We hoped to write the recipe in even amounts, using whole vegetables, one can of broth, one bottle of wine, and so on. But an entire bottle of wine proved overwhelming. The resulting sauce was dominated by acidity. Some testers also felt that the meat was tougher than in previous batches with less wine. We scaled the wine back to 2½ cups, about two thirds of a bottle, and were happy with the results. More than half of the wine is used to deglaze the pot between searing batches of veal shanks and thus the final dish is not as alcoholic or liquidy as it might seem.

With the wine and broth amounts settled, we needed to figure out how to best incorporate the tomatoes. Most tasters did not like too much tomato because they felt it easily overwhelmed the other flavors in the sauce. Fresh tomatoes are always a gamble outside of the summer months, so we chose canned diced tomatoes, thoroughly strained of their juice. This approach worked out well, and the strained tomatoes did not overwhelm the sauce.

We still needed to determine the ideal braising time. Several sources suggest cooking osso buco almost to the consistency of pulled pork. Tasters loved the meat cooked this way, but it was less than attractive—broken down and pot roast–like. We wanted compact meat firmly attached to the bone, so we cooked the meat until it was just fork-tender but still clinging to the bone. Two hours in the oven produced veal that was meltingly soft but still attached to the bone. With some of the larger shanks, the cooking time extended to about 2½ hours.

We experimented with oven temperature and found that 325 degrees reduced the braising liquid to the right consistency and did not harm the texture of the meat. While beef stews are best cooked at 300 degrees, veal shanks have so much collagen and connective tissue that they can be braised at a slightly higher temperature.

Just before serving, osso buco is sprinkled with gremolata, a mixture of minced garlic, parsley, and lemon zest. We were surprised to find variations on this classic trio. A number of recipes include orange zest mixed with lemon zest or on its own. Other recipes include minced anchovies. We tested three gremolatas: one traditional, one with orange zest mixed in equal part with lemon zest, and one with anchovies. Tasters liked all three dishes but favored the traditional version.

In some recipes the gremolata is used as a garnish, and in others it is added to the pot just before serving. We chose a compromise approach, stirring half the gremolata into the pot and letting it stand for five minutes so that the flavors of the garlic, lemon, and parsley permeated the dish. We sprinkled the remaining gremolata on individual servings for a hit of freshness.

WHAT WE LEARNED: **Choose medium-size shanks, tie them to keep the meat attached, and brown them in two batches to develop maximum flavor from this mild-tasting meat. Use a mix of chicken broth, white wine, and canned tomatoes as the braising liquid. Stir half of the gremolata (minced garlic, lemon, and parsley) into the stew and sprinkle the rest over individual portions.**

OSSO BUCO

Serves 6

To keep the meat attached to the bone during the long simmering process, tie a piece of twine around the thickest portion of each shank before it is browned. Use a zester, vegetable peeler, or paring knife to remove the zest from a single lemon, then mince it with a chef's knife. With the lid on the pot cracked, the braising liquid should reduce to a sauce-like consistency in the oven. Just before serving, taste the liquid and, if it seems too thin, simmer the liquid on the stovetop as you remove the strings from the osso buco and arrange them in individual bowls.

osso buco

- 4 tablespoons vegetable oil
- 6 veal shanks, 1½ inches thick (8 to 10 ounces each), patted dry with paper towels and tied around the equator with butcher's twine
  Salt and ground black pepper
- 2½ cups dry white wine
- 2 medium onions, cut into ½-inch dice (about 2 cups)
- 2 medium carrots, cut into ½-inch dice (about 1½ cups)
- 2 medium celery ribs, cut into ½-inch dice (about 1 cup)
- 6 medium garlic cloves, minced or pressed through a garlic press (about 2 tablespoons)
- 2 cups low-sodium chicken broth
- 2 small bay leaves
- 1 (14.5-ounce) can diced tomatoes, drained

gremolata

- 3 medium garlic cloves, minced or pressed through a garlic press (about 1 tablespoon)
- 2 teaspoons minced zest from 1 lemon
- ¼ cup minced fresh parsley leaves

1. FOR THE OSSO BUCO: Adjust an oven rack to the lower-middle position and heat the oven to 325 degrees. Heat 1 tablespoon of the oil in a large ovenproof Dutch oven over medium-high heat until shimmering. Meanwhile, sprinkle both sides of the shanks generously with salt and pepper to taste. Swirl to coat the pan bottom with the oil. Place 3 shanks in a single layer in the pan and cook until they are golden brown on one side, about 5 minutes. Using tongs, flip the shanks and cook on the second side until golden brown, about 5 minutes longer. Transfer the shanks

---

Q&A

What exactly is a simmer, and how does it differ from a boil?

Simmering is a key technique used to make stews, soups, sauces, and stocks. The idea is to cook foods slowly but gently. For instance, if stews boil, the meat will fall apart. Boiling also causes fat to break down into small globules that are harder to remove. The end result is a greasy boiled stew or stock.

So how do you distinguish a boil from a simmer?

A rapid boil occurs at 212 degrees (at sea level) and is characterized by large bubbles bursting all over the surface of the liquid. The bubbles appear to be rolling over each other—hence the term "a rolling boil." A steady simmer occurs between 206 and 211 degrees. Bubbles break over the surface of the liquid, but they do not roll over each other. More bubbles are found along the edges of the pot. Finally, a gentle simmer occurs between 198 and 205 degrees. Very few bubbles break the surface, and all of these bubbles are confined to the edges of the pot.

to a bowl and set aside. Off the heat, add ½ cup of the wine to the Dutch oven, scraping the pan bottom with a wooden spoon to loosen any browned bits. Pour the liquid into the bowl with the browned shanks. Return the pot to medium-high heat, add 1 more tablespoon of the oil, and heat until shimmering. Brown the remaining shanks, about 5 minutes for each side. Transfer the shanks to the bowl. Off the heat, add 1 cup of the wine to the pot, scraping the bottom to loosen the browned bits. Pour the liquid into the bowl with the shanks.

2. Set the pot over medium heat. Add the remaining 2 tablespoons oil and heat until shimmering. Add the onions, carrots, celery, ¼ teaspoon salt, and ⅛ teaspoon pepper and cook, stirring occasionally, until soft and lightly browned, about 9 minutes. Add the garlic and cook until lightly browned, about 1 minute longer. Increase the heat to high and stir in the broth, remaining 1 cup wine, accumulated veal juices in the bowl, and bay leaves. Add the tomatoes; return the veal shanks to the pot (the liquid should just cover the shanks). Bring the liquid to a full simmer. Cover the pot, cracking the lid just slightly, and transfer the pot to the oven. Cook the shanks until the meat is easily pierced with a fork but not falling off the bone, about 2 hours. (Can be refrigerated for up to 2 days. Bring to a simmer over medium-low heat.)

3. FOR THE GREMOLATA: Combine the garlic, lemon zest, and parsley in a small bowl. Stir half of the gremolata into the pot, reserving the rest for garnish. Season with salt and pepper to taste. Let the osso buco stand, uncovered, for 5 minutes.

4. Using tongs, remove the shanks from the pot, cut off and discard the twine, and place 1 veal shank in each of 6 bowls. Ladle some of the braising liquid over each shank and sprinkle each serving with the remaining gremolata. Serve immediately.

TASTING LAB: Bottled Water

IT IS RATHER BAFFLING THAT A SUBSTANCE AS FUNDA-mental and as abundant as water can form the basis of an astonishingly large business. In 2003, bottled water sales ballooned to $8.3 billion in the United States alone. Per capita consumption was more than 22 gallons, nearly double what it had been only a decade earlier, and sales and consumption of bottled water are only expected to grow further. To meet the demand, retailers have stocked their shelves with a multitude of brands, both domestic and foreign, many wearing labels that suggest pristine alpine springs or crisp, clean mountain air. That the bottles differ in labeling is clear; what is less apparent is the extent to which they differ in taste. To better understand what—if anything—distinguishes one bottled water from another, we conducted a blind tasting.

We collected nine brands that covered the still-water spectrum—both domestic and imported. We also included a water not expressly meant for drinking, ultrapure plasma-grade water. Used in sensitive chemistry applications, this water is double-distilled and virtually free of all minerals and impurities. We reasoned that by including in the tasting water in its near-purest form, we might gain some insight into what makes water taste good—its purity or its impurities, in a manner of speaking.

There are several types of bottled water, but three categories stand out: spring water, artesian water, and purified water. A bottle labeled "spring water" must contain water that came from an underground water source that flows naturally to the earth's surface. The location of the source must be identified. The water is collected either at the spring or through a hole that has been made to tap the source that feeds the spring. Spring water is sometimes bottled without additional treatment (this is true particularly of European bottled waters), but domestic bottlers often use carbon filtration to remove odors, micro- or ultrafiltration to remove fine particles and impurities, and/or ultraviolet light or ozonation to disinfect the water.

Some producers tap several springs, bottle each separately, yet sell all under the same brand name. This means that a bottle of brand X purchased on the East Coast may not be from the same source as a bottle of brand X purchased on the West Coast. This practice is common among domestic producers and allows suppliers to better meet demand and minimize the cost of transport. But it also means that the flavor profiles of the same brand may differ from one region of the country to another. Many European and foreign producers bottle water from a single source—and are proud of it. Of the nine brands we assembled for our tasting, six were spring waters—Arrowhead, Crystal Geyser, Dannon, Evian, Poland Spring, and Volvic.

Artesian water differs from spring water in that its source must be an underground formation known as a confined aquifer. The water is sandwiched between—or confined by—a top and bottom layer of impermeable rock. When the aquifer is tapped, natural internal pressure causes the water to flow. Is artesian water better than "regular" spring water? Not necessarily. While the U.S. Environmental Protection Agency says that water from artesian aquifers is often cleaner because the confining layers of rock and clay impede the movement of contaminants, there is no guarantee that artesian water is any more pure—or otherwise better—than spring water. The only artesian water in the tasting was Fiji, which is indeed imported from the Fiji Islands in the Pacific and is the second-best-selling imported brand.

Spring water and artesian water both contain dissolved solids (or minerals) such as calcium, magnesium, sulfates, silica, and chlorides. Mineral water is spring or artesian water that naturally contains at least 250 parts per million (ppm) of total dissolved solids (TDS). Evian was the only mineral water in the tasting, although it is not marketed as such. (A laboratory analysis we conducted did show that our sample of Fiji had TDS of more than 250 ppm, but to qualify as a mineral water, the water must, through repeated analysis, be shown to consistently contain 250 ppm of TDS. According to Fiji, its water has TDS of 210 ppm.)

Two purified waters, Pepsi-Cola's Aquafina and Coca-Cola's Dasani, were part of our tasting. Aquafina is the best-selling brand of bottled water in this country, and Dasani is number two. What is purified water? The simple definition is that purified water has been processed to remove contaminants and minerals before bottling. The source is often a municipal water supply. Pepsi and Coke tap municipal water sources in various parts of the country and filter the water in a process called reverse osmosis. Reverse osmosis removes most of the impurities, and the water is left nearly bereft of minerals. Such a tight filtration process means that no matter what the source, the taste of purified water is likely to be consistent from bottle to bottle.

Purified water is frequently criticized for being merely a highly filtered version of what flows when you open the home tap. Coke claims, however, that consumers are much more concerned about taste than source. For that reason, after reverse-osmosis processing, Coke adds minerals back to the purified water to obtain a particular flavor profile. Pepsi does not add minerals to Aquafina.

By contrast, a spring water's flavor profile is organically derived. As the water journeys from its origin as rainwater or snowmelt to the spring, a process that can take years, it travels through layers of rock, clay, gravel, and/or sand that filter out impurities. As the impurities are filtered out, the water also acquires dissolved minerals that in their specific combinations give the water its signature flavor.

The only water in the tasting that tasters unanimously rejected was the ultrapure plasma-grade water, which earned the lowest possible score because of its flat, vapid flavor. Though this water is of course unavailable to consumers, it did teach us something. Ostensibly, when it comes to water, absolute purity is a liability, not an asset. Some mineral content makes water likable and palatable.

Is spring water better than purified municipal water? The two purified waters we sampled, Aquafina and Dasani, earned respectable scores, coming in fourth and fifth, respectively, and beat out four spring waters. But they were not in the winners' circle. Two spring waters and the one artesian water in the tasting swept the pack, with win, place, and show. Volvic, a spring water from France, was the clear winner, with Fiji, the artesian water, close behind.

What should you buy? While most of our tasters will now purchase Volvic or Fiji when given the option, our results show that the flavor differences between bottled waters are not great. Unlike the differences between brands of chocolate or barbecue sauce, the distinctions between brands of bottled water are so modest that you are unlikely to be disappointed with any of those that we tasted.

TASTING LAB: Bottled versus Tap Water

WE WERE CURIOUS TO SEE HOW THE HIGHEST- AND lowest-rated bottled waters would fare against tap water, so we organized a second tasting in which we sampled Volvic (first place), Poland Spring (last place), Boston tap water, samples of water from the Metropolitan Water District (MWD) of Southern California in Los Angeles (because it has won awards in its category at international water tastings), and tap water from a residence in Los Angeles County.

Volvic and the MWD water were equally well liked, earning identical scores and accolades such as "fresh" and "clean." Poland Spring came in next, besting Boston tap water, which tasters described as metallic, musty, and stale. Residential Los Angeles County water was so chlorinated that it stopped tasters in their tracks. Why would the MWD water be so good and the residential water so bad? The MWD is a water wholesaler, and the water it has to offer is not necessarily the water that flows from area faucets. A phone call to the MWD revealed that it was, in fact, not the source of the residential tap water that we tasted.

What, then, did we learn from this tasting? That tap water can rival even the best bottled water (at least in theory), but that even our least-favorite bottled water was superior to water culled straight from two not-so-excellent taps in Boston and Los Angeles.

Rating Bottled Waters

TWENTY-THREE MEMBERS OF THE *COOK'S ILLUSTRATED* STAFF SAMPLED NINE DIFFERENT BRANDS OF STILL BOTTLED WATER. The waters were tasted at room temperature, which allows odors and flavors to be more perceptible than when tasted chilled. Total dissolved solids (TDS) analysis was conducted by an independent laboratory; the amounts listed below (in parts per million) may not be identical to amounts given by producers. The waters are listed in order of preference. Unless otherwise noted, the waters are available in supermarkets nationwide.

RECOMMENDED

Volvic Natural Spring Water

$1.29 for 1 liter

Source: Clairvic Spring, Volvic, France

TDS: 137 ppm

Tasters had a clear preference for this water, calling it very fresh, pure, and clean, with slight mineral flavors. One taster wrote, "smooth and velvety," while another declared it a favorite because it "tastes like water."

RECOMMENDED

Fiji Natural Artesian Water

$1.59 for 1 liter

Source: Viti Levu, Republic of Fiji

TDS: 260 ppm

Tasters appreciated the "nice and clean," "incredibly drinkable," "unadulterated" quality of this water. One taster hailed it as "perfect." It was also described as having a hint of sweetness and mineral flavor. A few detractors called it "dull."

RECOMMENDED

Dannon Natural Spring Water

$0.53 for 25 ounces

Source: Springs in Bellefonte, Pa.; Grand Prairie, Texas; Anaheim, Calif.; High Springs, Fla.; Mount Shasta, Calif. (sample tasted was from Bellefonte, Pa.)

TDS: 200 ppm

"Pure," "clean," "fresh," and "smooth" were the accolades. A couple tasters noted a sweetness. Negative comments included "stale" and "flat."

RECOMMENDED

Aquafina Purified Drinking Water

$0.99 for 1 liter

Source: Multiple municipal water supplies

TDS: 30 ppm

Most tasters found this water to be sweet, but there agreement ended. Comments like "fresh" and "lively" were countered with criticisms like "metallic" and "artificial."

RECOMMENDED

Dasani Purified Water

$1.19 for 1 liter

Source: Multiple municipal water supplies

TDS: 80 ppm

Nearly half of the tasters found this water to have distinct mineral flavors ("like licking a geode," said one). Though it was described as "clean," some found it "harsh."

RECOMMENDED

Arrowhead Mountain Spring Water

$1.09 for 1 liter

Source: Multiple springs in the U.S. and Canada

TDS: 120 ppm

Comments about this water, available in the West, ranged from positive ("nice taste" and "silky") to moderate ("not bad") to decidedly negative ("yuck, tap water"). Some tasters commented that this water had an aftertaste, and one said that the flavor "lingers on and on."

RECOMMENDED

Evian Natural Spring Water

$1.69 for 1 liter

Source: Cachat Spring, Evian, France

TDS: 360 ppm

This was a controversial water. "Soft, smooth, and supple" and "very refreshing" were the praises. "Heavy," "creamy," and "yuck" were criticisms. Most tasters agreed that this water had a notable sweetness and strong mineral flavors.

RECOMMENDED

Crystal Geyser

$0.69 for 1.5 liters

Source: Springs in Benton, Tenn., and Mount Shasta, Calif. (sample tasted was from Benton, Tenn.)

TDS: 180 ppm

Tasters mustered little excitement—positive or negative—about this water. "Pretty neutral and clean" and "a bit dull, but relatively clean" typified comments.

RECOMMENDED

Poland Spring

$0.89 for 1 liter

Sources: Springs in Hollis, Fryeburg, Poland Spring, and Poland, Maine (sample tasted was from Hollis)

TDS: 50 ppm

This water, which is widely available in the Northeast, was criticized for tasting "unnatural" and having "off flavors." More temperate tasters commented that it was "basic" but uninteresting. Several tasters noted a saltiness.

POLENTA

WHAT WE WANTED: Creamy, smooth polenta, achieved without lumps or constant stirring.

I f your mother ever complained about slaving over a hot stove, she was probably talking about making polenta. Nothing more than cornmeal mush, polenta is made from dried, ground corn cooked in liquid until the starches in the corn hydrate and swell into soft, balloon-like structures. For many purposes, this soft stage is the most delicious way to serve polenta.

The stiff polenta you often see in restaurants starts out as a soft mass but is spread into a thin layer on a baking sheet or marble surface, cooled until firm, sliced, and then sautéed, fried, or grilled until it resembles a crouton. These crisp rectangles are rarely more than a garnish. However, a smooth, piping-hot mound of soft polenta can be a meal. More commonly, soft polenta is used as a filler to stretch out meager game birds like quail or to cut the richness of sausages. Most stews and braised dishes—everything from osso buco to braised rabbit—can be ladled over a bowl of soft polenta.

Although making polenta sounds easy, the traditional Italian method for cooking it is a lot of work. The polenta must be slowly added to boiling salted water and stirred constantly (to prevent scorching) during the entire 30- to 40-minute cooking time. Within five minutes, you'll feel like you've been arm-wrestling Arnold Schwarzenegger. Thirty minutes of such constant stirring can seem like an eternity.

Of course, this assumes that you have avoided the biggest pitfall of all, the seizing problem at the beginning of the cooking process. Cornmeal is a starch, and starch thickens when mixed with water and heated. If this happens too quickly, the cornmeal seizes up into a solid, nearly immovable mass.

We tested adding cornmeal to cold water, using more water, using less water, and using different grinds of

cornmeal, all to no avail. Yes, we learned to prevent seizing (add the cornmeal very slowly), but we still needed to stir constantly for at least 30 minutes to prevent scorching.

This testing did, however, reveal some important information. We found that medium-grind cornmeal makes the best polenta. (For more information about cornmeal, see page 255.) Finely ground cornmeal, such as the Quaker brand sold in many supermarkets, is too powdery and makes gummy polenta. Cornmeal with a texture akin to granulated sugar, not table salt, makes the best polenta. We also discovered that a ratio of 4 parts water to 1 part cornmeal delivers the right consistency. As for salt, 1 teaspoon is the right amount for 1 cup of cornmeal.

At this point in our testing, we started to explore alternative cooking methods. The microwave was a bust, yielding sticky, raw-tasting polenta. The pressure cooker was even worse; the polenta took a long time to cook and then stuck firmly to the pot. We finally got good results when we prepared polenta in a double boiler. The polenta was cooked over simmering water so it didn't scorch or seize up the way it can when cooked over direct heat. It emerged with a soft, light texture and sweet corn flavor. There is only one drawback to this method, and it is a big one: time.

While a double boiler produced undeniably rich, creamy polenta, the cooking time was prohibitively long. Even with the minimum attention that the technique required, 1½ hours of cooking was simply impractical. We wondered whether we could produce similar results via more conventional methods. The double boiler method proved to us that slow, very gentle heat was the key to unlocking cornmeal's smooth texture, not vigilant stirring. Could we approximate a double boiler's low heat with a conventional saucepan?

Luckily, we could. A heavy-bottomed saucepan on the stove's lowest possible setting (or in conjunction with a flame tamer; see the recipe note) shielded the polenta from cooking too rapidly and allowed the starches to be released and the flavor of the cornmeal to develop. Keeping the cover on the pot held in moisture and reduced the risk of scorching the polenta, even when we stirred infrequently rather than constantly. Within ½ hour, a third of the time it took in the double boiler, we had creamy polenta ready for the table. We did find, however, that with the slightly higher temperature, stirring was a more significant issue. When we left the polenta unheeded for more than seven minutes, it tended to stick to the pot bottom and corners, where it remained immovably until washing. Stirring vigorously every five minutes prevented such mishaps.

WHAT WE LEARNED: Start with one part medium-grind cornmeal and four parts water for polenta with the right consistency. Slowly add the cornmeal to simmering water and then turn the heat down very low and cover so that the polenta can cook slowly without scorching or constant stirring.

BASIC POLENTA

Serves 4 to 6

If you do not have a heavy-bottomed saucepan, you may want to use a flame tamer to manage the heat. A flame tamer can be purchased at most kitchen supply stores, or one can be fashioned from a ring of foil (see the illustration on page 255). It's easy to tell whether you need a flame tamer or not. If the polenta bubbles or sputters at all after the first 10 minutes, the heat is too high, and you need one. Properly heated polenta will do little more than release wisps of steam. When stirring the polenta, make sure to scrape the sides and bottom of the pan to ensure even cooking. Use this polenta as the base for any stew or braise, especially osso buco (page 248). Cooked leafy greens also make excellent toppings for soft polenta.

6   cups water
    Salt
1½ cups medium cornmeal, preferably
    stone-ground
3   tablespoons unsalted butter, cut into large
    chunks
    Ground black pepper

1. Bring the water to a rolling boil in a heavy-bottomed 4-quart saucepan over medium-high heat. Reduce the heat to the lowest possible setting, add 1½ teaspoons salt, and pour the cornmeal into the water in a very slow stream from a measuring cup, all the while whisking in a circular motion to prevent lumps.

2. Cover and cook, vigorously stirring the polenta with a wooden spoon for about 10 seconds once every 5 minutes and making sure to scrape clean the bottom and corners of the pot, until the polenta has lost its raw cornmeal taste and becomes soft and smooth, about 30 minutes. Stir in the butter, season with salt and pepper to taste, and serve immediately.

POLENTA WITH PARMESAN AND BUTTER

Serves 4 to 6 as a first course or side dish

Follow the recipe for Basic Polenta, stirring in ¾ cup grated Parmesan cheese along with the butter. Divide the polenta among individual bowls and top each with a small pat of butter. Sprinkle generously with more grated Parmesan to taste and serve immediately.

POLENTA WITH GORGONZOLA

Serves 4 to 6 as a substantial first course or light entrée

Choose a Gorgonzola dolce or other mild, creamy blue cheese such as Saga Blue. Do not use an aged Gorgonzola for this dish. Other aged blue cheeses will also be too salty, crumbly, and pungent.

Follow the recipe for Basic Polenta, dividing the finished polenta among individual bowls. Top each bowl with a 1-ounce slice of Gorgonzola cheese and serve immediately.

TASTING LAB: Cornmeal

LARGE COMMERCIAL MILLS USE HUGE STEEL ROLLERS TO grind dent corn (a hard, dry corn) into cornmeal. This is how Quaker cornmeal, the leading supermarket brand, is produced. But some smaller mills scattered around the United States grind with millstones; this product is called stone-ground cornmeal. (If water is used as an energy source, the cornmeal may be labeled water-ground.) Stone-ground cornmeal is usually a bit coarser than cornmeal processed through steel rollers. The difference is like that between granulated sugar (which is a tiny bit coarse) and table salt (which is smooth and fine).

In addition, smaller millers often choose not to degerm, or remove all the germ, cleanly. This makes their product closer to whole-grain cornmeal. If the color is uniform, the germ has been removed. A stone-ground cornmeal with some germ has flecks that are both lighter and darker than the predominant color, whether yellow or white.

In our tests, we found the texture of polenta made with stone-ground meal more interesting, as the grind of the cornmeal was not uniform. More important, we found that polenta made with stone-ground cornmeal tasted much better than that made with the standard Quaker cornmeal. Stone-ground cornmeal gives polenta a sweeter, more intense corn flavor. Yellow cornmeal is traditional for polenta making and was the first choice among our tasters.

The higher moisture and oil content of stone-ground cornmeal causes it to go rancid rather quickly. Wrap stone-ground cornmeal tightly in plastic or put it into a moisture-proof container, then refrigerate or freeze it to prolong freshness. Degerminated cornmeals, such as Quaker, keep for a year if stored in a dry, cool place.

TECHNIQUE: Flame Tamer

A flame tamer is a metal disk that can be used as a buffer between a burner and a pot to maintain a gentle, low level of heat. A flame tamer is especially useful when trying to cook a stew or soup at the barest simmer for a long time. If you don't own a flame tamer, aluminum foil can be fashioned into a thick, slightly flattened ring and placed right on top of a gas burner.

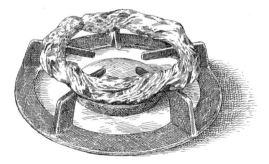

Cut a 3-foot length of foil and squeeze it into a ¾-inch-thick rope. Roll one end to form a ring the size of the burner. Twist the remaining foil rope around the ring to form a flame tamer. Set the ring on the burner, then place the pot on top.

Ceramic crocks are filled with onion soup and ready for their crusty cheese topping and a quick trip under the broiler.

BISTRO classics

Who doesn't like bistro food? It offers the panache of fine French cooking but in a casual setting. The dishes are rustic, hearty, and satisfying. And unlike so much restaurant cooking, bistro food makes sense at home. Most recipes rely on inexpensive, easy-to-find ingredients and basic techniques.

That doesn't always mean that bistro food is great. Casualness can sometimes translate as sloppiness. Who hasn't been served a bowl of watery French onion soup with crunchy onions and way too much gooey cheese? Or maybe the onions were cooked properly but the broth was way too salty?

A baked goat cheese salad is a delicate balance of textures (crunchy greens and creamy cheese), temperatures (cool lettuce and warm cheese), and flavors (sweet, tangy, bitter, and acidic) that is often out of kilter. Our goal for this chapter was simple. Take French onion soup and baked goat cheese salad and make stellar versions of these bistro favorites.

BAKED GOAT CHEESE SALAD

WHAT WE WANTED: To make this bistro classic at home with warm but not fluid goat cheese, tasty greens, and the right dressing.

Warm goat cheese salad has been a fixture of restaurant menus for years, featuring artisanal cheeses, organic baby field greens, barrel-aged vinegars, and imported oils. Marketing being what it is, the jargon is often more intriguing than the execution: tepid, crumb-dusted cheese on overdressed designer greens at a price that defies reason. When we've tried to prepare this salad at home, the results have been equally disappointing, albeit less expensive. We've usually ended up with flavorless warm cheese melted onto the greens. What we wanted was quite different: creamy cheese rounds infused with flavor and surrounded by crisp, golden breading, all cradled in lightly dressed greens.

Coating and heating the cheese is clearly the major challenge of this recipe. Techniques uncovered in the recipes we researched included pan-frying, broiling, and baking. We began by coating portions of goat cheese in herbs (thyme and chives), then dipping the goat cheese rounds in beaten egg (with a little Dijon mustard added for bite), and finally fresh bread crumbs (the most common option for coating). We tried pan-frying (the most frequent method in cookbook recipes and the classic restaurant technique). Although the bread crumbs crisped up nicely after a short stay in the hot oil, several problems arose. The worst problem was that the interior of the cheese rounds began to melt while the first side was browning, which made turning the disks a nightmare.

Nevertheless, we continued to pursue this method, chilling the rounds in the refrigerator for 30 minutes before they hit the oil, which we hoped would prevent the centers from overheating before the crust had crisped, but this, too, failed. One recipe suggested broiling the goat cheese rounds, but the rounds simply melted under the intense heat of the broiler.

It was time to try baking. Baking the cheese at temperatures ranging from 300 to 400 degrees for 4 to 7 minutes resulted in pallid, soggy crusts across the board, with varying degrees of unpleasant melting. Curious whether higher temperatures would yield the crust we were searching for, we turned the oven up to 475 degrees and ended up with goat cheese fondue.

Logic (or stubbornness) had persuaded us that higher temperatures had the potential to produce a crisp crust, but reality had shown that we needed a more durable breading. Then we hit upon the idea of using Melba toasts—perhaps these extremely dry (and extremely hard) crackers would work. We pulverized them, dunked the cheese in beaten egg, and then coated the rounds in the sandy crumbs. Appearing to fuse with the egg, the Melba crumbs formed a cohesive, shell-like barrier in the oven. Finally, our crust was crisp, although there still was some oozing of the cheese.

Theorizing that if the oven were blistering hot and the cheese arctic cold we would get a crispy crust and no oozing cheese, we placed our goat cheese rounds in the freezer rather than the refrigerator for 30 minutes. Baking our "frozen" cheese at 475 degrees for 7 minutes, we struck gold. Although a few kitchen naysayers found the Melba crust a bit dry, we found that a quick brush of olive oil onto the exterior of the breaded and chilled rounds solved this problem.

It was time to add the baked goat cheese rounds to a salad. Most tasters preferred a mix of heartier greens, such as arugula and frisée, and all tasters preferred a classic vinaigrette, as this dressing echoed and complemented the flavors of the goat cheese rounds. Given the fat in the cheese, we found that it's important to dress the greens lightly.

WHAT WE LEARNED: Ground Melba toasts make the crispest crust for the goat cheese, which should be frozen and then baked in a very hot oven to brown the exterior without causing the rounds to lose their shape.

SALAD WITH HERBED BAKED GOAT CHEESE AND VINAIGRETTE

Serves 6

The baked goat cheese should be served warm. Prepare the salad components while the cheese is in the freezer, then toss the greens and vinaigrette while the cheese cools a bit after baking.

goat cheese

3	ounces white Melba toasts (about 2 cups)
1	teaspoon ground black pepper
3	large eggs
2	tablespoons Dijon mustard
1	tablespoon chopped fresh thyme leaves
1	tablespoon chopped fresh chives
12	ounces firm goat cheese
	Extra-virgin olive oil

salad

2	tablespoons red wine vinegar
1	tablespoon Dijon mustard
1	teaspoon finely minced shallot
¼	teaspoon salt
6	tablespoons extra-virgin olive oil
	Ground black pepper
18	ounces (about 14 cups) mixed hearty greens, washed and dried

1. FOR THE CHEESE: In a food processor, process the Melba toasts to fine, even crumbs, about 1½ minutes; transfer the crumbs to a medium bowl and stir in the pepper. Whisk the eggs and mustard in another medium bowl until combined. Combine the thyme and chives in a small bowl.

2. Using dental floss or kitchen twine, divide the cheese into 12 equal pieces (see the photograph on page 260). Roll each piece of cheese into a ball; roll each ball in the combined fresh herbs to coat lightly. Transfer 6 pieces to the egg mixture and turn each piece to coat; transfer to the Melba crumbs and turn each piece to coat, pressing the crumbs

into the cheese. Flatten each ball gently with your fingertips into a disk about 1½ inches wide and 1 inch thick and set on a baking sheet. Repeat with the remaining 6 pieces of cheese. Transfer the baking sheet to the freezer and freeze the disks until firm, about 30 minutes. (The cheese may be wrapped tightly in plastic wrap and frozen up to 1 week.) Adjust an oven rack to the uppermost position; heat the oven to 475 degrees.

3. FOR THE SALAD: Meanwhile, combine the vinegar, mustard, shallot, and salt in a small bowl. Whisking constantly, drizzle in the olive oil; season with pepper to taste. Set aside.

4. Remove the cheese from the freezer and brush the tops and sides evenly with olive oil. Bake until the crumbs are golden brown and the cheese is slightly soft, 7 to 9 minutes (or 9 to 12 minutes if the cheese is completely frozen). Using a thin metal spatula, transfer the cheese to a paper towel–lined plate and cool 3 minutes.

5. Place the greens in a large bowl, drizzle the vinaigrette over them, and toss to coat. Divide the greens among individual plates; place 2 rounds of goat cheese on each salad. Serve immediately.

VARIATION

SALAD WITH APPLES, WALNUTS, DRIED CHERRIES, AND HERBED BAKED GOAT CHEESE

Plump 1 cup dried cherries in ½ cup hot water in a small bowl, about 10 minutes; drain. Quarter and core 2 medium Granny Smith apples and cut into ⅛-inch-thick slices. Follow the recipe for Salad with Herbed Baked Goat Cheese and Vinaigrette, replacing the red wine vinegar with 2 tablespoons cider vinegar and adding ¼ teaspoon sugar to the dressing. Proceed as directed, dividing cherries, apples, and ½ cup toasted and chopped walnuts among individual salad plates.

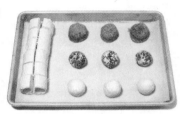

GETTING IT RIGHT:
Making the Goat Cheese Rounds

The goat cheese is divided into 12 equal pieces (left), rolled into balls (bottom), coated with herbs (middle), and then breaded (top). It's now ready to cook.

TASTING LAB: Goat Cheese

THE FRENCH ONCE HAD A CORNER ON THE GOAT cheese (or chèvre) market, but that's no longer the case. We conducted a tasting of three domestic and four readily available imported fresh goat cheeses. All were sold in log form ranging in size from 3.5 to 5 ounces.

Our tasters concluded that American producers have mastered the craft of making goat cheese. All of the domestic cheeses were well liked, but the clear favorite was Vermont Chèvre, from the Vermont Butter and Cheese Company. It was creamy and tangy but not overpowering.

Reviews of the imported cheese were mixed. Tasters were enthusiastic about Le Biquet from Canada, but many of the French cheeses were described as gamey or muttony, with a chalky, Spackle-like texture. A few adventurous tasters appreciated the assertive flavors of the imported cheeses, but the overall feeling was that the domestic cheeses were cleaner tasting, more balanced, and better suited for use in a baked goat cheese salad. (A head-to-head tasting of our favorite domestic and imported cheeses bore this out.)

Whether you like a mild or assertive goat cheese, when using goat cheese for salad look for a firm log with a relatively dry exterior. Softer cheeses are more difficult to portion evenly and don't lend themselves well to rolling and breading.

GETTING IT RIGHT: Cooking the Cheese

Pan-Fried	Baked at 350 Degrees	Baked at 475 Degrees

Pan-fried goat cheese develops a crisp crust, but it's very tricky to turn the rounds over without crushing the melting interior and causing the cheese to ooze out (left photo). Goat cheese coated with bread crumbs and baked in a 350-degree oven (center photo) is soggy and pale. Goat cheese coated with ground Melba crumbs, partially frozen, and baked at 475 degrees is crisp; it doesn't ooze; and it maintains its shape (right photo). It has all the benefits of pan-frying with none of the disadvantages.

Rating Goat Cheeses

TEN MEMBERS OF THE *COOK'S ILLUSTRATED* STAFF TASTED ALL OF THE CHEESES AS IS, WITH CRACKERS AND WATER offered to cleanse palates. The cheeses are listed in order of preference based on their scores in this tasting. Look for these cheeses in supermarkets and specialty markets.

HIGHLY RECOMMENDED
Vermont Butter & Cheese Company Chèvre

Websterville, Vermont   **$3.59 for 4 ounces**

The clear favorite was described by tasters as "creamy," "tangy," and "buttery."

HIGHLY RECOMMENDED
Le Biquet Plain Goat Cheese

Chesterville, Quebec   **$5.99 for 3.5 ounces**

The best imported goat cheese in the tasting. This cheese was well liked by tasters, who called it "well balanced" and "tangy."

RECOMMENDED
Capri, Westfield Farm Goat Cheese

Hubbardston, Massachusetts   **$5.49 for 5 ounces**

This cheese had a slightly "chalky" texture but a nice "nutty" flavor.

RECOMMENDED
Belmont Goat Cheese

Belmont, Wisconsin   **$3.59 for 4 ounces**

Tasters described this cheese as "lemony" and "tangy" with a texture "like thick cream cheese."

RECOMMENDED WITH RESERVATIONS
Chevron Goat Cheese

France   **$3.99 for 4 ounces**

This cheese had a quite strong flavor that was compared to feta cheese. Comments ranged from "tangy" to "sour."

RECOMMENDED WITH RESERVATIONS
Couturier Fresh Goat Cheese

France   **$3.99 for 4 ounces**

Tasters described this cheese as "bitter," and there were several complaints about the "Spackle-like" texture.

RECOMMENDED WITH RESERVATIONS
Montrachet Chèvre

France   **$3.79 for 5 ounces**

The texture of this cheese was deemed "chalky" and "starchy," and the flavor was described as either "grassy" or "like mutton."

FRENCH ONION SOUP

WHAT WE WANTED: French onion soup should have a dark, rich broth, intensely flavored by an abundance of seriously cooked onions and covered by a slice of French bread that is broth-soaked beneath and cheesy and crusty on top.

Making traditional French onion soup is easily a two-day affair, with one day spent making the beef stock and the next toiling over the onions to finish the soup. And there's no guarantee that it will turn out right. Over the years, we have consumed many crocks of flavorless onions floating in hypersalty beef bouillon and topped with globs of greasy melted cheese. We've also eaten weak, watery soups. We set out to develop a soup to obliterate these bad memories.

The first obstacle to success is the base. This soup is most commonly made with homemade beef stock. If the right stock is used, the results can be delicious. But making beef stock takes at least three hours. We wondered if there was a way to get around this step.

We tested soups made with homemade chicken stock (which takes considerably less time to prepare than beef stock) and canned broth. Both were too chickeny and just not right. Soups made with canned beef broth were terrible. Commercial beef broth does not have enough flavor to carry the day alone. After experimentation, we devised a formula for what we call "cheater" broth. By combining canned beef and chicken broths with red wine (the secret ingredient here), we came up with a broth that has enough good, rich flavor to make an excellent soup base.

The next obvious step was to examine the choice of onions. We found Vidalias to be disappointingly bland and boring, white onions to be candy-sweet and one-dimensional, and yellow onions to be only mildly flavorful, with just a slight sweetness. Red onions ranked supreme in our tests. They were intensely oniony and sweet but not cloying, with subtle complexity and nuance.

It was exasperating that the onions took so long—nearly an hour—to caramelize. On top of that, they required frequent stirring to keep them from sticking to the bottom of the pot and burning. We found that adding salt to the onions as they began to cook helped draw out some of the water in the onions and shaved about 10 minutes off the cooking time, but this didn't seem to be our answer. We also tried roasting the onions, thinking that the even, constant heat of the oven might be the answer. Wrong again. Opening and closing the oven door to stir the onions is an incredible hassle.

It was inattentiveness that caused us to let the drippings in the pot of a batch of onions go a little too far. The onions themselves weren't thoroughly caramelized, but all the goo stuck on the pot was. We were sure that the finished soup would taste burnt, but we were surprised to find that it was, in fact, as sweet, rich, and flavorful as the soups we had been making with fully caramelized onions. To refine the technique we had stumbled on, we decided that medium-high heat was the way to go and that the drippings should be very, very deeply browned. There's no way around frequent stirring, but this method cut about another 10 minutes off the onion-cooking time, bringing it down to just over 30 minutes.

With all those wonderful, tasty drippings stuck on the bottom of the pot, the deglazing process of adding the liquid and scraping up all the browned bits is crucial. Once the broth is added to the onions, we found that a simmering time of 20 minutes is needed to allow the onion flavor to permeate the broth and for the flavors to meld.

Many French onion soup recipes call for herbs. A couple of sprigs of fresh parsley, some thyme, and a bay leaf simmered in the soup rounded out the flavors and imparted freshness. Having arrived at a soup that was rich, well-balanced, and full of fabulous onion flavor, it was time to move on to the bread and the cheese.

Some recipes call for placing the bread in the bottom of the bowl and ladling the soup over it. We disagree. We opt to set the bread on top, so that only the bottom of the slice is moistened with broth while its top is crusted with cheese. The bread can then physically support the cheese and prevent it from sinking into the soup. To keep as much cheese as possible on the surface, we found it best to use two slices of bread to fill the mouth of the bowl completely. A baguette can be cut on the bias as necessary to secure the closest fit in the bowl.

Traditionally, French onion soup is topped with Swiss, Gruyère, or Emmentaler. We also ventured across the border to try Asiago. Plain Swiss cheese was neither outstanding nor offensive. It was gooey, bubbly, and mild in characteristic Swiss flavor. Both Gruyère and Emmentaler melted to perfection and were sweet, nutty, and faintly tangy, but they also were very strong and pungent, overwhelming many tasters' palates.

We surprised ourselves by favoring the subdued Italian Asiago. Its flavor, like that of Gruyère and Emmentaler, was sweet and nutty, but without the pungent quality.

Asiago is a dry, not a "melting," cheese, so although we were leaning toward it in flavor, we were left wanting in texture. The obvious answer was to combine cheeses. We tried a layer of Swiss topped with a grating of Asiago. A winning combination, hands down, of chewy goodness and nutty sweetness.

The final coup that weakens knees and makes French onion soup irresistible is a browned, bubbly, molten cheese crust. The quickest way to brown the cheese is to set the bowls on a baking sheet under the broiler, making heat-safe bowls essential. Bowls or crocks with handles make maneuvering easier. This is no soup for fine china.

WHAT WE LEARNED: Start with lots of red onions and cook them until very well browned. Use canned beef and chicken broth along with red wine to create a flavorful soup. Finish with a cheesy crouton (covered with Swiss and Asiago cheeses) that floats on top of individual bowls.

FRENCH ONION SOUP

Serves 6

Tie the parsley and thyme sprigs together with kitchen twine so they will be easy to retrieve from the soup pot. Slicing the baguette on the bias will yield slices shaped to fill the mouths of the bowls.

soup

2	tablespoons unsalted butter
5	medium red onions (about 3 pounds), halved and sliced thin
	Salt
6	cups low-sodium chicken broth
1¾	cups low-sodium beef broth
¼	cup dry red wine
2	sprigs fresh parsley
1	sprig fresh thyme
1	bay leaf
1	tablespoon balsamic vinegar
	Ground black pepper

cheese-topped crusts

1	baguette, cut on the bias into ½-inch slices (2 slices per serving)
4½	ounces Swiss cheese, sliced ¹⁄₁₆ inch thick
1½	ounces Asiago cheese, grated (about ¾ cup)

1. FOR THE SOUP: Melt the butter in a large stockpot or Dutch oven over medium-high heat; add the sliced onions and ½ teaspoon salt and stir to coat the onions thoroughly with the butter. Cook, stirring frequently, until the onions are reduced and syrupy and the inside of the pot is coated with a very deep brown crust, 30 to 35 minutes. Stir in the chicken and beef broths, red wine, parsley, thyme, and bay leaf, scraping the pot bottom with a wooden spoon to loosen the browned bits, and bring to a simmer. Simmer to blend the flavors, about 20 minutes, and discard the herbs. Stir in the balsamic vinegar and season with salt and pepper. (The soup can be cooled to room temperature and refrigerated in

an airtight container up to 2 days; return to a simmer before finishing the soup with the croutons and cheese.)

2. FOR THE CRUSTS: Adjust an oven rack to the upper-middle position and heat the oven to 350 degrees. Spread the bread out on a rimmed baking sheet and bake, flipping once, until lightly browned, about 15 minutes. Remove the bread from the oven. Turn the oven to broil.

3. Set heat-safe soup bowls or crocks on a rimmed baking sheet; fill each with about 1½ cups of the soup. Top each bowl with 2 toasted baguette slices and divide the Swiss cheese slices, placing them in a single layer, if possible, on the bread. Sprinkle each serving with about 2 tablespoons of the grated Asiago and broil until well browned and bubbly, 7 to 10 minutes. Cool 5 minutes and serve.

SCIENCE DESK: Blue Onion Soup?

RED ONIONS MAY BE THE BEST CHOICE IN TERMS OF flavor, but they can turn onion soup an unappetizing bluish-gray color. This is because they contain anthocyanin, a water-soluble pigment that also causes red cabbage to discolor when cooked. This pigment is present in some other reddish fruits and vegetables as well, such as cherries and radishes.

When the fruit or vegetable is cooked in liquid, the anthocyanin leaches out. If the liquid is alkaline (as is the case with our soup), the anthocyanin turns blue. Adding some acid, either lemon juice or vinegar, to the soup at the end helps it to regain its reddish color. This may sound improbable, but when we stirred in 1 tablespoon of balsamic vinegar, the soup returned to a deep reddish brown. The vinegar also brightens the flavors in the soup. So, whenever the color of cooked red onions becomes dull looking, add a little citrus juice or vinegar to restore their naturally vibrant color.

TECHNIQUE: Bouquet Garni

A bouquet garni is a classic French combination of herbs and spices used to flavor soups, stocks, and stews. Traditional recipes call for wrapping the herbs in cheesecloth for easy removal. A paper coffee filter works just as well. (Another option is a tea ball; see page 193.)

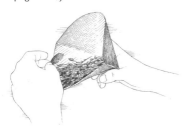

1. Place the herbs (usually bay leaves and thyme, either dried or fresh, and fresh parsley) and spices (usually black peppercorns) in the coffee filter.

2. Tie the end of the filter closed, catching the stems of the herbs as you do so.

3. Tie the other end of the string to the handle of the pot so you can easily retrieve the bouquet garni once the herbs and spices have given up their flavor.

For the best flavor and texture, the onions should be cooked until they become dark and syrupy, a process that will take about half an hour over medium-high heat. Make sure to use a heavy-bottomed pot, such as this Dutch oven.

EQUIPMENT CORNER: Santoku Knives

THE SANTOKU HAS LONG BEEN THE JAPANESE EQUIVALENT of a chef's knife—an all-purpose blade capable of performing any task in the kitchen. But only recently has this knife gained America's attention, as the darling of celebrity chefs such as Ming Tsai and Rachel Ray. With the popularity of Japanese minimalism in the culinary world at its apex, could this be a case of media hype, or were we missing something? We set out to see if the santoku could supplant our kitchen's workhorse, the classic 8-inch chef's knife.

What is a santoku knife? Compared with a classic chef's knife, the santoku, sometimes labeled in stores as an Asian or oriental chef's knife, is typically shorter and has a thinner blade, a stubbier tip, and a straighter edge. The santoku's slight size, believed to have evolved from the narrow, rectangular Japanese vegetable knife, equates to a great amount of blade control.

To fully evaluate the santoku, we bought 10 models, ranging in price from $30 to $100, with blades made from a variety of materials, from the conventional high-carbon stainless steel to the exotic, including ceramic and a titanium silver alloy. To be as thorough as possible, we ran them through a series of tests, using the Forschner (Victorinox) chef's knife (the winning model from an earlier test of chef's knives) for comparison. The tests included preparing onions, garlic, carrots, tomatoes, and boneless chicken breasts. We assessed each knife for precision, control, sharpness of blade, efficiency, comfort, price, and finally size, which proved to be very significant in these tests.

During the first test we conducted, mincing and chopping onions, the size of the santoku blade came into play. All of the santoku blades ranged in size from 6 to 7 inches, but the larger blades significantly outperformed their smaller counterparts. The 6-inch blade was so short that most of the testers ended up knuckle-deep in onions after just a few strokes. The larger-bladed santokus, on the other hand, performed very well during the onion test, with the Kershaw Shun ($99.95) taking home top honors over the Forschner chef's knife.

Where the Santokus really excelled was in more precise or delicate tasks. Julienned carrots rifled off the blade, and the chicken breasts practically butterflied themselves under the accurate blade of the santoku. Most testers found the santokus superior in these situations because their thin, short blades reduced friction and felt more exact against the dense flesh of the carrots and the chicken.

During mincing evaluations, the curve of the blade was the main factor mentioned by our testers. Because of the rocking motion used during mincing, the santokus with straighter edges tended to feel more jarring than those with more rounded edges. The straight-edged santokus seemed to be geared more toward slicing, and in fact, they performed very well while slicing tomatoes. A very telling test, slicing tomatoes calls for only the sharpest of blades. High-carbon stainless steel knives performed best in this test, followed by the ceramic-bladed Kyocera Ming Tsai ($99.95) that was adequately sharp, but not weighty enough to take top honors. Bringing up the rear in the tomato test was the titanium silver alloy Boker Cera-Titan I ($63.95) that was at once too thin, overly flexible, and disappointingly dull.

While most of the testers appreciated the performance and quality of many of the santoku knives, only two

EQUIPMENT CORNER:
Hollowed-Edge Santoku Knives

MANY SANTOKUS ARE AVAILABLE WITH EITHER A standard or a granton blade, the latter being hollow-ground and incorporating oval recesses along the blade. (This design was originally intended to make slicing meat easier.) Granton blades are often advertised as "nonstick."

Unfortunately, we quickly learned that these knives are not exactly nonstick. Minced garlic and cucumber slices will still cling vigilantly to the sides of a granton-style blade. However, as master bladesmith Robert Kramer explained to us, the hollows do help break the surface tension between the food and the blade surface. The hollows create air pockets between the breadth of the blade and the food, thus reducing the drag or friction between the two. So it was no coincidence that the two knives with the tallest hollows, the Mac and the Kershaw Shun, seemed to show the biggest decrease in friction when tested against their standard-edge versions. Even then, the differences didn't bowl us over.

A santoku with a granton edge typically costs $10 to $20 more than one with a standard edge. Knives with granton edges can be sharpened, although it takes a little more care because once sharpened into the hollows, the blade becomes slightly thinner. Given the less-than-eye-opening differences, we prefer santokus with the cheaper standard edge.

knives—the Mac Superior ($55) and the Kershaw Shun Classic—were consistently preferred to the Forschner chef's knife in the tests. Now, although this fact speaks highly of santoku knives in general, it could be argued that the tests we performed were geared toward the lightweight santokus. In preliminary tests, we attempted tasks such as butchering a whole chicken or halving acorn squash. In most cases, the santokus were deemed too small or lightweight for these operations, while the chef's knife tackled them with ease.

So should you run out to the nearest cutlery dealer and purchase the latest celebrity-endorsed santoku? Not necessarily. The santoku would certainly be a reliable addition to any kitchen—its lightweight and lightning quick blade feels right at home with vegetable preparations. However, due to its smaller size and delicate blade, the santoku comes up short in its ability to function as an all-purpose blade. A good santoku can complement—but not replace—a trusted chef's knife.

A BETTER EDGE?
A granton-style blade with oval recesses reduces friction ever so slightly. But this minor perk is not worth the higher price tag.

Rating Santoku Knives

SEVEN TEST COOKS AND ONE KITCHEN INTERN EVALUATED EACH KNIFE ACCORDING TO PERFORMANCE AND design. The knives were used to chop and dice onions, mince and slice garlic, thinly slice and julienne carrots, slice tomatoes, and butterfly boneless, skinless chicken breasts. The testers ran the gamut in terms of knife skills—from beginner to advanced—as well as hand size and strength. Only one tester was left-handed. Knives are listed in order of preference. See www.americastestkitchen.com for up-to-date prices and mail-order sources for top-rated products.

HIGHLY RECOMMENDED
MAC Superior Santoku $55

An ideal bridge between the cramped, smaller santokus and the larger chef's knife. Admired for being the most sharp and responsive, this knife was especially nimble, easy to control, and precise. As one tester gushed, "great with everything."

RECOMMENDED
Kershaw Shun Classic Santoku model DM-0702 $99.95

Praised as the Cadillac of the group, this knife felt "sturdy" and "solid." The curvature of the blade made it good at rocking while mincing, and the tip was sharp and decisive. We docked points for a handle that was uncomfortable for the left-handed tester.

RECOMMENDED
Wüsthof Grand Prix Oriental Cook's Knife $70

This model excelled at thin slicing and fine mincing. Its straight blade created a "see-saw" effect when rocking to mince or chop. Some testers applauded the Wüsthof's light feel as a smaller, quicker chef's knife. Others deemed it flimsy.

RECOMMENDED
Global Oriental Cook Knife $81.99

This could have been a perfect knife if not for a narrow, sleek stainless steel handle that made the grip feel unsteady. The sharp blade with a markedly curved edge and the tapered tip were useful—more like a chef's knife than a santoku.

RECOMMENDED
Zwilling Henckels Four Star Santoku $65

A sharp, relatively thick blade made this knife a strong, substantial slicer, but the blade's flat curve made its rocking motion shallow and somewhat jarring. This knife generally had an awkward, less maneuverable feel.

RECOMMENDED
Oxo Good Grips MV55-Pro Santoku $30

This model possessed decent sharpness and maneuverability but was best suited to slicing. The stubby, cleaver-shaped blade felt somewhat dead while mincing and coarse chopping. The fat handle on the Oxo was liked by many for its soft, grippy feel.

NOT RECOMMENDED
Kyocera Ming Tsai Santoku $99.95

This knife's notably sharp, short blade performed delicate knife work respectably but didn't have the weight behind it to handle all tasks. The white ceramic blade made it tricky to see light-colored foods (such as garlic) when working on a white plastic board. Overall, too small to be of much use.

NOT RECOMMENDED
Furi Pro East/West Santoku $70

This knife's blade was dull, fat, stubby, and clumsy—more like a cleaver. It had a decent rocking motion but lacked the capacity for delicate and precise work. The molded stainless steel handle was deemed too large and cumbersome.

NOT RECOMMENDED
Boker Cera-Titan I Santoku $63.95

Feather-light, flimsy, short, and cheap in feel was the overall consensus on this knife. Difficult control and a shallow, abrupt rocking motion were common complaints.

NOT RECOMMENDED
Forschner Santoku $35

Most testers found the Forschner's teeny, hobbit-size handle uncomfortable and difficult to control. Not enough clearance under the handle, so even those with small hands banged their knuckles when the blade came in full contact with the cutting board.

Best-ever sticky buns rise to the occasion.

ULTIMATE sticky buns

Sticky buns are things of breakfast-time debauchery. In bakeries, they are often plate-size buns, warm and glistening, heady with brown sugar and spices. In our opinion, anything less than a great one is not worth its calories.

A sticky bun should be neither dense nor bready, neither saturated with butter nor so sugary that it makes your heart race. The crumb should be tender and feathery and the sticky glaze gently chewy and gooey; the flavor should be warm and spicy, buttery and sweet—but just enough so that devouring one doesn't feel like a feat.

Home bakers rarely attempt them, probably because sticky buns, like many other sweet yeasted breads, are a project, requiring a substantial time commitment. But we think that's a shame. Sticky buns are worth the effort. We set out to develop a recipe that would be irresistible.

STICKY BUNS

WHAT WE WANTED: These bakery favorites are often too sweet, too big, too rich, and just too much. We wanted sticky buns that were impressive, not excessive.

In our search for the ultimate sticky bun, we looked at dozens of recipes. Our research turned up all manner of sticky buns. Of those that we tried, one was too lean—like a sugar-soaked baguette. One was cakey, with an insubstantial crumb, and it had a meager amount of sticky goo; another was doughy and had a hard sugar veneer. The most laborious recipe resulted—some 18 hours later—in overly rich sticky buns that weren't worth the time or the effort. Those recipes that contained nuts, which were baked beneath the buns, had in common soggy, steamy pecans or walnuts that contributed little to either flavor or texture.

The basic MO for sticky buns starts with a sugary glaze mixture that is put into a baking dish. The dough, after its first rise, is rolled, filled, and cut into buns. The buns are set on top of the glaze mixture, allowed a second rise, then baked, inverted, and devoured.

We began this multi-component preparation with the dough. From the start we knew that a lean dough, made with only flour and water, was out. It was an anomaly anyway. Most recipes involved fairly rich doughs with milk, butter, eggs, and sugar in addition to the requisite flour, yeast, and salt. First off, we tried different liquids. Water, milk, and buttermilk all worked, but the buttermilk dough was vastly superior to the others. In the baked buns, the tanginess of the buttermilk translated into a flavor complexity that the others simply lacked; its acidity, though not overt, made a nice counterpoint to the sugary sweetness. Both flavor and texture were rich without being heavy, and the crumb was tender and light. Nonfat and low-fat buttermilk succeeded equally, as did, to our surprise, powdered buttermilk (which is added as a dry ingredient, with water being substituted for the buttermilk).

For the four or so cups of flour in the dough, we tested varying quantities of butter and finally settled on 6 tablespoons. It turned out that melted, rather than softened, butter was not only easier to use but yielded superb results to boot. Next we experimented with eggs, starting with no eggs and going up to three whole eggs. With too few eggs, the texture of the buns lacked substance; the crumb was too soft and yielding, like a squishy sandwich bread. Egg-rich versions—namely, those made with three eggs—were the favorite. These were moist, with a nice, light, open crumb. They were also tender and yet had substantial structure and chew.

The rest of the dough fell into place. One-quarter cup of sugar gave it a light sweetness, and a hit of salt boosted flavor. One packet of instant yeast (2¼ teaspoons) worked to get the dough rising in a timely manner without leaving a distinct yeastiness in its wake (as an overabundance of yeast would). Bread flour didn't outperform all-purpose flour, so all-purpose it was.

After the dough's first rise, or fermentation, it is rolled out into a rectangle and filled. The spiced sugar filling, which creates the swirl in the shaped buns, was quickly settled. Brown sugar beat out granulated because it has more presence; its color is darker and its flavor more assertive. A healthy dose of ground cinnamon and a dash of ground cloves added warmth and fragrance. We were making quick progress.

Most recipes specify dark brown sugar for use in the glaze as well as the filling, but before too long we dropped dark brown sugar in favor of light brown for the glaze. During baking, dark brown sugar took on too much color, and, though it tasted fine, it made the buns look unattractive . . . just shy of singed.

At this point, progress slowed. In the batches we baked, the glaze invariably cooked up treacherously sticky and far too firm—ideal for ripping out dental work (which it did in fact do to one unfortunate taster). In combination with ¾ cup of brown sugar, we tried different amounts of

butter—2, 4, 6, 8, and even 10 tablespoons. We increased and decreased the brown sugar. We tried adding water to the glaze mixture. We shortened baking times and lowered oven temperatures so that the glaze faced less heat (heat is what causes it to cook and harden). All to no avail. We tried adding a dose of corn syrup. The glaze showed some improvement—it had a softer, chewier texture—but it was still rather stiff and taffy-like, and it lacked fluidity. With a thick, unctuous, but pourable, classic caramel sauce in mind (one made from caramelized sugar and heavy cream), we tried adding heavy cream—just 2 tablespoons—and it worked like magic. The topping was now sticky, gooey, and just a bit sauce-like. The downside to the cream was that it had a slight dulling effect on the flavor of the caramel, but tasters—and their fillings, bridges, and crowns—could live with that.

We tried different oven temperatures, and a 350-degree oven worked best, as did a 13 by 9-inch baking pan. Yet the buns were still far from perfect. They had a tacky, doughy, underdone surface, and the caramel glaze was a couple shades too light. One cookbook author suggested placing the baking dish on a preheated baking stone, a step that vastly improved the evenness of browning and allowed the bottoms of the buns (which, bear in mind, later become the tops) to bake through in spite of all the goo that they sat in. With

the baking stone in play, though, the baking pan's material became important. A nonstick metal pan proved the best choice (see page 275 for details). At first, we were inverting the hot sticky buns out of the pan as soon as they were done. After a few batches, though, we finally realized the merits of allowing them to cool for about 10 minutes before inversion. When hot, the caramel glaze was so molten that it quickly ran off the buns and pooled on the platter. Cooled for just a bit, however, the glaze was viscous enough to generously blanket the surface.

According to tasters, the sticky buns were close to being great, but they were missing something—nuts, pecans in particular. Instead of sprinkling chopped toasted pecans over the glaze in the baking dish, where we knew they would turn soggy, we introduced them to the filling. No good. Encased in the dough rather than sitting beneath it, the once toasty, crisp pecans still turned soft and soggy. The sticky buns were hardly better off for having them.

We recalled a recipe that had included an unusual postbake glaze. At first the idea of still more glaze seemed superfluous (enough sugar already!), but then we realized that it could form a sort of base for a topping . . . a toasted pecan topping. We formulated a mixture of more glaze ingredients—butter, light brown sugar, and corn syrup for fluidity—to which we added toasted chopped pecans and some vanilla for good measure. The relatively small amount of sugar in this topping gave the nuts some cohesion without oversweetening matters. We poured/spread the nut topping over the buns as soon as we turned them out of the pan. Crowned with pecans, the sticky buns had achieved greatness.

WHAT WE LEARNED: Start with an egg-rich, buttery dough, coat the pan with a caramel-like glaze made fluid by the addition of heavy cream, and then fill the dough with a simple mixture of brown sugar, cinnamon, cloves, and butter. For proper browning, use a nonstick metal pan placed on a preheated baking stone. To keep nuts crisp, use them in a second glaze to coat the baked buns, rather than adding them to the dough.

STICKY BUNS WITH PECANS

Makes 12 buns

This recipe has four components: the dough that is shaped into buns, the filling that creates the swirl in the shaped buns, the caramel glaze that bakes in the bottom of the baking dish along with the buns, and the pecan topping that garnishes the buns once they're baked. Although the ingredient list may look long, note that many ingredients are repeated; for example, butter is called for in all four components (for a total of 16 tablespoons, or 2 sticks), light brown sugar is called for in three (for a total of 1¾ cups, or about 12 ounces), and corn syrup in two (for a total of 6 tablespoons). If not using a baking stone or nonstick baking dish, see "Baking the Buns" on page 275. Leftover sticky buns can be wrapped in foil or plastic wrap and refrigerated for up to 3 days, but they should be warmed through before serving. They reheat quickly in a microwave oven (for 2 buns, about 2 minutes at 50 percent power works well).

dough

- 3 large eggs, at room temperature
- ¾ cup buttermilk, at room temperature
- ¼ cup (1¾ ounces) granulated sugar
- 1¼ teaspoons salt
- 2¼ teaspoons (1 envelope) instant yeast
- 4¼ cups (21¼ ounces) unbleached all-purpose flour, plus more for dusting the work surface
- 6 tablespoons (¾ stick) unsalted butter, melted and cooled until warm

caramel glaze

- 6 tablespoons (¾ stick) unsalted butter
- ¾ cup (5¼ ounces) packed light brown sugar
- 3 tablespoons light or dark corn syrup
- 2 tablespoons heavy cream
  Pinch salt

cinnamon–sugar filling

- ¾ cup (5¼ ounces) packed light brown sugar
- 2 teaspoons ground cinnamon
- ¼ teaspoon ground cloves
  Pinch salt
- 1 tablespoon unsalted butter, melted

pecan topping

- 3 tablespoons unsalted butter
- ¼ cup (1¾ ounces) packed light brown sugar
- 3 tablespoons light or dark corn syrup
  Pinch salt
- 1 teaspoon vanilla extract
- ¾ cup (3 ounces) pecans, toasted in a small, dry skillet over medium heat until fragrant and browned, about 5 minutes, then cooled and coarsely chopped

1. FOR THE DOUGH: In the bowl of a standing mixer, whisk the eggs to combine; add the buttermilk and whisk to combine. Whisk in the sugar, salt, and yeast. Add about 2 cups of the flour and the butter; stir with a wooden spoon or rubber spatula until evenly moistened and combined.

GETTING IT RIGHT: Problem Buns

We tested dozens of recipes and found that several recurring problems plagued most of them.

RUNAWAY GOO
Immediately after baking, the glaze is molten and will run off the buns if the pan is inverted too soon.

UNDERBROWNED
When baked in a glass Pyrex baking dish, the surface of the buns appears underbaked in color and texture.

SEEMINGLY BURNT
Using dark brown sugar in the glaze results in dark, almost burnt-looking sticky buns.

Add all but about ¼ cup of the remaining flour and knead with a dough hook at low speed 5 minutes. Check the consistency of the dough (the dough should feel soft and moist but should not be wet and sticky; add more flour, if necessary); knead at low speed 5 minutes longer (the dough should clear the sides of the bowl but stick to the bottom). Turn the dough out onto a lightly floured work surface; knead by hand about 1 minute to ensure that the dough is uniform (the dough should not stick to the work surface during hand kneading; if it does, knead in additional flour 1 tablespoon at a time).

2. Lightly spray a large bowl or plastic container with non-stick cooking spray. Transfer the dough to the bowl, spray the dough lightly with cooking spray, then cover the bowl tightly with plastic wrap and set in a warm, draft-free spot until doubled in volume, 2 to 2½ hours.

3. FOR THE GLAZE: Meanwhile, combine all the ingredients for the glaze in a small saucepan; cook over medium heat, whisking occasionally, until the butter is melted and the mixture is thoroughly combined. Pour the mixture into a nonstick metal 13 by 9-inch baking dish; using a rubber spatula, spread the mixture to cover the surface of the baking dish; set the baking dish aside.

4. TO ASSEMBLE AND BAKE THE BUNS: For the filling, combine the brown sugar, cinnamon, cloves, and salt in a small bowl and mix until thoroughly combined, using your fingers to break up any sugar lumps; set aside. Turn the dough out onto a lightly floured work surface. Gently shape the dough into a rough rectangle with a long side nearest you. Lightly flour the dough and roll to a 16 by 12-inch rectangle. Brush the dough with the 1 tablespoon melted butter, leaving a ½-inch border along the top edge; brush the sides of the baking dish with the butter remaining on the brush. Sprinkle the filling mixture over the dough, leaving a ¾-inch border along the top edge; smooth the filling in an even layer with your hand, then gently press the mixture into the dough to adhere. Beginning with the long edge nearest you, roll the dough into a taut cylinder. Firmly pinch the seam to seal and roll the cylinder seam-side down.

TECHNIQUE: Assembling Sticky Buns

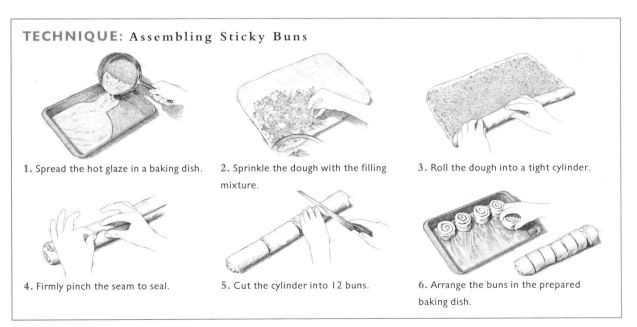

1. Spread the hot glaze in a baking dish.

2. Sprinkle the dough with the filling mixture.

3. Roll the dough into a tight cylinder.

4. Firmly pinch the seam to seal.

5. Cut the cylinder into 12 buns.

6. Arrange the buns in the prepared baking dish.

Very gently stretch to form a cylinder of even diameter and 18-inch length; push the ends in to create an even thickness. Using a serrated knife and gentle sawing motion, slice the cylinder in half, then slice each half in half again to create evenly sized quarters. Slice each quarter evenly into thirds, yielding 12 buns (the end pieces may be slightly smaller).

5. Arrange the buns cut-side down in the prepared baking dish; cover tightly with plastic wrap and set in a warm, draft-free spot until puffy and pressed against one another, about 1½ hours. Meanwhile, adjust an oven rack to the lowest position, place a baking stone (if using) on the rack, and heat the oven to 350 degrees.

6. Place the baking pan on the baking stone; bake until golden brown and the center of the dough registers about 180 degrees on an instant-read thermometer, 25 to 30 minutes. Cool on a wire rack 10 minutes; invert onto a rimmed baking sheet, large rectangular platter, or cutting board. With a rubber spatula, scrape any glaze remaining in the baking pan onto the buns; cool while making the pecan topping.

7. FOR THE TOPPING: Combine the butter, brown sugar, corn syrup, and salt in a small saucepan and bring to a simmer over medium heat, whisking occasionally to thoroughly combine. Off heat, stir in the vanilla and pecans until the pecans are evenly coated. Using a soup spoon, spoon a heaping tablespoon of nuts and topping over the center of each sticky bun. Continue to cool until the sticky buns are warm, 15 to 20 minutes. Pull apart or use a serrated knife to cut apart the sticky buns; serve.

VARIATIONS

HAND-KNEADED METHOD FOR STICKY BUNS

1. Using same ingredient list as for Sticky Buns with Pecans, in a large bowl, whisk the eggs to combine; add the buttermilk and whisk to combine. Whisk in the sugar, salt, and yeast. Add about 2 cups of the flour and the butter; stir with a wooden spoon or rubber spatula until evenly moistened and combined. Add all but about ¼ cup of the remaining flour and stir until the mixture forms a shaggy dough. Turn the dough out onto a lightly floured work surface and knead by hand 10 to 15 minutes, adding more flour as needed (after about 5 minutes, the dough should feel soft and moist but should not stick to the work surface).

2. Continue with the recipe from step 2.

OVERNIGHT STICKY BUNS

If you'd like to serve freshly baked sticky buns for a late breakfast or for a brunch and want to minimize early morning preparation, they can be made and shaped the night before and then refrigerated. The next morning, to help the buns rise in a timely manner, they should be set in a warm-water bath for 20 minutes and then allowed to complete their rise at room temperature.

1. Follow the recipe for Sticky Buns with Pecans; after forming and arranging the buns in the baking pan, cover the pan tightly with plastic wrap and refrigerate 10 to 14 hours.

2. Place the baking pan in a warm-water bath (about 120 degrees) in a kitchen sink or large roasting pan for 20

Q&A

What's the best way to clean up a sticky bowl lined with bits of dough?

Never wash bowls that have been used to make bread dough with hot water. The heat swells the starches in the flour, and they begin to harden. Cold water is a much better choice. To keep sponges from becoming clogged with dough, we save the mesh bags that onions are sold in and use them to scrub doughy bowls. Once the bowl is cleaned, we simply discard the mesh bag and all the dough attached to it.

minutes. Remove the baking dish from the water bath and let stand at room temperature until the buns look slightly puffy and are pressed against one another, about 1½ hours. About an hour before baking, adjust an oven rack to the lowest position, place the baking stone on the rack (if using), and heat the oven to 350 degrees.

3. Continue with the recipe from step 6.

GETTING IT RIGHT: Baking the Buns

The type of baking dish and the use of a baking stone make a difference in how well and how evenly the buns and topping brown in the oven.

BEST: Nonstick metal baking dish on 350-degree preheated baking stone.
We obtained the best results by baking the sticky buns in a nonstick metal baking pan on a preheated baking stone. Browning was uniform, and cleanup was a breeze.

RUNNER-UP: Traditional (not nonstick) metal baking dish on 400-degree preheated baking stone; reduce oven temperature to 350 degrees after placing buns in the oven.
A traditional reflective-finish baking pan and a slightly hotter baking stone work well, but the heat must be adjusted after the buns go into the oven.

HANDICAP: Nonstick metal baking dish on lowest oven rack at 350 degrees.
If using a baking stone is not an option, use a nonstick baking pan. The dark color of the nonstick finish aids in browning. (Note, however, that the buns will not brown as evenly as those baked on a stone.)

NO-GO: Glass baking dish
Baking the buns in a glass dish without the benefit of a baking stone gives them a doughy, underdone appearance; making them in a glass dish with the benefit of a baking stone is not a safe option.

SCIENCE DESK: Designer Yeast

LESAFFRE, THE PRODUCER OF RED STAR YEAST, MAKES a line of yeast called Nevada Gold Label ($6.50 for 15.85 ounces, available from www.bakerscatalogue.com)that is specifically designed for high-sugar doughs, and we thought that our sweet sticky buns would be an ideal candidate on which to test it. After baking two batches of rolls, we found that this designer yeast worked, decreasing the time required for the first rise by 33 percent and the second rise by 45 percent when compared with the standard SAF instant yeast. In total, this saved us more than an hour in rising time. Our curiosity was piqued.

It's not easy being unicellular yeast. Precious little separates their insides from the harsh world at large—no skin, no fat, just a membrane. Most bakers consider sugar food for yeast, but sugar in too high a concentration can be a killer. Yeast placed in a high-sugar dough can undergo osmotic stress, in which water wants to flow out of the yeast and into the dough, causing the yeast to dry out.

Nevada Gold Label yeast is designed to withstand this stress better than regular yeast. The dough we made with it performed particularly well in the second rise, when the rolls were shaped, cloaked in sugar, and exposed to the air—definitely a harsh environment for a moisture-loving organism. If you bake a lot of sweet breads, you may want to keep some Nevada Gold Label on hand.

TASTING LAB: Supermarket Coffees

IT WASN'T TOO LONG AGO THAT IF YOU WANTED A CUP of coffee, you had two choices: brew it yourself at home with a supermarket brand or buy a watery, tasteless cup at your local convenience store or diner. Today, specialty coffees abound, with boutique shops in every town selling "premium" beans so that quality coffee can be had at home. But what about those old stalwarts, the supermarket brands of yore? At just one-quarter the price of premium beans and widely available, there's no beating the cost or the convenience. Are any of these dinosaurs of an era past worth drinking?

After sampling eight brands of ground coffee from the supermarket (including Starbucks, a supposedly premium brand that is now available in supermarkets already ground), we can safely say no. The best anyone could say about our "winner" was that it was the "least offensive" of the lot.

We brewed all the coffees to the strength recommended by the Specialty Coffee Association, which is 1.6 grams of coffee per ounce of water, and used the same model of electric drip coffee maker for all of them. We tasted the coffees plain, without sugar or milk.

Only one coffee is recommended, and even that one received mostly negative comments from tasters, though a few found it palatable. The problem most of the tasters had with the coffees was the lack of depth; the overriding flavor in almost all of the samples was bitterness, with no floral, fruity, or chocolatey flavors that you would find in a good coffee. Chock Full o' Nuts (which also performed well in a previous tasting of French roast coffees) was less the most liked of the brands than the least hated of them. As for the rest of the pack—well, let's just say that no one wanted to save the leftovers for iced coffee.

So is this just a case of money buying quality? Will the $12-a-pound coffee you buy at the coffee shop always be better than the coffee you buy in the supermarket? Well, yes and no. Starbucks, a premium brand that is sold in most major supermarkets (as well as in dedicated coffee shops), placed second-to-last in our tasting, yet it costs more than three times as much as our top finisher, Chock Full o' Nuts. Our reasons for not liking Starbucks, however, are different than those for not liking the other supermarket brands. In our opinion, Starbucks tends to overroast their beans, which can lead to overtly bitter tones in the coffee, something our tasters didn't like.

There are two likely reasons we didn't like the supermarket brands, both having to do with the beans. The beans used by supermarket brands are of a lower quality than those used at coffee shops. The second factor is the grind; when you buy coffee at a coffee shop, the beans are ground when you purchase them (or shortly before). With supermarket coffee, the beans are ground far in advance of when you buy them. And with freshness goes much of the flavor.

Money, then, is not necessarily the best judge of coffee; rather, you should go for freshness first and always buy high-quality beans.

Rating Supermarket Coffees

TWENTY-THREE MEMBERS OF THE *COOK'S ILLUSTRATED* STAFF PARTICIPATED IN THE TASTING. WE BREWED THE COFFEES TO THE same strength (1.6 grams of coffee per ounce of water, the ratio recommended by the Specialty Coffee Association) and in the same model of electric drip coffee maker. The coffees were tasted plain—no sugar, no milk. The coffees are listed in order of preference based on their scores in this tasting. All brands are available in supermarkets.

RECOMMENDED WITH RESERVATIONS
Chock Full o' Nuts Original **$2.69 for 13 ounces**
No one got very excited by this brand, which was deemed the "least offensive." "Tastes like diner coffee," wrote one taster.

NOT RECOMMENDED
Melitta Traditional Roast **$3.99 for 11.5 ounces**
This brand costs more than other basic options and wasn't any better. "Very sour" and "no aroma" were typical comments.

NOT RECOMMENDED
Folgers Classic Roast **$2.79 for 13 ounces**
"Bursting with charcoal flavors, and nothing else," summed up the general reaction to this coffee.

NOT RECOMMENDED
Hills Bros. Original Blend Medium Roast **$2.79 for 13 ounces**
This sample had very little flavor. "Tastes like hot water, but at least the bitterness is in check."

NOT RECOMMENDED
Nescafé Taster's Choice (Instant) **$5.49 for 4 ounces**
Lack of flavor was the most common criticism of this instant coffee. "Sour," "greasy," and "tastes like nothing."

NOT RECOMMENDED
Maxwell House Original **$2.79 for 13 ounces**
"No depth" and "highly bitter" were typical criticisms of this familiar brand. So much for drinking the last drop.

NOT RECOMMENDED
Starbucks House Blend **$8.39 for 12 ounces**
Too much flavor—rather than too little—was the problem with this coffeehouse favorite, which is now sold in many supermarkets. "Smells like a forest fire," quipped one taster.

NOT RECOMMENDED
Chase & Sanborn Special Roast **$2.49 for 11.5 ounces**
The worst of the worst. "Tastes like something . . . dirt, maybe?"

EQUIPMENT CORNER:
New Generation Coffee Makers

IN OUR EXPERIENCE, AUTOMATIC-DRIP COFFEE MACHINES make coffee easily, but rarely well—often producing a burnt and bitter liquid reminiscent of stale truck stop coffee. Recently, appliance makers have introduced machines with improved technologies aimed at brewing better tasting coffee. The three main categories are: grind-and-brew machines, electric vacuum machines, and single-cup brewers similar to espresso machines. We selected seven of these machines, which range in price from $50 to $250, and rated them according to their price, coffee flavor, convenience, full pot brew time, and full pot temperature (when fresh, 30 minutes, and 60 minutes old).

According to the Specialty Coffee Association of America, the quality of a cup of coffee is affected by 10 primary variables, from the chemistry of the beans to the composition of the water and the method used to hold the finished beverage. Automatic brewers, whether drip or another type, should control at least four of the 10 variables. Those are brewing time (four to six minutes for a full pot using medium-grind coffee, optimally), temperature (195 to 205 degrees for brewing and 155 to 175 degrees for serving), delivery of water and resulting agitation of the grounds (large filter basket to provide room for grounds to swell without compacting), and holding conditions (assuming that you brew a partial or entire pot, as opposed to a single cup).

The first three machines that we tested, the grind-and-brew models, attempted to produce a better cup of coffee by grinding the beans immediately before brewing. Ideally, this would enhance the coffee by limiting the dissipation of flavorful chemical compounds caused by premature grinding. This would be an effective approach, but unfortunately, the 10- to 12-minute brewing cycles of these machines seemed to have an adverse effect on the coffee's aroma. Even so, tasters rated the Cuisinart ($149.99) and the Capresso ($199.99) coffee well. Where they did not impress was in convenience—both were difficult to clean and the latter lacked a thermal carafe that would preserve the brewed coffee.

The next style of machine, the electric vacuum brewer, has predecessors dating back to the mid-1800s. Consisting of two bowls sitting one on top of the other, this machine exploits the vacuum produced when steam forces boiling water from the bottom to the top bowl. From there, the water and coffee mix and drip back down through a filter to the bottom bowl. We tested two of these machines, a Black & Decker ($69.99) and a Bodum ($99.99) and found that they both produced a very hot and distinctly robust brew, which will appeal to many (but not all) coffee drinkers. The brew cycles on both machines were, respectably, in the four- to six-minute range, but neither model featured a thermal carafe. We gave top honors for the vacuum machines to the Black & Decker because it was easier to clean.

The final category, the espresso-method single-cup brewers, trumpeted a very intriguing development in the java world. Each time that you want a cup of coffee, you brew a fresh one—in less than one minute. These machines work much like an espresso machine; the units use pumps (typically air or steam powered) to force hot, pressurized water through packaged coffee grounds to extract maximum flavor in seconds. These machines also produced a distinct style of coffee. It was mild with a light body, basically what we think of as classic American coffee. The only drawback to these machines is that they only accept coffee cartridges, or pods, provided by the machine's manufacturer. The Keurig ($249.99), in all fairness, does offer almost 80 varieties of coffee, but the Melitta ($49.99) offers only six selections.

If you are a fan of a light, American-style coffee, we suggest the single-cup brewers over the grind-and-brew machines, largely because of the design idiosyncrasies among the latter. Because we like our coffee strong and full-bodied, we prefer the electric vacuum brewers, despite their lack of thermal carafes. If the R & D people were to produce a vacuum brewer that incorporated a thermal carafe, we'd buy it in a second. For now, we'll simply pour the brewed coffee into a separate thermal carafe.

Rating New Generation Coffee Makers

OUR TEST INCLUDED SEVEN ELECTRIC COFFEE MAKERS (OF WHICH THREE WERE PROTOTYPES BECAUSE PRODUCTION models were not available at testing time), each with designs or features aimed at improving the flavor of the coffee, ease of use, or both. Whenever possible, we chose models with a thermal carafe, which we prefer over a traditional glass carafe on a hot burner plate for keeping coffee hot and fresh tasting over time. For all of the machines except the single-cup brewers, we brewed three full pots and evaluated the coffee when fresh, after 30 minutes, and after 60 minutes. With the single-cup machines, we evaluated the coffee only when fresh. The machines are listed by type and in order of preference within each type. See www.americastestkitchen.com for up-to-date prices and mail-order sources for top-rated products.

GRIND AND BREW

RECOMMENDED WITH RESERVATIONS
Cuisinart Grind & Brew Thermal 10-Cup Coffee Maker, Model DGB-600
$149.99

Though the coffee was good, the unit was a nuisance to clean. It lacks a grind adjustment feature and maximum fill mark in the carafe. The grinder chamber is small.

RECOMMENDED WITH RESERVATIONS
Melitta Automatic Mill & Brew with Thermal Carafe, Model MEMB10T
$95

This model was very easy to use, and it features a large grinder/filter assembly that was easy to clean. Some tasters found this coffee to be bitter unless the grind was set to coarse.

RECOMMENDED WITH RESERVATIONS
Capresso CoffeeTEAM Luxe, Model 453th
$199.99

Although it brews a good pot of coffee, testers found this machine to be temperamental. You must change two settings to brew a partial pot, and the carafe must be positioned perfectly to prevent condensation from building in the coffee feeder channel.

VACUUM

RECOMMENDED
Black & Decker InFuze 10-Cup Vacuum-Brew Coffeemaker (PROTOTYPE)
$69.99

The Black & Decker was praised for its ease of use and cleaning. It brewed the hottest coffee of all the machines, but it lost points for not having a thermal carafe.

RECOMMENDED WITH RESERVATIONS
Bodum Santos Electric Vacuum Coffee Maker
$99.99

This model was easy to set up and use, but its narrow carafe made cleaning it a bit of a chore. Lost points for not having a thermal carafe.

SINGLE CUP

RECOMMENDED
Melitta One:One Java-Pod Coffee Maker, Model MESIW (PROTOTYPE)
$49.99

The Melitta produced tasty coffee while having a very modest price tag. Excellent value, but the flavored coffee "pods" Melitta offers are very limited. The coffee did tend to splash as it dispensed into the cup.

RECOMMENDED
Keurig B-100 Single-Cup Brewing System (PROTOTYPE)
$249.95

This was the sexiest of the machines—quick brewing, easy to clean, and a lovely design. The downside? This model lacks the ability to adjust the brew strength, and it was the most expensive of the coffee makers tested.

Erika whips up a batch of her all-American brownies.

BAKE SALE favorites

Every afternoon around three, editors come sniffing around the test kitchen looking for cookies fresh from the oven. Given how many cookies we make, our test cooks appreciate bar cookies. There's no measuring or shaping of the dough. Just spread the entire batter into the pan, bake, cool, and cut into squares. Bar cookies are understandably popular items at bake sales. They are easy to make and are always a hit.

But brownies and other bar cookies can be disappointing. Many brownies are rather dull, and blondies (as well as Congo bars, their coconut-flavored cousins) can be even worse, since they are even plainer. So when we created recipes for these favorite bake sale items, we kept the recipes simple (a bar cookie that required exotic ingredients or difficult techniques just wouldn't do) while developing superior flavor and texture. The result is brownies, blondies, and Congo bars so good that you'll want to bake two batches—one for the bake sale at school or church and one to keep at home.

CLASSIC BROWNIES

WHAT WE WANTED: A chewy, not over-the-top, yet chocolatey brownie. It should have intense flavor without being overly rich or candy-like.

These days, if you go to a bakery and order a brownie, chances are you'll end up with a heavy chunk of pure confection. While there's no denying that such brownies are sumptuous, they are also most often overwhelming. More candy than cake, such brownies are fine as infrequent treats, but many of us can look back to a time when the brownie was a much simpler affair, more chocolate bar than chocolate truffle, more bake sale than upscale café.

Our initial recipe testing was not a success. Either pale and dry or cloyingly sweet, all of the brownies we baked lacked substantial chocolate flavor. We wanted an old-fashioned brownie, but we also wanted serious chocolate flavor.

Before we embarked on our testing, there was one thing about all of the research recipes that we knew we wanted to change: the size. The recipes called for baking the brownies in skimpy 8-inch square pans. We wanted big brownies, and a lot of them, so a 13 by 9-inch baking pan was the size of choice. We then constructed a recipe with 4 ounces of unsweetened chocolate, two sticks of butter, 2 cups of sugar, four eggs, and 1¼ cups of all-purpose flour.

Our working recipe yielded brownies that were dense and a bit greasy. Cutting back on the butter seemed like an obvious way to make them less greasy. Going from two sticks to 1½ sticks did the trick, but it also produced an unanticipated side effect—an unpleasantly gritty texture. We suspected that the source of the problem might be in the starch in the recipe, not just from the all-purpose flour we'd been using but from the chocolate, which also contains starch. Not wanting to alter the amount of chocolate (our brownies needed more chocolate flavor, not less), we decreased the flour. The brownies were still too gritty. Next, we tried substituting cake flour for the entire amount of all-purpose flour. This solved the problem, producing nicely tender brownies. (Cake flour is milled from softer wheat than all-purpose flour and contributes less protein, or gluten, to a recipe. The result is a finer-textured product, which, in the case of these brownies, was preferred.) Here was our first big revelation: Cake flour makes tender brownies with a delicate chew.

Though tender, the brownies were still too compact. We thought an extra egg might provide more structure, but it made the brownies too cakey. Maybe baking powder would lighten the crumb. Well, too much baking powder produced a dry and cakey brownie, but a modest ¾ teaspoon was just right. The texture of the brownies was now nearly perfect, right in the middle between cakey and fudgy.

Our brownies now had the right texture—neither fudgy nor cakey, with a tender chew—but the flavor was a bit insipid. Although we didn't want the decadent texture of fudgy brownies, we did appreciate their assertive chocolate flavor. In search of a similar chocolate intensity, we added a little high-quality bittersweet chocolate to the unsweetened chocolate in our working recipe. These brownies were too sweet, too greasy, and too heavy. When we cut back on the sugar, the brownies were less sweet, but they remained heavy and soggy. In addition, tasters felt that the flavor was more reminiscent of milk chocolate (that is, very mild) than bittersweet chocolate. When we used considerably more bittersweet chocolate, the flavor was more intense but the texture now decidedly confection-like. Ounce for ounce, unsweetened chocolate has more chocolate flavor than bittersweet or semisweet chocolate (which are one third to one half sugar). To get enough flavor from these chocolates, you have to use a lot, and that made the brownies fudgy and rich—exactly what we did not want.

We tried adding cocoa, but in small amounts; it did nothing to pump up the chocolate flavor in our brownies.

Using ¼ cup cocoa in place of an equal amount of flour started to help, but now the texture was dense and pasty. We crossed cocoa off our list.

We wondered what would happen if we increased the amount of unsweetened chocolate in our working recipe. Using 6 ounces of unsweetened chocolate (rather than 4 ounces) gave us the desired flavor we were after—not too sweet, with profound chocolate notes. Although we had performed a lot of unnecessary tests, we now realized why most recipes call for unsweetened chocolate. We just needed to use more to make our recipe taste better. We also found that we needed a generous amount of salt and vanilla to enhance the chocolate flavor and give the brownies more depth.

Many recipes call for creaming the butter (beating it until light-textured), but our tests showed that this produced a light, dry texture. Much to our relief, the easiest method worked best: Melt the chocolate and butter, add the sugar, eggs, and vanilla, and then fold in the flour.

As simple as they are to mix, these brownies need to be baked just right to guarantee the perfect texture. An even temperature of 325 degrees baked them through without drying the edges, a problem when the oven temperature was higher. Close attention near the end of the baking time proved beneficial as well. Underbaking by just a couple of minutes resulted in a gummy (undercooked) center, and overbaking quickly dried them out. Because home ovens are notoriously fickle and poorly calibrated, the baking times in this recipe should be used only as a general guide.

When we mixed nuts into the batter before baking the brownies, they steamed and became soft. Sprinkling the nuts on top just before baking kept the nuts dry and crunchy; toasting them first made them even crunchier while also enhancing their flavor. That said, we decided to make the nuts—not everyone's preference in brownies—optional.

WHAT WE LEARNED: Use unsweetened chocolate— and a lot of it—for a potent chocolate punch. Cake flour and a little baking powder give the brownies a nice chew. Melt the butter, rather than creaming it, for a dense texture.

CLASSIC BROWNIES

Makes 24 brownies

Be sure to test for doneness before removing the brownies from the oven. If underbaked (the toothpick has batter clinging to it), the texture of the brownies will be dense and gummy; if overbaked (the toothpick comes out completely clean), the brownies will be dry and cakey.

    1   cup pecans or walnuts, chopped medium
         (optional)
    1¼   cups (5 ounces) plain cake flour
    ½   teaspoon salt
    ¾   teaspoon baking powder
    6   ounces unsweetened chocolate, chopped fine
    12   tablespoons (1½ sticks) unsalted butter, cut into
         six 1-inch pieces
    2¼   cups (15¾ ounces) sugar
    4   large eggs
    1   tablespoon vanilla extract

1. Adjust an oven rack to the middle position and heat the oven to 325 degrees. Line a 13 by 9-inch baking pan with two pieces of foil (see the illustration on page 288). Spray the foil-lined pan with nonstick cooking spray.

2. If using nuts, spread the nuts evenly on a rimmed baking sheet and toast in the oven until fragrant, 5 to 8 minutes. Set aside to cool.

3. In a medium bowl, whisk the flour, salt, and baking powder together until combined; set aside.

4. Melt the chocolate and butter in a large heatproof bowl set over a saucepan of almost-simmering water, stirring occasionally, until smooth. (Alternatively, in a microwave, heat the butter and chocolate in a large microwave-safe bowl on high for 45 seconds, then stir and heat for 30 seconds more. Stir again and, if necessary, repeat in 15-second increments; do not let the chocolate burn.) When the chocolate mixture is completely smooth, remove the bowl from the saucepan and gradually whisk in the sugar. Add the eggs, one at a time, whisking after each addition until thoroughly combined. Whisk in the vanilla. Add the flour mixture in 3 additions, folding with a rubber spatula until the batter is completely smooth and homogeneous.

5. Transfer the batter to the prepared pan; using a spatula, spread the batter into the corners of the pan and smooth the surface. Sprinkle the toasted nuts (if using) evenly over the batter. Bake until a toothpick or wooden skewer inserted into the center of the brownies comes out with a few moist crumbs attached, 30 to 35 minutes. Cool on a wire rack to room temperature, about 2 hours, then remove the brownies from the pan by lifting them out using the foil overhangs. Cut the brownies into 2-inch squares and serve. (Store leftovers in an airtight container at room temperature up to 3 days.)

CHOCOLATE-GLAZED MINT-FROSTED BROWNIES

These brownies have both a mint frosting and a chocolate glaze.

1. Follow the recipe for Classic Brownies, omitting the optional nuts; when the brownies are cool, leave them in the pan.

2. In the bowl of a standing mixer or with a handheld mixer, beat 8 tablespoons (1 stick) softened unsalted butter and 2 cups (8 ounces) confectioners' sugar at low speed until just incorporated, then increase the speed to medium and beat until smooth and fluffy, about 1½ minutes. Add 1 tablespoon milk and 1 teaspoon mint extract and continue to beat until combined, about 30 seconds, adding up to 1 additional tablespoon milk if necessary to achieve a soft spreadable consistency. Using an offset spatula, spread the mint frosting evenly onto the cooled brownies, cover with foil, and refrigerate until firm, about 1 hour.

3. Melt 4 ounces chopped bittersweet or semisweet chocolate and 4 tablespoons (½ stick) unsalted butter in a medium heatproof bowl set over a saucepan of barely simmering water, stirring occasionally, until smooth; set aside to cool slightly, about 10 minutes.

4. Pour the chocolate glaze on the frosted brownies; using an offset spatula, spread the glaze into an even layer. Cover with foil and refrigerate until firm, about 1 hour. Remove the brownies from the pan by lifting the foil overhang, cut into 2-inch squares, and serve. (Store leftovers in an airtight container in the refrigerator.)

CLASSIC BROWNIES WITH COCONUT-PECAN TOPPING

These brownies have the flavors of German chocolate cake.

1. Follow the recipe for Classic Brownies, toasting only ¾ cup pecans in step 2 and reserving the pecans for the topping (do not sprinkle the pecans over the batter before baking); when the brownies are cool, leave them in the pan.

2. Whisk 2 large egg yolks, ½ cup (3½ ounces) sugar, and ⅛ teaspoon salt in a small nonreactive saucepan until combined. Whisk in 4 tablespoons (½ stick) softened unsalted butter, then gradually whisk in ½ cup heavy cream and ½ teaspoon vanilla extract. Cook over low heat, stirring constantly, until the mixture is fluffy, begins to thicken, and registers about 180 degrees on an instant-read thermometer, 8 to 12 minutes. Off the heat, stir in the pecans and 1 cup lightly packed sweetened flaked coconut. Spread the topping evenly onto the cooled brownies, cover with foil, and refrigerate until set, about 2 hours. Remove the brownies from the pan by lifting the foil overhang, cut into 2-inch squares, and serve. (Store leftovers in an airtight container in the refrigerator.)

GETTING IT RIGHT: Developing a Brownie to Please Everyone

Seemingly minor changes in brownie recipes can yield quite different results.

Too Cakey

This recipe called for creaming the butter and sugar and for lots of baking powder, yielding brownies with a fluffy, cakey texture.

Too Fudgy

This recipe called for a lot of chocolate and no baking powder and produced a confection-like brownie that was extremely rich and dense.

Just Right

With a moderate amount of chocolate and a little baking powder, our brownie has good flavor and a moist texture that is neither cakey nor fudgy.

TASTING LAB: Boxed Brownie Mixes

ADMIT IT. IN A MOMENT OF DESPERATION YOU'VE reached for a boxed brownie mix. Maybe you forgot about tomorrow's school bake sale, or in a moment of haste you volunteered to make something for an office party. Why not use one of the countless pre-packaged comestibles available on supermarket shelves?

You know why not—most boxed brownies are not very good. But we wondered which brands were better than the others—and thought maybe one could rival homemade. (OK, that was a bit optimistic.) We purchased six brands, prepared each according to the instructions on the package, and rated them according to their texture, moistness, and chocolate flavor.

We came away with only one boxed brownie mix to halfheartedly recommend: Ghirardelli Double Chocolate Premium Brownie Mix. No one loved these brownies, but they had a decent amount of chocolate flavor (they are made with both cocoa and semisweet chips) and were the least offensive of the bunch. Tasters complained, loudly, about artificial flavors and excessive sweetness in the Pillsbury, Betty Crocker, and Duncan Hines mixes.

The two remaining brands were a bit different. In place of the typical water, vegetable oil, and egg additions that most mixes require, No-Pudge calls for nonfat yogurt and vanilla extract, and Dr. Oetker uses melted butter and eggs. Tasters felt both lacked chocolate flavor and had undesirable textures.

In the end, we can't be too enthusiastic about any of these choices, especially since homemade brownies are so easy to prepare. But if you must use a mix, at least now you know they're not all the same.

Rating Brownie Mixes

TWELVE MEMBERS OF THE *COOK'S ILLUSTRATED* STAFF tasted all of the brownie mixes, which were prepared and baked according to the package directions. Some packages come with directions for using the mix in pans of various sizes. If more than one option was listed on the package, we have listed the largest pan size below. The mixes are listed in order of preference based on their scores in this tasting. All the brands are available in supermarkets.

PASSABLE IN A PINCH
Ghirardelli Double Chocolate Brownie Mix
$2.79 for 20 ounces, yielding an 8-inch pan of brownies
These brownies were twice as thick as other brands and had the "best chocolate flavor." However, they were on the sweet side and "somewhat mushy."

NOT RECOMMENDED
Pillsbury Rich & Moist Fudge Brownie Mix
$1.79 for 19.5 ounces, yielding a 13 by 9-inch pan of brownies
These brownies were "bitter" with a "mild, fake chocolate flavor."

NOT RECOMMENDED
Betty Crocker Traditional Chewy Fudge Brownie Mix
$1.89 for 19.8 ounces, yielding a 13 by 9-inch pan of brownies
Tasters deemed these brownies "artificial" and said eating them was "like chewing on a chocolate chamois."

NOT RECOMMENDED
Duncan Hines Family-Style Chewy Fudge Brownies
$1.89 for 21 ounces, yielding a 13 by 9-inch pan of brownies
"Tastes totally commercial," said one taster about these brownies. Others called them "dry" and "chalky."

NOT RECOMMENDED
Dr. Oetker Simple Organics Organic Brownie Mix
$3.19 for 13.1 ounces, yielding an 8-inch pan of brownies
"Leaden," "tough," and "no flavor" was the consensus on these brownies.

NOT RECOMMENDED
No-Pudge Fat-Free Fudge Brownie Mix
$3.69 for 13.7 ounces, yielding an 8-inch pan of brownies
Tasters said these brownies were "like chewing gum" and had "no chocolate flavor."

BLONDIES

WHAT WE WANTED: Bakers like blondies because they are so simple to prepare, but many recipes are pretty flavorless. Is there a way to make a great blondie that's still quick and easy?

Blondies are first cousins to both brownies and chocolate chip cookies. Although blondies are baked in a pan like brownies, the flavorings are similar to those in chocolate chip cookies—vanilla, butter, and brown sugar, otherwise known as butterscotch. Blondies are sometimes laced with nuts and chocolate chips or butterscotch chips. Most of the time, blondies are pretty bland and need all the help they can get from additional ingredients. Dry, floury, flavorless—we have eaten them all. What does it take to make a good blondie?

The majority of the recipes we found had essentially the same ingredients but in different proportions that yielded blondies with dramatically different textures—from light and cakey to dense and buttery. Tasters preferred the latter, but with reservations. They felt that blondies could be too dense, as were some of the ones we tried. Super-dense blondies tasted of little more than raw flour and butter.

After baking a variety of blondie recipes, we found that the key to dense blondies that did not taste raw lay in how the butter was incorporated into the batter and the amount of flour in the batter. Melted butter produced a much denser blondie than creamed butter because the creaming process incorporates air into the batter. Melting the butter also meant that we could make the batter by hand rather than dirtying a food processor or electric mixer.

While we knew all-purpose flour would give us the chewiest, densest texture, the exact amount of flour was tricky to determine. Too much flour resulted in a dense, flavorless cookie, and too little produced a greasy cookie that oozed butter. After a dozen batches with the slightest variations in the amounts of flour, we finally settled on 1½ cups of all-purpose flour leavened with a small amount of baking powder. These bar cookies were definitely dense and very chewy, but they had risen just enough to prevent them from being gooey.

For sweetening and flavor, tasters favored light brown sugar, which lent the right amount of earthy, molasses flavor; dark brown sugar was overpowering. And combined with a substantial amount of vanilla extract and salt (to sharpen the sweetness), the light brown sugar developed a rich butterscotch flavor.

To add both texture and flavor to the cookies, we included chocolate chips and pecans. While the chips are traditional, pecans are not. Most recipes suggest walnuts, but tasters thought the pecans better complemented the butterscotch flavor.

We also tried butterscotch chips, but most tasters found that they did little for this recipe. On a whim, we included white chocolate chips with the semisweet chips, and we were surprised that they produced the best blondie yet. While white chocolate does not have cocoa, it does have cocoa butter, which highlighted both the vanilla and caramel flavors. These blondies now had a significantly deeper and richer flavor.

WHAT WE LEARNED: Use melted rather than creamed butter to create dense, chewy blondies. Light brown sugar (rather than dark brown sugar) and vanilla are the keys to creating a rich butterscotch flavor. A combination of semisweet and white chocolate chips adds a big boost of chocolate flavor.

BLONDIES

Makes 36 bars

If you have trouble finding white chocolate chips, chop a bar of white chocolate into small chunks.

1½	cups (7½ ounces) unbleached all-purpose flour
1	teaspoon baking powder
½	teaspoon salt
12	tablespoons (1½ sticks) unsalted butter, melted and cooled
1½	cups (10½ ounces) packed light brown sugar
2	large eggs
1½	teaspoons vanilla extract
½	cup semisweet chocolate chips
½	cup white chocolate chips
1	cup pecans, toasted and chopped coarse

1. Adjust an oven rack to the middle position and heat the oven to 350 degrees. Line a 13 by 9-inch baking pan with two pieces of foil (see the illustration on this page). Spray the foil-lined pan with nonstick cooking spray.

2. Whisk the flour, baking powder, and salt together in a medium bowl; set aside.

3. Whisk the melted butter and brown sugar together in a medium bowl until combined. Add the eggs and vanilla and mix well. Using a rubber spatula, fold the dry ingredients into the egg mixture until just combined. Do not overmix. Fold in the semisweet and white chocolate chips and the nuts and turn the batter into the prepared pan, smoothing the top with a rubber spatula.

4. Bake until the top is shiny and cracked and feels firm to the touch, 22 to 25 minutes. Place the pan on a rack and cool completely. Cut into 1½ by 2-inch bars.

VARIATION
CONGO BARS

Despite their name, Congo bars have nothing at all to do with Africa. In fact, they are little more than blondies enriched with coconut—an ingredient that was exotic in years past perhaps but is far from it these days. We tried adding both sweetened, flaked coconut and unsweetened, shredded coconut to our blondies, and tasters unanimously preferred the unsweetened. Sweetened coconut did little but make the bars overly sweet and unpleasantly chewy. We were able to extract a bit more flavor from the unsweetened coconut by toasting it golden brown before adding it to the blondie dough. If you have trouble locating unsweetened shredded coconut, try a natural food store or an Asian market. Keep a close eye on the coconut when toasting as it can burn quickly.

Toast 1½ cups unsweetened, shredded coconut on a rimmed baking sheet on the middle oven rack at 350 degrees, stirring 2 to 3 times, until light golden, about 4 to 5 minutes. Transfer to a small bowl to cool. Follow the recipe for Blondies, adding the toasted coconut with the chocolate chips and nuts in step 3.

TECHNIQUE:
Removing Bar Cookies from the Pan

1. Place two sheets of aluminum foil or parchment paper perpendicular to each other in the pan, pushing the foil or paper into the corner.

2. After the bars have baked and cooled, use the foil or paper to transfer them to a cutting board, then slice into individual portions.

Q & A

What is the difference between margarine and shortening?

Margarine is a manufactured product made with vegetable oil; it was developed in France in 1869 as a butter substitute when butter was scarce and more expensive. In order to make the oil solid at room temperature, it is hydrogenated (extra hydrogen atoms are added to unsaturated fat, a process that creates trans-fatty acids and converts the mixture to saturated fat). Regular margarine must contain 80 percent fat; the other 20 percent is liquid, coloring, flavoring, and other additives. There are many varieties, including butter-margarine blends, cholesterol-lowering blends, soft margarine, and whipped margarine. When used in baked goods in place of butter, margarine often compromises both flavor and texture.

Shortening is also a solid fat made from vegetable oils through the process of hydrogenation. Unlike margarine, shortening is 100 percent fat and is virtually flavorless. Shortening can be more stable than butter and therefore can help a less experienced baker work with certain doughs at room temperature. It can be especially helpful when making pie crust. Shortening generally won't compromise texture (in fact, it makes very flaky pie crust), but it can have a detrimental effect on the flavor of many baked goods.

EQUIPMENT CORNER: Baking Pans

HERE IN CAKE-AND-CASSEROLE-CRAZED AMERICA, THE shallow, rectangular 13 by 9-inch baking dish is a kitchen workhorse. As expected, there is a huge variety of options from which to choose, many with new designs, materials, finish colors, and baking surface textures, all taking aim at the tried-and-true pans of old—Pyrex and stoneware. These "improvements," of course, come at a cost.

Would our grandparents have spent nearly $100 on a baking pan? En route to determining the true value of these pans, we found ourselves knee-deep in cornbread, lasagna, raspberry squares, and gingerbread, all baked in each of 12 pans representing the major designs and materials, both old and new.

Though no longer common, rough stoneware and earthenware pans have been around since the days of communal bread ovens in the village square. Ovensafe glass, represented by the Pyrex brand, came to market in 1915 and in the years since has become a standard kitchen item familiar to almost every home cook.

Pans made from both materials performed well in our tests, browning cornbread deeply and evenly. (We put a high value on the enhanced flavor and texture of deeply browned exterior surfaces. Pans that did not brown well were marked down.) Like a trusty cast-iron skillet, stoneware has a huge capacity to absorb and retain heat. The story is similar for glass. Although it heats up slowly, once glass is hot, it stays that way. In both cases, that's good news for fans of deeply browned crusts.

Our group included six pans with nonstick surfaces. All but the Wearever CushionAir ($22.99), which is also insulated (more on this later), browned cornbread deeply. Previous bakeware tests have shown—and the cornbread baked in this test confirmed—that when it comes to browning, a dark surface color is more important than the material of the pan. Dark-colored surfaces absorb heat in the oven; bright surfaces do, too, but they also reflect it.

The nonstick pans did, however, present a serious practical consideration. Many dishes baked in a 13 by 9-inch pan, including the lasagna we tested, are customarily cut and served right from the pan. With a nonstick pan that's a problem, because the use and care recommendations usually advise against cutting in the pan to protect the nonstick coating. Though not officially part of this test, some old, poorly cared for pieces of nonstick bakeware brought in from home by several editors were scarred, chipped, and rusted, proving that it pays to follow the manufacturer's guidelines in this respect. In our view, not being able to cut in a pan is a strike against it.

In the last couple of years, some manufacturers, including Doughmakers and Emerilware, have introduced heavy-gauge aluminum pans with textured baking surfaces that are supposed to increase airflow beneath the baked good to improve browning and release. Although pure aluminum is known to conduct heat efficiently, previous tests of bakeware have shown that this advantage is offset by its shiny surface, which reflects some of the oven's radiant heat. (The crusts of cornbread baked in these pans were on the light side.) Also, when you grease a textured pan, excess lubricant clings to the ridges, which in our tests caused the bottom of the gingerbread cake to turn soggy.

In addition to subpar browning, aluminum pans have another limitation. Manufacturers recommend against preparing acidic foods (such as tomato-based products) in them because acid and aluminum can react, causing off flavors.

The Rolls-Royce of the aluminum group was the All-Clad. Though it was solid as a rock, this wallet-wilting $95 pan didn't brown cornbread or raspberry squares as well as some of its darker competitors. Yes, it's nonreactive, and, yes, you can put it under the broiler and use metal utensils with it, but this pan just costs too much for us to recommend it over less expensive alternatives that performed better.

Another design innovation that has surfaced in recent years is insulated bakeware, which incorporates an air layer between two sheets of metal. Although this pan has a dark nonstick finish on the cooking surface, it did a lousy job of browning. Part of the problem was the reflective, shiny exterior surface of the pan. The pan's main selling point, its insulating air layer, was the second problem. We found that it also prevents baked goods from browning—not a good thing.

The newest and most unexpected design in our group was the Kaiser Backform Noblesse springform ($31.99), which brings the removable sides of a classic round cheese-cake pan to a 13 by 9-inch size. This unique pan had both pros and cons. Removal of baked goods intact couldn't have been easier, but the seal between the sides and bottom was not tight enough to prevent some lasagna juices from leaking out and burning in the oven.

It turns out that our story ends almost right where it began, with Pyrex. This pan may not be perfect, but it did have five distinct advantages over the newcomers. First, it browned on a par with the dark-colored nonstick pans. Second, it is compatible with metal utensils. Third, it is nonreactive. Fourth, while it's no stunning beauty, most people we asked were perfectly willing to set it on a dining table at dinnertime, which allows it to pull double duty in sweet and savory baking. Last, at $8.95 it's inexpensive; only two other pans in the lineup cost less. The stoneware pan offers the same virtues but costs more. Of course, if your baking is usually of the sweet variety and you are willing to forgo cutting foods right in the pan, any of the recommended nonstick models will also serve you well.

Rating Baking Pans

WE TESTED TWELVE 13 X 9-INCH CAKE/BAKING PANS BY BAKING CORNBREAD, RASPBERRY SQUARES, GINGERBREAD, AND A simple lasagna. The pans were evaluated by a number of criteria, including price, performance, and pan restrictions. Performance differences among the pans that did well were minor enough to let us recommend any of them. Within the Recommended and Not Recommended categories, pans are listed in ascending order by price. See www.americastestkitchen.com for up-to-date prices and mail-order sources for top-rated products.

HIGHLY RECOMMENDED
Pyrex Bakeware 13 x 9 Baking Dish
$8.95

Produced deep and evenly golden brown cornbread and slightly dark edges on raspberry squares and gingerbread. The clear glass makes it easy to monitor browning.

RECOMMENDED
Baker's Secret Non-Stick Oblong Cake Pan
$6.29

Browns deeply and evenly, cleans up easily, and is inexpensive. Not the sturdiest pan but cheap enough to replace if need be.

RECOMMENDED
Chicago Metallic Professional Bake N' Roast Pan
$10.57

Produced handsome dark golden brown cornbread and raspberry squares but difficult to wash and dry.

RECOMMENDED
KitchenAid Sheet Cake Pan 13 x 9
$24.99

The oversized rims/handles on this pan make for especially easy handling.

RECOMMENDED
Calphalon Commercial Non-stick Bakeware Rectangular Cake Pan
$25.99

The absence of rims or handles made it a bit tricky to grab this model with oven mitts.

RECOMMENDED
Pampered Chef Family Heritage Stoneware Rectangular Baker
$30.75

Surprisingly, this pan did not retain food odors; however, it does require initial seasoning and cannot be washed with soap or detergents.

RECOMMENDED
Kaiser Backform Noblesse Quadro 13 x 9 Springform Pan
$31.99

Despite its super-easy release owing to the springform design, we wouldn't use this pan for dishes that might produce juices, for fear of leakage.

NOT RECOMMENDED
Wilton Performance Pan 13 x 9 Sheet
$7.69

This pan cooked raspberry squares less thoroughly than other pans and was not as easy to clean as nonstick pans.

NOT RECOMMENDED
Doughmakers 13 x 9 Cake Pan
$19.99

The crust of the cornbread and the base of the raspberry squares were lighter than examples baked in darker nonstick pans.

NOT RECOMMENDED
Wearever CushionAir Covered Oblong Baking Pan
$22.99

This pan produced pale, spongy cornbread, raspberry bars ranging from pale to raw, and leaden, underbaked gingerbread. Cannot be soaked in water—a minus for sure.

NOT RECOMMENDED
Emerilware 13 x 9 All Purpose Pan
$24.99

Cornbread crusts and raspberry square bottoms were lighter than we prefer, and the bottom of the gingerbread was soggy.

NOT RECOMMENDED
All-Clad Rectangular Cake Pan 13 x 9, #9004
$94.99

Browning of the cornbread crust and raspberry squares was acceptable but not stellar. Given the price, this pan should slice and butter your cornbread for you.

Chris knows which cookie
recipes have been naughty
and which have been nice.

HOLIDAY cookies

Making cookies is a favorite holiday activity. Many people who bake infrequently during the year throw themselves into marathon cookie projects. These occasional bakers need reliable recipes. Dough that sticks to the rolling pin, cookies that melt together in the oven, and glazes that refuse to set up just won't do. The holidays are stressful enough. You certainly don't need suspect cookie recipes.

We set out to create a foolproof rolled butter cookie dough that tasted great and could be turned into an array of different cookies. Could we create lots of cookies, with distinct flavors and shapes, from the same basic dough? And could we do it easily?

Nut crescents go by a variety of names, including Viennese crescents, butterballs, and Mexican wedding cakes. Whatever the name, these cookies always have two things in common—a melt-in-your-mouth texture and an attractive coating of powdered sugar. But they also can be dry, bland, and soggy. We aimed to avoid these pitfalls and create nut crescents that would taste as good as they looked.

HOLIDAY ROLLED COOKIES

WHAT WE WANTED: A roll-and-cut holiday cookie that is almost as easy as the slice-and-bake tubes of cookie dough in the supermarket—but without the glue-like flavor or pasty texture.

When we started our recipe development process, we knew what we wanted, but we didn't know how to get there. We wanted a buttery cookie dough that doesn't cling to the rolling pin or rip and tear. We wanted a simple one-hour process, not a half-day project. We wanted to develop a simple recipe that would yield a forgiving, workable dough and produce cookies that would be sturdy enough to decorate yet tender enough to be worth eating. And, to save even more time, we wanted a chameleon-like dough that could be transformed into distinctly different cookies with just a few additional ingredients.

We started our investigation by testing five recipes that called for similar ratios of flour to fat and followed the standard butter-and-sugar creaming method of cookie making. These recipes did vary slightly in their choice of ingredients. One used a combination of shortening and butter, one called for all confectioners' sugar, and another used all light brown sugar. Some added an egg or dairy component, while others utilized a leavener. Although these cookies were certainly edible, we still found ourselves in a sticky situation. Only one batch had been easy to handle, but that batch also tasted like powdery cardboard because it used so much confectioners' sugar. We realized that if we wanted the perfect holiday cookie dough, we would have to go back to basics.

The most important issue was the ratio of butter to flour. After extensive testing, we ended up with 2½ cups of flour to two sticks of butter. (Shortening adds no flavor to cookies and is not an option.) This was just enough butter to stay true to the nature of a butter cookie but not so much

that the dough would be greasy. Although the dough was not perfect (it still had a tendency to stick when rolled), we at least had a good jumping-off point for the rest of our recipe development.

Next we experimented with flour, first testing cake flour, which produced delicate cookies with a chalky texture. We got similar results when we tried replacing different amounts of all-purpose flour with equal parts of cornstarch, another common tenderizing technique. These cookies were also very fragile—not ideal when it's time to decorate. We came to the conclusion that a little bit of structure-providing gluten (the combination of proteins found in greater amounts in all-purpose flour than in cake flour or cornstarch) wasn't necessarily a bad thing.

Because these cookies would play host to glazes or sweet fillings, we did not want to add too much sugar to the dough—just enough to enhance their flavor. Confectioners' sugar was out because of its bland flavor and powdery texture, while brown sugar made the cookies too soft and chewy. But when we tried superfine sugar, we were surprised at the difference it made. Cookies made with regular granulated sugar had a crumb with larger holes and a flaky texture. The cookies made with superfine sugar, on the other hand, had a fine, even crumb and were compact and crisp—very definitely positive attributes. Liking these thin and crisp cookies, we ruled out the use of a leavener (which would make them puff in the oven) and eggs (which would add both moisture and chewiness). But we still needed to enrich the flavor of the cookies, so we tried adding flavorful dairy components to the dough: buttermilk, sour cream, and cream cheese. The buttermilk produced a crisp yet overly tangy cookie, and the sour cream made the dough far too wet. But the cream cheese—a surprise ingredient to be sure—was just right. It gave the cookies flavor and richness without altering their texture. With a pinch of salt and a dash of vanilla, we had obtained

a simple but top-notch flavor for our holiday cookies.

We had come a long way in terms of improving the flavor (rich but direct) and texture (fine and crisp) of the baked cookies, but we were still having trouble rolling out the dough. It was less sticky than the doughs we had made from other recipes, but we wanted a dough that was even easier to work with—something foolproof. All the recipes we had tested called for the creaming method, wherein butter and sugar are beaten into a fluffy union. What if we creamed the butter with the sugar and the flour? The dough came together in two minutes and was incredibly easy to handle: soft, pliable, and easy to roll. Even with less chilling time than before, the dough was easily rolled to a slight thickness of ⅛ inch, cut out into different shapes, and maneuvered to a baking sheet. (For more on why this technique works so well, see "Why Does Mixing Method Matter?" on page 298.)

As far as oven temperature goes, 375 degrees was best, as was using only one rack placed in the center of the oven. In the amount of time it took to cut out a second sheet of cookies, the first sheet was finished. But the final selling point was the baked result: thin, flat cookies that were both crisp and sturdy. They tasted great and were foolproof—what more could a holiday baker want?

WHAT WE LEARNED: Superfine sugar makes rolled cookies especially crisp, and all-purpose flour gives them some structure. Cream cheese makes them rich, and vanilla adds flavor. And to make the dough easy to roll out, add the butter to the dry ingredients rather than creaming it with the sugar alone.

GLAZED BUTTER COOKIES

Makes about 38 cookies

If you cannot find superfine sugar, you can obtain a close approximation by processing regular granulated sugar in a food processor for about 30 seconds. If desired, the cookies can be finished with sprinkles or other decorations immediately after glazing.

butter cookie dough

2½	cups (12½ ounces) unbleached all-purpose flour
¾	cup (5½ ounces) superfine sugar (see note)
¼	teaspoon salt
16	tablespoons (2 sticks) unsalted butter, cut into 16 pieces, softened but still cool
2	teaspoons vanilla extract
2	tablespoons cream cheese, at room temperature

glaze

1	tablespoon cream cheese, at room temperature
3	tablespoons milk
1½	cups (6 ounces) confectioners' sugar

1. FOR THE COOKIES: In the bowl of a standing mixer, or with a handheld mixer, mix the flour, sugar, and salt at low speed until combined, about 5 seconds. With the mixer running on low, add the butter 1 piece at a time; continue to mix until the mixture looks crumbly and slightly wet, about 1 minute longer. Add the vanilla and cream cheese and mix on low until the dough just begins to form large clumps, about 30 seconds.

2. Knead the dough by hand in the bowl for 2 to 3 turns to form a large, cohesive mass. Turn the dough out onto a work surface; divide it in half, pat each half into a 4-inch disk, wrap the disks in plastic, and refrigerate until they begin to firm up, 20 to 30 minutes. (The disks can be refrigerated up to 3 days or frozen up to 2 weeks; defrost in the refrigerator before using.)

3. Adjust an oven rack to the middle position and heat the oven to 375 degrees. Roll out 1 dough disk to an even ⅛-inch thickness between 2 large sheets of parchment paper; slide the rolled dough, still on the parchment, onto a baking sheet and refrigerate until firm, about 10 minutes. Meanwhile, repeat with the second disk.

4. Working with the first portion of rolled dough, cut into desired shapes using cookie cutters and place the shapes on a parchment-lined baking sheet, spacing them about 1½ inches apart. Bake until the cookies are light golden brown, about 10 minutes, rotating the baking sheet halfway through the baking time. Repeat with the second portion of rolled dough. (The dough scraps can be patted together, chilled, and rerolled once.) Cool the cookies to room temperature on a wire rack.

5. FOR THE GLAZE: Whisk the cream cheese and 2 tablespoons of the milk in a medium bowl until combined and no lumps remain. Whisk in the confectioners' sugar until smooth, adding the remaining milk as needed until the glaze is thin enough to spread easily. Drizzle or spread a scant teaspoon of glaze with the back of a spoon onto each cooled cookie, as desired.

VARIATIONS

JAM SANDWICHES

Makes about 30 cookies

See the illustrations on page 297 to prepare these cookies.

- 1 recipe Butter Cookie Dough, prepared through step 3
- 2 tablespoons turbinado, Demerara, or white decorating sugar
- 1¼ cups (12 ounces) raspberry jam, strained, simmered until reduced to 1 cup, and cooled to room temperature

1. Using a 2-inch fluted round cookie cutter, cut rounds from 1 piece of rolled dough and bake on a parchment-lined baking sheet in a 375-degree oven, rotating the baking sheet halfway through the baking time, until the cookies are light golden brown, 8 to 10 minutes.

2. Sprinkle the second piece of rolled dough evenly with the sugar.

3. Using a 2-inch round cookie cutter, cut out rounds of sugar-sprinkled dough and place them on a parchment-lined baking sheet. Using a ¾-inch fluted round cookie cutter, cut out the centers of the rounds. Bake, rotating the baking sheet halfway through the baking time, until the cookies are light golden brown, about 8 minutes.

4. When the cookies have cooled, spread 1 teaspoon jam on the top of each solid cookie, then cover with a cut-out cookie. Let the filled cookies stand until set, about 30 minutes.

LIME-GLAZED COCONUT SNOWBALLS

Makes about 40 cookies

See the illustrations on page 297 to prepare these cookies.

- 1 recipe Butter Cookie Dough, with 1 teaspoon grated lime zest added with the dry ingredients and prepared through step 1
- 1 recipe Glaze, with 3 tablespoons lime juice substituted for the milk
- 1½ cups sweetened shredded coconut, pulsed in a food processor until finely chopped, about fifteen 1-second pulses

1. Use your hands to roll the dough into 1-inch balls. Place the balls on parchment-lined baking sheets, spacing them about 1½ inches apart. Bake, one batch at a time, in a 375-degree oven until lightly browned, about 12 minutes. Cool to room temperature.

TECHNIQUE: One Dough, Many Cookies

Our butter cookie dough is not only foolproof but also the perfect vehicle for a number of different flavorings, shapes, and sizes. One easy-to-handle dough can be the basis for a wide assortment of holiday cookies. Here's how to make three of our favorite cookies with this dough.

Cutting and Filling Jam Sandwiches

1. Using a 2-inch fluted round cookie cutter, cut rounds from I piece of rolled dough.

2. Sprinkle the second piece of rolled dough evenly with turbinado sugar.

3. Cut out 2-inch rounds of sugar-sprinkled dough and place on a parchment-lined baking sheet. Using a ¾-inch fluted round cookie cutter, cut out the centers.

4. When the cookies have cooled, spread I teaspoon jam on the tops of each solid cookie, then cover with a cut-out cookie.

Shaping and Coating Lime–Glazed Coconut Snowballs

1. Use your hands to roll the dough into 1-inch balls. Place the balls on parchment-lined baking sheets.

2. Dip the tops of the baked and cooled cookies into the glaze and scrape away the excess, then dip them into the coconut. Set the cookies on a rack until the glaze dries.

Making Chocolate–Cherry Bar Cookies with Hazelnuts

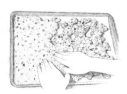   

1. Press the dough evenly into a 17 by 12-inch rimmed baking sheet that has been lined with parchment paper.

2. Immediately after removing the baking sheet from the oven, sprinkle evenly with the chocolate chips; let stand to melt, about 3 minutes.

3. Using an offset icing spatula, spread the chocolate into an even layer, then sprinkle the chopped hazelnuts evenly over the chocolate.

4. When the cookies have cooled slightly, use a pizza wheel to cut on the diagonal into 1½-inch diamonds.

2. Dip tops of the cookies into the glaze and scrape away the excess, then dip them into the coconut. Set the cookies on a rack and let stand until the glaze sets, about 20 minutes.

CHOCOLATE-CHERRY BAR COOKIES WITH HAZELNUTS

Makes about 50 cookies

See the illustrations on page 297 to prepare these cookies.

> 1 recipe Butter Cookie Dough, 1 cup chopped dried cherries added with the dry ingredients, prepared through step 1
> 1½ cups semisweet chocolate chips
> 1½ cups hazelnuts, toasted, skinned, and chopped

1. Press the dough evenly into a 17 by 12-inch rimmed baking sheet that has been lined with parchment paper. Bake on the lower-middle rack in a 375-degree oven until golden brown, about 20 minutes, rotating the baking sheet halfway through the baking time.

2. Immediately after removing the baking sheet from the oven, sprinkle evenly with the chocolate chips; let stand to melt, about 3 minutes.

3. Using an offset icing spatula, spread the chocolate into an even layer, then sprinkle the chopped hazelnuts evenly over the chocolate. Cool on a wire rack until just warm, 15 to 20 minutes.

4. Using a pizza wheel, cut on the diagonal into 1½-inch diamonds. Transfer the cookies to a wire rack to cool completely.

SCIENCE DESK:
Why Does Mixing Method Matter?

CREAMING IS A COMMON METHOD USED IN BAKING. Butter and sugar are whipped until light and fluffy, eggs are added, and then dry ingredients are incorporated gradually. This method delivers good results when making most cookies, but we found that it did not work well for rolled butter cookies, and we wondered why.

Our recipe has two striking features: It contains no leavener (we did not want the cookies to puff) and no liquid. Because the dough is somewhat dry, the flour did not incorporate well when added at the end of the mixing process. As a result, the dough was unevenly mixed, with

---

GETTING IT RIGHT: Chasing the Perfect Holiday Cookie

If your rolled cookies look like the three sorry samples on the left, we've figured out why. It's not your technique but your dough. If the dough is too sticky, the cookies will be misshapen (far left). If the dough contains too much butter, the cookies will bake up very fragile (second from left). If the dough contains too much sugar, the cookies will spread in the oven and look bloated (second from right). If you follow our "reverse creaming" method for making the dough, the cookies will roll out easily and bake up perfectly (far right).

Misshapen

Fragile

Bloated

Perfect

streaks of butter, which became sticky when handled. This streaking also had negative effects on the final baked product, as the pockets of butter led to puffed, uneven cookies. Butter is about 18 percent water, and when its temperature reaches 212 degrees Fahrenheit, this water turns to steam and expands dramatically, producing bubbles.

When we reversed the order of mixing and added the butter to the flour, the dough was much more uniform, without streaks of butter. Thus, the dough was neither sticky when rolled nor puffy when baked. The baked cookies had flat tops, ready for decorating.

STANDARD CREAMING   "REVERSE" CREAMING

An enormous bubble formed where the butter had not been mixed in completely using the standard creaming method (left). The cookie made using our "reverse" creaming method (right) was uniform throughout, indicating that the butter was evenly distributed.

Q & A

Can waxed paper be used in place of parchment paper?

Waxed paper cannot be substituted for parchment paper in many cases. Parchment can withstand temperatures up to 425 degrees without burning, while waxed paper will smoke when subjected directly to heat. So, for lining a cake pan, waxed paper will do. The batter will cover the paper and prevent burning. But for lining a baking sheet, waxed paper will smoke and parchment is the only choice.

Q & A

Can wet and dry measuring cups be used interchangeably?

First of all, 1 cup in a "dry" measuring cup is exactly the same volume as 1 cup in a "wet" measuring cup. The choice, then, of how to measure dry ingredients and wet ingredients comes down to convenience and accuracy.

Let's start by defining what we mean by "dry" and "wet" cups. Dry measuring cups are made from metal or plastic and can be leveled off with a straight edge. Wet measuring cups are made of heatsafe glass (such as Pyrex) or plastic and have a pouring spout. Whereas dry measures usually come in sizes from ⅛ or ¼ cup up to 1 cup, wet measures are available in sizes of 1, 2, 4, and 8 cups.

When using both dry and wet measuring cups to weigh dry ingredients—sugar and flour—we found the dry cups to be much easier to use. It is nearly impossible to get an accurate measure of 1 cup of flour in a liquid measure of any size (even 1 cup) because the top can't be leveled off. Dry ingredients, then, ought to be measured in dry measuring cups.

Wet ingredients, on the other hand, ought to be measured in wet measuring cups. Measuring liquids in a dry measuring cup is a messy business. You must fill the cup right up to the rim, and spills are likely. It is also important that a wet measuring cup be transparent. To get an accurate reading of an amount of liquid, you have to stoop down so that the measuring cup is at eye level and look through the cup at the surface of the liquid.

Finally, we are often asked what is the best way to measure honey, molasses, peanut butter, and other sticky, thick ingredients. The answer is the push-up style measuring cup (see page 49), which looks like a wide syringe. You pull out the plunger to set the proper quantity (say, ½ cup), fill the device with the item to be measured, and then simply push it out of the cup. Nothing is left behind (a problem with sticky ingredients in "regular" dry and wet measuring cups), so you can be sure that the measurement is accurate.

NUT CRESCENT COOKIES

WHAT WE WANTED: Nut crescents with a rich, nutty, buttery flavor and a delicate, melt-in-your-mouth texture.

Nut crescents, coated in a pasty layer of melting confectioners' sugar, can taste like stale, dry, floury, flavorless little chokeballs. They often fall short of the buttery, nutty, slightly crisp, slightly crumbly, melt-in-your-mouth nuggets they should be. But that is a shame. When they are well made, they are delicious. Their snowy white appearance also makes them festive enough for the holiday cookie platter.

We gathered recipe after recipe from large, authoritative books and small, pamphlet-size publications in our quest for the best nut crescent cookies. These cookies, round or crescent-shaped, go by different names: Viennese crescents, butterballs, and Mexican wedding cakes, as well as almond, pecan, or walnut crescents. All the recipes are surprisingly similar, differing mainly in the amount and type of sugar and nuts. The standard ratio of butter to flour is 1 cup to 2 cups, with the amount of flour in a few instances going as low as 1¾ cups or as high as 2½ cups. Across the board, the ingredients are simple: flour, sugar, butter, and nuts. Some add vanilla extract and salt. We chose four recipes and, with the input of a few tasters, formed a composite recipe to serve as the springboard for our testing.

Flour was our starting point. We certainly didn't need to go very far. Cookies made with 2 cups of all-purpose flour to 1 cup of butter were right on. The dough was easy to shape and handle, and the baked cookies were tender, delicate, and shapely. Any less flour and the rich cookies spread and lost some form in the oven; any more and they were dry and floury. We tried cake flour and cornstarch in place of some of the all-purpose flour, thinking that one or another would provide extra tenderness. Both were failures. The resulting cookies disintegrated unpleasantly in the mouth.

Next we zeroed in on sugar. Granulated sugar yielded a cookie that was tasty but coarse in both texture and appearance. Cookies made with confectioners' sugar were very tender, light, and fine-textured. Superfine sugar, however, proved superior, producing cookies that were delicate, lightly crisp, and superbly tender, with a true melt-in-your-mouth quality. In a side-by-side tasting, the cookies made with superfine sugar were nuttier and purer in flavor, while the cornstarch in the confectioners' sugar bogged down the flavor and left a faint pastiness in the mouth.

As we tinkered with the amount of sugar, we had to keep in mind that these cookies are coated in confectioners' sugar after they are baked. One-third cup gives them a mildly sweet edge when they're eaten plain, but it's the roll in confectioners' sugar that gives them their finished look and just the right amount of extra sweetness.

When to give the baked cookies their coat of confectioners' sugar is a matter of some debate. Some recipes say to dust or dip them while they're still hot or warm. The sugar melts a bit, and then they're usually given a second coat to even out their appearance and form a thicker coating. But we didn't like the layer of melting moistened confectioners' sugar, concealed or not. It formed a thin skin that was pasty and gummy and didn't dissolve on the tongue with the same finesse as a fine, powdery coat. We found it better to wait until the cookies had cooled to room temperature before coating them with confectioners' sugar.

Sifting sugar over the cooled cookies was tedious, and we weren't able to achieve a heavy enough coating on the tops, or any at all on the bottoms. What worked much better was simply rolling them in confectioners' sugar. One roll resulted in a rather thin layer that was a bit spotty, but a second coat covered any blemishes, giving them an attractive, thick, powdery white coating. If not served immediately, the cookies may lose a little in looks due to handling and storage. This problem can be easily solved by reserving the second coat of confectioners' sugar until just before serving.

While testing the nuts, we concluded that what affected the cookies most was not the taste of the nuts but whether they were oily or dry. We found that when they were ground, the two types of nuts affected the cookies in different ways.

The flavor of oily nuts like walnuts and pecans is strong and distinct. These nuts are easier to chop and grind and, when finely ground, become quite oily. This is a definite advantage when making nut crescents, because the dough becomes softer and the resulting cookies are incredibly tender and delicate. Dry nuts like almonds and hazelnuts taste rather subdued by comparison. Toasting brings out their maximum flavor and crunchiness. Although nut crescents made with almonds or hazelnuts are delicious, they just don't melt in your mouth with the same abandon as the pecan and walnut ones.

Chopped nuts were too coarse for the fine texture of the crescents and were quickly dismissed. Ground nuts, on the other hand, warranted further investigation. Ground nuts were flavorful, and because grinding really brought out the oils, they actually tenderized the cookies. We thought, though, that using a combination of ground and finely chopped nuts might tenderize, be flavorful, and add a pleasant crunch. Hands down, a combination of 1 cup of finely chopped and ¾ cup of ground nuts was the tasters' choice.

Recipes suggested baking temperatures ranging from a ridiculously low 300 degrees to a hot 400. At 400 degrees, the cookies browned too quickly, while at 300, they never achieved a nice golden hue, even after nearly half an hour of baking. Cookies baked at 350 degrees were good, but those baked at 325 degrees had a smoother, finer appearance and were more tender and evenly textured and colored.

WHAT WE LEARNED: Use superfine sugar for a delicate, melt-in-your-mouth texture. Pecans and walnuts give these cookies a stronger flavor than almonds or hazelnuts, although toasting can enhance the flavor of the milder nuts. As for the exterior coating of powdered sugar, wait until the cookies have cooled and roll them twice in the sugar for even coverage.

PECAN OR WALNUT CRESCENT COOKIES
Makes about 48 cookies

You can buy superfine sugar in most grocery stores. You can also process regular granulated sugar to superfine consistency in about 30 seconds in a food processor.

2	cups whole pecans or walnuts, chopped fine
2	cups (10 ounces) unbleached all-purpose flour
½	teaspoon salt
16	tablespoons (2 sticks) unsalted butter, softened but still cool
⅓	cup (2½ ounces) superfine sugar
1½	teaspoons vanilla extract
1½	cups confectioners' sugar for rolling cooled cookies

1. Adjust the oven racks to the upper- and lower-middle positions and heat the oven to 325 degrees. Line 2 large baking sheets with parchment paper.

2. Mix 1 cup of the chopped nuts, the flour, and salt in a medium bowl; set aside. Place the remaining chopped nuts in a food processor and process until they are the texture of coarse cornmeal, 10 to 15 seconds (do not overprocess); stir into the flour mixture and set aside. (To finely grind chopped nuts by hand, roll them between 2 large sheets of plastic wrap with a rolling pin, applying moderate pressure, until broken down to a coarse cornmeal-like texture.)

3. Either by hand or with an electric mixer, cream the butter and sugar until light and fluffy, about 1½ minutes; beat in the vanilla. Scrape the sides and bottom of the bowl with a rubber spatula; add the flour mixture and beat at low speed until the dough just begins to come together but still looks scrappy, about 15 seconds. Scrape the sides and bottom of the bowl again with the rubber spatula; continue beating at low speed until the dough is cohesive, 6 to 9 seconds longer. Do not overbeat.

4. Working with about 1 tablespoon of dough at a time, roll the dough in 1¼-inch balls. Following the illustrations on this page, roll each ball between your palms into a rope that measures 3 inches long. Place the ropes on the parchment-lined baking sheet and turn up the ends to form a crescent shape. Bake until the tops are pale golden and the bottoms are just beginning to brown, 17 to 19 minutes, rotating the baking sheets front to back and top to bottom halfway through the baking time.

5. Cool the cookies on the baking sheets about 2 minutes; remove with a wide metal spatula to a wire rack and cool to room temperature, about 30 minutes. Working with 3 or 4 cookies at a time, roll the cookies in the confectioners' sugar to coat them thoroughly. Gently shake off the excess. (They can be stored in an airtight container up to 5 days.) Before serving, roll the cookies in the confectioners' sugar a second time to ensure a thick coating and tap off the excess.

VARIATION
ALMOND OR HAZELNUT CRESCENT COOKIES

Choosing almonds for your cookies automatically presents you with a second choice: whether to use them raw for traditional almond crescent cookies that are light in both color and flavor or to toast them to enhance the almond flavor and darken the crescents. Toast the almonds or hazelnuts in a preheated 350-degree oven until very lightly browned, stirring twice during baking, 12 to 14 minutes. The hazelnuts should be skinned after they are toasted.

Follow the recipe for Pecan or Walnut Crescent Cookies, substituting a scant 1¾ cups whole blanched almonds (toasted or not) or 2 cups toasted, skinned hazelnuts for the pecans or walnuts. If using almonds, add ½ teaspoon almond extract along with the vanilla extract.

TECHNIQUE:
Making Nut Crescent Cookies

1. Working with 1 tablespoon of dough each time, roll the dough in 1¼-inch balls. Roll each ball between your palms into a rope that measures 3 inches long.

2. Place the ropes on a parchment-lined baking sheet and turn up the ends to form a crescent shape.

3. Rolling the cooled crescents in a bowl of confectioners' sugar creates a thicker, more attractive coating than sifting the sugar over the cookies.

EQUIPMENT CORNER:
Handheld versus Standing Mixers

CURIOUS ABOUT THE PERFORMANCE DIFFERENCES between our favorite handheld and standing mixers (both made by KitchenAid), we conducted side-by-side tests to establish general guidelines for their use. We whipped cream, beat egg whites for meringue, and made cookies, cakes, and buttercream frosting.

Although it took the handheld mixer 40 to 60 seconds longer than the standing mixer to whip cream and beat egg whites, it did just as good a job (both were fitted with the whisk attachment). When making oatmeal cookie dough, the standing mixer (with the paddle attachment) produced more volume in the batter, but the baked cookies were identical in number, texture, and flavor. Neither mixer had trouble mixing oatmeal and nuts into the stiff dough at low speed.

Our favorite yellow layer cake recipe baked up the same when made with both mixers, although the standing mixer created a slightly more voluminous batter. The same was true with génoise, a cake leavened by whole-egg foam, although the handheld mixer took nearly twice as long to beat the eggs to the right volume. For those partial to butter-cream frostings, we found that the handheld mixer actually worked better than the standing mixer because it was easier to keep the hot sugar syrup from clinging to the beaters.

OUR CONCLUSION: The standing mixer does offer greater flexibility and versatility. (Its dough hook is ideal for kneading bread, something a handheld mixer can't do.) Also, the solid base leaves your hands free to accomplish other tasks. We found, however, that with some adjustments for time and technique, the handheld mixer generally yields baked goods that are identical to those prepared in a standing mixer.

After performing these side-by-side kitchen tests with both standing and handheld mixers, we found some pointers to help ensure good results with both kinds of mixers.

When using a handheld mixer:
• Use a deep, narrow bowl to avoid flinging batter around your kitchen.
• Continuously move the beaters around the circumference of the bowl and through its center to incorporate all ingredients.
• Remove batter stuck to beaters by lifting the beaters out of the batter—but still keeping them below the lip of the bowl—and (very carefully) turning the mixer on medium for several seconds.
• Stabilize the mixing bowl by resting it within a damp towel twisted in a circle or on a piece of rubber shelf-liner.

When using a standing mixer:
• Avoid overbeating egg whites or cream by turning off the mixer, detaching the whisk attachment, removing the bowl from the mixer, and using the whisk attachment to make the last few strokes by hand.

• Prevent overbeating by resisting the impulse to push the speed lever all the way to the end when a recipe says, "Beat at high speed." To prevent overbeating on our powerful KitchenAid mixers, we rarely go above 8.
• Use the paddle attachment to cream butter and mix batters.
• Use the whisk attachment to whip heavy cream and egg whites.
• Use the hook attachment to knead bread dough.

No matter which mixer you use:
• Scrape down the sides and bottom of the bowl frequently with a rubber spatula to ensure that all the ingredients are incorporated.
• Start on low speed when adding ingredients and gradually increase the speed as necessary to avoid pushing the contents out of the bowl.

Chocolate Bundt cake might have a hole in the center, but when it comes to flavor it's not missing a thing.

THERE'S A HOLE
CHAPTER 24

in your cake

Cakes baked in Bundt pans and tube pans are popular for a variety of reasons. First of all, these pans make cakes that are especially attractive. Second, the cakes made in these pans are pretty simple to prepare; no complicated arrangement of layers or frosting. Most Bundt cakes require just a dusting of confectioners' sugar. Angel food cake, the recipe we prepare most often in our tube pan, is even simpler to decorate. Just cool and serve, adding some fresh berries or perhaps a scoop of ice cream.

Bundt pans and tube pans work with especially thick or heavy batters. The center tube conducts heat and helps the batter to rise. This promotes even cooking and ensures a moist texture.

In addition to angel food cake, we decided to develop a recipe for chocolate Bundt cake. With their short ingredient lists and easy preparation, these recipes are perfect for novice bakers. But that doesn't mean they always turn out right. Angel food cakes can be dry and cottony (or worse, they can fall), and chocolate Bundt cakes are often bland. We set out to perfect these cakes with the hole in the center.

CHOCOLATE BUNDT CAKE

WHAT WE WANTED: A cake that's not only attractive but moist and rich with chocolate flavor.

A Bundt cake is the pinnacle of cake-baking simplicity. With its decorative shape, this cake doesn't require frosting or fussy finishing techniques. What chocolate Bundt cakes do require, it turns out, is a major boost in flavor. Despite their tantalizing looks, most of these cakes have at best a muted chocolate presence. We wanted a cake that would deliver that moment of pure chocolate ecstasy when the first bite stops time. A chocolate Bundt cake should taste every bit as good as it looks, with a fine crumb, moist texture, and rich flavor.

Unfortunately, these sweet masters of disguise disappointed us so often in our initial taste tests that we almost relegated this recipe to the dustbin. Moist but pale, many of the cakes were devoid of any chocolate flavor. Others looked appealingly dark and mysterious but managed to capture only flat, bitter nuances of chocolate. An overly sweet, walnut-studded "tunnel of fudge" cake with a gummy, underbaked center was hardly worth the calories. A cake similar to a pound cake had great texture—dense and moist owing to the addition of sour cream—but the only thing that told tasters it was chocolate was its brown color.

Because the pound cake made with sour cream had come closest to our textural ideal, we started with a working recipe using roughly the same proportions of butter, sugar, eggs, and flour and using the traditional method of creaming the butter and sugar (beating them together) before adding the other ingredients. We then focused on boosting the virtually nonexistent chocolate flavor. The recipe included a small amount of cocoa powder, so we thought that a good dose of melted chocolate would be in order. We started with unsweetened chocolate, which has the most intense flavor. The resulting cake tasted bitter, and its texture was chalky, reminiscent of third-rate brownies. Trying both semisweet

and bittersweet chocolates, we noticed an improvement in texture, as both of these chocolates have added sugar and stabilizers that make them smoother and creamier than unsweetened. Tasters found the semisweet chocolate too sweet; the bittersweet added the right chocolate edge.

Now we had more chocolate flavor, but we wanted a deeper, more complex taste. This time, more cocoa powder seemed like a logical solution. We replaced a portion of the flour in our recipe with an equal amount of cocoa powder. We had to choose between Dutch-processed cocoa powder and natural cocoa powder. (The first is "alkalized"—treated so as to reduce acidity—and is thought to provide a smoother chocolate flavor with an intensely dark color. The second, natural or regular cocoa powder, is slightly acidic and has a lighter, reddish hue.) Tasters preferred the cakes made with natural cocoa. Its assertive flavor with fruity undertones stood up better to the sour cream in the recipe.

We came upon the real trick to developing the chocolate flavor of this cake, however, when we tried a technique that the test kitchen had earlier developed for devil's food cake. We poured boiling water over the cocoa and chocolate to dissolve them, a step that not only disperses the cocoa particles throughout the batter but also blooms the flavor.

Now we had great, complex chocolate flavor, but we also had a new problem—the cake was too dry. To remedy this, we first tried decreasing the flour by ½ cup. The resulting cake was more moist but still not moist enough, and we could not remove more flour without compromising its structure. We tried increasing the butter, but this merely made the cake greasy. We added an extra egg (most recipes call for just four; we went up to five), and that helped. Finally, we switched from granulated to light brown sugar, which not only added moistness but dramatically improved the flavor.

But even after all of these amendments to the recipe, we were still falling short of our goal of a really moist cake.

We decided to review the quantity of sour cream. When we increased it, the cake became greasy and overly acidic. We went back to the original recipes and found that many of them used either milk or buttermilk, which have a higher water content than sour cream. This tipped us off to a simple way to solve the problem: increasing the amount of boiling water added with the cocoa powder and chocolate. The resulting batter was looser and the baked cake significantly more moist—moist enough to finally satisfy our goal.

To finish the recipe, we dissolved a small amount of espresso powder along with the chocolate and cocoa and also added a healthy tablespoon of vanilla extract. Both flavors complemented the floral nuances of the chocolate. With the right pan and a ready batter, we baked cakes at temperatures of 325, 350, and 375 degrees. The cake baked at the highest temperature developed a thick upper crust and an uneven crumb. Finding little difference in the cakes baked at the other two temperatures, we opted for the quicker baking time at 350. At long last, we had reached chocolate heaven.

WHAT WE LEARNED: **Use both bittersweet chocolate and cocoa powder and intensify their flavor by melting them with boiling water. Sour cream makes the cake rich, dense, and moist, as does brown sugar.**

CHOCOLATE SOUR CREAM BUNDT CAKE

Serves 12 to 14

Natural (or regular) cocoa gives the cake a fuller, more assertive chocolate flavor than does Dutch-processed cocoa. In addition, Dutch-processed cocoa will result in a compromised rise. The cake can be served with just a dusting of confectioners' sugar but is easily made more impressive with Tangy Whipped Cream and Lightly Sweetened Raspberries (recipes follow). The cake can be made a day in advance; wrap the cooled cake in plastic and store it at room temperature. Dust with confectioners' sugar just before serving.

cake release

1	tablespoon unsalted butter, melted
1	tablespoon cocoa

cake

¾	cup (2¼ ounces) natural cocoa (see note)
6	ounces bittersweet chocolate, chopped
1	teaspoon instant espresso powder (optional)
¾	cup boiling water
1	cup sour cream, at room temperature
1¾	cups (8¾ ounces) unbleached all-purpose flour
1	teaspoon salt
1	teaspoon baking soda
12	tablespoons (1½ sticks) unsalted butter, at room temperature
2	cups (14 ounces) packed light brown sugar
1	tablespoon vanilla extract
5	large eggs, at room temperature
	Confectioners' sugar for dusting

1. FOR THE PAN: Stir together the butter and cocoa in a small bowl until a paste forms. Using a pastry brush, coat all the interior surfaces of a standard 12-cup Bundt pan. (If the mixture becomes too thick to brush on, microwave it for 10 to 20 seconds, or until warm and softened.) Adjust an oven rack to the lower-middle position and heat the oven to 350 degrees.

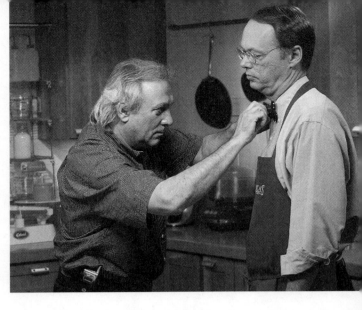

2. FOR THE CAKE: Combine the cocoa, chocolate, and espresso powder (if using) in a medium heatproof bowl. Pour the boiling water over and whisk until smooth. Cool to room temperature; then whisk in the sour cream. Whisk the flour, salt, and baking soda in a second bowl to combine.

3. In a standing mixer fitted with the flat beater, or with a handheld mixer, beat the butter, brown sugar, and vanilla on medium-high speed until pale and fluffy, about 3 minutes. Reduce the speed to medium and add the eggs one at a time, mixing about 30 seconds after each addition and scraping down the bowl with a rubber spatula after the first 2 additions. Reduce to medium-low speed (the batter may appear separated); add about one third of the flour mixture and half of the chocolate/sour cream mixture and mix until just incorporated, about 20 seconds. Scrape the bowl and repeat using half of the remaining flour mixture and all of the remaining chocolate mixture; add the remaining flour mixture and beat until just incorporated, about 10 seconds. Scrape the bowl and mix on medium-low until the batter is thoroughly combined, about 30 seconds.

4. Pour the batter into the prepared Bundt pan, being careful not to pour the batter on the sides of the pan. Bake until a wooden skewer inserted into the center comes out with a few crumbs attached, 45 to 50 minutes. Cool in the pan 10 minutes, then invert the cake onto a parchment-lined wire rack; cool to room temperature, about 3 hours. Dust with confectioners' sugar, transfer to a serving platter, and cut into wedges. Serve with Tangy Whipped Cream and Lightly Sweetened Raspberries, if desired.

TANGY WHIPPED CREAM
Makes about 2½ cups
This garnish is good either on its own or with the raspberries.

1	cup cold heavy cream
¼	cup sour cream
¼	cup packed light brown sugar
⅛	teaspoon vanilla extract

With an electric mixer, beat all the ingredients, gradually increasing the speed from low to high, until the cream forms soft peaks, 1½ to 2 minutes.

LIGHTLY SWEETENED RASPBERRIES
Makes about 3 cups
The berries are best served with the whipped cream garnish.

3	cups fresh raspberries, gently rinsed and dried
1–2	tablespoons granulated sugar

Gently toss the raspberries with the sugar, then let stand until the berries have released some juice and the sugar has dissolved, about 15 minutes.

TECHNIQUE:
Filling Tube and Bundt Pans

Batter can run down into the hole in the center of a tube or Bundt pan and burn. To prevent this, place a small paper cup over the center tube just before scraping the batter into the pan.

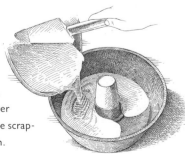

Q&A

Why do some baking recipes call for flour by weight?

Professional bakers measure all ingredients by weight rather than volume. As long as the scale is accurate, you can rest assured that 5 ounces of flour is always 5 ounces of flour.

Because of the different ways cooks use dry measuring cups, volume measures are far less accurate. If you spoon flour into a measuring cup then sweep off the excess, you will end up with about 25 percent less flour than if you dip the measuring cup into a container of flour and sweep off the excess. Even with the so-called dip-and-sweep method (which we use in the test kitchen), different cooks can obtain different amounts of flour. (We tested our staff and found the variance was about 10 percent.) Weighing flour and other dry ingredients, especially sugar, eliminates this problem and ensures consistent results.

According to our test kitchen standards, 1 cup of all-purpose flour should weigh 5 ounces. An equal amount of cake flour weighs 4 ounces. Granulated sugar and packed brown sugar weigh 7 ounces per cup.

TASTING LAB: Chocolate Ice Cream

IT'S HARD TO IMAGINE "BAD" CHOCOLATE ICE cream. But as any ice cream lover knows, some brands are a lot better than others. We tested seven leading brands to find out which ones have the scoop on the competition.

We found two clear winners—Häagen-Dazs and Double Rainbow, both of which were praised for their "intense" chocolate flavor and rich, creamy, dense texture. Both of these brands have a low overrun, a technical term that indicates how much air has been pumped into the ice cream during processing. Kids may want something sweeter and fluffier, but our adult tasters were in chocolate heaven.

The rest of the field ranged from "pretty good" to "barely decent." Tasters generally panned the fluffy-style ice creams sold in half-gallon containers. Yes, they are a lot cheaper than the good stuff that comes in small pint or quart containers, but then again you're paying for a lot of air. More important, brands at the bottom of our rankings did not pack enough chocolate flavor. If you want something cold and sweet, buy vanilla. But we think if you're going to buy chocolate ice cream, you'd better be able to taste the chocolate.

Rating Chocolate Ice Creams

TWENTY-EIGHT MEMBERS OF THE *COOK'S ILLUSTRATED* STAFF TASTED ALL SEVEN ICE CREAMS. THE ICE CREAMS ARE LISTED in order of preference based on their scores in this tasting. All brands are available in supermarkets.

RECOMMENDED

Häagen-Dazs Chocolate Ice Cream

$5.29 for I quart

Tasters responded to the "intense bittersweet chocolate" flavor and smooth, "dense" texture of this familiar premium brand. Several panelists praised the "lovely, fresh milk" flavor.

RECOMMENDED

Double Rainbow Ultra Chocolate Ice Cream

$3.49 for I quart

"Dark" chocolate flavor with a "clean" finish was the general consensus about this brand. The texture was described as "eggy" and "creamy." Not as potent as Häagen-Dazs but still an excellent value.

RECOMMENDED WITH RESERVATIONS

Brigham's Chocolate Ice Cream

$3.59 for I quart

Tasters liked this "refreshing but potent" ice cream, but it was deemed "too sweet" and "airy."

RECOMMENDED WITH RESERVATIONS

365 Every Day Value Chocolate Ice Cream

$4.49 for a half gallon

This store brand from Whole Foods markets was downgraded for its "robust cocoa powder" flavor and "gummy, powdery" texture.

RECOMMENDED WITH RESERVATIONS

Turkey Hill Dutch Chocolate Ice Cream

$2.50 for a half gallon

Tasters thought this inexpensive brand was "too sweet" and "artificial."

RECOMMENDED WITH RESERVATIONS

Breyers Chocolate Ice Cream

$3.99 for a half gallon

This popular brand received low scores for its "mild chocolate flavor" that reminded one taster of "cake batter." Tasters also panned the "icy" and "quick-to-melt" texture.

RECOMMENDED WITH RESERVATIONS

Edy's Grand Chocolate Ice Cream

$3.99 for a half gallon

Tasters compared the flavor to "chocolate milk" or "soft-serve" ice cream. Several complained about "malty," "artificial" flavor.

ANGEL FOOD CAKE

WHAT WE WANTED: A tall, perfectly shaped angel food cake with a snowy-white, tender crumb, encased in a thin, delicate, golden crust.

Although most angel food cakes contain no more than six ingredients, there are literally hundreds of variations on this basic theme. The type of flour used, the baking temperature, the type of sugar, and even the use of baking powder—a serious transgression, according to most experts—are all in dispute. What is not in dispute is that angel food cake requires a delicate balance of ingredients and proper cooking techniques. If leavened with just beaten egg whites (as is the custom), this cake can be fickle.

An angel food cake is distinguished by its lack of egg yolks, chemical leaveners, and fat. Other cakes also use beaten egg whites for leaveners, but there are differences. Chiffon cake contains egg yolks, which makes for a slightly heavier, moister cake. Sponge cake also includes whole or separated eggs; it, too, is denser and more yellow than angel food cake.

The six ingredients found in every angel food cake are egg whites, sugar, flour, cream of tartar, salt, and flavorings. Most recipes start by beating the egg whites. Mixer speed is critical for well-beaten whites. We found that starting at high speed will produce quick but inconsistent results. To create the most stable foam, beat the whites at low speed to break them up into a froth. Add the cream of tartar and salt, increase the speed to medium, and beat until the whites form very soft, billowy mounds. When large bubbles stop appearing around the edges, and with the mixer still on medium, add the sugar, a tablespoon at a time, until all the sugar has been incorporated and the whites are shiny and form soft peaks when the beater is lifted. The mass should still flow slightly when the bowl is tilted. Do not beat until the peaks are stiff; we found that this makes it difficult to fold in the flour, deflating the whites and therefore reducing volume.

Because there is no fat in angel food cake, sugar is critical to its taste and texture. We tested confectioners' sugar and found that the cornstarch in it makes the cake too dense. Superfine sugar is simply too fine, making a soft cake with little substance. We found that granulated sugar is best in this recipe.

Flour sets the cake batter, but because it also adds weight, the flour should be as light and airy as possible. We found that cake flour, which is finer than all-purpose flour, is easier to incorporate into the beaten whites without deflating them. The lower protein content of cake flour results in a more delicate, tender crumb, which we preferred. No matter what kind of flour is used, we found sifting to be essential; it makes the flour lighter in texture and easier to incorporate into the whites. Sift the flour twice—once before measuring and once before adding it to the beaten whites—for maximum lightness.

Egg whites, sugar, flour, and cream of tartar will produce a good-looking angel food cake that is sweet but bland. Salt is added for flavor and also helps stabilize the beaten whites. Other common additions are vanilla and almond extract (we like to use both), which add flavor without changing the basic chemistry of the batter. You can add grated citrus zest or a little citrus juice; we prefer the latter because zest can mar the perfectly soft texture and white color of the cake. We found that high-fat flavorings, such as grated chocolate and nuts, greatly affect the cake's texture, and we prefer to stick with simpler flavorings.

We tried using some baking powder for added leavening and stability but found that the resulting cake was not as white and had a coarser crumb. Adding baking powder also felt like cheating. If you separate and beat the egg whites properly, there should be no need to add baking powder.

Our most intriguing experiment involved oven temperatures. We baked the same recipe in the same pan at 300, 325, 350, and 375 degrees, baking each cake until it

tested done with a skewer and the top bounced back when pressed lightly. Surprisingly, all the cakes cooked evenly, but those baked at 350 and 375 degrees had a thicker, darker crust, while the cakes baked at 300 and 325 degrees had a more desirable, delicate, evenly pale golden crust. After many taste tests, we decided that 325 degrees was the ideal temperature.

The best tool we found to remove an angel food cake from the pan is a thin, flexible, nonserrated knife that is at least five inches long. Tilt the pan at a right angle to the counter to make it easy to work the knife around the sides. Insert the knife between the crust and the pan, pressing hard against the side of the pan, and work your way all around the cake. To cut around the central core of the pan, use a long, thin skewer. Invert the pan so that the cake slides out, then peel off the parchment or waxed paper. If using a pan with a removable bottom, slide the knife blade between the cake and the sides of the pan to release it. Present the cake sitting on its wide, crustier top, with the delicate and more easily sliced bottom crust facing up.

To cut the cake, use a long, serrated knife and pull it back and forth with a gentle sawing motion. When we tried using the specially made tool for cutting angel food cake—a row of prongs attached to a bar—it mashed and squashed this tender cake.

WHAT WE LEARNED: Beat the egg whites to soft peaks (not stiff peaks) so it's easier to incorporate the flour. Add cream of tartar and sugar to the egg whites to help stabilize them. For an ethereal texture, use cake flour (rather than all-purpose) and sift it twice.

ANGEL FOOD CAKE

Serves 10 to 12

Sift both the cake flour and the granulated sugar before measuring to eliminate any lumps and ensure the lightest possible texture.

1	cup (3 ounces) sifted plain cake flour
1½	cups (10½ ounces) sifted sugar
12	large egg whites (1¾ cups plus 2 tablespoons), at room temperature
1	teaspoon cream of tartar
¼	teaspoon salt
1½	teaspoons vanilla extract
1½	teaspoons juice from 1 lemon
½	teaspoon almond extract

1. Adjust an oven rack to the lower-middle position and heat the oven to 325 degrees. Have ready an ungreased large tube pan (9-inch diameter, 16-cup capacity), preferably with a removable bottom. If the pan bottom is not removable, line it with parchment paper or waxed paper.

Q&A

What's the best way to separate yolks from whites?

Many recipes, especially for cakes, call for room-temperature eggs. For example, angel food cake should be made with room temperature egg whites. But separating room-temperature eggs can be tricky, as the warm yolks can easily break and fall into the whites. Yolks are much more taut and less apt to break into the whites when cold. Always separate eggs straight from the refrigerator and then bring the eggs to room temperature if necessary. Also, it's always a good idea to separate each egg over a smaller bowl before adding the yolk and white to another bowl. That way, if a yolk breaks into a white, it won't ruin a big bowl of whites.

2. Whisk the flour and ¾ cup of the sugar in a small bowl. Place the remaining ¾ cup sugar in another small bowl next to the mixer.

3. In the bowl of a standing mixer, or with a handheld mixer, beat the egg whites at low speed until just broken up and beginning to froth. Add the cream of tartar and salt and beat at medium speed until the whites form very soft, billowy mounds. With the mixer still at medium speed, beat in the ¾ cup sugar, 1 tablespoon at a time, until all the sugar is added and the whites are shiny and form soft peaks. Add the vanilla, lemon juice, and almond extract and beat until just blended.

4. Place the flour-sugar mixture in a sifter set over waxed paper. Sift the flour-sugar mixture over the whites, about 3 tablespoons at a time, and gently fold in, using a large rubber spatula. Sift any flour-sugar mixture that falls onto the paper back into the bowl with the whites.

5. Gently scrape the batter into the pan, smooth the top with a spatula, and give the pan a couple of raps on the counter to release any large air bubbles.

6. Bake until the cake is golden brown and the top springs back when pressed firmly, 50 to 60 minutes.

7. If the cake pan has prongs around the rim for elevating the cake, invert the pan onto them. If the pan does not have prongs, invert the pan onto the neck of a bottle or funnel. Let the cake cool completely, 2 to 3 hours.

8. To unmold, run a knife around the edges of the pan, being careful not to separate the golden crust from the cake. Slide the cake out of the pan and cut the same way around the removable bottom to release, or peel off the parchment or waxed paper, if using. Place the cake, bottom-side up, on a platter. Cut slices by sawing gently with a large serrated knife. Serve the cake the day it is made.

Q&A

Is it necessary to sift presifted flour?

Flour companies sift their product to remove lumps and any foreign material. At home, bakers sift to aerate flour so that it will blend more easily into a batter. (Unsifted flour takes longer to incorporate into delicate batters and can lead to overmixing.) Presifted flour will become compact during shipping and should be sifted again if a recipe calls for sifted flour. This is especially important when making cakes.

Some recipes call for sifting dry ingredients in order to mix them evenly. This is especially true of older cookie recipes. We find this is unnecessary and instead use a wire whisk to combine dry ingredients for cookies. In this case, unsifted flour won't cause the dough to deflate or lose volume.

EQUIPMENT CORNER: Bundt Pans

UTTERLY SIMPLE TO MAKE, YET POSSESSING A DELICATE elegance, the Bundt cake is a staple of any bake sale or neighborhood get-together. Unlike other cakes, Bundt cakes need no adornment; their distinct shape and texture speak volumes about their content. So what makes this cake so special? Bundt pans, which were introduced by NordicWare (which is still in possession of the registered trademark) in the 1950s, are based on the traditional cast-iron kugelhopf molds of Eastern Europe. What defined kugelhopf cakes was the distinctive, decorative shape that the molds imparted on the dough. This tradition has continued, and to this day, more so than in any other savory or sweet preparation, the pan is the defining characteristic of a Bundt cake. Of course, quality ingredients and a great technique will dictate the cake's flavor, but only the perfect pan can create this distinctively ridged loaf with its perfectly bronzed, symmetrical curves. Having baked quite a few cakes in our time, we understand that not all pans are created equal, so we set out to find a Bundt pan capable of generating a beautiful and delicious cake worthy of its esteemed history.

In our search for pan perfection, we tested eight so-called nonstick pans that ranged in price from $9.99 to $27.99. Each pan had a simple ridged design and a minimum capacity of 12 cups. In order to assess their performance, we baked both our chocolate Bundt cake and a vanilla pound cake in each pan. Aside from evenness and depth of browning, the ease of release was our top concern. All of the chocolate cakes released easily, but some of the pound cakes did stick, most notably in the Kaiser ($17.99), Calphalon ($24.99), and NordicWare Bubble ($9.99). All of the pound cakes baked properly, but cooking times deviated by as much as 10 minutes and some of the cakes were not evenly browned—the Silicone Zone Pan ($19.99) baked a cake with no color at all. The KitchenAid ($24.99), Exeter ($14.99), Silicone Zone, and Kaiser lost points for design flaws—specifically, an unsightly crease where the center tube and the ring were joined. The NordicWare Platinum ($27.99) took top honors for best shape, deepest and most evenly browned exterior, and easiest release. The runner-up was the Baker's Secret, picked up at our local supermarket for a mere $11.99. Although it was made of lightweight material, it passed all of our tests with above-average results.

Rating Bundt Pans

WE TESTED EIGHT BUNDT PANS WITH A MINIMUM CAPACITY OF 12 CUPS. IN ADDITION TO PREPARING OUR chocolate Bundt cake in each pan, we baked vanilla pound cakes to test for evenness and depth of browning as well as ease of release. The pans are listed in order of preference. See www.americastestkitchen.com for up-to-date prices and mail-order sources for top-rated products.

HIGHLY RECOMMENDED
NordicWare Platinum Series, 12-Cup Bundt Pan
$27.99
Thick, durable, cast aluminum produced even browning and a clean, well-defined shape. The most expensive pan tested, but a winner across the board.

RECOMMENDED
Baker's Secret Non-Stick Fluted Tube Pan
$11.99
The best buy of the group, this inexpensive pan outperformed most others, including more expensive pans.

RECOMMENDED WITH RESERVATIONS
NordicWare "Colors," Bubble Non-Stick
$9.99
This flimsy pan had a nice shape but lost points in release tests.

RECOMMENDED WITH RESERVATIONS
Exeter Fluted 10-Inch Pan
$14.99
This poorly designed pan had decent browning but some sticking problems.

RECOMMENDED WITH RESERVATIONS
KitchenAid Fluted Cake Pan
$24.99
A wide rim made for easy handling, but the exterior was very slippery.

RECOMMENDED WITH RESERVATIONS
Kaiser Noblesse Bundform, 12-Cup Non-Stick
$17.99
Cakes clung to this lightweight pan with barely detectable ridges.

NOT RECOMMENDED
Calphalon Crown Bund Pan, Commercial Non-Stick
$24.99
Non-stick? Not in our tests. Cakes stuck seriously to this weighty pan, and they also failed to brown evenly.

NOT RECOMMENDED
Silicone Zone Bundform Pan
$19.99
This pliable pan was hard to handle and produced cakes with flattened tops. Because this pan is silicone and heat resistant, it does not brown the cake.

Jack explains the results of our cream cheese tasting as Chris tries several samples.

PUMPKIN cheesecake

Pumpkin cheesecake stands second to the traditional pumpkin pie as a holiday dessert. Those who suffer from pumpkin pie ennui embrace pumpkin cheesecake as "a nice change," but the expectations are low.

Undoubtedly, pumpkin cheesecake can be good in its own right, though it rarely is. The tendency is for extremes in texture—dry, dense, chalky cakes or wet, soft, mousse-like ones. Flavors veer from far too cheesy and tangy or pungently overspiced to noxiously sweet or totally bland. Merely mixing a can of pumpkin into a standard cheesecake batter doesn't work; the texture is amiss (leaden and sloppy), and the pumpkin flavor is thwarted. And then there are soggy, grease-leaching crumb crusts—a common problem in most every recipe we tried.

The promise of this recipe is so high, so we were willing to get to work. But we never figured it would take 30 cheesecakes—that's more than 11,000 grams of fat and 150,000 calories—to develop a great recipe worthy of the finest holiday dinner.

PUMPKIN CHEESECAKE

WHAT WE WANTED: A creamy cheesecake with a velvety smooth texture that tasted of sweet, earthy pumpkin as well as tangy cream cheese. And, of course, it had to have a crisp, buttery, cookie-crumb crust.

Pumpkin cheesecake has two distinct components—a crumb crust and a lush cream cheese filling. To make a crumb crust for pumpkin cheesecake, our options were ground-up vanilla wafers, animal crackers, gingersnaps, and graham crackers. The first two were too mild-flavored for the spicy filling. Gingersnaps were well liked for their spicy bittersweet molasses notes, which balanced well against the pumpkin flavor of the cake, but no matter the brand or the amount of butter and sugar we added—and despite prebaking—they refused to form a crust that retained its crispness.

With graham crackers we had success. Five ounces of crackers (nine whole ones), crushed to crumbs, formed a substantial crust. Too little butter and the crust was not cohesive; 6 tablespoons was just the right amount. Too little sugar and the crust was not adequately sweet; 3 tablespoons was a good amount. Pressed into the bottom of the springform pan and baked until browned around the edges, the graham crackers formed a sturdy, crisp, buttery crust. (Without prebaking, the crust became a pasty, soggy layer beneath the filling.) We then replaced the granulated sugar with dark brown sugar to replicate the molasses flavor of the gingersnaps, but the sugar's moisture caused sogginess, so we went back to granulated. To increase spiciness, we added doses of ground cinnamon, cloves, and ginger.

Anyone who has prepared fresh pumpkin for pumpkin pie can attest to the fact that cutting, seeding, peeling, and cooking fresh pumpkin is not time and effort well spent. Opening a can takes only a few seconds; preparing fresh pumpkin takes a few hours. Moreover, all pumpkin cheesecake recipes call for canned pumpkin.

With a working recipe pieced together, we found that one can of pumpkin and 1½ pounds of cream cheese made a tall, handsome cake with a balance of tang and earthy pumpkin flavor. We were using granulated sugar to sweeten the cheesecake, but we surmised that brown sugar, with its molasses flavor, would add depth and richness. We were wrong. Substituted for the entire amount of granulated sugar, brown sugar only mucked up and masked the flavor of the pumpkin while giving the cheesecake a dirty brown hue (this was especially true of dark brown sugar). We tried lesser and lesser amounts until eventually there was none.

According to recipes, most pumpkin cheesecakes, unlike plain ones, require neither sour cream nor heavy cream. No matter. We tried them both (after all, none of the recipes we had tried hit the mark). Sour cream, even in small amounts, was too assertive; its tang eclipsed the delicate flavor of the pumpkin. On the other hand, heavy cream—a cup of it—made the cheesecake feel and taste smooth and lush. It seemed to mitigate the slightly mealy fibrousness of the pumpkin and enrich the cheesecake without obscuring the pumpkin flavor. It did, however, affect the texture, making it loose and soft. Not wanting to compromise the richness, we attempted to remedy the problem by adjusting the eggs, but to no avail. We then tried flour and cornstarch in hopes that one would absorb excess moisture, but both resulted in a starchy, pasty, unappealing texture.

As we were reevaluating heavy cream as an essential ingredient, a colleague suggested cooking the pumpkin before adding it to the cheesecake. It then occurred to us that if we could remove some moisture from the pumpkin, perhaps we could improve the texture. We emptied a can of pumpkin into a nonstick skillet and cooked it until it had lost a surprising amount of moisture—nearly five ounces, or more than half a cup. The cheesecake made with this "dried" pumpkin had a thick, plush, velvety texture to match its rich flavor.

The downside to cooking the pumpkin, which involved frequent stirring and then a cooling period, was that it meant paying the pumpkin more attention than we wanted. Simply draining it did not work. In our numerous dealings with canned pumpkin, we noticed that it had cohesion and a nonstick quality. We spread the pumpkin onto a baking sheet lined with paper towels—like spreading frosting on a cake—and then pressed additional paper towels down on its surface to wick away more moisture. In seconds, the pumpkin shed enough liquid (about four ounces) to yield a cheesecake with a lovely texture, and the paper towels were peeled away almost effortlessly.

With the essential ingredients determined, we turned to eggs. After making some 10 cheesecakes with different amounts of egg in various configurations (whole eggs, egg whites, and egg yolks), we had discovered a surprising range of textures, from stiff and dry to waxy. Five whole eggs produced our favorite cheesecake, one that was satiny, creamy, and unctuous.

Finally, we worked on refining the flavorings. Vanilla and salt were good additions, as was a tablespoon of lemon juice for brightness. Sweet, warm cinnamon was favored at the fore; sharp, spicy ground ginger and small amounts of cloves, nutmeg, and allspice produced, in unison, a deep,

resounding flavor but not an overspiced burn.

In its springform pan, a cheesecake can be baked either directly on the oven rack like a regular cake or in a water bath like a delicate custard. The cake baked in a water bath was undeniably better than the version baked without a water bath. (For more information, see page 323.) We tried a few different oven temperatures, and 325 degrees worked best. At higher temperatures, the water in the bath reached a simmer; at lower temperatures the cheesecake took an inordinate amount of time to bake.

We sliced the cheesecake into neat wedges and served it with bourbon-and-brown-sugar-laced whipped cream (many at first decried this as over-the-top, but they were silenced after a single taste). At last, here was a pumpkin cheesecake that pleased the pumpkin pie traditionalists and that for the others was a nice change from "a nice change."

WHAT WE LEARNED: Start with a basic graham cracker crust that is flavored with ground ginger, cinnamon, and cloves. For the filling, dry canned pumpkin on paper towels to remove excess moisture and rely on heavy cream—not sour cream—for added richness. Add pumpkin-friendly spices to the filling and bake the cheesecake in a water bath for a smooth, creamy texture.

SPICED PUMPKIN CHEESECAKE

Serves 12 to 16

Depending on the oven and the temperature of the ingredients, this cheesecake may bake about 15 minutes faster or slower than the instructions indicate; it is therefore best to check the cake 1¼ hours into baking. Although the cheesecake can be made up to 3 days in advance, the crust will begin to lose its crispness after only 1 day. To make slicing the cheesecake easy and neat, use a knife with a narrow blade, such as a carving knife; between cuts, dip the blade into a pitcher of hot water and wipe it clean with paper towels. The cheesecake is good on its own, but the Brown Sugar and Bourbon Cream (recipe follows) is a grand addition.

crust

9	graham crackers (5 ounces), broken into large pieces
3	tablespoons sugar
½	teaspoon ground ginger
½	teaspoon ground cinnamon
¼	teaspoon ground cloves
6	tablespoons (¾ stick) unsalted butter, melted

filling

1⅓	cups (10⅓ ounces) sugar
1	teaspoon ground cinnamon
½	teaspoon ground ginger
¼	teaspoon ground nutmeg
¼	teaspoon ground cloves
¼	teaspoon ground allspice
½	teaspoon salt
1	(15-ounce) can pumpkin
1½	pounds cream cheese, cut into 1-inch chunks, at room temperature
1	tablespoon vanilla extract
1	tablespoon juice from 1 lemon
5	large eggs, at room temperature
1	cup heavy cream

1. FOR THE CRUST: Adjust an oven rack to the lower-middle position and heat the oven to 325 degrees. Spray the bottom and sides of a 9-inch springform pan evenly with nonstick cooking spray. Place the graham crackers, sugar, and spices in a food processor and process until evenly and finely ground, about fifteen 2-second pulses. Transfer the crumbs to a medium bowl, drizzle the melted butter over them, and mix with a rubber spatula until evenly moistened. Turn the crumbs into the prepared springform pan and spread the crumbs in an even layer, following the illustrations on page 321. Bake until fragrant and browned around the edges, about 15 minutes. Cool on a wire rack to room temperature, about 30 minutes. When cool, wrap the outside of the pan with two 18-inch-square pieces of heavy-duty foil; set the springform pan in a roasting pan.

2. FOR THE FILLING: Bring about 4 quarts water to a simmer in a stockpot. While the crust is cooling, whisk the sugar, spices, and salt in a small bowl; set aside. Line a baking sheet with a triple layer of paper towels. Spread the pumpkin on the towels and cover with a second triple layer of towels. Press firmly until the towels are saturated. Peel back the top layer of towels and discard. Grasp the bottom towels and fold the pumpkin in half; peel back the towels. Repeat and flip the pumpkin onto the baking sheet; discard the towels.

3. In the bowl of a standing mixer, or with a handheld mixer, beat the cream cheese at medium speed to break up and soften slightly, about 1 minute. Scrape the beater and the bottom and sides of the bowl well with a rubber spatula. Add about a third of the sugar mixture and beat at medium-low speed until combined, about 1 minute; scrape the bowl and add the remaining sugar in two additions, scraping the bowl after each addition. Add the pumpkin, vanilla, and lemon juice and beat at medium speed until combined, about 45 seconds; scrape the bowl. Add 3 of the eggs and beat at medium-low speed until incorporated, about 1 minute; scrape the bowl. Add the remaining 2 eggs and beat at medium-low speed until incorporated, about 45 seconds; scrape the bowl. Add the heavy cream and beat at low speed until combined, about 45 seconds. Using a rubber spatula, scrape the bottom and sides of the bowl and give a final stir by hand.

4. Pour the filling into the springform pan and smooth the surface; set the roasting pan in the oven and pour enough boiling water to come about halfway up the sides of the springform pan. Bake until the center of the cake is slightly wobbly when the pan is shaken and the center of the cake reads 150 degrees on an instant-read thermometer, about 1½ hours (see note). Set the roasting pan on a wire rack and cool until the water is just warm, about 45 minutes. Remove the springform pan from the water bath, discard the foil, and set on a wire rack; run a paring knife around the inside edge of the pan to loosen the sides of the cake and cool until barely warm, about 3 hours. Wrap with plastic wrap and refrigerate until chilled, at least 4 hours or up to 3 days.

5. TO SERVE: Remove the sides of the pan. Slide a thin metal spatula between the crust and pan bottom to loosen, then slide the cake onto a serving platter. Let the cheesecake stand at room temperature about 30 minutes, then cut into wedges (see note) and serve with Brown Sugar and Bourbon Cream, if desired.

VARIATION
PUMPKIN-BOURBON CHEESECAKE WITH GRAHAM-PECAN CRUST

Follow the recipe for Spiced Pumpkin Cheesecake, reducing the graham crackers to 3 ounces (5 whole crackers), processing 2 ounces chopped pecans (about ½ cup) with the crackers, and reducing the butter to 4 tablespoons. Omit the lemon juice from the filling, reduce the vanilla extract to 1 teaspoon, and add ¼ cup bourbon along with the heavy cream.

TECHNIQUE:
Pressing the Crumbs into the Pan

1. Use the bottom of a ramekin or drinking glass to press the crumbs into the bottom of a buttered springform pan. Press the crumbs as far as possible into the edges of the pan.

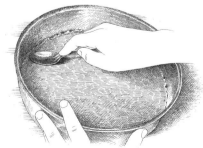

2. Use a teaspoon to neatly press the crumbs into the corners of the pan to create a clean edge.

BROWN SUGAR AND BOURBON CREAM

Makes about 3 cups

1 cup heavy cream
½ cup sour cream
⅓ cup (2⅓ ounces) packed light brown sugar
⅛ teaspoon salt
2 teaspoons bourbon

1. In the bowl of a standing mixer or with a handheld mixer, whisk the heavy cream, sour cream, brown sugar, and salt until combined. Cover with plastic wrap and refrigerate until ready to serve the cheesecake, at least 4 hours or up to 24, stirring once or twice during chilling to ensure that the sugar dissolves.

2. When ready to serve the cheesecake, add the bourbon and beat the mixture at medium speed until small bubbles form around the edges, about 40 seconds; increase the speed to high and continue to beat until fluffy and doubled in volume, about 1 minute longer. Spoon the cream onto individual slices of cheesecake.

TECHNIQUE: Chilling the Bowl to Make Whipped Cream

For the best results, you should chill a bowl before whipping cream in it. For many cooks, the freezer is either too small or too full to accommodate a large bowl. Here's how to accomplish this task outside of the freezer.

1. At least 15 minutes before whipping the cream, fill the bowl with ice cubes and cold water and place the whisk (or beaters from an electric mixer) in the ice water.

2. When ready to whip the cream, dump out the ice water, dry the bowl and whisk, and add the cream. The bowl will stay cold as you work, and the cream will whip up beautifully.

SCIENCE DESK:
Is a Water Bath Worth the Trouble?

A WATER BATH IS COMMONLY CALLED FOR IN THE BAKING of cheesecakes and custards. The theory is that a water bath moderates the temperature around the perimeter of the pan, preventing overcooking at the edges. To figure out exactly what's happening, we prepared two identical cheesecakes and baked one directly on the oven rack and the other in a water bath. Both were removed from the oven when their centers reached 147 degrees. The cake that had been baked in a water bath was even-colored and smooth; the other cake was browned and cracked. A quick comparison of the temperature at the edges of the cakes confirmed what we suspected. Upon removal from the oven, the cake that had had the benefit of a water bath was 184 degrees at the edges, whereas the edges of the cake baked without the water bath had climbed to 213 degrees.

Why was the cheesecake baked in a water bath 30 degrees cooler at the edges than the cake baked without a water bath? Although in both cases the oven had been set to 325 degrees, a water bath cannot exceed 212 degrees, as this is the temperature at which water converts to steam.

Why did the cheesecake baked in the water bath have an even and uncracked top? By moderating the temperature of the cheesecake, the water bath prevented the cheesecake top from inflating like a soufflé. In addition, the water bath added considerable moisture to the oven (more than four cups of water evaporated from the bath during cooking). The added moisture helped to keep the top of the cake supple, which discourages cracking.

TASTING LAB: Cream Cheese

SUPERMARKET SHELVES AREN'T EXACTLY OVERFLOWING with cream cheese options. Whenever we need cream cheese in the test kitchen, we instinctively reach for Philadelphia brand. But is Philadelphia the best or just the most familiar and widely available?

To find out, we gathered all the types of cream cheese we could find: a paltry five, three of which were Philadelphia products (Philadelphia ⅓ Less Fat, Philadelphia Whipped, and original Philadelphia); the other two were organic brands. We tasted them plain and in our New York Cheesecake—we figured the flavors in our Spiced Pumpkin Cheesecake would be distracting.

Tasters judged the cream cheeses on richness, tanginess, creaminess, and overall quality, and one product swept both the plain and cheesecake tastings in all categories: Philadelphia. Though some liked the easy spreadability of Philadelphia Whipped (we let the tasters try the cream cheese on bagels after they tasted each sample plain) and most were enthusiastic about buttery Organic Valley (our second-place finisher), overall the familiar Philadelphia held its place as the cream cheese of choice in the test kitchen.

GETTING IT RIGHT:
Most Cheesecakes Need a Water Bath

A water bath guarantees a cheesecake with a smooth, creamy texture. We baked two cheesecakes until the center reached 147 degrees. One was baked with a water bath; the other without. Note the differences in temperature at the edges of these two pieces. See Science Desk above for an explanation.

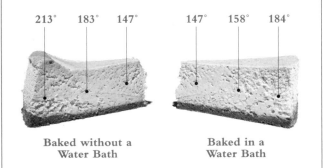

213° 183° 147°   147° 158° 184°

Baked without a   **Baked in a**
Water Bath   **Water Bath**

Although Philadelphia was the clear winner, all but one of the products tasted are recommended. Despite our hopes to the contrary, Philadelphia ⅓ Less Fat tanked, coming in last. While we would have been thrilled to offer low-fat cream cheese as a suitable substitution in our cheesecakes, the artificial flavor and stiff texture forced it out of consideration.

Q&A

How do you prevent cheesecakes from cracking?

Cracks are usually caused by overbaking and can be avoided by removing the cheesecake from the oven when the internal temperature taken on an instant-read thermometer reads 150 degrees. Running a paring knife around the inside of the springform pan as soon as the cheesecake comes out of the oven is also a good idea; if the edges stick to the pan, a crack can form as the cheesecake cools and shrinks.

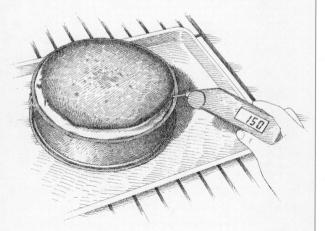

Note that if you take the temperature of the cheesecake multiple times you can do more harm than good. Puncturing the surface again and again will weaken the structure of the cheesecake and can cause cracks. Consequently, we recommend that you take the temperature of the cheesecake only once or, if necessary, take the temperature again through the initial thermometer hole at the center of the cake. You can eliminate this risk altogether by taking the temperature of the cheesecake from the side, approaching the center through the part of the cheesecake that rises above the pan.

Rating Cream Cheeses

FIFTEEN MEMBERS OF THE *COOK'S ILLUSTRATED* STAFF TASTED ALL OF THE CREAM CHEESES BOTH PLAIN AND baked in our New York Cheesecake. The cream cheeses are listed in order of preference based on their combined scores in the two tastings. All brands are available in supermarkets.

RECOMMENDED

Philadelphia Original Cream Cheese

$1.99 for 8 ounces

"Milky" and "very flavorful" was the overall assessment of this supermarket staple. This classic choice won both the plain and the cheesecake tastings, earning high marks for its creamy texture.

RECOMMENDED

Organic Valley Organic Cream Cheese

$2.45 for 8 ounces

Tasters called this sample "mild," "buttery," and "slightly waxy." It finished a strong second in the cheesecake tasting and was tied for second in the plain tasting. In both cases, panelists praised its creamy texture.

RECOMMENDED

Horizon Organic Spreadable Cream Cheese

$1.99 for 8 ounces

"Bland" and "not bad" was the general consensus about this brand, which performed better in the cheesecake tasting than when sampled plain.

RECOMMENDED

Philadelphia Whipped Cream Cheese

$2.99 for 12 ounces

Tasters liked the tangy flavor of this product but complained about its airy consistency. One taster wrote, "light texture—not what I want in a cream cheese." This sample fared better in the plain tasting than when baked in the cheesecake.

NOT RECOMMENDED

Philadelphia ⅓ Less Fat Than Cream Cheese

$1.99 for 8 ounces

"Chalky" and "pasty" were the two most common complaints about this reduced-calorie, reduced-fat Neufchâtel cheese. It fared OK in the plain tasting (although tasters wanted more creaminess), but tasters felt it compromised the quality of the cheesecake.

Our individual chocolate volcano cakes can be portioned into baking dishes a day in advance and then baked as needed.

FOUR-STAR desserts

When our test cooks eat in restaurants, they always come back to the kitchen and talk about the dessert. Dramatic and artful presentations rightfully garner a lot of attention. But we're most interested in how these desserts taste. Many modern pastry chefs include several components in their desserts, offering a mix of flavors, textures, and temperatures on one plate. These creations seem light-years ahead of the usual pies, cakes, and cookies we usually serve at home. But are they?

Over the years, we've discovered several spectacular four-star desserts that are actually pretty simple, at least in theory. Our goal was to identify two such modern classics and figure out ways to make them even more approachable for the home cook.

The first dessert, a molten chocolate cake paired with an espresso ice cream bombe, is a fresh interpretation of a well-worn (and sometimes tired) restaurant classic. The second dessert is more exotic. It starts with the common pairing of blue cheese and pears but then cooks the pears and uses a caramel sauce flavored with black pepper to unite the two main elements. Novel flavors with dramatic presentation. Could we really make these desserts suitable for a weekend dinner party?

IN THIS CHAPTER

THE RECIPES
Chocolate Volcano Cakes with Espresso Ice Cream

Caramelized Pears with Blue Cheese and Black Pepper–Caramel Sauce

EQUIPMENT CORNER
Handheld Mixers

CHOCOLATE VOLCANO CAKES WITH ESPRESSO ICE CREAM

WHAT WE WANTED: A warm chocolate cake with an intense chocolate flavor, served with a cooling scoop of equally potent espresso ice cream.

Restaurant menus often offer a molten chocolate cake, but we have had our share of bad molten cakes—usually raw-tasting and soggy or reheated and stale. That said, we were impressed with a version from Ixora restaurant in Whitehouse Station, New Jersey. Served straight out of the oven with a hot, rich, liquidy center, Ixora tempers its intensely flavored cake by serving a tiny, chocolate-coated, ice cream bombe alongside. The dramatic range in temperatures, powerful chocolate punch, and visual appeal make this dessert appear far more difficult and time-consuming than it really is. Using a durable cake batter and a minimal number of ingredients, this dessert can largely be prepared up to 24 hours in advance.

Combining the features of both a brownie and a fallen chocolate cake, the exterior walls of the individual cakes are toothsome and sturdy while the centers are smooth and creamy, and the tops become shiny and appealingly cracked as they bake. The batter has a high proportion of sugar and chocolate, like a fudgy brownie, yet the cake gets its basic structure from eggs and egg yolks, much like a fallen chocolate cake. The original recipe called for extra-bittersweet chocolate, which is somewhat difficult to find. We approximated the intense flavor by using both a supermarket bittersweet chocolate and a few ounces of unsweetened chocolate. With a little cornstarch to stabilize the chocolate and a complete absence of both chemical leavening (such as baking powder or soda) and whipped eggs (which could deflate over time), this batter has been engineered to be unfailingly successful regardless of how hot, hectic, or harried the restaurant's kitchen might get.

We found it easiest to portion the batter into individual ramekins as soon as it was mixed. The cakes can then be either baked right away or wrapped tightly with plastic wrap, refrigerated, and baked straight from the refrigerator at a moment's notice. Although the cakes could be served right in their ramekins, we preferred to unmold them onto individual plates so they could nuzzle up to the ice cream. To help the cakes fall right out of the hot ramekins without a struggle, we found it helpful to butter and sugar the ramekins before pouring in the batter.

Offering bites of relief from the intense, lava-hot cakes, the ice cream bombes are small domes of espresso ice cream coated with a thin shell of hardened chocolate, like a bonbon. After attempting to replicate these morsels on several occasions, we realized that this is one task best left to professionals. In order to thinly coat the ice cream, we found it took multiple dips into chocolate that was melted to a very specific temperature. If done any other way, the chocolate coating either became too thick or slid right off the ice cream. Instead, we liked a scoop of the espresso ice cream placed on the plate next to the hot cake.

The restaurant makes its own espresso ice cream, but in the spirit of home cooking, we found it just as satisfying to mix finely ground espresso beans into coffee-flavored ice cream. After the ice cream is softened on the counter for a few minutes, the ground espresso can be folded in using a rubber spatula. Lastly, we noted that a sprinkling of confectioners' sugar over the cake and plate not only helped prevent the scoop of ice cream from sliding around but also made the dessert look truly impressive.

WHAT WE LEARNED: Duplicate the flavor of hard-to-find extra-bittersweet chocolate by combining regular bittersweet chocolate with a little unsweetened chocolate. Cornstarch makes the batter remarkably stable and ensures that the cakes rise in the oven. To approximate the intense flavor of the restaurant's espresso ice cream, simply fold some finely ground espresso beans into store-bought coffee ice cream.

CHOCOLATE VOLCANO CAKES WITH ESPRESSO ICE CREAM

Serves 8

Use a bittersweet bar chocolate in this recipe, not chips—the chips include emulsifiers that will alter the cakes' texture. The cake batter can be mixed and portioned into the ramekins, wrapped tightly with plastic wrap, and refrigerated up to 24 hours in advance. The cold cake batter should be baked straight from the refrigerator.

espresso ice cream

2	pints coffee ice cream, softened
1½	tablespoons finely ground espresso beans

cakes

10	tablespoons unsalted butter, cut into ½-inch pieces, plus more for buttering the ramekins
1½	cups (10½ ounces) granulated sugar, plus more for dusting the ramekins
8	ounces bittersweet chocolate, finely chopped
2	ounces unsweetened chocolate, finely chopped
2	tablespoons cornstarch
3	large eggs, at room temperature
4	large egg yolks, at room temperature
2	teaspoons Grand Marnier (or other orange-flavored liqueur)
	Confectioners' sugar, for dusting the cakes

1. FOR THE ICE CREAM: Transfer the ice cream to a medium bowl and, using a rubber spatula, fold in the ground espresso until incorporated. Press a sheet of plastic wrap flush against the ice cream (see the illustration on this page) to prevent freezer burn and return it to the freezer. (The ice cream can be prepared up to 24 hours ahead.)

2. FOR THE CAKES: Lightly coat eight 4-ounce ramekins with butter. Dust with sugar, tapping out any excess, and set aside.

3. Melt the bittersweet and unsweetened chocolates and 10 tablespoons butter in a medium bowl over a medium saucepan of simmering water, stirring occasionally, until the chocolate mixture is smooth. In a large bowl, whisk the 1½ cups sugar and cornstarch together. Add the chocolate mixture and stir to combine. Add the eggs, egg yolks, and Grand Marnier and whisk until fully combined. Scoop ½ cup of the batter into each of the prepared ramekins. (The ramekins can be covered tightly with plastic wrap and refrigerated for up to 24 hours.)

4. Adjust an oven rack to the upper-middle position and heat the oven to 375 degrees. Place the filled ramekins on a rimmed baking sheet and bake until the tops of the cakes are set, have formed shiny crusts, and are beginning to crack, 16 to 20 minutes.

5. Transfer the ramekins to a wire rack and cool slightly, about 2 minutes. Run a paring knife around the edge of each cake. Using a towel to protect your hand from the hot ramekins, invert each cake onto a small plate, then immediately invert again right-side up onto 8 individual plates. Sift confectioners' sugar over each cake and the area of the plate where the ice cream will be placed. Remove the ice cream from the freezer and scoop a portion on top of the confectioners' sugar, next to the cake. Serve immediately.

TECHNIQUE:
Keeping Ice Cream Fresh

To prevent ice crystals from forming on the ice cream, press plastic wrap flush against the surface of the ice cream before covering it with a lid.

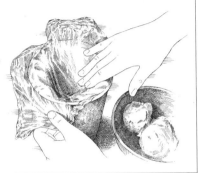

EQUIPMENT CORNER:
Handheld Mixers

IN HEAD-TO-HEAD COMPETITIONS IN OUR TEST KITCHEN, standing mixers always outperform handheld mixers (see page 302 for details). Simply put, a standing mixer offers greater flexibility and versatility. The most obvious difference is brute force. Any decent standing mixer can knead bread dough, but even the best handheld mixer fails miserably at this task. A standing mixer also frees up the cook to take on other tasks. While these two advantages are dramatic, for many day-to-day uses, handheld and standing mixers are actually quite similar. When making cake batters and cookie doughs, whipping cream, and beating egg whites, we have found that a handheld mixer can yield the same results as a standing mixer, albeit a little more slowly.

In addition, a handheld mixer costs a fraction of a standing mixer, and it's also compact and easily transported. If your workspace or budget is restricted, a handheld mixer can prove most valuable, especially if you don't want a mixer for bread making and you don't mind standing by the bowl as the mixer does its work. But this calculation only makes sense if you invest in a good handheld mixer—and that's easier said than done.

Over the years, we've been disappointed by many handheld mixers; they can be little more than glorified whisks. And who hasn't encountered the disconcerting smoky odor of a handheld mixer's motor as the beaters slog their way through a particularly stiff dough? These experiences notwithstanding, the promise of a good handheld mixer—reliable performance easily had, and at a low cost—beckoned. And so we assembled eight leading models to see if we could separate the wimps from the workhorses.

Lack of power isn't the only complaint we've had with handheld mixers. With a standing mixer, splattering isn't much of an issue because the whisk sits deep into the bowl. A handheld mixer, however, can spray both the counter and the cook as the beaters whirl away. When whipping cream,

we found that most mixers splattered on some level, but the best mixers kept the mess in the bowl; the worst managed to propel flecks of cream up to eye level, which was not appreciated.

All of the mixers were able to beat egg whites to stiff peaks. The main discrepancy resided in the "feel" of the mixer as it beat the whites; some felt unwieldy (and thus received a rating of "fair" on this task), while others felt controlled (and were rated "good"). We also found that certain beater styles were more efficient at beating egg whites. Actually, in recent years, many mixers have abandoned the old-style beaters with flat tines and a center post for a more streamlined wire beater without the hard-to-clean center post. Some manufacturers still offer both styles, while others are also throwing in a bonus whisk attachment. One model in our testing offered all three.

In our tests, we found that the wire beaters were the best choice as they were the most versatile of the three beater styles. They proved good for thin batters, thick doughs, and liquids and were the easiest to clean—by far. And not too far behind were the flat beaters with center posts (the classic attachment), which we found to be a decent choice. They creamed butter and sugar nicely, tending not to spread ingredients to the outskirts of the bowl. They also did a nice job beating egg whites quickly; however, the center post caused thick doughs to become clogged in the beaters. We did not like any of the whisk attachments tested. They were downright flimsy and inefficient and caused a significant amount of splattering.

On the whole, making pound cake seemed the perfect test for a mixer's effectiveness at creaming. Traditional pound cake contains no chemical leaveners; its rise comes from creaming the butter and sugar until they are light and fluffy. Proper aeration is key to avoiding an overly dense cake. The eight mixers tested made cakes that rose to heights within ¼ inch of one another—a range so negligible that this test counted for little in the overall ratings.

The test that really separated the winners from the losers was mixing peanut butter cookie dough. Unlike chocolate chip cookie dough, which is easy enough to mix by hand if necessary, thick, stiff peanut butter cookie dough requires a determined motor. Of the eight mixers tested, only the KitchenAid and the Braun did not hesitate once the dry ingredients were added to the sticky mix of peanut butter, eggs, and butter. Four of the mixers struggled but ultimately managed to tough it out as the dough began to come together or the mixing speed was increased. Two models could not complete this task and landed at the bottom of our ratings.

Somewhat to our surprise, wattage was not a good indicator of power. Of the mixers that fell into the run-of-the-mill category, one had the highest wattage of all eight mixers tested, another the lowest. KitchenAid, the maker of our winning mixer, did not even post the machine's wattage on its box or in its literature.

Because so many consumers judge the power of an appliance by its wattage, we asked KitchenAid about this. A representative explained that unlike most manufacturers, which use AC (alternating current) motors, KitchenAid uses a DC (direct current) motor, which it finds to be less heavy, less noisy, and more powerful than AC motors. The company also claims that this motor is more energy-efficient and requires less wattage to operate. (KitchenAid would not disclose the exact wattage required.) In sum, the KitchenAid representative said, wattage is not always the best measurement of power when buying small electrical appliances. Our science editor explained that wattage is a measure of input—the amount of power a motor is taking in to operate. If a motor is not designed to work efficiently, it can require more input, or wattage, without necessarily delivering more output—that is, a stronger performance.

Secondary to power, although still significant, was design. Most of the mixers weighed in at around 2 pounds, 2 ounces, but some felt much heavier than others and were more fatiguing to use. For example, mixers with angled handles let you relax your elbow at your side. Those with horizontal handles (parallel to the machine's body) make it necessary to lift your elbow in order to hold the machine

upright. This posture quickly proved tiring. Balance of weight and the shape of the handle grip also affected fatigue. The number of speeds didn't seem nearly as important as the range of power within those speeds. The Braun, for instance, with just three speeds, outperformed many models with seven speeds.

Both the KitchenAid and the Cuisinart came with an on/off switch, which we considered a welcome safety mechanism—just in case the machine gets plugged in before the beaters are inserted. We were also big fans of Oster's retractable cord (press a button and the cord automatically winds into the mixer's housing). A round cord design was also preferred to a flat cord with a crease up the center, because the former is much easier to wipe clean.

Overall—and as expected—most of the mixers we tested had their shortcomings. But the KitchenAid was the total package: powerful, quiet, controlled, and compact. It was a pleasure to use. Of course, this machine came with the highest price tag: $70. Braun, the runner-up, was cheaper by $20 but lacked the KitchenAid's finesse. Considering the proven versatility of this mixer and the fact that our favorite standing mixer sells for about $250, maybe $70 doesn't seem so unreasonable after all.

Rating Handheld Mixers

WE TESTED EIGHT HANDHELD MIXERS, EVALUATING EACH ACCORDING TO PRICE, ATTACHMENTS, DESIGN, AND performance in the following tests: whipping cream, beating egg whites, mixing pound cake batter, and mixing peanut butter cookie dough. The mixers are listed in order of preference. See www.americastestkitchen.com for up-to-date prices and mail-order sources for top-rated products.

HIGHLY RECOMMENDED
KitchenAid 7 Speed Artisan Mixer, Model KHM7T $69.99

This mixer never slowed or hesitated when mixing stiff peanut butter cookie dough. The mixing action was notably "neat," "smooth," and "controlled" compared with that of others. It took the longest of all mixers to whip cream and beat egg whites—admittedly, with barely any splattering.

HIGHLY RECOMMENDED
Braun MultiMix 4-in-1, Model M880 $49.99

This mixer worked through thick cookie dough without slowing. A total of three speeds could have felt limited if the rates didn't feel just right. A more angled handle with a narrower grip would have been more comfortable.

RECOMMENDED
Bosch TurboBeat Hand Mixer, Model MFQ2100UC $59.99

The beater design of this model is similar to Braun's and thus is extremely efficient at whipping. Its motor was quiet—"like a modern-day sewing machine"—and the overall operation felt smooth. The beaters slowed some when making cookie dough, but increasing the speed took care of this.

RECOMMENDED
Cuisinart SmartPower Electronic Hand Mixer, Model HTM-7L $49.95

An on/off switch, digital touchpad display, and good overall balance were clear design strengths of this mixer. It didn't "bite into the cookie dough," however, requiring the mixer to be pushed through the dough, at which point the beaters turned but didn't appear to be blending anything.

RECOMMENDED
Black & Decker PowerPro, Model #MX85 $19.99

This mixer began to smell when mixing peanut butter cookie dough. Increased speed helped, but the mixer still had to be pushed through the dough, as the beaters didn't grab it. It did just fine when it came to lighter jobs, such as whipping.

RECOMMENDED
Oster Easystore Hand Mixer, Model 2491 $24.99

The performance of this mixer was top-notch, but it couldn't handle the cookie dough, which became clogged inside the flat beaters. We loved the retractable cord for neat storage but found the handle hard to hold.

NOT RECOMMENDED
Hamilton Beach Power Deluxe Mixer, Model 62695 $29.99

The square edges on this mixer's wire beaters clanged and rattled against the sides of the bowl. Splatters from whipping cream reached eye level, and the beaters repeatedly bogged down in cookie dough as the motor emitted a burning odor. The mixer vibrated noticeably during use.

NOT RECOMMENDED
Farberware Hand Mixer, Model FPHM600 $24.99

While there was some bogging down of beaters during the cookie dough test, our biggest complaint was this mixer's tendency to fling ingredients around and out of the bowl. The handle was so thick that even a tester with large hands struggled to maintain his grip.

CARAMELIZED PEARS WITH BLUE CHEESE AND BLACK PEPPER–CARAMEL SAUCE

WHAT WE WANTED: A new spin on pears and cheese with caramelized, tender pears and a spicy caramel sauce.

When we first tasted this dessert from Tea Tray in the Sky in Cambridge, Massachusetts, we knew it was special. An updated version of the classic combination of pears and blue cheese, this dessert starts with pears that are caramelized, rendering them soft and golden. Although the pears are tasty on their own, it is the rich caramel sauce, surprisingly flavored with crushed black pepper, that really sets this dessert apart. Served on an early menu from the café, this incredible dessert sounded so delicious that we tracked down the chef and coerced the recipe from his memory.

At the café, the caramel sauce was made in advance, while the pears were cut, dipped in sugar, then seared in a hot nonstick pan to caramelize per order. This multipot method makes sense in a restaurant because it limits the amount of last-minute work during dinner service, but it

doesn't make sense for the home cook. To streamline the recipe, we found it easy to cook the pears right in the caramel sauce, saving time and eliminating some dirty dishes. We brought water and sugar (the basis for caramel sauce) to a boil in a skillet and slid the pears into the hot mixture and let them cook in the slowly browning caramel. Because this method actually cooks the pears in the sauce, we found it best to use firm pears that could take the extensive amount of heat. Also, we noted it was easiest to trim the bottom of the pears so that they stand upright on the plate before cooking them, as opposed to after.

With our first batch, we tried removing the pears from the pan before we stirred the heavy cream into the caramel to finish it. This didn't work so well: The pears turned unappetizingly sticky as they cooled, having been essentially cooked in sugar candy. For our next batch, we tried adding the cream to the pan around the pears as they finished caramelizing, which transformed the sticky sugar syrup into a smooth sauce that slid right off the pears. We let the pears drain for a few minutes on a wire rack set over a rimmed baking sheet before serving. After removing the pears, we were able to season the sauce left in the skillet with just the right amount of black pepper and salt.

The presentation of this elegant and sophisticated dessert can be as dramatic or casual as the mood dictates. Whether served individually with an attractive wedge of blue cheese and a fancy swirl of sauce or presented to the table family-style on a platter, passing the sauce and cheese separately, it is the surprising combination of flavors that makes this dessert so good.

WHAT WE LEARNED: Rather than making the caramel sauce in advance and cooking the pears to order in a separate pan (as a restaurant would do), cook the pears and caramel sauce together. It's essential to use firm pears that can withstand a fair amount of heat.

CARAMELIZED PEARS WITH BLUE CHEESE AND BLACK PEPPER–CARAMEL SAUCE

Serves 6

Any type of pear can be used in this recipe, as long as it is firm. See the illustrations on this page for tips on preparing the pears.

- ⅓   cup water
- ⅔   cup (4¾ ounces) sugar
- 3   firm pears, halved, seeds removed with a large melon baller, and ¼ inch trimmed off the bottom of each pear half so it will stand upright
- ⅔   cup heavy cream
      Salt
- ¼   teaspoon whole black peppercorns, roughly crushed (see the illustrations on page 335)
- 3   ounces strong blue cheese (such as Stilton), cut into 6 attractive wedges

1. Place the water in a 12-inch nonstick skillet and pour the sugar into the center of the pan, taking care not to let the crystals adhere to the sides of the pan. Bring to a boil over high heat, stirring occasionally, until the sugar is fully dissolved and the mixture is bubbling wildly. Add the pears to the skillet, cut-side down, cover, reduce the heat to medium-high, and cook until the pears are nearly tender (a paring knife inserted into the center of the pears feels slight resistance), 13 to 15 minutes.

2. Uncover, reduce the heat to medium, and cook until the sauce is golden brown and the cut sides of the pears are partly caramelized, 3 to 5 minutes. Pour the heavy cream around the pears and cook, shaking the pan back and forth, until the sauce is a smooth, deep caramel color and the cut sides of the pears are beautifully golden, 3 to 5 minutes.

3. Remove the pan from the heat. Using tongs, carefully remove the pears from the pan and place cut-side up on a wire rack set over a rimmed baking sheet. Cool slightly.

Season the sauce left in the pan with salt to taste and the crushed black pepper, then pour it into a liquid measuring cup.

4. Carefully (the pears will still be hot) stand each pear half upright on an individual plate and arrange a wedge of the blue cheese beside it. Drizzle the plate and some of the pear with the caramel sauce. Serve immediately. (Alternatively, the pears can be stood upright on a large serving platter, and the warm caramel sauce and the blue cheese can be passed separately.)

TECHNIQUE: Coring a Pear

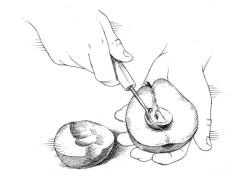

1. Cut the fruit in half from stem to blossom end. Use a melon baller to cut around the central core with a circular motion.

2. Draw the melon baller from the central core to the top of the pear, removing the interior portion of the stem as you go.

TECHNIQUE: Crushing Peppercorns

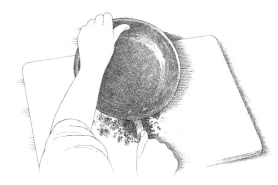

A. Chefs frequently use the back of a heavy pan and a rocking motion to grind peppercorns.

B. Or, you can spread the peppercorns in an even layer in a zipper-lock plastic bag and whack them with a rolling pin or meat pounder.

A NOTE ON CONVERSIONS

SOME SAY COOKING IS BOTH A SCIENCE AND AN ART. We would say that geography has a hand in it, too. Flour milled in the United Kingdom and elsewhere will feel and taste different from flour milled in the United States. So we cannot promise that the loaf of bread you bake in Canada or England will taste the same as a loaf baked in the States, but we can offer guidelines for converting weights and measures. We also recommend that you rely on instincts when making our recipes. Refer to the visual cues provided. If the bread dough hasn't "come together in a ball," as described, you may need to add more flour—even if the recipe doesn't tell you so. You be the judge. For more information on conversions and ingredient equivalents, visit our Web site at

www.cooksillustrated.com and type "conversion chart" in the search box.

The recipes in this book were developed using standard U.S. measures following U.S. government guidelines. The charts below offer equivalents for U.S., metric, and Imperial (U.K.) measures. All conversions are approximate and have been rounded up or down to the nearest whole number. For example:

1 teaspoon = 4.9292 milliliters, rounded up to 5 milliliters

1 ounce = 28.3495 grams, rounded down to 28 grams

Volume Conversions

U.S.	METRIC
1 teaspoon	5 milliliters
2 teaspoons	10 milliliters
1 tablespoon	15 milliliters
2 tablespoons	30 milliliters
¼ cup	59 milliliters
½ cup	118 milliliters
¾ cup	177 milliliters
1 cup	237 milliliters
1¼ cups	296 milliliters
1½ cups	355 milliliters
2 cups	473 milliliters
2½ cups	592 milliliters
3 cups	710 milliliters
4 cups (1 quart)	0.946 liter
1.06 quarts	1 liter
4 quarts (1 gallon)	3.8 liters

Weight Conversions

OUNCES	GRAMS
½	14
¾	21
1	28
1½	43
2	57
2½	71
3	85
3½	99
4	113
4½	128
5	142
6	170
7	198
8	227
9	255
10	283
12	340
16 (1 pound)	454

Conversions for Ingredients Commonly Used in Baking

Baking is an exacting science. Because measuring by weight is far more accurate than measuring by volume, and thus more likely to achieve reliable results, in our recipes we provide ounce measures in addition to cup measures for many ingredients. Refer to the chart below to convert these measures into grams.

INGREDIENT	OUNCES	GRAMS
1 cup all-purpose flour*	5	142
1 cup whole-wheat flour	5½	156
1 cup granulated (white) sugar	7	198
1 cup packed brown sugar (light or dark)	7	198
1 cup confectioners' sugar	4	113
1 cup cocoa powder	3	85
Butter†		
4 tablespoons (½ stick, or ¼ cup)	2	57
8 tablespoons (1 stick, or ½ cup)	4	113
16 tablespoons (2 sticks, or 1 cup)	8	227

*U.S. all-purpose flour, the most frequently used flour in this book, does not contain leaveners, as some European flours do. These leavened flours are called self-rising or self-raising. If you are using self-rising flour, take this into consideration before adding leavening to a recipe.

†In the United States, butter is sold both salted and unsalted. We generally recommend unsalted butter. If you are using salted butter, take this into consideration before adding salt to a recipe.

Oven Temperatures

FAHRENHEIT	CELSIUS	GAS MARK (IMPERIAL)
225	105	¼
250	120	½
275	130	1
300	150	2
325	165	3
350	180	4
375	190	5
400	200	6
425	220	7
450	230	8
475	245	9

Converting Temperatures from an Instant-Read Thermometer

We include doneness temperatures in many of our recipes, such as those for poultry, meat, and bread. We recommend an instant-read thermometer for the job. Refer to the table at left to convert Fahrenheit degrees to Celsius. Or, for temperatures not represented in the chart, use this simple formula:

Subtract 32 degrees from the Fahrenheit reading, then divide the result by 1.8 to find the Celsius reading.

EXAMPLE:
"Roast until the juices run clear when the chicken is cut with a paring knife or the thickest part of the breast registers 160 degrees on an instant-read thermometer." To convert:

160°F − 32 = 128°
128° ÷ 1.8 = 71°C (rounded down from 71.11)

INDEX

INDEX

Shrimp:
buying, 43
Pan-Seared, 79–80, *83*
with Chipotle-Lime Glaze,
80
with Garlic-Lemon Butter,
80
with Ginger-Hoisin Glaze,
80
and Sausage Gumbo, Creole-Style,
40–43, *96*
Side dishes:
Asparagus, Broiled, 142–43
Carrots, Glazed, 59–61, *197*
Cornbread, Southern, 128–30,
203
Ginger-Apple Chutney, Quick,
55
Macaroni and Cheese, Classic, *98,*
105–7
Polenta, *93,* 253–55
Potatoes, Herb-Roasted, 70–71
Rice, Mexican, *90,* 167–69
Sifting dry ingredients, 313
Simmering vs. boiling, 248
Soups, 15–32
chicken
Noodle, 21–22
with Orzo and Spring
Vegetables, 22
with Shells, Tomatoes, and
Zucchini, 22
Chicken Stock for, Quick, 16–18
freezing small portions of, 27
Lentil, Hearty, 30–32, *88*
with Fragrant Spices, 32
with Spinach, 32
Mulligatawny, 184–87
with Chicken, 186
with Lamb, 186–87
onion
bluish-gray (science desk), 264
French, *85,* 262–64
Pasta and Bean, Italian (Pasta e
Fagioli), 24–26, *199*
best pasta shapes for, 26
with Orange and Fennel, 26

Southeast Asian:
Beef Satay, 10–12
fish sauce, tasting of, 150–51
Spicy Peanut Dipping Sauce, 12
Thai Grilled Chicken with Spicy,
Sweet, and Sour Dipping Sauce,
146–49, *196*
Southern Cornbread, 128–30
Soy-Maple Glaze, 155
Spaghetti with Olive Pesto, 180–81
Spiced:
Nuts, 4–6
Pumpkin Cheesecake, *208,* 320–21
Spice grinders, rating of, 165
Spices:
bouquet garni for, 264
removing easily from finished dish,
193
Spinach Dip, 7–8
with Blue Cheese and Bacon, 8
Cilantro-Lime, with Chipotle
Chiles, 8
Creamy Herbed, 8
with Feta, Lemon, and Oregano, 8
Spot removers, rating of, 103–4
Stainless steel cookware, cleaning, 81–82
Stain removal products, rating of, 103–4
Sticky Buns with Pecans, *204,* 269–75
Hand-Kneaded Method for, 274
Overnight, 274–75
Stock:
Chicken, for Soup, Quick, 16–18
fat separators for, rating of, 19–20
freezing small portions of, 18
Sugar, creaming butter and (science
desk), 298–99

T

Tastings:
bacon, mail-order, 34–35
beef tenderloin, 138–39
brownie mixes, 286
chicken cutlets, 77–78
chocolate ice cream, 309–10
coffees, supermarket, 276–77
cornbread mixes, 130–31

Tastings *(cont.)*
cornmeal, 255
cream cheese, 323–25
curry powder, 188–89
egg noodles, 22–23
fish sauce, 150–51
goat cheese, 260–61
gravy additives, 58
lentils, 32–33
olives, black, 218
pasta sauces, jarred, 239–41
popcorn, microwave, 108–9
rice
basmati, 193
long-grain white, 45
for risotto, 237
saffron, 194
salsa, 12–13
tomatoes, sun-dried, 181
water, bottled, 249–52
white beans, canned, 27
Taylor Classic Oven Guide
Thermometer, 49
Texas-Style Barbecued Beef Ribs,
121–26
Barbecue Sauce for, 126
Thai Grilled Chicken with Spicy, Sweet,
and Sour Dipping Sauce, 146–49, *196*
Thermometers, recommended, 49
Timers, recommended, 48–49
Tomato(es):
Chicken Soup with Shells, Zucchini
and, 22
Pasta with Bacon, Onion and (Pasta
all'Amatriciana), *97,* 238–39
Sauce, 225, 227
sauce, raw, pasta with, 172–74
Farfalle with Tomatoes, Olives,
and Feta, 173
Fusilli with Tomatoes and Fresh
Mozzarella, 173
Orecchiette with Tomatoes,
Fennel, and Parmesan, 173
sun-dried
Pesto, Pasta with Arugula, Goat
Cheese and, 179–80
tasting of, 181

Tongs, recommended, 49

Tortillas:

    Chicken Enchiladas, *91,* 160–64

      rolling, 164

Trichinosis, 55

Tube pans, filling, 308

Tubetini, 26

V

Veal shanks, in Osso Buco, 246–49

Vegetable peelers, rating of, 33–34

W

Walnut Crescent Cookies, 301–2

Water, bottled:

    tap water vs., 251

    tasting of, 249–52

Water baths (science desk), 323

Waxed paper, parchment paper vs., 299

Whipped cream:

    Brown Sugar and Bourbon, 322

    chilling bowl for, 322

    Tangy, 308

White beans:

    canned, tasting of, 27

    Pasta e Fagioli (Italian Pasta and

      Bean Soup), 24–26, *199*

White chocolate, in Blondies, 287–88

White wine, non-alcoholic substitute

  for, in pan sauces, 77

Whole-wheat flour, in yeasted breads,
218

Wood chunks, soak-ahead, 125

Y

Yeast:

    designer (science desk), 275

    see also Breads, yeasted

Yogurt Sauce, 191, 192

Z

Zucchini, Chicken Soup with Shells,
  Tomatoes and, 22

ALSO BY THE EDITORS OF COOK'S ILLUSTRATED
HOME OF AMERICA'S TEST KITCHEN

The Best Recipe
The Best Recipe: American Classics
The Best Recipe: Grilling and Barbecue
The Best Recipe: Italian Classics
The Best Recipe: Soups and Stews
Perfect Vegetables
The Quick Recipe
Restaurant Favorites at Home

The America's Test Kitchen Cookbook
Here in America's Test Kitchen

The Best Kitchen Quick Tips

The Complete Book of Pasta and Noodles
The Cook's Illustrated Complete Book of Poultry

How to Barbecue and Roast on the Grill
How to Cook Chicken Breasts
How to Cook Chinese Favorites
How to Cook Garden Vegetables
How to Cook Shrimp and Other Shellfish
How to Grill
How to Make an American Layer Cake
How to Make Cookie Jar Favorites
How to Make Ice Cream
How to Make Muffins, Biscuits, and Scones
How to Make Pasta Sauces
How to Make Pot Pies and Casseroles
How to Make Salad
How to Make Sauces and Gravies
How to Make Simple Fruit Desserts
How to Make Soup
How to Make Stew
How to Sauté

To order any of our books,
visit us at http://www.cooksillustrated.com
or http://www.americastestkitchen.com
or call us at 800-611-0759

INSIDE AMERICA'S TEST KITCHEN

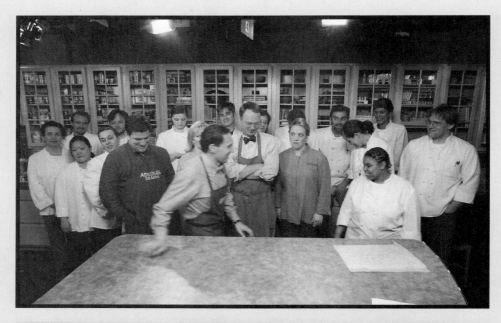

INSIDE

AMERICA'S TEST KITCHEN

BY THE EDITORS OF

COOK'S ILLUSTRATED

ILLUSTRATIONS
John Burgoyne

PHOTOGRAPHY
Carl Tremblay
Daniel Van Ackere

AMERICA'S TEST KITCHEN
BROOKLINE, MASSACHUSETTS

America's Test Kitchen
17 Station Street
Brookline, MA 02445

ISBN 0-936184-71-X
Library of Congress Cataloging-in-Publication Data
The Editors of *Cook's Illustrated*

Inside America's Test Kitchen: New Recipes and Product Ratings from Public Television's Favorite Cooking Show
1st Edition

ISBN 0-936184-71-X (hardback): $29.95
I. Cooking. I. Title
2003

Manufactured in the United States of America

Distributed by America's Test Kitchen, 17 Station Street, Brookline, MA 02445
Editor: Jack Bishop
Series Designer: Amy Klee
Director of Editorial Operations: Barbara Bourassa
Art Director: Robin Gilmore-Barnes
Graphic Designer: Nina Madjid
Jacket Designer: Julia Sedykh
Photographers: Carl Tremblay (color and documentary photography);
Daniel Van Ackere (silhouette photography)
Illustrator: John Burgoyne
Production Manager: Jessica Lindheimer Quirk
Associate Editor: Rebecca Hays
Copy Editor: India Koopman
Proofreader: Amy Monaghan
Indexer: Cathy Dorsey

CONTENTS

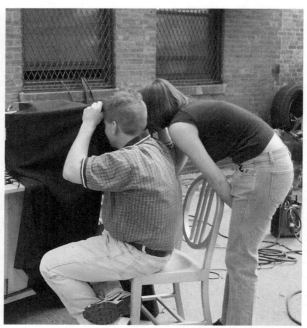

PREFACE

ARE YOUR "BLIND" TASTE TESTS REALLY BLIND? DO YOU really test a recipe 30 or 40 times? Is the "bad" food at the beginning of the show really that bad? Does the "good" food really taste as good as it looks? Do you ever make mistakes on camera that viewers don't see? Are you really having fun during filming?

The short answer to all of these questions is "Yes!" The tastings really are blind (I have no idea which brands are which when I taste them on camera), we do test recipes for weeks at a time, the "bad" food really is that bad, the "good" food really does taste good (in some cases so good that we keep eating after the camera is turned off), we make our share of mistakes on and off camera, and, yes, we really do have a lot of fun filming *America's Test Kitchen*.

Inside America's Test Kitchen not only brings you the recipes, taste tests, cookware ratings, and food science from our public television show, it also brings you *inside* our test kitchen, the place where we test recipes for *Cook's Illustrated* magazine and also film *America's Test Kitchen*. You get a front-row seat, watching the series unfold as we prep, sauté, bake, grill, taste, and test our way through another 26 episodes. It is indeed as much fun as it appears to be on television, and we hope that *Inside America's Test Kitchen* will become your behind-the-scenes guide to the show, the recipes, and the people who make it all work.

Cooking and music have a lot in common. I recently met a banjo player who loves old-time music—fiddle tunes that predate bluegrass and were popular at a time when most households could lay claim to a $5 banjo. One night last summer, I played along with her band in a house lit only by candles at the end of a long dirt road not far from our Vermont farm. We worked through some of the classic repertoire: "Shady Grove," "Waterbound," and "Barlow Knife." Like cooking, making old-time music seems like a hard thing to do, especially the fiddling, but also like cooking, it's easier to learn by watching other people do it. Once you see it done, the underlying structure of the tunes becomes clearer and you can really start to play.

What does this have to do with a cooking show? Well, watching *America's Test Kitchen* is a bit like watching a bunch of old-time fiddlers. The cast has played the old favorites hundreds, if not thousands, of times and is eager to share them with you, the viewer. You can just sit back and watch or sit up and pay really close attention and start to learn what makes these classic recipes tick. If nothing else, a good time should be had by all, fiddling away in the kitchen, trying to make a little magic with a few basic ingredients and more than our share of enthusiasm.

Thanks for watching *America's Test Kitchen*. We hope that you find the time to get into the kitchen to make a little music.

Christopher Kimball
Founder and editor, *Cook's Illustrated* magazine
Host, *America's Test Kitchen*
Brookline, Massachusetts, 2003

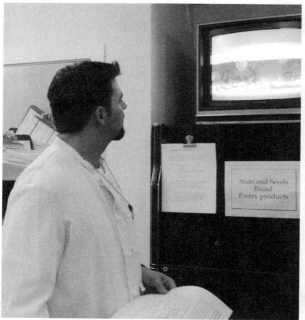

INSIDE AMERICA'S TEST KITCHEN

AMERICA'S TEST KITCHEN IS A GROUP OF EDITORS, RECIPE developers, test cooks, art directors, photographers, tasters, equipment testers, and scientists all working in pursuit of a single goal—foolproof versions of favorite recipes. We cook in a real kitchen located in Brookline, Massachusetts. This kitchen is home to *Cook's Illustrated* magazine, numerous cookbooks, including *The Best Recipe,* as well as our public television show, *America's Test Kitchen*. We are dedicated to—some might say, obsessed with—helping Americans to cook better.

What, exactly, happens in America's Test Kitchen? We start with favorite American recipes. This means old-fashioned comfort food like coconut cream pie, grilled steak, mashed potatoes, and chocolate chip cookies. It also means "new" classics—often from other cuisines—such as pad Thai, tarte Tatin, and strawberries with balsamic vinegar. We begin the recipe development process by talking about the problems we have encountered when preparing these dishes in the past. We draw up a list of common pitfalls with a particular recipe—say, sticky noodles when making pad Thai, or soggy crust when preparing coconut cream pie—and then we start researching possible solutions. We comb through dozens of cookbooks and magazines, looking for interesting or unusual strategies. We search the Internet and get on the phone with experts in the field.

After compiling a lengthy list of kitchen tests, we start cooking. We usually make about a half-dozen versions of a particular recipe to refine our goals and sort out the problems. After this diagnostic phase, we start testing the variables, one by one. Which types of potatoes are best for mashing—russets, Yukon Gold, all-purpose, or red? Should we boil the potatoes in their skins, or should we peel them and cut them into chunks? What's the best tool for mashing the potatoes—a food mill, ricer, or potato masher? Should we add milk, half-and-half, or cream, and how much dairy is the right amount?

As we answer these questions, our recipe begins to take shape. Along the way, other questions—usually regarding equipment, ingredients, or science—often present themselves. Does it matter which kind of vegetable peeler you use to peel the potatoes? Is salted or unsalted butter better? Why do some potato varieties become soupy when dairy is added to them while others turn fluffy and smooth?

When we have a recipe that we all agree is the best it can be, we test it again (and again) on different stoves, with different pots and pans, until we know that it will work for every cook in every kitchen.

The Cast

OUR TELEVISION SHOW HIGHLIGHTS THE BEST RECIPES developed in the test kitchen during the year—those recipes that our test kitchen staff makes at home over and over again. These recipes are accompanied by our most exhaustive equipment tests, our most shocking food-tasting results, and our most informative science experiments. These four elements—recipes, equipment tests, food tastings, and science experiments—are blended together to create television episodes that we hope are engaging and entertaining.

Christopher Kimball, the founder and editor of *Cook's Illustrated* magazine, is the ringmaster. He directs the presentation of these tests, tastings, and experiments. He is the host of the show and asks the questions you might ask. Why does sugar make beaten egg whites more stable? Which unsweetened chocolate makes the best brownies? What separates a great omelet from a mediocre one?

It's the job of our two executive chefs, Julia Collin Davison and Bridget Lancaster, to demonstrate our recipes. They show Chris what works, what doesn't, and explain why. In the process, they discuss (and show us) the best and worst examples from our development process—the cookies that burned, the cake that fell, and the chicken that was rubbery. As they cook, they reveal the findings from our exhaustive

kitchen work. They teach Chris (and the audience) the right way to mince an onion, why browning makes a tastier stew, and how to make salad.

Adam Ried, our equipment guru, shares the highlights from our detailed testing process in the Equipment Corner segments. He brings with him our favorite (and least favorite) gadgets and tools. He tells you which saucepan performed best in a dozen kitchen tests and shows why most grill brushes are nearly worthless. (Although he did find one unusual gem that makes cleaning the grill grate a pleasure—well, almost.) You learn why most vegetable choppers don't work and why every kitchen should be stocked with at least one kind of vegetable peeler.

Jack Bishop is our ingredient expert. He has Chris taste our favorite (and least favorite) brands of common food products—everything from canned tomatoes and olive oil to milk chocolate and mayonnaise. Chris may not always enjoy these exercises (it's not much fun tasting balsamic vinegar straight up), but he usually learns something as Jack explains what makes one brand superior to another. Good cooking starts with the right ingredients, and our Tasting Lab segments will help you shop efficiently.

The Crew

ONLY FIVE COOKS AND EDITORS APPEAR ON THE TELEVISION show, but another 50 people work to make the show a reality. During filming, executive chefs Erin McMurrer and Dawn Yanagihara ran the "back kitchen," where all the food that appeared on camera originated. Along with the on-air crew, Erin and Dawn also planned and organized the 26 television episodes shot in May 2003. India Koopman helped develop equipment segments, Keri Fisher organized tastings, John Olson wrote many of the science segments, and Melissa Baldino researched all of the "Food Facts."

During filming, chefs Erika Bruce, Matthew Card, Garth Clingingsmith, Keith Dresser, Sean Lawler, and Diane Unger-Mahoney were in the kitchen from early in the morning to late at night helping Erin and Dawn cook all of the food needed on the set. Nina West was charged with the Herculean task of making sure all of the ingredients we needed were on hand. Kitchen assistants Judy Davis, Laura Courtemanche, and Greg Wislocki also worked long hours peeling potatoes, making pies, and baking cookies. Keri Fisher, Rebecca Hays, and Susan Light helped coordinate the efforts of the kitchen with the activities on the set by readying props, equipment, and food.

Jim McCormack, vice president for operations and technology, and Rich Cassidy, systems administrator, supervised the building of the test kitchen and helped turn the kitchen into a shooting set. They made sure all of the wiring, computers, and ovens were ready to go. Barbara Bourassa, director of editorial operations, staffed the kitchen and made sure all of the resources we needed were in place.

The staff of A La Carte Communications turned our recipes, tastings, equipment tests, and science experiments into a lively television show. Special thanks to executive producer Geof Drummond; director and editor Herb Sevush; director of photography Dean Gaskill; camera operators Stephen Hussar and Michael McEachern; jib camera operator Peter Dingle; audio engineer Gilles Morin; video engineer Eliat Goldman; script supervisor/makeup specialist Brenda Coffey; second camera operator/gaffer Thomas Hamilton; gaffers Patrick Ruth and Jack McPhee; grips Robert Ouzounian and Aaron Frutman; production manager Elena Battista; and production assistant Yale Miller.

We also would like to thank Hope Reed, who handles station relations, and co-executive producer Nat Katzman. Sur La Table and Vendange Wines helped to underwrite the show, and we thank them for their support. Props for the show were supplied by Olga Russo at A. Russo & Sons; Mahoney's Garden Center of Cambridge, Massachusetts; and Sur La Table.

We hope this book gives you an inside look at the fun, the chaos, and the food that make *America's Test Kitchen* unique. We are passionate about our work, and we hope you enjoy making (and eating) our recipes as well as reading about the process by which they were created. Our mission is pretty simple. We want to help make you a better cook. We hope that our television show and this book will do just that. If you have comments or questions about the show or the book, contact us at www.americastestkitchen.com. Visit www.cooksillustrated.com for more information about *Cook's Illustrated* magazine.

INSIDE AMERICA'S TEST KITCHEN

Keri readies 14 red wine vinegars for an on-camera tasting.

SALAD 101

Salad seems so easy. Just dress some leafy greens and serve, right? Well, as with most simple kitchen tasks, success depends on the details. Here's how we make a basic leafy green salad with a vinaigrette dressing in the test kitchen.

1. Tear the greens into bite-size pieces.

2. Soak the greens in a bowl of cold water. (We use the bowl of a salad spinner.)

3. Spin the greens dry, adding paper towels to the spinner to blot up excess moisture. (The greens can be refrigerated in a spinner lined with paper towels for a day or so.)

4. Use good oil in the dressing, which usually means extra-virgin olive oil.

5. Use the right ratio of oil to vinegar in the dressing. In most cases, 3 parts oil to 1 part vinegar works best.

6. Whisk the vinegar and salt and pepper together and then whisk in the oil to emulsify the dressing.

7. Dress the greens in a large bowl—at least 50 percent larger than the amount of greens—so there's plenty of room for tossing.

8. Toss gently. You want to fluff the greens, not bruise them.

GREEK SALAD

WHAT WE WANTED: A salad with crisp ingredients and bold flavors, highlighted by briny olives and tangy feta, all married together with a bright-tasting dressing infused with fresh herbs.

Most pizza-parlor versions of Greek salad consist of iceberg lettuce, chunks of green pepper, and a few pale wedges of tomato, sparsely dotted with cubes of feta and garnished with one forlorn olive of questionable heritage. The accompanying dressing is loaded with musty dried herbs. How could we make this pizzeria staple worthy of the dinner table?

We started by testing different vinaigrette recipes, with ingredients ranging from vinegar and lemon juice to yogurt and mustard. Tasters thought that the yogurt-based dressing overwhelmed the salad and that the mustard and cider vinegar versions were just "wrong." Lemon juice was harsh and white wine vinegar was dull, but a dressing that combined lemon juice and red wine vinegar had the balanced flavor we were looking for. There was no place for dried herbs in this salad. Fresh herbs typically used in Greek cuisine include dill, oregano, parsley, mint, and basil. Tasters loved the idea of mint and parsley, but they lost their zip when mixed with the vinaigrette. Oregano's bold flavor stood up well to the vinegar and lemon juice and was the clear favorite. Pure olive oil and extra-virgin olive oil worked equally well, and the addition of a small amount of garlic gave the dressing the final kick it needed.

The next ingredients up for scrutiny were the vegetables. Although lettuce is not commonly found in traditional Greek salad, it is a main ingredient in the American version. The iceberg lettuce had to go. Romaine, which has the body and crunch of iceberg but also more color and flavor, was the natural choice. Tomatoes were also essential, and only the ripest ones would do. Green bell pepper got a unanimous thumbs-down. Everyone preferred the sweeter red variety, which was improved even further by being roasted. In the interest of saving time, we also tried jarred roasted red peppers, which tasters liked even better. The jarred peppers are packaged in a vinegary brine and have more depth of flavor than freshly roasted peppers do (for more information, see the Tasting Lab on page 6).

Onion was next. When the pungency of the raw onion sent some tasters running for breath mints, someone suggested soaking the onion in water to eliminate its caustic bite. We took that idea one step further: Why not marinate the onion in the vinaigrette? On a whim, we included some cucumber as well. The results were striking. The cucumber, which had been watery and bland just minutes before, was bright and flavorful, and the onion had lost its unpleasant potency.

Now the vinaigrette recipe was finalized and the vegetables selected, but something was still missing. We returned to the mint and parsley that had been eliminated from the vinaigrette. Instead, we simply mixed them with the vegetables, tossed this mixture together with the onion and cucumber that had been marinating in the vinaigrette, generously sprinkled the salad with feta and kalamata olives, and offered it to tasters. It was a hit. This was a Greek salad worthy of being served on china—not in an aluminum takeout container.

WHAT WE LEARNED: Use a combination of lemon juice and red wine vinegar in the dressing. Marinate the onion in this dressing to reduce its sting; marinate the cucumber in the dressing to flavor it. Use fresh herbs rather than dried, and replace dull iceberg lettuce with crisp, flavorful romaine.

GREEK SALAD Serves 6 to 8

Marinating the onion and cucumber in the vinaigrette tones down the onion's harshness and flavors the cucumber. For efficiency, prepare the other salad ingredients while the onion and cucumber marinate. Use a salad spinner to dry the lettuce thoroughly after washing; any water left clinging to the leaves will dilute the dressing.

vinaigrette

3	tablespoons red wine vinegar
1½	teaspoons juice from 1 lemon
2	teaspoons minced fresh oregano leaves
½	teaspoon salt
⅛	teaspoon ground black pepper
1	medium clove garlic, minced or pressed through a garlic press (about 1 teaspoon)
6	tablespoons olive oil

salad

½	medium red onion, sliced thin (about ¾ cup)
1	medium cucumber, peeled, halved lengthwise, seeded (see the illustration at right), and cut into ⅛-inch-thick slices (about 2 cups)
2	romaine hearts, washed, dried thoroughly, and torn into 1½-inch pieces (about 8 cups)
2	large vine-ripened tomatoes (10 ounces total), each tomato cored, seeded, and cut into 12 wedges
¼	cup loosely packed torn fresh parsley leaves
¼	cup loosely packed torn fresh mint leaves
6	ounces jarred roasted red bell peppers, cut into ½ by 2-inch strips (about 1 cup)
20	large kalamata olives, each olive pitted and quartered lengthwise
5	ounces feta cheese, crumbled (1 cup)

1. Whisk the vinaigrette ingredients in a large bowl until combined. Add the onion and cucumber and toss; let stand to blend flavors, about 20 minutes.

2. Add the romaine, tomatoes, parsley, mint, and peppers to the bowl with the onions and cucumbers; toss to coat with the dressing.

3. Transfer the salad to a wide, shallow serving bowl or platter; sprinkle the olives and feta over the salad. Serve immediately.

VARIATION
COUNTRY-STYLE GREEK SALAD

This salad, made without lettuce, is served throughout Greece, where it is known as country or peasant salad. It is excellent with garden-ripe summer tomatoes.

Follow the recipe for Greek Salad, reducing the red wine vinegar to 1½ tablespoons and the lemon juice to 1 teaspoon in the vinaigrette. Omit the lettuce and use 2 medium cucumbers, peeled, halved lengthwise, seeded, and cut into ⅛-inch-thick slices (about 4 cups) and 6 large tomatoes (about 2 pounds), each tomato cored, seeded, and cut into 12 wedges.

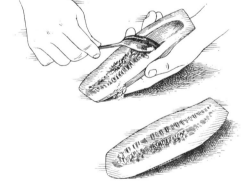

TECHNIQUE: Seeding Cucumbers

Halve the cucumber (already peeled if desired) lengthwise. Run a small spoon inside each cucumber half to scoop out the seeds and surrounding liquid.

TASTING LAB:
Jarred Roasted Red Peppers

JARRED PEPPERS ARE CONVENIENT, BUT ARE ALL BRANDS created equal? To find out, we collected five brands from local supermarkets. The contenders were Divina Roasted Sweet Peppers, Greek Gourmet Roasted Sweet Red Peppers, Lapas Sweet Roasted Peppers, Gaea Flame Roasted Red Peppers, and Peloponnese Roasted Florina Whole Sweet Peppers. Three of these brands identified the type of pepper used (Divina, Gaea, and Peloponnese all use Florina peppers), and we wondered if a company's willingness to identify the variety of pepper it was selling would be an indicator of the quality of the pepper. In other words, would tasters prefer the clearly identified Florina peppers over the generics (whose main ingredient was identified only as "peppers")? To identify their preferences, tasters tried the peppers "as is," straight from the jar.

What we found was that tasters did not necessarily prefer the peppers labeled Florina. What counted was the flavor and texture of the pepper itself as well as the flavor of the brine. The top two brands, Divina (roasted Florina pimento red peppers) and Greek Gourmet (fire-roasted peppers), were preferred for their "soft and tender texture" (the Divinas) and "refreshing," "piquant," "smoky" flavor (the Greek Gourmets). The other brands were marked down for their lack of "roasty flavor" and for the unpleasantly overpowering flavor of the brines. These peppers were described as having a "pepperoncini-like sourness" or a "sweet and acidic aftertaste"; one person said they tasted as if they'd been "buried under brine and acid."

The conclusion? Tasters preferred peppers with a full smoky, roasted flavor, a spicy but not too sweet brine, and a tender-to-the-tooth texture.

BEST JARRED ROASTED RED PEPPERS
Divina peppers (left) were the top choice of tasters. Greek Gourmet peppers (right) were a close second.

TASTING LAB:
Supermarket Red Wine Vinegars

THE SOURCE OF THAT NOTABLE EDGE YOU TASTE WHEN sampling any red wine vinegar is acetic acid, the chief flavor component in all vinegar and the byproduct of the bacterium *Acetobacter aceti*, which feeds on the alcohol in wine. The process of converting red wine to vinegar once took months, if not years, but now, with the help of an acetator (a machine that speeds the metabolism of the *Acetobacter aceti*), red wine vinegar can be made in less than 24 hours.

Does this faster, cheaper method—the one used to make most supermarket brands—produce inferior red wine vinegar? Or is this a case in which modern technology trumps Old World craftsmanship, which is still employed by makers of the more expensive red wine vinegars? To find out, we included in our tasting vinegars made using the fast process (acetator) and the slow process (often called the Orleans method, after the city in France where it was developed).

We first tasted 10 nationally available supermarket brands in two ways: by dipping sugar cubes in each brand and sucking out the vinegar (a method professionals use to cut down on palate fatigue) and by making a simple vinaigrette with each and tasting it on iceberg lettuce. We then pitted the winners of the supermarket tasting against four high-end red wine vinegars (see Tasting Lab: Gourmet Red Wine Vinegars, page 9).

Although no single grape variety is thought to make the best red wine vinegar, we were curious to find out if our tasters were unwittingly fond of vinegars made from the same grape. We sent the vinegars to a food lab for an anthocyanin pigment profile, a test that can detect the 10 common pigments found in red grapes. Although the lab was unable to distinguish specific grape varieties (Cabernet, Merlot, Pinot Noir, Zinfandel, and the like), it did provide us with an interesting piece of information: Some of the vinegars weren't made with wine grapes (known as *Vitus vinifera*) but with less expensive Concord-

FOOD ANALYSIS:
Supermarket Red Wine Vinegars

After our tasting of supermarket vinegars, we sent all 10 brands to a laboratory to determine the type of grapes used in each as well as their acidity. Results show that six vinegars are made from a blend of wine grapes (lab analysis could not identify the exact varieties), three are made from grapes in the Concord family (the kind of grapes used to make jams and bottled juices), and one is a mixture of both. Acidity ranges from 5.16 percent to 6.3 percent and turns out to be a less important factor than grape type.

Vinegar	Grape Type	Acidity (%)
Spectrum	Concord-type, wine	6.13
Pompeian	Concord-type, wine	5.16
Eden	Wine	5.30
Whole Foods	Concord-type	6.30
Star	Wine	5.18
Heinz	Concord-type	5.18
Four Monks	Wine	5.97
Colavita	Wine	6.28
Progresso	Wine	5.23
Regina	Wine	5.30

type grapes, the kind used to make Welch's grape juice.

Did the vinegars made with grape juice fair poorly, as might be expected? Far from it. The taste-test results were both shocking and unambiguous: Concord-type grapes not only do just fine when it comes to making vinegar, they may be a key element in the success of the top-rated brands in our tasting. Spectrum, our overall winner, is made from a mix of wine grapes and Concord grapes. Pompeian, which came in second among the supermarket brands, is made entirely of Concord-type grapes.

What else might contribute to the flavor of these vinegars? One possibility, we thought, was the way in which the acetic acid is developed. Manufacturers that mass-produce vinegar generally prefer not to use the Orleans method

Rating Supermarket Red Wine Vinegars

TWENTY STAFF MEMBERS OF *COOK'S ILLUSTRATED* TASTED THE VINEGARS USING TWO METHODS. FIRST, WE DIPPED slow-dissolving sugar cubes into the vinegars before tasting—this method cuts down on palate fatigue. Next, we made simple vinaigrettes and sampled them with lettuce. The vinegars are listed in order of preference. All vinegars are available in supermarkets nationwide.

HIGHLY RECOMMENDED
Spectrum Organic Red Wine Vinegar
$4.49 for 16.9 ounces

This peppery, sweet, "full-bodied" vinegar won first place in the vinaigrette tasting and had the highest score overall. It was liked for its fruity flavors, which reminded tasters of lemons, berries, cherries, and grapes.

HIGHLY RECOMMENDED
Pompeian Red Wine Vinegar
$2.29 for 16 ounces

Tasters liked this fruity, "bright and tangy" vinegar with grape and cherry highlights, giving it first place in the plain tasting. Some tasters thought the vinaigrette made with this vinegar was "lackluster," while others liked its mild flavors.

RECOMMENDED
Eden Selected Red Wine Vinegar
$2.59 for 16 ounces

This vinegar placed third in the vinaigrette tasting. It was praised for its mild, berry-like flavor. Tasters put it in eighth place in the plain tasting, calling it weak and "not strong or fruity enough."

RECOMMENDED
Whole Foods Red Wine Vinegar
$4.69 for 12.7 ounces

Tasters could easily detect the Concord grapes in this vinegar, along with blackberry and cherry flavors. Tasters were split on the vinaigrette, with comments ranging from "it's the only one worth eating" to "tastes like rancid Concord grapes."

RECOMMENDED
Star Red Wine Vinegar
$2.19 for 12 ounces

Tasters gave this vinegar second place in the vinaigrette tasting. It was liked it for its "bright but mild" flavor, though some tasters though it was "one-dimensional." It didn't do so well in the plain tasting, where it was described as rough.

RECOMMENDED
Heinz Gourmet Red Wine Vinegar
$2.79 for 12 ounces

While some tasters liked this vinegar's mellow flavor, others disliked its "insipid aroma" and lack of acidity and fruit flavors. Comments about the vinaigrette were divided, ranging from "not very complex" to "well seasoned."

RECOMMENDED
Four Monks Red Wine Vinegar
$2.69 for 12.7 ounces

Tasters liked this vinegar's subtle, light flavor and gave it second place in the plain tasting. These subtle characteristics were lost in the vinaigrette, which tasters found acidic and oily.

RECOMMENDED WITH RESERVATIONS
Colavita Red Wine Vinegar
$2.95 for 16.9 ounces

This vinegar placed in the bottom half of both taste tests. Tasters thought it had a fruity flavor, though most of them couldn't decide what fruit it tasted like, calling it "Kool-Aidy."

RECOMMENDED WITH RESERVATIONS
Progresso Red Wine Vinegar
$3.49 for 25 ounces

The mellow flavors of this vinegar reminded some tasters of apples and berries, though some thought it had a weak aroma and little flavor. Comments about the vinaigrette were uniformly negative.

RECOMMENDED WITH RESERVATIONS
Regina Red Wine Vinegar
$1.99 for 12 ounces

This vinegar placed next-to-last in the plain tasting and last in the vinaigrette tasting. Tasters disliked its sourness and "biting aftertaste," calling it "very harsh and unbalanced."

because it's slow and expensive. Spectrum red wine vinegar is produced with the Orleans method, but Pompeian is made in an acetator in less than 24 hours.

What, then, can explain why Spectrum and Pompeian won the supermarket tasting and beat the other gourmet vinegars? Oddly enough, for a food that defines sourness, the answer seems to lie in its sweetness. It turns out that Americans like their vinegar sweet (think balsamic vinegar).

The production of Spectrum is outsourced to a small manufacturer in Modena, Italy, that makes generous use of the Trebbiano grape, the same grape used to make balsamic vinegar. The Trebbiano, which is a white wine grape, gives Spectrum the sweetness our tasters admired. Pompeian vinegar is finished with a touch of sherry vinegar, added to give the red vinegar a more fruity, well-rounded flavor. Also significant to our results may be that both Spectrum and Pompeian start with wines containing Concord grapes, which are sweet enough to be a common choice when making jams and jellies.

When pitted against gourmet vinegars, Spectrum and Pompeian still came out on top. Which red wine vinegar should you buy? Skip the specialty shop and head to the supermarket.

TASTING LAB:
Gourmet Red Wine Vinegars

DURING OUR SEARCH FOR RED WINE VINEGARS, WE found gourmet vinegars made from a single grape variety (such as Zinfandel) that cost up to eight times as much as mass-market vinegars. Wondering if the difference in taste would match the difference in cost, we tasted four gourmet vinegars: "O" Zinfandel Vinegar ($7.99 for 6.8 ounces), Sparrow Lane Cabernet Sauvignon Vinegar ($11.95 for 12.75 ounces), Vinaigre de Banyuls ($29.95 for 25.5 ounces), and Martin Pouret Cabernet Franc Vinegar ($9.95 for 17.66 ounces). We tasted the vinegars plain and in a vinaigrette and then included the supermarket vinegar that

had won each of these tests (Pompeian and Spectrum, respectively).

"O" Zinfandel's distinct earthy, fruity flavor made it the clear winner of the plain tasting. Surprisingly, Pompeian placed second. Tasters thought it had a more balanced flavor than the other three gourmet vinegars.

In the vinaigrette test, Spectrum's "bright, sweet" flavors soundly beat out the gourmet brands. "O" Zinfandel placed second; tasters described it as "round and fully flavored" with a "lovely sweet-tart balance." The three remaining gourmet vinegars were called bland, harsh, and unremarkable.

SPINACH SALAD

WHAT WE WANTED: A rich but well-balanced salad that has plenty of bacon without being greasy.

We can't think of a better way to enjoy fresh spinach than to toss it with a rich, warm, sweet-tart dressing and then cover the lot with plenty of crisp bacon. Yet ordering a wilted spinach salad in a restaurant is a move we usually regret. The spinach, which is often drowned in an oily, bland dressing and sprinkled with minuscule bacon bits, leaves us perplexed—and still hungry. This salad can be made with a simple method and a short list of ingredients. Why, then, was a good one so hard to find?

The first hurdle—having to wash, dry, and trim mature curly spinach—was easily overcome. Kitchen tests determined that prewashed, bagged baby spinach works best in this salad, as it is both more tender and sweeter than the mature variety.

Aside from the spinach, bacon is the central ingredient, with the potential to provide plenty of smoky, salty flavor. We chose thick-cut bacon, finding that it offered more presence and textural interest than thin-cut. (Slab bacon can also be used, but it fries up chewy, not crispy.) The easiest way to achieve substantial, uniform pieces (and avoid tiny Baco-style bacon bits) was to cut the strips before frying them rather than crumbling them afterward. At this point, we also confirmed that hard-cooked egg wedges (a common ingredient) belonged in this salad. Their creamy yolks and cool whites formed a natural partnership with the bacon.

With plenty of mouthwatering bacon fat at the ready, we were loath to use another type of oil in the dressing, though some recipes call for either vegetable or olive oil. Happily, tests bolstered our conviction that dressing made solely with bacon grease not only had a lush texture but a hearty flavor; oil-based dressings tasted flat.

We found eight types of vinegar in the test kitchen cabinets and tested all of them, as well as lemon juice. Tasters criticized many of the choices, calling them boring and one-dimensional. Rice vinegar showed promise—its sweetness played well against the rich bacon fat—but it wasn't acidic enough and seemed a bit out of place for such an American recipe. More traditional cider vinegar, which is quite sharp, brightened the dressing considerably. A little sugar added a pleasing sweet element.

Most recipes for this salad call for a generous amount of fat (or oil) and a small amount of acid (vinegar). Typical ratios are 2, 3, or even 4 parts fat to 1 part acid, a standard formula for vinaigrette. We mixed up bacon fat and cider vinegar dressings using each proportion and were disappointed with all of them. To avoid being saddled with a fatty, lifeless mixture, we'd have to throw convention by the wayside. This meant cutting back on the bacon fat and elevating the vinegar level to counterbalance the fat and richness contributed by the fried bacon and egg yolks. After fiddling with the ratio, we settled on a dressing made with 3 tablespoons each of fat and vinegar.

We now had a great-tasting salad, but tasters asserted that it wasn't wilted enough. Because adding more dressing would only result in an overdressed, swampy salad, we weren't sure how to proceed. Luckily, the issue resolved itself when we sautéed a half-cup of onions and mixed them into the dressing. They added enough volume and heat to wilt the spinach perfectly after a few tosses. Wondering if yellow onions were the best choice, we also tested sautéed scallions, shallots, red onions, and garlic. Tasters preferred red onions and garlic, so we opted to use both.

WHAT WE LEARNED: For the best results, use baby spinach and thick-cut bacon. Cider vinegar tastes best with the bacon fat, and you need to use a lot more vinegar than you would in other salads. Finally, cook some onions and garlic in the bacon fat, which will add flavor to the dressing and help wilt the spinach properly.

WILTED SPINACH SALAD WITH WARM BACON DRESSING Serves 4 to 6 as a first course

This salad comes together quickly, so have the ingredients ready before you begin cooking. When adding the vinegar mixture to the skillet, step back from the stovetop—the aroma is quite potent.

    6   ounces baby spinach (about 8 cups)
    3   tablespoons cider vinegar
    ½   teaspoon sugar
    ¼   teaspoon ground black pepper
        Pinch salt
   10   ounces (about 8 slices) thick-cut bacon, cut
        into ½-inch pieces
    ½   medium red onion, chopped medium (about
        ½ cup)
    1   small clove garlic, minced or pressed through
        a garlic press (about ½ teaspoon)
    3   hard-cooked eggs (recipe follows), peeled and
        quartered lengthwise

1. Place the spinach in a large bowl. Stir the vinegar, sugar, pepper, and salt together in a small bowl until the sugar dissolves; set aside.

2. Fry the bacon in a medium skillet over medium-high heat, stirring occasionally, until crisp, about 10 minutes. Using a slotted spoon, transfer the bacon to a paper towel–lined plate. Pour the bacon fat into a bowl, then return 3 tablespoons bacon fat to the skillet. Add the onion to the skillet and cook over medium heat, stirring frequently, until softened, about 3 minutes. Stir in the garlic and cook until fragrant, about 15 seconds. Add the vinegar mixture, then remove the skillet from the heat. Working quickly, scrape the bottom of the skillet with a wooden spoon to loosen the browned bits. Pour the hot dressing over the spinach, add the bacon, and toss gently until the spinach is slightly wilted. Divide the salad among individual plates, arrange the egg quarters over each, and serve immediately.

FOOLPROOF HARD-COOKED EGGS Makes 3

We have always considered hard-cooking an egg to be a crapshoot. One cook's simmer might be another cook's boil, and the eggs can cook faster or slower depending on the water temperature. Because there's no way to watch the proteins cook under the brittle shell of an uncracked egg, this often leads to overcooked eggs with rubbery whites and chalky yolks. After trying various methods, we decided on this one, which is foolproof as long as you can recognize when water is at a boil and can time 10 minutes. You can double or triple this recipe as long as you use a pot large enough to hold the eggs in a single layer, covered by an inch of water.

    3   large eggs

1. Place the eggs in a medium saucepan, cover with 1 inch of water, and bring to a boil over high heat. Remove the pan from the heat, cover, and let sit for 10 minutes. Meanwhile, fill a medium bowl with 1 quart of water and 1 tray of ice cubes (or equivalent).

2. Transfer the eggs to the ice bath with a slotted spoon and let sit 5 minutes. Peel the eggs.

Matt brushes puff pastry with beaten eggs—
to help form a barrier against moisture from
the tomatoes—before baking the tart shell.

SUMMER tomatoes

CHAPTER 2

It's feast or famine when it comes to good tomatoes.

For most of the year, supermarkets stock pretty red orbs that have almost no flavor and are either mealy or rock-hard. The situation completely changes during the summer, when local tomatoes are available at farmers markets and roadside stands. These tomatoes may not always look perfect, but they are sweet and tangy, ripe and juicy—in short, everything a tomato should be.

What's the best way to enjoy summer tomatoes? It's hard to argue with a recipe that goes something like this: Slice, salt, and serve. Still, there are times when you want to use tomatoes in more elaborate dishes, and gazpacho and a cheesy tart are two of our favorite uses for summer tomatoes.

While these two recipes sound easy, we've had plenty of thick, bland gazpacho and soggy tomato tarts. Our goals when developing these summer recipes were simple: Keep the focus on the tomato flavor, and make sure the texture is correct. We wanted the soup to be chunky, not thick or porridge-like, and we wanted the tomato tart to be crisp, not watery or squishy.

GAZPACHO

WHAT WE WANTED: A chilled soup with clearly flavored, distinct pieces of vegetable in a bracing tomato broth.

azpacho is high summer in a bowl. Popular on both sides of the Atlantic, this ice-cold, uncooked vegetable soup, made principally of tomatoes (whole and juice), cucumbers, bell peppers, and onions and seasoned with olive oil and vinegar, is sometimes referred to as liquid salad in its native Spain. That slang name may be more apt on these shores, though, as many American gazpacho recipes simply instruct the cook to puree all the vegetables together in the blender. Needless to say, the resulting mixture is more a thin vegetable porridge with an anonymous vegetal flavor.

It's little wonder, then, that texture is one key to a great gazpacho. As you might imagine, philosophies about what is the right texture and how to achieve it vary considerably. Traditionally, gazpacho was thickened with water-soaked bread for extra body, but a number of the recipes we looked at skipped the bread altogether. Some recipes dictate that the mixture be put through a mesh strainer to create a silky smooth texture, while others leave it chunky. With gorgeous summer produce and ingredients that remained constant from recipe to recipe, we knew that the basic flavor profile would not be a problem here. That left thickening, method of manufacture as it related to texture and flavor both, and the seasonings as the most important questions to explore.

In deference to tradition, we started by trying a number of bread-thickened gazpachos. No matter what kind of bread was used or how long it was soaked, tasters consistently favored breadless brews. The consensus among our palates was that the bread-thickened soups had a subtle but inescapable pastiness. It was the same with the gazpachos that were passed—rather laboriously, we might add—through a strainer. Their texture was too uniform for a soup that featured fresh vegetables.

With our preference for a chunky-style soup established, we had to figure out the best method for preparing the vegetables. Although it was a breeze to use, the blender broke the vegetables down beyond recognition, which was not at all what we wanted. The food processor fared somewhat better, especially when we processed each vegetable separately. This method had distinct pros and cons. On the pro side were ease and the fact that the vegetables released some juice as they broke down, which helped to flavor the soup. The cons were that no matter how we finessed the pulse feature, the vegetable pieces were neither neatly chopped nor consistently sized. This was especially true of the tomatoes, which broke down to a pulp. The texture of the resulting soup was more along the lines of a vegetable slushy, which might be acceptable, given the ease of preparation, but was still not ideal. On balance, the food processor is a decent option, especially if you favor speed and convenience, so we've included a recipe based on its use.

Needless to say, we pressed on to the old-fashioned, purist method of hand chopping the vegetables. It does involve some extra work, but it went much more swiftly than we'd imagined, and the benefits to the gazpacho's texture were dazzling. Because the pieces were consistent in size and shape, they not only retained their individual flavors but also set off the tomato broth beautifully, adding immeasurably to the whole. This was just what we were after.

One last procedural issue we investigated was the resting time. Gazpacho is best served ice cold, and the chilling time also allows the flavors to develop and meld. We tasted every hour on the hour for eight hours and found that four hours was the minimum time required for the soup to chill and the flavors to blossom.

Several of the key ingredients and seasonings also bore some exploration. Tomatoes are a star player here, and we preferred beefsteak over plum because they were larger, juicier, and easier to chop. Gazpacho is truly a dish to make only when local tomatoes are plentiful. We made several batches using handsome supermarket tomatoes, but the flavor paled in comparison with those batches made with perfectly ripe, local farm-stand tomatoes. We considered skinning and seeding them, but not a single taster complained when we didn't, so we skipped the extra steps.

When it came to peppers, we preferred red over green for their sweeter flavor. But red was less popular in the onion department; tasters rejected red onions, as well as plain yellow, as too sharp. Instead, they favored sweet onions—such as Vidalia or Maui—and shallots equally. We did note, however, that any onion was overpowering if used in the quantities recommended in most recipes (especially in the leftovers the next day), and the same was true of garlic, so we

dramatically reduced the quantity of both. To ensure thorough seasoning of the whole mixture, we marinated the vegetables briefly in the garlic, salt, pepper, and vinegar before adding the bulk of the liquid. These batches had more balanced flavors than the batches that were seasoned after all the ingredients were combined.

The liquid component was also critical. Most recipes called for tomato juice, which we sampled both straight and mixed in various amounts with water and low-sodium chicken broth. The winning ratio was 5 cups of tomato juice thinned with 1 cup of water to make the 6-cup total we needed. The water cut the viscosity of the juice just enough to make it brothy and light but not downright thin. Given our preference for ice-cold gazpacho, we decided to add ice cubes instead of straight water. The ice cubes helped to chill the soup and then provided water as they melted. We also conducted a blind tasting of tomato juices in which Welch's and Fresh Samantha's showed very well.

Finally, a word about the two primary seasonings, vinegar and olive oil. Spain is a noted producer of sherry, so it follows that sherry vinegar is a popular choice for gazpacho. When we tasted it, along with champagne, red wine, and white wine vinegars, the sherry vinegar was our favorite by far, adding not only acidity but also richness and depth. If you find that your stock of sherry vinegar has run dry, white wine vinegar was the runner-up and can be substituted. The oil contributes both flavor and a lush texture to this simple soup, and, in a word, only extra-virgin will do. Liquid or not, would you dress a beautiful summer salad with anything less?

WHAT WE LEARNED: For the best texture, chop the vegetables by hand. If you want to speed up the process, use a food processor, but never a blender, which turns the vegetables to slush. Save the bread for croutons rather than for thickening the soup.

CLASSIC GAZPACHO Serves 8 to 10

Welch's and Fresh Samantha's are our favorite brands of tomato juice for this recipe—not too thick, with a bright, lively flavor. This recipe makes a large quantity because the leftovers are so good, but it can be halved if you prefer. Traditionally, diners garnish their own bowls with more of the same diced vegetables that are in the soup. If that appeals to you, cut some extra vegetables while you prepare those called for in the recipe. Additional garnish possibilities include croutons (see page 17), chopped pitted black olives, chopped hard-cooked eggs (page 11), and finely diced avocado.

3 ripe medium beefsteak tomatoes (about 1½ pounds), cored and cut into ¼-inch dice, following the illustrations on page 19 (about 4 cups)

2 medium red bell peppers (about 1 pound), cored, seeded, and cut into ¼-inch dice, following the illustrations on page 19 (about 2 cups)

2 small cucumbers (about 1 pound), one peeled and the other with skin on, both seeded and cut into ¼-inch dice, following the illustrations on page 19 (about 2 cups)

½ small sweet onion (such as Vidalia, Maui, or Walla Walla) or 2 large shallots, peeled and minced (about ½ cup)

2 medium cloves garlic, minced or pressed through a garlic press (about 2 teaspoons)

2 teaspoons salt

⅓ cup sherry vinegar
Ground black pepper

5 cups tomato juice

1 teaspoon hot pepper sauce, such as Tabasco (optional)

8 ice cubes
Extra-virgin olive oil for serving

1. Combine the tomatoes, bell peppers, cucumbers, onion, garlic, salt, vinegar, and pepper to taste in a large (at least 4-quart) nonreactive bowl. Let stand until the vegetables just begin to release their juices, about 5 minutes. Stir in the tomato juice, hot pepper sauce, if using, and ice cubes. Cover tightly and refrigerate to blend flavors, at least 4 hours and up to 2 days.

2. Adjust the seasonings with salt and pepper and remove and discard any unmelted ice cubes. Serve cold, drizzling each portion with about 1 teaspoon extra-virgin olive oil and topping with the desired garnishes (see note).

VARIATIONS

QUICK FOOD PROCESSOR GAZPACHO

Using the same ingredients and quantities as for Classic Gazpacho, core and quarter the tomatoes and process them in the workbowl of a food processor fitted with a steel blade until broken down into ¼- to 1-inch pieces, about twelve 1-second pulses; transfer to a large bowl. Cut the cored and seeded peppers and seeded cucumbers into rough 1-inch pieces and process them separately until broken down into ¼- to 1-inch pieces, about twelve 1-second pulses; add to the bowl with the tomatoes. Add the onion, garlic, salt, vinegar, and ground black pepper to taste; continue with the recipe as directed.

SPICY GAZPACHO WITH CHIPOTLE CHILES AND LIME

A garnish of finely diced ripe avocado is a must with this variation.

Follow the recipe for Classic or Quick Food Processor Gazpacho, omitting optional hot pepper sauce and adding 2½ tablespoons minced chipotle chiles in adobo sauce, ¼ cup minced fresh cilantro leaves, and 6 tablespoons lime juice and 2 teaspoons grated lime zest along with the tomato juice and ice cubes.

GARLIC CROUTONS Makes about 3 cups
These croutons can be stored in an airtight container at room temperature for a day or so.

- 3   medium cloves garlic, minced or pressed through a garlic press (about 1 tablespoon)
- ¼   teaspoon salt
- 3   tablespoons extra-virgin olive oil
- 3   cups ½-inch white bread cubes (from a baguette or country white loaf)

Adjust an oven rack to the middle position and heat the oven to 350 degrees. Combine the garlic, salt, and oil in a small bowl; let stand 20 minutes, then pour through a fine-mesh strainer into a medium bowl. Discard the garlic. Add the bread cubes to the bowl with the garlic oil and toss to coat. Spread the bread cubes in an even layer on a rimmed baking sheet and bake, stirring occasionally, until golden, about 15 minutes. Cool on the baking sheet to room temperature.

SCIENCE DESK: Why Does Cold Food Require More Seasoning?

FLAVOR IS PERCEIVED BY OUR BRAINS PREDOMINANTLY BY the combined effort of our senses of taste and smell. The human ability to detect odor is outstanding; we recognize thousands of them. Our keen sense of smell makes good biological sense because we depend on it when we are hunting for food—be it in a forest or in the produce section at the grocery store. Taste is a much less complex sensation because it tells us the quality of what we have already selected and put in our mouth. There are just four fundamental tastes: sweet, salty, bitter, and sour. (Some experts argue for a fifth taste called *umami*, which is perceived as savory.) The way a food smells accounts for the vast majority of the flavor we perceive, probably more than 70 percent.

A problem occurs when we eat cold food. Smell needs volatile compounds to reach our nasal cavity. When the temperature of food drops, very little vapor is released; consequently, a cold food does not have much odor. This is a stroke of good fortune because if the corollary were true our refrigerators would stink. Unfortunately, without the

---

GETTING IT RIGHT: Texture Matters

Gazpacho is all about texture and temperature. For this reason, we recommend that you hand-chop the vegetables.

BLENDED
Too much time in the blender yields a smooth tomato slush.

OVERPROCESSED
Overpulsing creates uneven, pulpy vegetable bits. If pulsed lightly, vegetables can be chopped in a food processor with better results.

HAND-CHOPPED
Cutting the vegetables with a knife retains their vibrant color and firm texture.

odor component the flavor of cold food is dramatically reduced. How do we keep cold food interesting?

One solution is to use flavorings that are particularly pungent. These might include garlic or citrus. The other is to focus on the sensation in our mouths, considering sweet, salty, bitter, and sour as the predominant flavorings. Vinegar is often found in cold recipes such as pickles, soups, and dressings because its acidity can be detected even at a low temperature. Sugar is commonly added in large quantities to cold desserts such as ice cream. Our sensitivity to salt is relatively uniform throughout the temperature spectrum, so we add similar quantities to both cold and warm foods. That said, it's always a good idea to check cold foods just before serving to see if they require more salt. An additional measure can be used to heighten sensation at low temperatures—the introduction of contrasting flavors. Try sprinkling salt on cold pineapple to emphasize the sweetness by providing a counterpoint. In short, to make that cold dish interesting, select strong-smelling seasonings and, when tasting, focus on the flavors sweet, sour, bitter, and/or salty.

TECHNIQUE:
Keeping a Cutting Board Stable

Chefs often use a no-skid mat beneath a cutting board to keep it from slipping all over the counter. If you don't own a mat, place a damp paper towel on the counter, then put the cutting board on top. The damp towel holds the board in place and can be used to wipe down the counter when you're done.

TECHNIQUE: Cutting Vegetables into Perfect Dice

1.

1.

1.

2.

2.

2.

CUCUMBERS	PEPPERS	TOMATOES
1. Cut a 3/4-inch section off both ends of the cucumbers. Halve the cucumbers lengthwise and scoop out the seeds with a dinner spoon. Cut each seeded half lengthwise into 1/4-inch strips.	1. Slice a 3/4-inch section off both the tip and stem ends of the peppers. Make one slice through the wall of each pepper, lay the pepper skin-side down on a board, and open the flesh, exposing the seeds and membranes.	1. Core the tomatoes, halve them pole to pole, and, working over a bowl to catch all the juices, scoop out (and reserve) the inner pulp and seeds with a dinner spoon. Cut the pulp into 1/4-inch pieces.
2. Turn the strips 90 degrees and cut into even 1/4-inch pieces.	2. Cut away and discard the seeds and membranes. Cut the flesh into 1/4-inch strips. Turn the strips 90 degrees and cut them into even 1/4-inch pieces. Finally, cut the tips and tops into even 1/4-inch pieces.	2. Cut the empty tomato halves into 1/4-inch strips. Turn the slices 90 degrees and cut them into even 1/4-inch pieces.

TOMATO TART

WHAT WE WANTED: A recipe we could easily make at home with a solid (not soggy) bottom crust and great vine-ripened flavor.

Falling someplace in between pizza and quiche, tomato and mozzarella tart shares the flavors of both but features problems unique unto itself. For starters, this is not fast food, as some sort of pastry crust is required. Second, the moisture in the tomatoes almost guarantees a soggy crust. Third, tomato tarts are often tasteless, their spectacular open faces offering false promises. We wanted something foolproof and simple.

The first thing we learned is that tomato and mozzarella tarts come in all shapes and sizes—everything from overwrought custardy pies resembling quiche to stripped-down, minimalist models that are more like pizza. A test kitchen sampling of these various styles delivered dismal results—sodden bottoms and tired toppings across the board—but we did agree that one recipe stood out: a simple construction of tomatoes and cheese shingled across a plain, prebaked sheet of puff pastry. Unwilling to make puff pastry from scratch (who is?), we grabbed some store-bought puff pastry and started cooking.

The winning recipe from the taste test consisted of a flat sheet of puff pastry with a thin border to contain the topping (tomatoes easily slip off a flat sheet of anything) and a thick glaze of egg wash to seal the dough tightly against the seeping tomatoes. From a single rectangular sheet of pastry dough (we found Pepperidge Farm to be the most available; two pieces of dough come in a single box), we trimmed thin strips of dough from the edges and cemented them with egg wash to the top of the sheet to create a uniform 1-inch border. This single tart shell looked large enough for two to three servings. With scarcely any more effort, we found we could serve twice as many by joining the two pieces of dough that came in the box (we sealed the

seam tightly with egg wash and rolled it flat) and making a long rectangular version (roughly 16 by 8 inches). Once assembled, the tart got a heavy brushing with beaten egg.

From the initial test results, we knew that prebaking the crust would be essential to give it a fighting chance against the moisture from the tomatoes. Following the recipe on the back of the Pepperidge Farm box, we baked the enlarged tart shell at 400 degrees until it was light, airy, and golden brown. Now we ran into our first problem. The shell was too frail to support a heavy, wet filling. Baked at 350 degrees, the shell was noticeably squatter—and thus better suited to a heavy filling—but it was also unpleasantly tough and chewy. We wondered if a two-step baking method might be more successful: a high temperature for initial lift and browning, then a lower temperature to dry out the shell for maximum sturdiness. When started at 425 degrees (and held there until puffed and light golden, about 15 minutes) and finished at 350 degrees (and held there until well browned, 15 minutes longer), the crust was flaky yet rigid enough for a test cook to hold it aloft while holding onto just one end.

Now we had half-solved the problem of the soggy crust, but there was still work to do. The egg wash coating had proven only deflective, not impermeable. Liquid soaked through to the puff pastry, albeit at a slower rate than uncoated pastry. Egg wash was part of, but not the whole, solution.

Our next thought was that a layer of cheese might help. We gathered up a trio of mozzarellas for a tasting: fresh cow's milk, low-moisture part-skim cheese from the supermarket, and low-moisture whole milk cheese, also shrink-wrapped and from the supermarket. Fresh mozzarella won accolades for flavor, but its high moisture content rendered the crust mushy (even after pressing the cheese to extrude excess moisture). Part-skim mozzarella was deemed "a little bland," though its dry constitution fit the tart's needs. Whole milk mozzarella packed a fuller, creamier flavor and most pleased tasters; it was clearly the best choice. A scant half pound of grated cheese melted into a smooth, seemingly watertight layer across the tart's bottom. When the entire tart was assembled and baked, the bottom crust was vastly improved, but the tomatoes still gave off too much water, affecting the texture of the crust and the overall flavor of the tart.

Our first thought was to use tomatoes with a relatively low water content. We limited our tests to standard beefsteak (round) and Roma (plum) tomatoes as they are the two most readily available. A quick side-by-side test ruled out beefsteaks as excessively high in liquid. As we had suspected, Romas were the better choice for this recipe.

As for extracting the tomatoes' juices, roasting was an obvious choice, but we ruled it out as too time- and labor-intensive. Besides, we wanted the brighter flavor of lightly cooked tomatoes. Salting worked well but not perfectly. We sprinkled sliced tomatoes with salt and left them to drain on paper towels for 30 minutes. The underlying toweling was soaked through, but the tomatoes were still juicy to the touch. Increasing the amount of salt and time accomplished frustratingly little. A little gentle force, however, worked magic: We sandwiched the salted slices between paper towels and

pressed down with enough force to extrude any remaining juices (and the seeds) but not enough to squish the slices flat. They were as dry as could be, yet still very flavorful.

Baked quick and hot to melt the cheese and preserve the tomatoes' meaty texture (425 degrees turned out to be the best temperature), the tart looked ready for the cover of a magazine, especially when slicked with a garlic-infused olive oil and strewn with fresh basil leaves. But just a few minutes from the oven, the horrible truth revealed itself: The crust was soggy. Despite the egg wash, the melted mozzarella, and the drained and pressed tomatoes, the tart continued to suffer the ills of moisture.

Discouraged but not undone, we kept turning the same image over in our mind: bits of hard-baked Parmesan cheese on bread sticks or those dreadful prebaked "pizza crusts." We wondered if a solid layer of crisply baked Parmesan, on top of the egg wash but beneath the mozzarella, would seal the base more permanently. We sprinkled finely grated Parmesan over the tart shell for the prebake and crossed our fingers. The cheese melted to such a solid (and deliciously nutty tasting) layer that liquid rolled right off, like rain off a duck's back.

We assembled a whole tart and were stunned by the results: Slices could be lifted freely and consumed like pizza, even hours from the oven. Rich in flavor and sturdy in form, this tart had character to match its good looks—and we could make it pretty quickly, too. Ready-made dough and minimal ingredients kept preparation brief, and total cooking time was less than an hour and a half. Not only was this tart better than we expected, it was also simpler.

WHAT WE LEARNED: Prebake the puff pastry crust, sealing it first with an egg wash and then grated Parmesan cheese to keep out the moisture from the tomatoes. Salt the sliced tomatoes and press them lightly to remove as much liquid as possible.

TOMATO AND MOZZARELLA TART Serves 4 to 6

The baked tart is best eaten warm within two hours of baking. If you prefer to do some advance preparation, the tart shell can be prebaked through step I, cooled to room temperature, wrapped in plastic wrap, and kept at room temperature for up to two days before being topped and baked with the mozzarella and tomatoes. Use a low-moisture, shrink-wrapped supermarket cheese rather than fresh mozzarella. To keep the frozen dough from cracking, it's best to let it thaw slowly in the refrigerator overnight.

Flour for the work surface
1   (1.1-pound) box frozen puff pastry (Pepperidge Farm), thawed in its box in the refrigerator overnight
1   large egg, beaten
2   ounces Parmesan cheese, finely grated (1 cup)
1   pound Roma tomatoes (about 3 to 4 medium), cored and cut crosswise into ¼-inch-thick slices Salt
2   medium cloves garlic, minced or pressed through a garlic press (about 2 teaspoons)
2   tablespoons extra-virgin olive oil Ground black pepper
8   ounces low-moisture whole milk mozzarella, shredded (2 cups)
2   tablespoons coarsely chopped fresh basil leaves

1. Adjust an oven rack to the lower-middle position and heat the oven to 425 degrees. Dust the work surface with flour and unfold both pieces of puff pastry onto the work surface. Following the illustrations on page 24, form 1 large sheet with a border, using the beaten egg as directed. Sprinkle the Parmesan evenly over the bottom of the shell. Using a fork, uniformly and thoroughly poke holes in the bottom. Bake 15 minutes, then reduce the oven temperature to 350 degrees. Continue to bake until golden brown and crisp, 15 to 17 minutes longer. Transfer the baking sheet to a wire rack. Increase the oven temperature to 425 degrees.

2. While shell bakes, place the tomato slices in a single layer on a double layer of paper towels and sprinkle them evenly with ½ teaspoon salt; let stand 30 minutes. Place a second double layer of paper towels on top of the tomatoes and press firmly to dry the tomatoes. Combine the garlic, olive oil, and a pinch each of salt and pepper in a small bowl; set aside.

3. Sprinkle the mozzarella evenly over the bottom of the warm (or cool, if made ahead) baked shell. Shingle the tomato slices widthwise on top of the cheese (about 4 slices per row). Brush the tomatoes with the garlic oil.

4. Bake until the shell is deep golden brown and the cheese is melted, 15 to 17 minutes. Cool on a wire rack 5 minutes, sprinkle with the basil, slide onto a cutting board or serving platter, cut into pieces, and serve.

GETTING IT RIGHT: Good Tart, Bad Tart

If you neglect to salt the tomatoes and fail to brush the dough with egg wash, the baked tart will be soggy and limp (top right). If you take both of these precautions *and* add a layer of grated Parmesan, individual slices will be firm and dry, having enough structural integrity to hold their shape (bottom left).

Semisoft cheeses such as cheddar and mozzarella can stick to a box grater and cause a real mess. To keep the holes from becoming clogged, coat the box grater with a light film of nonstick cooking spray. The cooking spray will keep the cheese from sticking to the surface of the grater.

VARIATIONS

TOMATO AND MOZZARELLA TART WITH PROSCIUTTO

Follow the recipe for the Tomato and Mozzarella Tart, placing 2 ounces of thinly sliced prosciutto in a single layer on top of the mozzarella before arranging the tomato slices.

TOMATO AND SMOKED MOZZARELLA TART

Follow the recipe for the Tomato and Mozzarella Tart, substituting 6 ounces smoked mozzarella for the whole milk mozzarella.

TASTING LAB: Puff Pastry

PUFF PASTRY IS A SUPERFLAKY DOUGH WITH HUNDREDS of buttery layers. It is made by wrapping a simple pastry dough around a stick of cold butter, rolling the dough, folding the dough over itself at least four times, and chilling the dough for at least one hour between each fold. When baked, the water in the butter creates steam, which causes the dough to puff into flaky, delicate layers.

Almost no one—not even chefs at fine restaurants—makes puff pastry. Home cooks have one, maybe two commercial options in the freezer case. Pepperidge Farm Puff Pastry Sheets (made with vegetable oil, not butter) are available in almost every supermarket. Better supermarkets and gourmet shops might carry Classic Puff Pastry from Dufour Pastry Kitchens. When pitted in the test kitchen against Pepperidge Farm, the all-butter pastry was easy to pick out and was the clear favorite. That said, tasters felt that Pepperidge Farm was pretty good. Each brand has different size sheets, so we decided to use the more widely available Pepperidge Farm puff pastry to develop our tart recipe.

TASTING LAB: Supermarket Mozzarella

MOST HOME COOKS MAKE PIZZA OR LASAGNA EVERY NOW and then, and the array of baked pasta dishes and casseroles served under a blanket of melted mozzarella certainly doesn't end there. They are, in fact, almost as numerous as the seemingly endless mozzarella choices in most supermarkets, which typically include whole blocks and pouches of preshredded cheeses, both of which can be made from whole milk or skim milk (hence the moniker "part skim"). In addition, some supermarket (and most gourmet shops) sell fresh cheese floating in liquid. Like many of you, we've been warned about the pitfalls of using preshredded cheese, but unlike many of you, we have the time and inclination to put those warnings to the test. So we organized a blind tasting of 13 nationally available mozzarellas covering each of the four main variables—part-skim, whole milk, preshredded, and block—as well as three "fresh" mozzarellas (see pages 26 and 27) and tasted each one raw and melted on pizza.

All mozzarella, be it the supermarket variety or fresh cheese purchased at a specialty shop, falls into a cheese category called *pasta filata*. This means the cheese is made by stretching (or pulling, spinning, or "stringing"—the translation of *filata*) the curds to give the final product a fine layered effect and elastic texture. This process, according to Bill Wendorff, professor and chair of the food science department at the University of Wisconsin, Madison, aligns the proteins into long chains. The result is multiple layers of curd and a stringy texture; when you peel back a layer of the cheese, it resembles a cooked chicken breast.

The technical designation for fresh mozzarella sold floating in liquid (usually water or brine, opaque from whey that leaches out of the cheese) is "high moisture," which the U.S. Food and Drug Administration (FDA) defines as having a moisture content of at least 52 percent but not more than 60 percent by weight. Fresh, high-moisture mozzarella, however, is highly perishable and therefore poorly suited to long storage times and lengthy supermarket stays.

That brings us to the mozzarella typically found in supermarkets, melted on takeout pizza, and tasted in this test—a second variety designated "low moisture," with an

TECHNIQUE: Assembling the Tart Shell

1. Brush the beaten egg along one edge of one sheet of puff pastry. Overlap with a second piece of dough by 1 inch and press down to seal the pieces together.

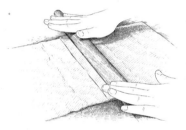

2. Using a rolling pin, smooth out the seam. The dough should measure about 18 by 9 inches. Use a pizza wheel or knife to trim the edges straight.

3. With a pizza wheel or knife, cut a 1-inch strip from one long side of the dough. Cut another 1-inch strip from the same side.

4. Cut a 1-inch strip from one short side of the dough. Cut another 1-inch strip from the same side. Transfer the large piece of dough to a parchment-lined baking sheet and brush with the beaten egg.

5. Gently press the long strips of dough onto each long edge of the dough and brush the strips with egg. Gently press the short strips of the dough onto each short edge and brush the strips with egg.

6. With a pizza wheel or knife, trim the excess dough from the corners.

FDA-mandated moisture content of 45 percent to 52 percent. This drier cheese is less perishable than the fresh version and therefore better suited to wide distribution and commercial uses. Many of the experts we contacted referred to low-moisture mozzarella as "pizza cheese," though that is not an official, FDA-recognized designation. They also mentioned that it is a uniquely American product, developed for the burgeoning U.S. pizza industry.

If only the differences in mozzarella ended with moisture. But they don't. Milk fat content also varies. We limited our tasting to whole milk mozzarella, which the FDA states must have a minimum milk fat content of 45 percent of the weight of the solids, and part-skim mozzarella, in which the milk fat content must be between 30 and 45 percent.

We broke our tasting into four parts. The first three were dedicated to low-moisture mozzarella: first the preshredded cheeses, then the block cheeses, and, finally, a face-off between the winners in each of these categories. In every case, we tasted the products both raw and melted (on our thin-crust pizza), and we included both part-skim and whole milk cheeses in each stage of the game. A fourth tasting included three types of fresh mozzarella and our favorite low-moisture cheese from the supermarket.

The tasters' impressions confirmed what anyone who has ever eaten a pizza already knows about mozzarella: It's pretty bland stuff. All of our samples had almost the same short ingredient list: pasteurized milk (and/or part-skim milk), cheese cultures, salt, and enzymes (as well as vinegar, in the case of the Polly-O cheeses and the Sorrento block cheeses). We found that these ingredients do indeed result in a neutral product. Don't count on finding much complexity or depth of flavor in any mozzarella. As a matter of fact, a quick glance at the charts on pages 26 and 27 reveals that none of the cheeses were met with much enthusiasm by tasters. "Mild," "milky," and "creamy" were the highest praises mustered for the winners.

That said, we were shocked to find that preshredded cheeses scored on par with their counterparts in block form. On a scale of 1 (worst) to 10 (best), the overall scores of the shredded cheeses varied from a high of 6.9 to a low of 4.24. These numbers were closely mirrored by the block cheese ratings—a high of 6.73 and a low of 4.08. In our tests, the experts' warnings about the horrors of preshredded cheese turned out to be for naught—as long as you choose the right brand. Tasters found cheeses in both categories—shredded and block—that they liked and disliked.

Tasters' comments indicated that the shredded cheeses' reasonably good showing was due more to their texture when melted than to any particularly positive flavor characteristics. All of the shredded cheeses were packed with anti-caking agents, usually potato or rice starch and/or powdered cellulose. Cheese expert Barry Swanson, a professor in the department of food science and human nutrition at Washington State University, explained that the starches and cellulose, an indigestible glucose fiber that gives most plant tissues their structure, bind moisture in the cheese, helping to keep the shreds separate in the package. The anti-caking agents were a disadvantage for the shredded cheeses when tasted raw, however, causing tasters to make frequent use of the adjectives "chalky," "powdery," and "dusty." Honestly, though, no one we know would eat preshredded cheese raw anyway, so this factor is negligible.

The winning shredded cheese was Kraft part-skim, which beat out brands with Italian-sounding names as well as three samples made with whole milk. But for this surprising exception, our tasters generally ruled in favor of whole milk cheeses, at least when compared with the part-skim cheese made by the same company. Again, excepting Kraft, tasters found that the whole milk cheeses were creamier and less bland than their part-skim counterparts. Many whole milk mozzarellas contain an extra 10 calories and just 1 gram of fat per serving, so we'll take any flavor advantage we can get, especially if the alternative saves so few calories.

Among the block cheeses we considered, Dragone rose as the overall champ. It also won the whole shebang when we pitted it against Kraft, the winner of the preshredded competition. If you don't mind shredding a block of cheese yourself, we think you'll get the very best flavor and texture

Rating Shredded Mozzarella

WE SELECTED FIVE WIDELY AVAILABLE BRANDS OF "SUPERMARKET," OR LOW-MOISTURE, MOZZARELLA AND SAMPLED those made with part-skim or whole milk. Because the most common use for this type of cheese is quick and convenient melting, we decided to include both preshredded and block forms (see right). Fifteen *Cook's Illustrated* staff members tasted these cheeses both raw and melted on pizza. Separate tests were performed in this manner, one for the category of shredded cheeses, and the other for block cheeses. The cheeses are listed below in order of preference, based on the combined scores of the raw and the pizza tests.

RECOMMENDED
Kraft Shredded Low Moisture Part-Skim Mozzarella
$2.50 for 8 ounces

This cheese was the clear winner in both the raw and the pizza tests. When tasted raw, it was found to be "rich" and "tangy," with only a "slight chalkiness." On pizza, tasters found it to be "mild and lean," yet "tasty," "fresh," and "flavorful."

RECOMMENDED WITH RESERVATIONS
Polly-O Shredded Low Moisture Whole Milk Mozzarella
$3.29 for 8 ounces

While this cheese rated overall as the tasters' second favorite, eaten raw it was found to be "nondescript" and "a little boring." But on pizza its true character came through: It was seen as having a "nice melted texture" with a "sharp flavor like cheddar."

RECOMMENDED WITH RESERVATIONS
Sargento Chef Style Natural Low Moisture Whole Milk Mozzarella
$2.50 for 8 ounces

Considered "quite salty" but with a "nice chewiness" raw, this shredded cheese was a little "greasy" and "slightly acidic" when melted on pizza.

RECOMMENDED WITH RESERVATIONS
Sorrento Shredded Low Moisture Whole Milk Mozzarella (known west of the Mississippi as Precious)
$2.39 for 8 ounces

This cheese was "soft and mild" and "non-chalky." It was considered to have a "nice texture" but "very little flavor" on pizza.

RECOMMENDED WITH RESERVATIONS
Sorrento Shredded Low Moisture Part-Skim Mozzarella (known west of the Mississippi as Precious)
$2.39 for 8 ounces

"Holy powder" was one taster's comment when eating this cheese raw; others called it "pasty" and "artificial tasting." The cheese was better on pizza—one taster remarked on its "full cheesy flavor"—but it was nonetheless "a bit greasy" with "spotty melting characteristics."

NOT RECOMMENDED
Sargento Chef Style Natural Low Moisture Part-Skim Mozzarella
$2.50 for 8 ounces

This shredded mozzarella was rejected because of its "sour," "tangy" flavor. It tasted "almost lemony" on pizza. The texture was described as "pasty" and "rubbery."

NOT RECOMMENDED
Polly-O Shredded Low Moisture Part-Skim Mozzarella
$3.29 for 8 ounces

We found it interesting that this cheese took last place considering the high marks its whole milk counterpart received. The one redeeming quality was the thickness of the individual shreds of cheese, but the texture was "plasticky" and "gummy" with an "innocuous flavor."

from a block of Dragone whole milk mozzarella. But if you are pressed for time, you'll do fine with a bag of Kraft preshredded, low-moisture part-skim mozzarella.

TASTING LAB: Fresh Mozzarella

IT'S PRETTY COMMON KNOWLEDGE THAT FRESH mozzarella is best in salads and sandwiches, being creamier, more tender, and more flavorful than low-moisture supermarket mozzarella. But what about on pizzas and tarts? Many experts say that fresh cheeses make these dishes watery and ruin crisp pizza crust. We wondered if this was true. The local pizza parlor certainly doesn't use fresh mozzarella.

To find out, we pitted the winner of our supermarket low-moisture mozzarella test (Dragone whole milk block cheese) against three brands of fresh mozzarella: BelGioioso (widely available in supermarkets, $3.29 for a 7-ounce container with 4 ounces of actual cheese), Calabro (made locally with Vermont cow's milk, $7.95 per pound), and mozzarella di bufala (made by Mandara from Italy, with water buffalo milk, as all mozzarellas were originally, and priced at $7.95 for an 8-ounce ball). All four cheeses were tested both raw and on pizza.

Not surprisingly, all three fresh mozzarellas were preferred over the Dragone whole milk block mozzarella when eaten raw. However, we were surprised by the results on the pizza test. Only one fresh cheese, the BelGioioso, made a poor showing on pizza. The Calabro and the mozzarella di bufala easily beat the supermarket cheese on pizza. Panelists thought they both tasted "real" and had the most "milk flavor." A few tasters objected to the gamy flavor of the mozzarella di bufala, so it finished in second place. Calabro was our favorite for flavor and texture, and it also was the least expensive of the three fresh cheeses we tasted. This cheese is not available nationally (no fresh cow's milk mozzarella is), but based on these results we suggest that you look for a high-quality, locally made fresh mozzarella. It will taste great in salads and sandwiches, and it may surprise you on pizza or a tart.

Dawn prepares pots (and pots) of chili in the back kitchen for the next day's shoot.

ONE-POT wonders

CHAPTER 3

The notion of dinner made in a single pot is certainly alluring. Chili is probably America's favorite one-pot supper, but this dish can be plagued with problems. The meat can be tough, the beans are often either undercooked or mushy, the chili can be either much too spicy or boringly bland, and, more often than not, the whole thing is swimming in a pool of orange grease. The "experts" generally complicate matters by using a combination of meats and homemade chili powder (made by toasting, seeding, and grinding dried chiles). We wanted great chili, but it had to be simple. We wanted something all-American that would appeal to everyone in the family.

No one thinks of a clambake as a one-pot wonder. The traditional recipe requires a sandy beach and a pit that takes hours to dig. After you've gathered stones to hold in the heat and harvested seaweed from the ocean, you've still got a lot of cooking to do. Although a real clambake is a treat, we love the flavors of the seafood, sausage, corn, and potatoes too much to relegate this dish to a once-in-a-lifetime event. Could we make an indoor clambake simple enough to prepare even on a busy weeknight?

BASIC CHILI

WHAT WE WANTED: A basic all-American chili made with supermarket staples—ground meat, tomatoes, chili powder, and canned beans—that was easy to make and delicious.

Like politics, chili provokes heated debate. Some purists insist that a chili that contains beans or tomatoes is just not chili. Others claim that homemade chili powder is essential or that ground meat is taboo. But there is one kind of chili that almost every American has eaten (or even made) at one time or another. It's the kind of chili you liked as a kid and still see being served at Super Bowl parties. Made with ground meat, tomatoes, and chili powder, this thick, fairly smooth chili is spiced but not spicy. It's basic grub (and it can be great grub) that's not intended to fuel impassioned exchanges over the merits of ancho versus New Mexico chiles.

Although this simple chili should come together easily, it should not taste as if it did. The flavors should be rich and balanced, the texture thick and lush. Unfortunately, many "basic" recipes yield a pot of underspiced, underflavored chili reminiscent of Sloppy Joes. Our goal was to develop a no-fuss chili that tasted far better than the sum of its common parts.

Most of the recipes for this plain-spoken chili begin by sautéing onions and garlic. Tasters liked red bell peppers added to these aromatics but rejected other options, including green bell peppers, celery, and carrots. After this first step, things became less clear. The most pressing concerns were the spices (how many and what kind) and the meat (how much ground beef and whether or not to add another meat). There were also the cooking liquid (what kind, if any) and the proportions of tomatoes and beans to consider.

Our first experiments with these ingredients followed a formula we had seen in lots of recipes: 2 pounds ground beef, 3 tablespoons chili powder, 2 teaspoons ground cumin, and 1 teaspoon each red pepper flakes and dried oregano. Many recipes add the spices after the beef has been browned, but we knew from work done in the test kitchen on curry that ground spices taste better when they have direct contact with hot cooking oil.

To see if these results would apply to chili, we set up a test with three pots of chili—one with the ground spices added before the beef, one with the spices added after the beef, and a third in which we toasted the spices in a separate skillet and added them to the pot after the beef. The batch made with untoasted spices added after the beef tasted weak. The batch made with the spices toasted in a separate pan was better, but the clear favorite was the batch made with spices added directly to the pot before the meat. In fact, subsequent testing revealed that the spices should be added at the outset—along with the aromatics—to develop their flavors fully.

Although we didn't want a chili with killer heat, we did want real warmth and depth of flavor. Commercial chili powder is typically 80 percent ground dried red chiles with the rest a mix of garlic powder, onion powder, oregano, ground cumin, and salt. To boost flavor, we increased the amount of chili powder from 3 to 4 tablespoons, added more cumin and oregano, and tossed in some cayenne for heat. We tried some more exotic spices, including cinnamon (which was deemed "awful"), allspice (which seemed "out of place"), and coriander (which "added some gentle warmth"). Only the coriander became part of our working recipe.

It was now time to consider the meat. The quantity (2 pounds) seemed ideal when paired with two 16-ounce cans of beans. Tests using 90 percent, 85 percent, and 80 percent lean ground beef showed that there is such a thing as too much fat. Pools of orange oil floated to the top of the chili made with ground chuck (80 percent lean beef). At the other end of the spectrum, the chili made with 90 percent lean beef was a tad bland—not bad, but not as full flavored as the chili made with 85 percent lean beef, which was our final choice.

We wondered if another type of meat should be used in place of some ground beef. After trying batches of chili made with ground pork, diced pork loin, sliced sausage, and sausage removed from its casing and crumbled, tasters preferred the hearty flavor and creamy texture of an all-beef chili. (The exception was one batch to which we added bacon; many tasters liked its smoky flavor, so we made a version with bacon and black beans as a variation on the master recipe.)

Some of us have always made chili with beer and been satisfied with the results. Nodding to the expertise of others, we tried batches made with water (too watery), chicken broth (too chickeny and dull), beef broth (too tinny), wine (too acidic), and no liquid at all except for that in the tomatoes (beefy tasting and by far the best). When we tried beer, we were surprised to find that it subdued that great beefy flavor. Keep the beer on ice for drinking with dinner.

Tomatoes were definitely going into the pot, but we had yet to decide on the type and amount. We first tried two small (14-ounce) cans of diced tomatoes. Clearly not enough tomatoes. What's more, the tomatoes were too chunky, and they were floating in a thin sauce. We tried two 28-ounce cans of diced tomatoes, pureeing the contents of one can in the blender to thicken the sauce. Although the chunkiness was reduced, the sauce was still watery. Next we paired one can of tomato puree with one can of diced tomatoes and, without exception, tasters preferred the thicker consistency. The test kitchen generally doesn't like the slightly cooked flavor of tomato puree, but this recipe needed the body it provided. In any case, after the long simmering time, any such flavor was hard to detect. (For more information about buying tomato puree, see the Tasting Lab on page 33. For more information about buying diced tomatoes, see the Tasting Lab on page 222.)

We tried cooking the chili with the lid on, with the lid off, and with the lid on in the beginning and off at the end. The chili cooked with the lid on was too soupy, that cooked with the lid off too dense. Keeping the lid on for half of the cooking time and then removing it was ideal—the consistency was rich but not too thick. Two hours of gentle simmering was sufficient to meld the flavors; shorter cooking times yielded chili that was soupy or bland—or both.

Most recipes add the beans toward the end of cooking, the idea being to let them heat through without causing them to fall apart. But this method often makes for very bland beans floating in a sea of highly flavorful chili. After testing several options, we found it best to add the beans with the tomatoes. The more time the beans spent in the pot, the better they tasted. In the end, we preferred dark red kidney beans or black beans because both keep their shape better than light red kidney beans, the other common choice.

With our recipe basically complete, it was time to try some of those offbeat additions to the pot that other cooks swear by, including cocoa powder, ground coffee beans, raisins, chickpeas, mushrooms, olives, and lima beans. Our conclusion? Each of these ingredients was either weird tasting or too subtle to make much difference. Lime wedges, passed separately at the table, both brightened the flavor of the chili and accentuated the heat of the spices. Our chili was now done. Although simple, it is, we hope, good enough to silence any debate.

WHAT WE LEARNED: Cook the spices before the meat to bring out their flavor, and use all ground beef. Don't add any stock, beer, or water—the liquid from the tomatoes should be sufficient. Add the beans early in the process (not just before serving, as directed in most recipes), so they can soak up the flavors of the chili.

BEEF CHILI WITH KIDNEY BEANS

Makes about 3 quarts, serving 8 to 10

Good choices for condiments include diced fresh tomatoes, diced avocado, sliced scallions, chopped red onion, chopped cilantro leaves, sour cream, and shredded Monterey Jack or cheddar cheese. If you are a fan of spicy food, consider using a little more of the red pepper flakes or cayenne—or both. The flavor of the chili improves with age; if possible, make it a day or up to five days in advance and reheat before serving. Leftovers can be frozen for up to a month.

2	tablespoons vegetable or corn oil
2	medium onions, chopped fine (about 2 cups)
1	medium red bell pepper, stemmed, seeded, cut into ½-inch dice
6	medium cloves garlic, minced or pressed through a garlic press (about 2 tablespoons)
¼	cup chili powder
1	tablespoon ground cumin
2	teaspoons ground coriander
1	teaspoon red pepper flakes
1	teaspoon dried oregano
½	teaspoon cayenne pepper
2	pounds 85 percent lean ground beef
2	cans (15 ounces each) dark red kidney beans, drained and rinsed
1	can (28 ounces) diced tomatoes, with juice
1	can (28 ounces) tomato puree
	Salt
2	limes, cut into wedges

1. Heat the oil in a large heavy-bottomed nonreactive Dutch oven over medium heat until shimmering but not smoking. Add the onions, bell pepper, garlic, chili powder, cumin, coriander, pepper flakes, oregano, and cayenne and cook, stirring occasionally, until the vegetables are softened and beginning to brown, about 10 minutes. Increase the heat to medium-high and add half the beef. Cook, breaking up pieces with a wooden spoon, until no longer pink and

just beginning to brown, 3 to 4 minutes. Add the remaining beef and cook, breaking up pieces with a wooden spoon, until no longer pink, 3 to 4 minutes.

2. Add the beans, tomatoes, tomato puree, and ½ teaspoon salt. Bring to a boil, then reduce the heat to low and simmer, covered, stirring occasionally, for 1 hour. Remove the lid and continue to simmer 1 hour longer, stirring occasionally (if the chili begins to stick to the bottom of the pot, stir in ½ cup water and continue to simmer), until the beef is tender and the chili is dark, rich, and slightly thickened. Adjust the seasoning with additional salt. Serve with lime wedges and condiments (see note), if desired.

VARIATION

BEEF CHILI WITH BACON AND BLACK BEANS

Cut 8 ounces bacon (about 8 strips) into ½-inch pieces. Fry the bacon in a large heavy-bottomed nonreactive Dutch oven over medium heat, stirring frequently, until browned, about 8 minutes. Pour off all but 2 tablespoons fat, leaving the bacon in the pot. Follow the recipe for Beef Chili with Kidney Beans, substituting the bacon fat in the Dutch oven for the vegetable oil and an equal amount of canned black beans for kidney beans.

EQUIPMENT CORNER: Slow Cookers

SLOW COOKERS (BETTER KNOWN AS CROCK-POTS, A name trademarked by the Rival company) may be the only modern kitchen convenience that saves the cook time by using more of it rather than less. To see if these appliances could cook not just slowly but also well, we purchased five of them, all 6-quart oval cookers, a size and shape offering the most options in terms of the amount and type of food that can be prepared. The contestants included three "standard" cookers, the Rival Crock-Pot ($39.99), the Farberware Millennium Slow Cooker ($39.99), and the Hamilton Beach Portfolio Slow Cooker ($34.99); one with a new "programmable" feature, the Rival Smart-Pot ($49.99); and one with a completely revamped design, the West Bend Versatility Cooker ($54.99).

All five models had the standard slow cooker temperature settings of low, high, and keep warm. To test the functioning of each setting, we cooked the pot roast recipe (page 102) on low for eight hours and the chili recipe (page 32) on high for four hours; we then set each pot of chili on "keep warm" for two hours. All five cookers produced good renditions of the pot roast and the chili, and all five kept the chili plenty warm for two hours. (The lowest temperature reached during warming was a piping-hot 187 degrees, by the West Bend cooker; the other four cookers maintained the chili at close to 200 degrees.)

What do we recommend? In the "standard slow cooker with no fancy features" category, both the Farberware Millennium and the Rival Crock-Pot performed admirably. The Hamilton Beach cooker showed slight scorching of the chili in the bottom corners of the crockery pot and so was slightly downgraded.

How did the two novel cookers fare? Rival's Smart-Pot is the only cooker on the market that lets you select a specific time and heat setting and then automatically shifts to the warm setting when the cooking time is up. Theoretically, this buys you a couple more hours at the mall or at work before you have to come home and tend the pot. Two hours after switching from high to warm, however, the Smart-Pot had brought the temperature of the chili down by just 10 degrees, from 205 to 195. We're not sure this feature is worth the extra money.

West Bend's Versatility Cooker is a standout because its pot is made from aluminum with a nonstick interior coating, which means you can use it to cook foods on the stove-top, just as you would any other conventional pot. Both our chili and pot roast recipes start out with instructions for browning on the stovetop, and it was nice to brown foods in the same pot we ultimately used for slow cooking. While a crockery-less crockery pot does seem a little odd, this expensive model does get the job done, and then some.

BEST SLOW COOKERS
The Farberware Millennium (left) and the Rival Crock-Pot (middle) were the best basic models tested. The West Bend Versatility Cooker (right) has a stovetop-worthy pot made of aluminum rather than the classic ceramic. See www.americastestkitchen.com for up-to-date prices and mail-order sources for these top-rated products.

TASTING LAB: Tomato Puree

IN THE FAMILY OF CANNED TOMATO PRODUCTS, TOMATO puree is the neglected middle child, often overlooked in favor of its older sibling, whole peeled tomatoes, or its hot-shot younger sibling, diced tomatoes. The reason is clear: While whole and diced tomatoes prove a passable substitute for fresh tomatoes (they are simply skinned and processed), tomato puree is cooked and strained, thereby removing all seeds and all allusions to freshness. That's not to say that tomato puree doesn't have a role in most kitchens, it's just that puree performs best in long-cooked dishes where the thick, even texture of puree is important and fresh tomato flavor is not.

Although we haven't developed many recipes using tomato puree, we did find it to be necessary to achieve full tomato flavor and a smooth richness in our Beef Chili with Kidney Beans. But which brand is best? We gathered eight popular brands of tomato puree and tasted them plain. We then

Rating Tomato Purees

FIFTEEN MEMBERS OF THE *COOK'S ILLUSTRATED* STAFF TASTED ALL EIGHT PUREES STRAIGHT FROM THE CAN. WE ALSO tasted the winner and loser of this tasting in a slow-simmering chili and found the differences to be negligible. The purees are listed in order of preference based on their scores in the plain tomato puree tasting. Because differences between brands fade with prolonged cooking, all brands are recommended.

RECOMMENDED
Progresso Tomato Puree
$1.50 for 28 ounces
Tied for first place, this puree was "thick" and "strong," with a "fresh," "mild" flavor.

RECOMMENDED
Hunt's Tomatoes Puree
$.99 for 29 ounces
Hunt's, one of the two top-rated purees, was favored for its "nice and thick" texture and "tomatoey" flavor, though some tasters found it "too sweet."

RECOMMENDED
Cento Tomato Puree
$1.19 for 28 ounces
Most tasters found this puree "balanced," with a "good flavor," though many found it "slightly bitter."

RECOMMENDED
Muir Glen Organic Tomato Puree
$2.59 for 28 ounces
The lone organic sample in the tasting, this puree was deemed "thick and strong," with "good flavor."

RECOMMENDED
Pastene Tomato Puree
$1.69 for 28 ounces
Though some found this brand "fresh tasting," many tasters thought it tasted slightly "tinny."

RECOMMENDED
Redpack Tomato Puree
$1.19 for 29 ounces
Some praised its "velvety smooth texture," while others agreed with the one taster who deemed it "middle of the road in every aspect."

RECOMMENDED
Contadina Tomato Puree
$1.29 for 29 ounces
"Where's the salt?" wrote one taster of this puree, which many found "thin" and "bland." Others, however, praised its "good balance."

RECOMMENDED
Rienzi Tomato Puree
$.99 for 28 ounces
Though it had strong "vegetable flavor," most found it "a bit flat" and "very thin."

tasted the winner and loser of the plain tasting in our chili.

We had a tie in the straight puree tasting, with Progresso and Hunt's sharing top honors. Hunt's was praised for "layers of flavor," while Progresso won points for its "strong tomato flavor." Coming in last was Rienzi, unanimously criticized as too thin and watery, though a handful of tasters liked the "vegetal" flavor that one taster described as being like "wicked salty V-8."

For part two of our tasting, we pitted Progresso against Rienzi in our chili recipe. Although it was easy to judge the winners and losers of the straight puree tasting, we wondered how clear the differences would be once the puree had been simmered for two hours with a half-dozen spices. The answer: not very clear. While some tasters found the batch made with Progresso "thicker" and "more full-flavored" and some found the batch made with Rienzi "slightly meatier" and "fresher and sweeter," most agreed with the taster who wrote, "I would use either one." Given that most recipes calling for tomato puree involve long cooking times and lots of ingredients, it's safe to say that using one particular brand over another is not going to make much of a difference in the final dish.

INDOOR CLAMBAKE

WHAT WE WANTED: We wanted to re-create the great flavors of a clambake without help from the sand or the sea.

A clambake is a rite of summer along the East Coast. At this festive beach party, loads of shellfish and a variety of vegetables are steamed in a wide, sandy pit using seaweed and rocks warmed from a nearby campfire. This feast usually takes a day or more to prepare—digging the pit is no small chore—and hours to cook. Though some may mock the idea of a kitchen clambake, it is nonetheless a simple and efficient way (taking a mere half-hour) to prepare a fantastic shellfish dinner—complete with corn, potatoes, and sausage—for a hungry crowd.

An indoor clambake is not a novel idea. We found dozens of recipes in our cookbook library. While the methods used to put one together vary dramatically, the ingredients, in keeping with tradition, are fairly consistent, including clams, mussels, lobsters, potatoes, corn, onions, and spicy sausage. Some recipes tell the cook to partially cook each ingredient separately and then finish things together on the grill, while others recommend specific systems for layering the ingredients in a stockpot. Some recipes use seaweed or corn husks for extra flavor, while others tout the importance of smoky bacon. The goal of all of these recipes, however, is to manage the process such that the various components are cooked perfectly and ready to serve at the same time. Taking note of these different clambake styles, we began our testing.

It soon became apparent which methods were worthwhile and which simply made a mess. Partially cooking the ingredients separately before combining them on the grill was time-consuming and produced a clambake without that authentic clambake flavor. Layering the various ingredients in a stockpot, on the other hand, was both easy to do and produced tasty results. With the stockpot set over high heat, the components steamed and infused one another with their flavors. This method was not without problems,

however, as the onions turned out slimy, and half of the ingredients wound up submerged in shellfish-flavored water. Using this one-pot method as a point of departure, we began to tinker with the technical details and the ingredients.

Although every recipe we read called for adding water to the pot to create steam for cooking, we found the shellfish released enough of their own liquid to make adequate steam. When placed over high heat, the shellfish took only a few minutes to release the moisture needed to steam the whole pot, with a cup or more left over to use as a broth for the clams and mussels. We took advantage of those first few minutes when the pot was dry by lining it with sliced sausage, giving it a chance to sear before the steam was unleashed. We tested several kinds of sausage, and tasters preferred mild kielbasa. The light smoke flavor of this sausage works well with seafood, and the sausage is fairly juicy and fatty, making it perfectly suited to this cooking method.

With the sausage layered on the bottom, we played with the order in which to add the remaining ingredients. We found it best to lay the clams and mussels right on top of the sausage because they provide most of the necessary liquid for the steam and needed to be close to the heat source. Wrapping them loosely in a cheesecloth sack makes them easy to remove when done. Although potatoes actually take the longest to cook, they were best laid on top of the clams and mussels, close to the heat source yet easily accessible with a prodding knife to test their doneness. We shortened their cooking time by cutting the potatoes into 1-inch pieces. Corn, with a layer of husk left on, was placed on top of the potatoes. The husk, we found, protects the delicate corn from becoming infused with too much shellfish flavor. The husk also protects the corn from any foam released by the lobsters, which we placed on top of the corn. We decided to omit the onions, which no one had eaten anyway; the bacon, which smoked out the delicate flavor of the shellfish; and the seaweed, which was hard to find and unnecessary for flavor.

Layered in this fashion, the clambake took just 17 to 20 minutes to cook through completely over high heat. Surprisingly, the shellfish liquid is quite salty and naturally seasons all the ingredients. After taking a couple of minutes to remove the ingredients from the pot and arrange them attractively on a platter, we had a feast that had been made from start to finish in half an hour.

WHAT WE LEARNED: Don't bother to precook ingredients—they can all go into the pot at the same time. Success depends on how you layer the ingredients in the pot. Line a large pot with sliced sausage, following with the clams and mussels, the potatoes, the corn, and, finally, the lobsters.

TECHNIQUE: Debearding Mussels

Mussels often contain a weedy beard protruding from the crack between the two shells. It's fairly small and can be difficult to tug out of place. To remove it easily, trap the beard between the side of a small knife and your thumb and pull to remove it. The flat surface of the paring knife gives you some leverage to remove the beard.

INDOOR CLAMBAKE Serves 4 to 6

Choose a large, narrow stockpot in which you can easily layer the ingredients. The recipe can be cut in half and layered in an 8-quart Dutch oven, but it should cook for the same amount of time. We prefer small littlenecks for this recipe. If your market carries larger clams, use 4 pounds.

2   pounds small littleneck or cherrystone clams, scrubbed (see the illustration on page 42)
2   pounds mussels, shells scrubbed and beards removed (see the illustration above)
1   pound kielbasa, sliced into 1/3-inch-thick rounds
1   pound small new or red potatoes, scrubbed and cut into 1-inch pieces
4   medium ears corn, silk and all but the last layer of husk removed (see the illustrations on page 37)
2   live lobsters (about 1 1/2 pounds each)
8   tablespoons salted butter, melted

TECHNIQUE:
Preparing Corn for a Clambake

1. Remove all but the innermost layer of husk.

2. Use scissors to snip off the tassel.

1. Place the clams and mussels on a large piece of cheese-cloth and tie the ends together to secure; set aside. In a large, heavy-bottomed, 12-quart stockpot, layer the sliced kiel-basa, the sack of clams and mussels, the potatoes, the corn, and the lobsters on top of one another. Cover with the lid and place over high heat. Cook until the potatoes are tender (a paring knife can be slipped into and out of the center of a potato with little resistance), and the lobsters are bright red, 17 to 20 minutes.

2. Remove the pot from the heat and remove the lid (watch out for scalding steam). Remove the lobsters and set aside until cool enough to handle. Remove the corn from the pot and peel off the husks; arrange the ears on a large platter. Using a slotted spoon, remove the potatoes and arrange them on the platter with the corn. Transfer the clams and mussels to a large bowl and cut open the cheesecloth with scissors. Using a slotted spoon, remove the kielbasa from the pot and arrange it on the platter with the potatoes and corn. Pour the remaining steaming liquid in the pot over the clams and mussels. Using a kitchen towel to protect your hand, twist and remove the lobster tails, claws, and legs (if desired). Arrange the lobster parts on the platter. Serve immediately with melted butter and napkins.

Julia and Chris shape crab cakes into thick rounds, which will go into the refrigerator to firm up before they are pan-fried.

EAST COAST seafood

Clam chowder and crab cakes are available in most every seafood restaurant in the country. These dishes both have their origins along the East Coast and have been subjected to numerous changes (most not for the better) as they became more popular.

How many times have you ordered clam chowder in a restaurant only to be served a thin, runny soup? At the other end of the spectrum, many chowders are so thick that a spoon can stand up in the bowl.

Crab cakes can be mixed and shaped in a matter of minutes. But this simple recipe usually goes wrong long before that step, when the ingredients are chosen. Most restaurants use low-quality frozen or (gasp) imitation crabmeat. Better restaurants may use the real deal—fresh jumbo lump crabmeat—but they stretch this pricey ingredient with fillers, such as bread crumbs. Yes, the crab must be bound to form cohesive cakes, but in the end you want to taste the crab, not the binder.

We knew our test kitchen could get these simple dishes right. We also wanted to figure out the best tool and method for opening another East Coast favorite, oysters.

NEW ENGLAND CLAM CHOWDER

WHAT WE WANTED: A delicious, traditional chowder that was economical, would not curdle, and could be prepared quickly.

We love homemade clam chowder almost as much as we love good chicken soup. After all, our test kitchen is located just outside of Boston, in the heart of chowder country. But we must confess that many cooks (including some that work in our test kitchen) don't make their own chowder. While they might never buy chicken soup, they seem willing to make this compromise. We wondered why.

Time certainly isn't the reason. You can prepare clam chowder much more quickly than you can a pot of good chicken soup. The reason why many cooks don't bother making their own clam chowder is the clams. First of all, clams can be expensive. Second, clams are not terribly forgiving—you must cook them soon after their purchase (chickens can be frozen), and then the chowder itself must be quickly consumed (again, chicken soup can be frozen or at least refrigerated for another day). Last, chowders are more fragile (and thus more fickle) than most soups. Unless the chowder is stabilized in some way, it's likely to curdle, especially when brought to a boil.

Before testing chowder recipes, we explored our clam options. Chowders are typically made with hard-shell clams (rather than soft-shell clams, such as steamers), so we purchased (from smallest to largest) cockles, littlenecks, cherrystones, and chowder clams, often called quahogs (pronounced ko-hogs).

Although they made delicious chowders, we eliminated littlenecks and cockles, both of which were just too expensive to toss into a chowder pot. Chowders made with the cheapest clams, however, weren't satisfactory. The quahogs we purchased for testing were large (4 to 5 inches in diameter), tough, and strong flavored. Their oversized bellies (and the contents therein) gave the chowder an overbearing mineral taste, detracting from its smooth, rich flavor.

Though only a little more expensive than quahogs, cherrystones offered good value and flavor. The chowder made from these slightly smaller clams was distinctly clam flavored, without an inky aftertaste. Because there are no industry sizing standards for each clam variety, you may find some small quahogs labeled cherrystones or large cherrystones labeled quahogs. Regardless of designation, clams much over 4 inches in diameter will deliver a distinctly metallic, inky-flavored chowder.

Some recipes suggest shucking raw clams and then adding the raw clam bellies to the pot. Other recipes steam the clams open. We tested both methods and found that steaming the clams open is far easier than shucking them. After seven to nine minutes over simmering water, the clams open as naturally as budding flowers. Ours did not toughen up as long as we pulled them from the pot as soon as they opened and didn't let them cook too long in the finished chowder.

Although many chowder recipes instruct the cook to soak the clams in salt water spiked with cornmeal or baking powder to remove grit, we found the extra step of purging or filtering hard-shell clams to be unnecessary (see the Science Desk on page 43 for more details). All of the hard-shells we tested were relatively clean, and what little sediment there was sank to the bottom of the steaming liquid. Getting rid of the grit was as simple as leaving the last few tablespoons of broth in the pan when pouring it from the pot. If you find that your clam broth is gritty, strain it through a coffee filter.

At this point, we turned our attention to texture. We wanted a chowder that was thick but still a soup rather than a stew. Older recipes call for thickening clam chowder with crumbled biscuits; bread crumbs and crackers are modern stand-ins.

Chowders thickened with bread crumbs failed to impress. We wanted a smooth, creamy soup base for the potatoes, onions, and clams, but no matter how long the chowder simmered, neither the bread crumbs nor crackers ever completely dissolved into the cooking liquid. Heavy cream alone, by contrast, did not give the chowder enough body. We discovered fairly quickly that flour was necessary not only as a thickener but also as a stabilizer; unthickened chowders separate and curdle.

Most recipes for chowder call for potatoes, some of them calling specifically for starchy baking potatoes, which tend to break down when boiled and so can double as a thickener. In our tests, these potatoes did not break down sufficiently but instead simply became soft and mushy. We found waxy red boiling potatoes to be best for creamy-style chowders. They have a firm but tender texture, and their red skins look appealing.

We now had two final questions to answer about New England clam chowder. First, should it include salt pork or bacon, and, if the latter, did the bacon need to be blanched? Second, should the chowder be enriched with milk or cream?

Salt pork and bacon both come from the pig's belly. Salt pork is cured in salt, while bacon is smoked, and salt pork is generally fattier than bacon. Salt pork is the more traditional choice in chowder recipes, although bacon has become popular in recent decades, no doubt because of its availability. Jasper White writes in *Fifty Chowders* (Scribners, 2000), his definitive book on the subject, that chowders made years ago with salt pork often had a smoky flavor because they were also cooked over an open hearth. For modern cooks, bacon adds both the pork and the smoky flavor.

We made clam chowder with both salt pork and bacon, and tasters liked both versions. Frankly, we ended up using such small amounts of pork in our final recipe that either salt pork or bacon is fine. Bacon is more readily available and, once bought, easier to use up. Blanching the bacon makes it taste more like salt pork, but we rather liked the subtle smokiness of the chowder made with unblanched bacon.

As for the cream versus milk issue, we found that so much milk was required to make the chowder look and taste creamy that it began to lose its clam flavor and became more like mild bisque or the clam equivalent of oyster stew. Making the chowder with almost all clam broth (5 cups of the cooking liquid from the steaming clams), then finishing the stew with a cup of cream, gave us what we were looking for: a rich, creamy chowder that tasted distinctly of clams.

WHAT WE LEARNED: Use medium-size clams and then steam them open to create the liquid base for the chowder. Thicken the chowder with flour rather than potatoes; the flour also prevents the dairy from curdling. Use bacon rather than the traditional salt pork for a nice smoky flavor.

NEW ENGLAND CLAM CHOWDER Serves 6

We like waxy potatoes (with red skins) in this recipe because they hold up much better than high-starch russets.

7	pounds medium-size hard-shell clams, such as cherrystones, washed and scrubbed clean (see the illustration at right)
4	slices thick-cut bacon (about 4 ounces), cut into ¼-inch pieces
1	large Spanish onion, chopped medium
2	tablespoons all-purpose flour
3	medium boiling potatoes (about 1½ pounds), scrubbed and cut into ½-inch dice
1	large bay leaf
1	teaspoon fresh thyme leaves or ¼ teaspoon dried thyme
1	cup heavy cream
2	tablespoons minced fresh parsley leaves
	Salt and ground black or white pepper

1. Bring 3 cups water to a boil in large stockpot or Dutch oven. Add the clams and cover with a tight-fitting lid. Cook for 5 minutes, uncover, and stir with a wooden spoon. Quickly cover the pot and steam until the clams just open, 2 to 4 minutes (see illustration 1 on page 43). Transfer the clams to a large bowl; cool slightly. Open the clams with a paring knife, holding the clams over a bowl to catch any juices (see illustration 2 on page 43). With the knife, sever the muscle that attaches the clam to the shell (see illustration 3 on page 43) and transfer the meat to a cutting board. Discard the shells. Mince the clams; set aside. Pour the clam broth into a 2-quart Pyrex measuring cup, holding back the last few tablespoons of broth in case of sediment; set the clam broth aside. (You should have about 5 cups. If not, add bottled clam juice or water to make this amount.) Rinse and dry the stockpot or Dutch oven, then return the pot to the burner.

2. Fry the bacon in the empty pot over medium-low heat until the fat renders and the bacon crisps, 5 to 7 minutes.

Add the onion and cook, stirring occasionally, until softened, about 5 minutes. Add the flour and stir until lightly colored, about 1 minute. Gradually whisk in the reserved clam broth. Add the potatoes, bay leaf, and thyme and simmer until potatoes are tender, about 10 minutes. Add the clams, cream, parsley, and salt (if necessary) and ground pepper to taste; bring to simmer. Remove from the heat, discard the bay leaf, and serve immediately.

VARIATION

QUICK PANTRY NEW ENGLAND CLAM CHOWDER

From late summer through winter, when clams are plentiful, you'll probably want to make fresh clam chowder. But if you're short on time or find clams scarce and expensive, the right canned clams and bottled clam juice deliver a chowder that's at least three notches above canned chowder in quality. We

---

TECHNIQUE: Scrubbing Clams

Many recipes instruct the cook to scrub clams. Don't skip this step; many clams have bits of sand embedded in their shells that can ruin a pot of chowder. We like to scrub clams under cold, running water using a soft brush, sometimes sold in kitchen shops as a vegetable brush.

TECHNIQUE: Steaming Clams for Chowder

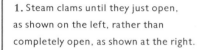

1. Steam clams until they just open, as shown on the left, rather than completely open, as shown at the right.

2. Using a paring knife, open the clams carefully, holding each one over a bowl to catch any juices that are released.

3. When open, discard the top shell and use the knife to sever the muscle that connects the clam to the bottom shell.

tested seven brands of minced and small whole canned clams and preferred Doxsee Minced Clams teamed with Doxsee brand clam juice as well as Snow's clams and its clam juice. These clams were neither too tough nor too soft, and they had a decent natural clam flavor.

Follow the recipe for New England Clam Chowder, substituting for the fresh clams 4 cans (6½ ounces each) minced clams, juice drained and reserved and clam meat reserved in small bowl, along with 1 cup water and 2 bottles (8 ounces each) clam juice in medium bowl. Add reserved clam meat and juice at same points when fresh clam meat and broth would be added.

SCIENCE DESK:
Why Are Some Clams So Sandy?

CLAMS ARE EASY TO COOK. WHEN, THEY OPEN, THEY are done. But perfectly cooked clams can be ruined by lingering sand. Straining the juices through cheesecloth after cooking will remove the grit, but it's a pain. Plus, you lose some of the juices to the cheesecloth. Worse still, straining will not remove bits of sand still clinging to the clam meat. Rinsing the cooked clams washes away flavor.

That's why so many clam recipes start by soaking clams in cold salted water for several hours. We tried various soaking regimens—such as soaking in water with flour, soaking in water with baking powder, soaking in water with cornmeal, and scrubbing and rinsing in five changes of water. If the clams were dirty at the outset, none of these techniques really worked. Even after soaking, many clams needed to be rinsed and the cooking liquid strained.

However, during the course of this testing, we noticed that some varieties of clams were extremely clean and free of grit at the outset. A quick scrub of the shell exterior and these clams were ready for the cooking pot, without any tedious soaking. The cooked clams were free of grit and the liquid was clean. If you want to make sure that your clams will be clean (and that your chowder will be free of grit), you must shop carefully.

Clams can be divided into two categories—hard-shell varieties (such as quahogs, cherrystones, and littlenecks) and soft-shell varieties (such as steamers and razor clams). Hard-shells live along sandy beaches and bays; soft-shells in muddy tidal flats. We have found that this modest difference in location makes all the difference in the kitchen.

When harvested, hard-shells remain tightly closed. In our tests, we found the meat inside to be sand-free. The exteriors should be scrubbed under cold running water to remove any caked-on mud, but otherwise these clams can be cooked without further worry about gritty broths.

Soft-shell clams gape when they are alive. We found that they almost always contain a lot of sand. While it's worthwhile to soak them in several batches of cold water to remove some of the sand, you can never get rid of it all. In the end, you must strain the cooking liquid (we find that a paper coffee filter works best). It's a good idea to rinse the cooked clams, too.

SCIENCE DESK:
Must Onions Make You Cry?

WHEN AN ONION IS CUT, THE CELLS THAT ARE DAMAGED in the process release sulfuric compounds as well as various enzymes, notably one called sulfoxide lyase. Those compounds and enzymes, which are separated when the onion's cell structure is intact, activate and mix to form the real culprit behind crying, a volatile new compound called thiopropanal sulfoxide. When thiopropanal sulfoxide evaporates in the air, it irritates the eyes, causing us to cry.

Over the years, we've collected more than 20 ideas from readers, books, and conversations with colleagues all aimed at reducing tears while cutting onions. We decided to put those ideas to the test. They ranged from the common sense (work underneath an exhaust fan or freeze onions for 30 minutes before slicing) to the comical (wear ski goggles or hold a toothpick in your teeth).

Overall, the methods that worked best were to protect our eyes by covering them with goggles or contact lenses or to introduce a flame near the cut onions. The flame, which can be produced by either a candle or a gas burner, changes the activity of the thiopropanal sulfoxide by completing its oxidization. Contact lenses and goggles form a physical barrier that the thiopropanal cannot penetrate. So if you want to keep tears at bay when handling onions, light a candle or gas burner or put on some ski goggles.

EQUIPMENT CORNER: Oyster Knives

OYSTERS ARE A DELICACY ENJOYED UP AND DOWN THE East Coast, as well as along the Gulf and Pacific Coasts. Of course, fresh oysters must be shucked before eating, and this task inspires fear even among intrepid cooks. Most everyone we know worries that the process will take forever or that the knife will somehow end up cutting their hand. Keeping a folded dish towel between your hand and the oyster should keep you safe (see the illustrations on page 45), but what about speed? Does your choice of knife affect the rate and ease with which the oysters can be opened?

To find out, we rounded up 12 knives in various lengths and styles. We also included a church-key can opener, a household staple that some cooks swear by. The bad news first. We couldn't open a single oyster with the church-key opener. The good news is that we found three oyster knives that we liked quite a lot (even novice shuckers were impressed), and they have some common features.

Oyster knives tend to come in various styles named for cities along the East and Gulf Coast. A Boston-style oyster knife has a long blade that tapers to a roundish tip. A Providence-style knife has a wide, thin blade that ends in a pointed tip. A New Haven–style knife has a wide, thin blade with an angled, pointed tip. Finally, a Galveston-style knife has a long, wide blade with a rounded tip. Both the experienced and inexperienced shuckers in the test kitchen preferred the New Haven–style knife. Its angled, pointed tip easily penetrated the hinge between the bottom and top shells and popped the oyster open. The flat or rounded tips on the other knives were less adept at this crucial task.

The other key factor in our ratings was the handle. Knives with contoured or textured handles consistently received high marks, while knives with slick or wooden handles were downgraded.

TECHNIQUE: Shucking Oysters

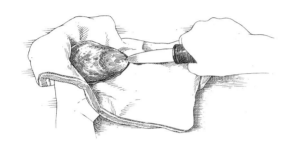

1. Start by holding the oyster cupped-side down in a dish towel. Keep the oyster flat as you work to keep the flavorful juices from spilling out of the shell. Locate the hinge with the tip of the knife.

2. Push between the edges of the shells, wiggling the knife back and forth to pry them open.

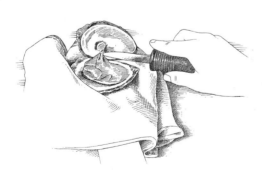

3. Detach the meat from the top shell and discard the shell.

4. To make eating easier, sever the muscle that holds the meat of the oyster to the bottom shell. As you do all of this, work over a bowl to catch the precious oyster liquor that is released.

Rating Oyster Knives

BOTH NOVICE AND EXPERIENCED SHUCKERS ATTEMPTED TO OPEN OYSTERS WITH 12 DIFFERENT BRANDS OF OYSTER knives plus a church-key can opener (which did not work—we couldn't open a single oyster with it). Models that opened the oysters easily, quickly, and safely received high marks. The knives are listed in order of preference. See www.americastestkitchen.com for up-to-date prices and mail-order sources for top-rated products.

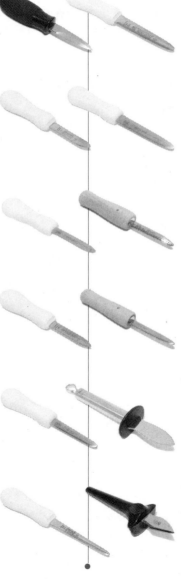

RECOMMENDED
Oxo Good Grips Oyster Knife
$6.99
Nonslip handle is comfortable, and the slightly angled blade and pointed tip were the easiest to work with.

RECOMMENDED
Dexter-Russell S121 Oyster Knife
$13.75
This 2³/₄-inch New Haven–style knife has a slightly angled tip that makes opening oysters a breeze.

RECOMMENDED
Mundial 5673 Oyster Knife
$8.00
Another good example of the New Haven style, with a slightly angled tip that we liked.

RECOMMENDED WITH RESERVATIONS
Dexter-Russell S126 Oyster Knife
$13.95
Nice, firm grip, and blade has pointed tip that's the perfect length. If the tip were angled, this knife would be perfect.

RECOMMENDED WITH RESERVATIONS
Mundial 5672 Oyster Knife
$8.00
Textured grip feels secure and the blade is thin and sharp. The tip on this Boston-style knife could be more pointed, though.

RECOMMENDED WITH RESERVATIONS
Dexter-Russell S120 Oyster Knife
$12.50
This Boston-style knife has a nice handle, but the 4-inch blade seems too long, and the tip is blunt and thick.

RECOMMENDED WITH RESERVATIONS
Dexter-Russell S137 Oyster Knife
$14.60
This Galveston-style knife has a good textured grip, but the 4-inch blade is thick and blunt.

RECOMMENDED WITH RESERVATIONS
Mundial 5674 Oyster Knife
$8.40
This Galveston-style knife has an excellent contoured grip, but the blade is too long and too thick.

RECOMMENDED WITH RESERVATIONS
Capco 3712 Oyster Knife
$3.95
This New Haven–style knife, with an angled tip, has a round wooden handle that testers found uncomfortable.

RECOMMENDED WITH RESERVATIONS
Capco 3711 Oyster Knife
$3.95
Testers found the round wooden handle on this knife to be uncomfortable. The blade is thin but not as effective as others.

NOT RECOMMENDED
Carlo Giannini Oyster Knife
$11.00
The slick handle is awkward to use, and the short, wide blade is not very effective.

NOT RECOMMENDED
Wüsthof Oyster Knife
$22.40
Awkward finger guard severely limits maneuverability, and the blade is too short.

MARYLAND CRAB CAKES

WHAT WE WANTED: A crab cake that tastes like the star ingredient, not the binder. The exterior would be crisp and brown, while the interior would be creamy and moist.

Good crab cakes taste first and foremost of sweet crabmeat. Too many restaurants serve crab-flecked dough balls. That's why the crab cake is especially suited to home cooking.

Great crab cakes begin with top-quality crabmeat. We tested all of the options and found the differences between them to be stark. Canned crabmeat is horrible; like canned tuna, it bears little resemblance to the fresh product. Frozen crabmeat is stringy and wet. Fresh pasteurized crabmeat is a bit watery but far better than the other options. Our top choice is fresh crabmeat, preferably "jumbo lump," which indicates the largest pieces and highest grade. This variety costs a couple of dollars more per pound than other types of fresh crab meat, but a 1-pound container is enough to make crab cakes for four; in our opinion, it's money well spent.

Fresh lump blue crab is available year-round but tends to be most expensive from December to March. The meat should never be rinsed, but it does need to be picked over to remove any shells or cartilage the processors may have missed.

Once we figured out what type of crab to use, our next task was to find the right binder. None of the usual suspects worked. Crushed saltines were a pain to smash into small-enough crumbs, potato chips added too much richness, and fresh bread crumbs blended into the crabmeat a little too well. We finally settled on fine dry bread crumbs. Their flavor is mild, and it's easy to mix them into the crabmeat. The trickiest part is knowing when to stop; crab cakes need just enough binder to hold them together but not so much that the filler overwhelms the seafood. We started out with ¾ cup crumbs but ended up reducing it down to just 2 tablespoons for our final recipe.

The other ingredients we adopted are also pretty basic.

Good, sturdy commercial mayonnaise (we like Hellmann's) keeps the crabmeat moist (a homemade blend can be too liquidy), and a whole egg, unbeaten, makes the crab, crumbs, and seasonings meld together both before and during cooking.

Classic recipes call for spiking crab cakes with everything from Tabasco to Worcestershire sauce, and those are both fine. But we've decided the best blend of tradition and trendiness is Old Bay seasoning combined with freshly ground white pepper and chopped fresh herbs.

Just as essential as careful seasoning is careful mixing. We found a rubber spatula works best, used in a folding motion rather than stirring. You want to end up with a chunky consistency. Those lumps aren't cheap.

We were pleased with our basic recipe on most fronts, but we still had trouble keeping the cakes together as they cooked. Our final breakthrough came when we tried chilling the shaped cakes before cooking. As little as half an hour in the refrigerator made an ocean of difference. The cold firmed up the cakes so that they fried into perfect plump rounds without falling apart. We found that formed cakes can be kept, refrigerated and tightly wrapped, for up to 24 hours.

We also tried different cooking methods. After baking, deep-frying, and broiling, we settled on pan-frying in a cast-iron skillet over medium-high heat. This method is fast and also gives the cook complete control over how brown and how crisp the cakes get. We first tried frying in butter, but it burned as it saturated the crab cakes. The ideal medium turned out to be plain old vegetable oil. It can be heated without burning and smoking, it creates a crisp crust, and it never gets in the way of the crab flavor.

WHAT WE LEARNED: Use fresh jumbo lump crabmeat, bind the crab with the minimum amount of dry bread crumbs, add mayonnaise for richness, and chill the shaped cakes thoroughly so they will hold their shape when cooked. Pan-frying in oil is the only way to cook crab cakes.

MARYLAND CRAB CAKES Serves 4

The amount of bread crumbs you add will depend on the crab-meat's juiciness. Start with the smallest amount, adjust the seasonings, then add the egg. If the cakes won't bind at this point, add more bread crumbs, 1 tablespoon at a time. If you can't find fresh jumbo lump crabmeat, pasteurized crabmeat, though not as good, is a decent substitute.

- 1 pound fresh jumbo lump crabmeat, picked over to remove cartilage or shell
- 4 scallions, green part only, minced (about ½ cup)
- 1 tablespoon chopped fresh herb, such as cilantro, dill, basil, or parsley
- 1½ teaspoons Old Bay seasoning
- 2–4 tablespoons plain dry bread crumbs
- ¼ cup mayonnaise
    Salt and ground white pepper
- 1 large egg
- ¼ cup all-purpose flour
- ¼ cup vegetable oil
    Lemon wedges or dipping sauce (recipes follows)

1. Gently mix the crabmeat, scallions, herb, Old Bay, 2 table-spoons bread crumbs, and mayonnaise in a medium bowl, being careful not to break up the lumps of crab. Season with salt and white pepper to taste. Carefully fold in the egg with a rubber spatula until the mixture just clings together. Add more crumbs if necessary.

2. Divide the crab mixture into four portions and shape each into a fat, round cake, about 3 inches across and 1½ inches high. Arrange the cakes on a baking sheet lined with waxed or parchment paper; cover with plastic wrap and chill at least 30 minutes. (The crab cakes can be refrigerated up to 24 hours.)

3. Put the flour on a plate or in a pie tin. Lightly dredge the crab cakes in the flour. Heat the oil in a large, preferably non-stick skillet over medium-high heat until hot but not smoking. Gently place chilled crab cakes in the skillet; pan-fry until the outsides are crisp and browned, 4 to 5 minutes per side. Serve immediately with lemon wedges or dipping sauce.

TARTAR SAUCE Makes generous ¾ cup

The classic sauce with seafood.

- ¾ cup mayonnaise
- 1½ tablespoons minced cornichons (about 3 large), plus 1 teaspoon cornichon juice
- 1 tablespoon minced scallion
- 1 tablespoon minced red onion
- 1 tablespoon capers, minced

Mix all of the ingredients in a small bowl. Cover and refrigerate until the flavors blend, at least 30 minutes. (The sauce can be refrigerated for several days.)

CREAMY CHIPOTLE CHILE SAUCE

Makes about ½ cup

The addition of sour cream makes this sauce richer than traditional tartar sauce. The chipotles add smoky and spicy flavors. This sauce is our favorite with crab cakes.

¼ cup mayonnaise

¼ cup sour cream

2 teaspoons minced canned chipotle chiles in adobo sauce

1 small clove garlic, minced or pressed through a garlic press

2 teaspoons minced fresh cilantro leaves

1 teaspoon juice from 1 lime

Mix all of the ingredients in a small bowl. Cover and refrigerate until the flavors blend, about 30 minutes. (The sauce can be refrigerated for several days.)

FOOD ANALYSIS: Mayonnaise

All eight brands that we tasted were also sent to a food lab and analyzed for oil, egg yolk, and total egg content, which are listed below as percentages of total weight. For comparison, the *Cook's* recipe for homemade mayo (with ¾ cup oil for each large egg yolk) contains 82.2 percent oil and 10.0 percent egg yolk (also 10.0 percent total egg).

Mayonnaise	Oil Content (%)	Egg Yolk Content (%)	Total Egg Content (%)
Hellmann's	78.8	2.9	8.8
Kraft	80.2	2.6	4.4
Trader Joe's	81.7	6.9	12.6
Hain	83.3	3.7	8.5
Kraft Miracle Whip	40.0	4.0	6.3
365	78.5	5.3	11.5
Whole Foods	85.3	5.7	11.5
Spectrum	81.8	2.0	9.6

TASTING LAB: Mayonnaise

MAYONNAISE MIGHT NOT BE THE MOST EXCITING ITEM IN the refrigerator, but given that it is a $1 billion industry, one thing is for certain: Americans buy the creamy, white condiment on a regular basis. And chances are that the jar in most refrigerators is either Hellmann's (sold under the Best Foods label west of the Rockies) or Kraft mayonnaise. Together they account for 78 percent of mayonnaise sales. But a product that dominates the market isn't necessarily the best product. With the surge in popularity of preservative-free, unsweetened, and healthier mayos, we were curious to see if any of these newer spreads could challenge the favorites.

Our taste test included seven nationally available brands of mayonnaise along with Kraft Miracle Whip. Even though the U.S. Food and Drug Administration does not recognize Miracle Whip as a real mayonnaise, we included in our tasting because of its resounding popularity (Kraft sells more Miracle Whip than it does regular mayonnaise). Why is Miracle Whip considered a salad dressing and not a mayonnaise? The FDA defines mayonnaise as an emulsified semi-solid food that is at least 65 percent vegetable oil by weight, at least 2.5 percent acidifying ingredient (vinegar and/or lemon juice) by weight, and contains whole eggs or egg yolks. Miracle Whip, which is also sweeter than regular mayo, weighs in with only 40 percent soybean oil. (Water makes up the difference.)

When you make mayonnaise at home, you whisk together egg yolks and seasonings (lemon juice, salt, mustard, etc.), then slowly whisk in oil until the mixture is emulsified. The ingredients for commercial mayonnaise are premixed and then processed through a colloid mill, a machine that breaks the mixture down into tiny, uniform droplets and creates a stable emulsion with a light consistency. The biggest variations in brands of commercial mayonnaise concern the amount and type of oil, the amount and type of egg (both whole eggs and yolks are used in most products), and flavorings.

The results of our tasting mirrored the sales in America's grocery stores. Hellmann's placed first and Kraft finished second. No other brand was even close. What explains such a strong showing by Hellmann's and Kraft, given that there are few ingredients in mayonnaise and that most commercial mayonnaises are manufactured in similar fashion? We sent the mayonnaises to our food lab to test for oil, egg content (both whole eggs and yolks), acidity, and total fat.

The first suspect that we thought might explain our tasting results also happens to be the first item on the list of ingredients: oil. The oil content for the group ranged from 78.5 percent to 85.3 percent, well above the minimum 65 percent required by the FDA. The only exception, of course, was Kraft Miracle Whip, which has about half the oil of commercial mayonnaise. Oil level alone didn't yield any revealing information (Whole Foods had the most oil and 365 had the least oil, and they both scored poorly).

With that in mind, we went back to the lab results to see if we could find another trend, but the information was ambiguous. Acidity levels were similar (with the exception of tangy Miracle Whip), and total fat did not vary much. As we pored over the data, we noticed that Hellmann's and Kraft both had a very low egg yolk content, while Trader Joe's, our third-place finisher, had the highest egg yolk content (making it the most similar of all the contestants to the test kitchen recipe for homemade mayonnaise).

At this point we turned to tasters' comments on their tasting sheets. A good mayonnaise will have clear egg flavor and a touch of acidity to offset the significant amount of fat from the added oil. Hellmann's was liked for having that balance, and Kraft was thought to be "flavorful but not overpowering." Still, what tasters seemed to like most about these products was that they tasted like "what mayonnaise should taste like." Paul Rozin, a noted food psychologist from the University of Pennsylvania, wasn't surprised by our findings. "A blind taste test isn't blind to your past," he said. "The participant's first exposure to a food will usually become the standard to judge all others against. In the case of mayonnaise, many people grew up eating Hellmann's and Kraft. People like familiar tastes."

Well, if it's all about Hellmann's and Kraft, which one should you buy? In a bread tasting, Kraft beat out Hellmann's by a negligible margin, but in macaroni salad trials, Hellmann's placed second (behind Trader Joe's), while Kraft came in fifth. We recommend Hellmann's, but the difference between the two contenders is not overwhelming. If you are interested in a preservative-free, unsweetened brand, try Trader Joe's. Our tasters liked its bold egg flavor, and, what's more, it's the least expensive brand we tested.

Finally, is it possible for a light mayo to be as flavorful as the full-fat original? We put five brands to the test: Kraft Light Mayonnaise, Hellmann's Light Mayonnaise, Miracle Whip Light Salad Dressing, Spectrum Light Canola Mayonnaise, and Nayonaise (a soy-based sandwich spread), all with a fat content of 3 to 5 grams per serving. To see if our tasters could tell the difference, we also threw the winner of the full-fat tasting into the mix (Hellmann's Real Mayonnaise, 11 grams of fat per serving). As in the mayonnaise tasting, we sampled these products spread on bread and tossed in macaroni salad.

The results? Last place went to Nayonaise. Tasters were unanimous in thinking it bore no resemblance to mayonnaise. One taster said it tasted like "a cross between pureed cottage cheese and tofu." Miracle Whip ("overly sweet" and "pasty") and Spectrum ("bland" and "artificial") didn't fare much better. Tasters thought Kraft was too sweet but made a fairly decent macaroni salad. Hellmann's Light came in second place, very nearly beating out the winner, Hellmann's Real Mayonnaise. Although the light version had a pastier texture than regular Hellmann's, the bright, balanced flavors were similar when tasted on bread, and the two products were virtually identical in the macaroni salad. Even our most finicky taster admitted that the salad made with Hellmann's Light was "not bad."

Rating Mayonnaises

NINETEEN MEMBERS OF THE *COOK'S ILLUSTRATED* STAFF TASTED THE MAYONNAISES TWO WAYS: SPREAD ONTO PLAIN white sandwich bread and tossed in a simple macaroni salad that contained only pasta, mayonnaise, onion, celery, parsley, and pickles. Mayonnaises are listed in order of preference based on their combined scores in the two tests. All mayonnaises are available in supermarkets nationwide.

HIGHLY RECOMMENDED
Hellmann's Real Mayonnaise (known west of the Rockies as Best Foods)
$3.29 for 32 ounces

The majority of tasters felt that Hellmann's was "what mayonnaise should taste like." It was liked for its bright, well-seasoned, and balanced flavors. Those classic flavors made macaroni salad that was mild, though some complained that it was "neutral tasting" and "not tangy enough."

HIGHLY RECOMMENDED
Kraft Real Mayonnaise
$2.99 for 32 ounces

This "flavorful but not overpowering" mayonnaise was another that panelists found to taste like "what you expect mayonnaise to taste like." Most liked its tangy, eggy flavors, while others called it "pleasant but bland" and "unremarkable."

HIGHLY RECOMMENDED
Trader Joe's Real Mayonnaise
$1.79 for 32 ounces

According to the label, this salty, tangy mayonnaise is "preservative free and unsweetened." It has bold egg and vinegar flavors that came through well in the macaroni salad. Tasters thought it had "a good mix of flavors" and "nicely balanced salt and vinegar."

RECOMMENDED
Hain Safflower Mayonnaise
$3.69 for 24 ounces

The only mayonnaise made with safflower oil, Hain was described as tart and sweet, with one taster calling it "clean and straightforward." Others thought it had "unbalanced sugar and vinegar."

RECOMMENDED
Kraft Miracle Whip Salad Dressing
$3.39 for 32 ounces

The panelists were divided into two distinctly different camps: Some thought this dressing had a nice, tangy flavor, while others said it tasted like "white BBQ sauce." Some liked it for making the macaroni salad taste "like store-bought salad"; others disliked it for the same reason. Everyone agreed on one thing: This brand was the sweetest of those tasted.

RECOMMENDED WITH RESERVATIONS
365 Mayonnaise
$1.99 for 32 ounces

While some tasters liked its assertiveness, most thought this brand was too tart, with excessive egg flavor. Those dominating flavors were better received in the macaroni salad, which tasters thought had a nice, balanced flavor and was "pleasantly tangy."

RECOMMENDED WITH RESERVATIONS
Whole Foods Canola Mayonnaise
$1.99 for 16 ounces

Tasters thought that this mayonnaise was "faintly eggy," with a "sharp vinegar flavor." The macaroni salad was bland, and when tasted on bread the mayonnaise was described as "dull" and "boring."

RECOMMENDED WITH RESERVATIONS
Spectrum Canola Mayonnaise
$2.99 for 16 ounces

This mayonnaise was judged to be the blandest of the bunch. The macaroni salad "wasn't vinegary enough" and "needed sharper flavor." When tasted plain, this brand was thought to be too sweet; it also "lacked depth" and had an off, musty taste.

Bridget shows Chris the secret to
great jambalaya—batch cooking the
ingredients in a Dutch oven.

NEW ORLEANS menu

Few cities are as much fun as New Orleans. The music is great, and the food is rightly famous. Jambalaya and bananas Foster are two of our favorite dishes from New Orleans. Although we've had delicious versions of both classics in New Orleans, our attempts to replicate these results in our Boston test kitchen have been less than successful.

Many jambalaya recipes yield soggy, sticky rice punctuated with dry pieces of chicken and rubbery shrimp. The dish demands a careful balance of flavor and attention to detail—as little as an extra quarter cup of liquid can ruin the rice.

Bananas Foster is high drama (the bananas and sauce are usually flambéed tableside in restaurants). That said, this dish has very few ingredients, and it seems like it should be easy to pull off at home (and it is). However, in our testing we found that most recipes are way too boozy. Yes, New Orleans is a party town, but we think you should be able to taste the fruit and the rich brown sugar sauce. We knew the test kitchen could figure out how to make this dish simply and safely at home.

JAMBALAYA

WHAT WE WANTED: Most recipes ask a lot from the home cook and provide no more than mushy rice, rubbery shrimp, and dry chicken in return. We wanted to make great jambalaya in one hour.

With chicken, sausage, shrimp, rice, tomatoes, and a laundry list of herbs and spices, jambalaya may sound more like a weekend project than a weeknight dinner. But done right, jambalaya is a one-pot meal that can be on the table in about an hour. Like New Orleans, the city from which it came, jambalaya has a combination of sweet, spice, and smoke that makes it a standout. But when poorly executed, jambalaya is no better than the Vegas version of New Orleans: an imposter with gummy rice, overcooked shrimp, and tough, dry chicken.

We started by testing a half-dozen recipes, all of which followed the same protocol: In a large Dutch oven, brown the chicken and remove; brown the sausage and remove; sauté the vegetables; add the cooking liquid, tomatoes, seasonings, and rice; return the chicken and sausage to the pot; and, finally, add the shrimp when the rice is about half done. Our conclusion? We wanted fluffier rice, more succulent chicken, more delicate shrimp, a more modest amount of tomato, and fresher flavors. In addition, we wanted a streamlined method that would bring the dish together more easily.

Although most jambalaya recipes call for a whole chicken cut up into parts, we opted to use chicken thighs instead. We knew this would save us the time it takes to cut up a chicken, but we also thought that using thighs, which are composed of relatively fatty dark meat, might solve the problem of dry chicken, as white meat is more apt to dry out.

We started by searing both sides of the chicken (with the skin on to provide extra fat to flavor the dish) in just 2 teaspoons of hot vegetable oil, then removed it from the pot, set it aside to cool, and peeled off the skin (chicken skin becomes soggy and unappetizing when cooked in liquid).

Rice and liquid went into the pot, followed by the chicken, and, after just 25 minutes, the chicken and rice were perfectly cooked through. But there was something clumsy about eating the chicken off the bone. For our next test, we tried cooking the chicken in exactly the same way, but instead of serving the thighs whole, we shredded them. Now the dish looked and tasted much more appealing, offering a bite of chicken in every forkful.

Next we took on the sausage. After comparing the classic choice, andouille, with tasso, chorizo, and linguiça, we decided that nothing tastes like andouille—a Cajun sausage that infuses the other ingredients in the pot with spice and smoke (see Tasting Lab: Pork Products, on page 56). We browned ¼-inch pieces of andouille in the chicken fat and then set them aside, planning to add them back to the pot along with the liquid, rice, and chicken.

Vegetables were the next item on our roster. Because the trio of minced bell pepper, onion, and celery is key to Cajun cooking, we included all three in our recipe. However, after sampling bitter-tasting green peppers (the classic choice) side by side with sweet red peppers, we unabashedly chose the reds. We also decided to add 2 tablespoons of minced garlic to give the jambalaya more punch. Most recipes use artificial-tasting garlic powder or too little fresh garlic to make much of an impact.

Now approaching our tenth test, we began to dread the task of chopping and mincing the vegetables and garlic. So we took out the food processor and gave the vegetables a whirl. What a difference! Not only did the food processor get the job done in seconds, but the vegetables were cut into smaller pieces than when hand-chopped and so sautéed more quickly in the pan and contributed more flavor.

For the rice, we started with 2 cups of water to 1 cup of long-grain white rice, the liquid ratio recommended on the back of the rice box. But our rice turned out gummy, and there wasn't enough to serve four to six people. We decided to increase the rice to 1½ cups, using only 2¼ cups water instead of the traditional 3 cups. The rice was now too dry, so we bumped up the water to 2¾ cups. This rice was the perfect compromise between fluffy pilaf (too light for jambalaya) and sticky risotto (too heavy).

Most jambalaya recipes call for homemade chicken stock, but we found that canned chicken broth was fine given the other strong flavors in the dish. We also tried combining clam juice with the chicken broth, hoping that it might bring out the sweetness of the shrimp. Although the clam juice/chicken broth duo was pleasing, the rice needed more punch. To boost the flavor of the rice, we substituted ¼ cup of tomato juice (from a can of diced tomatoes) for an equal amount of water. Now the rice was perfect: flavorful and cohesive without being gummy, heavy, or sticky.

The next step was to find a way to keep the shrimp tender and sweet. We seared the shrimp in a hot pan, set them aside, and then added them back to the jambalaya when the chicken was halfway done. This batch was a failure. The shrimp were tough, and they took on a smoky flavor from the searing that provided little contrast with the andouille. For the next test, we added the raw shrimp just five minutes before the chicken and rice were finished. After removing the lid, we could see that the shrimp were perfectly cooked to a blushing pink, still tender and succulently sweet.

This jambalaya was smoky and sweet, spicy and savory, with perfectly tender shrimp, moist chicken, flavorful sausage, and rice cooked just so. You'd never have guessed we were eating it in our Boston test kitchen and not on Bourbon Street.

WHAT WE LEARNED: For the best flavor, use chicken thighs and andouille sausage. Cook the rice in a mixture of canned chicken broth, clam juice, and the juice from canned tomatoes. Add the shrimp once the rice is nearly done so that they don't overcook.

CHICKEN AND SHRIMP JAMBALAYA
Serves 4 to 6

Because andouille varies in spiciness, we suggest tasting a piece of the cooked sausage and then adjusting the amount of cayenne in the jambalaya to suit your taste. If you can't find andouille, try tasso, chorizo, or linguiça; if using chorizo or linguiça, consider doubling the amount of cayenne. The onion, celery, bell pepper, and garlic can be chopped by hand instead of in the food processor. The shrimp don't need to be deveined, but you can do so if you prefer. If you're serving only four people, you may choose to skip the shredding step and serve each person one piece of chicken on the bone.

1   medium onion, peeled, ends trimmed, and quartered lengthwise
1   medium rib celery, cut crosswise into quarters
1   medium red bell pepper, stem removed, seeded, and quartered lengthwise
5   medium cloves garlic, peeled
2   teaspoons vegetable oil
4   bone-in, skin-on chicken thighs
8   ounces andouille sausage, halved lengthwise and cut into ¼-inch pieces
1½ cups (10 ounces) long-grain white rice
1   teaspoon salt
½   teaspoon minced fresh thyme leaves
¼   teaspoon cayenne pepper (see note)
1   can (14.5 ounces) diced tomatoes, drained, ¼ cup juice reserved
1   cup bottled clam juice
1½ cups low-sodium chicken broth
2   large bay leaves
1   pound medium-large shrimp (31 to 35 shrimp per pound), shelled
2   tablespoons minced fresh parsley leaves

1. In food processor, pulse the onion, celery, red pepper, and garlic until chopped fine, about six 1-second pulses, scraping down the sides of the bowl once or twice. Do not over-process; the vegetables should not be pureed (see the photo on page 58).

2. Heat the oil in a large heavy-bottomed Dutch oven over medium-high heat until shimmering but not smoking. Add the chicken, skin-side down, and cook until golden brown, about 5 minutes. Using tongs, turn the chicken and cook until golden brown on the second side, about 3 minutes longer. Transfer the chicken to a plate and set aside. Reduce the heat to medium and add the andouille; cook, stirring frequently, until browned, about 3 minutes. Using a slotted spoon, transfer the sausage to a paper towel–lined plate and set aside.

3. Reduce the heat to medium-low, add the vegetables, and cook, stirring occasionally and scraping the bottom of the pot with a wooden spoon, until the vegetables have softened, about 4 minutes. Add the rice, salt, thyme, and cayenne; cook, stirring frequently, until the rice is coated with fat, about 1 minute. Add the tomatoes, reserved tomato juice, clam juice, chicken broth, bay leaves, and browned sausage to the pot; stir to combine. Remove and discard the skin from the chicken; place the chicken, skinned-side down, on the rice. Bring to a boil, reduce the heat to low, cover, and simmer for 15 minutes. Stir once, keeping the chicken on top, skinned-side down. Replace the cover and continue to simmer until the chicken is no longer pink when cut into with a paring knife, about 10 minutes more; transfer the chicken to a clean plate and set aside. Scatter the shrimp over the rice, cover, and continue to cook until the rice is fully tender and the shrimp are opaque and cooked through, about 5 minutes more.

4. While the shrimp are cooking, shred chicken (see the illustration above). When the shrimp are cooked, discard the bay leaves; off heat, stir in the parsley and shredded chicken, and serve immediately.

TECHNIQUE: Shredding Chicken

Hold one fork in each hand, with the prongs down and facing toward each other. Insert the prongs into the chicken meat and gently pull the forks away from each other, breaking the meat apart and into long, thin strands.

TASTING LAB: Pork Products

ANDOUILLE, A SEASONED SMOKED SAUSAGE, IS THE MOST authentic choice for jambalaya, with tasso, also known as Cajun ham, a close second. (Tasso is a lean chunk of highly seasoned pork or sometimes beef that is cured and then smoked.) Because andouille and tasso can sometimes be hard to find in supermarkets, we tested the two against chorizo and linguiça (Spanish and Portuguese sausages, respectively), which are more widely available.

After making a batch of jambalaya with each sausage, tasters agreed there ain't nothing like the real thing. Andouille was perfection. It had intense heat and the bold flavor of garlic and herbs, and it imparted a noticeable yet manageable amount of smokiness to the dish. While well-seasoned and flavorful, tasso was ultrasmoky and had a strange, gristly texture that no one liked. Linguiça was bland and added little heat to the finished product; chorizo was slightly more piquant but still dull.

Andouille is clearly the best choice for jambalaya, but we wondered if all andouille were created equal. So we gathered five brands available nationally in supermarkets and by mail-order and put them to the test. Here are the results, with brands listed in order of preference:

Chef Paul's regular andouille (sometimes called "mild") took the crown, one vote shy of a sweep. Its "smoky," "rich," and "earthy" flavors and "balanced heat level" are the perfect accompaniment to the other big flavors in jambalaya.

Jacob's andouille was big, dark, and jerky-esque, with a strange muscled grain. Despite its aesthetic shortcomings, Jacob's andouille was our runner-up. It had a "deeply smoky," almost sweet flavor.

Chef Paul's hot andouille was so spicy it masked the sausage's other flavors.

Poche's andouille had little flavor to offer, and its texture was "chewy," "rubbery," and "tough."

North Country Smokehouse andouille was excessively spicy and had a strange "tinny" flavor.

The conclusion is clear: If you can find Chef Paul's regular andouille, buy it.

GETTING IT RIGHT:
The Best Pork for Jambalaya

Some traditional jambalaya recipes call for tasso, while others use andouille sausage. We tested both. Tasters thought tasso had great flavor, but they did not like its gristly texture and found its smokiness overpowering. Andouille is a better choice for jambalaya: spicy, bold, smoky, and perfectly textured.

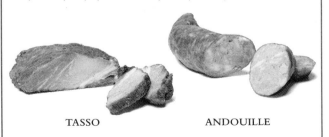

TASSO   ANDOUILLE

TASTING LAB: Vegetable Broth

WE DON'T LIKE CANNED VEGETABLE BROTH. THAT WAS our assumption, at least, when we began this tasting. Usually thin, metallic, and overly sweet and/or salty, canned vegetable broth was a good idea in theory, we thought, but when it came time to prepare vegetable soups, sauces, and risottos (as well as dishes such as jambalaya), we instinctively reached for canned chicken broth.

But after one too many arguments around the editorial table about making vegetable dishes completely meat-free, we decided to review our preconceptions. We gathered nine popular brands of packaged vegetable broth and tasted them in three different applications: warmed, in an enriched vegetable soup stock, and in asparagus risotto.

The winner of the straight broth tasting, Swanson, was praised for its "nice sweet-sour-salty balance," though some tasters noted the "barely perceptible vegetable flavor." Second-place Better than Bouillon was deemed "good, nicely flavored," and "very tasty," but many found it "very sour," with "strong metallic flavors." Coming in at the bottom of the tasting was Kitchen Basics, which lost points for a sweet molasses flavor that one taster likened to "honey tea." It's no surprise that top-ranked Swanson had one of the highest sodium levels, with 970 milligrams per cup, compared with 330 milligrams per cup for Kitchen Basics, the lowest sodium level. Salt is perceived as flavorful, whereas the less salty broths were deemed bland and flavorless.

Our winning vegetable broth had a mean score of 5.3 out of 10—perfectly average, but not exactly high praise. That's OK—we're not advocating drinking straight vegetable broth. But how would canned vegetable broth fare in a recipe where it was not the leading lady but instead a strong supporting character?

For the second test, we enriched the canned vegetable broth with roasted vegetables and garlic. We pitted the winner, Swanson, and the loser, Kitchen Basics, of our straight broth tasting against each other. Swanson eked out a win,

with a saltier flavor that most tasters preferred. Kitchen Basics was praised by some as "flowery," "earthy," and "more vegetal," though it was those same qualities that some tasters listed as negatives in the plain broth tasting. Neither soup was bad; each had different flavor characteristics that worked in this application.

In the asparagus risotto, the results were surprising. We threw in what we thought would be a ringer—Swanson reduced-sodium chicken broth, the winner of our canned chicken broth tasting—to compete against Swanson and Kitchen Basics vegetable broths. Swanson vegetable broth was the tasters' favorite, praised as "well balanced," with "round, full flavors." The darkest colored of all the original broths in the tasting, Kitchen Basics, was liked by some for its "rich and hearty" flavor, though most tasters found the "muddy" color distracting, giving this broth a last-place finish. The chicken broth finished a strong second.

Though there was a clear winner and loser in the straight broth tasting, the varied results in other applications lead us to believe that the differences between the broths are subtle. If you are using canned vegetable broth in a recipe with lots of other strong flavors, it probably doesn't matter which broth you use. If the flavors of the broth are going to be more up front, as they are in a simple brothy soup or risotto, you should probably use Swanson. And if you are sensitive to salt, you may want to check the sodium level before you buy. As for our jambalaya recipe, you could use vegetable broth instead of chicken broth—it won't make a huge difference.

GETTING IT RIGHT:
Properly Cut Vegetables

Using the pulse button on the food processor yields finely chopped vegetables in seconds. Don't overprocess or puree the vegetables—they should remain in distinct pieces.

Rating Vegetable Broths

EIGHTEEN MEMBERS OF THE *COOK'S ILLUSTRATED* STAFF TASTED ALL THE BROTHS WARMED BUT OTHERWISE STRAIGHT from the package. We also tested our favorite and least favorite broths in a hearty vegetable soup and an asparagus risotto. The broths are listed in order of preference based on their scores in the plain broth tasting. Note that when the broths were used in soup or risotto, some (but not all) of these differences faded away. All brands are sold in supermarkets nationwide.

RECOMMENDED
Swanson Vegetable Broth
$.99 for 14.5 ounces
970mg sodium per cup
This top-rated broth had the most flavor, though some tasters found it too salty.

RECOMMENDED WITH RESERVATIONS
Better than Bouillon Vegetable Base
$4.99 for 8 ounces (enough to make 38 cups of broth)
560mg sodium per cup
Most tasters liked this thick liquid base, deeming it "good, nicely flavored, and salty"; some tasters nonetheless found it "sour" and "wheaty."

RECOMMENDED WITH RESERVATIONS
Herb-Ox Granulated Vegetable Bouillon Cubes
$2.39 for 3.33 ounces (enough to make 25 cups of broth)
980mg sodium per cup
With the highest level of sodium, this powdered base earned one taster's comment: "Tastes like a veggie-flavored salt lick."

RECOMMENDED WITH RESERVATIONS
Morga Instant Vegetable Broth
$7.99 for 5 ounces (enough to make 35 cups of broth)
520mg sodium per cup
The prettiest of the bunch, with flakes of parsley floating in a pale gold broth, this powdered base produced broth that was "pale and nondescript," though some found it "quite vegetabley."

RECOMMENDED WITH RESERVATIONS
Health Valley Vegetable Broth
$2.39 for 32 ounces
360mg sodium per cup
While some tasters found the flavor "cardboardy," others praised the "natural," "oniony" taste.

RECOMMENDED WITH RESERVATIONS
College Inn Garden Vegetable Broth
$1.19 for 13.75 ounces
780mg sodium per cup
"Pretty good," wrote one taster about this supermarket standby, but others found it "too sour" and "very bland."

RECOMMENDED WITH RESERVATIONS
Pacific Foods Organic Vegetable Broth
$2.99 for 32 ounces
530mg sodium per cup
Though it had "some depth and richness," many tasters found it "too strong and manufactured tasting."

RECOMMENDED WITH RESERVATIONS
Hain Vegetable Broth
$2.15 for 14.5 ounces
480mg sodium per cup
Several tasters detected a "thick, nutmeg flavor," with a scent like "allspice and clove." Other tasters found this broth to be "very tomatoey," with "almost no flavor at all."

RECOMMENDED WITH RESERVATIONS
Kitchen Basics Vegetable Stock
$2.39 for 32 ounces
330mg sodium per cup
This last-place broth, deemed "supersweet," with an earthy vegetal flavor, had the lowest sodium content of all the brands.

BANANAS FOSTER

WHAT WE WANTED: A quick, reliable dessert with tender yet not mushy bananas and a flavorful yet not boozy sauce.

Bananas Foster is a classic, simple dessert that hails from New Orleans. The dish is often made tableside at restaurants (or at home, for guests) in a chafing dish. Bananas are cooked in a caramel-type sauce of melted butter and brown sugar, then flambéed with rum, brandy, banana liqueur, or a combination of liquors. The luscious mixture is then spooned over scoops of vanilla ice cream.

Although bananas Foster is quick and simple, with very few ingredients, it can go wrong. Sometimes the bananas are overcooked and mushy. The sauce can be too thin, overly sweet, or taste too strongly of alcohol.

To begin our testing, we first settled on the amounts of dark brown sugar and butter. Sauces made with high ratios of butter to sugar were thin, greasy, and not sweet enough, while too little butter made a sauce that was sugary and sticky. Four tablespoons of butter to ½ cup of brown sugar created a slightly thickened, buttery (but not greasy) sauce.

We pulled brandy, rum, and banana liqueur from the test kitchen liquor cabinet to determine which would be best for this dish. We chose to use dark rum; its full-bodied flavor was a perfect foil for the sweetness of the bananas and brown sugar.

The recipes we had uncovered called for anywhere from 1 tablespoon to a whopping 2 cups of spirits. We started with 1 tablespoon of dark rum and worked our way up to 4 tablespoons, which was just enough to impart a definite rum flavor but not so much as to turn the dessert into an after-dinner drink. We decided to add 1 tablespoon of the rum to the sauce and use the rest to flambé the bananas.

WHAT WE LEARNED: Use the proper ratio of brown sugar to butter so the sauce will be nice and thick but not too sweet. Rum is the best liquor for this dish, and a little cinnamon and lemon zest add complexity to the sauce.

BANANAS FOSTER Serves 4

While the bananas cook, scoop the ice cream into individual bowls so they are ready to go once the sauce has been flambéed. Before flambéing, make sure to roll up long shirt sleeves, tie back long hair, turn off the exhaust fan (otherwise the fan may pull the flames up), and turn off any lit burners (this is critical if you have a gas stove).

- 4 tablespoons unsalted butter
- ½ cup packed (3½ ounces) dark brown sugar
- 1 cinnamon stick
- 1 strip lemon zest, 2 inches long by about ½ inch wide
- 4 tablespoons dark rum
- 2 large, firm, ripe bananas, peeled and halved lengthwise and then crosswise
- 1 pint vanilla ice cream, divided among four bowls

1. Place the butter, sugar, cinnamon stick, lemon zest, and 1 tablespoon rum in a heavy-bottomed 12-inch skillet. Turn the heat to medium-high and cook, stirring constantly, until the sugar dissolves and the mixture is thick, about 2 minutes.

2. Reduce the heat to medium and add the bananas to the pan, spooning some sauce over each piece. Cook until the bananas are glossy and golden on the bottom, about 1½ minutes. Turn the bananas and continue cooking until very soft but not mushy or falling apart, about 1½ more minutes.

> **FOOD FACT: Bananas**
> Americans consume an average of 28 pounds of bananas every year. With three medium bananas weighing about a pound, the average American eats about 84 bananas every year.

3. Remove the skillet from the heat. Add the remaining 3 tablespoons rum and wait until the rum has warmed slightly, about 5 seconds. Wave a lit match over the pan until the rum ignites, shaking the pan to distribute the flame over the entire pan. When the flames subside (this will take 15 to 30 seconds), divide the bananas and sauce (discarding the cinnamon stick and lemon zest) among the four bowls of ice cream and serve.

EQUIPMENT CORNER: Ice Cream Scoops

WE'VE ALL STRUGGLED WITH AN INTRACTABLE PINT OF rock-hard ice cream. That's where a good ice cream scoop comes in handy; it can release even hard-frozen ice cream from bondage. We gathered 10 readily available scoops and dipped our way through 20 pints of vanilla to find the best one. We tested three basic types of scoop: classic, mechanical-release (or spring-loaded), and spade-shaped. Prices ranged from $3.99 to $22.

Classic ice cream scoops sport a thick handle and curved bowl. They can be used by lefties and righties with equal comfort. There are a few variations on the theme; among the classic scoops we purchased, one had a pointed "beak" scoop, another offered a "comfort grip" rubber handle, and another contained a self-defrosting liquid. Testers were unanimous in assigning first place—in both its own category and overall—to the Zeroll Classic Ice Cream Scoop ($22). Its thick handle was comfortable for large and small hands, and its nonstick coating and self-defrosting liquid (which responds to heat from the user's hand) contributed to perfect release, leaving only traces of melted cream inside the scoop. The defrosting fluid and the elegantly curved bowl allowed the scoop to take purchase immediately, curling a perfect scoop with minimal effort. Only one caveat: Don't run this scoop through the dishwasher, as it will lose its magical defrosting properties.

Coming in second among the other classic scoops tested was the Oxo Beak Scoop ($11.99). The beak point dug into ice cream with ease, and the ice cream curled up

nicely. Our only minor quibble was the short handle, which forced testers with larger hands to choke up close to the head. If price is a concern, you might consider this model.

Mechanical-release scoops come in various sizes and operate with a spring-loaded, squeezable handle (or thumb trigger) that connects to a curved steel lever inside the scoop. When the handle or lever is released, the ice cream pops out in a perfectly round ball. Although we frequently use a mechanical-release scoop to measure out even portions of cookie dough and muffin batter, we found these scoops to be less than ideal when it came to ice cream. They are designed for right-handed users only, and their thin, straight-edged handles were distinctly uncomfortable when considerable pressure was applied. Of the four models we tested, none was worthy of recommendation.

Spades, with their flat, paddle-type heads, are useful when you need to scoop a lot of ice cream quickly, say, for an ice cream cake or sandwiches, but they are too big to fit into pint containers. If you make frozen desserts frequently or need to work your way through multiple gallon-size containers of ice cream, a spade might be for you. Our preferred model, made by the same manufacturer as our winning scoop, is the Zeroll Nonstick Ice Cream Spade ($19.60).

BEST ICE CREAM SCOOPS
The Zeroll Classic Ice Cream Scoop (left) was the favorite model tested. If you need to scoop a lot of ice cream for an ice cream cake, you might consider the Zeroll Nonstick Ice Cream Spade (right), but this tool is too big to fit into pint containers.

Chris quizzes Bridget about the names of Italian pasta shapes and their literal translations. This one seems pretty easy—shells anyone?

FREEDOM FROM
red sauce

Tired of the same old marinara sauce? Tomatoes and pasta are a classic (and delicious) pairing, but sometimes you want a change. Vegetable sauces, like the two included in this chapter, one with mushrooms and one with broccoli rabe, are appealing options—at least in theory.

We've had plenty of mushroom pasta dishes that seem like little more than noodles and cream of mushroom soup. We were confident that we could create something special if we started with good, fresh (not canned) mushrooms.

Pasta with broccoli rabe is common in southern Italy. When made in this country, it's often too oily or the broccoli rabe is too wilted and mushy. We wanted to investigate this classic (and very simple) recipe and figure out how to make it right.

PASTA WITH MUSHROOMS

WHAT WE WANTED: We wanted a woodsy, creamy sauce that would enhance the pasta and be ready to serve as quickly as possible.

Transforming an ordinary box of pasta and a package of mushrooms into something special is weeknight cooking at its best: quick, simple, and delicious. But that doesn't mean that it's easy. Mushrooms easily turn out slippery, pale, and watery, not unlike those packed in a tin can. When this dish is done right, however, the mushrooms are woodsy, distinctive, and full-flavored. We'd need to figure out how to cook them properly and then choose a sauce that would marry them best with pasta.

We soon discovered that there is no definitive recipe for this dish; cookbook and Internet research turned up limitless options. We chose four recipes representing the most common mushroom sauce preparations. Pasta with mushrooms simmered in tomato sauce was unanimously dismissed; the delicate mushrooms took a back seat to the tomatoes, and we all wanted a stronger mushroom presence. A sauce made with rehydrated dried mushrooms had intense mushroom flavor, but tasters wanted something fresher and lighter in color (the dried mushrooms had stained the pasta an unappealing dark brown). An Alfredo-like recipe of mushrooms cloaked in a dense cream sauce showed promise—the milky sauce nicely offset the earthy mushrooms. The problem was that it was too heavy and rich, curbing tasters' appetites after just a few forkfuls. A simple topping of sautéed mushrooms, garlic, and herbs made an intoxicating sauce but left the pasta itself dry and bland. If we could find a way to combine the intense flavor of these sautéed mushrooms with a lightened version of the cream sauce, we'd be in business.

Clearly, our next step was to choose the mushrooms. Not willing to shell out $18 per pound on exotic mushrooms, we limited ourselves to cultivated mushrooms that could be purchased for modest prices at the supermarket. The list included white button mushrooms, portobellos, cremini, and shiitakes. A quick taste test confirmed the obvious: White button mushrooms have the least flavor of the group. We also found that portobellos are tasty, but they darken sauces unless the gills are removed, a tedious process. We settled on a combination of cremini and shiitakes; tasters enjoyed the rich and meaty nature of cremini, while shiitakes have a hearty flavor and a pleasant chewy texture.

From experience, we knew the basics of mushroom cookery: They leach liquid a few minutes after exposure to high heat and then, after the moisture evaporates, they begin to brown. We cranked the heat on the stove and threw in a chunk of butter, followed by very thinly sliced mushrooms. The mushrooms quickly absorbed all of the butter and burned slightly. We started anew, adding a good drizzle of olive oil to reduce the risk of burning, but keeping some butter for flavor and slicing the mushrooms thicker. This time they cooked the way we expected them to, ending up lightly browned.

We turned to other variables to refine our technique. Salt draws moisture out of vegetables, and we suspected it might do the same with mushrooms. In a side-by-side test, mushrooms salted at the onset of sautéing released more liquid than an unsalted batch, which was a bonus. The more juices that were released, the more deeply the mushrooms browned (dry food always browns more readily than moist). Because shiitakes contain more moisture than cremini, we gave them a two-minute head start in the pan. (Note that it is possible to overcook mushrooms; we learned to keep them in the skillet just until they are browned; any longer and they become tough and rubbery.) A traditional skillet is our usual choice for sautéing, but we wondered if a nonstick pan was better for delicate mushrooms. A head-to-head test proved that the traditional skillet was best because the resulting fond (the browned bits on the bottom of the pan)

We knew from the first recipes we tested that we wanted a light creamy sauce. We removed the mushrooms from the skillet and made a quick pan sauce by deglazing the pan with chicken broth and then tested a few additions. Sour cream caused the sauce to separate, and it was too tangy. A swirl of heavy cream, however, did the trick, creating a smooth, mild sauce. However, with ½ cup chicken broth and ½ cup cream, the pasta turned dry within minutes of saucing. We added more chicken broth in ¼ cup increments and ended up using quite a bit more than we had expected; 1¼ cups creates a saucy, but not soupy consistency. An acidic element (alcohol, citrus, or vinegar) is often the key ingredient in a recipe—it sharpens and refines competing flavors. We tried small amounts of white wine, vermouth, Marsala, sherry, Madeira, balsamic vinegar, and lemon juice, the latter being the test kitchen favorite.

Chunky sauces pair well with stubby, molded pasta shapes that have crevices in which the sauce can nestle. We found the best choices to be an unusual, frilly, flower-shaped pasta called campanelle and the readily available farfalle (bow ties). Rather than reducing the sauce and tossing it with the pasta, we simmered al dente pasta in the sauce for a couple of minutes. This way, the pasta and sauce became fully integrated, with the pasta absorbing a good amount of flavor. The sauce also thickens slightly during this step as the pasta leaches starch. As with many pasta dishes, this one is improved by a handful of grated Parmesan cheese, a speck of black pepper, and chopped fresh parsley.

contribute flavor to the sauce. (Nonstick skillets produce little fond.) When we added dried porcinis, the resulting sauce was richer, but rehydrating dried mushrooms complicated this otherwise simple recipe and the fresh shiitakes and cremini on their own were just fine.

Garlic and thyme have a natural affinity with mushrooms, so we added generous amounts of both, saving other herbs for variations. Adding the thyme after the mushrooms were fully cooked preserved its pungency. We also experimented with a variety of choices from the onion family and settled on mild shallots, which didn't compete with the mushrooms.

WHAT WE LEARNED: Use a combination of shiitake and cremini mushrooms for optimum flavor and texture. Cook the mushrooms in a skillet (not in the sauce) to improve their flavor. Create the pasta sauce by adding chicken broth and cream to the browned bits left in the skillet after the mushrooms have been removed. Use a pasta shape that cradles the mushrooms.

PASTA WITH SAUTÉED MUSHROOMS AND THYME Serves 4 as a main course or 6 to 8 as side dish

Vegetable broth can be substituted for the chicken broth to make this dish vegetarian. If you add the pasta to the boiling water at the same time the cremini go into the skillet, the pasta and sauce will finish at the same time.

	Salt
1	pound campanelle or farfalle pasta
2	tablespoons unsalted butter
2	tablespoons extra-virgin olive oil
3–4	large shallots, chopped fine (about 1 cup)
3	medium cloves garlic, minced or pressed through garlic press (about 1 tablespoon)
10	ounces shiitake mushrooms, stems discarded, caps wiped clean and sliced ¼ inch thick
10	ounces cremini mushrooms, wiped clean and sliced ¼ inch thick
1	tablespoon plus 1 teaspoon minced fresh thyme leaves
1¼	cups low-sodium chicken broth
½	cup heavy cream
1	tablespoon juice from 1 lemon
	Ground black pepper
2	ounces finely grated Parmesan (1 cup)
2	tablespoons minced fresh parsley leaves

1. Bring 4 quarts water to a rolling boil, covered, in a stockpot; add 1 tablespoon salt and the pasta, stir to separate, and cook until just shy of al dente. Drain and return the pasta to the stockpot.

2. Meanwhile, heat the butter and oil over medium heat in a 12-inch skillet until foaming. Add the shallots and cook, stirring occasionally, until softened and translucent, about 4 minutes. Add the garlic and cook until fragrant, about 30 seconds. Increase the heat to medium-high; add the shiitakes and cook, stirring occasionally, for 2 minutes. Add the cremini and ½ teaspoon salt; cook, stirring occasionally, until the moisture released by the mushrooms has evaporated and the mushrooms are golden brown, about 8 minutes. Stir in the thyme and cook 30 seconds. Transfer the mushrooms to a bowl and set aside. Add the chicken broth to the skillet and bring to a boil, scraping up the browned bits on the bottom of the pan; off heat, stir in the cream, lemon juice, and salt and pepper to taste.

GETTING IT RIGHT: Mushroom Cooking 101

1. Raw mushrooms initially soak up all the fat in a pan. Don't give in to temptation and add more oil and butter.

2. After several minutes, the mushrooms begin to release a significant amount of liquid, which will evaporate with continued cooking.

3. The liquid has evaporated and the mushrooms turn golden brown. They are done. If the mushrooms continue to cook, they become dry and rubbery.

3. Add the mushrooms, chicken broth/cream mixture, cheese, and parsley to the pasta in the stockpot. Toss over medium-low heat until the cheese melts and the pasta absorbs most of the liquid, about 2 minutes; serve immediately.

VARIATIONS

PASTA WITH MUSHROOMS, PEAS, AND CAMEMBERT

Follow the recipe for Pasta with Sautéed Mushrooms and Thyme, omitting the thyme and adding 1 cup frozen peas, thawed, to the skillet along with the chicken broth; substitute 6 ounces Camembert cut into ½-inch cubes (do not remove the rind) for the Parmesan, and 2 tablespoons finely chopped chives for the parsley.

PASTA WITH MUSHROOMS, PANCETTA, AND SAGE

Cook 4 ounces pancetta, cut into ¼-inch cubes, in 2 tablespoons olive oil, stirring occasionally, until lightly browned and crisp, about 6 minutes. Using a slotted spoon, transfer the pancetta to a paper towel-lined plate. Follow the recipe for Pasta with Sautéed Mushrooms and Thyme, substituting the fat in the skillet for the butter and olive oil and an equal amount minced fresh sage leaves for the thyme; add the pancetta to the pasta along with the sautéed mushrooms.

SCIENCE:
Why Are Shiitake Stems So Tough?

FORGET TO REMOVE THE STEMS FROM SHIITAKES BEFORE cooking, and you'll spend a good part of the dinner hour picking inedible, chewy bits from your plate. Seasoned cooks know to either discard the stems or save them for stock, but most learned this lesson the hard way. Why are shiitake stems so tough while white button and other cultivated mushrooms have tender, edible stems?

Many of the experts we contacted suggest that a sturdy stem with a tightly packed cellular structure evolved over

---

FOOD FACT: Mushrooms

Of the more than 5,000 known varieties of mushroom, about 100 are poisonous. Every year, about 9,000 cases of mushroom poisoning are reported to the American Association of Poison Control Centers.

---

time to support the shiitake's wide cap, which can range from the size of a quarter to 5 inches in diameter. Two experts—Judy Rogers, mycologist and executive secretary of the North American Mycological Association, and David Ellis, associate professor of mycology at the University of Adelaide in Australia—concur that the way shiitakes are grown also contributes to the sturdy composition of their stems.

Shiitakes are cultivated on either natural hardwood logs or on man-made sawdust logs. Mushrooms grown this way are called wood-decomposing fungi, a family of mushrooms in which tough, woody stems are characteristic. For these mushrooms, woody stems are a necessity; a tender, flimsy stem would not be able to establish growth in the tough environment of a log. (This hardiness amounts to more long-lived mushrooms, too; shiitakes exist in nature for several weeks without rotting and are slower to rot in the refrigerator than white mushrooms.)

Common white button mushrooms, on the other hand, are raised in composted and sterilized manure. These materials decompose quickly by nature, and the mushrooms grown in them are significantly more delicate with respect to texture and longevity; all but the very ends of their stems are perfectly edible.

EQUIPMENT CORNER: Herb Choppers

IS THERE AN EASIER WAY TO ACHIEVE FINELY MINCED PILES of parsley, basil, and mint than rocking a chef's knife back and forth a hundred times? We tested several kinds of herb choppers and mincers to find out.

The first gadgets tested were herb mills, a stainless

steel mill by KüchenProfi and a plastic mill by Zyliss. Each has a hopper in which you put the herbs and a series of small blades that chop them when you turn a hand crank. For all of the herb choppers tested we used basil, parsley, rosemary, and garlic. The seemingly solid KüchenProfi gagged on the herbs, and they had to be pinched and pried out of the hopper. The Zyliss didn't choke, but it could not mince either. Shreds of leafy herb and shards of garlic would be more like it.

Next in line were herb rollers, which depend on a row of wheel-like blades that are pushed back and forth over the item to be minced by means of a handle (as in the Oxo we tested) or some sort of protective casing (as in the International Cutlery). Rollers are comfortable, easy to use, and fast—so fast that they crushed and bruised the parsley and basil leaves into a slimy green mush in about 30 seconds. The rosemary and garlic didn't fare much better, being reduced to odd-shaped bits and pieces, and the garlic tended to stick to the blades.

The most newfangled entry in our lineup was the Rev'n Chef by Chef'n, a round plastic case with a ripcord inside that, when pulled and released, turned a blade that tore up everything we gave it into large, rough, unevenly

sized pieces. And more pulls of the ripcord didn't help much. A beat-up clove of garlic looked much the same after 75 pulls as it did after 25.

The only worthwhile alternative to a chef's knife was the mezzaluna, a cutting tool named for its half-moon shape that has been in use for hundreds of years. We tried three styles: one with a single blade and a single handle meant to be used in a wooden bowl, one with a single blade and two handles, and one with two blades and two handles. The first of these minced well but was a bit awkward to use as well as labor-intensive. The latter pair, each with a handle on either end, let you get a rocking motion going that cut through herbs—especially tough, woody rosemary—cleanly and quickly. The double-bladed mezzaluna was faster (usually 30 to 60 seconds faster than the single blade when producing ¼ cup of minced herbs), but it was tough on the basil, bruising it badly. Neither mezzaluna could mince garlic as perfectly as a garlic press.

What do we recommend? If your knife skills aren't quite what you'd like them to be, try a single-bladed, two-handled mezzaluna. It's not only effective, it's fun. And purchase one with a 7-inch blade rather than a 6-inch blade. The 7-inch really rocks.

Rating Herb Choppers

WE TESTED EIGHT HERB CHOPPERS BY MINCING BASIL, PARSLEY, ROSEMARY, AND GARLIC WITH EACH DEVICE. The choppers are listed in order of preference based on their performance in these tests as well as their ease of use and design. See www.americastestkitchen.com for up-to-date prices and mail-order sources for the top-rated product.

RECOMMENDED
Henckels 7-Inch Single-Blade Mezzaluna
$17.99
With a handle at either end, this tool rocked through piles of herbs—especially tough, woody rosemary—cleanly and quickly.

RECOMMENDED WITH RESERVATIONS
Schaaf Double-Blade Mezzaluna
$55.00
With two blades, this mezzaluna works especially fast, but it was tough on the basil, bruising it badly.

RECOMMENDED WITH RESERVATIONS
KüchenProfi Single-Blade Mezzaluna (with Wooden Bowl)
$31.95
With just a single handle that sits on top of the blade, this tool is designed for use inside a wooden bowl. Although it produces nicely minced herbs, testers found it awkward to use.

NOT RECOMMENDED
Zyliss Herb Mill
$12.95
Although better than the KüchenProfi mill, this plastic mill shredded herbs rather than mincing them.

NOT RECOMMENDED
KüchenProfi Herb Mill
$14.99
This seemingly solid stainless steel tool gagged on every herb.

NOT RECOMMENDED
Oxo Rolling Herb Mincer
$6.50
The parsley and basil were badly bruised. The garlic was oddly chopped and stuck to the blade.

NOT RECOMMENDED
International Cutlery Rolling Mincer/Vegetable Cutter
$12.50
Turned delicate herbs into a slimy green mush in seconds but could not mince them.

NOT RECOMMENDED
Chef'n Rev'n Chef Herb Processor
$19.74
The ripcord design is intriguing, but the results—roughly torn leaves—weren't very impressive. A beat-up garlic clove looked much the same after 75 pulls as it did after 25.

PASTA WITH BROCCOLI RABE AND SAUSAGE

WHAT WE WANTED: A quick sauce that yields properly cooked broccoli rabe in a moist and flavorful (but not oily) pasta dish.

Southern Italy is renowned for its pasta dishes, and one of these is the combination of broccoli rabe (also known as *rapini*, *cime de rape*, *rape*, *raab*, and *brocoletti*) and orecchiette, which loosely translates as "little ears." With the addition of sausage, this pasta dish from Puglia, located in the heel of Italy's boot, quickly makes a satisfying meal.

A search of Italian cookbooks turned up a number of recipes for orecchiette with broccoli rabe. After several tests, we identified some common problems with these recipes. The first was that they used three pans to cook a dish with just a handful of ingredients. The second was that the sauces were bland. The third was that the pasta was dry. We wanted to rectify these problems and streamline the cooking process without sacrificing flavor.

The first issue we tackled was the cooking procedure. Most recipes call for blanching the broccoli rabe in one pot, sautéing the sausage in another pan, and, finally, cooking the pasta in a third pot. Thinking we could eliminate the pot in which the rabe was blanched, we tried several cooking methods.

Our first thought was to add the rabe directly to the pot with the pasta. While this worked, we found it hard to judge the proper time to put the rabe in the pot; it was difficult to cook through both ingredients without overcooking either. We next tried cooking the rabe in the pan in which we cooked the sausage. Sautéing the rabe in the hot pan along with the sausage did not work; some of the rabe was fully cooked while other pieces were undercooked. It was obvious that the rabe required moist-heat cooking, such as steaming, rather than dry-heat cooking (sautéing). So we tried adding a small amount of liquid to the hot pan after we browned the sausage. Because the pan was quite hot, it created a fair amount of steam. By covering the pan, we captured this steam to cook the rabe. This method of pan-steaming turned out to be the solution. We eliminated the extra pot and still had consistently cooked pasta and rabe.

Now that we had mastered a cooking method for the rabe, we focused on the problems of bland flavor and dry pasta. The blanching of the rabe in previous tests resulted in loss of flavor, and our new cooking method seemed to alleviate this problem, but not fully. We therefore decided to steam the rabe in chicken broth rather than water. This did the trick. As the broth reduced, it added richness and depth to the dish. In addition, it moistened the pasta without making it oily or heavy.

Tasters preferred spicy Italian sausage to the sweet version, and most wanted even more heat (remember, the pasta is bland), so we added some hot red pepper flakes. A hefty dose of garlic (we ended up adding six cloves) was also a must. A dusting of grated Parmesan finished off the dish nicely.

WHAT WE LEARNED: Brown the sausage, add the broccoli rabe and chicken broth, and then cover the pan to steam the rabe with the other sauce ingredients. Besides eliminating the need for a separate pot to blanch the rabe, this cooking method won't wash away the pleasantly bitter flavor of this Italian vegetable.

FOOD FACT: Pasta Consumption

The average American eats about 20 pounds of pasta every year. Italians consume three times as much. Italian authorities have recorded more than 500 different pasta shapes, from common shapes such as spaghetti and linguine to the exotic, such as gemelli (the name means "twins" and refers to the two identical strands of pasta that are twisted together to form this shape) and orecchiette (which means "little ears" and refers to their curved bowl shape, which resembles the human ear).

ORECCHIETTE WITH BROCCOLI RABE AND SAUSAGE Serves 4

If you prefer to use broccoli instead of broccoli rabe in this recipe, use 2 pounds broccoli cut into 1-inch florets and increase the cooking time by several minutes. If you prefer a less spicy dish, use sweet Italian sausage.

Salt
1 pound orecchiette
8 ounces hot Italian sausage, casings removed
6 medium cloves garlic, minced or pressed through a garlic press (2 tablespoons)
½ teaspoon hot red pepper flakes
1 bunch broccoli rabe (about 1 pound), trimmed and cut into 1½-inch lengths (see the illustrations below)
½ cup low-sodium chicken broth
1 tablespoon extra-virgin olive oil
½ cup (1 ounce) grated Parmesan cheese

1. Bring 4 quarts water to a rolling boil in a large pot. Add 1 tablespoon salt and the pasta, stir to separate, and cook until al dente. Drain and return the pasta to the pot.

2. While the pasta is cooking, cook the sausage until browned in a large nonstick skillet over medium-high heat, breaking it into ½-inch pieces with a wooden spoon, about 3 minutes. Stir in the garlic, red pepper flakes, and ½ teaspoon salt. Cook, stirring constantly, until the garlic is fragrant and slightly toasted, about 1½ minutes. Add the broccoli rabe and chicken broth, cover, and cook until the broccoli rabe turns bright green, 2 minutes. Uncover and cook, stirring frequently, until most of the broth has evaporated and the broccoli rabe is tender, 2 to 3 minutes.

3. Add the sausage-rabe mixture, oil, and cheese to the pot with the pasta and toss to combine. Serve immediately.

TASTING LAB:
Boutique Extra-Virgin Olive Oil

ONE OF THE ENDURING MYTHS ABOUT PURCHASING food products, especially gourmet foods, is that price and

---

TECHNIQUE: Preparing Broccoli Rabe

1. The thick stalk ends of broccoli rabe should be trimmed and discarded. Use a sharp knife to cut off the thickest part (usually the bottom 2 inches) of each stalk.

2. Cut the remaining stalks and florets into bite-sized pieces about 1 ½ inches long.

packaging indicate something about the quality of the product. Sometimes this is true. A boutique brand of chocolate such as Scharffen Berger is indeed much better than Baker's, at least in the opinion of our tasters. But this is by no means any sort of universal rule. In fact, price and packaging often have virtually nothing to do with quality. Take the case of premium extra-virgin olive oils.

Many food experts make a big deal about pricey olive oils. To find out if these boutique oils (all made in relatively small quantities) are worth those big bucks, we purchased eight different bottles of expensive extra-virgin olive oils, with prices ranging from $27 to $80 per liter. We also threw in Da Vinci extra-virgin olive oil, winner of a previous tasting of supermarket oils and priced at just $8.50 per liter.

The cheap supermarket oil, Da Vinci, took fourth place, and the two least expensive boutique oils (Antica Azienda Raineri,

$32 per liter, and Columela-Hojiblanca, $27 per liter) took first and second place. One of the most expensive oils, Salvatore Mirisola ($80 per liter) came in next to last. How can this be?

All of the oils were, in fact, pretty good. To earn the designation "extra-virgin," an olive oil must meet a number of criteria and be free from defects. Technically, all of the oils we tasted were fine. They were, however, very different. Some were grassy and mild, others sharp and peppery. In large measure, personal taste will determine favorites. Our panel did object to flavor traits in several oils, especially those that were especially aggressive, but these oils might be delicious when drizzled over grilled vegetables or a spicy soup. In the end, you have to taste for yourself and find an oil that you like. Of course, choosing an inexpensive supermarket oil (such as Da Vinci) is a good option and will save you the bother and expense of holding your own tasting.

Rating Boutique Extra-Virgin Olive Oils

ELEVEN TASTERS SAMPLED NINE BRANDS OF OLIVE OIL STRAIGHT FROM CUPS. THE LINEUP INCLUDED EIGHT EXPENSIVE oils sold in gourmet shops and Italian markets as well as our favorite supermarket olive oil, Da Vinci. The olive oils are listed in order of preference based on scores from the tasting. See www.americastestkitchen.com for up-to-date prices and mail-order sources for top-rated products.

RECOMMENDED
Antica Azienda Raineri Extra-Virgin Olive Oil
$31.99 for 1 liter

This top-rated oil, which hails from northern Italy, won points for its "smooth, easy flavor" and "fruity finish."

RECOMMENDED
Columela-Hojiblanca Extra-Virgin Olive Oil
$13.49 for 500 ml ($26.98 per liter)

This "very dark green" oil was praised for its "strong olive taste" and "fruity aroma." Some, however, found it "rubbery" and "very mild." This Spanish oil was the cheapest boutique oil that we tested and offers a good value.

RECOMMENDED
Olio Verde Extra-Virgin Olive Oil
$21.99 for 500 ml ($43.98 per liter)

"Smells like freshly cut grass," wrote one taster. Most approved of the "grassy" flavor, though some found it "metallic" and "sour."

RECOMMENDED
Da Vinci Extra-Virgin Olive Oil
$8.49 for 1 liter

The least expensive of the bunch, this supermarket staple won points for its "light, natural olive flavor" and "fruity, mild aroma," although several tasters found it "bland." You certainly can't go wrong for the price.

RECOMMENDED WITH RESERVATIONS
Frantoio Galantino Extra-Virgin Olive Oil
$40.00 for 500 ml ($80.00 per liter)

With its "light taste" and "very faint olive aroma," most tasters found this oil "uninteresting" and "unremarkable."

RECOMMENDED WITH RESERVATIONS
Piccolo Molino-Dolce Verde Extra-Virgin Olive Oil
$24.99 for 500 ml ($49.98 per liter)

Though many tasters found this oil "full-bodied" and "grassy," several described it as "bitter," with a "slightly medicinal aroma."

RECOMMENDED WITH RESERVATIONS
Exentia Extra-Virgin Olive Oil
$32.99 for 500 ml ($65.98 per liter)

Tasters found this oil "medicinal tasting," with a "pine-forest scent" and a "hit of pepper at the back of the throat."

RECOMMENDED WITH RESERVATIONS
Salvatore Mirisola Extra-Virgin Olive Oil
$40.00 for 500 ml ($80.00 per liter)

Detractors of this oil likened the flavor to "paint thinner" and "motor oil." Kinder tasters simply found it "flat" and "not very fruity."

RECOMMENDED WITH RESERVATIONS
Rendola Extra-Virgin Olive Oil
$34.99 for 750 ml ($46.55 per liter)

"Like furniture polish," wrote one taster of this "mineral-ly," "woody," and "one-dimensional" oil.

Chris drains pasta before it's al dente—it will finish cooking in the oven with the four cheeses.

QUICK pasta

CHAPTER 7

Everyone knows pasta is quick. That's one of the reasons Americans (and Italians) love it. Some pasta dishes, however, take a considerable amount of time to prepare. We wanted to take two such recipes—bolognese, a slow-simmering tomato and meat sauce, and baked four-cheese pasta—and figure out how to make them less than an all-day—or even all-afternoon—affair.

True bolognese simmers lazily for half a day on the stove. The real deal is rich and delicious. Many short-cut recipes are nothing more than browned ground beef and tomatoes. These recipes may be quick, but they have none of the finesse or complexity of the original.

Baked four-cheese pasta often yields overcooked pasta in a stringy, curdled sauce. Given all the work involved (grating and shredding all those cheeses, making the sauce, cooking the pasta, and then baking the casserole for half an hour or more), this dish should be better.

BOLOGNESE SAUCE

WHAT WE WANTED: A lush, decadent, unctuous meat sauce ready in less than an hour rather than the usual three hours.

Bolognese gets its big flavor from the braising of ground meat and softened vegetables in slowly reducing liquids—most often milk and wine—and then, finally, tomatoes. The process is often given as much as three hours, but the result is a bold, meaty pasta sauce with sweet resonance and ultra-tender meat.

Just try to short-cut the process and you'll be left with bits of rubbery meat floating in a subpar tomato sauce. We wanted to make bolognese weeknight-friendly. If perfect, it would be everything that we expected from the long-cooked sauce, but we wanted this sauce on table in less than an hour.

There is not exactly a wealth of "quick" bolognese recipes. We found only two, one of them no more than ground beef and jarred tomato sauce. We decided to take the test kitchen's favorite bolognese sauce, which uses the traditional slow-cooking technique, and try to pare the cooking time. Armed with a pitifully small amount of knowledge, we went into the test kitchen, started the clock, and began to cook.

The original test kitchen recipe calls for equal parts ground beef, pork, and veal, and, unfortunately, we found all three to be necessary. We were, however, able to avoid buying several packages of meat by purchasing the trusty super-market "meatloaf mix" made from equal parts of each. To boost the flavor of our quick-cooked sauce, we tested additions such as pancetta, prosciutto, and even porcini mushrooms. Prosciutto was out owing to its salty flavor and big price tag, but pancetta was a perfect fit—a little went a long way. Porcini mushrooms had such an amazingly beefy impact on the sauce that we just couldn't refuse them.

Vegetables were next under the microscope. Our favorite three-hour recipe called for celery, carrots, and onion, but we found celery could go by the wayside. Garlic found a home, but tasters thought herbs were distracting. Either butter or olive oil can be used to sauté the vegetables, but we chose butter for its richer flavor.

Tomatoes add sweetness to the sauce, and their juice is used to braise the meat. We tried all kinds—crushed, diced, sauce—and in the end liked the juicier whole canned tomatoes best because they come packed in so much juice. To provide some deeper, slow-cooked tomato flavor, we added some tomato paste.

Now hold on a minute! Our goal was to shorten this recipe, not to complicate it with an epic ingredient list. We could already count at least 10 minutes of prep time. The solution? We whipped out a food processor and used it to chop just about everything: carrots, onions, mushrooms, tomatoes, even the pancetta. Only the garlic was spared from the food processor (it never chopped up completely), but a garlic press made quick work of that step, too. Now what had been taking 10 minutes was being accomplished in less than two.

In a true bolognese, liquids are reduced slowly one at a time to tenderize the meat and develop the characteristic sweetness of the sauce. Because we didn't have all day, we had to find a quicker method. To sweeten the sauce, we added a pinch of sugar. But it wasn't until we started thinking outside the box and tried sweeter white wines like Riesling and Gewürztraminer in place of the traditional dry Sauvignon Blanc that our sauce achieved the proper sweetness. We even tried a white Zinfandel—the "other" white wine—often snubbed for its grapey-sweet flavor. Guess what? It worked beautifully.

Now all we had to do was get around that slow simmer. Sure, cooking everything at a raging boil was an obvious option, but the meat (which was still tough) became downright springy when boiled. Our trick for minimizing cooking time was to reduce the wine on the side in a separate skillet; 1¼ cups went down to 2 tablespoons in 20 minutes.

Now meaty, sweet, and fast, this 45-minute sauce had everything going for it—well, almost. The meat still presented itself in the form of little rubber pellets, and no sauce, however good, could mask that.

A hint of an answer came when we thought about the milk. In Italian cooking, milk and meat are often braised together, producing very tender results. What if we soaked the ground meat in milk before cooking? We tried it. After sautéing the vegetables, we added the milk-soaked meat to the hot pan and watched as the meat disintegrated into grainy, mushy bits. OK, this was not the perfect solution, but at least the meat wasn't tough.

Next we added the meat directly to the pan along with the milk (no soaking). Same as before, the meat fell apart into bits, but this time, no mush. Sure that we were on the right track, the next time we added the meat to the pan we quickly broke it into large pieces with a wooden spoon (letting it spend no more than a minute in the pan alone) and then added the milk. We stirred the two together to break up the meat and—success! This meat was incredibly tender. Actually, it made sense. As any fan of steak tartare will tell you, raw ground meat is already tender. Because we weren't browning the meat, it never obtained that tough crust that takes hours upon hours to return to its tender state.

So we had done it. Making no sacrifices in flavor, texture, or our pride, we had made a sauce that was rich and meaty, sweet and bold, luxuriously tender, and on the table in 45 minutes.

WHAT WE LEARNED: Beef up the flavor of the ground meats with pancetta and dried porcini mushrooms. Use the food processor to prepare the ingredients. Don't brown the meat and cook it through in milk. Use a sweet white wine and sugar to achieve the flavor traditionally imparted by prolonged simmering.

WEEKNIGHT BOLOGNESE SAUCE Serves 4 to 6

Sweet white wines such as Gewürztraminer, Riesling, and even white Zinfandel work especially well in this sauce. To obtain the best texture, be careful not to break up the meat too much when cooking it with the milk in step 4. With additional cooking and stirring, it will continue to break up. Just about any pasta shape complements this meaty sauce, but spaghetti and linguine are the test kitchen favorites. If using pancetta that has been sliced thin rather than cut into 1-inch chunks, reduce the processing time in step 3 from 30 seconds to about 5 seconds.

½	ounce dried porcini mushrooms
1¼	cups sweet white wine (see note)
½	small carrot, peeled and chopped into rough ½-inch pieces (about ½ cup)
½	small onion, chopped into rough ½-inch pieces (about ¼ cup)
3	ounces pancetta, cut into 1-inch pieces
1	can (28 ounces) whole tomatoes with juice
1½	tablespoons unsalted butter
1	small clove garlic, minced or pressed through a garlic press (about ½ teaspoon)
1	teaspoon sugar
1¼	pounds meatloaf mix (or equal amounts 80 percent lean ground beef, ground veal, and ground pork)
1½	cups whole milk
2	tablespoons tomato paste
	Salt
⅛	teaspoon ground black pepper
1	pound pasta
	Grated Parmesan cheese, for serving

1. Cover the porcini mushrooms with ½ cup water in a small microwave-safe bowl; cover the bowl with plastic

Transfer the vegetables to a small bowl. Process the softened porcini until well ground, about 15 seconds, scraping down the bowl if necessary. Transfer the porcini to the bowl with carrot and onion. Process the pancetta until the pieces are no larger than ¼ inch, 30 to 35 seconds, scraping down the bowl if necessary; transfer to a small bowl. Pulse the tomatoes with juice until chopped fine, six to eight 1-second pulses.

4. Heat the butter in a 12-inch skillet over medium-high heat; when the foaming subsides, add the pancetta and cook, stirring frequently, until well browned, about 2 minutes. Add the carrot, onion, and porcini; cook, stirring frequently, until the vegetables are softened but not browned, about 4 minutes. Add the garlic and sugar; cook until fragrant, about 30 seconds. Add the ground meats, breaking the meat into 1-inch pieces with a wooden spoon, about 1 minute. Add the milk and stir to break the meat into ½-inch bits; bring to a simmer, reduce the heat to medium, and continue to simmer, stirring to break up the meat into small pieces, until most of the liquid has evaporated and the meat begins to sizzle, 18 to 20 minutes. Stir in the tomato paste and cook until combined, about 1 minute. Add the tomatoes, reserved porcini soaking liquid, ¼ teaspoon salt, and pepper; bring to a simmer over medium-high heat, then reduce the heat to medium and simmer until the liquid is reduced and the sauce is thickened but still moist, 12 to 15 minutes. Stir in the reduced wine and simmer to blend the flavors, about 5 minutes.

wrap, cut a few steam vents with a paring knife, and microwave on high power for 30 seconds. Let stand until the mushrooms have softened, about 5 minutes. Using a fork, lift the porcini from the liquid and transfer to a second small bowl; pour the soaking liquid through a paper towel–lined mesh strainer. Set the porcini and the strained liquid aside.

2. Bring the wine to simmer in a 10-inch nonstick skillet over medium heat; reduce the heat to low and simmer until the wine is reduced to 2 tablespoons, about 20 minutes. Set the reduced wine aside.

3. Meanwhile, pulse the carrot in a food processor until broken down into rough ¼-inch pieces, about ten 1-second pulses. Add the onion; pulse until the vegetables are broken down into ⅛-inch pieces, about ten 1-second pulses.

5. Meanwhile, bring 4 quarts water to a rolling boil, covered, in a stockpot. Add 1 tablespoon salt and the pasta, stir to separate, and cook until al dente. Drain, reserving ¼ cup pasta cooking water, and return the pasta to the stockpot. Add 2 cups sauce and 2 tablespoons pasta water to the pasta; toss well, adding the remaining pasta water, if necessary, to help distribute the sauce. Divide the pasta among individual bowls and top each portion with about ¼ cup remaining sauce. Serve immediately, passing the Parmesan separately.

SCIENCE DESK:
Why Does Milk Make Meat Tender?

BROWNING ADDS FLAVOR, BUT IT ALSO CAUSES THE PROTEIN molecules in ground meat to denature (unwind). As the proteins unwind, they link up to create a tighter network and squeeze out some of the water in the meat. Long simmering allows some of that liquid to be reabsorbed. But if you skip the browning and cook the meat in milk (or any other liquid) at the outset, you limit the temperature of the meat to about 212 degrees (browning occurs in dry heat and at higher temperatures). As a result, meat cooked in milk does not dry out and toughen but remains tender. This means you can simmer the sauce just until the liquid has reduced to the right consistency rather than waiting for the meat to soften.

TASTING LAB: Tomato Paste

A CELEBRATED INGREDIENT IN ITS POST–WWII HEYDAY, when the long-cooked tomato sauce was king, tomato paste has fallen by the wayside as discerning cooks have favored fresher, more brightly flavored tomato sauces. These days, our use of tomato paste comes with a more conservative hand. We reserve it for occasions when a deep tomato flavor is warranted, such as in a chili or our slow-simmering bolognese sauce.

Given this limited use, we wondered if it mattered which brand we used. To find out, we went to local supermarkets to gather seven brands for a tasting: six American brands in small cans and an Italian import in a toothpaste-like tube. We asked tasters to try the tomato paste as is—no cooking, no sauce.

Every brand did well in providing a big tomato punch, but the Amore brand, imported from Italy, was the unanimous winner owing to its "intense" and "fresh" flavor. Amore is the only tomato paste tested that contains fat, which could account for its bigger flavor. The Amore brand

also scored points because of its tube packaging. Just squeeze out what you need and store the rest in the refrigerator. No fuss, no waste.

How did the flavor of this tomato paste hold up in cooking? We tasted it, along with Hunt's, the brand that came in last, in our bolognese recipe, to see if we could detect a difference. We did indeed pick out (and downgrade) the distinct dried herb flavor of the Hunt's paste. On the other hand, we liked the sauce made with the Amore tomato paste for its deep, round tomato flavor.

GETTING IT RIGHT: The Pan Matters

When the sauce is simmered in a Dutch oven, it doesn't reduce quickly enough, and the consistency is watery (left). When the sauce is simmered in a 12-inch skillet, the texture is thicker, and the sauce reduces more quickly (right).

COOKED IN DUTCH OVEN   COOKED IN SKILLET

GETTING IT RIGHT: Pancetta

Just like bacon, pancetta comes from the belly of the pig, but it has a very different flavor. American bacon is cured with salt, sugar, and spices and then smoked. Pancetta is not smoked, and the cure does not contain sugar—just salt, pepper, and, usually, cloves. As a result, pancetta has a richer, meatier flavor than bacon. Pancetta is rolled tightly, packed in casing, and then sliced thin or thick as desired.

Rating Tomato Pastes

ELEVEN MEMBERS OF THE *COOK'S ILLUSTRATED* STAFF TASTED SEVEN TOMATO PASTES STRAIGHT FROM THE CAN OR TUBE. Tasters were asked to evaluate each sample for intensity of tomato flavor, freshness, sweetness, and saltiness. The tomato pastes are listed in order of preference based on tasters' scores. All brands are sold in supermarkets nationwide.

HIGHLY RECOMMENDED
Amore Italian Tomato Paste
$2.49 for 4.5 ounces

Tasters described this paste-in-a-tube as "intense" and "fresh." The only sample tasted that contains fat. No-fuss, no-waste packaging is appealing.

RECOMMENDED
Redpack California Tomato Paste
$.60 for 6 ounces

This familiar brand finished a distant second. Panelists commented on its "sweet," "bold" flavor, but it was not as fresh tasting as the winner.

RECOMMENDED
Cento Tomato Paste
$.50 for 6 ounces

"Good tomato flavor" was the general consensus about this brand, which showed fairly well.

RECOMMENDED WITH RESERVATIONS
Rienzi Tomato Paste
$.75 for 6 ounces

This Italian brand elicited mixed reviews. Some tasters praised its "fruity" flavor, but quite a few thought it was "unbalanced" and "too strong."

RECOMMENDED WITH RESERVATIONS
Muir Glen Organic Tomato Paste
$.99 for 6 ounces

Tasters were not impressed with this brand, which has scored well in our tastings of other tomato products. "OK" and "dull" were typical comments.

NOT RECOMMENDED
Contadina Tomato Paste
$.50 for 6 ounces

This brand was deemed "bland" and "lifeless," and it tied for last place in the scoring. Tasters had no positive comments about this sample.

NOT RECOMMENDED
Hunt's Tomato Paste
$.99 for 6 ounces

Tasters demonstrated a real aversion to the "fishy," "herbal" flavors in this paste. Many tasters picked up strong hits of dried herbs.

BAKED FOUR-CHEESE AND PASTA CASSEROLE

WHAT WE WANTED: We set out to make a creamy casserole with great flavor, properly cooked pasta, and a crisp bread-crumb topping—all in record time.

Pasta ai quattro formaggi, the classic Italian pasta dish with four cheeses and heavy cream, is a great idea in theory. In reality, however, it often turns into an inedible mess: tasteless, stringy, heavy, and greasy. We wanted to discover what made this dish great in the first place, delivering a pasta dinner that was silky smooth and rich but not heavy—a grown-up, sophisticated version of macaroni and cheese with Italian flavors.

The cheese was first up for consideration, in terms of both flavor and texture. We were committed to Italian cheeses, but this barely diminished our choices; research turned up varying combinations and amounts (1 cup to 6½ cups cheese per 1 pound pasta) of Asiago, Fontina, Taleggio, Pecorino Romano, mascarpone, mozzarella, Gorgonzola, Parmesan, and ricotta. Initial testing reduced the scope quickly: Mascarpone and ricotta added neither flavor nor texture, and Asiago was bland. Pasta tossed with mozzarella was gooey and greasy, whereas Taleggio was not only difficult to obtain but also made the pasta too rich and gluey. After testing numerous combinations of the remaining cheeses, tasters favored a 2½-cup combination of Italian Fontina (which is creamier and better-tasting than versions of this cheese made elsewhere), Gorgonzola, Pecorino Romano, and Parmesan.

The techniques of heating the cheeses and cream together and of adding the cheeses separately to the hot pasta both produced nasty messes. Each attempt caused the cheeses to curdle, separate, and/or turn greasy. Some recipes solved this problem by beginning with a *besciamella* (known in French as a *béchamel*). This basic white sauce starts by cooking butter and flour and then adding milk or cream. The cheeses can then be added to the white sauce, which, because of the flour, will not separate. As we soon found out, the white sauce kept the sauce from breaking, but it also had an unintended side effect: The flavor of the cheeses was diminished. The solution was to radically reduce the amount of flour and butter to two teaspoons each instead of the usual three to four tablespoons each. Now the sauce was silky and smooth and allowed the flavor of the cheeses to stand out.

After making this recipe a half-dozen more times, we were bothered by the notion of heating the cheeses ahead of time with the béchamel. We wanted to cook the cheeses as little as possible for the best flavor, so we put the shredded/crumbled/grated cheeses in a large bowl and added the hot pasta and hot béchamel. A quick toss melted the cheeses without cooking them. We had now both simplified the recipe and produced a cleaner tasting, more flavorful dish.

We found that the sauce worked best with tubular pasta shapes (penne was ideal), which could be coated inside and out. Many recipes suggest cooking the pasta fully and then baking it for 30 minutes. This approach not only consumes extra time but is a recipe for mushiness. To keep the pasta from overcooking, we found it necessary to drain the pasta several minutes before it was al dente and then minimize the baking time. Just seven minutes in a 500-degree oven (the pasta heats more quickly in a shallow baking dish) is enough to turn the pasta and sauce into a casserole.

Many recipes add a bread crumb topping that browns and crisps in the oven. We tried this casserole with and without the crumb topping, and tasters unanimously voted for the topping. It contrasts nicely with the creamy pasta and helps balance the richness of the sauce.

WHAT WE LEARNED: To preserve the fresh flavor of the cheeses, don't cook them along with the sauce and use just a tiny bit of roux (cooked butter and flour) to stabilize the sauce. Undercook the pasta and then bake the casserole in a very hot oven for just seven minutes to prevent mushiness.

CREAMY BAKED FOUR-CHEESE PASTA

Serves 4 to 6 as main course, 6 to 8 as side dish

To streamline the process, prepare the bread-crumb topping and shred, crumble, and grate the cheeses while you wait for the pasta water to come to a boil. This dish can be on the table in about half an hour.

bread-crumb topping

3–4	slices white sandwich bread with crusts, torn into quarters
¼	cup (½ ounce) grated Parmesan cheese
¼	teaspoon salt
⅛	teaspoon ground black pepper

pasta and cheese

4	ounces Italian Fontina cheese, shredded (about 1 cup)
3	ounces Gorgonzola cheese, crumbled (about ¾ cup)
½	cup (1 ounce) grated Pecorino Romano cheese
¼	cup (½ ounce) grated Parmesan cheese
1	pound penne
	Salt
2	teaspoons unsalted butter
2	teaspoons all-purpose flour
1½	cups heavy cream
¼	teaspoon ground black pepper

1. FOR THE TOPPING: Pulse the bread in a food processor until the mixture resembles coarse crumbs, about ten 1-second pulses (you should have about 1½ cups). Transfer to a small bowl; stir in the Parmesan, salt, and pepper. Set the mixture aside.

2. FOR THE PASTA: Adjust an oven rack to the middle position and heat the oven to 500 degrees.

3. Bring 4 quarts water to a rolling boil in a stockpot. Combine the cheeses in a large bowl; set aside. Add the pasta and 1 tablespoon salt to the boiling water; stir to separate the pasta. While the pasta is cooking, melt the butter in a small saucepan over medium-low heat; whisk the flour into the butter until no lumps remain, about 30 seconds. Gradually whisk in the cream, increase the heat to medium, and bring to a boil, stirring occasionally; reduce the heat to medium-low and simmer 1 minute to ensure that the flour cooks. Stir in ¼ teaspoon salt and pepper; cover the cream mixture to keep hot and set aside.

4. When the pasta is almost al dente (when bitten into, the pasta should be opaque and slightly underdone at the very center), drain about 5 seconds, leaving the pasta slightly wet. Add the pasta to the bowl with the cheeses; immediately pour the cream mixture over, then cover the bowl with foil or a large plate and let stand 3 minutes. Uncover the bowl and stir with a rubber spatula, scraping the bottom of the bowl, until the cheeses are melted and the mixture is thoroughly combined.

5. Transfer the pasta to 13 by 9-inch baking dish, then sprinkle evenly with the reserved bread crumbs, pressing down lightly. Bake until the topping is golden brown, about 7 minutes. Serve immediately.

VARIATIONS

BAKED FOUR-CHEESE PASTA WITH TOMATOES AND BASIL

Follow the recipe for Creamy Baked Four-Cheese Pasta, adding one 14½-ounce can diced tomatoes, drained, to the pasta along with the cream mixture and stirring in ¼ cup coarsely chopped fresh basil leaves just before transferring the pasta to the baking dish.

BAKED FOUR-CHEESE PASTA WITH PROSCIUTTO AND PEAS

Follow the recipe for Creamy Baked Four-Cheese Pasta, omitting the salt from the cream mixture and adding 4 ounces prosciutto, chopped, and 1 cup frozen peas to the pasta along with the cream mixture.

Classic Gazpacho **page 16**

Chicken Provençal **page 152**

Tomato and Mozzarella Tart **page 22**

Chicken and Shrimp Jambalaya **page 55**

Wilted Spinach Salad with Warm Bacon Dressing **page 11**

87

Pan-Roasted Chicken Breast with Sage-Vermouth Sauce **page 133**

88

Beef Chili with Kidney Beans **page 32**

Pad Thai **page 194**

90

Charcoal-Grilled Filet Mignon **page 158** with Lemon, Garlic, and Parsley Butter **page 159**

Stir-Fried Pork, Green Beans, and Red Bell Pepper with Gingery Oyster Sauce **page 186**

Charcoal-Grilled Steak Tips **page 172**

Maple-Glazed Pork Roast **page 114**

94

Wild Rice Pilaf with Pecans and Dried Cranberries **page 117**

Chicken with 40 Cloves of Garlic **page 144**

Stir-Fried Beef and Broccoli with Oyster Sauce **page 182**

Pot Roast with Root Vegetables **page 102**

98

POT roast

Pot roast can be the ultimate comfort food or a huge waste of time. When it comes out right, pot roast is tender, succulent, and richly flavored. When it turns out wrong, the meat is dry, gray, tough, and full of fat and sinew.

Good pot roast begins at the market. Some cuts will never make good pot roast. But there's more to pot roast than careful shopping. We've found that technique matters just as much as the cut. We bought a dozen kinds of roasts and tested as many cooking methods to develop our foolproof recipe for pot roast. Green beans are a natural accompaniment to pot roast, and we've developed an unusual technique to cook and sauce them in just one skillet.

POT ROAST

WHAT WE WANTED: Tender, moist, flavorful meat floating in a savory liquid that becomes a sauce.

A good pot roast by definition entails the transformation of a tough (read cheap), nearly unpalatable cut of meat into a tender, rich, flavorful main course by means of a slow, moist cooking process called braising. It should not be sliceable; rather, the tension of a stern gaze should be enough to break it apart. Nor should it be pink or rosy in the middle—save that for prime rib or steak.

The meat for pot roast should be well marbled with fat and connective tissue to provide the dish with flavor and moisture. Recipes typically call for roasts from the sirloin (or rump), round (leg), or chuck (shoulder). When all was said and done, we cooked a dozen cuts of meat to find the right one.

The sirloin roasts tested—the bottom rump roast and top sirloin—were the leanest of the cuts and needed longer cooking to be broken down to a palatable texture. The round cuts—top round, bottom round, and eye of round—had more fat running through them than the sirloin cuts, but the meat was chewy. The chuck cuts—shoulder roast, boneless chuck roast, cross rib, chuck mock tender, seven-bone roast, top-blade roast, and chuck-eye roast—cooked up the most tender, although we gave preference to three of these cuts (see "Getting It Right: Chuck Roasts" on page 104). The high proportion of fat and connective tissue in these chuck cuts gave the meat much-needed moisture and superior flavor.

Tough meat, such as brisket, can benefit from the low, dry heat of oven roasting, and it can be boiled. With pot roast, however, the introduction of moisture by means of a braising liquid is thought to be integral to the breakdown of the tough muscle fibers. (We also tried dry-roasting and boiling pot roast just to make sure. See page 103 to find out why braising was the winner.) It was time to find out what kind of liquid and how much was needed to best cook the roast and supply a good sauce.

Before we began the testing, we needed to deal with the aesthetics of the dish. Because pot roast is traditionally cooked with liquid at a low temperature, the exterior of the meat will not brown sufficiently unless it is first sautéed in a Dutch oven on the stovetop. High heat and a little oil were all that were needed to caramelize the exterior of the beef and boost both the flavor and appearance of the dish.

Using water as the braising medium, we started with a modest ¼ cup, as suggested in a few recipes. This produced a roast that was unacceptably fibrous, even after hours of cooking. After increasing the amount of liquid incrementally, we found that the moistest meat was produced when we added liquid halfway up the sides of the roast (depending on the cut, this amount could be between 2 and 4 cups). The greater amount of liquid also accelerated the cooking process, shaving nearly one hour off the cooking time needed for a roast cooked in just ¼ cup of liquid.

Next we tested different liquids, hoping to add flavor to the roast and sauce. Along with our old standby, water, we tested red wine, low-sodium canned chicken broth, and low-sodium canned beef broth. Red wine had the most startling effect on the meat, penetrating it with a potent flavor that most tasters agreed was "good, but not traditional pot roast." However, tasters did like the flavor of a little red wine added to the sauce after the pot roast was removed from the pan. Each of the broths on their own failed to win tasters over completely—the chicken broth was rich but gave the dish a characteristic poultry flavor, while the beef broth tasted sour when added solo. In the end, we found that an equal amount of each did the job, with the beef broth boosting the depth of flavor and the chicken broth tempering any sourness. Because different amounts of liquid would have to be added to the pot depending on the size and shape of each individual roast, we chose to be consistent in the amount of chicken and beef broth used—1 cup each—

and to vary the amount of water to bring the liquid level halfway up the roast.

Trying to boost the flavor of the sauce even more, we added carrot, celery, onion, and garlic to the pot as the meat braised. Unfortunately, the addition of raw vegetables made the pot roast taste more like a vegetable stew. We then tried sautéing them until golden brown and found that the caramelized flavor of the vegetables added another layer of flavor to the sauce. Tomato paste, an ingredient found in several recipes, was not a welcome addition. Tasters appreciated the sweetness it added but not the "tinny" flavor. A little sugar (2 teaspoons) added to the vegetables as they cooked gave the sauce the sweetness tasters were looking for.

Some recipes thicken the sauce with a mixture of equal parts butter and flour (beurre manié); others use a slurry of cornstarch mixed with a little braising liquid. Both techniques made the sauce more gravy-like than we preferred, and we didn't care for the dilution of flavor. We chose to remove the roast from the pot, then reduce the liquid over high heat until the flavors were well concentrated and the texture more substantial.

As for the best cooking method for pot roast, there are two schools of thought: on the stove or in the oven. After a few rounds of stovetop cooking, we felt that it was too difficult to maintain a steady, low temperature, so we began pot-roasting in the oven, starting out at 250 degrees. This method required no supervision, just a turn of the meat every 30 to 40 minutes to ensure even cooking. We then tested higher temperatures to reduce the cooking time. Heat levels above 350 degrees boiled the meat to a stringy, dry texture because the exterior of the roast overcooked before the interior was cooked and tender. The magic temperature turned out to be 300 degrees—enough heat to keep the meat at a low simmer while high enough to shave a few more minutes off the cooking time.

As said above, pot roast is well-done meat—meat cooked to an internal temperature above 165 degrees. Up to this point, we were bringing the meat to an internal temperature of 200 to 210 degrees, the point at which the fat and connective tissue begin to melt. In a 300-degree oven, the roast came up to that temperature in a neat 2½ hours, certainly by no means a quick meal but still a relatively short time in which to cook a pot roast. But we still had not achieved our goal of fall-apart tenderness. We went back and reviewed our prior testing to see what we might have missed.

Once in a great while in the test kitchen we happen upon a true "Eureka!" moment, when a chance test result leads to a breakthrough cooking technique. Some days before, we had forgotten to remove one of the roasts from the oven, allowing it to cook one hour longer than intended. Racing to the kitchen with our instant-read thermometer, we found the internal temperature of the roast was still 210 degrees, but the meat had a substantially different appearance and texture. The roast was so tender that it was starting to separate along its muscle lines. A fork poked into the meat met with no resistance and nearly disappeared into the flesh. We took the roast out of the pot and "sliced" into it. Nearly all the fat and connective tissue had dissolved into the meat, giving each bite a soft, silky texture and rich, succulent flavor. We "overcooked" several more roasts. Each roast had the same great texture. The conclusion? Not only do you have to cook pot roast until it reaches 210 degrees internally, but the meat has to remain at that temperature for a full hour. In other words, cook the pot roast until it's done—and then keep on cooking!

WHAT WE LEARNED: Start with a cut from the chuck and brown the meat to build flavor and enhance its appearance. Use chicken and beef broths as the braising medium and cook the pot roast until the internal temperature reaches 210 degrees, and then cook it another hour. It's hard to overcook pot roast but easy to undercook it.

SIMPLE POT ROAST Serves 6 to 8

Our favorite cut for pot roast is a chuck-eye roast. Most markets sell this roast with twine tied around the center (see the photo on page 104); if necessary, do this yourself. Seven-bone and top-blade roasts are also good choices for this recipe. Remember to add only enough water to come halfway up the sides of these thinner roasts, and begin checking for doneness after 2 hours. If using a top-blade roast, tie it before cooking (see the illustrations on page 105) to keep it from falling apart. Mashed or boiled potatoes are a good accompaniment to pot roast.

 1 boneless chuck-eye roast (about 3½ pounds)
    Salt and ground black pepper
 2 tablespoons vegetable oil
 1 medium onion, chopped medium
 1 small carrot, chopped medium
 1 small rib celery, chopped medium
 2 medium cloves garlic, minced
 2 teaspoons sugar
 1 cup low-sodium chicken broth
 1 cup low-sodium beef broth
 1 sprig fresh thyme
1–1½ cups water
 ¼ cup dry red wine

1. Adjust an oven rack to the middle position and heat the oven to 300 degrees. Thoroughly pat the roast dry with paper towels; sprinkle generously with salt and pepper.

2. Heat the oil in a large heavy-bottomed Dutch oven over medium-high heat until shimmering but not smoking. Brown the roast thoroughly on all sides, reducing the heat if the fat begins to smoke, 8 to 10 minutes. Transfer the roast to a large plate; set aside. Reduce the heat to medium; add the onion, carrot, and celery to the pot and cook, stirring occasionally, until beginning to brown, 6 to 8 minutes. Add the garlic and sugar; cook until fragrant, about 30 seconds. Add the chicken and beef broths and thyme, scraping the

bottom of the pan with a wooden spoon to loosen the browned bits. Return the roast and any accumulated juices to the pot; add enough water to come halfway up the sides of the roast. Place a large piece of foil over the pot and cover tightly with a lid; bring the liquid to a simmer over medium heat, then transfer the pot to the oven. Cook, turning the roast every 30 minutes, until fully tender and a meat fork or sharp knife easily slips in and out of the meat, 3½ to 4 hours.

3. Transfer the roast to a carving board; tent with foil to keep warm. Allow the liquid in the pot to settle about 5 minutes, then use a wide spoon to skim the fat off the surface; discard the thyme sprig. Boil over high heat until reduced to about 1½ cups, about 8 minutes. Add the red wine and reduce again to 1½ cups, about 2 minutes. Season to taste with salt and pepper.

4. Using a chef's or carving knife, cut the meat into ½-inch-thick slices, or pull apart into large pieces; transfer the meat to a warmed serving platter and pour about ½ cup sauce over the meat. Serve, passing the remaining sauce separately.

VARIATIONS
POT ROAST WITH ROOT VEGETABLES

In this variation, carrots, potatoes, and parsnips are added near the end of cooking to make a complete meal.

1. Follow the recipe for Simple Pot Roast. In step 2, when the roast is almost tender (a sharp knife should meet little resistance), transfer the roast to a cutting board. Pour the braising liquid through a mesh strainer and discard the solids. Return the liquid to the empty pot and let it settle for 5 minutes; use a wide spoon to skim the fat off the surface. Return the roast to the liquid and add 1½ pounds (about 8 medium) carrots, sliced ½ inch thick (about 3 cups), 1½ pounds small red potatoes, halved if larger than 1½ inches in diameter (about 5 cups), and 1 pound (about

5 large) parsnips, sliced ½ inch thick (about 3 cups), submerging them in the liquid. Continue to cook until the vegetables are almost tender, 20 to 30 minutes.

2. Transfer the roast to a carving board; tent with foil to keep warm. Add the wine and salt and pepper to taste; boil over high heat until the vegetables are fully tender, 5 to 10 minutes. Using a slotted spoon, transfer the vegetables to a warmed serving bowl or platter; using a chef's or carving knife, cut the meat into ½-inch-thick slices or pull apart into large pieces; transfer to the bowl or platter with the vegetables and pour about ½ cup sauce over. Serve, passing the remaining sauce separately.

POT ROAST WITH MUSHROOMS, TOMATOES, AND RED WINE

This recipe is based on stracotto, an Italian pot roast with tomatoes and red wine.

1. Follow the recipe for Simple Pot Roast, adding 10 ounces white button mushrooms, cleaned and quartered, to the Dutch oven along with the onion, carrot, and celery in step 2. Decrease the chicken and beef broths to ½ cup each and add ½ cup dry red wine and 1 can (14½ ounces) diced tomatoes, with juice, along with the broths.

2. After skimming fat off the liquid in step 3, add 1 sprig fresh rosemary; omit the red wine. Boil the liquid over high heat until reduced to 1½ cups; discard the rosemary and thyme sprigs. Season to taste with salt and pepper.

3. Using a chef's or carving knife, cut the meat into ½-inch-thick slices or pull apart into large pieces; transfer the meat to a warmed serving platter or bowl, pour the sauce and vegetables over the meat, and serve.

SCIENCE DESK:
How Does Braising Work?

BRAISING—SEARING MEAT, PARTIALLY SUBMERGING IT IN liquid in a sealed pot, and then cooking it until fork-tender—is a classic technique used with tough cuts of meat. A variety of cooks have put forward theories about why and how braising works (as opposed to roasting or boiling). We set out to devise a series of experiments that would explain the mystery of braising.

Before kitchen testing began, we researched the meat itself to better understand how it cooks. Meat (muscle) is made up of two major components: muscle fibers, the long thin strands visible as the "grain" of meat, and connective

---

GETTING IT RIGHT: Roasting versus Braising

A distinctive pattern of fat and connective tissue runs through the meat of a chuck roast (left). When cooked in dry heat, or roasted (middle), the fat and sinew do not break down sufficiently, even after many hours in the oven. Cooking the meat in moist heat, or braising (right), promotes a more complete breakdown of the fat and connective tissue, yielding very tender meat.

tissue, the membranous, translucent film that covers the bundles of muscle fiber and gives them structure and support. Muscle fiber is tender because of its high water content (up to 78 percent). Once meat is heated beyond about 120 degrees, the long strands of muscle fiber contract and coil, expelling moisture in much the same way that it's wrung out of a towel. In contrast, connective tissue is tough because it is composed primarily of collagen, a sturdy protein that is in everything from the cow's muscle tendons to its hooves. When collagen is cooked at temperatures exceeding 140 degrees, it starts to break down to gelatin, the protein responsible for the tender, rich meat and thick sauces of braised dishes.

In essence, then, meat both dries out as it cooks (meat fibers lose moisture) and becomes softer (the collagen melts). That is why (depending on the cut) meat is best either when cooked rare or pot-roasted—cooked to the point at which the collagen dissolves completely. Anything in between is dry and tough, the worst of both worlds.

This brings us to why braising is an effective cooking technique for tough cuts of meat. To determine the relative advantages of roasting, braising, and boiling, we constructed a simple test. One roast was cooked in a 250-degree oven, one was braised, and one was simmered in enough liquid to cover it. The results were startling. The dry-cooked roast never reached an internal temperature of more than 175 degrees, even after four hours, and the meat was tough and dry (see "Roasting versus Braising" on page 103). To our great surprise, both the braised and boiled roasts cooked in about the same amount of time, and the results were almost identical. Cutting the roasts in half revealed little difference—both exhibited nearly full melting of the thick bands of connective tissue. As far as the taste and texture of the meat, tasters were hard pressed to find any substantial differences between the two. Both roasts yielded meat that was exceedingly tender, moist, and infused with rich gelatin.

The conclusion? Dry heat (roasting) is ineffective because the meat never gets hot enough to fully melt the collagen. It does not appear that steam heat (braising) enjoys

---

GETTING IT RIGHT: Chuck Roasts

The seven-bone pot roast (left) is a well-marbled cut with an incredibly beefy flavor. It gets its name from the bone found in the roast, which is shaped like the number seven. Because it is only 2 inches thick, less liquid and less time are needed to braise this roast. Do not buy a seven-bone pot roast that weighs more than 3 1/2 pounds, as it will not fit into a Dutch oven. This roast is also sometimes referred to as a seven-bone steak.

The top-blade pot roast (middle) is also well-marbled with fat and connective tissue, which make this roast very juicy and flavorful. Even after thorough braising, this roast retains a distinctive strip of connective tissue, which is not unpleasant to eat. This roast may also be sold as a blade roast.

The chuck-eye roast (right) is the fattiest of the three roasts and the most commonly available. Its high proportion of fat gives pot roast great flavor and tenderness. Because of its thicker size, this roast takes the longest to cook.

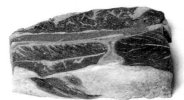

SEVEN-BONE POT ROAST

TOP-BLADE POT ROAST

CHUCK-EYE ROAST

any special ability to soften meat over boiling. Braising has one advantage over simmering or boiling, however—half a pot of liquid reduces to a sauce much faster than a full pot.

SCIENCE DESK:
What's So Special about Collagen?

COLLAGEN IS THE PREDOMINANT PROTEIN IN CONNECTIVE tissue and is quite tough to chew. It is found in abundance in tough cuts of meat. Braising is a slow cooking technique that is applied to tough cuts of meat. The meat is covered halfway with cooking liquid and heated, covered, at a low temperature. By the time the meat reaches 150 degrees the muscle tissue has tightened fully and has expelled a great deal of its moisture into the braising liquid. If the meat is pulled from the pot at this temperature it will be dry and tough, but the braising liquid will be rich and flavorful.

Upon further heating, the collagen in the muscle will break down progressively into soft gelatin. The tightened muscle tissue strands can then separate a little, and moisture from the cooking liquid will accumulate between the fibers. Now, though the finished product still is tough muscle tissue, it is more succulent owing to the conversion of collagen to soft gelatin and to the resultant opening of gaps between the tough strands of muscle.

TECHNIQUE: How to Tie a Top-Blade Roast

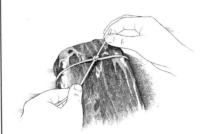

1. Slip a 6-foot piece of twine under the roast and tie a double knot.

2. Hold the twine against the meat and loop the long end of twine under and around the roast.

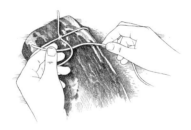

3. Run the long end through the loop.

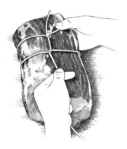

4. Repeat this procedure down the length of the roast.

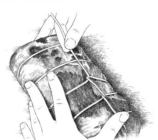

5. Roll the roast over and run the twine under and around each loop.

6. Wrap the twine around the end of the roast, flip the roast, and tie to the original knot.

EQUIPMENT CORNER:
Vegetable Choppers

EVERY NIGHT OWL HAS SEEN THE MIDNIGHT INFOMERCIALS advertising do-it-all food preparation devices that will "make superfresh salads, pizza, coleslaw, tacos, and more in seconds!" Real people give testimonials in which they claim these gadgets quickly and effortlessly chop, mince, slice, dice, julienne, and shred.

Such gadgets would probably not tempt cooks with a sharp knife and passable skill in its use. But there are countless cooks with dull knives or limited time, interest, or facility who might well part with their hard-earned cash for the lure of easily and speedily dispatching all manner of foodstuffs. Wondering how well they'd be served by these devices, we gathered eight models—several of them courtesy of the toll-free number on the television screen—and repaired to the test kitchen to chop, mince, slice, and shred everything from garlic and parsley to cheese and potatoes.

The models tested showcased a variety of designs. Of the five units intended to chop and mince, three—the Zyliss, Gemco, and Dalla Piazza—use a chamber to contain the food and a pump-operated, rotating, zigzag-shaped blade that descends over the food to chop it. The first few pumps chop the food roughly; continued pumping minces it. The New & Improved Quick Chopper operates like a hand-cranked food processor, with a blade spinning in a workbowl. The last of the five chopper models, the Kitchen Magic, combines a nonadjustable slicing blade mounted in the handle with a series of circular blades, which you roll back and forth over the slices you've made to chop them.

The remaining three models slice and shred. The Culinary 2000 Rocket Chef, like the Quick Chopper, is a hand-cranked manual food processor that includes slicing and shredding blades. The Presto Salad Shooter pushes food through a feed tube onto a rotating, cone-shaped slicing or shredding blade, and the Veg-o-Matic makes the cook push food through blades using a plunger and two hands.

In the course of running 11 separate tests on each unit, it didn't take long to reach the conclusion that this bunch of kitchen gadgets is unimpressive. The shortcomings include uneven processing, whether chopping, shredding, or slicing; poor design in terms of rinsing, cleaning, and even safety; and lackluster manufacturing quality.

First, the cutting quality. Not one machine did a decent job on parsley, and several choked when we tried to chop nuts. In general, we found it best to process small amounts of food at one time because ½ cup of nuts or even a small onion brought several units to a halt.

Cleaning or rinsing these units between runs through the dishwasher (so they could be used on different foods being prepared for the same meal) was no walk in the park. Most designs included numerous hard-to-reach nooks and crannies and multiple pieces. Only the Zyliss opened up to reveal the entire blade, which made it easy to clean.

Because our test cooks are not the target consumer for these products—we have both a sharp knives and enough skill to use them comfortably—we expanded the testing to include four less experienced cooks who work in the production and accounting departments at *Cook's Illustrated* magazine. We asked each individual to finely chop an onion and to mince a knob of ginger, using both a freshly honed 8-inch chef's knife and the winning chopper.

It goes almost without saying that average onion-chopping times with the machine were much faster than those with the knife—one minute, 19 seconds, versus four minutes, 45 seconds, respectively. But, like our test cooks, three of the four novice testers were not pleased with the quality (fineness and evenness) of the chop. To be fair, the tester who took the longest to get through the onion and ginger with a knife was very enthusiastic about the chopper.

All in all, we would rather see money spent on a decent chef's knife (which can be had for about $30) and an adult education course in knife skills than on any of these machines. That said, if you are really averse to using a knife and think that one of these machines might help you out, the Zyliss is the one to go for.

Rating Vegetable Choppers

WE RATED EIGHT FOOD CHOPPER/SLICER/SHREDDER DEVICES AND EVALUATED THEM IN 11 TESTS: CHOPPING GARLIC, ginger, parsley, chocolate, almonds, dried apricots, and onion, and slicing or shredding cheddar cheese, carrots, tomatoes, and potatoes. We've divided the devices into two categories based on their intended uses. The devices are listed in order of preference in each category based on their performance in these tests as well as ease of use and ease of cleaning. See www.americastestkitchen.com for up-to-date prices and mail-order sources for top-rated products.

FOOD CHOPPERS

BEST CHOPPER
Zyliss Comfort Food Chopper $19.99
Clever design and best performance by a wide margin make this a handy kitchen tool if you hate to use a knife. Parsley was the only test it failed.

RECOMMENDED WITH RESERVATIONS
Gemco—The Chopper $4.99
Simple, cheap, and a bit flimsy, but it might be worth keeping around if you chop a lot of chocolate. Good with dried fruit, but lousy on ginger, garlic, nuts, and parsley.

RECOMMENDED WITH RESERVATIONS
Dalla Piazza Brushed Stainless Steel Food Chopper $22.00
Performance was acceptable in some cases (nuts and chocolate), mediocre in most.

NOT RECOMMENDED
New & Improved Quick Chopper $14.95
Performance in key tests ranged from subpar to terrible.

NOT RECOMMENDED
Kitchen Magic Chopper $17.25
Two words characterize this unit best: "dangerous" and "useless."

FOOD SLICERS/SHREDDERS

NOT RECOMMENDED
Presto 2972 Pro Salad Shooter/Shredder $49.92
Shredding is its strong suit; slicing performance is fickle.

NOT RECOMMENDED
K-Tel Veg-o-Matic Food Cutter $22.35
Flimsy, unstable, and a disgracefully poor performer.

NOT RECOMMENDED
Culinary 2000 New Rocket Chef & Supreme Ice Cream $28.99
The phrase "piece of junk" could have been coined for this unit.

GREEN BEANS

WHAT WE WANTED: To skip the traditional, multipot method and cook the beans and sauce together in a skillet.

For eleventh-hour cooks (like us), the conventional frigmarole for cooking green beans—boiling, shocking in ice water, drying, and, finally, reheating in a separately made sauce—simply takes too long and dirties too many dishes. We wanted a streamlined technique that would yield tender beans and a flavorful sauce.

The plan was to steam the beans in a covered skillet with a little water, remove the lid part way through to evaporate the water, then build a quick pan sauce around the beans as they finished cooking. The beans, however, steamed in only eight minutes, leaving little time to make a decent sauce after the water had evaporated. Switching the cooking order, we then tried making the sauce first. Building good flavor and texture by sautéing aromatics (such as garlic and onion) and a little flour, we then stirred in broth and some fresh herbs. Adding the beans right to the sauce, we covered the skillet and cooked them until almost tender (omitting the water altogether), then removed the lid to thicken the sauce. Not only did these beans turn out more flavorful, but by removing the lid near the end of cooking, we were able to closely monitor the doneness of the beans.

When made in a nonstick skillet, these beans are easy to gussy up with some toasted bread crumbs or glazed nuts. The toppings are made first, then the pan is simply wiped clean with paper towels and returned to the stove. Putting this one-pan technique to the ultimate test, we also re-create a green bean "casserole," complete with a mushroom cream sauce and fried shallots.

WHAT WE LEARNED: Build a sauce in the skillet with aromatics, broth, and a little flour; add the beans, cover, and steam until almost done; then uncover during the final phase of cooking to thicken the sauce.

QUICK GREEN BEAN "CASSEROLE" Serves 8

- 3 large shallots, sliced thin (about 1 cup)
  Salt and ground black pepper
- 3 tablespoons all-purpose flour
- 5 tablespoons vegetable oil
- 10 ounces cremini mushrooms, stems discarded, caps wiped clean and sliced ¼-inch thick
- 2 tablespoons unsalted butter
- 1 medium onion, minced (about 1 cup)
- 2 medium cloves garlic, minced
- 1½ pounds green beans, stem ends trimmed
- 3 sprigs fresh thyme
- 2 bay leaves
- ¾ cup heavy cream
- ¾ cup low-sodium chicken broth

1. Toss the shallots with ¼ teaspoon salt, ⅛ teaspoon pepper, and 2 tablespoons flour in a bowl. Heat 3 tablespoons oil in a 12-inch nonstick skillet over medium-high heat until smoking; add the shallots and cook, stirring frequently, until golden and crisp, about 5 minutes. Transfer the shallots with the oil to a baking sheet lined with paper towels.

2. Wipe out the skillet and return to medium-high heat. Add the remaining 2 tablespoons oil, mushrooms, and ¼ teaspoon salt; cook, stirring occasionally, until the mushrooms are well browned, about 8 minutes. Transfer to a plate and set aside.

3. Wipe out the skillet. Heat the butter in the skillet over medium heat; when the foaming subsides, add the onion, and cook, stirring occasionally, until the edges begin to brown, about 2 minutes. Stir in the garlic and remaining 1 tablespoon flour; toss in the green beans, thyme, and bay. Add the cream and chicken broth, increase the heat to medium-high, cover, and cook until the beans are partly tender but still crisp at the center, about 4 minutes. Add the mushrooms, and continue to cook, uncovered, until the green beans are tender, about 4 minutes. Off heat, discard the bay and thyme; adjust the seasonings with salt and pepper. Transfer to a serving dish, sprinkle evenly with the shallots, and serve.

GARLIC-LEMON GREEN BEANS WITH TOASTED BREAD CRUMBS Serves 8

3 tablespoons unsalted butter
2 slices high-quality sandwich bread, ground fine in a food processor
   Salt and ground black pepper
2 tablespoons grated Parmesan cheese
6 medium cloves garlic, minced
2 teaspoons all-purpose flour
1/8 teaspoon red pepper flakes
1 teaspoon minced fresh thyme leaves
1 1/2 pounds green beans, stem ends trimmed
1 cup low-sodium chicken broth
1 tablespoon juice from 1 lemon

1. Heat 1 tablespoon butter in a 12-inch nonstick skillet over medium-high heat; when melted, add the bread crumbs and cook, stirring frequently, until golden brown, 3 to 5 minutes. Transfer to a medium bowl, stir in 1/4 teaspoon salt, 1/8 teaspoon pepper, and the Parmesan; set aside.

2. Wipe out the skillet. Add the remaining 2 tablespoons butter, garlic, and 1/4 teaspoon salt; cook over medium heat, stirring constantly, until the garlic is golden, 3 to 5 minutes. Stir in the flour, pepper flakes, and thyme, then toss in the green beans. Add the broth and increase the heat to medium-high; cover and cook until the beans are partly tender but still crisp at the center, about 4 minutes. Uncover and cook, stirring occasionally, until the beans are tender, about 4 minutes. Stir in the lemon juice; adjust the seasonings with salt and pepper. Transfer to a serving dish, sprinkle with bread crumbs, and serve.

GREEN BEANS WITH ORANGE ESSENCE AND TOASTED MAPLE PECANS Serves 8

3/4 cup pecans (about 1 3/4 ounces), chopped coarse
3 tablespoons unsalted butter
2 tablespoons maple syrup
   Salt
2 medium shallots, minced (about 1/2 cup)
1/2 teaspoon grated zest plus 1/3 cup juice from 1 large orange
   Pinch cayenne
2 teaspoons all-purpose flour
1 1/2 pounds green beans, stem ends trimmed
2/3 cup low-sodium chicken broth
1 teaspoon minced fresh sage leaves
   Ground black pepper

1. Toast the pecans in a 12-inch nonstick skillet over medium-high heat, stirring occasionally, until golden brown and fragrant, about 3 minutes. Off heat, stir in 1 tablespoon butter, maple syrup, and 1/8 teaspoon salt. Return the skillet to medium heat and cook, stirring constantly, until the nuts are dry and glossy, about 45 seconds; transfer to a large plate and set aside.

2. Wipe out the skillet. Heat the remaining 2 tablespoons butter in the skillet over medium heat; when the foaming subsides, add the shallots, orange zest, and cayenne and cook, stirring occasionally, until the shallots are softened, about 2 minutes. Stir in the flour until combined, then toss in the green beans. Add the chicken broth and orange juice; increase the heat to medium-high, cover, and cook until the beans are partly tender but still crisp at the center, about 4 minutes. Uncover and cook, stirring occasionally, until the beans are tender and the sauce has thickened slightly, about 4 minutes. Off heat, adjust the seasonings with salt and pepper. Transfer to a serving dish, sprinkle evenly with the pecans, and serve.

Maple-glazed pork loin is browned on the stovetop and then finished—still in its skillet—in the oven.

MAPLE-GLAZED
pork roast

CHAPTER 9

The marketing of the "other white meat" would be amusing if today's pork weren't so lean and flavorless. Pork producers have worked so hard to remove fat from their pigs that most pork roasts have little character. Glazing a pork roast with maple syrup is an attractive way to boost flavor, but all too often the meat becomes too sweet and candyish. We wanted to perfect this simple recipe, figuring out how to apply the glaze as well as how to cook this lean roast without having the meat dry out.

Wild rice is as all-American as maple syrup. Too bad, then, that most wild rice dishes are better fed to farm animals than human beings. Most wild rice is mushy and starchy or tough and crunchy. And forget about those horrible boxed mixes. We wanted to develop a simple pilaf that would showcase the unusual flavor and texture of this indigenous ingredient.

MAPLE-GLAZED PORK ROAST

WHAT WE WANTED: Tender, juicy pork with a rich, clingy glaze that packs a lot of pure maple flavor—all in less than an hour.

From pancakes to pineapple, New Englanders will slather maple syrup on just about anything. Among the multitude of dishes done right by a dash of maple, classic New England maple-glazed pork roast is one of our favorites. Sweet maple, with its delicate flavor notes of smoke, caramel, and vanilla, makes an ideal foil for pork, which has a faint sweetness of its own. The result of this marriage is a glistening maple-glazed pork roast, which, when sliced, combines the juices from tender, well-seasoned pork with a rich maple glaze to create complex flavor in every bite.

When we tested five different recipes, however, we found that this dish often falls short of its savory-sweet promise. Of course, many of the roasts turned out dry (a constant concern when cooking today's lean pork), but we were surprised to discover that the glazes presented even bigger problems. Most of them were too thin to coat the pork properly, some were so sweet that they required a hotline to the dentist's office, and none of them had a pronounced maple flavor.

Good maple-glazed roast pork starts out as good plain roast pork. We wanted a boneless cut, of which there are four popular choices: the blade roast, which is cut from the animal's shoulder; the blade-end loin roast, cut from the loin near the shoulder blade; the center loin roast, cut from the center of the loin; and the sirloin roast, cut from the posterior of the loin. Tasters preferred the blade-end loin roast for its flavor and juiciness, which it receives in part from a deposit of fat that separates the two muscle sections at one end of the roast.

As is the custom in our test kitchen, we tried brining the meat (soaking it in a saltwater solution to season and boost juiciness), and brining did, indeed, yield tender, juicy,

well-seasoned pork. On the other hand, the unbrined pork was almost as good (as long as we took care not to overcook it), and it was nice to dispense with the 2½-hour brining time. Tasters also noted that the minor improvements realized by brining were lost to the assertively sweet glaze, so brining was out. We also ran a series of tests using "enhanced" pork, a common supermarket product that has been injected with a solution of water, salt, and sodium phosphate to season the meat and add moisture. Tasters were put off by the flood of liquid these roasts released when they were sliced, as well as by the overly wet, spongy texture of the meat.

In cooking more than a dozen roasts up to this point, we had learned that the real key to juicy pork is simple. Don't overcook it. In the old days, when pork had more fat and the trichinosis parasite was a more persistent threat, pork was routinely cooked to an internal temperature of 160 degrees. Today, pork is considerably leaner, and the possibility of contamination with trichinosis has been reduced to almost nil. This means that pork can be safely served at 145 to 150 degrees (measured in the center of the roast). If, however, you take the roast out of the oven once it reaches this temperature, it will be overcooked. The reason is simple: The temperature of the roast continues to rise, by as much as 15 degrees. The thing to do is to remove the roast when it hits a mere 135 degrees and then let it rest on the cutting board before slicing.

Innumerable tests in the kitchen have proven that roasts with a deep brown, caramelized crust look and taste better than those without. Trying to brown the meat using high oven heat at the beginning or end of roasting produced marginal results, so we decided to sear it on the stovetop. Because the meat was tied into a neat bundle, it fit well in a skillet, which made for great browning and gave us lots of control over the process. From the hot skillet, the loin went onto a rack in a roasting pan placed in a 325-degree oven, which proved to be the temperature of choice for even cooking.

Now it was time to get serious about developing maple flavor. The recipes we had researched touted dozens of glaze concoctions and methods for marrying them to the pork. Most of the flavoring ingredients added to the maple syrup either diluted it (so that it was too thin to use as a glaze) or were simply unwelcome. This list included soy sauce, vinegar, lemon juice, cranberry juice, cider, and bourbon for liquid ingredients and herbs, spices, jams, jellies, brown sugar, maple sugar, mustards, and chiles for flavor boosters. (We reserved the best of these flavorings for recipe variations.) Everyone agreed, however, that small amounts of complementary spices added subtle dimension to the maple, thus cinnamon, ground cloves, and cayenne all found their way into the glaze recipe. Still, we wanted more maple flavor and a glaze that would really stick to the meat. We even tried brining one loin in maple syrup and wrapping another with maple-flavored bacon. The former added no discernible maple flavor, while the latter tasted mildly artificial. We finally hit upon a simple solution to enhance flavor when we reduced the maple syrup in a saucepan. But we were frustrated when it dripped down off the roast onto the bottom of the roasting pan and burned.

Then we had an idea. Remember the hot pan we had left from searing the roast? How about putting it to additional use? We decided to use it to flash-reduce the maple syrup. We removed the loin from the pan after searing, poured off excess fat, added the syrup, and let it heat for 30 seconds. This allowed us to use the drippings that had formed in the pan when the meat seared and also eliminated the extra pan we had been using to reduce the syrup. Next we decided to lose the roasting pan (as well as the basting brush, which we invariably trashed with the sticky glaze) in favor of using the same skillet. Instead of pouring the glaze mixture over the pork in the roasting pan, where it would run to the edges and scorch, we returned the seared loin to the skillet with the syrup, twirled the pork around in the glaze a couple of times with tongs, and then popped the whole thing into the oven, with the skillet serving as the roasting pan.

The smaller surface area of the skillet prevented the glaze from spreading out and burning. This pan also made it easier to coat the pork thoroughly because it was sitting right in the glaze, like a belle in her bath. The roast emerged from the oven with a thick, uniform, glistening coating of glaze and an impressive, concentrated maple flavor. We had managed to turn this into a one-pan dish by searing, reducing the glaze, and roasting all in the same skillet. And there was yet another bonus. Starting with a hot skillet shaved a little time off the whole process. This skillet-roasted, burnished beauty was now out of the oven in 45 minutes or less.

WHAT WE LEARNED: Use a blade-end pork loin. Brown the meat in a large skillet, remove it to reduce the syrup and the spices, then return the meat to the pan and pop the whole thing—pan and all—into the oven.

MAPLE-GLAZED PORK ROAST Serves 4 to 6

A nonstick ovenproof skillet will be much easier to clean than a traditional one. Whichever you use, remember that the handle will be blistering hot when you take it out of the oven, so be sure to use a pot holder or oven mitt. Note that you should not trim the pork of its thin layer of fat. The flavor of grade B maple syrup (sometimes called "cooking maple") is stronger and richer than grade A, but grade A syrup will work well, too. This dish is unapologetically sweet, so we recommend side dishes that take well to the sweetness. Garlicky sautéed greens, braised cabbage, and soft polenta are good choices.

⅓   cup maple syrup, preferably grade B
⅛   teaspoon ground cinnamon
     Pinch ground cloves
     Pinch cayenne pepper
1   boneless blade-end pork loin roast (about 2½ pounds), tied at even intervals along length with 5 pieces butcher's twine (see the photo on page 115)
¾   teaspoon salt
½   teaspoon ground black pepper
2   teaspoons vegetable oil

1. Adjust an oven rack to the middle position; heat the oven to 325 degrees. Stir the maple syrup, cinnamon, cloves, and cayenne together in a measuring cup or small bowl; set aside. Pat the roast dry with paper towels, then sprinkle evenly with the salt and pepper.

2. Heat the oil in a heavy-bottomed ovenproof 10-inch nonstick skillet over medium-high heat until just beginning to smoke, about 3 minutes. Place the roast fat-side down in the skillet and cook until well browned, about 3 minutes. Using tongs, rotate the roast one-quarter turn and cook until well browned, about 2½ minutes; repeat until the roast is well browned on all sides. Transfer the roast to a large plate. Reduce the heat to medium and pour off the fat from the skillet; add the maple syrup mixture and cook until fragrant, about 30 seconds (the syrup will bubble immediately). Turn off the heat and return the roast to the skillet; using tongs, roll the roast to coat with glaze on all sides.

3. Place the skillet in the oven and roast until the center of the roast registers about 135 degrees on an instant-read thermometer, 35 to 45 minutes, using tongs to roll and spin the roast to coat with glaze twice during roasting time. Transfer the roast to a carving board; set the skillet aside to cool slightly to thicken the glaze, about 5 minutes. Pour the glaze over the roast and let rest 15 minutes longer (the center of the loin should register about 150 degrees on an instant-read thermometer). Snip the twine off the roast, cut into ¼-inch slices, and serve immediately.

FOOD FACT: Pancake Syrup

Many pancake syrups sold in supermarkets do not contain a drop of maple syrup. In fact, they are nothing more than corn syrup with artificial colors and flavors.

VARIATIONS

MAPLE-GLAZED PORK ROAST WITH ROSEMARY

Follow the recipe for Maple-Glazed Pork Roast, substituting 2 teaspoons minced fresh rosemary for the cinnamon, cloves, and cayenne.

MAPLE-GLAZED PORK ROAST WITH ORANGE ESSENCE

Follow the recipe for Maple-Glazed Pork Roast, adding 1 tablespoon grated orange zest to the maple syrup along with the spices.

MAPLE-GLAZED PORK ROAST WITH STAR ANISE

Follow the recipe for Maple-Glazed Pork Roast, adding 4 star anise pods to the maple syrup along with the spices.

MAPLE-GLAZED PORK ROAST WITH SMOKED PAPRIKA

Follow recipe for Maple-Glazed Pork Roast, adding 2 teaspoons smoked hot paprika to maple syrup along with spices.

SCIENCE DESK:
Why Brown and Glaze a Roast?

IT MIGHT SEEM A LITTLE RIDICULOUS TO GO TO THE TROUBLE of browning a pork roast when all of that beautiful color ends up being covered in a thick maple glaze. But pork requires extra attention to flavor development because the meat alone is plain. Our pork roast develops great flavor from two different reactions, both involving sugar.

The first reaction happens when we brown the meat and is called the Maillard reaction. Heat from the pan denatures proteins on the surface of the meat, and these proteins recombine with the natural sugars present in the meat to cause browning. This combination of protein with sugar has hundreds of possible chemical outcomes, leading to exceptional flavor depth.

The second reaction happens when the sugar in the maple glaze reaches a temperature of about 310 degrees, which generates hundreds of new compounds by means of caramelization. No wonder caramel is so much more interesting than sugar.

GETTING IT RIGHT:
The Importance of Tying

Straight from the supermarket packaging, most pork loins will lie flat in the pan and cook unevenly (left). Tying the roast not only yields more attractive slices but ensures that the roast will have the same thickness from end to end so that it cooks evenly (right).

GETTING IT RIGHT:
Don't Buy Enhanced Pork

Many markets sell enhanced pork, which has been injected with a water/salt/sodium phosphate solution meant to season the meat and improve juiciness. During testing, we found that an enhanced roast exuded nearly one and a half times as much juice as a regular roast when carved. We recommend buying regular pork.

JUICES LOST FROM ENHANCED PORK   JUICES LOST FROM REGULAR ROAST

MAPLE-GLAZED PORK ROAST 115

WILD RICE

WHAT WE WANTED: Too often, this American grain resembles mulch and has a taste to match. We wanted to figure out how to tame the flavor and turn out properly cooked rice every time.

Like a couture evening gown, wild rice is slinky black, demurely elegant, and exorbitantly pricey. But like the dress, the rice's inky sheath is no guarantee of what lies underneath. More often than not, that sleek ebony coating masks a chewy interior tasting of little but the marsh from whence the rice came. The question before us was how to make wild rice taste as good as it looks.

Properly cooked wild rice is a study in contrasts: chewy yet tender and cottony—like popcorn. Ideally, the cooked grains remain discreet, doubling to quadrupling in size from their uncooked state. Undercooked rice is tough and, quite literally, hard to chew. At the other end of the spectrum, overcooked wild rice is gluey.

To find the best cooking method, we first tried steaming and boiling, but both methods produced poorly cooked wild rice. Research revealed the best approach to be slow simmering, although the timing varied from batch to batch. The key is to stop the cooking process at just the right moment; otherwise the texture goes quickly from

tough to gluey. The solution? Once the rice had simmered for 35 minutes, we checked it for doneness every couple of minutes.

Finding good flavor was another story. Plain water made for distinctly bad-tasting rice, and the addition of wine only accentuated the off flavor. Beef broth was overwhelming, but chicken broth was a revelation. Mild yet rich, the chicken broth tempered the rice's muddy flavor to a pleasant earthiness and affirmed its subdued nuttiness. Bay leaves and thyme added finesse and complexity.

Although it was now perfectly cooked, tasters found the wild rice alone to be overwhelming. Perhaps it could be better appreciated if complemented by a mellower grain, such as brown or white rice. Brown rice offered too little contrast, so we quickly settled on white. Cooking both rices in the same pot (adding the white rice midway through the simmer) caused the texture of the white rice to suffer, so an additional pot was called for. To make the most of this second saucepan, we decided to add flavoring ingredients in the style of a pilaf, a simple technique that guarantees flavorful, fluffy rice. Aromatics are first softened in oil or butter, and then the rice is lightly toasted in the pan, after which the liquid is added (in a smaller amount than for conventional cooking) and the rice steamed until tender. The winning pilaf ingredients turned out to be onions, carrots, dried cranberries, and toasted pecans.

WHAT WE LEARNED: Simmer wild rice in plenty of chicken broth and check the pot often as it nears completion to make sure the grains do not overcook. Mellow the intense flavor of wild rice with some white rice pilaf.

FOOD FACT: Wild Rice

While wild rice (*Zizania aquatica*) and traditional cultivated rice (*Oryza sativa*) are both members of the grass family, wild rice is not considered a cereal grass (as are wheat, corn, oats, barley, rye, and traditional cultivated rice). Truly "wild" wild rice is native to the northern Great Lakes, where it is still harvested. But most so-called wild rice is now cultivated on farms in California. Cultivated wild rice grown in man-made paddies costs between $3 and $5 per pound, while hand-harvested rice from lakes and streams in Minnesota and Canada costs about $9 per pound.

WILD RICE PILAF WITH PECANS AND DRIED CRANBERRIES Serves 6 to 8

Wild rice goes quickly from tough to pasty, so begin testing the rice at the 35-minute mark and drain the rice as soon as it is tender.

1¾   cups low-sodium chicken broth

2   bay leaves

8   sprigs thyme, divided into 2 bundles, each tied together with kitchen twine

1   cup wild rice, rinsed well in a strainer and picked over

1½   cups long-grain white rice

3   tablespoons unsalted butter

1   medium onion, chopped fine (about 1¼ cups)

1   large carrot, chopped fine (about 1 cup)

    Salt

¾   cup sweetened or unsweetened dried cranberries

¾   cup pecans, toasted in small dry skillet over medium heat until fragrant and lightly browned, about 6 minutes, then chopped coarse

1½   tablespoons minced fresh parsley leaves

    Ground black pepper

1. Bring the chicken broth, ¼ cup water, bay leaves, and 1 bundle thyme to a boil in a medium saucepan over medium-high heat. Add the wild rice, cover, and reduce the heat to low; simmer until the rice is plump and tender and has absorbed most of the liquid, 35 to 45 minutes. Drain the rice in a mesh strainer to remove excess liquid. Return the rice to the now-empty saucepan; cover to keep warm and set aside.

2. While the wild rice is cooking, place the white rice in a medium bowl and cover with 2 of inches water; gently swish the grains to release excess starch. Carefully pour off the water, leaving the rice in the bowl. Repeat about 5 times, until the water runs almost clear. Drain the rice in a mesh strainer.

3. Heat the butter in a medium saucepan over medium-high heat until foam subsides, about 2 minutes. Add the onion, carrot, and 1 teaspoon salt; cook, stirring frequently, until softened but not browned, about 4 minutes. Add the rinsed white rice and stir to coat the grains with the butter; cook, stirring frequently, until the grains begin to turn translucent, about 3 minutes. Meanwhile, bring 2¼ cups water to a boil in a small saucepan or a microwave. Add the boiling water and the second thyme bundle to the rice; return to a boil, then reduce the heat to low, sprinkle the cranberries evenly over the rice, and cover. Simmer until all of the liquid is absorbed, 16 to 18 minutes. Off the heat, fluff the rice with a fork.

4. Combine the wild rice, white rice mixture, toasted pecans, and parsley in a large bowl; toss with a rubber spatula until ingredients are evenly mixed. Adjust the seasonings with salt and pepper to taste; serve immediately.

GETTING IT RIGHT: The Texture Matters

Undercooked wild rice is tough and hard to chew. At the other end of the spectrum, overcooked wild rice bursts, revealing the pasty starch concealed beneath the glossy coat. Perfectly cooked wild rice is chewy but tender, the individual grains plumped but intact.

UNDERCOOKED   PERFECTLY COOKED   OVERCOOKED

EQUIPMENT CORNER:
Food Storage Containers

CIRCA 1950, LEFTOVERS WENT INTO TUPPERWARE. . . period. Today, some 50 years later, you can store leftovers in any number of containers made from plastic, glass, or metal and including features such as vacuum sealing, stain resistance, locking lids, and special venting. We wanted to find out if any of the newer models offered a higher level of protection for your food, more useful features, or significantly better design.

"Food storage containers?" grimaced one test kitchen skeptic, "Just how do you rate those?" After much discussion, we came up with several reliable, if slightly unconventional, methods to test the seal between the container and its lid. The "sink test" was first. We filled each container with 2 pounds of pie weights topped with a layer of sugar and, with the lid in place, submerged the whole thing in water. Then we fished out the container, dried it, and inspected the sugar inside. To further assess the seal, we devised the "shake test." We filled each container with soup, fixed the lid in place, and shook vigorously. If we ended up wearing soup, the seal wasn't tight enough.

Preventing the transfer of food odors is also largely up to the seal between container and lid. After all, you don't want your last few bites of chocolate mousse to smell like the anchovies next to it in the fridge, do you? To gauge odor protection, we conducted "stink tests" by loading slices of white sandwich bread into each container, positioning the lids, and storing them in the fridge with a huge, uncovered bowl of diced raw onions. Over the course of five days, we sniffed the bread daily to see if we could detect any "eau de allium."

We chose chili to test stain resistance, refrigerating it in the containers for three days, microwaving it to serving temperature (about three minutes), and then immediately running the containers through the dishwasher. Last, to mimic the ravages of time, we ran the containers through 100 cycles in the dishwasher, and then repeated every test.

Our lineup of 12 containers included Tupperware, two Rubbermaid models (Seal'n Saver and Stain Shield), several competing plastic containers, two inexpensive disposable containers, two vacuum-sealing models, and models made from both ovensafe glass and metal. The Genius VakSet container, with its pump-operated vacuum seal, performed impressively in the sink, shake, and stink tests. Several other containers with tight-fitting lids, particularly the Tupperware, both Rubbermaid models, and the Tramontina stainless steel, held their own against the vice grip of the Genius.

The "stink tests" produced no clear pattern among the odor control champs, including the Genius, GladWare, Tupperware, Tramontina, Betty Crocker, and Rubbermaid Seal'n Saver, which just edged out the Rubbermaid Stain Shield. The Pyrex glass container was a loser in both the stink and sink tests.

The results of the staining tests, on the other hand, did reveal a pattern. The winners were made of the hardest materials. The glass Pyrex and stainless steel Tramontina containers proved stain resistant, though the same cannot be said of the latter's plastic lid. Among the plastic containers, those made from hard, clear polycarbonate (the same stuff used for lightweight eyeglass lenses and compact disks), including the Tupperware, Rubbermaid Stain Shield, Genius, and Snapware, resisted stains best in our tests. The remaining plastic containers were made of polypropylene, a somewhat softer polymer that seems more susceptible to staining, as we observed in our tests.

To our surprise, several containers matched or surpassed the performance of the reigning king, Tupperware. Strictly speaking, the vacuum-sealed Genius VakSet edged out the Tupperware by one point in the performance tests. Yet despite stellar performance, we'd still hesitate to buy it because of its design. We fear that some cooks will lose the pump and the containers will become useless. Also, no one in our test kitchen could figure out how to release the vacuum seal without first reading the instruction manual. Throwing leftovers in the fridge shouldn't be any hassle at all. That's why our nod goes to the Tupperware, followed closely by the two Rubbermaid models. Their performance was excellent, and you don't have to think twice to use them.

Rating Food Storage Containers

WE TESTED 12 FOOD STORAGE CONTAINERS, ASSESSING THE QUALITY OF THE SEAL BETWEEN THE CONTAINER AND LID, the resistance of the sealed container to food odors, and the resistance of the container to staining. Containers are listed in order of preference based on results from these tests, tests performed after the containers went through the dishwasher 100 times, and design features. See www.americastestkitchen.com for up-to-date prices and mail-order sources for top-rated products.

RECOMMENDED
Tupperware Rock 'N Serve Medium Deep Container
$12.99
Well designed (handles, flat lid, vent for microwaving) with performance to match.

RECOMMENDED
Rubbermaid Stain Shield Square Container
$4.99
Lives up to the marketing claims of stain resistance. Odor-control performance was not perfect, though.

RECOMMENDED
Genius VakSet: Four Vacuum Storage Containers with Pump
$57.99/set of four
Its impressive performance comes with some hassle factor, and the containers are rendered useless if you lose the pump.

RECOMMENDED
Rubbermaid Seal'n Saver
$4.99
Staining was the only problem we encountered in this sturdy container with an excellent seal.

RECOMMENDED WITH RESERVATIONS
Betty Crocker Servables Container
$3.99
A decent container that didn't stand up well to the submersion and staining tests.

RECOMMENDED WITH RESERVATIONS
GladWare Containers/Deep Dish Size
$2.89/package of three
Despite some staining and minor leaking, a good overall performer, which surprised us given its flimsy feel. A good value.

RECOMMENDED WITH RESERVATIONS
Ziploc Brand Containers/Large Rectangle
$2.99/package of two
Only odor protection was truly subpar. We're not crazy for the flimsy feel, but you can't argue with the performance.

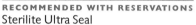

RECOMMENDED WITH RESERVATIONS
Sterilite Ultra Seal
$3.29
Less leakage, less staining, and better odor protection after 100 dishwasher cycles.

RECOMMENDED WITH RESERVATIONS
Snapware Snap N' Serve Stainproof Six-Piece Storage Container Set
$19.97
Cracked during the 100 dishwasher cycles, which impaired the seal. We're concerned about durability.

NOT RECOMMENDED
Tramontina Stainless Steel Gourmet Collection Storage Containers
$29.75
Despite good performance, testers found it so difficult to affix the lid to the container securely that we would avoid this model.

NOT RECOMMENDED
Pyrex Storage Plus/Rectangle Dish
$5.99
Stain resistant for sure, but also heavy, hard to handle when hot, and seals poorly.

NOT RECOMMENDED
SK Enterprises Vacuum Seal Storage Containers
$19.94/set of three
Midway through the testing, the vacuum mechanism broke and never worked again.

Becky and Susan check to make sure that all the food and equipment are on the set.

TRUCK STOP favorites

Truckers often know where to find the best home cooking. After long days on the road, most would rather tuck into real food, prepared from scratch, than the prefab food offered by roadside chains. And what could be better than chicken-fried steak with cream gravy and real coconut cream pie?

Chicken-fried steak can go wrong in many places. If you use the wrong cut of meat, the steak will be tough. If you don't bread and fry the steak properly, the coating can be pale, soggy, or greasy. And, if you don't take care with the gravy, it will be no better than the canned version.

Coconut cream pie almost always looks good. More often than not, it tempts with mile-high looks but then disappoints with lackluster flavor (some versions taste nothing like coconut) or gummy texture. And let's not even think about that soggy crust. The test kitchen wanted to perfect these roadside classics.

CHICKEN-FRIED STEAK

WHAT WE WANTED: Thin cutlets of beef that have been breaded and fried until crisp and golden brown. The creamy gravy that accompanies the steaks would be well seasoned and not too thick.

Although this truck-stop favorite often gets a bad rap, chicken-fried steak can be delicious when cooked just right. When cooked wrong, however, the dry, rubbery steaks snap back with each bite and are coated in a damp, pale breading and topped with a bland, pasty white sauce.

The first question we encountered on the road to good chicken-fried steak was what type of steak to use. By design, chicken-fried steak is a technique used with only the cheapest of cuts. No one would use strip steaks or filet mignon in this recipe, but steaks from the round, chuck, and sirloin are all contenders. We tested cube, Swiss, top-round, bottom-round, eye-round, chuck, and top sirloin steaks and came up with one winner. The cube steak was our favorite. This steak is lean yet tender; most of the other cuts tested were either fatty or difficult to chew.

Cube steak is usually cut from the round and tenderized (cubed) by the butcher, who uses a special machine to give the steak its unique, bumpy texture. We found that this lean, tender steak required little trimming and was easy to pound out to a thin cutlet, about ⅓ inch thick. Regular top, bottom-, and eye-round steaks, on the other hand, were thick and tough, requiring lots of muscle to pound out and chew. Swiss and chuck steaks, which come from the shoulder, were slightly less tough but still chewy and resilient. Top sirloin tasted great and had a nice texture, but the meat was laced with wide strips of gristle. Trimming the gristle reduced this steak to small, awkwardly sized pieces, making for unusual portions and cooking times.

What really makes chicken-fried steak great is the coating and subsequent frying. But what kind of coating is best?

To find out, we tested straight flour against various contenders, including cornflakes, Melba toast, cornmeal, matzo crumbs, ground saltines, and panko (Japanese bread crumbs). Straight flour was light and clung well to the steak but was simply too delicate for the toothsome meat and cream gravy. Cornflakes and Melba toast both burned and became tough, while the grittiness of cornmeal was simply out of place. Matzo, saltines, and panko all tasted great but quickly grew soggy under the rich, cream gravy.

We figured our single-breading technique might to be blame and decided to try double (or bound) breading. With single breading, meat is dipped into egg and then into flour, while double breading starts off with an initial dip in flour, then into egg, and again into flour (or into a coating such as those we tried with the steak). In side-by-side tests, we were surprised to discover that single breading was actually messier than double. When initially dipped in flour, the meat became dry and talcum-smooth, allowing the egg to cling evenly to the surface. The double breading also produced a more substantial base coat that didn't become overly thick or tough. Seasoned flour and a double-breading technique yielded a much improved crust.

Although this double breading was far superior to any other breading so far, we were still left wanting a heartier and crunchier crust. We wondered if we could bolster the egg wash with some buttermilk, baking soda, and baking powder, something that we knew worked well with fried chicken. Sure enough, these ingredients turned the egg wash into a thick, foamy concoction. This created a wet yet airy layer that stuck to and hydrated both layers of flour. This wet-looking, skin-like coating fried up to an impressive dark mahogany color and had a resilient texture that didn't weaken under the gravy. Because the coating is such a big part of the dish, we found it necessary to season it heavily with salt, black pepper, and cayenne.

After frying a few batches of these steaks, we found the

flavor of peanut oil preferable to that of vegetable oil or even shortening. Because the steaks are thin, they fry evenly in just 1 inch of oil. To keep splattering to a minimum, we used a deep Dutch oven. We also noted that the steaks fried to a dark, beautiful brown without tasting too greasy when the oil was heated initially to 375 degrees. Although the thick breading offers substantial protection from the hot oil, the steaks usually cook through completely within the time it takes for the crust to brown, about 2½ minutes per side.

Equally important to the crust is the cream gravy made from the fried drippings. Not wanting to waste any time while the fried steaks were kept warm in the oven, we found it easy to strain the small amount of hot oil used to fry the steaks right away. Adding the strained bits of deep-fried crumbs back to the Dutch oven, we were ready to make gravy. Most recipes simmer the drippings with some milk and thicken it with flour. To avoid making a floury-tasting sauce, we decided to cook the flour in the fat (that is, to

make a roux) and then add the milk, along with a splash of chicken stock. We found this technique quick and easy, and it also produced an authentic-tasting sauce.

We tested recipes using cream, half-and-half, and evaporated milk, but tasters preferred the fresh, clean flavor and lighter texture of whole milk. Onions and cayenne are traditional seasonings for the gravy, but tasters also liked small additions of thyme and garlic (neither of which is authentic). Topped with the light, well-seasoned gravy, this chicken-fried steak is the best any trucker has ever tasted.

WHAT WE LEARNED: Start with cube steaks pounded to an even thickness. Double-bread the steaks, dredging them in heavily seasoned flour, dipping in a thick buttermilk and egg mixture aerated with baking power and baking soda, and then returning to the seasoned flour for a second coat. Build flavor in the cream sauce by using the fried bits that fall off the steaks as they cook and by making a roux.

CHICKEN-FRIED STEAK Serves 6

Getting the initial oil temperature to 375 degrees is key to the success of this recipe. An instant-read thermometer with a high upper range is perfect for checking the temperature; a clip-on candy/deep-fry thermometer is also fine. If your Dutch oven measures 11 inches across (as ours does), you will need to fry the steaks in two batches.

steak

3	cups unbleached all-purpose flour
	Salt and ground black pepper
⅛	teaspoon cayenne
1	large egg
1	teaspoon baking powder
½	teaspoon baking soda
1	cup buttermilk
6	cube steaks, about 5 ounces each, pounded to ⅓-inch thickness
4–5	cups peanut oil

cream gravy

1	medium onion, minced
⅛	teaspoon dried thyme
2	medium cloves garlic, minced or pressed through a garlic press
3	tablespoons unbleached all-purpose flour
½	cup low-sodium chicken broth
2	cups whole milk
¾	teaspoon salt
¼	teaspoon ground black pepper
	Pinch cayenne

1. FOR THE STEAKS: Measure the flour, 5 teaspoons salt, 1 teaspoon black pepper, and cayenne into a large shallow dish. In a second large shallow dish, beat the egg, baking powder, and baking soda; stir in the buttermilk (the mixture will bubble and foam).

2. Set a wire rack over a rimmed baking sheet. Pat the steaks dry with paper towels and sprinkle each side with salt and pepper to taste. Drop the steaks into the flour and shake the pan to coat. Shake excess flour from each steak, then, using tongs, dip the steaks into the egg mixture, turning to coat well and allowing the excess to drip off. Coat the steaks with flour again, shake off the excess, and place them on the wire rack.

3. Adjust an oven rack to the middle position, set a second wire rack over a second rimmed baking sheet, and place the sheet on the oven rack; heat the oven to 200 degrees. Line a large plate with a double layer of paper towels. Meanwhile, heat 1 inch of oil in a large (11-inch diameter) Dutch oven over medium-high heat to 375 degrees. Place three steaks in the oil and fry, turning once, until deep golden brown on each side, about 5 minutes (oil temperature will drop to around 335 degrees). Transfer the steaks to the paper towel–lined plate to drain, then transfer them to the wire rack in the oven. Bring the oil back to 375 degrees and repeat the cooking and draining process (use fresh paper towels) with the three remaining steaks.

4. FOR THE GRAVY: Carefully pour the hot oil through a fine-mesh strainer into a clean pot. Return the browned bits from the strainer along with 2 tablespoons of frying oil back to the Dutch oven. Turn the heat to medium, add the onion and thyme, and cook until the onion has softened and is beginning to brown, 4 to 5 minutes. Add the garlic and cook until aromatic, about 30 seconds. Add the flour to the pan and stir until well combined and starting to dissolve, about 1 minute. Whisk in the broth, scraping any browned bits off the bottom of the pan. Whisk in the milk, salt, pepper, and cayenne; bring to a simmer over medium-high heat. Cook until thickened (gravy should have a loose consistency—it will thicken as it cools), about 5 minutes.

5. Transfer the chicken-fried steaks to individual plates. Spoon a generous amount of gravy over each steak. Serve immediately, placing any remaining gravy in a small bowl.

EQUIPMENT CORNER: Meat Pounders

IN BOXING, WEIGHT MATTERS SO MUCH THAT IT SETS THE contenders apart; it just wouldn't be fair to put a heavyweight in the ring with a lightweight. In our test of five "official" meat pounders plus a couple of ringers (a rubber mallet and a small skillet), we learned that weight matters in this arena, too, but the advantage doesn't necessarily go to the big guys.

The challenge was to flatten halved boneless chicken breasts into ¼-inch-thick paillards and to pound 1½-inch-thick slices of pork tenderloin into ½-inch cutlets. What counted was efficiency (as judged by the number of strokes it took to get the job done), quality (we wanted even, perfectly smooth cutlets and paillards, without marred or torn surfaces), and comfort and ease of use. Here are the results, by category.

Lightweights: More featherweight than lightweight and very cheap at $2.99, the 5-ounce wood hammer was the least efficient tool we tried, needing an average of about 90 strokes to produce one paillard and close to 40 for a pork cutlet. It was easy enough to use (we flattened the meat with its flat rectangular sides; the teeth on the square sides of the head are for tenderizing), but the sharp edges on the corners of the head tore into the meat a bit. This was not the performance we were looking for.

Also in this category was an 11-ounce rubber and metal pounder from Oxo, available for $9.95. It was more effective than the wood pounder—needing about 60 strokes for a paillard and 35 for a cutlet—but it also tore the meat, if very slightly.

Middleweight: The one entrant in this category was a standout. It may look a little odd, with its offset handle, but the 1-pound, 10-ounce Norpro meat pounder, which costs just $14.99, produced flawlessly smooth paillards (about 35 strokes) and cutlets (about 20) with a modicum of effort. Its moderate weight and offset handle make it very easy to control.

Heavyweights: The performance of two stainless steel tools from Mouli—the disk pounder and the square pounder—suffered from their excesses. The disk, which was not cheap at $44.95, weighed in at 3 pounds, 3 ounces. It produced very nice paillards and cutlets in relatively few strokes (35 and 20, respectively), but it felt so heavy compared with the Norpro, which was also much cheaper. *Cheap* is not a word that applies to Mouli's 2-pound, 4-ounce square pounder, which costs $99.95. It did a very good job and required very few strokes (about 25 for the paillards and only 12 for the cutlets), but even if we could use it as a snow shovel as well as a meat pounder, we'd have a hard time justifying that price. Its large size (12 inches tall with a 4-inch-square head) also made it a little hard to handle, with the corners of the head sometimes missing the meat and hitting the countertop.

Ringers: If you're not in the mood to bring yet another tool into your kitchen, we found that you can make do with a rubber mallet (20 strokes for paillards, 13 for cutlets) or a sturdy 8-inch skillet (25 strokes for paillards, 15 for pork). The skillet may not be as elegant or ergonomic as the Norpro (our top choice among models tested), but it will suffice for any home cook who rarely takes to pounding meat.

BEST MEAT POUNDERS
The Norpro Offset Pounder (left) was the clear favorite in our tests. Its offset handle and moderate weight make it both effective and easy to control. If you don't want to buy a meat pounder, we found that a small skillet (right) works pretty well if not terribly elegantly.

COCONUT CREAM PIE

WHAT WE WANTED: A dreamily soft, delicately perfumed, luscious filling nestled in a crisp crust.

Coconut cream pie evokes happy thoughts—a fluffy cloud of a dessert, a sweet finish to a satisfying home-cooked meal. But imagining the taste of a perfect coconut cream pie can be a much different experience from eating a piece that's right in front of you. We discovered this first-hand when we whipped up a few recipes. These coconut cream pies did not have the smooth and satiny fillings and crisp crusts we had hoped for. Instead, they were disappointingly heavy, leaden, pasty, noxiously sweet, bland vanilla puddings in soggy pie shells. Hardly what we had in mind.

First, we went to work on the crust. Though a plain pastry crust is typical of a coconut cream pie, we were not the least bit wowed. The crust was fully prebaked and started out perfectly crisp, but when the filling went in, it quickly became soggy. For cream pies, we have in the past advocated rolling out a basic pie pastry in graham cracker crumbs. This speckled crust stayed crispy longer than the plain pie pastry, but we still had misgivings, mostly about its texture. It was a crust made entirely of graham crackers—a somewhat unorthodox but not completely odd option—that was the crowd-pleaser. Its crisp, sandy texture, sturdy construction, and substantial presence was the perfect contrast to the creamy smooth filling. Its sweet, toasty flavor also complemented the mild flavor of the filling.

It occurred to us, though, that the flavor of the graham cracker crust could be heightened and made to better fit its role by adding some coconut to it. In our next attempts, we toasted some shredded coconut until it was golden brown, then processed it along with the graham crackers so that it could be broken down into the finest bits. The coconut was a welcomed addition; though it offered only a little flavor, ¼ cup of it dispersed throughout the cracker crumbs gave the crust that characteristic fibrous, nubby coconut crunch.

Coconuts are exotic tropical nuts (seeds, actually). They hail from lands of balmy breezes, palm trees, and ocean air, but recipes for coconut cream pie fillings are often boring and domesticated. They consist of no more than eggs, sugar, cornstarch or flour, and cream or milk. In a nutshell, they are vanilla cream pies garnished with a spray of toasted shredded coconut. We wanted to breathe some life into this downtrodden pie by pumping the filling full of true coconut flavor.

As with other cream pies, the filling for coconut cream pie is made on the stovetop in the same manner as a home-cooked pudding. In developing a filling, the first thing we needed to do was find the right kind of cream or "milk" to use. We made versions with half-and-half, whole milk, and coconut milk. As we expected, the first two made for boring, bland puddings. The coconut milk filling had a delicate coconut flavor and aroma, but it was far too rich to be palatable. We pulled back on the coconut milk and tried a filling made with one 14-ounce can of coconut milk cut with a cup of whole milk. Much better, but still we felt we needed to work in more coconut flavor.

We stirred some toasted shredded coconut into the filling, but the long stringy shreds suspended in the otherwise smooth filling were unappealing. Next, we took the advice of a recipe that suggested steeping unsweetened shredded coconut (which comes shredded in fine flecks and is available in natural foods and Asian grocery stores) in the milk to extract some of its flavor; the coconut was then strained out and pressed to remove any liquid that it was withholding. Though this technique didn't yield the results expected—the steeped mixture didn't have much more flavor and was a nuisance to boot—we did make the fortuitous discovery that the unsweetened shredded coconut itself had good, pure coconut flavor. We captured this delicate coconut flavor by leaving the tiny bits in the filling. The coconut also

As for eggs, some recipes called for whole eggs, some for just yolks, and a few for both. The number called for ranged from two to six. Our preference was for five yolks. This number made a filling with a smooth, lush, supple texture and a full, deep flavor. By comparison, fillings made with whole eggs—even with whole eggs plus yolks—had a leaner, gummier texture and a hollow flavor. In addition, their color wasn't as appealing as that of the all-yolk filling.

We were now very close to a final recipe. The last adjustments were to add some salt and vanilla to heighten and round out the flavors. Some butter whisked into the hot filling just before pouring it into its shell was the final touch that smoothed out any rough edges and made the coconut cream superbly creamy, rich, and silky—yet not so unctuous as to make one slice—topped with a puff of whipped cream—a challenge to eat.

Operationally, our coconut cream pie came together seamlessly. First, we made and prebaked the crust. While it sat cooling, we made the filling. As soon as the filling was done, we poured it—hot—into the cooled shell, covered the surface flush with plastic wrap (so that it didn't form a "skin"), and shuttled it into the refrigerator. Three or so hours later, when the pie was chilled and firm and ready to serve, we whipped up the cream with a bit of sugar and some vanilla (and some dark rum for those who cared for it), piled the cream on top, and gave it a sprinkle of toasted coconut. Finally, a truly memorable coconut cream pie that lived up to our notions of what it should be.

offered up its gritty coconut crunch. One-half cup of coconut in the filling was good; any more and it overran the smoothness of the filling.

Next we tasted one filling thickened with cornstarch and another with flour. The cornstarch, as we expected, made a filling with a lighter, more natural feel; the flour made a heavy and starchy goo. One-quarter cup of cornstarch was just the right amount to allow the filling to set up into a firm texture. When chilled, the pie sliced neatly and cleanly. The filling had just enough resistance to keep it from slipping and sliding onto the plate.

WHAT WE LEARNED: A graham cracker crust flavored with shredded coconut may not be traditional, but it is crisp, sweet, and, to our way of thinking, just what this pie needs. For the best flavor, use coconut milk and unsweetened shredded coconut in the filling. For the best texture, use cornstarch (not flour) and egg yolks (rather than whole eggs) to thicken the filling.

COCONUT CREAM PIE Serves 8 to 10

When toasting the coconut, keep a close eye on it because it burns quite easily.

coconut–graham cracker crust

5	tablespoons unsweetened shredded coconut
10	graham crackers (5 ounces, or 1 package), broken into rough pieces
2	tablespoons sugar
5	tablespoons unsalted butter, melted

coconut cream filling

1	can (14 ounces) coconut milk, well stirred
1	cup whole milk
½	cup (1¼ ounces) unsweetened shredded coconut
⅔	cup (4¾ ounces) sugar
¼	teaspoon salt
5	large egg yolks
¼	cup (1 ounce) cornstarch
1½	teaspoons vanilla extract
2	tablespoons unsalted butter, cut into 4 pieces

whipped cream topping

1½	cups heavy cream, chilled
1½	tablespoons sugar
1½	teaspoons dark rum, optional
½	teaspoon vanilla extract

1. FOR THE CRUST: Adjust an oven rack to the middle position and heat the oven to 325 degrees. Spread the 5 tablespoons coconut in a 9-inch Pyrex glass pie plate and toast in the oven until golden brown, about 9 minutes, stirring 2 or 3 times. When cool enough to handle, reserve 1 tablespoon for garnishing the finished pie.

2. Pulse the graham crackers and the remaining 4 tablespoons toasted coconut in a food processor until the crackers are broken down into coarse crumbs, about ten 1-second pulses. Process the mixture until evenly fine crumbs form, about 12 seconds. Transfer the crumbs to a medium bowl and stir in the sugar to combine; add the melted butter and toss with a fork until the crumbs are evenly moistened. Wipe out the now-empty pie plate and empty the crumb mixture into it. Using the bottom of a ramekin or measuring cup, press the crumbs evenly into the bottom and up the sides. Bake the crust until deep golden brown and fragrant,

---

TECHNIQUE:
Whipping Cream to Soft and Stiff Peaks

SOFT PEAKS
Cream whipped to soft peaks droops slightly from the ends of the beaters or whisk.

STIFF PEAKS
Cream whipped to stiff peaks clings tightly to the ends of the beaters or whisk and holds its shape.

---

about 22 minutes. Cool the crust on a wire rack while making the filling.

3. FOR THE FILLING: Bring the coconut milk, milk, shredded coconut, ⅓ cup sugar, and salt to a simmer in a medium saucepan over medium-high heat, stirring occasionally with a wooden spoon to dissolve the sugar. When the mixture reaches a simmer, whisk the egg yolks in a medium bowl to break them up, then whisk in the remaining ⅓ cup sugar and cornstarch until well-combined and no lumps remain. Gradually whisk the simmering liquid into the yolk mixture to temper it, then return the mixture to the saucepan, scraping the bowl with a rubber spatula. Bring the mixture to a simmer over medium heat, whisking constantly, until 3 or 4 bubbles burst on the surface and the mixture is thickened, about 30 seconds. Off heat, whisk in the vanilla and butter. Pour the filling into the cooled crust, press a sheet of plastic wrap directly on the surface of the filling, and refrigerate until the filling is cold and firm, at least 3 hours.

4. FOR THE TOPPING: Just before serving, whip the cream, sugar, rum, and vanilla in a chilled bowl with chilled beaters on low speed until small bubbles form, about 30 seconds. Increase the speed to medium and continue beating until beaters leave a trail, about 30 seconds longer. Increase the speed to high and beat until the cream is nearly doubled in volume and forms soft peaks, 30 to 60 seconds longer.

5. TO SERVE: Spread or pipe the whipped cream over the chilled pie filling. Sprinkle the reserved 1 tablespoon toasted coconut over the cream. Cut the pie into wedges and serve.

TASTING LAB: Graham Cracker Crusts

SAVING TIME IS ALWAYS A GOOD IDEA—JUST AS LONG AS you're not sacrificing quality. With this in mind, we thought we'd see if store-bought graham cracker pie crusts were worth their weight in pie tins. All you have to do is fill, chill, then serve. We sampled three such crusts (Nabisco Honey Maid Graham Pie Crust, Keebler Graham Cracker Ready Crust, and our local supermarket brand) and unanimously rejected all of them. Tasters described them as pale in color, with a "chalky," "sandy" texture, and "bland," "artificial" flavor. This could be attributed to the fact that all are made with vegetable shortening (already present in the graham cracker itself, but in much less quantity).

After this test, it was obvious to us that adding real butter to ground graham crackers was the best way to get a good-flavored crust and was well worth the few extra minutes. But are all graham crackers the same?

After experimenting with the three leading brands, we discovered subtle but distinct differences between them and found that these differences carried over into crumb crusts made with each kind of cracker. Our favorite was Nabisco Original Graham Crackers. Tasters liked the hardy molasses flavor in these crackers. The two other brands tested (Nabisco Honey Maid and Keebler Graham Crackers) both use honey and yielded crusts that were on the sweet side. We did find that packaged graham cracker crumbs are an acceptable substitute to making your own (they don't have the off flavors we found in premade crusts), but we could not find them made with Nabisco Original's.

BEST GRAHAM CRACKERS
Nabisco Original Graham Crackers have a hardy molasses flavor and make the best-tasting pie crust. Other graham crackers can be used, but don't bother with store-bought crusts—they are made with shortening rather than butter and taste terrible.

Once the chicken breasts have been roasted, it takes just five minutes to make a sauce in the empty skillet.

CHICKEN
CHAPTER II
in a skillet

A skillet can turn out hundreds of chicken dinners. For most Americans, chicken breasts are the holy grail of weeknight cooking. (We think thighs are more flavorful, but that's another story.) We like to cook split breasts (with the bones and skin still attached) as well as boneless, skinless cutlets. Adding a quick pan sauce enhances the split breasts, and a coating turns cutlets into something special.

Although these chicken dinners are quick to prepare, they can go terribly wrong. Part of the problem is the chicken itself—the breast meat has very little fat and will become dry and chalky if overcooked. The other major source of trouble is improper cooking methods. If you try to brown skin-on chicken breasts in a nonstick skillet, they won't produce the lovely browned bits that later must flavor the sauce. Likewise, if you use bad technique, it's easy to turn out breaded chicken cutlets that are greasy, soggy, and/or poorly browned.

Because Americans eat so much chicken, we decided to tackle these issues with some creativity. The inspired recipes that follow are foolproof and intriguing—a combination that is sure to please, night after night after night.

PAN-ROASTED CHICKEN BREASTS

WHAT WE WANTED: Crisp skin, moist meat, and a quick pan sauce.

Bone-in, skin-on chicken breasts look primitive compared with their boneless, skinless, trimmed, and filleted brethren, and the best way to cook them is primitive as well—over a live fire on a hot grill. But during the colder months of the year, cooking them becomes a challenge. Oven-roasting fails to impress us because the delicate white meat cooks faster than the skin can crisp. This cut of chicken is also difficult to sauté or cook through on the stovetop because it has great girth on one end and is thin and tapered on the other. If overcooked, it becomes dry and takes on the texture of overchewed bubble gum. And last, this piece of chicken has a mild—some might say bland—flavor that could certainly use a boost.

Our immediate thought was to try pan-roasting, a restaurant technique in which food is browned in a skillet on the stovetop and then placed, skillet and all, in a hot oven to finish cooking. We often employ this technique to cook a whole cut-up chicken and wondered if pan-roasting could be adapted to breasts only, where the meat is thicker and more prone to drying out than in the legs and thighs. The goal was to produce moist, tender, and crisp-skinned, bone-in chicken breasts.

The first problem we encountered was the packaging and quality of chicken breasts in the supermarket. Curiously, bone-in, skin-on split chicken breasts are often sold three to a package. (This makes no sense from either an anatomical or culinary perspective.) More problematic are the facts that split chicken breasts are often covered only by shreds of skin and that large portions of the meat near the breastbone are often missing. An additional reason not to buy split chicken breasts is that the pieces within one package can differ greatly in size (we found 9-ounce and 13-ounce pieces in one pack). Obviously, smaller pieces cook more quickly, so when cooking pieces of divergent sizes, we were forced to closely monitor them and pull the smaller breasts out earlier. Not ideal. Consequently, we found we prefer to purchase whole chicken breasts and split them ourselves so that we'd have more control over their size, quantity, and condition.

With these matters resolved, we tried brining the chicken—soaking it in a saltwater solution—before cooking it. It was no surprise that this chicken was superior—more moist and better seasoned than unbrined chicken. Brining also mitigated the dryness and blandness typical of chicken breasts. The sugar that the test kitchen typically likes in brines was omitted because it caused scorching in the skillet. We also found it necessary to rinse the brined chicken before cooking; otherwise the skin was unpalatably salty.

When it came to browning, we heated a mere teaspoon of vegetable oil in the skillet until it was smoking and then browned both sides of the chicken before transferring the skillet to the oven. We tried oven temperatures from 375 degrees up to 500. Five hundred caused profuse smoking and sometimes singed drippings. Temperatures on the lower end meant protracted cooking times. At 450, however, the skin was handsomely brown and crackling crisp.

The bonus of pan-roasting is that the skillet is left with caramelized drippings, or fond. To let the fond go to waste would be criminal; it is ideal for making a rich, flavorful pan sauce to accompany the chicken. Shallots, wine, chicken broth, herbs, and butter, or a variation on this combination, created pan sauces that added flavor interest and made these crisp-skinned, pan-roasted chicken breasts as good as, if not better than, their grilled incarnations.

WHAT WE LEARNED: Buy whole breasts and split them yourself to control their size, brine the breasts for maximum moistness, and then sear on the stovetop before letting them cook through in a 450-degree oven.

PAN-ROASTED CHICKEN BREASTS WITH SAGE-VERMOUTH SAUCE Serves 4

We prefer to split whole chicken breasts ourselves because store-bought split chicken breasts are often sloppily butchered. However, if you prefer to purchase split chicken breasts, try to choose 10- to 12-ounce pieces with skin intact. If split breasts are of different sizes, check the smaller ones a few minutes early to see if they are cooking more quickly, and remove them from the skillet if they are done ahead.

chicken

- 1   cup kosher salt (or ½ cup table salt)
- 2   whole bone-in, skin-on chicken breasts, about 1½ pounds each, split in half along breast bone and trimmed of rib sections
       Ground black pepper
- 1   teaspoon vegetable oil

sage-vermouth sauce

- 1   large shallot, minced (about 4 tablespoons)
- ¾   cup low-sodium chicken broth
- ½   cup dry vermouth
- 4   medium fresh sage leaves, each leaf torn in half
- 3   tablespoons unsalted butter, cut into 3 pieces
       Salt and ground black pepper

1. FOR THE CHICKEN: Dissolve the salt in 2 quarts cold water in a large container or bowl; submerge the chicken in the brine and refrigerate until fully seasoned, about 30 minutes. Rinse the chicken pieces under running water and pat dry with paper towels. Season the chicken with pepper.

2. Adjust an oven rack to the lowest position and heat the oven to 450 degrees.

3. Heat the oil in a heavy-bottomed 12-inch ovenproof skillet over medium-high heat until beginning to smoke; swirl the skillet to coat with the oil. Brown the chicken skin-side down until deep golden, about 5 minutes; turn the chicken and brown until golden on the second side, about 3 minutes longer. Turn the chicken skin-side down and place the skillet in the oven. Roast until the juices run clear when the chicken is cut with a paring knife, or the thickest part of the breast registers 160 degrees on an instant-read thermometer, 15 to 18 minutes. Transfer the chicken to a platter, and let it rest while making the sauce. (If you're not making the sauce, let the chicken rest 5 minutes before serving.)

4. FOR THE SAUCE: Using a potholder to protect your hands from the hot skillet handle, pour off most of the fat from the skillet; add the shallot, then set the skillet over medium-high heat and cook, stirring frequently, until the shallot is softened, about 1½ minutes. Add the chicken broth, vermouth, and sage; increase the heat to high and simmer rapidly, scraping the skillet bottom with a wooden spoon to loosen the browned bits, until slightly thickened and reduced to about ¾ cup, about 5 minutes. Pour the accumulated chicken juices into the skillet, reduce the heat to medium, and whisk in the butter 1 piece at a time; season to taste with salt and pepper and discard the sage. Spoon the sauce around the chicken breasts and serve immediately.

VARIATIONS

PAN-ROASTED CHICKEN BREASTS WITH GARLIC-SHERRY SAUCE

Peel 7 medium cloves garlic and cut crosswise into very thin slices (you should have about 3 tablespoons). Follow the recipe for Pan-Roasted Chicken Breasts with Sage-Vermouth Sauce, substituting the sliced garlic for the shallots and cooking the garlic until light brown, about 1½ minutes; also, substitute dry sherry for the vermouth and 2 sprigs fresh thyme for the sage. Add ½ teaspoon lemon juice along with the salt and pepper.

PAN-ROASTED CHICKEN BREASTS WITH SWEET-TART RED WINE SAUCE

This sauce is a variation on the Italian sweet-sour flavor combination called *agrodolce*.

Follow the recipe for Pan-Roasted Chicken Breasts with Sage-Vermouth Sauce, substituting ¼ cup each red wine and red wine vinegar for the vermouth and 1 bay leaf for the sage leaves. Add 1 tablespoon sugar and ¼ teaspoon ground black pepper to the skillet with chicken broth.

PAN-ROASTED CHICKEN BREASTS WITH ONION AND ALE SAUCE

Brown ale gives this sauce a nutty, toasty, bittersweet flavor. Newcastle Brown Ale and Samuel Smith Nut Brown Ale are good choices.

Follow the recipe for Pan-Roasted Chicken Breasts with Sage-Vermouth Sauce, substituting ½ medium onion, sliced very thin, for the shallot; cook the onion until softened, about 3 minutes. Also, substitute brown ale for the vermouth and 1 sprig fresh thyme for the sage. Add 1 bay leaf and 1 teaspoon brown sugar along with the chicken broth. Add ½ teaspoon cider vinegar along with the salt and pepper.

SCIENCE DESK:
When Is the Pan Hot Enough?

COOKS COMMONLY USE A DROP OF WATER TO HELP decide if the pan is warm enough to begin searing; when the drop begins to dance around the pan, the meat is added. But how often have you added the meat to the pan only to discover that it won't brown? Simple math tells us why. We all know that water boils at 212 degrees; what we may not know is that meat begins to brown well at above 310 degrees—that's a difference of about 100 degrees between the boiling point and the browning point.

Oil begins to break down when exposed to high heat and will release an acrid smoke. Olive oil smokes at about 375 degrees, peanut oil at about 440 degrees. If a drop of oil placed in the bottom of your pan is beginning to smoke, the temperature of the pan is plenty hot enough for good browning. We generally add food to the pan just as oil begins to smoke.

EQUIPMENT CORNER:
Traditional Skillets

HAVE YOU SHOPPED FOR A SKILLET RECENTLY? THE choices in material, weight, brand, and price—from $10 to $140—are dizzying. Preliminary tests on a lightweight discount store special selling for $10 confirmed our suspicions that cheap was not the way to go. But how much do you need to spend on this vital piece of kitchen equipment? To find out what more money buys, we zeroed in on a group of eight pans from well-known manufacturers, ranging in price from $60 to more than twice that, and sautéed our way to some pretty surprising conclusions.

All of the pans tested had flared sides, a design that makes it easier to flip foods in the pan (accomplished by jerking the pan sharply on the burner). Oddly, this design feature has created some confusion when it comes to nomenclature. Different manufacturers have different names for their flare-sided pans, including sauté pan, skillet, frypan, chef's pan, and omelet pan. In the test kitchen, we refer to flare-sided pans as skillets and to pans with straight sides (and often lids as well) as sauté pans. All of the pans tested also fall into a category we refer to as traditional—that is, none of the pans were nonstick. Most had uncoated stainless steel cooking surfaces, which we prize for promoting a *fond* (the brown, sticky bits that cling to the interior of the pan when food is sautéed and that help flavor sauces). We also included a Le Creuset model made from enameled cast iron.

The pans tested measured 12 inches in diameter (across the top) or as close to that as we could get from each manufacturer. We like this large size in a skillet because it can accommodate a big steak or all of the pieces cut from a typical 3½-pound chicken. Because the pan walls slope inward, the cooking surface of each pan is considerably smaller than 12 inches. In fact, we found that a loss of even ¼ inch of cooking space could determine whether all of the chicken pieces fit without touching and therefore how well they would brown. (If a pan is too crowded, the food tends to steam rather than brown.) For instance, the All-Clad, with its 9¼-inch cooking surface, accommodated the chicken pieces without incident, whereas the 9-inch cooking surface of the Viking caused the pieces to touch.

Skillet construction also varies, and our group included the three most popular styles: clad, disk bottom, and cast. The All-Clad, Viking, Calphalon, Cuisinart, and KitchenAid units are clad, which means that the whole pan body, from the bottom up through the walls, is made from layers of the same metal that have been bonded under intense pressure and heat. These layers often form a sandwich. The "filling" is made of aluminum, which has the fourth highest thermal conductivity of all metals, behind silver, copper, and gold, and each slice of "bread" is made of stainless steel, which is attractive, durable, and nonreactive with acidic foods but is also a lousy heat conductor on its own.

In the disk-bottom construction style, only the pan bottom is layered and the walls are thus thinner than the bottom. In our group, the Farberware has an aluminum sandwich base and the Emerilware has disks of both aluminum and copper in its base.

Casting is the third construction style, represented here by Le Creuset, in which molten iron is molded to form the pan, body and handle alike. Cast iron pans are known to be heavy, to heat up slowly, and to retain their heat well. The French Le Creuset pans are also enameled, which makes them nonreactive inside and out.

Did we uncover any significant differences in performance based on these three construction styles? Although some manufacturers tout the benefits of cladding, our kitchen testing did not support this. The two skillets with disk bottoms, the Farberware and the Emerilware, did heat up a little faster than the rest of the field, but it was easy to accommodate this difference by adjusting the stovetop burner.

To get a more precise answer to our question, we set up an experiment. Around the perimeter of pans of each construction type (and in the lightweight $10 pan mentioned earlier), we placed rings of solder with a melting point of 361 degrees and heated them from dead center. Over the course of several trials, we averaged the time it took the pans to reach 361 degrees all around (that is, the time it took all of the solder beads to melt). The difference between the clad and disk-bottomed pans was less than 15 percent (they all reached 361 degrees in four to five minutes), with the disk-bottomed pans heating up a little faster than the clad pans. This difference was of little significance.

We checked our observations with an industry expert, who, after expressing the desire to remain anonymous, admitted to reaching the same conclusion about skillets after trying many different models over the years. Because you cook on the bottom of a skillet (not the sides), cladding is not that important. It may be more important in saucepans and Dutch ovens, in which it's common practice to cook liquids, which are of course in contact with the sides of the pan.

The weight of the pans turned out to be more important than construction, especially in our solder tests. The lightweight (1 pound, 1 ounce) aluminum budget pan was the quickest to reach 361 degrees, at an average of 2.8 minutes, while the heavy 6.5-pound Le Creuset was the slowest, at an average of 10.1 minutes. The lightweight pan performed poorly in kitchen tests, while Le Creuset did well. Still, cast iron does have its disadvantages. The heavy Le Creuset pan is difficult to lift on and off the burner and to handle while cleaning. If your strength is limited, these factors can mean a lot. In addition, the pan's iron handle gets just as hot as the rest of the pan, so it's necessary to use a potholder both during and just after use.

We concluded that a range of 3 to 4 pounds is ideal in a 12-inch skillet. The medium-weight pans (especially those from All-Clad, Viking, and Calphalon) brown foods beautifully, and most testers handled them comfortably. These pans have enough heft for heat retention and structural integrity but not so much that they are difficult to lift or manipulate.

Which skillet should you buy? For its combination of excellent performance, optimum weight and balance, and overall ease of use, the All-Clad was our favorite. But the Calphalon and Farberware nearly matched the All-Clad and did so for less than half the price, making these pans best buys.

Rating Traditional Skillets

WE TESTED EIGHT TRADITIONAL SKILLETS WITH A 12-INCH DIAMETER (OR AS CLOSE TO IT AS WE COULD FIND IN THAT manufacturer's line) in six applications (cooking crêpes, searing steaks, simmering a pan sauce, browning stew meat, pan-roasting chicken, and sautéing onions). The skillets are listed in order of preference based on their performance in these tests as well as design factors. See www.americastestkitchen.com for up-to-date prices and mail-order sources for top-rated products.

HIGHLY RECOMMENDED
All-Clad Stainless 12-Inch Fry Pan $125.00
From crêpes to steak to chicken, this pan browned foods perfectly. Sometimes, however, more fond stuck to the pan than was left on the food. Spacious and easy to handle. A star performer.

HIGHLY RECOMMENDED
Viking 7-Ply 11-Inch Frying Pan $140.00
Eight pieces of chicken were a trifle crowded, but that was the only misstep in an otherwise excellent performance. Good news for the most expensive pan in the group.

BEST BUY
Calphalon Tri-Ply Stainless 12-Inch Omelette Pan $63.95
Really shines when it heats up for heavy searing and browning. Onions and crêpes, both cooked at moderate heat, were a tad pale but still acceptable. Easy to lift and maneuver. A fine pan at an attractive price.

BEST BUY
Farberware Millennium 18/10 Stainless Steel 12-Inch Covered Skillet $69.99
Easy to manipulate and wide open in terms of space, but this pan sautés a bit too quickly, which can lead to very dark fond when browning meat. Watch it carefully and adjust the heat if necessary.

RECOMMENDED WITH RESERVATIONS
Emerilware Stainless 12-Inch Frypan $59.99
Does well in higher-heat applications, such as searing steak and browning chicken, but sauté speed is fast, so keep an eye on the heat. Runs a little hot and is a bit heavy to lift, but by no means a bad pan.

RECOMMENDED WITH RESERVATIONS
Cuisinart MultiClad Stainless 12.5-Inch Skillet $99.99
A respectable performer with ample space for large batches, but required some attention to control the sauté speed. Plenty of space and a helper handle, but you have to watch the heat and take care with the handle, which ran hot in some tests.

RECOMMENDED WITH RESERVATIONS
KitchenAid Hi-Density Hard Anodized 12-Inch Skillet $119.00
Despite reliable performance, this pan was downgraded because the chicken was a bit crowded, the handle heated up, and the pan felt bulky and poorly balanced in the hands of some testers.

RECOMMENDED WITH RESERVATIONS
Le Creuset 12-Inch Iron Handle Skillet $85.50
Spacious and terrific at searing meat but also heavy, unwieldy, and hot-handled. Requires extra preheating time, and the pan's dark surface can make it difficult to judge fond development. Retains heat like a pro, but have a potholder handy and be prepared for some heavy lifting.

NUT-CRUSTED CHICKEN CUTLETS

WHAT WE WANTED: To create a new kind of breaded chicken cutlet, with nuts taking the place of bread crumbs. We also wanted to add a salad to make the dish a complete meal.

Sautéed chicken cutlets are basic fare in most every cook's repertoire. In many homes, they appear on the dinner table at least once a week. Although fast to prepare, sautéed cutlets can become a bit boring. By replacing bread crumbs with nuts, a simple breaded chicken cutlet can be quickly transformed. Yet, for the transformation to be a success, we had to make a few adjustments to our technique.

Using boneless skinless chicken breasts, we began by adapting our standard breading technique: dredge the chicken in flour, dip it in an egg wash, then coat with bread crumbs. We first tried replacing the bread crumbs with sliced almonds, but the thin almond slices refused to stick to the chicken. We had more success when the almonds were processed into fine crumbs in the food processor, but even then the crust tasted dense, oily, and sodden after it was cooked. In an effort to lighten the crust, we mixed the nuts with some bread crumbs. Testing various ratios of nuts to bread crumbs, we landed on a ratio of 2 parts freshly ground nuts to 1 part crumbs. We also found that the light, crispy Japanese-style bread crumbs called panko worked especially well.

Because the nut/bread crumb mixture was so dense, we wondered if the initial step of flouring the chicken was necessary. In cooking two nut-crusted pieces of chicken, one floured and one flourless, side by side, we found the differences to be minor; in the spirit of streamlining, we decided to omit the flouring step. It is sufficient just to dip the cutlets (already trimmed of excess fat and any tough tendons) in beaten egg and then in the nut-bread crumb mixture.

Cooking the chicken turned out to be fairly straightforward. The keys were to use a skillet large enough to comfortably cook four pieces of chicken and to use plenty of oil. Much like regular breaded chicken, the cutlets need to be pan-fried in a fair amount of oil rather than sautéed in a wisp of oil. We found that four cutlets are best cooked in six tablespoons of vegetable oil in a 12-inch skillet. When pan-frying almost anything, we have found that a nonstick skillet is best because there's no chance that any food or coating will cling to the pan surface. In addition, cleaning a nonstick surface is much easier; pan-frying can really make a mess in a conventional skillet.

As for flavor, we were surprised to find that the nut crust tasted relatively mild. To spruce it up, we tried flavoring the egg wash by introducing ingredients such as Dijon mustard and/or citrus zest; this was both easy and effective.

Noticing how well the nut-crusted chicken tasted with fruit, it was a short jump to pair the chicken with a wilted spinach salad with fruit-based dressings. Holding the chicken warm in a 200-degree oven, we simply wiped the oil out of the pan and returned it to the stovetop to make a warm dressing, which served to lightly wilt baby spinach without it turning wet or slimy. Cooked from start to finish in merely 45 minutes, this exotic-tasting meal is far from your average chicken and salad supper.

WHAT WE LEARNED: Ground almonds paired with panko create a rich-tasting crust for chicken that is light and crisp. Pan-fry the chicken for the best results. To make a quick side dish, heat some fruit and dressing in the empty pan and use it to wilt spinach salad.

FOOD FACT: Panko

Japanese bread crumbs, called panko, have a coarser texture than ordinary breadcrumbs, and they make for a much lighter and crunchier casserole topping and coating for deep-fried foods like tempura. We also like to use panko as a coating for breaded chicken cutlets.

ALMOND-CRUSTED CHICKEN CUTLETS WITH WILTED SPINACH–ORANGE SALAD

Serves 4

It should take about 10 seconds to process the almonds into fine crumbs—don't overprocess or the nuts will become oily. If you like, serve with couscous.

2   large eggs
1   teaspoon Dijon mustard
1¼ teaspoons grated zest from 1 orange, zested orange cut into 4 wedges
     Salt and ground black pepper
1   cup sliced almonds, processed into fine crumbs in the food processor
½   cup panko (Japanese-style bread crumbs)
4   boneless, skinless chicken cutlets (5 to 6 ounces each), trimmed (see the illustrations on page 139) and dried thoroughly with paper towels
½   cup vegetable oil
5   ounces baby spinach (about 6 cups)
2   medium oranges, peel and pith removed (see the illustrations at right), and then quartered through the ends and sliced crosswise into ¼-inch-thick pieces
1   small shallot, minced (about 2 tablespoons)

1. Lightly beat the eggs, mustard, 1 teaspoon orange zest, ½ teaspoon salt, and ¼ teaspoon pepper together in a shallow dish. Mix the almonds and panko in a separate shallow dish. Working with one piece of chicken at a time, dip the chicken into the egg mixture using tongs, turning to coat well and allowing excess to drip off. Drop the chicken into the nut mixture and press the nuts into the chicken with your fingers. Transfer the breaded chicken to a wire rack set over a baking sheet and repeat with the remaining chicken. Adjust an oven rack to the middle position and heat the oven to 200 degrees.

2. Heat 6 tablespoons oil in a heavy-bottomed, 12-inch nonstick skillet over medium-high heat until just smoking.

Place the chicken in the skillet gently and cook until golden brown and crisp on the first side, about 2½ minutes. Using tongs, flip the chicken; reduce the heat to medium and continue to cook until the meat feels firm when pressed gently, the second side is deep golden brown and crisp, and the chicken is no longer pink in the center, about 2 minutes longer. Transfer the chicken to a paper towel–lined plate and place the plate in the oven. Discard the oil in the skillet and, using tongs and paper towels, wipe the skillet clean.

> ### TECHNIQUE:
> #### Removing the Peel and Pith from Oranges
>
>
>
> 1. Start by slicing a small section, about ½ inch thick, from the top and bottom ends of the orange.
>
>
>
> 2. Use a very sharp paring knife to slice off the rind, including all of the bitter white pith. Slide the knife edges from the top to the bottom of the orange, following the outline of the fruit as closely as possible to minimize waste.

3. Place the spinach in a large bowl. Heat 1 tablespoon oil in the cleaned skillet over high heat until just smoking. Add the orange slices and cook until lightly browned around the edges, 1½ to 2 minutes. Remove the pan from the heat and add remaining 1 tablespoon oil, shallot, remaining ¼ teaspoon zest, ¼ teaspoon salt, and ⅛ teaspoon pepper and allow residual heat to soften the shallot, 30 seconds. Pour the warm dressing with the oranges over the spinach and toss gently to wilt. Remove the chicken from the oven and serve it immediately with the salad and orange wedges.

VARIATION

MACADAMIA NUT–CRUSTED CHICKEN BREASTS WITH WILTED SPINACH–PINEAPPLE SALAD

Buy peeled and cored pineapple at the supermarket to save time. Round out the meal with white rice.

Follow the recipe for Almond-Crusted Chicken Breasts with Wilted Spinach-Orange Salad, omitting the mustard. Substitute lime zest and lime wedges for the orange zest and orange wedges and macadamia nuts for the almonds. Substitute 2 cups fresh pineapple cut into ¾-inch dice for the orange slices in step 3, sautéing the pineapple for 2 minutes.

TECHNIQUE:
Trimming Chicken Cutlets

1. Place each cutlet tenderloin-side down and smooth the top with your fingers. Any fat will slide to the periphery, where it can be trimmed with a knife.

2. To remove the tough, white tendon, turn the cutlet tenderloin-side up and peel back the thick half of the tenderloin so it lies top-down on the work surface. Use the point of a paring knife to cut around the top of the tendon to expose it, then scrape the tendon free with a knife.

TECHNIQUE: Freezing Small Portions

1. Place two portions of food (such as two chicken cutlets) in different locations inside a large zipper-lock freezer bag. Flatten the bag, forcing the air out in the process, so that the portions do not touch.

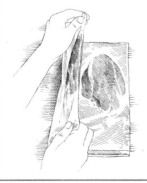

2. Fold the bag over in the center and freeze. The bag divides the two portions so they will freeze separately. Best of all, you have the option of using one or both frozen portions.

The back kitchen is filled with food being prepared for use on the set.

CHICKEN
in a pot

Herbert Hoover may have promised Americans a chicken in every pot, but no one said that chicken couldn't be French. In fact, French country cooking has a way with chicken in a pot, whether it's the famous chicken with 40 cloves of garlic or the lesser-known chicken Provençal with tomatoes and olives. When made correctly, these dishes take chicken to new heights.

But these dishes can also go astray. The 40 cloves of garlic may be raw tasting and harsh, or the sauce may be thin and vapid. Chicken Provençal can be greasy or overwhelmed by a thick, sweet tomato sauce. The goal for the test kitchen was simple: Rework these French classics so that all Americans would welcome such chickens into their pots.

CHICKEN WITH 40 CLOVES OF GARLIC

WHAT WE WANTED: Well-browned, crisp-skinned chicken paired with sweet, nutty garlic and a savory sauce.

Poulet à quarante gousses d'ail, or chicken with 40 cloves of garlic, is a classic Provençal dish that entered into the American culinary consciousness several decades ago, when our interest in French gastronomy was sparked. But since its introduction, chicken with 40 cloves of garlic has failed to make it onto many dinner tables or into many cooks' repertoires . . . and not without reason.

Recipes for chicken with 40 cloves of garlic involve a whole or cut-up chicken. Sometimes the chicken is browned, sometimes not. It is put into a pot along with raw garlic cloves (most often unpeeled), some liquid (usually wine and/or chicken broth), sometimes onions and other aromatic vegetables and herbs, and then the lot is cooked, covered, for an hour or more. The garlic becomes soft and spreadable, but its flavor is spiritless, not like that of sweet, sticky roasted garlic. With such prolonged cooking, the chicken becomes tender, but the breast meat takes on a dry chalky quality, and the flavor of the chicken in general is vapid, as if it had been washed out into the liquid. In addition, as cannot be helped in moist heat cookery, the chicken skin is soggy, flabby, and wholly unappealing, even if the chicken had first been browned.

A diagnostic test of several recipes found all tasters in agreement. We all sought richer, more concentrated flavors like those imparted by roasting, not braising. We wanted the chicken browned, full-flavored, and crisp-skinned, the garlic browned, sweet, and nutty. And we wanted a savory sauce to unite the elements.

Our first decision was to use a cut-up chicken rather than a whole bird because it cooks faster and more evenly. We brined the chicken, browned it in a large skillet, tossed in the unpeeled garlic cloves from three medium heads (42 cloves, so pretty true to the name), and slipped the skillet into a hot oven. About 12 minutes later, the chicken was fully cooked; we removed the chicken pieces, leaving the garlic in the skillet, and made a pan sauce with the drippings, wine, chicken broth, and butter. The gravest offense of this attempt came from the garlic: The cloves were far from done. Although they were browned, they were neither creamy nor spreadable, and they had a raw, fiery flavor. The second problem was that the chicken, though flavorful and crisp-skinned, seemed divorced from the other elements. Third, the sauce lacked depth and tasted of neither the chicken nor the garlic. Despite its demerits, this technique showed enough promise that we were compelled to pursue it.

We grappled with the garlic first. We knew that to soften and gain color the cloves would have to roast in dry heat, but they would require considerably more time to roast than was built into the pan-roasting technique. Hence, they would need to be at least partially roasted by the time they joined the chicken. Some tests later, we arrived at roasting the garlic cloves, tossed with a little olive oil, salt, and pepper, in a small baking dish for 40 minutes in a 400-degree oven. For the first 30 minutes, they cooked under foil to speed things along. For the final 10 minutes, they went uncovered to finish browning. At this point, the garlic cloves were soft, sweet, and mellow but could still withstand some additional cooking with the chicken and sauce. Because the garlic could be roasted while the chicken was being brined and browned, this step did not add time to the recipe.

We then focused on refining the cooking technique. In a braise, the chicken cooks half-submerged in simmering liquid, and an exchange of flavors thereby occurs to the benefit of both the chicken and the liquid that becomes the sauce. This made us think to modify the pan-roasting technique. After we browned the chicken, we poured off the rendered fat, added chicken broth and dry vermouth (we came to use vermouth because it is herbaceous, slightly

sweet, and more flavorful than most white wines of the same price), added the roasted garlic cloves, returned the chicken skin-side up, and then put the skillet into the 400-degree oven from which the garlic had emerged. Things were slightly improved with this pan-roasting/braising technique. The sauce had better flavor, although it was still mousy, especially in texture, and the chicken seemed to be more a part of the dish. The skin, however, had turned soggy from the moisture.

To counter the effects of the moisture, we tried increasing the oven temperature to 450 degrees. This produced acceptably crisp skin. The ultimate solution, however, was a quick blast of broiler heat, which crisped the skin very nicely in less than five minutes. Because cooks with drawer-type gas broilers might find this step inconvenient, if not impossible, we made it optional. We were nonetheless pleased with the results of this hybrid pan-roasting/braising technique.

Now a different issue came into play. The brined chicken, cooked in the liquid that eventually becomes the sauce, seemed to exude juices that resulted in an overseasoned sauce, even for those tasters who love salt. We pulled back on the salt in the brine until we were using only ¼ cup of table salt per 2 quarts of water. Unsure that this small amount was of any benefit to the dish as a whole, we compared it with a batch made with unbrined chicken. Even this weak brine improved the flavor and juiciness of the cooked chicken.

Finally, we worked on the flavor of the sauce. Inspired by those recipes that included onions, we roasted some shallots—milder in flavor than onions—with the garlic cloves to see if they would affect the flavor of the sauce. Indeed they did. The sauce tasted fuller and rounder. Some tasters even found the roasted shallots to be good eating. Herbs—thyme, rosemary, and bay—all had pleasing effects on the flavor of the sauce, offering depth and complexity.

We had seen in another recipe the recommendation of mashing a few of the garlic cloves and adding them back to the sauce. Using a mesh sieve and rubber spatula, we made a paste of a dozen or so peeled garlic cloves and whisked it into the sauce (peeling the cloves and then mashing them on a cutting board with the back of a fork is another effective method). What an extraordinarily good idea. The garlic paste endowed the sauce with the velvety texture of a well-made gravy, and the sauce was now richly flavored with garlic as well as chicken and wine. Last, a couple tablespoons of butter to enrich the sauce met with applause. *Enfin, un nouveau poulet à quarante gousses d'ail est arrivé.*

WHAT WE LEARNED : **To give this dish the complete overhaul it needs, brown a cut-up chicken in a skillet, build a sauce in the pan with roasted garlic and shallots, and then roast the chicken (now back in the pan) in the oven. Then give the chicken a final run under the broiler to ensure crisp skin. Finally, puree some of the garlic to thicken and flavor the sauce.**

CHICKEN WITH 40 CLOVES OF GARLIC

Serves 3 to 4

Try not to purchase heads of garlic that contain enormous cloves; if unavoidable, increase the foil-covered baking time to 40 to 45 minutes so that the largest cloves soften fully. A large Dutch oven can be used in place of a skillet, if you prefer. Broiling the chicken for a few minutes at the end of cooking crisps the skin, but this step is optional. Serve the dish with slices of crusty baguette; you can dip them into the sauce or spread them with the roasted garlic cloves.

    Salt
1   chicken (3½ to 4 pounds), cut into 8 pieces
    (4 breast pieces, 2 thighs, 2 drumsticks) and
    trimmed of excess fat
    Ground black pepper
3   medium heads garlic (about 8 ounces), outer
    papery skins removed, cloves separated and
    unpeeled
2   medium shallots, peeled and quartered pole to
    pole
1   tablespoon olive oil
2   sprigs fresh thyme
1   sprig fresh rosemary
1   bay leaf
¾   cup dry vermouth or dry white wine
¾   cup low-sodium chicken broth
2   tablespoons unsalted butter

1. Adjust an oven rack to the middle position and heat the oven to 400 degrees. Dissolve ¼ cup salt in 2 quarts cold tap water in a large container; submerge the chicken pieces in the brine and refrigerate until fully seasoned, about 30 minutes. Rinse the chicken pieces under running water and thoroughly pat dry with paper towels. Season both sides of the chicken pieces with pepper.

2. Meanwhile, toss the garlic and shallots with 2 teaspoons olive oil and salt and pepper to taste in a 9-inch pie plate; cover tightly with foil and roast until softened and beginning to brown, about 30 minutes, shaking the pan once to toss the contents after 15 minutes (the foil can be left on during tossing). Uncover, stir, and continue to roast, uncovered, until browned and fully tender, 10 minutes longer, stirring once or twice. Remove from the oven and increase the oven temperature to 450 degrees.

GETTING IT RIGHT: Developing the Flavor of the Garlic

Remove the outer papery skins from three heads of garlic and separate but do not peel the individual cloves (far left). Lightly oil the cloves and roast them in a pie plate covered with foil; remove the foil (second from left) and continue to roast until the cloves are fully tender. Add the roasted cloves to the braising liquid in the skillet (center), return the chicken to the pan, and place the skillet in the oven. When the chicken is done, use a rubber spatula to push a dozen garlic cloves through a mesh sieve to remove the skins and obtain a smooth paste (second from right). Whisk the garlic paste into the sauce just before serving (right).

3. Using kitchen twine, tie together the thyme, rosemary, and bay; set aside. Heat remaining 1 teaspoon oil in a 12-inch heavy-bottomed ovenproof skillet over medium-high heat until beginning to smoke; swirl to coat the pan with oil. Brown the chicken pieces skin-side down until deep golden, about 5 minutes; using tongs, turn the chicken pieces and brown until golden on second side, about 4 minutes longer. Transfer the chicken to a large plate and discard the fat; off heat, add the vermouth, chicken broth, and herbs, scraping the bottom of the skillet with a wooden spoon to loosen browned bits. Set the skillet over medium heat, add the garlic/shallot mixture, then return the chicken, skin-side up, to the pan, nestling the pieces on top of and between the garlic cloves.

4. Place the skillet in the oven and roast until an instant-read thermometer inserted into the thickest part of the breast registers about 160 degrees, 10 to 12 minutes. If desired, increase the heat to broil and broil to crisp the skin, 3 to 5 minutes. Using potholders or oven mitts, remove the skillet from oven and transfer the chicken to a serving dish. Remove 10 to 12 garlic cloves to a mesh sieve and reserve; using a slotted spoon, scatter the remaining garlic cloves and shallots around the chicken and discard the herbs. With a rubber spatula, push the reserved garlic cloves through a sieve and into a bowl; discard the skins. Add the garlic paste to the skillet. Bring the liquid to a simmer over medium-high heat, whisking occasionally to incorporate the garlic; adjust the seasoning with salt and pepper to taste. Whisk in the butter; pour the sauce into a sauceboat, and serve.

TECHNIQUE: Cutting Up a Chicken

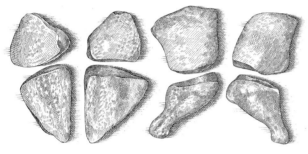

For chicken with 40 cloves of garlic, cut a whole chicken into two drumsticks, two thighs, and four breast pieces. Discard the wings and back or save them for making stock.

TECHNIQUE: An Extra-Large Trivet

There never seem to be enough spots in the kitchen to place a hot pan or pot. To solve this problem, we place an overturned rimmed baking sheet on the counter and use it as a trivet on which to rest a hot roasting pan, Dutch oven, or skillet.

EQUIPMENT CORNER: Kitchen Shears

A PAIR OF KITCHEN SHEARS IS NOT AN ESSENTIAL KITCHEN implement. But when you need to butterfly or trim chicken, there is no better tool. To test their versatility, we also used kitchen shears to cut lengths of kitchen twine, trim pie dough, and cut out parchment paper rounds. We found two pairs to recommend.

Wüsthof Kitchen Shears ($27.99) made easy, smooth cuts even through small chicken bones and completed all tasks flawlessly. The size and proportion of the shears felt ideal—the blades could open wide for large jobs and to

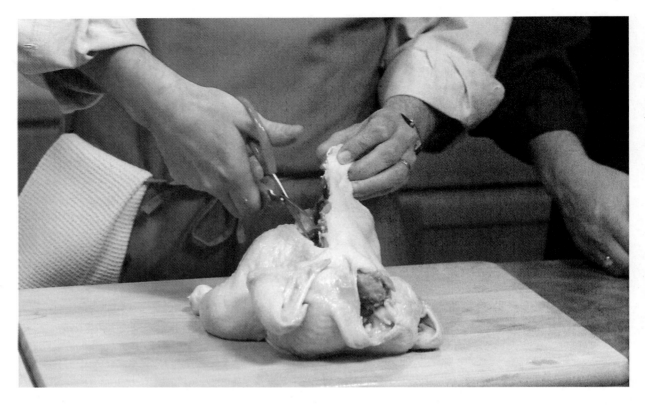

achieve more forceful cutting, but the shears were also suited to smaller, more detailed tasks such as snipping pieces of twine. These shears boasted heft, solid construction, and textured handles that were comfortable, even when wet and greasy. They were also suitable and comfortable for left-handed users.

Messermeister Take Apart Kitchen Shears ($16.99) were also great performers, though the blades didn't have quite the spread of those on the Wüsthof. These shears, too, made clean, easy cuts and accomplished all tasks without hesitation. The Messermeister shears came apart for cleaning, which we found to be neither a benefit nor a disadvantage. The soft, rubber-like handles proved extremely comfortable but were clearly designed for right-handed users.

Three pairs of shears fall into the category of "recommended with reservations." The first pair is Henckels Twin M Kitchen Shears ($39.99). These shears were of nice size and proportion and made smooth, clean, easy cuts. They were also handsome—in fact, too much so. The design of the handle seemed to sacrifice comfort for style. More effort was needed to butterfly a chicken with the Chicago Cutlery Walnut Signature Kitchen Scissors ($9.95). When making cuts requiring some force, the handles were hard and unforgiving. Joyce Chen Scissors ($18.00) cut through chicken bones with ease but slipped when cutting through skin, and their relatively diminutive size sometimes made the cutting motion feel more like a snipping motion. Given their size and feather weight, these scissors were suitable to more detailed tasks, such as cutting parchment paper rounds.

The two pairs of shears that we cannot recommend are F. Dick Come-Apart Kitchen Scissors ($31.60) and Oxo Good Grips Kitchen Scissors ($11.95). The F. Dick pair failed miserably at butterflying a chicken. The handles were actually painful to use and slippery when greasy and wet. Their ponderous weight was also a disadvantage, particularly for smaller, finer cutting. The Oxo Kitchen Scissors struggled to get through the chicken and were the only pair that had trouble snipping kitchen twine. The spring-loaded design made the scissors feel rather uncontrollable and difficult to use with precision.

Rating Kitchen Shears

WE TESTED SEVEN PAIRS OF KITCHEN SHEARS IN A VARIETY OF KITCHEN TASKS—EVERYTHING FROM BUTCHERING A chicken to trimming pie dough. The shears are listed in order of preference based on their performance in these tests as well as on design and ease of use. See www.americastestkitchen.com for up-to-date prices and mail-order sources for top-rated products.

RECOMMENDED
Wüsthof Kitchen Shears
$27.99
These shears made smooth, easy cuts through bones and performed all tasks flawlessly. Suitable and comfortable for both lefties and righties.

RECOMMENDED
Messermeister Take Apart Kitchen Shears
$16.99
These shears cut cleanly in all tests. Righties found the soft rubber-like handles comfortable, but lefties were less enthusiastic. An excellent value.

RECOMMENDED WITH RESERVATIONS
Henckels Twin M Kitchen Shears
$39.99
Excellent performance but uncomfortable handles bothered most testers. Sharp edges between the two handles gave pause to some users.

RECOMMENDED WITH RESERVATIONS
Chicago Cutlery Walnut Signature Kitchen Scissors
$9.95
Butterflying a chicken required some force, and the handles were hard and unforgiving.

RECOMMENDED WITH RESERVATIONS
Joyce Chen Scissors
$18.00
These small scissors are better suited to snipping chives than cutting up a chicken.

NOT RECOMMENDED
F. Dick Come-Apart Kitchen Scissors
$31.60
Handles are painful to use and slippery when greasy or wet. Heavier than the rest of the pack and less comfortable to use.

NOT RECOMMENDED
Oxo Kitchen Scissors
$11.95
These spring-loaded scissors struggled to snip kitchen twine; forget about cutting through bone.

TASTING LAB: Garlic

GARLIC FALLS INTO TWO PRIMARY CATEGORIES: HARDNECK and softneck. The garlic that most of us cook with is soft-neck, so called because its neck is soft and braidable. Softneck garlic contains a circle of plump cloves shrouding a second circle of smaller cloves, all enveloped by many papery layers. Because softneck garlic is heat tolerant and produces and stores well, it has become the favored commercial garlic. Supermarket garlics are almost invariably softneck.

Hardneck, which is the original cultivated garlic variety, is distinguished by its stiff center staff, around which large uniform cloves hang. Hardneck garlic has a relatively sparse parchment wrapper that makes it easier to peel (and damage) than softneck. It is considered superior in flavor—more complex and intense than softneck. Its thinly wrapped cloves lose moisture quickly, however, and do not winter over, as do the cloves of the robust softneck.

We tasted eight garlic varieties, softneck and hardneck, raw and cooked, and found a wide range of flavors. We enjoyed several softneck and hardneck varieties, but our favorites were Porcelain Zemo and Rocambole Carpathian, both of which are hardnecks.

HARDNECK GARLIC   **SOFTNECK GARLIC**

Hardneck garlic has a stiff center staff around which its large, uniformly sized cloves hang. Softneck garlic, the kind found most commonly in supermarkets, has cloves of varying sizes (larger on the outside, smaller near the center) and no central staff.

TASTING LAB: Dry Vermouth

THOUGH IT'S OFTEN USED IN COOKING, AND EVEN MORE often in martinis, dry vermouth is a potable that is paid very little attention. Imagine our surprise, then, when we did a little research and turned up nearly a dozen different brands. We pared them down to eight and tasted the vermouths straight (chilled) and in simple pan sauces for chicken (containing only shallots, chicken broth, and butter in addition to the vermouth).

First, a quick description of what dry vermouth is. Its base is a white wine, presumably not of particularly high quality, as evidenced by the relatively low prices of most vermouths. The wine is fortified with neutral grapes spirits that hike the alcohol level up a few percentage points to 16 to 18 percent, and it is "aromatized," or infused with "botanicals," such as herbs, spices, and fruits. In this country, dry vermouth, also called extra-dry vermouth, is imported from France and Italy (Italian vermouths being most common here) or is made domestically in California.

Two vermouths found their way into the top three in both tastings: Gallo Extra Dry and Noilly Prat Original French Dry. Gallo is the fruitier of the two and made the favorite pan sauce, which tasters called balanced, complex, smooth, and round. Noilly Prat is more woodsy and herbaceous and made a pan sauce that tasted fresh and balanced.

Rating Dry Vermouths

WE GATHERED EIGHT DRY VERMOUTHS MADE IN CALIFORNIA, FRANCE, AND ITALY, AND NINE TASTERS SAMPLED THEM straight (chilled) and in a simple pan sauce for chicken made with just chicken broth, shallots, butter, and vermouth. Panelists were asked to rate each vermouth and describe its aroma and flavor. The vermouths are listed below in order of preference based on their combined scores from the two tastings.

RECOMMENDED

Gallo Extra Dry Vermouth (California)

$5.00 for 750 ml

Simple but floral and fruity, with hints of melons and apples.

RECOMMENDED

Noilly Prat Original French Dry Vermouth (France)

$6.79 for 750 ml

Honeyed, herbaceous, and woodsy, with faint anise notes and a subtle bitterness.

NOT RECOMMENDED

Boissiere Vermouth (Italy)

$6.99 for 1 liter

Floral aroma and flavors, and a sherry-like finish. The pan sauce tasted sweet and stale.

NOT RECOMMENDED

Martini & Rossi Extra Dry Vermouth (Italy)

$6.79 for 750 ml

Medicinal and harsh tasted straight. The vermouth made a sweet-sour pan sauce.

NOT RECOMMENDED

Cinzano Extra Dry Vermouth (Italy)

$6.79 for 750 ml

Sweet, woodsy, and tannic. The pan sauce was dull and unremarkable.

NOT RECOMMENDED

Stock Extra Dry Vermouth (Italy)

$6.79 for 1 liter

Fruity nose, very dry, and slightly tart. Acidic and vinegary in a pan sauce.

NOT RECOMMENDED

Tribuno Extra Dry Vermouth (California)

$4.99 for 1 liter

Harsh, bitter, and alcoholic tasted straight. Harsh and acidic in a pan sauce.

NOT RECOMMENDED

Vya Extra Dry Vermouth (California)

$19.99 for 750 ml

Smoky, earthy, and spicy. Sour, woodsy, and a bit unbalanced in a pan sauce.

CHICKEN PROVENÇAL

WHAT WE WANTED: A chicken dish that was meltingly tender, moist, and flavorful, napped in an aromatic, garlicky tomato sauce that we could mop up with a good loaf of crusty bread.

Chicken Provençal may represent the best of French peasant cooking—chicken pieces on the bone simmered in a liquid flavored with tomatoes, garlic, herbs, and olives—but it is not well known here in the United States. We soon discovered why. The handful of recipes we tested produced rubbery, dry chicken, dull and muddy flavors, and a sauce that was too thick or too thin, too sweet or too greasy.

Most recipes we reviewed began with browning a cut-up whole chicken, removing the parts from the pot, sautéing some aromatic vegetables, deglazing the pot with white wine or dry vermouth, adding stock, tomatoes, olives, and herbs, and then simmering the chicken in the liquid until it was cooked. When we used a whole cut-up chicken, we encountered several problems. First, the breast pieces always dried out and lacked flavor after cooking. Second, the skin, although crisp after browning, turned soggy and unappealing after braising. Finally, the wings contained mostly inedible skin and very little meat. We tried again, using only dark meat, which, with its extra fat and connective tissue, was better suited to braising. The meat turned out tender, moist, and flavorful—far more appealing than either the breasts or the wings. We had used whole legs for this first test with dark

meat, but because tasters preferred the meatier thighs to the drumsticks, we decided to make the dish with thighs only.

Next we addressed the skin. Its flabby texture after cooking made it virtually inedible. When we began with skinless thighs, however, they stuck to the pan, the outer layer of meat becoming tough and dry with browning. The skin, it turns out, acts as a necessary cushion between the meat and the pan, so we left it on for browning and then discarded it. We also wondered if the amount of browning mattered. A side-by-side taste test—one batch made with lightly browned thighs, the other with deeply browned thighs—revealed that more browning renders more fat and results in more chicken flavor.

We assumed that olive oil was essential to this dish (it is ostensibly from Provence, after all), but most recipes (which use about three tablespoons) were too greasy. We browned a batch of thighs in a meager 1 tablespoon of oil and found that the skin quickly rendered a couple of additional tablespoons of fat. But even with this reduced amount of fat, tasters found the final dish to be greasy. Pouring off all but 1 tablespoon of fat after browning the chicken eliminated the greasiness, but now the flavor of the sauce was lacking. We were throwing flavor out with the rendered fat. We tried another test using just 1 teaspoon of oil. Sure enough, using less olive oil at the beginning allowed for a stronger chicken flavor in the final dish because we were discarding less chicken fat. We had one more test in mind—drizzling 2 teaspoons of extra-virgin olive oil over the finished dish just before serving. Tasters approved of the additional fruity olive flavor.

Our final tests with the chicken focused on the cooking method. Almost by definition, chicken Provençal is braised (browned and then cooked in a tightly covered pot in a small amount of liquid over low heat for a lengthy period of time). Stovetop braising proved unreliable. The cooking time varied, and, despite the fact that we set the

---

FOOD FACT: Chicken Provençal

The term Provençal refers to the dishes prepared in the style of Provence, a region in southeastern France. Garlic, tomatoes, and olive oil are the trademarks of Provençal cooking. Onions, olives, mushrooms, anchovies, and eggplant also play a prominent part in many of these dishes.

---

flame at the same heat level every time, the heat transfer was not uniform. Braising in a 300-degree oven was much more reliable, producing a predictably even, consistent level of heat. Next we tested the optimal braising time. Technically, thighs are considered done when they reach an internal temperature of 170 degrees, or after 30 minutes of braising. Unfortunately, 30 minutes of braising produced thighs that were not as meltingly tender as desired, and the chicken did not have enough flavor. What if we were to cook them longer? Would they dry out?

To our great surprise, after trying longer and longer cooking times, we ended up keeping the dish in the oven for a whopping 1½ hours. At this point, the meat simply falls off the bone; it is exceedingly tender and flavorful, and the thighs did not seem overcooked. Additional tests, however, revealed that slightly less time—1¼ hours, wherein the meat reaches an internal temperature of 210 degrees—was perfect, as the meat then stays on the bone. Why this long cooking time? The long stay in the oven breaks down the connective tissue in the thighs, much as it does in a pot roast, yielding more tender meat. (White meat contains little connective tissue, so there's no benefit to cooking it longer.) In addition, thighs have plenty of fat that keeps them moist as they braise away.

Many recipes call for browning onions after the chicken is browned and taken out of the pot. Tasters approved of some onion, but not a lot, commenting that a modest amount of its pungent flavor was enough to balance the sweetness of the tomatoes. Garlic is most often added next and sautéed briefly to bring forth its flavor. Preliminary tests showed that both dry white wine and dry vermouth work well for deglazing the pan, but the wine turned out to be the favorite among tasters. The vermouth seemed to exaggerate the acidity of the tomatoes.

Crushed and pureed canned tomatoes each produced a thick, sweet, overbearing sauce reminiscent of a bad Italian restaurant. Canned diced tomatoes, though more promising, presented the opposite problem: Even when drained they contain a fair amount of liquid, and the resulting sauce was too thin. We added a few tablespoons of tomato paste to the diced tomatoes and the texture improved dramatically—now the sauce coated the chicken without overwhelming it. Chicken broth rounded out the flavors.

Whole niçoise olives appeared in just about every recipe, but tasters complained about the pits. Niçoise are so small that pitting by hand with a knife is unreasonable. We tried kalamatas, gaetas, and oil-cured olives, but none of them sufficed. The flavors of their brine or oil were too strong and inappropriate. While discussing this predicament with colleagues, a solution surfaced that involved a mallet and clean kitchen towels (see the illustration on page 152). Olives are best stirred in at the end of cooking, just before serving.

As for seasonings, the combination of dried herbs referred to as herbes de Provence (lavender, marjoram, basil, fennel seed, rosemary, sage, summer savory, and thyme) seemed like a shoe-in. But tasters said that when used alone, these dried herbs were too strong, giving the sauce a flavor that bordered on medicinal. Fresh thyme, oregano, and parsley with a bay leaf were preferred, and a teaspoon of the dried blend became an optional item. A pinch of cayenne balanced the sweet tomatoes.

Inspired by one of the better initial recipes tested, we tried adding a teaspoon of minced anchovies before deglazing. Although tasters could not identify the ingredient, everyone agreed the sauce tasted richer and fuller. The final item on our list was lemon zest, a common and, as it turned out, welcome addition. We found that the zest is best added at two points: first to the braising liquid while it is being reduced (just before serving) and second to the finished dish itself, sprinkled on top along with the parsley.

WHAT WE LEARNED: Use chicken thighs for the best flavor and texture. Brown the thighs in a sheer film of oil and then spoon off excess fat to keep the sauce from becoming greasy. Braise the chicken until it is meltingly tender—about one and one-quarter hours, which is far longer than most recipes suggest.

CHICKEN PROVENÇAL Serves 4

This dish is often served with rice or slices of crusty bread, but soft polenta is also a good accompaniment. Niçoise olives are the preferred olives here; the flavor of kalamatas and other types of brined or oil-cured olives is too potent.

8 bone-in, skin-on chicken thighs (about 3 pounds), trimmed of excess skin and fat
  Salt
1 tablespoon extra-virgin olive oil
1 small onion, chopped fine (about ⅔ cup)
6 medium cloves garlic, minced or pressed through a garlic press (about 2 tablespoons)
1 anchovy fillet, minced (about 1 teaspoon)
⅛ teaspoon cayenne
1 cup dry white wine
1 cup low-sodium chicken broth
1 can (14.5 ounces) diced tomatoes, drained
2½ tablespoons tomato paste
1½ tablespoons chopped fresh thyme leaves
1 teaspoon chopped fresh oregano leaves
1 bay leaf
1 teaspoon herbes de Provence (optional)
1½ teaspoons grated zest from 1 lemon
½ cup niçoise olives, pitted (see the illustration at right)
1 tablespoon chopped fresh parsley leaves

1. Adjust an oven rack to the lower-middle position; heat the oven to 300 degrees. Sprinkle both sides of the chicken thighs with salt to taste. Heat 1 teaspoon oil in a large Dutch oven over medium-high heat until shimmering but not smoking. Add 4 chicken thighs, skin-side down, and cook without moving them until the skin is crisp and well browned, about 5 minutes. Using tongs, turn the chicken pieces and brown on the second side, about 5 minutes longer; transfer to a large plate. Add the remaining 4 chicken thighs to the pot and repeat, then transfer them to a plate and set aside. Discard all but 1 tablespoon of fat from the pot.

2. Add the onion to the fat in the Dutch oven and cook, stirring occasionally, over medium heat until softened and browned, about 4 minutes. Add the garlic, anchovy, and cayenne; cook, stirring constantly, until fragrant, about 1 minute. Add the wine and scrape up browned bits from the pan bottom with a wooden spoon. Stir in the chicken broth, tomatoes, tomato paste, thyme, oregano, bay, and herbes de Provence (if using). Remove and discard the skin from the chicken thighs, then submerge the chicken pieces in the liquid and add the accumulated chicken juices to the pot. Increase the heat to high, bring to a simmer, cover, then set the pot in the oven; cook until the chicken offers no resistance when poked with the tip of a paring knife but is still clinging to the bones, about 1¼ hours.

3. Using a slotted spoon, transfer the chicken to a serving platter and tent with foil. Discard the bay leaf. Set the Dutch oven over high heat, stir in 1 teaspoon lemon zest, bring to

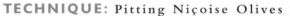

TECHNIQUE: Pitting Niçoise Olives

Removing the pits from tiny niçoise olives by hand is not an easy job. We found the following method to be the most expedient. Cover a cutting board with a clean kitchen towel and spread the olives on top, about 1 inch apart from each other. Place a second clean towel over the olives. Using a mallet, pound all of the olives firmly for 10 to 15 seconds, being careful not to split the pits. Remove the top towel, and, using your fingers, press the pit out of each olive.

a boil, and cook, stirring occasionally, until slightly thickened and reduced to 2 cups, about 5 minutes. Stir in the
olives and cook until heated through, about 1 minute.
Meanwhile, mix the remaining ½ teaspoon zest with the
parsley. Spoon the sauce over the chicken, drizzle the
chicken with the remaining 2 teaspoons olive oil, sprinkle
with the parsley mixture, and serve.

CHICKEN PROVENÇAL WITH SAFFRON, ORANGE, AND BASIL

Follow the recipe for Chicken Provençal, adding ⅛ teaspoon saffron threads along with the wine and substituting
orange zest for the lemon zest and 2 tablespoons fresh
chopped basil for the parsley.

Erin carries hot coals to the outdoor "test kitchen."

STEAK
CHAPTER 13
& potatoes

It's hard to beat steak and mashed potatoes for both simplicity and flavor. When you've purchased a good steak and cooked it properly, it needs little more than salt and pepper, and, of course, a side of spuds. Unfortunately, many of the inexpensive steaks labeled "great for grilling" at supermarkets turn out tough and dry and have little flavor.

We think premium steaks—the strip, rib-eye, and filet—are worth the extra money, but you certainly don't want to spend big bucks and then use the wrong grilling technique. We know many home cooks have trouble timing steaks on the grill—it can be a struggle to achieve a browned, crisp crust and a perfectly cooked center at the same time. We knew the test kitchen could fire up the grill and solve this problem.

When the steak is special, we think the potatoes should be, too. But all too often, mashed potatoes are gluey or runny. We wanted potatoes with perfect texture and big flavor—something unusual to accompany a great steak and a good bottle of wine.

GRILLED STEAKS

WHAT WE WANTED: A sure-fire technique for grilling the three most popular premium steaks—strip, rib-eye, and filet.

Grilled steaks have many attractive qualities: rich, beefy flavor; a thick, caramelized crust; and almost no prep or cleanup for the cook. But sometimes a small bonfire fueled by steak fat can leave expensive steaks charred and tasting of resinous smoke. And sometimes the coals burn down so low that the steaks end up with those pale, wimpy grill marks and just about no flavor at all. In those cases, you try leaving the steaks on the grill long enough to develop flavor, but they just overcook.

We went to work, promising ourselves we'd figure out how to use the grill to get the results we were after: meat seared evenly on both sides so that the juices are concentrated into a powerfully flavored, dark brown, brittle coating of crust; the juicy inside cooked a little past rare; and the outside strip of rich, soft fat crisped and browned slightly on the edges.

We decided to focus on the steaks from the short loin and rib sections of the animal that we think are the best the cow has to offer—the strip and filet mignon (both from the short loin) and the rib-eye (from the rib section). We figured these steaks were bound to take to pretty much the same cooking technique because they were all cut from the same general part of the cow.

Early on in our testing, we determined that we needed a very hot fire to get the crust we wanted without overcooking the steak. We could get that kind of heat by building the charcoal up to within 2 or 2½ inches of the grilling grate. But with this arrangement, we ran into problems with the fat dripping down onto the charcoal and flaming. We had already decided that a thick steak—at least 1½ inches thick, to be precise—was optimal because at that thickness we got a tasty contrast between the charcoal flavoring on the outside of the steak and the beefy flavor on the inside. The problem was that we couldn't cook a thick steak over consistently high heat without burning it.

After considerable experimentation, we resolved this dilemma: We had to build a fire with two levels of heat. Once we realized that we needed a fire with a lot of coals on one side and far fewer coals on the other, we could sear the steak properly at the beginning of cooking, then pull it onto the cooler half of the grill to finish cooking at a lower temperature. And we could use the dual heat levels to cook thin steaks as well as thick ones properly. The system also provided insurance against bonfires—if a steak flared up, we simply moved it off the high heat.

We found we could be sure we had the right levels of heat on both sides of the fire by holding a hand about five inches over the cooking grate. When the hot side of the grill was hot enough for searing, we could hold a hand over the grill for only about two seconds. For the cooler side of the grill, we could count four to five seconds. (This is how we adapted our recipes for a gas grill, using burners set to high and medium.)

Common cooking wisdom suggests that bringing meat to room temperature before grilling will cause it to cook

---

FOOD FACT: Steak Names

Steaks have curious names, and many of these names have interesting histories. Legend has its that England's King Henry VIII was so impressed with meat from the sirloin that he dubbed it "Sir Loin." (The more likely source for this word is the French *surlonge*, which translates as "over the loin.") The châteaubriand, the premium portion of the filet mignon, takes its name from the French statesman François Châteaubriand. The term *porterhouse* comes from the early 1800s, when travelers stopped to dine on steak and ale at coach stops, which were also known as porter houses.

---

more evenly and that letting it rest for five minutes after taking it off the grill will both preserve the juices and provide a more even color. We tested the first of these theories by simultaneously grilling two similar steaks, one straight from the refrigerator and a second that stood at room temperature for one hour. We noticed no difference in the cooked steaks except that the room temperature steak cooked a couple of minutes faster than the other. The second test was more conclusive. Letting a cooked steak rest for five minutes does indeed help the meat retain more juices when sliced and promotes a more even color throughout the meat.

We tried lightly oiling steaks before grilling to see if they browned better that way and tried brushing them with butter halfway through grilling to see if the flavor improved. Although the oiled steaks browned a tiny bit better, the difference wasn't significant enough to merit the added ingredient. (The filets mignons were an exception; oiling them improved browning in these leaner steaks.) As for the butter, we couldn't taste any difference.

We did find proper seasoning with salt and pepper before grilling to be essential. Seasonings added after cooking sit on the surface and don't penetrate as well as salt and pepper added before cooking. Be liberal with the salt and pepper. A fair amount falls off during the cooking process. Finally, consider using coarse sea salt or kosher salt. In our tests, tasters consistently preferred steaks sprinkled with coarse salt before grilling compared with those sprinkled with table salt. The larger crystals are easier to pick up and sprinkle evenly over the meat.

WHAT WE LEARNED: Cook these premium steaks over a two-level fire, searing them first over a high stack of coals and then moving them to a cooler part of the grill to cook through. Oil lean filets mignons to encourage browning, but otherwise don't fuss with these steaks before cooking them—salt and pepper are all that they need.

CHARCOAL-GRILLED STRIP OR RIB STEAKS Serves 4

Strip and rib steaks, on or off the bone, are our first choice for individual steaks. A steak that's between 1 1/4 to 1 1/2 inches thick gives you a solid meat flavor as well as a little taste of the grill; cut any thicker and the steak becomes too thick for one person to eat. If your guests are more likely to eat only an 8-ounce steak, grill two 1-pounders, slice them, and serve each person a half steak. The most accurate way to judge doneness is to stick an instant-read thermometer through the side of the steak deep into the meat, so that most of the shaft is embedded in the steak (see the illustration on page 159).

4   strip or rib steaks, with or without the bone,
     1¼ to 1½ inches thick (12 to 16 ounces each),
     patted dry
     Salt and ground black pepper

1. Light a large chimney starter filled with hardwood charcoal (about 6 quarts) and allow to burn until all the charcoal is covered with a layer of fine gray ash. Build a two-level fire by stacking most of the coals on one side of the grill for a medium-hot fire and arranging the remaining coals in a single layer on the other side of the grill for a medium-low fire. Set the cooking rack in place, cover the grill with the lid, and let the rack heat up, about 5 minutes. Use a wire brush to scrape clean the cooking rack.

2. Meanwhile, sprinkle both sides of the steaks with salt and pepper to taste. Grill the steaks, uncovered, over the hotter part of the fire until well browned on one side, 2 to 3 minutes. Turn the steaks; grill until well browned on the other side, 2 to 3 minutes. (If the steaks start to flame, pull them to the cooler part of the grill and/or extinguish the flames with a squirt bottle.)

3. Once the steaks are well browned on both sides, slide them to the cooler part of grill. Continue grilling, uncovered, to the desired doneness, 5 to 6 minutes more for rare (120 degrees on an instant-read thermometer), 6 to 7 minutes for medium-rare on the rare side (125 degrees), 7 to 8 minutes for medium-rare on the medium side (130 degrees), or 8 to 9 minutes for medium (135 to 140 degrees).

4. Remove the steaks from the grill and let rest for 5 minutes. Serve immediately.

VARIATION
GAS-GRILLED STRIP OR RIB STEAKS

Depending on the heat output of your gas grill, you may need to cook the steaks over the cooler part of the grill for an extra minute or two.

Turn on all burners to high, close the lid, and heat the grill until very hot, about 15 minutes. Scrape the grill grate clean with a grill brush. Leave one burner on high and turn the other burner(s) to medium. Follow the recipe for Charcoal-Grilled Strip or Rib Steaks from step 2.

CHARCOAL-GRILLED FILETS MIGNONS
Serves 4

Filet mignon steaks are cut from the tenderloin, which is, as the name indicates, an extremely tender portion of meat. Though tender, the steaks are not extremely rich. To prevent the steaks from drying out on the grill and to encourage browning, we found it helpful to lightly rub each steak with a little oil before grilling. We suggest that you drizzle the grilled steaks with olive oil and serve them with lemon wedges, or serve the steaks with one of the flavored butters on page 159.

- 4   center-cut filets mignons, about 1½ to 2 inches thick (7 to 8 ounces each), patted dry
- 4   teaspoons olive oil
     Salt and ground black pepper

1. Light a large chimney starter filled with hardwood charcoal (about 6 quarts) and allow to burn until all the charcoal is covered with a layer of fine gray ash. Build a two-level fire by stacking most of the coals on one side of the grill for a medium-hot fire. Arrange the remaining coals in a single layer on the other side of the grill for a medium-low fire. Set the cooking rack in place, cover the grill with the lid, and let the rack heat up, about 5 minutes. Use a wire brush to scrape clean the cooking rack.

2. Meanwhile, lightly rub the steaks with the oil and sprinkle both sides of the steaks with salt and pepper to taste. Grill the steaks, uncovered, over the hotter part of the fire until well browned on one side, 2 to 3 minutes. Turn the steaks; grill until well browned on the other side, 2 to 3 minutes.

3. Once steaks are well browned on both sides, slide them to the cooler part of the grill. Continue grilling, uncovered,

---

GETTING IT RIGHT:
The Eight Primal Cuts of Beef

If you want to buy beef, it helps to understand the anatomy of a cow. Butchers divide the meat into eight primal cuts. Steaks generally come from six places on the cow—not from the brisket or plate. We find that best steaks come from the rib and short loin sections.

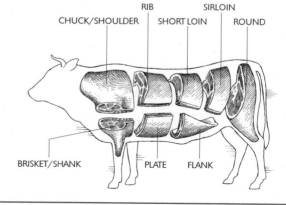

to the desired doneness, 6 minutes more for rare (120 degrees on an instant-read thermometer), 7 minutes for medium-rare on the rare side (125 degrees), 8 minutes for medium-rare on the medium side (130 degrees), or 9 to 10 minutes for medium (135 to 140 degrees).

4. Remove the steaks from the grill and let rest for 5 minutes. Serve immediately.

VARIATION
GAS-GRILLED FILETS MIGNONS

Depending on the heat output of your gas grill, you may need to cook the steaks over the cooler part of the grill for an extra minute or two.

Turn on all burners to high, close the lid, and heat the grill until very hot, about 15 minutes. Scrape the grill grate clean with a grill brush. Leave one burner on high and turn the other burner(s) to medium. Follow the recipe for Charcoal-Grilled Filets Mignons from step 2.

ROASTED RED PEPPER AND SMOKED PAPRIKA BUTTER

Makes 4 tablespoons, enough for 4 steaks
Serve this butter with filets mignons.

- 4 tablespoons unsalted butter, softened
- 2 tablespoons very finely minced jarred roasted red bell peppers (about 1 ounce)
- 1 tablespoon minced fresh thyme leaves
- ¾ teaspoon smoked paprika
- ½ teaspoon salt
  Ground black pepper

Using a fork, beat all of the ingredients, including pepper to taste, together in a small bowl until combined. Just before serving the steaks, spoon about 1 tablespoon butter onto each and serve.

LEMON, GARLIC, AND PARSLEY BUTTER

Makes 4 tablespoons, enough for 4 steaks
This is a variation on maître d'hôtel butter, a classic French accompaniment to meat, fish, and vegetables. It works well with filets.

- 4 tablespoons unsalted butter, softened
- ½ teaspoon grated lemon zest
- 1 tablespoon minced fresh parsley leaves
- 1 medium clove garlic, minced to a puree or pressed through a garlic press (about 1 teaspoon)
- ½ teaspoon salt
  Ground black pepper

Using a fork, beat all of the ingredients, including pepper to taste, together in a small bowl until combined. Just before serving the steaks, spoon about 1 tablespoon butter onto each and serve.

TECHNIQUE:
Judging When Steaks Are Done

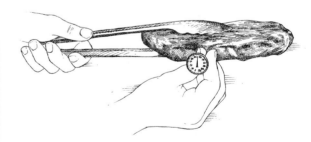

Hold the steak with a pair of tongs and push the tip of the thermometer through the edge of the steak until most of the shaft is embedded in the meat and not touching any bone. Pull the steak off the grill when it registers 120 degrees for rare; 125 to 130 degrees for medium-rare; and 135 to 140 degrees for medium. Note that the internal temperature will rise another 5 degrees or so as the steak rests.

SCIENCE DESK:
Why Do Juicy Meats Seem Tender?

THE SENSATION OF TENDERNESS IN MEAT HAS A LOT TO do with the condition of the muscle fiber. Loss of water invariably leads to toughness (just think about beef jerky). Meats such as turkey or ham are often "enhanced" by the injection of water. When these meats are cooked, they seem more tender than when untreated because they retain more moisture.

Why does extra water make us think "tender"? One reason could be that as meat cooks the muscle cells contract and water is expelled. What was once a moist, thick cut of meat is now more thin and sinewy. The net effect is that you need to (specifically, your jaw needs to) expend more effort to bite through the same number of cells over a shorter distance. Juiciness, or water content, also affects the structure of the cells. A normal, healthy cell has suppleness primarily because of the presence of water; the contents can readjust their position because water serves as a lubricant. When water is eliminated through cooking, the cell becomes more rigid.

Thus, loss of water may contribute to the sensation of toughness in two ways. First, cells become smaller and denser, and, second, they become less supple. It is not surprising that "tender" and "juicy" have become inseparable partners in the cook's mind.

TASTING LAB: Mail-Order Steaks

TO CONNOISSEURS, STEAKS ARE THE STARS OF THE BEEF world, and strip steaks are the divas. Long and lean, with a heartier chew and a lot more flavor, strip steaks put their more popular brethren, filets mignons, to shame. Beef is a tricky business, however, and too often you can find your steak more dud than stud. To guarantee quality, more and more people are looking beyond the confines of their local

supermarket butcher case and buying their steaks through mail-order sources. These outlets promise all-star beef with a price tag to match. But do the mail-order steaks really outshine the ones you can get around the corner?

We gathered seven widely available mail-order strip steaks and two from local supermarkets (Coleman Natural—hormone- and antibiotic-free—from our local Whole Foods market and choice steak from the regular market). Our candidates included Niman Ranch, a high-end, all-natural, restaurant favorite; Peter Luger, a New York steakhouse that many consider to be the best in the country; Omaha, probably the most well-known mail-order steak company, with two steaks in the running (their "private reserve" as well as their standard); Allen Brothers, a Chicago-based company that supplies many of this country's steakhouses; and Lobel's, a New York butcher shop. In

Rating Mail-Order Steaks

TWENTY-THREE MEMBERS OF THE *COOK'S ILLUSTRATED* STAFF TASTED SEVEN MAIL-ORDER STEAKS ALONG WITH TWO supermarket samples. All samples were boneless strip steaks, pan-seared in a thin film of vegetable oil and then sliced for the tasting. (The steaks were not seasoned with salt or pepper.) The steaks are listed in order of preferences based on their scores in this tasting. Prices do not include shipping, which can add another $15 to $30 to the overall cost. See www.americastestkitchen.com for up-to-date prices and mail-order sources for top-rated products.

HIGHLY RECOMMENDED
Lobel's Wagyu (Kobe-Style) Boneless Strip Steak (from Oakleigh Ranch, Australia) **$68.00 per pound**
"Incredibly tender" and "awesome." The clear favorite, but incredibly expensive.

HIGHLY RECOMMENDED
Niman Ranch New York Steak **$22.00 per pound**
Tasters thought this steak, which is a favorite with chefs, had "good flavor" and was "very tender."

HIGHLY RECOMMENDED
Coleman Natural Boneless Strip Steak **$14.00 per pound**
This all-natural supermarket option was praised by tasters for its "great flavor" and "rich, meaty" quality.

HIGHLY RECOMMENDED
Peter Luger Strip Steak **$29.00 per pound**
This steak from the famed Brooklyn steakhouse was "extremely tender" and "mild."

RECOMMENDED
Lobel's Boneless Strip Steak **$34.00 per pound**
The steak from this famous New York butcher was "juicy" and "chewy."

RECOMMENDED
Allen Brothers Dry-Aged Boneless Sirloin Strip Steak **$35.00 per pound**
"Very tender" but "kind of bland" was the consensus on this steak.

RECOMMENDED
Stop & Shop Choice Boneless Strip Steak **$10.00 per pound**
"Very juicy" but "not much flavor" was how most tasters judged this supermarket steak.

NOT RECOMMENDED
Omaha Boneless Strip Steak **$25.00 per pound**
This basic steak from the famed mail-order company was judged "beefy but generic" and "too thin."

NOT RECOMMENDED
Omaha Private Reserve Boneless Strip Steak **$45.00 per pound**
This premium offering from Omaha was "a little chewy" and "tough and stringy."

addition to Lobel's boneless strip steak we included Lobel's Wagyu, or Kobe-style, steak from Oakleigh Ranch in Australia. Kobe beef comes from Wagyu cattle raised to certain specifications in Kobe, Japan. Considered the foie gras of beef, the meat is extremely well-marbled, tender, and rich. Wagyu is the more generic name for the same type of beef, but not from Japan. Although few of us could afford the hefty $68/pound price tag for Wagyu beef, we wanted to see if it was really worth that much.

Well, it was. After pan-searing three dozen steaks (four of each type for perhaps the largest tasting turnout in the test kitchen), we found that money can buy you happiness, if happiness for you is the best steak you ever ate.

"Wow," wrote one happy taster of our first-place Wagyu steak. "This is unlike any strip that I've had." Others deemed the Wagyu steak "tender like a filet" and "very rich and meaty." But the overwhelming richness—which one taster likened to "foie gras–infused beef"—was not everyone's cup of tea. A minority of tasters agreed with the one who wrote, "This doesn't taste like beef at all."

Three steaks shared the spot for second place: Niman Ranch ($22 per pound), praised for its "good flavor" and "nice texture"; Coleman Natural, deemed "very robust"; and Peter Luger, described as having "strong beef flavor" and "great juiciness."

Unfortunately, the brand most people turn to when ordering steak through the mail took the last two spots in our tasting. The Omaha strip steak had "off flavors" and was "grainy tasting," while the Omaha Private Reserve (at almost twice the price) finished last, with tasters finding it "a little chewy" and "very dry."

The good news is that you don't have to spend a small fortune (or pay for shipping) to get a great steak. Coleman Natural steak, available at all-natural supermarkets, tied for second place and was a comparative bargain at $14 per pound (just $4 more than the low-ranked Stop & Shop beef). If you want to sample true steak greatness, however, we recommend splurging on the Wagyu beef...at least once.

MASHED POTATOES

WHAT WE WANTED: Mashed potatoes packed with enough flavor to stand as an equal partner with a great grilled steak.

When it comes to mashed potatoes, most cooks (including those here in the test kitchen) worry so much about getting the texture right that they forget about flavor. Butter and half-and-half make for mashed potatoes that are rich tasting but not terribly exciting. Giving flavor second-tier status is fine if the potatoes are going to be smothered with gravy, but with just a bit of help they can stand proudly on their own.

Based on work done in the test kitchen a few years ago, we knew how to make potatoes with great texture. The formula is simple: Use russets for the fluffiest texture (other varieties turn out soggy, heavy mashed potatoes), boil them whole and in their skins to keep them from soaking up water, add melted butter to coat the starch molecules, and finish with half-and-half. A ricer or food mill delivers the smoothest (and best) texture, but a potato masher can be used if you don't mind lumps. With our method for cooking and mashing the potatoes decided, our goal was to jazz up the flavor.

We tried multiple flavor combinations and found that adding too many ingredients served only to muddy the flavor of the potatoes. Tasters preferred simple pairings of contrasting but complementary flavors. Sweet caramelized onions balance the tang and sharpness of blue cheese. The richness of smoked cheddar is cut with the vinegary bite of grainy mustard. Scallions add a fresh, light onion flavor to potatoes spiked with spicy horseradish. The warmth of toasted garlic softens the smoky edge of Spanish paprika.

WHAT WE LEARNED: A few well-chosen ingredients can elevate mashed potatoes to star status.

MASHED POTATOES WITH BLUE CHEESE AND PORT-CARAMELIZED ONIONS Serves 4

We especially like this dish with Roquefort cheese.

onions

- 1½ teaspoons unsalted butter
- 1½ teaspoons vegetable oil
- ¼ teaspoon salt
- ½ teaspoon light brown sugar
- 1 pound yellow onions, sliced ¼ inch thick
- ⅓ cup port, preferably ruby port

potatoes

- ¾ cup half-and-half
- 1 teaspoon chopped fresh thyme leaves
- 2 pounds russet potatoes, unpeeled and scrubbed
- 6 tablespoons unsalted butter, melted
- 1¼ teaspoons salt
- ½ teaspoon ground black pepper
- 4 ounces blue cheese, crumbled

1. FOR THE ONIONS: Heat the butter and oil in an 8-inch nonstick skillet over high heat; when the foam subsides, stir in the salt and sugar. Add the onions and stir to coat; cook, stirring occasionally, until the onions begin to soften and release some moisture, about 5 minutes. Reduce the heat to medium; cook, stirring frequently, until the onions are deeply browned and sticky, about 35 minutes longer (if the onions are sizzling or scorching, reduce the heat; if the onions are not browning after 15 minutes, increase the heat). Stir in the port; continue to cook until the port reduces to a glaze, 4 to 6 minutes. Set the onions aside.

2. FOR THE POTATOES: While the onions are cooking, bring the half-and-half and thyme to boil in a small saucepan; cover to keep warm.

3. Place the potatoes in a large saucepan with water to cover by 1 inch. Bring to a boil over high heat, reduce the heat to medium, and simmer until the potatoes are just tender (a paring knife can be slipped into and out of the potato with very little resistance), 20 to 30 minutes. Drain.

4. Set a food mill or ricer over the now-empty but still-warm saucepan. Spear the potato with a dinner fork, then peel back the skin with a paring knife; repeat with the remaining potatoes. Working in batches, cut the peeled potatoes into rough chunks and drop them into the hopper of a food mill or ricer. Process or rice the potatoes into the saucepan, or mash the potatoes with a potato masher directly in the saucepan.

5. Stir the butter into the potatoes until just incorporated. Sprinkle the salt and pepper over the potatoes. Add the warm half-and-half and blue cheese; stir until just combined. Serve immediately, topping individual servings with a portion of the onions.

MASHED POTATOES WITH SCALLIONS AND HORSERADISH Serves 4

Prepared horseradish gives the potatoes a vinegary kick, while fresh horseradish adds a sweeter, more mellow horseradish flavor without pungency.

   2 pounds russet potatoes, unpeeled and scrubbed
   8 tablespoons (1 stick) unsalted butter, melted
1½ teaspoons salt
   ½ teaspoon ground black pepper
   2 tablespoons prepared hot horseradish
   ¼ cup grated fresh horseradish
   3 medium scallions, green parts only, minced (about ½ cup)
   1 cup half-and-half, warm

1. Place the potatoes in a large saucepan with water to cover by 1 inch. Bring to a boil over high heat, reduce the

heat to medium, and simmer until the potatoes are just tender (a paring knife can be slipped into and out of the potato with very little resistance), 20 to 30 minutes. Drain.

2. Set a food mill or ricer over the now-empty but still-warm saucepan. Spear the potato with a dinner fork, then peel back the skin with a paring knife; repeat with the remaining potatoes. Working in batches, cut the peeled potatoes into rough chunks and drop into the hopper of a food mill or ricer. Process or rice the potatoes into the saucepan or mash the potatoes with a potato masher directly in the saucepan.

3. Stir the butter into the potatoes until just incorporated. Sprinkle the salt and pepper over the potatoes. Whisk the horseradish and scallions into the warm half-and-half; add the mixture to the potatoes and stir until just combined. Serve immediately.

MASHED POTATOES WITH SMOKED CHEDDAR AND GRAINY MUSTARD Serves 4

Because of the cheese, this recipe uses a bit less salt. Coarse Dijon mustard is ideal in this recipe.

   2 pounds russet potatoes, unpeeled and scrubbed
   8 tablespoons (1 stick) unsalted butter, melted
1¼ teaspoons salt
   ½ teaspoon ground black pepper
   1 cup half-and-half, warm
   2 tablespoons grainy mustard
   3 ounces smoked cheddar cheese, grated (1 cup)

1. Follow the recipe for Mashed Potatoes with Scallions and Horseradish through step 2.

2. Stir the butter into the potatoes until just incorporated. Sprinkle the salt and pepper over the potatoes; add the warm half-and-half, mustard, and cheese and stir until just combined. Serve immediately.

MASHED POTATOES WITH SMOKED PAPRIKA AND TOASTED GARLIC Serves 4

Smoked paprika is a Spanish specialty. It gives these mashed potatoes a flavor that is deep, earthy, and complex, with a mild smokiness. Sweet paprika can be substituted, but the flavor won't be quite the same.

2   pounds russet potatoes, unpeeled and scrubbed
1   teaspoon sweet or bittersweet smoked paprika
8   tablespoons (1 stick) unsalted butter
3   medium-large cloves garlic, minced or pressed through a garlic press (about 1 generous tablespoon)
1½   teaspoons salt
½   teaspoon ground black pepper
1   cup half-and-half, warm

1. Follow the recipe for Mashed Potatoes with Scallions and Horseradish through step 2.

2. While the potatoes are cooking, toast the paprika in a small dry skillet over medium heat, stirring frequently, until fragrant, about 2 minutes. (Do not let the paprika burn, or it will taste bitter.) Transfer to a small bowl; set aside. Heat the butter in a small saucepan over medium-low heat; when melted, add the garlic and reduce the heat to low. Cook, stirring frequently, until the garlic begins to brown, 12 to 14 minutes; remove the saucepan from the heat immediately and set aside for 5 minutes (the garlic will continue to brown). Pour the butter mixture through a mesh strainer; reserve the butter and set the toasted garlic aside.

3. With a wooden spoon, stir the reserved butter into the mashed potatoes until just incorporated. Sprinkle the potatoes with salt, pepper, and toasted paprika; add the warm half- and-half and stir until just combined. Serve immediately, sprinkling individual servings with a portion of the reserved toasted garlic.

EQUIPMENT CORNER:
Large Saucepans

WHEN COOKING MOST VEGETABLES, WE REACH FOR A three- to four-quart saucepan. Which begs an obvious question: Does the brand of pan matter? With prices for these large saucepans ranging from $24.99 for a Revere stainless-steel model with thin copper cladding at the base up to $140 for an All-Clad pan with a complete aluminum core and stainless-steel interior and exterior cladding, a lot of money is riding on the answer. To let us offer guidance, we tested eight models, all between three and four quarts in size, from well-known cookware manufacturers.

The tests we performed were based on common cooking tasks and designed to highlight specific characteristics of the pans' performance. Sautéing minced onions illustrated the pace at which the pan heats up and sautés. Cooking white rice provided a good indication of the pan's ability to heat evenly as well as how tightly the lid sealed. Making pastry cream let us know how user-friendly the pan was—was it shaped such that a whisk reached into the corners without trouble, was it comfortable to pick up, and could we pour liquid from it neatly? These traits can make a real difference when you use a pan day in and day out.

Of the tests we performed, sautéing onions was the most telling. In our view, onions should soften reliably and evenly (and with minimal attention and stirring) when sautéed over medium heat. In this regard, the All-Clad, Calphalon, KitchenAid, and Sitram pans all delivered. The Chantal and Cuisinart pans sautéed slightly faster, necessitating a little more attention from the cook, but still well within acceptable bounds. Only the Revere and Farberware Millennium sautéed so fast that we considered them problematic.

Incidentally, the Revere and Farberware pans that sautéed onions too fast for us were the lightest pans of the bunch, weighing only 1 pound 10 ounces and 2 pounds 6 ounces, respectively. This indicates that they were made from thinner metal, which is one reason they heat quickly.

On the flip side of the weight issue, however, we found that too heavy a pan, such as the 4-pound Calphalon, could be uncomfortable to lift when full. The ideal was about 3½ pounds; pans near this weight, including the All-Clad, KitchenAid, Chantal, Sitram, and Cuisinart, balanced good heft with easy maneuverability.

While none of the pans failed the rice test outright, there were performance differences. In the Sitram, Revere, and Farberware pans, the rice stuck and dried out at the bottom, if only a little bit. Although this did not greatly affect the texture, the flavor, or the cleanup, we'd still choose a pan for which this was not an issue.

Every pan in the group turned out perfect pastry cream. During this test, we did observe one design element that made it easy to pour liquid from the pan neatly, without dribbles and spills. A rolled lip that flares slightly at the top of the pan helped control the pour. Only two pans in the group did not have a rolled lip: the All-Clad and the Calphalon.

So which pan do you want to buy? That depends largely on two things: your budget and your attention span. Based on our tests, we'd advise against really inexpensive pans—those that cost less than $50. For between $50 and $100, you can get a competent pan such as the Chantal, Sitram, or Cuisinart. The only caveat is that you may have to watch them carefully; they offer less room for error than our favorite pans, made by All-Clad, Calphalon, and KitchenAid.

Rating Large Saucepans

WE TESTED EIGHT LARGE SAUCEPANS, EACH WITH A CAPACITY OF THREE TO FOUR QUARTS, IN THREE APPLICATIONS: sautéing onions, steaming rice, and preparing pastry cream. The pans are listed in order of preference based on their performance in these tests as well as on design factors. See www.americastestkitchen.com for up-to-date prices and mail-order sources for top-rated products.

RECOMMENDED
All-Clad Stainless Steel 3 Quart Saucepan
$139.99
Performed beautifully, but why not include a rolled lip for neat pouring? A long, indented handle helps the cook maintain a secure grip when lifting this pan.

RECOMMENDED
Calphalon Commercial Hard-Anodized 3½ Quart Saucepan
$110.99
The bruiser of the group—are we cooking or weight-training here? Performed well but has minor design shortcomings, including a lip that is not rolled.

RECOMMENDED
KitchenAid Stainless Steel 3 Quart Saucepan
$119.00
The rolled lip makes for neat pouring, but the handle is too short for some testers. Otherwise, a solid performer.

RECOMMENDED WITH RESERVATIONS
Chantal 3 Quart Saucepan #35-200S
$89.99
Sautés at a faster than usual clip, so it requires a bit of extra attention. Nothing unacceptable, however.

RECOMMENDED WITH RESERVATIONS
Sitram Professional Induction 3.17 Quart Saucepan
$56.90
Especially light lid allowed steam to escape, so rice began to stick to the pan bottom. Otherwise, a decent pan.

RECOMMENDED WITH RESERVATIONS
Cuisinart Everyday Stainless 3¾ Quart, Model 919-20
$79.99
Watch the sauté speed, which is a little faster than we like. Otherwise, a very serviceable saucepan.

NOT RECOMMENDED
Revere Stainless Steel Copper Clad Bottom 3 Quart Saucepan
$24.99
This featherweight heats up and sautés exceptionally fast, so it can be difficult to control. Lid allowed significant steam to escape so rice browned and stuck a bit.

NOT RECOMMENDED
Farberware Millennium 3 Quart Saucepan
$44.99
The handle was hot at the base and the performance far from ideal; this pan turned out dry rice and over-browned onions.

Geof keeps Chris on his toes as the crew
lights our outdoor grilling location.

STEAK tips
CHAPTER 14

Steak tips and steak fries sound like bad menu offerings from your local low-rent steakhouse. The meat is tough and weirdly seasoned, and the thick fries are pale and soggy. No doubt the restaurant has used the cheapest scraps of meat for the steak tips (you really don't want to think about that), and the fries probably came frozen from their food purveyor.

But there is something appealing about taking a relatively inexpensive cut of meat and making it special. And there's no reason why steak fries have to be greasy and bland. If you started out with decent quality meat and fresh potatoes, could you make this humble fare special? The test kitchen felt confident that we could rescue these dishes from the clutches of the fast food empire and turn them into something you would actually welcome into your home.

STEAK TIPS

WHAT WE WANTED: A way to turn this inexpensive cut into something worth grilling.

Steak tips have never been on our list of favorite meats. It's not that we're premium steak snobs, but we were skeptical about a cut of meat that has long been the darling of all-you-can-eat restaurant chains, where quantity takes precedence over quality. There is also some confusion about what constitutes a steak tip. Some steak tips are sautéed and served with a sauce (these are often called pub-style steak tips), some are marinated and grilled (known as tailgate tips). We were drawn to grilling and so began by testing five such recipes.

The recipes differed in the ingredients used to marinate the meat and in the marinating time. The simplest recipe marinated the tips in a bottled Italian-style salad dressing for 24 hours. The most complex marinated the meat for three days in a mixture that included aromatics and herbs. Despite such variations in time and ingredients, none of these grilled tips was very good. Some were mushy, but most were tough and dry. At this point, steak tips still seemed like a cheap cut of meat, with promising beefy flavor but poor texture.

Thinking that the problem might be the cut of meat, we went to the supermarket only to discover a confusing array of meats—cubes, strips, and steaks—labeled "steak tips." Still more confusing, these cubes, strips, and steaks could be cut from a half-dozen different parts of the cow.

After grilling more than 50 pounds of tips, it became clear that the only cut worth grilling is one referred to by butchers as flap meat. (For more information, see "Buying Steak Tips," page 172.) When we grilled whole flap meat steaks and then sliced them on the bias before serving, tasters were impressed. Although the meat was still a bit chewy, choosing the right cut was a start.

We now turned to marinades. Given the long-held belief that acidic marinades tenderize tough meat, we created four recipes using four popular acids: yogurt, wine, vinegar, and fruit juice. To determine the best timing, we let the meat sit in each marinade for four hours and for 24 hours. Curious about marinades' other claim to fame—flavoring—we added aromatics, spices, and herbs.

The yogurt marinade was the least favorite, producing dry meat that was chewy and tough. Tasters also panned the wine-based marinade. The meat was tough and dry, the flavors harsh and bland. Some tasters liked the complex flavor of the vinegar marinade, but everyone found the tips to be "overly chewy." The marinade prepared with pineapple juice was the favorite. Both the four-hour and 24-hour versions yielded juicy, tender, flavorful meat.

Why did pineapple juice make the best marinade? Our first thought was proteases, enzymes that help to break down proteins. Proteases are found in pineapple, papaya, and other fruits. One of them, *papain*, from papayas, is the active component of meat tenderizers such as Adolph's. The juice we had been using was pasteurized, however, and the heat of pasteurization is thought to disable such enzymes. To see if proteases were in fact at work, we devised three tests in which we made three more marinades: one with pasteurized pineapple juice from the supermarket; a second with pasteurized pineapple juice heated to the boiling point and then cooled; and a third with fresh pineapple pureed in a food processor.

The result? The fresh juice was a much more aggressive "tenderizer," so much so that it turned the meat mushy on the inside and slimy on the outside. We had learned three things: proteases do break down meat, but they don't make it any better (tasters universally disapproved of these tenderized tips); pasteurization does kill this enzyme (the fresh juice was much more powerful than the supermarket variety); and proteases were not responsible for the strong showing made by the original pineapple marinade. Why, then, did tasters prefer the pineapple marinade to those made with yogurt, wine, and vinegar?

After rereading the ingredient list in our pineapple marinade, we devised a new theory. The pineapple marinade included soy sauce, an ingredient that is packed with salt and that was not used in any of the other marinades. Was the soy sauce tenderizing the meat by acting like a brine of salt and water? In the past, the test kitchen has demonstrated the beneficial effects of brining on lean poultry and pork.

To answer these questions, we ran another series of tests, trying various oil-based marinades made with salt or soy sauce (in earlier tests, we had determined that oil helped to keep the meat moist and promoted searing). To use salt in a marinade, we first had to dissolve it. Because salt doesn't dissolve in oil, we used water, but the liquid prevented the meat from browning properly. That said, brining did make these steak tips tender and juicy.

We concluded that soy sauce, not pineapple juice, was the secret ingredient in tasters' favorite marinade. The salt in soy sauce improved the texture of the meat, and the soy sauce also promoted browning. We experimented with brining times and found that an hour was optimal. It allowed the thicker parts of the meat to become tender while preventing the thinner sections from becoming too salty.

We then went to work on flavor variations, adding garlic, ginger, orange zest, hot pepper, brown sugar, and scallions for an Asian marinade and making a Southwest-inspired marinade that included garlic, chili powder, cumin, cayenne, brown sugar, and tomato paste. We found that a squeeze of fresh citrus served with the steak provided a bright acidic counterpoint.

Because this relatively thin cut of meat cooks quickly, high heat is necessary to achieve a perfect crust. The uneven thickness of many of the steak tips presented a problem, though. The exterior would scorch by the time the thick portions were cooked, and the thin parts would be overcooked. A two-level fire, with more coals on one side of the grill to create hotter and cooler areas, solved the problem. We started cooking the tips over high heat to sear them and then moved them to the cooler area to finish cooking.

We prefer steaks grilled rare, so we were surprised to find that when cooked rare the meat was rubbery, whereas longer cooking gave it a tender chew—without drying out the meat. Even when cooked until well done, these tips were exceptionally juicy. We had the brine to thank again: The salty soy marinade helped the meat hold onto its moisture.

Conventional wisdom prompted one more test. We grilled two more batches of tips and sliced one immediately after it came off the grill and the other five minutes later. Sure enough, the rested tips were both more juicy and more tender. Finally, a recipe for steak tips as pleasing to the palate as they are to the pocketbook.

WHAT WE LEARNED: Buy flap meat sirloin tips, marinate the meat for at least an hour in a soy-based marinade, grill over a two-level fire, let the meat rest for five minutes, then slice thinly against the grain for meat that is tender and flavorful.

CHARCOAL-GRILLED STEAK TIPS Serves 4 to 6

A two-level fire allows you to brown the steak over the hot side of the grill, then move it to the cooler side if it is not yet cooked through. If your steak is thin, however, you may not need to use the cooler side of the grill. The times in the recipe below are for relatively even, 1-inch-thick steak tips. When grilling, bear in mind that even those tasters who usually prefer rare beef preferred steak tips cooked medium-rare to medium because the texture is firmer and not quite so chewy. Serve lime wedges with the Southwestern-marinated tips and orange wedges with the tips marinated in garlic, ginger, and soy sauce.

   1   **recipe marinade (recipes follow)**
   2   **pounds flap meat sirloin steak tips, trimmed of excess fat**
       Lime or orange wedges for serving

1. Combine the marinade and meat in a gallon-size zipper-lock bag; press out as much air as possible and seal the bag. Refrigerate for 1 hour, flipping the bag after 30 minutes to ensure that the meat marinates evenly.

2. About halfway through the marinating time, light a large chimney starter filled with hardwood charcoal (about 6 quarts) and allow to burn until all the charcoal is covered with a layer of fine gray ash. Build a two-level fire by stacking most of the coals on one side of the grill for a medium-hot fire. Arrange the remaining coals in a single layer on the other side of the grill for a medium-low fire. Set the cooking rack in place, cover the grill with the lid, and let the rack heat up, about 5 minutes. Use a wire brush to scrape clean the cooking rack.

3. Remove the steak tips from the marinade and pat dry with paper towels. Grill, uncovered, until well seared and dark brown on the first side, about 4 minutes. Using tongs, flip the steak tips and grill until the second side is well seared and the thickest part of the meat is slightly less done than

desired, 4 to 5 minutes for medium-rare (about 130 degrees on instant-read thermometer), 6 to 8 minutes for medium (about 135 degrees); if the exterior of the meat is browned but the steak is not yet cooked through, move the steak tips to the cooler side of the grill and continue to grill to the desired doneness.

4. Transfer the steak tips to a cutting board; tent the tips loosely with foil and let rest for 5 minutes. Slice the steak tips very thinly on the bias; serve immediately with the lime or orange wedges.

VARIATION
GAS-GRILLED STEAK TIPS

Follow the recipe for Charcoal-Grilled Steak Tips through step 1. When about 15 minutes of marinating time remains, turn all of the burners on the gas grill to high, close the lid, and heat the grill until hot, about 15 minutes. Continue with the recipe from step 3, grilling the steak tips covered.

GETTING IT RIGHT: Buying Steak Tips

Steak tips can be cut from a half-dozen muscles and are sold in three basic forms: cubes, strips, and steaks. To make sure that you are buying the most flavorful cut (called flap meat sirloin tips by butchers and pictured at right), buy whole steaks.

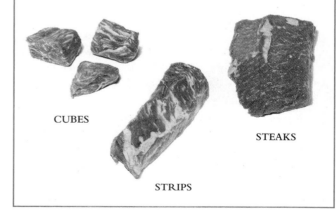

CUBES

STRIPS

STEAKS

SOUTHWESTERN MARINADE

Makes enough for 2 pounds of steak tips

⅓   cup soy sauce
⅓   cup vegetable oil
3   medium cloves garlic, minced or pressed
    through a garlic press (about 1 tablespoon)
1   tablespoon dark brown sugar
1   tablespoon tomato paste
1   tablespoon chili powder
2   teaspoons ground cumin
¼   teaspoon cayenne

Combine all of the ingredients in a small bowl.

GARLIC, GINGER, AND SOY MARINADE

Makes enough for 2 pounds of steak tips

⅓   cup soy sauce
3   tablespoons vegetable oil
3   tablespoons toasted sesame oil
3   medium cloves garlic, minced or pressed
    through a garlic press (about 1 tablespoon)
1   piece (1 inch) fresh ginger, minced (about 1
    tablespoon)
2   tablespoons dark brown sugar
2   teaspoons grated zest from 1 orange
½   teaspoon red pepper flakes
1   medium scallion, sliced thin

Combine all of the ingredients in a small bowl.

TASTING LAB: Steak Tips

STEAK TIPS CAN COME FROM TWO AREAS OF THE COW. One kind comes from tender, expensive cuts in the middle of the cow, such as the tenderloin. These tips are a superior cut but not what we consider to be a true steak tip, which should be a more pedestrian cut that is magically transformed into a desirable dish through marinating and cooking. If the steak tips at your market cost $8 to $10 per pound, the meat likely comes from the tenderloin.

True steak tips come from various muscles in the sirloin and round and cost about $5 per pound. After tasting 50 pounds of cheap steak tips, tasters had a clear favorite: a single muscle that butchers call flap meat and that is typically labeled "sirloin tips." A whole piece of flap meat weighs about 2½ pounds. One piece can range in thickness from ½ inch to 1½ inches and may be sold as cubes, strips, or small steaks. It has a rich, deep beefy flavor and a distinctive longitudinal grain.

We found that it's best to buy flap meat in steak form rather than cubes or strips, which are often cut from nearby muscles in the hip and butt that are neither as tasty nor as tender. Because meat labeling is so haphazard, you must visually identify this cut; buying it in steak form makes this easy.

SCIENCE DESK: How to Infuse Meat with Moisture and Flavor

IN BRINING, TWO NATURAL PHENOMENA COMBINE TO yield great-tasting meat: osmosis and diffusion. Osmosis controls the movement of water. In brining, the net flow of water is into the meat, producing moister meat after cooking. Diffusion is the movement of molecules from an area of higher concentration to one of lower concentration. In brining, salt penetrates the meat through diffusion. It serves a cook well to remember diffusion when placing food in a liquid. Soaking, simmering, and marinating all present the cook with a golden opportunity to infuse any flavor—not just that of salt—into food simply by adding it to the liquid. The net result is always more flavor. A little patience is required, though, because diffusion can be quite slow. Our steak tips, for example, need a full hour for complete flavor development.

EQUIPMENT CORNER: Grill Brushes

ANYONE WHO HAS GRILLED A RACK OF STICKY BARBECUED ribs has had to deal with the task of removing the sugary, burned-on mess that gets left behind. The ideal time to do this is soon after your food comes off the grill, but, if you're like most of us, you close the lid, walk away, and save the mess for the next time grill duty calls. We set out to find a grill brush that could make the tedious task of cleaning a gunked-up grill grate more efficient. And we did not want to exert superhuman strength to get the job done.

To test the brushes, we concocted a "paint"—a mixture of honey, molasses, mustard, and barbecue sauce—that we could burn onto our grates. We coated the grates four times, baking them for one hour in the test kitchen ovens between coats. The result was a charred mess that would be sure to challenge even the hardiest of brushes. The grates were put back on the grills, which were then heated so we could test the brushes under real-life conditions.

The seven brushes we tested were chosen based on the construction and design of the handle and the scrubbing head. The handle of the stainless steel model was decidedly the heaviest and looked to be the most durable, but it absorbed heat at an alarming rate. Plastic performed adequately if you didn't spend too much time in one place on the grill (melting occurred) and if the handle was long enough. One plastic-handled brush, the Grill Pro, with a skimpy 5-inch handle, didn't even make it through the first test. The handle was so short that we couldn't get the brush to the far side of the grill without getting burned. A combination plastic/aluminum brush handle was so flexible it caused burnt knuckles when pressed with any strength. The material of choice for grill brush handles is clearly wood, which is relatively comfortable and durable.

In terms of the scrubbing heads, six of the seven brushes tested had brass bristles. Among these six, those with stiffer bristles fared better than their softer counterparts, but none of them worked all that well. The bristles on most bent after a few strokes and trapped large quantities of gunk, thereby decreasing their efficiency.

In the end, only one brush was able to successfully clean our molten mess down to the grill grate in a reasonable number of strokes. The unusual but incredibly effective Grill Wizard has no brass bristles to bend, break, or clog with unwanted grease and grime. Instead, this brush comes equipped with two large woven mesh stainless steel "scrubbie" pads. The pads are able to conform to any grill grate's spacing, size, and material, including porcelain. Best of all, the pads are detachable, washable, and replaceable. The 14-inch handle, made of poplar, is smooth, with rounded edges (unlike its square-cut competitors), with a hook for easy storage.

The one downside to this brush was the two-page instruction sheet that came affixed to the underside of the scrubbie head (yes, a grill brush with instructions). Had we not seen a corner of the instructions sticking out, we would have used the brush and burned the instructions. Not only do the instructions need better placement, but operating a grill brush should not be made to seem as difficult as programming a DVD player. Still, though the instructions were confusing, the process of replacing the scrubbies was fairly easy.

Rating Grill Brushes

WE TESTED SEVEN GRILL BRUSHES ON GRILL GRATES WE HAD DIRTIED WITH A BAKED-ON MIXTURE OF HONEY, molasses, mustard, and barbecue sauce. The brushes were rated on effectiveness, design, and ease of use and are listed in order of preference. See www.americastestkitchen.com for up-to-date prices and mail-order sources for top-rated products.

HIGHLY RECOMMENDED
Grill Wizard China Grill Brush $19.99
The most-odd looking of the bunch, with no bristles; instead, stainless steel "scrubbie" pads are held in place by stainless bars. The hardwood handle is very comfortable and smooth. The Grill Wizard cleaned the grate completely in 40 strokes. The scrubbies were very dirty after the test, but they can be removed and washed (or replaced for $2.50). After being cleaned, the scrubbies were in great shape.

RECOMMENDED WITH RESERVATIONS
Weber 18-Inch Grill Brush $6.99
This classic brush with brass bristles and a hardwood handle cleaned fairly well, but the bristles showed wear and tear in our tests.

NOT RECOMMENDED
Brushtech Wide-Faced, Industrial Quality Grill Brush $12.99
The bristles on this wide brush were the stiffest of the lot, but they wore down to the metal in just 70 strokes. The plastic handle was too flexible and the unusual design did not win any fans among our testers.

NOT RECOMMENDED
Grill Pro Two-Sided Grill Brush $10.00
The bristles looked bad after 50 strokes. The scrubber on the other side did not work at all; it just burned. The scraper did not work because of the location of both scrubber and bristles.

NOT RECOMMENDED
Original Char Buster Grill Brush $7.95
This brush did not clean at all. The short brass bristles collapsed during testing, and we ended up scraping the grill with the brush head. The 12-inch plastic handle was fairly comfortable though.

NOT RECOMMENDED
Mr. BBQ Premium Grill Brush $9.99
Even after 150 strokes, this brush could not clean the grill. The soft bristles collapsed almost immediately after we started using this brush. The metal handle absorbed too much heat and became impossible to hold.

NOT RECOMMENDED
Grill Pro Grill Brush $3.83
The 5-inch plastic handle is so short that we could not complete the test without risking serious burns on our hands. Yes, this brush is cheap, but its design makes absolutely no sense to us.

STEAK FRIES

WHAT WE WANTED: Much like good french fries, good steak fries should be crisp on the outside and tender on the inside. They should never be oily, dry, mealy, or soggy.

Steak fries are the rustic, country cousin to french fries. With their skin left on and their shape determined largely by the shape of the potato, these wedge-shaped fries are easier to prepare and less wasteful than the typical french fry, where much effort is expended to obtain a ruler-perfect consistency of shape. They are much easier for the home cook to prepare.

As with regular french fries, we found that starchy russets fried up beautifully. Their dense, starchy texture cooked to a consistently tender interior while the thick skin fried up good and crisp. Russets we bought in 5-pound bags, however, came in various sizes and were difficult to cut into uniformly sized wedges. We found that the russets sold loose, in bins, are more consistent in size and are easier to cut into same-size wedges for more consistent cooking times. After cooking up fries of various thicknesses, we found that we preferred wedges with an outside edge measuring ¾ inch wide; this works out to one large potato cut into 12 wedges. Any thicker or thinner, and the ratio of tender interior to crisp exterior was thrown off.

Many recipes for deep-fried potatoes suggest refrigerating the raw wedges before frying them, and we found this step to be crucial. Cooling the potatoes down before plunging them in the hot oil allows them to cook more slowly and evenly. By soaking the wedges in a refrigerated bowl of ice water for at least 30 minutes, we were able to ensure that the inner pulp was fully cooked before the outside turned overly brown.

Like most who've fried potatoes before us, we found that simply dunking the chilled, raw fries in hot oil and cooking them until they are done will not produce a good fry. By the time the inside of the fry is cooked and the outside is well browned, the fry itself is wooden and overcooked. We first par-fried them at a relatively low temperature to help them cook through without much browning. We then gave them a brief repose to cool off before refrying them quickly in oil at a higher temperature until nicely browned. In combination with the ice water bath, this technique worked like a dream. The thick wedges of potato were evenly cooked, with tender middles and crisp, browned exteriors.

What is the right fat for making perfect steak fries? To find out, we experimented with lard, vegetable shortening, canola oil, corn oil, and peanut oil. Lard and shortening make great fries, but we figured that many cooks won't want to use these products. We moved on to canola oil, the ballyhooed oil of the '90s, but we were unhappy with the results: bland, almost watery fries. Corn oil was the most forgiving oil in the test kitchen. It rebounded well from temperature fluctuations and held up very well in subsequent frying, and the fries tasted marvelous. A potato fried in peanut oil is light, and the flavor is rich but not dense. The earthy flavor of the potato is there, as with corn oil, but is not overbearing. It is our top choice.

WHAT WE LEARNED: Cut russet potatoes into ¾-inch wedges, soak them in ice water for at least 30 minutes, and then fry the potatoes twice (the first time to cook through the centers and the next time to brown and crisp the exteriors) in peanut oil.

FOOD FACT: Potatoes

Potatoes are America's favorite vegetable, easily outpacing tomatoes, which are in second place. Each man, woman, and child in this country consumes about 135 pounds of potatoes every year. What's our favorite way to eat potatoes? French fries are king. In fact, 13 percent of Americans eat French fries every day.

STEAK FRIES Serves 4

See the illustrations below for tips on cutting potatoes into wedges. The potatoes must be soaked in cold water, fried once, cooled, and then fried a second time—so start this recipe at least one hour before dinner.

4 large russet potatoes (about 10 ounces each), scrubbed and cut lengthwise into ¾-inch-thick wedges (about 12 wedges per potato)
2 quarts peanut oil
Salt and ground black pepper

1. Place the cut fries in a large bowl, cover with cold water by at least 1 inch, and then cover with ice cubes. Refrigerate at least 30 minutes or up to 3 days.

2. In a 5-quart pot or Dutch oven fitted with a clip-on candy thermometer, or in a large electric fryer, heat the oil over medium-low heat to 325 degrees. (The oil will bubble up when you add fries, so be sure you have at least 3 inches of room at the top of the pot.)

3. Pour off the ice and water, quickly the wrap potatoes in a clean kitchen towel, and thoroughly pat them dry. Increase the heat to medium-high and add the fries, one handful at a time, to the hot oil. Fry, stirring with a Chinese skimmer or large-holed slotted spoon, until the potatoes are limp and soft and have turned from white to gold, about 10 minutes. (The oil temperature will drop 50 to 60 degrees during this frying.) Use a skimmer or slotted spoon to transfer the fries to a triple thickness of paper towels to drain; let rest at least 10 minutes. (The fries can stand at room temperature up to 2 hours or be wrapped in paper towels, sealed in a zipper-lock bag, and frozen up to 1 month.)

4. When ready to serve the fries, reheat the oil to 350 degrees. Using the paper towels as a funnel, pour the potatoes into the hot oil. Discard the paper towels and line a wire rack with another triple thickness of paper towels. Fry the potatoes, stirring fairly constantly, until medium brown and puffed, 8 to 10 minutes. Transfer to the paper towel–lined rack to drain. Season to taste with salt and pepper. Serve immediately.

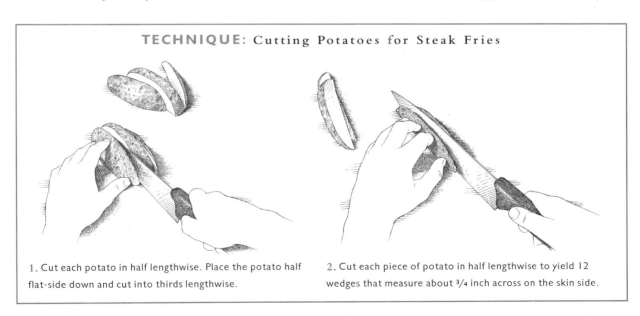

TECHNIQUE: Cutting Potatoes for Steak Fries

1. Cut each potato in half lengthwise. Place the potato half flat-side down and cut into thirds lengthwise.

2. Cut each piece of potato in half lengthwise to yield 12 wedges that measure about ¾ inch across on the skin side.

Ingredients are assembled for the pork and eggplant stir-fry.

STIR-FRY 101

Ordering Chinese take-out is like playing Russian roulette. Once in a great while, those little white cartons deliver tasty morsels of stir-fried meat and vegetables in a lightly thickened, potent, and savory sauce, with the flavors of garlic and ginger clean and invigorating. Unfortunately, the reality is usually something quite different. The meat is tough, the vegetables are overcooked, and the sauce is thick and gloppy. The garlic and ginger taste scorched and the sauce is bland, greasy, or overly sweet.

We think the best stir-fries are made at home, where it's easier to pay attention to detail and the food can be served immediately. Over the years, the test kitchen has developed some foolproof guidelines that guarantee great stir-fries.

STIR-FRIED BEEF AND BROCCOLI

WHAT WE WANTED: Tender beef and jade green, crisp-tender broccoli coated (not smothered) in a deeply flavored, silky sauce.

Order beef and broccoli in most restaurants and you are served a pile of chewy, gray "beef" surrounded by a forest of giant, overcooked army-issue broccoli. Worst of all is the thick-as-pudding brown sauce (more suitable for meatloaf than stir-fry), which, aside from being flavored with burnt garlic, is otherwise tasteless.

We turned to several recipes in cookbooks for help. Although most produced that gloppy, tasteless mass of beef and broccoli that we were trying to avoid, a couple of recipes showed promise. In these recipes, we found that each component of the dish—the beef, the broccoli, and even the sauce—was distinct and cooked to the best of its ability. Grateful for this glimmer of hope, we grabbed a 12-inch, nonstick skillet (our pan of choice when it comes to stir-frying because its flat surface perfectly matches the surface of the American stovetop) and started cooking.

Although flank steak—a chewy cut from the underbelly beneath the loin—is most often called for, in this stir-fry, we also tested a few other boneless cuts. Tender and expensive filet mignon (from the tenderloin) was mushy and dull flavored in this application. Strip steak (from the loin) was good, but not as good as the flank. A blade steak (cut from the shoulder blade area of the chuck) was similar to the tenderloin—too soft and too mild tasting. Flank steak clearly offered the biggest beefy taste. Slicing the steak thinly across the grain made it tender, but when we used a less than razor-sharp knife (like the knives found in most home kitchens), the steak tugged on the blade. We threw the steak in the freezer for 20 minutes to stiffen it up enough to make slicing easier.

Having recently discovered that using soy sauce in a marinade aids in tenderizing meat (see Chapter 14, "Steak Tips"), we tested one batch of unmarinated flank steak against batches marinated in soy sauce for two hours, one hour, and ten minutes. The results were dramatic. Two hours was overkill; the steak became gummy and spongy. One hour was perfect. The steak was tender and full of great soy flavor. Just a few minutes of marinating, however, made a big difference, which is good news if you don't have the full hour to marinate the steak.

But marinating introduced a new problem. The soaked beef expunged its liquid well before the meat had time to brown. We found that the best way to counter this was to limit the time the beef spent in the pan. The skillet had to be incredibly hot so that the meat would begin to brown in seconds. Also, many recipes simply throw all of the beef at once into the pan. The result was beef that steamed in its own juices and never browned (ergo the gray mass). We found it best to cook the beef in two batches and give it plenty of room to sear. Finally, getting rid of some of the marinade by way of draining the soaked beef before cooking helped immensely.

Cooking the broccoli evenly was the next test, and our first decision here was to get rid of those gargantuan pieces of broccoli we found in both the restaurant and recipe versions of this dish. Fork-friendly 1-inch pieces of broccoli floret seemed right, and by trimming the tough exterior from the broccoli stems and slicing them into thin ⅛-inch slices, we were able to cook the stems right along with the florets.

Most recipes cook the broccoli either by straightforward stir-frying or by steaming or blanching. While the former technique produced unevenly cooked broccoli, steaming or blanching made for tender broccoli every time. Unfortunately, this technique required an additional pan. In an effort to avoid this, we modified our use of the pan we'd already been using. After cooking the beef and removing it from the skillet, we stir-fried the broccoli for a few seconds, added water to the pan, and covered it tightly in hopes of

steaming the broccoli. This greatly simplified the recipe and produced superior broccoli—steamed to perfect tenderness and a brilliant emerald hue.

As for other vegetables, tasters wanted to keep this dish true to its name, save for the addition of red bell pepper, which added sweetness and vivid color. After removing the broccoli, we tossed the peppers into the hot pan and cooked them briefly to retain their crispness.

Garlic was a must, but we had to figure out the best way to add it to the mix. Added to the marinade, the garlic scorched in the skillet as it cooked with the beef. Added with the broccoli, it tasted raw. In the end we added minced garlic (along with some well-received ginger) to the skillet when the red peppers were nearly finished cooking.

Oyster-flavored sauce is the typical base for the sauce in this dish. Indeed, in some restaurants, it is referred to as "beef and broccoli in oyster sauce." We found no need to depart from the tradition of oyster sauce, as its deep, earthy notes provided the right flavor base and its thick consistency (think ketchup) added great body to the sauce. Soy sauce was next up for consideration, but we found it unnecessary; there was already enough in both the oyster sauce and the beef marinade. Rice vinegar and sherry are common additions, but only the latter was approved for its warm flavor.

Chicken stock was also welcomed to balance the flavors. Just a little toasted sesame oil and light brown sugar and the sauce took a sweet and nutty turn for the better.

Finally, satisfied with the flavor of the sauce, we added it to the pan along with the browned beef and steamed broccoli. We tossed the mixture together, but the sauce pooled on the bottom of the skillet. Clearly, the sauce wasn't thick enough, so we reluctantly returned to an often used but frequently troublesome ingredient: cornstarch. While many recipes (including some used in our early failed tests) called for a tablespoon or more of this thickener, we started more modestly. With a tentative hand, we stirred in the cornstarch until we had used only 1 teaspoon.

And now we had it: a sensuous sauce that barely clung to the deeply browned, tender beef and perfectly cooked jade green broccoli. The kitchen was studded with the heady aroma of garlic, and we knew that Chinatown had come home.

WHAT WE LEARNED: Use thinly sliced flank steak for the best texture and flavor, marinate it in soy sauce to improve on that texture and flavor, stir-fry the meat in batches to make sure it browns, and then coat with an oyster sauce mixture that is lightly thickened with cornstarch.

STIR-FRIED BEEF AND BROCCOLI WITH OYSTER SAUCE Serves 4

To make slicing the flank steak easier, freeze it for about 20 minutes before slicing. Steamed white rice is the perfect accompaniment for this stir-fry.

1	pound flank steak, sliced according to the illustrations at right
3	tablespoons soy sauce
1	tablespoon dry sherry
2	tablespoons low-sodium chicken broth
5	tablespoons oyster sauce
1	tablespoon light brown sugar
1	teaspoon Asian sesame oil
1	teaspoon cornstarch
6	medium cloves garlic, minced or pressed through a garlic press (about 2 tablespoons)
1	piece (1 inch) ginger, minced (about 1 tablespoon)
3	tablespoons peanut or vegetable oil
1¼	pounds broccoli, florets cut into bite-sized pieces, stems trimmed, peeled, and cut on the diagonal into ⅛-inch-thick slices
⅓	cup water
1	small red bell pepper, cored, seeded, and diced
3	medium scallions, sliced ½ inch thick on the diagonal

1. Combine the beef and soy sauce in a medium bowl; cover with plastic wrap and refrigerate at least 10 minutes or up to 1 hour, stirring once. Meanwhile, whisk the sherry, chicken broth, oyster sauce, sugar, sesame oil, and cornstarch in a measuring cup. Combine the garlic, ginger, and 1½ teaspoons peanut oil in a small bowl.

2. Drain the beef and discard the liquid. Heat 1½ teaspoons peanut oil in a 12-inch nonstick skillet over high heat until smoking. Add half of the beef to the skillet and break up clumps; cook without stirring, 1 minute, then stir and cook

until the beef is browned about the edges, about 30 seconds. Transfer the beef to a medium bowl. Add 1½ teaspoons peanut oil to the skillet, heat until just smoking, and repeat with the remaining beef.

3. Add 1 tablespoon peanut oil to the now-empty skillet; heat until just smoking. Add the broccoli and cook 30 seconds; add the water, cover the pan, and lower the heat to medium. Steam the broccoli until tender-crisp, about 2 minutes; transfer to a paper towel–lined plate. Add the remaining 1½ teaspoons peanut oil to the skillet; increase the heat to high and heat until just smoking. Add the bell

---

TECHNIQUE:
Slicing Flank Steak for Stir-Fries

1. Slice the partially frozen flank steak into 2-inch-wide pieces.

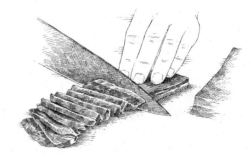

2. Cut each piece of flank steak against the grain into very thin slices.

---

pepper and cook, stirring frequently, until spotty brown, about 1½ minutes. Clear the center of the skillet; add the garlic and ginger to the clearing and cook, mashing the mixture with a spoon, until fragrant, about 15 to 20 seconds, then stir the mixture into the peppers. Return the beef and broccoli to the skillet and toss to combine. Whisk the sauce to recombine, then add to the skillet; cook, stirring constantly, until the sauce is thickened and evenly distributed, about 30 seconds. Transfer to a serving platter, sprinkle with the scallions, and serve.

TECHNIQUE: Stir-Frying 101

Whether you are making beef and broccoli, kung pao shrimp, or chicken with ginger, there are six key steps you should follow to turn out a perfect stir-fry. Use very little oil, preferably peanut, at each step listed below—no more than 1 tablespoon and less when possible.

1. Preparing the ingredients in advance is key. While the meat, seafood, or chicken is marinating, whisk the sauce ingredients together in a measuring cup and add a small amount of oil to the garlic and ginger.

2. Heat the oil in a 12-inch nonstick skillet until smoking. Drain the meat, seafood, or chicken and add half to the pan. Cook until well browned. Remove to a large bowl and repeat with more oil and the remaining meat, seafood, or chicken.

3. Stir-fry long-cooking vegetables— such as broccoli, asparagus, or green beans—in oil in the empty pan, add a little water, cover, and then steam. Once the vegetables are crisp-tender, transfer them to a bowl.

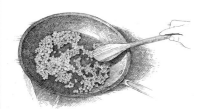

4. Stir-fry short-cooking vegetables— such as peppers or onions—for a minute or two in oil in the empty pan.

5. When the vegetables are slightly browned, add the garlic and ginger to the center of the pan. Cook until fragrant (15 to 20 seconds), and then stir the aromatics into vegetables.

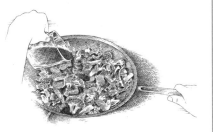

6. Add the meat and long-cooking vegetables back to the skillet. Whisk the sauce to recombine, then pour it into the skillet and toss with the meat and vegetables. Once everything is hot (30 to 60 seconds), serve immediately.

TASTING LAB: Broccoli Relations

BESIDES SUPERMARKET STANDARD BROCCOLI, WE TESTED some other "broccoli" options in our beef and broccoli recipe and found that all worked well.

Chinese broccoli, sometimes referred to as Chinese kale or *gai lan*, is the broccoli called for in many authentic recipes. Made of mostly thick stems and leaves, it has a mildly bitter flavor that tastes of bell pepper. Trim the yellowed or bruised leaves and bottom 1 inch of the stem from 1 pound of Chinese broccoli, then cut into 2-inch-long pieces. Chinese broccoli can be cooked exactly like regular broccoli in the recipe.

Broccoli rabe, also known as *rapini*, is actually a type of turnip green. Also made mostly of leaves and stems, broccoli rabe has a much stronger flavor. Cut off the bottom 2 inches of the stems from 1 pound of broccoli rabe, then cut into 2-inch-long pieces. Cook according to the recipe instructions, increasing the steaming time to 3 minutes.

Baby broccoli, also sold under the trademarked names Broccolini or Asperation, looks like a mix of broccoli and asparagus, but it's actually a cross between broccoli and Chinese broccoli. Very mild in flavor, the stalks are tender and do not need to be peeled. Remove any leaves from 1 pound of baby broccoli, then cut into 2-inch-long pieces. Baby broccoli may be cooked exactly according to recipe.

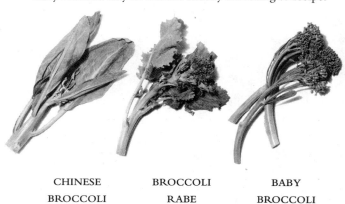

CHINESE BROCCOLI   BROCCOLI RABE   BABY BROCCOLI

TASTING LAB: Oyster Sauce

OYSTER SAUCE, WHICH IS ACTUALLY CALLED OYSTER-FLAVORED sauce, is a rich, concentrated mixture of oyster extracts, soy sauce, brine, and assorted seasonings. This brown sauce is thick, salty, and strong tasting. It is used sparingly to enhance the flavor of many dishes, including those—like some of the stir-fries in this chapter—without any seafood.

A trip to our local grocery store and Asian market turned up five different brands of bottled oyster sauce. Lee Kum Kee dominated the shelves with three varieties: Choy Sun, Panda Brand, and Premium Brand. Coin Tree and Sa Cheng rounded out the list. Although oyster sauce is too strong to be used as a condiment, we thought it important to take note of the raw, unadulterated flavor of each bottle before using it in a recipe. Each brand of the potent sauce received the same standard comments: "salty," "biting," and "fishy." However, when we mixed the bottled oyster sauces with other ingredients—sherry, soy sauce, sesame oil, sugar, and freshly ground black pepper—and then made simple stir-fries, our tasters were able to detect a wider range of flavors.

The most authentic of the group was undoubtedly Lee Kum Kee's Premium Brand Oyster Flavored Sauce with Dried Scallop. Admittedly intense and somewhat fishy, it was the only sauce with true depth of flavor; its saltiness was balanced by sweet caramel undertones, and the oyster flavor was strong. However, this sauce is not for the faint of heart, as one taster proclaimed, "My American taste buds can't take it." According to Jason Wong, president of AsiaFoods.com, Lee Kum Kee's Premium sauce is the favorite among the Asian-American population and the "only one" used in restaurants. It is also the most expensive sauce we tested ($5.79 for an 18-ounce bottle). All of this notwithstanding, the other favorite among tasters was Sa Cheng Oyster Flavored Sauce ($1.59 for a 15-ounce bottle), preferred because it was mild and "gravylike." The other three bottled sauces we tried didn't seem to add much to our stir-fries. As one taster put it, they "may just as well have been soy sauce."

PORK AND VEGETABLE STIR-FRIES

WHAT WE WANTED: Stir-fries with tender, flavorful pork and perfectly cooked vegetables. They would taste authentic but would not have epic ingredient lists.

From a pork and vegetable stir-fry—homemade or ordered out—we usually expect nothing more than tough, tasteless pork and barely cooked vegetables in a thick, slithery sauce. We set out to make pork and vegetable stir-fries that were both tasty and tender without being labor-intensive.

Pork shoulder is often called for in authentic pork stir-fry recipes, but because pieces weighing less than several pounds can be difficult to find, we excluded pork shoulder as a possibility. Instead, we tried stir-frying the more sensible options: boneless loin chops and tenderloin, both cut into strips small enough to eat with a piece or two of vegetable. The loin chops cooked into dry, tight, tough pieces not unlike shoe leather. The tenderloin was the uncontested winner. Tender and yielding, it had the textural quality of a filet mignon.

The next task was to determine whether marinating the pork was worth the trouble. We tossed one plain batch of tenderloin strips unceremoniously into the skillet and a second batch with some soy and sherry to marinate a few minutes before cooking. The marinade, which boosted flavor quickly and easily, was the clear winner. But it also dealt

us a setback when the pork failed to brown properly, even in the hottest skillet. The reason? Pork tenderloin is almost always sold in shrink-wrapped packages and therefore contains a lot of moisture (and we were adding more). We discovered that the answer was to cook the pork in batches over high heat. This way, the moisture that the pork released evaporated rapidly, and, after it did, the pork was free to take on color. Each batch needed to cook for only 2 minutes—quite a flash in the pan.

With the pork out of the skillet and set aside in a bowl, we worked on the vegetables and flavorings. Because different vegetables cook at different rates, batch cooking was necessary (batch cooking also prevents overcrowding, so that the vegetables, too, can brown their way to good flavor). We added various mixes of aromatics (such as garlic and ginger) using our standard stir-fry method (add at the end of cooking to a clearing in the center of the skillet, where they can cook long enough to develop their flavors but not long enough to burn).

We were not after an abundance of sauce, just enough light-bodied liquid to cling to the pork and vegetables and provide succulence. If we added enough soy sauce or fish sauce to provide the bulk of the sauce, saltiness or fishy pungency prevailed. If we added water, the flavor was hollow. Chicken broth was the solution. It provided a liquid element that gave the sauce backbone and did not dilute flavor. We also found that a small addition of acid—lime juice or rice vinegar—did a lot to brighten flavors. Finally, just a teaspoon of cornstarch allowed the sauce to lightly cloak the meat and vegetables instead of pooling at the bottom of the plate.

WHAT WE LEARNED: Use pork tenderloin for the best texture, marinate the meat to improve its flavor, stir-fry it in batches to promote browning, and cloak everything in potently flavored sauce that has been lightly thickened with cornstarch.

FOOD FACT: Rice

Americans don't eat much rice, at least compared with rest of the world. Our per capita consumption of rice is about 20 pounds per year. In many Asian countries, annual per capita consumption runs about 300 pounds, and, in the United Arab Emirates, that figure is an astonishing 450 pounds. The French, who eat about 10 pounds of rice per person every year, are one of the few peoples to eat less rice than Americans do.

STIR-FRIED PORK, EGGPLANT, AND ONIONS WITH GARLIC AND BLACK PEPPER

Serves 4 as a main dish with rice

This classic Thai stir-fry is not for those with timid palates.

12	ounces pork tenderloin, prepared according to the illustrations on page 188
1	teaspoon plus 2½ tablespoons fish sauce
1	teaspoon plus 2½ tablespoons soy sauce
2	tablespoons low-sodium chicken broth
2	teaspoons juice from 1 lime
2½	tablespoons light brown sugar
1	teaspoon cornstarch
12	cloves garlic, minced or pressed through a garlic press (about 3½ tablespoons)
2	teaspoons ground black pepper
3½	tablespoons peanut or vegetable oil
1	pound eggplant, cut into ¾-inch cubes
1	large onion, cut into ¼- to ⅜-inch wedges
½	cup fresh cilantro leaves, chopped coarse

1. Combine pork, 1 teaspoon fish sauce, and 1 teaspoon soy sauce in a small bowl. Whisk remaining 2½ tablespoons each fish sauce and soy sauce, chicken broth, lime juice, sugar, and cornstarch in a measuring cup. Combine the garlic, pepper, and 1 tablespoon oil in a small bowl.

2. Heat 1½ teaspoons oil in a 12-inch nonstick skillet over high heat until smoking; add half of the pork to the skillet and cook, stirring occasionally and breaking up clumps, until well-browned, about 2 minutes. Transfer the pork to a medium bowl. Repeat with an additional 1½ teaspoons oil and the remaining pork. Add 1 tablespoon oil to the now-empty skillet; add the eggplant and cook, stirring every 30 seconds, until browned and no longer spongy, about 5 minutes; transfer to the bowl with the pork. Add the remaining 1½ teaspoons oil to the skillet; add the onion and cook, stirring occasionally, until beginning to brown and soften, about 2 minutes. Clear the center of the skillet, add the

garlic/pepper mixture to the clearing; cook, mashing the mixture with a spoon, until fragrant and beginning to brown, about 1½ minutes, then stir the mixture into the onions. Add the pork and eggplant; toss to combine. Whisk the sauce to recombine, then add to the skillet; cook, stirring constantly, until the sauce is thickened and evenly distributed, about 30 seconds. Transfer to a serving platter; sprinkle with the cilantro and serve.

STIR-FRIED PORK, GREEN BEANS, AND RED BELL PEPPER WITH GINGERY OYSTER SAUCE

Serves 4 as a main dish with rice

See page 184 for more information on oyster sauce.

12	ounces pork tenderloin, prepared according to the illustrations on page 188
2	teaspoons soy sauce
2	teaspoons plus 1 tablespoon dry sherry
⅓	cup low-sodium chicken broth
2½	tablespoons oyster sauce
2	teaspoons toasted sesame oil
1	teaspoon rice vinegar
¼	teaspoon ground white pepper
1	teaspoon cornstarch
2	cloves garlic, minced or pressed through a garlic press (about 2 teaspoons)
1	piece (about 2 inches) fresh ginger, grated (about 2 tablespoons)
3	tablespoons peanut or vegetable oil
12	ounces green beans, cut on the diagonal into 2-inch lengths
¼	cup water
1	large red bell pepper, cut into ¾-inch squares
3	medium scallions, sliced thin on the diagonal

1. Combine the pork, soy sauce, and 2 teaspoons sherry in a small bowl. Whisk the remaining 1 tablespoon sherry, chicken broth, oyster sauce, sesame oil, rice vinegar, white pepper, and cornstarch in a measuring cup. Combine the garlic, ginger, and 1½ teaspoons peanut oil in a small bowl.

2. Heat 1½ teaspoons peanut oil in a 12-inch nonstick skillet over high heat until smoking; add half of the pork to the skillet and cook, stirring occasionally and breaking up clumps, until well-browned, about 2 minutes. Transfer the pork to a medium bowl. Repeat with an additional 1½ teaspoons peanut oil and the remaining pork. Add 1 tablespoon peanut oil to the now-empty skillet; add the green beans and cook, stirring occasionally, until spotty brown, about 2 minutes. Add the water, cover the pan, and lower the heat to medium. Steam until the beans are tender-crisp, 2 to 3 minutes; transfer beans to the bowl with the pork. Add the remaining 1½ teaspoons oil to the skillet; add the bell pepper and cook, stirring frequently, until spotty brown, about 2 minutes. Clear the center of the skillet, then add the garlic/ginger mixture to the clearing; cook, mashing the mixture with a spoon, until fragrant, about 45 seconds, then stir the mixture into the peppers. Add the pork and green beans; toss to combine. Whisk the sauce to recombine, then add to the skillet; cook, stirring constantly, until the sauce is thickened and evenly distributed, about 30 seconds. Transfer to a serving platter; sprinkle with the scallions and serve.

SPICY STIR-FRIED PORK, ASPARAGUS, AND ONIONS WITH LEMON GRASS

Serves 4 as a main dish with rice

To use lemon grass, peel off the tough outer leaves to reveal a creamy white interior, then trim off the bottom inch of the stalk. Of what remains, the bottom 4 or 5 inches can be minced.

12	ounces pork tenderloin, prepared according to the illustrations on page 188
1	teaspoon plus 2 tablespoons fish sauce
1	teaspoon soy sauce
⅓	cup low-sodium chicken broth
2	teaspoons juice from 1 lime
1	tablespoon light brown sugar
1	teaspoon cornstarch
2	medium cloves garlic, minced or pressed through a garlic press (about 2 teaspoons)
¼	cup minced lemon grass from 2 stalks (see note)
¾	teaspoon red pepper flakes
3½	tablespoons peanut or vegetable oil
1	pound asparagus, cut on the diagonal into 2-inch pieces
¼	cup water
1	large onion, cut into ¼- to ⅜-inch wedges
¼	cup chopped fresh basil leaves

1. Combine the pork, 1 teaspoon fish sauce, and soy sauce in a small bowl. Whisk the remaining 2 tablespoons fish sauce, chicken broth, lime juice, sugar, and cornstarch in a measuring cup. Combine the garlic, lemon grass, red pepper flakes, and 1 tablespoon oil in a small bowl.

2. Heat 1½ teaspoons oil in a 12-inch nonstick skillet over high heat until smoking; add half of the pork to the skillet and cook, stirring occasionally and breaking up clumps, until well browned, about 2 minutes. Transfer the pork to a medium bowl. Repeat with an additional 1½ teaspoons oil and remaining pork. Add 1 tablespoon oil to the now-empty skillet; add the asparagus and cook, stirring every 30 seconds, until lightly browned, about 2 minutes. Add the water, cover the pan, and lower the heat to medium. Steam the asparagus until tender-crisp, about 2 minutes; transfer the asparagus to the bowl with the pork. Add the remaining 1½ teaspoons oil to the skillet; add the onion and cook, stirring occasionally, until beginning to brown and soften, about 2 minutes. Clear the center of the skillet, add the garlic/lemon grass mixture to the clearing; cook, mashing the mixture with a spoon, until fragrant, about 1 minute, then stir the mixture into the onion. Add the pork and asparagus; toss to combine. Stir the sauce to recombine, then add to the skillet; cook, stirring constantly, until the sauce is thickened and evenly distributed, about 30 seconds. Transfer to a serving platter; sprinkle with the basil and serve.

EQUIPMENT CORNER: Electric Woks

WE'VE SAID IT PLAINLY SEVERAL TIMES: WE DON'T LIKE woks. The relatively small base of a wok means only modest burner contact, which translates to less than maximal heat. Quite simply, the design of a wok is not meant for cooking on a Western stovetop, where a large open skillet is much more successful at achieving optimum sizzle and sear.

We wondered, however, if electric woks offered advantages over stovetop woks. We collected six of them, ranging in price from $30 to $100, then stir-fried and deep-fried in each, looking for differences in heating ability and design. To our surprise, one wok—and a modestly priced one at that—excelled in all areas and another did quite well.

The runaway winner was the Maxim Nonstick Electric Wok with Dome Cover ($60). It stir-fried on par with a skillet, and it managed the oil for deep-frying like a pro. The temperature dial was accurate and easy to read. The size of this wok is generous (14 inches in diameter, 6½-quart capacity), and the long-handled design makes it possible to simultaneously empty and scrape ingredients out of the wok when cooking in batches.

The runner-up was the Toastmaster High Performance Electric Wok ($30). This wok had the heat output of the winner, but it was not nearly as commodious (12¾ inches in diameter, with a 4½-quart capacity). With use, its temperature dial became hot to the touch, and the wok's two short handles made it impossible to scrape out food while turning the wok to empty it.

The remaining four woks tested weren't worth the space they occupied on the countertop. Problems included flimsy construction, odd design, and hot spots. Moreover, none of these woks had good heat output—in fact, three couldn't get the oil for deep-frying above 350 degrees, though their thermostats were set for 375 and indicated that the temperature had been reached. In comparison, our favorite woks maintained temperatures of 365 to 375 degrees, ideal for deep-frying.

Should you purchase an electric wok? If you're a frequent fryer or you like to use a bamboo steamer (which requires a wok of some sort, electric or not), our winning model, the Maxim, might be a worthwhile investment. However, if stir-frying is your limit, stick with a large, heavy, totally utilitarian nonstick skillet.

TECHNIQUE:
Slicing Pork Tenderloin for Stir-Fries

1. Pork tenderloin is easier to slice when partially frozen. Freeze the tenderloin until firm but not frozen solid, 45 minutes to 1 hour. Cut the tenderloin crosswise into ¼-inch slices.

2. Cut the slices into ¼-inch strips.

Rating Electric Woks

WE TESTED SIX ELECTRIC WOKS BY STIR-FRYING AND DEEP-FRYING IN EACH ONE. WE PREHEATED EACH WOK AND THEN prepared a batch of our stir-fried pork with eggplant. We also heated peanut oil in each wok, with the temperature dial set to 375 degrees, and then deep-fried chicken wings. The woks are listed in order of preferences based on their performance in these tests as well as their heating ability and design. See www.americastestkitchen.com for up-to-date prices and mail-order sources for top-rated products.

RECOMMENDED
Maxim Nonstick Electric Wok with Dome Cover
$60.00
This large wok stir-fries like a skillet and is perfect for deep-frying. We particularly like the long handle (which makes it easy to pick up) and the no-fuss cleanup. The temperature dial was accurate and easy to read.

RECOMMENDED WITH RESERVATIONS
Toastmaster High Performance Electric Wok
$30.00
This wok heats up quite well but is considerably smaller than our top choice. The two short handles are not ideal, but the nonstick interior made cleanup a snap. Also, the temperature dial became hot to the touch as the wok heated up.

NOT RECOMMENDED
Rival Stainless Steel Electric Wok
$90.00
Food stuck horribly to the stainless steel surface of this flawed wok, which did not get hot enough to deep-fry properly.

NOT RECOMMENDED
West Bend Electric Wok
$48.00
This wok heated very unevenly and erratically, and it was difficult to brown foods evenly. Better at deep-frying than stir-frying.

NOT RECOMMENDED
Martin Yan Professional Wok
$90.00
This pricey wok had little sizzle, and food browned only moderately. After 15 minutes of heating, oil only reached 312 degrees, much too low for proper deep-frying.

NOT RECOMMENDED
Circulon Hard Anodized Electric Wok
$100.00
This expensive wok was slow to heat and cooled down quickly when food was added. Small surface grooves ensnared small bits of food. Could not achieve high enough temperature to deep-fry.

Bean sprouts, stored and stacked,
are ready for use in our pad Thai recipe.

ASIAN noodles

We no longer think of noodles as just Italian. Asian noodles are everywhere, from slippery udon noodles in Japanese soups to delicate cellophane noodles in Vietnamese salads. Pad thai and cold sesame noodles are two of our favorite Asian noodle recipes, but both have fallen victim to their popularity. We've been served more bad Americanized versions of these dishes than we care to admit. More often than not, the noodles are much too starchy (Asian noodles cannot be handled as if they were Italian pasta) and the sauces are sweet or greasy.

We decided to take matters in our own hands in the test kitchen. We figured that authentic ingredients would be part of the answer, and we were willing to make special shopping expeditions to Asian markets to find the pantry staples we needed. We also wanted to better understand the fundamental cooking techniques associated with the noodles.

PAD THAI

WHAT WE WANTED: A fresh, vibrant version of this Thai classic, not the greasy, soggy, candy-sweet dish served in so many restaurants.

Pad thai is a remedy for a dead, jaded palate. Hot, sweet, and pungent Thai flavors tangled in an un-Western jumble of textures awaken all of the senses that have grown weary of the usual grub. We have downed numerous platefuls of pad thai, many from an excellent Thai restaurant only a few blocks away from our test kitchen. What we noticed was that from one order to the next, pad thai prepared in the same reliable restaurant kitchen was inconsistent. If it was perfect, it was a symphony of flavors and textures. It balanced sweet, sour, and spicy, and the tender, glutinous rice noodles ensnared curls of shrimp, crisp strands of bean sprouts, soft curds of fried egg, and sturdy bits of tofu. Sometimes, however, it tasted weak and flat, as if seasoned too timidly. At its worst, pad thai suffers from indiscriminate amounts of sugar, from slick, greasy noodles, or from sticky, lifeless strands that glom onto one another to form a chaotic skein.

We have become so enamored of pad thai and so tired of disappointment that we have attempted it several times in the test kitchen with only moderate success, and that we attribute to luck. The recipes were unclear, the ingredient lists daunting, and we stumbled through the steps only to produce dry, undercooked noodles and unbalanced flavors. Happily, though, our pad thai was loaded with plump, sweet shrimp (not the paltry four or five per typical restaurant order), and the flavors tasted clean and fresh. Our goal was to build on these positives and produce a consistently superlative pad thai.

Rice sticks, the type of noodles used in pad thai, are often only partially cooked, particularly when used in stir-fries. We found three different methods of preparing them: soaking in room-temperature water, soaking in hot tap water,

and boiling. We began with boiling and quickly realized that this was bad advice. Drained and waiting in the colander, the noodles glued themselves together. When we managed to stir-fry them, they wound up soggy and overdone. Noodles soaked in room-temperature water remained fairly stiff. After lengthy stir-frying, they eventually became tender, but longer cooking made this pad thai drier and stickier. Finally, we tried soaking the rice sticks in hot tap water for about 20 minutes. They "softened," turning limp and pliant, but were not fully tender. Drained, they were loose and separate, and they cooked through easily with stir-frying. The result? Noodles that were at once pleasantly tender and resilient.

Sweet, salty, sour, and spicy are the flavor characteristics of pad thai, and none should dominate; they should coexist in harmony. Although the cooking time is short, the ingredient list isn't, and many components will appear foreign to some. Fish sauce supplies a salty-sweet pungency, sugar gives sweetness, the heat comes from ground chiles, vinegar provides acidity, and tamarind rounds out the dish with its fruity, earthy, sweet-tart molasses-tinged flavor. Garlic and sometimes shallots contribute their heady, robust flavors. Some recipes call for ketchup (sounds dubious but probably worth trying) and some for soy sauce.

With these ingredients in hand, we set off to find out which ones were key to success and how much of each to use to achieve balanced flavor. For 8 ounces of rice sticks, 3 tablespoons of fish sauce and the same amount of sugar were ideal. Three-quarters of a teaspoon of cayenne (many recipes call for Thai chiles, but for the sake of simplicity, we opted not to use them) brought a low, even heat—not a searing burn—and 1 tablespoon of rice vinegar (preferred in pad thai for its mild acidity and relatively complex fermented-grain flavor) greatly vivified the flavors.

Tasters liked the garlic at 1 tablespoon minced. Shallots had a surprising impact on flavor. Just one medium shallot (about 3 tablespoons minced) produced such a round, full

sweetness and depth of flavor that we just couldn't say no. To coax the right character out of these two aromatics, we found that cooking them to the point of browning was critical; they tasted mellow, sweet, and mildly toasty.

Tamarind was the most enigmatic ingredient on our list. Tamarind is a fruit that grows as a round brown pod about 5 inches long and is often sold as a paste (a hard, flat brick) or as a sticky concentrate. (For more information, see page 195.) Although we eschew hard-to-find ingredients in the test kitchen, we came to the conclusion that tamarind is central—if not essential—to the unique flavor of pad thai. Testing showed that tamarind paste has a fresher, brighter, fruitier flavor than concentrate, which tasted dull by comparison. For those who cannot obtain either tamarind paste or concentrate, we worked out a formula of equal parts lime juice and water as a stand-in. This mixture produces a less interesting and less authentic dish, but we polished off several such platefuls with no qualms.

We tried a little ketchup, but its vinegary tomato flavor was out of place. As for soy sauce, even just a mere tablespoon was a big bully—its assertive flavor didn't play nicely with the others.

The other ingredients in pad thai are sautéed shrimp, scrambled eggs, chopped peanuts, bean sprouts, and scallions.

For more textural intrigue and to achieve authentic pad thai flavor, dried shrimp and Thai salted preserved radish are worthy embellishments (both sold in Asian grocery stores). Dried shrimp are sweet, salty, and intensely shrimpy, and they add tiny bursts of incredible flavor. We used 2 tablespoons of the smallest dried shrimp we could find and chopped them up finer still, because tasters asked that their firm, chewy texture be mitigated. Thai salted preserved radish is brownish-yellow in color, dry, and a bit wrinkled, and it is sold in long sections (think daikon radish) folded into a flimsy plastic package. Two tablespoons of chopped salted radish added piquant, savory bits with a good crunch.

Oddly, after consuming dozens of servings of pad thai, we did not feel glutted. We were addicted. These days, if we order it in a restaurant, we prepare ourselves for disappointment. We've come to think that pad thai is not unlike chocolate chip cookies: It's always best homemade.

WHAT WE LEARNED: Soak the rice noodles in hot water before stir-frying them. Tamarind paste is the key flavor in the sauce, although lime juice and water make an adequate substitute. Fish sauce, sugar, and rice vinegar are the other key components in the sauce, and browned garlic and shallot add tremendous flavor.

PAD THAI Serves 4 as a main dish

A wok might be the implement of choice in restaurants and the old country, but a large 12-inch skillet (nonstick makes cleanup easy) is more practical for home cooks. Although pad thai cooks very quickly, the ingredient list is long, and everything must be prepared and within easy reach at the stovetop when you begin cooking. For maximum efficiency, use the time during which the tamarind and noodles soak to prepare the other ingredients. Tofu is a good and common addition to pad thai. If you like, add 4 ounces of extra-firm tofu or pressed tofu (available in Asian markets) cut into 1/4-inch cubes (about 1 cup) to the noodles along with the bean sprouts.

- 2 tablespoons tamarind paste or substitute (see "Tasting Lab: Tamarind Options" on page 195)
- 3/4 cup boiling water
- 3 tablespoons fish sauce
- 1 tablespoon rice vinegar
- 3 tablespoons sugar
- 3/4 teaspoon cayenne pepper
- 4 tablespoons peanut or vegetable oil
- 8 ounces dried rice stick noodles, about 1/8 inch wide (the width of linguine)
- 2 large eggs
- 1/4 teaspoon salt
- 12 ounces medium (31/35 count) shrimp, peeled and deveined, if desired
- 3 cloves garlic, minced or pressed through a garlic press (about 1 tablespoon)
- 1 medium shallot, minced (about 3 tablespoons)
- 2 tablespoons dried shrimp, chopped fine (optional)
- 2 tablespoons chopped Thai salted preserved radish (optional)
- 6 tablespoons chopped roasted unsalted peanuts
- 3 cups (6 ounces) bean sprouts
- 5 medium scallions, green parts only, sliced thin on a sharp diagonal
- 1/4 cup loosely packed cilantro leaves (optional)
  Lime wedges

GETTING IT RIGHT: Soaking the Noodles

STIFF NOODLES
Soaking the rice sticks in room-temperature water yields hard noodles that take too long to stir-fry.

STICKY NOODLES
Fully cooking the rice sticks in boiling water results in soft, sticky, gummy, overdone noodles.

PERFECT NOODLES
Soaking the rice sticks in hot water yields softened noodles. When stir-fried, they are tender but resilient.

1. Rehydrate the tamarind paste in boiling water (see the instructions in "Tasting Lab: Tamarind Options" at right). Stir the fish sauce, rice vinegar, sugar, cayenne, and 2 tablespoons oil into the tamarind liquid and set aside.

2. Cover the rice sticks with hot tap water in a large bowl; soak until softened, pliable, and limp but not fully tender, about 20 minutes. Drain the noodles and set aside. Beat the eggs and ⅛ teaspoon of the salt in a small bowl; set aside.

3. Heat 1 tablespoon oil in a 12-inch skillet (preferably nonstick) over high heat until just beginning to smoke. Add the shrimp and sprinkle with the remaining ⅛ teaspoon salt; cook, tossing occasionally, until the shrimp are opaque and browned about the edges, about 3 minutes. Transfer the shrimp to a plate and set aside.

4. Off heat, add the remaining tablespoon oil to the skillet and swirl to coat; add the garlic and shallot, set the skillet over medium heat, and cook, stirring constantly, until light golden brown, about 1½ minutes; add the eggs to the skillet and stir vigorously with a wooden spoon until scrambled and barely moist, about 20 seconds. Add the noodles and the dried shrimp and salted radish (if using) to the eggs; toss with 2 wooden spoons to combine. Pour the fish sauce mixture over the noodles, increase the heat to high, and cook, tossing constantly, until the noodles are evenly coated. Scatter ¼ cup peanuts, bean sprouts, all but ¼ cup scallions, and cooked shrimp over the noodles; continue to cook, tossing constantly, until the noodles are tender, about 2½ minutes (if not yet tender add 2 tablespoons water to the skillet and continue to cook until tender).

5. Transfer the noodles to a serving platter, sprinkle with the remaining scallions, 2 tablespoons peanuts, and cilantro; serve immediately, passing lime wedges separately.

TASTING LAB: Tamarind Options

SWEET-TART, BROWNISH-RED TAMARIND IS A NECESSARY ingredient for a pad thai that looks and tastes authentic. It's commonly sold in paste (also called pulp) and in concentrate form. But don't fret if neither is available—you can still make a very good pad thai using lime juice and water. Here are your three options.

Tamarind Paste or Pulp: Tamarind paste, or pulp, is firm, sticky, and filled with seeds and fibers. We favored this product because it had the freshest, brightest flavor. To use it in the pad thai recipe, soak 2 tablespoons in ¾ cup boiling water for about 10 minutes, then push it through a mesh strainer to remove the seeds and fibers and extract as much pulp as possible.

Tamarind Concentrate: Tamarind concentrate looks more like a scary pomade than a foodstuff. It's black, thick, shiny, and gooey. Its flavor approximates that of tamarind paste, but it tastes less fruity and more "cooked," and it colors the pad thai a shade too dark. To use in the pad thai recipe, mix 1 tablespoon with ⅔ cup hot water.

Lime Juice and Water Substitute: If tamarind is out of the question, combine ⅓ cup lime juice and ⅓ cup water and use it in its place; use light brown sugar instead of granulated to give the noodles some color and a faint molasses flavor. Because it will already contain a good hit of lime, do not serve this version with lime wedges.

TAMARIND PASTE   TAMARIND CONCENTRATE   LIME

EQUIPMENT CORNER:
Flat-Bottom Woks

WE DON'T LIKE STOVETOP WOKS—AT LEAST NOT conventional rounded models. The traditional wok is designed to sit in an open cooking pit with flames licking the sides of the vessel. Of course, on a flat American stovetop, a round wok wobbles and has little direct contact with the heat source. For these reasons, we prefer a 12-inch nonstick skillet for stir-frying. When we decided to revisit the wok issue yet again, this time with flat-bottom woks, we thought we'd wait to pass judgment. We needn't have bothered. We can now safely say that we don't like stovetop woks, period.

There are dozens of flat-bottom woks on the market, which are also sold as stir-fry pans. To narrow the field, we set a few guidelines. First was size. We chose woks that had a diameter of at least 12 inches when measured across the top. Second was interior material. We like to use a nonstick pan in stir-fries, so we limited our field to nonstick woks only. We found eight popular brands of nonstick flat-bottom woks and brought them into the kitchen for a marathon stir-fry session, making batch after batch of beef and broccoli. The woks ranged in price from $16.99 to $139.99. Did price correlate to quality? Not at all.

The best performer, the 14-inch Joyce Chen Original Stir Fry Pan ($43.95), held a roomy 6½ quarts and measured 6½ inches across the bottom (the widest bottom area we could find). The wok was balanced, sturdy, and easy to use, though it was a bit heavy for one petite tester. The best part about this wok was that it got hot and stayed hot, taking a respectable three minutes to get the oil smoking initially and a quick 49 seconds to get it smoking for the second batch of beef. That heat is key to developing a brown crust on the beef, which this wok achieved to some degree, though not quite as nicely as our trusty 12-inch skillet. A 12-inch skillet has twice as much surface in direct contact with the heating source as the Joyce Chen wok. This larger area allows for the meat to be spread in an even layer, ensuring even browning.

Our second-place finisher, the Anolon Classic Stir Fry Pan ($39.99), had the same size bottom as the Joyce Chen but was significantly smaller overall, with a 12-inch diameter at the top and a 5-quart capacity. Beef and broccoli browned somewhat, but the wok's tipsy and unstable design made us nervous. This thin wok didn't hold heat well; it took almost twice as long as the Joyce Chen wok to get the oil hot for the second batch of beef.

The woks that fared worst in our tests were the Scanpan Ergonomic Stir Fry Pan ($139.99) and the Circulon Steel Stir Fry Pan ($39.99). Neither browned the beef or the broccoli at all. The large-capacity Scanpan was sturdy and easy to work with, but its relatively small bottom (5¾-inches) made browning difficult; instead of lying in an even layer across the bottom, the pieces of meat stacked up into a pile, oozing juice and steaming rather than searing. Despite the heft of this wok, it didn't hold heat at all; at 2 minutes, 15 seconds, it took the longest to get hot again after searing the first batch of beef.

One tester described last-place finisher Circulon as a "mixing bowl with a handle." The Circulon pan's tippy design made it difficult to work with, and its 5½-inch flat bottom never gave the beef a chance.

Though the Joyce Chen Stir Fry Pan fared the best in our testing, we'd still reach first for a 12-inch nonstick skillet when stir-frying. If you were using a bamboo steamer, for which you need a wok, or cooking a large batch of fried rice, the Joyce Chen might come in handy. But if you're sticking to stir-fry, stick to your skillet. Its large, flat bottom is better suited for flat Western stovetops.

Rating Flat-Bottom Woks

WE TESTED EIGHT WOKS WITH FLAT BOTTOMS, PREPARING A BEEF AND BROCCOLI STIR-FRY IN EACH. THE WOKS ARE listed in order of preference based on their ability to brown foods, the time it took them to heat up, and their design. For up-to-date prices and mail-order sources for the top-rated product see www.americastestkitchen.com.

RECOMMENDED WITH RESERVATIONS
Joyce Chen Original Stir Fry Pan
$43.95
Best browning with large capacity. Better than the rest of the pack but not as good as a 12-inch nonstick skillet.

NOT RECOMMENDED
Anolon Classic Stir Fry Pan with Lid
$39.99
This small wok did not heat up well, and the tipsy designed was worrisome. "Feels cheap," wrote one tester.

NOT RECOMMENDED
Excalibur (Williams-Sonoma) Nonstick Wok with Lid
$59.00
Decent browning, but this pan was slightly awkward to use.

NOT RECOMMENDED
Calphalon Commercial Nonstick Flat Bottom Wok
$99.99
Decent browning, but this model was tipsy and unbalanced.

NOT RECOMMENDED
Asian Traditions (Target) Nonstick Stir Fry Pan
$16.99
This wok got very hot, very fast, but lost its heat as soon as we put food in it.

NOT RECOMMENDED
Anolon Professional Stir Fry Pan
$31.99
Slight browning, but this pan was very wobbly.

NOT RECOMMENDED
Scanpan Ergonomic Stir Fry Pan
$139.99
Stable and sturdy, but no browning in this expensive pan.

NOT RECOMMENDED
Circulon Steel Stir Fry Pan
$39.99
Small flat bottom means that very little browning can occur. High handle is awkward.

COLD SESAME NOODLES

WHAT WE WANTED: We set out to avoid the sticky noodles, gloppy texture, and lackluster flavor typically found in this Chinese classic.

Much like a Chinese finger trap that lures by appearing to be a toy, sesame noodles are not what they seem. You may think of them as merely a humble bowl of cold noodles, but don't be fooled—just one bite and you're hooked on these Chinese wheat noodles with shreds of tender chicken, all tossed with a fresh sesame sauce. And now you've got a real problem: Once you get the hankering, good versions of the dish are hard to find. The cold noodles have a habit of turning gummy, the chicken often dries out, and the sauce is notorious for turning bland and pasty. We wanted a recipe that could not only quell a serious craving but could do it in less time than it would take to grab a bus to Chinatown.

Though immediately drawn to the softer texture and milder flavor of fresh Chinese wheat noodles, we conceded that dried spaghetti could serve as a second-string substitute. The trouble with both types of noodles, however, was that after being cooked and chilled, they gelled into a rubbery skein. After trying a number of ways to avoid this problem, we found it necessary to rinse the noodles under cold tap water directly after cooking. This not only cooled the hot noodles immediately but washed away much of their sticky starch. To further forestall any clumping, we tossed the rinsed noodles with a little toasted sesame oil; this kept them slack and separated for hours.

Boneless, skinless chicken breasts are quick to cook and easy to shred; the real question is how to cook them. The microwave seemed easy in theory, but we found the rate of cooking difficult to monitor. Many recipes suggested poaching the chicken in water or broth, but this chicken had a washed-out flavor. Roasting caused the outer meat to dry out before the interior was fully cooked. Cooking under the broiler, however, worked perfectly. We found it necessary to position the chicken six inches from the broiler; any closer and the exterior of the cutlets will burn before the middle is cooked through. Once the internal temperature of chicken reaches 160 degrees, the cutlets are done.

To be authentic, the sesame sauce should be made with an Asian sesame paste (not to be confused with Middle Eastern tahini), but most recipes substitute peanut butter because it's easier to find. Somewhat surprisingly, tasters preferred chunky peanut butter over smooth, describing its flavor as fresh and more peanutty. We had been making the sauce in a blender and realized that the chunky bits of peanuts were being freshly ground into the sauce, resulting in the cleaner, stronger flavor. We found the flavors of both fresh garlic and ginger necessary, along with soy sauce, rice vinegar, hot sauce, and brown sugar. We then stumbled on the obvious way to keep the sauce from being too thick or pasty: Thin it out with water.

Although the sauce was good, tasters still complained that there was not enough sesame flavor. We tried adding toasted sesame seeds. Blended into the sauce along with the peanut butter, the sesame seeds added the final kick of authentic sesame flavor we were all hankering for.

FOOD FACT: Peanuts

Two American presidents were peanut farmers. Most of us remember Jimmy Carter on his Georgia peanut farm, but Thomas Jefferson also farmed peanuts on his Virginia plantation.

WHAT WE LEARNED: Use fresh Chinese noodles or dried spaghetti, but rinse and then oil the cooked noodles to keep them from sticking together. Use toasted sesame seeds and chunky peanut butter to build flavor in the sauce, which should be thinned with hot water to achieve the proper consistency.

SESAME NOODLES WITH SHREDDED CHICKEN
Serves 4 to 6 as a main course

In our experience, chicken takes longer to cook in a gas broiler than in an electric one, which is why the cooking times in the recipe range widely. Although our preference is for fresh Chinese egg noodles, we found that dried spaghetti works well, too. Because dried pasta swells so much more than fresh pasta during cooking, 12 ounces of dried spaghetti can replace one pound of fresh noodles.

¼   cup sesame seeds
¼   cup chunky peanut butter
2   medium cloves garlic, minced or pressed through a garlic press (about 2 teaspoons)
1   piece (1-inch) fresh ginger, grated or minced (about 1 tablespoon)
5   tablespoons soy sauce
2   tablespoons rice vinegar
1   teaspoon hot sauce (such as Tabasco)
2   tablespoons lightly packed light brown sugar
    Hot water
3   boneless, skinless chicken breast halves (1½ pounds), trimmed of excess fat
1   tablespoon salt
1   pound fresh Chinese egg noodles or 12 ounces dried spaghetti
2   tablespoons Asian sesame oil
4   scallions, sliced thin on the diagonal
1   medium carrot, peeled and grated on large holes of box grater (about ⅔ cup)

1. Toast the sesame seeds in a medium skillet over medium heat, stirring frequently, until golden and fragrant, about 10 minutes. Reserve 1 tablespoon sesame seeds in a small bowl. In a blender or food processor, puree the remaining 3 tablespoons sesame seeds, peanut butter, garlic, ginger, soy sauce, vinegar, hot sauce, and sugar until smooth, about 30 seconds. With the machine running, add hot water 1 tablespoon at a time until the sauce has the consistency of heavy

cream, about 5 tablespoons; set the mixture aside (it can be left in the blender jar or food processor workbowl).

2. Bring 6 quarts water to a boil in a stockpot over high heat. Meanwhile, adjust an oven rack to 6 inches from the broiler element; heat the broiler. Spray the broiler pan top with vegetable cooking spray; place the chicken breasts on top and broil the chicken until lightly browned, 4 to 8 minutes. Using tongs, flip the chicken over and continue to broil until the thickest part is no longer pink when cut into and registers about 160 degrees on an instant-read thermometer, 6 to 8 minutes. Transfer to a cutting board and let rest 5 minutes. Using 2 forks, shred the chicken into bite-sized pieces and set aside. Add the salt and noodles to the boiling water; boil the noodles until tender, about 4 minutes for fresh and 10 minutes for dried. Drain, then rinse with cold running tap water until cool to the touch; drain again. In a large bowl, toss the noodles with the sesame oil until evenly coated. Add the shredded chicken, scallions, carrot, and sauce; toss to combine. Divide among individual bowls, sprinkle each bowl with a portion of reserved sesame seeds, and serve.

SESAME NOODLES WITH SWEET PEPPERS AND CUCUMBERS

Core, seed, and cut into ¼-inch slices 1 medium red bell pepper; peel, halve lengthwise, seed, and cut crosswise into ⅛-inch slices 1 medium cucumber. Follow the recipe for Sesame Noodles with Shredded Chicken, omitting the chicken, adding the bell pepper and cucumber to the noodles along with the sauce, and sprinkling each bowl with a portion of 1 tablespoon chopped fresh cilantro leaves along with the sesame seeds.

SCIENCE DESK: Why Do Some Peanut Butters Separate?

THE FIRST FEW STEPS IN MAKING ANY TYPE OF PEANUT butter are essentially the same. Raw, shelled peanuts are roasted, cooled by industrial-strength suction fans, skinned, and ground.

After being ground, natural peanut butters are immediately jarred and shipped. When emulsified peanut butters are made, the peanuts must be ground once more, this time with salt, sweeteners, and hydrogenated stabilizers. During this grinding, the stabilizers trap the oil that is extracted from the peanuts in what scientists call a beta-prime polymorph. In layman's terms, this is a lattice-like structure that holds the peanut oil in its weave, suspending it throughout the creamed mass and protecting it from exposure to oxygen, which is the cause of rancidity. This is why hydrogenated peanut butters have a longer shelf life than natural peanut butters.

TASTING LAB: Peanut Butter

PEANUT BUTTER IS A CUPBOARD STAPLE, USED FOR EVERYTHING from sandwiches and cookies to sesame noodles. In the United States alone, peanut butter accounts for more than $630 million in sales annually, which is pretty amazing considering that just 150 years ago the peanut was thought fit only as fodder for pigs. Because we are constantly turning to peanut butter as a flavor booster for cookies, sauces, and sandwiches, we decided to find out which brand is best.

To do so, we first took a look at how all those brands got onto our supermarket shelves. Early peanut butters were (like today's "natural" versions) essentially just nuts ground into a paste. Because of the peanut's high fat content, these butters turned rancid easily and so were basically local products, with most producers supplying only their home city. In the early 1920s, Swift & Company introduced the first emulsified peanut butter, E. K. Pond, to American consumers. Emulsification made not only for a smoother, more spreadable product but also increased peanut butter's shelf

Rating Peanut Butters

TWENTY MEMBERS OF THE *COOK'S ILLUSTRATED* STAFF TASTED EIGHT PEANUT BUTTERS IN THREE APPLICATIONS—PLAIN, in peanut sauce, and in peanut butter cookies. Tasters evaluated the peanut butters and the sauces for intensity of peanut flavor and texture (mealy, smooth, pasty, gritty, and the like). The cookies were evaluated for peanut flavor, texture, and appearance. The peanut butters are listed in order of preference based on the combined scores from the three tastings. All brands are sold in supermarkets nationwide.

HIGHLY RECOMMENDED
Skippy Creamy Peanut Butter
$2.09 for 18 ounces

Overall, tasters felt that Skippy had a "good sweet/salty balance" and "tasted just like peanut butter should." Skippy made a tender and crisp cookie and a satisfying peanut sauce.

RECOMMENDED
Jif Creamy Peanut Butter
$1.99 for 18 ounces

Many tasters described second-place Jif as having the "perfect thickness" and being "sweet, but not obnoxiously so." Its texture was "silky and smooth," and it produced cookies with brown sugar undertones. In the peanut sauce, however, Jif was relatively sweet.

RECOMMENDED
Teddie Smooth Old Fashioned Peanut Butter
$2.39 for 16 ounces

Teddie Old Fashioned was the only natural peanut butter to rank in the upper echelons of the tasting. In its raw state, one taster complained that she "couldn't even swallow" it. In the cookie and sauce, however, it was described as "peanutty perfection."

RECOMMENDED
Reese's Creamy Peanut Butter
$1.88 for 18 ounces

Even though Reese's didn't fare too well in the sauce (tasters found it "unbalanced") or the cookies (it was deemed "gritty," with a "loose, shattery crumb"), tasters loved it raw. Most found it sweet and silky smooth, with a delicious flavor.

RECOMMENDED
Simply Jif Creamy Peanut Butter
$2.19 for 17.3 ounces

With only two-thirds of the sugar and less than half of the sodium per serving of other brands, Simply Jif scored surprisingly well. Many tasters thought it was very peanutty (albeit a little bland). In the sauce, it was called "fairly peanutty," but in the cookie this peanut butter failed to impress.

RECOMMENDED WITH RESERVATIONS
Freshly ground peanuts from a natural foods store
$1.99 for 16 ounces

Tasters found the cookies made with this product to be "meaty," with "lots of peanut flavor." When tasted raw, it was thought very bland, with the texture of "cardboard." The sauce made with it was found lacking in "character."

NOT RECOMMENDED
Peter Pan Creamy Peanut Butter
$2.19 for 18 ounces

Peter Pan was criticized for its "artificial" and "unbalanced" flavor. It gave the sauce a bitter, "fake" flavor, while it made a cookie that was sandy, dry, and generally unpleasant.

NOT RECOMMENDED
Smucker's Natural Creamy Peanut Butter
$2.79 for 16 ounces

Tasters just couldn't get past the texture when it came to eating the peanut butter raw, calling it "gritty," "grainy," and "pasty." In the sauce it was criticized for being too salty, and the cookie made with it was described as "dense," "tough," and very dry.

life. (See the Science Desk on page 200 for an explanation.) As a result, E. K. Pond became the first nationally available brand of peanut butter. In 1928, Swift changed the E. K. Pond label to Peter Pan; in 1932, a disgruntled Swift employee left the company to make his own brand of peanut butter, which he called Skippy; in 1958, Procter & Gamble lined market shelves with its new brand, Jif.

Over the years, the peanut butter scene hasn't changed much. Shoppers can choose natural, or "old-fashioned," peanut butter, or they can opt for a smooth emulsified peanut butter with a long shelf life.

We decided to focus our tasting on the top-selling peanut butters in grocery stores nationwide. This decision led us to include both natural and emulsified peanut butters, but only in their "creamy" form; "crunchy" peanut butter accounts for only 26 percent of peanut butter sales. In addition, our tasting would confine itself to "real" peanut butters as defined by the Food and Drug Administration: those that contain at least 90 percent peanuts. We tasted the peanut butters raw, in a sauce, and in a baked peanut butter cookie. After many long hours of tasting, we concluded that the peanut butter you choose might well depend on how you plan to use it.

When sampling the peanut butters straight from the jar, tasters chose Reese's as their favorite, with Jif only one point behind and Skippy trailing a distant third. When we checked the labels to try to explain this, we found that Reese's and Jif were the only two brands to include molasses. This, it seemed, added a caramel-like facet to their flavor profiles—an attribute tasters valued.

In the peanut sauce tasting, emulsified peanut butter once again stole the show. The rather grainy texture of the natural peanut butters was at odds with what should be the silky mouthfeel of the sauce. But this time Skippy took the lead, getting twice as many votes as the runner-up, Jif. Both the Jif and Reese's sauces were described by tasters as "very sweet" and "rather unbalanced." We concluded that this was the result of combining the already sweet ingredients in the sauce, which included coconut milk, with the molasses in the peanut butter.

It was in the cookie category, though, that we observed the most dramatic differences from brand to brand. The textures of the cookies were quite distinct. The cookies made with the natural peanut butters (Teddie and Smucker's) and those made with freshly ground peanut butter were hearty and thick, just what you would expect of a "natural" cookie. The cookies made with Reese's and Simply Jif (a version of Jif with reduced salt, molasses, and sugar) were sandy and delicate, while those made with regular Jif were of medium build, with soft, chewy centers and crisp edges. We attributed the semipliant character of the cookies made with regular Jif to the presence and amount of molasses, a hygroscopic substance that helps to retain moisture, giving the cookie its chewy quality. But if the Jif cookie was slightly soft, why wasn't the cookie made with Reese's, which also contains a significant amount of molasses? We once again compared the ingredient lists of Jif and Reese's and found our answer: Reese's contains cornstarch and less fat (1 gram). Robert Parker, a professor in the division of nutritional sciences at Cornell University, explained that the cornstarch in the peanut butter bound the water in the dough, leading to a dry cookie.

When it came to flavor, tasters slightly preferred the cookie made with Skippy, which they described as "tender and crisp." But the cookies made with natural peanut butters (one of which earned second and another third place in the cookie tasting) were consistently called more "peanutty" in flavor. The reason, according to University of Maryland lipids expert Elizabeth Boyle-Roden, is that natural peanut butters have not been doctored with hydrogenated oils, starches, sweeteners, or mono- or diglycerides, which can interfere with the peanut flavor in a cookie after it is baked.

Given all this information, what peanut butter should you buy? If you're looking for an all-purpose peanut butter, you can't go wrong with Skippy—and regular Jif comes in a close second. But if you eat your peanut butter on crackers, in sandwiches, or on an apple more often than you cook with it, you might prefer Reese's for its molasses-enhanced, caramel-like sweetness.

To remove chicken alla diavola from
the grill without tearing the crisp skin,
grasp the ends of the drumsticks
with sturdy tongs.

ITALIAN classics

Americans love Italian food—and rightly so. When prepared correctly (and authentically), most Italian dishes are light, simple, and quick. Italian cooks know that simpler is better, especially if you are starting with good ingredients. Luckily, there seem to be an endless number of appealing Italian dishes that make sense for the American home cook.

The recipes in this chapter start with three staple ingredients—cheese, chicken, and strawberries—but use them in interesting ways to create an easy but unusual Italian menu. Of course, the fact that a dish is simple (or Italian) doesn't mean that it will taste good. It's easy to incinerate chicken on the grill, and berries with balsamic vinegar often turn into a harsh, acidic affair. We wanted to explore these classic Italian dishes and get them right.

FRICO

WHAT WE WANTED: Thin, crisp cheese wafers to serve with cocktails.

Frico is probably the simplest and most addictive snack you'll ever eat. It is a thin, golden, flavorful cheese crisp. Classically made from a cheese called Montasio, this snack hails from the region of Friuli in northern Italy. It is nothing more than grated cheese sprinkled into a pan, melted, and then browned to form a crisp wafer. When made well, frico is light and airy, with a heavenly and intense cheese flavor. More often than not, however, it turns out chewy, bitter, and overly salty. Wondering what the key to this one-ingredient wonder was, we set out to make the perfect frico.

Although most of the recipes we researched were similar, we did encounter minor differences in technique. Some recipes call for a regular skillet and butter, while others call for olive oil and a well-seasoned cast-iron pan. After making a few rounds in the test kitchen, we found it easiest to use a medium (10-inch) nonstick skillet. The nonstick surface repels any fat released from the melting cheese, which ensures a smooth and effortless release without the use of butter or olive oil.

As we made and ate batches of frico, we picked up a few more tips for success. First, we discovered an easy way to flip the frico midway through cooking to brown the second side. After the first side browned, we simply removed the pan from the heat for several seconds to cool. As the cheese wafer began to cool and set up, it was easy to flip without tearing or stretching. We then quickly returned the pan to the heat and continued to brown the frico on the second side.

Using the right level of heat is also essential. If the pan is too hot, the cheese cooks too fast and turns bitter. But when cooked slowly over low heat, the cheese dries out, becomes crunchy, and turns a beautiful, golden color. We

found it necessary to adjust the heat between medium-high and medium between flips.

Last, we tried using a variety of cheeses other than Montasio, which can be difficult to find in the United States. While many of the recipes we found recommended Parmesan, we found aged Asiago to be a more appropriate substitution. When tasted side by side, the frico made with Parmesan was salty and harsh, while the frico made with aged Asiago was smooth and clean. But for the ultimate frico, with a deep, complex flavor that is neither too bitter nor too salty, a good hunk of Montasio is worth tracking down.

WHAT WE LEARNED: Montasio cheese makes the best frico and Asiago is a better substitute than Parmesan. Use a 10-inch nonstick skillet set over medium-high heat. To flip the frico, remove the pan from the burner once the first side has browned, cool briefly, flip with a fork and spatula, and return to the burner on medium heat to finish cooking on the second side.

FRICO Makes 8 large wafers

Serve frico with drinks and a bowl of marinated olives or marinated sun-dried tomatoes.

1 **pound Montasio or aged Asiago cheese, finely grated**

Sprinkle 2 ounces (about ½ cup) grated cheese over the bottom of a 10-inch nonstick skillet set over medium-high heat. Use a heat-resistant rubber spatula or wooden spoon to tidy the lacy outer edges of the cheese (see the illustration at right). Cook, shaking the pan occasionally to ensure an even distribution of the cheese over the pan bottom, until the edges are lacy and toasted, about 4 minutes. Remove the pan from the heat and allow the cheese to set for about 30 seconds. Using a fork and a heatproof spatula (see the illustration at right), carefully flip the cheese wafer and return the pan to medium heat. Cook until the second side is golden brown, about 2 minutes. Slide the cheese wafer out of the pan and transfer to a plate. Repeat with the remaining cheese. Serve the frico within 1 hour.

TECHNIQUE: Making Frico

1. After sprinkling the cheese into the skillet, use a heat-resistant spatula or wooden spoon to gently push the scattered shreds of cheese around the edges inward to form a tidy rim.

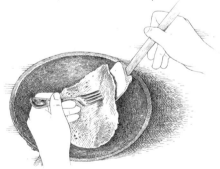

2. Once the first side is browned, remove the pan from the heat and let cool for 30 seconds to allow the frico to firm slightly. Using a fork and a heatproof spatula, carefully flip the cheese wafer and return the pan to medium heat to cook the second side.

CHICKEN ALLA DIAVOLA

WHAT WE WANTED: Chicken that was pleasantly spicy (not searingly hot) and nicely grilled (not charred).

Pounded flat, seasoned with a wicked amount of peppery spice, and pinned beneath a brick over a bed of fiery coals, "devil's chicken" often sounds better than it tastes (or looks). Although its namesake implies plenty of heat, many recipes for chicken alla diavola produce dreary, bland main courses, while others blast the taste buds with raw bits of untamed spice. In addition, this mysterious method of grilling a butterflied chicken under the weight of a brick often left us with a hopelessly charred bird. What we wanted was a reliable grilling technique and a well-rounded diavola flavor that was spicy but not overwhelming. We began by focusing on flavor.

Most chicken alla diavola recipes can be divided into two camps, touting either ground black pepper or red pepper flakes as crucial to both flavor and heat. But no matter what their party alignment in this regard, all recipes develop flavor by marinating the chicken in a traditional mixture of olive oil, lemon juice, garlic, salt, and the party-line pepper, brushing more marinade onto the chicken during the last few minutes of grilling. Not wanting to overlook the benefits of brining (soaking in a saltwater solution), we first tested brined chickens against chickens that had been marinated overnight, brushing both types with marinade as they finished cooking. The marinated-only birds tasted bland and boring compared with the moist, well-seasoned, brined chickens. We now wanted to add some spicy diavola flavor to the brine and tried using both types of pepper, with little luck. (No peppery flavors made their way into the chicken.) By crushing garlic and bay leaves into the brine, however, we were able to make the chicken pleasantly fragrant and reasonably flavorful, albeit not spicy.

Although the marinade was ineffective for marinating, we were still brushing the grilled chicken with it during the last minutes of cooking. We thought that boosting the flavor in the marinade-turned-basting-sauce might be the answer. After many tests, we found that a combination of black and red pepper flakes tasted far better than either on its own. Noting that a quarter cup of oil made plenty of brushing sauce for one chicken, we added teaspoon after teaspoon of both spices to find a good balance of flavor and heat. But instead of getting more flavor with each teaspoon, we merely turned the basting sauce into a crude-textured paste that offered little beyond a burnt tongue and heartburn. The way around this problem was simple enough: We steeped the spices in warm oil and discovered the well-rounded, intense, yet sophisticated flavor we had been looking for (see the Science Desk on page 211 for more information on releasing the flavor of spices). Just 2 teaspoons each of ground black pepper and red pepper flakes did the trick. Tasters liked the additional flavor of garlic. We tried adding lemon to the basting sauce, but this flavor didn't come across. Instead, we served the grilled chicken with fresh wedges of lemon, and this was a huge hit.

Up until now we had been brushing the sauce on the chicken during the last few minutes of grilling. We wondered if brushing it on at the beginning or rubbing it underneath the skin would make a difference. When we brushed the sauce onto the skin before grilling, the garlic and peppers burned. Rubbing it under the skin, however, worked wonders. The rubbed chicken had a fuller, rounder flavor, as the spices were able to seep directly into the meat. We then tried dabbing extra sauce onto the meat after it had been rubbed, grilled, and carved, and hit pay dirt. The fresh kick of garlic and pepper ensured that every bite tasted spicy without going overboard.

To butterfly a chicken, you remove the backbone with poultry shears or a chef's knife, then press the bird flat. Some cooks remove the breastbone, but we found this maneuver to be both tricky and fruitless. It leaves the breast meat

unprotected on the grill and prone to overcooking. Keeping the breastbone intact, we tried pressing the chicken flat with our hands, but this caused the chicken to bow on the grill, resulting in uneven cooking and uneven grill marks. Pounding the chicken flat with a mallet worked well.

So far, we were having little success on the grill. We were consistently burning chickens even though we had yet to weight them down with a brick (a technique that would probably make burning more—not less—likely). To get to the bottom of this problem, we decided to investigate the best method for setting up a charcoal grill.

A charcoal fire can be set up in three basic ways: single level, two level, or modified two level. A single-level fire spreads the coals evenly over the bottom of the grill, a two-level fire spreads a thin layer of coals over the grill and then banks the rest to one side, and a modified two-level fire banks all of the coals to one side of the grill and leaves the other side completely empty. When cooking over a two-level fire (which is often used when grilling meat), you use the hot side of the grill first for searing, then the cooler side to finish the cooking. We placed a foil-wrapped brick on top of the chicken and then tried all three setups to see which worked best. The result? A parade of incinerated chickens. No matter what the type of fire or the heat level, tall menacing flames licked the chickens until they were fully blackened—the devil's chicken, indeed.

Although these last tests were utter failures, they clearly illustrated the problem inherent to grilling chicken alla diavola over a charcoal fire: The oil-based marinade (or, in this case, sauce) seeps out of the chicken (particularly under

the weight of the brick) and onto the hot coals, thereby creating unmanageable infernos. Because we were rubbing the sauce underneath the skin, the chicken burned mostly when it was skin-side down. How, then, could we grill the chicken skin-side down without charring it? We tried a modified two-level fire—backward—grilling the chicken skin-side down over the empty side of the grill and flipping it skin-side up over the coals to finish cooking. Although this technique did prevent the skin from burning, it also prevented the skin from receiving any color at all. The empty side of the grill was just too cool. To increase the level of heat without placing any coals directly under the chicken, we tried banking the coals on either side of the grill, leaving the center completely empty. We put the chicken in the center of the cooking grate and then covered the grill to help retain the heat. Finally, we produced a great grilled chicken with a gorgeous brown skin. To render the skin completely crisp, we found it necessary to cook the chicken skin-side down, covered, for the entire 30- to 40-minute grilling time. Developing a technique for the gas grill was no problem. We simply grilled the chicken skin-side down over medium-low heat, covered, until it was done and crisp. There were no flare-ups.

Throughout these tests we faithfully employed the brick, but we had come to find its repeated removal and replacement a real nuisance when checking the chicken. Testing the difference between a bricked chicken and an unbricked chicken with our newfound grilling methods, we suddenly felt like the punch line to an old Italian prank. The brick, it turned out, was little more than a conversation starter.

WHAT WE LEARNED: Brine the chicken in a mixture of salt, water, garlic, and bay leaves as the first flavor-building step. Rub spicy garlic oil (heated first to intensify the flavors of the garlic as well as the black and hot red pepper) under the skin before grilling the chicken, and then drizzle the bird with more of this oil right before serving. Finally, grill the bird over moderate heat and without bricks, which press oil out of the bird and promote flare-ups.

CHARCOAL-GRILLED CHICKEN ALLA DIAVOLA Serves 3 to 4

Before building the fire, make sure that the grill is cleaned of residual ash from previous use; if left in the bottom, residual ash catches fat drippings and causes flare-ups that can singe the chicken. For this recipe, we prefer the even, slower heat generated by charcoal briquettes over faster-burning hardwood charcoal.

chicken and brine

- 2 medium garlic heads
- 3 bay leaves, crumbled
- ½ cup salt
- 1 whole chicken (3 to 3½ pounds), butterflied and pounded according to the illustrations below

garlic-pepper oil

- 4 medium garlic cloves, minced or pressed through garlic press (about 4 teaspoons)
- 2 teaspoons ground black pepper
- 2 teaspoons red pepper flakes
- ¼ cup olive oil

- Vegetable oil for grill grate
- 1 lemon, cut into wedges, for serving

1. TO BRINE THE CHICKEN: Combine the garlic heads, bay leaves, and salt in a gallon-size zipper-lock bag; press out the air and seal the bag. Using a rubber mallet or meat pounder, pound the mixture until the garlic cloves are crushed; transfer the mixture to a large container or stockpot and stir in 2 quarts cold water until the salt is dissolved. Immerse the chicken in the brine and refrigerate until fully seasoned, about 2 hours.

2. FOR THE GARLIC-PEPPER OIL: While the chicken is brining, heat the garlic, black pepper, pepper flakes, and oil in a small saucepan over medium heat until the garlic is fragrant and sizzling and the mixture registers about 200 degrees on an instant-read thermometer, about 3 minutes. Remove from the heat and cool to room temperature, about

---

TECHNIQUE: Butterflying a Chicken

1. With the breast side down and the tail of the chicken facing you, use poultry shears to cut along the entire length of one side of the backbone.

2. With the breast side still down, turn the neck end to face you and cut along the other side of the backbone and remove it.

3. Turn the chicken breast side up. Open the chicken out on the work surface. Use the palm of your hand to flatten the chicken, then pound it with the flat side of a mallet to a fairly even thickness.

---

40 minutes. Measure 2 tablespoons garlic-pepper oil into 2 small bowls and set aside.

3. TO FLAVOR THE CHICKEN: Remove the chicken from the brine and thoroughly pat dry with paper towels. Slip your fingers underneath the skin of the breast and legs to loosen the membrane and rub 2 tablespoons of the infused oil beneath the skin.

4. TO GRILL THE CHICKEN: Light a large chimney starter filled with charcoal briquettes (about 6 quarts) and allow to burn until all the charcoal is covered with a layer of fine gray ash. Empty the coals into the grill and bank half of the coals on either side of the grill, leaving the midsection of the grill free of coals. Set the cooking rack in place, cover the grill with the lid, and let the rack heat up, about 5 minutes. Use a wire brush to scrape clean the cooking rack. Lightly dip a small wad of paper towels in vegetable oil; holding the wad with tongs, wipe the grill rack. Position the chicken skin-side down on the grill rack over area with no coals; cover the grill and fully open the lid vents.

5. Cook until an instant-read thermometer inserted into the thickest part of the thigh registers 170 to 175 degrees, 30 to 40 minutes. Transfer the chicken to a cutting board; let rest 10 minutes. Carve the chicken, cutting the bird into 10 pieces (two wings, two drumsticks, two thighs, and four breast quarters), and transfer the pieces to a platter. Drizzle the chicken with the remaining infused oil and serve with the lemon wedges.

VARIATION

GAS-GRILLED CHICKEN ALLA DIAVOLA

To prevent flare-ups that can char the chicken, make sure that the gas grill's fat drainage system is in place. Lava rocks can intensify flare-ups, so be especially vigilant if making this recipe on a grill with these ceramic briquettes. Keep a squirt bottle filled with water near the grill to extinguish any flare-ups.

Follow the recipe for Charcoal-Grilled Chicken alla Diavola through step 3. Turn all burners on a gas grill to high, close the lid, and heat until the grill is very hot, about 15 minutes. Scrape the grill grate clean with a wire brush; lightly dip a small wad of paper towels in vegetable oil and, holding the wad in tongs, wipe the grill grate. Turn all burners to medium-low, position the chicken skin-side down on the center of the grill grate, cover, and continue with the recipe from step 5.

SCIENCE:
How to Pry Flavor Out of Spices

AS WE DEVELOPED OUR RECIPE FOR CHICKEN ALLA diavola, we were curious as to why we weren't able to extract much flavor from either the ground black pepper or the red pepper flakes when they were added to the brine or a room-temperature marinade. We were further intrigued when their flavor blossomed, becoming deep and fragrant, after being briefly steeped in warm oil. After some research, we learned that it's simply a matter of solubility.

The essential oils in both black pepper and red pepper flakes are oil-soluble as opposed to water-soluble. This means that they dissolve in oil rather than water. As they dissolve, these flavorful essential oils are released from a solid state into solution form, where they mix and interact, thereby producing a more complex flavor. Like most substances, these essential oils dissolve faster and to a greater extent in a hot solvent (in this case, olive oil) than in a cold solvent. However, if the oil is too hot, the spices can scorch. We prepared five batches of marinade, bringing them to temperatures of 150, 200, 250, 300, and 400 degrees. The differences were dramatic. The 150-degree batch tasted flat and boring, while the marinades brought to 250, 300, and 400 degrees tasted increasingly burnt. When heated to 200 degrees, however, the marinade tasted perfectly spicy and well rounded.

STRAWBERRIES AND BALSAMIC VINEGAR

WHAT WE WANTED: A simple dessert, with vinegar enhancing but not overwhelming the flavor of the berries.

Strawberries with balsamic vinegar may sound like an odd combination or even a bit trendy. But this dessert is neither. At its best, balsamic vinegar is akin to fine port—something to sip in a glass rather than toss in a salad. A few drops of the slightly sweet vinegar enhances the sweetness and fragrant qualities of fresh fruit. As for trendiness, artisan-made balsamic vinegar has been produced in parts of northern Italy for hundreds of years and served over berries for nearly as long.

True balsamic vinegars have brilliantly complex flavors with hints of spice, honey, and caramel. Used primarily as a condiment or liqueur, they are soft, mellow, and not at all acidic. A 3½-ounce bottle of artisan-made balsamic vinegar, otherwise referred to as *tradizionale* or *extra-vecchio tradizionale aceto balsamico*, can fetch up to $300. Of course, most Americans are familiar with industrial balsamic vinegars that cost just a few dollars a bottle. These vinegars are thinner, more acidic, and less complex than the traditional vinegars. Such commercial vinegars are perfectly suited for salads and pan sauces, but would they work in this recipe?

Curious to see how the best supermarket balsamic vinegar would fare, we started with 365 Every Day Value balsamic vinegar, which won our tasting of leading commercial vinegars (see the Tasting Lab on page 213). The result was not totally surprising. The vinegar was somewhat mellow and had a hint of vanilla flavor, but it lacked body and, frankly, tasted like—well—vinegar. As most Americans are not willing to lay down a couple hundred dollars for the real McCoy, we wanted to find some way to use commercial vinegar so that it would approximate the syrupy texture and complex but mellow flavor of aged traditional vinegar.

The obvious solution was to simmer the vinegar to improve its texture and to add sugar and perhaps seasonings to improve its flavor. Reducing the supermarket vinegar by almost half improved its texture and created a syrupy sauce—a major improvement over the straight vinegar. A tiny bit of sugar tempered its acidity. We also tried reducing the vinegar with vanilla and honey, hoping to create a sauce with more personality. The vanilla was overpowering, and the honey was not noticeably different from the sugar. Finally, we tried a squirt of lemon juice to brighten the flavors; this was well received by tasters.

Now that we had found a viable solution to the vinegar problem, we focused our attention on the strawberries. The strawberries must be sweetened; sugar accentuates the flavors of the berries and balances the balsamic syrup. We found that ¼ cup was ideal for 3 pints of strawberries. Traditionally, strawberries and balsamic vinegar are sweetened with white granulated sugar. We tested different sweeteners, hoping to find a sweetener that might enhance the flavors of the vinegar. Honey produced a funny aftertaste and was distracting. Dark brown sugar was too strong and so also distracting. We tried a coarse natural sugar but found no appreciable difference in flavor over white sugar. Light brown sugar, however, added gentle hints of molasses without being overpowering. Though the difference was subtle, tasters felt that light brown sugar was slightly preferable to granulated white sugar.

After mixing the sliced berries and sugar, we found that it took 10 to 15 minutes for the sugar to dissolve and the berries to release some juice. Don't let the berries macerate for much longer. We found that they will continue to soften and become mushy rather quickly.

WHAT WE LEARNED: Simmer an inexpensive vinegar with some sugar to approximate the syrupy texture of aged balsamic vinegar. Toss the berries with light brown sugar—rather than the traditional granulated sugar—for the most complex flavor.

STRAWBERRIES WITH BALSAMIC VINEGAR

Serves 6

If you don't have light brown sugar on hand, sprinkle the berries with an equal amount of granulated white sugar. Serve the berries and syrup as is or with a scoop of vanilla ice cream or a dollop of lightly sweetened mascarpone cheese.

⅓   cup balsamic vinegar
2   teaspoons granulated sugar
½   teaspoon lemon juice
3   pints strawberries, hulled and cut lengthwise into ¼-inch-thick slices (small strawberries can be halved or quartered)
¼   cup packed light brown sugar
     Ground black pepper

1. Bring the vinegar, granulated sugar, and lemon juice to a simmer in a small heavy-bottomed saucepan over medium heat. Simmer until the syrup is reduced by half (to approximately 3 tablespoons), about 3 minutes. Transfer the vinegar syrup to a small bowl and cool completely.

2. With a spoon, lightly toss the berries and brown sugar in a large bowl. Let stand until the sugar dissolves and the berries exude some juice, 10 to 15 minutes. Pour the vinegar syrup over the berries, add pepper to taste, and toss to combine. Divide the berries among individual bowls or goblets and serve immediately.

TASTING LAB: Balsamic Vinegar

YOU CAN BUY A DECENT BOTTLE OF NONVINTAGE French table wine for $8, or you can invest in a bottle of 1975 Château Lafite Rothschild Bordeaux for $300—but no one would ever compare the two. They are two different beasts. The same holds true for balsamic vinegars. There are balsamic vinegars you can buy for $2.50 and those that nudge the $300 mark. The more expensive vinegars bear the title *tradizionale* or *extra-vecchio tradizionale aceto balsamico* (traditional or extra-old traditional). According to Italian law, these traditional vinegars must come from the northern Italian provinces of Modena or Reggio Emilia and be created and aged in the time-honored fashion.

Unfortunately, American consumers cannot really be sure that the industrial-style balsamic vinegar they purchase in their grocery or specialty foods store is a high-quality product. Unlike the makers of trademark-protected products of Italy, including tradizionale balsamico, Parmigiano-Reggiano, and Prosciutto di Parma (all from the Reggio Emilia region), Italian producers of commercial balsamic vinegars failed to unite before market demand for their products ballooned in the United States in the early 1980s. The result has been high consumer demand with little U.S. regulation—the perfect scenario for producers who take advantage of the system by misleading consumers about the integrity of their products.

For hundreds of years, tradizionale balsamico vinegar has been made from Trebbiano grapes grown in the Modena or Reggio Emilia regions of northern Italy. The grapes are crushed and slowly cooked into *must* over an open flame. The must begins mellowing in a large wooden barrel, where it ferments and turns to vinegar. The vinegar is then passed through a series of barrels made from a variety of woods. To be considered worthy of the tradizionale balsamico title, the vinegar must be moved from barrel to barrel for a minimum of 12 years. An extra-vecchio vinegar must be aged for at least 25 years.

Because of its complex flavor and high production cost, tradizionale balsamico is used by those in the know as a condiment rather than an ingredient. The longer the vinegar ages, the thicker and more intensely flavored it becomes, maturing from a thin liquid into a spoon-coating, syrupy one—perfect for topping strawberries or cantaloupe. This is the aristocrat of balsamic vinegars.

The more common varieties—those with a price tag under $30—are categorized as commercial or industrial balsamic vinegars. These vinegars are the kind with which most

Americans are familiar and are often used to complete a vinaigrette or flavor a sauce. The flavor profile of commercial balsamic vinegars ranges widely from mild, woody, and herbaceous to artificial and sour, depending on the producer and the style in which the vinegar was made. Commercial balsamic vinegar may or may not be aged and may or may not contain artificial caramel color or flavor.

We wondered how bad—or good—inexpensive commercial balsamic vinegars would be when compared in a blind tasting. To level the playing field—and ease the burden on our budget—we limited the tasting to balsamic vinegars that cost $15 or less. We included some vinegars from supermarkets (we held a preliminary supermarket balsamic vinegar tasting and included the three most favored by our tasters in the final tasting) and some from mail-order sources and specialty foods stores. We also included samples of the many production styles, including some aged in the traditional fashion, some with added caramel color and flavor, and some made from a blend of aged red wine vinegar and grape must.

We found that a higher price tag did not correlate with a better vinegar. In addition, age seemed to play a less important role than we had expected. There were young vinegars among the winners as well as older vinegars among the losers.

Across the board, tasters found balsamic vinegars containing caramel color or flavor to be "sour" and "uninteresting." The top brands from our tasting contain no artificial colors or flavors whatsoever. Our findings led us to believe that much as *fond* (the browned bits left in a pan after food

has been sautéed) is instrumental in creating a high-quality pan sauce, *must* is paramount to making a full-flavored balsamic vinegar. As the must ages, it becomes thick and sweet, contributing a character almost like sherry or port. Producers who substitute artificial color and flavor for must end up with a shallow product that was routinely derided by our tasters. Some connoisseurs might argue that the only balsamic vinegars worth buying are aged ones, but we found that age didn't make nearly as big a difference as artificial additives did.

Given this information, how can you figure out what type of balsamic vinegar to buy? The easy answer is to check the label. If it discloses that artificial ingredients have been added, don't buy it. Unfortunately, it's not only commonplace but legal for the ingredient label to skirt the issue and completely avoid publishing the contents of the vinegar. This is because Italian law dictates that "Balsamic Vinegar of Modena"—which is how 9 out of 10 vinegars are labeled—is itself an ingredient and product, so no further description of the vinegar's contents is required. Label specifications from the U.S. Food and Drug Administration require only that the producer indicate whether or not the vinegar contains sulfites, a preservative that produces a severe allergic reaction in some people.

"Whatever you want to call a balsamic vinegar, you can call a balsamic vinegar," says John Jack, vice president of sales and marketing for Fiorucci Foods in Virginia. "It's become very much of a commodity-oriented business." Even if a vinegar is labeled "Balsamic Vinegar of Modena," a title that conveys the idea of quality to consumers, it may not have been produced in, or even near, Modena. In fact, several manufacturers bottle their vinegar right here in the United States. Young vinegars can bear the balsamic title, too. As a result of the less-than-stringent regulations, many producers and importers look forward to the passage of a new regulation in Italy that would make it illegal to label a vinegar younger than three years *balsamic*.

For now, check the label. If the vinegar contains artificial color or sweetener, look further.

Rating Inexpensive Balsamic Vinegars

TWENTY-ONE MEMBERS OF THE *COOK'S ILLUSTRATED* STAFF AND NINE CHEFS RATED EIGHT VINEGARS FOR COLOR, bouquet, flavor, body, and density. The balsamic vinegars were tasted in their natural state, with bread and water provided to cleanse the palate between samples. The vinegars are listed in order of preference. All vinegars are available in supermarkets nationwide.

HIGHLY RECOMMENDED
365 Every Day Value Balsamic Vinegar
$3.99 for 16.9 ounces
MADE IN MODENA

Started from must; blend of older (up to five years) and younger balsamic vinegars.

Tasters described this vinegar as chocolate brown, with a medium thickness. They loved its vanilla, fruit, and caramel-like underpinnings as well as its "balanced acidity."

HIGHLY RECOMMENDED
Masserie Di Sant'Eramo Balsamic Vinegar
$10.95 for 8.5 ounces
MADE IN MODENA

Started from must; aged a minimum of five years.

This vinegar was dark reddish-brown in color. Tasters liked its fruit and honey notes as well as its "balanced spice and acidity." One taster called it "demure" and "floral"; another found it "sherry-like."

HIGHLY RECOMMENDED
Fiorucci Riserva Balsamic Vinegar
$8.99 for 8.5 ounces
MADE IN MODENA

Aged wine vinegar blended with must; aged six years.

Described as "translucent brown," the Fiorucci vinegar was called "mellow" and "tangy-sweet" in flavor, reminding some tasters of plums and apples.

RECOMMENDED
Cavalli Balsamic Seasoning
$15.00 for 8.5 ounces
MADE IN REGGIO EMILIA

Started from must; aged three years.

This was an interesting, "enormously complex" sample, scoring either as a favorite or as a most detested balsamic—which lands it in the middle of the rankings. It had big vanilla and honey attributes, but some tasters couldn't get past the "strange but alluring" cedar/balsam notes.

RECOMMENDED
Fini Balsamic Vinegar
$10.50 for 8.5 ounces
MADE IN MODENA

Started from must; aged two years.

Note: Contains caramel color.

Tasters called this sample "cloudy" and "muddy," with many objecting to the presence of sediment. It was characterized as having a fermented flavor somewhat reminiscent of soy sauce or raisins.

RECOMMENDED
Colavita Balsamic Vinegar
$8.49 for 16.9 ounces
MADE IN MODENA

Aged wine vinegar blended with must; aged one year.

Note: Contains caramel color and flavor.

Although this vinegar wasn't considered very complex, tasters were fond of its "fig," "burnt nut," and "tobacco" flavors. It was downgraded for being overly harsh, acidic, and "fleeting."

NOT RECOMMENDED
Regina Balsamic Vinegar
$2.79 for 12 ounces
GRAPES FROM MODENA, BOTTLED IN THE UNITED STATES

Wine vinegar blended with must; aged two to four years.

Note: Contains caramel color and flavor.

Called a "thin, mousy, unassuming little vinegar," Regina was disliked for its "artificial" qualities.

NOT RECOMMENDED
Giuseppe Giusti Balsamic Vinegar
$11.95 for 8.5 ounces
MADE IN MODENA

Started from must; aged approximately six years.

Note: May contain caramel color and flavor (an industry representative was unable to confirm or deny their presence in this product).

Tasters called it "salty," "harsh," and "sharp."

Becky readies cassoulet for its final sprinkling with croutons and baking in the oven.

FRENCH · FOOD
in a flash

Americans seem to have a love/hate relationship with all things French, including their food. There's no denying that French cuisine is marvelous, but many traditional dishes are best made by an army of sous chefs. Preparing favorite dishes such as cassoulet (a bean and pork stew showered with a crisp bread crumb topping) or tarte Tatin (a caramelized apple tart) calls for a lot of patience and time. By the time you've completed these projects, the day is gone and your kitchen is a mess.

We wondered if we could find ways to simplify these recipes without sacrificing the qualities that make them great. Does a cassoulet really require all of those exotic meats? What about using canned beans rather than dried? Can you make good tarte Tatin with store-bought puff pastry? Do you need to caramelize the apples and bake the pastry in the skillet at the same time?

We decided to roll up our sleeves and rethink these French classics. After much trial and error, the test kitchen developed two novel versions of these dishes that eliminate much of the work but still deliver high-quality results.

CASSOULET

WHAT WE WANTED: Great cassoulet made in a few hours (rather than a few days) that didn't sacrifice the deep, melded flavors that are characteristic of this dish.

Every once in a while, a dish comes around that is so robust, so satisfying to every sense that we deem it comfort food. It warms us from the inside out and assures us that this winter, too, shall pass. Cassoulet is such a dish.

But for most cooks, the reasons to eat cassoulet outnumber the reasons to make it. Cassoulet can take three days to make, and the ingredients can be both hard to find and difficult to prepare.

The cassoulet originated in Languedoc, France, and each area of the region touts its recipe as "the real thing." All versions of the dish contain white beans, but that is where the agreement ends. Some prefer pork loin in their cassoulet, others use a shoulder of lamb, while still others use a combination of both. Mutton, duck, pheasant, garlic sausage, and even fish can be found in the different variations.

But the best known and most often replicated type of cassoulet hails from Toulouse. This cassoulet must start with the preparation of confit. Meat or poultry, most often goose legs (the region of Toulouse also houses the foie gras industry, so goose is plentiful), is placed in a large container, sprinkled heavily with salt, and cured for 24 to 48 hours. This both preserves and tenderizes the meat. After this sojourn in salt, the meat is slowly simmered in its own fat, so that the flavor of the fat penetrates the spaces previously occupied by the juices. The finished confit may be used immediately or stored in an airtight container, covered in its own fat.

But the intricacy of cassoulet doesn't end with the confit. Pork loin and mutton must be slow-roasted for hours to become fully tender, and garlic sausages freshly made. The beans must be presoaked and then simmered with pork rinds to develop flavor. Finally, the entire mixture has to be combined in an earthenware pot, topped with bread crumbs, and placed in a low-temperature oven to simmer slowly for several hours.

The result is nothing short of divine. But while this classic French peasant dish can be replicated at restaurants, it is definitely not a dish for the casual home cook. The time investment alone is impractical, and it can be difficult to achieve a perfect balance of flavors. On more than one occasion we have eaten cassoulets that were overwhelmed by salt or swimming in fat, most often because of the confit and sausages. All the same, we love this dish so much that we decided it would be worth the effort to try to streamline it without compromising its essential nature.

We decided to accept the hardest of the challenges first and conquer the confit. We eliminated the notion of confit made from scratch as far too time-consuming. Assessing our other options, we created three cassoulets. One was prepared with braised duck leg confit (goose leg confit is less widely available) purchased through our butcher. The others we made with no confit at all, starting one version with sautéed and braised duck legs and the other with sautéed and braised chicken thighs, which we wanted to use because they're so easy to find in the supermarket. The results were disheartening, although not surprising. The cassoulet made with the purchased confit was the clear favorite. Those made without it produced dishes more reminiscent of duck and chicken stews.

Unfortunately, ready-made confit is not widely available, so we wanted to develop a recipe that wouldn't rely on it. Somewhat ironically, we arrived at the solution to the problem with some help from the confit itself.

Because confit is salt-cured and then cooked in its own fat, it retains an intense duck flavor when added to the cassoulet, contributing a rich, slightly smoky flavor that was noticeably absent from the dishes prepared with the sautéed duck and chicken. The texture of the dish made with confit was superior as well, the flesh plump with flavor yet tender to the bite; the sautéed and braised duck and chicken became tough and gave up all of their flavor to the broth. Taking an educated guess, we decided to adopt an approach often used in the test kitchen and brine the chicken. Because we had found when making other dishes that brining resulted in poultry that was both more moist and more flavorful, we reasoned that brining the chicken might bring it closer to the tender texture of confit. To approximate the confit's light smokiness, we decided to cook the thighs in bacon fat.

We quick-soaked the chicken thighs for one hour in a concentrated salt and sugar solution, sautéed them quickly in rendered bacon fat, then braised them with the rest of the cassoulet ingredients. What resulted was just what we were hoping for: a suitable substitute for duck confit. The bacon added a smoky flavor, and it enhanced the flavors of the pork and sausage added later. The texture was spot-on for the confit; the chicken thighs were plump and juicy; and the broth became well seasoned because of the brine. With this "mock" confit in hand, we proceeded.

Our next test involved figuring out which meats to use and how to avoid slow roasting. We knew that we wanted to be true to the original recipe and use either fresh pork or lamb. We decided to try stewing the meat in liquid entirely on top of the stove. This method yielded great results in terms of tenderness, but the meat had none of the depth of flavor that occurs with roasting. Searing the meat in some of the rendered bacon fat that we had used with the chicken thighs took care of that problem.

Because we were now stewing the meat, we needed to use cuts that were appropriate for this method. We tried pork loin, the choice in so many cassoulet recipes, but the loin became waterlogged and tasteless during stewing. A suggestion from our butcher led us to try a blade-end roast, which is the part of the loin closest to the shoulder. The blade-end roast, which has more internal fat than the center loin, retained the moisture and flavor. To facilitate quicker cooking, we cut the roast into 1-inch pieces. We used similar testing with the lamb. Lamb shoulder is the best cut for stewing, but it can be difficult to find in markets. We bought instead thick lamb shoulder chops, which we also cut into 1-inch pieces. Finally, perfectly tender meat without the effort of roasting.

Cassoulets traditionally use white beans. We wanted to make sure that the beans would retain their shape while adding a soft texture to the dish. Canned beans fell apart quickly, so we opted for dried. We tested four varieties, and the winner was the pale green flageolet bean. These small, French, kidney-shaped beans have a creamy, tender texture and delicate flavor that perfectly enhanced the cassoulet. We also cooked the beans on top of the stove along with bacon and the aromatics to let them absorb additional flavor.

The last major decision we had to make concerned the sausage. After ruling out the use of hard-to-find French sausages (and not willing to take the time to make our own), we found that both kielbasa and andouille sausages intensified the smoky flavor that we so desired.

With the major problems out of the way, we were able to concentrate on streamlining the technique used to cook the dish. This proved to be quite simple. With the chicken, meat, and beans now modified for cooking on the stovetop, oven braising became unnecessary. Cooking the dish entirely on the stove at a low simmer, with a quick finish in the oven to brown the bread crumbs, produced perfect results in a short amount of time. At last we had it: a quick cassoulet that was worthy of the name.

WHAT WE LEARNED: Use brined chicken thighs cooked in bacon fat to approximate the duck confit traditionally used in this recipe. Stew the meat rather than roast it and use fattier cuts of pork or lamb from the shoulder area. Dried beans are a must (canned beans will turn to mush), and flageolets are our favorites.

SIMPLIFIED CASSOULET WITH PORK AND KIELBASA Serves 8

This dish can be made without brining the chicken, but we recommend that you do so. To ensure the most time-efficient preparation of the cassoulet, while the chicken is brining and the beans are simmering, prepare the remaining ingredients. Look for dried flageolet beans in specialty food stores. If you can't find a boneless blade-end pork loin roast, a boneless Boston butt makes a fine substitution. Additional salt is not necessary because the brined chicken adds a good deal of it. If you skip the brining step, add salt to taste before serving.

chicken

- ½ cup salt
- 1 cup sugar
- 10 bone-in skinless chicken thighs (about 3½ pounds), excess fat removed

beans

- 1 pound dried flageolet or great Northern beans, picked over and rinsed
- 1 medium onion, peeled and left whole
- 1 medium head garlic, outer papery skin removed and top ½ inch sliced off
- 1 teaspoon salt
- ½ teaspoon ground black pepper

- 6 ounces (6 slices) bacon, chopped medium
- 1 pound boneless blade-end pork loin roast, trimmed of excess fat and cut into 1-inch pieces
- 1 small onion, chopped fine
- 2 medium garlic cloves, minced or pressed through garlic press
- 1 can (14.5 ounces) diced tomatoes, drained
- 1 tablespoon tomato paste
- 1 large sprig fresh thyme
- 1 bay leaf
- ¼ teaspoon ground cloves

Ground black pepper
- 3½ cups low-sodium chicken broth
- 1½ cups dry white wine
- ½ pound kielbasa, halved lengthwise and cut into ¼-inch slices

croutons

- 6 slices good-quality white sandwich bread, cut into ½-inch dice (about 3 cups)
- 3 tablespoons unsalted butter, melted

1. FOR THE CHICKEN: In a gallon-size zipper-lock plastic bag, dissolve the salt and sugar in 1 quart cold water. Add the chicken, pressing out as much air as possible; seal and refrigerate until fully seasoned, about 1 hour. Remove the chicken from the brine, rinse thoroughly under cold water, and pat dry with paper towels. Refrigerate until ready to use.

2. FOR THE BEANS: Bring the beans, whole onion, garlic head, salt, pepper, and 8 cups water to a boil in a stockpot or

TECHNIQUE:
Sorting Dried Beans with Ease

It is important to rinse and pick over dried beans to remove any stones or debris before cooking. To make this task easier, sort dried beans on a white plate or cutting board. The neutral background makes any unwanted matter easy to spot and discard.

Dutch oven over high heat. Cover, reduce the heat to medium-low, and simmer until the beans are almost fully tender, 1¼ to 1½ hours. Drain the beans and discard the onion and garlic.

3. While the beans are cooking, fry the bacon in a Dutch oven over medium heat until just beginning to crisp and most of the fat has rendered, 5 to 6 minutes. Using a slotted spoon, add half of the bacon to the pot with the beans; transfer the remaining bacon to a paper towel–lined plate and set aside. Increase the heat to medium-high; when the bacon fat is shimmering, add half of the chicken thighs, fleshy-side down; cook until lightly browned, 4 to 5 minutes. Using tongs, turn the chicken pieces and cook until lightly browned on the second side, 3 to 4 minutes longer. Transfer the chicken to a large plate; repeat with the remaining thighs and set aside. Drain off all but 2 tablespoons fat from the pot. Return the pot to medium heat; add the pork pieces and cook, stirring occasionally, until lightly browned, about 5 minutes. Add the chopped onion and cook, stirring occasionally, until softened, 3 to 4 minutes. Add the minced garlic, tomatoes, tomato paste, thyme, bay leaf, cloves, and pepper to taste; cook until fragrant, about 1 minute. Stir in the chicken broth and wine, scraping up the browned bits off the bottom of the pot with a wooden spoon. Submerge the chicken in the pot, adding any accumulated juices.

GETTING IT RIGHT:
Blade versus Center Loin Pork

Because the pork is stewed, the blade end of the loin is preferable to the leaner center loin.

BLADE	**CENTER LOIN**

FOOD FACT: Pigs

To stop free-roaming pigs from rampaging through their grain fields, New York residents built a long wall on the northern edge of what is now Lower Manhattan. The street that came to border the wall was named Wall Street.

Increase the heat to high and bring to a boil, then reduce the heat to low, cover, and simmer about 40 minutes. Remove the cover and continue to simmer until the chicken and pork are fully tender, 20 to 30 minutes more. Using tongs and a slotted spoon, remove and discard the chicken skin.

4. FOR THE CROUTONS: While the chicken is simmering, adjust an oven rack to the lower-middle position and heat the oven to 400 degrees. Mix the bread crumbs and butter in a small baking dish. Bake, tossing occasionally, until light golden brown and crisp, 8 to 12 minutes. Cool to room temperature; set aside.

5. Gently stir the kielbasa, drained beans, and reserved bacon into the pot with the chicken and pork; remove and discard the thyme and bay leaf and adjust the seasonings with salt and pepper. Sprinkle the croutons evenly over the surface and bake, uncovered, until the flavors have melded and the croutons are deep golden brown, about 15 minutes. Let stand 10 minutes and serve.

VARIATION
SIMPLIFIED CASSOULET WITH LAMB AND ANDOUILLE SAUSAGE

Lamb, with its robust, earthy flavor, makes an excellent substitute for the pork. Andouille sausage adds a peppery sweetness that tasters loved.

Follow the recipe for Simplified Cassoulet with Pork and Kielbasa, substituting 2 pounds lamb shoulder chops, trimmed, boned, and cut into 1-inch pieces, for the pork, and substituting 8 ounces andouille sausage for the kielbasa.

TASTING LAB: Canned Diced Tomatoes

IN LATE SUMMER AND EARLY FALL, SUN-RIPENED LOCAL tomatoes abound. But fast-forward to mid-February... what are you going to use in your sauce now? The pale, hard, flavorless orbs that pass for fresh tomatoes during the off season—which is most of the year here in New England—won't get you far in the flavor department, and the handsome "on-the-vine" and deep red hydroponic specimens usually look better than they taste.

The conventional wisdom holds that canned tomatoes surpass fresh for much of the year because they are packaged at the height of ripeness. After side-by-side tests of fresh, off-season tomatoes and canned tomatoes while we were developing recipes for cream of tomato soup, pasta all'Amatriciana (pasta with tomatoes, bacon and onion), and shrimp fra diavolo, among others, we agree. But the many brands of canned tomatoes available beg an obvious question: Which brand tastes best? Having sampled eight brands of canned diced tomatoes, both plain and cooked in a simple sauce, we have the answer.

According to both Bob Graf, president of the California League of Food Processors, and representatives of Small Planet Foods, distributors of Muir Glen tomato products, canned diced tomatoes emerged on the market in the early 1990s. Sales of diced tomatoes have since come to dominate the category of canned processed tomato products, outselling tomato paste, whole and crushed tomatoes, and tomato sauce and puree, all products that have been around for generations.

Depending on the season and growing location, more than 50 varieties of tomatoes are used to makes these products, according to Graf and Dr. Diane Barrett, fruit and vegetable products specialist in the department of food science and technology at the University of California, Davis. Graf said that while tomato varieties are generally not genetically engineered, they are refined for traits that will satisfy growers (yield and harvesting characteristics), processors (ease of skinning and solid-to-liquid ratio), and consumers (color and flavor) alike.

Packers generally reserve the ripest, best-colored specimens for use as whole, crushed, and diced tomatoes, products in which consumers demand vibrant color and fresher flavor. Lower-grade tomatoes are generally used in cooked products, such as paste, puree, and sauce.

Before processing, the tomatoes are peeled by means of either steam—always the choice of Muir Glen, the only organic brand in our lineup—or a hot lye bath, which many processors currently favor. Because temperatures in lye peeling are not as high as those in steaming, many processors believe that lye leaves the layer of flesh just beneath the skin in better condition, giving the peeled tomato a superior appearance. Our tasters, however, could not detect specific flavor characteristics in the canned tomatoes based on this aspect of processing. Two of our three highly recommended products, Muir Glen and S&W, use steam, while the third, Redpack, uses lye.

After peeling, the tomatoes are sorted again for color and the presence of obvious deficiencies, and then they're diced. After the dice is sorted, the cans are filled with the tomatoes and topped off with salt and filler ingredients (usually tomato juice, but sometimes puree—read on). Finally, the lids are attached to the cans and the cans are cooked briefly for sterilization, and then cooled and dried so they can be labeled.

The flavor of a ripe, fresh tomato balances elements of sweetness and tangy acidity. The texture should be somewhere between firm and pliant, and certainly not mushy. Ideally, canned diced tomatoes should reflect the same combination of characteristics. Indeed, tasters indicated that excessive sweetness or saltiness (from the salt added during processing), along with undesirable texture qualities, could make or break a can of diced tomatoes. If the tasters thought that any one of these characteristics was out of whack, they downgraded that sample. In fact, two of the eight brands in the tasting were deemed to have major flaws in both flavor and texture that landed them in the lowest echelon of the ratings.

The downfall of Hunt's, the lowest rated brand of the eight, was saltiness. According to the label on the can, one serving of Hunt's diced tomatoes contains 380 milligrams of sodium; the other brands tested average just over 240 milligrams per serving. That's a good 50% more salt, a characteristic that tasters easily detected and didn't appreciate.

Cento, the only other brand besides Hunt's that tasters relegated to the "Not Recommended" category, suffered from a triple whammy of flavor and texture problems, according to our tasters. First, it was the only product in the bunch that was packed in tomato puree, rather than the more common tomato juice. This led to complaints about the flavor, which some tasters perceived as "way cooked," "like candy," and "ketchupy." By comparison, the thin, watery juice in which the other canned diced tomatoes are packed tasted lighter and more natural. Puree is heavier and pulpier than juice, and must be heated longer to achieve its specified concentration. In short, more cooking equals less freshness. The heavy puree is probably also responsible for tasters' impressions that Cento tomatoes were overly sweet, another significant point against them.

Cento was also the only brand in the lineup that didn't include calcium chloride among its ingredients. According Diane Barrett, the calcium in this compound helps the tomato pieces maintain a firm texture by stabilizing the pectin network in the tomato tissue. Because calcium is divalent, that is, it has an electrical charge of +2, it acts as a bridge between two long chains of pectin, in effect bonding them together. Based on our results, the absence of calcium chloride made a difference, as tasters described the Cento tomatoes as "mealy," "very broken down," and "squishy."

Oddly, no one flavor profile dominated. The three highly recommended brands, Muir Glen, S&W, and Redpack, displayed a range of flavor characteristics. Muir Glen led the ratings with a favorable balance of sweetness and saltiness and a notably "fresh" flavor in the sauce. Redpack also ranked high for its fresh flavor in the sauce. The same group of tasters, however, gave the thumbs up to S&W tomatoes, a brand noted for its bracing acidity and powerful, almost exaggerated, tomato flavor. What link these three brands, then? Well, it's more about what characteristics they don't have than what they do. None of them exhibited major flavor flaws, the likes of which landed some other brands down in the ratings. The three winners were neither too sweet, like Cento, nor too salty, like Hunt's. Likewise, they tasted neither bitter nor metallic.

On the topic of winning texture, however, tasters were in accord. Both Muir Glen and S&W placed in the middle of pack in terms of firmness, while Redpack was rated firmest of all. Clearly, our tasters frowned on mushy canned tomatoes.

TASTING LAB: Petite Diced Tomatoes

WHILE WE WERE SHOPPING FOR CANNED DICED tomatoes for the tasting, we noticed a new product on the shelves: petite diced canned tomatoes. Was this just a tweak by manufacturers' marketing departments to boost sales or a genuinely useful product? Because we often find pieces of regular diced tomatoes to be too large for certain recipes and are forced to break them up with our fingers or a knife, we wanted to see if petite tomatoes could save us the trouble.

We picked a widely available recommended brand, Del Monte (the only other brand we saw at press time was Hunt's), and made quick tomato sauces with both regular and petite diced tomatoes. (The regular dice measured 7/8 inch, the petite dice 3/8 inch.) The result? We were surprised to find that we unanimously preferred the sauce made with the petite diced tomatoes. The differences between the sauces resided not in their flavor but in their texture: Small, uniformly cut pieces of tomato created a cohesive sauce that clung to the strands of pasta. The regular diced tomato sauce was separated and watery, and the large firm chunks of tomatoes easily evaded our forks. That is not to say the petite diced tomatoes are always preferable to regular. For quick preparations, such as this tomato sauce, the petite diced worked very well, but for recipes that call for longer cooking times, such as chili or stew, you may want beefier chunks of tomato.

Rating Canned Diced Tomatoes

TWENTY MEMBERS OF THE *COOK'S ILLUSTRATED* STAFF TASTED EIGHT DIFFERENT BRANDS OF CANNED DICED TOMATOES. The tomatoes were tasted two ways; plain, to get opinions of overall flavor, texture, and size, and cooked, in a simple sauce with garlic, olive oil, sugar, and salt. The tomatoes are listed in order of preference based on the combined results of both tastings.

RECOMMENDED

Muir Glen Organic Diced Tomatoes

$1.99 for 28 ounces

A few tasters thought these tomatoes were "bland" and "mellow" when tasted plain, but for these same reasons this brand rated number one in the sauce tasting. "Sweet," "fresh tasting," and "most like fresh tomatoes" were some of the comments that explained why this brand received high marks.

RECOMMENDED

S&W "Ready Cut" Premium Peeled Tomatoes

$2.46 for 28 ounces

This West Coast brand was liked for its "tangy," "vibrant" flavor. It was rated as "very acidic" in both the plain and the sauce tasting, and made one of the saltiest sauces. Tasters also commented on the "concentrated" flavor, which was "like tomato paste."

RECOMMENDED

Redpack "Ready Cut" Diced Tomatoes (Known as Redgold on the West Coast)

$1.19 for 28 ounces

These tomatoes did not score very high in the plain tasting and were considered "bland" by some. But they were also judged the firmest tomatoes, which may have contributed to their jump to second place in the sauce tasting, where they exhibited a "fresh tomato-y taste," and a texture that "did not break down at all."

RECOMMENDED WITH RESERVATIONS

Del Monte Diced Tomatoes

$1.79 for 28 ounces

The flavor of these tomatoes was slightly "musty" and "sweet" to some and "bright and balanced" to others when eaten raw but became "like stewed tomatoes" in sauce. This brand may be better suited for raw sauces; when cooked, the tomatoes turned "mushy."

RECOMMENDED WITH RESERVATIONS

Contadina "Recipe Ready" Diced Tomatoes

$1.39 for 28 ounces

While some tasters thought these tomatoes tasted "bright and fresh," the overall consensus was that they were too "soft and fleshy." The sauce had a "nice balance of sweet/salty," but was "very broken down" and looked as if "it had cooked for a very long time." These tomatoes tasted "very, very sweet."

RECOMMENDED WITH RESERVATIONS

Furmano's Diced Tomatoes

$1.39 for 28 ounces

This highly acidic and salty brand secured a decent rating in the sauce tasting because the "tomatoes retained their texture" and "bright flavor" when cooked. When tasted raw, however, they were viewed as "bitter," "with the taste of a tin can."

NOT RECOMMENDED

Cento "Chef's Cut" Tomatoes

$1.59 for 28 ounces

The only brand without calcium chloride in the ingredient list was very mushy. Tasters commented on the addition of basil only in the raw tasting; some welcomed it, others thought it tasted of "stale herbs." The sauce was described as too sweet, "like ketchup."

NOT RECOMMENDED

Hunt's Diced Tomatoes

$1.59 for 28 ounces

The word "hypersalty" sums up these tomatoes. Eaten raw, they tasted like V-8, with an unpleasant metallic aftertaste. And things only got worse in the sauce, which tasted "like soy sauce" to several people, with a "fermented," "burnt" flavor. To top it off, tasters found the texture "mealy" and "mushy."

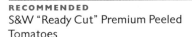

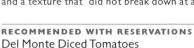

TARTE TATIN

WHAT WE WANTED: Caramelized apples resting in a buttery, flaky pastry—but without the usual hassles.

Making a true tarte Tatin is a labor of love. First, you need to make the puff pastry, a multi-hour endeavor requiring dexterity with a rolling pin and a no-fear attitude of incorporating hundreds of layers of butter within a single sheet of dough. Once the pastry is made, the apples go into a heavy-bottomed hot pan to caramelize. The pastry tops the browned apples, and the entire pan goes into the oven where the apples will caramelize further, their juices bubbling into the dough as the pastry puffs like an inflatable pillow. With a pot holder in one hand and a plate in the other, fearless Tatin-makers invert the tart onto the plate. In a perfect world, the apples fall from the pan and perfectly nestle into the pastry.

If this process sounds stressful, you're right, it is. Not only do you have to worry about making puff pastry and caramelizing the apples in a pretty concentric circle (so that when they're inverted onto the pastry, they retain an orderly look), but the entire inverting process can spawn a rational fear of spitting hot caramel dripping from the pan and down your arm.

Our goal was to whittle the Tatin process down to a manageable affair. We still wanted to retain the flavor of sticky-sweet caramelized apples and the flakiness of buttery puff pastry, but didn't want to be chained to the kitchen for hours to do so. So we came up with an idea—could the apples and puff pastry be made separately and then married together just before serving? It was definitely worth a try.

We started by simplifying the puff pastry—rather than making it from scratch, we bought pre-made puff pastry from the grocery store. We popped it in the oven for about 12 minutes and took it out when it was golden and inflated. Easy enough.

We then focused on the apples, melting butter in a large pan, sprinkling in some sugar, and laying quartered apples on top of it all. We allowed the apples to caramelize for about 10 minutes, flipped them over, and browned the other side. We then removed the apples, piece by piece with tongs, and arranged them in pretty overlapping rows on the baked puff pastry square.

We spooned about ¾ of the leftover caramelized juices in the pan over the tart. To the remaining juices, we added a few tablespoons of the whipped sour cream topping that gets served alongside the tart. This makes an instant caramel sauce that provides a nice tangy contrast to the sweet, syrupy juices of the tart. In just 30 minutes, we created a faux Tatin that even Francophiles will like.

WHAT WE LEARNED: Cook the apples and caramel separately on top of the stove. Bake the crust in the oven (using store-bought puff pastry), and then assemble the tart just before serving.

30-MINUTE TARTE TATIN Serves 6 to 8

To get this dessert on the table in 30 minutes, peel the apples while the oven preheats and the pastry thaws, and then bake the pastry while the apples are caramelizing. If the pastry rises unevenly in the oven, press it flat immediately after removing it from the oven. Some of the whipped sour cream topping is stirred into the caramelized apple juices left in the pan to make a caramel sauce. The remaining whipped sour cream topping is dolloped over individual portions of the tart.

puff pastry

1   sheet (9 by 9½ inches) frozen commercial puff pastry, thawed on the counter for 10 minutes

caramelized apples

8   tablespoons unsalted butter
¾   cup (5¼ ounces) sugar
2   pounds Granny Smith apples (6 medium or 4 large), peeled, quartered, and cored

whipped sour cream topping

½   cup sour cream
1   cup heavy cream
2   tablespoons liqueur, optional (spiced rum, Calvados apple liqueur, or Grand Marnier orange liqueur)

1. FOR THE PASTRY: Adjust an oven rack to the middle position and heat the oven to 400 degrees. Line a rimmed baking sheet with parchment paper. Place the puff pastry on the parchment, prick all over with a fork, and bake until golden brown and puffed, 10 to 12 minutes. Using a wide metal spatula, transfer the baked pastry shell to a cutting board or to a flat serving platter.

2. FOR THE APPLES: Meanwhile, melt the butter in a 12-inch heavy-bottomed skillet. Remove the pan from the heat and sprinkle evenly with the sugar. Place the apples in the skillet so they are all resting flat side down. Return the skillet to high heat and cook until the juices in the pan turn a rich amber color, 10 to 12 minutes. Using tongs, turn the apples over to the other flat side. Continue to caramelize the apples for an additional 5 minutes.

3. FOR THE TOPPING: Whip the sour cream and heavy cream to soft peaks in the bowl of a standing mixer. Add the liqueur (if desired) and continue to whip to medium-stiff peaks.

4. TO ASSEMBLE: Using tongs, remove the apple slices from the pan one at a time and place in 3 overlapping horizontal rows on the baked pastry square. Spoon about three-quarters of the pan juices over the top of the apples (you can use a pastry brush to dab some of the liquid onto the edges of the pastry). To the leftover liquid in the pan whisk in 2 tablespoons whipped sour cream topping.

5. TO SERVE: Cut the tart in half vertically down the center, and then horizontally into 3 or 4 rows (to serve 6 or 8, respectively). Transfer portions to individual plates and top each with a dollop of whipped sour cream and a drizzle of caramel sauce from pan. Serve immediately.

VARIATION

TARTE TATIN WITH PEARS

Follow the recipe for 30-Minute Tarte Tatin, substituting 2 pounds Anjou or Bartlett pears (6 to 8 medium) for the apples. You may need to increase the caramelization time in step 2 to 15 minutes for the first side, and to 8 minutes for the second side. Poire William is best liqueur to use in the whipped sour cream.

FOOD FACT: Puff Pastry

Although the French claim to have invented puff pastry, the first documented recipe is actually Italian. When prepared by the classical method, puff pastry has 729 separate layers (3 layers per fold with a total of 6 folds, or 3 to the sixth power).

Weeknight Bolognese Sauce **page 77**

Green Beans with Orange Essence and Toasted Maple Pecans **page 109**

Pasta with Sautéed Mushrooms and Thyme **page 66**

Sesame Noodles with Shredded Chicken **page 199**

230

Charcoal-Grilled Chicken Alla Diavola **page 210**

Corn and Apricot Muffins with Orange Essence **page 262**

232

Oatmeal Scones **page 245**

233

German Apple Pancake **page 278**

234

Blueberry Pancakes **page 272**

235

Simple Carrot Cake with Cream Cheese Frosting **page 306**

236

Summer Berry Pie **page 295**

Thin, Crispy Chocolate Chip Cookies **page 284**

Chocolate-Dipped Triple-Coconut Macaroons **page 289**

Lemon Cheesecake **page 315**

240

Chocolate Sheet Cake with Creamy Milk Chocolate Frosting **page 309**

241

Lemon Pound Cake with Lemon Glaze **page 249**

242

TEATIME

CHAPTER 19

In the test kitchen, we think afternoon (or morning) tea is an excellent excuse to whip up a batch of scones or a golden loaf of lemon pound cake. Making these simple baked goods at home certainly yields better results than what you can buy.

Most American scones have strayed far from the British original and are either much too sweet (scones are not cookies or muffins) or oversized, dense, and heavy (scones are biscuits and should be light in texture and small in size).

Pound cake dates back several centuries and was originally made from 1 pound each of eggs, butter, sugar, and flour. This recipe may be easy to remember, but we found that it yields a leaden cake that does not suit modern palates. On the other hand, contemporary pound cakes, especially store-bought versions that come in foil containers, are often gummy and riddled with artificial ingredients and flavors. Could we make this classic cake appeal to modern tastes and still keep the process simple?

OATMEAL SCONES

WHAT WE WANTED: The dry, fat-free triangles passed off as scones at coffeehouses would make better paperweights. Is it possible to bake a rich, toasty oatmeal scone that's tender and flaky?

Scones in America—unlike their diminutive English counterparts—have the reputation of being thick, heavy, dry bricks. To enhance their appeal, they are often disguised under a sugary shellac of achingly sweet glaze or filled with chopped ginger, chopped fruit, or chocolate chips. Despite these feeble attempts to dress them up, it is no secret that today's coffeehouse confections are a far cry from what a scone should be: tender and flaky, like a slightly sweetened biscuit.

Still, creating the perfect scone didn't seem like enough of a challenge. We were up for revamping the heaviest, densest, driest variation of them all: the oatmeal scone. The first few recipes we tried confirmed our worst fears about scones. There was the lean, mean whole-wheat flour oatmeal scone, which was gritty and dense, and the dried fruit–laden scone, which was like a thick cookie. Luscious cream scones were liked for their rich flavor but ultimately rejected for their gummy texture. And while scones made from a melted butter batter were tender, they were too cakey and delicate. Although tasters had different preferences when it came to texture, all agreed on the need for a stronger oat flavor. Our goal, then, was to pack the chewy nuttiness of oats into a moist and tender breakfast pastry, one that wouldn't require a fire hose to wash down the crumbs.

The first hurdle was deciding what type of oat to use. Because they take at least 30 minutes to cook, steel-cut oats were quickly ruled out—the baking time of the scones would not be long enough to cook these crunchy oats through. Instant oats turned out soft and gooey scones, which left us with two choices: rolled (or old-fashioned) and quick. This was not an easy decision, as each had qualities to recommend it. The whole rolled oats gave the scones a deeper, nuttier flavor (a few tasters even asked if there was peanut butter in the scones), whereas the smaller flaked quick oats gave the scones a softer texture, which was considered more palatable by some. We finally decided that either would do.

Next we had to figure out how to pack in the most oat flavor without sacrificing texture. We were sure we could achieve this by simply processing the oats into the flour. But this made for a horrible texture, very gluey and dense. Leaving the oats intact, we found that equal parts oats and flour combined good flavor with a decent texture. (Most of the recipes we tested called for much smaller proportions of oats, thus their wimpy oat flavor.) But we were still yearning for a nuttier taste, so we toasted the oats before mixing them with the flour. We tried toasting them in butter on the stovetop and on a baking sheet in the oven and found that while both methods worked well, throwing oats into the preheated oven required much less effort.

Wary of scones that were too sweet, we tried to keep the sugar content to a minimum—just enough to tenderize the scones while enhancing the oat flavor. We wanted to use a minimal amount of leavener to avoid the off flavors detected in many of the preliminary tests. We settled on just 2 teaspoons of baking powder, a much smaller amount than the tablespoon or more called for in the test recipes.

Moving on to the butter, we quickly realized why so many scones are so dry: They don't have nearly enough fat. A lean scone, we decided, is simply not worth eating, so we used 10 tablespoons of butter, which added flavor as well as making the scones tender. As for how to add the butter to the dough, we tried cutting cold butter into the dry ingredients (a standard biscuit-making technique), and we tried stirring in melted butter. Tasters preferred the lightness of the former to the cakiness of the latter.

We knew that heavy cream alone would create gummy scones, while milk alone would give us lean scones. The solution? Use a mixture of milk and heavy cream (or half-and-half) for a rich oatmeal scone that doesn't double as a paper-weight. As with biscuits, we found it important not to overwork the dough. It should be mixed just until the ingredients come together. Overmixing will yield tough, flat scones.

In keeping with the recommendations of the test recipes, we baked scones at temperatures ranging from 350 degrees all the way up to 425 degrees—and every 25-degree increment in between. The best of the lot were those baked at 425 degrees, but they were not ideal. We tried pushing the oven temperature to 450 degrees (a bit of a gamble, as the sugar in the recipe might burn) and were rewarded. These scones had a dramatic rise and a deep, golden brown crust. And this is what sold tasters on them. In such high heat, the cold butter melted quickly and produced steam, which created the light texture we were looking for. The intensity of the rise also gave the scones a cracked, craggy, rustic look. This higher temperature also meant that the scones spent less time in the oven, depriving them of the opportunity to dry out.

Until this point, our tests had shown that good scones follow the three basic rules of biscuit making: plenty of cold fat, a light hand when mixing, and a high oven temperature. Would we spoil our good luck by adding an egg, something rarely included in biscuit recipes? Perhaps scones are not exactly biscuits after all. We added one egg to our recipe, and this version won hands down for its richness. Finally, we had a scone that was hearty and flavorful from toasty whole oats, yet light enough to be consumed in one sitting without having to wash it down with a giant-size latte.

WHAT WE LEARNED: Use old-fashioned or quick oats (not instant) and toast them for a nutty oat flavor. Use a lot of butter (scones with too little butter are not worth eating) and a blend of milk and cream for richness without gumminess. Finally, bake the scones in a very hot oven to achieve maximum rise and deep browning.

OATMEAL SCONES Makes 8 scones

This recipe was developed using Gold Medal unbleached all-purpose flour; best results will be achieved if you use the same or a similar flour, such as Pillsbury unbleached. King Arthur flour has more protein; if you use it, add an extra 1 to 2 tablespoons milk. Half-and-half is a suitable substitute for the milk/cream combination.

1½	cups (4½ ounces) old-fashioned rolled oats or quick oats
¼	cup whole milk
¼	cup heavy cream
1	large egg
1½	cups (7½ ounces) unbleached all-purpose flour
⅓	cup (2¼ ounces) sugar, plus 1 tablespoon for sprinkling
2	teaspoons baking powder
½	teaspoon salt
10	tablespoons cold unsalted butter, cut into ½-inch cubes

1. Adjust an oven rack to the middle position and heat the oven to 375 degrees. Spread the oats evenly on a baking sheet and toast in the oven until fragrant and lightly browned, 7 to 9 minutes; cool on a wire rack. Increase the oven temperature to 450 degrees. Line a second baking sheet with parchment paper. When the oats are cooled, measure out 2 tablespoons (for dusting the work surface and the dough) and set aside.

2. Whisk the milk, cream, and egg in a large measuring cup until incorporated; remove 1 tablespoon to a small bowl and reserve for glazing.

3. Pulse the flour, ⅓ cup sugar, baking powder, and salt in a food processor until combined, about four 1-second pulses.

Scatter the cold butter evenly over the dry ingredients and pulse until the mixture resembles coarse cornmeal, twelve to fourteen 1-second pulses. Transfer the mixture to a medium bowl; stir in the cooled oats. Using a rubber spatula, fold in the liquid ingredients until large clumps form. Mix the dough by hand in the bowl until the dough forms a cohesive mass.

4. Dust the work surface with half of the reserved oats, turn the dough out onto the work surface, and dust the top with the remaining oats. Gently pat into a 7-inch circle about 1 inch thick. Using a bench scraper or chef's knife, cut the dough into 8 wedges and set on the parchment-lined baking sheet, spacing them about 2 inches apart. Brush the surfaces with the reserved egg mixture and sprinkle with 1 tablespoon sugar. Bake until golden brown, 12 to 14 minutes; cool the scones on the baking sheet on a wire rack for 5 minutes, then remove the scones to a rack and cool to room temperature, about 30 minutes. Serve.

VARIATIONS
CINNAMON-RAISIN OATMEAL SCONES
Follow the recipe for Oatmeal Scones, adding ¼ teaspoon ground cinnamon to the dry ingredients and ½ cup raisins to the flour/butter mixture along with the toasted oats.

APRICOT-ALMOND OATMEAL SCONES
Follow the recipe for Oatmeal Scones, reducing the oats to 1 cup, toasting ½ cup slivered almonds with the oats, and adding ½ cup chopped dried apricots to the flour/butter mixture along with the toasted oats and nuts.

OATMEAL SCONES WITH DRIED CHERRIES AND HAZELNUTS
Follow the recipe for Oatmeal Scones, reducing the oats to 1¼ cups, toasting ¼ cup coarsely chopped skinned hazelnuts with the oats, and adding ½ cup chopped dried sour cherries to the flour/butter mixture along with the toasted oats and nuts.

GLAZED MAPLE-PECAN OATMEAL SCONES
Follow the recipe for Oatmeal Scones, toasting ½ cup chopped pecans with the oats, whisking ¼ cup maple syrup into the milk/cream/egg mixture, and omitting the sugar. When the scones are cooled, whisk 3 tablespoons maple syrup and ½ cup confectioners' sugar in a small bowl until combined; drizzle the glaze over the scones.

GETTING IT RIGHT: Hotter Is Better

The scone on the left was baked in a moderate oven and did not rise as much as the scone on the right, which was baked in a very hot oven. The intense heat quickly turns the moisture in the dough into steam, and the resulting scones rise dramatically and have a craggy, well-browned top.

BAKED AT 350 DEGREES   BAKED AT 450 DEGREES

LEMON POUND CAKE

WHAT WE WANTED: Although made from only a handful of ingredients, pound cake can be a finicky, disappointing dessert prone to disaster. We set out to construct a foolproof recipe.

Making a wedding cake is hard. Making a multi-layered Dobos torte out of génoise sponge cake and buttercream is daunting. But lemon pound cake? Well, that's easy, isn't it? After all, it's made only of eggs, butter, sugar, flour, and lemon mixed together and baked in a loaf pan. But if it's so easy, why do pound cakes often turn out spongy, rubbery, heavy, and dry rather than fine-crumbed, rich, moist, and buttery? In addition, most pound cake recipes call for creaming the butter, a tricky method that demands the ingredients be at just the right temperature to achieve a silken cake batter. So our goal was twofold: Produce a superior pound cake while making the process as simple and foolproof as possible.

We started with a pound cake recipe developed in the test kitchen many years ago that was known for being excellent in its results but finicky in its preparation. The cake was top-notch, with a submissive crumb and a golden, buttery interior. In fact, it was everything we wanted from a pound cake, except for one thing—the preparation method was anything but foolproof. The method—calling for the traditional creaming of the butter and sugar until fluffy and pale—was so exacting that even the smallest diversion curdled the batter. To achieve perfection, the ingredients had to be at an unforgiving 67 degrees, the butter and sugar beaten together for exactly five minutes to aerate, and the eggs drizzled into the batter over a period of three to five minutes. All of these precautions were advised to eliminate the danger of "breaking" the batter (a pound cake has so many eggs that keeping them in emulsion can be tricky when using the creaming method), which can make the crust look mottled and leave the cake's interior dense and tough.

We knew there had to be a simpler way to achieve greatness. First we tried cutting softened butter into flour using a standing mixer. Once the butter and flour resembled knobby crumbs, we added some of the eggs, beat the mixture until cohesive, then added the rest of the eggs and beat the batter further until thick, fluffy, and lush. We often favor this method for cakes because it produces a velvety texture and a superfine crumb. Although the pound cake batter assembled in this way looked great, the baked cake was too open-grained and tender. It looked more like a yellow cake than it did a pound cake.

Next we tried melting the butter, a method often used in making quick breads. The liquids are combined and the dry ingredients then mixed into the wet by hand. This method was quick and easy. Melting the butter eliminated all of the temperature issues associated with creaming. Best of all, the batter could be pulled together and put into the oven in five minutes.

With a tight grain, a perfect swell and split in its center, and a nice, browned exterior, this cake showed promise. When we made it a second time, however, it sagged in the center. Additional tests yielded varying results. The problem may have been in the mixing method; perhaps inconsistent mixing produced inconsistent cakes. The solution? A food processor would do a better job of emulsification and also standardize the process. We added the eggs, sugar, and vanilla to the food processor bowl, combining them enough to integrate the sugar and eggs, and then drizzled the melted butter in through the feed tube. We transferred the watery base to a large bowl and sifted in flour and salt, then whisking in these ingredients by hand.

This method was a success. The cake had a split dome that afforded a peek inside at the marvelously yellow color of its interior. Just to be sure, we made the cake again and again, with the same results. Recognizing that some home cooks don't have a food processor, we tried the method in a blender. Although the cake was a bit more dense, the differences were so minimal that we can recommend either approach. With the method determined, we focused on the cake's texture and flavor.

Our objective was to make the cake just a bit lighter—but not so light as to resemble a yellow cake. (Pound cakes are by definition heavier and more dense than layer cakes.) When we tested cake flour against all-purpose, the former was superior, making the cake more tender. But the cake still needed more lift and less sponginess.

We were at this point using two sticks of melted butter. Thinking that more butter might improve the texture, we increased the amount, but the cake turned out greasy. Next we turned to the eggs. The original test kitchen recipe called for three eggs plus three yolks, so we tried four whole eggs instead (an equivalent liquid amount), thinking that the additional white might add some lift. The cake was better but still on the dense side. Without success, we tried adding cream (this cake turned out heavy) and reducing the flour (this one was greasy). Four whole eggs had gotten us close, but the texture was still not ideal.

In the oldest of recipes (from the 1700s), eggs were the only ingredient in pound cake that gave it lift. In the 1850s, however, many cooks began adding the new wonder ingredient—baking powder—to achieve a lighter texture and a higher rise. Although traditionalists might scoff at the addition of chemical leavening, we were willing to give it a try. With just 1 teaspoon, we instilled enough breath into the cake to produce a consistent, perfect crumb. Now that we had simplified the method and achieved the right texture, it was time to concentrate on lemon flavor.

In all of our prior tests, we had experienced difficulty keeping the lemon zest afloat. In cake after cake, the zest came together in large yellow clumps. The solution turned out to be simple. When the lemon zest was pulsed with the sugar before the eggs were added to the food processor bowl, the baked cake came out evenly dotted throughout with perfect specks of zest. We also added lemon juice to the batter to boost flavor.

While some prefer their lemon pound cake plain, or with only a simple shower of confectioners' sugar, we like a blast of lemon flavor. A quick glaze—made by bringing sugar and lemon juice to a boil—tasted great in the pan but failed to migrate into the nooks and crannies of the cake's crumb when simply brushed on top. We used an old trick to help the glaze on its way, poking small holes in the cake's top crust and sides with a toothpick. The glaze now penetrated to the interior of the cake, distributing plenty of lemon flavor. Finally, we had a quick, foolproof recipe that delivered a great crumb and great lemon flavor. Pound for pound, this cake's a winner.

WHAT WE LEARNED: Melt the butter instead of creaming to foolproof the recipe. Assemble the batter in the food processor to make sure the melted butter is evenly incorporated. Use cake flour for maximum tenderness and a bit of baking powder for lift. Grind the lemon zest with the sugar so it remains evenly distributed in the cake, and brush the cake with lemon glaze as it cools.

LEMON POUND CAKE

Makes one 9 by 5-inch cake, serving 8

You can use a blender instead of a food processor to mix the batter. To add the butter, remove the center cap of the lid so it can be drizzled into the whirling blender with minimal splattering. This batter looks almost like a thick pancake batter and is very fluid. The Lemon Glaze (recipe follows) makes the pound cake especially moist and flavorful.

16	tablespoons (2 sticks) unsalted butter, plus 1 tablespoon, softened, for greasing pan
1½	cups (6 ounces) cake flour, plus 1 tablespoon for dusting pan
1	teaspoon baking powder
½	teaspoon salt
1¼	cups (8¾ ounces) sugar
2	tablespoons grated zest plus 2 teaspoons juice from 2 medium lemons
4	large eggs
1½	teaspoons vanilla extract

1. Adjust an oven rack to the middle position and heat the oven to 350 degrees. Grease a 9 by 5-inch loaf pan with 1 tablespoon softened butter; dust with 1 tablespoon flour, tapping out the excess. In a medium bowl, whisk together the flour, baking powder, and salt; set aside.

2. In a glass measuring cup or microwave-safe bowl, microwave the butter, covered with plastic wrap, at full power until melted, 1 to 2 minutes. (Alternatively, melt the butter in a small saucepan over medium heat.) Whisk the melted butter thoroughly to reincorporate any separated milk solids.

3. In a food processor, process the sugar and zest until combined, about five 1-second pulses. Add the lemon juice, eggs, and vanilla; process until combined, about 5 seconds. With the machine running, add the melted butter through the feed tube in a steady stream (this should take about 20

seconds). Transfer the mixture to a large bowl. Sift the flour mixture over the eggs in three steps, whisking gently after each addition until just combined.

4. Pour the batter into the prepared pan and bake 15 minutes. Reduce the oven temperature to 325 degrees and continue to bake until deep golden brown and a skewer inserted in the center comes out clean, about 35 minutes, rotating the pan halfway through the baking time. Cool in the pan for 10 minutes, then turn onto a wire rack and brush on the Lemon Glaze, if desired. Cool to room temperature, at least 1 hour. (The cooled cake can be wrapped tightly in plastic wrap and stored at room temperature for up to 5 days.)

LEMON GLAZE Enough to glaze one 9 by 5-inch cake
Brush this glaze onto the warm cake to give it a fresh, sweet-tart lemon kick.

- ½ cup (3½ ounces) sugar
- ¼ cup juice from 1 or 2 medium lemons

While the cake is cooling, bring the sugar and lemon juice to a boil in a small nonreactive saucepan, stirring occasionally to dissolve the sugar. Reduce the heat to low and simmer until thickened slightly, about 2 minutes. After removing the cake from the pan, poke the top and sides of the cake throughout with a skewer or long toothpick. Brush the top and sides of the cake with the glaze and cool to room temperature.

VARIATION
LEMON–POPPY SEED POUND CAKE
Follow the recipe for Lemon Pound Cake through step 1. Toss 1 tablespoon flour mixture with ⅓ cup poppy seeds in a small bowl; set aside. Continue with the recipe from step 2, folding the poppy seed mixture into the batter after the flour is incorporated.

EQUIPMENT CORNER:
Citrus Juicers and Reamers

CITRUS JUICERS AND REAMERS OFFER A QUICK, SIMPLE way to juice a lemon or two, with a modicum of fuss. The working part of both of these tools is a ridged, conical head. In the case of the reamer, the tool is turned; with the juicer, the lemon is turned. Are all juicers and reamers created alike? Of course not. After testing nine models, we found that the better models have a pointed tip, which effectively pierces the flesh of the lemon and grabs hold. Without the pointed tip, the lemon slips right off the head. The second important feature is the sharpness of the ridges. Those models with sharp, pointed ridges "gripped" the lemon well, making it easy to extract maximum juice with minimum effort, while those with rounded ridges allowed the lemon to slide around, making for difficult juicing.

The two winners were the plastic Oxo Good Grips Citrus Juicer and the Fox Run Wood Lemon Reamer. They both juiced the lemons quickly and efficiently. The Oxo Citrus Juicer features a unique design with two open ridged heads (for both larger and smaller citrus fruit) and a nonskid bowl for juice collection. The Fox Run reamer has a classic design and an especially comfortable handle.

The remaining reamers and juicers tested were less successful. Two models of Oxo Good Grips Citrus Reamers (one featuring a black plastic head, the other an aluminum head) and the Harold Stainless Steel Citrus Reamer featured relatively sharp tips, but their dull ridges caused lemons to slip. The other models all failed to pierce or grab lemons effectively owing to rounded heads and dull ridges.

Rating Citrus Juicers and Reamers

WE TESTED NINE JUICERS AND REAMERS BY JUICING HALVED LEMONS WITH EACH DEVICE. THE JUICERS AND REAMERS are listed in order of preference based on their effectiveness (that is, the amount of juice they extracted) and their ease of use. See www.americastestkitchen.com for up-to-date prices and mail-order sources for top-rated products.

RECOMMENDED—BEST JUICER

Oxo Good Grips Citrus Juicer

$11.99

The pointed tip and sharp ridges make for maximum juice extraction. A unique design accommodates lemons and oranges equally well.

RECOMMENDED—BEST REAMER

Fox Run Wood Lemon Reamer

$2.99

A pointed tip, sharp ridges, comfortable handle, and low price—what more could you ask for?

RECOMMENDED WITH RESERVATIONS

Oxo Good Grips Lemon Reamer

$4.99

The tip on this plastic reamer with a comfortable black plastic handle is pointed, but the ridges are rounded, so the lemons tend to slip and slide.

RECOMMENDED WITH RESERVATIONS

Oxo Silver Lemon Reamer

$8.50

The tip on this aluminum reamer with a comfortable black plastic handle is pointed, but the ridges are rounded and dull. The lemons tended to slip and slide on this model.

RECOMMENDED WITH RESERVATIONS

Harold Stainless Steel Lemon Reamer

$10.00

The pointed tip pierces lemons, but the rounded ridges allow too much slippage.

NOT RECOMMENDED

Mason Cash Vitrified Ceramic Reamer

$6.95

This ceramic reamer did a poor job at both piercing and holding onto lemons.

NOT RECOMMENDED

Endurance Citrus Juicer

$12.99

This stainless steel juicer has two strikes against it—a rounded tip and rounded ridges.

NOT RECOMMENDED

SCI Cuisine Internationale Citrus Juicer

$8.95

This glass juicer has a rounded head and ridges that we didn't like, although the pour spout is a nice touch.

NOT RECOMMENDED

Zyliss Fruit Juicer

$11.95

This plastic juicer has a rounded head and dull ridges and doesn't juice very effectively.

TASTING LAB: Supermarket Teas

TEA IN THE UNITED STATES HAS BEEN RUNNER UP IN THE hot beverage pageant ever since our founding fathers turned Boston Harbor into the world's largest cup of tea more than 200 years ago. Today, tea is making a bit of a comeback. While nowhere near as ubiquitous as coffee shops, tea shops have sprouted, with menus featuring dozens (and sometimes hundreds) of different teas and blends.

But what about the old standby, traditional supermarket tea? With most around 3 cents per bag, there's no beating the price or the convenience.

Unless otherwise labeled, supermarket offerings contain black tea. There are three basic types of tea: green, black,

and oolong. (Herbal teas are not actually teas at all but rather a blend of leaves, flowers, and/or herbs.) Green teas contain leaves that have been steamed and dried, black teas contain fermented leaves, and oolong teas fall right in the middle, fermented for a shorter period of time than black teas. The two major categories of black teas are leaf and broken, and each category is then further broken down by size. Of the leaf category, orange pekoe refers to the largest leaf size.

If you look closely at a box of supermarket tea, you'll likely see the words "Orange Pekoe and Pekoe Cut Teas." That means that the tea bags contain large and small pieces of tea. Most supermarket teas are a blend of black teas. While all teas come from the same basic plant, regional variances in climate and soil make for more than 3,000 varieties of tea.

We tasted five popular national brands of supermarket

Rating Supermarket Teas

TWELVE MEMBERS OF THE *COOK'S ILLUSTRATED* STAFF TASTED FIVE NATIONAL BRANDS OF TEA BAGS AS WELL AS A generic store brand. All tea bags were steeped in boiled water for four minutes and tasted plain. The teas are listed in order of preference based on scores from the tasting. With the exception of the Stop & Shop tea, all brands are sold in supermarkets nationwide.

HIGHLY RECOMMENDED
Lipton Tea $2.99 for 100 individually wrapped bags
Tasters described this familiar brand as "well bodied," "smoky," and "rich." The clear winner.

RECOMMENDED
Salada Tea Bags $3.19 for 100 bags
The runner-up received generally favorably comments, such as "full, smooth flavor," but a few tasters complained about a "dusty" flavor.

RECOMMENDED
Tetley Classic Blend $3.19 for 100 bags
Depending on the taster, this popular brand was described as "mellow and smooth" or "weak" and "watery."

NOT RECOMMENDED
Twinings Ceylon Orange Pekoe Tea $2.99 for 25 individually wrapped bags
This "premium" brand was roundly dismissed by tasters as "fishy" and "slightly bitter."

NOT RECOMMENDED
Red Rose Tea $3.19 for 100 bags
This tea was described as "thin and bitter" as well as "soapy and harsh."

NOT RECOMMENDED
Stop & Shop Original Tea Bags $1.49 for 48 individually wrapped bags
This supermarket brand received the lowest scores and harshest assessment from tasters, with comments like "sour" and "absolutely heinous."

tea, as well as the generic store brand from our local supermarket. Directions on the packages called for the tea to steep for three to five minutes in boiled water. We held a quick preliminary test to determine the best steeping time. At three minutes teas were deemed too flat, while at five minutes they were too strong. Tea steeped for four minutes had just the right balance. Most of the teas cost just above 3 cents per bag; the cheapest tea (at less than 3 cents per bag) ranked higher than our lone double-digit tea (at less than 12 cents per bag).

A significant range of scores separated our first- and last-place finishers. Lipton was the favorite, praised for its "smooth" and "slightly musty" flavor and "complexity." Fans of our second-place finisher, Salada, called it "earthy," "musty," and "floral," while detractors deemed it "nasty," "bitter," and "very average." At the bottom of the ranking were a generic store brand and Red Rose. One taster said of the generic brand, "It tastes like brown recycled paper towels." Though one taster described Red Rose as "light, with a good round flavor," most agreed with the two tasters who wrote, "Yuck."

Keith and Erin examine the long
prep list in the back kitchen.

SUNDAY brunch

Sunday brunch sounds so civilized. Every other day of the week breakfast happens in seconds. You eat a bowl of cereal as you dress, or you grab a bagel on the way to work. But one day a week you spend the morning preparing eggs, baking muffins, and squeezing fresh juice. All that extra work better be worth the time and effort.

But all too often that Denver omelet is rubbery, with raw chunks of vegetable poking holes in its surface, and the corn muffins turn out like the sticky-sweet cakes or dry hockey pucks you get in bad coffee shops. You wonder why you should bother. Cold cereal looks pretty good compared with such disappointing fare.

We figure that if you're going to make a real breakfast, it better be really good. Our recipes for Denver omelets and corn muffins are special enough to make you long for Sunday mornings.

DENVER OMELET

WHAT WE WANTED: A hearty American omelet with properly cooked vegetables and tender eggs.

While we love soft, delicately flavored French omelets, we also have a weakness for lightly browned diner-style omelets bursting at the seams with filling. And our favorite is the Denver omelet, a mixture of sautéed bell peppers, onions, and ham with a generous handful of melted Monterey Jack cheese. Unfortunately, like too much diner food, Denver omelets are often ill-prepared and lacking in flavor. We set out to remedy this problem and make a refined Denver omelet worthy of cooking at home.

As we see it, the two biggest problems facing Denver omelets are undercooked filling and overcooked eggs. And the two together can be quite off-putting: crunchy, vegetal-tasting peppers sandwiched between layers of tough eggs. The filling proved the easiest place to start. We wanted a well-cooked, slightly browned filling that brought out the natural sweetness in the peppers. And we wanted the ham's smokiness to cut through the rich creaminess of the eggs and cheese. To emphasize the peppers' sweetness and build complexity of flavor, we used both red and green peppers, which also made for a more attractive filling. We first tried julienning the vegetables, as done in many diners do, but

tasters complained that the vegetables were hard to eat and the peppers' skins added an unpleasant, fibrous quality to the filling. So we switched to a dice, which was easier to eat, and the peppers' thick skins no longer marred the texture. To keep the cooking time short, we diced everything fairly small. The vegetables softened and lightly browned with about six minutes of cooking over medium-high heat.

After trying several different kinds of ham, including ham steaks, canned ham, and sliced deli ham, we found they all worked fine, but ham steaks proved the easiest to dice and provided the deepest, smokiest flavor. We first tried adding the ham to the vegetables long enough to just warm through but found that the filling did not take on the ham's potent flavor. When the ham was added midway through cooking, however, the smokiness infused the vegetables and the diced ham browned at the edges.

Although we had overcome the hurdle of under-cooked vegetables, the filling tasted one-dimensional. Borrowing from the classic Basque dish of piperade—a mixture of ham, peppers, and onions from which the Denver filling is clearly derived—we added a hint of garlic and parsley. The garlic sharpened the robust flavors, and the parsley added some freshness. The final touch was a dash of hot pepper sauce, which accented the flavors without necessarily tasting spicy.

With our filling perfected, we moved on to the eggs. There are probably more techniques for cooking omelets than for any other dish under the sun. We tested a variety and came up with a relatively foolproof method. First off, a good-quality, nonstick pan is crucial; otherwise you are guaranteed to produce scrambled eggs instead of an omelet. For these big, overstuffed omelets, we found that a 10-inch pan worked best, allowing the eggs to spread out to provide plenty of surface area for the filling. After experimenting with different heat levels, medium-high seemed to work the best because the eggs set quickly. At

> **FOOD FACT: Eggs**
> Annual per capita consumption of eggs in the shell has dropped from 283 eggs in 1966 to 177 today. During that same period, annual per capita consumption of processed eggs (in baked good, cookies, etc.) has risen from 30 eggs to 73. Although we are eating fewer eggs in total per year (313 in 1966 versus 250 today), the numbers are less dramatic when you look at the total egg picture, not just consumption of whole eggs purchased in supermarkets.

lower heat, they tended to get rubbery. The sizzling point of the butter added to the pan proved a good indicator of when the pan was hot enough to receive the eggs (the butter added great flavor as well).

With the eggs in the pan, we quickly stirred them with a heat-safe rubber spatula until they just began to set, a matter of a few seconds. Then, gingerly, we lifted up the edges of the set eggs with the spatula and tilted the pan, allowing the uncooked eggs to run underneath and cook. When the eggs were almost fully set—just a little runny on top—we added the cheese. We discovered that once the cheese was almost melted, the bottom had lightly browned and was ready to come out of the pan. We quickly covered half the omelet with the warm pepper filling, slid the omelet onto a plate, filled-side first, and, with a slight twist of the wrist, flipped the empty half over the filled half. (We tried folding the omelet in the pan with the spatula, but this method occasionally ripped the omelet.)

We were pleased with the technique and the egg's light browning, but the omelet itself was a little dense and tough. Because the omelet cooked longer than a French-style omelet, the eggs were robbed of moisture. To increase the moisture, we tried adding milk, cream, and water to the beaten eggs. Milk and cream worked equally well, but water diluted the omelet's subtle flavor. As little as 1 tablespoon of cream or milk to 3 eggs was just right. The interior stayed fluffy and moist, while the exterior was lightly browned.

WHAT WE LEARNED: Dice the pepper and onion so they cook quickly and don't poke through the eggs. Add diced ham steak, garlic, parsley, and hot sauce to enliven the vegetable filling. Add milk or cream to keep the eggs moist as they cook and make sure to use a nonstick pan set over medium-high heat.

DENVER OMELET Serves 1

Prepare the filling (recipe follows) and then begin making the omelet. The filling recipe makes enough for two omelets and can be doubled. See the illustrations on page 259 for tips on folding an omelet. You can make one omelet after another in the same pan, although you may need to reduce the heat. For the best results, serve all omelets, including this one, on warmed plates.

3	large eggs
1	tablespoon cream or milk
	Salt and ground black pepper
½	tablespoon unsalted butter
2	ounces Monterey Jack cheese, shredded (about ½ cup)

1. Beat the eggs, cream or milk, and salt and pepper to taste with a fork in a small bowl until thoroughly combined.

2. Heat the butter in a 10-inch nonstick skillet over medium-high heat. When the foaming subsides and the butter just begins to turn color, pour in the eggs. Cook until the edges begin to set, about 2 to 3 seconds, then, with a rubber spatula, stir in a circular motion until slightly thickened, about 10 seconds. Use the spatula to pull the cooked edges in to the center, then tilt the pan to one side so that the uncooked egg runs to the edge of the pan. Repeat until the omelet is just set but still moist on the surface, 1 to 2 minutes.

3. Sprinkle the cheese evenly across the surface of the omelet and allow to partially melt, 15 to 20 seconds. With the handle of the pan facing you, spoon the filling over the left side of the omelet. Slide the omelet onto a warmed plate, filled-side first, and, with a slight twist of the wrist, invert the pan so that the other side of the omelet folds over the filling. Serve immediately.

FILLING FOR DENVER OMELET

Makes enough to fill 2 omelets

A ham steak is our top choice for this recipe, although canned ham and sliced deli ham will work. (If using sliced deli ham, add it with the garlic, parsley, and hot sauce.) If you can find them, Cook's brand ham steaks are our favorite.

1	tablespoon unsalted butter
½	medium red bell pepper, stemmed, seeded, and diced
½	medium green bell pepper, stemmed, seeded, and diced
1	small onion, diced
¼	teaspoon salt
4	ounces ham steak, diced (about 1 cup)
1	tablespoon minced fresh parsley leaves
½	teaspoon hot pepper sauce, such as Tabasco

Heat the butter in a medium nonstick skillet over medium-high heat. When the foaming subsides, add the peppers, onions, and salt. Cook, stirring occasionally, until the onions begin to soften, about 4 minutes. Add the ham and cook until the peppers begin to brown lightly, about 2 minutes. Add the garlic, parsley, and hot sauce and cook for 30 seconds. Transfer to a small bowl and cover to keep warm.

TASTING LAB: Eggs

WE WERE CURIOUS HOW EGGS FROM DIFFERENT sources might stack up when tasted side-by-side. Despite marketing hype to the contrary, a kitchen taste-test proved that shell color has no effect on flavor. Brown eggs and white eggs from similar sources taste the same.

But what about organic or farm-fresh eggs? To find out, we put the following four varieties to the test by cooking each sunny-side up: farm-fresh eggs (less than a week old), Egg Innovations organic eggs ("free roaming"), Eggland's Best brand eggs from hens raised on vegetarian feed (the labels says these eggs are guaranteed to possess "25% less saturated fat than regular eggs" and "100 mg of omega 3 fatty acids"), and standard supermarket eggs. The farm-fresh eggs were standouts from the get-go. The large yolks were shockingly orange and sat very high above the comparatively small white. Their flavor was exceptionally rich and complex. The organic eggs followed in second place, with eggs from hens raised on a vegetarian diet in third and the standard supermarket eggs last.

Our conclusion? If you have access to eggs fresh from the farm, by all means buy them; they are a special treat. Otherwise, organic eggs are worth the premium—about a dollar more than standard supermarket eggs—especially if you frequently eat them on their own or in simple recipes such as an omelet.

We also wondered how freshness affected flavor. Egg cartons are marked with both sell-by and "pack dates" (the

---

GETTING IT RIGHT: Egg Sizes

Eggs come in six sizes—jumbo, extra-large, large, medium, small, and peewee. Most markets carry only the top four sizes—small and peewee are generally reserved for commercial use. There's little mystery about size—the bigger the chicken, the bigger the egg. All of our recipes are tested with large eggs, but substitutions are possible when large quantities of eggs are used. See the chart for help in making accurate calculations. For example, four jumbo eggs are equivalent to five large eggs because their weight (10 ounces) is the same.

EGG SIZES AND WEIGHTS

Size	Weight
Medium	1.75 ounces
Large	2.00 ounces
Extra-Large	2.25 ounces
Jumbo	2.50 ounces

latter is a three number code printed just below the sell-by date and it runs consecutively from 001, for January 1, to 365, for December 31). The sell-by date is the legal limit to which eggs may be sold and is within 30 days of the pack date. The pack date is the day the eggs were graded and packed, which is generally within a week of being laid but, legally, may be as much as 30 days. In short, a carton of eggs may be up two months old by the end of the sell-by date. Even so, according to the U.S. Department of Agriculture, they are still fit for consumption three to five weeks past the sell-by date. The dates, then, are by no means an exact measure of an egg's freshness; they provide vague guidance at best.

So how old is too old? We tasted two- and three-month-old eggs that were perfectly palatable, though at four months, the white was very loose and the yolk "tasted faintly of the refrigerator"—though it was still edible. Our advice? Use your discretion: if the egg smells odd or displays discoloration, pitch it. Older eggs also lack the structure-lending properties of fresh eggs, so beware when baking. Both the white and yolk becomes looser. We whipped four-month old eggs and found they rapidly deflated.

TECHNIQUE: Folding a Denver Omelet

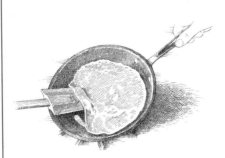

1. Push the cooked eggs along the edges of the pan toward the center, tilting the pan so that any uncooked egg runs to the pan's edges.

2. Sprinkle the cheese evenly across the surface of the omelet and let it melt slightly. With the handle facing you, spoon the filling over the left side of the omelet.

3. Slide the filled half of the omelet onto a warm plate. With a slight turn of the wrist, slightly invert the pan so the other side of the omelet folds over the filling.

CORN MUFFINS

WHAT WE WANTED: A muffin that won't set off sucrose alarms, a pronounced but not overwhelming cornmeal flavor, and a moist and tender crumb. And all of this goodness has to be capped off with a crunchy, golden, craggy muffin top.

We have a love/hate relationship with corn muffins, and it seems to be getting harder to find any to love. Whether too coarse, dry, and crumbly, too sticky and sweet, or just too fluffy and cupcake-like, the majority of corn muffins on the market today just don't make the cut. What do we want? To find out, we started by testing an assortment of recipes (see "Corn Muffins," page 262) from various cookbooks. Although their ingredient lists were similar, the end results were not. Some were too chewy, too short, and too puck-shaped, while others had too little corn flavor or were just plain too sweet or savory. Two recipes, however, stood out. One produced muffins that were tall and rustic; the other made muffins with a pleasant, wholesome cornmeal flavor. Working with these recipes as a starting point, we began to test variables.

There are two basic methods used to mix muffins. The creaming method calls for beating softened butter and sugar together, adding eggs one at a time, then adding dry and wet ingredients alternately to complete the batter. In the quick-bread (or straight) method, the dry and wet ingredients are combined separately and then mixed together. First, we tried creaming, which produced a high-rise muffin, but the crumb was too light and fluffy, much like a layer cake. (Air is whipped into the butter and sugar during creaming.) We then tried the quick-bread method, which turned out a muffin with not only good height but also a more substantial crumb. The quick-bread method, in its use of melted rather than creamed butter, apparently introduced less air to the batter, and the resulting muffin was less cupcake-like.

Because we wanted a sturdy muffin, not an airy confection, this suited us just fine. As an added bonus, the quick-bread method was also both easier and quicker than creaming: Just melt the butter, pour, and stir.

With our mixing method down, it was now time to focus on the choice of cornmeal. We tested three brands: Quaker, Arrowhead Mills, and Hodgson Mill. Quaker cornmeal, the most common brand in supermarkets, is degerminated. During processing, the dried corn is steel-rolled, which removes most of the germ and husk. Because the germ contains most of the flavor and natural oils, this process results in a drier, less flavorful cornmeal. When baked into a corn muffin, Quaker offered an unremarkable corn flavor and, because of its dryness, an unpleasant "crunch."

Arrowhead Mills and Hodgson Mill are similar in that both are whole-grain cornmeals, made from the whole corn kernel. Hodgson Mill, which is stone-ground (the dried corn is ground between two stones), has a coarse, inconsistent texture, while Arrowhead Mills, which is hammer-milled (pulverized with hammers), has a consistent, fine texture. Both brands delivered a more wholesome and complex corn flavor than Quaker. However, the Hodgson Mill cornmeal made the muffins coarse, dry, and difficult to chew. Arrowhead Mills produced by far the best corn muffin, with a consistently fine texture and real cornmeal flavor. The conclusion? Use a whole-grain cornmeal in a fine grind, such as Arrowhead Mills.

At this point, our muffins had the right texture and good flavor, but they were too dry. Some recipes suggest mixing the

> **FOOD FACT: Corn Muffins**
> We knew there was a reason why America's Test Kitchen was based in Massachusetts. The corn muffin was designated the official state muffin in 1986. But what about other local favorites, such as blueberry and cranberry muffins?

buttermilk, sour cream, and yogurt. We tried them all, using different amounts of each. Our initial thought was "butter, butter, butter," with enough milk added to hit the right consistency. When tested, however, these muffins were lacking in moisture. We then tried using buttermilk in place of the milk. This muffin packed more flavor into each bite, but it was still on the dry side. What finally produced a superior muffin was sour cream paired with butter and milk. These muffins were rich, light, moist, and tender, but they were no dainty cupcakes, either. We were curious to see how a muffin made with whole milk yogurt would stand up to the muffin made with sour cream. The difference was slight. The muffin made with whole milk yogurt was leaner but still moist and delicious. Muffins made with low-fat yogurt, on the other hand, were too lean and dry. Based on these tests, we concluded that a moist muffin requires fat and the tenderizing effect of acidity, both of which are found in sour cream.

The leavener used in most muffins is baking powder and/or baking soda, and we found that a combination of 1½ teaspoons baking powder and 1 teaspoon baking soda delivered the ideal height. We tested temperatures from 325 to 425 degrees and found that 400 degrees delivered the crunchy, crispy, golden crust we were looking for.

So, with the right cornmeal and the addition of sour cream, butter, and milk, it is possible to bake a tender, moist, and delicious corn muffin. By decreasing the amount of sugar and adding a few savory ingredients, you can serve these muffins with dinner as well as for breakfast. Either way, they beat the coffee-shop variety by a country mile.

cornmeal with a hot liquid before adding it to the batter. This method allows the cornmeal to absorb the liquid while expanding and softening the grain. The other wet ingredients are then added to the mush and combined with the dry ingredients. This seemed like a good way to make a moister muffin—or so we thought. Unfortunately, tasters found these muffins too dense and strong-tasting, more like cornbread than corn muffins, which should be lighter.

Back to square one. We made a list of the ingredients that might help produce a moist muffin: butter, milk,

WHAT WE LEARNED: **Use the quick-bread method rather than the creaming method to assemble the batter. Use whole-grain cornmeal that has been finely ground for the best flavor and texture. Butter and sour cream make the crumb tender and moist, and baking at 400 degrees delivers a crunchy top.**

CORN MUFFINS Makes 12 muffins

Whole-grain cornmeal has a fuller flavor than regular corn-meal milled from degerminated corn. To determine what kind of cornmeal a package contains, look closely at the label. See page 263 for more tips about buying cornmeal.

2	cups (10 ounces) unbleached all-purpose flour
1	cup (4½ ounces) fine-ground, whole-grain yellow cornmeal
1½	teaspoons baking powder
1	teaspoon baking soda
½	teaspoon salt
2	large eggs
¾	cup (5¼ ounces) sugar
8	tablespoons (1 stick) unsalted butter, melted
¾	cup sour cream
½	cup milk

1. Adjust an oven rack to the middle position and heat the oven to 400 degrees. Spray a standard muffin tin with non-stick cooking spray.

2. Whisk the flour, cornmeal, baking powder, baking soda, and salt in a medium bowl to combine; set aside. Whisk the eggs in a second medium bowl until well combined and light-colored, about 20 seconds. Add the sugar to the eggs; whisk vigorously until thick and homogenous, about 30 seconds; add the melted butter in 3 additions, whisking to combine after each addition. Add half the sour cream and half the milk and whisk to combine; whisk in the remaining sour cream and milk until combined. Add the wet ingredients to the dry ingredients; mix gently with a rubber spatula until the batter is just combined and evenly moistened. Do not over-mix. Using an ice cream scoop or large spoon, divide the batter evenly among muffin cups, dropping it to form mounds. Do not level or flatten the surface of the mounds.

3. Bake until the muffins are light golden brown and a skewer inserted into the center of the muffins comes out clean, about 18 minutes, rotating the muffin tin from front to back halfway through the baking time. Cool the muffins in the tin for 5 minutes; invert the muffins onto a wire rack, stand the muffins upright, cool 5 minutes longer, and serve warm.

VARIATIONS

CORN AND APRICOT MUFFINS WITH ORANGE ESSENCE

Apricots in the batter and a dusting of orange sugar makes these muffins are our favorites in the test kitchen.

GETTING IT RIGHT: Corn Muffins

Despite the simplicity of corn muffins, a lot can wrong when making them. Here are some of the worst muffins we encountered in our testing, from left to right: (A) This flat muffin contains too much cornmeal and tastes like cornbread. (B) This pale muffin contains no butter and relies on egg whites as the leavener. (C) This hockey puck-like muffin starts with cornmeal mixed with hot water. (D) This cupcake-like muffin resembles many store-bought muffins and is made with too much sugar and leavener.

A. Squat and Corny

B. Dense and Tough

C. Small and Wet

D. Fluffy and Cakey

1. In a food processor, process ⅔ cup granulated sugar and 1½ teaspoons grated orange zest until pale orange, about 10 seconds. Transfer to a small bowl and set aside.

2. In a food processor, pulse 1½ cups (10 ounces) dried apricots for ten 2-second pulses, until chopped fine. Transfer to a medium microwave-safe bowl; add ⅔ cup orange juice to the apricots, cover the bowl tightly with plastic wrap, and microwave on high until simmering, about 1 minute. Let the apricots stand, covered, until softened and plump, about 5 minutes. Strain the apricots; discard the juice.

3. Follow the recipe for Corn Muffins, substituting ¼ cup packed dark brown sugar for an equal amount granulated sugar and stirring ½ teaspoon grated orange zest and strained apricots into the wet ingredients before adding to the dry ingredients. Before baking, sprinkle a portion of the orange sugar over each mound of batter. Do not invert the baked muffins; use a paring knife to lift the muffins from the tin one at a time and transfer to a wire rack. Cool muffins 5 minutes longer; serve warm.

BACON-SCALLION CORN MUFFINS WITH CHEDDAR CHEESE

Because these muffins contain bacon, store leftovers in the refrigerator wrapped in plastic. Bring them to room temperature or re-warm the muffins before serving.

1. Grate 8 ounces cheddar cheese (you should have 2 cups); set aside. Fry 3 slices bacon (about 3 ounces), cut into ½-inch pieces, in a small skillet over medium heat until crisp and golden brown, about 5 minutes. Add 10 to 12 medium scallions, sliced thin (about 1¼ cups), ¼ teaspoon salt, and ⅛ teaspoon ground black pepper; cook to heat through, about 1 minute. Transfer the mixture to a plate to cool while making the muffins.

2. Follow the recipe for Corn Muffins, reducing the sugar to ½ cup. Stir 1½ cups grated cheddar cheese and bacon/scallion mixture into the wet ingredients, then add to the dry ingredients and combine. Before baking, sprinkle a portion of additional ½ cup cheddar over each mound of batter.

GETTING IT RIGHT: Buying Cornmeal

Cornmeal can vary greatly in texture (depending on how the corn kernels are ground) and flavor (depending on whether the kernels are whole grain or degerminated). We found that whole-grain Arrowhead Mills cornmeal (left) makes the best corn muffins. Its texture resembles slightly damp fine sand. Whole-grain Hodgson Mills cornmeal (middle) has great flavor, but the texture is coarser (akin to kosher salt), making corn muffins that are too coarse. Degerminated Quaker cornmeal (right) has a fine texture (similar to table salt) and makes muffins that are bland and dry.

TASTING LAB: Baking Powder

DOUBLE-ACTING BAKING POWDER IS COMPRISED OF BAKING soda (the single acting ingredient), another rise ingredient (such as sodium aluminum sulfate and/or calcium phosphate), and cornstarch (a buffer to keep the ingredients separate in the can). Baking powder goes to work immediately when mixed with a liquid, and then gets its second lift when it hits the heat of an oven. You do have a choice of baking powders at the supermarket, so we put four nationally available brands to the test.

Two brands, Davis and Clabber Girl, contain both sodium aluminum sulfate and calcium phosphate. Calumet contains both of these ingredients along with calcium sulfate, which according to the label "maintains leavening," while Rumford has just calcium phosphate. We wondered if these leaveners would perform differently. Also, some experts say baking powders with aluminum can give baked goods an off flavor. Is this true? To find out, we tested each brand in carrot cake (with lots of sugar and spices) and in plain biscuits (made with just flour, salt, baking powder, and cream).

Well, when it comes to cake, you've got one less thing to worry about. All four baking powders lifted the cake to nearly equal heights (the cake made with Clabber Girl had a slight depression on top, but it was not big enough to affect the texture of the cake). Also, tasters could not detect any off flavors in any of the cakes. We wondered if the spices in the cake were hindering the tasting process, so we baked up four batches of cream biscuits. The biscuits were nearly identical in appearance. A couple of sensitive tasters did notice a very faint chemical taste in the biscuits made with Clabber Girl, but admitted that if they hadn't been looking for it, they wouldn't have noticed it at all. Our conclusion is to forget about brand when choosing baking powder, but do make sure your powder is fresh.

EQUIPMENT CORNER:
Rubber Spatulas

GOOD RUBBER SPATULAS AND PLACID, WELL-ADJUSTED people have two things in common. Both are firm enough to stay the course, yet flexible enough to hug the curves and contours (of the mixing bowl and of life). We all know that it takes years of experience for people to achieve that delicate balance, but you can buy a spatula with those traits this afternoon. While a rubber spatula is not a particularly costly kitchen purchase, the few dollars you spend should get you a comfortable, efficient utensil. To that end, we identified four design factors—two each for the blade and the handle—that make for a great spatula.

The group of 10 spatulas displayed blades of different shape, size, and flexibility. Given that the two most important tests were folding whipped egg whites into pastry cream to make soufflé batter and scraping down the sides of a mixing bowl as we prepared cookie dough, size and flexibility proved most important.

When folding whipped egg whites, the idea is to work gently and efficiently to avoid bursting the bubbles that constitute the foam. Larger spatula blades moved more of the mixture at once, thereby decreasing the number of strokes necessary to integrate the beaten whites and reducing the risk of deflating the foam. The Rubbermaid, Le Creuset, KitchenAid, Oxo, and Rösle spatulas had the largest blades. It's worth noting, however, that a smaller spatula is also useful for scraping the last bits of something out of a small- or narrow-mouthed jar or for reaching crevices that a large blade can't touch. That said, if you buy only one spatula, make it a large one.

Blending chocolate chips into stiff cookie dough and scraping the mixture down the sides of the bowl illustrated the importance of the relative flexibility and stiffness of the blade. Every spatula but one was flexible enough to conform to the curve of the mixing bowl. That one was the Farberware, which was so soft that the blade bent over on itself when we pushed it against the dough, rendering it nearly useless. In a related observation, we noticed that the blades with relatively thin, sharp edges, like those of the Rubbermaid, KitchenAid, Pyrex, Cuisipro, and Oneida, cut through the mixture a little more efficiently and left the bowl walls slightly cleaner. In our minds, then, stiffer blades with thinner edges make better spatulas.

Among the 10 spatulas tested, only two, the Henckels and the Farberware, are made of rubber. The other eight blades are made of silicone, a polymer that is similar to rubber. Silicone is supposed to be more heat-resistant than rubber, making silicone spatulas the choice when cooking. To find out if this is true, we tested the heat resistance of all

Rating Rubber Spatulas

WE TESTED 10 RUBBER OR SILICONE SPATULAS IN FOUR APPLICATIONS—FOLDING, HEAVY SCRAPING, LIGHT SCRAPING, and simmering tomato sauce (the latter was designed to judge heat damage, staining, and odor absorption). Spatulas are listed in order of preference based on their overall performance in these tests as well as their design. See www.americastestkitchen.com for up-to-date prices and mail-order sources for the top-rated product.

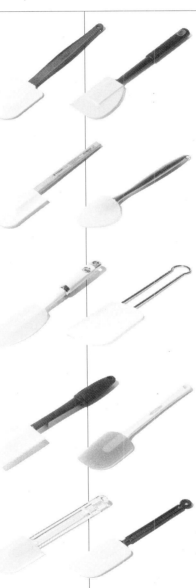

HIGHLY RECOMMENDED
Rubbermaid 13.5-inch High Heat Scraper
$13.95
Long, rigid handle is great for leverage and firm, thin-edged blade is great for scraping. Just don't leave it in the sauce.

HIGHLY RECOMMENDED
Le Creuset Heatproof 13-inch (Large) Spatula
$12.50
Wooden handle is rigid but slightly less comfortable than thicker, more rounded plastic handles. Also, blade edge is slightly thicker and more blunt than is ideal. The abuse champ of the group.

HIGHLY RECOMMENDED
KitchenAid Silicone Mixing Spatula
$9.99
Handle was fine for many testers, but too bulky for some. Long blade reached into deep bowls, but motivated some staffers to refer to this spatula as "the oar."

HIGHLY RECOMMENDED
Oxo Good Grips Silicone Turner Spatula
$8.99
Performed well, but the handle grip aroused controversy. Some testers felt it forced their hand into the wrong position; others were not bothered by it.

RECOMMENDED WITH RESERVATIONS
Pyrex Professional All Purpose Spatula—Silicone Head
$5.99
This would be a great spatula if it weren't for the sharp, midhandle protrusion Pyrex calls a bowl rest. It's possible, though, to place fingers around it and march on.

RECOMMENDED WITH RESERVATIONS
J.A. Henckels Rubber Spatula
$5.99
Not quite as efficient for folding as those spatulas with large blades, but otherwise fine. No real advantage to the deeply curved shape of the blade.

NOT RECOMMENDED
Cuisipro Silicone Spatula
$13.95
Pointed blade gets into the corners of a saucepan but is too small to fold very efficiently. Stainless steel handle looks and feels good, but don't tap it too hard the rim of a ceramic or glass mixing bowl.

NOT RECOMMENDED
Rösle 12.5-Inch Silicone Spatula
$19.00
Large blade would be great if it weren't rendered almost useless by a torturous handle, which is an example of how high style can fail no-nonsense cooks.

NOT RECOMMENDED
Oneida Silicone Head Spatula
$1.99
Flexible handle offers no leverage against stiff mixtures. Forget about most heavy-duty tasks with the Gumby-handle.

NOT RECOMMENDED
Farberware Classic Series 2 Piece Spoon Spatula Set
$5.99
Blade is much too flexible to scrape nearly any type of mixture very efficiently. Short handle can lead to sticky hands.

10 models by leaving them in a pan of tomato sauce cooking over medium-high heat for an hour. None of them showed significant heat damage. The silicone may be more heat resistant, but in normal, everyday cooking, rubber spatulas are unlikely to melt.

The tomato sauce test pointed out another problem with spatulas—staining and odor absorption. On this front, we have bad news to report. Even after multiple trips through the dishwasher, every spatula—whether made from rubber or silicone—was still stained and smelled of tomato.

A poorly designed handle turned out to be the Achilles heel of several otherwise good spatulas. In fact, several of the handles were so bad as to be considered fatal flaws—reason enough not to buy the spatula.

When testing was complete, the two traits we came to prize in spatula handles were rigidity and comfort. Handles that were too flexible, like those on the Oneida and Farberware models, bent when we dug into a batch of cookie dough, thus pushing our patience more than the dough. Stiff handles provided more leverage, which translates into much more efficient scraping, folding, and stirring.

No matter what the task, it was always more pleasant to use a spatula with a comfortable handle. The key here was simplicity of design. The Rubbermaid and Le Creuset spatulas, for example, had straight handles with rounded edges that were comfortable for all testers. Handles with sharp bowl rests, odd grips, or uncomfortable shapes (such as those made from stainless steel wire) were downgraded.

Which spatula, then, do you want in your kitchen? If you are going to buy only one spatula, go for one with a large, relatively stiff blade (preferably with a thin edge) and a rigid, rounded handle. Taken together, these factors can make your next trip through a batch of egg white foam or down the sides of a mixing bowl filled with chocolate chip cookie dough as efficient and comfortable as can be.

EQUIPMENT CORNER: Spoonulas

TRULY A FUSION UTENSIL IF EVER THERE WAS ONE, THE spoonula, as some manufacturers call it, is a spoon/spatula hybrid that marries the concave shape of a spoon with the material and overall form of a spatula. But to what effect, we wondered? The answer, it turned out, depends on whom you ask. Every day in the test kitchen we use both spatulas and spoonulas by the dozen, and we tested four spoonulas (Pyrex, Oneida, Le Creuset, and Farberware) along with our lineup of spatulas for this article.

Spoonula detractors make two main claims. The first is that the mixture you are stirring, scraping, or folding sticks in the shallow bowl of the blade and is difficult to remove. Others among us do not find that to be the case. Sticky mixtures show no preference for one utensil over the other; they stick to spatulas and spoonulas equally. The second claim is that spoonulas do not fold as well as spatulas, again because the mixture sticks in the depression of the blade, thereby creating drag. Although many tests cooks were unable to detect excess drag during the folding tests, several test cooks were adamant that a thinner, flatter blade is better suited to gliding through a delicate mixture—to their minds, a spoonula is a blunt instrument.

Several test cooks noted that they use the two utensils differently, choosing a regular spatula for folding and scraping batters and egg whites and using a spoonula in place of a wooden spoon to stir simmering sauces, soups, and stews. Most spoonula blades are broader than the heads of many wooden spoons, so they are more efficient at moving the mixture being stirred.

Our recommendation is simple. A spoonula is really a replacement for a wooden spoon. For folding, we feel that a spatula is the better instrument.

With eager anticipation, Chris watches Julia as she puts the finishing touch—a light dusting of confectioners' sugar—on her German apple pancake.

THE PANCAKE show

Few recipes deliver so much pleasure for so little work as pancakes. The batter comes together in minutes, and the cooking time is brief. Why, then, do most Americans never make pancakes from scratch? Frozen pancakes, with their cardboard-like texture and dull flavor to match, are the standard offering in most homes. Pancake mixes yield slightly better results than frozen products, but it hardly takes more time to measure your own flour, salt, and leavener.

The test kitchen decided to develop two great recipes that would tempt even die-hard microwavers to make pancakes from scratch. Our recipes for blueberry pancakes and German apple pancake rely on ingredients you likely already have on hand. Once you've tasted the real thing, we doubt you'll ever buy frozen pancakes or packaged mixes again.

BLUEBERRY PANCAKES

WHAT WE WANTED: Fluffy, flavorful pancakes that were easy to make at any time of the year.

Plain old pancakes may be a dime a dozen, but when it comes to blueberry pancakes, we say stack 'em high and bring on the maple syrup. When perfect, they're light and fluffy, sweet and tangy, and studded with juicy bursts of summer's best berry. Unfortunately, most blueberry pancakes are either are so tough and rubbery that they snap back and smack you in the face or are so cottony and tasteless that they must be accompanied by a very tall glass of milk. As for the blueberries—well, those sweet little berries leak into the batter without fail. The result? A gray, marbled pancake.

We decided to remedy this problem once and for all and began by cooking up a big stack of pancake recipes. The test kitchen came to a few conclusions. One: We like our pancakes tender and fluffy. Two: A good blueberry pancake starts with a great pancake. Three: Even though we were after the best blueberry pancake, we wanted to avoid any nonsensical techniques or ingredients that required a jaunt to the grocery store, especially given that we would likely be making these pancakes early in the morning, with only one eye open and one cup of coffee running through our veins.

Before we even thought about blueberries, we wanted to get the pancake part out of the way. First up was flour, and because this no-nonsense recipe would not put up with a blend of flours, we pitted cake flour, bleached all-purpose flour, and unbleached all-purpose flour against one another. The pancake made with cake flour lacked structure, and the flour gave the pancake a strange, chemical taste. The pancake made with bleached all-purpose flour had a similar "off" flavor, so unbleached flour—usually the test kitchen standard—was the winner.

Sugar was next, and the question was not whether to add but how much. We like pancakes on the sweet side. Starting at 1 teaspoon of sugar, we worked our way up until tasters cried "enough" at 2 tablespoons. As for leavener, we were hoping to use just baking powder, but, sure enough, tasters preferred the golden brown color that baking soda provided, so in the end we had to use them both. Two teaspoons of baking powder and ½ teaspoon of baking soda did the job. Finally, a little salt went in to make everything taste better.

In most pancake recipes, the dry ingredients are measured out, and the wet ingredients, such as eggs, melted butter, and dairy (usually milk or buttermilk), are added to the dry ingredients. Most recipes call for 2 eggs per 2 cups of flour, but tasters unanimously found these cakes to be too eggy. Using an egg and a fraction thereof (one whole egg plus one egg yolk) was too fussy for our recipe, so we simply used one egg. What about butter—was it truly necessary? One quick test later we found the answer to be an emphatic yes. Without butter, the pancakes were more evenly colored (no spots of scorched butter), but they had the cottony interior that we just couldn't stomach. In went 3 tablespoons of melted butter, and everyone was happy.

As for the dairy, we tested milk and buttermilk and also threw half-and-half into the mix to see what would happen. To no one's surprise, buttermilk took first place. This tangy, thick liquid produced a pancake with great flavor and beat-all fluffiness. But to be true to our "rule number three," we couldn't pretend that buttermilk would be found on most people's lists of basic pantry ingredients. We needed a substitute.

A quick search on the Internet led us to a few buttermilk impostors, usually a little white distilled vinegar, cream of tartar, or lemon juice stirred into regular milk, then left to sit for a few minutes to thicken. This faux buttermilk method mimics the effects of the modern process of making buttermilk, which is produced by injecting milk with acidic bacterial cultures. The cultures not only give buttermilk that characteristic tang, but they also thicken it. When we compared the buttermilk pancakes with pancakes made

with the lemon and milk mixture, we were surprised to find that those made with lemon juice had a tang that was similar to that provided by the buttermilk ("sour" was the word for those made with vinegar or cream of tartar). Even more surprising was that tasters preferred the pancakes made with lemon juice and whole milk over those made with buttermilk. One tablespoon of lemon juice per 2 cups of milk was the right amount. After allowing the mixture to sit for a few minutes, it thickened to a consistency much like that of buttermilk. (If you have buttermilk on hand, however, go ahead and use it.)

We had a good idea that overmixing was likely to produce a tough, rubbery pancake. Boy, were we right. When we whisked the batter until no lumps of flour were detectable, the pancakes were tough. We cannot emphasize enough that a less thorough mixing is needed here, just until the ingredients are blended. A few lumps or streaks of flour here and there, and you know that you've done it correctly.

OK. We had a great pancake recipe. But what about those berries? We found that the size of the berry really mattered. If possible, choose small, fresh, wild blueberries; they are much sweeter than their bigger blueberry cousins. We also found that if you can't find good blueberries in the produce section, you should head right for the frozen foods. One particular brand of frozen blueberries, Wyman's, tasted nearly as good as (and in some cases better than) fresh berries. If you keep a stash of frozen blueberries on hand, you're always ready to make these pancakes.

Now, how to avoid those mottled berry pancakes. Stirring the berries into the batter proved unsuccessful for two reasons. One, no matter how carefully we stirred, a few berries would invariably break and produce blue-gray pancakes. Two, extra stirring was a no-no; the more we stirred, the tougher the pancake. The best method was simply to ladle out some batter onto the hot skillet, then scatter a handful of berries on top.

And speaking of skillet, we wasted a couple of cups of batter using a regular skillet. No matter how well we oiled the pan (butter scorched every time), the pancakes would stick and the blueberries would rip open. Do yourself a favor and use a nonstick skillet.

So there they were. Fluffy, tender, flavorful, and very simple blueberry pancakes, without a broken berry in sight. Good enough to eat without maple syrup, you ask? Sure, but why on earth would you want to do that?

WHAT WE LEARNED: Use a mixture of lemon juice and milk to create that buttermilk tang without having to run out to the store. Leave a few streaks of flour in the batter; if you mix more, the pancakes will be tough. Add small wild berries directly to the pancakes in the skillet, not to the batter, to keep them from dying everything blue.

BLUEBERRY PANCAKES

Makes about sixteen 4-inch pancakes, serving 4 to 6

When local blueberries are not in season, frozen blueberries are a better alternative (see the Tasting Lab on page 274). To make sure that frozen berries do not bleed, rinse them under cool water in a mesh strainer until the water runs clear, and then spread them on a paper towel–lined plate to dry. If you have buttermilk on hand, use 2 cups instead of the milk and lemon juice. To keep pancakes warm while cooking the remaining batter, see the tip at right.

  1 tablespoon juice from 1 lemon
  2 cups milk
  2 cups (10 ounces) unbleached all-purpose flour
  2 tablespoons sugar
  2 teaspoons baking powder
½ teaspoon baking soda
½ teaspoon salt
  1 large egg
  3 tablespoons unsalted butter, melted and cooled slightly
1–2 teaspoons vegetable oil
  1 cup fresh or frozen blueberries, preferably wild, rinsed and dried (see note)

1. Whisk the lemon juice and milk in a medium bowl or large measuring cup; set aside to thicken while preparing the other ingredients. Whisk the flour, sugar, baking powder, baking soda, and salt in a medium bowl to combine.

2. Whisk the egg and melted butter into the milk until combined. Make a well in the center of the dry ingredients in the bowl; pour in the milk mixture and whisk very gently until just combined (a few lumps should remain). Do not overmix.

3. Heat a 12-inch nonstick skillet over medium heat for 3 to 5 minutes (see the photos on page 273 for tips on gauging when the pan is properly heated); add 1 teaspoon oil and brush to coat the skillet bottom evenly. Pour ¼ cup batter onto 3 spots on the skillet; sprinkle 1 tablespoon blueberries over each pancake. Cook the pancakes until large bubbles begin to appear, 1½ to 2 minutes. Using a thin, wide spatula, flip the pancakes and cook until golden brown on second side, 1 to 1½ minutes longer. Serve immediately, and repeat with the remaining batter, using the remaining vegetable oil only if necessary.

VARIATION

LEMON-CORNMEAL BLUEBERRY PANCAKES

Follow the recipe for Blueberry Pancakes, adding 2 teaspoons grated lemon zest to the milk along with the lemon juice and substituting 1½ cups stone-ground yellow cornmeal for 1 cup flour.

GETTING IT RIGHT:
Keeping Pancakes Warm

A large skillet can turn out only three pancakes at a time, so if you want everyone to eat at the same time, you must keep the first few batches warm. After testing various methods in cookbooks (most of which suggest covering the pancakes, causing them to become steamed and rubbery), we discovered that pancakes will hold for 20 minutes when placed on a greased rack set on a baking sheet in a 200-degree oven. The warm oven keeps the pancakes hot enough to melt a pat of butter, and leaving the pancakes uncovered prevents them from becoming soggy.

EQUIPMENT CORNER:
Electric Griddles

WITH COUNTERTOP REAL ESTATE SO VALUABLE, WE'RE wary about buying "extra" appliances, such as an electric griddle. But after standing in front of what must have been our 40th batch of blueberry pancakes, we gave electric griddles a second thought. Many electric griddles have a bigger cooking surface than even a large 12-inch skillet (which will fit only three pancakes at a time comfortably). The possible payoff—less time cooking—was too good to resist.

We bought the four largest models we could find. They were seemingly identical: All had an electric probe with an indicator light that turned off when the selected temperature was reached, all were fully immersible or dishwasher-safe (except for the electric probe control), all were made of cast aluminum with a nonstick coating, all had a hole or channel so that excess fat would drain into a removable grease tray. After heating each griddle to 350 degrees, we poured on the batter (each griddle fit eight pancakes at a time) and checked the pancakes for even browning. We also cooked bacon on each griddle.

The BroilKing Extra Large Griddle ($49.99), which measured a whopping 21 inches by 12 inches and was the only griddle that could comfortably hold a full pound of bacon (16 strips), was the clear winner. Good thing that it also had one of the largest grease trays. Its only downfall was the excruciating 12½ minutes it took to heat up to 350 degrees. But this could be due to the thickness of the aluminum griddle. After it reached the proper temperature, there was very little temperature fluctuation. As a result, pancakes were evenly cooked every time.

The West Bend Cool Touch Electric Griddle ($39.99) was the runner-up. The cooking surface measured 20½ inches by 10½ inches and could hold 12 strips of bacon. The West Bend heated up to 350 degrees in 6½ minutes and cooked pancakes very evenly. One minor drawback: The grease channel was slightly cumbersome to wash.

The remaining two models, the Rival Electric Griddle ($29.99) and the Presto Cool Touch Electric Griddle ($38.99), were the same size as the West Bend, and both heated up to 350 degrees in 5½ minutes. The cooking surfaces on both models heated unevenly, however, and some pancakes were lighter in color than others. Also, some of the pancakes spread out very thin because of cool spots.

Are electric griddles worth the counter space? If you find yourself making stacks of pancakes and pounds of bacon every weekend, you can't beat the speedy delivery they provide.

GETTING IT RIGHT: Is the Pan Ready?

 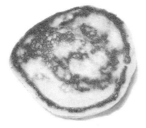

The only way to know when the pan is ready is to make a test pancake about the size of a half-dollar (use 1 tablespoon of batter). If after 1 minute the pancake is blond in color (left), the pan is not hot enough. If after 1 minute the pancake is golden brown, the pan is heated correctly. Speeding up the process by heating the pan at a higher temperature will result in a dark, unevenly cooked pancake (right).

BEST ELECTRIC GRIDDLE
The BroilKing griddle took top honors in our testing, in part because it is so big. It also demonstrated even browning, without any of the cool spots that plagued two other models.

soda. Gluten is a mix of very long proteins that are disorganized in structure. Once gluten is dissolved in water, these proteins can more easily rearrange their structure. Kneading or mixing gluten elongates the proteins and somewhat organizes them, an action similar to combing the strands of your hair. As the proteins start to lie more or less parallel to each other, the dough becomes elastic and less tender. By reducing the mixing time of your batter, you give the gluten less opportunity to organize.

Baking soda (either on its own or as part of the baking powder formula) creates the bubbles that make pancakes rise. When baking soda encounters an acid, carbon dioxide is formed to produce the bubbles in the batter. The stirring of the pancake batter speeds bubble formation by moving the baking soda and acid together. Unfortunately, stirring also causes the release of carbon dioxide gas by bringing formed bubbles to the surface of the mixture. Just a little too much stirring and the bubble-forming capacity of the baking soda will be quickly exhausted. To make the fluffiest pancakes possible, then, you should stir the batter until the ingredients are just incorporated—and not one stir more!

TASTING LAB: Blueberries

WHEN LOCAL BERRIES ARE NOT IN SEASON, WHAT KIND of blueberries should you buy? Should you rely on fresh berries imported from South America (often at a cost of $5 for a dry half-pint container) or frozen berries? If you choose the latter, should you pick cultivated or wild frozen berries? And what about price? A January cobbler that costs $25 seems, well, silly. Likewise, spending $5 on berries for pancakes seems excessive.

During the winter, the test kitchen tried fresh berries from Chile as well as five frozen brands. Easily beating the fresh imported berries as well as the other frozen contenders were Wyman's frozen wild berries. (Compared with cultivated berries, wild berries are smaller, more intense in color, firmer in texture, and more sweet and tangy in flavor.) The

SCIENCE DESK:
Why Does Lumpy Pancake Batter Produce Fluffier Pancakes?

THERE ARE TWO FACTORS THAT PROMOTE FLUFFINESS IN pancake batter, underdeveloped gluten and dissolved baking

Rating Blueberries

NINE MEMBERS OF THE *COOK'S ILLUSTRATED* STAFF TRIED FIVE KINDS OF BLUEBERRIES COOKED IN A SIMPLE COMPOTE to compare their flavor. (Because many of these berries were frozen, we were not concerned with texture, although juiciness was a consideration.) The brands are listed below in order of preference. All brands are available in supermarkets nationwide.

HIGHLY RECOMMENDED
Wyman's Frozen Wild Blueberries
$2.19 for 12 ounces

These small blueberries were intense in color and flavor, with a pleasing balance of sweetness and tang and a clean, fresh berry finish.

RECOMMENDED
Fresh (South American) Blueberries
$5.00 for 4 ounces

Nice, plump berries lacked that "picked at peak ripeness" sweet flavor you get with local fresh berries. However, these out-of-season berries were still sweet and juicy, with a nice level of tartness. But look at the price.

RECOMMENDED
Cascadian Farms 100% Organic Frozen Blueberries
$3.79 for 10 ounces

This mix of berries contains several varieties, including one that is "wild." The berries had the tart punch characteristic of wild berries and a pleasant "jammy" sweetness.

RECOMMENDED WITH RESERVATIONS
365 Grade A Fancy Frozen Blueberries
$2.99 for 16 ounces

These cultivated berries were very sweet, with just a hint of tartness. Compared with the other brands of frozen berries, they lacked complexity.

NOT RECOMMENDED
Shaw's Individually Quick Frozen Whole Blueberries
$2.59 for 16 ounces

Of all the frozen berries tasted, this supermarket brand was the most disappointing. The berries were watery, bland, and flat tasting, with a mushy consistency.

---

fresh imported berries tied for second place with Cascadian Farms frozen berries, which includes a mix of cultivated and wild berries. Frozen cultivated berries trailed in the tasting.

Flavor aside, the average cost of these frozen berries is $8 for a small cobbler versus the above-mentioned $25 for the fresh South American berries. You could make three cobblers using the frozen berries for that price, and the money would also buy you better quality.

Why did the frozen wild blueberries beat the fresh imported berries? Well, the imported berries are picked before they have a chance to fully ripen to help them survive the long trip north. As a result, they are often tart and not so flavorful. Frozen blueberries have been picked at the peak time—when perfectly ripe—and are then put through a cleaning and sanitation process before being sent to the freezer tunnel, where they are individually quick frozen (IQF) at a temperature of minus 20 degrees. The quick freezing preserves their sweetness, making it possible to enjoy them year-round—and at a price that even a humble test cook can afford.

GERMAN APPLE PANCAKE

WHAT WE WANTED: This Old World classic combines the best qualities of a popover and a pancake. Could we make a version that had both great apple flavor and perfect puff-pancake texture?

Started on the stove and finished in the oven, German apple pancakes (similar to puff pancakes, Panaküchen, and Dutch babies) bear little resemblance to their American cousin, fluffy flapjacks. Unlike the American version, which owes its cakelike texture to baking powder or baking soda, the German pancake has more in common with a popover, getting its dramatic rise from eggs and a hot oven. A German apple pancake is also prone to the same pitfalls as a popover: insufficient rise, leaden texture, and too much egg flavor. The perfect German apple pancake should have crisp, lighter-than-air edges and a custard-like center, with buttery sautéed apples baked right into the batter.

We started our research by going to a local diner chain known for its German apple pancake. The dinner plate–sized version arrived at the table sparsely scattered with pale pieces of apple and dusted with confectioners' sugar. We tasted it. The pancake had little flavor, and the apples were soggy, blond, and bland. We knew that the test kitchen could do better.

German pancake batter is composed of three main ingredients: flour, eggs, and liquid (usually milk). We began by experimenting with different types of liquid, making pancakes with half-and-half, heavy cream, and a combination of sour cream and milk. The pancake made with heavy cream was leaden and flat, while the sour cream/milk version had a strange, tart flavor. Half-and-half turned out to be the perfect solution. It has just enough butterfat to give the pancake a rich flavor without sacrificing the texture. After trying various ratios of half-and-half, eggs, and flour, we found that a combination of two eggs, ⅔ cup half-and-half,

and ½ cup all-purpose flour made a nicely puffed pancake. The addition of a little sugar, salt, and vanilla gave it just the right balance of flavors.

The next step was to find the perfect oven temperature. Like a popover, this pancake relies on steam (instead of chemical leavening) for its explosive rise. Because the batter is poured into a preheated pan and placed immediately into a hot oven, the surfaces of the batter set first. While in the oven, the liquid in the batter turns to steam, creating pockets of air that cause the pancake to rise, much like an inflating balloon. We tried baking the pancake at 400, 425, and 450 degrees. The pancake baked at 400 degrees never rose high enough, and even at 450 degrees the airy texture we were looking for was lacking. In desperation, we cranked up the temperature to 500 degrees. It puffed spectacularly, but both the bottom and top of the pancake were charred. We tried preheating the oven to 500 degrees and lowering it to a more moderate 425 degrees when the pancake went into the oven. The initial high heat gave the batter the quick rise it needed, and the more moderate heat cooked the pancake to perfection.

Now that the pancake was rising so dramatically, the expanding batter was pushing some of the apples out of the pan and onto the oven floor. To solve this problem, we poured the batter around the perimeter of the pan first, then over the apples. This ring of batter along the edge of the pan, which added a cushion between the apple slices and the pan, kept the apples from jumping ship.

Our next task was to figure out how to cook the apples. Apples cooked with granulated sugar were sweet but flat tasting, while those cooked with either light or dark brown sugar were fabulous. When the light brown sugar combined with the butter and apples, it made a great sauce that enhanced the apples' clean flavor. Dark brown sugar did the same, producing a slightly smokier caramel with molasses highlights. Adding a little cinnamon and some

lemon juice made the apples at once earthy and bright. We tried other apple-friendly spices (nutmeg, allspice, and cloves), but they all made the apple pancake taste like apple pie. Not bad, but not what we were going for. As for the size of the apple slices, we found that cutting the apples into ½-inch-thick pieces kept them from getting mushy during cooking.

Our last task was to figure out which kind of apple to use. We chose 10 widely available varieties and made pancakes with each. The pancake made with Golden Delicious—the first choice of many bakers—was liked for its simple fruity character, though some tasters found it cloyingly sweet. Empires, Southern Roses, and Royal Galas didn't have enough apple flavor to stand up to the brown sugar, and both McIntosh and Red Delicious became too soft when sautéed. Fujis were sweet but tasted more like pears than apples. Tasters unanimously disliked the pancake

made with Red Romes; these apples were bitter and dry and had a texture that reminded one taster of cardboard. With their perfect balance of sweetness and tartness, Granny Smith apples were the favorite. Braeburns were also liked; they were more sugary-sweet, with just the slightest hint of lemony brightness.

Inverted onto a serving platter and covered with a snowy dusting of confectioners' sugar (and a generous drizzle of maple syrup or caramel sauce), this German apple pancake was ideal.

WHAT WE LEARNED: Use half-and-half in the batter for a rich flavor and a light texture. For maximum rise without burning the edges, preheat the pan in a 500-degree oven, add the batter to the hot pan, and then reduce the oven temperature to 425 degrees. As for the apples, use Granny Smiths and cook them with brown sugar for the best flavor.

GERMAN APPLE PANCAKE Serves 4

A 10-inch ovenproof skillet is necessary for this recipe; we highly recommend using a nonstick skillet for the sake of easy cleanup, but a regular skillet will work. You can also use a cast-iron pan; if you do, set the oven temperature to 425 degrees in step 1, and when cooking the apples in step 3, cook them only until just barely golden, about 6 minutes. Cast iron retains heat better than stainless steel, making the higher oven temperature unnecessary. If you prefer tart apples, use Granny Smiths; if you prefer sweet ones, use Braeburns. For serving, dust the apple pancake with confectioners' sugar and pass warm maple syrup or Caramel Sauce (recipe follows) separately, if desired.

½ cup (2½ ounces) unbleached all-purpose flour
1 tablespoon granulated sugar
½ teaspoon salt
2 large eggs
⅔ cup half-and-half
1 teaspoon vanilla extract
2 tablespoons unsalted butter
1¼ pounds Granny Smith or Braeburn apples (3 to 4 large apples), peeled, quartered, cored, and cut into ½-inch-thick slices
¼ cup packed light or dark brown sugar
¼ teaspoon ground cinnamon
1 teaspoon lemon juice from 1 lemon
Confectioners' sugar for dusting
Maple syrup or Caramel Sauce for serving

1. Adjust an oven rack to the upper-middle position and heat the oven to 500 degrees.

2. Whisk to combine the flour, granulated sugar, and salt in a medium bowl. In a second medium bowl, whisk the eggs, half-and-half, and vanilla until combined. Add the liquid ingredients to the dry ingredients and whisk until no lumps remain, about 20 seconds; set the batter aside.

3. Heat the butter in a 10-inch ovenproof nonstick skillet over medium-high heat until sizzling. Add the apples, brown sugar, and cinnamon; cook, stirring frequently with a heatproof rubber spatula, until the apples are golden brown, about 10 minutes. Off heat, stir in the lemon juice.

4. Working quickly, pour the batter around the edge of the pan and then over the apples. Place the skillet in the oven and immediately reduce the oven temperature to 425 degrees. Bake until the pancake edges are brown and puffy and have risen above the edges of the skillet, about 18 minutes.

5. Using oven mitts to protect your hands, remove the hot skillet from the oven and loosen the pancake edges with a

---

GETTING IT RIGHT:
Choosing the Right Apple

MCINTOSH APPLES
These apples collapse when cooked and are the wrong choice for German apple pancake.

GRANNY SMITH APPLES
These apples keep their shape when cooked and are a better choice for German apple pancake.

heatproof rubber spatula; invert the pancake onto a serving platter. Dust with confectioners' sugar, cut into wedges, and serve with syrup or Caramel Sauce.

CARAMEL SAUCE Makes about 1 ½ cups

To prevent undissolved sugar crystals from marring the sauce, we prefer to cook the sugar with some water in a covered pot. The trapped moisture ensures that the sugar will dissolve. Make sure to remove the cover during the final minute or two so you can monitor the progress of the sugar syrup. When the hot cream mixture is added in step 3, the hot sugar syrup will bubble vigorously (and dangerously), so don't use a smaller saucepan. If you make the caramel sauce ahead, reheat it in the microwave or a small saucepan over low heat until warm and fluid.

½	cup water
1	cup (7 ounces) granulated sugar
1	cup heavy cream
⅛	teaspoon salt
½	teaspoon vanilla extract
½	teaspoon lemon juice from 1 lemon

1. Place the water in a heavy-bottomed 2-quart saucepan; pour the sugar in the center of the pan, taking care not to let the sugar crystals adhere to the sides of the pan. Cover and bring the mixture to a boil over high heat; once boiling, uncover and continue to boil until the sugar syrup is thick and straw-colored (it should register 300 degrees on a candy thermometer), about 7 minutes. Reduce the heat to medium and continue to cook until the syrup is deep amber (it should register 350 degrees on a candy thermometer), about 1 to 2 minutes.

2. Meanwhile, bring the cream and salt to a simmer in a small saucepan over high heat (if the cream boils before the sugar syrup reaches a deep amber color, remove the cream from the heat and cover to keep warm).

3. Remove the pan with the sugar syrup from the heat; very carefully pour about one quarter of hot cream into it (the mixture will bubble vigorously), and let the bubbling subside. Add the remaining cream, vanilla, and lemon juice; whisk until the sauce is smooth. (The sauce can be cooled and refrigerated in an airtight container for up to 2 weeks.)

SCIENCE DESK: Why Are Some Apples Mushy When Cooked?

AS ANYONE WHO HAS MADE APPLESAUCE OR AN APPLE PIE knows, some apple varieties are ideal for cooking while others are best eaten raw. When testing different types of apples in the German apple pancake, we found that some turned to mush in the pan while others remained toothsome, maintaining their shape and texture.

So why does this happen? The texture of an apple depends on three things: the thickness and composition of the cell walls, the amount of acid in the apple, and the amount of air between the apple cells.

The first factor is the composition of the cell walls, which are made of cellulose and are held together with pectin. The crunchier, crispier varieties (such as Granny Smith) contain more cellulose. Even before cooking, you can clearly see the difference between crunchy Granny Smith apples and softer McIntoshes. As an apple is cooked, the pectin melts and the cells fall apart. The varieties with more cellulose will remain more firm, while those with less cellulose will become softer.

The next factor is acid. Acid strengthens pectin and keeps it from dissolving so readily when heated. Naturally acidic apples, such as Granny Smiths, are thus more likely to hold their shape than other varieties.

Finally, the air. Apples have lots of air pockets between their cells (25 percent or more of their volume may consist of air), which is why they float. When apples are cooked, the air escapes and the air pockets collapse. As a result, there is a loss of firmness and volume. The less air an apple has to begin with, the firmer it will be, both before and after cooking.

Can store-bought cookie dough compare to homemade? We baked up piles of cookies to find out.

COOKIE JAR *favorites*

Good cookies don't really require any more work than bad cookies. Unless, of course, you are willing to consider dry, crumbly, tasteless packaged cookies from the supermarket—but we aren't. Although easy to prepare, most cookie recipes are notoriously fickle. A minor ingredient change or fluctuation in oven temperature can yield unexpected results. Our goal was simple: Take two favorite cookies and develop reliable recipes that taste great.

We love the buttery crunch of thin, crisp chocolate chip cookies. These aren't the soft, chewy cookies that have become all the rage in malls. These are the kind of cookies our grandmothers might have kept in a tin above the refrigerator. Almost delicate, these cookies are a study in restraint.

Macaroons may seem a bit old-fashioned, but we think few cookies can rival a well-made coconut macaroon. We wanted something that would be both rich with coconut flavor and chewy. Our macaroons would not be dry or crumbly, our macaroons would be easy to shape (no pastry bags, please), and they would be sturdy enough to withstand a partial dip in melted chocolate.

CRISP CHOCOLATE CHIP COOKIES

WHAT WE WANTED: A flat, almost praline-like cookie with plenty of crunch and packed with the flavors of butter, caramelized sugar, and chocolate.

Rich and buttery, with their soft, tender cores and crispy edges, Toll House cookies are the American cookie-jar standard. As such, they serve as the springboard for all other versions of the chocolate chip cookie. A popular variation, thin and crispy, embodies one of the Toll House cookie's textural extremes.

We could see the thin, crisp cookies clearly. They would be very flat, almost praline in appearance, and they would pack a big crunch without either breaking teeth or shattering into a million pieces when eaten. They'd have the simple, gratifying flavors of deeply caramelized sugar and rich butter, along with agreeable amounts of salt and vanilla. The chips—always tender and super-chocolatey—would not overwhelm but leave plenty of room for enjoyment of the surrounding cookie. Finally, these cookies would be resilient enough for pantry storage and worthy of five consecutive appearances in a school lunchbox.

To get our bearings, we first surveyed a handful of recipes for thin and crispy chocolate chip cookies, taking inventory of the ingredient lists and ratios. We were hoping to find the key to what might make these cookies thinner and crispier than the classic Toll House. Our collection of test recipes featured the same basic ingredients—butter, flour, sugar, flavorings, and chocolate chips—but widely varying ratios and yields. As a result, the cookies were all quite different when baked. While all of the cookies tasted good, tasters were dissatisfied with the various textures, which they found too brittle, too crumbly, too dense, or too greasy. Believe it or not, we were pleased with the mixed reactions. The ingredients we had to work with held promise; we just needed to understand the role of each one and tweak the proportions to arrive at a cookie with the texture we wanted.

Whether chewy or crispy, nearly all chocolate chip cookies contain a mixture of granulated and brown sugars. Aside from contributing sweetness, sugar also affects the texture, flavor, and color of the cookies. Doughs high in granulated sugar yield crispy cookies. As the cookies cool, the sugar crystallizes and the cookies harden. Brown sugar is quite different from granulated. It contains 35 percent more moisture and is also more hygroscopic (that is, it more readily absorbs moisture from the atmosphere). Consequently, cookies made with brown sugar come out of the oven tender and pliable and often soften further as they stand. These characteristics were the opposite of what we were looking for. Nevertheless, we knew the recipe had to include some brown sugar, because it alone is responsible for the irresistible butterscotch flavor we associate with chocolate chip cookies.

With this understanding, we went on to test various proportions of sugar. Too much granulated sugar produced cookies with no butterscotch flavor. Too much brown sugar produced cookies that were delicious but too soft. Desperate to retain the flavor of the brown sugar, we shifted from dark brown to light brown. Light brown sugar, we knew, had the potential to crisp the cookies because it contains half the molasses—and therefore less moisture—than dark brown sugar does. But we were skeptical because its flavor is weaker. We needn't have worried; the cookies were much improved, producing a flavor that fully satisfied tasters. After a little more tinkering, we settled on 1/3 cup light brown sugar and 1/2 cup granulated sugar, yielding cookies with a notable butterscotch flavor and sufficient crunch.

Satisfied with the crispness of the cookies, we turned our attention to their thickness. Throughout earlier testing, we hadn't been totally happy with the way the cookies spread in the oven. They were never as thin as we wanted them to be. This was important not just for appearance' sake

but because we had noticed that the flatter the cookies were, the more delicate and tender they became; we wanted them crisp, without being tough.

After some research, we returned to the kitchen armed with the understanding that a cookie's spread is determined largely by the type, treatment, and melting properties of fat in the dough. Butter, which is key in this recipe, has both a low melting point and outstanding flavor. Initial test recipes advised creaming butter and sugar, but we noticed that cookies made with this technique came out of the oven with a slight lift. We were certain that creaming was the culprit.

When butter and sugar are creamed, rigid sugar crystals cut into the butterfat and create air cells. As the remaining ingredients are incorporated into the airy mixture, the air cells get locked up in the dough and capture moisture from the butter (and other ingredients) as it vaporizes in the oven. The cells expand, and the cookies rise. Our other option, melting the butter, was much more successful. Because melted butter, unlike creamed, does not accommodate air cells, the moisture from various ingredients has nowhere to go except out. Working our way down from 12 tablespoons, we found that the cookies spread evenly and effortlessly at 8 tablespoons (one stick) of melted butter. To get them thinner still, we added a couple of tablespoons of

milk to the dough. The cookies were flatter than pancakes.

Having spent all of our time thus far perfecting the cookies' texture and spread, we were surprised to notice that they were looking slightly pallid and dull. The light brown sugar we had introduced to the recipe was the problem: It has less browning power than dark brown sugar. Knowing that corn syrup browns at a lower temperature than sugar, we tried adding a few tablespoons. As it happened, the corn syrup made the surface of the cookies shiny and crackly. Despite their new spiffy, dressed-up look, though, they remained a little pale. We rectified the situation by adding a bit of baking soda, which enhances browning reactions in doughs. With only a few tests at various amounts, the cookies went from washed out to a beautiful deep golden brown.

Finally, after a few last-minute adjustments to the amount of salt and vanilla, we turned a full recipe of the finished dough onto two parchment-lined baking sheets and tested baking times and temperatures. Much to our disappointment, these cookies did not spread properly and were slightly chewy. After a few batches, we found that these cookies, like Greta Garbo, wanted to be alone, baked one sheet at a time. In 12 uninterrupted minutes at 375 degrees, they spread, flattened, caramelized, and cooled into thin, crispy, and delicious chocolate chip cookies.

Now we just had to find out if these cookies had staying power. We stored a batch in an airtight container for a week to test their longevity. After the wait, tasters gathered to give them a final critique. The cookies were still a hit, as crisp and flavorful as they had been on day one. In fact, some commented that the crunch had improved with time.

WHAT WE LEARNED: Use melted butter and milk to make a batter that will spread in the oven. Add a bit of corn syrup for a nice sheen and baking soda for better browning. Finally, bake the cookies one sheet at time to achieve maximum crispness.

THIN, CRISPY CHOCOLATE CHIP COOKIES

Makes about forty 2-inch cookies

The dough, en masse or shaped into balls and wrapped well, can be refrigerated up to 2 days or frozen up to 1 month. Be sure to bring it to room temperature before baking.

1½	cups (7½ ounces) unbleached all-purpose flour
¾	teaspoon baking soda
¼	teaspoon salt
8	tablespoons (1 stick) unsalted butter, melted and cooled
½	cup (3½ ounces) granulated sugar
⅓	cup packed (2¾ ounces) light brown sugar
2	tablespoons light corn syrup
1	large egg yolk
2	tablespoons milk
1	tablespoon vanilla extract
¾	cup (4½ ounces) semisweet chocolate chips

1. Adjust an oven rack to the middle position and heat the oven to 375 degrees. Line two baking sheets with parchment paper.

2. Whisk the flour, baking soda, and salt in a medium bowl until thoroughly combined; set aside.

3. In the bowl of a standing mixer fitted with the paddle attachment, beat the melted butter, granulated sugar, light brown sugar, and corn syrup at low speed until thoroughly blended, about 1 minute. Add the yolk, milk, and vanilla; mix until fully incorporated and smooth, about 1 minute, scraping the bottom and sides of the bowl with a rubber spatula as necessary. With the mixer running on low speed, slowly add the dry ingredients and mix until just combined. Do not overbeat. Add the chips and mix on low speed until distributed evenly throughout the batter, about 5 seconds.

4. Leaving about 2 inches between each ball, scoop the dough onto the parchment-lined baking sheets with a 1¼-inch (1 tablespoon capacity) ice cream scoop. Bake, one sheet at a time, until the cookies are deep golden brown and flat, about 12 minutes.

5. Cool the cookies on the baking sheet for 3 minutes. Using a wide metal spatula, transfer the cookies to a wire rack and let sit until crisped and cooled to room temperature.

TASTING LAB:
Refrigerator Cookie Dough

TAKE A WALK DOWN THE REFRIGERATOR AISLE OF YOUR local supermarket and you'll be amazed at the plethora of options for cookie lovers. Ready-to-bake cookie dough comes in a variety of shapes and sizes, dotted with everything from traditional chocolate chips to pink and purple flowers. The commercials for these products promise just-like-homemade cookies with almost no effort—just slice and bake, or, with many of the newer cookies, just break and

---

TECHNIQUE: Softening Brown Sugar

To bring hardened brown sugar back to life, place a cup or so of it in a glass pie plate or bowl, cover with a small piece of waxed paper, then top with a slice of bread to provide a bit of moisture. Loosely cover the pie plate or bowl with plastic wrap and microwave until softened, about 30 seconds.

Rating Refrigerator Cookie Dough

FIFTEEN MEMBERS OF THE *COOK'S ILLUSTRATED* STAFF TASTED EIGHT BRANDS OF READY-TO-BAKE CHOCOLATE CHIP cookie dough sold in supermarket refrigerator cases. All of the cookies were baked according to the package instructions. The cookie doughs are listed in order of preference based on scores in this test. All brands are sold in supermarkets.

RECOMMENDED WITH RESERVATIONS

Nestlé Toll House Break & Bake Chocolate Chip Cookies **$3.19 for 18 ounces**

Though the most processed of the bunch, these cookies were praised for their "good flavor and texture" and for being "not too sweet." Long list of unrecognizable ingredients, plus molasses, eggs, margarine, and cornstarch.

RECOMMENDED WITH RESERVATIONS

600-Lb. Gorillas Chocolate Chip Cookie Dough Balls **$3.99 for 18 ounces**

This brand, available only in the Northeast, was deemed "deliciously chocolatey," though some thought it had a "weird aftertaste." Made with just flour, chocolate, butter, brown sugar, oil, water, eggs, salt, and baking soda.

RECOMMENDED WITH RESERVATIONS

Mrs. Fields Semi-Sweet Chocolate Chip Cookie Dough **$5.19 for 16 ounces**

Many tasters praised these cookies because they were "not overly sweet." Though this cookie is ubiquitous in malls, distribution of the frozen dough is limited. Made with chocolate chips, flour, butter, sugar, brown sugar, eggs, vanilla, salt, and baking soda.

RECOMMENDED WITH RESERVATIONS

Tom's Chocolate Chip Cookie Dough **$3.69 for 16 ounces**

Many tasters liked these "buttery" cookies, noting that the "flavor tastes almost homemade." Others, however, found them "dry and ugly." Made with wheat flour, chocolate chips, brown sugar, sugar, butter, eggs, whole oats, baking powder, vanilla, and salt.

NOT RECOMMENDED

Pillsbury Ready-to-Bake Chocolate Chip Cookies **$2.50 for 18 ounces**

Most tasters rejected these processed, preformed cookies as "artificial tasting" and "too sweet." Among their long list of mostly unrecognizable ingredients were partially hydrogenated vegetable oil, molasses, eggs, sodium aluminum phosphate, and nut flours (peanut, walnut, and macadamia nut).

NOT RECOMMENDED

Pillsbury Chocolate Chip Cookies (log) **$2.99 for 18 ounces**

There were few fans of this popular brand, which was deemed "too oily" and "bland." Another long list of unrecognizable ingredients, plus partially hydrogenated vegetable oil, molasses, and eggs.

NOT RECOMMENDED

Nestlé Toll House Chocolate Chip Cookie Dough (log) **$2.99 for 18 ounces**

Although the preformed version of this brand won the tasting, the traditional log was found to be "too greasy," with a "chemical taste." A long list of unrecognizable ingredients, plus molasses, eggs, and margarine.

NOT RECOMMENDED

Maury's Chocolate Chip Cookie Dough **$4.99 for 18 ounces**

Despite the short list of organic ingredients (just organic flour, sugar, chocolate, butter, eggs, and baking soda), this cookie from a well-known New York bakery was rejected as tasting "fake" and having an off-putting "butterscotch flavor."

bake. Do any of these cookies really deliver homemade flavor? We gathered eight popular brands of ready-to-bake chocolate chip cookies to find out.

Our selection included the traditional (Pillsbury and Nestlé Toll House logs of dough), the newfangled (Pillsbury and Nestlé Toll House portioned blocks of dough—just break and bake), the classic (Mrs. Fields), the all-natural (Maury's and Tom's), and the local start-up (600-Lb. Gorillas). Most of the cookies sampled are available nationwide, with the exception of 600-Lb. Gorillas, a brand available only in the Northeast, and Mrs. Fields, available in some, but not all, areas of the country.

Nestlé Toll House portioned cookies won the tasting, with comments ranging from "tastes sort of homemade" to "not homemade tasting at all, but good." Our last-place finisher, Maury's, which came from the local Whole Foods Market, was deemed "not very chocolatey," "way too crisp," and "greasy." So was this a matter of choosing the lesser of all evils, or can Nestlé Toll House cookies really hold a candle to homemade? Well, both.

Our *Cook's* tasters, who have eaten much more than their fair share of good and bad chocolate chip cookies (and, sadly, have the waistlines to prove it), weren't thrilled with any of the prefab cookies. Most agreed with the taster among them who picked the Toll House block cookies as his favorite but wrote, "None of them are good, though."

We realized, however, that these ready-to-bake chocolate chip cookies aren't really marketed to us, they're marketed to kids. So we brought in a dozen fifth- and sixth-graders from the Atrium School in Watertown, Mass., and asked them to taste our homemade cookie alongside the winner and loser of our ready-to-bake cookies (we didn't tell them that any of the three were homemade). Maury's again suffered a landslide loss. Toll House block cookies managed to hold their own against our homemade cookies, with votes evenly split between the two. "This cookie is not sweet enough," wrote one young taster of the Toll House block cookies, while another found them "very good in one part, OK in the other." Of our homemade cookies, one

taster (who may be looking ahead to career in food writing) wrote, "My taste buds went to heaven with a side trip to paradise." We couldn't agree more.

Why did Toll House Break & Bake cookies top our tasting? We don't know. We would have bet our money on one of the all-natural brands (the only cookies with a completely recognizable list of ingredients: flour, butter, sugar, etc.). In our mayonnaise tasting (see page 49), we discovered that taste preferences are predisposed toward the familiar, which explained why most tasters chose Hellmann's or Kraft—in short, the brand they grew up with. That could explain the results of this tasting. No matter how active our parents were in the kitchen, we probably all grew up with Nestlé Toll House morsels, either in homemade cookies or the ready-to-bake dough. Perhaps our tasters chose what was most familiar to them. Though why tasters chose Nestlé Break & Bake, which includes stabilizers like cornstarch, over the company's traditional log of dough, is a mystery.

Of course, for the top chocolate chip cookie, we recommend our own: They're easy to make and delicious to boot. But if you absolutely, positively must buy ready-to-bake cookies, go with the one that tasters young and not-so-young agree is the best of the lot: Nestlé Toll House Break & Bake cookies. After all, 6 out of 12 fifth- and sixth-graders can't be wrong.

COCONUT MACAROONS

WHAT WE WANTED: Most coconut macaroons are achingly sweet, sticky mounds of semicooked dough that don't taste much like coconut. We set out to make something better—much better.

Coconut macaroons are a bit like broughams. In the age of horse-pulled transport, a brougham was a light closed carriage with seating for either two or four. When Detroit got hold of this term, realizing that nobody had a clue as to what a real brougham was, they appropriated it, transforming the brougham from an elegant 19th-century conveyance into a rather pedestrian, motor-powered two-door sedan. Macaroons have undergone a similar transformation. Hundreds of years ago they were baked almond paste, and by the 19th century they had become quite elegant (and very popular) cone-shaped cookies flavored with real coconut. But today they have deteriorated into lackluster mounds of beaten egg whites and coconut shreds or, at their worst, nothing more than a baked mixture of condensed milk and sweetened coconut.

When we began looking at recipes for modern coconut macaroons, we found that they varied widely. In addition to different kinds of coconut and sweeteners, they often called for one or more of a wide range of ingredients, including extracts such as vanilla or almond, salt, flour, sugar, sweetened condensed milk, and even an egg or two (in extreme variations).

We were sure that somewhere among these second-rate cookies was a great coconut macaroon waiting to be found, with a pleasing texture and real, honest coconut flavor. We decided to find it.

The initial recipe testing included five recipes. What came out of the oven that day ranged from dense, wet cookies to light, if not dry, mounds of coconut. In the former category were recipes that used unbeaten egg whites mixed with sweetened coconut and sugar. (One of them, a Brazilian macaroon, even included whole eggs and produced a gooey, cavity-inducing cookie with a strong caramel flavor but nary a hint of coconut.) A recipe calling for beaten egg whites resulted in a light, airy, meringue-style cookie, pleasantly delicate but totally lacking in coconut flavor or chew. The test winners were simple enough: unbeaten egg whites mixed with sugar, unsweetened coconut, salt, and vanilla. But even these lacked coconut flavor and were a bit on the dry side, not sufficiently chewy or moist. We set out to find a happy medium among our test recipes.

Our tests had shown us that the use of sweetened versus unsweetened coconut has a major effect on texture. The unsweetened variety resulted in a less sticky, more appealing texture, but it made the cookies just a bit too dry. Flour—we tried both cake and all-purpose—was helpful in eliminating the stickiness of cookies made entirely with sweetened coconut, but it also made the cookies a bit too dense. Looking for a way past this roadblock, we decided to test a combination of sweetened and unsweetened coconut. This worked very well, giving the cookies a more luxurious texture without making them wet or heavy.

We also found, to our surprise, that the sweetened coconut had more flavor than unsweetened, so the coconut flavor was turned up a notch. A scientist who works with the Baker's brand of coconut, which is sweetened and flaked, explained this phenomenon. He said that fresh coconut is 53 percent moisture; unsweetened, which is dried, is 3 to 5 percent moisture; and sweetened and flaked coconut (which is dried before being flaked and then rehydrated) is 9 to 25 percent moisture. Unlike most fruits that are quite sweet, coconut is mostly fat and, when dried, is rather tasteless, unlike, say, dried apples or apricots. Hydrating dried coconut therefore adds flavor, as does the addition of sugar. Although one could add more moisture and more sweetness to a macaroon batter and then use dried, unsweetened coconut, the coconut itself would still be less flavorful than sweetened coconut flakes.

Another key issue was the ratio of coconut to unbeaten egg whites. Testing showed that cookies made with 3½ cups of coconut and only one egg white were dense and heavy; 3 cups of coconut to 4 egg whites, however, seemed like a better ratio.

To add still more moisture to the cookies, we tried using corn syrup instead of sugar as a sweetener and found that the cookies were slightly more moist, held together a bit better, and were pleasantly chewy. Melted butter was tried but discarded because it masked the flavor of the coconut, as did sweetened condensed milk.

We still felt that the cookies were a bit light in coconut flavor. To remedy this, we tried adding cream of coconut, and we hit the jackpot. The coconut flavor was superior to any of the cookies we had made to date. Finally, a coconut macaroon with real coconut flavor. (Because cream of coconut is sweetened, we did have to decrease the amount of corn syrup. For more information on this and similar products, see the Tasting Lab on page 289.)

Putting these cookies together is easy. There is no need to even whip the egg whites. The liquid ingredients are whisked together, the dry ingredients are mixed, and then the two are combined. We found it best to refrigerate this dough for 15 minutes to make it easier to work with, but in a pinch you can skip this step. In an effort to produce a nicely browned, crisp exterior, we experimented with oven temperatures and finally settled on 375 degrees; the bottoms tended to overcook at 400 degrees, and lower temperatures never produced the sort of browning we were after.

We also found that these cookies are great when the bottom third is dipped in chocolate. Because the cookie is not overly sweet, the chocolate is a nice complement.

WHAT WE LEARNED: For the best flavor, use three kinds of coconut—unsweetened, sweetened, and cream of coconut. Corn syrup adds more moisture to the batter than granulated sugar and is preferred.

> **FOOD FACT: Macaroons**
>
> Macaroons were first developed in Italy during the Renaissance. They originally were biscuits made of marzipan and served at banquets. During the 18th and 19th centuries, macaroons became especially popular in Britain at teatime.

TRIPLE-COCONUT MACAROONS

Makes about 4 dozen 1-inch cookies

Cream of coconut, available canned, is a very sweet product commonly used in piña colada cocktails. Be sure to mix the can's contents thoroughly before using, as the mixture separates upon standing. Unsweetened desiccated coconut is commonly sold in natural food stores and Asian markets. If you are unable to find any, use all sweetened flaked or shredded coconut, but reduce the amount of cream of coconut to ½ cup, omit the corn syrup, and toss 2 tablespoons cake flour with the coconut before adding the liquid ingredients. For larger macaroons, shape haystacks from a generous ¼ cup of batter and increase the baking time to 20 minutes.

1	cup cream of coconut
2	tablespoons light corn syrup
4	large egg whites
2	teaspoons vanilla extract
½	teaspoon salt
3	cups (8 ounces) unsweetened, shredded, desiccated (dried) coconut
3	cups (8 ounces) sweetened flaked or shredded coconut

1. Adjust the oven racks to the upper-middle and lower-middle positions and heat the oven to 375 degrees. Line two baking sheets with parchment paper and lightly spray the parchment with nonstick vegetable cooking spray.

2. Whisk together the cream of coconut, corn syrup, egg whites, vanilla, and salt in a small bowl; set aside. Combine the unsweetened and sweetened coconuts in a large bowl;

for beauty

toss together, breaking up clumps with your fingertips. Pour the liquid ingredients into the coconut and mix with a rubber spatula until evenly moistened. Chill for 15 minutes.

3. Drop heaping tablespoons of batter onto the parchment-lined baking sheets, spacing them about 1 inch apart. With moistened fingertips, form the cookies into loose haystacks. Bake until light golden brown, about 15 minutes, turning the baking sheets from front to back and switching from the top to bottom racks halfway through baking.

4. Cool the cookies on the baking sheets until slightly set, about 2 minutes; remove to a wire rack with a metal spatula.

VARIATION

CHOCOLATE-DIPPED TRIPLE-COCONUT MACAROONS

Using the two-stage melting process for the chocolate helps ensure that it will be at the proper consistency for dipping the cookies.

Follow the recipe for Triple-Coconut Macaroons. Cool the baked macaroons to room temperature, about 30 minutes. Line two baking sheets with parchment paper. Chop 10 ounces semisweet chocolate; melt 8 ounces in a small heat-proof bowl set over a pan of almost-simmering water, stirring once or twice, until smooth. (To melt the chocolate in a microwave, heat at 50 percent power for 3 minutes and stir. If the chocolate is not yet entirely melted, heat an additional 30 seconds at 50 percent power.) Remove from the heat; stir in the remaining 2 ounces of chocolate until smooth. Holding the macaroon by its pointed top, dip the bottom and ½ inch up the sides in the chocolate, scrape off the excess with your finger, and place the macaroon on the prepared baking sheet. Repeat with the remaining macaroons. Refrigerate until the chocolate sets, about 15 minutes.

TASTING LAB: Coconut Milk, Coconut Cream, and Cream of Coconut

COCONUT MILK IS NOT THE THIN LIQUID FOUND INSIDE the coconut itself—that is called coconut water. Coconut milk is a product made by steeping equal parts shredded coconut meat and either warm milk or water. The meat is pressed or mashed to release as much liquid as possible, the mixture is strained, and the result is coconut milk. The same method is used to make coconut cream, but the ratio of coconut meat to liquid is higher, about 4 to 1. (The cream that rises to the top of coconut milk after it sits a while is also referred to as coconut cream.) Finally, cream of coconut—not to be confused with coconut cream—is a sweetened product based on coconut milk that also contains thickeners and emulsifiers. Cream of coconut and coconut cream are not interchangeable in recipes, as the former is heavily sweetened and the latter is not.

To find out firsthand how coconut milk, coconut cream, and cream of coconut stack up, we made coconut milk and cream in the test kitchen and compared them with commercial products. For the first test batch, we made coconut milk with water. (One cup of fresh coconut meat was ground in a food processor with 1 cup of warm water. The mixture steeped for one hour and then was strained.) Next we made a batch with milk, using the same method. The coconut cream was made using the same method, but with a higher ratio of meat to water: 2 cups of fresh coconut meat to ½ cup of water. We then did a blind taste test, pitting our homemade products against canned cream of coconut and canned coconut milk.

Both the canned and the homemade coconut milks were very thin, with only a modest amount of coconut flavor (although the coconut milk made with cow's milk rather than water was superior). The homemade coconut cream, though made with water, was quite good: thicker, creamier, and somewhat more flavorful than the coconut milk. The canned cream of coconut was very sweet and syrupy, really inedible right out of the can, with sugar being the predominant flavor. However, we found that it can be used in baking with good results.

EQUIPMENT CORNER: Potholders

IN PROFESSIONAL KITCHENS, A TRUSTY, ALBEIT FLIMSY, side towel folded over a few times offers protection from things hot. Home cooks, however, whose hands are not as hardened as the vocational cook's, prefer to protect their paws with potholders. And, lucky for them, there is a panoply of potholders from which to choose, from simple terry-cloth swatches to high-tech silicone to plush leather squares. We selected six different potholders (we purchased two of each type) and used them when handling the handles on a tea kettle, stockpot, and heavy skillet (which had been in a 450-degree oven for 15 minutes), when removing a soufflé from the oven, and when manipulating hot pie plates and cake pans in the oven.

All potholders were adequately heat-resistant. The attributes of a winning potholder were softness, thinness, and suppleness, all of which allow a potholder to conform to the shape of the hand, making it comfortable to use and easy to grasp a hot object, whatever its shape.

The three best were the LamsonSharp Leather Handiholder ($12.95 each), a very basic potholder made by Ritz ($2.99 each), and the Ritz Sterling Pocket Mitt ($4.95 each). The washable suede Handiholder was uniquely soft and supple and afforded the user a very good, secure grip, but at 9½ inches square it seemed excessively large, which was a minor annoyance given its tendency to flop around. Both Ritz potholders were made of terry cloth and had a comfortable, broken-in feel from the get-go, but we slightly preferred the plain potholder over the Pocket Mitt because of its compact size (about 8½ inches square before washing, about 8 inches square after three washes) and its thinner, more svelte feel. But the Pocket Mitt was good as well, just a bit bulkier.

We recommend Pyro Guard potholders ($3.95 each) with reservations. They were decent, not exceptional, performers whose shiny metallic side felt slippery in some tasks and whose overall feel was on the stiff side of acceptable. Of greater concern, however, was the fact that these potholders are not machine-washable. The label says to wipe clean with a damp sponge or cloth. Knowing how grungy potholders can become with use, we wondered about the life expectancy of these potholders.

Two potholders fell into the "not recommended" category. The Kitchensafe potholders ($9.99 each), made of a washable, flame-resistant fabric and dotted on one side with "hot dots" that offer a no-slip surface, were far too rigid,

Rating Potholders

WE TESTED SIX SETS OF POTHOLDERS IN VARIOUS KITCHEN APPLICATIONS, INCLUDING PICKING UP HANDLES ON A HOT tea kettle, stockpot, and heavy skillet; removing a soufflé dish from the oven; and turning pie plates and cake pans in the oven. The potholders are listed in order of preference based on their performance in these tests. See www.americastestkitchen.com for up-to-date prices and mail-order sources for top-rated products.

RECOMMENDED
LamsonSharp Leather Handiholder
$12.95 each
This washable suede potholder is soft and supple and so conforms to any shape handle or pot. Very secure in testers' hands.

RECOMMENDED
Ritz Potholder
$2.99 each
This terry-cloth potholder is reliable if not terribly sexy. Compact size is a plus.

RECOMMENDED
Ritz Sterling Pocket Mitt
$4.95 each
This terry-cloth mitt has a nice, broken-in feel and performed well in tests. A bit bulkier than we like, though.

RECOMMENDED WITH RESERVATIONS
Pyro Guard Potholders
$3.95 each
The shiny metallic side is somewhat slippery and a bit too stiff. Not machine-washable, which is a big drawback given how dirty potholders get.

NOT RECOMMENDED
Kitchensafe Potholders
$9.99 each
The washable, flame-resistant fabric is far too rigid, making it difficult to grasp small handles or rims.

NOT RECOMMENDED
HotSpot Silicone Potholders
$7.95 each
The material on these high-tech potholders is too springy, and it became very slippery when coated with even a drop of fat.

even after three washes. They did not conform easily to the movements and shape of the hand, which made grasping the small rims on pie plates and cake pans difficult; securing a good grasp on the narrow girth of a skillet handle was nearly impossible. The look of the newfangled HotSpot silicone potholders ($7.95 each) elicited wows, but they failed to impress when pressed into service. Though bendable, these potholders possessed a springy nature that made them awkward to use. On most surfaces, the HotSpot silicone potholders afforded the user a firm, no-slip grip. But even a small drop of fat on the potholders or the item being grasped can render them slick and slippery, as one test cook discovered when using one to grasp a skillet whose handle had been lightly splattered with grease.

Garth and Adam have the scoop on the latest
high-tech ice cream machines.

SUMMER BERRY
desserts
CHAPTER 23

When local berries are in season, we like to showcase them in simple desserts. While berries and ice cream make a fine dessert, on occasion we like to attempt something a bit more challenging. But an all-day battle with pastry isn't our idea of summer fun.

We especially like to use summer berries in a no-bake pie. Unfortunately, most recipes are nothing more than berries suspended in gelatin, with a can of "whipped cream" as garnish. We wanted a no-bake pie that was every bit as appealing as a traditional double-crust pie—but without all of the work.

Sabayon is a frothy dessert sauce made with egg yolks, sugar, and flavorings. It takes just minutes to prepare and can transform a bowl of berries into a real dessert. Like many custards, however, sabayon can be fickle. We wanted to figure out the dos and don'ts when making this classic sauce.

SUMMER BERRY PIE

WHAT WE WANTED: No-bake pies can be soupy, chewy, or tasteless. Could we make a pie with great texture and flavor—and still keep it simple?

We love summer fruit pies, but the prospect of wrestling with buttery pie dough in a 90-degree kitchen is not especially appealing. We also find that berries are spectacular when not baked at all. But the alternatives to baked pies hardly inspired us. Most quick "no-bake" pies consist mainly of rubbery Jell-O or viscous pudding garnished with Cool Whip. Our idea for this summer dessert was closer to the bright flavors of a berry tart; we just wanted it in the more substantial form of a pie.

Our first round of tests with no-bake pies was disheartening. The first recipe called for "red" flavored gelatin and a cornstarch-thickened syrup that were poured over fresh berries in a premade crust. It had only one redeeming quality: neat slices. Other attempts to use cornstarch as a thickener left us with a soupy, cinnamon-laden blueberry "icebox" pie and an overly sweet mixed-berry mash in soggy pastry dough. The best recipe called for merely tossing the mixed berries in melted raspberry jam and then pouring them into a prebaked graham cracker crust. The problem with this method became readily apparent: Once the pie was sliced, the berries spilled out, making it impossible to serve neatly and difficult to eat. Exasperated, we set

out to find a technique for making a fresh, flavorful pie with good texture and neat slices.

We did learn one thing from these initial tests: A graham cracker crust is not only easy to make but pairs nicely with tangy sweet berries. Our first thought was to give store-bought graham cracker pie crusts a chance. It quickly became apparent that this was not going to be an option (see the Tasting Lab on page 129), so we decided to make our own.

Some recipes call for simply pressing the crumbs in place and chilling the crust before filling it, but we found that prebaking dramatically improved the flavor of the crust and gave it more structure by melting the butter and sugar together. As we continued testing, it became clear that a careful balance of the three ingredients—crumbs, butter, and sugar—would also be crucial to texture and flavor. If we added too much butter, the sides of the crust slid down as it baked, causing the crust to pool in the center of the pan. If we added too much sugar, the crust became too hard and exceedingly sweet. The right proportions were 5 table-spoons of butter and 2 tablespoons of sugar to 1 cup of crumbs. We found that it was much easier to press the crumbs into the pan when the butter was very warm.

The biggest issue now before us was figuring out how to hold the berries together. We needed a binder that would give the pie enough structure to stand up to slicing without interfering with the pure flavor of the fruit.

Early on we found that combining a berry puree with whole berries was best for optimal flavor; using Jell-O or some other commercial filler resulted in poor flavor and less than ideal texture. But we still needed to thicken the puree somehow. An early test recipe called for cornstarch, which seemed like a good idea, but that recipe also added orange juice, which made the pie soupy. Our plan was simple: Lose the juice but keep the cornstarch (or another thickener). We would briefly cook the puree with the thickener, sugar, and salt, and then season with lemon juice at the end. After

---

FOOD FACT: Graham Crackers

Graham crackers were created by dietary reformer Sylvester Graham in 1829 and originally made with whole-wheat flour (sometimes called graham flour in older cookbooks). Today's graham crackers are often made with bleached white flour, something that would surely distress Graham, who regarded refined flour as one of the world's great dietary evils. He also believed that mustard and ketchup caused insanity. Go figure.

---

cooling this mixture slightly, we would pour it over the whole berries in the prebaked crust. The pie would then go into the refrigerator to set up.

But which thickener would be best? We started our tests with tapioca, which, because of the short stovetop cooking time, turned out an unpleasantly grainy filling. (We wanted to keep the cooking time as short as possible to retain the fresh berry flavor.) Potato starch produced a gummy filling. In the end, cornstarch worked just fine, producing a good texture without adding any off flavors. But we still had some kinks to work out—namely, the seeds that kept sticking between our teeth. The obvious solution was to strain the filling before cooking, a step that took only a couple of minutes and made a huge difference.

So far, so good, but now that it was time to assemble the pie, we found that pouring the puree over sun-sweetened whole berries made the filling dark and murky looking. And merely tossing the berries on top of the thickened puree was no way to turn heads either. This pie needed some gloss. So we borrowed a trick from tart making: glazing the fresh whole berries with a thin layer of melted seedless jam. Because we weren't interested in a precise arrangement of berries (we wanted a fast and unfussy pie), gently tossing them with the glaze (rather than painting them with it, as is often done when making tarts) was a quick solution. We had managed to gussy them up and enhance their flavor at the same time. When we poured the glazed berries over the puree, the result was a truly attractive berry pie. Better yet, it tasted fresh, sliced well, and was a whole lot easier to make than a traditional American pie.

WHAT WE LEARNED: Skip the Jell-O and the Cool Whip, make a berry puree thickened with cornstarch to hold the whole berries together, toss the whole berries with warm jam for a glossy finish, and pour the puree and then the berries into a freshly made graham cracker crust.

SUMMER BERRY PIE
Makes one 9-inch pie, serving 8 to 10

Berries are not sold in standard half-pint containers. When shopping for ingredients, use the weights on the containers as a guideline but make sure to measure out the berries (gently, to avoid bruising). If you wind up short on one type of berry but have extras of another type, make up the difference with the extras. If blackberries are not available, use 3 cups each of raspberries and blueberries. When pureeing the berries, be sure to process them for a full minute; otherwise, the yield on the puree may be too small. Apple jelly can be substituted if red currant jelly is unavailable. If you have a salad spinner, line the basket with paper towels, add the berries, and spin until dry.

graham cracker crust

9	graham crackers, broken into rough pieces
2	tablespoons sugar
5	tablespoons unsalted butter, melted and warm

berry filling

2	cups (about 9 ounces) raspberries
2	cups (about 11 ounces) blackberries
2	cups (about 10 ounces) blueberries
½	cup (3½ ounces) granulated sugar
3	tablespoons cornstarch
⅛	teaspoon salt
1	tablespoon juice from 1 lemon
2	tablespoons red currant jelly

whipped cream

1	cup cold heavy cream
1	tablespoon sugar
1	teaspoon vanilla extract

1. FOR THE CRUST: Adjust an oven rack to the middle position and heat the oven to 325 degrees.

2. In a food processor, process the graham crackers until evenly fine, about 30 seconds (you should have 1 cup crumbs). Add the sugar and pulse to combine. Continue to pulse while adding the warm melted butter in a steady stream; pulse until the mixture resembles wet sand. Transfer the crumbs to a 9-inch glass pie plate. Using a ½-cup dry measuring cup, press the crumb mixture into the place. Use your thumb to square off the top of the crust. Bake the crust until fragrant and beginning to brown, 15 to 18 minutes; transfer to a wire rack and cool completely while making the filling.

3. FOR THE FILLING: Combine the berries in a large colander and gently rinse (taking care not to bruise them); spread the berries on a paper towel–lined rimmed baking sheet and gently pat dry with additional paper towels.

4. In a food processor, puree 2½ cups mixed berries until smooth and fully pureed, about 1 minute. Strain the puree through a mesh strainer into a small nonreactive saucepan, scraping and pressing on the seeds to extract as much puree as possible (you should have 1¼ to 1½ cups). Whisk the sugar, cornstarch, and salt in a small bowl to combine, then whisk the mixture into the puree. Bring the puree to a boil over medium heat, stirring constantly with a wooden spoon; when the mixture reaches a boil and is thickened to the consistency of pudding, remove from the heat, stir in the lemon juice, and set aside to cool slightly.

5. While the puree is cooling, place the remaining berries in a medium bowl. Heat the jelly in a second small saucepan over low heat until fully melted. Drizzle the melted jelly over the berries and toss gently with a rubber spatula to coat. Pour the slightly cooled puree into the cooled pie shell and smooth the top with a spatula. Distribute the glazed berries evenly over the puree and gently press them into the puree. Loosely cover the pie with plastic wrap; refrigerate until chilled and the puree has set, about 3 hours or up to 1 day.

6. FOR THE WHIPPED CREAM: Just before serving, beat the cream, sugar, and vanilla with an electric mixer on low speed until small bubbles form, about 30 seconds. Increase the speed to medium; continue beating until the beaters leave a trail, about 30 seconds longer. Increase the speed to high; continue beating until the cream is smooth, thick, nearly doubled in volume, and forms soft peaks, about 30 to 60 seconds.

7. Cut the pie into wedges and serve with whipped cream.

EQUIPMENT CORNER:
Ice Cream Machines

FRUIT DESSERTS AND HOMEMADE ICE CREAMS ARE natural pairings. If you're in the market for an ice cream maker, you've got several options. We tested seven models, ranging in price from a fairly modest $50 to a whopping $600. They fell into three basic categories: expensive machines that don't require the use of a freezer, midpriced machines with an electric motor and a removable canister that must be frozen in advance, and midpriced machines with a hand crank and a removable canister that must be frozen in advance.

The two canister-free models were also the most expensive, and they produced smooth, creamy ice cream. They have two distinct advantages over the other models tested (some of which also produced high-quality ice cream): volume and ready-to-serve ice cream (it was frozen fully and could be eaten right from the machine). The Lussino Dessert Maker from Musso ($594.95, 1½-quart capacity) contains a built-in refrigerator unit and is the Cadillac of ice cream makers. It lets you make endless batches of ice cream without having to wait 12 hours for a freezer canister to get back down to the proper temperature. The White Mountain Ice Cream Maker ($199.95, 4-quart capacity) produces a whole gallon of great ice cream in one shot, but it requires 10 pounds of ice as well as rock salt. This

Rating Ice Cream Machines

WE TESTED SEVEN ICE CREAM MACHINES, EVALUATING THE QUALITY OF THE ICE CREAM THAT EACH PRODUCED AS WELL as ease of use. The ice cream machines are listed in order of preference based on these tests. See www.americastestkitchen.com for up-to-date prices and mail-order sources for top-rated products.

HIGHLY RECOMMENDED
Lussino Dessert Maker from Musso
$594.95

This quiet 1 1/2 quart-machine makes top-notch ice cream, and there's no need to freeze a canister in advance—it contains a built-in refrigerator. But you have to pay dearly for these conveniences.

RECOMMENDED
Krups La Glacière
$59.95

This electric machine is pretty quiet and turns out really good ice cream. Although you need to freeze the canister overnight before making ice cream and the churned ice cream will require further harden-ing in the freezer, this machine offers the best value.

RECOMMENDED
Cuisinart Flavor Duo Frozen Yogurt/Ice Cream/Sorbet Maker
$99.95

This machine comes with two 1-quart canisters so you can make vanilla and chocolate ice cream on the same day. Otherwise, it's similar to the other Cuisinart model tested.

RECOMMENDED
Cuisinart Automatic Frozen Yogurt and Ice Cream Maker
$49.95

This machine is similar to the Krups (both come with 1 1/2 quart-canisters) but is a bit noisier. The ice cream, however, is very good.

RECOMMENDED WITH RESERVATIONS
White Mountain Ice Cream Maker
$199.95

The huge 4-quart capacity is a plus, as is the superior quality of the ice cream, but this electric machine requires 10 pounds of ice and rock salt, and it's extremely noisy. Great as a weekend project on the back porch.

NOT RECOMMENDED
Donvier Ice Cream Maker
$49.95

Although this hand-cranked machine turns out ice cream quickly, the quality is only so-so. Given the price tag, the ice cream should be better.

NOT RECOMMENDED
Chilly by William Bounds
$69.99

The machine makes grainy, icy, dense ice cream. For the money, you can do much better.

machine is unbearably loud to boot, better suited to a back porch than a kitchen.

The three electric models with canisters that must go in the freezer overnight made delectably smooth, creamy ice cream in less than 30 minutes. The ice cream was quite soft, however, and benefited from a few hours in the freezer to firm it up before eating. The Krups La Glacière ($59.95, 1½-quart capacity) was quieter than both the Cuisinart one-canister machine ($49.95, 1½-quart capacity) and the Cuisinart two-canister machine ($99.95, 2-quart capacity). Given its modest price and size (and immodestly good ice cream), the Krups machine is an excellent choice.

The two manual models tested—the Donvier ($49.95, 1-quart capacity) and the Chilly by William Bounds ($69.99, 1-quart capacity)—made ice cream in just 15 to 20 minutes (once the canisters had been chilled overnight). While it seemed miraculous that ice cream could be made so quietly and so quickly with so little hand churning, the ice cream was grainy, icy, and dense. If you can buy a model with a built-in motor for about the same price, why settle for hand-cranked, inferior ice cream?

BERRY GRATIN WITH SABAYON

WHAT WE WANTED: A medley of summer fruit warmed slightly and topped with frothy sabayon and a delicate, caramelized sugar crust.

Fruit and egg yolk foam (called *sabayon* in French or *zabaglione* in Italian) are simple summertime pleasures. Most recipes start with a mixture of sugared berries, which are then topped with chilled sabayon and served in goblets. We wanted something a bit different—warming the fruit in a gratin dish so that the juices would run. The sabayon would be spooned over the fruit and then sprinkled with sugar, which we would caramelize with a torch. Although still simple, this dish is far more elegant than the typical frothy zabaglione and berries served in old-fashioned Italian restaurants.

We started with the fruit. Tasters liked a mixture of raspberries, blackberries, and blueberries. We tried sugaring the berries as well as flavoring them with liqueur or vanilla, but tasters objected. They wanted pure berry flavor. In any case, a brief stay in the oven heated the berries and released their juices, so the sugar was not needed for this purpose.

Sabayon is a thick, slightly frothy, and creamy dessert sauce made of nothing but whipped egg yolks, sugar, and wine (often Marsala) or lemon juice. We began by testing the various flavoring options. Tasters quickly chose lemon as the best complement to the fruit; alcohol seemed to overpower the delicate berries. A mixture of zest and juice was best, providing the most complex lemon flavor.

Next we focused on the ratio of egg yolks to lemon juice. Three egg yolks and a scant half cup of lemon juice produced a sauce with the correct consistency—light and frothy, not loose and watery—but the lemon flavor was overwhelming. We solved this problem by cutting the lemon juice with water.

As for the sugar, we began with ½ cup (an amount that seemed typical in most research recipes), but tasters thought the sauce was too sweet. We reduced the sugar tablespoon by tablespoon, ultimately deciding that ⅓ cup was enough to sweeten the sauce without overwhelming it. (Remember, we wanted to add a crunchy layer of caramelized sugar to finish this dessert.) A pinch of salt rounded the flavors in the sabayon.

With the ingredients chosen, it was time to refine our technique. There are two main goals when heating sabayon ingredients: to dissolve the sugar fully and to whip enough air into the sauce to create the desired frothy texture. Whisking the egg yolks and sugar together in a bowl, off heat, dissolved most of the sugar. Setting the bowl over a pan of simmering water for a minute while continuing to whisk dissolved the rest of the sugar.

At this point, we added the lemon juice, lemon zest, water, and salt and continued whisking. We found that five to seven minutes of constant whisking yielded a threefold increase in volume. We tried whisking occasionally but ended up with scrambled eggs. If the mixture is not in constant motion, the yolks in direct contact with the bowl (where the heat is most intense) will overcook and curdle (see the Science Desk on page 300 for more details). For this reason, it is necessary to whisk the mixture constantly while it is on the stovetop. Once the sabayon thickens properly, it should be removed from the heat immediately. We found it best to continue whisking for 30 seconds to cool off the sabayon.

With the sabayon made and the berries warmed, the dessert came together very quickly. We simply spooned the sabayon over the warmed fruit and then added a sprinkling of sugar, which we quickly caramelized with a kitchen torch.

WHAT WE LEARNED: Warm the berries—without sugar or flavorings—to release their juices. Use lemon juice and zest to brighten the flavor of the sabayon, and whisk constantly to prevent the sauce from curdling.

BERRY GRATIN WITH LEMON SABAYON

Serves 6

When making the sabayon, make sure the heat under the simmering water is not set too high. If the egg yolks overheat, they will scramble. Constant whisking is also required. Although we prefer to make this recipe with a mix of raspberries, blackberries, and blueberries, you can use three cups of just one berry if that's what you have on hand.

lemon sabayon

- ¼   cup water
- ½   teaspoon grated zest and 3 tablespoons juice from 1 large lemon
-     Pinch salt
- 3   large egg yolks
- ⅓   cup (2⅓ ounces) sugar

berries

- 1   cup raspberries
- 1   cup blackberries
- 1   cup blueberries

- 3   tablespoons sugar for caramelized crust

1. FOR THE SABAYON: Adjust an oven rack to the upper-middle position and heat the oven to 400 degrees.

2. Combine the water, lemon zest, lemon juice, and salt in a small bowl and set aside.

3. Whisk the egg yolks and sugar in a medium bowl until frothy, about 1 minute. Set the bowl over a pan of simmering water. Continue whisking until the mixture begins to thicken, about 1 minute. Gradually whisk in the lemon mixture and continue cooking, whisking constantly, until the mixture is thick, light yellow, and tripled in volume, 5 to 7 minutes. Remove the bowl from the saucepan, whisk constantly for about 30 seconds to cool, then set aside while preparing the berries, occasionally whisking the mixture.

4. FOR THE BERRIES: Combine the berries in a wide, shallow 2-quart broiler-safe gratin dish or divide among 6 ramekins or individual gratin dishes set on a rimmed baking sheet. Bake the berries until the fruit is warm and just beginning to release its juices, about 8 minutes. Remove the berries from the oven. Spoon the lemon sabayon over the berries and sprinkle with the sugar. Ignite a kitchen torch and caramelize the sugar. Serve immediately.

SCIENCE DESK:
Why Do Egg Yolk Foams Require Heat?

ACCORDING TO LEGEND, THE FROTHY SAUCE KNOWN AS *zabaglione* in Italian and *sabayon* in French was created in the Medici court in Florence in the 16th century. It is one of the few recipes still prepared in the modern kitchen that makes use of egg yolk foam. Foams made from egg whites are routine: just place the whites in a bowl and beat in air (see the Science Desk on page 334 for more information). If this method is attempted with egg yolks, however, very little air will be incorporated. In fact, if even a small amount of egg yolk contaminates egg whites, the whites will not foam. Why?

While egg whites are essentially protein and water, egg yolks are about 34 percent fat, and it is the fat that spells disaster for egg white foam. Foams are the result of egg proteins denaturing, or unfolding, and associating with adjacent proteins to form a web; this web stabilizes the foam structure. In the case of egg white foam, your arm (and a whisk) or a mixer can provide enough energy to reorganize the protein structure, but with egg yolks this is not the case. Instead, a significant amount of heat is required to encourage the yolk proteins to form a sturdy matrix. Specifically, the yolk must be heated above 140 degrees to get good foam formation. Caution must be taken, however. If the temperature of the foam rises above 160 degrees, the proteins will begin to coagulate, an irreversible process wherein the proteins tighten, leaving the cook with a serving of sweet scrambled eggs.

Rows and rows of cakes are ready to be frosted and filmed.

EASY
CHAPTER 24
sheet cakes

A sheet cake is like a two-layer cake with training wheels—it's hard to fall off. Unlike regular cakes, which often require trimming and decorating skills to ensure that the cake doesn't turn out lopsided, domed, or altogether amateurish, sheet cakes are single-story and easy to frost. These are the sorts of cakes made for church suppers, old home days, bake sales, and Fourth of July picnics, decorated with red, white, and blue frosting.

But sheet cakes are still cakes. They can still turn out dry, sticky, or flavorless and, on occasion, can even sink in the middle. The test kitchen decided to tackle two popular sheet cakes—carrot and chocolate—and produce simple recipes (a complicated sheet cake makes no sense) that would deliver superior results. We think we've succeeded.

CARROT CAKE

WHAT WE WANTED: A streamlined recipe that was moist (but not soggy) and rich (but not oily).

A relic of the health food craze, carrot cake was once heralded for its use of vegetable oil in place of butter and carrots as a natural sweetener. But healthy or not (and we doubt that it ever was), we have never been a fan of this cake. Sure, the carrots add some sweetness, but they also add a lot of moisture, which is why carrot cake is invariably soggy. And oil? It makes this cake dense and, well, oily. Save for the mercifully thick coating of cream cheese frosting, many of us in the test kitchen think carrot cake is nothing but a good spice cake gone bad.

But other colleagues spun stories about the ultimate carrot cake. They spoke of moist (not soggy) cakes that were rich (not greasy). The crumb should be relatively tight and tender, while the spices should be nicely balanced. And what about the cake's namesake? They admitted that it was not all that important to taste the carrots, but they did want to know on first glance that what they were eating was carrot cake. As a group, we reasoned that if we were going to make this cake, it had better be simple—from ingredient list to mixing method.

Our initial research turned up numerous recipes, and we chose several that seemed promising. Some of these recipes were not in our desired sheet-cake form, but at this point we figured it was worth testing all kinds of recipes. To our dismay, all of these initial test cakes were, with the exception of one, very bad (see Getting It Right, page 307). But the test wasn't a complete wash, as we learned two very important things.

First, shape mattered. Layer cakes could hardly be considered part of our "simple" plan. Loaf-shaped was easy but looked more like quick bread than cake. A Bundt-shaped cake was easy as well as attractive but difficult to ice with a thick coating of cream cheese frosting (a must, if you remember). No, for our purposes, there was nothing easier than a sheet cake baked in a standard 13 by 9-inch pan, and this round of testing had confirmed our opinion.

Second, there are carrot cakes out there made with just about anything and everything. Canned crushed pineapple, toasted coconut, wheat germ, raisins, and nuts all made appearances in the cakes. The first three were unanimously voted out, but the raisins and nuts were liked well enough to make them an option.

All-purpose flour worked better than cake flour (the latter proved too delicate for this sturdy American classic), and we used 2½ cups as the base for our tests. We quickly found that this cake would need healthy amounts of baking soda and baking powder—1 and 1¼ teaspoons, respectively (nearly twice the amount found in many recipes)—to give it sufficient lift and a beautiful brown color. Four eggs gave the cake a slight spring and a tender crumb. As for sugar, this cake clearly benefited from both granulated and light brown sugar, the former giving the cake clean sweetness, the latter bringing out the warmth of the spices. While many recipes use handfuls of every baking spice in the pantry, we found that a conservative touch with cinnamon, along with a little help from nutmeg and cloves, won the approval of tasters.

Now that we had a reasonably simple working recipe, we introduced carrots to the mix. We rejected any idea of first boiling, steaming, or pureeing the carrots, as called for in some recipes. It was just too much work. Grating the carrots was clearly the way to go, but it took a few failed efforts before we realized that just the right amount of carrots was paramount, as their high moisture content could determine whether a cake was moist or soggy. After baking cakes with as few cups of grated carrots as 1 (no carrot presence) and as many as 5 (soaking-wet cake), we found that 3 cups gave the cake a pleasantly moist texture. To hasten the grating (as well as to spare ourselves a few grazed knuckles), we put away the box grater and plugged in the food processor.

About 99 percent of carrot cake recipes use oil instead of softened butter in the batter, and while the idea of not having to wait on softened butter fit into our simple approach, the thought of using oil gave us some pause. As a compromise, we tested melted butter versus oil. We were shocked to find that tasters preferred the cleaner taste of the cake made with oil. Any more than 1½ cups of oil and the cake was too dense and greasy; any less and tasters found the cake too lean.

Just as we would with a butter-based cake, we beat the oil with the sugar and the eggs in a standing mixer before adding the dry ingredients and the carrots. This cake was good, but we still weren't happy about two things. First, the bottom of the cake was too dense. Second, we weren't thrilled with the idea of pulling out both the food processor and standing mixer to bake a "simple" cake. Deciding to work with the easier problem first, we examined our mixing method. Because we were using the food processor to grate the carrots, we wondered if we could use it to mix the cake. We processed the eggs and oil together with sugar,

then added the dry ingredients and finally the carrots. This cake was tough from the beating of the flour and jack-o'-lantern orange from the processing of the carrots. Next time around we again processed the eggs, oil, and sugar but then transferred the mixture to another bowl, into which we could stir the carrots and dry ingredients. This was much better, but we still had to deal with that annoyingly dense bottom.

On a whim, we wondered if gradually adding the oil to the sugar and eggs while the machine was running (much like making a mayonnaise) would have any impact on the cake. You bet it did. By first creating this stable emulsion of eggs and oil, we were breaking up the oil into tiny particles that were less likely to sink to the bottom, instead dispersing themselves evenly throughout the cake. No more soggy bottom, no more heavy texture. This cake was light, tender, and pleasantly moist.

Our cake was now good enough to eat on its own, but there was no way we were going to pass up the frosting. Made with cream cheese, butter, and confectioners' sugar, cream cheese frosting is one of those things that even when it's bad, it's still good. So we made (and happily ate) several frostings made with various proportions of each ingredient. We added vanilla for depth of flavor, but it wasn't until we added a little sour cream that the frosting really shone on top of the cake.

WHAT WE LEARNED: This cake is best made with all-purpose flour and plenty of leavener to give it lift. Neutral-tasting oil works better than butter with the flavor of the carrots. For the best texture, beat the sugar and eggs in a food processor (which is also used to grate the carrots) and then add the oil in a steady stream. By using the same method to mix the cake that you would to mix mayonnaise, the oil gets broken into tiny droplets, and the texture of cake is moist throughout but neither soggy nor heavy.

SIMPLE CARROT CAKE WITH CREAM CHEESE FROSTING Makes one 13 by 9-inch cake

If you like nuts in your cake, stir 1 1/2 cups toasted chopped pecans or walnuts into the batter along with the carrots. Raisins are also a good addition; 1 cup can be added along with the carrots. If you add both nuts and raisins, the cake will need an additional 10 to 12 minutes in the oven.

carrot cake

2½	cups (12½ ounces) unbleached all-purpose flour
1¼	teaspoons baking powder
1	teaspoon baking soda
1¼	teaspoons ground cinnamon
½	teaspoon ground nutmeg
⅛	teaspoon ground cloves
½	teaspoon salt
1	pound (6 to 7 medium) carrots, peeled
1½	cups (10½ ounces) granulated sugar
½	cup (3½ ounces) packed light brown sugar
4	large eggs
½	cups safflower, canola, or vegetable oil

cream cheese frosting

8	ounces cream cheese, softened but still cool
5	tablespoons unsalted butter, softened but still cool
1	tablespoon sour cream
½	teaspoon vanilla extract
1¼	cups (4½ ounces) confectioners' sugar

1. FOR THE CAKE: Adjust an oven rack to the middle position and heat the oven to 350 degrees. Spray a 13 by 9-inch baking pan with nonstick cooking spray. Line the bottom of the pan with parchment and spray the parchment.

2. Whisk together the flour, baking powder, baking soda, cinnamon, nutmeg, cloves, and salt in a large bowl; set aside.

3. In a food processor fitted with a large shredding disk, shred the carrots (you should have about 3 cups); transfer

the carrots to a bowl and set aside. Wipe out the food processor workbowl and fit with the metal blade. Process the granulated and brown sugars and eggs until frothy and thoroughly combined, about 20 seconds. With the machine running, add the oil through the feed tube in a steady

TECHNIQUE:
Transporting a Frosted Cake

The common method for keeping plastic wrap from touching gooey frosting or glaze is to stick the cake with toothpicks and place the wrap over the toothpicks. Occasionally, though, the sharp points of the toothpicks puncture the wrap, which can then slide down and stick to the frosting. To keep the wrap securely above the frosting, try this method.

1. Place a miniature marshmallow over the end of each toothpick.

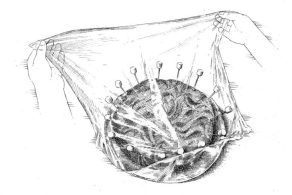

2. Insert the toothpicks into the cake with the marshmallows facing up. Lay the plastic wrap over the marshmallows.

stream. Process until the mixture is light in color and well emulsified, about 20 seconds longer. Scrape the mixture into a medium bowl. Stir in the carrots and the dry ingredients until incorporated and no streaks of flour remain. Pour into the prepared pan and bake until a toothpick or skewer inserted into the center of the cake comes out clean, 35 to 40 minutes, rotating the pan halfway through the baking time. Cool the cake to room temperature in the pan on a wire rack, about 2 hours.

4. FOR THE FROSTING: When the cake is cool, process the cream cheese, butter, sour cream, and vanilla in a clean food processor workbowl until combined, about 5 seconds, scraping down the bowl with a rubber spatula as needed. Add the confectioners' sugar and process until smooth, about 10 seconds.

5. Run a paring knife around the edge of the cake to loosen from the pan. Invert the cake onto a wire rack, peel off the parchment, then invert again onto a serving platter. Using an icing spatula, spread the frosting evenly over the surface of the cake. Cut into squares and serve. (Cover leftovers and refrigerate for up to 3 days.)

SPICED CARROT CAKE WITH VANILLA BEAN–CREAM CHEESE FROSTING
The Indian tea called chai inspired this variation.

Follow the recipe for Simple Carrot Cake with Cream Cheese Frosting, substituting an equal amount ground black pepper for the nutmeg, increasing the cloves to ¼ teaspoon, and adding 1 tablespoon ground cardamom along with the spices. For the frosting, using a paring knife, halve and scrape the seeds from 2 vanilla beans and add the seeds to the food processor along with the vanilla extract.

GINGER-ORANGE CARROT CAKE WITH ORANGE–CREAM CHEESE FROSTING
Follow the recipe for Simple Carrot Cake with Cream Cheese Frosting, reducing the cinnamon to ½ teaspoon, adding 1½ teaspoons ground ginger along with the spices, adding ½ cup finely chopped crystallized ginger along with the carrots, and processing 1 tablespoon grated orange zest along with the sugar and eggs. For the frosting, substitute an equal amount orange juice for the sour cream and 1 tablespoon grated orange zest for the vanilla.

GETTING IT RIGHT: Some Failed Carrot Cakes

We uncovered a number of problems in our initial round of testing. Pureed carrots gave one cake (left) an odd texture. The curved Bundt shape (center) was hard to ice, and the cake was bland. One layer cake (right) was so delicate that we had to slice it cold.

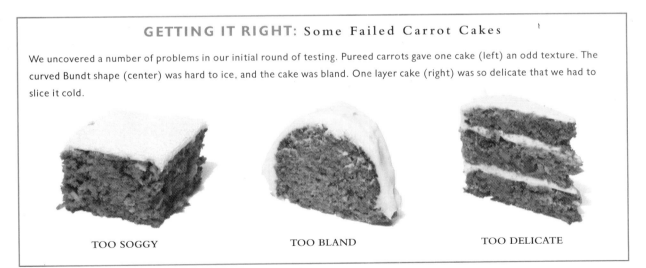

TOO SOGGY   TOO BLAND   TOO DELICATE

CHOCOLATE SHEET CAKE

WHAT WE WANTED: The simplest, most dependable recipe for a chocolate sheet cake—one that was moist yet also light and chocolatey.

A basic chocolate sheet cake is used as the foundation for Mississippi mud cake (just add a layer of marshmallow cream and chocolate frosting) and is also referred to as Texas sheet cake. It's arguably America's most popular sheet cake, served at birthday parties, picnics, and potluck suppers.

We started our kitchen work by preparing a test batch of five different recipes that required a variety of mixing techniques, everything from creaming butter to beating yolks, whipping whites, and gently folding everything together at the end. The best of the lot was the most complicated to make. But we were taken with another recipe that simply whisked together the ingredients without beating, creaming, or whipping. Although the recipe needed work, its approach was clearly a good match for the simple, all-purpose nature of a sheet cake.

The recipe called for 2 sticks of butter, 4 eggs, 1½ cups flour, 2 cups sugar, ½ cup cocoa, 1 teaspoon vanilla, and ⅛ teaspoon salt. Our first change was to add buttermilk, baking powder, and baking soda to lighten the batter, as the cake had been dense and chewy in its original form. To increase the chocolate flavor, we reduced the sugar and flour, increased the cocoa, and decreased the butter. To further deepen the chocolate taste, we decided to use semisweet chocolate in addition to the cocoa.

With this revised recipe and our simple mixing method, we actually had a cake that was superior to those whose recipes called for creaming butter or whipping eggs.

The only significant problem came when we tested natural versus Dutch-processed cocoa and discovered that the cake fell a bit in the center when we used the former. A few tests later, we eliminated the baking powder entirely, relying instead on baking soda alone, and the problem was fixed. (Natural cocoa is more acidic than Dutch-processed, and when it was combined with baking powder, which also contains acid, it produced an excess of carbon dioxide gas. This in turn caused the cake to rise very fast and then fall like a deflated balloon.)

Also of note is the low oven temperature—325 degrees—which, combined with a relatively long baking time of 40 minutes, produced a perfectly baked cake with a lovely flat top. Using a microwave oven rather than a double boiler to melt the chocolate and butter also saved time and hassle.

This cake can be frosted with almost anything—a buttercream, an Italian meringue, a sour cream or whipped cream frosting—but we developed a classic American milk chocolate frosting that pairs well with the darker flavor of the cake. Unlike a regular two-layer cake, this cake is a snap to frost.

WHAT WE LEARNED: Use both semisweet chocolate and cocoa powder for depth of flavor and buttermilk to give the cake a tender crumb. Bake at a low oven temperature so the cake rises slowly and finishes up with a nice flat top that is easy to frost.

CHOCOLATE SHEET CAKE Serves 10 to 12

Melting the chocolate and butter in the microwave is quick and neat, but it can also be done in a heatproof bowl set over a saucepan containing 2 inches of simmering water. We prefer Dutch-processed cocoa for the deeper chocolate flavor it gives the cake. The baked and cooled cake can be served simply with lightly sweetened whipped cream or topped with any frosting you like. We particularly like Creamy Milk Chocolate Frosting (recipe follows).

12 tablespoons (1½ sticks) unsalted butter, plus 1 tablespoon for greasing the baking pan
¾ cup cocoa, preferably Dutch-processed
1¼ cups (6¼ ounces) unbleached all-purpose flour
½ teaspoon baking soda
¼ teaspoon salt
8 ounces semisweet chocolate, chopped
4 large eggs
1½ cups sugar
1 teaspoon vanilla extract
1 cup buttermilk

1. Adjust an oven rack to the middle position and heat the oven to 325 degrees. Grease the bottom and sides of a 13 by 9-inch baking pan with 1 tablespoon butter.

2. Sift together the cocoa, flour, baking soda, and salt in a medium bowl; set aside. Heat the chocolate and remaining 12 tablespoons butter in a microwave-safe bowl covered with plastic wrap for 2 minutes at 50 percent power; stir until smooth. (If not fully melted, heat 1 minute longer at 50 percent power.) Whisk together the eggs, sugar, and vanilla in a medium bowl. Whisk in the buttermilk until smooth.

3. Whisk the chocolate into the egg mixture until combined. Whisk in the dry ingredients until the batter is smooth and glossy. Pour the batter into the prepared pan; bake until firm in the center when lightly pressed and a toothpick inserted in the center comes out clean, about 40 minutes. Let the cake cool on a wire rack to room temperature, at least 1 hour; serve, or ice with frosting, if desired. (The cake can be wrapped in plastic and stored at room temperature for up to 2 days.)

CREAMY MILK CHOCOLATE FROSTING

Makes about 2 cups, enough to ice one 13 by 9-inch cake

This frosting needs about an hour to cool before it can be used, so begin making it when the cake comes out of the oven. Use the best-quality milk chocolate you can find—it will make a big difference in this recipe. See the Tasting Lab on page 310 for specific recommendations.

½ cup heavy cream
   Pinch salt
1 tablespoon light or dark corn syrup
10 ounces milk chocolate, chopped
½ cup (2 ounces) confectioners' sugar
8 tablespoons (1 stick) cold unsalted butter, cut into 8 pieces

1. Heat the cream, salt, and corn syrup in a microwave-safe measuring cup on high until simmering, about 1 minute, or bring to a simmer in a small saucepan over medium heat.

2. Place the chocolate in the workbowl of a food processor fitted with the steel blade. With the machine running, gradually add the hot cream mixture through the feed tube; process 1 minute after the cream has been added. Stop the machine; add the confectioners' sugar to the workbowl and process to combine, about 30 seconds. With the machine running, add the butter through the feed tube one piece at a time; process until incorporated and smooth, about 20 seconds longer.

3. Transfer the frosting to a medium bowl and cool at room temperature, stirring frequently, until thick and spreadable, about 1 hour.

SCIENCE DESK: To Sift or Not to Sift?

SIFTING FLOUR IS A CHORE. THIS IS ESPECIALLY TRUE when sifting into a measuring cup because you inevitably end up sifting twice as much as you need to fill the cup. Many bakers skip this step, thinking it insignificant. Here's why you shouldn't, especially when the recipe says to do so.

Sifting reduces the overall amount of flour (in weight) that goes into the recipe. Because sifting aerates the flour, 1 cup of sifted cake flour weighs in at about 3 ounces, whereas 1 cup of cake flour measured straight from the bin using the dip-and-sweep method (the test kitchen's standard, in which you dip the measure into the flour and then level it by sweeping with a straight-edged spatula) weighs around 4 ounces. To see what effect this difference in amount of flour has on the finished product, we baked two cakes—one with sifted flour, one with unsifted. The cake made with sifted flour baked up perfectly flat, a dream to frost and layer because it required no trimming or leveling. The cake made with unsifted flour, however, mounded in the center and, though still very tasty, was also a bit drier.

Recipes with cocoa powder, such as our chocolate cake, often call for sifting. In this case, sifting breaks up small clumps of cocoa that form as the powder sits in the package. Sifted cocoa can be evenly distributed throughout a cake batter; with unsifted cocoa this isn't always the case.

TASTING LAB: Milk Chocolate

IF LIFE IS LIKE A BOX OF CHOCOLATES, THEN THE MILK chocolates are childhood. Sweet and simple, milk chocolate is the first choice for a kid in a candy store but rarely sought after as an ingredient in grown-up chocolate desserts. In 10 years at *Cook's Illustrated*, we have developed only one recipe using milk chocolate. That recipe, Milk Chocolate Frosting, doesn't specify a brand of chocolate, so we wondered if we could detect any significant differences in the widely available brands. And, to be perfectly honest, some of us really like to eat milk chocolate. When we reach for a bar of milk chocolate in a candy store, we want to be sure we grab the best one.

We gathered nine brands of milk chocolate, ranging from supermarket favorites, such as Hershey's and Nestlé, to boutique brands, such as Valrhona and Callebaut. We tasted them plain and in our Milk Chocolate Frosting (there was no shortage of tasters for these tests).

In the straight chocolate tasting, Lindt took first place, its flavor described as "very rich" and "just about perfect." Close behind was Perugina (a European brand owned by Nestlé), which won points for its "creamy, firm texture," though one taster described it as "waxy." Falling at the bottom of our tasting was boutique brand Valrhona, which was deemed "bitter," "chalky," and "weird." Valrhona has strong fruit and floral notes that many tasters found disagreeable.

There was some shuffling in our Milk Chocolate Frosting tasting, which again saw Perugina and Lindt among the top three (first and third, respectively) but also saw Nestlé jump from fourth to second place. Nestlé was praised for its "deep chocolate flavor" and "smooth texture," though some found the flavor "slightly fake." Valrhona again took the bottom berth (by a wide margin), with its "slightly rancid flavor" that led one taster to wonder, "Is this from one of those tubs?"

If you're looking for an eating chocolate, we recommend splurging on Lindt or Perugina. For baking, when the subtle nuances are much more difficult to detect, save your money. At less than half the price of the top finishers, and with a much wider availability (both Lindt and Perugina could be found only at specialty food stores), Nestlé is a good choice.

Rating Milk Chocolates

TWENTY-TWO MEMBERS OF THE *COOK'S ILLUSTRATED* STAFF TASTED NINE BRANDS OF MILK CHOCOLATE IN TWO WAYS— plain and in a simple frosting. The chocolates are listed below in order of preference based on their combined scores in both tastings. Most brands are sold in supermarkets. A few are available only in gourmet shops with good chocolate selections or in candy stores.

HIGHLY RECOMMENDED
Perugina Milk Chocolate **$2.49 for 3.5 ounces ($11.38/pound)**
This "well-rounded" chocolate was the overall winner. Several tasters called it "honey-like."

HIGHLY RECOMMENDED
Lindt Excellence Extra Creamy Milk Chocolate **$2.49 for 3.5 ounces ($11.38/pound)**
A close second, this chocolate was described as "super soft and creamy" and "deep and rich."

HIGHLY RECOMMENDED
Nestlé Superior Quality Milk Chocolate **$1.50 for 5 ounces ($4.80/pound)**
This chocolate offers an excellent value and is readily available. "Nice balance" was the general consensus, although a few tasters thought it "too sweet."

RECOMMENDED
Callebaut Milk Chocolate **$6.99 for 1 pound**
This premium Belgian chocolate was deemed "really milky" and "somewhat flat."

RECOMMENDED WITH RESERVATIONS
Hershey's Milk Chocolate **$1.19 for 5 ounces ($3.81/pound)**
Many tasters thought this American favorite had a "rich chocolate flavor," but others disagreed and found it "kind of boring."

RECOMMENDED WITH RESERVATIONS
Ghirardelli Milk Chocolate Premium Baking Bar **$2.10 for 4 ounces ($8.76/pound)**
This supermarket brand was described as "sweet" and "harmless," but several tasters complained that it had "no depth."

RECOMMENDED WITH RESERVATIONS
Newman's Own Organics Milk Chocolate **$1.89 for 2.8 ounces ($10.80/pound)**
Tasters were neither wowed nor disappointed by this natural foods store brand. "Buttery" and "not too bad" were typical comments.

RECOMMENDED WITH RESERVATIONS
Cadbury Dairy Milk Milk Chocolate **$1.39 for 4.5 ounces ($4.94/pound)**
This chocolate has a "nice sweet flavor," but tasters also found it "very chewy."

NOT RECOMMENDED
Valrhona Jivara Lactee Milk Chocolate **$10.99 for 1 pound**
Most tasters derided the "gummy" texture and "odd," "fruity" flavors in this premium French chocolate, although it did have a few defenders.

Lemon zest is a key ingredient in our cheesecake recipe. To keep the zest's fibrous texture from marring the smooth cheesecake, it is ground fine with some sugar.

LEMON cheesecake

Although some would never dare to adulterate plain cheesecake, there are plenty of variations out there: some good, some bad, some ugly. Standing out against a Ben & Jerry's–style menu of flavors such as chocolate chip and cappuccino (and many more deplorable variations), lemon is the one version that serves a function by cutting through the cloying nature of this rich dessert.

During our initial recipe testing, we discovered a host of different lemon cheesecake styles. One was a towering soufflé made by separating the eggs, whipping the whites, and folding them in at the end. Another had a pasty texture owing to the addition of sweetened condensed milk. And in all cases the lemon flavor was either too fleeting or too harsh. What we wanted was a light, creamy-textured cheesecake, a style that everyone in the test kitchen felt would be a good partner with the flavor of lemon.

LEMON CHEESECAKE

WHAT WE WANTED: A light, creamy cheesecake with a bracing but not overpowering lemon flavor.

We began our kitchen testing with the foundation of the cheesecake: the crust. Most cheesecakes have a sweet and spicy graham cracker crust that remains crunchy under the weight of the heavy filling. But after our first few attempts, we realized that the strong molasses flavor of the graham crackers overpowered the lemon. We experimented with several types of crumb crusts and ended up preferring one made with biscuit-type cookies. Of all the brands that we tried, Nabisco's Barnum's Animals Crackers were the surprise favorite (see the Tasting Lab on page 317).

We based our filling on our favorite creamy cheesecake recipe, which, although a bit heavy, came closest to our ideal. Our first move was to lighten it by reducing the amount of cream cheese from 2 pounds to 1½. Next we eliminated the sour cream because the addition of lemon provided a tangy counterpoint to the cream cheese. To our surprise, a bit more heavy cream was a good thing, producing a luscious texture.

As for the lemon flavor, we discovered that one can have too much of a good thing by using too much lemon juice. Zest provided a balanced lemon flavor, but it came with a hitch: The fibrous texture of the zest marred the creamy smoothness of the filling. To solve this problem, we tried processing the zest and sugar together before adding them to the cream cheese. This produced a wonderfully potent lemon flavor by breaking down the zest and releasing its oils, but it also caused the cheesecake to become strangely dense. After many trials, we realized that the food processor was wreaking havoc with the sugar, breaking down its crystalline structure (necessary for the aeration of the cream cheese) as well as melding it with the oils from the lemon zest. By processing only ¼ cup of the sugar with the zest and then stirring in the remaining sugar by hand, we solved the problem.

Baking this cheesecake in a water bath at a low oven temperature of 325 degrees was also key to achieving a creamy texture. We were surprised to find that when we used hot tap water instead of boiling water (we like shortcuts), the result was a more evenly baked cheesecake (and about 10 minutes of extra baking time). We also discovered that an additional hour in the oven, with the heat off and the door ajar, was crucial to a consistent texture. When we tried to skip this step, the cheesecake set up on the edges but remained gooey in the center.

Our cheesecake was certainly lemony, but we wanted more pizzazz. We found it by revisiting a test recipe that had included a topping of lemon curd. We found we could make a curd in just five minutes and let it set up in the refrigerator while the cheesecake was baking and cooling.

Based on previous work done in the test kitchen for a lemon tart recipe, we knew three things about lemon curd: There must be enough acid to denature the proteins in the eggs and thereby form the curd; sugar helps to prevent the eggs from overcooking; and butter helps to emulsify the ingredients, creating a smoother product. Many recipes called for only yolks in the curd, but these were too rich. Curd made

---

FOOD FACT: Animal Crackers

In the late 1800s these animal-shaped cookies were first imported to the United States from England, answering a demand for fancy baked goods. In 1902, Nabisco designed a box that looked just like a circus wagon cage and even attached a string so the box could be hung from the Christmas tree. Called Barnum's Animals, these crackers have remained popular for a century. Today the company bakes 19 animals into cracker likenesses. The newest animal to join the collection is the koala, which beat out the penguin, walrus, and cobra in recent voting by consumers.

with just two whole eggs was pale in color and lacked depth of flavor. Just one extra yolk gave the curd the right color and amount of richness. The only problem remaining was the curd's slightly acidic edge. To curb it, we mixed in 1 tablespoon of heavy cream at the end of cooking, along with a dash of vanilla. Cold cubed butter, also added at the end, served both to cool the curd (and prevent overcooking) and to form a smoother emulsion. The curd now complemented the cheesecake perfectly, adding a bit of easy showmanship to this otherwise plain dessert.

WHAT WE LEARNED: Use biscuit-type cookies, such as animal crackers, to create a mild-tasting crust that will let the lemon flavor of the cheesecake shine. Grind the zest with some of the sugar to release its flavor and improve its texture. Add heavy cream for richness, and bake the cake in a water bath for ultimate creaminess. Finally, top off the cake with lemon curd for another layer of lemon flavor.

LEMON CHEESECAKE Serves 12 to 16

While this recipe takes several hours from start to finish, the actual preparation is simple, and baking and cooling proceed practically unattended. Chill the finished cheesecake at least 4 hours before attempting to slice it. The cheesecake can be made up to a day in advance; leftovers can be refrigerated for up to 4 days, although the crust will become soggy.

cookie-crumb crust

5   ounces Nabisco's Barnum's Animals Crackers or Social Tea Biscuits
3   tablespoons sugar
4   tablespoons unsalted butter, melted and kept warm

filling

1¼ cups (8¾ ounces) sugar
1   tablespoon grated zest plus ¼ cup juice from 1 or 2 lemons
1½ pounds (three 8-ounce packages) cream cheese, cut into rough 1-inch chunks and left to stand at room temperature 30 to 45 minutes
4   large eggs, room temperature
2   teaspoons vanilla extract
¼   teaspoon salt
½   cup heavy cream

lemon curd

⅓   cup juice from 2 lemons
2   large eggs plus 1 large egg yolk
½   cup (3½ ounces) sugar
2   tablespoons unsalted butter, cut into ½-inch cubes and chilled
1   tablespoon heavy cream
¼   teaspoon vanilla extract
    Pinch salt

1. FOR THE CRUST: Adjust an oven rack to the lower-middle position and heat the oven to 325 degrees. In a food processor, process the cookies to fine, even crumbs, about 30 seconds (you should have about 1 cup). Add the sugar and pulse 2 or 3 times to incorporate. Add the warm melted butter in a slow, steady stream while pulsing; pulse until the mixture is evenly moistened and resembles wet sand, about ten 1-second pulses. Transfer the mixture to 9-inch springform pan; using the bottom of a ramekin or a dry measuring cup, press the crumbs firmly and evenly into the pan bottom, keeping the sides as clean as possible. Bake until fragrant and golden brown, 15 to 18 minutes. Cool on a wire rack to room temperature, about 30 minutes. When cool, wrap the outside of the pan with two 18-inch-square pieces of heavy-duty foil; set the springform pan in the roasting pan.

2. FOR THE FILLING: While the crust is cooling, process ¼ cup sugar and lemon zest in a food processor until the sugar is yellow and the zest is broken down, about 15 seconds, scraping down the bowl if necessary. Transfer the lemon sugar to a small bowl; stir in the remaining 1 cup sugar.

3. In a standing mixer fitted with the paddle attachment, beat the cream cheese on low to break up and soften slightly, about 5 seconds. With the machine running, add the sugar mixture in a slow steady stream; increase the speed to medium and continue to beat until the mixture is creamy and smooth, about 3 minutes, scraping down the bowl with a rubber spatula as needed. Reduce the speed to medium-low and add the eggs 2 at a time; beat until incorporated, about 30 seconds, scraping the sides and bottom of the bowl well after each addition. Add the lemon juice, vanilla, and salt and mix until just incorporated, about 5 seconds; add the heavy cream and mix until just incorporated, about 5 seconds longer. Give the batter a final scrape, stir with a rubber spatula, and pour into the prepared springform pan; fill the roasting pan with enough hot tap water to come halfway up the sides of the springform pan. Bake until the center jiggles slightly, the sides just start to puff, the surface is no longer shiny, and an instant-read thermometer inserted in the center of the cake registers 150 degrees, 55 to 60 minutes. Turn off the oven and prop open the oven door with a potholder or wooden spoon handle; allow the cake to cool in the water bath in the oven for 1 hour. Transfer the springform pan without the foil to a wire rack; run a small paring knife around the inside edge of the pan to loosen the sides of the cake, and cool the cake to room temperature, about 2 hours.

GETTING IT RIGHT: Judging When the Curd Is Done

At first, the curd will appear thin and soupy, as shown at left. When the spatula leaves a clear trail in the bottom of the saucepan (which quickly disappears), the curd is ready to come off the heat (center). If the curd continues to cook, it will become too thick and pasty, and a spatula will leave a wide clear trail (right).

4. FOR THE LEMON CURD: While the cheesecake bakes, heat the lemon juice in a small nonreactive saucepan over medium heat until hot but not boiling. Whisk the eggs and yolk in a medium nonreactive bowl; gradually whisk in the sugar. Whisking constantly, slowly pour the hot lemon juice into the eggs, then return the mixture to the saucepan and cook over medium heat, stirring constantly with a wooden spoon, until the mixture registers 170 degrees on an instant-read thermometer and is thick enough to cling to a spoon, about 3 minutes (see the photos on page 316 to gauge doneness). Immediately remove the pan from the heat and stir in the cold butter until incorporated; stir in the cream, vanilla, and salt, then pour the curd through a fine-mesh strainer into a small nonreactive bowl. Cover the surface of the curd directly with plastic wrap; refrigerate until needed.

5. TO FINISH THE CAKE: When the cheesecake is cool, scrape the lemon curd onto the cheesecake still in the springform pan; using an offset icing spatula, spread the curd evenly over the top of the cheesecake. Cover tightly with plastic wrap and refrigerate for at least 4 hours or up to 24 hours. To serve, remove the sides of the springform pan and cut the cake into wedges.

GETTING IT RIGHT: Chill Thoroughly

If the cheesecake is not thoroughly chilled, it will not hold its shape when sliced (left). After four hours in the refrigerator (preferably longer), the cheesecake has set up and can be sliced neatly (right).

TASTING LAB: Cookies for Crumb Crusts

AFTER REJECTING GRAHAM CRACKERS IN FAVOR OF something more delicate, we decided to try shortbread cookies in the crust for our lemon cheesecake. Walkers Shortbread, Nabisco's Lorna Doones, and Keebler Sandies all produced crusts that were dense and chewy, with a toffee-like flavor that was too rich and sweet. Next we used digestive biscuits to make the crust. Although this crust was too sweet and a little gritty (these biscuits contain whole-wheat flour), the dryness of the biscuit produced the best-textured crust to complement the creamy cheesecake; it also let us add more butter to the crust, which resulted in a better flavor. After testing all of the biscuit-type cookies we could find, the surprising favorite was Barnum's Animals Crackers from Nabisco. Nabisco's Social Tea Biscuits were a close second.

BEST COOKIES FOR CRUMB CRUST
Biscuit-type cookies, especially Barnum's Animals Crackers from Nabisco, beat out shortbread cookies, digestive biscuits, and graham crackers in our tasting of 10 cookies for the crumb crust.

TASTING LAB: Lemon Substitutes

FACED WITH THE TASK OF SQUEEZING LEMONS FOR BAKED goods, we wondered if there was an easier alternative. We found several possible timesaving products at the grocery store: Minute Maid frozen lemon juice made from concentrate and bottled reconstituted lemon juice made by ReaLemon and Concord Foods; both of the latter two products contain preservatives and lemon oil as well as lemon juice from concentrate. Would it be possible to make decent baked goods with these products, or would they result in cookies that tasted as plastic as the lemon-shaped squeeze bottle?

To give all three products a thorough testing, we tasted them two different ways: in lemonade and in glazed lemon cookies—intense, lemony cookies. The results of the lemonade tasting were no surprise. Tasters overwhelmingly preferred lemonade made with the freshly squeezed lemons. The lemonade made with frozen juice wasn't bad but "tasted like store-bought lemonade," and the reconstituted

juices tasted artificial and weak. When baked into cookies and made into a glaze, the differences were smaller but still noticeable. Tasters thought the cookies made with reconstituted juices were "acidic but not very lemony" and had the least amount of flavor. The frozen juice fared slightly better—the cookies had more lemon flavor. No surprise—the

TECHNIQUE: Juicing Lemons

Everyone has a trick for juicing lemons. After testing dozens of methods, we think this one extracts the most juice from lemons as well as limes.

1. Start by rolling the lemon on a hard surface, pressing down firmly with the palm of your hand to break the membranes inside the fruit.

2. Cut the lemon in half. Use a reamer with a pointed tip (see the Equipment Corner on page 250) to extract the juice. To catch the seeds, place a mesh strainer over the bowl.

TECHNIQUE: Cleaning the Food Processor Workbowl

The easiest way to clean bowls is to soak them with sudsy water before washing. However, the hole in the center of a food processor workbowl makes this impossible, unless you plug up that hole. Here's how we do it in the test kitchen.

1. Remove the bowl cover and blade. Set an empty 35mm film canister upside down over the hole in the workbowl.

2. Now you can fill the bowl with warm, soapy water and allow it to soak.

cookies made with fresh lemon juice were "nice and tangy" and "tasted the most like lemons."

The verdict? Get out your cutting board and lemon reamer. It's best to squeeze your own lemon juice, even for baked goods.

SCIENCE DESK:
Why Bother with a Water Bath?

A WATER BATH IS COMMONLY CALLED FOR WHEN BAKING cheesecakes and custards. The theory is that the water bath moderates the temperature around the perimeter of the pan, preventing overcooking at the edges. To figure out exactly what's happening, we prepared two identical cheesecakes; one was placed in an oven alone while the other was placed in a water bath before baking. Both were taken from the oven when their centers reached 147 degrees. The cake that had

been baked in a water bath was even-colored and smooth, while the other had browned and cracked. A quick comparison of the temperature at the edges of the cakes confirmed what we suspected. The cake that had had the benefit of a water bath was 184 degrees at the edge, while the cake baked without the water bath had climbed to 213 degrees.

Why was the cheesecake baked in a water bath 30 degrees cooler at the edges than the cake baked without the water bath? Although the oven had been set to 325 degrees, a water bath can never exceed 212 degrees, as this is the temperature at which water converts to steam. In fact, more than half of the water in the bath had indeed evaporated, resulting in quite a humid oven. The increased water content of the air in the oven served to keep the top of the cake moist and to prevent cracking. For five minutes of work, then, our water bath protected the edges of the cake by keeping the temperature low and protected the top of the cake through added humidity.

EQUIPMENT CORNER: Springform Pans

ALTHOUGH SELDOM USED IN MOST HOME KITCHENS, A springform pan is essential if you want to make cheesecake, chocolate mousse cake, or any other cake that would be impossible to release intact from a standard cake pan. We baked cheesecake and chocolate mousse cake in six (9-inch) springform pans, ranging in price from $9 to $38, to see if more money bought a better pan.

An ideal pan, we thought, would release the cakes from the sides and bottom of the pan effortlessly. All six pans tested had acceptable side release, but dislodging a cake from the pan bottom was trickier. Here, the top-performing pans were the Kaiser Bakeware Noblesse and the Frieling Glass Bottom, each of which has a rimless bottom; the other four pans tested have a ridge around the outside edge that can get in the way of cake removal. We also found that pans with rimless bottoms are much easier to clean.

Another valuable quality in a springform pan is its resistance to leakage when placed in a water bath. To test leakage, we baked cheesecakes in a water bath tinted with green food coloring, our theory being that the less secure the seal of the pan, the more water would seep through and the greener the cheesecake. This was a tough test. Even the best-performing pan in this test, the Kaiser Noblesse, showed an edge of green that traveled in a ring around one third of the cake. The worst performers here were the Kaiser Bakeware Tinplate and the Cuisipro Tall Tinned pan, in which the green made a complete circle around the outside edge of the cake. Of all the pans tested, these two also had the most flimsy construction and were the cheapest, priced at $8.99 and $9.99, respectively. The Frieling pan as well as the Roscho Commercial ($12.99) and the Exeter Non-Stick ($11.49) showed decent performance in this test. Because no pan demonstrated a perfect seal, we recommend wrapping the bottom of a springform pan with foil when baking in a water bath.

The good news is that we found two pans we like quite a lot. The bad news is that they were the priciest pans tested.

Rating Springform Pans

WE TESTED SIX 9-INCH SPRINGFORM PANS BY BAKING A CHEESECAKE AND A CHOCOLATE MOUSSE CAKE (SEE RECIPE ON page 326) in each pan. We rated the pans for ease of release (from the sides as well as the bottom), leakage (we dyed a water bath green to see how much water was getting into each pan), and design (including their overall construction). The pans are listed in order of preference based on scores from these tests. See www.americastestkitchen.com for up-to-date prices and mail-order sources for top-rated products.

RECOMMENDED

Kaiser Bakeware Noblesse Springform Pan

$19.80

This well-made pan won the leak test. It is well constructed and well designed. The rimless bottom means removing cakes is especially easy.

RECOMMENDED

Frieling Handle-It Glass Bottom Springform Pan

$31.95

The handles come in handy when lifting this pricey pan out of a water bath. The rimless bottom means removing cakes is especially easy.

RECOMMENDED WITH RESERVATIONS

Roscho Commercial Springform Pan

$12.99

Decent performance in the leak test, but the rimmed bottom gets in the way when trying to remove cakes at serving time.

RECOMMENDED WITH RESERVATIONS

Exeter Non-Stick Springform Pan

$11.49

Minimal leaking, but the rimmed bottom makes removal of neat slices somewhat tricky. The rim also makes cleanup more tedious than is necessary.

NOT RECOMMENDED

Kaiser Bakeware Tinplate Springform Pan

$8.99

This pan performed poorly in the leak test (the green food dye made a complete circle around the edge of the cake), and it does not seem well constructed.

NOT RECOMMENDED

Cuisipro Tall Tinned Springform Pan

$9.99

Flimsy construction and serious leaking sunk this pan to the bottom of the ratings. Again, the rimmed bottom made it difficult to remove neat slices from this pan.

Foil collars are attached to ceramic ramekins so that individual chilled lemon soufflés can rise high above the rims of the dishes.

SHOWSTOPPER *desserts*

CHAPTER 26

In the test kitchen, we tend to favor simple, homespun desserts. Most of us would rather make a batch of really good cookies than a fancy cake or tart. That said, we all recognize the need for showy desserts, especially when entertaining. A plate of chocolate chip cookies just won't do after some meals.

On these occasions, we like desserts that look more complicated to prepare than they really are. A chocolate mousse cake requires a minimum of ingredients and comes together in minutes, but it is sure to elicit the proper oohs and aahs from guests. A chilled lemon soufflé is made from ingredients that probably are in your kitchen right now—eggs, milk, lemon, sugar, and cream. Even better, this soufflé must be prepared in advance, making it far more suitable for entertaining than the more familiar baked soufflés that must go straight from oven to table. We hope these two easy but special desserts will become favorites in your home.

CHOCOLATE MOUSSE CAKE

WHAT WE WANTED: Chocolate mousse cake runs the gamut from fluffy, insubstantial layer cake to dense-as-a-brick, fudge-like slab. Could we make one that maintained the qualities of a perfect chocolate mousse—rich, creamy, and full of chocolate flavor?

Chocolate mousse is comfort food dressed up for company, like pudding for grownups. Less familiar to most home cooks is the chocolate mousse cake. After investigating local bakeries, we discovered that this dessert has two distinct styles. One was a fancy, fluffy chocolate sponge layer cake, brushed with syrup, with mousse sandwiched between the layers. The other was essentially chocolate mousse baked in a cake pan, almost cheesecake-like in density. Before deciding on one style, we'd have to make both.

The sponge cake/mousse combination was incredibly time-consuming (make the cake, cool the cake, cut the cake, make the syrup, soak the cake, make the mousse, assemble the cake, chill the cake—whew). An enormous sinkful of dishes and several grueling hours later, we tasted the cake. Its elegant appearance couldn't make up for its lack of chocolate flavor. This cake was a dud—all show and no substance. Although we could work on improving the flavor, we decided not to try. This cake was simply too much work for the home cook.

The baked mousse was much simpler—a major benefit—but it came out of the oven a dense, homely mess. Texture and appearance aside, however, this ugly duckling showed promise. The flavor was excellent: fudgy, chocolatey, and very, very rich. With a more mousse-like texture and a bit of a facelift, this cake could be a winner.

The ingredient list for chocolate mousse cake is short: chocolate, sugar, butter, eggs, vanilla, and salt. We tackled the most important ingredient first: the chocolate. We tried grocery-store brands as well as a few high-end boutique chocolates and determined that Hershey's Special Dark made a great cake with nicely balanced chocolate flavor. Baker's Bittersweet Chocolate was less successful, having an artificial aftertaste that tasters rejected. Other, more expensive brands worked, but we decided to stick to the more widely available Hershey's, which had also done well in a previous tasting of bittersweet chocolates.

But bittersweet chocolate alone didn't bring the intensity we were looking for. We tried cocoa, but it gave the cake a sour flavor. After some experimentation, we found that adding a mere ounce of unsweetened chocolate to 12 ounces of bittersweet provided a deep, chocolatey taste and a darker, slightly more sophisticated quality. (See the Tasting Lab on page 327 for information about buying unsweetened chocolate.)

Butter and egg yolks are the ingredients that give this cake its melt-in-your-mouth texture. Twelve tablespoons was the perfect amount of butter. Any more made the cake unpalatably greasy; less made it dry. As for egg yolks, we made cakes using as few as four and as many as 10. The 10-yolk version remained a little too damp in the middle, even when thoroughly baked. Eight was the magic number. Some vanilla and a pinch of salt heightened the chocolate flavor even more. The vanilla does double duty: It rounds out the smokiness of the chocolate, giving the cake slightly fruity overtones, while taming the egginess of the yolks.

The final ingredient in this cake is beaten egg whites, which are folded into the batter just before it goes into the oven. But folding the beaten egg whites into the chocolate mixture was proving problematic. The delicate whites collapsed under the weight of the chocolate, giving the cake a dense, bricklike texture. Was there anything we could do to make the whites sturdier? We tried beating the egg whites further, until they were almost rigid. That wasn't the answer; it just made the cake unappealingly dry. Maybe beating the whites less rigorously was the answer. No such luck. That

temperature for most cakes. Not for this one. It turned into a giant mushroom that collapsed after cooling. A more gentle heat was clearly necessary. We tried lowering the temperature, but even at 300 degrees the outside of the cake was overdone while the center remained raw. Baking the mousse cake in a water bath—an extra complication we had hoped to avoid—might do the trick. We placed the mousse-filled springform pan in a roasting pan, filled the roasting pan with hot water, and put it all in the oven. Once again, we tried baking the cake at 350, 325, and 300 degrees. The cake baked at 325 degrees was perfect. It rose evenly and had a velvety, creamy texture throughout. That extra step was definitely worth the effort.

Now we had a cake with great texture, but there was still something missing. The chocolate flavor was intense but still a little too sweet and one-dimensional. Perhaps reducing the sugar was the answer. Not so. It only made the cake slightly bitter. On a whim, we tried using light brown sugar instead of granulated white sugar. The flavor was fabulous, with just the right amount of sweetness and a tiny hint of smokiness from the molasses. Brown sugar offered an additional bonus. The molasses in brown sugar is slightly acidic, eliminating the need for cream of tartar (another acid) to stabilize the egg whites. When beaten together, the whites and brown sugar turned into a glossy, perfect meringue.

Our chocolate mousse cake was rich and creamy, with tremendous chocolate flavor, and it was also pretty easy to make. What more could a chocoholic ask?

made the cake even more dense. We looked again at the mousse cake recipes we had found in our initial research. All of them called for the sugar to be added to the yolks and chocolate. We decided to add the sugar, along with a pinch of cream of tartar, to the whites instead. (Sugar creates a thicker, more stable egg foam, and acids, such as cream of tartar, help prevent egg foams from collapsing.) Finally, we had uncovered the secret to the perfect texture. This method produced a creamy meringue that held up well when folded into the chocolate mixture and produced a baked mousse cake that was moist, rich, and creamy.

We tried baking the cake at 350 degrees, the standard

WHAT WE LEARNED: For the best chocolate punch, use bittersweet chocolate mixed with a bit of unsweetened chocolate. Beat the egg whites with brown sugar for hint of smoky molasses flavor. The acidity in the brown sugar also stabilizes the beaten whites, so they can folded into the heavy batter without collapsing. Finally, bake the cake in a water bath for a velvety, creamy texture.

BITTERSWEET CHOCOLATE MOUSSE CAKE

Makes one 9-inch cake, serving 12 to 16

Because it is available in most supermarkets and has scored highly in past tastings, Hershey's Special Dark is the chocolate of choice in this recipe. Other bittersweet chocolates will work, but because the amounts of sugar and cocoa butter differ from brand to brand, they will produce cakes with slightly different textures and flavors. When crumbling the brown sugar to remove lumps, make sure that your fingers are clean and grease-free; any residual fat from butter or chocolate might hinder the whipping of the whites. If you like, dust the cake with confectioners' sugar just before serving or top slices with a dollop of lightly sweetened whipped cream. To make slicing easier, freeze the cake for 30 minutes just before serving.

12 tablespoons (1½ sticks) unsalted butter, cut into 12 pieces, plus 1 teaspoon softened butter for greasing pan
    Flour for dusting pan
12 ounces bittersweet chocolate (such as Hershey's Special Dark), chopped
1 ounce unsweetened chocolate, chopped
1 tablespoon vanilla extract
8 large eggs, separated
⅛ teaspoon salt
⅔ cup (4½ ounces) packed light brown sugar, crumbled with fingers to remove lumps (see note)

1. Adjust an oven rack to the lower-middle position and heat the oven to 325 degrees. Butter the sides of a 9-inch springform pan; flour the sides and tap out the excess. Line the bottom of the pan with a parchment or waxed paper round. Wrap the bottom and sides of the pan with a large sheet of foil.

2. Melt 12 tablespoons butter and the chocolates in a large bowl over a large saucepan containing about 2 quarts barely simmering water, stirring occasionally, until the chocolate mixture is smooth. Cool the mixture slightly, then whisk in the vanilla and egg yolks. Set the chocolate mixture aside, reserving the hot water, covered, in the saucepan.

3. In the clean bowl of a standing mixer fitted with the whisk attachment, beat the egg whites and salt at medium speed until frothy, about 30 seconds; add half of the crumbled brown sugar, beat at high speed until combined, about 30 seconds, then add the remaining brown sugar and continue to beat at high speed until soft peaks form when the whisk is lifted (see photo on page 334), about 2 minutes longer. Using a whisk, stir about one third of the beaten egg whites into the chocolate mixture to lighten it, then fold in the remaining egg whites in 2 additions, using the whisk. Gently scrape the batter into the prepared springform pan, set the springform pan in a large roasting pan, then pour the hot water from the saucepan into the roasting pan to a depth of 1 inch. Carefully slide the roasting pan into the oven; bake until the cake has risen, is firm around the edges, the center has just set, and an instant-read thermometer inserted into the center registers about 170 degrees, 45 to 55 minutes.

4. Remove the springform pan from the water bath, discard the foil, and cool on a wire rack 10 minutes. Run a thin-bladed paring knife between the sides of the pan and cake to loosen; cool the cake in the springform pan on a wire rack until barely warm, about 3 hours, then wrap the pan in plastic wrap and refrigerate until thoroughly chilled, at least 8 hours. (The cake can be refrigerated for up to 2 days.)

5. To unmold the cake, remove the sides of the pan. Slide a thin metal spatula between the cake and pan bottom to loosen, then invert the cake onto a large plate, peel off the parchment, and re-invert onto a serving platter. To serve, use a sharp, thin-bladed knife, dipping the knife in a pitcher of hot water and wiping the blade before each cut.

VARIATION
CHOCOLATE-ORANGE MOUSSE CAKE

Follow the recipe for Bittersweet Chocolate Mousse Cake, reducing the vanilla extract to 1 teaspoon and adding 1 tablespoon orange liqueur and 1 tablespoon finely grated orange zest to the chocolate mixture along with the vanilla and egg yolks.

TASTING LAB: Unsweetened Chocolate

LIKE HOLLYWOOD, THE WORLD OF CHOCOLATE HAS celebrities, some of whom earn their fame through stellar performances, while others simply coast on favorable publicity. We wanted to see if all of the fuss over premium chocolates was based on quality or hype. We selected unsweetened chocolate (rather than semi- or bittersweet) because it is a building-block ingredient in countless desserts, most notably brownies and chocolate cake. Not for nibbling, it is pure, unadulterated chocolate, or solidified chocolate liquor, produced without added sugar or flavorings (see "Chocolate Glossary" on page 329 for more definitions). Seven brands were rated: the four American supermarket standbys—Baker's, Ghirardelli, Hershey's, and Nestlé; the premium American brand, Scharffen Berger; and two brands used largely by candy makers and pastry chefs, Callebaut from Belgium and Valrhona from France. We

conducted a blind tasting, sampling a classic American brownie and a chocolate sauce.

Our assumption going into this tasting (based on prior taste tests) was that, in general, the more expensive brands would prevail. In fact, this was the outcome. However, we found a surprising range of taste differences from one brand to the next. If unsweetened chocolate is pure chocolate, how could one brand be so different from another? We spent weeks searching for the answer to this question, encountering red herrings, unhelpful company representatives, and conflicting stories along the way.

The first thing we learned was that most chocolate companies don't like to talk about their product in detail. With the exception of Scharffen Berger, the companies we contacted were distinctly vague. The response from Marie Olson of Nestlé said it all: "Most of what we do is proprietary. Nestlé has established a certain flavor profile, and we blend beans from various sources based on availability and cost to match our profile."

We turned to outside experts to uncover the trade secrets of chocolate manufacturers. One was Maricel Presilla, author of *The New Taste of Chocolate: A Cultural and Natural History of Cacao with Recipes* (Ten Speed Press, 2001). "Normally," she told us, "companies use a lower-priced bulk bean—from Malaysia, Indonesia, the Dominican Republic, or the Ivory Coast—for their unsweetened. I would not use a company's unsweetened as a barometer for the quality of any brand. With a few notable exceptions, that is not where a company uses their best beans." A cacao trader who sells to most of the major chocolate companies and wished to remain unnamed agreed. "They don't use their best beans for unsweetened. After all, you don't put your best burgundy in a coq au vin." The irony of this practice is that there is more chocolate in unsweetened than in any other type, so the quality of the beans may matter more, not less.

Every expert we contacted told us that the flavor of unsweetened chocolate is largely determined before it gets to the chocolate processor. Country of origin and specific bean blend are the most critical factors. In fact, the above-mentioned cacao trader said, "If you gave Scharffen Berger Nestlé's beans and they put it through their process, the chocolate would taste like Nestlé." Scharffen Berger cofounder Robert Steinberg concurred, adding, "A processor can ruin a good bean but cannot make good chocolate from an inferior one." Both comments underscore a simple fact: When it comes to making chocolate, you have to start with good ingredients. If this is the case, however, then why don't all companies purchase the highest quality beans?

Cacao beans come mainly from West Africa, Indonesia, Brazil, and Malaysia, with smaller amounts coming from other South American countries and the Caribbean. Each region has diverse outputs and characteristics. If a flavor profile includes, say, the taste of coffee, a company would select West African beans; for floral notes, Ecuadorian arriba; for fruity flavor, beans from Venezuela and Trinidad; and for citrus flavor, beans from Madagascar.

Scharffen Berger's Steinberg allows that taste is his company's priority when it comes to buying beans, and he is willing to pay more to secure that taste. "Without exception," he said "we are paying above-market prices for our beans." But some companies can't afford the luxury of buying the best-flavored beans, and it's not necessarily because of the price. Large companies may use 10,000 tons of beans per year, so what is most important to them is supply. They need to buy chocolate from a region that consistently produces a large amount, such as West Africa. They cannot risk a short supply from Venezuela, for instance, which produces a tiny amount of some of the best beans.

FOOD ANALYSIS:
Unsweetened Chocolates

After our tasting of unsweetened chocolates, we sent all seven brands to a laboratory to determine the amount of fat in each as well as its pH (acidity). The results were mixed. While three of the four top-rated chocolates—Scharffen Berger, Callebaut, and Valrhona—did have slightly more fat than most of the other brands, fifth-place Nestlé had the highest fat content of all. As for pH, there was no correlation at all with the results of our tasting.

Chocolate	Fat Content (%)	pH
Scharffen Berger	53.12	5.36
Callebaut	53.96	5.62
Ghirardelli	48.92	5.51
Valrhona	54.94	5.36
Nestlé	58.42	5.91
Baker's	50.03	5.48
Hershey's	52.73	5.60

We concluded that the really big players in the unsweetened chocolate business use a more limited mix of beans because their volume demands exclude smaller suppliers. This in turn may make the flavor profile of their product less interesting.

If the quality of a bean is one important determinant of flavor, the blend of beans selected is another. "One great bean can give you a flat taste, whereas a blend of many can give you more depth," said the cacao trader. Greg Ziegler, associate professor of food science at Penn State University, agreed, pointing out that roasting is yet another key step in the process. Of most interest, according to Ziegler, is whether a company roasts bean types individually or together.

Other experts agree that roasting varieties of beans separately allows the roaster to be more selective and to both preserve and concentrate flavor. Beans vary in size, moisture content, and acidity, and as a result they require different roasting temperatures and times. "If you mix everything

together," said Presilla, "you're not doing justice to any bean; you destroy the nuances. Beans should be roasted independently." Of the companies whose chocolate we tasted, Scharffen Berger is the only one that would confirm that it roasts beans separately by type. Although many experts vouch for roasting independently, our tasting results suggest it's not the only way to produce a high-quality chocolate. In fact, a spokesperson for third-place Ghirardelli noted that the company roasts all types of beans together.

One final production issue is conching, which aerates and homogenizes the chocolate, thereby mellowing the flavor and making its texture smooth and creamy. While eating chocolates are always conched, only Scharffen Berger and Valrhona conch their unsweetened chocolate, and these chocolates finished first and third in our chocolate sauce tasting, where smooth texture was an important consideration.

What do we recommend? The more expensive chocolates—Scharffen Berger, Callebaut, Ghirardelli, and Valrhona—were all well liked and received similar scores. If you are willing to buy in bulk by mail, Callebaut turns out to be a best buy. Of the three mass-market brands (Nestlé, Baker's, and Hershey's), Nestlé received more positive comments and significantly higher scores. In fact, there were so many negative comments about Baker's and Hershey's that we cannot recommend either chocolate. It's important to remember, though, that chocolate, much like coffee, is a matter of personal preference, so consider each brand to find a chocolate that suits your palate. The gamut of flavors runs from "nutty" and "cherry" to "smoky," "earthy," and "spicy."

CHOCOLATE GLOSSARY

HERE ARE DEFINITIONS FOR VARIOUS KINDS OF CHOCOLATE as well as the products that are precursors in the process of making eating chocolates.

Cacao Beans: Seeds harvested from fleshy yellow pods that grow on cacao trees.

Nibs: The meats of cacao beans, which get ground into chocolate liquor.

Chocolate Liquor: The thick, nonalcoholic liquid that results when the roasted, hulled beans (nibs, see above) are ground.

Cocoa Butter: The fat that can be extracted from chocolate liquor. It is not a dairy product.

Cocoa Powder: The solids that remain after the cocoa butter is extracted. When the solids are dried, they are processed and then either "Dutched" (treated with alkali) or left as is.

Unsweetened Chocolate: Solidified pure chocolate liquor that contains between 50 percent and 60 percent cocoa butter.

Bittersweet/Semisweet Chocolate: Chocolate that contains at least 35 percent chocolate liquor. The remainder is sugar, vanilla and/or lecithin.

Milk Chocolate: Chocolate made primarily from sugar, at least 10 percent chocolate liquor, milk solids, vanilla and/or lecithin.

Rating Unsweetened Chocolates

TWENTY MEMBERS OF THE *COOK'S ILLUSTRATED* STAFF AND FOUR PASTRY CHEFS TASTED THE CHOCOLATES IN TWO applications. Because unsweetened chocolate, which does not contain sugar or milk solids, is an ingredient that is not eaten in its raw form, we tested it in brownies and in chocolate sauce. The chocolates are listed in order of preference based on the combined scores from these two tests. These chocolates are sold in gourmet shops or supermarkets.

RECOMMENDED

Scharffen Berger Unsweetened Pure Dark Chocolate $8.95 for 275 grams ($14.78/pound)

Scharffen Berger chocolate is made in small batches from high-quality beans from small producers with refurbished vintage equipment from Europe. Tasters described this American chocolate as "fruity" and "nutty," with a "deep, caramelized flavor."

RECOMMENDED

Callebaut Unsweetened Chocolate $11.95 for 1 kilogram ($5.43/pound)

Belgian Callebaut is the number one chocolate manufacturer in the world and a favorite of pastry chefs. In both tests, our tasters ranked this chocolate second and described it as "nutty," with hints of "cinnamon" and "cherry." One devotee called it "spicy," while another said it had "deep, chocolate flavor."

RECOMMENDED

Ghirardelli Unsweetened Chocolate Baking Bar $2.19 for 4 ounces ($8.76/pound)

Testers regularly used the adjectives "coffee," "rich," and "earthy" when commenting on this sample. One panelist described the Ghirardelli brownie as "normal," which may explain its top finish in that test.

RECOMMENDED

Valrhona Cacao Pâte Extra $25.00 for 1 kilogram ($11.36/pound)

A French chocolate available in unsweetened only in bulk, it often elicited the words "cherry," "fruity," "wine," and "rich." One detractor said that it "tasted more like flowers than chocolate," while another found it "dull."

RECOMMENDED

Nestlé Unsweetened Baking Chocolate Bars $1.99 for 8 ounces ($3.98/pound)

The only chocolate in our group processed with alkali; our lab found it significantly higher in pH (or lower in acidity). Its fat content was the highest at 58.42%. A basic chocolate that fans called "earthy" and "nutty" and detractors described as "smoky," "scorched," or "dull."

NOT RECOMMENDED

Baker's Unsweetened Baking Chocolate Squares $2.39 for 8 ounces ($4.78/pound)

The unsweetened chocolate we all have in our kitchens was considered "smoky," "acidic," and "bitter," but a few fans found it "rich" and "earthy." One taster described it as "dry and mealy," while another said it "didn't have much chocolate flavor."

NOT RECOMMENDED

Hershey's Unsweetened Baking Chocolate $2.19 for 8 ounces ($4.38/pound)

Hershey's adds cocoa to its unsweetened chocolate, which came in last in both tastings. Tasters found it "acidic," "muted," and "chemical-y." One described its flavor as having a "hint of anchovy," while another said it was "plain and dull."

CHILLED LEMON SOUFFLÉ

WHAT WE WANTED: An ethereal, creamy dessert that dissolves on the tongue and satisfies with a complex lemon flavor.

Based on a classic Bavarian cream, chilled lemon soufflé is most often a mixture of a custard base, gelatin, whipped cream, beaten egg whites, sugar, and lemon flavorings. But like any good mongrel American classic, "chilled lemon soufflé" covers a wide range of recipes, from baked pudding cakes, which are cooled and served at room temperature, to nothing more than lemon juice, sugar, and beaten whites, with no egg yolks and no whipped cream.

Given these various guises, it's hard to know exactly how this dessert should taste. For us, a chilled lemon soufflé is an unusual marriage of cream and foam, of sweet and sour, of high lemony notes and lingering, rich custard. It starts at the tip of the tongue with the sharp tingle of lemon zest and then slides slowly down the throat, filling the mouth with cream and pudding and a soft, long finish. At least that's what it is supposed to do. The question is, how can a home cook make this delicate balance of ingredients and technique turn out just right? We set out to test as many recipes as possible to find out.

After testing several recipes, we discovered that there are five basic approaches to this dessert. The most elaborate begins with a custard base that is then combined with gelatin, whipped cream, and beaten egg whites. Many recipes, however, leave out the custard, using only beaten egg yolks and sugar as the base, while some classic French versions of this dish also leave out the egg whites. Other recipes omit the egg yolks altogether, using just sugar, lemon juice, whipped cream, and beaten egg whites. If the whipped cream is eliminated in a further act of reductionism, you have what is known as a lemon snow pudding. We also looked up recipes for lemon mousse and found that mousse is usually made without gelatin, the key ingredient in chilled lemon soufflé.

We began our testing with the simplest approach, just beaten egg whites, gelatin, sugar, and lemon juice. The result was a foamy confection, much like being served a mound of beaten egg whites. This dessert needed some fat for texture and flavor. We then thought we would try a recipe with whipped cream as well. This was quite good, rated number one by some tasters. It had lots of lemon punch but a somewhat airy, foamy texture that called for a bit more fat. Next, we added beaten egg yolks to the mixture, perhaps the most common approach to chilled lemon soufflé, but the texture of this version of the dessert was tough. We tried a second variation on this theme and were still unsatisfied with the texture. We then left out the egg whites and produced a dense, rubbery lemon dome, the sort of dessert that might hold up nicely in Death Valley in July. Finally, we started with a custard base made with sugar, egg yolks, milk, lemon juice, and gelatin and then added this to the whipped cream and beaten whites. This was highly rated, but the lemon flavor was a bit muted by the fat in the milk and egg yolks.

Upon reviewing the test results, we decided that a compromise might be reached between the two test

winners. The lemon juice/whipped cream/beaten egg-white dessert was light and lemony but too foamy; the custard base dessert had a better finish and mouthfeel but was lacking the bright, clear flavor of lemon. We worked up a new master recipe that called for softening one package of gelatin in a half cup of lemon juice. (We tried two packages of gelatin and ended up with a rubbery orb.) Next, a cup of milk was heated with sugar while we beat two egg yolks with an extra 2 tablespoons of sugar. The milk and the beaten yolks were combined on top of the stove and heated until the mixture began to steam. Finally, the cooled custard was folded into ¾ cup of whipped heavy cream, and six beaten egg whites were folded into the result. This was the best variation to date, but it still needed a few refinements.

First, we cut back the whites from six to five to give the dessert less air and more substance. Next, we added just ¼ teaspoon of cornstarch to the custard mixture to prevent the yolks from curdling too easily, and we added grated lemon zest to the custard mixture to pump up the lemon flavor. We also discovered that to maintain a more consistent texture it

was better to whisk a small part of the beaten egg whites into the custard base before folding the mixture together.

Although many recipes call for individual ramekins, we decided to make one large and impressive soufflé and save the individual portions for a variation. To make this chilled dessert look even more like its baked cousin, we added a simple collar of aluminum foil and increased the recipe to the point where the mixture would rise above the rim of the dish, much like a real soufflé. We were also curious about how well this dessert would hold up in the refrigerator. After one day, it was still good but slightly foamy, losing the creamy, tender undercurrent that is the hallmark of this dessert when well made. After two and three days, it quickly deteriorated. This is one dessert that is best served the day it is made.

WHAT WE LEARNED: Start with a silky custard base (milk, egg yolks, sugar, and lemon juice) and lighten it with whipped cream and beaten egg whites. Stabilize the mixture with gelatin and use grated lemon zest for an extra citrus punch.

¾ cup sugar

5 large egg whites, plus 2 yolks, at room
temperature

¼ teaspoon cornstarch
Pinch cream of tartar

¾ cup heavy cream
Mint, raspberries, confectioners' sugar, or finely
chopped pistachios for garnish (optional)

1. Place the lemon juice in a small nonreactive bowl; sprinkle the gelatin over. Set aside.

2. Heat the milk and ½ cup sugar in a medium saucepan over medium–low heat, stirring occasionally, until steaming and the sugar is dissolved, about 5 minutes. Meanwhile, whisk together the yolks, 2 tablespoons sugar, and cornstarch in a medium bowl until pale yellow and thickened. Whisking constantly, gradually add the hot milk to the yolks. Return the milk-egg mixture to the saucepan and cook, stirring constantly, over medium–low heat until the foam has dissipated to a thin layer and the mixture thickens to the consistency of heavy cream and registers 185 degrees on an instant-read thermometer, about 4 minutes. Pour the mixture through a mesh sieve and into a medium bowl; stir in the lemon juice mixture and zest. Set the bowl with the custard in a large bowl of ice water; stir occasionally to cool.

3. While the custard mixture is chilling, in the bowl of a standing mixer fitted with the whisk attachment, beat the egg whites and cream of tartar on medium speed until foamy, about 1 minute. Increase the speed to medium-high; gradually add the remaining 2 tablespoons sugar and continue to beat until glossy and the whites hold soft peaks when the beater is lifted, about 2 minutes longer. Do not overbeat. Remove the bowl containing the custard mixture from the ice water bath; gently whisk in about one third of the egg whites, then fold in the remaining whites with a large rubber spatula until almost no white streaks remain.

CHILLED LEMON SOUFFLÉ Serves 4 to 6

To make this lemon soufflé "soufflé" over the rim of the dish, use a 1-quart soufflé dish and make a foil collar for it as follows: Cut a piece of foil 3 inches longer than the circumference of the soufflé dish and fold it lengthwise into fourths. Wrap the foil strip around the upper half of the soufflé dish and secure the overlap with tape. Tape the collar to the soufflé dish as necessary to prevent it from slipping. Spray the inside of the foil collar with vegetable cooking spray. When ready to serve, carefully remove the collar.

For those less concerned with appearance, this dessert can be served from any 1½-quart serving bowl. For best texture, serve the soufflé after 1½ hours of chilling. It may be chilled up to 6 hours; though the texture will stiffen slightly because of the gelatin, it will taste just as good.

½ cup lemon juice from 2 or 3 lemons, plus
2½ teaspoons grated zest

1 packet (¼ ounce) unflavored gelatin

1 cup whole milk

4. In the same mixer bowl (washing is not necessary), using the whisk attachment, beat the cream on medium-high speed until soft peaks form when the beater is lifted, 2 to 3 minutes. Fold the cream into the custard and egg-white mixture until no white streaks remain.

5. Pour into the prepared soufflé dish (see note) or bowl. Chill until set but not stiff, about 1½ hours; remove the foil collar, if using, and serve, garnishing if desired.

VARIATIONS

CHILLED LEMON SOUFFLÉ WITH WHITE CHOCOLATE

The white chocolate in this variation subdues the lemony kick. The difference is subtle, but the sweeter, richer flavor and texture was popular among tasters.

Follow the recipe for Chilled Lemon Soufflé, adding 2 ounces chopped white chocolate to the warm custard before adding the lemon juice mixture and the zest. Stir until melted and fully incorporated.

INDIVIDUAL CHILLED LEMON SOUFFLÉS

Follow the recipe for Chilled Lemon Soufflé, dividing the batter equally among eight ¾-cup ramekins (filled to the rim) or six ¾-cup ramekins with foil collars.

SCIENCE DESK: Why Add Cream of Tartar When Beating Egg Whites?

IN MOST KITCHENS, IN THE BACK OF THE SPICE CUPBOARD, you will find an aged tin of cream of tartar covered with some dust. We obediently add it when whipping egg whites, but otherwise leave this curious white powder alone.

What is cream of tartar and how does it work? Its technical name is acid potassium tartrate, and it is derived from a crystalline acid deposited on the inside of wine barrels as the wine ferments. It is known as an acid salt, that is, an acid that has been partially neutralized to leave a weakly acidic salt.

Egg whites have the miraculous ability to increase their volume over eight-fold when provided with enough energy by means of a strong arm or a good mixer. Mechanical energy causes strands of the protein albumin to partially unfold and connect with one another. These interconnected albumin strands can wrap around air bubbles and lead to foam development.

As anyone who has made egg foams can tell you, it is an imperfect art ripe with opportunities for collapse. Cream of tartar, because of its acidic nature, gives the cook a leg up by lowering the alkaline pH of the egg whites from about 9 to 8. This change in pH helps neutralize certain proteins that tend to repel each other and encourages their association. The result is easier development of a more stable foam.

Our kitchen tests have confirmed that egg whites beaten with cream of tartar achieve greater volume than egg whites beaten on their own. In addition, egg whites beaten with cream of tartar will not collapse as quickly as egg whites beaten on their own. When it comes time to beat egg whites, we suggest that you dust off that tin of cream of tartar.

GETTING IT RIGHT: Beating Egg Whites

The egg whites should be beaten until they appear smooth and creamy. When the beater is lifted out of the bowl, the egg whites should hold a soft peak (left). If the egg whites are beaten too long, they will look dry and grainy and will begin to separate (right).

INDEX

Corn:
Indoor Clambake, 35–37
muffins, 260–63
Apricot, with Orange Essence,
232, 262–63
Bacon-Scallion, with Cheddar
Cheese, 263
best cornmeal for, 263
food fact about, 260
Master Recipe for, 262
problems with, 262
Cornmeal:
Lemon Blueberry Pancakes, 272
tasting of, 263
Crab Cakes, Maryland, 47–48
Creamy Chipotle Sauce for, 48
Tartar Sauce for, 47
Cranberries, Dried, Wild Rice Pilaf with
Pecans and, *95,* 116–17
Cream:
Coconut, Pie, 126–29
Gravy, 124
whipped
chilling bowl for, 298
Topping, 128
Topping, Sour Cream, 226
Cream Cheese Frosting, *236,* 306–7
Orange, 307
Vanilla Bean, 307
Creaming method, 249
Cream of tartar, egg whites and, 334
Creole. *See* New Orleans menu
Crock-Pots (slow cookers), rating of,
32–33
Croutons, 220–21
Garlic, 17
Crusts:
Cookie-Crumb, 315–16
tasting of cookies for, 317
Graham Cracker, 295–96
Coconut, 128–29
store-bought, tasting of, 129
Cucumbers:
cutting into perfect dice, 19
gazpacho, 14–17
Classic (Master Recipe), 16, *83*
Garlic Croutons for, 17
origins of, 16
Quick Food Processor, 16
Spicy, with Chipotle Chiles and
Lime, 16–17
texture of, 17

Cucumbers: *(cont.)*
Greek salad, 4–5
Country-Style, 5
Master Recipe for, 5
seeding, 5
Sesame Noodles with Sweet Peppers
and, 200
Curd, Lemon, 315–16
Cutting boards, keeping stable, 18

D
Denver Omelet, 256–58
Filling for, 258
folding, 259
Desserts, 281–335
Apple Pancake, German, *234,* 276–79
Caramel Sauce for, 278–79
choosing right apple for, 279
Bananas Foster, 60–61
Berry Gratin with Lemon Sabayon,
299–300
Berry Pie, Summer, *237,* 294–96
Coconut Cream Pie, 126–29
lemon cheesecake, 313–21
chilling thoroughly, 317
judging when curd is done for,
316
Master Recipe for, *240,* 315–17
rating of springform pans for,
320–21
water bath for, 319
lemon soufflé(s), chilled, 331–34
Individual, 334
Master Recipe for, 333–34
with White Chocolate, 334
Strawberries with Balsamic Vinegar,
212–13
Tarte Tatin, 225–26
with Pears, 226
30-Minute (Master Recipe), 226
Whipped Cream Topping, 128
chilling bowl for, 298
Sour Cream, 226
see also Cakes; Cookie(s); Frostings
Dicing vegetables, 19
Diners, food facts about, 129
Dressings:
Bacon, Warm, 10–11, *87*
vinaigrettes, 3
for Greek Salad, 5
Dutch ovens, simmering sauces in skillets
versus, 79

E
Egg(s):
consumption of, 256
Denver Omelet, 256–58
Filling for, 258
folding, 259
Hard-Cooked, Foolproof, 11
sizes and weights of, 258
tasting of, 258–59
whites, beating
with cream of tartar, 334
getting it right, 334
yolk foams, science of, 300
Eggplant, Stir-Fried Pork, Onions and, with
Garlic and Black Pepper, 186
Equipment:
cutting boards, keeping stable, 18
food processors
chopping vegetables in, 58
cleaning workbowl of, 318
mixing pound cake batter in,
249
microwave, softening brown sugar in,
284
pans, determining when hot enough
for browning meat, 134
for pancakes, 273
pans, for simmering sauces, skillets
versus Dutch ovens, 79
ratings of
citrus juicers and reamers,
250–51
food storage containers, 118–19
griddles, electric, 273
grill brushes, 174–75
herb choppers, 67–69
ice cream machines, 296–98
ice cream scoops, 61
meat pounders, 125
oyster knives, 44–46
potholders, 290–91
saucepans, large, 165–67
shears, kitchen, 145–47
skillets, traditional, 134–36
slow cookers, 32–33
spatulas, rubber, 264–66
spoonulas, 266
springform pans, 320–21
vegetable choppers, 106–7
woks, electric, 188–89
woks, flat-bottom, 196–97
trivets, extra-large, improvising, 145

Mushrooms: *(cont.)*
  sautéed, pasta with, 64–67
    with Pancetta and Sage, 67
    with Peas and Camembert, 67
    and Thyme (Master Recipe),
      66–67, *229*
  shiitake, tough stems of, 67
Mussels:
  debearding, 36
  Indoor Clambake, 35–37
Mustard, Grainy, Mashed Potatoes with
  Smoked Cheddar and, 164

N

New England (cooking):
  clam chowder, 40–43
    Master Recipe for, 42
    Quick Pantry, 42–43
    scrubbing clams for, 42
    steaming clams for, 43
  maple-glazed pork roast, 112–15
    Master Recipe for, *94,* 114
    with Orange Essence, 115
    with Rosemary, 115
    with Smoked Paprika, 115
    with Star Anise, 115
New Orleans menu, 53–61
  Bananas Foster, 60–61
  Chicken and Shrimp Jambalaya, 54–56,
    86
    chopping vegetables in food pro-
      cessor for, 58
    shredding chicken for, 56
    tasting of pork products for, 56–57
Noodles:
  Pad Thai, *90,* 192–95
    soaking noodles for, 194
  sesame, cold, 198–200
    with Shredded Chicken (Master
      Recipe), 199, *230*
    with Sweet Peppers and
      Cucumbers, 200
  see also Pasta
Nut(s):
  -crusted chicken cutlets, 137–39
    Almond-Crusted, with Wilted
      Spinach–Orange Salad (Master
      Recipe), 138–39
    Macadamia Nut–Crusted, with
      Wilted Spinach–Pineapple Salad,
      139
  see also specific nuts

O

Oatmeal scones, 244–46
  Apricot-Almond, 246
  Cinnamon-Raisin, 246
  with Dried Cherries and Hazelnuts,
    246
  Glazed Maple-Pecan, 246
  Master Recipe for, *233,* 245–46
  oven temperature for, 246
Oils:
  Garlic-Pepper, 210
  olive, boutique extra-virgin, tasting of,
    71–73
  smoking point of, 134
Olive oil, boutique extra-virgin, tasting of,
  71–73
Olives, Niçoise, pitting, 152
Omelet, Denver, 256–58
  Filling for, 258
  folding, 256–58
Onion(s):
  and Ale Sauce, Pan-Roasted Chicken
    Breasts with, 134
  crying from, science of, 44
  Denver Omelet, 256–58
    Filling for, 258
  Port-Caramelized, Mashed
    Potatoes with Blue Cheese
    and, 163–64
  Spicy Stir-Fried Pork, Asparagus and,
    with Lemon Grass, 187
  Stir-Fried Pork, Eggplant
    and, with Garlic and
    Black Pepper, 186
Orange(s):
  Chicken Provençal with Saffron, Basil
    and, 153
  Chocolate Mousse Cake, 327
  essence
    Corn and Apricot Muffins with,
      232, 262–63
    Green Beans with Toasted Maple
      Pecans and, 109, *228*
    Maple-Glazed Pork Roast with,
      115
  –Cream Cheese Frosting, Ginger Carrot
    Cake with, 307
  removing peel and pith from, 138
  Wilted Spinach Salad, 138–39
Orecchiette with Broccoli Rabe and
  Sausage, 70–71
Oyster knives, rating of, 44–46

Oyster sauce:
  Gingery, Stir-Fried Pork, Green Beans,
    and Red Bell Pepper with, *92,*
    186–87
  Stir-Fried Beef and Broccoli with, *97,*
    182–83
  tasting of, 184
Oysters, shucking, 45

P

Pad Thai, *90,* 192–95
  soaking noodles for, 194
Pancake(s), 269–79
  Apple, German, *234,* 276–79
    Caramel Sauce for, 278–79
    choosing right apple for, 279
  blueberry, 270–72
    Lemon-Cornmeal, 272
    Master Recipe for, *235,* 272
  keeping warm, 272
  knowing when pan is ready for, 273
  promoting fluffiness in, 274
  rating of electric griddles for, 273
Pancake syrups, 114
Pancetta, 79
  Pasta with Mushrooms, Sage and, 67
Panko, 137
Pans:
  determining when hot enough
    for browning meat, 134
    for pancakes, 273
  for simmering sauces, Dutch ovens
    versus skillets, 79
Paprika, smoked:
  Maple-Glazed Pork Roast with, 115
  Mashed Potatoes with Toasted Garlic
    and, 165
  and Roasted Red Pepper Butter, 159
Parmesan, in creamy baked four-cheese
  pasta, 81–82
  Master Recipe for, 82
  with Prosciutto and Peas, 82
  with Tomatoes and Basil, 82
Parsley, Lemon, and Garlic Butter, *91,* 159
Parsnips, in Pot Roast with Root Vegetables,
  98, 102–3
Pasta, 63–82
  Bolognese Sauce, Weeknight, 76–78,
    227
    braising meat in milk for, 77, 79
    choosing right pan for, 79
    tasting of tomato pastes for, 79–80

Pound cake:
    lemon, 247–50
        Lemon Glaze for, 250
        Master Recipe for, *242*, 249–50
        Poppy Seed, 250
    mixing methods for, 249
Prosciutto:
    Baked Four-Cheese Pasta with Peas
        and, 82
    Tomato and Mozzarella Tart with, 23
Provençal (cuisine):
    chicken, 150–53
        Master Recipe for, *84*, 152–53
        with Saffron, Orange, and Basil, 153
    Chicken with 40 Cloves of Garlic, *96*,
        142–45
        cutting up chicken for, 145
        developing flavor of garlic for, 144
    use of term, 150
Puff pastry:
    assembling tart shell with, 24
    food fact about, 226
    Tarte Tatin, 225–26
        with Pears, 226
        30-Minute (Master Recipe), 226
    tasting of, 23

R

Raisin-Cinnamon Oatmeal Scones, 246
Raspberries, in Summer Berry Pie, *237*, 294–96
Ratings. *See* Equipment—ratings of; Tastings
Reamers, rating of, 250–51
Red wine:
    Pot Roast with Mushrooms, Tomatoes
        and, 103
    Sauce, Sweet-Tart, Pan-Roasted
        Chicken Breasts with, 133–34
Red wine vinegars:
    food analysis of, 7
    tastings of
        gourmet, 9
        supermarket, 7–9
Rib steaks, grilled, 156–59
    Charcoal- (Master Recipe), 157–58
    Gas-, 158
Rice:
    Chicken and Shrimp Jambalaya, 54–56, *86*
        chopping vegetables in food pro-
            cessor for, 58
        shredding chicken for, 56
        tasting of pork products for, 56–57
    consumption of, 185

Rice stick noodles, in Pad Thai, *90*, 192–95
    soaking noodles for, 194
Roasting, braising versus, 103
Root Vegetables, Pot Roast with, *98*, 102–3
Rosemary, Maple-Glazed Pork Roast with,
    115

S

Sabayon, Lemon, Berry Gratin with, 299–300
Saffron, Chicken Provençal with Orange,
    Basil and, 153
Sage:
    Pasta with Mushrooms, Pancetta and, 67
    Vermouth Sauce, Pan-Roasted Chicken
        Breasts with, *88*, 133
Salad dressings:
    Bacon, Warm, 10–11, *87*
    vinaigrettes, 3
        for Greek Salad, 5
Salads, 3–11
    Greek, 4–5
        Country-Style, 5
        Master Recipe for, 5
    leafy green, with vinaigrette, 3
    spinach, wilted
        Orange, 138–39
        Pineapple, 139
        problems with, 11
        with Warm Bacon Dressing,
            10–11, *87*
Salt, seasoning cold food with, 18
Saucepans, large, rating of, 165–67
Sauces:
    Bolognese, Weeknight, 76–78, *227*
        braising meat in milk for, 77, 79
        choosing right pan for, 79
        tasting of tomato pastes for, 79–80
    Caramel, 278–79
    for chicken (pan)
        Garlic-Sherry, 133
        Onion and Ale, 134
        Red Wine, Sweet-Tart, 133–34
        Sage-Vermouth, *88*, 133
    Chipotle Chile, Creamy, 49
    Tartar, 48
Sausage:
    andouille
        Cassoulet with Lamb and,
            Simplified, 221
        Chicken and Shrimp Jambalaya,
            54–56, *86*
        tasting of, 56–57

Sausage: *(cont.)*
    kielbasa
        Cassoulet with Pork and,
            Simplified, 220–21
        Indoor Clambake, 35–37
        Orecchiette with Broccoli Rabe and,
            70–71
Scallion(s):
    Bacon Corn Muffins with Cheddar
        Cheese, 263
    Mashed Potatoes with Horseradish and,
        164
Science of cooking:
    apples, cooking and texture of, 279
    braising, 103–5
    cold food, seasoning, 17–18
    collagen, 105
    cream of tartar, beating egg whites with,
        334
    egg yolk foams, 300
    flour, sifting, 310
    meat, infusing with moisture and flavor,
        173
    meat tenderness
        cooking in milk and, 79
        juiciness and, 160
    onions, crying from, 44
    pancakes, promoting fluffiness in, 274
    pans, determining when hot enough to
        begin searing, 134
    peanut butters, separation of, 200
    pork roasts, browning and glazing, 115
    spices, prying flavor out of, 211
    water baths, 319
Scones, oatmeal, 244–46
    Apricot-Almond, 246
    Cinnamon-Raisin, 246
    with Dried Cherries and Hazelnuts, 246
    Glazed Maple-Pecan, 246
    Master Recipe for, *233*, 245–46
    oven temperature for, 246
Seafood, 39–49
    Crab Cakes, Maryland, 47–48
        Creamy Chipotle Sauce for, 48
        Tartar Sauce for, 47
    Indoor Clambake, 35–37
    oysters, shucking, 45
        rating of oyster knives for, 44–46
    sauces for
        Creamy Chipotle Chile, 49
        Tartar, 48
    see also Clam(s); Shrimp

ALSO BY THE EDITORS OF COOK'S ILLUSTRATED

The Best Recipe
The Best Recipe: Grilling & Barbecue
The Best Recipe: Soups & Stews

365 Quick Tips

The Complete Book of Pasta and Noodles
The Cook's Illustrated Complete Book of Poultry

How to Barbecue and Roast on the Grill
How to Cook Chicken Breasts
How to Cook Chinese Favorites
How to Cook Garden Vegetables
How to Cook Holiday Roasts and Birds
How to Cook Potatoes
How to Cook Shrimp and Other Shellfish
How to Grill
How to Make a Pie
How to Make an American Layer Cake
How to Make Cookie Jar Favorites
How to Make Holiday Desserts
How to Make Ice Cream
How to Make Muffins, Biscuits, and Scones
How to Make Pasta Sauces
How to Make Pizza
How to Make Pot Pies and Casseroles
How to Make Quick Appetizers
How to Make Salad
How to Make Sauces
How to Make Simple Fruit Desserts
How to Make Soup
How to Make Stew
How to Sauté
How to Stir-Fry

http://www.cooksillustrated.com

THE AMERICA'S TEST KITCHEN COOKBOOK

THE AMERICA'S TEST KITCHEN COOKBOOK

BY THE EDITORS OF
COOK'S ILLUSTRATED

Photography by Carl Tremblay
Illustrations by John Burgoyne

 BOSTON COMMON PRESS   BROOKLINE, MASSACHUSETTS

Boston Common Press
17 Station Street
Brookline, MA 02445

ISBN 0-936184-54-X
Library of Congress Cataloging-in-Publication Data
The Editors of Cook's Illustrated

The America's Test Kitchen Cookbook:
The Recipes, Equipment Ratings, Food Tastings, and Science Experiments from the Hit Public Television Show.
1st edition

ISBN 0-936184-54-X (hardback): $29.95
1. Cooking. 1. Title
2001

Manufactured in the United States of America

Distributed by Boston Common Press, 17 Station Street, Brookline, MA 02445

Designed by Amy Klee
Edited by Jack Bishop

CONTENTS

PREFACE

IN OUR SMALL TOWN IN VERMONT, CHARLIE BENTLEY, THE venerable selectman and local farmer, was recently injured in a farming accident involving a tractor and a disk harrow. A pancake breakfast was quickly organized to raise money to pay for his medical bills. I cooked 35 pounds of breakfast sausage, neighbors made more than 500 pancakes, the country store provided gallons of free orange juice, and we raised more than $10,000 in a town of 350 residents.

Now, that may not sound like much money to many, but that morning was an act of community. Hundreds of locals showed up—including one farmer I hadn't seen in 35 years—and everyone pitched in. The silent auction offered homemade bluebird houses, quilts, jams, candies, toy tractors, wagon rides, and even a telephone that was shaped like a duck. It was, by all accounts, a great success.

America's Test Kitchen is not unlike my small country town. It is a place where collaboration rules, where the sense of community overrides any notion of individual taste. We cook together, we test together, we taste together, and we work on the show together. But, unlike much of what is on television today, this is not a performance. The cameras give you an honest, if slightly more lively, view of how we work in our test kitchen. The set you see on the show is, in fact, a real working kitchen. This is where we live, Monday through Friday, developing recipes for *Cook's Illustrated* magazine.

It is our opinion that viewers are well served by an honest approach to cooking. To that end, we show you bad food—dry turkey meat, greasy fried chicken, and pie shells that sink when baked—as well as good food. We know what you know: Recipes rarely turn out perfectly at home. We all make mistakes, and America's Test Kitchen—through both the TV show and the cookbook—is for those of you who want to understand why recipes fail so that you can improve your chances for success.

My first day on the job at a local dairy farm, I was asked to bring in a cow with her newborn calf. Being nine years old and inexperienced, I confidently strode out through the pasture with the notion of a quick roundup. Instead, I spent the next half-hour being chased around the field, often ducking under barbed wire to escape a pair of long, untrimmed horns. That is often the story with home cooking. We set out with confidence only to quickly discover what we don't know. At America's Test Kitchen, we hope to give you the culinary knowledge to make your next trip into the kitchen a success.

America's Test Kitchen is the culmination of a dream come true for everyone on the staff here in Boston. For me, that dream began in 1980 when I founded the original *Cook's Magazine* with a lot more enthusiasm than money. My wife and partner, Adrienne, worked for the magazine for almost 20 years. Others, such as Jack Bishop (our food tasting expert) and "Doc" Willoughby (at the science desk), have been with us for more than a dozen years. Other editors—Mark Bittman and Pam Anderson in particular—have long histories with *Cook's* and have left their enthusiasm and their mark on the magazine as they have gone on to distinguished careers in the culinary world.

I would say, if asked, that the one thing that sets us apart is that we are not fancy cooks. We love good home cooking, and the show and this book have given us the opportunity to reach out into your kitchens, to start a discussion about the best way to roast a chicken or grill a hamburger. We may not always agree, but I hope that you will enjoy cooking along with us. You are part of the America's Test Kitchen community, and we welcome you into our home.

Christopher Kimball
Founder and editor, *Cook's Illustrated* magazine
Boston, Massachusetts, 2001

ACKNOWLEDGMENTS

IN ADDITION TO ALL THE PEOPLE WHO WORKED ON THE television show are the many individuals who contributed to this book.

Editor Jack Bishop took the recipes, techniques, food tastings, equipment testings, and science segments from the television show and turned them into a cookbook.

Art director Amy Klee designed a book that reflects the spirit and energy of America's Test Kitchen. Carl Tremblay spent countless hours on the set to capture the black-and-white images that appear throughout the book, and John Burgoyne's illustrations bring many key techniques to life. Thank you also to Daniel Van Ackere for the silhouette photography of equipment that appears throughout the book.

India Koopman copyedited the manuscript, and Becky Hays and Jessica Quirk shepherded the text and images through the production process.

The following individuals on the editorial and production staffs also worked on the book: Ron Bilodeau, Barbara Bourassa, Rich Cassidy, Mary Connelly, Daniel Frey, Jim McCormack, Jen McCreary, and Nicole Morris. We would also like to thank proofreader Jana Branch and indexer Diane Brenner.

And without help from members of the marketing and circulation departments, readers might never find our books. Steven Browall, Adam Dardeck, Connie Forbes, Jason Geller, Robert Lee, David Mack, and Jacqui Valerio all contributed to marketing and distribution efforts.

Thank you also to Sharyn Chabot, Henrietta Murray, Juliet Nusbaum, and Mandy Shito.

Clockwise from top left: test cooks Bridget Lancaster and Julia Collin; executive producer Geoffrey Drummond; script supervisor/makeup specialist Brenda Coffey, director/editor Herb Sevush, and technical engineer Eliat B. Goldman; host Chris Kimball; *Cook's Illustrated* editors Shannon Blaisdell and Shona Simkin; coordinating producer Kimberly Nolan and director of photography Dean Gaskill; *Cook's Illustrated* editor Becky Hays, Shona, Bridget, Julia, Herb, and chef Raquel Pelzel.

INSIDE AMERICA'S TEST KITCHEN

AMERICA'S TEST KITCHEN IS MORE THAN JUST A TELEVISION show. It's a real place—the test kitchen at *Cook's Illustrated* magazine, located just outside Boston, Massachusetts. Founded in 1980, *Cook's Illustrated* (formerly *Cook's Magazine*) is dedicated to finding the best and most foolproof methods for preparing home-cooked food. Now public television takes you inside our kitchen to give you an insider's view of how we develop recipes, test cookware, taste foods, and even perform scientific experiments. America's Test Kitchen is not, however, about celebrity chefs or restaurant cooking. The show features the staff of *Cook's Illustrated* magazine—editors, writers, test cooks, and researchers—and real food—burgers, brownies, and mashed potatoes.

Our goal is to help you make Tuesday night dinner quickly, easily, and reliably. To do this, we ask lots of questions, such as what's the best chocolate for brownies, which potato is the best choice for mashing, or what's the best pan for searing steaks. For example, to develop a recipe for brownies that are fudgy and moist, we baked more than three dozen batches. We tested cocoa (both natural and Dutch-processed), unsweetened chocolate, semisweet chocolate, and bittersweet chocolate. We tested different brands of chocolates as well as baking pans. We made brownies with melted butter and creamed butter. We tried brownies made with one egg, two eggs, and three eggs. We even tried both cake flour and all-purpose flour. In the end, we produced a fudgy brownie that we hope you will consider the "best" (or at least darn good) by your standards as well as ours.

The Four Corners

AMERICA'S TEST KITCHEN IS BUILT ON FOUR SEPARATE components: the recipe workshop, the equipment corner, the tasting lab, and the science desk. Christopher Kimball, the founder and editor of *Cook's Illustrated* magazine, acts as host,

introducing the show, asking the questions, and helping to cook. Julia Collin and Bridget Lancaster demonstrate the recipes, highlighting what worked and what didn't in the recipe development process. They demonstrate the missteps (those brilliant-sounding ideas that resulted in awful, inedible food) as well as the right steps (the secret techniques and tips we discovered along the way). As you watch Julia and Bridget cook, you might learn the best way to roll out pie dough (chill the dough thoroughly and use a tapered rolling pin) or discover why an overnight rise in the refrigerator is the secret to shatteringly crisp pizza (the extra time lets the dough relax, so it can be rolled superthin).

Even the best recipes can fail if you use the wrong equipment. Adam Ried is the America's Test Kitchen cookware expert. If you need to find the best vegetable peeler, Adam will round up 25 models along with crates of potatoes, squash, and apples. After peeling all day, Adam will discover which peeler is the best choice and why. (It turns out that every home cook would be better off with two different kinds of peelers. See page 185 for details.) Because *Cook's Illustrated* magazine does not accept advertising, Adam and his colleagues in the equipment corner share their no-nonsense opinions freely. If a food processor lumbers across the counter as it attempts to knead bread dough, Adam will say so. If one saucepan really outshines the rest, Adam will quote you the model and price. And because seasoned cooks test all of this equipment, our recommendations are based on performance, not just good looks.

Jack Bishop uses the same standards when evaluating common kitchen ingredients in the tasting lab. Which brand of canned chicken broth tastes best? Does one kind of heavy cream whip up better than the rest? Are American pastas as good as Italian brands? Can anything in the supermarket beat fresh-squeezed orange juice? Which hot dog is the top dog? To answer these questions, Jack conducts blind tastings. We often invite experts from the Boston food community—

chefs, cooking teachers, owners of gourmet stores, food purveyors—to participate. Tasters write down their reactions to taste, texture, and appearance and rank the brands being tested in order of preference. No talking is allowed. Each individual vote reflects the perspective of a different palate. Results are tabulated, and the collective opinion of the tasting panel is captured in the final results. Once our tasting results have been confirmed, our reporters and researchers start talking to food scientists and manufacturers to understand the findings. Why did the beef broths with the most sodium win the tasting? Why didn't tasters object to ice creams made with artificial vanilla? What does protein content have to do with the performance of all-purpose flours?

In America's Test Kitchen, we are curious to know why something works, not just how. John "Doc" Willoughby is our resident science expert. He has spent years working with and talking to food scientists and can translate even physics and chemistry into an easy-to-understand demonstration. Don't know why your salad dressing always separates? Why does whipped cream become grainy and curdled if beaten too long? Do marinades really tenderize meat? What you learn can be applied to all kinds of recipes, not just those featured on the show and in this cookbook. Our goal is to help you become a more informed cook, one who understands why heat tames the bitter flavors in garlic or why butter must be properly softened before creaming.

A Collective Effort

SO MANY COOKBOOKS AND TELEVISION SHOWS ARE showcases for the thoughts and creations of a single individual. At America's Test Kitchen, every recipe developed is the result of a group effort. This collaboration goes well beyond the six personalities featured on camera during the show.

Executive chefs Kay Rentschler and Dawn Yanagihara ran the "back kitchen" for the show, where all the food that appeared on camera originated. They also were responsible for turning recipes and testing information from the magazine

Left to right: Adam Ried (equipment corner), John "Doc" Willoughby (science desk), Jack Bishop (tasting lab).

Left to right: executive chefs Kay Rentschler and Dawn Yanagihara, chef Raquel Pelzel.

into lively television segments. Kay and Dawn developed many of the favorite recipes demonstrated on the show.

Dawn and Kay were not alone in the back kitchen. Chefs Matthew Card, Ian Davison, Kate Neave, Raquel Pelzel, and Meg Suzuki and assistants Ginger Hawkins, Pring Ram, and Shelley Rashotsky peeled apples, roasted turkeys, and sliced potatoes from early in the morning to late at night so that the cast of the show would have plenty of pies—good, bad, and ugly—to use in their segments. Shannon Blaisdell, Becky Hays, Raquel Pelzel, and Shona Simkin helped develop science, tasting, and equipment segments for the show. They tested ice cream scoops, ran beef broth tastings, and researched the science of emulsions.

Architect Tim Mulavey of Mulavey Studios designed the test kitchen. Jim McCormack, vice president for operations and technology at *Cook's,* and Rich Cassidy, our systems administrator, were responsible for the building of the test kitchen and for keeping it up and running. They figured out how to make the wiring in our 19th-century office building supply enough power to operate eight wall ovens, two ranges, 16 cooktop burners, three dishwashers, six refrigerators, and one chest freezer—plus all the lights, cameras, and air conditioning units brought in by the television crew.

David Mack, vice president for marketing, enjoyed his 15 minutes of television fame as a pizza delivery man.

The staff of A La Carte Communications did a wonderful job producing, directing, and filming America's Test Kitchen. Special thanks to executive producer Geoffrey Drummond; coordinating producer Kimberly Nolan; director/editor Herb Sevush; director of photography Dean Gaskill; camera operators Jan Maliszewski and Stephen Hussar; jib camera operator Michael Mulvey; alternate camera operator Michael McEachern; technical engineer Eliat B. Goldman; audio engineer Chris Bresnahan; script supervisor/makeup specialist Brenda Coffey; grip/gaffers Tommy Hamilton, Patrick Ruth, Jack McPhee, and Aaron Frutman; and production assistant Leland Drummond.

We hope that our television shows captures the spirit of the special place America's Test Kitchen has become. We invite you to come into our kitchen, pull up a stool, and watch great food being prepared. We're confident that you'll take away information and recipes that will make you a better cook and be entertained in the process. Contact us at www.americastestkitchen.com if you have questions or comments about the show. For information about *Cook's Illustrated* magazine, visit www.cooksillustrated.com.

THE AMERICA'S TEST KITCHEN COOKBOOK

PUREED vegetable soups

CHAPTER 1

Soup recipes always seem so easy. Most can be boiled down to one line: Cook chopped ingredients in liquid until tender. Pureed soups have an added instruction—puree until smooth—a step that almost promises to hide any imperfections in the soup by turning the ingredients into a uniform, thickened liquid.

But as any cook knows, even the simplest of soups can go very wrong. Who hasn't had cream of tomato soup that was much too thick and devoid of tomato flavor? The same holds true for pea soup and mushroom soup. The soup looks fine—it's smooth and pretty—but tastes bland. Many pea soups are so flavorless that a blindfolded taster would be hard-pressed to identify peas as an ingredient.

As far as we are concerned, pureed vegetable soups should taste like vegetables. The trick is to coax flavor from the vegetables and then highlight that flavor—not to overwhelm it with lots of other ingredients. As for texture, pureed soups should be velvety and smooth. They should have good body without being floury or gummy.

Adam, our resident equipment guru, put nine blenders through a series of tests before deciding that simpler (and cheaper) is better when it comes to this kitchen workhorse.

TOMATO SOUP

WHAT WE WANTED: **A perfectly smooth soup with rich color and great tomato flavor.**

Rainy Saturdays in late winter bring to mind the grilled cheese sandwiches and tomato soup of childhood. Long after our affection for other soups wrapped in that famous red and white label has waned, our nostalgia for Campbell's cream of tomato soup persists. Few of us really eat canned tomato soup these days, but some of us do have a vision of the perfect tomato soup. Our vision was a soup of Polartec softness, rich color, and a pleasing balance of sweetness and acidity.

To get a dose of reality, we opened a can of Campbell's. Though rich and tomatoey, it was also cloyingly sweet, almost a cream of ketchup soup. So we moved on to develop a soup that would be as good as we remembered.

For our first set of tests, we used fresh out-of-season tomatoes. The tomatoes were cosmetically peerless, with gleaming red skins and crisp, upright stems. Their taste was a different matter. Without exception, the soups they produced were anemic and completely lacking in tomato flavor. Soups containing flavor boosters, such as carrots, celery, and onions, failed perhaps even more strikingly to suggest a tomato soup. One made with a *roux* (a paste of butter and flour) had the characteristics of a tomato gravy.

Not content to develop a recipe that would be worth making only during the one or two months of the year when tomatoes are in prime form, we turned to canned tomatoes. For our soup we selected fine canned organic diced tomatoes and added shallots, a bit of flour to give the finished product some body, a spoon of tomato paste and some canned chicken broth to enrich the flavor, a helping of heavy cream and a little sherry for refinement, and a pinch of sugar for good measure. Though the resulting soup was dramatically better than those made with fresh winter tomatoes, it still failed to make the cut; the flavor simply wasn't robust enough.

How do you get bigger flavor from canned tomatoes? If they were fresh and ripe, you might roast them: The caramelization of sugar that occurs during roasting concentrates flavors. In the test kitchen, where almost any experiment is considered worth trying, we decided to roast the canned tomatoes. We hoped that intense dry heat might evaporate the surface liquid and concentrate the flavor.

Leaving the above recipe otherwise unchanged, we switched from diced to whole tomatoes for ease of handling, drained and seeded them (reserving the juice for later), then laid them on a foil-covered sheet pan. We then sprinkled them with brown sugar, which we hoped would induce surface caramelization. Only minutes after sliding our tray of tomatoes into a 450-degree oven, the test kitchen was filled with real tomato fragrance, and we knew we had done something right. The roasting made an extraordinary difference, intensifying the tomato flavor and mellowing the fruit's acidity. The rest of the soup could be prepared while the tomatoes roasted, so this step didn't add to the overall preparation time.

Only one minor visual detail marred our efforts. The intense flavor we'd achieved by roasting the tomatoes was not mirrored in the soup's color. The deep coronation red we admired while the soup simmered on the stovetop gave way to a faded circus orange following a round in the blender. The mechanical action of combining solids and liquids had aerated the soup and lightened the color. This wouldn't do. We decided to leave most of the rich tomato broth behind in the saucepan while pureeing the solids with just enough liquid to result in a soup of perfect smoothness. With a finish of heavy cream, our vision of tomato soup had come to life.

WHAT WE LEARNED: **For best flavor, roast canned whole tomatoes. For best color, puree the solids with a minimal amount of liquid.**

CREAM OF TOMATO SOUP   serves 4

Make sure to use canned whole tomatoes packed in juice. Use the packing juice as well as the liquid that falls from the tomatoes when they are seeded to obtain 3 cups of juice.

- 2   (28-ounce) cans whole tomatoes packed in juice, drained, 3 cups juice reserved
- 1½   tablespoons dark brown sugar
- 4   tablespoons unsalted butter
- 4   large shallots, minced (about ½ cup)
- 1   tablespoon tomato paste
       Pinch ground allspice
- 2   tablespoons all-purpose flour
- 1¾   cups homemade chicken stock or canned low-sodium chicken broth
- ½   cup heavy cream
- 2   tablespoons brandy or dry sherry
       Salt and cayenne pepper

1. Adjust oven rack to upper-middle position and heat oven to 450 degrees. Line rimmed baking sheet with foil. With fingers, carefully open whole tomatoes over strainer set in bowl and push out seeds, allowing juices to fall through strainer into bowl. Spread seeded tomatoes in single layer on foil. Sprinkle evenly with brown sugar. Bake until all liquid has evaporated and tomatoes begin to color, about 30 minutes. Let tomatoes cool slightly, then peel them off foil; transfer to small bowl and set aside.

2. Heat butter over medium heat in large saucepan until foaming. Add shallots, tomato paste, and allspice. Reduce heat to low, cover, and cook, stirring occasionally, until shallots are softened, 7 to 10 minutes. Add flour and cook, stirring constantly, until thoroughly combined, about 30 seconds. Gradually add chicken stock, whisking constantly to combine; stir in reserved tomato juice and roasted tomatoes. Cover, increase heat to medium, and bring to boil. Reduce heat to low and simmer, stirring occasionally, to blend flavors, about 10 minutes.

3. Pour mixture through strainer and into medium bowl; rinse out saucepan. Transfer tomatoes and solids in strainer to blender; add 1 cup strained liquid and puree until smooth. Place pureed mixture and remaining strained liquid in saucepan. Add cream and warm over low heat until hot, about 3 minutes. Off heat, stir in brandy and season with salt and cayenne. Serve immediately. (Soup can be refrigerated in an airtight container for up to 2 days. Warm over low heat until hot; do not boil.)

TASTING LAB: Canned Whole Tomatoes

CANNED WHOLE TOMATOES ARE THE CLOSEST PRODUCT to fresh. Whole tomatoes, either plum or round, are steamed to remove their skins and then packed in tomato juice or puree. We prefer tomatoes that are packed in juice; they generally have a fresher, more lively flavor. Puree has a cooked tomato flavor that can impart a slightly stale, tired taste to the whole can.

To find the best canned whole tomatoes, we tasted 11 brands, both straight from the can and in a simple tomato sauce. Muir Glen (an organic brand available in most supermarkets and natural foods stores) and Progresso finished at the head of the pack. Either brand is an excellent choice in cream of tomato soup or any recipe that calls for canned whole tomatoes.

TECHNIQUE:
Pureeing Hot Soup Safely
Blending hot soup can be dangerous. To prevent mishaps, don't fill the blender jar past the halfway point, and hold the lid in place with a folded kitchen towel.

PEA SOUP

WHAT WE WANTED: A velvety soup with real pea flavor, made with readily available ingredients and a minimum of tedious work.

Classic sweet pea soup was originally prepared by briefly stewing fresh blanched peas, leeks, and tendrils of lettuce in butter, moistening them with homemade veal stock, and passing them through a fine-mesh strainer. The soup was then finished with cream and seasoned with fresh chervil.

We wanted a quick and delicious version of this soup, minus the laborious techniques, so we looked at several modern versions. Some introduced new ingredients, largely dismissing the veal stock in favor of chicken stock and adding split peas or sugar snap peas to the mix. Most also moved into the arena of frozen peas. Lacking in gelatinous veal stock, these recipes were obliged to include a bit of thickener in the form of egg yolk, potatoes, or flour. Fresh mint typically replaced chervil. Of the handful of such recipes that we tried, most either completely lacked pea flavor or attained it only by sacrificing color or body.

What we were looking for was something different— an easy version of this popular soup that had the same fundamental virtues as the original. Flavor, color, and texture all bear equally on the success or failure of this soup. Our challenge was to cook the peas quickly enough to preserve their vivid color and to achieve a puree of spectacular smoothness without incurring the loss of flavor sometimes associated with sieving away vegetable bits in short-cooked soups.

The obvious starting point was the pea itself. For those of us without gardens, the long-awaited season of fresh peas is often disappointing. Grocery-store pods can conceal tough, starchy pellets worthy of neither the price they command nor the effort they occasion. So when we began this recipe, we headed not down the garden path but up the frozen foods aisle.

From the pea, we ventured to aromatics. Because the flavor of peas is delicate and easily overwhelmed, we wanted to minimize additions. After experimenting with several aromatics—onions, leeks, and shallots sautéed in butter (unquestionably the most pea-compatible fat in terms of flavor)—we found onions too strong but shallots and leeks equally agreeable. They were delicate and sweet, like the peas themselves.

The means of introducing peas to the soup now became critical. The fun of eating whole peas—breaking through the crisp, springy hull to the sweet pea paste—goes missing in a smooth pea soup, where the listless hulls become an impediment to enjoyment and so must be removed altogether. Simmering peas first to soften their skins, we invariably overcooked them. Additions of sugar snap peas or snow peas sounded interesting but actually added little flavor.

It occurred to us that if we pureed the peas before putting them in the soup and infused them briefly in the simmering liquid, we might get to the heart of the pea right off. Toward that end, we processed partially frozen peas in a food processor and simmered them briefly in the soup base to release their starch and flavor quickly. At this juncture, finding the puree a trifle thin, we doubled back and added 2 tablespoons of flour to the sautéed aromatics to give the base a little body. A few ounces of Boston lettuce added along with the peas gave the soup a marvelous frothy texture when pureed. (To achieve optimal texture, the soup still had to be passed through a strainer.) Some heavy cream, salt, and pepper were the only finishing touches required.

WHAT WE LEARNED: Frozen peas make excellent soup. For maximum pea flavor, grind the frozen peas in a food processor before adding them to the soup pot. Keep the other seasonings simple—just shallots, chicken stock, lettuce, and cream—so the focus stays on the peas.

CREAMY PEA SOUP serves 4 to 6

A few croutons (at right) are the perfect embellishment.

 4 tablespoons unsalted butter
 8 large shallots, minced (about 1 cup), or
   2 medium leeks, white and light green parts
   chopped fine (about 1⅓ cups)
 2 tablespoons all-purpose flour
 3½ cups homemade chicken stock or canned
   low-sodium chicken broth
 1½ pounds frozen peas (about 4½ cups), partially
   thawed at room temperature for 10 minutes
 12 small leaves Boston lettuce (about 3 ounces)
   from 1 small head, leaves washed and dried
 ½ cup heavy cream
   Salt and ground black pepper

1. Heat butter in large saucepan over low heat until foaming. Add shallots or leeks and cook, covered, until softened, 8 to 10 minutes, stirring occasionally. Add flour and cook, stirring constantly, until thoroughly combined, about 30 seconds. Gradually add chicken stock, whisking constantly. Increase heat to high and bring to a boil. Reduce heat to medium-low and simmer 3 to 5 minutes.

2. Meanwhile, in workbowl of food processor fitted with steel blade, process partially thawed peas until coarsely chopped, about 20 seconds. Add peas and lettuce to simmering stock. Increase heat to medium-high, cover, and return to simmer; cook for 3 minutes. Uncover, reduce heat to medium-low, and continue to simmer 2 minutes longer.

3. Working in batches, puree soup in blender until smooth (see illustration on page 5). Strain soup through fine-mesh strainer into large bowl; discard solids. Rinse out and wipe saucepan clean. Return pureed mixture to saucepan and stir in cream. Warm soup over low heat until hot, about 3 minutes. Season to taste with salt and pepper and serve immediately.

BUTTERED CROUTONS makes about 3 cups

Either fresh or stale bread can be used in this recipe, although stale bread is easier to cut and crisps more quickly in the oven. To use stale bread, reduce the baking time by about two minutes. Croutons made from stale bread will be more crisp than those made from fresh. Be sure to use regular or thick-sliced bread.

 6 slices white bread (about 6 ounces), crusts
   removed and slices cut into ½-inch cubes
   (about 3 cups)
   Salt and ground black pepper
 3 tablespoons unsalted butter, melted

1. Adjust oven rack to upper-middle position and heat oven to 400 degrees. Combine bread cubes and salt and pepper to taste in medium bowl. Drizzle with butter and toss well with rubber spatula to combine.

2. Spread croutons in single layer on rimmed baking sheet or in shallow baking dish. Bake croutons, turning over at halfway mark, until golden brown and crisp, 8 to 10 minutes. After cooling, croutons can be stored in an airtight container or plastic bag for up to 3 days.

EQUIPMENT CORNER: Blenders

THE TEXTURE OF A PUREED SOUP SHOULD BE AS SMOOTH and creamy as possible. With this in mind, we tried pureeing several soups with a food mill, a food processor, a hand-held immersion blender, and a regular countertop blender.

Forget using the food mill for this purpose. We tried all three strainer plates (coarse, medium, and fine), and the liquid ran right through each plate as we churned and churned only to produce baby food of varying textures.

The food processor does a decent job of pureeing, but some small bits of vegetables can get trapped under the blade and remain unchopped. Even more troubling is the tendency of a food processor to leak hot liquid. Fill the workbowl more than halfway and you are likely to see liquid running down the side of the food processor base.

The immersion blender has appeal because it can be brought to the pot, eliminating the need to ladle hot ingredients from one vessel to another. However, we found that this kind of blender leaves unblended bits of food behind.

We found that a standard blender turns out the smoothest pureed soups. The blade on the blender does an excellent job with soups because it pulls ingredients down from the top of the container. No stray bits go untouched by the blade. And as long as plenty of headroom is left at the top of the blender, there is no leakage.

Many modern blenders have electronic touch-pad controls, a wide range of speeds, and new jar designs. We wondered how these newfangled options compared with the features on a basic blender. We put nine blenders through a series of tests to find out.

We found that blender jars with flutes (vertical protrusions on the inside of the container) were especially efficient at pureeing soups. These flutes cause the vortex created by the spinning blade to collapse, thus redirecting food matter being thrown against the jar walls back down onto the blade. A modification to the standard angled shape of the classic blender jar was not received as positively in the test

kitchen. Some companies now make a wide-mouth blender with straight sides. Because these jars are wider at the base, there's more room between the blade and the walls of the jar. Extra space gives bits of food a place to hide, and the texture of soups can suffer. In contrast, the tapered bottom on the standard blender jar is quite narrow and thus promotes more contact between food and blade.

An apparent wide range of speeds (as indicated by countless buttons) did not necessarily track with the actual range of speeds observed by our test cooks. Some blenders with just two speeds (high and low) actually had more (and less) power than blenders with 15 speeds.

Our test cooks also remained unimpressed by electronic touch-pad controls. The flat touch pad is easier to clean than a control panel with raised buttons, but it is not easier to operate. On several models, we found it necessary to press down on the electronic touch pad quite forcefully.

In the end, we preferred basic models from Oster and Hamilton Beach (both around $40) to more expensive brands.

BLENDERS

Many new blenders (left) have a wide mouth with straight sides. On a classic blender (right), the jar tapers at the bottom. In our tests, we found that the classic design promotes a smoother consistency in pureed soups.

MUSHROOM SOUP

WHAT WE WANTED: A richly textured pureed soup, neither too thick nor too thin, with deep mushroom flavor.

Traditional French mushroom soups (and mushroom soups are traditionally French) use white button mushrooms sautéed in butter with onions or shallots. The sautéed mushrooms are simmered in a white veal or chicken stock, pureed, and then finished with cream and sherry. Nutmeg or thyme provides the narrow range of flavoring options. Such a soup must have a faultlessly smooth texture and taste of mushrooms. That's it. Additional "stuff" simply takes the soup off course.

We ruled out any combination of fresh wild mushrooms for the base of the soup: They are expensive and can be difficult to find. Instead, we wanted a recipe that would call on the very real virtues of the white mushroom, a readily available ingredient that is often underestimated. On the other hand, a soupçon of dried mushrooms seemed a reasonable option if the flavor needed encouragement.

We began our testing with the mushrooms themselves. In the past we had "sweated" sliced mushrooms in butter in a covered pan to soften them up and release their juices. But we were interested in seeing how roasting would affect their flavor in a soup. Roasted mushrooms appealed to us not only because they are a sublime eating experience but also because we saw them as a means of losing the chop-chop segment of the recipe altogether.

So against 2 pounds of roasted mushrooms we sliced and sautéed 2 pounds of raw mushrooms. Both batches were simmered in chicken stock and pureed, finished with cream, and tasted. To our surprise, the roasted mushroom soup was less flavorful than the soup made with sautéed mushrooms. Juices released during roasting had browned on the pan and were, for all intents and purposes, irretrievable.

Our next attempt to minimize chopping was more mundane. We pulsed the mushrooms in a food processor before sautéing them. The unevenly sliced scraps became bruised and watery; the finished soup had a blackish hue and an unfulfilled flavor. We would need to chop mushrooms by hand.

The sliced mushrooms required an initial toss in hot melted butter (which bore the translucent shimmer and perfume of sautéed shallots and garlic and had been dusted with ground nutmeg), followed by prolonged cooking over low heat in a covered Dutch oven. This half-moist/half-dry heat in close quarters brought out the flavors and was far superior to boiling a vegetable away in broth or water until softened. In contrast, a soup made with sliced mushrooms that were sautéed in an uncovered skillet, and thus stripped of their liquid and browned, suffered in much the same way as the roasted mushrooms.

After the initial cooking of the white mushrooms, we added chicken stock and a pinch of dried porcini mushrooms, which torqued up the flavor a notch or two. (Water alone, we discovered, would not produce the trophy flavor that even watery canned broth managed to impart.) Fifteen minutes of measured simmering drained every last bit of fiber and flavor from the mushrooms and fused the small family of flavors together.

Once run through the blender, the soup took on a beautiful deep taupe color, provoking tasters to fantasize about paint colors and loveseat sofa fabric (a stark contrast with the institutional flecked beige that blights most mushroom soups). With no thickening to mar its innocence, the texture of the soup was light, but it had body from the puréed mushrooms and heavy cream. The cream and the splash of Madeira added with it at the close of business rounded out the flavors and added just the right touch of sweetness.

WHAT WE LEARNED: For best flavor, slice mushrooms by hand and then sweat them in a covered pot with butter and shallots. Add dried porcini for still more mushroom flavor, and enrich the soup with cream and Madeira.

CREAMY MUSHROOM SOUP serves 6 to 8

To make sure that the soup has a fine, velvety texture, puree it hot off the stove, but do not fill the blender jar more than halfway, as the hot liquid may cause the lid to pop off the jar.

6	tablespoons unsalted butter
6	large shallots, minced (about ¾ cup)
2	small cloves garlic, minced
½	teaspoon freshly grated nutmeg
2	pounds white mushrooms, wiped clean and sliced ¼ inch thick
3½	cups homemade chicken stock or canned low-sodium chicken broth
4	cups hot water
½	ounce dried porcini mushrooms, rinsed well
⅓	cup Madeira or dry sherry
1	cup heavy cream
2	teaspoons lemon juice
	Salt and ground black pepper
1	recipe Sautéed Wild Mushrooms for garnish (recipe follows)

1. Heat butter in large stockpot or Dutch oven over medium-low heat. When foaming subsides, add shallots and sauté, stirring frequently, until softened, about 4 minutes. Stir in garlic and nutmeg and cook until fragrant, about 1 minute longer. Increase heat to medium, add sliced mushrooms, and stir to coat with butter. Cook, stirring occasionally, until mushrooms release some liquid, about 7 minutes. Reduce heat to medium-low, cover pot, and cook, stirring occasionally, until mushrooms have released all their liquid, about 20 minutes. Add chicken stock, water, and porcini mushrooms. Cover, bring to simmer, then reduce heat to low and simmer until mushrooms are fully tender, about 20 minutes.

2. Puree soup in batches in blender until smooth, filling the blender jar only halfway for each batch (see illustration on page 5). Rinse and dry pot. Return soup to pot. Stir in Madeira and cream and bring to simmer over low heat. Add lemon juice and season to taste with salt and pepper. (Soup can be refrigerated in an airtight container for up to 4 days. Warm over low heat until hot; do not boil.) Serve, garnishing each bowl with some sautéed wild mushrooms.

SAUTÉED WILD MUSHROOMS makes enough to garnish 6 to 8 bowls of soup

Float a few sautéed mushrooms in each bowl of soup for visual, textural, and flavor appeal. Delicate enoki mushrooms are also a nice addition. If you like, add an ounce or two of enoki mushrooms to the pan during the final minute of the cooking time in step 2.

2	tablespoons unsalted butter
8	ounces shiitake, chanterelle, oyster, or cremini mushrooms, stems trimmed and discarded, mushrooms wiped clean and sliced thin
	Salt and ground black pepper

1. Heat butter in medium skillet over low heat. When foam subsides, add mushrooms and sprinkle with salt and pepper to taste. Cover and cook, stirring occasionally, until the mushrooms release their liquid, about 10 minutes for shiitakes and chanterelles, about 5 minutes for oysters, and about 9 minutes for cremini.

2. Uncover and continue to cook, stirring occasionally, until liquid released by mushrooms has evaporated and mushrooms are browned, about 2 minutes for shiitakes, about 3 minutes for chanterelles, and about 2 minutes for oysters and cremini. Use mushrooms immediately as garnish for bowls of soup.

TASTING LAB:
Commercial Chicken Broth

COMMERCIAL CHICKEN BROTH WON'T MAKE VERY GOOD matzo ball soup, but it's fine in a pureed vegetable soup. That said, you want to use a broth that comes as close to homemade as possible. Unfortunately, few of the 15 commercial broths we tasted came close to the full-bodied consistency of a successful homemade stock. Many lacked even a hint of chicken flavor.

Interestingly, the top four broths were all products of the Campbell Soup Company, of which Swanson is a subsidiary. In order, they were Swanson Chicken Broth, Campbell's Chicken Broth, Swanson Natural Goodness Chicken Broth (with 33 percent less sodium than regular Swanson chicken broth), and Campbell's Healthy Request Chicken Broth (with 30 percent less sodium than regular Campbell's chicken broth). The remaining broths were decidedly inferior and hard to recommend.

We tried to find out more about why Campbell's broths were superior to so many others, but the giant soup company declined to respond to questions, explaining that its recipes and cooking techniques are considered proprietary information. Many of the answers, however, could be found in the products' ingredient lists. The top two broths happened to contain the highest levels of sodium. Salt has

been used for years in the food industry to make foods with less than optimal flavor tastier. The top two products also contained the controversial monosodium glutamate (MSG), a very effective flavor enhancer. Most of the products that had lower levels of salt and did not have the benefit of other food industry flavor enhancers tasted like dishwater.

Ingredients aside, we found one more important reason why most commercial broths simply cannot replicate the full flavor and body of a homemade stock. Most broths are sold canned, which entails an extended heating process carried out to ensure a sterilized product. The immediate disadvantage of this processing is that heat breaks down the flavorful compounds found in chicken protein. And prolonged heating, which is necessary for canning, destroys other volatile flavors at the same time that it concentrates flavor components that are not volatile, such as salt.

A few national brands of chicken broth have begun to offer the option of aseptic packaging. Compared with traditional canning, in which products are heated in the can for up to nearly an hour to ensure sterilization, the process of aseptic packaging entails a flash heating and cooling process that is said to help products better retain both their nutritional value and their flavor.

We decided to hold another tasting to see if we could detect more flavor in the products sold in aseptic packaging. We tasted Swanson's traditional and Natural Goodness chicken broths sold in cans and in aseptic packages. The results fell clearly in favor of the aseptically packaged broths; both tasted cleaner and more chickeny than their canned counterparts. So if you are truly seeking the best of the best in commercial broths, choose one of the two Swanson broths sold in aseptic packaging.

One drawback of the aseptic packages is the fact that they contain more than two cans' worth of broth, making them impractical for cooks who keep commercial broth on hand for the occasional recipe that calls for a small amount of broth. Still, an opened aseptic package will keep in the refrigerator for up to two weeks, whereas broth from a can will keep in the refrigerator for only a few days.

For great carbonara, first pour the cheese and eggs over the hot pasta. Then, add the bacon and toss again. Since the pasta is already sticky from the cheese and eggs, the bits of bacon will cling to the noodles rather than fall to the bottom of the bowl.

PESTO, CARBONARA, & salad

CHAPTER 2

Everyone has a recipe for the classic Italian basil sauce known as pesto. And there certainly are plenty of prepared options in supermarkets and gourmet shops. But more often than not, this sauce only hints at basil flavor, and the garlic takes center stage. Good pesto should knock your socks off with a strong basil punch, and the garlic should be muted. The test kitchen developed a clever method for playing up the basil while toning down the garlic.

Few home cooks, however, have a well-thumbed copy of a recipe for carbonara, a rich pasta sauce made with eggs, cheese, and bacon. While it is popular in restaurants from Rome to Los Angeles, no one seems to make this dish at home—even though it can be on the table 20 minutes after you walk into the kitchen. Most home cooks worry that the sauce will turn out clumped or curdled. And even when things go right, all the delicious bacon usually falls to the bottom of the serving bowl. We wanted to figure out how to create a silky, rich sauce and then get the bits of bacon to adhere to the spaghetti, not the bowl.

A leafy salad dressed with vinaigrette complements either of these pasta dishes. (It also works with a spaghetti and meatball supper; see page 27.) After making enough salad to feed a small army, we have unlocked the secrets of a basic oil-and-vinegar dressing and figured out the right ratio of vinaigrette to salad greens.

IN THIS CHAPTER

THE RECIPES
Bow-Tie Pasta with Pesto

Spaghetti alla Carbonara

Basic Vinaigrette
Balsamic Vinaigrette
Walnut Vinaigrette
Mediterranean Vinaigrette
Mixed Herb Vinaigrette

Leafy Green Salad
Tricolor Salad with Balsamic
   Vinaigrette
Arugula Salad with Walnut
   Vinaigrette

EQUIPMENT CORNER
Salad Spinners

TASTING LAB
Supermarket Extra-Virgin Olive
   Oils
Vinegars and Citrus Juices in Salad
   Dressings

PESTO

WHAT WE WANTED: A smooth sauce with potent basil flavor and a mild hit of garlic and cheese.

Pesto is a pounded basil sauce that comes from Liguria, a coastal area in northwestern Italy. Traditionally, the sauce is made with a mortar and pestle from basil leaves, raw garlic, extra-virgin olive oil, pine nuts, grated cheese, and salt.

In our experience, the bright herbal fragrance of basil always hinted at more flavor than it really delivered. The raw garlic can also be a problem, having a sharp, acrid taste that bites through the other flavors in the sauce. We also wondered about the nuts. Some sources suggest that only pine nuts are authentic, while others mention walnuts as an alternative. Our goals when testing pesto were simple—heighten the flavor of the basil, mellow the punch of the garlic, and figure out how to handle the nuts.

We started our tests by using a mortar and pestle to make pesto. The advantage of this method was that it produced a silky paste with an unusually full basil flavor. The disadvantage was that it required 15 minutes of constant pounding and a piece of equipment not found in many home kitchens. The blender and food processor are more practical for making pesto. Of the two, we found that the food processor makes a sauce with a finer, more consistent texture.

We decided to use the food processor for our recipe but wondered how to get the full basil flavor of pesto made with a mortar and pestle. Because the basil was completely broken down in the mortar and pestle, it released its full range of herbal and anise flavors in a way that the chopping action of a food processor alone could not accomplish. Attempting to approximate that fuller flavor, we tried separate tests of chopping, tearing, and bruising the leaves (packed in a sealable plastic bag) with a meat pounder before processing. Bruising released the most flavor from the basil leaves, so we stuck with this method.

Garlic is a star player in pesto, but we often find that this star shines a little too brightly. Wondering how to cut the raw garlic edge, we tried roasting it, sautéing it, and even infusing its flavors into olive oil, but none of these methods were ideal. Blanching whole garlic cloves in boiling water turned out to be the best solution for several reasons—it's quick (the garlic needs less than a minute in boiling water), it loosens the papery skin from cloves for easy peeling, and it eliminates the raw garlic sting.

With the basil flavor boosted and the garlic toned down, we began to experiment with nuts. We often toast nuts when using them in recipes and found that toasting the nuts in a dry skillet until fragrant also brings out their flavor in pesto. Pine nuts, walnuts, and almonds all work well. Almonds are relatively sweet, which worked beautifully with the basil, but they are also hard, so they gave pesto a coarse, granular texture. Walnuts break down a little more, but they still remained distinctly meaty in flavor and texture. Pine nuts were the favorite for the vast majority of our tasters. They became very creamy when processed and gave the pesto an especially smooth, luxurious texture.

Tasters preferred the combination of Parmesan and sharper Pecorino Romano than either cheese alone. But the pesto made with all Parmesan was a close second, so, in a nod to convenience, we made the Pecorino Romano optional. (See page 28 for information on Parmesan.)

When using pesto to sauce pasta, we found it imperative to use some of the cooking liquid to thin out the consistency. Thinning the pesto with up to ½ cup of pasta cooking water allowed for good distribution of the sauce over the noodles, it softened and blended the flavors a bit, and highlighted the creaminess of the cheese and nuts.

WHAT WE LEARNED: Bruise the basil in a plastic bag with a meat mallet or rolling pin to unlock its flavor, and tame the sting of the garlic by blanching unpeeled cloves.

BOW-TIE PASTA WITH PESTO serves 4

Basil usually darkens in homemade pesto, but you can boost the green color by adding the optional parsley. For sharper flavor, substitute 1 tablespoon finely grated Pecorino Romano cheese for 1 tablespoon of the Parmesan. For a change from bow-tie pasta, try long, thin pasta such as linguine or curly shapes, such as fusilli, which can trap bits of the pesto.

¼   cup pine nuts, walnuts, or almonds
3   medium cloves garlic, threaded on skewer
2   cups packed fresh basil leaves
2   tablespoons fresh flat-leaf parsley leaves (optional)
7   tablespoons extra-virgin olive oil
    Salt
¼   cup finely grated Parmesan
1   pound farfalle (bow-tie pasta)

1. Toast nuts in small, heavy skillet over medium heat, stirring frequently, until just golden and fragrant, 4 to 5 minutes.

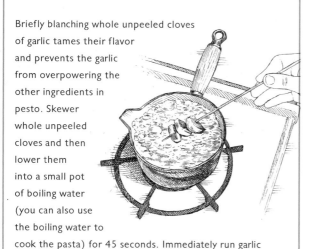

TECHNIQUE: Blanching Garlic

Briefly blanching whole unpeeled cloves of garlic tames their flavor and prevents the garlic from overpowering the other ingredients in pesto. Skewer whole unpeeled cloves and then lower them into a small pot of boiling water (you can also use the boiling water to cook the pasta) for 45 seconds. Immediately run garlic under cold water to stop the cooking process.

2. Meanwhile, bring 4 quarts of water to boil in large pot. Lower skewered garlic into water and boil for 45 seconds (see illustration below). Immediately run garlic under cold water. Remove from skewer; peel and mince.

3. Place basil and parsley (if using) in heavy-duty, quart-size, sealable plastic bag; pound with flat side of meat pounder or a rolling pin until all leaves are bruised (see illustration on page 16).

4. Place nuts, garlic, basil, oil, and ½ teaspoon salt in workbowl of food processor fitted with steel blade; process until smooth, stopping as necessary to scrape down sides of bowl. Transfer mixture to small bowl, stir in cheese, and adjust salt. (Surface of pesto can be covered with sheet of plastic wrap or thin film of oil and refrigerated for up to 5 days.)

5. Add 1 tablespoon salt and pasta to boiling water. Cook until al dente. Reserve ½ cup pasta cooking water; drain pasta and transfer back to cooking pot. Mix in ¼ cup reserved cooking water and pesto; use remaining ¼ cup cooking water as needed to moisten. Divide among 4 warmed pasta bowls and serve immediately.

TASTING LAB:
Supermarket Extra-Virgin Olive Oils

WHEN YOU BUY A SUPERMARKET EXTRA-VIRGIN OLIVE OIL, you're not buying a boutique oil produced and bottled in the small production plant of an olive grower just outside a quaint Tuscan village. You are buying a big-name producer's mass-marketed extra-virgin brand, usually made from olives shipped into Italy from different countries—or even different continents—for bottling. (An extra-virgin oil can be called Italian even if it is only bottled in Italy.)

This leads to differences not only in price and quality but in what you may or may not know about the oil. When you purchase an artisanal oil in a high-end shop, certain

Bruising herb leaves in a zipper-lock plastic bag with a meat pounder (or rolling pin) is a quick but effective substitute for hand-pounding with a mortar and pestle and helps to release the herbs' flavor.

cold pressed comes into play, meaning that the olives are pressed into a paste using mechanical wheels or hammers and are then kneaded to separate the oil from the fruit.) Third, it must pass taste and aroma standards as defined by groups such as the International Olive Oil Council (IOOC), an intergovernmental olive oil regulatory committee that sets the bar for its member countries.

Tasting extra-virgin olive oil is much like tasting wine. The flavors of these oils range from citrusy to herbal, musty to floral, with every variable in between. And what one taster finds particularly attractive—a slight briny flavor, for example—another person might find unappealing. Also like wine, the flavor of a particular brand of olive oil can change from year to year, depending on the quality of the harvest and the olives' place of origin.

We chose to taste extra-virgin olive oil in its most pure and unadulterated state: raw. Tasters were given the option of sampling the oil from a spoon or on neutral-flavored French bread and were then asked to eat a slice of green apple—for its acidity—to cleanse the palate between oils. The olive oils were evaluated for color, clarity, viscosity, bouquet, depth of flavor, and lingering of flavor.

Whereas in a typical tasting we are able to identify a clear "winner" and "loser," this time around we could not draw such a distinct line. In fact, the panel seemed to quickly divide itself into those who liked a gutsy olive oil with bold flavor and those who preferred a milder, more mellow approach. Nonetheless, in both camps one oil clearly had more of a following than any other—the all-Italian-olive Davinci brand. Praised for its rounded and buttery flavor, it was the only olive oil we tasted that seemed to garner across-the-board approval with olive oil experts and in-house staff alike. Consequently, it is the only supermarket extra-virgin olive oil we could rate as "highly recommended."

informational perks are expected (and paid for). These typically include written explanations of the character and nuances of the particular oil as well as knowledgeable staff who can assist you in your purchase. But in a supermarket, it's just you and a price tag. How do you know which supermarket extra-virgin oil best suits your needs? To provide some guidance, we decided to hold a blind tasting of the nine best-selling extra-virgin oils typically available in American supermarkets.

The label "extra-virgin" denotes the highest quality of olive oil, with the most delicate and prized flavor. (The three other grades are "virgin," "pure," and "olive pomace." "Pure" oil, often labeled simply "olive oil," is the most commonly available.) To be tagged as extra-virgin, an oil must meet three basic criteria. First, it must contain less than 1 percent oleic acid per 100 grams of oil. Second, the oil must not have been treated with any solvents or heat. (Heat is used to reduce strong acidity in some nonvirgin olive oils to make them palatable. This is where the term

Among tasters who preferred full-bodied, bold oils, Colavita and Filippo Berio also earned high marks. Tasters in the mild and delicate camp gave high scores to Pompeian and Whole Foods oils.

SPAGHETTI ALLA CARBONARA

WHAT WE WANTED: Restaurant carbonara is often an unctuous, congealed mass of cheese, eggs, and bacon. We set out to make the sauce silky and smooth.

A pasta dish quintessentially Roman in nature, carbonara taunts us with food taboos. It begins with a sauce made from eggs and cheese that cooks into velveteen consistency from only the heat of the just-drained pasta that it drapes. Shards of Italian bacon punctuate the dish with enough presence to make one give silent thanks to the pig. And just when you think that it can't get any better, the bright punch of hot garlic kicks in. This is no diet food, but the indulgent nature of carbonara is one reason it is featured on every trattoria menu.

Far from this heavenly marriage of sauce and pasta, the run-of-the-mill carbonara is a lackluster dish of spaghetti smothered in a heavy, dull, cream-laden sauce that makes you wonder if you ordered Alfredo by mistake. Even worse are variations loaded with cheese that refuses to melt and

sticks to the pasta in dry, abrasive pieces. Even a well-made carbonara can be destroyed by a waitperson. If the dish is not brought to the table immediately, the sauce congeals and the carbonara turns sticky and rubbery.

Searching Italian cookbooks for the solutions to these problems provided little help. Most recipes deviated little in the ingredient list, and the technique was similar throughout: Make a raw sauce with eggs and cheese, render bacon, cook pasta, add hot pasta to sauce and bacon, and toss until the mixture is hot and creamy. The only noticeable difference we found was in the ratio of ingredients, especially the eggs and cheese. That ratio, we reasoned, must be the key to a successful carbonara.

Eggs form the base of the lush, silky sauce that binds the other ingredients to the slender strands of pasta. Only the heat from the cooked pasta is necessary to cook the eggs to the right consistency, so we knew a precise amount of egg would be critical to both the texture and the richness of the dish. Basing our recipe on 1 pound of pasta, we started out with two eggs. Mixed with 1 cup grated cheese, this sauce was thick and clumped when introduced to the hot pasta. Four eggs made a sauce too soupy and wet to stick to the pasta. Three eggs were just right. The sauce was silky in texture, had the fortitude to cling to the spaghetti, and was moist and rich.

Next, the cheese. When in Rome, the cheese of choice is Pecorino Romano, an aged sheep's milk cheese with a distinctly sharp, tangy flavor. On its own, 1 cup of Pecorino Romano proved too strong for our taste. But reducing the amount of cheese in the hope of softening the strong flavor yielded a dish that lacked richness.

We tried substituting a cup of Parmigiano-Reggiano for the Pecorino Romano. While the Parmigiano-Reggiano gave the dish a sweet, nutty flavor that was well received, tasters now longed for a little of the potency from the Pecorino Romano. We found that a blend of cheeses—¼ cup Pecorino Romano and ¾ cup Parmesan—brought just the right amount of flavor from both. It also made for a perfect ratio of cheese to eggs to create the smooth, creamy sauce we'd been looking for.

Many carbonara recipes dictate the addition of ½ cup heavy cream to the sauce. Our tasters immediately rejected this lack of discretion. The heavy cream dulled the mouth with a fatty coating, and it deadened the flavor of the cheeses. Tablespoon by tablespoon, we reduced the amount of cream in the recipe, but tasters were satisfied only when the cream was omitted altogether.

On the other hand, the sweet punch of garlic was a welcome addition. At first we sautéed a few minced cloves in a little olive oil before adding it to the sauce, but this sautéed garlic lacked the fortitude to counterbalance the heavy weight of the eggs and cheese. Adding raw garlic to the mixture was just the trick. A brief exposure to the heat of the pasta allowed the garlic flavor to bloom and gave the dish a pleasing bite.

In Rome, carbonara is traditionally made with guanciale—salt-cured pork jowl. You can't buy this product in the United States, so we centered the testing around available bacons—pancetta (Italian bacon) and American bacon. Pancetta, like American bacon, comes from the belly of the pig, but rather than being smoked, pancetta is cured only with salt, pepper, and spice, usually cloves. American bacon is recognizably smoked and has a distinct sweetness from the sugar that's added during the curing process.

The pancetta gave the carbonara a substantial pork flavor. It was distinctly seasoned with the salt and pepper of the cure. But tasters weren't crazy about its meaty texture. Even though the pancetta was thinly sliced and fried until crisp, the pieces became chewy after a short time in the sauce. The American bacon managed to retain much of its crisp texture, and it added a pleasantly sweet and smoky flavor to the dish that tasters preferred overwhelmingly.

In an effort to find the absolutely best carbonara, we tried a dry red wine (a common ingredient in authentic recipes), vermouth (which appeared in only one recipe but piqued our interest), and a dry white wine, which was favored by the majority of the recipes we had found.

The red wine wasn't unpleasant, but the overall flavor wasn't bright enough to stand up to the smoky flavor of the bacon. The vermouth offered a distinct herbal flavor that tasters voted down. White wine created the most impact and resonance. It was full-flavored, and the acidic nature of the wine cut through the taste of the bacon, brightening the flavor of the dish.

Up to this point, we had been making the carbonara in the traditional method. We mixed the eggs and cheese in the bottom of the serving bowl along with the fried bacon, then dumped the hot, drained pasta on top and tossed the mixture thoroughly. But this method had flaws. It was difficult to distribute the egg and cheese mixture evenly throughout the pasta, and, try as we might to keep the bacon pieces afloat, gravity pulled them back to the bottom of the bowl.

Mixing the eggs and cheese together in a separate bowl, then pouring the mixture over the hot pasta, ensured even coverage. In addition, by choosing not to mix the eggs and cheese in the bottom of the serving bowl, we were able to preheat the bowl—a step that keeps the pasta warm. Finally, we found that tossing the hot pasta with the egg mixture first, then gently tossing in the bacon, worked best. The bacon adhered nicely to the sticky coating of sauce.

We found that carbonara will not maintain its creamy consistency if the cooked pasta is allowed too much time to drain. We ultimately allowed it to sit in the colander for only a few seconds before mixing it with the sauce. (To ensure that proper moisture from the pasta was not lost, we found it a good practice to reserve ⅓ cup of the pasta cooking water to add if the noodles became dry or sticky.) Even with these precautions, the carbonara thickened up considerably if left to cool for even a short time. It's best for hungry diners to wait for the carbonara, not the other way around.

WHAT WE LEARNED: **Use a blend of cheeses for the right flavor, combine the cheeses and eggs in a small bowl, and pour this mixture over the hot pasta for even coverage. Use regular American bacon, white wine, and raw garlic to balance the richness of the eggs and cheese.**

SPAGHETTI ALLA CARBONARA serves 4 to 6

Add regular table salt to the pasta cooking water, but use sea salt flakes, if you can find them, to season the dish. We like the full flavor they bring to the carbonara. Note that while either table salt or sea salt can be used when seasoning in step 3, they are not used in equal amounts.

¼ cup extra-virgin olive oil
½ pound bacon (6 to 8 slices), slices halved lengthwise, then cut crosswise into ¼-inch pieces
½ cup dry white wine
3 large eggs
¾ cup finely grated Parmesan (about 2 ounces)
¼ cup finely grated Pecorino Romano (about ¾ ounce)
3 small cloves garlic, minced to paste or pressed through garlic press
1 pound spaghetti
Salt (see note) and ground black pepper

1. Adjust oven rack to lower-middle position, set heatproof serving bowl on rack, and heat oven to 200 degrees. Bring 4 quarts water to rolling boil in large stockpot.

2. While water is heating, heat oil in large skillet over medium heat until shimmering, but not smoking. Add bacon and cook, stirring occasionally, until lightly browned and crisp, about 8 minutes. Add wine and simmer until alcohol aroma has cooked off and wine is slightly reduced, 6 to 8 minutes. Remove from heat and cover to keep warm. Beat eggs, cheeses, and garlic together with fork in small bowl; set aside.

3. When water comes to boil, add pasta and 1 tablespoon table salt; stir to separate pasta. Cook until al dente; reserve ⅓ cup pasta cooking water and drain pasta for about 5 seconds, leaving pasta slightly wet. Transfer drained pasta to warm serving bowl; if pasta appears dry, add some reserved cooking water and toss to moisten. Immediately pour egg mixture over hot pasta, sprinkle with 1 teaspoon sea salt flakes or ¾ teaspoon table salt; toss well to combine. Pour bacon mixture over pasta, season generously with black pepper, and toss well to combine. Serve immediately.

LEAFY SALAD WITH VINAIGRETTE

WHAT WE WANTED: A basic dressing that is neither harsh nor oily and salad greens that glisten with dressing but are not wilted.

A leafy salad sounds simple. Take some lettuce and dress with oil and vinegar. But this is a case where little adjustments in the recipe can make a big difference in the results. We've all had soggy, overdressed salads as well as salads ruined by poorly made dressings.

Vinaigrette is the most popular dressing for salads. While it is possible to dress a salad by adding the oil and vinegar separately, the results are quite different when the ingredients are combined before being poured over greens. To demonstrate this difference, try this test we conducted in the test kitchen. Dress a simple green salad first with oil, then with a mixture of vinegar, salt, and pepper. The result will be harsh, with a prominent vinegar bite. If you are using a good vinegar, you may like this result.

For the sake of comparison, take another batch of greens and the same dressing ingredients. Mix the salt and pepper into the vinegar and then whisk in the oil until the dressing is translucent. When this emulsified dressing is poured over greens, the flavor will be smoother, with a greater emphasis on the oil.

The science of emulsions explains why the same ingredients can taste so different. In the first oil-then-vinegar salad, the oil and vinegar don't mix, so both race up the tongue. The less viscous vinegar wins, hence this salad tastes more acidic. In the emulsion, the oil is whipped into tiny molecules that surround dispersed droplets of vinegar. The oil is in the so-called continuous phase of the emulsion and is tasted first. The tongue is coated with fat droplets that cushion the impact of the acid.

The best ratio of oil to vinegar is open to much discussion and can depend on the acidity of the vinegar as well as the flavor of the oil. In general, we prefer a ratio of 4 parts oil to 1 part acid, but this can vary, especially when using citrus juices or rice vinegar, both of which are much less acidic than common vinegars.

We find that either a fork or small whisk generates the whipping action necessary to break up the oil and vinegar into small droplets. (You can also shake ingredients together in a sealed jar.) In any case, the emulsion will break rather quickly, so it is necessary to rewhisk (or reshake) the dressing just before pouring it over salad greens. We like to add the salt and pepper to the vinegar because the vinegar mutes these flavors a bit and prevents them from becoming too overpowering. On the other hand, we prefer to add herbs to the finished dressing to maximize their impact.

We find that ¼ cup of vinaigrette is sufficient to dress 2 quarts of salad greens, enough for four servings. Any more dressing turns the salad greens soggy. Salad greens can be tricky to measure. We lightly pack a 4-cup plastic measure to obtain consistent amounts.

Because they grow so close to the ground, salad greens are often quite sandy. Thorough washing in a deep bowl or sink filled with cold water is a must. Swish the greens in the water to loosen any sand, then lift them out of the dirty water. Once the bottom of bowl is free of grit (you may need to drain the bowl and add clean water several times), dry greens in a salad spinner and then use paper or kitchen towels to blot off any remaining moisture. It's imperative to remove all visible moisture. Dressing slides off damp greens and pools at the bottom of the salad bowl.

Once a leafy salad is dressed, the clock is ticking. Our tests showed that waiting even 15 minutes to eat the salad causes significant loss in freshness and crispness.

WHAT WE LEARNED: In most cases, 4 parts oil to 1 part vinegar produces the best balance of flavors in a vinaigrette. The ingredients can be mixed with a fork or small whisk or shaken together in a jar.

BASIC VINAIGRETTE makes about ½ cup, enough to dress 4 quarts (8 servings) of salad greens

Salt and pepper are mixed first with the vinegar, which subdues their sometimes harsh bite. If you like, you can adjust the seasonings after the salad has been dressed by sprinkling additional salt and pepper directly onto the greens. Extra dressing can be refrigerated for several days. Variations that contain fresh herbs should be used within several hours for maximum freshness.

- 1½ tablespoons red wine vinegar
- ¼ teaspoon salt
- ⅛ teaspoon ground black pepper
- 6 tablespoons extra-virgin olive oil

Combine vinegar, salt, and pepper in bowl with fork. Add oil, then whisk or mix with fork until smooth, about 30 seconds. The dressing will separate after 5 to 10 minutes, so use immediately or cover and refrigerate; mix again before tossing with greens.

VARIATIONS

BALSAMIC VINAIGRETTE

Follow recipe for Basic Vinaigrette, reducing red wine vinegar to 1½ teaspoons and combining with 1½ tablespoons balsamic vinegar.

WALNUT VINAIGRETTE

Follow recipe for Basic Vinaigrette, replacing vinegar with 2 tablespoons lemon juice and replacing olive oil with 4 tablespoons canola oil mixed with 2 tablespoons walnut oil.

MEDITERRANEAN VINAIGRETTE

Follow recipe for Basic Vinaigrette, replacing vinegar with 2¼ teaspoons lemon juice, increasing pepper to ¼ teaspoon, and decreasing oil to 4 tablespoons. Whisk 1 tablespoon drained and minced capers, 1 tablespoon minced fresh parsley leaves, 1 teaspoon minced fresh thyme leaves, and 1 medium garlic clove, minced fine, into finished dressing.

MIXED HERB VINAIGRETTE

Follow recipe for Basic Vinaigrette, adding 1 tablespoon minced fresh basil leaves, 1½ teaspoons minced fresh parsley leaves, and 1 teaspoon minced fresh oregano leaves to finished dressing.

TASTING LAB: Vinegars and Citrus Juices in Salad Dressings

WE FIND THAT THE FOLLOWING VINEGARS WORK BEST IN salad dressings. Lower-acidity vinegars work best with mild greens, such as Bibb or Boston lettuce; higher-acidity vinegars can be matched with stronger greens, such as arugula or mizuna. Citrus juice and zest add a distinct flavor and less acid.

red wine vinegar: The most versatile choice in salads. Its flavor is sharp but clean. Domestic brands tend to have an acidity around 5 percent, imported red brands often about 7 percent. In our tasting of red wine vinegars, Heinz beat other domestic brands as well as imports, some of which cost 10 times as much.

white wine vinegar: Similar to red wine vinegar but often not quite as complex. Our choice when a pink-colored vinaigrette made with red wine vinegar might seem odd.

balsamic vinegar: This rich, sweet, oaky vinegar is best used in combination with red wine vinegar in salads. Real balsamic vinegar is aged at least a dozen years and can cost $50 an ounce. Cheaper supermarket versions vary tremendously in quality. Some are nothing more than caramel-colored red wine vinegar. Others follow the traditional process (unfermented white grape juice, called must, is fermented in wood casks) but cut back on the aging time. Our advice is to avoid products with artificial colors and flavors—they were deemed harsh and unpleasant in our tasting of leading brands. It's usually a good sign if the word "must" appears on the label.

rice vinegar: A natural choice in Asian dressings, this low-acidity (about 4.5 percent), clear vinegar is quite mild. Use it when you want to keep acidity in check but also want to avoid the distinctive flavor of citrus juices.

sherry vinegar: This Spanish vinegar is usually quite strong (often with 7 percent acidity) but has a rich, oaky, nutty flavor.

citrus juices: Orange, lime, and lemon juices can all be used in salad dressing. They add acidity (although not as much as most vinegars) as well as flavor. Lemon and lime juices are more acidic and can stand on their own. Orange juice is usually combined with vinegar. To add more citrus flavor without disturbing the ratio of acid to oil, stir in some grated zest.

LEAFY GREEN SALAD serves 4

For best results, use at least two kinds of greens. A blend of mild, delicate greens, such as Boston and leaf lettuces, and peppery greens, such as arugula and watercress, is ideal. Romaine adds crunch and texture and is welcome in most salads. If you like, add mild fresh herbs, such as chives, tarragon, or basil, in small amounts.

    2   quarts salad greens, washed and dried
  ¼ cup Basic Vinaigrette or any variation
       (page 21)

Place greens in large salad bowl. Drizzle dressing over greens and toss to coat evenly, about 1 minute. Serve immediately.

VARIATIONS
TRICOLOR SALAD WITH BALSAMIC VINAIGRETTE

Dress 4 cups arugula, 1 small head radicchio, cored and leaves torn, and 2 small heads Belgian endive, stems trimmed and leaves cut crosswise into thirds, with ¼ cup Balsamic Vinaigrette.

ARUGULA SALAD WITH WALNUT VINAIGRETTE

We prefer to toast nuts in a dry skillet over medium heat until fragrant, which takes four or five minutes. Make sure to shake the pan occasionally to turn the nuts.

Dress 2 quarts arugula and 3 tablespoons toasted and coarsely chopped walnuts with ¼ cup Walnut Vinaigrette.

EQUIPMENT CORNER: Salad Spinners

THE BASIC DESIGN OF ALL SALAD SPINNERS IS SIMILAR. A perforated basket is fitted into a larger outer bowl, and gears connected to the mechanism in the lid spin the basket rapidly, creating centrifugal force that pulls the greens to the sides of the basket and the water on the leaves through the perforations into the outer bowl. Beyond this, however, there are three important ways in which various models can differ.

First is the lid. Some are solid, and some have a hole that lets water run directly into the basket while it spins. Second is the outer bowl. Some, like the lids, are solid, while others are perforated so water can flow through. Third is the mechanism that makes the basket spin: pull cord, turning crank, lever crank, or pump knob.

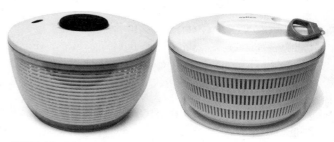

BEST SALAD SPINNERS
With its non-skid base and push-button brake, the Oxo Good Grips spinner (left) requires just one hand to operate. The Zyliss Salad Spinner (right) is especially sturdy and dried greens exceptionally well in our tests.

To be fair, all of the eight spinners we tested did a reasonably good job of drying wet lettuce leaves and parsley, though none dried the greens so thoroughly that they wouldn't benefit from a quick blotting with paper towels before being dressed. Since the differences between them in terms of drying performance are not terribly dramatic, what you really want in your kitchen is a spinner that is well designed, easy to use, and sturdy.

We didn't like the spinners with flow-through lids. The greens we cleaned by running water into the basket tended to bruise from the rushing water and never got clean enough. We also didn't like models with bowls that had holes in the bottom so the water could flow right out. Again, we did not consider this a benefit, in part because it assumes you have an empty sink in which to place the spinner. Second, we like to use the outer bowl of the spinner to soak the leaves clean, something you can't do if there are holes in the bowl.

As for the turning mechanism, the real standout in terms of design and ease of use was the spinner made by Oxo. You can use the Oxo with just one hand because of its clever no-skid base and the pump knob by which it operates. Pushing the pump down both makes the basket spin and pushes the whole unit down onto the counter.

Among the other models tested, the pull cord on the Zyliss model was the easiest to grip, and it did in fact get the greens a tad drier than other spinners, including the Oxo. The Zyliss and the Oxo, each of which can be purchased for about $25, were also the sturdiest of the bunch.

SPAGHETTI & meatballs

CHAPTER 3

A spaghetti and meatball dinner is an American classic, beloved by children and adults alike. Start with spaghetti, coated with thick tomato sauce and topped with savory meatballs. Add garlic bread, crusty and heady with garlic and butter. You might round out the meal with a leafy green salad (see page 22).

Although this meal sounds simple (and it is), much can go wrong. Who hasn't tasted leaden meatballs capable of sinking the *Titanic* or squishy garlic bread devoid of crunch or character?

Our goals for this hearty supper were clear: Produce moist, creamy meatballs and a quick, robust tomato sauce for the pasta. Figure out how to make crisp garlic bread that's neither bland nor so strong tasting that it overpowers everything else on the table.

With the right techniques and recipes, a spaghetti supper can rival any fancy meal. This is honest, good food.

We tested whole, diced, and crushed canned tomatoes before determining that spaghetti and meatballs requires the kind of smooth sauce that only crushed tomatoes can deliver.

SPAGHETTI AND MEATBALLS

WHAT WE WANTED: Moist, light meatballs and a tomato sauce that's easy to prepare yet packed with flavor.

Many cooks think of meatballs as hamburgers with seasonings (cheese, herbs, garlic) and a round shape. This is partly true. However, unlike hamburgers, which are best cooked rare or medium-rare, meatballs are cooked until well-done—at which point they've often turned into dry, tough golf balls.

Our goal was to create meatballs that were moist and light. We also wanted to develop a quick tomato sauce that was loaded with flavor. We focused on the meatballs first.

Meatballs start with ground meat but require additional ingredients to keep them moist and lighten their texture. Meatballs also require binders to keep them from falling apart in the tomato sauce.

A traditional source of moisture in meatballs is egg. We tested meatballs made with and without egg and quickly determined that the egg was a welcome addition. It made the meatballs both moister and lighter.

The list of possible binders included dried bread crumbs, fresh bread crumbs, ground crackers, and bread soaked in milk. We found that bread crumbs and ground crackers soaked up any available moisture, making the meatballs harder and drier when cooked to well-done. In comparison, the meatballs made with bread soaked in milk were moist, creamy, and rich. Milk was clearly an important part of the equation.

We liked the milk but wondered if we could do better. We tried adding yogurt but had to thin it with some milk in order to mix it with the bread. Meatballs made with thinned yogurt were even creamier and more flavorful than those made with plain milk. We also tried buttermilk, and the results were just as good, with no need to thin the liquid.

With the dairy now part of our working recipe, we found the meatball mixture a tad sticky and hard to handle. By eliminating the egg white (the yolk has all the fat and emulsifiers that contribute smoothness), we eliminated the stickiness.

It was finally time to experiment with the crucial ingredient: the meat. Ground round was too lean. We preferred fattier chuck in this recipe. We tried blending in some ground veal but decided it was not worth the bother; these meatballs tasted bland. Ground pork was another matter. It added another flavor dimension.

With our ingredients in order, it was time to test cooking methods. We tried roasting, broiling, and the traditional pan-frying. Roasting yielded dry, crumbly meatballs, while broiling was extremely messy and also tended to produce dry meatballs. Pan-frying produced meatballs with a rich, dark crust and moist texture.

We wondered if we could save some cleanup time and build more flavor into the tomato sauce by making it in the same pan used to fry the meatballs. We emptied out the vegetable oil used to fry the meatballs (olive oil is too expensive for this task and doesn't add much flavor), then added a little fresh olive oil (olive oil is important to the flavor of the sauce) before adding garlic and tomatoes. Not only did this method prove convenient, but it gave the sauce depth, as the browned bits that had formed when the meatballs were fried loosened from the pan bottom and dissolved in the sauce.

Meatballs need a thick, smooth sauce—the kind produced by canned crushed tomatoes. Sauces made with whole or diced tomatoes were too chunky and more liquidy; they didn't meld with the meatballs and made them soggy.

WHAT WE LEARNED: White bread soaked in buttermilk is the best binder for meatballs, giving them a creamy texture and an appealing tang. An egg yolk keeps meatballs moist and light, and a mixture of ground beef and ground pork tastes best. Pan-frying browns the exterior of the meatballs while keeping the interior moist. Finally, building the tomato sauce on top of the browned bits left in the pan after frying the meatballs makes for a hearty, robust-tasting sauce.

SPAGHETTI AND MEATBALLS   serves 4 to 6

The shaped meatballs can be covered with plastic wrap and refrigerated for several hours ahead of serving time, if you like. Fry the meatballs and make the sauce at the last minute.

meatballs

2 slices white sandwich bread (crusts discarded), torn into small pieces
½ cup buttermilk or 6 tablespoons plain yogurt thinned with 2 tablespoons whole milk
1 pound ground meat (preferably ¾ pound ground chuck and ¼ pound ground pork)
¼ cup freshly grated Parmesan cheese
2 tablespoons finely minced fresh parsley leaves
1 large egg yolk
1 teaspoon finely minced garlic
¾ teaspoon salt
   Ground black pepper
   About 1¼ cups vegetable oil for pan-frying

smooth tomato sauce

2 tablespoons extra-virgin olive oil
1 teaspoon minced garlic
1 (28-ounce) can crushed tomatoes
1 tablespoon minced fresh basil leaves
   Salt and ground black pepper

1 pound spaghetti
   Freshly grated Parmesan cheese

1. FOR THE MEATBALLS: Combine bread and buttermilk in small bowl and let stand, mashing occasionally with fork, until smooth paste forms, about 10 minutes.

2. Place ground meat, cheese, parsley, egg yolk, garlic, salt, and pepper to taste in medium bowl. Add bread-milk mixture and combine until evenly mixed. Shape 3 tablespoons of mixture into 1½-inch-round meatball. (When forming meatballs use a light touch. If you compact the meatballs too

much, they can become dense and hard.) You should be able to form about 14 meatballs.

3. Pour vegetable oil into 10- or 11-inch sauté pan to depth of ¼ inch. Turn flame to medium-high. After several minutes, test oil with edge of meatball. When oil sizzles, add meatballs in single layer. Fry, turning several times, until nicely browned on all sides, about 10 minutes (see illustration below). Regulate heat as needed to keep oil sizzling but not smoking. Transfer browned meatballs to plate lined with paper towels and set aside.

4. Bring 4 quarts water to a boil in large pot for pasta.

5. FOR THE SAUCE: Meanwhile, discard oil in pan but leave behind any browned bits. Add olive oil for tomato sauce along with garlic and sauté over medium heat, scraping up browned bits, just until garlic is golden, about 30 seconds. Add tomatoes, bring to boil, and simmer gently until sauce thickens, about 10 minutes. Stir in basil and salt and pepper to taste. Add meatballs and simmer,

TECHNIQUE: Browning Meatballs

We found that meatballs taste best when browned evenly on all sides. Their round shape makes this a challenge. Our solution is to brown the two broader sides of the meatballs first and then use tongs to stand the meatballs on their sides. If necessary, lean the meatballs up against one another as they brown.

turning them occasionally, until heated through, about 5 minutes. Keep warm over low flame.

6. Meanwhile, add 1 tablespoon salt and pasta to boiling water. Cook until al dente, drain, and return to pot. Ladle several large spoonfuls of sauce (without meatballs) over spaghetti and toss until noodles are well coated. Divide pasta among individual bowls and top each with a little more tomato sauce and 2 or 3 meatballs. Serve immediately with grated cheese passed separately.

VARIATION
SPAGHETTI AND CHICKEN MEATBALLS
If you want to trim some fat from this recipe, ground chicken is a decent alternative to ground beef and pork. We found that meatballs made from chicken are a tad soft, so they must be refrigerated for an hour before being fried to keep them from sticking to the pan or falling apart.

Follow recipe for Spaghetti and Meatballs, replacing ground meat with 1 pound ground chicken. After shaping meatballs in step 2, place on platter, cover with plastic wrap, and refrigerate until firm, about 1 hour. Proceed as directed.

TASTING LAB: Parmesan Cheese

WHEN IT COMES TO GRATED PARMESAN CHEESE, THERE'S A wide range of options—everything from the whitish powder in green jars to imported cheese that costs $14 a pound. You can buy cheese that has been grated, or you can pick out a whole hunk and grate it yourself. We wondered if the "authentic" Parmigiano-Reggiano imported from Italy would be that much better when tasted side by side with a domestic Parmesan at half the price.

Parmesan is a *grana,* a hard, grainy cheese. The grana cheese category is composed mostly of Italian grating cheeses. Parmigiano-Reggiano is the most famous (and expensive) of the granas, and its manufacture dates back 800

years. Parmigiano-Reggiano has become an increasingly regulated product; in 1955 it became what is known as a certified name (not a brand name). Since that time the name has indicated that the cheese was made within a specific region of northern Italy and approved by a certifying consortium.

American cheese makers have been making Parmesan only since the beginning of the century and need not abide by any more stringent regulations than basic U.S. Department of Agriculture standards. There is no lack of pregrated products, but only a handful of domestic Parmesans come in wedges. Other granas considered Parmesan types are Grana Padano (from Italy) and Reggianito (from Argentina).

The samples in our tasting included five pregrated Parmesan cheeses (domestic and imported), three wedges of domestic Parmesan, a wedge of Grana Padano, one of Reggianito, and two of Parmigiano-Reggiano. To see if differences in storage and handling could affect the quality of the latter two, we purchased one at a specialty cheese store, where the humidity and temperature of the storage room are controlled and the wedges are cut from the wheel per order, and the other at a large supermarket, where the cheese is sold precut and wrapped in plastic. All of the cheeses were tasted grated, at room temperature.

To get an idea of what tasters might want to look for when tasting the different cheeses, we spoke to a number of cheese experts. All recommended that the tasters rate the cheeses on the basics: aroma, flavor (particularly depth of flavor and saltiness versus sweetness), and overall texture. The experts also said the Parmesans should be left to sit on tasters' tongues to see if they would melt smoothly into creaminess in the mouth. All of the experts we spoke to expressed confidence that Parmigiano-Reggiano would be the hands-down winner. This time the experts were correct. Parmigiano-Reggiano had a depth and complexity of flavor and a smooth, melting texture that none of the others could match.

Parmigiano-Reggiano owes much of its flavor to the unpasteurized milk used to produce it. It is a "controlled-district" cheese, which means not only that it must be made within the boundaries of this zone but also that the milk

weighs 75 to 90 pounds; domestic Parmesan wheels average 24 pounds.)

The low-salt content of Parmigiano-Reggiano makes it more perishable than other cheeses once cut from the wheel. Once cut, the cheese will also begin to dry out. This was evident in the Parmigiano-Reggiano sample purchased at the grocery store. Tasters rated this a few tenths of a point lower than the sample purchased at the specialty cheese store because of a chalky finish. This drying effect was even more glaring with the chalky pregrated products, which received consistently poor ratings.

Another benefit of the larger wheel is that it gives the cheese more time to age. Parmigiano-Reggiano ages for about 24 months, while domestic Parmesan ages for about 10 months. The longer aging allows more complex flavors and aromas to develop. The aging also makes a difference in texture, creating a distinctive component that tasters described as "crystal crunch." The crunch stems from proteins breaking down into free amino acid crystals during the latter half of the aging process. The crystals are visible, appearing as white dots in the cheese. No other Parmesan showed this effect.

Other textural differences are created by the fact that the curds for Parmigiano-Reggiano are cut into fragments the size of wheat grains, which is much finer than the fragments cut in the manufacture of domestic Parmesan. The benefit of smaller curds is that they drain more effectively. Domestic Parmesans are mechanically pressed to rid them of excess moisture. The consequence, as our tasting panel discovered with several domestic Parmesans that were not pregrated, is a cheese that is much more dense. Tasters characterized these cheeses as "rubbery," "tough," and "squeaky."

One domestic Parmesan scored well enough to be recommended. This was Wisconsin-made DiGiorno. The other less expensive options paled in comparison with the real thing. The pregrated cheeses received especially low ratings and harsh comments from our panel. Most were much too salty and marred by odd off flavors. Most everyone agreed that these poor imitations could actually ruin a dish.

used to make it and even the grass, hay, and grain fed to the cows that make the milk must come from the district. Consequently, just like good wine, a lot of character comes from the soil and climate where the cheese was made. In the tasting we found that none of the other cheeses had the sweet, nutty, creamy flavor of Parmigiano-Reggiano.

Most of the cheeses in the tasting—except the Parmigiano-Reggiano—were extremely salty. In fact, Parmigiano-Reggiano contains about two-thirds less sodium than the other Parmesans. This is because the wheels of Parmigiano-Reggiano are so large that they do not become as saturated with salt during the brining process that is one of the final steps in making the cheese. (The average wheel is about 9 inches high and 16 to 18 inches in diameter and

TASTING LAB: Jarred Tomato Sauces

WE WONDERED IF ANY TOMATO SAUCE FROM A JAR could compete with a simple homemade recipe. We assembled a sampling of 11 leading brands of marinara-style sauces containing tomatoes, garlic, herbs (usually basil and/or oregano), and sometimes onions and tasted them blind against our sauce.

While tasters clearly expressed varied preferences when it came to the ideal consistency of the sauces, they all agreed on the driving component—freshness of flavor. In this department, our homemade sauce was the only one considered to taste "extremely fresh" and the only one that tasters really liked. Several jarred sauces were deemed acceptable, but we judged the rest not worth eating.

We found several probable reasons for the stale taste of most of the jarred sauces. Apart from those which placed first and second (Barilla and Classico, respectively), all of the supermarket jarred tomato sauces listed tomato puree as their main ingredient and diced tomatoes second. We find that tomato puree diminishes the fresh tomato flavor. This results from the fact that puree is a concentrate requiring higher temperatures and longer cooking times to process than simple cooked tomatoes, whether whole or diced.

The freshness and purity of other ingredients in a sauce also contribute to the success of the final product. Barilla, a market leader in pasta and jarred sauces in Italy, uses primarily fresh ingredients that are diced at the plant. Some other producers use dried spices and even dried vegetables. Barilla's sauce is minimally cooked, really just enough to prevent the growth of bacteria. The problem for many manufacturers, however, is not excessive cooking but the prolonged time that a sauce stays hot before it is jarred and cooled. To avoid this, Barilla expedites the final stage by rapidly cooling the sauce and filling the jars.

A few of the sauces tried to make up for their deficiency in tomato flavor with excessive sweetness. These efforts failed. Our tasters typically labeled these sauces as

"kids' food." Notably, Barilla and Classico were the only supermarket brands to put onions before sugar (or corn syrup in some cases) on their list of ingredients.

In the end, most jarred tomato sauces don't taste very good. Some are acceptable; most are not.

GARLIC BREAD

WHAT WE WANTED: Crisp toasted bread with sweet, nutty garlic flavor.

So simple to make, yet so often a soggy, greasy disappointment, garlic bread should have a lightly toasted surface with a crisp crust that shatters when bitten. The bread within should be warm and chewy, light and yet substantial. Butter, which we chose over olive oil for this American-style bread, should be plentiful but not excessive, and the garlic flavor should be full and prominent without being harsh. But garlic bread rarely lives up to this ideal. Sometimes there is so much garlic you can taste it for days; other times there is so little you can't taste it at all. Worse yet, the bread is often completely saturated with butter.

We started out by tasting several garlic breads made according to different recipes and methods. From this came an interesting revelation: Even though most of the breads had too little garlic oomph (they ranged from a single clove to six cloves per 1-pound loaf of bread), all the tasters complained about the raw garlic flavor in every recipe. We definitely had to deal with this. Tasters made several other helpful observations. First, there was unanimous preference for wide loaves of bread, such as Italian, which yielded large slices. Second, tasters preferred their loaf sliced with the insides exposed to the oven to crisp up rather than cut in vertical slices left attached at the bottom, as specified in many recipes. The latter method left the slices soggy and a bit harsh-tasting.

The cry for a full, resonant garlic flavor necessitated the use of many more cloves than the usual two or three. But upping the ante created another problem—near overpowering harshness from all that raw garlic. Because the flavor of garlic mellows with heat, precooking seemed like a good plan.

To keep the testing consistent, we used six medium garlic cloves (about two tablespoons), minced, per 1-pound loaf of bread and tried two methods of precooking the garlic. First, we sautéed minced garlic in butter, but the resulting bread lacked character and depth, failing to win over any of the tasters. Next, we tried toasting unpeeled cloves in a dry skillet over medium heat until they were just fragrant. This cooked the garlic just enough to highlight its rich, sweet, nutty flavor, and the resulting bread was judged a unanimous winner. After a few experiments, we settled on 8 minutes of toasting; at 10 minutes the garlic was a little too docile, and at 5 minutes it still had more raw punch than we liked.

Toasting allowed us to use far more garlic than recipes generally allow. Most tasters favored 10 medium cloves, which equaled three generous tablespoons, minced, for each 1-pound loaf.

Not surprising for a dish largely about bread, the type of bread used makes a huge difference. The whole wheat and sourdough loaves we tried tasted out of place, and the long, narrow shape and relatively open texture of French bread produced slices that were too small to be truly satisfying. So we stuck with football-shaped loaves of hearty white Italian bread. We found it worthwhile to buy the highest quality loaf available to us. The sturdy texture, satisfying chew, and well-developed yeasty flavor of the bakery-purchased, artisan Italian loaves we tried made the supermarket variety seem fluffy, unsubstantial, and bland.

The right amount of butter would make the garlic bread moist, not soggy or saturated. Many recipes call for a stick or more, which made the bread spongy and slightly greasy. Less butter—6 tablespoons—did the trick, giving the bread ample richness without marring its texture. Melting the butter proved unnecessary, while also adding to the process an unnecessary step and utensil (a brush to distribute it on the bread). Softened butter that we could spread easily with a rubber spatula worked best.

We also checked out an arsenal of additional ingredients common to many recipes. Red wine, olive oil, paprika, hot pepper sauce, cayenne, garlic powder, garlic salt, mustard, and lemon juice all failed to impress, but 2 tablespoons of grated Parmesan cheese added depth and complexity without interfering with the garlic flavor. Even for the basic recipe, we recommend the cheese. You won't even know it's there but for the subtle flavor boost it gives the bread.

The last areas of inquiry were the cooking method and temperature. Many recipes recommend wrapping the loaf in foil for all or part of the baking time. Our tests proved foil wrapping to be a counterproductive extra step. We consistently found the wrapped breads to be soggy, with a slightly harsh flavor and an unwelcome steamed taste. It turned out that exposing the cut-and-buttered surface to the oven heat helped to mellow the garlic's flavor by dehydrating the molecules somewhat. This changes their structure and, with it, their flavor. Wrapping the loaf in foil, or for that matter reassembling it so the cut sides faced each other, deprived

the garlic of some heat, thereby diminishing the desirable flavor change.

The oven setting most commonly listed in the recipes we looked at was 350 degrees, but that wasn't hot enough to give the bread the supercrisp, toasted exterior layer we were after. We tested and retested, increasing the temperature by 25 degrees each time until getting to 500 degrees, which produced a beautifully crunchy crust and a nicely browned surface in just nine minutes or so, with no broiling involved. We did find it necessary to set the bread on a baking sheet, though, to avoid scorching the bottom.

WHAT WE LEARNED: **Toast whole garlic cloves to tame their harshness. Use softened butter rather than melted butter. Add a bit of Parmesan cheese for depth and complexity of flavor. Select a football-shaped loaf of Italian bread, slice it horizontally, and then leave the bread unwrapped as it bakes to achieve the crispiest crust.**

AMERICAN GARLIC BREAD serves 6 to 8

Plan to pull the garlic bread from the oven when you are ready to serve the other dishes. Garlic bread is best served piping hot.

9–10   medium cloves garlic (about the size of a plump cashew nut), skins left on
6   tablespoons unsalted butter, softened
2   tablespoons grated Parmesan cheese
½   teaspoon salt
1   whole loaf high-quality Italian bread (about 1 pound, football-shaped), halved lengthwise Ground black pepper

1. Adjust oven rack to middle position and heat oven to 500 degrees. Meanwhile, toast garlic cloves in small skillet over medium heat, shaking pan occasionally, until fragrant and color of cloves deepens slightly, about 8 minutes (see illustration at right). When cool enough to handle, skin and mince cloves (you should have about 3 tablespoons). Using dinner fork, mash garlic, butter, cheese, and salt in small bowl until thoroughly combined.

2. Spread cut sides of loaf evenly with butter mixture; season to taste with pepper. Transfer loaf halves, buttered side up, onto rimmed baking sheet; bake, reversing position of baking sheet in oven from front to back halfway through baking time, until surface of bread is golden brown and toasted, 5 to 10 minutes. Cut each half into 2-inch slices; serve immediately.

VARIATIONS
CHIPOTLE GARLIC BREAD

Canned chipotle chiles packed in adobo sauce add a smoky, spicy flavor that made this the hands-down favorite of everyone who tasted these variations.

Follow recipe for American Garlic Bread, mashing 1½ chipotle chiles en adobo (about 1 tablespoon) and 1 teaspoon adobo sauce into garlic butter mixture. Increase baking time by a minute or two.

HERB GARLIC BREAD

Follow recipe for American Garlic Bread, mashing 1 tablespoon each minced fresh basil and chives and ½ tablespoon each minced fresh thyme and oregano into garlic butter mixture.

PARMESAN AND ASIAGO CHEESE GARLIC BREAD

Follow recipe for American Garlic Bread, decreasing salt to ¼ teaspoon, increasing Parmesan cheese to ¼ cup, and mashing ¼ cup grated Asiago cheese and 2 teaspoons Dijon mustard into butter along with garlic.

EQUIPMENT CORNER: Bread Knives

A BREAD KNIFE SHOULD EASILY BREAK THROUGH THE top crust on a loaf, no matter how thick that crust is. It should also slice neatly through the crumb, clean through to the bottom of the loaf. Finally, the handle should provide enough space for fingers, especially as you get close to the bottom of the loaf. Ideally, you won't scrape your knuckles

TECHNIQUE: Dry-Toasting Garlic

Place unpeeled garlic cloves in a dry skillet over medium heat. Toast, shaking the pan occasionally, until the skins are golden brown, about 8 minutes.

against the cutting board every time you cut through bread.

To find out which features really matter, we tested 10 bread knives, slicing through 30 loaves of crusty peasant bread, five dozen bagels, and 25 pounds of tomatoes, whose surprisingly tough skin is a perfect subject for serrated knives. Here's what we learned.

When it comes to a bread knife, we found that longer is better. Knives with 10-inch blades could cut through the entire width of a medium-sized peasant bread. The 8-inch blades were particularly frustrating because the tips of their blades tended to catch in the crumb of loaves.

There are two different styles of serration—pointed and wavy. On blades with pointed serrations, the points touch the food first. Between each point is an arched cutting edge that helps the knife cut through foods once the points have made contact. Wavy serrations are just the opposite—the arched cutting edges make up most of the cutting blade.

We found that pointed serrations give a blade a good grip on tough crusts, allowing the knife to cut into loaves easily. The points also preserve overall blade sharpness because they are the first part of the knife to touch all surfaces—be it a bread crust or a cutting board—thereby minimizing the contact the rest of the edge has with any surface. Our favorite knives had pointed serrations, although knives with extremely pronounced serrations caught on tomato skins and soft bread and caused some ripping.

With wavy serrations, more of the cutting edge comes into contact with the food. In our tests on crusty bread, this blade type failed to get the same sure grip as knives with pointed serrations. The wavy serrations tended to slide a little more than we liked, especially when trying to make that initial cut into a crusty loaf.

Another important aspect of blade design is the curvature of the cutting edge. We found that curved cutting edges allow for a gentle rocking motion that helps cut through tough bottom crusts and separates each slice neatly. By contrast, knives with straight cutting edges required more manipulation—sometimes sawing with the tip of the blade, twisting, and even ripping—to get through the bottom crust and free the slice. A slightly curved blade also allows a little extra room under the handle for fingers.

In terms of flexibility, we found that knives with very flexible blades can be unsteady when trying to slice through thick crusts. Rigid blades are more stable and easier to work with.

Finally, our test cooks preferred textured plastic handles to wood because the former felt especially stable in the hand. More important, our testers liked knives with handles that were offset, or raised above the blade. This design keeps fingers above the level of the cutting board, preventing knuckle scrapes even when cutting through the bottom crust.

BREAD KNIVES

Bread knives can have curved (top) or straight (bottom) cutting edges. In our tests, we found that a curved cutting edge allows for a gentle rocking motion that helps cut through tough bottom crusts. Knives with straight cutting edges require more sawing, twisting, and tearing to separate slices of bread.

SCIENCE DESK: Taming Garlic

HUNDREDS OF CHEMICAL COMPOUNDS ARE RESPONSIBLE for the flavor and odor of garlic. The two harshest tasting and smelling chemical groups, glucose inolates and sulfur-containing isothiocyanates, are activated when the garlic cloves are cut, but they are also the first to dissipate when the garlic is heated. Heat, therefore, tames the harshness of garlic, eliminating its unpleasant raw edge and helping to accentuate its sweet, nutty flavors.

Raquel uses a long-handled peel to slide a thin-crust pizza into a hot oven. If you don't own a peel, use a rimless baking sheet or the back of a rimmed baking sheet to move thin-crust pizza in and out of the oven.

PIZZA night

CHAPTER 4

Good pizza can be defined largely by what it is not. A good pizza is neither puffy, bland white bread under a sea of overly sweet tomato sauce nor tough cardboard stamped into a circle and topped with a mountain of blistering, rubbery, tasteless cheese. A good pizza is not damp, molten, saucy, greasy, or messy. Unfortunately, most pizza parlor pies fall into at least one of the above categories. Matters become even worse once you start talking about takeout pizza. Sure, it's nice to have a hot pizza delivered to your door in 30 minutes. But when that pizza tastes like a chemical-laden sponge, we think convenience has come at too high a price.

Thankfully, good pizza can be made at home. As long as you invest $15 in a large ceramic pizza stone, a regular home oven can turn out remarkably good pies. In the test kitchen, we are evenly divided into two camps—those who like their pizza thick and rich and those who like it light and lean. To satisfy everyone, we've developed two pizza recipes—a deep-dish pizza that bakes in a pan as well as a cracker-thin pie that's in and out of the oven in just 10 minutes.

DEEP-DISH PIZZA

WHAT WE WANTED: Something better than take-out pizza that wouldn't require Herculean effort.

Deep-dish pizza is about 75 percent crust, so the crust must be great. We wanted it to be rich, substantial, and moist, with a tender, yet slightly chewy crumb and a well-developed flavor, like that of a good loaf of bread. We also thought a crust should be crisp and nicely browned without being dry or tough. Knowing how time-consuming pizza making can be, we also wanted a pizza dough that could be made in as little time as possible without sacrificing quality.

After scouring various cookbooks, the test kitchen made five different pizza doughs and baked them in deep-dish pans. To our disappointment, none delivered the flavorful, crisp brown crust that we felt was needed.

After these initial tests, we tried dozens of variations. We played around with the ratio of water to flour, the amount of oil, the type of flour, and just about every other variable we could think of. But we weren't satisfied until we finally widened the field and tried a recipe for focaccia that used boiled, riced potatoes to add moisture and flavor to the dough. This dough was just what we were hoping for: very wet and yet easy to handle, light, and smooth. When baked, it was soft and moist, yet with a bit of chew, sturdiness, and structure that was not present in the previous doughs.

Now that we had found a dough that we liked, the challenge was to come up with a rising and baking method suited to deep-dish pizza. We placed the pizza dough in a barely warmed oven for the first rise, reducing the initial rising time from 1 hour to 35 minutes and producing dough that tasted no different from the dough that rose at room temperature for a full hour.

Next we tried reducing—even eliminating—the amount of time allowed for the second rise. The dough given a full 30 minutes of rising time was vastly better than doughs given a second rise of only 15 minutes or given no second rise at all. The flavor was more complex, and the texture of the pizza crust was softer and lighter, making this second rise too important to pass up or shorten.

After some testing, we discovered that a crust baked at 425 degrees in a pan placed on a baking stone was almost perfect; the bottom and sides of the pizza were well-browned, and the interior crumb was moist, light, and evenly cooked through. The exterior of this crust was, however, slightly tough. To combat this, we began lining the pizza pan with oil. After some experimentation, we found that the pizzas made with a generous amount of oil lining the pan (¼ cup was optimal) had a far more desirable crust than those made with little or no oil in the pan. Lightly "frying" the dough in the pan made for a rich, caramelized exterior; this added a good amount of flavor and a secondary texture to the crust, without drying it out or making it tough.

Now it was time for the toppings. On most pizzas, the toppings can simply be placed on raw dough and baked, since the crust bakes in about the same amount of time as the toppings. But we found that the weight of the toppings prevented the crust from rising in the oven, resulting in a dense, heavy crust, especially in the center of the pie. So we tried prebaking crusts from 5 minutes up to 15 minutes to develop some structure before adding the toppings. The pizza prebaked for 15 minutes, then topped, was perfect. This scheme gave the pizza a chance at an initial rise in the oven without the weight or moisture of the toppings, and the toppings had just enough time to melt and brown by the time the crust was baked through.

WHAT WE LEARNED: Add potato to the dough for a soft, chewy crust and prebake the crust before adding the toppings to encourage maximum rise.

DEEP-DISH PIZZA   makes one 14-inch pizza, serving 4 to 6

Prepare the topping while the dough is rising so the two will be ready at the same time. Baking the pizza in a deep-dish pan on a hot pizza stone will help produce a crisp, well-browned bottom crust. If you don't have a pizza stone, use a heavy rimless baking sheet (do not use an insulated baking sheet). If you have only a rimmed baking sheet, turn it upside down and bake the pizza on the rimless side. The amount of oil used to grease the pan may seem excessive, but it helps brown the crust while also preventing sticking.

1	medium baking potato (about 9 ounces), peeled and quartered
3½	cups (17.5 ounces) unbleached all-purpose flour
1½	teaspoons rapid-rise or instant yeast
1¾	teaspoons salt
1	cup (8 ounces) warm water (105 to 115 degrees)
6	tablespoons extra-virgin olive oil, plus more for oiling bowl
1	recipe topping (recipes follow)

1. Bring 1 quart water and potato to boil in a small saucepan over medium-high heat; cook until tender, 10 to 15 minutes. Drain and cool until potato can be handled comfortably; press through fine disk on potato ricer or grate through large holes on box grater. Measure 1⅓ cups lightly packed potato; discard remaining potato.

2. Adjust one oven rack to highest position, other rack to lowest; heat oven to 200 degrees. Once oven reaches 200 degrees, maintain heat for 10 minutes, then turn off heat.

3. Combine flour, yeast, and salt in workbowl of food processor fitted with steel blade. With motor running, add water and process until dough comes together in a shaggy ball. Add 2 tablespoons oil and process several more seconds, until dough is smooth and slightly sticky. Transfer dough to

lightly oiled medium bowl, turn to coat with oil, and cover tightly with plastic wrap. Place in warm oven until dough is soft and spongy and doubled in size, 30 to 35 minutes.

4. Oil bottom of 14-inch deep-dish pizza pan with remaining 4 tablespoons olive oil. Remove dough from oven and gently punch down; turn dough onto clean, dry work surface and pat into 12-inch round. Transfer round to oiled pan, cover with plastic wrap, and let rest until dough no longer resists shaping, about 10 minutes.

5. Place pizza stone or rimless baking sheet on low oven rack (do not use insulated baking sheet; see note) and heat oven to 500 degrees. Uncover dough and pull up into edges and up sides of pan to form 1-inch-high lip. Cover with plastic wrap; let rise in warm draft-free spot until doubled in size, about 30 minutes. Uncover dough and prick generously with fork. Reduce oven temperature to 425, place pan with pizza on preheated stone or baking sheet, and bake until dry and lightly browned, about 15 minutes. Add desired toppings; bake on stone or baking sheet until cheese melts, 10 to 15 minutes (5 to 10 minutes for 10-inch pizzas). Move pizza to top rack and bake until cheese is spotty golden brown, about 5 minutes longer. Let cool 5 minutes, then, holding pizza pan at angle with one hand, use wide spatula to slide pizza from pan to cutting board. Cut into wedges and serve.

VARIATIONS

10-INCH DEEP-DISH PIZZAS

If you don't own a 14-inch deep-dish pizza pan, divide the dough between two 10-inch cake pans.

Follow recipe for Deep-Dish Pizza through step 3. Grease bottom of two 10-inch cake pans with 2 tablespoons olive

oil each. Turn dough onto clean, dry work surface and divide in half. Pat each half into 9-inch round; continue with recipe, reducing initial baking time on lowest rack to 5 to 10 minutes and dividing topping evenly between pizzas.

FRESH TOMATO TOPPING WITH MOZZARELLA AND BASIL

4   medium ripe tomatoes (about 1½ pounds), cored, seeded, and cut into 1-inch pieces
2   medium cloves garlic, minced
      Salt and ground black pepper
6   ounces whole milk mozzarella cheese, shredded (about 1½ cups)
1¼ ounces Parmesan cheese, grated (about ½ cup)
3   tablespoons shredded fresh basil leaves

1. Mix together tomatoes and garlic in medium bowl; season to taste with salt and pepper and set aside.

2. Top partially baked crust evenly with tomato mixture, followed by mozzarella, then Parmesan. Bake as directed in step 5 of recipe for Deep-Dish Pizza. Scatter basil over fully baked pizza before cutting into wedges.

FOUR-CHEESE TOPPING WITH PESTO

For the pesto, follow the recipe on page 15 for Bow-Tie Pasta with Pesto through step 4.

½   cup pesto
6   ounces mozzarella cheese, shredded (about 1½ cups)
4   ounces provolone cheese, shredded (about 1 cup)
1¼ ounces grated Parmesan cheese (about ½ cup)
1¼ ounces blue cheese (about ¼ cup, crumbled)

Spread partially baked crust evenly with pesto; sprinkle with mozzarella, followed by provolone, Parmesan, and blue cheese. Bake as directed in step 5 of recipe for Deep-Dish Pizza.

TASTING LAB: Mozzarella Cheese

IF YOU'RE GOING TO THE TROUBLE OF MAKING YOUR own pizza, you certainly don't want to wreck things by using inferior mozzarella. We wondered if you could use preshredded cheese or whether premium buffalo mozzarella (made from water buffalo milk and imported from Italy) was worth the added expense. Could you even compare these cheeses?

To find out which kinds of mozzarella work best in pizza, tasters sampled six different brands, including three shrink-wrapped low-moisture cheeses from the supermarket (two made from whole milk, one from part skim milk), a preshredded part-skim cheese also from the supermarket, one salted fresh mozzarella made at a local cheese shop, and one salted fresh buffalo mozzarella imported from Italy. We sampled each cheese raw and cooked on a deep-dish pizza. Tasters were asked to rate each cheese on overall flavor (both raw and melted), texture, and melting properties.

When tasted raw, the results were quite clear. Tasters liked the gamey, barnyard flavor of the buffalo mozzarella. The fresh cow's milk mozzarella also performed quite well. Among the supermarket cheeses, there was a clear bias for the whole milk cheeses over those made with part skim milk. The preshredded cheese had a rubbery texture and grainy mouthfeel. (Most tasters noted that even when cooked it was chalky or grainy.) Preshredded cheese is coated with powdered cellulose to prevent clumping. Some tasters felt that the preshredded cheese was drier, attributable to the cellulose or from having been shredded months ago.

Tasted on pizzas, the cheeses produced the same results (at least in terms of flavor), but moisture was now a factor. The fresh cheeses exuded a lot of liquid that flooded the surface of the pizza. Unless the fresh mozzarella is pressed of excess liquid before cooking (we had success weighting the shredded cheese for an hour prior to cooking in a strainer set in a bowl), it is unsuitable for pizza.

Because most cooks (ourselves included) don't want to weight cheese, we think the shrink-wrapped supermarket cheeses make more sense for sprinkling on pizzas. Stick with a whole milk cheese and try to choose a brand with a bit more moisture than the rest of the pack. Our favorite supermarket cheese was Calabro brand whole milk mozzarella (from Connecticut), which was softer and moister than the other supermarket offerings. Certainly, don't use preshredded cheese. The convenience is simply not worth the sacrifice in taste and texture.

SCIENCE DESK: How Yeast Works

YEAST IS A PLANT-LIKE LIVING ORGANISM. ITS FUNCTION in a bread dough is to consume sugars and starches in the flour and convert them into carbon dioxide and alcohol, which give bread its lift and flavor. This process is known as fermentation. Flavor compounds and alcohol—byproducts of fermentation—give bread its characteristic aroma and flavor.

A small amount of honey or sugar is sometimes added to bread dough to enhance the fermentation process—yeast grows faster and better when it has enough sugar to feed on. Warm water (about 110 degrees) is also necessary to activate dry yeast. Very warm water (in excess of 130 degrees) will kill the yeast, and yeast will not activate well in cool water.

Heat is generated during fermentation and rising, and punching the dough down mixes the warmer dough (in the center) with the cooler dough (on the outside edges), thus normalizing the overall temperature. Punching down also releases any excess carbon dioxide, breaks apart yeast particles that are clinging together, and redistributes the sugars, giving the yeast a refreshed food source. After punching down, the dough is often given a second rise, which happens more quickly since there is more yeast at work.

During the first few minutes of baking, the alcohol (formed earlier during fermentation) evaporates, gasses expand, and bubbles enlarge, fostering more rise. This is referred to as oven spring. The yeast cells are killed off during the first few minutes in the oven.

THIN-CRUST PIZZA

WHAT WE WANTED: A crackling-crisp pizza with big flavor that could be rolled superthin with a minimum of effort.

We think a pizza should be thick, soft, and chewy (like our deep-dish pizza) or thin and crisp—not in between. Our goal for thin-crust pizza was simple: a shatteringly crisp, wafer-thin crust with a deeply caramelized flavor and no trace of raw yeast or flour and toppings that were sleek, light, and off the charts in flavor.

We knew that this crust must not only taste remarkably good, it must be easy to produce and cooperative as well. Pizza is casual fare and should shape up easily. Our first inclination, therefore, was to advance to the food processor and give it a whirl against the standing mixer and hand methods. It buried the competition for ease and speed, producing gorgeous, supple doughs in about 30 seconds, or faster than you could say "large pepperoni."

We were keen to make a big, free-form pizza, and we knew that a thin crust would need every bit of conventional oven heat it could get in the 10 minutes or so it would take to bake. That meant 500 degrees and a giant pizza stone with an hour's head start to preheat. (Though we tested a slightly lower oven heat as well, the extra minutes the pizza needed to brown left the finished crust more tough than crisp.) Wanting the crackerlike simplicity of a rich burnished crust, we dressed the pizzas with sauce and mozzarella only.

A handful of the pizza recipes we reviewed offered ideas that contributed significantly to the success of our final recipe. Overnight fermentation (the dough's first long rise) in the refrigerator was a key first precept. The dough is put to bed in chilly quarters—where it rises at its leisure—and is then stretched and baked the following day.

The chilled, rested dough handled easily, having become more pliant and less sticky in the intervening hours. Even better, we could toss the dough into the fridge and forget about it altogether until the next day—we didn't need to wait around to punch it down after a two- or three-hour rise at room temperature. By letting the dough rest overnight, we were also able to use less yeast and gain more flavor from fermentation. As a result of using warm water to make the dough, the yeast got enough of a jump to take off in the cold climate of the refrigerator. The refrigerated dough holds for up to two days without depleting the energy of just ½ teaspoon of yeast. (Granted, this approach removes home pizza making from the world of whimsy and impulse, but the fact that the dough was so easy to handle and the baked pizza so flavorful and crisp more than made up for the delay.)

The second precept was that a soft, supple, and frankly moist dough produces a light, crisp crust. This proved true time after time. Surprisingly, and to our everlasting relief, moist doughs were also easier to work with than drier ones.

Having long been fans of the neo-Neapolitan-style pizza, which is just a couple of hairs thinner than the original thin-crust pizza of Naples, we knew the only instrument equal to the task of achieving a crust as thin as a credit card was a rolling pin. Armed with our overnight-rested, food-processor dough and a tapered French rolling pin, we lightly dusted a large sheet of parchment paper with flour and commenced rolling as one would with a pie dough.

The dough was fully compliant under the pin until we made an effort to turn it like a regular pie dough. At that point, the dough gripped the parchment for dear life. Though it continued to roll thinner and wider, we could not shake it loose from the parchment. A potentially maddening situation morphed into a saving grace when we realized the parchment could accompany the dough to the oven. As the pizza baked, it loosened from the paper automatically, and the stone remained clean. Best yet, the tackiness of the dough held it securely to the parchment, preventing it from springing and shrinking back and eliminating the need for excess flouring when rolling out.

Eventually, we refined this technique by positioning an 18-inch piece of plastic wrap directly onto the top surface of the dough during rolling. Thus insulated, the dough could be rolled effortlessly and flipped about like a sandwich. It did not dry out. Once the dough was rolled, the plastic wrap peeled off easily; the thin round could be dressed and hurried into the oven without further ado.

While Americans have a propensity for using high-protein flour in breads, our research indicated that Italians use fairly soft flour. Here at the test kitchen, King Arthur all-purpose is generally our flour of choice. A fairly strong all-purpose flour with no chemical additives, King Arthur has outstanding flavor. We had been using it throughout testing, occasionally in combination with softer flours such as cake or rye to lighten the dough (these flour combinations produced unexceptional pizzas). But doughs made exclusively with King Arthur were occasionally less than cracker-crisp, especially during damp weather.

At the suggestion of Maggie Glezer, a baker certified by the American Institute of Baking and a wizard with yeast, we switched from King Arthur all-purpose flour at 11.7 percent protein to Gold Medal unbleached all-purpose flour at 10.5 percent protein. Flours with a higher protein content require more vigorous kneading to create structure in the dough and more water to achieve proper hydration. The lower-protein Gold Medal flour yielded uniformly light doughs that were as full-flavored as those made with King Arthur.

Working initially with measures of volume—2 cups flour to ¾ cup water—the results became unpredictable enough to convince us to switch to weights. We discovered stunning discrepancies between liquid measuring cups at that volume (up to a tablespoon), and with our meager dough ball, a few drops of water more or less made quite an impact.

We found that thin-crust pizzas are best topped simply—tomato sauce and good mozzarella are sufficient. If you want to get fancier, tread carefully. A thin crust cannot bear the weight and water of raw vegetables or a stifling canopy of four cheeses. During their stay in the oven, the crust and topping must become one, sustaining temperatures

that drive off moisture as they toast the crust mahogany, bake the sauce to a lacquer, and graft cheese to the top. If you want to add some embellishments, try caramelized onions, roasted mushrooms, or strips of roasted red peppers added before baking. Thin-crust pizza can also be "flavored" after baking with a thin layer of pesto or tapenade, arugula tossed with olive oil, or thin medallions of goat cheese.

A final note or two: Force of habit persuaded us to transfer the hot, sliced pizza to a cooling rack. Though the pizza rarely survived long enough to underscore the merits of this method, on the occasions that it did, the air circulating under the crust kept it crisp. In fact, the crusts generally became more crisp in the few minutes after being removed from the oven—like a cookie might. And although a 14-inch pizza may sound extra-large, one of these will satisfy only two restrained, polite adults.

WHAT WE LEARNED: Use a low-protein, unbleached all-purpose flour, let the dough rise slowly overnight in the refrigerator, and roll the dough between parchment and plastic to prevent sticking and the need for additional flour.

CRISP THIN-CRUST PIZZA makes two 14-inch pizzas
All-purpose unbleached flour with a protein percentage no higher than 10.5, such as Gold Medal, makes the lightest, crispiest pizzas. We recommend weighing the flour and water, but because many factors affect the flour's capacity to absorb water, heed visual and tactile clues to achieve a dough with the proper consistency. For rolling out the dough, we prefer commercial-sized parchment paper sheets, though parchment sold in rolls 14 inches wide also works. Keep in mind that it is more important for the rolled dough to be of even thinness than to be a perfect circle. For topping the pizzas, we recommend buying whole milk mozzarella and shredding it by hand with a box grater; do not use fresh or prepackaged shredded mozzarella, and resist the temptation to sprinkle on more cheese than is recommended.

- 2 cups (10 ounces) unbleached all-purpose flour, preferably Gold Medal or Pillsbury, protein content no higher than 10.5 percent
- ½ teaspoon rapid-rise or instant yeast
- ½ teaspoon honey
- ½ teaspoon salt
- ¾ cup plus 2 teaspoons (6.2 ounces) water, preferably filtered or spring, 100 to 105 degrees
- ¼ cup olive oil

- 1 cup Quick Tomato Sauce for Pizza (recipe follows)
- 8 ounces whole milk mozzarella, shredded (about 2 cups)

day 1
1. Combine flour, yeast, honey, and salt in workbowl of food processor fitted with steel blade. With machine running, add all but 2 teaspoons water through feed tube. With machine still running, add olive oil through feed tube and process until dough forms ball, about 30 seconds. Turn dough out onto work surface. Use technique recommended on page 45 to see if dough needs more water and to finish kneading.

2. Divide dough in half and place each piece in gallon-sized, heavy-duty zipper-lock plastic bag and seal. Refrigerate overnight or up to 48 hours.

day 2
1. Adjust oven rack to lowest position, set baking stone on rack, and heat oven to 500 degrees. Heat baking stone 1 hour before proceeding.

2. Remove dough from plastic bags. Set each half in center of lightly floured large sheet parchment paper. Cover each with two 18-inch lengths plastic wrap overlapping in center (alternatively, use one 18-inch length of extrawide plastic wrap); let doughs rest 10 minutes.

3. Setting one dough aside, roll the other into 14-inch round with even thinness of ¹⁄₃₂ inch, using tackiness of dough against parchment to help roll. If parchment wrinkles, flip dough sandwich over and smooth wrinkles with metal dough scraper.

4. Peel plastic wrap off top of rolled dough. Use soup spoon to spread and smooth ½ cup tomato sauce to edges of dough. Sprinkle with about 1 cup cheese. With scissors, trim excess parchment so that it is just larger than dough.

5. Slip dough with parchment onto pizza peel, inverted rimmed baking sheet, or rimless baking sheet. Slide pizza, parchment and all, onto hot baking stone. Bake until deep golden brown, about 10 minutes. Remove from oven with pizza peel or pull parchment with pizza onto baking sheet. Transfer pizza to cutting board, slide parchment out from under pizza; cut pizza into wedges and slide onto wire rack. Let cool 2 minutes until crisp; serve.

6. While first pizza is baking, repeat steps 3 and 4 to roll and sauce second pizza; allow baking stone to reheat 15 minutes after baking first pizza, then repeat step 5 to bake second pizza.

CRISP THIN-CRUST PIZZA WITH ARUGULA

Since dressed arugula will wilt, it's best to prepare the topping for each pizza as needed. For two pizzas, double the amounts listed below.

Toss 5 ounces arugula, stemmed (about 1 cup lightly packed), with 1 tablespoon extra-virgin olive oil and salt and pepper to taste. Follow recipe for Crisp Thin-Crust Pizza, preparing pizza as directed and baking for 8 minutes. Sprinkle arugula over pizza and return to oven for 2 minutes more. Slice as directed and cool.

CRISP THIN-CRUST PIZZA WITH TAPENADE

For best presentation, spoon eight equal portions of tapenade (each about 1 teaspoon) evenly over baked pizza and cut so each slice has one portion. You can do the same thing with pesto (see recipe on page 15 and follow steps 1 through 4).

Follow recipe for Crisp Thin-Crust Pizza, spooning 8 teaspoons Tapenade (recipe follows) over each pizza as soon as it comes out of the oven.

QUICK TOMATO SAUCE FOR PIZZA

makes about 1 ½ cups

For pizza, you want the smoothest possible sauce. Start with crushed tomatoes and puree them in a food processor before cooking the tomatoes with garlic and oil. This recipe makes a bit more sauce than needed to sauce two thin-crust pizzas.

1   can (14.5 ounces) crushed tomatoes
1   large clove garlic, minced or pressed through garlic press
1   tablespoon olive oil
    Salt and ground black pepper

1. Process tomatoes in workbowl of food processor fitted with steel blade until smooth, about five 1-second pulses.

2. Heat garlic and oil in medium saucepan over medium heat until garlic is sizzling, about 40 seconds. Stir in tomatoes; bring to simmer and cook, uncovered, until sauce thickens enough to coat wooden spoon, about 15 minutes. Season to taste with salt and pepper.

TECHNIQUE: How to Achieve the Proper Dough Consistency

  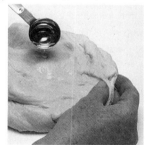 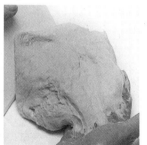

A freshly processed dough with adequate water will look shaggy and stick to the counter. A few "throws" against the counter will help the dough become supple and fine-textured.	A freshly processed dough that is too dry will form a clean ball, feel more oily than moist, and look slightly curdy on the surface.	To moisten a processed dough that is too dry, add 1 teaspoon water and throw the dough against the counter 10 times. The dough may take up to 2 teaspoons additional water.	A properly kneaded dough with enough water will be supple and fine-textured. Though moist and sticky, the dough should have structure and not feel "batter-like."

TAPENADE makes 1 cup

Spread extra tapenade on small toasts for a quick appetizer or use tapenade as a sandwich spread—it works especially well with fresh mozzarella and either sliced tomatoes or roasted peppers.

3	tablespoons extra-virgin olive oil
1½	cups pitted kalamata olives
2	tablespoons shredded fresh basil leaves
2	teaspoons fresh rosemary leaves
1	tablespoon capers, rinsed
4	anchovy fillets, rinsed

Place ingredients in workbowl of food processor. Process, stopping as necessary to scrape down sides of bowl, until mixture is finely minced and forms a chunky paste, about 1 minute. Transfer mixture to small bowl. (Surface of tapenade can be covered with plastic wrap or film of olive oil and refrigerated for up to 3 days.)

THIN-CRUST PIZZA ON HOLD

OUR RECIPE MAKES TWO PAPER-THIN 14-INCH PIZZAS. If you're hungry for just one pizza, make the full recipe anyway. Roll out both doughs, but roll one of them to 15 inches. Dress the dough rolled to the standard 14 inches with sauce and topping and bake it; poke the larger dough everywhere with a fork, but leave it undressed. Bake the undressed dough on the stone for 2 minutes, then remove it from the parchment and cool it on a rack. (The dough will look like a large flour tortilla and will have shrunk to 14 inches.) Wrap well and freeze on a baking sheet (yes, it is pretty big, but the sheet can be balanced on top of other frozen goods). When you're in the mood for pizza, heat up the stone for an hour, defrost and dress the frozen dough, slide it onto parchment, and bake it for nine minutes. Pizzas done this way were so good our tasters could not distinguish them from fresh. A frozen crust will keep nicely for up to three weeks in the freezer—but can you wait that long to have another pizza?

EQUIPMENT CORNER: Box Graters

A BOX GRATER IS ONE OF THOSE UNFORTUNATE KITCHEN tools—it occupies significant cabinet or counter space, is used infrequently, yet is absolutely essential. While food processors come complete with a grater attachment, not everyone has one, and it's doubtful that those who do would dirty the entire contraption to grate a handful of mozzarella. That said, there are a number of graters on the market, from nonstick to heavy-grade stainless steel. We wanted to find out if there was a significant difference between these models. Did we need to spend $20 on a grater, or would a $6 grater do the job?

We tested eight different box graters, ranging in price from $6.48 to $19.99. We grated items of varying texture and firmness, all of which we grate frequently in the test kitchen—mozzarella cheese, celeriac, carrots, and ginger.

The winning box grater would need to rate well in all categories. It would be fast (efficient and sharp, requiring little effort and pressure), stable (no rocking or sliding), comfortable (a good grip on the handle), and easy to clean (a single trip through the dishwasher or a quick scrub with soapy water—all models were dishwasher-safe). With those standards in mind, we grated and rated.

We soon found that most graters had little problem with speed and sharpness. From carrots to cheese, the shreds were clean and uniform, falling quickly from the grater. Ginger proved a problem for two models, which sported only the punched, raised-spike holes for grating smaller items. Those spiked teeth grabbed onto the ginger fibers, leaving juice on the counter and negligible scrapings of actual ginger meat. Graters with miniature versions of the large-holed side were much more successful with ginger.

Stability proved an essential component of a quality box grater. While many models slid a bit if set atop a smooth countertop, testers found sliding to be the lesser of evils. Grated knuckles, the unwelcome result of tipping and rocking, were a common (and unacceptable) occurrence with poorly balanced, flimsy graters. The graters with the largest bases sat

firmly on the countertop, allowing fast, safe grating.

Several graters boasted "slipfree" rubber bases, which we found to be both a help and a hindrance. When grating soft items that required little pressure (such as cheese), the bases indeed kept the grater firmly in place. But when grating firmer items (such as carrots) that required more pressure, the immovable graters tipped, endangering fingers. Additionally, testers preferred a smooth surface for making uninterrupted passes with the cheese or vegetable. The models with rubber or plastic bases and tops were not composed of a single piece of metal, so the grated item had to pass over or be halted by the attached base or top. The attached base also acted as a trap for juices or tiny bits of grated material.

Comfort was similarly affected by the size of the grater's base; there was no need for a tight grip as long as the grater was well-balanced. The most stable graters required merely a hand resting on the top. As a bonus, larger bases offered wider openings at the top, enabling a clear view of the progress.

Most of the graters were easy to clean. A simple scrub by hand or a single run through the dishwasher removed all traces of cheese or vegetables. However, the two models that trapped the ginger fibers had significant problems. The fibers were thoroughly enmeshed in the teeth, proving a true challenge for washing by hand, and they remained firmly in place after a heavy-duty dishwasher run, quickly drying into an intractable mess. The fibers had to be delicately plucked by hand from the sharp teeth.

On your next trip to the kitchen store, look for box graters with extra wide bases, preferably composed of a single piece of metal, with one side offering tiny raised holes for smaller items. We found the more expensive graters tended to be better. The top-rated graters were the Küchenprofi 6-Sided ($15; see photo on page 49), Amco Professional Performance ($19.99), and Progressive International Perfect Prep ($16.99). You can justify the extra expense and cabinet space with the savings you'll reap in Band-Aids.

SIMPLE sandwiches

CHAPTER 5

Although the sandwich was named in England for the Earl of Sandwich, we rightly think of sandwiches as particularly American creations. Packed in a lunch box, eaten at a picnic table, or nibbled in front of the television, there's something comforting about a sandwich.

Of course, just because Mom used to make sandwiches doesn't mean that this humble American mainstay is always shown the proper respect today. Mushy, bland tuna salad is the rule rather than the exception. Individually wrapped cheese singles have all but ruined the grilled cheese sandwich.

But there's something special about a well-made sandwich. It shows that you care about the details and can enjoy life's small pleasures. With good ingredients and some easy-to-master techniques, great sandwiches are within reach.

Lunch is ready in the test kitchen. Two classics—tuna salad and grilled cheese—along with a fancy steak sandwich are being served. Bring on the chips and pickles.

When making grilled cheese sandwiches, we found that grated cheese melts better than sliced and also covers the bread more evenly.

TUNA SALAD SANDWICHES

WHAT WE WANTED: A technique that would eliminate the twin problems that plague most tuna salad: watery texture and bland flavor.

Grade-school lunches, hospital cafeterias, and second-rate delis have given tuna salad a bad name with mixtures that are typically mushy, watery, and bland. But these poor examples should not cause cooks to lose hope for this old standard. We tackled tuna salad in the test kitchen and came up with three simple preparation and flavoring tricks that guarantee a tuna salad that is evenly moist, tender, flaky, and well-seasoned every time.

A first-rate tuna salad begins with the best canned tuna. All comers favored solid white tuna over chunk light for its meaty texture and delicate flavor. Among the five brands we tried, StarKist reigned supreme, so we made it the basis of all our subsequent testing. (See the Tasting Lab on page 52 for more details.)

In a dish as simple as tuna salad, the finer points of preparation make a real difference. For instance, most cooks simply squeeze out a bit of the packing water by pressing the detached can lid down lightly on the fish. Tasters consistently deemed all of the salads made with tuna prepared in this manner "soggy" and "watery." Taking the minor extra step of draining the tuna thoroughly in a colander before mixing it with other ingredients gave the salads a toothsome, less watery texture.

Breaking the tuna apart with a fork was another standard procedure we dumped. In salads made with tuna prepared this way, we'd invariably bite into a large, dry, unseasoned chunk that the fork had missed. With the tuna in the colander, we decided to break down the larger chunks with our fingers until the whole amount was fine and even in texture. This gave the finished salad a smooth, even, flaky texture that all of our tasters appreciated.

Seasoning was the last problem we addressed. All too often, tuna salad tastes dull and lifeless because of careless seasoning or, even worse, no seasoning at all. Salt and pepper were critical to making the most of tuna's delicate flavor. An acidic seasoning, such as lemon or lime juice or vinegar, was equally important, adding some much needed brightness to the flavor.

We also found that the order in which we mixed the ingredients made a difference. We first tried mixing the basic seasonings and flavorings with the tuna alone before adding the mayonnaise. Next we tried adding the seasonings, flavorings, and mayonnaise all at once. Our tasters agreed that preseasoning the tuna resulted in a more deeply flavored, lively tuna salad.

After settling on these three basic techniques, we were unanimous in finding mayonnaise to be the binder of choice and found other salad ingredients to be largely a matter of taste. We nonetheless agreed that trace amounts of garlic and mustard added dimension to the overall flavor and that a modest amount of minced pickle provided a touch of piquancy, not to mention a link to tradition. (In fact, tuna takes well to a wide range of flavorings; see some of our variations for inspiration.)

So forget the sopping, mushy salad you ate in your last beleaguered, institutional tuna sandwich. The next time the cold cuts run out, or even before, reach for the canned tuna that graces even the emptiest pantry, take a little extra care with the contents, and find out how satisfying a well-made tuna salad sandwich can be.

WHAT WE LEARNED: Thoroughly drain the tuna in a colander and break it up with your fingers for the optimal texture. For the best flavor and even distribution of ingredients, season the tuna and add flavorings before mixing with mayonnaise.

CLASSIC TUNA SALAD makes about 2 cups, enough for 4 sandwiches

See the Tasting Lab on page 52 for information on brands of tuna and the one we recommend.

2	(6-ounce) cans solid white tuna in water
2	tablespoons juice from 1 lemon
½	teaspoon salt
¼	teaspoon ground black pepper
1	small rib celery, minced (about ¼ cup)
2	tablespoons minced red onion
2	tablespoons minced dill or sweet pickles
½	small clove garlic, minced or pressed through garlic press (about ⅛ teaspoon)
2	tablespoons minced fresh parsley leaves
½	cup mayonnaise
¼	teaspoon Dijon mustard

Drain tuna in colander and shred with fingers until no clumps remain and texture is fine and even. Transfer tuna to medium bowl and mix in lemon juice, salt, pepper, celery, onion, pickles, garlic, and parsley until evenly blended. Fold in mayonnaise and mustard until tuna is evenly moistened. (Can be covered and refrigerated up to 3 days.)

VARIATIONS

TUNA SALAD WITH BALSAMIC VINEGAR AND GRAPES

Follow recipe for Classic Tuna Salad, omitting lemon juice, dill (or pickles), garlic, and parsley and adding 2 tablespoons balsamic vinegar, 6 ounces halved red seedless grapes (about 1 cup), ¼ cup lightly toasted slivered almonds, and 2 teaspoons minced thyme leaves to tuna along with salt and pepper.

CURRIED TUNA SALAD WITH APPLES AND CURRANTS

Follow recipe for Classic Tuna Salad, omitting dill (or pickles), garlic, and parsley and adding 1 medium firm, juicy apple, cut into ¼-inch dice (about 1 cup), ¼ cup currants, and 2 tablespoons minced fresh basil leaves to tuna along with lemon juice, salt, and pepper; mix 1 tablespoon curry powder into mayonnaise before folding into tuna.

TUNA SALAD WITH LIME AND HORSERADISH

Follow recipe for Classic Tuna Salad, omitting lemon juice, dill (or pickles), and garlic and adding 2 tablespoons juice and ½ teaspoon grated zest from 1 lime and 3 tablespoons prepared horseradish to tuna along with salt and pepper.

TUNA SALAD WITH CAULIFLOWER, JALAPEÑO, AND CILANTRO

Follow recipe for Classic Tuna Salad, omitting dill (or pickles), garlic, and parsley and adding 4 ounces cauliflower florets cut into ½-inch pieces (about 1 cup), 1 medium jalapeño chile, minced (about 2 tablespoons), 2 medium scallions, minced (about ¼ cup), and 2 tablespoons minced fresh cilantro leaves to tuna along with lemon juice, salt, and pepper.

EQUIPMENT CORNER: Can Openers

WE PURCHASED FOUR MANUAL CAN OPENERS LABELED "safety" can openers and six standard can openers with varying grips and features. We tested these can openers on standard 14.5 ounce cans of beans. We judged each opener on its comfort, ease of operation, and safety.

In terms of comfort, we took into account both the grip and the turning mechanism. Can openers having an ergonomic grip and a comfortable turning mechanism were preferred over models that pinched our fingers or forced an uncomfortable hand angle.

Ease of operation hinged on time—if more than one rotation around the can was necessary, or if we had to pause and restart turning, the opener was downgraded.

Determining safety was clear-cut. If the opened can had smooth edges and little handling of sharp-edged tops was necessary, the opener earned the top rating. If the operation endangered fingers or produced ragged edges on the can or its top, the opener received a poor rating.

In the end, the simplest models won. Perhaps it was our lifelong use of standard can openers, but we simply could not get used to a different hand position, a two-part operation, or a locking handle—particularly if the opener in question was stiff and difficult to operate, which most of them were. Standard, simple models may not result in perfectly smooth edges, but we're willing to use a bit of extra caution in exchange for ease, speed, and comfort.

Our favorite models were the Oxo Good Grips ($9.95), with a great grip and comfortable turning mechanism, and Swing Away ($6.99), a classic stainless steel opener with plastic coated handles for extra comfort. Of the safety-oriented models, the Culinare MagiCan Auto Release ($9.99) received the best marks. This all-plastic opener magnetically attaches itself to the lid and then ejects the lid with the push of a button. However, testers found this model messy to use (liquid spilled out as cans were opened), and we can only recommend it with reservations.

TASTING LAB: Canned Tuna

WE SELECTED THE 10 BEST-SELLING CHUNK-LIGHT AND solid white tunas packed in water and assembled 25 tasters in the test kitchen. We drained the tuna and lightly blended it with mayonnaise. No seasonings were added.

In most of our blind taste tests, taste has predictably reigned. But when it came to canned tuna, texture set the pace. Most canned tuna is bland—that's why tuna salad is so heavily seasoned. But some brands could be chewed, while others were more suitable to gumming.

Chunk light was the least expensive of the two varieties in our tasting, costing about 41 cents a can less than solid white. This may explain why it is also the top-selling type of canned tuna. Certainly our tasting results do not explain it, since tasters found only one of the five chunk-light samples (Geisha) acceptable. In general, chunk light tuna is made of skipjack tuna or yellowfin tuna or both; skipjack contributes a stronger flavor than yellowfin. Each can contains several small pieces of tuna as well as some flakes.

While our tasters were not wild about the more pronounced flavor of chunk light (which often included an aftertaste of tin), what really upset the balance between the white and light tunas was texture. White tuna you could eat, even pierce, with a fork; the light version was more appropriately scooped with a spoon. When blended with mayonnaise, the small flakes of chunk light tuna quickly broke down even further, taking on a texture that reminded many tasters of cat food. Tasters not only disliked this lack of chew but found that the small shreds of fish held moisture too well, which created a sopping, mushy consistency.

Solid white, on the other hand, consists of one large piece of loin meat from albacore tuna. Though known as "white" tuna, albacore can vary from nearly white to light pink or even beige. Solid white was the tuna of choice among tasters for its mild flavor, milky-white appearance, and chunky texture. StarKist took top honors, followed by 3 Diamonds, Chicken of the Sea, Bumble Bee, and Geisha.

GRILLED CHEESE SANDWICHES

WHAT WE WANTED: Buttery, golden sandwiches with a lacy-crisp exterior and perfectly melted, oozing cheese.

Anyone with kids makes a lot of grilled cheese sandwiches. Rarely are they as good as they could be. Quite simply, most parents are often rushed. The skillet's too hot, the butter is cold, and the cheese is difficult to slice—especially when the block has been whittled down to a nub.

We set some time aside to figure out exactly how to make consistently great grilled cheese sandwiches—hot and buttery, with a golden, lacy-crisp exterior and a tender interior oozing with melted cheese.

What we've come to understand is that making a grilled cheese sandwich with an evenly golden, crispy exterior and a molten interior has less to do with your choice of cheese, bread, and skillet than with what you do with your cheese, bread, and skillet. What's most important is how (pardon the expression) to cut the cheese, how and where to apply the fat, and what level of heat to use when cooking the sandwich.

When it comes to grilled cheese sandwiches, the filling is largely a question of personal taste. What tradition does firmly suggest is that the cheese be cut into thin, even slices for even melting. Unfortunately, achieving such perfectly sliced cheese can be problematic. Cheese planes don't work well on soft, rubbery cheeses. (Besides, not everyone has a cheese plane.) Achieving thin slices with a knife requires patience, practice, and a relatively hard block of cheese. We usually end up with a pile of small, uneven pieces, suitable for placing together like a mosaic.

With all this in mind, we opted for the common box grater. Grating is quick and efficient, and it always delivers a uniform mass of cheese, whether it's hard or soft, from a big hunk or a tiny nub. And grated cheese covers the entire slice of bread in one even layer.

Choosing the right bread is like choosing the right pillow. Some people like theirs soft, while others prefer theirs firm. The test kitchen's favorite is Pepperidge Farm Toasting White Bread for its ½-inch-thick slices, delicate flavor, tender yet firm texture, and crumb with craterlike pockets that cradle the melted cheese perfectly.

Having tried the full range of fats, from vegetable spray to mayonnaise to clarified butter, we chose to work with (salted) butter for its superior flavor and ability to turn the bread deeply golden. We also preferred buttering the bread instead of adding butter to the skillet, where the butter tends to burn and is absorbed unevenly by the bread. For this approach, melted butter was the logical choice. This method eliminates any risk of tearing the bread's tender crumb and allows the entire surface to be evenly coated, thus ensuring a uniform toasty golden-brown color.

A heavy-gauge skillet with a flat bottom is your best choice for cooking grilled cheese sandwiches. The real key when it comes to cooking, though, is low heat. We found we could leave the sandwich in the skillet over low heat for an astonishing 30 minutes on one side before the bread became too dark. Few of us have that kind of time to spend making a simple sandwich. But the fact is, the longer it takes the bread to turn golden, the more developed and crispy the exterior will be. The level of heat may be raised slightly, but no higher than medium-low. The least amount of time you can get away with to achieve a golden-crisp exterior is about five minutes per side, though eight to ten minutes is optimal. At higher temperatures, the bread will burn long before the cheese melts.

WHAT WE LEARNED: To make sure the cheese is evenly distributed, grate rather than slice it. For a uniformly golden crust, brush the bread with melted butter rather than melting butter in a hot pan. To make sure that the crust is also lacy-crisp, cook the sandwich over low heat.

CLASSIC GRILLED CHEESE SANDWICHES

serves 2

The traditional grilled cheese sandwich usually uses a mild cheddar cheese, but our technique for this sandwich works with most any cheese. Grilled cheese sandwiches are best served hot out of the pan, though in a pinch they can be held, unsliced, for about 20 minutes in a warm oven. If you want to make more than two sandwiches at once, get two skillets going or use an electric griddle, set at medium-low (about 250 degrees), grilling 10 minutes per side. The possible variations on the basic grilled cheese sandwich are endless, but the extras are best sandwiched between the cheese. Try a few very thin slices of baked ham, prosciutto, turkey breast, or ripe, in-season tomato. Two to three tablespoons of caramelized onions also make a nice addition. Condiments such as Dijon mustard, pickle relish, or chutney can be spread on the bread instead of sandwiched in the cheese.

> 3 ounces cheese (preferably mild cheddar) or combination of cheeses, grated on large holes of box grater (about ¾ cup)
> 4 slices (½ inch-thick) firm white sandwich bread, such as Pepperidge Farm Toasting White
> 2 tablespoons butter (preferably salted), melted

1. Heat heavy 12-inch skillet over low to medium-low heat. Meanwhile, sprinkle a portion of cheese over two bread slices. Top each with a remaining bread slice, pressing down gently to set.

2. Brush sandwich tops completely with half of melted butter; place each sandwich, buttered-side down, in skillet. Brush remaining side of each sandwich completely with remaining butter. Cook until crisp and deep golden brown, 5 to 10 minutes per side, flipping sandwiches back to first side to reheat and crisp, about 15 seconds. Serve immediately.

VARIATION

GRILLED FRESH MOZZARELLA SANDWICHES WITH BLACK OLIVE PASTE AND ROASTED RED PEPPERS

If you prefer not to roast fresh peppers, use jarred; for the olive paste, try our recipe for tapenade on page 46 or use a prepared paste.

Cut 2 ounces roasted red peppers into ½-inch strips; set aside. Follow recipe for Classic Grilled Cheese Sandwiches, substituting European-style country bread for sandwich white and 3 ounces fresh mozzarella for cheddar. Spread 1 teaspoon tapenade on each slice of bread. Sprinkle half of cheese over two bread slices; top each with portion of roasted pepper strips and few grinds of black pepper, then remaining cheese. Continue with recipe, substituting extra-virgin olive oil for butter and rubbing toasted sandwiches with clove raw garlic.

FLANK STEAK SANDWICHES

WHAT WE WANTED: An upscale steak sandwich that would be easy to execute.

We love flank steak. It's relatively inexpensive, lean, and tender as long as the meat is cooked and sliced correctly. (For more information on this cut, see the Tasting Lab on page 158.) Although we usually grill flank steak, for sandwiches we like to pan-sear the meat—it seems a shame to limit this recipe to the grill, which is dependent on warm weather.

We found that searing flank steak is easy as long as you follow a couple of basic rules. You must use a heavy-bottomed pan that has been preheated over high heat for four minutes. (A 12-inch cast-iron skillet is the ideal choice.) The meat won't brown properly in cooler, lighter pans. Although many steaks have enough fat to pan-sear with little or no oil, we discovered that lean flank steak requires a tablespoon of vegetable oil. Once the steak is well browned on both sides, it's imperative to let the meat rest (see the Science Desk on page 158) before slicing. To make the sandwiches easy to eat, slice the meat very thin across the grain; thicker slices will be unpleasantly tough and chewy.

With the meat element of our sandwich ready, we focused on the bread and greens. A baguette was our first choice, and it tested well in the kitchen. We tried both mild and spicy greens, and most tasters preferred the latter, especially arugula, watercress, or mizuna. Tasters also responded well to a little thinly sliced red onion, which added crunch and bite.

Mayonnaise is the classic dressing for this kind of sandwich. It is usually spiked with herbs and/or spices. After testing several possibilities, we decided on Asian-inspired seasonings—soy sauce, garlic, ginger, and sesame oil.

We experimented with both homemade and commercial mayonnaise. (For information on our favorite brands, see the Tasting Lab on page 96.) Although commercial mayonnaise was fine, it could not compete with the richness and silky texture of homemade. We decided to do some testing to perfect our recipe for homemade mayonnaise.

The old-fashioned way of making mayonnaise is to whisk together oil, lemon juice, and egg yolk into a thick creamy sauce known as an emulsion. The egg yolk stabilizes the emulsion and prevents the oil and lemon juice from reverting to their liquid form. At least this is what is supposed to happen. But homemade mayonnaise often separates into a greasy mess as the cook attempts to stretch as much as ¾ cup oil around a single egg yolk and teaspoon of lemon juice. We found that whisking the egg yolk and lemon juice thoroughly (the egg yolk itself contains liquid and fat materials that must be emulsified) helps to stabilize the mayonnaise. Adding the oil very, very slowly is also key.

Given the perils of whisking, many modern cooks turn to the food processor when making mayonnaise. We wondered how the two methods would compare. Although we eventually perfected a whisk method, the food processor is more foolproof, in part because it's easier to add the oil slowly through the feed tube when both hands are free. (When whisking, you must balance the measuring cup with oil in one hand, while whisking constantly with the other. This takes some practice.)

But making mayonnaise in a food processor necessitates some changes to the basic recipe. Because of the size of the workbowl, it's not possible to make a small amount, using just one egg yolk. Many sources suggest using one whole egg and twice as much oil, while others recommend two egg yolks and twice as much oil. We tested both methods and preferred the whole-egg mayonnaise for its lightness and creaminess. Rather than doubling the oil to 1½ cups, we found we could use just 1¼ cups oil.

WHAT WE LEARNED: Sear the flank steak in an extremely hot, heavy skillet for maximum browning. Use the food processor to make an especially stable, creamy mayonnaise.

FLANK STEAK AND ARUGULA SANDWICHES WITH RED ONION serves 4

If you prefer, grill the flank steak according to the directions on page 157.

1½ pounds flank steak, trimmed of excess fat and patted dry with paper towels
Salt and ground black pepper
1 tablespoon vegetable oil
1 baguette, cut into four 5-inch lengths, each piece split into top and bottom pieces
½ cup Garlic-Soy Mayonnaise (recipe follows)
½ small red onion, sliced thin
1 bunch arugula, stemmed, washed, and dried (about 3 cups)

1. Heat heavy-bottomed, 12-inch skillet over high heat until very hot, about 4 minutes. While skillet is heating, season steak generously with salt and pepper. Add oil to pan and swirl to coat bottom. Lay steak in pan and cook without moving it until well browned, about 5 minutes. Using tongs, flip steak; cook until well browned on second side,

about 5 minutes longer. Transfer steak to cutting board, tent with foil, and let rest 10 minutes. Cut steak into ¼-inch slices on the bias against the grain.

2. Spread each baguette piece with 1 tablespoon mayonnaise; portion out steak over bottom pieces of bread and sprinkle with salt and pepper. Add portion of red onion and arugula; place tops of baguette on top and serve.

QUICK FOOD PROCESSOR MAYONNAISE
makes about 1½ cups

Extra mayonnaise can be refrigerated in an airtight container for up to several days.

2 teaspoons juice from 1 lemon
Salt
¼ teaspoon Dijon mustard
Dash Tabasco sauce
Dash Worcestershire sauce
Pinch ground black pepper
1 large egg
1¼ cups vegetable, canola, or light olive oil

1. Process lemon juice, generous ¼ teaspoon salt, mustard, Tabasco, Worcestershire, pepper, and egg in food processor until combined and mixture turns light yellow, about 30 seconds.

2. With machine running, pour oil in thin, steady stream through feed tube until fully incorporated, thick, and emulsified, about 1 minute.

VARIATION
GARLIC-SOY MAYONNAISE makes ½ cup

If you prefer, start with commercial mayonnaise instead of homemade.

½ cup Quick Food Processor Mayonnaise
1 tablespoon soy sauce
½ teaspoon honey

1   very small clove garlic, minced or pressed
     through garlic press (about ½ teaspoon)
1   piece (⅓ inch) ginger, minced (about 1 teaspoon)
½   teaspoon Asian sesame oil

Mix all ingredients together in small bowl. (Can be covered
and refrigerated for up to 1 day.)

SCIENCE DESK:
Mayonnaise Emulsification

AN EMULSION IS A MIXTURE OF TWO OR MORE THINGS
that don't ordinarily mix, such as oil and water, or the
stuffed monster and Barbie doll that Doc is using to demonstrate this phenomenon in the photo above. The only way
to mix them is to stir or whisk so strenuously that one of
the two ingredients breaks down into tiny droplets. In the
case of mayonnaise, the oil is broken down into tiny droplets

(called the dispersed phase of the emulsion) that are suspended in the lemon juice (called the continuous phase).
Light cannot make its way through the many suspended
droplets, and this is why the mixture appears to be creamy.

Such a mixture will start to fall out of emulsion (or separate) because the droplets move around. As they move
around, they run into each other and stick, becoming bigger
and bigger, until the oil and lemon juice return to their previously separate states.

One way to sustain an emulsion is to add some sort of
emulsifier. Egg yolks act as an emulsifier by preventing the oil
droplets from sticking together. The active emulsifying
ingredient in egg yolks is lecithin. Whereas most substances
are either attracted to water (hydrophilic) or repelled by
water (hydrophobic), lecithin is both. One end of the
lecithin molecule is hydrophilic, and the other end is
hydrophobic. The hydrophobic ends coat the oil droplets,
preventing the oil droplets from coming together and falling
out of suspension.

The combined forces of cognac and flame bring out the deepest, sweetest flavor in shrimp and imbue our fra diavolo recipe with the spirit's richness and complexity.

SHRIMP classics

CHAPTER 6

Cooking shrimp is a relatively straightforward process. As soon as the meat turns pink (which can happen in just two to three minutes in the presence of intense heat), the shrimp are done. How the shrimp are handled before cooking actually generates more confusion. Should they be peeled? Should the vein that runs down the back of each shrimp be removed?

Shopping for shrimp is equally thought-provoking. Are some shrimp varieties better than others? Is it worth the extra money to buy larger shrimp? Are frozen shrimp a viable option?

We cooked pound after pound of shrimp to answer these questions and to develop recipes for classic dishes such as shrimp cocktail, shrimp scampi, shrimp fra diavolo, and grilled shrimp. Our recipes are easy to follow, but they do rely on some unusual techniques to obtain optimal results. Step into the test kitchen and learn how to become the shrimp expert in your home.

SHRIMP COCKTAIL

WHAT WE WANTED: Plump, tender, flavorful shrimp accompanied by a zesty cocktail sauce.

Nothing is more basic than shrimp cocktail: "boiled" shrimp served cold with "cocktail" sauce, typically a blend of bottled ketchup or chili sauce spiked with horseradish. Given its simplicity, few dishes are more difficult to improve. Yet we set out to do just that and believe we succeeded.

It's easy enough to change the basic pattern to produce a more contemporary cold shrimp dish; you could, for example, grill shrimp and serve them with a fresh tomato salsa. But there is something refreshing and utterly classic about traditional shrimp cocktail.

We saw two ways to challenge the traditional method of preparing shrimp cocktail to produce the best-tasting but still recognizable version of this dish. One, work on the flavor of the shrimp; two, produce a great cocktail sauce.

The shrimp in shrimp cocktail can be ice-cold strings of protein, chewy or mushy, or they can be tender, flavorful morsels that barely need sauce. To achieve the latter, you need to start with the best shrimp you can find and give them as much flavor as they can handle without overwhelming them.

If you start with good shrimp and follow a typical shrimp cocktail recipe—that is, simmer the shrimp in salted water until pink—the shrimp will have decent but rarely intense flavor. The easiest way to intensify the flavor of shrimp is to cook them in their shells. But, as we found out, this method has its drawbacks. First of all, it's far easier to peel shrimp when they are raw than when they have been cooked in liquid. More important, however, the full flavor of the shells is not extracted during the relatively short time required for the shrimp to cook through. It takes a good 20 minutes for the shells to impart their flavor, and this is far too long to keep shrimp in a pot.

It's better, then, to make shrimp stock, using just the shrimp shells, and then cook the shrimp in that stock. To improve on the results of this process, every time you use shrimp for any purpose, place the peels in a pot with water to cover, then simmer them for 20 minutes. Cool, strain, and freeze the resultant stock. Use this stock as the cooking liquid for your next batch of shrimp peels. Naturally, this stock will become more and more intensely flavored each time you add to it.

Next, we thought, it would be best to see what other flavors would complement the shrimp without overpowering it. Our first attempt was to use beer and a spicy commercial seasoning, but this was a near disaster; the shrimp for cocktail should not taste like a New Orleans crab boil. Next we tried a classic court bouillon, the traditional herb-scented stock for poaching fish, but quickly discovered that the result wasn't worth the effort; we wanted a few quick additions to our shrimp stock that would add complexity of flavor without making a simple process complicated. Court bouillon was a good idea, but we wanted to reduce the laundry list of ingredients called for in classic recipes.

After trying about 20 different combinations, involving wine, vinegar, lemon juice, and a near-ludicrous number of herbs and spices, we settled on the mixture given in the recipe here. It contains about 25 percent white wine, a dash of lemon juice, and a more-or-less traditional herb combination. Variations are certainly possible, but we caution against adding more wine or lemon juice; both were good up to a point, but after that their pungency became overwhelming.

Although we were pleased at this point with the quality of the shrimp's flavor, we thought it could be still more intense. We quickly learned, however, that the answer to this problem was not to keep pouring flavorings into the cooking liquid; that was self-defeating because we eventually lost the flavor of the shrimp. We decided to keep the shrimp in contact with the flavorings for a longer period of time.

We tried several methods to achieve this, including

near-perfect form in the supermarket. Again, there are more interesting tomato-based sauces than ketchup, but they're not ketchup.

So we decided the best thing we could do was to find the bottled ketchup or chili sauce we liked best and season it ourselves. First we had to determine which made the better base, ketchup or chili sauce. The answer to this question was surprising but straightforward: ketchup. Bottled chili sauce is little more than vinegary ketchup with a host of seasonings added. The less expensive chili sauces have the acrid, bitter taste of garlic powder, monosodium glutamate, and other dried seasonings. The more expensive ones have more honest flavors but still did not compare with the cocktail sauce we whipped up in three minutes using basic store-bought ketchup. In addition, chili sauce can be four to eight times as expensive as ketchup.

Our preference in cocktail sauce has always been to emphasize the horseradish. But ketchup and horseradish, we knew, were not enough. Cocktail sauce benefits from a variety of heat sources, none of which overpower the other, and the sum of which still allow the flavor of the shrimp to come through. We liked the addition of chili powder. We also liked some bite from cayenne. Black pepper plays a favorable role as well (as does salt, even though ketchup is already salty). Finally, after trying high-quality wine vinegar, balsamic vinegar, rice vinegar, sherry vinegar, and distilled vinegar, we went back to lemon, the gentlest and most fragrant acidic seasoning. In sum, the keys to good cocktail sauce include ordinary ketchup, fresh lemon juice, horseradish (fresh is best—even month-old bottled horseradish is dim when compared with a just-opened bottle), and chili powder.

starting the shrimp in cold water with the seasonings and using a longer cooking time at a lower temperature. But shrimp cook so quickly that these methods only served to toughen the meat. What worked best, we found, was to bring the cooking liquid to a boil, turn it off, and add the shrimp. Depending on their size, we could leave them in contact with the liquid for up to 10 minutes (even a little longer for jumbo shrimp), during which time they would cook through without toughening, while taking on near perfect flavor.

Improving traditional cocktail sauce proved to be a tricky business. We wanted to make a better sauce, but we still wanted it to be recognizable as cocktail sauce. Starting with fresh or canned tomatoes, we discovered, just didn't work. The result was often terrific (some might say preferable), but it was not cocktail sauce. It was as if we had decided to make a better version of liver and onions by substituting foie gras for veal liver—it might be "better," but it would no longer be liver and onions.

We went so far as to make American-style ketchup from scratch, an interesting project but not especially profitable in that the effect was to duplicate something sold in

WHAT WE LEARNED: For best flavor, cook the shrimp in a potent but not overpowering liquid. We used shrimp shells to make stock and then flavored the stock with herbs and wine. To maximize flavor absorption, bring the liquid to a boil, turn off the heat, and add the shrimp. Stick with ketchup as the base for cocktail sauce but liven things up with horseradish, chili powder, cayenne pepper, and lemon juice.

HERB-POACHED SHRIMP serves 4

When using larger or smaller shrimp, increase or decrease cooking times for shrimp by one to two minutes, respectively. When using such large shrimp, we find it wise to remove the large black vein.

  1 **pound very large (16 to 20 per pound) shrimp, peeled, deveined, and rinsed, shells reserved**
  1 **teaspoon salt**
  1 **cup dry white wine**
  4 **peppercorns**
  5 **coriander seeds**
  ½ **bay leaf**
  5 **sprigs fresh parsley**
  1 **sprig fresh tarragon**
  1 **teaspoon juice from 1 small lemon**

1. Bring reserved shells, 3 cups water, and salt to boil in medium saucepan over medium-high heat; reduce heat to low, cover, and simmer until fragrant, about 20 minutes. Strain stock through sieve, pressing on shells to extract all liquid.

2. Bring stock and remaining ingredients except shrimp to boil in 3- or 4-quart saucepan over high heat; boil 2 minutes. Turn off heat and stir in shrimp; cover and let stand until firm and pink, 8 to 10 minutes. Drain shrimp, reserving stock for another use. Plunge shrimp into ice water to stop cooking, then drain again. Serve shrimp chilled with cocktail sauce.

COCKTAIL SAUCE makes about 1 cup

Use horseradish from a freshly opened bottle and mild chili powder for the best flavor.

  1   **cup ketchup**
  2½ **teaspoons prepared horseradish**
  ¼   **teaspoon salt**
  ¼   **teaspoon ground black pepper**
  1   **teaspoon ancho or other mild chili powder**
        Pinch cayenne pepper
  1   **tablespoon juice from 1 small lemon**

Stir all ingredients together in small bowl; adjust seasonings as necessary.

TASTING LAB: Buying Shrimp

IT'S SAFE TO SAY THAT ANY SHRIMP YOU BUY HAVE BEEN frozen (and usually thawed by the retailer), but not all shrimp are the same—far from it. The Gulf of Mexico supplies about 200 million pounds of shrimp annually to the United States, but three times that amount is imported, mostly from Asia and Central and South America.

After tasting all of the commonly available varieties of shrimp several times, we had little trouble declaring two winners: Mexican whites *(Panaeus vannamei)*, from the Pacific coast, are usually the best. A close second, and often

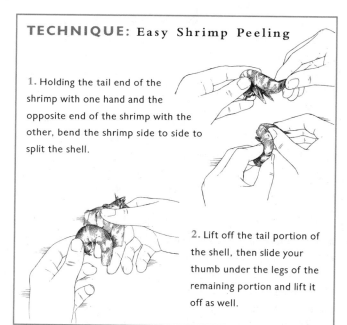

TECHNIQUE: Easy Shrimp Peeling

1. Holding the tail end of the shrimp with one hand and the opposite end of the shrimp with the other, bend the shrimp side to side to split the shell.

2. Lift off the tail portion of the shell, then slide your thumb under the legs of the remaining portion and lift it off as well.

just as good, are Gulf whites *(P. setiferus)*. Either of these may be wild or farm-raised. Unfortunately, these are rarely the shrimp you're offered in supermarkets. The shrimp most commonly found in supermarkets is Black Tiger, a farmed shrimp from Asia. Its quality is inconsistent, but it can be quite flavorful and firm. And even if you go to a fishmonger and ask for white shrimp, you may get a farm-raised, less expensive, and decidedly inferior shrimp from China *(P. chinensis)*. (There are more than 300 species of shrimp in the world and not nearly as many common names.)

All you can do is try to buy the best shrimp available, and buy it right. Beyond choosing the best species you can find, there are a number of factors to consider.

Because almost all shrimp are frozen after the catch, and thawed shrimp start losing their flavor in just a couple of days, buying thawed shrimp gives you neither the flavor of fresh nor the flexibility of frozen. We recommend buying frozen shrimp rather than thawed. We found that shrimp stored in the freezer retain peak quality for several weeks, deteriorating very slowly after that until about the three-month point, when we detected a noticeable deterioration in quality. If you do buy thawed shrimp, they should smell of saltwater and little else, and they should be firm and fully fill their shells.

Avoid prepeeled and deveined shrimp; cleaning before freezing unquestionably deprives shrimp of some of their flavor and texture; everyone we asked to sample precleaned shrimp found them to be nearly tasteless. In addition, precleaned shrimp may have added tripolyphosphate, a chemical that aids in water retention and can give shrimp an off flavor.

Shrimp should have no black spots, or melanosis, on their shells, which indicate that a breakdown of the meat has begun. Be equally suspicious of shrimp with yellowing shells or those that feel gritty. Either of these conditions may indicate the overuse of sodium bisulfite, a bleaching agent sometimes used to retard melanosis.

Despite the popularity of shrimp, there are no standards for size. Small, medium, large, extra-large, jumbo, and other size classifications are subjective and relative. Small shrimp of 70 or so to the pound are frequently labeled "medium," as are those twice that size and even larger. It pays, then, to judge shrimp size by the number it takes to make a pound, as retailers do. Shrimp labeled "16/20," for example, require 16 to 20 (usually closer to 20) individual specimens to make a pound. Those labeled "U-20" require fewer than 20 to make a pound. Large shrimp (21 to 25 per pound) usually yield the best combination of flavor, ease of preparation, and value (really big shrimp usually cost more).

One more note about size: Larger shrimp generally have larger veins, which should be removed. The veins in smaller shrimp are often so negligible that it's not worth removing them. Either way, we find the issue of removing the vein to be one of aesthetics. It neither harms nor improves the flavor of the shrimp. We tested several shrimp deveiners and found that some models work better than others but none beats a regular paring knife. We recommend that you save money (and drawer space) and live without this gadget that is of little real use.

SCIENCE DESK: Why Shrimp Turn Pink

MOST COOKS KNOW THAT WHEN YOU THROW A BATCH of shrimp into a pot of boiling water or a hot skillet, they change color almost immediately. The gray-white shells and flesh are transformed into a bright red/orange/pink. The color comes from a carotene-like pigment called astaxanthin, found not only in shrimp but also in salmon, lobster, crabs, crawfish, red sea bream, and some fish eggs.

Usually astaxanthin is the reddish color we associate with salmon and most crustaceans. But in shrimp, astaxanthin is bound to a protein that masks the color, making the shrimp appear gray, not pink, when raw. When heat is applied, a chemical reaction occurs, and the bond between the protein and the pigment is broken, allowing the reddish color to show through.

Astaxanthin does more than provide a pretty pink hue—it is also a powerful antioxidant. In aquatic species, it plays a role in immune system functions and reproduction.

SHRIMP SCAMPI AND SHRIMP FRA DIAVOLO

WHAT WE WANTED: Two Italian-American favorites with tender shrimp and plenty of delicious sauce.

The perfect shrimp scampi is surrounded by an ample amount of sauce flavored with garlic and lemon. We find that most recipes are too oily and that the garlic (which generally goes into the pan first) burns by the time the shrimp have cooked through. Most sauces are too thin, and there's not nearly enough to sop up with a chewy piece of bread. In addition, most recipes overcook the shrimp.

To start, we sautéed the shrimp quickly in batches. This prevented them from overcooking and becoming rubbery. With the shrimp cooked and reserved, we built a sauce in the sauté pan. Beginning with butter, we simply heated the garlic through before adding the lemon juice and a little vermouth, which gave the sauce a nice depth of flavor. Adding the liquid also kept the garlic from burning.

The sauce was delicious but thin. We mounted the sauce with more butter and finished it with parsley, both of which gave the sauce body, and added a pinch of cayenne. We returned the shrimp and their juices to the pan and the dish was done. Nothing complicated, but perfect nonetheless.

Shrimp fra diavolo, a seriously garlicky, spicy, winey tomato sauce studded with shrimp and served over pasta, is an Italian restaurant standard that's easy to make at home. But all too often, the garlic flavor is unpleasantly sharp, even acrid. In this dish, the garlic needs to be mellower than in scampi. And all too often the shrimp themselves contribute little to the overall flavor of the sauce, serving merely as a bulky, lifeless garnish.

Most fra diavolo recipes add raw shrimp to the almost finished sauce. While the shrimp remain tender, our tasters agreed that their flavor was barely developed. We improved the situation by seasoning the shrimp with some olive oil, salt, and red pepper flakes and searing them quickly in a very hot pan. Then we set the seared shrimp aside while making the sauce and added the shrimp back to heat through in the sauce just before serving. Every taster noted that both the shrimp and the sauce had much more flavor. The sear also benefited the red pepper flakes on the shrimp, as they now offered not only heat but a notably earthy, toasty note as well.

Shrimp and cognac have a well-established culinary affinity, and a number of fra diavolo recipes call for stirring cognac in with the other liquid sauce ingredients. We thought we might bring out still more flavor from the shrimp if we flambéed them in the cognac. As we'd hoped, the combined forces of cognac and flame brought out the shrimp's deepest, sweetest flavor and imbued our fra diavolo with the spirit's own richness and complexity.

We wanted enough garlic to make the devil proud, and we were frankly surprised to find that tasters agreed, preferring sauces that packed the wallop of 10 large cloves. But there was a caveat: We had to mitigate the bitterness. We experimented with cutting the garlic in slices and slivers, grating it, pureeing it, and adding it to the sauce at varying times, none of which eliminated the bitterness completely. Then we tried sautéing the garlic slowly, over low heat, until it turned golden, sticky, mellow, and nutty. The bitterness was gone, and the sauce had acquired an even sweeter, deeper dimension. We reserved a tablespoon of raw garlic to add to the sauce at the end of cooking, along with a splash of raw olive oil. Tasters appreciated the bright, fruity, high flavor notes that these raw ingredients added to the dish.

Tasters were united behind white wine for this sauce, preferring it to red wine and vermouth. All along, though, we had been bothered by the compounded acidity of the tomatoes and wine, so we tried adding a little brown sugar, which we found balanced the acidity perfectly.

WHAT WE LEARNED: Bring out the flavor of the shrimp and keep them tender by sautéing them separately, and tame the harshness of the garlic by treating it gently.

SHRIMP SCAMPI serves 4 to 6

Serve scampi with plenty of chewy bread to soak up extra juices.

    2   tablespoons olive oil
    2   pounds large shrimp (21 to 25 per pound),
        peeled and deveined if desired
    3   tablespoons unsalted butter
    4   medium cloves garlic, minced
    2   tablespoons juice from 1 lemon
    1   tablespoon dry vermouth
    2   tablespoons minced fresh parsley leaves
        Pinch cayenne
        Salt and ground black pepper

1. Heat 12-inch skillet over high heat until hot, 2 to 3 minutes. Add 1 tablespoon oil and swirl to coat bottom of pan. Add 1 pound shrimp and cook, stirring occasionally, until just

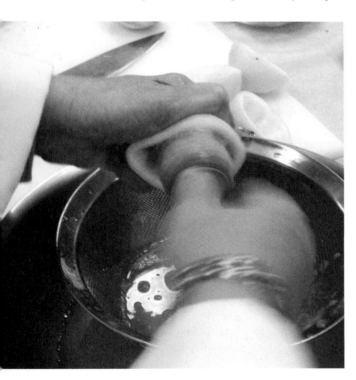

opaque, about 1 minute; transfer to medium bowl. Return pan to heat and repeat process with remaining oil and shrimp.

2. Return empty skillet to medium-low heat; melt 1 tablespoon butter. Add garlic and cook, stirring constantly, until fragrant, about 30 seconds. Off heat, add lemon juice and vermouth. Whisk in remaining 2 tablespoons butter; add parsley and cayenne, and season to taste with salt and pepper. Return shrimp and accumulated juices to skillet. Toss to combine; serve immediately.

SHRIMP FRA DIAVOLO WITH LINGUINE
serves 4 to 6

Tongs are the ideal tool for moving the shrimp in the pan. One teaspoon of red pepper flakes will give the sauce a little kick, but you may want to add more depending on your taste for fire.

    1   pound medium shrimp (31 to 35 per pound),
          peeled and deveined if desired
    1   teaspoon crushed red pepper flakes
          (or more, to taste)
    6   tablespoons extra-virgin olive oil
    1½   tablespoons salt
    ¼   cup cognac or brandy
    ¼   cup minced garlic (about 20 small, 12 medium,
          10 large, or 5 extra-large cloves) from
          1 or 2 heads
    ½   teaspoon sugar
    1   (28-ounce) can diced tomatoes, drained
    1   cup dry white wine, such as Sauvignon Blanc
    1   pound dried linguine or spaghetti
    ¼   cup minced fresh parsley leaves

1. Bring 4 quarts water to a boil in large Dutch oven or stockpot.

2. While water is heating, heat 12-inch heavy-bottomed skillet over high heat for 4 minutes. Meanwhile, toss shrimp with half of red pepper flakes, 2 tablespoons olive oil, and

until garlic foams and becomes sticky and straw colored, 7 to 10 minutes. Add remaining red pepper flakes and ¾ teaspoon salt, sugar, tomatoes, and wine, increase heat to medium-high, and simmer until thickened and fragrant, about 8 minutes longer. Stir in reserved shrimp (with accumulated juices), remaining 1 tablespoon garlic, and parsley and simmer until shrimp have heated through, about 1 minute longer. Off heat, stir in remaining 1 tablespoon olive oil.

4. Meanwhile, add linguine or spaghetti and 1 tablespoon salt to boiling water, stir to separate pasta, and cook until al dente; reserve ⅓ cup pasta cooking water and drain pasta. Transfer drained pasta back to now empty Dutch oven or stockpot; add about ½ cup sauce (sauce only, no shrimp) and 2 to 3 tablespoons reserved pasta cooking water; toss to coat. Divide pasta among warm serving plates, top with a portion of sauce and shrimp, and serve immediately.

VARIATIONS

SCALLOPS FRA DIAVOLO WITH LINGUINE

The scallops, as well as the monkfish in the recipe below, leave more *fond*—dark, sticky drippings—in the pan than do the shrimp. This is good, because fond is flavorful, but it can make the garlic appear straw colored before it has really finished cooking. Make sure that the garlic is fragrant, looks sticky, and has cooked for the full 7 to 10 minutes.

Follow recipe for Shrimp Fra Diavolo with Linguine, substituting 1 pound sea scallops, with small, crescent-shaped muscles removed, for shrimp.

MONKFISH FRA DIAVOLO WITH LINGUINE

See the note above for Scallops Fra Diavolo.

Follow recipe for Shrimp Fra Diavolo with Linguine, substituting 1-pound monkfish fillet, cut into 1-inch pieces, for shrimp.

¾ teaspoon salt. Add shrimp to hot skillet and quickly arrange in single layer; sear until bottom of shrimp forms small spot of crust, about 30 seconds. Remove skillet from heat, turn shrimp over, and add cognac; pause until cognac has warmed slightly, about 5 seconds, and return to high heat. Wave lit match over pan until cognac ignites, shaking pan. When flames subside, 15 to 30 seconds later, remove shrimp to medium bowl and set aside.

3. Allow empty skillet to cool, off heat, for 2 minutes; return to burner over low heat; add 3 tablespoons olive oil and 3 tablespoons garlic and cook, stirring constantly,

TASTING LAB: Dried Pasta

IN THE NOT-SO-DISTANT PAST, AMERICAN PASTA HAD A poor reputation, and rightly so. It cooked up gummy and starchy, and experts usually touted the superiority of Italian brands. We wondered if this was still the case.

To find out, we tasted eight leading brands of spaghetti—four American and four Italian. American brands took two of the three top spots, while two Italian brands landed at the bottom of the rankings. It seems that American companies have mastered the art of making pasta.

American-made Ronzoni was the top finisher, with tasters praising its "nutty, buttery" flavor and superb texture. Mueller's, another American brand, took third place. Tasters liked its "clean," "wheaty" flavor.

DeCecco was the highest-scoring Italian brand, finishing second in the tasting. It cooked up "very al dente" (or with a good bite) and was almost chewy. Other Italian brands did not fare quite so well. Martelli, an artisanal pasta that costs nearly $5 a pound, finished in next-to-last place, with comments like "gritty" and "mushy" predominating on tasters' score sheets. Another Italian brand, Delverde, sank to the bottom of the ratings.

Our conclusion: Save your money and don't bother with most imported pasta—American pastas are just fine. If you must serve Italian pasta in your home, stick with DeCecco.

EQUIPMENT CORNER: Garlic Presses

MOST COOKS DISLIKE THE CHORE OF MINCING GARLIC, and many turn to garlic presses. We know that many professional cooks sneer at this tool, but we have a different opinion. In hundreds of hours of use in our test kitchens, we have found that this little tool delivers speed, ease, and a comfortable separation of garlic from fingers.

And there are other advantages. First is flavor, which changes perceptibly depending on how the cloves are broken down. The finer a clove of garlic is cut, the more flavor is released from its broken cells (see the Science Desk on page 68 for more on this reaction). Fine mincing or pureeing, therefore, results in a fuller, more pungent garlic flavor. A good garlic press breaks down the cloves more than the average cook would with a knife. Second, a good garlic press ensures a consistently fine texture, which in turn means better distribution of the garlic throughout the dish.

The question for us, then, was not whether garlic presses work but which of the many available presses work best. Armed with 10 popular models, we pressed our way through a mountain of garlic cloves to find out.

Most garlic presses share a common design, consisting of two handles connected by a hinge. At the end of one handle is a small perforated hopper; at the end of the other is a plunger that fits snugly inside that hopper. The garlic cloves in the hopper get crushed by the descending plunger when the handles are squeezed together; the puree is extruded through the perforations in the bottom of the hopper.

Some presses employ a completely different design—a relatively large cylindrical container with a tight-fitting screw-down plunger. These presses are designed for large capacity, but this unusual design failed to impress us. The screw-type plungers required both pressure and significant repetitive motion, which we felt contributed to hand fatigue. This seemed like a lot of work just to press garlic. Matters did not improve when the hoppers were loaded

BEST GARLIC PRESS
We found that this Zyliss press can handle two cloves at once, producing very finely pureed garlic in a flash.

with multiple garlic cloves. Even greater effort was required to twist down the plungers, and the texture of the garlic puree produced was coarse and uneven.

A good garlic press should not only produce a smooth, evenly textured puree but should also be easy to use. To us, this means that different users should be able to operate it without straining their hands. With several notable exceptions, all of our presses performed reasonably well in this regard.

Several of our test cooks wondered if we could make an easy task even easier by putting the garlic cloves through the presses without first removing their skins. Instructions on the packaging of the Zyliss and Bodum presses specified that it was OK to press unpeeled cloves, and our tests bore out this assertion. Though the directions for several other presses did not address this issue specifically, we found that the Oxo and the Endurance also handled unpeeled garlic with ease. We did note, however, that the yield of garlic puree was greater across the board when we pressed peeled cloves. While we were at it, we also tried pressing chunks of peeled, fresh ginger. The Zyliss, Kuhn Rikon, and Oxo were the only three to excel in this department, and we found

that smaller chunks, about ½ inch, were crushed much more easily than larger, 1-inch pieces.

When all was said and pressed, the traditionally designed, moderately priced Zyliss ($12.99) turned out to be comfortable and consistent, and it produced the finest, most even garlic puree. In addition, it handled unpeeled garlic and small chunks of fresh ginger without incident. While other presses got the job done, the Zyliss just edged out the field in terms of both performance and design.

SCIENCE DESK: Changing Garlic's Flavor

IT MAY SEEM UNLIKELY, BUT THE WAY IN WHICH GARLIC IS prepared—whether sliced, chopped, or minced—influences the flavor it contributes to a dish. Raw garlic cloves contain a sulfur-based compound called alliin and an enzyme called alliinase. These two compounds are not in contact in raw garlic, which is why a head of garlic has almost no aroma. When the garlic is cut, the enzyme comes into contact with the alliin and converts it to allicin, a new and very pungent compound that gives garlic its typical aroma. This compound also gives garlic its characteristic bite.

When you slice garlic, only a small amount of enzyme and sulfur-compound come into contact with each other, so just a small amount of allicin is produced. The result is a mild garlic flavor. When you mince garlic, however, more allicin is produced because there's more contact between the sulfur-compound and the enzyme. More allicin means more aroma and flavor.

For the strongest garlic flavor, put the cloves through a press or mince them into a smooth paste. Doc is making just this point to Chris in the photo on the opposite page, by using packing peanuts to represent the amount of allicin that is released when the garlic is pressed or minced fine.

Because heat breaks down the enzyme alliinase, roasting or toasting garlic cloves before adding them to a dish will pretty much eliminate the development of any harsh garlic flavor.

TECHNIQUE: Mincing Garlic to a Paste

Mince the garlic as you normally would on a cutting board with a chef's knife. Sprinkle the minced garlic with salt and then drag the side of the chef's knife over the garlic-salt mixture to form a fine puree. Continue to mince and drag the knife as necessary until the puree is smooth. If possible, use kosher or coarse salt; the larger crystals do a better job of breaking down the garlic than fine table salt.

GRILLED SHRIMP

WHAT WE WANTED: Tender, juicy shrimp that tastes like it was cooked on the grill.

Throwing some shrimp on the barbie sounds easy. But even the simplest grilled dish requires proper technique. More often than not, grilled shrimp are tough and dry. And grilled shrimp rarely pick up the tantalizing flavors of wood or smoke.

After some initial tests, we concluded that shrimp destined for the grill should not be peeled. The shell shields the meat from the intense heat and helps to keep the shrimp moist and tender. Try as we might, we found it impossible to grill peeled shrimp without overcooking them and making the meat dry and tough, especially the exterior layers. The only method that worked was to intentionally undercook the shrimp; but that left the inside a little gooey, something that no one enjoyed.

Another reason to grill shrimp with the shells on is flavor. Peeled shrimp cooks so quickly that it doesn't have much time

to pick up any grill flavor. With the peel on, the grilling time is slightly longer; hence the shrimp tastes a bit smokier. Also, the shell contributes a lot of flavor to the shrimp meat as it cooks. If the shells are discarded before cooking, the transfer of flavor from shell to meat cannot occur.

To make it easier to eat the unpeeled, grilled shrimp, we found it useful to slit the shell open prior to cooking with a pair of manicure scissors. The shell still protects the meat as the shrimp cook, but the shell comes right off at the table.

Even with the shell on, though, tasters found the shrimp a tad too dry. We wondered if brining the shrimp before cooking would help. (We have found that soaking other delicate foods, especially chicken, in a mixture of water, salt, and sugar before cooking helps them to retain moisture.) It did. Our tests revealed that brined shrimp may gain as much as 10 percent in water weight. At its most successful, brining turns mushy shrimp into plump, juicy specimens with the chewy texture of a lobster tail. Even top-quality shrimp are improved by this process. We tested various concentrations of salt and brining times and in the end settled on soaking shrimp in a strong salt solution (1 cup kosher salt dissolved in 2 quarts water) for 30 minutes.

Once the shrimp have been brined, they can be threaded onto skewers and grilled. We found that shrimp should be cooked quickly to prevent them from toughening. This means using a very hot fire. Thankfully, grilling is simple—as soon as the shrimp turn pink, they are done.

We like to coat the shrimp with a paste or marinade before grilling. The flavorings adhere to the shell beautifully. When you peel the shrimp at the table, the seasonings stick to your fingers and are in turn transferred directly to the meat as you eat it. Licking your fingers also helps.

WHAT WE LEARNED: Shrimp must be grilled in their shells to prevent dryness. To increase flavor, firmness, and moisture, brine shrimp before grilling them.

CHARCOAL-GRILLED SHRIMP serves 4 to 6

We recommend that you brine the shrimp before grilling. This makes them especially plump and juicy. To keep the shrimp from dropping through the grill rack onto the hot coals, thread them onto skewers. This recipe (and the one that follows) are rather plain but still delicious. The variations on pages 72 and 73 are more complex-tasting and require only minimal additional work.

> 1 cup kosher salt or ½ cup table salt
> ½ cup sugar
> 2 pounds large shrimp (21 to 25 per pound)
> 2 tablespoons extra-virgin olive oil
>   Lemon wedges

1. Pour 2 quarts very cold water into large bowl. Add salt and sugar and stir until dissolved. Add shrimp and let stand in refrigerator for 30 minutes. Drain shrimp. Open shells with manicure scissors (see illustration 1 at right) and devein if desired (see illustration 2 at right). Toss shrimp and oil in medium bowl to coat.

2. Meanwhile, light large chimney starter filled with hard-wood charcoal (about 2½ pounds) and allow to burn until charcoal is covered with layer of fine gray ash. Spread coals evenly over grill bottom for medium-hot fire. (See how to gauge heat level on page 133.) Set cooking rack in place, cover grill with lid, and let rack heat up, about 5 minutes. Scrape rack clean with wire brush.

3. Thread shrimp on skewers (see illustration on page 73). Grill shrimp, uncovered, turning skewers once, until shells are barely charred and bright pink, 4 to 6 minutes. Serve hot or at room temperature with lemon wedges.

TECHNIQUE: Preparing Shrimp

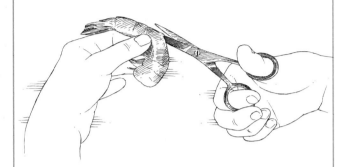

1. When grilling shrimp, we find it best to keep the shrimp in their shells. The shells hold in moisture and also flavor the shrimp as they cook. However, eating shrimp cooked in their shells can be a challenge. As a compromise, we found it helpful to slit the back of the shell with manicure or other small scissors with a fine point. When ready to eat, each person can quickly and easily peel away the shells.

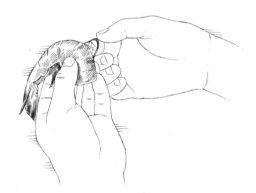

2. Slitting the back of the shell makes it easy to devein the shrimp as well. Except when the vein is especially dark and thick, we found no benefit to deveining in our testing. If you choose to devein shrimp, slit open the back of the shell as in step 1. Invariably you will cut a little into the meat and expose the vein as you do this. Use the tip of the scissors to lift up the vein and then grab it with your fingers and discard.

GAS-GRILLED SHRIMP   serves 4 to 6

There's only one difference between grilling shrimp over char-coal and gas—in the latter, the lid is kept down to concentrate the heat.

  1   cup kosher salt or ½ cup table salt
  ½   cup sugar
  2   pounds large shrimp (21 to 25 per pound)
  2   tablespoons extra-virgin olive oil
       Lemon wedges

1. Pour 2 quarts very cold water into large bowl. Add salt and sugar and stir until dissolved. Add shrimp and let stand for 30 minutes. Drain shrimp. Open shells with manicure scissors (see illustration 1 on page 71) and devein if desired (see illustration 2 on page 71). Toss shrimp and oil in medium bowl to coat.

2. Preheat grill with all burners set to high and lid down until grill is very hot, about 15 minutes. Scrape cooking rack clean with wire brush. Leave burners on high.

3. Thread shrimp on skewers (see illustration on page 73). Grill shrimp, covered, turning skewers once, until shells are barely charred and bright pink, 5 to 6 minutes. Serve hot or at room temperature with lemon wedges.

VARIATIONS

GRILLED SHRIMP WITH SPICY GARLIC PASTE

The garlic paste adheres perfectly and will coat your fingers as you peel and eat the grilled shrimp.

Mince 1 large garlic clove with 1 teaspoon salt to form smooth paste (see illustration on page 68). Combine garlic paste with ½ teaspoon cayenne pepper, 1 teaspoon sweet paprika, 2 tablespoons extra-virgin olive oil, and 2 teaspoons lemon juice in medium bowl. Follow recipe for Charcoal-Grilled or Gas-Grilled Shrimp, tossing brined and drained shrimp with garlic mixture instead of oil to coat well. Thread shrimp on skewers and grill as directed.

GRILLED SHRIMP WITH LEMON, GARLIC, AND OREGANO PASTE

The fresh oregano in this recipe can be replaced with other fresh herbs, including chives, tarragon, parsley, or basil.

Mince 1 large garlic clove with 1 teaspoon salt to form smooth paste (see illustration on page 68). Combine garlic paste with 2 tablespoons extra-virgin olive oil, 2 teaspoons lemon juice, and 2 teaspoons chopped fresh oregano leaves in a medium bowl. Follow recipe for Charcoal-Grilled or Gas-Grilled Shrimp, tossing brined and drained shrimp with garlic mixture instead of oil to coat well. Thread shrimp on skewers and grill as directed.

GRILLED SHRIMP WITH SOUTHWESTERN FLAVORS

Serve these shrimp with warm cornbread.

Heat 2 tablespoons extra-virgin olive oil in small skillet over medium heat. Add 2 minced garlic cloves, 2 teaspoons chili powder, and ¾ teaspoon ground cumin and sauté until

---

TECHNIQUE: Skewering Shrimp

Thread shrimp on a skewer by passing the skewer through the body near the tail, folding the shrimp over, and passing the skewer through the body again near the head end. Threading the shrimp twice keeps them in place (they won't spin around) and makes it easy to cook them on both sides by turning the skewer just once.

---

garlic is fragrant, 30 to 45 seconds. Scrape mixture into heat-proof bowl and cool to room temperature. Mix in 2½ tablespoons lime juice and 2 tablespoons minced fresh cilantro leaves. Follow recipe for Charcoal-Grilled or Gas-Grilled Shrimp, tossing brined and drained shrimp with garlic mixture instead of oil to coat well. Thread shrimp on skewers and grill as directed. Serve with lime wedges instead of lemon wedges.

NEW ORLEANS–STYLE GRILLED SHRIMP

Shrimp are tossed with a spicy paste, grilled, and drizzled with a rich butter-garlic mixture. For a classic Creole meal, serve with steamed white rice.

1	teaspoon dried thyme
1	teaspoon dried oregano
1	teaspoon sweet paprika
1	teaspoon garlic powder
	Pinch cayenne pepper
½	teaspoon salt
4	tablespoons unsalted butter
2	medium cloves garlic, minced
1	recipe Charcoal-Grilled or Gas-Grilled Shrimp (omit olive oil)
1½	tablespoons vegetable oil

1. Mix thyme, oregano, paprika, garlic powder, cayenne, and salt together in small bowl.

2. Melt butter in small saucepan over medium heat. When butter begins to sizzle, add garlic and cook for 30 seconds. Remove pan from heat, cover, and keep warm.

3. Prepare shrimp as directed in recipe for Charcoal-Grilled or Gas-Grilled Shrimp, tossing them with vegetable oil and spice mixture instead of olive oil. Grill shrimp and arrange skewers on platter. Drizzle with butter mixture and serve with lemon wedges.

STEAK frites

CHAPTER 7

When bistro food is as good as seared steak with red wine sauce and a piping-hot pile of extra-crisp fries, who needs haute cuisine? Nothing could be simpler or more satisfying.

So why, then, do steaks seared at home often turn out pallid? And why do restaurant sauces taste so much better than sauces made at home?

When it comes to searing steaks, most home cooks are timid about the heat. We found that you need a really hot pan to brown steaks properly. As for sauces, home cooks don't have the arsenal of gelatinous stocks that chefs rely on for so much of their cooking. But there must be a way to turn canned broth into a memorable sauce. In the test kitchen, we were determined to find out.

Despite what you may think, French fries really are best made at home, where you can control the timing and enjoy the fries the minute they emerge from the hot oil. Good fries aren't pale blondes, like those served at fast-food restaurants. They have a rich golden brown color and are crisp—really crisp. You'll learn how to make fries worthy of the finest Parisian bistro, and it's surprisingly easy.

For great French fries, we discovered that you must soak the cut potatoes in ice-cold water for at least 30 minutes. The water chills the exterior of each piece so that when the potatoes are drained and fried the interior has plenty of time to cook through before the exterior starts to brown.

PAN-SEARED STEAKS

WHAT WE WANTED: Steaks cooked on the stove that were every bit as good as those cooked on the grill.

Steaks must be cooked so that the entire surface caramelizes to form a rich, thick crust. The intense heat of the grill makes it easy to obtain such a crust. But sometimes grilling is impractical. We wanted to get the same result from pan-searing.

We decided to focus on boneless steaks. Bone-in steaks, such as T-bones and porterhouses, really should be grilled; when pan-seared it's the bone, not the meat, that makes contact with the pan, and the result is poor coloring and no crust development. We tested a dozen boneless steaks and found two that everyone in the test kitchen could agree on—rib-eye and strip steaks.

Rib steaks are cut from the rib roast (or prime rib) and come with the curved bone attached. More often, you will see boneless steaks from the rib, called rib-eye steaks. Rib-eyes are tender and smooth-textured, with a distinctive, robust, beefy taste. They are very rich, with good-sized pockets of fat. Rib eye is also known as Delmonico steak in New York or Spencer steak in the West.

The strip steak is cut from the short loin area of the cow. Also called shell, Kansas City strip, New York strip, or top loin, strip steak has a noticeable grain and a moderate amount of chew. The flavor is excellent and the meat a bit less fatty than in rib-eye steaks. Strips steaks are also slightly more expensive than rib-eyes.

It was obvious to us from the beginning that the key to browning the steaks was going to be preheating the pan, so that when the steaks hit the pan, the surface would be hot enough to sear the steaks before they overcooked. In this regard, we wondered if different types of pans would heat and cook differently.

We found that a cast-iron skillet did an excellent job of browning the steaks, but we feared pan sauces would suffer.

Many sources discourage the use of cast-iron pans because of the iron's tendency to react with acidic foods, giving them a metallic, off flavor. Sure enough, when we prepared a red wine pan sauce in a cast-iron skillet, it tasted tinny.

Next, we tried searing steaks in a nonstick skillet, but the browned bits that a good sear leaves behind in the pan and that make sauces so delicious did not materialize. The resulting sauces were anemic and weakly flavored. Pan sauces made in regular nonreactive pans were rich both in flavor and color. We had good results with heavy-bottomed pans made by All-Clad and Calphalon.

We had been searing the steaks over high heat to promote browning, but tasters noticed that the sauces tasted bitter. To avoid this problem, we heated the pan over high heat and then reduced the heat to medium-high once the steaks went into the pan. This worked fine as long as the pan was fully preheated (three minutes over high heat worked best) before the steaks were added. We found that strip and rib-eye steaks had enough fat to be seared without oil.

Over the course of testing, we noticed a few more factors that ensured the formation of a good crust on the steak and of richly flavored brown bits in the pan. (Called *fond*, these brown bits are crucial to the flavor of the sauce.) There should be at least ¼ inch of space between each steak if they are to sear, not steam. At the same time, the pan should not be too large because that encourages burning. A 12-inch skillet is the right size for four steaks. We also noticed that it was not a good idea to move the steaks around in the pan. This interrupted the browning process and resulted in steaks that lacked good caramelization. The steaks browned much better when moved only once, just to turn them over to the other side.

WHAT WE LEARNED: Sear boneless strip or rib-eye steaks in a preheated, heavy-bottomed, nonreactive 12-inch skillet, reducing the heat once the steaks go into the pan to keep the fond from burning.

PAN-SEARED STEAKS serves 4

Serve these steaks with either the red wine or shallot butter sauce on page 79.

4   boneless strip or rib-eye steaks, 1 to 1¼ inches thick (about 8 ounces each), thoroughly dried with paper towels
    Salt and ground black pepper

1. Heat heavy-bottomed, nonreactive 12-inch skillet over high heat until very hot, about 3 minutes. Meanwhile, season both sides of steaks with salt and pepper.

2. Lay steaks in pan, leaving ¼ inch of space between them; reduce heat to medium-high, and cook, not moving steaks until well browned, about 4 minutes. Using tongs, flip steaks; cook 4 minutes more for rare, 5 minutes more for medium-rare, and 6 minutes more for medium. Transfer steaks to large plate, tent with foil, and let rest 5 minutes while preparing pan sauce (recipes follow).

TASTING LAB: Prime, Choice, or Select Beef

THE U.S. DEPARTMENT OF AGRICULTURE (USDA) RECOGnizes eight grades of beef, but most everything available to consumers falls into the top three: Prime, Choice, and Select. The grades classify meat according to fat marbling and age, which are relatively accurate predictors of palatability; they have nothing to do with freshness or purity. Grading is voluntary on the part of the meat packer. If the meat is graded, it should bear a USDA stamp indicating the grade, but it may not be visible. Ask the butcher when in doubt.

We pan-seared rib-eye steaks from all three grades and tasted them blind. Prime ranked first for its tender, buttery texture and rich beefy flavor; it was discernibly fattier. Choice came in second, with solid flavor and a little more chew. The Select steak was tough and stringy, with flavor that was only "acceptable." The lesson here is that you get what you pay for. Prime steaks are worth the extra money, but Choice steaks that exhibit a moderate amount of marbling are a fine and more affordable option.

CONSUMER BEEF GRADES

PRIME

Prime meat is heavily marbled with intramuscular fat (seen as white streaks within the meat in this drawing), which makes for a tender, flavorful steak. About 2 percent of graded beef is considered Prime. Prime meats are most often served in restaurants or sold in high-end butcher shops.

CHOICE

The majority of graded beef is Choice. While the levels of marbling in Choice beef can vary, it is generally moderately marbled with intramuscular fat.

SELECT

Select beef has little marbling. The small amount of intramuscular fat can make Select meats drier, tougher, and less flavorful than the two higher grades.

PAN SAUCES FOR STEAK

WHAT WE WANTED: Two great sauces for steak—one heady with red wine and stock, the other a simple emulsion of butter and shallots.

Ever wonder how restaurants make the thick, rich red wine sauce they pour over a seared rib-eye steak? How about that creamy shallot-butter sauce drizzled over a seared strip steak? Chances are these sauces are made in the pan used to cook the steak. They begin with fond, the caramelized browned bits that sit on the bottom of the pan after the meat is seared.

Pan sauces are generally made by adding liquid (usually stock) to the pan and dissolving the fond (a process known as deglazing), reducing the liquid, then enriching and thickening the sauce with butter. These sauces are heavenly when made well—full-bodied, complex, balanced in flavor, rich in color, and thick enough to coat the steak and form a nice pool of sauce into which you can dip the meat. If you've properly seared the steak (see recipe on page 77), there will be plenty of browned bits to start a pan sauce.

A great red wine pan sauce starts with the right wine (see Tasting Lab on page 79). But even the right wine can produce a poor sauce. We found that wine doesn't react well to changes in temperature, making it a tricky ingredient to handle. As wine is heated, delicate flavor compounds known as esters break apart, turning fruity flavors and aromas sour and bitter. The higher the heat, the more rapidly the esters break down.

Transferring this knowledge to cooking, it would seem reasonable to assume that low, slow heat is better for wine than hot and fast heat. To test this assumption, we made two classic steak pan sauces, one made with rapidly simmered wine and the other made with slowly reduced wine. The results were so radically different that tasters thought the sauces had been made from different wines altogether. The rapidly simmered wine was tart and edgy, while the slowly

reduced wine was smooth and round. This surprised many of us who have learned to cook pan sauces the traditional way.

Classically, wine is added to a hot pan (the same pan in which the meat was just cooked) and reduced quickly over high heat while scraping up the tasty browned bits off the pan's bottom. We found that deglazing the hot pan with stock, not wine, and finishing the sauce with wine that had been slowly reduced in a separate pan, made a much better pan sauce—one unlike any we had made before. It was rich and voluptuous, with complex layers of flavor.

As we tested a few more pan sauces using this method, we discovered another trick. The wine reduction takes on an extra dimension and polished texture when small amounts of aromatic vegetables are added. Treating the wine almost like a stock, we steeped shallots, carrots, mushrooms, and herbs in the reducing wine, then strained them out before adding the reduction to the sauce.

By comparison, a shallot butter sauce is easy to prepare. It makes sense to think of this sauce as a melted version of compound butter. Compound butters are made by rolling butter (seasoned with shallots, herbs, spices, mustard, etc.) into a log, chilling the log, and then slicing off a round to melt over a cooked steak. Although delicious, a compound butter does not take advantage of the browned bits left in the pan used to sear the steaks.

For this reason, we like to add shallots to the empty skillet, then throw in the cold butter to create a quick, light sauce. Some lemon juice and parsley round out the flavor. Make sure the butter is cold when it goes into the pan. We found that cold butter gives a sauce more body than softened butter.

WHAT WE LEARNED: When making a red wine pan sauce, reduce the wine separately over low heat to preserve its delicate flavors. When making a shallot butter sauce, add cold, not softened, butter to the sautéed shallots to give the sauce body.

RED WINE SAUCE (FOR PAN-SEARED STEAKS)

makes enough for 4 steaks

Start cooking the steaks when the wine has almost finished reducing, then keep the steaks warm on a plate in a 200-degree oven as you make the pan sauce. Use a smooth, medium-bodied, fruity wine, preferably made from a blend of grapes, such as a Côtes du Rhône. For more information about choosing a red wine for cooking, see the Tasting Lab below.

wine reduction

1 small carrot, peeled and chopped fine (about 2 tablespoons)
1 medium shallot, minced (about 2 tablespoons)
2 white mushrooms, chopped fine (about 3 tablespoons)
1 small bay leaf
3 sprigs fresh parsley
1 cup red wine

sauce

1 medium shallot, minced (about 2 tablespoons)
½ cup canned low-sodium chicken broth
½ cup canned low-sodium beef broth
3 tablespoons unsalted butter, cut into 6 pieces
½ teaspoon fresh thyme leaves
Salt and ground black pepper

1. FOR THE WINE REDUCTION: Heat carrot, shallot, mushrooms, bay leaf, parsley, and wine in 12-inch nonstick skillet over low heat; cook, without simmering (liquid should be steaming but not bubbling) until entire mixture reduces to 1 cup, 15 to 20 minutes. Strain through fine-mesh strainer and return liquid (about ½ cup) to clean skillet. Continue to cook over low heat, without simmering, until liquid is reduced to 2 tablespoons, 15 to 20 minutes. Transfer reduction to bowl.

2. FOR THE SAUCE: Follow recipe for Pan-Seared Steaks, transferring plate with steaks to 200-degree oven to keep

warm. To same skillet used to cook steaks (do not clean skillet or discard accumulated fat), add shallot and cook over low heat until softened, about 1 minute. Turn heat to high; add chicken and beef broths. Bring to a boil, scraping up browned bits on pan bottom with wooden spoon until liquid is reduced to 2 tablespoons, about 6 minutes. Turn heat to medium-low, gently whisk in reserved wine reduction and any accumulated juices from plate with steaks. Whisk in butter, one piece at a time, until melted and sauce is thickened and glossy; add thyme and season with salt and pepper. Spoon sauce over steaks and serve immediately.

SHALLOT BUTTER SAUCE (FOR PAN-SEARED STEAKS)

makes enough for 4 steaks

2 large shallots, minced (about ⅓ cup)
4 tablespoons cold unsalted butter, cut into 4 pieces
1 teaspoon lemon juice from 1 lemon
1 teaspoon minced fresh parsley leaves
Salt and ground black pepper

Follow recipe for Pan-Seared Steaks. To same skillet used to cook steaks (do not clean skillet or discard accumulated fat), add shallots and cook over low heat until softened, about 1 minute. Turn heat to medium-low; stir in butter, scraping up browned bits on pan bottom with wooden spoon. When butter is just melted, stir in lemon juice and parsley; season to taste with salt and pepper. Spoon sauce over steaks and serve immediately.

TASTING LAB: Red Wines for Cooking

WHEN A RECIPE CALLS FOR RED WINE, THE TENDENCY IS to grab whatever is inexpensive, close at hand, or already open on the counter. But as with any ingredient, the type of wine you cook with can make a big difference. The wrong wine can turn a good sauce bad. Yet because wines range enormously in flavor, body, and astringency, choosing a good one for the kitchen can be a shot in the dark.

What defines a good red cooking wine? It is appropriate for a wide range of recipes, easy to find at the local store, and consistent through the years. To help determine which red wines are good cookers, we set up a series of three cooking tests—a quick tomato sauce, a long-cooked beef stew, and a pan sauce for steak—through which we could test numerous bottles.

Organizing the overwhelming body of red wine into manageable groups, we assigned four categories based on flavor, body, and style: light/fruity, smooth/mellow, hearty/robust, and nondescript jug wine. Ironically, the only type of wine not represented is the "cooking wine" found on most supermarket shelves. In the past, we found that these low-alcohol concoctions have no flavor, a high-pitched acidity, and an enormous amount of salt, which renders them both undrinkable and a very poor choice for cooking.

We began by cooking with a representative from each category: a light/fruity Beaujolais, a smooth/mellow Merlot, a hearty/robust Cabernet Sauvignon, and a jug of Paul Mason Mountain Burgundy. The results were drastically different. The Beaujolais made refreshingly fruity but wimpy sauces, while the Merlot made for balanced sauces with an overcooked, jamlike flavor. The Cabernet Sauvignon produced an astringent, woody bite that bullied other ingredients out of the way, and the Paul Masson made sweet, simple sauces that neither offended nor impressed anyone.

Although none of the four groups "won" this first round of testing, what emerged were some important attributes of a good cooking wine and some characteristics to be wary of. The light wine made weak sauces, and the hearty wine made sauces that were too muscular. Oak flavors (from barrel aging) did not soften as they cooked but wound up tasting bitter and harsh. Fruity characteristics, on the other hand, mingled well with the other sauce ingredients and complemented their flavors.

Narrowing our focus to smooth, fruity, medium-bodied wines with little oak influence, we put four more types of

wine through the trio of recipes: a Chianti, a Zinfandel, a Pinot Noir, and a Côtes du Rhône. The Chianti tasted great in the tomato sauce but made an astringent pan sauce and cardboard-tasting stew. The Zinfandel tasted overcooked and jammy in the tomato sauce and turned the pan sauce bitter. While both the Côtes du Rhône and Pinot Noir turned in impressive results across the board, the Côtes du Rhône was stellar. When compared with the sauces made with Pinot Noir (a wine made from just one type of grape), the Côtes du Rhône (a blend of grapes) had a fuller, more even-keeled flavor. Varietals within the blend compensated for each others' shortcomings. The resulting sauces were potent but well-rounded. Besides Côtes du Rhône, there are many fruity, medium-bodied, blended wines, including wines from the greater Rhône Valley, Languedoc (near the Mediterranean), Australia, and the United States.

We found a strong correlation between price and quality when it comes to red wine. Tests demonstrated that a $5 bottle cooked much differently from bottles costing $10, $20, or $30. As a wine cooks and reduces, it becomes a more intensely flavored version of itself, and defining characteristics become unbearably obvious. The sweet, bland, $5 wines cooked down to candy-like sauces, while the $10, $20, and $30 bottles were increasingly smooth, with multiple layers of flavor. Although the higher-end wines tasted more balanced and refined, none of the tasters thought the flavor difference between the $10 and $20 or $30 bottles was worth the extra money. What's more, limiting the price to around $10 does not restrict your options when shopping. We found plenty of good blends from California, Australia, and France.

EQUIPMENT CORNER: Corkscrews

YOU WANT A CORKSCREW THAT REQUIRES A MINIMUM OF force to operate. A corkscrew should work just as well with fresh, tight-fitting corks as with dry, older corks that may crumble. Most of all, a corkscrew must be reliable. It should remove the cork each and every time.

We tested 18 different corkscrews on a variety of wine bottles. Some bottles had standard rims; others the wider rims common on flanged bottles. We worked with corks that were brittle and falling apart as well as firm, newer corks. There are three basic designs for a corkscrew—worm, air pump, and prong—and we tested several versions of each.

Most corkscrews have a spiraling metal shaft called a worm. The worm has a pointed end that can be driven through the cork. Air pump corkscrews have a syringe-like needle that pierces the cork and allows the user to pump air into the bottle. Once enough air has been pumped into the bottle, the pressure pushes the cork up and out with a pop. Prong corkscrews have thin prongs, usually of uneven length, that the user is supposed to insert between the cork and the glass. Once the prongs are inserted, a twisting motion pulls up the cork.

We quickly dismissed the corkscrews without the familiar worm. The air pump models were easy enough to use but felt odd. It took a fair amount of strength to pierce the cork with the needle, followed by an average of 16 pumps per bottle to lift up the cork.

We also dismissed the corkscrews with two prongs. One of our testers consistently pushed corks into bottles when trying to wiggle the prongs between cork and glass. Though other testers had better luck, none felt that these corkscrews were reliable. Practice made the process more comfortable, but we preferred the models with worms.

The best worm-style corkscrews had several traits in common. First and foremost, models that operate by continually turning after the worm fully penetrates the cork are preferable to models that stop turning once the worm is in the cork. The latter rely on a lever to lift up the impaled cork. For example, the classic waiter's corkscrew, with a hinged arm that swings out to brace against the rim of the bottle, works fine but it takes some practice to master.

In contrast, novices can uncork a bottle the first time they use a corkscrew with a continuously turning worm (often called a screwpull). These corkscrews rely on continued turning action (called torque) after the worm has already gone all the way through the cork. The cork rides up the worm, so there's no yanking involved. These models have an extra-long shaft so that the cork has some place to go.

We also liked the nonstick surface on the continuously turning models we tested. The slick coating reduces resistance as the worm works its way through the cork. Finally, most models that operate by continuous turning usually have worms encased in frames, which slip over the bottle neck and guide the worm straight into the cork.

As for worm-style corkscrews with neither lever nor continuous turning, the less said the better. Even if you can jab the worm into the cork, most people don't have the strength necessary to pull out the cork.

FRENCH FRIES

WHAT WE WANTED: Long, straight, crisp fries with sides neatly cut at right-angles; golden brown fries with a nice crunch on the outside and an earthy potato taste.

A good French fry requires the right potato. Would it be starchy (like a baking potato) or waxy (like a boiling potato)? We tested two of the most popular waxy potatoes, and neither was even close to ideal, both being too watery. During frying, the water inside the potato evaporated, leaving hollows that would fill with oil, making the finished fries greasy.

Next we tested the starchy potato most readily available nationwide, the russet. This potato turned out to be ideal, frying up with all the qualities that we were looking for.

Many sources suggest chilling the sliced potatoes in ice water before frying them, and we found this step was crucial. With a 30-minute chill, the potatoes are nearly frozen when they first enter the hot oil; this allows for a slow, thorough cooking of the inner potato pulp. When we tried making fries without prechilling, the outsides started to brown well before the insides were fully cooked.

What is the right fat for making perfect French fries? To find out, we experimented with lard, vegetable shortening, canola oil, corn oil, and peanut oil. Lard and shortening make great fries, but we assumed that many cooks wouldn't want to use these products. Canola oil, the ballyhooed oil of the 1990s, produced bland, almost watery fries. Corn oil rebounded well from temperature fluctuations, and the fries tasted very good. Potatoes fried in peanut oil, however, were even better: light, with a flavor that was rich but not dense. The earthy flavor of the potato was there, too. Although corn oil is fine for frying potatoes, tasters gave the edge to the peanut oil.

At this point, we were very close to the perfect fry, and yet there was still something missing. The high flavor note, which is supplied by the animal fat in lard, was lacking. We tried a dollop of strained bacon grease in peanut oil, about two generous tablespoons per quart of oil. The meaty flavor came through. At last, an equivalent to lard.

Now it was time to get down to the frying, which actually means double-frying. First, we par-fried the potatoes at a relatively low temperature to release their rich and earthy flavor. The potatoes are then quick-fried at a higher temperature until nicely browned and served immediately.

The garden variety cookbook recipe calls for par-frying at 350 degrees and final frying at 375 to 400 degrees. We found these temperatures to be far too aggressive. We prefer an initial frying at 325 degrees, with the final frying at 350 degrees. Lower temperatures allowed for easier monitoring; with higher temperatures the fries can get away from the cook.

For the sake of convenience, we also attempted a single, longer frying. Like many cooks before us, we found that with standard French fries (as opposed to the much thinner shoestring fries), we could not both sear the outside and properly cook the inside with a single visit in the hot fat.

WHAT WE LEARNED: Use russet potatoes, soak them in ice water, and fry in peanut oil twice—first to cook the potatoes through, then to make them crisp and golden brown. For an old-fashioned, meaty flavor, add a little strained bacon grease to the pot.

FRENCH FRIES serves 4

We prefer to peel the potatoes. A skin-on fry keeps the potato from forming those little airy blisters that we like. Peeling the potato also allows removal of any imperfections and greenish coloring. Once the potatoes are peeled and cut, plan on at least an hour before the fries are ready to eat.

4   large russet potatoes, peeled and cut into
    ¼ inch by ¼-inch lengths (reserve nonuniform
    pieces for another use)
2   quarts peanut oil
4   tablespoons strained bacon grease (optional)
    Salt and ground black pepper

1. Place cut fries in large bowl, cover with at least 1 inch of water, then cover with ice cubes. Refrigerate at least 30 minutes or up to 3 days.

2. In 5-quart pot or Dutch oven fitted with clip-on candy thermometer, or in larger electric fryer, heat oil over medium-low heat to 325 degrees. (Oil will bubble up when you add fries, so be sure you have at least 3 inches of room at top of pot.) Add bacon grease, if using.

3. Pour off ice and water, quickly wrap potatoes in clean kitchen towel, and thoroughly pat dry. Increase heat to medium-high and add fries, one handful at a time, to hot oil. Fry, stirring with Chinese skimmer or large-hole slotted spoon, until potatoes are limp and soft and have turned from white to gold, about 10 minutes. (Oil temperature will drop 50 to 60 degrees during this frying.) Use skimmer or slotted spoon to transfer fries to triple thickness of paper towels to drain; let rest at least 10 minutes. (Can stand at room temperature up to 2 hours or be wrapped in paper towels, sealed in zipper-lock bag, and frozen up to 1 month.)

4. When ready to serve fries, reheat oil to 350 degrees. Using paper towels as funnel, pour potatoes into hot oil. Discard paper towels and line wire rack with another triple thickness of paper towels. Fry potatoes, stirring fairly constantly, until medium brown and puffed, about 1 minute. Transfer to paper towel–lined rack to drain. Season to taste with salt and pepper. Serve immediately.

SCIENCE DESK: Storing Potatoes

SINCE POTATOES SEEM ALMOST INDESTRUCTIBLE COMpared with other vegetables, little thought is generally given to their storage. But because various problems can result from inadequate storage conditions, we decided to find out how much difference storage really makes. We stored all-purpose potatoes in five environments: in a cool (50–60 degrees), dark place; in the refrigerator; in a basket near a sunlit window; in a warm (70–80 degrees), dark place; and in a drawer with some onions at room temperature. We checked all the potatoes after four weeks.

As expected, the potatoes stored in the cool, dark place were firm, had not sprouted, and were crisp and moist when cut. There were no negative marks on the potatoes stored in the refrigerator, either. Although some experts say that the sugar level dramatically increases in some potato varieties under these conditions, we could not see or taste any difference between these potatoes and the ones stored in the cool, dark but unrefrigerated environment.

Our last three storage tests produced unfavorable results. The potatoes stored in sunlight, in warm storage, and with onions ended up with a greenish tinge along the edges. When potatoes are stressed by improper storage, the level of naturally occurring toxins increases, causing the greenish tinge known as solanine. Because solanine is not destroyed by cooking, any part of the potato with this greenish coloring should be completely cut away before cooking. In addition, the skin of the potatoes stored in sunlight became gray and mottled, while the potatoes stored in a warm place and those stored with onions sprouted and became soft and wrinkled. Sprouts also contain increased levels of solanine and should be cut away before cooking.

A Dutch oven may seem like an unlikely choice for frying chicken. But this pot is deep enough to prevent splatters and comes with a lid that traps moisture during the first half of the cooking time, helping to keep the chicken moist.

FRIED CHICKEN,
CHAPTER 8
& fixin's

Fried chicken is so patently American, so perennially "in," that it travels with a band of icons. It's not possible to think of biscuits or gravy, coleslaw or ham, or Grandma without thinking about fried chicken.

But making good fried chicken is harder than it seems. There's a reason why the Colonel kept his recipe a secret. Not only must you get the chicken right—it should be juicy, tender, and incredibly well seasoned—but the coating has to be perfect. For us, the ultimate fried chicken is shatteringly crisp. Softness and sogginess have no place in this recipe.

Our fried chicken recipe is the result of five years' work and incorporates many unusual techniques. We soak the chicken in a mixture of buttermilk, salt, sugar, and spices; air-dry the pieces to make the skin taut; coat them with flour; and then fry them in a Dutch oven rather than a skillet. The results put fast-food chicken to shame.

Our oven-fried chicken—designed for those cooks who are trying to reduce fat content or want to avoid creating a mess in the kitchen—is pretty darn good, too.

Coleslaw is the classic accompaniment to fried chicken. Coleslaw should be crisp and tangy. The dressing should coat the cabbage lightly and not become watery as the coleslaw sits on the picnic table.

CRISPY FRIED CHICKEN

WHAT WE WANTED: Chicken with a crackling crisp crust and tender, moist, seasoned meat.

What makes fried chicken great? First come, first served: the crust. Crisp and crackling with flavor, the crust must cleave to the chicken itself, not balloon away or flake off in chips like old radiator paint. In addition, it should carry a deep, uniform mahogany without spots or evidence of greasiness. As for the chicken itself, tender, moist, and flavorful are the descriptors of the day. Served hot, it should be demonstrably juicy; served room temperature, it should be moist. On no account should it be punishingly dry or require a salt shaker as a chaperone.

The truth is that frying chicken at home is a daunting task, a messy tableau of buttermilk dip and breading, hot fat, and splatters one hopes will end at the stove's edge. The results are often tantamount to the mess: greasy, peeling chicken skin and dry, unseasoned meat that's a long way from Grandma's.

It was no surprise to us that the chicken we were frying had to be premium quality to be worth the effort. Packaged chicken parts were irregular and disappointing, containing mismatched pieces in shabby dress with tattered skin, cut without a nod to basic anatomy. Given this situation, we thought it wise to spend a few minutes cutting a whole 3½-pound broiler into 12 manageable pieces (see page 89).

In our first stove-side excursion, we fried up several batches of chicken with different coatings, oils, and so on. But our real interest resided beneath the skin: half of the chickens had been brined for two hours; the other half had not. A brine is at minimum a mixture of salt and water. When soaked in a brine, chicken (as well as other poultry and meat) absorbs some of the salt and some of the water, thereby becoming more flavorful and more juicy once cooked. The tasting results bore out these benefits of brining: However glorious the crust, however perfectly fried the piece, the unbrined chicken earned marks far below its brined competition. Who wants to bite through a crisp, rich, seasoned crust only to hit dry, white Styrofoam? Another benefit of brining presented itself during cooking. Our brined chicken parts fried at equal rates, relieving us of the need to baby-sit the white meat or pull the wings out of the fat early.

While brining per se may not be common practice when preparing fried chicken, soaking the pieces in some kind of liquid—particularly buttermilk—is traditional. This process is thought to tenderize the meat (a mistaken assumption) and add flavor. We examined a number of soaking solutions and found the bright acidic flavor and clinging viscosity of buttermilk to produce the best flavor accents and richest browning during cooking.

Appreciating the tang of a buttermilk soak but unwilling to forgo the succulence of brined chicken, we found ourselves whispering "buttermilk brine." Instead of soaking the chicken in buttermilk alone, why not add the saline blast of a brine, doubling the rewards and minimizing the number of steps? To get a leg up on the idea, we made it a flavored brine, adding a mountain of crushed garlic, a couple of crushed bay leaves, and some sweet paprika.

This remarkable "twofer" won high marks indeed, well above those garnered by a unilateral soak or brine. The buttermilk and paprika showed spirit, garlic and bay crept into the crust, and the meat was tender and seasoned. We also spiked the brine with ¼ cup of sugar—not enough to sweeten but enough to bring other flavors out of hiding.

Fried foods taste irresistibly good when dressed in crumbs or flour, not only because their insides are protected from damaging temperatures but also because hot, enveloping fat performs minor miracles on the flavor of the flour or crumbs. But what kind of coating is best?

To find out, we tested straight flour against a panoply of contenders: matzo crumbs, ground saltines, cornflakes, Melba toast, cornmeal, and panko (Japanese) bread crumbs.

In the end, plain flour—requiring in this instance no seasoning whatsoever since the chicken had been brined—surpassed all other options for the integrity and lightness of the crust it produced.

Many fried chicken recipes use a single breading process in which the chicken is dipped first into beaten egg, then into flour or crumbs. A double, or bound, breading dips the chicken into flour first, then into egg, and finally into flour or crumbs. In side-by-side tests, we found that the double breading offered a superior base coat—more tenacious in its grip, more protective in its bearing—without being overly thick or tough.

Another practice that has made its way into many fried chicken recipes is that of air-drying breaded chicken before frying it. Rather than becoming soggy in the refrigerator, as might be expected, the breading toughens up over time to produce a fried chicken of superior crispiness.

We were also curious about the effect of air-drying on unbreaded chicken. We have come to favor the laser-crisp and taut skin of roasted birds that have been air-dried and wanted to see if an analogous effect could be achieved by refrigerating our brined, unbreaded chicken on a rack for a couple of hours. We were reasonably confident this would allow the buttermilk to dry just enough to maintain a protective and flavorful posture and the chicken to bread nicely without first being dabbed or dried, frying up dry and crisp.

We tested the effects of air-drying the chicken before and after breading and compared the results with chicken that underwent no air-drying. Both air-dried versions were superior in terms of crust, but each was distinctly different from the other. The chicken that was breaded and then air-dried had a heartier, more toothsome crust—crunchy to some, hard to others. The chicken that was air-dried and then breaded was lighter and crispier, flaky, more shattery. We preferred this traditionally Southern crust. Though it initially seemed ideal, we noticed that its delicate crispiness succumbed to sandiness and porosity over the course of a few hours. This was not acceptable.

The memory of a particularly light but resilient crust

on a chicken-fried steak recipe we had made persuaded us to add baking soda and baking powder to an egg wash bolstered with buttermilk. We hoped the sandiness in the crust that developed over time might thus be offset. Stirred into the wash, ½ teaspoon of soda and 1 teaspoon of powder produced just enough carbon dioxide to lighten the breading to perfection. Not only did it bronze to a shattery filigree in the hot fat, it also remained crisp as it cooled.

One of the most important requirements of fat as a frying medium is that it offer nothing of its own flavor—and, in fact, have none to offer. This means that the oil must be refined—in other words, cleansed and sanitized. Another requirement is that the oil perform at temperatures below its smoke point (the temperature at which it emits smoke and acrid odors) to maintain thermal stability. With the relatively moderate temperatures required by our recipe, all refined vegetable oils stayed well below their smoke points. In the end, peanut oil edged out Crisco shortening by virtue of its marginally more neutral and clean flavor.

A cast-iron Dutch oven covered during the first half of the frying reduced splatters to a fine spray, maintained the oil temperature impeccably, and fried the chicken through in about 15 minutes total versus the 20 minutes per side recommended in many recipes.

Drying the gleaming, bronzed statuettes was the most satisfying test. Paper bags are simply not porous enough to keep the chicken out of a gathering pool of grease. We found that paper towels absorbed excess fat quickly and that rolling the pieces over onto a bare rack thereafter kept them crisp.

WHAT WE LEARNED: Soak chicken parts in a seasoned buttermilk brine for ultimate flavor and juiciness. Air-dry the brined chicken parts before coating with crumbs to create a light, crisp crust. Flour makes the crispest coating. Peanut oil can withstand the demands of frying and has the most neutral flavor of all the oils tested. Shortening was a close runner-up. With its high sides and lid, a Dutch oven minimizes splatters and retains heat that helps the chicken cook through.

CRISPY FRIED CHICKEN serves 4 to 6

Maintaining an even oil temperature is key to the success of this recipe. An instant-read thermometer with a high upper range is perfect for checking the temperature; a clip-on candy/deep-fry thermometer is fine, though it can be clipped to the pot only for the uncovered portion of frying.

1¼	cups kosher salt or ½ cup plus 2 tablespoons table salt
¼	cup sugar
2	tablespoons paprika
3	medium heads garlic, cloves separated
3	bay leaves, crumbled
2	quarts low-fat buttermilk
1	whole chicken (about 3½ pounds), giblets discarded, cut into 12 pieces (see illustrations on page 89)
4	cups all-purpose flour
1	large egg
1	teaspoon baking powder
½	teaspoon baking soda
3–4	cups refined peanut oil or vegetable shortening

1. In large zipper-lock plastic bag, combine salt, sugar, paprika, garlic cloves, and bay leaves. With rubber mallet or flat meat pounder, smash garlic into salt and spice mixture thoroughly. Pour mixture into large plastic container or nonreactive stockpot. Add 7 cups buttermilk and stir until salt is completely dissolved. Immerse chicken, cover with plastic wrap, and refrigerate until fully seasoned, 2 to 3 hours. Remove chicken from buttermilk brine and shake off excess; place in single layer on large wire rack set over rimmed baking sheet. Refrigerate uncovered for 2 hours. (After 2 hours, chicken can be covered with plastic wrap and refrigerated up to 6 hours longer.)

2. Measure flour into large shallow dish. Beat egg, baking powder, and baking soda in medium bowl; stir in remaining 1 cup buttermilk (mixture will bubble and foam). Working in batches of 3, drop chicken pieces in flour and shake pan to coat. Shake excess flour from each piece. Then, using tongs, dip chicken pieces into egg mixture, turning to coat well and allowing excess to drip off. Coat chicken pieces with flour again, shake off excess, and return to wire rack.

3. Adjust oven rack to middle position, set second wire rack over second rimmed baking sheet, and place on oven rack; heat oven to 200 degrees. Line large plate with double layer of paper towels. Meanwhile, heat oil (oil should have 2½-inch depth in pan) to 375 degrees over medium-high heat in large 8-quart cast-iron Dutch oven with a diameter of about 12 inches. Place half of chicken pieces skin-side down in oil, cover, reduce heat to medium, and fry until deep golden brown, 6 to 8 minutes; after about 3 minutes, lift chicken pieces with tongs to check for even browning; rearrange if some pieces are browning faster than others. (Spot-check oil temperature; after first 6 minutes of frying, oil should be about 325 degrees. Adjust burner if necessary.) Turn chicken pieces over and continue to fry, uncovered, until chicken pieces are deep golden brown on second side, 6 to 8 minutes longer. Using tongs, transfer chicken to paper towel–lined plate; let stand 2 minutes to drain, then transfer to rack in warm oven. Replace paper towel lining on plate. Return oil to 375 degrees and fry remaining pieces, transferring pieces to paper towel–lined plate to drain, then transferring to wire rack. Cool chicken pieces on wire rack (outside oven) about 5 minutes and serve.

TECHNIQUE: Cutting Up a Chicken for Frying

Chicken destined for the fry pot should be cut into fairly small pieces. Instead of the standard eight pieces (two breasts, two wings, two thighs, and two legs), we cut each breast piece in half and sever the wing at the main joint (the skin cooks better when thus separated, and the wings pieces are easier to eat) to yield a total of 12 pieces.

1. With a sharp chef's knife, cut through the skin around the leg where it attaches to the breast.

2. Using both hands, pop the leg joint out of its socket.

3. Use a chef's knife to cut through the flesh and skin to detach the leg from the body.

4. A line of fat separates the thigh and drumstick. Cut through the joint at this point. Repeat steps 1 through 4 with the other leg.

5. Bend the wing out from the breast and use a boning knife to cut through the joint. Repeat with the other wing.

6. Cut through the cartilage around the wing tip to remove it. Discard the tip. Cut through the joint to split. Repeat with the other wing.

7. Using poultry shears, cut along the ribs to completely separate the back from the breast. Discard backbone.

8. Place the knife on the breast-bone, then apply pressure to cut through and separate the breast into halves.

9. Cut each breast in half crosswise.

SCIENCE DESK: Successful Frying

MANY COOKS SHY AWAY FROM FRYING, THINKING THAT the technique adds loads of fat to their food. Taking nothing for granted, we put this notion to the test. We heated 3 cups of peanut oil to 375 degrees in a 12-inch Dutch oven and pan-fried a whole chicken in two batches. To our delight, we poured back almost exactly three cups of fat after frying. Each time the test was repeated, we ended up with virtually the same amount of fat before and after.

The explanation is simple: If the water in the food you are frying is kept above the boiling point (212 degrees), the outward pressure of the escaping water vapor keeps oil from soaking into the hot food. If the frying oil is not hot enough, the oil will seep into the food, making it greasy. The key is to get the oil hot enough before adding food (375 degrees worked well) so that you maintain a temperature (around 325 degrees) that keeps the moisture in the food boiling.

EQUIPMENT CORNER: Best Pots for Frying Chicken

A SKILLET MIGHT SEEM THE NATURAL CHOICE FOR FRYING CHICKEN, BUT THE DEEP SIDES OF A DUTCH OVEN MINIMIZE splattering and create a veil of condensation that tenderizes the chicken. (All-Clad refers to its pan as a stockpot, but it functions well as a Dutch oven.)

CAST-IRON SKILLET
The lid for this squat skillet basically sat on top of the chicken, giving the hot, moist air nowhere to go. After turning, the top of the chicken became soggy.

LODGE CAST-IRON DUTCH OVEN
The thick walls of this pot took 10 minutes to heat, but once they did, the pot maintained the oil's temperature and fried the chicken to perfection.

ALL-CLAD STOCKPOT
This sturdy entry took on heat quickly but lost it, and failed to recover it, once the chicken entered the fat. The chicken did not color easily.

LE CREUSET ENAMELED DUTCH OVEN
The thinner cast-iron walls of this beauty heated up fast and stayed that way. Cleanup was a cinch with its slick enamel surface.

OVEN-FRIED CHICKEN

WHAT WE WANTED: "Fried" chicken with real crunch and good flavor.

We've always thought of oven-fried chicken as ersatz fried chicken—only for those who were afraid to mess up their kitchen or consume too much fat. Depending on the liquid or crumb coating, this chicken could be bland, soggy, rubbery-skinned, greasy, artificially flavored, dry, or crumbly. Was it possible, we wondered, to make a decent alternative to the real thing?

After reading many recipes, we realized that the coatings—both the moist one that helps the crumbs stick and the dry one that provides crunch—were the key issues to examine.

Since the moist coating comes first, we started there. (For information on dry coatings, see page 92.) Before testing, we assumed this wet dunk did little more than help the crumbs adhere to the chicken. After testing, however, it became clear that this initial coat plays a larger role. A good first coat, we discovered, should offer flavor, attract the right proportion of crumbs to form an impressive, uniform crust, and, finally, help the crust stay crunchy during baking.

To find the best moist coating, we baked 13 drumsticks, keeping the dry coating constant while varying the moist coating: water, whole milk, evaporated milk, cream, buttermilk, yogurt, sour cream, milk beaten with egg, egg beaten with lemon juice, and egg with Dijon mustard. In addition, we tried legs coated with ranch dressing, mayonnaise, and butter.

Because many recipes for oven-fried chicken start by rolling chicken parts in butter, we thought the fat coatings would perform well. Not so. All of them—butter, mayonnaise, and ranch dressing—created a slick surface that prevented the crumbs from adhering properly. In addition, none of the fats did anything to crisp up the crumbs.

With the exception of buttermilk and evaporated milk, moreover, none of the dairy coatings impressed us. Buttermilk and evaporated milk did attract decent crusts and give a subtle flavor dimension to the chicken, but they didn't result in the crispness we wanted.

The egg beaten with lemon did result in a crisp coating. Unfortunately, it also contributed too much lemon flavor with an overcooked egg aftertaste. But a change of just one ingredient made all the difference. Chicken coated with beaten egg and Dijon mustard was our favorite. This not-too-thick, not-too-thin moistener not only attracted a uniform, impressive layer of crumbs, it also gave the meat a wonderfully subtle flavor. Unlike many of the wet coatings, which made the crumbs either soggy or barely crisp, this one took the crumbs to an almost crunchy level.

Over the course of testing, we found that we much preferred legs and thighs to breasts because they don't dry out as quickly. As expected, the buttermilk brine that worked so well in our crispy fried chicken recipe did wonders here, too. The meat was more moist and better seasoned after a two-hour brine. We also discovered that we didn't like the skin on oven-fried chicken. Unlike fried chicken, in which hot oil causes the fat to render and the skin to crisp up, oven heat simply softens the skin and makes it rubbery. We decided to remove the skin before coating the pieces.

Oven temperature was a simple matter. We started baking at 400 degrees, and all of the chicken pieces were cooked through and rich golden brown in about 40 minutes. A wire rack set over a rimmed baking sheet allows heat to circulate around the chicken during baking, allowing the chicken to crisp without being turned.

In the end, this "fried" chicken was pretty darn good. Perhaps not as crispy as the real thing, but a close runner-up.

WHAT WE LEARNED: Soak chicken legs and thighs in buttermilk brine to achieve maximum juiciness and flavor in the meat. A mixture of eggs and mustard helps the crumbs stick to the chicken and encourages the formation of a crunchy crust. Melba toast crumbs make the crispest coating.

OVEN-FRIED CHICKEN   serves 4

To make Melba toast crumbs, place the toasts in a heavy-duty plastic freezer bag, seal, and pound with a meat pounder or other heavy blunt object. Leave some crumbs in the mixture the size of pebbles, but most should resemble coarse sand.

chicken

- 1¼ cups kosher salt or ½ cup plus 2 tablespoons table salt
- ¼ cup sugar
- 2 tablespoons paprika
- 3 medium heads garlic, cloves separated
- 3 bay leaves, crumbled
- 7 cups low-fat buttermilk
- 4 whole chicken legs, separated into drumsticks and thighs (see illustration 4 on page 89) and skin removed

coating

- ¼ cup vegetable oil
- 1 box (about 5 ounces) plain Melba toast, crushed
- 2 large eggs
- 1 tablespoon Dijon mustard
- 1 teaspoon dried thyme
- ¾ teaspoon salt
- ½ teaspoon ground black pepper
- ½ teaspoon dried oregano
- ¼ teaspoon garlic powder
- ¼ teaspoon cayenne (optional)

1. FOR THE CHICKEN: In large zipper-lock plastic bag, combine salt, sugar, paprika, garlic cloves, and bay leaves. With rubber mallet or flat meat pounder, smash garlic into salt and spice mixture thoroughly. Pour mixture into large plastic container or nonreactive stockpot. Add buttermilk and stir until salt is completely dissolved. Immerse chicken and refrigerate until fully seasoned, 2 to 3 hours. Remove chicken from buttermilk brine and shake off excess; place in single layer on large wire rack set over rimmed baking sheet. Refrigerate

uncovered for 2 hours. (After 2 hours, chicken can be covered with plastic wrap and refrigerated up to 6 hours longer.)

2. Adjust oven rack to upper-middle position and heat oven to 400 degrees. Line sheet pan with foil and set large flat wire rack over sheet pan.

3. FOR THE COATING: Drizzle oil over Melba toast crumbs in a shallow dish or pie plate; toss well to coat. Mix eggs, mustard, thyme, salt, pepper, oregano, garlic powder, and optional cayenne with a fork in a second shallow dish or pie plate.

4. Working one piece at a time, coat chicken on both sides with egg mixture. Set chicken in Melba crumbs, sprinkle crumbs over chicken, and press to coat. Turn chicken over and repeat on other side. Gently shake off excess and place on rack. Bake until chicken is deep nutty brown and juices run clear, about 40 minutes.

TASTING LAB: Dry Coatings

WE STARTED WITH 20 DRY COATINGS OR COMBINATIONS, all from published recipes. After baking and tasting them all, there wasn't a single one we thought was perfect.

Of the cereal coatings, cornflakes were the best, offering good color and crunch, but they also had too much sweet corn flavor. Ditto for bran flakes, but their distinct flavor was even more pronounced. Unprocessed bran looked like kitty litter, while Grape-Nuts looked (worse) like hamster food.

Crackers didn't work, either. Both saltines and Ritz were too soft; the Ritz, in addition, were too sweet. Cracker meal delivered a bland blond shell. In the bread department, stuffing mix scored well in crunch but struck out in flavor. Fresh bread crumbs, on the other hand, tasted great but lacked the crunch we had come to like.

The meals and flours, as to be expected, did not show well. Cornmeal tasted raw, and it chipped off the chicken like flecks of old paint. Our grocery store's house brand of Shake 'n Bake was vile, tasting of liquid smoke and bad hot dogs.

Although this first round of tests did not produce a strong winner, it did help us to clarify what it was that we wanted—a coating that was crunchy (not just crisp) and flavorful (but not artificial tasting) and that baked up a rich copper brown.

With a clear ideal in mind, we found a whole new range of coating possibilities in the specialty/international cracker section of our grocery store, including Melba toast, pain grillé (French crisp toast), Swedish crisps, lavash (crisp flat bread), bread sticks, bagel chips, Italian toasts, and pita chips.

This series of tests delivered oven-fried chicken that was much closer to our ideal. The rather surprising winner, it turned out, was Melba toast. It scored the best in all three major categories—texture, flavor, and color.

EQUIPMENT CORNER: Cutting Boards

WHAT SEPARATES GOOD CUTTING BOARDS FROM BAD ones? Is it material? Size, thickness, or weight? Whether the board warps or retains odors with use?

To sort all of this out, we gathered boards made from wood, polyethylene (plastic), acrylic, glass, and Corian (the hard countertop material) and used them daily in our test kitchen for eight weeks. We found the two most important factors to be size and material.

In terms of size, large boards provide ample space for both cutting and pushing aside cut foods and waste. The disadvantage of really large boards is that they may not fit in the dishwasher. We are willing to make that sacrifice for the extra work area. If you are not, buy the largest board that will fit in your dishwasher. No matter the dimensions, a board should be heavy enough for stability but not so heavy (or thick and bulky) to impede its easy movement around the kitchen. We found boards in the range of 3 to 4 pounds to be ideal.

Material is important primarily in terms of the way the board interacts with the knife, but it is also relevant to odor retention and warping. We disliked cutting on hard acrylic, glass, and Corian boards because they don't absorb the shock of the knife strike. Plastic and wood boards are softer and therefore cushion the knife's blow, making for more controlled cutting.

There is one advantage to hard boards—they don't retain odors like plastic and wood can. A dishwasher will remove odors from plastic boards as well as specially treated dishwasher-safe wood boards. (Unless treated by the manufacturer with a waterproof coating, wood boards should never go in the dishwasher.)

If your boards are too large to fit in the dishwasher, use one for onions, garlic, and the like; another for raw poultry, fish, and meat; and a third for other foods. To remove most odors and bacteria, wash with hot soapy water after each use and then sanitize with a light bleach solution (1 tablespoon of bleach to 1 gallon of water).

Many plastic and wood boards will warp over time. Makers of wood boards advise consumers to season their boards with mineral oil to build up water resistance and, thereby, resist warping. As none of the cooks we know will go this extra mile, plastic boards probably make the most sense for home cooks. Keep plastic boards away from the dishwasher's heating element to prevent warping.

COLESLAW

WHAT WE WANTED: A crisp salad with creamy dressing that would be neither watery nor harsh-tasting.

Despite its simplicity, coleslaw has always bothered us for two reasons: the pool of watery dressing that appears at the bottom of the bowl after a few hours, and the salad's sharp flavor, no matter what kind or quantity of vinegar is used. Our slaw always seemed to taste better when we tried it again the next day, but by then the dressing was the consistency of skim milk.

While most recipes instruct the cook to toss the shredded cabbage immediately with dressing, a few add an extra step. Either the shredded (or merely quartered) cabbage is soaked in ice water for crisping and refreshing, or it is salted, drained, and allowed to wilt.

We soaked cabbage in ice water and found it to be crisp, plump, and fresh. If looks were all that mattered, this cabbage would have scored high next to the limp, salted cabbage in the neighboring colander. But its good looks were deceiving. Even though we drained the ice water–soaked cabbage and dried it thoroughly, the dressing didn't really adhere. Within minutes, the cabbage shreds started to lose their recently acquired water, making for not a small but a large puddle of water to dilute the creamy dressing. The stiff cabbage shreds were strawlike, making them difficult to get onto a fork and even more difficult to get into the mouth without leaving a creamy trail.

Quite unlike the ice-water cabbage, the salted shreds lost most of their liquid while sitting in the salt, leaving the cabbage wilted but pickle-crisp. Because the cabbage had already lost most of its own liquid, there was little or no liquid for the salt in the dressing to draw out. We had found the solution to the problem of watery dressing. In addition, we found that this cabbage, having less water in it, absorbed more flavor from the dressing, and, unlike the stiff, icy shreds, this limp cabbage was also easier to eat.

We did discover that the salting process leaves the cabbage a bit too salty, but a quick rinse washes away the excess. After the cabbage has been rinsed, just pat it dry with paper towels and refrigerate until ready to combine with the dressing. If the coleslaw is to be eaten immediately, rinse it quickly in ice water rather than tap water, then pat it dry. Coleslaw, at least the creamy style, should be served cold.

Having figured out how to keep the cabbage from watering down the dressing, we were ready to tackle the problem of acidity in the dressing. We found a few creamy coleslaw recipes in which the cabbage was tossed with sour cream only, or a combination of mayonnaise and sour cream—no vinegar. Although we were looking for ways to tone down the tang, a mix of sour cream and mayonnaise proved too mild for our taste. Other recipes called for lemon juice rather than vinegar. Although the lemon juice–flavored coleslaw was pleasantly tart, it lacked the depth that vinegar could offer. We decided to give low-acidity rice vinegar a try. We drizzled a bit of rice vinegar over the mayonnaise-tossed cabbage and found its mild acidity to be perfect for coleslaw.

Although there are several styles of coleslaw, the two that follow are classics—one mild and creamy, the other sweet-and-sour. Adjust either recipe to your taste. If sour cream is a must for your creamy slaw, then substitute it for some or all of the mayonnaise. And feel free to embellish our recipe. Add green pepper or celery, red onions, or apples. Try caraway seeds or fresh dill, radishes, or nuts.

WHAT WE LEARNED: Don't soak the shredded cabbage; that just makes the dressing watery. Do salt the shredded cabbage; removing excess water keeps the dressing thick and creamy. A combination of mayonnaise and low-acidity rice vinegar creates a dressing that's flavorful but not harsh.

CREAMY COLESLAW serves 4

If you like caraway or celery seeds, add 1/4 teaspoon of either with the mayonnaise and vinegar. You can shred, salt, rinse, and pat the cabbage dry a day ahead, but dress it close to serving time. If you like a tangier slaw, replace some or all of the mayonnaise with an equal amount of sour cream. For tips on handling cabbage, see illustrations at right.

- 1 pound (about ½ medium head) red or green cabbage, shredded fine or chopped (6 cups)
- 1 large carrot, peeled and grated
- 2 teaspoons kosher salt or 1 teaspoon table salt
- ½ small onion, minced
- ½ cup mayonnaise
- 2 tablespoons rice vinegar
  Ground black pepper

1. Toss cabbage and carrots with salt in colander set over medium bowl. Let stand until cabbage wilts, at least 1 hour and up to 4 hours.

2. Dump wilted cabbage and carrots into bowl. Rinse thoroughly in cold water (ice water if serving slaw immediately). Pour vegetables back into colander, pressing, but not squeezing, to drain. Pat dry with paper towels.

3. Pour cabbage and carrots back again into bowl. Add onion, mayonnaise, and vinegar; toss to coat. Season with pepper to taste. Cover and refrigerate until ready to serve. (Can be refrigerated for up to 2 days.)

SWEET-AND-SOUR COLESLAW serves 4

The presence of the sugar in this recipe makes it unnecessary to rinse the salt from the cabbage, as is ordinarily the case. For tips on handling cabbage, see illustrations at right.

- 1 pound (about ½ medium head) red or green cabbage, shredded fine or chopped (6 cups)
- 1 large carrot, peeled and grated

TECHNIQUE: Shredding Cabbage

1. Cut a whole head of cabbage in quarters. Cut away the hard piece of the core attached to each quarter.

2. Separate the cored cabbage quarters into stacks of leaves that flatten when pressed lightly.

3. Use a chef's knife to cut each stack of cabbage diagonally into long, thin pieces. Or, roll the stacked leaves crosswise to fit them into the feed tube of a food processor fitted with the shredding disk.

½ cup sugar
2 teaspoons kosher salt or 1 teaspoon table salt
¼ teaspoon celery seeds
6 tablespoons vegetable oil
¼ cup rice vinegar
  Ground black pepper

1. Toss cabbage and carrots with sugar, salt, and celery seeds in colander set over medium bowl. Let stand until cabbage wilts, at least 1 hour and up to 4 hours.

2. Pour draining liquid from bowl; rinse bowl and dry. Dump wilted cabbage and carrots from colander into bowl.

3. Add oil and vinegar; toss to coat. Season with pepper to taste. Cover and refrigerate until ready to serve. (Can be refrigerated for up to 2 days.)

VARIATION

CURRIED COLESLAW WITH APPLES AND RAISINS serves 6
Follow recipe for Sweet-and-Sour Coleslaw, adding 1 teaspoon curry powder, 1 medium apple, peeled and cut into small dice, and ¼ cup raisins (optional) with oil and vinegar.

SCIENCE DESK:
Where There's Salt, There's Water

VEGETABLES THAT SOAK IN ICE WATER CRISP UP, WHILE salted and drained vegetables go limp. These phenomena are evidence of the cell structure of most foods, including vegetables. Cells are filled with liquid, and their walls are semipermeable, meaning they allow some things, like water, to flow into and out of the cell. The water will flow to whichever side of the wall has a higher concentration of salt.

Cabbage is a pretty tough vegetable, but when soaked in ice water, its shreds become even stiffer and crisper. In this case, the cabbage cells have a greater concentration of salt than the ice water. The ice water is drawn into the cabbage cells, causing the shreds to plump up. Watching a scored radish blossom into a radish rose when soaked in ice water is an even more dramatic example of this principle.

When shredded cabbage is salted, on the other hand, the concentration of salt is greater outside the cabbage than inside the cells. The cell water is drawn out by the clinging salt. This partially dehydrated cabbage is limp but still crisp.

TASTING LAB: Mayonnaise

WHILE HOMEMADE MAYONNAISE IS A DELICIOUS ADDItion to salads, many cooks prefer the convenience and safety of commercial brands made without raw eggs. In dishes such as coleslaw, good commercial mayonnaise is a fine addition.

Two brands dominate the mayo market—Hellmann's (also known as Best Foods in some parts of the country) and Kraft. Each company makes several products—full fat, reduced fat, and low- or no-fat. We tasted six kinds of mayonnaise (three from each company) and tasters were unanimous in their first choice.

Hellmann's Real Mayonnaise was the creamiest in the bunch, with an excellent balance of flavors. Many tasters felt it was as good, if not better, than most homemade mayonnaise. Hellmann's Light (a reduced-calorie product with about half the fat of Hellmann's Real) took second place. Most tasters thought this product was almost as creamy as the winner.

Kraft Real Mayonnaise finished in third place, right behind Hellmann's Light. It was a bit less creamy and not as flavorful as the top finishers.

The remaining reduced-fat and no-fat products fared poorly in our tasting. Most were too acidic and lacked the sheen of a good mayonnaise. If you want to cut calories and fat, Hellmann's Light is a fine option, but don't try to trim any more fat grams—what you lose in calories just isn't worth what you lose in flavor.

Creamy Mushroom Soup with Sautéed Wild Mushrooms **page 10**

97

Spaghetti and Meatballs **page 27**

Deep-Dish Pizza **page 39** with Fresh Tomato Topping **page 40**

Crisp Thin-Crust Pizza page 44

100

Spaghetti alla Carbonara **page 19**

Grilled Fresh Mozzarella Sandwiches with Black Olive Paste and Roasted Red Peppers page 54

102

Breaded Chicken Cutlet page 119

Herb-Poached Shrimp with Cocktail Sauce **page 62**

Stuffed Chicken Cutlets **page 122** with Broiled Asparagus and Smoked Mozzarella Cheese Filling **page 123**

Grilled Hamburger page 128

106

French Fries **page 83**

Chunky Guacamole page 155

Classic Fajitas **page** 157 and Grilled Corn **page** 135

Green Beans with Toasted Hazelnuts and Brown Butter **page 187**

Pommes Anna **page 184**

CHICKEN cutlets 101

It's no secret that most Americans prefer white meat to dark meat chicken. Meat from the breast is lean and tender. Since most Americans don't like to deal with skin and bones, it makes sense that cutlets (otherwise known as boneless, skinless breasts) have become the preferred cut of chicken.

Although cutlets can be delicious, they can also be tough and dry. Because white meat contains very little fat, it can be the trickiest part of the bird to prepare.

For this episode, we take three classic preparations—Marsala, breaded, and stuffed—and explore ways to make these dishes really good. Chicken should be more than just serviceable. It should be something you look forward to and enjoy.

Bridget gathers flour, eggs, and fresh bread crumbs to make the crisp coating for our breaded cutlets.

CHICKEN MARSALA

WHAT WE WANTED: A rich, potent sauce to coat browned mushrooms and perfectly cooked chicken cutlets.

Marsala has never been a glamorous wine. It bears the name of its hometown, a seaport on the western coast of Sicily, once mockingly dubbed "the dump" by Italians from neighboring wine-making regions. In the early 1800s, a marketing campaign touted Marsala as a less expensive alternative to Madeira and sherry. As sales soared, it quickly made its way into Italian kitchens, where classic dishes such as chicken Marsala were created. Nowadays, chicken Marsala is an Italian restaurant staple. After having several disappointing encounters with this dish involving watery sauces, flaccid mushrooms, and pale, stale chicken, we realized that chicken Marsala was being taken for granted. It was in need of a rescue.

While all of the recipes we found listed the same three ingredients—breast of chicken, mushrooms, and Marsala—the cooking methods differed. Some called for simmering the chicken and mushrooms in Marsala, which resulted in flavors that were waterlogged and bland. Others recommended cooking everything in separate pans, creating not only a messy kitchen but a dish with disjointed flavors. Yet others had the cook sauté everything in the same pan, but sequentially. The clear winner turned out to be the classic, in which the meat is sautéed first and then moved to a warm oven while the browned bits left in the pan are splashed with wine and mounted with butter to create a sauce. With this decided, we focused on perfecting the sautéed chicken and developing the sauce.

When sautéing, the most important steps include getting the skillet incredibly hot and patting the chicken dry with paper towels before dusting with a light coating of flour. Using these pointers as a guide, we sautéed with a variety of oils and with butter to find that vegetable oil was the least likely to burn and splatter.

Our next task was to figure out how to get the mushrooms crisp and brown without burning the drippings left from the sautéed chicken. One way to do this, we thought, would be to add more fat to the pan and scrape the browned bits off the bottom before cooking the mushrooms. One way to add both fat and flavor was to cook small pieces of pancetta (Italian bacon that has been cured but not smoked) directly after the chicken. Just as we had thought, the fat rendered from the pancetta prevented the chicken drippings from burning while providing the oil necessary for sautéing the mushrooms—not to mention adding a meaty, pepper-flavored punch to the sauce.

Because several types and grades of Marsala wine can be found on the market, we conducted a taste test before doing any cooking, trying imported and California brands of both the sweet and dry varieties. We favored an imported wine, Sweet Marsala Fine, for its depth of flavor, smooth finish, and reasonable price tag. By reducing the wine, we found the silky, plush texture we were looking for in the final sauce. Knowing that stock is traditionally added to pan sauces for depth of flavor and body, we tested a variety of stock-to-Marsala ratios. Again and again, tasters preferred a sauce made only from wine, slightly reduced. The stock simply got in the way of the Marsala's distinctive zip.

All we needed to do now was round out the final flavors. Some lemon juice tempered the Marsala's sweetness, while one clove of garlic and a teaspoon of tomato paste rounded out the middle tones. Last, we found that 4 tablespoons of unsalted butter whisked in at the end added a dreamlike finish and beautiful sheen. Here was a chicken Marsala Sicilians could be proud of.

WHAT WE LEARNED: Add pancetta to help moisten the mushrooms as they cook and to add meatiness to the sauce. Use sweet Marsala wine (without any stock) for the richest-tasting sauce.

CHICKEN MARSALA   serves 4

Our wine of choice for this dish is Sweet Marsala Fine, an imported wine that gives the sauce body, soft edges, and a smooth finish.

1	cup all-purpose flour
4	boneless, skinless chicken breasts (5 to 6 ounces each), fat trimmed (see illustration below)
	Salt and ground black pepper
2	tablespoons vegetable oil
2½	ounces pancetta (about 3 slices), cut into pieces 1 inch long and ⅛ inch wide
8	ounces white mushrooms, sliced (about 2 cups)
1	medium clove garlic, minced (about 1 teaspoon)
1	teaspoon tomato paste
1½	cups sweet Marsala
1½	tablespoons juice from 1 small lemon
4	tablespoons unsalted butter, cut into 4 pieces
2	tablespoons minced fresh parsley leaves

1. Adjust oven rack to lower-middle position, place large heatproof dinner plate on oven rack, and heat oven to 200 degrees. Heat 12-inch heavy-bottomed skillet over medium-high heat until very hot (you can hold your hand 2 inches above pan surface for 3 to 4 seconds), about 3 minutes. Meanwhile, place flour in shallow baking dish or pie plate. Pat chicken breasts dry. Season both sides of breasts with salt and pepper; working one piece at a time, coat both sides with flour. Lift breast from tapered end and shake to remove excess flour; set aside. Add oil to hot skillet and heat until shimmering. Place floured cutlets in single layer in skillet and cook until golden brown, about 3 minutes. Using tongs, flip cutlets and cook on second side until golden brown and meat feels firm when pressed with finger, about 3 minutes longer. Transfer chicken to heated plate and return plate to oven.

2. Return skillet to low heat and add pancetta; sauté, stirring occasionally and scraping pan bottom to loosen browned bits until pancetta is brown and crisp, about 4 minutes. With slotted spoon, transfer pancetta to paper towel–lined plate. Add mushrooms and increase heat to medium-high; sauté, stirring occasionally and scraping pan bottom, until liquid released by mushrooms evaporates and mushrooms begin to brown, about 8 minutes. Add garlic, tomato paste, and cooked pancetta; sauté while stirring until tomato paste begins to brown, about 1 minute. Off heat, add Marsala; return pan to high heat and simmer vigorously, scraping browned bits from pan bottom, until sauce is slightly syrupy and reduced to about 1¼ cups, about 5 minutes. Off heat, add lemon juice and any accumulated juices from chicken; whisk in butter 1 tablespoon at a time. Season to taste with salt and pepper, and stir in parsley. Pour sauce over chicken and serve immediately.

TECHNIQUE: Trimming Cutlets

Most cutlets have a little yellow or white fat still attached to the breast meat. Lay each cutlet tenderloin-side down and smooth the top with your fingers. Any fat will slide to the edges of the cutlet, where it can be trimmed with a knife.

EQUIPMENT CORNER: Pepper Mills

PEPPER MILLS COME IN A VAST RANGE OF STYLES AND materials, but what really matters to us and other serious home cooks is performance. Is the fine-ground pepper truly fine? Is the medium grind really medium, or are there coarse particles mixed in? And how about output? Will you have to turn and turn and turn until your arm needs a brace to produce a teaspoon of ground pepper? To answer these questions, we rounded up 12 widely available mills.

Most pepper mills work by similar means. Peppercorns are loaded into a central chamber, through which runs a metal shaft. Near the bottom of the mill, the shaft is connected to a grinding mechanism that consists of a rotating, grooved "male" head that fits into a stationary, grooved "female" ring. Near the top of the male piece, large grooves crack the peppercorns and then feed the smaller pieces downward to be ground between the finer grooves of the male and female components.

Generally, the finer the grind, the more even the distribution of pepper throughout a dish. Thus the quality of a mill's fine grind is more important than options for an endless range of grinds beyond fine, medium, and coarse.

The industry experts we queried explained that the specifics of the grinding mechanism are key to grind quality. Jack Pierotti, president of Chef Specialties, maker of the Windsor mill, named the size, number, and angle of teeth in both male and female grinder components as factors in performance. A related consideration, according to Tom David, president of Tom David, Inc., maker of the Unicorn Magnum Plus mill, is how well the male and female grinding pieces are machined (the process used to cut the grooves). Sharper teeth combined with a very tight tolerance between the pieces yields a better grind, which to us means finer fine-ground pepper. Unfortunately, none of these details is evident upon inspecting a pepper mill in a kitchen store.

In addition to having an excellent grind quality, Unicorn Magnum Plus managed an awesome output. In one minute

of grinding, the Magnum produced an incredible average of 7.3 grams, or about 3½ teaspoons, of fine-ground pepper. By comparison, honors for the next highest average output went to the Oxo Grind It, at 5.1 grams, while about half the pack hovered around the two-grams-or-less mark (which, at roughly one teaspoon in volume, is perfectly acceptable).

Grind quality and speed are only half the battle—especially if most of your peppercorns land on the floor when you try to fill the mill. So we appreciated mills with wide, unobstructed filler doors that could accommodate the tip of a wide funnel or, better yet, the lip of a bag or jar so that we could dispense with the funnel altogether.

The ease of adjusting the grind was another factor we considered. Changing the grind from fine to coarse involves changing the tolerances of, or distances between, the male and female grinding components. The more space between them, the larger the pepper particles and the coarser the grind. Traditionally, a knob at the top of the mill called the finial is used to adjust the grind. This was our least favorite design for two reasons. First, the finial must be screwed down very tight for a fine grind, which not only requires

BEST PEPPER MILLS
The Unicorn Magnum Plus (far left) has a huge capacity and awesome speed. The East Hampton Industries Peppermate (second from left) has a detachable cup that captures ground pepper and makes measuring easy. The Oxo Good Grips Grind It (second from right) is lightning-fast, but it can be tricky to adjust the grind on this mill. The Zyliss Large Mill (far right) has a huge capacity and excellent range of grinds but is slower than the other top mills.

significant finger strength but also makes the head (or the crank) of the mill more difficult to turn. Second, the finial usually has to be removed entirely to fill the mill, which means you have to readjust the grind with each filling. We preferred mills like the Unicorn Magnum Plus, which use a screw or dial at the base of the grinding mechanism.

More than half of the mills tested did their jobs well, but the Unicorn Magnum Plus was the superstar. At $45, however, this mill was one of the two most expensive in the test (the second-place EHI Peppermate was $40). If your budget is a bit more restricted, we recommend both the Oxo Grind It ($19.99) and the Zyliss Large Pepper Mill ($27.50).

SCIENCE DESK:
The Role of Fond in Pan Sauces

EVER WONDER HOW RESTAURANTS MAKE THICK, RICH sauces to accompany sautéed cutlets and steaks? Chances are it's a pan sauce, made with the delicious caramelized browned bits (called fond) that sit on the bottom of the pan after the meat has been sautéed or pan-seared.

Pan sauces are usually made by adding liquid (stock, wine, or juice) to the pan once the cooked cutlets or steaks have been transferred to a plate to rest. The liquid dissolves the fond (a process known as deglazing) and incorporates it into the sauce.

So what makes those browned bits so delicious, so valuable? When meat or chicken browns, a process called the Maillard reaction occurs. This process is named after the French chemist who first described this reaction about one hundred years ago. When the amino acids (or protein components) and natural sugars in meat are subjected to intense heat, like that found in a skillet, they begin to combine and form new compounds. These compounds in turn break down and form yet more new flavor compounds, and so on and so on. The process is like rabbits multiplying. The browned bits left in the pan once the meat has been cooked are packed with complex flavors, which in turn are carried over to the pan sauce once the fond has been dissolved.

BREADED CHICKEN CUTLETS

WHAT WE WANTED: Tender, well-seasoned chicken with an evenly browned, crisp crust.

Tender boneless chicken breast pan-fried with a cloak of mild-flavored crumbs has universal appeal. Chicken Milanese, with grated Parmesan cheese added to the coating, is arguably the most popular incarnation of this technique. Yet this simple dish can fall prey to a host of problems. The chicken itself may be rubbery and tasteless, and the coating—called a bound breading and arguably the best part of the dish—often ends up uneven, greasy, pale, or even burnt.

For a breaded chicken cutlet to be great, the chicken itself better hold up its end of the bargain. According to our tasters, that means starting with a premium chicken cutlet rather than a mass-market supermarket brand. Since the test kitchen is fiercely devoted to the benefits of brining poultry, we wondered what effect soaking the cutlets in a mixture of salt, sugar, and water would have. The brined cutlets were a hit, exceptionally juicy and seasoned all the way to the center. The brining step is easy to execute and takes just 30 minutes, during which time you can pull together other components of the recipe. It's not often that so little work yields such big benefits.

Throughout this first series of tests, we noticed that the thin tip of the cutlet and the opposite end, which was much more plump, cooked at different rates. This problem was a cinch to fix—all we had to do was pound the chicken breasts gently to an even ½-inch thickness with a meat pounder or the bottom of a small saucepan. To promote even cooking, we also found it best to remove the floppy tenderloin from the underside of each cutlet before pounding.

During the crumb testing (see Tasting Lab on page 120), we made several important observations about the breading process. First, we learned that the cutlets had to be thoroughly dried after brining. We also learned that we could not dispense with the coating of flour that went onto the chicken before the egg wash and crumbs. If the cutlets were even slightly moist, or if we skipped the flour coat, the breading would peel off the finished cutlets in sheets. Dry cutlets also produced the thinnest possible coating of flour, which mitigated any floury taste when the cutlets were cooked and served. In addition, we found that it was essential to press the crumbs onto the cutlets to assure an even, thorough cover. Finally, we discovered that it was best to let the breaded cutlets rest for about five minutes before frying them, again to help bind the breading to the meat.

The bread crumbs are attached to the floured cutlets by means of a quick dip into beaten egg. But beaten eggs are thick and viscous, and they tend to form too heavy a layer on the meat, giving the breading a thick, indelicate quality. Thinning the egg with oil, water, or both is a common practice that allows excess egg to slide off the meat more easily, leaving a thinner, more delicate coat. We tried all three routines, and honestly, we couldn't detect much difference in the flavor or texture of the finished breading. In repeated tests we did notice that the breading made with oil-thinned egg wash seemed to brown a little more deeply than that made with water-thinned wash, so we added a tablespoon of oil to our two beaten eggs and moved on.

Last we explored the details of pan-frying. In any breaded preparation, the oil in the pan should reach one-third to one-half way up the food for thorough browning. We pitted pure olive oil against vegetable oil, and top billing went to the vegetable oil for its light, unobtrusive presence. The olive oil contributed too much of its own flavor.

WHAT WE LEARNED: Brine the cutlets for 30 minutes to make them moist and juicy; pound to an even thickness for even cooking; and dip in flour, egg wash, and fresh bread crumbs, then fry in batches in vegetable oil, for the crispiest coating.

BREADED CHICKEN CUTLETS serves 4

If you'd rather not prepare fresh bread crumbs, use panko, extra-crisp Japanese bread crumbs. The chicken is cooked in batches of two because the crust is noticeably more crisp if the pan is not overcrowded. We found it pays to use a premium brand of chicken. We particularly like Bell & Evans cutlets.

4   boneless, skinless chicken breasts (5 to 6 ounces each), tenderloins removed and reserved for another use, fat trimmed (see illustration on page 115)
½   cup kosher salt or ¼ cup table salt
½   cup sugar
5–8 slices high-quality white bread, such as Pepperidge Farm, crusts removed and torn into rough 1½-inch pieces
    Ground black pepper
¾   cup all-purpose flour
2   large eggs
1   tablespoon plus ¾ cup vegetable oil
    Lemon wedges for serving

1. Use rubber mallet, meat pounder, or rolling pin to pound chicken breasts to even ½-inch thickness. Dissolve salt and sugar in 1 quart cold water in gallon-sized zipper-lock plastic bag. Add cutlets and seal bag, pressing out as much air as possible; refrigerate 30 minutes. Line rimmed baking sheet with triple layer of paper towels.

2. Remove cutlets and lay in single layer on baking sheet; cover with another triple layer paper towels and press firmly to absorb moisture. Allow cutlets to dry for 10 minutes. Process bread in food processor until evenly fine-textured, 20 to 30 seconds (you should have about 1¼ cups fresh bread crumbs). Transfer crumbs to pie plate. Carefully peel paper towels off cutlets, sprinkle cutlets with pepper, and set aside.

3. Adjust oven rack to lower-middle position, set heatproof plate on rack, and heat oven to 200 degrees. Spread flour in second pie plate. Beat eggs with 1 tablespoon oil in third pie plate.

4. Working one at a time, dredge cutlets thoroughly in flour, shaking off excess. Using tongs, dip both sides of cutlets in egg mixture, taking care to coat thoroughly, allowing excess to drip back into pie plate to ensure very thin coating. Dip both sides of cutlets in bread crumbs, pressing crumbs with fingers to form even, cohesive coat. Place breaded cutlets in single layer on wire rack set over baking sheet and allow coating to dry about 5 minutes.

5. Meanwhile, heat 6 tablespoons remaining oil in heavy-bottomed 10-inch nonstick skillet over medium-high heat until shimmering but not smoking, about 2 minutes. Lay two cutlets gently in skillet; cook until deep golden brown and crisp on first side, gently pressing down on cutlets with wide metal spatula to help ensure even browning, about 2½ minutes. Using tongs, flip cutlets, reduce heat to medium, and continue to cook until meat feels firm when pressed gently and second side is deep golden brown and crisp, 2½ to 3 minutes longer. Line warmed plate with double layer paper towels and set cutlets on top; return plate to oven.

6. Discard oil in skillet and wipe skillet clean using tongs and large wad paper towels. Repeat step 5 using remaining 6 tablespoons oil and now-clean skillet to cook remaining cutlets; serve along with first batch with lemon wedges.

VARIATIONS

CHICKEN MILANESE

Though Parmesan is classic in this dish, use Pecorino Romano if you prefer a more tangy flavor. Keep a close eye on the cutlets as they brown to make sure the cheese does not burn.

Follow recipe for Breaded Chicken Cutlets, substituting ¼ cup finely grated Parmesan cheese for an equal amount of bread crumbs.

PECAN-CRUSTED CHICKEN CUTLETS WITH INDIAN SPICES

Keep a close eye on the cutlets as they cook to make sure the nuts in the coating do not burn. If you prefer the pure flavor of pecans, feel free to leave out the spice mixture.

Mix 1 teaspoon garam masala, ¼ teaspoon ground cumin, and ¼ teaspoon ground coriander in small bowl. Follow recipe for Breaded Chicken Cutlets, rubbing each side of each cutlet with scant ¼ teaspoon of spice mixture before dredging in flour, and substituting 6 tablespoons very finely ground pecans for an equal amount of bread crumbs.

BREADED CHICKEN CUTLETS WITH GARLIC AND OREGANO

Follow recipe for Breaded Chicken Cutlets, beating 3 tablespoons very finely minced fresh oregano leaves and 8 medium garlic cloves, pressed through garlic press, grated, or minced to puree, into egg mixture in step 3.

DEVILED BREADED CHICKEN CUTLETS

Follow recipe for Breaded Chicken Cutlets, rubbing each side of each cutlet with generous pinch cayenne before dredging in flour, and beating 3 tablespoons Dijon mustard, 1 tablespoon Worcestershire sauce, and 2 teaspoons very finely minced fresh thyme leaves into egg mixture in step 3.

TASTING LAB: Bread Crumbs

THE IDEAL BREADING SHOULD TASTE MILD AND comforting, but not dull, and certainly not greasy. To explore the possibilities, we pan-fried cutlets coated with fine, fresh bread crumbs (made from fresh sliced sandwich bread ground fine in the food processor), dry bread crumbs, and Japanese panko crumbs.

The dry bread crumbs had an unmistakably stale flavor, while the panko crumbs rated well for their shattering crispness and wheaty flavor. But the fresh bread crumbs swept the test, with a mild, subtly sweet flavor and a light, crisp texture. We went on to test crumbs made from different kinds of white bread, including premium sliced sandwich bread, Italian, French, and country style. The sliced bread was the sweetest, and therefore, the favorite.

STUFFED CHICKEN CUTLETS

WHAT WE WANTED: A filling that is creamy without being runny, flavorful without overpowering the chicken. A crust that is crisp all over, without burnt spots, and that completely seals in the filling so that none leaks out.

Cutlets that are stuffed and breaded are special-occasion food. The filling coats the chicken from the inside with a creamy, tasty sauce, while the crust makes a crunchy counterpoint. They can be very good, but these little bundles pose a number of problems for the cook.

We first focused on the cooking method. We wanted to develop a technique that would crisp the exterior without overbrowning it before the center was fully cooked. Deep-frying was the obvious answer, but this option is really better suited to restaurants than home kitchens. We tested roasting, broiling, sautéing, and combinations of these methods. We found that two approaches warranted further exploration: Complete cooking in a skillet on the stovetop and stovetop browning followed by roasting.

We ran our next test on the stovetop, sautéing the breasts in just enough vegetable oil to generously coat the bottom of a sauté pan. This test revealed a number of problems. First, it was difficult to arrive at a heat level that would cook the chicken through without burning it. And the cutlets often stuck to the pan. Furthermore, even though the breasts in the pan were of only slightly different weights, their rates of cooking were different enough to be worrisome.

It seemed logical that the two-step method—a preliminary pan-frying on top of the stove followed by roasting in the even heat of the oven—would solve the twin problems of overbrowning and undercooking. We sautéed the next batch in oil that came one-third to halfway up the sides of the chicken, cooking until the chicken was well-browned all over. Then, to combat the sogginess we had observed in roasted breasts during the initial round of testing, we baked the chicken on a rack in a rimmed baking sheet so that hot air could circulate underneath the breasts.

The results were much improved: The breasts didn't stick to the pan; they came out of the oven evenly browned, with an excellent, crunchy coating; and the meat inside was not soggy but instead almost uniformly moist, with only the skinny tips of the breasts slightly dry. Because the time in the oven didn't significantly darken the crust, we could rely on this method for a perfect crust every time as long as we carefully supervised the stovetop browning.

We turned our attention to the stuffing. After several false starts, we concluded that pounding the breasts thin and rolling them up around the filling produced the most even distribution of filling and the most even cooking of the meat.

As for the content of the filling, we wanted something creamy but thick. Cheese was the obvious choice. After several tests, we concluded that beaten cream cheese provided the creamy consistency we wanted. It was thick and smooth. For flavor, we turned to more potent cheeses, such as cheddar and gorgonzola, along with seasonings such as browned onions, garlic, and herbs.

But there was still a problem. These stuffed cutlets had to be secured with toothpicks—sometimes multiple toothpicks in a single breast—all of which then had to be removed before the cutlets were sliced into medallions.

Luckily, getting over this hurdle turned out to be easier than we anticipated. We found that wrapping the breasts in aluminum foil and refrigerating them for one hour before breading and cooking cooled the cheese enough to hold the roll together. It also kept the cheese from seeping out of the crust during baking, all without any toothpicks.

WHAT WE LEARNED: Pound chicken breasts thin, then roll them up around a cheese filling. Refrigerate the filled cutlets before breading and cooking to prevent leaks. Sauté the stuffed cutlets to brown and crisp them, but finish them in the oven for even, thorough cooking.

STUFFED CHICKEN CUTLETS serves 4

The cutlets can be filled and rolled in advance, then refrigerated for up to 24 hours. To dry fresh bread crumbs, spread them out on a baking sheet and bake in a 200-degree oven, stirring occasionally, for 30 minutes. Removing some moisture from the crumbs cuts down on splattering when the breaded cutlets are pan-fried.

  4   boneless, skinless chicken breasts (5 to 6 ounces each), tenderloins removed and reserved for another use, fat trimmed (see illustration on page 115)
      Salt and ground black pepper
  1   recipe filling (recipes follow)
  ¾   cup all-purpose flour
  2   large eggs
  1   tablespoon plus ¾ cup vegetable oil
  1½ cups fresh bread crumbs, dried (see note)

1. Place each chicken breast on large sheet of plastic wrap, cover with second sheet, and pound with rubber mallet, meat pounder, or rolling pin until ¼ inch thick throughout. Each pounded breast should measure roughly 6 inches wide and 8¼ inches long. Cover and refrigerate while preparing filling.

2. Place cutlets smooth-side down on work surface; season with salt and pepper. Fill, roll, and wrap each breast (see illustrations on page 123). Refrigerate until filling is firm, at least 1 hour.

3. Adjust oven rack to lower-middle position; heat oven to 450 degrees. Spread flour in pie plate. Beat eggs with 1 tablespoon oil in second pie plate. Spread bread crumbs in third pie plate. Unwrap chicken breasts and roll in flour; shake off excess. Using tongs, roll breasts in egg mixture; let excess drip off. Transfer to bread crumbs; shake pan to roll breasts in crumbs, then press with fingers to help crumbs adhere. Place breaded cutlets on large wire rack set over baking sheet and allow coating to dry about 5 minutes.

4. Heat remaining ¾ cup oil in heavy-bottomed 10-inch nonstick skillet over medium-high heat until shimmering, but not smoking, about 4 minutes; add chicken, seam-side down, and cook until medium golden brown, about 2 minutes. Turn each roll and cook until medium golden brown on all sides, 2 to 3 minutes longer. Transfer chicken rolls, seam-side down, to wire rack set over rimmed baking sheet; bake until deep golden brown and instant-read thermometer inserted into center of a roll registers 155 degrees, about 15 minutes. Let stand 5 minutes before slicing each roll crosswise diagonally with serrated knife into 5 medallions; arrange on individual dinner plates and serve.

HAM AND CHEDDAR CHEESE FILLING
enough to stuff 4 cutlets

  1   tablespoon unsalted butter
  1   small onion, minced
  1   small clove garlic, minced
  4   ounces cream cheese, softened
  1   teaspoon minced fresh thyme leaves
  2   ounces cheddar cheese, shredded (about ½ cup)
      Salt and ground black pepper
  4   slices (about 4 ounces) thin-sliced cooked deli ham

1. Heat butter in medium skillet over low heat until melted; add onion and sauté, stirring occasionally, until deep golden brown, 15 to 20 minutes. Stir in garlic and cook until fragrant, about 30 seconds longer; set aside.

2. In medium bowl using hand mixer, beat cream cheese on medium speed until light and fluffy, about 1 minute. Stir in onion mixture, thyme, and cheddar; season with salt and pepper and set aside. To stuff cutlets, place one slice ham on top of cheese on each cutlet, folding ham as necessary to fit onto surface of cutlet.

ROASTED MUSHROOMS AND PROVOLONE CHEESE FILLING WITH ROSEMARY

To cook mushrooms, toss 10 ounces stemmed and quartered white mushrooms with 2 tablespoons olive oil and salt and pepper to taste on large rimmed baking sheet, then roast in 450-degree oven, turning once, until mushrooms are well browned, 20 to 25 minutes.

Follow recipe for Ham and Cheddar Cheese Filling, replacing cheddar cheese with 2 ounces shredded provolone (about ½ cup) and adding 1 tablespoon chopped fresh rosemary to cheese mixture. Replace ham with roasted mushrooms.

BROILED ASPARAGUS AND SMOKED MOZZARELLA CHEESE FILLING

To cook asparagus for this filling, toss trimmed spears with 2 teaspoons olive oil and salt and pepper to taste on a rimmed baking sheet, then broil until tender and browned, 6 to 8 minutes, shaking pan to rotate spears halfway through cooking time.

Follow recipe for Ham and Cheddar Cheese Filling, replacing cheddar cheese with 2 ounces shredded smoked mozzarella (about ½ cup). Replace ham with 16 medium asparagus, trimmed to 5-inch lengths and broiled. Place 4 asparagus spears horizontally on top of cheese on each cutlet, spacing them about 1 inch apart and trimming off ends if necessary.

GORGONZOLA CHEESE FILLING WITH WALNUTS AND FIGS

Two tablespoons of dried cherries or cranberries can be substituted for the figs.

Follow recipe for Ham and Cheddar Cheese Filling, replacing cheddar cheese with 2 ounces crumbled gorgonzola (about ½ cup). Stir in ¼ cup chopped toasted walnuts, 3 medium dried figs, stemmed and chopped (about 2 tablespoons), and 1 tablespoon dry sherry along with gorgonzola. Omit ham.

TECHNIQUE:
Preparing Stuffed Chicken Cutlets

1. Place each cutlet smooth-side down on work surface, season, and spread with one-quarter of cheese mixture.

2. Roll up each cutlet from the tapered end, folding in the edges to form a neat cylinder. To help seal the seams, wrap each stuffed cutlet in foil and twist the ends of the foil in opposite directions.

ALL-AMERICAN cookout

CHAPTER 10

The backyard cookout is a ritual of summer. You light the grill, gather friends and family, and throw some burgers and dogs over the coals. While this scene may conjure up visions of American life circa 1955, the food often pales in comparison to the memory.

Who hasn't made burgers that were overcooked or, worse still, glued to the grill rack? Even if you manage to remove the burgers from the grill safely and at the right time, they can puff up into round balls that roll right off the buns. How can something so simple be so hard to cook right?

Ever notice how the hot dogs disappear long before the burgers? That said, lots of hot dogs have a mushy texture or just don't taste good. In our Tasting Lab, we figure out which brands are the top dogs.

Finally, what's a summer cookout without some grilled veggies? But which vegetables respond best to grilling, and how do you keep delicate vegetables from scorching or sticking to the grill?

Take a deep breath. Summer cooking is supposed to be fun. We've moved the test kitchen out back and made these favorite dishes foolproof.

The alley behind the test kitchen was turned into the staging ground for our outdoor cooking segments. Julia reads through her notes, Shannon readies the burgers, and Dawn tends the fire, while the television crew takes a breather.

GRILLED HAMBURGERS

WHAT WE WANTED: A juicy, meaty tasting burger that cooks up level, not puffy.

I f you have the right ground beef, a perfect hamburger can be ready in less than 15 minutes, assuming you season, form, and cook it right. The biggest difficulty for many cooks, though, may be finding the right beef.

To test which cut or cuts of beef cook into the best burger, we ordered chuck, round, rump, sirloin, and hanging tenderloin, all ground to order with 20 percent fat. (Although we would question fat percentages in later testing, we needed a standard for these early tests. From past experience, this percentage seemed right.) After a side-by-side taste test, we quickly concluded that most cuts of ground beef are pleasant but bland when compared with the robust flavored ground chuck. Pricier ground sirloin, for example, cooked up into a particularly boring burger.

So pure ground chuck—the cut of beef that starts where the ribs end and moves up to the shoulder and neck, ending at the foreshank—was the clear winner. We were ready to race ahead to seasonings, but before moving on we stopped to ask ourselves, "Will cooks buying ground chuck straight out of the supermarket meat case agree with our choice?" Our efforts to determine whether supermarket ground chuck and ground-to-order chuck were even remotely similar took us along a culinary blue highway from kitchen to packing plant, butcher shop, and supermarket.

According to the National Live Stock and Meat Board, the fat content of beef is checked and enforced at the retail level. If a package of beef is labeled 90 percent lean, then it must contain no more than 10 percent fat, give or take a point. Retail stores are required to test each batch of ground beef, make the necessary adjustments, and keep a log of the results. Local inspectors routinely pull ground beef from a store's meat case for a fat check. If the tested meat is not within 1 percent of the package sticker, the store is fined.

Whether a package labeled ground chuck is, in fact, 100 percent ground chuck is a different story. We surveyed a number of grocery store meat department managers, who said that what was written on the label did match what was in the package. For instance, a package labeled "ground chuck" would contain only chuck trimmings. Same for sirloin and round. Only "ground beef" would contain mixed beef trimmings.

We got a little closer to the truth, however, by interviewing a respected butcher in the Chicago area, who spoke candidly. Of the several grocery stores and butcher shops he had worked at over the years, he had never known a store to segregate meat trimmings. In fact, in his present butcher shop, he sells only two kinds of ground beef—sirloin and chuck. He defines ground sirloin as ground beef (mostly but not exclusively sirloin) that's labeled 90 percent lean and chuck as ground beef (including a lot of chuck trimmings) that's labeled 85 percent lean.

Only meat ground at federally inspected plants is guaranteed to match its label. At these plants, an inspector checks to see if labeled ground beef actually comes from the cut of beef named on the label and if the fat percentage is correct.

Since retail ground beef labeling can be deceptive, we suggest buying a chuck roast and having the butcher grind it for you. Even at a local grocery store, the butcher was willing to grind to order. Some meat always gets lost in the grinder, so count on losing a bit (2 to 3 percent).

Because mass-ground beef also stands a greater chance of being contaminated by bacteria than nonground beef, it made theoretical sense to recommend grinding beef at home for those who want to reduce their odds of eating beef tainted with the bacterium E. coli. It doesn't make much practical sense, though. Not all cooks own a grinder. And even if they did, we thought home grinding demanded far too much setup, cleanup, and effort for a food meant to be so simple.

To see if there was an easier way, we tried chopping by

hand and grinding in the food processor. The hibachi-style (two knives, one in each hand) method of chopping was just as time-consuming and more messy than the traditional grinder. The food processor, however, did a good job grinding meat. We thought the steel blade would raggedly chew the meat, but to our surprise, the meat was evenly chopped and fluffy. (See the Equipment Corner on page 130.)

For those who buy a chuck roast for grinding, we found the average chuck roast to be about 80 percent lean. To check its leanness, we bought a chuck roast—not too fatty, not too lean—and ground it in the food processor. We took our ground chuck back to the grocery store for the butcher to check its fat content in the Univex Fat Analyzer, a machine the store uses to check the beef it grinds. A plug of our ground beef scored an almost perfect 21 percent fat when tested in the fat analyzer.

Up to this point, all of our beef had been ground with approximately 20 percent fat. A quick test of burgers with less and more fat helped us decide that 20 percent fat, give or take a few percentage points, was good for burgers. Any higher, and the burgers are just too greasy. Any lower, and you start compromising the beef's juicy, moist texture.

Working with fresh-ground chuck, seasoned with salt and pepper, we now moved into shaping and cooking. To test the warnings against overpacking and overhandling that you see in many recipes, we thoroughly worked a portion of ground beef before cooking it. The resulting burger had a well-done exterior that was nearly as dense as a meat pâté; its less well-done interior was compact and pasty.

All the same, it's actually pretty hard to overhandle a beef patty, especially if you're trying not to overhandle it. After dividing the meat into portions, we found that tossing the meat from one hand to another helped bring it together into a ball without overworking it. We made one of our most interesting discoveries when we tested various shaping techniques for the patties. A divot in the center of each burger ensures that they come off the grill with an even thickness instead of puffed up like a tennis ball. (See the Science Desk on page 130.)

We were now nearly done with our testing. We simply needed to perfect our grilling method. Burgers require a real blast of heat if they are to form a crunchy, flavorful crust before the interior overcooks. While many of the recipes we looked at advise grilling burgers over a hot fire, we suspected we'd have to adjust the heat because our patties were quite thin in the middle. Sure enough, a superhot fire made it too easy to overcook the burgers. We found a medium-hot fire formed a crust quickly while also providing a wider margin of error in terms of cooking the center. Nonetheless, burgers cook quickly—needing only 2 to 4 minutes per side. Don't walk away from the grill when cooking burgers.

One last finding from our testing: Don't ever press down on burgers as they cook. Rather than speeding their cooking, pressing on the patties serves only to squeeze out their juices and make the burgers dry.

WHAT WE LEARNED: **Don't buy beef that's already been ground. Instead, grind your own chuck in the food processor, or ask the butcher to do this for you. Make a divot in the center of each burger to prevent puffing. Grease the cooking rack to prevent sticking and grill over a medium-hot fire.**

CHARCOAL-GRILLED HAMBURGERS   serves 4

For those who like their burgers well-done, we found that poking a small hole in the center of the patty before cooking helped the center to cook through before the edges dried out. See illustrations on page 129 for tips on shaping burgers.

1½ pounds 100 percent ground chuck (about 80 percent lean)
1 teaspoon salt
½ teaspoon ground black pepper
Vegetable oil for grill rack
Buns and desired toppings

1. Light large chimney starter filled with hardwood charcoal (about 2½ pounds) and allow to burn until all charcoal is covered with layer of fine gray ash. Spread coals evenly over bottom of grill for medium-hot fire. (See how to gauge heat level on page 133.) Set cooking rack in place, cover grill with lid, and let rack heat up, about 5 minutes. Scrape cooking rack clean with wire brush.

2. Meanwhile, break up chuck to increase surface area for seasoning. Sprinkle salt and pepper over meat; toss lightly with hands to distribute. Divide meat into four equal portions (6 ounces each); with cupped hands, toss one portion back and forth to form loose ball. Pat lightly to flatten meat into ¾-inch-thick burger that measures about 4½ inches across. Press center of patty down with your fingertips until about ½ inch thick, creating well in center of patty. Repeat with remaining portions of meat.

3. Lightly dip a wad of paper towels in vegetable oil; holding wad with tongs, wipe grill rack (see illustration on page 130). Grill burgers, uncovered and without pressing down on them, until well seared on first side, about 2½ minutes. Flip burgers with wide metal spatula. Continue grilling to desired doneness, about 2 minutes for rare, 2½ minutes for medium-rare, 3 minutes for medium, or 4 minutes for well-done. Serve immediately.

GAS-GRILLED HAMBURGERS   serves 4

1½ pounds 100 percent ground chuck (about 80 percent lean)
1 teaspoon salt
½ teaspoon ground black pepper
Vegetable oil for grill rack
Buns and desired toppings

1. Preheat grill with all burners set to high and lid down until grill is very hot, about 15 minutes. Scrape cooking rack clean with wire brush. Leave both burners on high.

2. Meanwhile, break up chuck to increase surface area for seasoning. Sprinkle salt and pepper over meat; toss lightly with hands to distribute. Divide the meat into four equal portions (6 ounces each); with cupped hands, toss one portion back and forth to form loose ball. Pat lightly to flatten meat into ¾-inch-thick burger that measures about 4½ inches across. Press center of patty down with your fingertips until about ½ inch thick, creating well in center of patty. Repeat with remaining portions of meat.

3. Lightly dip a wad of paper towels in vegetable oil; holding wad with tongs, wipe grill rack (see illustration on page 130). Grill burgers, covered and without pressing down on them, until well seared on first side, about 3 minutes. Flip burgers with wide metal spatula. Continue grilling, covered, to desired doneness, about 3 minutes for rare, 3½ minutes for medium-rare, 4 minutes for medium, or 5 minutes for well-done. Serve immediately.

VARIATIONS
GRILLED CHEESEBURGERS
We like grating cheese into the raw beef. Since the cheese is evenly distributed, a little goes much further than when a big hunk of cheese is melted on top.

Follow recipe for Charcoal-Grilled Hamburgers or Gas-Grilled Hamburgers, sprinkling 3½ ounces cheddar, Swiss, Monterey Jack, or blue cheese, shredded or crumbled as necessary, over ground chuck along with salt and pepper.

GRILLED HAMBURGERS WITH GARLIC, CHIPOTLES, AND SCALLIONS
Toast 3 medium unpeeled garlic cloves in small dry skillet over medium heat, shaking pan occasionally, until fragrant and color deepens slightly, about 8 minutes. When cool enough to handle, skin and mince garlic. Follow recipe for Charcoal-Grilled Hamburgers or Gas-Grilled Hamburgers, mixing garlic, 1 tablespoon minced chipotle chile in adobo sauce, and 2 tablespoons minced scallions into meat along with salt and pepper.

GRILLED HAMBURGERS WITH COGNAC, MUSTARD, AND CHIVES
Mix 1½ tablespoons cognac, 2 teaspoons Dijon mustard, and 1 tablespoon minced fresh chives in small bowl. Follow recipe for Charcoal-Grilled Hamburgers or Gas-Grilled Hamburgers, mixing cognac mixture into meat along with salt and pepper.

GRILLED HAMBURGERS WITH PORCINI MUSHROOMS AND THYME
Cover ½ ounce dried porcini mushroom pieces with ½ cup hot tap water in small microwave-safe bowl; cover with plastic wrap, cut several steam vents with paring knife, and microwave on high power for 30 seconds. Let stand until mushrooms soften, about 5 minutes. Lift mushrooms from liquid with fork and mince using chef's knife (you should

---

TECHNIQUE: Shaping Hamburgers

1. With cupped hands, toss one portion of meat back and forth from hand to hand to shape it into a loose ball.

2. Pat lightly to flatten the meat into a ¾-inch-thick burger that measures about 4½ inches across. Press the center of the patty down with your fingertips until it is about ½ inch thick, creating a well in the center. Repeat with the remaining portions of ground meat.

have about 2 tablespoons). Follow recipe for Charcoal-Grilled Hamburgers or Gas-Grilled Hamburgers, mixing porcini mushrooms and 1 teaspoon minced fresh thyme leaves into meat along with salt and pepper.

EQUIPMENT CORNER:
Food Processor as Grinder

EVEN THOUGH WE HAVE A MEAT GRINDER IN THE kitchen, we don't regularly grind meat ourselves. The setup, breakdown, and washing up required to grind a 2-pound chuck roast just isn't worth the effort. Besides, hamburgers are supposed to be impromptu, fast, fun food.

To our surprise, though, the food processor does a respectable grinding job, and it's much easier to use than a grinder. The key is to make sure the roast is cold, cut into small chunks, and processed in small batches.

For a 2-pound roast, cut the meat into 1-inch chunks. Divide the chunks into four equal portions. Place one portion of meat in the workbowl of a food processor fitted with a steel blade. Pulse the cubes until the meat is ground, fifteen to twenty 1-second pulses. Repeat with the remaining portions of beef. Then shape the ground meat as directed.

SCIENCE DESK: Why Hamburgers Puff

ALL TOO OFTEN, BURGERS COME OFF THE GRILL WITH A domed, puffy shape that makes it impossible to keep condiments from sliding off. Fast-food restaurants produce burgers with an even surface, but these burgers are usually extremely thin. We wondered if there was a way to produce a heftier burger at home that was the same thickness from edge to edge, with no puffing.

We shaped 6-ounce portions of ground beef into patties that were 1 inch, ¾ inch, and ½ inch thick. Once cooked, all these burgers looked like tennis balls. After talking to several food scientists, we understood why this happens.

The culprit responsible for puffy burgers is the connective tissue, or collagen, ground up along with the meat. When the connective tissue in the patty heats up to roughly 130 degrees, it shrinks. This happens on the top and bottom flat surfaces first, and then on the sides, where the tightening acts like a belt. When the sides tighten, the interior meat volume is forced up and out, so the burger puffs.

One of the cooks in the test kitchen suggested a trick she had picked up when working in a restaurant. We shaped patties ¾ inch thick but then formed a slight depression in the center of each one so that the edges were thicker than the center. On the grill, the center puffed so that it was now the same height as the edges. Finally, a level burger that could hold onto toppings.

TECHNIQUE: Oiling the Grill Rack

We find it helpful to oil the grill rack just before cooking foods that are prone to sticking, such as burgers, fish, and some vegetables. Dip a large wad of paper towels in vegetable oil, grab the wad with tongs, and wipe the grill rack thoroughly to lubricate it and prevent sticking. Wiping the grill rack also cleans off any residue you may have missed when scraping it with a wire brush—something we recommend that you do each time you grill.

TASTING LAB: Ketchup

FOR MANY PEOPLE, A BURGER ISN'T DONE UNTIL IT HAS been coated liberally with ketchup. This condiment originated in Asia as a salty, fermented medium for pickling or preserving ingredients, primarily fish. Early versions were made with anchovies and generally were highly spiced.

Tomato-based ketchup has its origins in 19th-century America. We now consume more than 600 million pints of ketchup every year, much of it landing on top of burgers. But as any ketchup connoisseur knows, not all brands are created equal. To find out which is the best, we tasted 13 samples, including several fancy mail-order ketchups and one that we made from scratch in our test kitchen.

It wasn't much of a surprise that the winner was Heinz. For all tasters but one, Heinz ranked first or second and was described as "classic" and "perfect." A tiny bit sweeter than Heinz, Del Monte took second place, while Hunt's (the other leading national brand, along with Heinz and Del Monte) took third place.

What about the mail-order, organic, fruit-sweetened, and homemade ketchups? Most tasters felt these samples were overly thick and not smooth enough. Some were too spicy, others too vinegary. Our homemade ketchup was too chunky, more like "tomato jam" that ketchup. In color, consistency, and flavor, none of these interlopers could match the ketchup archetype, Heinz.

EQUIPMENT CORNER: Hamburger Presses

WE HAVE FORMED PLENTY OF HAMBURGERS IN OUR TEST kitchen. While we don't consider patting a burger out by hand to be a problem, we wondered about all the gadgets specifically designed for this task. Could they make a simple task even simpler?

We rounded up four models and began testing. All of the presses easily accommodated 6-ounce portions of ground meat. That said, the only general advantage we could find to these gadgets was that they kept your hands from becoming overly greasy by limiting contact with the meat. As advantages go, this was pretty weak. You still have to touch the meat and thus wash your hands well. We suggest that you save your money and cabinet space for something more useful.

TASTING LAB: Hot Dogs

WHAT'S A BACKYARD BARBECUE WITHOUT SOME HOT dogs? We tasted nine brands of nationally available all-beef hot dogs, along with a deli-style hot dog sold in links at a local supermarket and made with natural casings. Since kids are such a big market for hot dogs, we departed from tradition with this tasting and assembled two panels instead of one. The first comprised 15 adults; the second a dozen third- and fifth-grade children. To make things easier for the kids, we served them just three brands of hot dogs—the top two finishers from the adult tasting and one of the adults' lowest rated dogs.

Hot dogs are made from meat trimmings, the same meat that would go into hamburger or other sausages. Trimmings should not be confused with variety meats—hearts, kidney, liver, etc. If variety meats are used, which nowadays is uncommon for hot dogs, the manufacturer is required by federal law to state on the front of the package "with variety meats" or "with meat byproducts." Hot dogs can contain nonmeat binders, such as nonfat dry milk, cereal, dried whole milk, or isolated soy protein. These must also be identified in the ingredients list.

Other hot dog ingredients include water (added in the form of ice) and curing or preserving agents—salt, nitrite, sugar, spices, and seasonings (typically coriander, garlic, ground mustard, nutmeg, and white pepper). Nitrite is a chemical that interacts with muscle pigment, myoglobin, to create the hot dog's characteristic pink color. It also lends a characteristic flavor. Most important, though, it prevents the growth of organisms that can cause botulism.

The process of making hot dogs is a source of intrigue for most eaters. Basically, meat trimmings are ground into a paste and then placed in a high-speed mixer along with spices, ice chips (to keep the meat cold), and curing ingredients. This forms a thick liquid that is pumped into casings. Most brands use inedible plastic casings, which are later removed. Traditional natural casings are costly and therefore less common. The filled casings are then moved to a smokehouse, where they are fully cooked. Finally, they are showered in cool water, sent to an automatic peeler to be stripped of the casings (if not natural casings), and vacuum-sealed.

What seemed to make or break a hot dog for our panels of tasters was meaty flavor with a balance of seasonings. They also required decent chewability. The deli-style dog was indisputably the top pick among the adult tasters. The manufacturer, a supermarket chain in the Northeast, was reluctant to give away any recipe secrets as to what made this hot dog stand out. A spokesman did say it was formulated after an old-fashioned hot dog with natural casings and "quality ingredients." The children were not quite as enthusiastic about the deli-style dog. The flavor and chew were a little too adult for their tastes.

The kids chose Ball Park franks as their favorite (the second-place finisher among adults). For similar reasons as the adults, the kids decisively rejected the dog that received the worst rating from adults.

All but one of the hot dogs that received poor ratings were unpalatably mushy and weak on beef flavor. The very worst of all the dogs was a brand purchased at a large natural foods chain store. The meat was uncured and contained no nitrites. Unlike its cohorts in the reject bin, it had chew. This was not much help, however, as tasters likened it to both leather and a spicy rubber sausage.

Aside from the obvious differences in products, such as the amount and type of spices used, there are more complex differences. The heart of a hot dog's flavor intensity is carried in the fat, so less fat often means less flavor. This was obvious in the flavorless low-fat product we tasted, but we found no particular correlation between fat and flavor in the regular dogs. As for texture, the addition of nonmeat binders, such as nonfat dry milk and cereal starches, seem to make a hot dog less firm. Significantly, the leading two hot dogs did not contain any such binders.

Cooking hot dogs is remarkably simple as long as you avoid the most common pitfall—burning the dogs. We found it best to grill hot dogs over a medium-hot fire (the same temperature we use to cook burgers). Avoid a scorching hot fire, which is likely to singe hot dogs. Let the hot dogs cook for two minutes, or until they plump and begin to show grill marks. At this point, start turning the hot dogs every 30 seconds to promote even browning. After a total of about four minutes over a medium-hot fire, hot dogs will be plump, lightly browned, and ready to serve.

TECHNIQUE:
Judging the Heat Level of a Grill Fire

Test the temperature of the grill by holding your hand 5 inches above the grill rack. If you can hold your hand there for three to four seconds, the fire is medium-hot. If you can hold your hand there for only three seconds, the fire is hot. If you can hold your hand there for two seconds or less, the fire is very hot.

GRILLED VEGETABLES

WHAT WE WANTED: Vegetables that are lightly streaked with grill marks and cooked just until crisp-tender.

Grilling vegetables should be easy. You've made a fire to grill a couple of steaks, some swordfish, or maybe a few burgers and hot dogs. There are some vegetables in the fridge, and you want to turn them into a side dish without having to heat up your kitchen. It sounds simple, but a number of questions immediately arise. Do you have to precook the vegetables? How thick should each vegetable be sliced? What's the best temperature for grilling them?

We decided at the outset that we wanted to develop guidelines for grilling as many kinds of vegetables as possible without precooking them. Blanching, baking, or microwaving is not hard, but each does add an extra step and time to what should be a simple process. In addition, blanching and baking heat up the kitchen. We wanted to blanch only when absolutely necessary.

Vegetables don't respond well to blazing fires—incineration is a real possibility. We found that most vegetables are best cooked over a medium or medium-hot fire. We played around with wood chips (both hickory and mesquite) and found no perceptible change in flavor. Vegetables do not cook long enough to pick up any wood flavor. If you happen to have chips on the grill to cook something else, they won't do any harm, but don't expect them to add great flavor to the vegetables.

A better way to season vegetables is to brush them with flavored oil just before grilling. (Marinating is not advised because the acids will make vegetables soggy; portobello mushrooms are the one exception.) Make sure to use a good-quality olive or peanut oil. (We found that vegetables brushed with canola, corn, or other bland oils were boring.) Try adding fresh herbs, garlic, and/or grated citrus zest to the oil, or purchase one that is already flavored. Seasoning with salt and pepper both before and after grilling is another way to maximize flavor.

A lot of equipment exists out there for grilling, much of it designed for vegetables. We tried grilling vegetables in a hinged metal basket and didn't find it to be very practical. One part of the grill is always hotter or colder than another, and, invariably, some vegetables are ready to be turned before others. Large vegetables (everything from asparagus spears to sliced zucchini) are best cooked right on the grill rack.

You can skewer smaller items (like cherry tomatoes and white mushrooms) to keep them from falling through the rack. Wooden skewers are generally quite thin (which is good), but they can burn. Metal skewers are a better option. Just make sure they are thin. Thick metal skewers are fine for meat but will tear mushrooms and cherry tomatoes.

The other option is to grill small vegetables on a grill grid or vegetable grid. This gadget prevents the vegetables from falling through the rack but allows you to turn each piece of food individually when it has browned sufficiently. A grill grid is typically made out of crosshatched wires or a single sheet of perforated metal. The grid goes right on top of the cooking rack. Once the grid is hot, small vegetables can be cooked on it.

Whether cooking vegetables on the grill surface or a grid, make sure the surface is clean. Vegetables will pick up any off flavors from the grill, so scrape the surface with a wire brush just before placing the vegetables on the grill.

If using a charcoal grill, cook the vegetables with the cover off to prevent them from picking up any stale smoke odors. If using a gas grill, cook the vegetables with the cover down to concentrate the heat.

WHAT WE LEARNED: Cook vegetables over a moderate fire to prevent burning, coat them with olive oil or peanut oil to boost flavor and prevent sticking, and don't bother with a hinged vegetable basket.

GRILLED CORN   serves 4 to 8

While grilling husk-on corn delivers great pure corn flavor, it lacks the smokiness of the grill; essentially, the corn is steamed in its protective husk. By leaving only the innermost layer, we were rewarded with perfectly tender corn graced with the grill's flavor. Prepared in this way, the corn does not need basting with oil.

> 8 ears fresh corn, prepared according to
>   illustrations below
>   Salt and ground black pepper
>   Butter (optional)

TECHNIQUE: Preparing Corn

1. Remove all but the innermost layer of the husk. The kernels should be covered by, but visible through, the last husk.

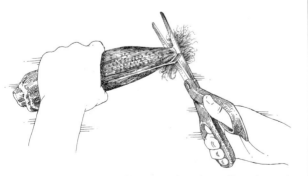

2. Use scissors to snip off the tassel, or long silk ends, at the tip of the ear.

---

1. Grill corn over a medium-hot fire (see how to gauge heat level on page 133), turning ears every 1½ to 2 minutes, until dark outlines of kernels show through husk and husk is charred and beginning to peel away from tip to expose some kernels, 8 to 10 minutes.

2. Transfer corn to platter; carefully remove and discard charred husk and silk. Season corn with salt and pepper to taste and butter, if desired. Serve immediately.

VARIATIONS

GRILLED CORN WITH HERB BUTTER

Brush with herb butter just before serving.

Melt 6 tablespoons unsalted butter in small saucepan. Add 3 tablespoons minced fresh parsley, thyme, cilantro, basil, and/or other fresh herbs and salt and pepper to taste; keep butter warm. Follow recipe for Grilled Corn, brushing herb butter over grilled corn in step 2.

GRILLED CORN WITH GARLIC BUTTER AND CHEESE

The buttery, nutty flavor of Parmesan cheese works surprisingly well with the flavor of grilled corn.

Melt 6 tablespoons unsalted butter in small saucepan over medium heat until bubbling. Add 1 minced garlic clove and cook until fragrant, about 30 seconds. Remove pan from heat and stir in ¼ teaspoon salt. Follow recipe for Grilled Corn, brushing butter over grilled corn in step 2. Sprinkle with ¼ cup grated Parmesan cheese and serve immediately.

TECHNIQUE: Preparing Endive

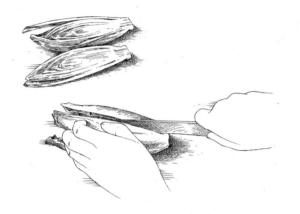

With a knife, shave off the discolored end of the endive. Cut the endive in half lengthwise through the core. Cut this way, the halves stay intact for easy grilling.

TECHNIQUE: Preparing Radicchio

Remove any brown outer leaves. Cut the radicchio in half through the core. Cut each half again through the core to make four wedges.

GRILLED BELGIAN ENDIVE   serves 8

Although we generally think of crisp and crunchy Belgian endive in terms of salads, it grills beautifully. The texture softens, but the vegetable holds its shape. Best of all, the bitter flavor mellows a bit when exposed to intense heat.

    8   medium heads Belgian endive, prepared
        according to illustration at left
    3   tablespoons extra-virgin olive oil or basting oil
        (see page 138)
        Salt and ground black pepper

1. Toss endive halves in large bowl with oil and season with salt and pepper to taste.

2. Grill endive over medium-hot fire (see how to gauge heat level on page 133), turning once, until dark grill marks appear and center of each is crisp-tender, 5 to 7 minutes. Serve hot, warm, or at room temperature.

GRILLED RADICCHIO   serves 4

To prevent radicchio from burning, it is necessary to brush the pieces with a fair amount of olive oil. For maximum grill flavor, turn each wedge of radicchio twice so that each side spends some time facing the fire.

    3   medium heads radicchio, cut into quarters with
        core intact (see illustration at left)
    4   tablespoons extra-virgin olive oil or basting oil
        (see page 138)
        Salt and ground black pepper

1. Place radicchio wedges on large rimmed baking sheet and brush all sides with oil. Season with salt and pepper to taste.

2. Grill radicchio over a medium-hot fire (see how to gauge heat level on page 133), turning every 1½ minutes, until edges are browned and wilted but centers remain slightly firm, about 4½ minutes total. Serve immediately.

GRILLED FENNEL serves 4

Fennel grills beautifully. Its anise flavor is complemented by the caramelization of natural sugars on the surface of the vegetable. The trickiest part is cutting the fennel so that it does not fall through the rack. We found that slicing it vertically into sections 1/4 inch thick, with a piece of the core still attached, keeps the layers intact.

 2 medium fennel bulbs (about 2 pounds), prepared according to illustrations below
 3 tablespoons extra-virgin olive oil or basting oil (see page 138)
    Salt and ground black pepper

1. Toss fennel and oil together in large bowl. Season with salt and pepper to taste.

2. Grill fennel over medium-hot fire (see how to gauge heat level on page 133), turning once, until tender and streaked with dark grill marks, 7 to 9 minutes. Serve hot, warm, or at room temperature.

GRILLED PORTOBELLO MUSHROOMS serves 4

Because of their dense, meaty texture, portobellos—unlike other vegetables—can be marinated. If you can find only smaller portobellos (say, about 4 inches across), use six mushrooms (and six pieces of foil) and reduce the grilling time wrapped in foil to 9 minutes.

 1/2 cup extra-virgin olive oil
   3 tablespoons juice from 1 lemon
   6 medium cloves garlic, minced fine (about 2 tablespoons)
 1/4 teaspoon salt
   4 medium portobello mushrooms, each 5 to 6 inches (or about 6 ounces each), stems removed and discarded, caps wiped clean

1. Combine oil, lemon juice, garlic, and salt in large zipper-lock bag. Add mushrooms; seal bag and gently shake to coat mushrooms with marinade. Refrigerate until seasoned, about 1 hour.

2. Cut four 12-inch-square pieces of foil. Remove mushrooms from marinade and place foil squares on work surface. Set one mushroom on top of each piece of foil, gill-side up, and fold foil edges over to enclose mushroom and seal edges.

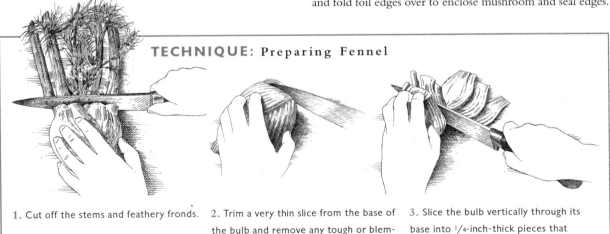

TECHNIQUE: Preparing Fennel

1. Cut off the stems and feathery fronds.

2. Trim a very thin slice from the base of the bulb and remove any tough or blemished outer layers.

3. Slice the bulb vertically through its base into 1/4-inch-thick pieces that resemble fans.

3. Grill mushrooms, with sealed sides of foil packets facing up, over medium-hot fire (see how to gauge heat level on page 133), until juicy and tender, 10 to 12 minutes. Using tongs, unwrap mushrooms and discard foil; set unwrapped mushrooms on rack gill-side up and cook until grill-marked, 30 to 60 seconds. Serve mushrooms hot.

VARIATION

GRILLED PORTOBELLO MUSHROOMS WITH TARRAGON

This variation is great served with burgers.

Combine 2 teaspoons rice vinegar, 1 minced garlic clove, 1 tablespoon chopped fresh tarragon leaves, ¼ teaspoon salt, and 2 tablespoons vegetable oil in medium bowl. Add Grilled Portobello Mushrooms and ground black pepper to taste. Toss to coat and serve immediately or cover with plastic wrap and let stand at room temperature for up to 30 minutes.

GARLIC BASTING OIL FOR VEGETABLES
makes about ½ cup

For extra flavor, use this basting oil, or the one that follows, instead of plain olive oil when cooking endive, fennel, or radicchio. These flavored oils work well with other vegetables, too, including peppers, onions, mushrooms, asparagus, and zucchini.

  ½   cup extra-virgin olive oil
  1   small clove garlic, minced to a paste or pressed through garlic press

Combine ingredients in small bowl; let stand to infuse flavors, about 10 minutes. Use while fresh and discard any unused oil.

LEMON-ROSEMARY BASTING OIL FOR VEGETABLES   makes about ½ cup

  ½   cup extra-virgin olive oil
  1   teaspoon minced fresh rosemary leaves
  1   teaspoon grated zest plus 1 tablespoon juice from 1 lemon

Combine ingredients in small bowl; let stand to infuse flavors, about 10 minutes. Use while fresh and discard any unused oil.

EQUIPMENT CORNER: Gas Grills

GAS GRILLS NOW ACCOUNT FOR 6 OUT OF 10 GRILLS sold in this country. The reasons for their increasing popularity are clear: The fire is easy to light and control. While there are few options when buying a charcoal grill, there are dozens and dozens of gas grills on the market. We tested six from the leading manufacturers and came to the following conclusions.

In general, we found that you get what you pay for. Inexpensive gas grills, priced at $200 or less, are generally inferior. If you are willing to spend more money (about $400), you can buy a gas grill that works extremely well, with results that can compete with a charcoal grill.

There are several features and design elements that separate a good grill from a poor one. A built-in thermometer that registers real numbers (not just low, medium, and hot) is essential. A gauge that tells you how much gas is left in the tank is also a plus.

As you might expect, a large grill offers the cook more possibilities. Unless the cooking surface has an area of at least 400 square inches, you will need to cook one slab of ribs at a time. (If the grill comes with a warming rack, you can cook a second slab there.)

In addition to size, the number of burners is critical. It's not possible to cook by indirect heat on a grill with only one burner, because the burner is usually positioned in the center of the grill and the "cool" parts of the grill are too small to fit most foods. You need a grill with at least two burners. With one burner on and one burner off, at least half of the grill will be cool enough for slow cooking.

The heat should be evenly distributed across the entire surface of the grill. We found that most gas grills are plenty hot. A bigger problem is that gas grills are often unable to sustain temperatures low enough for barbecuing. Many of the cheaper grills we tested were unable to barbecue a brisket without burning the exterior before the meat was tender. A good grill will heat up to 600 degrees and maintain a temperature of 250 degrees when the lid is down and just one burner is lit and turned to low.

Perhaps the most shocking conclusion we came to during our testing of gas grills concerns the cause of flare-ups. We found that lava rocks soak up dripping fat and catch fire as soon as there is some sort of flare-up. Several times we moved flaming chicken parts to the cool side of the grill (without a lit burner), and they still flamed from below for several minutes. It wasn't the chicken that was on fire, rather, the lava rocks had caught fire even though the burner underneath those rocks was cool.

Lava rocks are not the sole reason for flare-ups. Poor design that traps grease on the bottom of the grill doesn't help either. We consider a drainage system mandatory. The bottom of the cooking chamber should be sloped so that fat runs through an opening in the center and into a drip pan below.

Weber grills do not have lava rocks. Bars, made from steel coated with porcelain-enamel and shaped like an upside down V, channel fat down into the bottom of the grill and eventually into a drip pan attached to the underside of the cooking chamber. We find this drainage system far superior to others. For this (and the reasons stated above), these grills are our favorites.

If you entertain a lot, you will want the bigger and more expensive Weber Genesis Silver B with three burners. If your needs (or budget) are more modest, the two-burner Weber Genesis Silver A is an excellent choice.

Most gas grills come with two temperature controls, each regulating a separate burner. You can use the dials to change the heat level on the entire grill, turning it from high to medium once food has been seared. The dials can also be manipulated to create two heat levels on the cooking surface at the same time. For instance, you may set one burner at high for searing and set the other at medium to cook foods through or to have a place to move foods if they ignite.

Another note about gas grills. Unlike charcoal grills, the inside of the cover stays fairly clean because there is no buildup of resinous smoke. The grill cover can thus be used in recipes that call for a cover to cook foods through, such as grilled chicken breasts.

To make sure a gas grill is good and hot, always preheat with all burners turned to high and the lid down for 15 minutes. Then adjust the burners as directed in recipes, scrape the grill surface clean with a wire brush, and place the food on the grill to cook.

Unless you know you are going to need it, you may want to remove the warming rack before lighting the grill. On most grills, the rack is very close to the cooking surface, and it can be hard to reach foods on the back of the grill without burning your hands on the hot metal.

MIDDLE EASTERN barbecue

CHAPTER 11

The backyard barbecue always seems so familiar, so American. But grilling is practiced in almost every country around the globe. Shish kebab—skewers of lamb and vegetables—is perhaps the greatest "barbecue" dish from Turkey and the Middle East. When done right, the lamb is well browned but not overcooked, and the vegetables are crisp and tender. Everything is perfumed with the flavor of smoke.

When we make shish kebab, we like to offer other popular Middle Eastern dishes. Rice is a natural partner for shish kebab, and we think rice pilaf is the best choice. If you've only had rice pilaf from a box, you don't know how good this dish can be. Real rice pilaf is fluffy and fragrant. The grains are long and separate, tender but not mushy. The flavors of warm spices, nuts, and dried fruits take "plain rice" to new heights.

To start the meal, we serve baba ghanoush—the region's famous eggplant dip. Although this dip ends up in a bowl, the recipe begins on the grill, where the eggplant is cooked and flavored. The challenge here is to keep the focus on the eggplant, complementing it by adding just the right amount of garlic, sesame, and lemon.

Trays of eggplants are ready to be grill-roasted and then made into baba ghanoush.

SHISH KEBAB

WHAT WE WANTED: Lamb that cooks at the same rate as the vegetables on the skewer so that neither is raw or charred.

Shish kebab's components cook at different rates—either the vegetables are still crunchy when the meat is cooked perfectly to medium-rare, or the lamb is long overdone by the time the vegetables have been cooked properly. Our efforts to resolve this dilemma led us to explore which cut of lamb and which vegetables serve the kebab best. Getting the grill temperature just right was another challenge. Too hot, and the kebabs charred on the outside without being fully cooked; too cool, and they cooked without the benefit of flavorful browning.

Lamb can be expensive, so we searched for a cut that would give us tender, flavorful kebabs without breaking the bank. We immediately ruled out high-end cuts like loin and rib chops, which fetch upward of $14.99 per pound. Sirloin and shoulder chops are meatier and far more reasonable at $4.99 per pound. Each of these, however, requires cutting the meat off the bone before trimming and cubing. The best cut turned out to be the shank end of a boneless leg of lamb. It requires little trimming, yields the perfect amount of meat for four to six people, and can be purchased for about $6.99 per pound.

Lamb has a supple, chewy texture that behaves best when cut into small pieces. We found 1-inch pieces of lamb to be the optimal size for kebabs. With the meat cut and ready to go, we could now focus on the vegetables.

Many vegetables don't cook through by the time the lamb reaches the right temperature. This can be particularly ugly if you're using eggplant, mushrooms, or zucchini. We tried precooking the vegetables, but they turned slimy and were difficult to skewer. We thought about cooking them separately alongside the lamb on the grill, but that's just not shish kebab. Other vegetables, such as cherry tomatoes, initially looked great on the skewer but had a hard time hanging on once cooked.

As we worked our way through various vegetables, we came up with two that work well within the constraints of this particular cooking method. Red onions and bell peppers have a similar texture and cook through at about the same rate. When cut fairly small, these two vegetables were the perfect accompaniments to the lamb, adding flavor and color to the kebab without demanding any special attention.

What these handsome kebabs needed now was a little seasoned help, so we tried a variety of spices, dry rubs, and marinades on the meat. Spice rubs tasted good but left the surface of the meat chalky and dry; kebabs just aren't on the fire long enough for their juices to mix with the dried spices and form a glaze. Marinades, on the other hand, added a layer of moisture that kept the kebabs from drying out on the grill while their flavors penetrated the meat. Two hours in the marinade was sufficient time to achieve some flavor, but it took a good eight hours for these flavors to really sink in. Marinating for 12 hours, or overnight, was even better.

We were aware of the pitfalls of a mismanaged grill. The idea was to get a nice caramelization around the edges of the kebab without overcooking the interior of the small pieces of meat. A medium fire didn't work, turning the lamb an unappealing gray while leaving no grill marks behind. By the time the medium-hot fire turned out some decent grill marks, the meat was overcooked and a bit dry. A sizzling hot fire turned out to be the ticket, cooking the kebabs perfectly in only seven to eight minutes, about two minutes per side for medium-rare to medium. Tasters agreed that these kebabs tasted best when the meat was cooked to medium-rare; well-done lamb tasted "too muttony."

WHAT WE LEARNED: Use boneless leg of lamb, marinate for best flavor, limit vegetables to onions and peppers, and cook quickly over high heat.

CHARCOAL-GRILLED SHISH KEBAB serves 6

Cutting up the onion so the pieces will stay together on skewers is a little tricky. After substantial testing, we found that this method works best: Trim away stem and root end and cut the onion into quarters. Peel the three outer layers of the onion away from the inner core. Working with the outer layers only, cut each quarter—from pole to pole—into three strips of equal width. Cut each of the 12 strips crosswise into three pieces. (You should have 36 small stacks of three layers each.)

  1   recipe marinade (recipes follow)
2¼   pounds boneless leg of lamb (shank end),
      trimmed of fat and silver skin and cut into
      1-inch pieces
  3   medium bell peppers, 1 red, 1 yellow, and
      1 orange (about 1½ pounds), each cut into
      twenty-four 1-inch pieces
  1   large red onion (about 12 ounces), cut into
      thirty-six ¾-inch pieces (see note)
      Lemon or lime wedges for serving (optional)

1. Toss marinade and lamb in gallon-sized zipper-lock plastic bag or large, nonreactive bowl; seal bag, pressing out as much air as possible, or cover bowl and refrigerate until fully seasoned, at least 2 hours and up to 24 hours.

2. Ignite about 6 quarts (1 large chimney, or 2½ pounds) hardwood charcoal and burn until covered with light gray ash, 20 to 30 minutes. Spread coals over grill bottom, then spread 6 more quarts unlit charcoal over lit coals. Position grill rack over coals and heat until very hot, about 15 minutes. (See how to gauge heat level on page 133.)

3. Meanwhile, starting and ending with meat, thread 4 pieces meat, 3 pieces onion (three 3-layer stacks), and 6 pieces pepper in mixed order on 12 metal skewers.

4. Grill kebabs, uncovered, until meat is well browned all over, grill-marked, and cooked to medium-rare, about 7 minutes (or 8 minutes for medium), turning each kebab one-quarter turn every 1¾ minutes to brown all sides. Transfer kebabs to serving platter, squeeze lemon or lime wedges over kebabs if desired, and serve immediately.

GAS-GRILLED SHISH KEBAB serves 6

  1   recipe marinade (recipes follow)
2¼   pounds boneless leg of lamb (shank end),
      trimmed of fat and silver skin and cut into
      1-inch pieces
  3   medium bell peppers, 1 red, 1 yellow, and
      1 orange (about 1½ pounds), each cut into
      twenty-four 1-inch pieces
  1   large red onion (about 12 ounces), cut into
      thirty-six ¾-inch pieces (see note under
      Charcoal-Grilled Shish Kebab)
      Lemon or lime wedges for serving (optional)

1. Toss marinade and lamb in gallon-sized zipper-lock plastic bag or large, nonreactive bowl; seal bag, pressing out as much air as possible, or cover bowl and refrigerate until fully seasoned, at least 2 hours and up to 24 hours.

2. Turn all burners on gas grill to high, close lid, and heat grill until hot, 10 to 15 minutes.

3. Meanwhile, starting and ending with meat, thread 4 pieces meat, 3 pieces onion (three 3-layer stacks), and 6 pieces pepper in mixed order on 12 metal skewers.

4. Grill kebabs, covered, until meat is well browned all over, grill-marked, and cooked to medium-rare, about 8 minutes (or 9 minutes for medium), turning each kebab one-quarter turn every 2 minutes to brown all sides. Transfer kebabs to serving platter, squeeze lemon or lime wedges over kebabs if desired, and serve immediately.

WARM-SPICED PARSLEY MARINADE WITH GINGER   enough for 1 recipe of shish kebab

- ½ cup (packed) fresh parsley leaves
- 1 jalapeño chile, seeded and chopped coarse
- 1 (2-inch) piece fresh ginger, peeled and chopped coarse
- 3 medium cloves garlic, peeled
- 1 teaspoon ground cumin
- 1 teaspoon ground cardamom
- 1 teaspoon ground cinnamon
- ½ cup olive oil
- 1 teaspoon salt
- ⅛ teaspoon ground black pepper

Process all ingredients in workbowl of food processor fitted with steel blade until smooth, about 1 minute, stopping to scrape sides of workbowl with rubber spatula as needed.

GARLIC AND CILANTRO MARINADE WITH GARAM MASALA   enough for 1 recipe of shish kebab

- ½ cup (packed) fresh cilantro leaves
- 3 medium cloves garlic, peeled
- ¼ cup dark raisins
- ½ teaspoon garam masala
- 1½ tablespoons juice from 1 lemon
- ½ cup olive oil

- 1 teaspoon salt
- ⅛ teaspoon ground black pepper

Process all ingredients in workbowl of food processor fitted with steel blade until smooth, about 1 minute, stopping to scrape sides of workbowl with rubber spatula as needed.

SWEET CURRY MARINADE WITH BUTTERMILK   enough for 1 recipe of shish kebab

- ¾ cup buttermilk
- 1 tablespoon juice from 1 lemon
- 3 medium cloves garlic, minced
- 1 tablespoon brown sugar
- 1 tablespoon curry powder
- 1 teaspoon crushed red pepper flakes
- 1 teaspoon ground coriander
- 1 teaspoon chili powder
- 1 teaspoon salt
- ⅛ teaspoon ground black pepper

Combine all ingredients in gallon-sized, zipper-lock plastic bag or large, nonreactive bowl in which meat will marinate.

ROSEMARY-MINT MARINADE WITH GARLIC AND LEMON   enough for 1 recipe of shish kebab

- 10 large fresh mint leaves
- 1½ teaspoons chopped fresh rosemary
- 2 tablespoons juice plus ½ tablespoon minced zest from 1 lemon
- 3 medium cloves garlic, peeled
- ½ cup olive oil
- 1 teaspoon salt
- ⅛ teaspoon ground black pepper

Process all ingredients in workbowl of food processor fitted with steel blade until smooth, about 1 minute, stopping to scrape sides of workbowl with rubber spatula as needed.

SCIENCE DESK: Do Marinades Work?

CAN TOUGH CUTS OF BEEF, LAMB, AND PORK YIELD TENDER results if marinated long enough? Many cookbooks suggest tenderizing meat in acidic marinades, often for several days. The theory here is pretty straightforward: Acids, such as lemon juice, vinegar, and wine, cause protein strands to break apart. Over time, as more and more proteins disassemble, the meat softens. What actually happens in the refrigerator under real-life conditions is another question. We went into the test kitchen to find out.

We took a cut of steak from the round that is often used for London broil (a particularly lean cut and therefore prone to being tough when cooked), cut it into 2-inch cubes, and marinated the cubes in various solutions for 24 hours. Marinades with little or no acid had no affect on the texture of the meat. (Above, Doc is setting up toy cowboys and Indians to explain the standoff that occurs as meat soaks in a non-acidic marinade.) When we used more acid, the outer layer of the meat turned gray and dry—it had "cooked."

While some might call the texture tender, we found the meat to be mushy and the flavor of the acid to be overpowering. Our conclusion was simple—if you want tender meat, you must pay attention to the cut you purchase and the cooking method and forget about tenderizing with marinades.

Although marinades may not tenderize meat, they can give it a delicious flavor, as long as you soak the food for an appropriate amount of time. We marinated cubes of beef, lamb, and pork, as well as chicken parts, flounder, and tuna in low-acid marinades for varying amounts of time. As might be expected, fish picked up flavor rather quickly, in as little as 15 minutes for flounder and 30 minutes for the firmer tuna. Chicken was somewhat slower to become fully flavored, with skinless pieces taking about three hours and skin-on pieces taking at least eight hours. Dense meat takes even more time to absorb marinades. It took eight hours for the flavor to penetrate beyond the surface of beef, lamb, and pork, and meat marinated for 24 hours absorbed even more flavor. After a day, we found that meat gained little extra flavor. Although you can leave meat in a low-acid marinade for days, we don't see the point.

BABA GHANOUSH

WHAT WE WANTED: A smoky, creamy dip with real eggplant flavor.

The driving force behind baba ghanoush is grill-roasted eggplant, sultry and rich. Its beguiling creaminess and haunting flavor come from sesame tahini paste, cut to the quick with a bit of garlic, brightened with lemon juice, and flounced up with parsley. In Middle Eastern countries baba ghanoush is served as part of a mezze platter—not unlike an antipasto in Italy—which might feature salads, various dips, small pastries, meats, olives, other condiments, and, of course, bread.

There is no doubt that the eggplant is a majestic fruit—shiny, sexy, brilliantly hued. But its contents can be difficult to deal with. Baba ghanoush can be bitter and watery, green and raw, metallic with garlic, or occluded by tahini paste.

The traditional method for cooking eggplant for baba ghanoush is to scorch it over a hot, smoky grill. There the purple fruit grows bruised, then black, until its insides fairly slosh within their charred carapace. The hot, soft interior is scooped out with a spoon and the outer ruins discarded.

We realized that baba made with eggplant not cooked to the sloshy soft stage simply isn't as good. Undercooked eggplant, while misleadingly soft to the touch (eggplant has, after all, a yielding quality), will taste spongy-green and remain unmoved by additional seasonings.

Another question was whether a decent baba ghanoush could be made without a grill. Taking instruction from the hot fire we had used, we roasted a few large eggplants in a 500-degree oven. It took about 45 minutes to collapse the fruit and transform the insides to pulp. Though the babas made with grill-roasted eggplant were substantially superior to those made with oven-roasted, the latter were perfectly acceptable.

Eggplant suffers from persistent rumors that it is bitter. Most baba ghanoush recipes call for discarding the seedbed. But the insides of the eggplants we were roasting were veritably paved with seeds. We thought it impractical and wasteful to lose half the fruit to mere rumor, so we performed side-by-side tests comparing versions of the dip with and without seeds. We found no tangible grounds for seed dismissal. The dip was not bitter. The seeds stayed.

Other sources suggest one variety of eggplant over another, so we made baba ghanoush with standard large globe eggplants, with compact Italian eggplants, and with long, lithe Japanese eggplants. All were surprisingly good. The globe eggplants made a baba that was slightly more moist. The Italian eggplants were drier and contained fewer seeds. The Japanese eggplants were also quite dry. Their very slenderness allowed the smoke to permeate the flesh completely, and the resulting dip was meaty and delicious. (Given a choice, we would definitely select Italian or Japanese eggplant.)

Once the eggplants are roasted and scooped, you are about five minutes away from removing your apron. The eggplant can be mashed with a fork, but we prefer the food processor, which makes it a cinch to add the other ingredients and to pulse the eggplant, leaving the texture slightly coarse.

As for the proportions of said ingredients, tests indicated that less was always more. Minced garlic gathers strength on-site and can become aggressive when added in abundance. Many recipes we saw also called for tahini in amounts that overwhelmed the eggplant. Likewise with lemon juice: Liberal amounts dash the smoky richness of the eggplant with astringent tartness.

If you're serving a crowd, the recipe can easily be doubled or tripled. Time does nothing to improve the flavor of baba ghanoush, either. An hour-long stay in the refrigerator for a light chilling is all that's needed.

WHAT WE LEARNED: For the best flavor, grill-roast eggplant until it has completely collapsed. Don't bother discarding the seeds, but do use a gentle hand with the garlic, tahini, and lemon juice.

BABA GHANOUSH, CHARCOAL-GRILL
METHOD makes about 2 cups

When buying eggplants, select those with shiny, taut, and unbruised skins and an even shape (eggplants with a bulbous shape won't cook evenly). We prefer to serve baba ghanoush only lightly chilled. If yours is cold, let it stand at room temperature for about 20 minutes before serving. Baba ghanoush does not keep well, so plan to make it the day you want to serve it. Pita bread, black olives, tomato wedges, and cucumber slices are nice accompaniments.

2   pounds eggplant (about 2 large globe eggplants, 5 medium Italian eggplants, or 12 medium Japanese eggplants), each eggplant poked uniformly over entire surface with fork to prevent it from bursting
1   tablespoon juice from 1 lemon
1   small clove garlic, minced
2   tablespoons tahini paste
     Salt and ground black pepper
1   tablespoon extra-virgin olive oil, plus extra for serving
2   teaspoons chopped fresh parsley leaves

1. Ignite about 6 quarts (1 large chimney, or 2½ pounds) hardwood charcoal and burn until completely covered with thin coating of light gray ash, 20 to 30 minutes. Spread coals evenly over grill bottom, then spread additional 6 quarts unlit charcoal over lit coals. Position grill rack and heat until very hot, about 20 minutes. (See how to gauge heat level on page 133.)

2. Grill eggplants until skins darken and wrinkle on all sides and eggplants are uniformly soft when pressed with tongs, about 25 minutes for large globe eggplants, 20 minutes for Italian eggplants, and 15 minutes for Japanese eggplants, turning every 5 minutes and reversing direction of eggplants on grill with each turn. Transfer eggplants to rimmed baking sheet and cool 5 minutes.

3. Set small colander over bowl or in sink. Trim top and bottom off each eggplant. Slit eggplants lengthwise and use spoon to scoop hot pulp from skins and place pulp in colander (you should have about 2 cups packed pulp); discard skins. Let pulp drain 3 minutes.

4. Transfer pulp to workbowl of food processor fitted with steel blade. Add lemon juice, garlic, tahini, ¼ teaspoon salt, and ¼ teaspoon pepper; process until mixture has coarse,

choppy texture, about eight 1-second pulses. Adjust seasoning with salt and pepper; transfer to serving bowl, cover with plastic wrap flush with surface of dip, and refrigerate 45 to 60 minutes. To serve, use spoon to make trough in center of dip and spoon olive oil into it; sprinkle with parsley and serve.

VARIATIONS

BABA GHANOUSH, GAS-GRILL METHOD

Turn all burners on gas grill to high, close lid, and heat grill until hot, 10 to 15 minutes. Follow recipe for Baba Ghanoush, Charcoal-Grill Method, from step 2.

BABA GHANOUSH, OVEN METHOD

Adjust oven rack to middle position and heat oven to 500 degrees. Line rimmed baking sheet with foil, set eggplants on baking sheet, and roast, turning every 15 minutes, until eggplants are uniformly soft when pressed with tongs, about 60 minutes for large globe eggplants, 50 minutes for Italian

eggplants, and 40 minutes for Japanese eggplants. Cool eggplants on baking sheet 5 minutes, then follow recipe for Baba Ghanoush, Charcoal-Grill Method, from step 3.

BABA GHANOUSH WITH SAUTÉED ONION

Sautéed onion gives the baba ghanoush a sweet, rich flavor.

Heat 1 tablespoon extra-virgin olive oil in small skillet over low heat until shimmering; add 1 small onion, chopped fine, and cook, stirring occasionally, until edges are golden brown, about 10 minutes. Follow recipe for Baba Ghanoush, Charcoal-Grill, Gas-Grill, or Oven Method, stirring onion into dip after processing.

EQUIPMENT CORNER: Grill Tongs

GRILLING TODAY CAN BE COMPLICATED. EACH GRILLING season brings with it a truckload of snazzy new barbecue utensils. We wondered if any of these often expensive gadgets was worth a second look.

Testing all manner of tongs, we groped and grabbed kebabs, asparagus, chicken drumsticks, and 3-pound slabs of ribs and found tong performance differed dramatically. Grill tongs by Progressive International, Charcoal, Lamson, Oxo Good Grips, and AMC Rosewood were heavy and difficult to maneuver, and their less delicate pincers couldn't get a grip on asparagus. Other problems included sharp, serrated edges that nicked the food, flimsy arms that bent under the strain of heavy food, and pincers whose spread could not even accommodate the girth of a chicken leg. A new tong on the scene, the Lamson multipurpose, had a spatula in place of one pincer, rendering its grasp almost useless.

The winner was a pair of 16-inch stainless steel kitchen tongs by Amco. Not only did they grip, turn, and move food around the grill easily, but they also were long enough to keep the cook a safe distance from the hot coals. So forget about all those flashy new grill utensils and simply bring your kitchen tongs outside.

RICE PILAF

WHAT WE WANTED: Perfectly steamed, fragrant, fluffy rice that is tender while still retaining an al dente quality.

According to most culinary sources, rice pilaf is simply long-grain rice that has been cooked in hot oil or butter before being simmered in hot liquid, typically either water or stock. In Middle Eastern cuisines, however, the term pilaf also refers to a more substantial dish in which the rice is cooked in this manner and then flavored with other ingredients—spices, nuts, dried fruits, and/or chicken or other meat. To avoid confusion, we decided to call the simple master recipe for our dish "pilaf-style" rice, designating the flavored versions as rice pilaf.

The logical first step in this process was to isolate the best type of rice for pilaf. We immediately limited our testing to long-grain rice, since medium and short-grain rice inherently produce a rather sticky, starchy product, and we were looking for fluffy, separate grains. Searching the shelves of our local grocery store, we came upon a number of different choices: plain long-grain white rice, converted rice, instant rice, jasmine, basmati, and Texmati (basmati rice grown domestically in Texas). We took a box or bag of each and cooked them according to a standard, stripped-down recipe for rice pilaf, altering the ratio of liquid to rice according to each variety when necessary.

Each type of rice was slightly different in flavor, texture, and appearance. Worst of the lot was the instant rice, which was textureless and mushy and had very little rice flavor. The converted rice had a very strong, off-putting flavor, while the jasmine rice, though delicious, was a little too sticky for pilaf. Plain long-grain white rice worked well, but basmati rice was even better: Each grain was separate, long, and fluffy, and the rice had a fresh, delicate fragrance. Though the Texmati produced similar results, it cost three times as much as the basmati per pound, making the basmati rice the logical choice. That said, we would add that you can use plain long-grain rice if basmati is not available.

Most sources indicate that the proper ratio of rice to liquid for long-grain white rice is 1 to 2, but many cooks use less water. After testing every possibility, from 1:1 to 1:2, we found that we got the best rice using 1⅔ cups of water for every cup of rice. To make this easier to remember, as well as easier to measure, we increased the rice by half to 1½ cups and the liquid to 2½ cups.

With our rice/water ratio set, we were ready to test the traditional methods for making pilaf, which called for rinsing, soaking, or parboiling the rice before cooking it in fat and simmering it to tenderness. Each recipe declared one of these preparatory steps to be essential in producing rice with distinct, separate grains that were light and fluffy.

We began by parboiling the rice for three minutes in a large quantity of water, as you would pasta, then draining it and proceeding to sauté and cook it. This resulted in bloated, waterlogged grains of rice. To be sure that we weren't adding more liquid than necessary, we weighed the rice before and after parboiling to measure the amount of water the rice had absorbed, then subtracted that amount from the water in which the final cooking was done. After trying this with both basmati and domestic long-grain white rice and still coming up with waterlogged rice, we eliminated parboiling as part of our cooking method.

Rinsing the rice, on the other hand, made a substantial difference, particularly with basmati rice. We simply covered 1½ cups of rice with water, gently moved the grains around using our fingers, and drained the water from the rice. We repeated this process four or five times until the rinsing water was clear enough for us to see the grains distinctly. We then drained the rice and cooked it in oil and liquid (decreased to 2¼ cups to compensate for the water that had been absorbed by or adhered to the grains during rinsing). The resulting rice was less hard and more tender, and it had a slightly shinier, smoother appearance.

We also tested soaking the rice before cooking it. We rinsed three batches of basmati rice and soaked them for five minutes, one hour, and overnight, respectively. The batch that soaked for five minutes was no better than the one that had only been rinsed. Soaking the rice for an hour proved to be a still greater waste of time, since it wasn't perceptibly different from the rinsed-only version. Soaked overnight, however, the rice was noticeably better. It was very tender, less starchy, and seemed to have longer, more elegant grains than the other batches we'd prepared. Though the difference was subtle, this batch of rice was definitely more refined than the others. (Keep in mind that rice soaked overnight needs to be cooked in only 2 cups of liquid, compensating for the amount of water absorbed while it soaks overnight). Soaking overnight takes some forethought, of course, so if you don't think of it a day ahead of time, simply rinse the rice well; this also delivers a good pilaf.

Thus far, we had allowed the rice to steam an additional 10 minutes after being removed from the heat to ensure that the moisture was distributed throughout. We wondered if a longer or shorter steaming time would make much of a difference in the resulting pilaf. We made a few batches of pilaf, allowing the rice to steam for 5 minutes,

10 minutes, and 15 minutes. The rice that steamed for 5 minutes was heavy and wet. The batch that steamed for 15 minutes was the lightest and least watery. We also decided to try placing a clean dish towel between the pan and the lid right after we took the rice off the stove. We found this produced the best results of all, while reducing the steaming time to only 10 minutes. It seems that the towel prevents condensation and absorbs the excess water in the pan during steaming, producing drier, fluffier rice.

We were surprised to see that many Middle Eastern recipes called for as much as ¼ cup butter per cup of rice. Using butter (since we like the extra flavor that it lends to the rice), we tried from 1 to 4 tablespoons per 1½ cups rice. Three tablespoons turned out to be optimal. The rice was rich without being overwhelmingly so, and each grain was shinier and more distinct than when cooked with less fat.

We also wondered if sautéing the rice for different amounts of time would make a difference, so we sautéed the rice over medium heat for one minute, three minutes, and five minutes. The pan of rice that was sautéed for five minutes was much less tender than the other two. It also had picked up a strong nutty flavor. When sautéed for one minute, the rice simply tasted steamed. The batch sautéed for three minutes was the best, with a light nutty flavor and tender texture.

At the end comes the fun part—adding the flavorings, seasonings, and other ingredients that give the pilaf its distinctive character. We found that dried spices, minced ginger, and garlic, for example, are best sautéed briefly in the fat before the raw rice is added to the pan. Saffron and dried herbs are best added to the liquid as it heats up, while fresh herbs and toasted nuts should be added to the pilaf just before serving to maximize freshness, texture (in the case of nuts), and flavor. Dried fruits such as raisins, currants, or figs can be added just before steaming the rice, which gives them enough time to heat through and plump up without becoming soggy.

WHAT WE LEARNED: Use basmati rice, rinse well, sauté in plenty of butter, and then steam, with a dish towel under the lid, once the rice is done.

BASIC PILAF-STYLE RICE serves 4

If you like, olive oil can be substituted for the butter depending on what you are serving with the pilaf. Soaking the rice overnight in water results in more tender, separate grains. If you'd like to try it, add enough water to cover the rice by 1 inch after the rinsing process in step 1, then cover the bowl with plastic wrap and let it stand at room temperature 8 to 24 hours; reduce the amount of water to cook the rice to 2 cups. For the most evenly cooked rice, use a wide-bottomed saucepan with a tight-fitting lid.

1½	cups basmati or long-grain rice
2½	cups water
1½	teaspoons salt
	Ground black pepper
3	tablespoons unsalted butter
1	small onion, minced (about ½ cup)

1. Place rice in medium bowl and add enough water to cover by 2 inches; using hands, gently swish grains to release excess starch. Carefully pour off water, leaving rice in bowl. Repeat four or five times, until water runs almost clear. Using a colander or fine-mesh strainer, drain water from rice; place colander over bowl and set aside.

2. Bring water to boil, covered, in small saucepan over medium-high heat. Add salt and season with pepper; cover to keep hot. Meanwhile, heat butter in large saucepan over medium heat until foam begins to subside; add onion and sauté until softened but not browned, about 4 minutes. Add rice and stir to coat grains with butter; cook until edges of rice grains begin to turn translucent, about 3 minutes. Stir hot seasoned water into rice; return to boil, then reduce heat to low, cover, and simmer until all liquid is absorbed, 16 to 18 minutes. Off heat, remove lid, and place kitchen towel folded in half over saucepan (see illustration at right); replace lid. Let stand 10 minutes; fluff rice with fork and serve.

VARIATIONS

RICE PILAF WITH CURRANTS AND PINE NUTS

Toast ¼ cup pine nuts in small dry skillet over medium heat until golden and fragrant, about 5 minutes; set aside. Follow recipe for Basic Pilaf-Style Rice, adding ½ teaspoon turmeric, ¼ teaspoon ground cinnamon, and 2 medium garlic cloves, minced, to sautéed onion; cook until fragrant, about 30 seconds longer. When rice is off heat, before covering saucepan with towel, sprinkle ¼ cup currants over rice in pan (do not mix in). When fluffing rice with fork, toss in toasted pine nuts.

INDIAN-SPICED RICE PILAF WITH DATES AND PARSLEY

Follow recipe for Basic Pilaf-Style Rice, adding 2 medium garlic cloves, minced, 2 teaspoons grated fresh ginger, ⅛ teaspoon ground cinnamon, and ⅛ teaspoon ground cardamom to sautéed onion; cook until fragrant, about 30 seconds longer. When rice is off heat, before covering saucepan with towel, add ¼ cup chopped dates and 2 tablespoons chopped fresh parsley (do not mix in); continue with recipe.

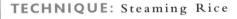

TECHNIQUE: Steaming Rice

After the rice is cooked, cover the pan with a clean dish towel and allow it to sit on a cool burner for 10 minutes.

FAJITAS & margaritas

CHAPTER 12

Guacamole, fajitas, and margaritas are standard-issue fare, even at non-Mexican restaurants, which might explain why they are generally so terrible. Who hasn't been served watery or gray guacamole overpowered by onions and an array of seasonings?

Fajitas is another dish often ruined by unnecessary complexity. The meat must be perfectly cooked, with a rosy interior and browned crust. The accompaniments must be flawless—strips of grilled vegetables, warm tortillas, and guacamole.

Finally, what's a Cinco de Mayo celebration or night out on the town without some margaritas? Too bad most Americans have never tasted the real thing—made with fresh citrus juice. Most bartenders rely on low-quality mixes and compensate with a surfeit of alcohol and the froth added by the blender. We wanted something more refined.

This Mexican meal, simple enough to prepare on a weeknight, is the real thing. The flavors are clean, crisp, and totally appealing.

After a long day of margarita testing, Ian uses a wine bottle to mash leftover lemons and limes to make lemon-limeade.

GUACAMOLE

WHAT WE WANTED: A chunky dip with an emphasis on the avocado, not the seasonings.

Guacamole has traveled a long road. Once a simple Mexican avocado relish, it has become one of America's favorite party dips. It's also an essential element when making fajitas, which is perhaps America's favorite Mexican entrée. Unfortunately, the journey has not necessarily been kind to this dish. The guacamole we are served in restaurants, and even in the homes of friends, often sacrifices the singular, extraordinary character of the avocado—the culinary equivalent of velvet—by adding too many other flavorings. Even worse, the texture of the dip is usually reduced to an utterly smooth, listless puree.

We wanted our guacamole to be different. First, it should highlight the dense, buttery texture and loamy, nutty flavor of the avocado. Any additions should provide bright counterpoints to the avocado without overwhelming it. Just as important, the consistency of the dip should be chunky.

Since good guacamole must begin with good avocados, we began our research with an avocado tasting. We focused on the two most familiar market varieties, the small, rough-skinned Hass (also spelled Haas), grown primarily in California and Mexico, and the larger, smooth-skinned Fuerte, grown mostly in Florida. The tasters were unanimous in their preference for Hass, compared with which the Fuerte tasted "too fruity," "sweet," and "watery."

Regardless of their origin, many supermarket avocados are sold rock hard and unripe. Because these fruits ripen off the tree, that's fine; in two to five days, your avocados are ready to eat. We tested all the supposed tricks to accelerate ripening, from burying the avocados in flour or rice to enclosing them in a brown paper bag, with and without another piece of fruit. We also tried putting them in different areas in the kitchen: light spots and dark, cool spots and warm. In the end, we found that most of these efforts made

little difference. The fastest ripening took roughly 48 hours and occurred in a warm, dark spot, but the advantage was minor. From now on, we won't think twice when tossing hard avocados into the fruit bowl on the counter.

Determining ripeness was also straightforward. The skins of Hass avocados turn from green to dark, purply black when ripe, and the fruit yields slightly to a gentle squeeze when held in the palm of your hand.

Now having the proper ripe avocados, we turned to the mixing method. Most guacamole recipes direct you to mash all the avocados, and some recipes go so far as to puree them in a blender or food processor. After making dozens of batches, we came to believe that neither pureeing nor simple mashing was the way to go. Properly ripened avocados break down very easily when stirred, and we were aiming for a chunky texture. To get it, we ended up mashing only one of the three avocados in our recipe lightly with a fork and mixing it with most of the other ingredients, then dicing the remaining two avocados into substantial ½-inch cubes and mixing them into the base using a very light hand. The mixing action breaks down the cubes somewhat, making for a chunky, cohesive dip.

Other problems we encountered in most recipes were an overabundance of onion and a dearth of acidic seasoning. After extensive testing with various amounts of onion, tasters found that 2 tablespoons of finely minced or grated onion gave guacamole a nice spike without an overwhelming onion flavor. We also tried guacamoles with various amounts of fresh lemon and lime juice. The acid was absolutely necessary, not only for flavor but also to help preserve the mixture's green color. Tasters preferred two tablespoons of lime juice in our three-avocado guacamole.

WHAT WE LEARNED: Use ripe, pebbly-skinned avocados. Mash just one with a fork, and dice the other two. Keep the onion to a minimum, but don't skimp on lime juice.

CHUNKY GUACAMOLE makes 2½ to 3 cups

To minimize the risk of discoloration, prepare the minced ingredients first so they are ready to mix with the avocados as soon as they are cut. Ripe avocados are essential here. To test for ripeness, try to flick the small stem off the end of the avocado. If it comes off easily and you can see green underneath it, the avocado is ripe. If it does not come off or if you see brown underneath after prying it off, the avocado is not ripe. If you like, garnish the guacamole with diced tomatoes and chopped cilantro just before serving.

3   medium, ripe avocados (preferably pebbly-
     skinned Hass)
2   tablespoons minced onion
1   medium clove garlic, minced
1   small jalapeño chile, stemmed, seeded, and
     minced
¼   cup minced fresh cilantro leaves
     Salt
½   teaspoon ground cumin (optional)
2   tablespoons lime juice

1. Halve one avocado, remove pit, and scoop flesh into medium bowl. Mash flesh lightly with onion, garlic, chile, cilantro, ¼ teaspoon salt, and cumin (if using) with tines of fork until just combined.

2. Halve, pit, and cube remaining two avocados, following illustrations at right. Add cubes to bowl with mashed avocado mixture.

3. Sprinkle lime juice over diced avocado and mix entire contents of bowl lightly with fork until combined but still chunky. Adjust seasonings with salt, if necessary, and serve. (Guacamole can be covered with plastic wrap, pressed directly onto surface of mixture, and refrigerated up to 1 day. Return guacamole to room temperature, removing plastic wrap at last moment, before serving.)

VARIATION

GUACAMOLE WITH BACON, SCALLIONS, AND TOMATO

Follow recipe for Chunky Guacamole, substituting 3 large scallions, sliced thin (about ⅓ cup), for onion and adding 6 slices cooked, drained, and crumbled bacon with 1 teaspoon rendered fat and ½ medium tomato, seeded and diced small.

TECHNIQUE: Dicing an Avocado

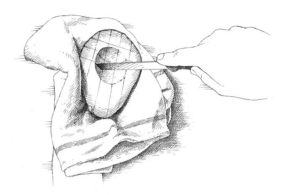

1. Use a dish towel to hold the avocado steady. Make ½-inch crosshatch incisions in the flesh of each avocado half with a dinner knife, cutting down to but not through the skin.

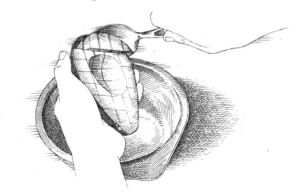

2. Separate the diced flesh from skin using a spoon inserted between the skin and flesh, gently scooping out the avocado cubes.

FAJITAS

WHAT WE WANTED: Perfectly cooked flank steak accompanied by grilled onions and peppers, warm tortillas, and great guacamole.

Thanks to fajitas, flank steak has become the darling of Tex-Mex fans from New York to California and everywhere in between. Although this dish was originally made with skirt steak (see page 158 for more information), flank steak is much more available and has become the steak of choice for this recipe.

But there are good reasons for the popularity of flank steak in addition to mere culinary fashion. Like other steaks cut from the chest and side of the cow, flank has a rich, full, beefy flavor. Also, because it is very thin, it cooks quickly.

Although the idea of grilling flank steak is a pretty straightforward proposition, we still had some questions about what was exactly the best way to go about it. All of them were directed at the achievement of two very simple goals: getting a good sear on the outside of this thin cut of meat before overcooking on the inside, and keeping it tender. We wondered whether the meat should be marinated or rubbed with spices, how hot the fire should be, and how long the meat should be cooked.

Virtually every recipe we found for flank steak called for marinating. Most sources ballyhooed the marinade as a means of tenderizing the meat as well as adding flavor. We found that marinades with a lot of acid eventually made this thin cut mushy and unappealing. If we left out the acid, we could flavor the meat, but this took at least 12 hours.

We eventually decided that the easiest, most effective way to flavor this cut of meat was with a squeeze of lime juice just before grilling and a generous seasoning with salt and pepper. With grilled vegetables and guacamole, this dish has plenty going on without the addition of spicy distractions. Everyone in the kitchen felt it was best to play up the beefy flavor of the meat.

To achieve tenderness (the reason many sources recommend marinating in the first place), we found that cutting the cooked steaks thinly and against the grain did the trick. When the steaks were cut up this way, there was virtually no difference between those that were marinated and those that were not. We concluded that flank steak can be seasoned in seconds, without compromising tenderness.

Every source we checked was in the same camp when it came to cooking the flank steak, and it is the right camp. These steaks should be cooked over high heat for a short period of time. We tried lower heat and longer times, but the meat inevitably ended up being tough.

Flank steak is so thin that it's impossible to check its temperature with a meat thermometer, so you need to resort to the most primitive (but ultimately the most effective) method of checking for doneness: Cut into the meat and see if it is done to your liking. Remember that carryover heat will continue to cook the steak after it comes off the grill for a much-needed rest (see the Science Desk on page 158). So if you want the steak medium-rare, take it off the heat when it looks rare, and so on. Because cooking flank steak beyond medium-rare toughens it, we advise against it. In fact, if you like your meat more than medium, you might want to choose another cut.

With the flank steak cooked and guacamole in hand, the rest of the recipe goes quickly. As the meat rests, the onions and peppers can be grilled. At the last minute, the tortillas are warmed around the edges of the fire (which should have cooled, if using charcoal, or which can be lowered, if using gas).

WHAT WE LEARNED: Don't bother marinating flank steak; it will be plenty tender as long as you slice it thin across the grain. Do let the meat rest (it will be juicier and more tender) before slicing, and grill the vegetables while the steak reposes.

CLASSIC FAJITAS serves 8

The ingredients go on the grill in order as the fire dies down: steak over a medium-hot fire, vegetables over a medium fire, and tortillas around the edge of a medium to low fire just to warm them. (Alternatively, the tortillas can be wrapped together in a clean, damp dish towel and warmed in a microwave oven for about 3 minutes at full power; keep them wrapped until you're ready to use them.) Flank steak is best when cooked rare or medium-rare at most. Because flank is a thin cut, it is very important for the meat to rest after it comes off the grill. Make sure to cover the grilled but unsliced flank steak with foil; it will take you at least 10 minutes to get the vegetables and tortillas ready. If you can find skirt steak (see Tasting Lab on page 158), it can be grilled just like flank steak.

1	flank steak (about 2½ pounds)
¼	cup lime juice
	Salt and ground black pepper
1	very large onion, peeled and cut into ½-inch rounds
2	very large red or green bell peppers, prepared following illustration at right
16	flour tortillas (each 10 to 12 inches in diameter)
1	recipe Chunky Guacamole (page 155)

TECHNIQUE: Cutting Peppers

Remove a ¼-inch-thick slice from the top and bottom of each pepper. Remove the stem from the top lobe. Reach into the pepper and pull out the seeds in a single bunch. Slice down one side of the pepper, then lay it flat, skin-side down, in a long strip. Slide a sharp knife along the inside of the pepper to remove all the white ribs and any remaining seeds.

1. Light a large chimney starter filled with hardwood charcoal (about 2½ pounds) and allow to burn until all charcoal is covered with layer of fine gray ash. Spread coals evenly over bottom of grill for medium-hot fire. (See how to gauge heat level on page 133). (If using gas grill, preheat grill with all burners set to high and lid down until grill is very hot, about 15 minutes.) Scrape cooking rack clean with wire brush.

2. Generously sprinkle both sides of steak with lime juice and salt and pepper to taste. Grill steak over coals until well seared and dark brown on one side, 5 to 7 minutes. Flip steak using tongs; continue grilling on other side until interior of meat is slightly less done than you want it to be when you eat it, 2 to 5 minutes more for medium-rare (depending on heat of fire and thickness of steak). (If using gas grill, grill steak, covered, until well seared and brown, 4 to 6 minutes. Flip and continue grilling another 2 to 5 minutes.) Transfer meat to cutting board; cover loosely with foil, and let rest for 10 minutes.

3. While meat rests and charcoal fire has died down to medium or gas burners have been adjusted to medium, grill onions and peppers, turning occasionally, until onions are lightly charred, about 6 minutes, and peppers are streaked with grill marks, about 10 minutes. Remove vegetables from grill and cut into long, thin strips; set aside. Arrange tortillas around edge of grill; heat until just warmed, about 20 seconds per side. Wrap tortillas in towel to keep warm and place in a basket.

4. Slice steak very thin on bias against grain; adjust seasonings with additional salt and pepper. Arrange sliced meat and vegetables on large platter; serve immediately with tortillas and guacamole passed separately.

TASTING LAB: Three Flat Steaks

LIKE FLANK STEAKS, THE OTHER TWO CUTS MOST SIMILAR to it—skirt steak and hanger steak—have also recently become fashionable. These three popular steaks share the distinction of coming from the chest and side of the animal. Hanger and flank both come from the rear side, while skirt comes from the area between the abdomen and the chest cavity. In addition to location, these steaks share certain other basic qualities: All are long, relatively thin, quite tough, and grainy, but with rich, deep, beefy flavor.

Of course, these flavorful steaks also have their individual distinctions. Hanger, a thick muscle that is attached to the diaphragm, derives its name from the fact that when a cow is butchered, this steak hangs down into the center of the carcass. Because it is a classic French bistro dish, this cut is highly prized in restaurants and therefore difficult to find in butcher shops. We don't think this is a great loss since the hangers we sampled had the toughest texture and least rich flavor of these three cuts.

Fortunately, flank steak is easy to find in any supermarket. It has a great beef flavor and is quite tender if cooked rare or medium-rare and sliced thin against the grain. Because of the popularity of fajitas, flank steak has become somewhat expensive, often retailing for $7 a pound.

Skirt steak, which was the cut originally used for fajitas, can be hard to locate, even in butcher shops. This is a real pity because skirt steak has more fat than flank steak, which makes it juicier and richer tasting. At the same time, it has a deep, beefy flavor that outdoes either hanger or flank steak. If you see skirt steak, buy it, and cook it like flank.

SCIENCE DESK: Why Meat Should Rest

A FINAL BUT VERY IMPORTANT STEP WHEN COOKING flank steak—and all red meats—is allowing it to rest after it comes off the heat. As the proteins in the meat heat up during cooking they coagulate, which basically means they uncoil and then reconnect, or bond with each other, in a different configuration. When the proteins coagulate, they squeeze out part of the liquid that was trapped in their coiled structures and in the spaces between the individual molecules. The heat from the cooking source drives these freed liquids toward the center of the meat.

This process of coagulation explains why experienced chefs can tell how done a piece of meat is by pushing on it and judging the amount of resistance: The firmer the meat, the more done it is. But the coagulation process is apparently at least partly reversible, so as you allow the meat to rest and return to a lower temperature after cooking, some of the liquid is reabsorbed by the protein molecules as their capacity to hold moisture increases. As a result, if given a chance to rest, the meat will lose less juice when you cut into it, which in turn makes for much juicier and more tender meat.

This is common wisdom among cooks, but to be sure it was correct, we cooked two more flank steaks, sliced one up immediately after it came off the fire, and allowed the second to rest for 10 minutes before slicing it. Not only did the first steak exude almost 40 percent more juice than the second when sliced, it also looked grayer and was not as tender. In this case, it is crucial to follow the conventional wisdom: Give your steak a rest.

MARGARITAS

WHAT WE WANTED: Fresh-tasting margaritas with an emphasis on the citrus, not just the tequila.

America's obsession with margaritas has helped make the United States the world's leading consumer of tequila. Unfortunately, the typical margarita tends to be a slushy, headache-inducing concoction made with little more than ice, tequila, and artificially flavored corn syrup. At their best, though, margaritas are the perfect balance of tequila, orange liqueur, and fresh lime juice, shaken briskly with crushed ice and served on the rocks (with salt if preferred). We wanted to see if we could produce this ideal cocktail, balancing the distinctive flavor of tequila with a hint of orange and a bright burst of citrus.

As tequila is a margarita's most important ingredient, we started the testing there. We made margaritas with all types of tequila, using both superpremium 100 percent blue agave (agave is the plant from which tequila is distilled) as well as mixed tequilas, to which cane or corn syrup is often added.

Two types of tequila, known as silver (or white) and gold, are not aged; their young alcoholic flavor gave the margaritas we made a raw, harsh flavor. Margaritas made with the prized aged and very aged tequilas were extremely smooth, but their distinct tannic taste, produced as they age up to six years in oak casks, dominated the cocktail. Reposado, or "rested," tequila, made from 100 percent blue agave and aged for 12 months or less, was the favorite. Its slightly mellow flavor blended perfectly with the other ingredients.

Next we tested orange-flavored liqueurs. Both Grand Marnier and Cointreau were delicious, but many tasters thought their robust flavor too pronounced and "boozy" for a margarita. Triple Sec, an orange liqueur with a lower alcohol content, made a more delicate contribution.

Margaritas are traditionally made with lime juice, but some tasters thought the flavor too acidic. Those made with only lemon juice ended up tasting too much like lemonade. An equal mixture of both lime and lemon juice produced a margarita that was refreshing but too mild.

We turned to a technique we had used in the test kitchen to make lemonade. For that recipe, we found that mashing thinly sliced lemons extracted their full flavor. While this technique boosted the citrus flavor in the margaritas, the oil from the white pith was too bitter, giving the drink a medicinal flavor. Steeping just the grated zest of the lime and lemon in their juices for 24 hours deepened the citrus flavor without adding bitterness. (We later discovered that the steeping period could be reduced to four hours.) Adding sugar to the steeping mixture countered any remaining harshness from the citrus.

In testing the proportions of the three main ingredients, we found that tasters favored an equal portion of each, quite different from the tequila-heavy concoctions we had consumed in the past. Our last test was to try the margarita in a salt-rimmed glass. This was clearly a question of individual taste. So salt the glass or not, as you and your guests prefer.

WHAT WE LEARNED: For the ultimate margarita, mix premium tequila with fresh juice and zest. Use Triple Sec for a bright orange flavor that's not too alcoholic.

FRESH MARGARITAS makes about 1 quart, serving 4 to 6

The longer the zest and juice mixture is allowed to steep, the more developed the citrus flavors in the finished margaritas. We recommend steeping for the full 24 hours, although the margaritas will still be great if the mixture is steeped for only the minimum four hours. If you're in a rush and want to serve margaritas immediately, omit the zest and skip the steeping process altogether.

4	teaspoons grated zest plus ½ cup juice from 2 or 3 medium limes
4	teaspoons grated zest plus ½ cup juice from 2 or 3 medium lemons
¼	cup superfine sugar
	Pinch salt
2	cups crushed ice
1	cup 100 percent agave tequila, preferably reposado
1	cup Triple Sec

1. Combine lime zest and juice, lemon zest and juice, sugar, and salt in large liquid measuring cup; cover with plastic wrap and refrigerate until flavors meld, 4 to 24 hours.

2. Divide 1 cup crushed ice between 4 or 6 margarita or double old-fashioned glasses. Strain juice mixture into 1-quart pitcher or cocktail shaker. Add tequila, Triple Sec, and remaining crushed ice; stir or shake until thoroughly combined and chilled, 20 to 60 seconds. Strain into ice-filled glasses; serve immediately.

VARIATIONS

FRESH PINEAPPLE MARGARITAS

Peel and core 1 small ripe pineapple (about 3½ pounds); cut half of pineapple into rough 2-inch chunks (reserve remaining half for another use). Puree in workbowl of food processor fitted with steel blade until smooth and foamy, about 1 minute. Follow recipe for Fresh Margaritas, omitting zest and steeping process, reducing lemon and lime juices to ¼ cup each, and adding ½ cup pureed pineapple to juice mixture.

FRESH RASPBERRY MARGARITAS

To make strawberry margaritas, substitute an equal amount of hulled strawberries for the raspberries.

Follow recipe for Fresh Margaritas, omitting zest and steeping process and pureeing 1 cup fresh raspberries, lime and lemon juices, sugar, and salt in workbowl of food processor fitted with steel blade until smooth. Strain mixture into pitcher or cocktail shaker; continue with recipe, reducing Triple Sec to ½ cup and adding ½ cup Chambord (or desired raspberry liqueur) to juice and tequila mixture in pitcher.

EQUIPMENT CORNER: Zesters

WHAT'S THE BEST TOOL FOR REMOVING THE COLORED peel from limes, lemons, and oranges while leaving behind the bitter white pith? It depends on how you want your zest. Traditional zesters remove the peel in long, thin strips, which can be left as is (for garnish) or minced. Box graters and other similar tools yield tiny bits of moist zest.

Armed with bags of lemons and oranges, we set out to find the best tool for zesting. We assembled seven utensils. We not only wanted to determine which tool was the easiest to use but which produced zest without any pith and left the least amount of zest in the grater itself.

Traditional citrus zesters have short handles and stainless steel heads with beveled, sharp holes at the top. You must bear down with the tool and scrape away long strips of zest, turning the fruit as you go. Comfort and sharpness were the key issues when testing these models. The Oxo zester performed best—its ergonomic grip was not only soft but also short enough to nestle perfectly in testers' palms, allowing greater ease of movement. The sharp holes on this zester raced through the fruits cleanly and yielded long strips of oil-rich zest.

For grated zest, most cooks turn to four-sided box graters. This old kitchen standby usually has one side reserved for zesting, which consists of small holes with raised teeth. Another choice is a small paddle with small, raised holes. The newest grater/zester on the market is modeled after the traditional woodworking rasp, with tiny razor-sharp teeth set in a long, flat stainless steel base.

We quickly concluded that the box grater is a poor choice for zesting fruits. It mangled lemons and oranges, and most of the zest became trapped in the grater holes. We needed a toothbrush to remove the last stubborn bits of zest. The flat grater with raised teeth was only slightly easier to use. The rasplike Microplane (see photo, left) was the fastest and easiest grater/zester we tested. It created tiny fluffs of perfect zest, leaving pith and fruit intact.

An unusual butchering technique gets a 12-pound turkey out of the oven in less than two hours and delivers supercrisp skin and evenly cooked meat.

THANKSGIVING dinner

The only certain things in life are death, taxes, and turkey at Thanksgiving. Over the years, we have cooked hundreds of turkeys in the test kitchen to figure out how to bring the most flavorful, most beautiful bird to the holiday table.

Never ones to rest on our laurels, we are always looking for new and different ways to deal with the holiday turkey, always with improvement in mind. After a successful round of roasting chickens in a scorching hot 450-degree oven (the skin was the crispiest ever), we began to wonder if this method could be applied to turkey. After all, the goals are the same: dark, crisp skin; evenly cooked, moist meat; and quick cooking. We reasoned that if high-heat roasting was good enough for chicken, then it was good enough for turkey, too.

So we went into the kitchen, rolled up our sleeves, cranked up the oven, and started roasting turkeys. Several scorched turkeys later, and a panicked call from the boss to the test kitchen about the billows of smoke filling the air, we met with success. We had a turkey with crackling crisp skin and moist meat on the table with just two hours of work on Thanksgiving Day. We even figured out how to get the dressing and gravy done at the same time.

IN THIS CHAPTER

THE RECIPES
Crisp-Skin High-Roast Butterflied
    Turkey with Sausage Dressing
Golden Cornbread
Turkey Gravy

Basic Cranberry Sauce
Cranberry-Orange Sauce
Cranberry Sauce with Pears
    and Fresh Ginger

EQUIPMENT CORNER
Saucepans

SCIENCE DESK
How Brining Works

TASTING LAB
Boxed Stuffing

CRISP-SKIN HIGH-ROAST TURKEY

WHAT WE WANTED: A turkey in and out of the oven—and on the table with dressing and gravy—in less than 2 hours—given some prep time the day before.

We have cooked hundreds of turkey in the test kitchen, always with improvement in mind. In our latest effort, we put the emphasis on high roasting—a method that uses oven temperatures of at least 450 degrees. We had heard that high-roasting would produce a turkey with juicy meat and crisp skin in record time—less than two hours. This was clearly an opportunity we couldn't afford to pass up.

For our initial test, we placed the turkey (a 12-pound bird), breast-side up on a V-rack, placed the rack in a roasting pan, and roasted the turkey at 500 degrees, undisturbed, until the thigh meat registered around 175 degrees—in this case just under 2 hours. There was crisp skin as promised, but only a modicum of it. The recipe never called for rotating the turkey in the oven, so it was only the skin over the breast meat that was crisp. In addition, the breast meat had overcooked by the time the thighs had cooked. Even worse, the kitchen filled with black smoke caused by burnt pan drippings. Still, even with the outward failure of this initial attempt, we were encouraged by the short amount of time needed to roast the turkey.

Tackling the problem of the unevenly cooked meat first, we started the turkey breast down, then flipped the turkey from side to side, finally finishing breast-side up. This method yielded evenly cooked meat, but since each side of the turkey spent less time face up, the skin was not very crisp.

In their natural form, turkeys are not designed to roast evenly. The cathedral ceiling–shaped bone structure of the breast promotes faster cooking, while the legs lag behind. Because dark meat tastes best when cooked to a higher temperature than lean white meat (175 degrees for dark meat versus about 165 degrees for the breast), turkeys are not terribly well designed. You want the white meat to cook more slowly than the dark meat, not the other way around.

If we had any hope of getting the turkey in and out of the oven quickly and with crisp skin, we decided, a turkey redesign was in order. We butterflied the turkey—a technique in which the backbone is removed, then the bird is opened up and flattened. Logic stated that with the turkey flattened and all of the meat facing up at the same time, the turkey would cook more evenly, and the skin would have equal time to crisp. This method worked beautifully and had one additional benefit. Because the legs were now in contact with part of the breast, essentially shielding it, they prevented the white meat from overcooking. The thighs and the breast reached their target temperatures of 175 and 165 degrees, respectively, at the same time. Perfect!

Butterflying a chicken requires only a pair of good scissors to cut out the backbone. However, scissors are no match for the sturdier bone structure of the turkey. We found a good-quality chef's knife was necessary to cut along either side of the backbone. Even with a sharp blade, we still needed to apply some serious pressure to cut through the thicker bones, sometimes literally hacking down the backbone. Once the backbone was removed, we found that the sturdy rib cage would not flatten under the heel of a hand. We reached for a heavy-duty rolling pin, placed the turkey breast-side up, and whacked the breastbone until it flattened—aggressive culinary therapy, if you will.

We now had evenly cooked meat and crisp skin, but what to do about the profusion of smoke? Filling the roasting pan with water to keep the fat from hitting the bottom of the hot pan would work, but, instead of water, we turned to dressing. The dressing soaked up the drippings from the turkey—thereby eliminating the smoke while also picking up great flavor. For this test, we had been using our favorite cornbread dressing recipe, but we found a little

With the technical problems of high-roasting a turkey solved, we were now able to move on to flavor—or lack thereof. As is tradition here in the test kitchen, we turned to brining—a process in which the turkey is soaked in a salt/sugar/water solution (see the Science Desk on page 171). The salt in the solution makes its way into the meat and seasons it. The brine also gives the turkey needed moisture, which protects the meat from overcooking. But with this moisture comes soggy skin. Air-drying the brined turkey in the refrigerator the night before it was roasted allowed the moisture in the skin to evaporate, and once again the skin was crackling crisp. For those not inclined to brine, we also found that air-drying a kosher bird works well. Because it is salted during processing, a kosher turkey has a similar flavor to brined turkey.

Now we had great turkey and dressing, but what about the gravy? We had always made gravy using the precious pan drippings from the turkey, but in this recipe the dressing soaked up the drippings. Gravy made from a stock flavored only with giblets was weak tasting. We had to find a way to pump flavor into the gravy.

We butterflied yet another turkey, this time saving the backbone. We chopped it into small pieces and threw it into a roasting pan along with the neck and giblets and some celery, carrots, onion, and garlic. We roasted the bones and vegetables at 450 degrees until well browned. Then we placed them in a saucepan along with some chicken stock, white wine, and water and made a stock. After the stock cooled down, we removed the fat and reserved it. We used the reserved fat to make a roux—a flour and fat mixture that is used to thicken a sauce or gravy. This gravy was big on flavor, and by making the stock ahead of time, while the turkey was brining, we had less work to do on Thanksgiving day, when time is always at a premium.

tweaking was necessary. The dressing was greasy when left to soak up the drippings, so we lowered the fat in the recipe by reducing the amount of butter from 8 tablespoons to 2 and cutting the amount of half-and-half and sausage by half. We also found it necessary to reduce the amount of stock used in the original recipe; the dressing got the moisture it needed from the juices of the turkey. Now turkey and dressing were on the table in less than two hours.

All we needed now was a proper roasting pan to suit our two-story arrangement of butterflied bird and dressing. A broiler pan would have been ideal, since the slotted top would prevent the dressing from drying out and burning and would also keep the bird elevated enough so that it wasn't nesting in the dressing. But while the broiler pan top was the perfect size to hold the turkey, the bottom held only enough dressing for four—what about leftovers? After going through the kitchen's battalion of roasting pans to use with the broiler pan top, we resorted to using a disposable rectangular aluminum roasting pan. Big enough to hold plenty of dressing, sturdy enough to support the broiler pan top, and easy to clean up—just throw it away.

WHAT WE LEARNED: To get crisp skin and evenly cooked meat, butterfly the turkey and roast it at 450 degrees. To keep your kitchen from filling with smoke, line the roasting pan with dressing.

CRISP-SKIN HIGH-ROAST BUTTERFLIED TURKEY WITH SAUSAGE DRESSING

serves 10 to 12

If you prefer not to brine your turkey, we recommend a kosher bird. The dressing can be made with cornbread or white bread, but note that they are not used in equal amounts. The turkey is roasted in a 12 by 16-inch disposable roasting pan, sitting on a broiler pan top or a sturdy flat wire rack covered with foil. If using a wire rack, choose one that measures about 11 by 17 inches so that it will span the roasting pan and sit above the dressing in the pan. Cover with foil, cut slits in the foil for fat drainage, and spray with nonstick cooking spray. Serve turkey and dressing with gravy (see page 169).

turkey

- 2 cups kosher salt or 1 cup table salt
- 1 cup sugar
- 1 turkey (12 to 14 pounds gross weight), rinsed thoroughly; giblets, neck, and tailpiece removed and reserved for gravy; and turkey butterflied (see illustrations 1 through 5 on page 167)
- 1 tablespoon unsalted butter, melted

sausage dressing

- 12 cups cornbread (recipe follows) broken into 1-inch pieces (include crumbs), or 18 cups 1-inch challah or Italian bread cubes (from about 1½ loaves)
- 1¾ cups chicken stock or canned low-sodium chicken broth
- 1 cup half-and-half
- 2 large eggs, beaten lightly
- 12 ounces bulk pork sausage, broken into 1-inch pieces
- 3 medium onions, chopped fine (about 3 cups)
- 3 ribs celery, chopped fine (about 1½ cups)
- 2 tablespoons unsalted butter
- 2 tablespoons minced fresh thyme leaves
- 2 tablespoons minced fresh sage leaves
- 3 medium cloves garlic, minced
- 1½ teaspoons salt
- 2 teaspoons ground black pepper

1. TO BRINE TURKEY: Dissolve salt and sugar in 2 gallons cold water in large stockpot or clean bucket. Add turkey and refrigerate or set in very cool spot (about 40 degrees) for 8 hours.

2. TO PREPARE DRESSING: While the turkey brines, adjust one oven rack to upper-middle position and second rack to lower-middle position and heat oven to 250 degrees. Spread bread in even layers on 2 rimmed baking sheets and dry in oven 50 to 60 minutes for cornbread or 40 to 50 minutes for challah or Italian bread.

TECHNIQUE: Preparing the Turkey

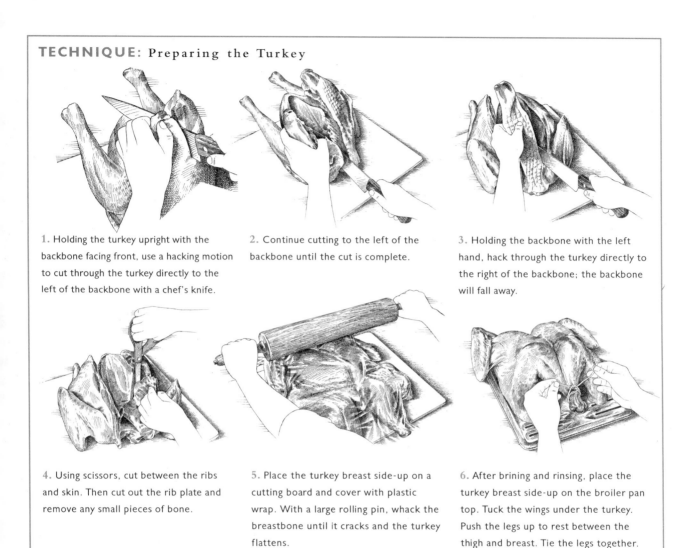

1. Holding the turkey upright with the backbone facing front, use a hacking motion to cut through the turkey directly to the left of the backbone with a chef's knife.

2. Continue cutting to the left of the backbone until the cut is complete.

3. Holding the backbone with the left hand, hack through the turkey directly to the right of the backbone; the backbone will fall away.

4. Using scissors, cut between the ribs and skin. Then cut out the rib plate and remove any small pieces of bone.

5. Place the turkey breast side-up on a cutting board and cover with plastic wrap. With a large rolling pin, whack the breastbone until it cracks and the turkey flattens.

6. After brining and rinsing, place the turkey breast side-up on the broiler pan top. Tuck the wings under the turkey. Push the legs up to rest between the thigh and breast. Tie the legs together.

---

3. Place bread in large bowl. Whisk together stock, half-and-half, and eggs in medium bowl; pour over bread and toss very gently to coat so that bread does not break into smaller pieces. Set aside.

4. Heat heavy-bottomed, 12-inch skillet over medium-high heat until hot, about 1½ minutes. Add sausage and cook, stirring occasionally, until sausage loses its raw color, 5 to 7 minutes. With slotted spoon, transfer sausage to medium bowl. Add about half the onions and celery to fat in skillet; sauté, stirring occasionally, over medium-high heat until softened, about 5 minutes. Transfer onion mixture to bowl with sausage. Return skillet to heat and add 2 tablespoons butter; when foam subsides, add remaining celery and onions and sauté, stirring occasionally, until softened, about 5 minutes. Stir in thyme, sage, and garlic; cook until fragrant, about 30 seconds; add salt and pepper. Add this mixture along with sausage and onion mixture to bread and stir gently to combine (try not to break bread into smaller pieces).

TECHNIQUE: Carving the Turkey

1. With a sharp carving knife, cut both leg quarters off the turkey.

2. Cut both wing pieces off the breast section.

3. Slice straight down along the breast-bone. Continue to slice down, with the knife hugging the rib bones, to remove the breast meat.

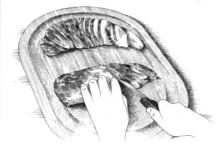

4. Beginning at the narrow end of the breast, slice the meat across the grain, about 1/4 inch thick.

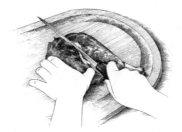

5. Pull the thigh and the drumstick apart and locate the joint. Cut through the joint, separating the two pieces.

6. Remove the largest pieces of meat from the thigh and slice the meat across the grain, about 1/4 inch thick.

5. Spray disposable aluminum 12 by 16-inch roasting pan with nonstick cooking spray. Transfer dressing to roasting pan and spread in even layer. Cover pan with foil and refrigerate while preparing turkey.

6. TO PREPARE TURKEY FOR ROASTING: Remove turkey from brine and rinse well under cool running water. Following illustration 6 on page 167, position turkey on broiler pan top or foil-lined rack; thoroughly pat surface of turkey dry with paper towels. Place broiler pan top or rack with turkey on top of roasting pan with dressing; refrigerate, uncovered, 8 to 24 hours.

7. TO ROAST TURKEY WITH DRESSING: Adjust oven rack to lower-middle position and heat oven to 450 degrees. Remove broiler pan top with turkey and foil cover over roasting pan; replace broiler pan top with turkey. Brush turkey with 1 tablespoon melted butter. Place roasting pan with turkey on broiler pan top in oven and roast until turkey skin is crisp and deep brown and instant-read thermometer registers 165 degrees when inserted in thickest part of breast and 175 degrees in thickest part of thigh, 80 to 100 minutes, rotating pan from front to back after 40 minutes.

8. Transfer broiler pan top with turkey to cutting board, tent loosely with foil, and let rest 20 minutes. Meanwhile, adjust oven rack to upper-middle position, place roasting pan with dressing back in oven, and bake until golden brown, about 10 minutes. Cool dressing 5 minutes, then spoon into bowl or onto turkey serving platter. Carve turkey (see illustrations on page 168) and serve.

GOLDEN CORNBREAD makes about 16 cups
crumbled cornbread

You need about three-quarters of this recipe for the dressing; the rest is for nibbling.

4	large eggs
1⅓	cups buttermilk
1⅓	cups milk
2	cups yellow cornmeal, preferably stone-ground
2	cups (10 ounces) unbleached all-purpose flour
4	teaspoons baking powder
1	teaspoon baking soda
2	tablespoons sugar
1	teaspoon salt
4	tablespoons unsalted butter, melted, plus extra for greasing baking dish

1. Adjust oven rack to middle position and heat oven to 375 degrees. Grease 9 by 13-inch baking dish with butter.

2. Beat eggs in medium bowl; whisk in buttermilk and milk.

3. Whisk cornmeal, flour, baking powder, baking soda, sugar, and salt together in large bowl. Push dry ingredients up sides of bowl to make a well, then pour egg and milk mixture into well and stir with whisk until just combined; stir in melted butter.

4. Pour batter into greased baking dish. Bake until top is golden brown and edges have pulled away from sides of pan, 30 to 40 minutes.

5. Transfer baking dish to wire rack and cool to room temperature before using, about 1 hour.

TURKEY GRAVY makes about 1 quart

Because this gravy doesn't use drippings from the roasted turkey but instead uses the trimmings from butterflying the bird, the gravy can conveniently be made a day in advance (while the turkey brines and air-dries in the refrigerator) and then reheated before serving. When roasting the trimmings and vegetables, make sure to use a roasting pan that can go over the stovetop. The bottom of a broiler pan works well, too.

	Reserved giblets (do not use liver), neck, tailpiece, and backbone and breast bones from turkey
1	medium carrot, cut into 1-inch pieces
1	rib celery, cut into 1-inch pieces
2	small onions, chopped coarse
6	cloves garlic, unpeeled
3½	cups chicken stock or canned low-sodium chicken broth
2	cups dry white wine
6	sprigs fresh thyme
¼	cup all-purpose flour
	Salt and ground black pepper

1. Heat oven to 450 degrees. Place turkey trimmings, carrot, celery, onions, and garlic in large flameproof roasting pan or broiler pan bottom. Spray lightly with vegetable oil spray and toss to combine. Roast, stirring every 10 minutes, until well-browned, 40 to 50 minutes.

2. Remove pan from oven, and place over burner(s) set at high heat; add chicken stock and bring to boil, scraping up browned bits on bottom of pan with wooden spoon.

3. Transfer contents of pan to large saucepan. Add wine, 3 cups water, and thyme; bring to boil over high heat. Reduce heat to low and simmer until reduced by half, about 1½ hours. Strain stock into large measuring cup or container. Cool to room temperature; cover with plastic wrap, and refrigerate until fat congeals on surface, about 2 hours.

4. Skim fat from stock using soup spoon; reserve fat. Pour stock through fine-mesh strainer to remove remaining bits of fat; discard bits in strainer. Bring stock to simmer in medium saucepan over medium-high heat.

5. In second medium saucepan, heat 4 tablespoons reserved turkey fat over medium-high heat until bubbling; whisk in flour and cook, whisking constantly, until combined and honey-colored, about 2 minutes. Continuing to whisk constantly, gradually add hot stock; bring to boil, then reduce heat to medium-low and simmer, stirring occasionally, until slightly thickened, about 5 minutes. Season to taste with salt and pepper. (Gravy can be refrigerated up to 3 days. After turkey comes out of oven, heat gravy in medium saucepan over medium heat until hot, about 8 minutes.)

SCIENCE DESK: How Brining Works

WE FIND THAT SOAKING TURKEYS (AS WELL AS CHICKEN and even pork chops) in a saltwater solution before cooking best protects delicate white meat. Whether we are roasting a turkey or grilling chicken parts, we have consistently found that brining keeps the meat juicier. Brining also gives delicate (and sometimes mushy) poultry a meatier, firmer consistency and seasons the meat down to the bone. (We also find that brining adds moisture to pork and shrimp and improves their texture and flavor when grilled.)

To explain these sensory perceptions, we ran some tests. We started by weighing several 11-pound turkeys after they had been brined for 12 hours and found an average weight gain of almost ¾ pound. Even more impressive, we found that brined birds weighed 6 to 8 ounces more after roasting than a same-sized bird that had not been brined.

Our taste buds were right: Brined birds are juicier.

How does brining work? Brining promotes a change in the structure of the proteins in the muscle. The salt causes protein strands to become denatured, or unwound. This is the same process that occurs when proteins are exposed to heat, acid, or alcohol. When protein strands unwind, they get tangled up with one another, forming a matrix that traps water. Salt is commonly used to give processed meats a better texture. For example, hot dogs made without salt would be limp.

In most cases, we add sugar to the brine. Sugar has little if any effect on the texture of the meat, but it does add flavor and promotes better browning of the skin.

We usually list both kosher and regular table salt in recipes that call for brining. Because of the difference in the size of the crystals, cup for cup, table salt is about twice as concentrated as kosher salt.

TASTING LAB: Boxed Dressings

AFTER CHOPPING, MINCING, DICING, DRYING, AND CUBING our way through countless batches of homemade dressing, we wondered if there was an easier, less time-consuming way to make this dish. To answer this question, we held a blind taste test of seven leading brands of commercial dressing. We prepared each according to the package directions.

Not surprisingly, all of these commercial stuffings received disappointing scores. Most were too salty and greasy and much too bland. After reading ingredient labels, this is easy to understand. On all labels, wheat flour is listed first, followed by corn syrup, salt, and soybean oil.

Bell's Family Style Dressing was the best of the lot; tasters liked its "herby" and "sweet" flavor. Kellogg's Croquettes was a distant second, followed by Arnold Premium Sage & Onion and Pepperidge Farm Cubed Herb.

Our conclusion: The high amounts of sugar, salt, and fat in boxed dressings will not mask the absence of fresh ingredients like onions, celery, eggs, and stock. For dressing that tastes great, take the time to make homemade.

CRANBERRY SAUCE

WHAT WE WANTED: A well balanced sauce—neither too sweet or tart—with a soft gel-like texture and some whole berries.

Although cranberry jelly, molded in the shape of the can and sliced into neat disks, is one of the test kitchen's guilty pleasures, it's usually not our first choice for the holiday table. There, a soft, tart-sweet sauce with plenty of whole berries reigns. The best cranberry sauce has a clean, pure cranberry flavor, with enough sweetness to temper the assertively tart fruit but not so much that the sauce is cloying or candylike. The texture should be that of a soft gel, neither too liquidy nor too stiff, cushioning some softened but still intact berries.

Because simple cranberry sauce has only three ingredients—cranberries, sweetener, and liquid—the variables to test were relatively straightforward. Though many of the recipes we researched called for 1 pound of cranberries, we wanted to base ours on 12 ounces of berries simply because all the bags in stores are that size; we couldn't see the point of opening a second bag to use only a third of it.

Most cranberry sauce recipes use granulated sugar as a sweetener, but we also tried brown sugar, honey, maple syrup, and corn syrup. Granulated sugar was the tasters' favorite because it balanced the tartness of the berries with a direct sweetness, without adding a strong flavor profile of its own. The corn syrup tasted flat and bland, while the flavors of the maple syrup, brown sugar, and honey were too pronounced, compromising that of the berries. The amount of sugar called for in the recipes we turned up during our research ranged from ⅜ cup to 1½ cups for 12 ounces of berries. Tasters unanimously favored 1 cup of sugar.

The liquids used to make the sauce ran a wide gamut. We tried batches made with apple juice and cider, white and dark grape juice, orange juice, pineapple juice, cranberry juice cocktail, 7-Up, red wine, white wine, port, and champagne. Tasters agreed that none of these liquids—even the orange juice, which is traditional—offered a significant flavor advantage over plain water. In testing different amounts of water, we found that ¾ cup provided the ideal sauce-to-berry ratio once the sauce had reached serving temperature.

Tests of the various cooking times revealed that less is more. About five minutes over medium heat was all it took to achieve a supple, just-firm-enough set in the cooled sauce. Cranberries are high in pectin, a naturally occurring carbohydrate in many fruits. In the presence of sugar and acid (cranberries contain both), the large pectin molecules bond with each other to produce the characteristic jelled consistency. Since pectin molecules are released as the cells of the fruit break down during cooking, the longer the fruit cooks, the more pectin is released (and the more liquid is evaporated), and the stiffer the finished gel becomes. Cooking the sauce for 10 minutes, for instance, resulted in a gel you could slice with a knife. We also tested using a skillet instead of a saucepan and high heat rather than medium heat. We could see no advantage either way and decided to leave well enough alone.

The last round of tests focused on seasoning. Many recipes call simply for cranberries, water, and sugar, while others specify additions such as lemon juice, almond or vanilla extract, and salt. Lemon juice was much too tart, and both extracts left tasters cold, but we were amazed by the dramatic improvement a little salt could make. Just ¼ teaspoon of salt revealed heretofore unknown sweetness in the cranberries and heightened the flavor of the sauce overall, letting loose a full range of high and low flavor notes.

WHAT WE LEARNED: Keep it simple—just water, granulated sugar, and cranberries make the best sauce. Keep it short—simmering for more than five minutes results in a stiff, sliceable gel. And don't forget the salt.

BASIC CRANBERRY SAUCE   makes 2¼ cups

If you've got frozen cranberries, do not defrost them before use; just pick through them and add about 2 minutes to the simmering time.

    ¾   cup water
    1   cup sugar
    ¼   teaspoon salt
    1   (12-ounce) bag cranberries, picked through

Bring water, sugar, and salt to boil in medium nonreactive saucepan over high heat, stirring occasionally to dissolve sugar. Stir in cranberries; return to boil. Reduce heat to medium; simmer until saucy, slightly thickened, and about two-thirds of berries have popped open, about 5 minutes. Transfer to nonreactive bowl, cool to room temperature, and serve. (Can be covered and refrigerated up to 7 days; let stand at room temperature 30 minutes before serving.)

VARIATIONS

CRANBERRY-ORANGE SAUCE

Orange juice adds little flavor, but we found that zest and liqueur pack the orange kick we were looking for in this sauce.

Follow recipe for Basic Cranberry Sauce, heating 1 tablespoon grated orange zest with sugar mixture. Off heat; stir in 2 table-spoons orange liqueur (such as Triple Sec or Grand Marnier).

CRANBERRY SAUCE WITH PEARS AND FRESH GINGER

Peel, core, and cut 2 medium-sized firm, ripe pears into ½-inch chunks; set aside. Follow recipe for Basic Cranberry Sauce, heating 1 tablespoon grated fresh ginger and ¼ tea-spoon ground cinnamon with sugar mixture and stirring pears into liquid along with cranberries.

EQUIPMENT CORNER: Saucepans

A MEDIUM SAUCEPAN (2 TO 2½ QUARTS) IS BEST FOR preparing cranberry sauce. You'll also use this pan to blanch small amounts of vegetables, prepare rice, or make pastry cream. To find out whether it's necessary to spend a lot of money on this pan, we tested seven leading brands. We sautéed minced onion in butter to judge sauté speed. We also tested the pans' ability to cook evenly by preparing rice in each vessel. To assess which pans could cook without the burning or scorching caused by inferior material or hot spots, we scalded milk in each saucepan and made pastry cream.

Our tests turned out a wide range of results. We found that really lightweight pans are prone to scorching and that heavy copper or enameled cast-iron saucepans are hard to maneuver because they weigh too much. We recommend a pan with some heft (two to three pounds is ideal for this size pan), but don't go overboard. Also look for pans with han-dles that won't become scorching hot. Hollowed-out stain-less steel handles or even cheap plastic handles (a saucepan never goes into the oven, so there's no need to buy some-thing ovenproof anyway) are better than solid metal handles, which became hot very quickly during our tests.

Our favorite saucepans were the All-Clad Stainless fol-lowed by Tramontina. Both had good conductivity, were easy to maneuver, and sautéed reasonably well. Both of these pans are made from stainless steel with a layer of aluminum sandwiched inside for increased heat conduction. On the All Clad pan, the aluminum layer runs across the bottom and up the entire side of the pan; on the Tramontina, the aluminum layer is only on the bottom. Expect to spend about $45 for the Tramontina pan and nearly $120 for All-Clad.

One final note. Although not an issue with cranberry sauce, many of the other jobs that a medium saucepan is suited for (making rice or oatmeal, heating milk for cocoa) involve ingredients that stick and leave a mess in the pan, even when the recipe comes out right. For this reason, you might want to consider buying a nonstick 2-quart saucepan.

CHRISTMAS dinner

CHAPTER 14

Christmas dinner is not the time to experiment with
new recipes or techniques. What every cook needs is foolproof recipes
for family favorites. Holiday cooks also need a streamlined menu with
as little last-minute work as possible.

For us, prime rib with potatoes and green beans is the perfect
Christmas dinner. It's festive (how often do you make prime rib at home?)
but relatively easy to prepare. In fact, you can probably prepare this entire
menu with just an hour or so of kitchen work on Christmas Day.

Of course, just because a menu is easy to prepare doesn't mean it's
good. Prime rib that's overcooked isn't going to make anyone jolly. Each
slice should be rosy from the center all the way to the crust.

Christmas dinner also needs great side dishes. Pommes Anna, an
elegant French potato cake, is a great choice. Like so many classic
French recipes, this one needed some updating for American kitchens.

And for cooks who want to pull out all the stops, you might start
things off with Creamy Mushroom Soup (page 10) and conclude with
our Bittersweet Chocolate Roulade (page 341).

IN THIS CHAPTER

THE RECIPES
Prime Rib

Pommes Anna

Blanched Green Beans
Green Beans with Sautéed
    Shallots and Vermouth
Green Beans with Toasted
    Hazelnuts and Brown Butter

EQUIPMENT CORNER
Roasting Pans
Vegetable Peelers

SCIENCE DESK
Why Aging Tenderizes Beef
Why Potatoes Turn Brown

TASTING LAB
Prime Rib
Commercial Beef Broth

Chris hurries from the prime rib in the oven to the potatoes on the stove.

PRIME RIB

WHAT WE WANTED: A foolproof method for roasting prime rib that delivers juicy, tender, rosy slices of meat.

A prime rib is a little like a turkey: You probably cook only one a year, usually for an important occasion such as Christmas. Although you know there are alternative cooking methods that might deliver a better roast, they're too risky. You don't want to be remembered as the cook who carved slices of almost raw standing rib or delayed dinner for hours waiting for the roast to finish cooking. Rather than chance it, you stick with the standard 350 degrees for X minutes per pound. A roast cooked this way, you decide, will at least not embarrass you. But a roast cooked this way won't be great either.

Other than using general terms like juicy and tender, we weren't quite sure how to define perfect prime rib when we started testing, so we had no preconceived ideas about what techniques or methods would deliver a superior roast. In addition to our normal cookbook research, we decided to interview a few of the thousands of chefs who cook prime rib every day. Between what we found in books and what we learned from these chefs, we came up with a dozen or so fairly different methods. Although there were minor issues, such as whether the roast needed to be tied or whether it should be roasted on a rack, one big question needed answering: At what temperature should prime rib be roasted?

We started with oven temperatures. Suggested roasting temperatures ranged from a tepid 250 degrees to a bold 425 degrees. Other recipes recommended an initial high-temperature sear (450 to 500 degrees), then reduced the oven temperature to a more moderate 350 degrees for actual roasting. Wanting to test the full range, we roasted prime ribs at temperatures ranging from 250 to 500 degrees.

All prime ribs roasted at oven temperatures exceeding 300 degrees looked pretty much the same. Each slice of carved beef was well-done around the exterior, medium toward the center, and a beautiful, pink medium-rare at the center. We might have been tempted to report that roasting temperature doesn't much matter if we hadn't tried cooking prime rib at oven temperatures under 300 degrees. The results surprised us, although it certainly wasn't love at first sight.

About halfway through the cooking time of the first roast tested at 250 degrees, we wrote in our notes, "Though the meat looks virtually raw, the internal temperature registers 110 degrees, and very little of its fat has rendered." But we changed our minds as soon as we carved the first slice. This roast was as beautiful on the inside as it was anemic on the outside. Unlike the roasts that cooked at higher temperatures, this one was rosy pink from the surface to the center—the juiciest and most tender of all the roasts we had cooked. This was restaurant prime rib at its best.

In addition to being evenly cooked, the prime rib roasted in a 250-degree oven had another thing going for it: Its internal temperature increased only a degree or two during its resting period. (Roasts are allowed to rest when they come out of the oven both to distribute the heat evenly and to allow the juices to reabsorb back into the outer layers of the meat. For more information on this phenomenon, see the Science Desk on page 158.) A roast cooked to 128 degrees, for example, moved only to 130 degrees after a 45-minute rest.

Not so with the roasts cooked at higher temperatures. Their internal temperatures increased much more dramatically out of the oven. As a matter of fact, we noticed a direct correlation between oven temperature and the increase in the temperature of the roast while resting. Prime ribs roasted at moderate temperatures (325 to 350 degrees) increased, on average, 14 degrees during resting. In other words, if pulled from the oven at a rare 126-degree internal temperature, these roasts moved up to a solid medium (140 degrees) by the end of the resting period. Meanwhile, the prime rib roasted at 425 degrees increased a whopping 24 degrees (from 119 to 143) during its rest. We considered a smaller increase in postcooking temperature a definite advantage. It let us pull the roast from the oven at the temperature we wanted instead of having to speculate as to how many degrees the temperature would climb during resting.

In addition to its more stable internal temperature, prime rib roasted at 250 degrees lost less weight during cooking than prime rib roasted at higher temperatures. A 6¾-pound roast cooked in a 250-degree oven weighed just over 6¼ pounds when it came out of the oven, a loss of less than half a pound. By contrast, similar roasts cooked in a 325-degree oven lost just more than a pound, while roasts cooked at 350 degrees lost 1½ pounds. The prime rib cooked at 425 degrees lost a shocking 2 pounds. Part of the weight loss is fat, but certainly a good portion is juice. This test confirmed our suspicions that the beef roasted at 250 degrees was indeed juicier than beef roasted at higher temperatures.

Because members of a trade group called National Cattlemen's Beef Association would not endorse an oven-roasting temperature below 300 degrees, we decided to check the safety of this low-heat method before getting too sold on it. After conversations with a number of food scientists across the country, we determined that low-temperature roasting is as safe a cooking method as higher-temperature roasting. And though the odds of finding bacteria inside a prime rib roast are close to nil, the only way to guarantee a bacteria-free slab of prime rib is to cook it to an internal temperature of 160 degrees, no matter what cooking method is used, low temperature or high. Unfortunately, at 160 degrees, the meat is gray, tough, and unappetizing.

The only thing that bothered us about the slow-roasted prime rib was its raw-looking, fatty exterior. We solved this problem by searing the meat on top of the stove before low-roasting it, giving it a beautiful crusty brown exterior.

As we expected, our tests with various seasonings demonstrated that simpler is better. Good prime rib needs nothing other than salt and pepper. We did discover that aging the beef at home—keeping it uncovered on a rack over a pan in the refrigerator—will improve the flavor and texture of the meat. (For more information on aging, see the Science Desk on page 179.)

As nebulous as the meaning of "perfect prime rib" had been to us at the beginning of our tests, it became crystal clear the moment we carved off that first slice of low-roasted prime rib. We immediately recognized it as the beef you get at a great prime rib restaurant. As it turns out, many such restaurants slow-roast their meat. They use special ovens that roast the meat at 250 degrees until it reaches an internal temperature of 120 degrees. At that time, the oven heat is decreased to 140 degrees, causing the meat's internal temperature to increase to 130 degrees and remain there until ready to serve (up to 24 hours later). Unfortunately, few home cooks can use this method since most home oven thermostats do not go below 200 degrees. But by following our recipe, home cooks can very closely approximate the superb prime rib served in the country's best restaurants.

WHAT WE LEARNED: Roast prime rib in a 250-degree oven for meat that cooks evenly and yields rosy slices. To promote a brown crust, pan-sear the roast on top of the stove before it goes into the oven.

PRIME RIB serves 6 to 8

Even if you don't purchase the roast a week ahead of time as the instructions suggest, a day or two of aging in the refrigerator will help. (See the Science Desk on page 179 for more information on aging beef.)

1 **(3-rib) standing rib roast (about 7 pounds), aged up to 1 week, set at room temperature for 1 hour, and tied with kitchen twine at both ends, twine running parallel to bone (see illustration below left)**
   Salt and ground black pepper

1. Adjust oven rack to low position and heat oven to 250 degrees. Heat large roasting pan over two burners set at medium-high heat until hot, about 4 minutes. Place roast in hot pan and cook on all sides until nicely browned and about ½ cup fat has rendered, 6 to 8 minutes.

2. Remove roast from pan. Set wire rack in pan, then set roast on rack. Generously season with salt and pepper.

3. Place roast in oven and roast until meat registers 130 degrees (for medium-rare) on instant-read thermometer, 3 to 3½ hours. Remove roast from oven and tent with foil. Let

stand 20 to 30 minutes to allow juices to redistribute themselves evenly throughout roast.

4. Remove twine and set roast on cutting board, rib bones at 90-degree angle to board. Carve (see illustrations below right), and serve immediately.

TASTING LAB: Prime Rib

BUTCHERS TEND TO CUT A RIB ROAST, WHICH CONSISTS of ribs 6 through 12 if left whole, into two distinct cuts. The more desirable of the two cuts consists of ribs 10 through 12. Since this portion of the roast is closer to the loin end, it is sometimes called the "loin end." Other butchers call it the "small end" or the "first cut." Whatever it is called, it is more desirable because it contains the large, single rib-eye muscle and is less fatty. A less desirable cut, which is still an excellent roast, consists of ribs 6 to 9, closer to the chuck end, and sometimes called the second cut. The closer to the chuck, the more multimuscled the roast becomes. Since muscles are surrounded by fat, this means a fattier roast. While some cooks may prefer this cut because the fat adds flavor, the more tender and more regularly formed loin end is considered the best.

TECHNIQUE: Tying Up Prime Rib

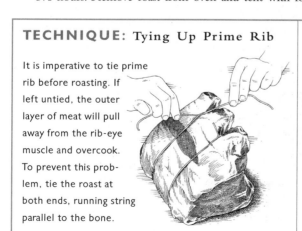

It is imperative to tie prime rib before roasting. If left untied, the outer layer of meat will pull away from the rib-eye muscle and overcook. To prevent this problem, tie the roast at both ends, running string parallel to the bone.

TECHNIQUE: Carving Prime Rib

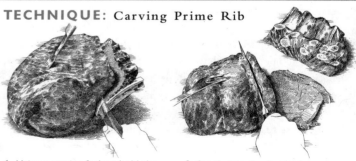

1. Using a carving fork to hold the roast in place, cut along the rib bones to sever the meat from the bones.

2. Set the roast cut-side down; carve the meat across the grain into thick slices.

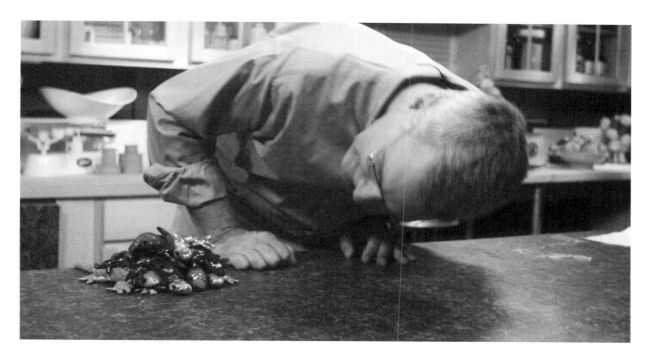

SCIENCE DESK:
Why Aging Tenderizes Beef

MEAT IS AGED TO DEVELOP ITS FLAVOR AND IMPROVE ITS texture. This process depends on certain enzymes, whose function in a live animal is to digest proteins. (In the above photo, Doc is using hungry toy lizards to represent these enzymes.) After the animal is slaughtered, the cells that contain these enzymes start to break down, releasing the enzymes into the meat where they attack the cell proteins and break them down into amino acids, which have more flavor. The enzymes also break down the muscles, so the tissue becomes softer. This process can take from one to several weeks. (For the sake of safety, meat should not be aged for more than one week at home; beyond that time it must be done under carefully controlled conditions.)

Traditionally, butchers have hung carcasses in the meat locker to age their beef. Today, some beef is still aged on hooks (this process is called dry aging), but for the most part beef is wet-aged in vacuum-sealed packets. We wondered if it was worth it to the home cook to go the extra mile for dry-aged beef, so we ordered both a dry-aged and wet-aged prime rib roast from a restaurant supplier in Manhattan. The differences between the two roasts were clear-cut.

Like a good, young red wine, wet-aged beef tasted pleasant and fresh on its own. When compared with the dry-aged beef, though, we realized its flavors were less concentrated. The meat tasted washed out. The dry-aged beef, on the other hand, engaged the mouth. It was stronger, richer, and gamier-tasting, with a pleasant tang. The dry-aged and wet-aged beef were equally tender, but the dry-aged beef had an added buttery texture.

Unfortunately, most butchers don't dry-age beef anymore because hanging quarters of beef take up valuable refrigerator space. Dry-aged beef also dehydrates (loses weight) and requires trimming (loses more weight). That weight loss means less beef costs more money. Wet-aged beef loses virtually no weight during the aging process, and it comes prebutchered, packaged, and ready to sell. Because beef is expensive to begin with, most customers opt for the less expensive wet-aged beef. Why does dry aging work better than wet aging? The answer is simple: air. Encased in plastic, wet-aged beef is shut off from oxygen—the key to flavor development and concentration.

Because availability and price pose problems, you may simply want to age beef yourself. It's just a matter of making room in the refrigerator and remembering to buy the roast ahead of time, up to one week before you plan on roasting it. When you get the roast home, pat it dry and place it on a wire rack set over a paper towel–lined cake pan or plate. Set the racked roast in the refrigerator and let it age until you are ready to roast it, up to seven days. (Aging begins to have a dramatic effect on the roast after three or four days, but we also detected some improvement in flavor and texture after just one day of aging.) Before roasting, shave off any exterior meat that has completely dehydrated. Between the trimming and dehydration, a 7-pound roast will lose a pound or so during a week's aging.

TASTING LAB: Commercial Beef Broth

BEEF BROTH IS A TRADITIONAL EUROPEAN AND AMERICAN staple, a key ingredient in many classic sauces as well as the basis for popular beef soups. In the past several years, however, sales of beef broth have lagged. The most recent statistics for annual sales show that more than four times as many cans of chicken broth are sold than cans of beef broth.

When we tasted commercial beef broths, it became obvious why this situation has developed: Most beef broths simply do not deliver full-bodied, beefy flavor. There might be subtle beef suggestions, but after tasting nearly all of the selected broths—bouillon-based, canned, gourmet, and organic—there remained one nagging question: "Where's the beef?"

As things stand, U.S. regulations for beef broth do not require much beef. A commercial beef broth need contain only 1 part protein to 135 parts moisture, according to the U.S. Department of Agriculture's standards. That translates to less than about an ounce of meat (or about one-quarter of a hamburger) to 1 gallon of water. Most commercial products are very close to that limit, strictly because of economics. Generally, manufactured beef broth derives its flavor from bare beef bones and a boost of various additives. A glance at the label on the side of any canned broth or boxed bouillon cubes will confirm this.

We wanted to talk to the manufacturers of beef broths to verify our impressions of the way they make their products, but calls to broth giants Hormel Foods and Campbell Soup Company were dead ends. Both declined to answer questions as to how their commercial beef broths are made. But beef bones plus additives would certainly explain why of the 12 commercial broths we tasted, none came even close to the full-bodied, beefy flavor of our homemade stock recipe—made with 6 pounds of meat. Nearly all of the commercial broths were thin and flavorless, with the exception of "off" or artificial flavors.

What seems to distinguish most supermarket broths from homemade, gourmet, or natural foods store broths is a riddling of flavor additives. Monosodium glutamate (MSG) can be found in nearly all supermarket beef broths. Disodium guanylate and disodium isonate, which are both yeast-based, hydrolyzed soy protein, are also typically added to commercial broths. Other yeast extracts also find their way into most of these broths. All approved by the U.S. Food and Drug Administration (FDA), these additives are intended to "enhance" flavor. As one FDA spokesperson explained, "You've got something that's kind of 'blah,' so to give it a little more taste they add these things."

Salt—and lots of it—also adds to the flavor of these broths. Most beef broth products contain about 35 percent of the daily allowance for sodium per serving. Salt is also added to help extract the needed protein from the bones.

The preferred product in our commercial broth tasting was a jarred beef base, Superior Touch Better Than Bouillon, but even this "winner" had an unflattering score of 4.6 on a scale of 0 to 10. Herb Ox Beef Bouillon Cubes lagged not too far behind. Forget about the more expensive gourmet and organic commercial broths, which not only failed to deliver beef flavor but also proved among the least palatable of the pack. Even if you get your hands on one of the "top finishers," we do not recommend that you use them in a recipe where the flavor of beef broth predominates, as it does in beef soup. They serve reasonably well when used as background flavor in a sauce or gravy and when heavily doctored up.

EQUIPMENT CORNER: Roasting Pans

THOUGH MOST COOKS HAUL OUT THEIR ROASTING PAN infrequently, when you need this large pan, nothing else will do. A roasting pan is a must for prime rib.

A roasting pan should promote deep, even browning of food. It should be easy to maneuver in and out of the oven. And it should be able to travel from oven to stovetop, so that you can deglaze the pan and loosen drippings.

Roasting pans can be made from stainless steel, enameled steel, nonstick-coated aluminum, or anodized aluminum, all of which we tested. We decided not to test pans lined with copper, which are prohibitively expensive; cast-iron pans, which when loaded with food are too heavy to lift; and pans made from Pyrex, ceramic, or stoneware, all of which seem better suited to lasagne and casseroles because they can't be used on top of the stove.

We tested eight roasting pans and preferred the materials we like in other cookware—stainless steel and anodized aluminum. These materials are heavy (though not prohibitively so) and produce good browning. Although nonstick coatings made cleanup easier, roasting racks slid around in these pans. For instance, when one test cook tilted a nonstick pan ever so slightly to remove it from the oven, a turkey and rack slid sharply to one side, which threw off her balance and nearly landed the hot turkey at her feet.

Roasting pans generally come in two different styles— upright handles and side handles (see photos, right). Upright handles tend to be square in shape, while side handles are generally oval loops. We found upright handles to be easier to grip. The problem with side handles is that their position, coupled with the large size of the pan, can cause you to bring your forearms perilously close to the hot oven walls. We tested one pan without handles, which was by far the most difficult to take out of the oven.

We tested pans ranging in length from 16 to 20 inches and in width from 11 to 14 inches. We preferred pans that measured about 16 inches long and 12 to 14 inches across. Larger pans made for an awkward fit in the oven, and, because of their large surface area, tended to burn pan drippings more easily.

In terms of weight, heavier pans performed better in all tests, especially on top of the stove. Lightweight pans buckled, and the meat browned quite spottily.

To summarize, heavy-duty pans made from stainless steel or anodized aluminum work best to brown foods, especially if the pan is to be used on top of the stove as well as in the oven, as is the case with our prime rib recipe. Expect to spend $150 on these top-flight pans.

ROASTING PANS
The handles on the roasting pan above are upright and easy to grasp. Side handles, like those on the roasting pan below, are more difficult to grasp than upright handles and seem more likely to cause burns.

POMMES ANNA

WHAT WE WANTED: A foolproof, simplified method for preparing this elegant potato cake that wouldn't sacrifice the buttery flavor and crisp texture that makes this dish so special.

Imagine thin potato slices layered meticulously in a skillet with nothing but butter, salt, pepper, and more butter, left to cook until the inverted dish reveals a potato cake with a lovely crisp, deep brown, glassine crust belying the soft, creamy potato layers within. This is pommes Anna, the queen of potato cookery.

Legend has it that Anna was a fashionable woman who lived during the reign of Napoleon III. Whoever Anna was, the creator of this dish was, to be sure, a chef with an inordinate amount of time on his hands, as the recipe requires painstaking procedures and the patience of Job. Given the amount of effort required to make just one dish of pommes Anna, it was particularly irritating when, in our preliminary recipe testing, those we made suffered a 50 percent rate of failure to release cleanly from the pan. It's no surprise, then, that pommes Anna is rarely seen on menus or home dinner tables and that recipes for it are sequestered in only the staunchest of French cookbooks.

We hoped to find a means of simplifying and foolproofing this classic. If we could do away with some of the maddening work and guarantee more than a crapshoot's chance of perfect unmolding, pommes Anna could find her way back onto the culinary map. . . and certainly onto the dining room table.

First we needed a pan for the perilous pommes. Of the four different cooking vessels we employed in tests—a cast-iron skillet, a copper pommes Anna pan, a heavy-bottomed skillet with a stainless steel cooking surface, and a heavy-bottomed nonstick skillet—only the nonstick effortlessly released the potatoes onto the serving platter. As reluctant as we were to make such specific equipment requisite for

pommes Anna, a nonstick skillet is essential to the dish's success. After all, once having expended the effort of slicing and arranging the potatoes, it is both enraging and mortifying to later witness them clinging stubbornly to the pan.

Most, if not all, recipes for pommes Anna begin with clarified butter. To make it, butter is melted, the foamy whey is spooned off the top, and the pure butterfat is poured or spooned off of the milky casein at the bottom. Since it lacks solids and proteins, clarified butter has a higher smoking point (and so is more resistant to burning) than whole butter, but it also lacks the full, buttery flavor that those solids and proteins provide. We have always been annoyed by clarified butter because of the time required to make it, the waste involved (typically, about 30 percent of the butter is lost with clarifying), and the loss of flavor. But pommes Anna, which spends a substantial amount of time cooking at moderately high temperatures, is always made with clarified butter. Our big coup, we thought, would be to circumvent its necessity, so we made a pommes Anna with whole butter to see if we couldn't prove false the centuries-old maxim that says clarified butter is a must. Sure enough, the surface of the potatoes was dotted with unappealing black flecks. Still, as a few tasters noticed, the whole butter gave the potatoes a richer, fuller flavor that we missed in the versions made with clarified butter.

We thought to replace the butter in the bottom of the skillet with oil, then drizzle melted whole butter between potato layers. This worked better than we could have hoped. Our newfangled pommes Anna had a lovely crisp brown crust rivaling that of any made with clarified butter.

Thinly sliced potatoes are a defining characteristic of pommes Anna, as is the overlapping arrangement of the slices in concentric circles. In the early stages of our testing, we preferred to slice the potatoes by hand (for no good reason), but as numbers increased, we took to a food processor fitted with a fine slicing disk that could get the job done

with effortless speed. If you own and are adept with a mandoline, it offers another quick means of slicing the potatoes.

Slicing wasn't the only obstacle presented by the potatoes. Because they will discolor if peeled and sliced and then kept waiting to be arranged in the skillet, they must be soaked in water, which in turn means that the slices must be dried before being layered. To avoid this incredible inconvenience, we opted to slice and arrange the potatoes in batches, making sure each group of slices was arranged in the skillet before slicing the next batch. This method prevented discoloration, but it was also awkward and inefficient. Someone suggested tossing the sliced potatoes in the melted butter to prevent them from discoloring (see the Science Desk on page 184.) We tried this, and though the butter did not prevent the discoloration, it did slow it down to the extent that all slices could be layered in the skillet before severe discoloration set in. That the butter no longer required drizzling between each layer was a bonus.

Most pommes Anna recipes have the cook start layering potato slices in the skillet as it heats on the stovetop. It may sound dangerous, but it isn't, really, and it saves much time. After all the slices are in, the skillet is transferred to a hot oven or left on the stovetop to complete cooking. After many tests, we determined that the potatoes—started in a cold skillet—require 30 minutes on the stovetop at medium-low heat, then—after a firm pressing with the bottom of a cake pan to compact the potatoes into a cohesive cake—25 minutes more in a 450-degree oven. The time on the stovetop gets the browning going on the bottom, and the oven time cooks through the potatoes' thickness while completing the bottom browning. Now, not only was a nonstick skillet necessary, but a nonstick ovenproof skillet was required to do the job.

The final step of pommes Anna is, of course, unmolding. If only it could be so easy as inverting a layer cake onto a cooling rack, but with a heavy, hot-handled skillet, the process is awkward and clumsy and can make an experienced cook feel like a bumbling one. Rather than trying to invert the potatoes directly onto a serving platter, where they cannot be unmolded in dead center because of the skillet's protruding handle, we lined the back of a baking sheet (a rimless cookie sheet will do) with lightly greased foil. We inverted the potatoes onto this surface, much as we would invert a cake onto a cooling rack, then slid them onto the serving platter. We found this technique a little less dangerous and much less complicated than going straight from pan to serving dish.

A last word on pommes Anna. Even simplified and streamlined, this recipe requires a good amount of patience, but it is no less a tour de force of culinary art and engineering than the classic rendition.

WHAT WE LEARNED: Skip the clarified butter and instead toss the sliced potatoes with melted butter. To keep the bottom layer from burning, coat the pan with oil. Use a nonstick skillet to prevent sticking and guarantee perfect release, and press down on the potatoes with a cake pan to compact them.

POMMES ANNA serves 6 to 8

Do not slice the potatoes until you are ready to start assembling. Remember to start timing when you begin arranging the potatoes in the skillet—no matter how quickly you arrange them, they will need 30 minutes on the stovetop to brown properly.

- 3 pounds russet, Yukon Gold, or white potatoes, peeled and sliced ⅟₁₆ to ⅛ inch thick
- 5 tablespoons unsalted butter, melted
- ¼ cup vegetable or peanut oil, plus additional for greasing baking sheet
  Salt and ground black pepper

1. Toss potato slices with melted butter in large bowl until potatoes are evenly coated. Adjust oven rack to lower-middle position and heat oven to 450 degrees.

2. Pour oil into 10-inch heavy-bottomed ovenproof non-stick skillet; swirl to coat pan bottom and set skillet over medium-low heat. Begin timing, and arrange potato slices in skillet, using nicest slices to form bottom layer. To start, place one slice in center of skillet. Overlap more slices in circle around center slice, then form another circle of overlapping slices to cover pan bottom. Sprinkle evenly with scant ¼ teaspoon salt and ground black pepper to taste. Arrange second layer of potatoes, working in opposite direction of first layer; sprinkle evenly with scant ¼ teaspoon salt and ground black pepper. Repeat, layering potatoes in opposite directions and sprinkling with salt and pepper, until no slices remain (broken or uneven slices can be pieced together to form single slice; potatoes will mound in center of skillet); continue to cook over medium-low heat until 30 minutes elapse from time you began arranging potatoes in skillet.

3. Using bottom of 9-inch cake pan, press potatoes down firmly to compact. Cover skillet and place in oven. Bake until potatoes begin to soften, about 15 minutes. Uncover and continue to bake until potatoes are tender, when paring knife can be easily inserted in center and edge of potatoes near skillet is browned, about 10 minutes longer. Meanwhile, line rimless baking sheet or back of rimmed baking sheet with foil and coat very lightly with oil. Drain off excess fat from potatoes by pressing bottom of cake pan against potatoes while tilting skillet. (Be sure to use heavy potholders or oven mitts.)

4. Set foil-lined baking sheet on top of skillet. With hands protected by oven mitts or potholders, hold baking sheet in place with one hand and carefully invert skillet and baking sheet together. Lift skillet off potatoes. Carefully slide potatoes from baking sheet onto platter. Cut into wedges and serve immediately.

SCIENCE DESK:
Why Potatoes Turn Brown

AS MANY OF US FIND OUT THE HARD WAY, PEELED AND sliced potatoes take on a brick-red hue when left to sit out for several minutes before cooking. This was of particular concern in our pommes Anna recipe, because the peeled, sliced potatoes must wait to be layered in the skillet. We consulted spud expert Dr. Alfred Bushway, professor of food science at the University of Maine, to find out what causes potatoes to turn color. He explained that with slicing and peeling, potato cells are broken down and the enzyme polyphenol oxidase (PPO) is released. Two major substrates, chlorogenic acid and tyrosine, are also released.

The enzyme and substrates combine with oxygen, and they are then oxidized into a compound called ortho-quinone. The orthoquinone quickly polymerizes (a process in which many molecules link up to form a chain of more complex material with different physical properties) and creates the dark pink-red color that we see in the potatoes.

Tossing the potatoes with butter, as in the pommes Anna recipe, helps limit oxygen exposure and therefore retards discoloration. We had also noted that certain potatoes

discolor more rapidly than others. Bushway said that from cultivar to cultivar and over the storage season, potatoes vary in their enzyme and/or substrate concentrations and enzyme activity, so differences in discoloration rates can be expected. In our experience, russet potatoes seem to discolor most rapidly, so if you're a slow hand, opt for Yukon Golds or white potatoes for pommes Anna.

EQUIPMENT CORNER:
Vegetable Peelers

YOU MIGHT IMAGINE THAT ALL VEGETABLE PEELERS ARE pretty much the same. Not so. In our research, we turned up 25 peelers, many with quite novel features. The major differences were the fixture of the blade, either stationary or swiveling; the material of the blade, carbon stainless steel, stainless steel, or ceramic; and the orientation of the blade to the handle, either straight in line with the body or perpendicular to it. The last arrangement, with the blade perpendicular to the handle, is called a harp, or Y, peeler because the frame looks like the body of a harp or the letter Y. This type of peeler, which is popular in Europe, works with a pulling motion rather than the shucking motion of most American peelers.

To test the peelers, we recruited several cooks and asked them to peel carrots, potatoes, lemons, butternut squash, and celery root. In most cases, testers preferred the Oxo Good Grips peeler with a sharp stainless steel blade that swivels. Peelers with stationary blades are fine for peeling carrots, but they have trouble hugging the curves on potatoes. As for blade material, we found peelers made from stainless steel, carbon steel, and ceramic that were sharp and dull. We concluded that sharpness is a factor of quality control during the manufacturing process and not blade material.

The Y-shaped peelers tested well, although they removed more flesh along with the skin on potatoes, lemons, and carrots and therefore did not rate as well as the Oxo Good Grips. This liability turned into an asset with butternut squash, where these Y-shaped peelers took off the skin as well as the greenish-tinged flesh right below the skin in one pass. With the Oxo Good Grips, it was necessary to go over the peeled flesh once the skin had been removed. Among Y-shaped peelers, testers preferred the Kuhn Rikon. Because both the Oxo Good Grips and Kuhn Rikon peelers can be had for less than $10, we recommend that you purchase both.

BEST PEELERS

The Oxo Good Grips (left) is our favorite all-purpose peeler. The blade is sharp and great on curves. However, testers in the kitchen with very small hands did complain about the bulky handle. The Kuhn Rikon (right) is our favorite Y-shaped peeler. Because this type of peeler removes more skin than a conventional peeler, it's an especially good choice for peeling butternut squash or celery root.

GREEN BEANS

WHAT WE WANTED: A foolproof way of cooking beans ahead of time and then simply reheating and seasoning them just before serving.

Every cook who has prepared a big holiday meal knows the swell of frenzied activity in the final moments before serving. The last thing anyone wants to deal with at that point is preparing and cooking the requisite green bean side dish. That's why we wanted to identify the best way to cook green beans ahead, so that all they would need is a quick finish before serving. To do so, we had to determine the best cooking method and how long the beans could be held before they were finished and served.

Our test kitchen experiments on cooking methods included blanching, steaming, and braising the beans. We concluded that blanching, or boiling them briefly, was the way to go for two reasons. First, blanched beans cooked more evenly than steamed ones, and second, blanching made it easier to add salt to the beans as they cooked, thereby seasoning them more deeply.

For the finished, dressed beans to arrive at the table with a properly tender-crisp texture, we found that it was especially important not to overcook them. This meant halting their cooking abruptly and completely with a dunk in ice water, a process known as shocking. After that, we had to determine how long the beans could be refrigerated. To find out, we blanched, shocked, and dried a big batch of beans, stored them in the refrigerator, and sampled them twice a day to test for flavor and texture retention. None of the tasters noted any deterioration until the morning of the fourth day, so we concluded that it is fine to blanch the beans up to three days in advance of serving.

Just as flavorful ingredients contribute to the unique flavor and texture of each of the green bean dishes presented here, so too does the treatment of the butter. Butter adds a sweet, rich flavor and lush, refined mouthfeel, but it can bring even more to the party depending on how it is handled.

In the green beans with sautéed shallots and vermouth, the butter melts as it becomes incorporated into the sauce but is not cooked any further. Such gentle treatment preserves the butter's sweet, fresh flavor notes and works well with the delicate shallots. In the green beans with toasted hazelnuts and brown butter, on the other hand, the butter is cooked until its color deepens visibly. This causes the proteins in the butter to brown and take on a deep nutty flavor and more complex character. This stark transformation is accomplished in just 5 minutes over medium heat. Browned butter has the necessary richness and flavor to stand up to toasted hazelnuts.

As we developed these recipes, we reheated plenty of chilled beans and learned a thing or two about the process. Most important was to add a little bit of water—¼ cup will do—to the pan with the beans as they heat. This small amount of water will come to a boil quickly and evaporate almost completely, helping to heat the beans in just a minute or two. We found that tongs are the tool best suited to tossing the beans in the pan and arranging them on the platter.

WHAT WE LEARNED: For maximum flexibility and flavor, blanch beans in salted water, shock in ice water to stop the cooking process, then towel dry and refrigerate until needed. To serve, reheat beans with a little water and flavor with butter sauce.

BLANCHED GREEN BEANS enough for 4 to 6 servings

Blanched and cooled beans can be refrigerated in a zipper-lock plastic bag for up to 3 days. To blanch, dress, and serve the beans without holding them first, increase the blanching time to 5 to 6 minutes and don't bother shocking them in ice water. Instead, quickly arrange the warm, drained beans on a serving platter and top them with the sauce you've prepared as the beans blanch.

1 teaspoon salt
1 pound green beans, stem ends snapped off

Bring 2½ quarts water to boil in large saucepan over high heat; add salt and green beans, return to boil, and cook until beans are bright green and tender-crisp, 3 to 4 minutes. Drain beans in colander set in sink; transfer beans immediately to large heatproof bowl filled with ice water. When beans no longer feel warm to touch, drain in colander again and dry thoroughly with paper towels. Set aside until needed.

GREEN BEANS WITH SAUTÉED SHALLOTS AND VERMOUTH serves 4 to 6

4 tablespoons unsalted butter
4 large shallots (about 8 ounces), sliced thin (about 2 cups)
1 recipe Blanched Green Beans
   Salt and ground black pepper
2 tablespoons dry vermouth

1. Heat 2 tablespoons butter in small skillet over medium heat until foaming. Add shallots and cook, stirring frequently, until golden brown, fragrant, and just crisp around the edges, about 10 minutes. Set skillet aside, off heat.

2. Heat ¼ cup water and beans in 12-inch skillet over high heat; cook, tossing frequently, until warmed through, 1 to 2 minutes. Season with salt and pepper to taste and arrange neatly on warm serving platter.

3. Meanwhile, return skillet with shallots to high heat, stir in vermouth, and bring to simmer. Whisk in remaining 2 tablespoons butter, 1 tablespoon at a time; season with salt and pepper to taste. Top beans with shallots and sauce and serve immediately.

GREEN BEANS WITH TOASTED HAZELNUTS AND BROWN BUTTER serves 4 to 6

4 tablespoons unsalted butter
½ cup hazelnuts (about 2½ ounces), chopped fine and toasted in small skillet over medium heat until just fragrant, 3 to 4 minutes
   Salt and ground black pepper
1 recipe Blanched Green Beans

1. Heat butter in small, heavy-bottomed saucepan over medium heat and cook, swirling frequently, until nut brown and fragrant, 4 to 5 minutes. Add hazelnuts and cook, stirring constantly, until fragrant, about 1 minute. Season with salt and pepper to taste.

2. Meanwhile, heat ¼ cup water and beans in 12-inch skillet over high heat; cook, tossing frequently, until warmed through, 1 to 2 minutes. Season with salt and pepper to taste and arrange neatly on warm serving platter. Top beans with hazelnut butter and serve immediately.

WINTER supper

In America's Test Kitchen, winter is the time for rich braises and stews. Braised short ribs are a favorite choice, not only because they are so delicious but also because short ribs are relatively inexpensive, appealing to our sense of Yankee frugality.

But cheap isn't necessarily good. Short ribs are full of fat—that's what gives them such great flavor. But all that fat can ruin the sauce. The challenge is to cook the short ribs until they are fall-off-the-bone tender while removing as much of the grease as possible.

What goes better with braised short ribs than mashed potatoes? Of course, any old mashed spuds won't do. They must be incredibly creamy, with a great potato flavor and plenty of buttery richness. We've worked out all the details so you can produce mashed potatoes worthy of a four-star restaurant. We've also perfected a foolproof method for roasting carrots that takes just 20 minutes and relies on just three ingredients.

We found that boiling whole potatoes
in their skins prevents them from absorbing
excess water and greatly improves the
texture of mashed potatoes. To peel hot
potatoes, spear them with a fork and remove
the skin with a paring knife.

SHORT RIBS

WHAT WE WANTED: A cooking method that removes the grease from these fatty but flavorful ribs while braising them to perfect tenderness.

In the supermarket meat case, short ribs are often over-looked, seldom understood, rather intimidating hunks of meat and bone that are frequently turned a cold shoulder. But braise them, and they become yielding, tender, and succulent. Then douse them with a velvety sauce containing all the rich, bold flavors from the braise, and they are as satisfying as beef stew, but with much more panache. All of this, however, comes at a price: Short ribs are outrageously fatty. The challenge is to get them to give up their fat.

The first step in most braises is browning the meat. Browning adds color and flavor, but in the case of short ribs it also presents an opportunity to render some of the fat. We tried browning both on the stovetop and in the oven and quickly became a proponent of oven browning. As long as you own a roasting pan large enough to hold all of the ribs in a single layer, you can use the oven to brown them in just one batch. This eliminates the need to brown in multiple batches on the stove, which can create a greasy, splattery mess and result in burnt drippings in the bottom of the pot. In the oven, the ribs can brown for a good long time to maximize rendering.

Braising liquids required only a cursory investigation. Homemade beef stock was out of the question because just about no one makes it. Based on previous tastings in the test kitchen, we also discounted canned beef broth. Canned chicken broth, however, offered sufficient backbone and, when enriched by the flavor and body contributed by the short ribs themselves, made for a rich, robust sauce. We began using a combination of red wine, chicken broth, and water. We eventually eliminated water, but the sauce, despite the abundance of aromatics and herbs, remained strangely hollow and lacking. All along we had been using a cheap, hardly potable wine. After stepping up to a good, solid one worthy of drinking, the sauce improved dramatically; it had the complexity and resonance that we were looking for.

If the braising liquid were to transform itself into the sauce we were after, it would need some thickening. After various experiments, we found that adding flour to the sautéed vegetables before pouring in the liquid resulted in a sauce that was lustrous and had the perfect consistency.

As they braise, the browned short ribs continue to release fat, which means that the braising liquid must be defatted before it is palatable. We found the easiest technique to be a two-day process, necessitating some forethought. Braise the ribs, let them cool in the liquid so that the meat does not dry out, remove them, strain the liquid, and then chill the ribs and the liquid separately. The next day, spoon the solidified fat off the liquid's surface, and heat the liquid and the ribs together.

WHAT WE LEARNED: Browning in the oven rather than on the stovetop is neater and more effective. A really good red wine is crucial to a rich-tasting braising liquid. Preparing the braise a day in advance makes for the easiest, most efficient way to defat the sauce.

SHORT RIBS BRAISED IN RED WINE WITH BACON, PARSNIPS, AND PEARL ONIONS

serves 6

If braising and serving the ribs on the same day, bypass cooling the ribs in the braising liquid; instead, remove them from the pot straight out of the oven, strain the liquid, then let it settle so that the fat separates to the top. With a wide shallow spoon, skim off as much fat as possible and continue with the recipe. Though this recipe and the one that follows calls for the widely available English-style short ribs, both recipes will also work with flanken-style short ribs. (We actually prefer flanken-style ribs, but they are more expensive and difficult to find.) We like to serve these short ribs with mashed potatoes (see page 195), but they also taste good over egg noodles. For information about roasting pans, see the Equipment Corner on page 181. For information about Dutch ovens, see the Equipment Corner on page 192.

short ribs

6	pounds bone-in English-style short ribs, trimmed of excess fat and silver skin, or bone-in flanken-style short ribs (see Tasting Lab on page 193) Salt and ground black pepper
3	cups dry full-bodied red wine
3	large onions, chopped medium
2	medium carrots, chopped medium
1	large celery stalk, chopped medium
9	medium cloves garlic, chopped (about 3 tablespoons)
¼	cup all-purpose flour
4	cups chicken stock or canned low-sodium chicken broth
1	(14.5 ounce) can diced tomatoes, drained
1½	tablespoons minced fresh rosemary leaves
1	tablespoon minced fresh thyme leaves
3	medium bay leaves
1	teaspoon tomato paste

bacon, pearl onion, and parsnip garnish

6	slices bacon (about 6 ounces), cut into ¼-inch pieces
8	ounces frozen pearl onions (do not thaw)
4	medium parsnips (about 10 ounces), peeled and cut diagonally into ¾-inch pieces
¼	teaspoon sugar
¼	teaspoon salt
6	tablespoons minced fresh parsley leaves

1. FOR THE SHORT RIBS: Adjust oven rack to lower-middle position and heat oven to 450 degrees. Arrange short ribs bone-side down in single layer in large flameproof roasting pan; season with salt and pepper. Roast until meat begins to brown, about 45 minutes; drain off all liquid and fat with bulb baster. Return pan to oven and continue to cook until meat is well browned, 15 to 20 minutes longer. (For flanken-style short ribs, arrange ribs in single layer in large roasting pan; season with salt and pepper. Roast until meat begins to brown, about 45 minutes; drain off all liquid and fat with bulb baster. Return pan to oven and continue to cook until browned, about 8 minutes; using tongs, flip each piece and cook until second side is browned, about 8 minutes longer.) Transfer ribs to large plate; set aside. Drain off fat to small bowl and reserve. Reduce oven temperature to 300 degrees. Place roasting pan on two stovetop burners set at medium heat; add wine and bring to simmer, scraping up browned bits with wooden spoon. Set roasting pan with wine aside.

2. Heat 2 tablespoons reserved fat in large Dutch oven over medium-high heat; add onions, carrots, and celery. Sauté, stirring occasionally, until vegetables soften, about 12 minutes. Add garlic and cook until fragrant, about 30 seconds. Stir in flour until combined, about 45 seconds. Stir in wine from roasting pan, chicken stock, tomatoes, rosemary, thyme, bay leaves, tomato paste, and salt and pepper to taste. Bring to boil and add short ribs, completely submerging meat in liquid; return to boil, cover, place in oven, and simmer until ribs are tender, about 2 to 2½ hours.

Transfer pot to wire rack and cool, partially covered, until warm, about 2 hours.

3. Transfer ribs from pot to large plate, removing excess vegetables that may cling to meat; discard loose bones that have fallen away from meat. Strain braising liquid into medium bowl, pressing out liquid from solids; discard solids. Cover ribs and liquid separately with plastic wrap and refrigerate overnight. (Can be refrigerated up to 3 days.)

4. FOR THE GARNISH AND TO FINISH DISH: In Dutch oven, cook bacon over medium heat until just crisp, 8 to 10 minutes; remove with slotted spoon to plate lined with paper towel. Add to Dutch oven pearl onions, parsnips, sugar, and salt; increase heat to high and sauté, stirring occasionally, until browned, about 5 minutes. Spoon off and discard solidified fat from reserved braising liquid. Add defatted liquid to Dutch oven and bring to simmer, stirring occasionally; adjust seasoning with salt and pepper. Submerge ribs in liquid; return to simmer. Reduce heat to medium and cook, partially covered, until ribs are heated through and vegetables are tender, about 5 minutes longer; gently stir in bacon. Divide ribs and sauce among individual bowls, sprinkle each with 1 tablespoon parsley, and serve.

PORTER-BRAISED SHORT RIBS WITH PRUNES, BRANDY, AND LEMON ESSENCE

Brandy-soaked prunes take the place of vegetables here, so this version is particularly suited to a mashed root vegetable or potato accompaniment. Use a dark, mildly assertive beer, not a light lager.

brandy, prune, and lemon essence garnish

½	cup brandy
8	ounces pitted prunes, each prune halved
2	teaspoons brown sugar
2	teaspoons grated zest from 1 lemon
6	tablespoons minced fresh parsley leaves

1. Follow recipe for Short Ribs Braised in Red Wine with Bacon, Parsnips, and Pearl Onions, substituting 3 cups porter beer for the red wine, eliminating rosemary, and substituting 2 tablespoons Dijon mustard and 2 teaspoons Worcestershire sauce for the tomato paste. Continue with recipe through step 3.

2. TO PREPARE GARNISH AND FINISH DISH: Bring brandy to boil in small saucepan; off heat, add prunes and let stand until plump and softened, about 15 minutes. Meanwhile, spoon off and discard solidified fat from braising liquid. Bring braising liquid to boil in Dutch oven over medium-high heat, stirring occasionally. Add prunes, brandy, and brown sugar; adjust seasoning with salt and pepper. Submerge ribs in liquid and return to simmer. Reduce heat to medium-low and cook until ribs are heated through, about 5 minutes longer; gently stir in lemon zest. Divide ribs and sauce among individual bowls, sprinkle each with 1 tablespoon parsley, and serve.

EQUIPMENT CORNER: Dutch Ovens

A DUTCH OVEN IS NOTHING MORE THAN A WIDE, DEEP pot with a cover. It was originally manufactured with "ears"

192 THE AMERICA'S TEST KITCHEN COOKBOOK

on the side (small, round tabs used to pick up the pot) and a top that had a lip around the edge. The latter design element was important because a Dutch oven was heated through coals placed both underneath and on top of the pot. The lip kept the coals on the lid from falling off. One could bake biscuits, cobblers, beans, and stews in this pot. It was, in the full sense of the word, an oven. This useful pot supposedly came to be called "Dutch" because at some point the best cast iron came from Holland.

Now that everyone in America has an oven, the Dutch oven is no longer used to bake biscuits or cobblers. However, it is essential for dishes that start on top of the stove and finish in the oven. (For this reason, the handles on a Dutch oven must be ovenproof.) To make some recommendations about buying a modern Dutch oven, we tested 12 models.

We found that a Dutch oven should have a capacity of at least six quarts to be useful. Eight quarts is even better. As we cooked in the pots, we came to prefer wider, shallower Dutch ovens because it's easier to see and reach inside them, and they offer more bottom surface area to accommodate larger batches of meat for browning. This reduces the number of batches required to brown a given quantity of meat, and, with it, the chances of burning the flavorful pan drippings. Ideally, a Dutch oven should have a diameter twice as wide as its height.

We also preferred pots with a light-colored interior finish, such as stainless steel or enameled cast iron. It is easier to judge the caramelization of the drippings at a glance in these pots. Dark finishes can mask the color of the drippings, which may burn before you realize it. Our favorite pot is the 8-quart All-Clad Stainless Stockpot (despite the name, this pot is a Dutch oven). The 7-quart Le Creuset Round French Oven, which is made of enameled cast iron, also tested well. These pots are quite expensive, costing at least $150, even when on sale. A less expensive alternative is the seven-quart Lodge Dutch Oven, which is made from cast iron. This pot is extremely heavy (making it a bit hard to maneuver), it must be seasoned (wiped with oil) regularly, and the dark interior finish is not ideal, but it does brown food quite well and costs just $45.

TASTING LAB: Short Ribs

SHORT RIBS ARE JUST WHAT THEIR NAME SAYS THEY ARE—"short ribs" cut from any part along the length of the cow's ribs. They can come from the lower belly section or higher up toward the back, from the shoulder (or chuck) area, or the forward midsection.

When we started testing short ribs, we went to the local grocery store and bought out their supply. What we brought back to the test kitchen were 2- to 4-inch lengths of wide flat rib bone, to which a rectangular plate of fatty meat was attached (see photo below left). We also ordered short ribs from the butcher. Imagine our confusion when these turned out to be long, continuous pieces of meat, about ¾ inch thick, that had been cut across the ribs and grain and that included two or three segments of rib bone (see photo below right). The former, we learned, are sometimes called English-style short ribs, and the latter are called flanken-style ribs.

BONE

ENGLISH-STYLE   FLANKEN-STYLE

We began by braising both types of ribs. The ones from the butcher were favored by most tasters because the relatively thin, across-the-grain cut made the meat more pleasant to eat; the supermarket ribs were a bit stringier because they contained longer segments of "grain." Both types were equally tender and good, but considering the cost ($5.99 versus $2.99 per pound) and effort (special order) required to procure the butcher-cut specimens, we decided to go with the supermarket variety.

MASHED POTATOES

WHAT WE WANTED: Mashed potatoes that are perfectly smooth and creamy, with a great potato flavor and plenty of buttery richness.

Most of us who make mashed potatoes would never consider consulting a recipe. We customarily make them by adding chunks of butter and spurts of cream until our conscience—or a backseat cook—tells us to stop. Not surprisingly, we produce batches of mashed potatoes that are consistent only in their mediocrity.

Great stew deserves great spuds. The right mashed potatoes can transform the humblest stew or braise (like short ribs) into a meal fit for a king. For us, the consummate mashed potatoes are creamy, soft, and supple, yet with enough body to stand up to sauce from a stew. As for flavor, the sweet, earthy, humble potato comes first, then the buttery richness that keeps you coming back for more.

We determined that high-starch potatoes, such as russets, are best for mashing (see the Science Desk on page 197 for more information.) Next, we needed to figure out the best way to cook the potatoes. We started by peeling and cutting some potatoes into chunks to expedite their cooking while cooking others unpeeled and whole. Even when mashed with identical amounts of butter, half-and-half (recommended by a number of trustworthy cookbooks), and salt, the two batches were wildly different. The potatoes that had been peeled and cut made mashed potatoes that were thin in taste and texture and devoid of potato flavor, while those cooked whole and peeled after cooking yielded mashed potatoes that were rich, earthy, and sweet.

We talked to several food scientists, who explained that peeling and cutting the potatoes before simmering increases the surface area through which they lose soluble substances, such as starch, proteins, and flavor compounds, to the cooking water. The greater surface area also enables lots of water molecules to bind with the potatoes' starch molecules. Combine these two effects and you've got bland, thin, watery mashed potatoes.

Next were the matters of butter and dairy. Working with 2 pounds of potatoes, which serves four to six, we stooped so low as to add only 2 tablespoons of butter. The potatoes ultimately deemed best in flavor by tasters contained 8 tablespoons. They were rich and full and splendid.

When considering dairy, we investigated both the kind and the quantity. Heavy cream made heavy mashed potatoes that were sodden and unpalatably rich, even when we scaled back the amount of butter. On the other hand, mashed potatoes made with whole milk were watery, wimpy, and washed out. When we tried adding more butter to compensate for the milk's lack of richness, the mixture turned into potato soup. Half-and-half, which we'd used in our original tests, was just what was needed, and 1 cup was just the right amount. The mashed potatoes now had a lovely light suppleness and a full, rich flavor that edged toward decadent.

The issues attending butter and dairy did not end there. We had heard that the order in which they are added to the potatoes can affect texture and that melted butter makes better mashed potatoes than softened butter. Determined to leave no spud unturned, we threw several more pounds into the pot. As it turns out, when the butter goes in before the dairy, the result is a silkier, creamier, smoother texture than when the dairy goes first; by comparison, the dairy-first potatoes were pasty and thick. Using melted rather than softened butter made the potatoes even more creamy, smooth, and light.

With our curiosity piqued by the significant textural differences effected by minor differences in procedure, we again contacted several food scientists, who explained that when the half-and-half is stirred into the potatoes before the butter, the water in it works with the starch in the potatoes to make the mashed potatoes gluey and heavy. When the butter is added before the half-and-half, the fat coats the starch molecules, inhibiting their interaction with the water in the half-and-half added later and thereby yielding silkier, creamier mashed potatoes. The benefit of using melted butter results from its liquid form, which enables it to coat the starch molecules quickly and easily. This buttery coating not only affects the interaction of the starch molecules with the half-and-half, it also affects the starch molecules' interaction with each other. All in all, it makes for smoother, more velvety mashed potatoes. (Melting the butter, as well as warming the half-and-half, also serves to keep the potatoes warm.)

There is more than one way to mash potatoes. In our testing, we had been using either a ricer or a food mill. We preferred the food mill because its large hopper accommodated half of the potatoes at a time. A ricer, which resembles an oversized garlic press, required processing in several batches. Both, however, produced smooth, light, fine-textured mashed potatoes.

A potato masher is the tool of choice for making chunky mashed potatoes, but it cannot produce smooth mashed potatoes on a par with those processed through a food mill or ricer. With a masher, potatoes mashed within an inch of their lives could not achieve anything better than a namby-pamby texture that was neither chunky nor perfectly smooth. Since the sentiment among our tasters was that mashed potatoes should be either smooth or coarse and craggy, a masher is best left to make the latter.

There are two styles of potato mashers—one is a disk with large holes in it, the other a curvy wire loop. We found the disk to be more efficient for reducing both mashing time and the number of lumps in the finished product.

WHAT WE LEARNED: To prevent the potatoes from absorbing too much water, boil them whole and unpeeled. Use a food mill or ricer for the smoothest texture imaginable. (A potato masher can be used if you prefer lumps.) Add melted butter before the half-and-half for the smoothest, creamiest texture.

MASHED POTATOES   serves 4 to 6

Russet potatoes make fluffier mashed potatoes, but Yukon Golds have an appealing buttery flavor and can be used. Mashed potatoes become gluey as they cool, so they are best served piping hot. If you must hold mashed potatoes, place them in a heatproof bowl, cover the bowl tightly with plastic wrap, and set the bowl over a pot of simmering water. The potatoes will remain hot and soft-textured for up to one hour. This recipe yields smooth mashed potatoes. If you don't mind lumps, use a potato masher, as directed in the variation.

2   pounds russet potatoes, scrubbed
8   tablespoons unsalted butter, melted
1   cup half-and-half, warmed
1½   teaspoons salt
     Ground black pepper

1. Place potatoes in large saucepan with cold water to cover by about 1 inch. Bring to boil over high heat, reduce heat to medium–low, and simmer until potatoes are just tender when pricked with thin-bladed knife, 20 to 30 minutes. Drain water from pan and remove potatoes.

2. Set food mill or ricer over now empty but still warm saucepan. Spear potato with dinner fork, then peel back skin with paring knife (see illustration 1 on page 196). Repeat with remaining potatoes. Working in batches, cut peeled potatoes into rough chunks and drop into hopper of food mill or ricer (see illustration 2 on page 196). Process or rice potatoes into saucepan.

3. Stir in butter with wooden spoon until incorporated. Gently whisk in half-and-half, salt, and pepper to taste. Serve immediately.

VARIATIONS

GARLIC MASHED POTATOES

Toasted garlic contributes the truest, purest garlic flavor imaginable to mashed potatoes. Best of all, the garlic can be peeled after toasting, when the skins will slip right off. Just make sure to keep the heat low and to let the garlic stand off heat until fully softened.

Toast 22 small to medium-large garlic cloves (about ⅔ cup), skins left on, in a small covered skillet over lowest possible heat, shaking pan frequently, until cloves are dark spotty brown and slightly softened, about 22 minutes. Remove pan from heat and let stand, covered, until cloves are fully softened, 15 to 20 minutes. Peel cloves and, with paring knife, cut off woody root end. Follow recipe for Mashed Potatoes, dropping peeled garlic cloves into food mill or ricer with peeled potatoes.

LUMPY MASHED POTATOES

We prefer silky, smooth mashed potatoes and therefore recommend using a food mill or ricer. If you prefer chunky mashed potatoes, use a potato masher instead.

Follow recipe for Mashed Potatoes, dropping peeled potato chunks back in warm saucepan and mashing with potato masher until fairly smooth. Proceed as directed, reducing half-and-half to ¾ cup.

MASHED POTATOES WITH PARMESAN AND LEMON

Follow recipe for Mashed Potatoes, stirring in 1 cup grated Parmesan cheese and minced or grated zest from 1 lemon along with half-and-half, salt, and pepper.

MASHED POTATOES WITH ROOT VEGETABLES

Most root vegetables are more watery than potatoes, so you will need less than the full cup of half-and-half.

Follow recipe for Mashed Potatoes, replacing 1 pound of potatoes with 1 pound of parsnips, rutabagas, celery root, carrots, or turnips that have been peeled and cut into 1½-inch to 2-inch chunks. Add half-and-half ¼ cup at a time until desired consistency is obtained.

BUTTERMILK MASHED POTATOES

Buttermilk gives mashed potatoes a pleasing tang and rich texture, even when less butter is used. If you are interested in mashed potatoes with less fat, this is your best option.

Follow recipe for Mashed Potatoes, reducing butter to 1 tablespoon and replacing half-and-half with 1 cup warmed buttermilk.

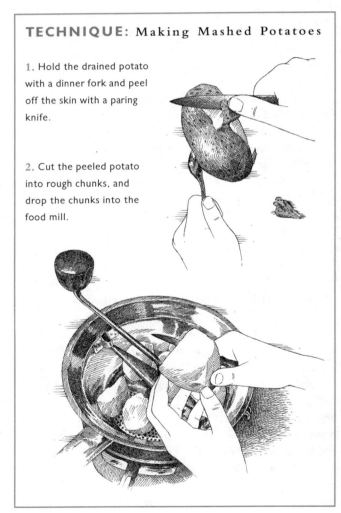

TECHNIQUE: Making Mashed Potatoes

1. Hold the drained potato with a dinner fork and peel off the skin with a paring knife.

2. Cut the peeled potato into rough chunks, and drop the chunks into the food mill.

SCIENCE DESK: Starch in Potatoes

POTATOES ARE COMPOSED MOSTLY OF STARCH AND water. The starch is in the form of granules, which in turn are contained in starch cells. The higher the starch content of the potato, the fuller the cells. In high-starch potatoes (russets are a good example), the cells are completely full—they look like plump little beach balls. In medium-starch (Yukon Golds) and low-starch potatoes (Red Bliss), the cells are more like underinflated beach balls. The space between these less-than-full cells is taken up mostly by water.

In our tests, we found that the full starch cells of high-starch potatoes are most likely to maintain their integrity and stay separate when mashed, giving the potatoes a delightfully fluffy texture. In addition, the low water content of these potatoes allows them to absorb milk, cream, and/or butter without becoming wet or gummy. Starch cells in lower-starch potatoes, on the other hand, tend to clump when cooked and break more easily, allowing the starch to dissolve into whatever liquid is present. The broken cells and dissolved starch tend to make sticky, gummy mashed potatoes.

However, the high moisture content of red potatoes makes them an excellent choice for dishes such as potato salad, where you want the potatoes to hold their shape. Because they contain a fair amount of moisture, they don't absorb much water as they boil. In contrast, low-moisture russets suck up water when boiled and fall apart. The resulting potato salad is starchy and sloppy-looking.

EQUIPMENT CORNER: Food Mills

A FOOD MILL IS NO LONGER A FIXTURE IN AMERICAN kitchens, but it is a terrific tool to have on hand. Think of it as part food processor, refining soft foods to a puree, and part sieve, separating waste such as peels, seeds, cores, and fiber from the puree as you go. And it accomplishes all of this with the simple turn of a crank, which rotates a gently angled, curved blade. The blade catches the food and forces it down through the holes of a perforated disk at the bottom of the mill. The separation of unwanted material from the puree is the food mill's raison d'être, but another benefit is that it does not aerate the food as it purees, as do food processors and blenders, so you are able to avoid an overly whipped, lightened texture. (In the case of potatoes, a food processor or blender would create a gummy texture.)

Since you can spend as little as $15 and as much as $100 on a food mill (some really huge mills cost as much as $200), we wondered if some were better than others. So we gathered six different models (including an electric one) and used them to make mashed potatoes and applesauce. Honestly, there was very little difference among the purees—they were all fine, smooth, and free of unwanted material. Thus, we evaluated the mills more on design factors, such as how easy it was to turn the crank, how efficiently the food was processed, and whether the mills offered adjustments in the texture of the puree produced.

The best mills in the group were the stainless steel Cuisipro, the VEV Vigano, and the white plastic Moulinex. Each was easy to crank and efficient and all came with fine, medium, and coarse disks. The top performer was the Cuisipro, but at $80, it was also the most expensive. The $15 Moulinex did nearly as well, so it became the pick of the pack for its combination of low price and high performance. The plastic is surely not as strong as the Cuisipro's stainless steel, but for occasional use, it was just fine.

Both the Foley and the Norpro mills were noticeably less efficient; their blades pushed the food around instead of forcing it through the perforated disk. In addition, neither one offered additional disks for different textures. There was just one medium disk, fixed in place. But the real loser was the Kenwood Passi Electric food mill. Though it was easier than hand-cranking, the power button did not have an "on" position, so you had to hold it in place. And it took forever to process the food. Also, the blade could not be cranked in the reverse direction (as it could on all of the manual models), so there was no way to loosen the food when it got stuck.

ROASTED CARROTS

WHAT WE WANTED: Perfectly caramelized carrots that are smooth and tender inside.

Roasted carrots' sublime nature lies in their rustic charm. Simple, sweet, and pure, their perfectly caramelized outer layer gently gives way to a smooth, tender interior—unless they are undercooked and have a crisp, bitter center or, on the opposite end of the spectrum, are subjected to such intense heat that they become wan, limp, and utterly unpalatable. Our ideal roasted carrot recipe, we decided, would be one that let us throw a couple of ingredients together, toss the carrots into the oven, and let them roast until they were done—a simple and painless side dish.

We started with the basic question of what type of carrot to use. We tested bunch carrots (those with greens still attached), bagged carrots, and bagged baby carrots. The bagged whole carrots were too toothy, fibrous, and bitter. Baby and bunch carrots were the best—sweet and tender. While the flavor and presentation of bunch carrots edged out the bagged babies (bunch carrots were breathtaking when roasted whole with just a nub of green stem left attached), the baby carrots needed no peeling, trimming, or chopping. They were effortless and easy, just what we had in mind.

Still, without a little help from a fatty cohort, we knew that the glossy, bronzed carrots we envisioned would not be possible. So we tossed batches of carrots with vegetable oil, olive oil, extra-virgin olive oil, butter, and clarified butter and roasted them. We were surprised to discover that our favorite was plain olive oil; it neither masked the carrots' sweetness, as did extra-virgin olive and vegetable oils, nor changed their texture, as did the butter.

We next examined possible roasting methods, times, and temperatures. We tried covering the broiler pan with foil to help keep the carrots moist and hasten the roasting,

but when we pulled these carrots out from their sealed bed, they had become reminiscent of cafeteria carrots: slightly bitter, pale, and soggy. Carrots covered for only part of the roasting time fared little better. The best batch was the most straightforward: roasted at 475 degrees, uncovered, for 20 minutes, until the carrots were brown and caramel colored.

We proceeded to roast carrots in different sorts of pans to see which would give us the best color and the easiest cleanup. After pitting broiler-pan bottoms against cookie sheets and roasting pans against Pyrex glass dishes and non-stick aluminum pans, we found the broiler-pan bottom to be the best for browning the carrots without burning them.

During this testing, we came to wonder just what a baby carrot was. Bagged baby carrots are made by taking long, thin carrots (usually carrot varieties grown for their high sugar and beta carotene content, which makes them sweet and bright in color) and forcing them through a carrot-trimming machine that peels the carrots and cuts them down to their ubiquitous baby size.

Real baby carrots are varieties of carrots that are miniature in size when mature; contrary to popular belief, they are not carrots of the standard length that are picked early. Unfortunately, real baby carrots are available only through specialty produce purveyors that sell to restaurants and other professional kitchens. If you are lucky enough to spy true, greens-still-attached, tapered baby carrots in your grocery store or farmer's market, buy them in the cooler months and roast according to our recipe. Baby carrots harvested in the warmer spring and summer months tend to be less sweet and have more of a metallic, turpentine-like flavor.

WHAT WE LEARNED: With a broiler pan and a hot oven, you can produce perfectly cooked, caramelized roasted carrots in just 20 minutes.

BASIC ROASTED CARROTS serves 8 as a side dish

Inspect your bag of baby carrots carefully for pockets of water. Carrots taken from the top of the supermarket's carrot pile are often waterlogged. This not only makes carrots mealy, it also dashes any hopes of caramelization in the oven.

2 pounds baby carrots (two 16-ounce bags)
2 tablespoons olive oil
½ teaspoon salt

Adjust oven rack to middle position and heat oven to 475 degrees. Toss carrots, oil, and salt in broiler-pan bottom. Spread into single layer and roast for 12 minutes. Shake pan to toss carrots; continue roasting about 8 minutes longer, shaking pan twice more, until carrots are browned and tender.

VARIATIONS

ROASTED MAPLE CARROTS WITH BROWNED BUTTER

Follow recipe for Basic Roasted Carrots, decreasing oil to 1½ teaspoons. After carrots have roasted 10 minutes, heat 1 tablespoon butter in small saucepan over medium heat, swirling occasionally, and simmer until deep gold, about 1 minute. Off heat, stir in 1 tablespoon maple syrup and drizzle mixture over carrots after 12 minutes of roasting; shake pan to coat, and continue roasting according to recipe.

ROASTED CARROTS WITH GINGER-ORANGE GLAZE

Follow recipe for Basic Roasted Carrots. After carrots have roasted 10 minutes, bring 1 heaping tablespoon orange marmalade, 1 tablespoon water, and ½ teaspoon grated fresh ginger to simmer in small saucepan over medium-high heat. Drizzle mixture over carrots after 12 minutes of roasting; shake pan to coat, and continue roasting according to recipe.

GREEN-TOPPED ROASTED CARROTS

Long, slender roasted carrots (no thicker than ½ inch) with little green stems still attached make a stunning table presentation. If you like, you can apply the instructions below to the preceding variations.

Follow recipe for Basic Roasted Carrots, replacing baby carrots with 2 pounds slender bunch carrots, trimmed of all but ½ inch of green stems. Increase total roasting time by 5 to 7 minutes.

ROASTED CARROTS, POTATOES, AND SHALLOTS

Give the potatoes a head start so they will be done at the same time as the carrots and shallots.

1 pound baby red potatoes, cut in half lengthwise
2 tablespoons olive oil
1 teaspoon salt
1 pound baby carrots (one 16-ounce bag)
6 shallots (about 6 ounces), peeled and cut in half lengthwise

1. Heat oven to 425 degrees. Place potatoes in broiler-pan bottom, add 1 tablespoon olive oil and ½ teaspoon salt; toss to coat. Arrange potato halves so cut sides face down, cover pan with aluminum foil, and roast 20 minutes.

2. Remove foil. Add carrots, shallots, remaining 1 tablespoon olive oil, and ½ teaspoon salt to potatoes. Toss to mix all ingredients together (it's OK if potatoes are not facing down), spread in single layer, and increase oven temperature to 475 degrees. Roast for 12 minutes. Shake pan to toss vegetables; continue roasting about 8 minutes longer, shaking pan twice more, until carrots are browned and tender.

After just 30 seconds of kneading,
the dough for our cream biscuits
is ready to be patted into a circle,
cut into rounds, and baked.

HAM, BISCUITS, & greens

CHAPTER 16

Southern food has a special place in the test kitchen.
For many of us, this is comfort food. A favorite meal is ham, biscuits, and greens. But we aren't content with just any old ham, biscuits, and greens.

We ventured into new territory when one of our staff members suggested soaking fresh ham in cola. After figuring out how to brine, season, roast, and glaze a fresh ham, we created our own version of cola ham. Many cooks in the test kitchen say it's the best pork roast they ever tasted.

Ham needs biscuits. But if not handled properly, biscuits can turn out flat and tough. Part of the problem is the fat, which must be at the ideal temperature to be worked evenly into the flour. Many cooks have hot hands or overwork the dough, and the results are disappointing. To avoid this problem, we developed a cream biscuit—without any butter or shortening—that's nearly foolproof.

What's a southern meal without a mess o' greens? But if the greens are soupy, tired, and bland, what's the point? We wanted to make greens as good as the rest of the meal. Our recipes for great greens are easy and quick.

ROAST FRESH HAM

WHAT WE WANTED: A new centerpiece roast to serve as an alternative to the more traditional turkey or leg of lamb.

Although this roast is called a ham, it gains much of its undeniable appeal from the fact that it's not really a ham at all—or at least not what most of us understand the term to mean. It's not cured in the fashion of a Smithfield ham or salted and air-dried like prosciutto. It's not pressed or molded like a canned ham, and it's not smoked like a country ham. In fact, the only reason this cut of pork is called a ham is because it comes from the pig's hind leg.

Even before we began roasting, we had decided that a full fresh ham, weighing in at about 20 pounds, was too much for all but the very largest feast. So we decided to use one of the two cuts into which the leg is usually divided—the sirloin, which comes from the top of the leg, or the shank, from the bottom of the leg (see page 205). We also decided that we wanted our ham skin-on (we couldn't see giving up the opportunity for cracklings). Fortunately, this is how these roasts are typically sold.

From our experiences with other large roasts, we knew that the big problem would be making sure the roast cooked all the way through while the meat stayed tender and moist. In our first set of tests, then, we wanted to assess not only the relative merits of sirloin and shank but also the best oven temperature and cooking time.

Early on in this process, we determined that the roast needed to be cooked to a lower final internal temperature than some experts recommend. We found that we preferred the roast pulled from the oven at 145 to 150 degrees—at this point, the meat is cooked to about medium and retains a slight blush. While the roast rests, its residual heat brings the temperature up to approximately 155 to 160 degrees.

That determined, we started testing different oven temperatures. First to come out of the oven was a ham from the sirloin end of the leg that we had roasted at a high temperature, 400 degrees, for its entire stay in the oven. Carving this ham was akin to whittling wood: Olympics-worthy agility with the carving knife was required to get around the aitchbone (part of the hip), the cracklings were more suited for tap shoes than consumption, and the meat was dry, dry, dry. We moved on to roasting a shank-end ham at a low heat the whole way through. This ham tasted like a wrung-out washcloth, with no cracklings in sight. What we did appreciate was the straightforward bone composition of the shank end, which simplified carving and convinced us to use this end of the fresh ham for the remainder of our tests.

Next we roasted a shank-end ham by starting it at a low temperature (325 degrees) and finishing it at a higher one (400 degrees), hoping to end up with both moist meat and crispy cracklings. To our dismay, this ham was also rather dry, which we attributed to the ham's long stay in the oven, made necessary by the low cooking temperature. What's more, the brief hike in the temperature at the end of cooking didn't help to crisp the skin.

Again, we figured we ought to try the opposite: starting the ham at a high temperature to give the meat a head start and get the skin on its way to crisping, then turning down the heat for the remainder of the roasting time to cook the meat through. Although meat cooked according to this method was slightly chalky and dry, the skin was close to our goal, crispy enough to shatter between our teeth yet tender enough to stave off a trip to the dentist. We decided that this would be our master roasting method.

Hoping to solve the dry meat dilemma, we brined a shank-end ham, immersing it in a solution of saltwater and spices to tenderize and flavor it. More than slightly biased from the positive results we achieved in past brining experiments with turkey, chicken, shellfish, and other cuts of pork, we expected brining to make the meat incredibly juicy. The salt in a brine causes the protein structure in meat to unravel and trap water in its fibers; brining also encourages the unwound proteins to gel, forming a barrier that helps seal in moisture. Together, these effects allow the cook to increase the roasting temperature, thus speeding the roasting process without fear of drying out the meat. Our estimations proved accurate: The brined shank emerged from the oven succulent and flavorful, with meat tender enough to fall apart in your mouth.

Just when we thought the ham couldn't possibly get any better, we decided to try roasting one shank face-down on a rack set in a roasting pan rather than letting it sit directly in the pan. This adjustment kept the cut end from becoming tough and leathery from direct contact with the hot pan. Rack roasting also allowed the heat to circulate around the ham constantly, promoting faster and more even cooking.

With our timing and temperature firmly in place, we turned to tweaking the flavor of the roast and obtaining the type of cracklings we had heard of but never really tasted. Not content with the infusion of flavor from the brine, we turned to spice rubs to further develop the flavor of the roast. Fresh thyme, sage, rosemary, garlic, brown sugar, cloves, dried mustard, juniper berries, peppercorns, and salt were all given an equal opportunity to complement the pork. We liked the combination of sage's earthy sweetness and garlic's pungent bite as well as the edge of fresh parsley, peppercorns, and kosher salt. Since our composed rub didn't lean strongly in the direction of any one particular spice, we were left with a wide-open field of glazing options.

While some recipes we tried called for simply basting the roast in its own drippings, we veered in the direction of sugary glazes, opting for sugar's ability to crisp, caramelize, and sweeten the skin. Starting the ham at 500 degrees negated glazing it at the outset: The sugary glaze would definitely char black before the roast had been in the oven very long. We decided to let the roast cook unglazed at 500 degrees for the first 20 minutes. We then turned the oven temperature down to 350 degrees and began to brush the roast liberally with glaze. We continued to do so in 45-minute intervals, which amounted to three bastings during the

roasting period. This ham was the one: flavorful meat with sweetened, crunchy skin.

More than one person in the test kitchen proclaimed this ham was the best roast pork they'd ever eaten. Rich and tender, with an underlying hint of sweetness, the meat had the power to quiet a room full of vocal, opinionated cooks and editors. Perhaps even better was the sweet, slightly salty, crisp, and crunchy skin that intensifies to a deep crimson by the time the roast is done. It was attacked with precision and proprietary swiftness during our trials in the test kitchen. Unbelievably succulent, tender, and uncomplicated, this culinary gem will leave you wondering how you could have gotten along so far without it.

WHAT WE LEARNED: Use the shank end, brine the meat, rub it with herbs and garlic, then roast in a hot oven for 20 minutes before lowering the temperature and applying a sweet glaze.

ROAST FRESH HAM serves 8 to 10

Fresh ham comes from the pig's hind leg. Because a whole leg is quite large, it is usually cut into two sections. The sirloin, or butt, end is harder to carve than our favorite, the shank end. If you don't have room in your refrigerator, brine the ham in an insulated cooler or a small plastic garbage can; add five or six freezer packs to the brine to keep it well cooled.

roast

    1   bone-in fresh half ham with skin, 6 to 8
         pounds, preferably shank end, rinsed

brine

    4   cups kosher salt or 2 cups table salt
    3   cups packed dark or light brown sugar
    2   heads garlic, cloves separated, lightly crushed
         and peeled
   10   bay leaves
    ½   cup black peppercorns, crushed

garlic and herb rub

    1   cup lightly packed sage leaves from 1 large
         bunch
    ½   cup parsley leaves from 1 bunch
    8   medium cloves garlic, peeled
    1   tablespoon kosher salt or 1½ teaspoons
         table salt
    ½   tablespoon ground black pepper
    ¼   cup olive oil

glaze

    1   recipe glaze (recipes follow)

1. FOR THE ROAST: Carefully slice through skin and fat with serrated knife, making 1-inch diamond pattern. Be careful not to cut into meat.

2. FOR THE BRINE: In large (about 16-quart) bucket or stockpot, dissolve salt and brown sugar in 1 gallon hot tap water. Add garlic, bay leaves, crushed pepper, and 1 gallon cold water. Submerge ham in brine and refrigerate 8 to 24 hours.

3. Set large disposable roasting pan on baking sheet for extra support; place flat wire rack in roasting pan. Remove ham from brine; rinse under cold water and dry thoroughly with paper towels. Place ham, wide cut-side down, on rack. (If using sirloin end, place ham skin-side up.) Let ham stand, uncovered, at room temperature 1 hour.

4. FOR THE RUB: Meanwhile, adjust oven rack to lowest position and heat oven to 500 degrees. In workbowl of food processor fitted with steel blade, process sage, parsley, garlic, salt, pepper, and oil until mixture forms smooth paste, about 30 seconds. Rub all sides of ham with paste.

5. Roast ham at 500 degrees for 20 minutes. Reduce oven temperature to 350 degrees and continue to roast, brushing ham with glaze every 45 minutes, until center of ham registers 145 to 150 degrees on instant-read thermometer, about 2½ hours longer. Tent ham loosely with foil and let stand until center of ham registers 155 to 160 degrees on thermometer, 30 to 40 minutes. Carve, following illustrations on page 205, and serve.

VARIATION

COCA-COLA HAM serves 8 to 10

Although cooking with Coke may seem unconventional, you haven't lived until you've tried cola pork. Cola pork was born when a member of our staff mentioned the southern tradition of Coca-Cola glaze and joked that we should try brining the meat in it. After giving this joke fair consideration, we dumped 6 liters of Coca-Cola Classic into a bucket, added kosher salt, and let the ham soak overnight. The next day we cooked it according to our recipe. The outcome was the talk of the kitchen. It was juicy; it was unusual; it was fantastic. The Coke had added its own unique flavor to the ham while tenderizing the meat even more than our regular brine. The meat was falling off the bone and unbelievably tender.

Follow recipe for Roast Fresh Ham, substituting 6 liters Coke Classic for both hot and cold water in brine, omitting sugar, and reducing salt to 3 cups kosher salt or 1½ cups table salt. Proceed as directed, rubbing ham with garlic and herb mixture and using Coca-Cola Glaze with Lime and Jalapeño.

GLAZES

CIDER AND BROWN SUGAR GLAZE
makes about 1⅓ cups, enough to glaze ham

- 1 cup apple cider
- 2 cups packed dark or light brown sugar
- 5 whole cloves

Bring cider, brown sugar, and cloves to boil in small nonreactive saucepan over high heat; reduce heat to medium-low and simmer until syrupy and reduced to about 1⅓ cups, 5 to 7 minutes. (Glaze will thicken as it cools between bastings; cook over medium heat about 1 minute, stirring once or twice, before using.)

SPICY PINEAPPLE-GINGER GLAZE makes about 1⅓ cups, enough to glaze ham

- 1 cup pineapple juice
- 2 cups packed dark or light brown sugar
- 1 (1-inch) piece fresh ginger, grated (about 1 tablespoon)
- 1 tablespoon red pepper flakes

Bring pineapple juice, brown sugar, ginger, and red pepper flakes to boil in small nonreactive saucepan over high heat; reduce heat to medium-low and simmer until syrupy and reduced to about 1⅓ cups, 5 to 7 minutes. (Glaze will thicken as it cools between bastings; cook over medium heat about 1 minute, stirring once or twice, before using.)

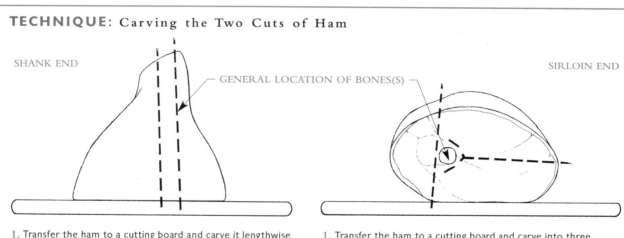

TECHNIQUE: Carving the Two Cuts of Ham

SHANK END   — GENERAL LOCATION OF BONES(S) —   SIRLOIN END

1. Transfer the ham to a cutting board and carve it lengthwise alongside the bone, as indicated with the two dotted lines in the illustration above.

2. Lay the large boneless pieces that you have just carved flat on the cutting board and slice into ½-inch pieces.

1. Transfer the ham to a cutting board and carve into three pieces around the bones, as indicated with the dotted lines in the illustration above.

2. Lay the large boneless pieces that you have just carved flat on the cutting board and slice into ½-inch pieces.

ORANGE, CINNAMON, AND STAR ANISE
GLAZE makes about 1⅓ cups, enough to glaze ham

- 1 cup juice plus 1 tablespoon grated zest from 2 large oranges
- 2 cups packed dark or light brown sugar
- 4 pods star anise
- 1 (3-inch) cinnamon stick

Bring orange juice, brown sugar, star anise, and cinnamon to boil in small nonreactive saucepan over high heat; reduce heat to medium-low and simmer until syrupy and reduced to about 1⅓ cups, 5 to 7 minutes. (Glaze will thicken as it cools between bastings; cook over medium heat about 1 minute, stirring once or twice, before using.)

COCA-COLA GLAZE WITH LIME AND
JALAPEÑO makes about 1⅓ cups, enough to glaze ham

- 1 cup Coke Classic
- ¼ cup juice from 2 limes
- 2 cups packed dark or light brown sugar
- 2 medium jalapeño chiles, cut crosswise into ¼-inch-thick slices

Bring Coke Classic, lime juice, brown sugar, and jalapeños to boil in small nonreactive saucepan over high heat; reduce heat to medium-low and simmer until syrupy and reduced to about 1⅓ cups, 5 to 7 minutes. (Glaze will thicken as it cools between bastings; heat over medium heat about 1 minute, stirring once or twice, before using.)

CREAM BISCUITS

WHAT WE WANTED: Great homemade biscuits without the bother of cutting fat into the flour.

Many cooks are intimidated by biscuits. They are not comfortable with the process of cutting butter into flour. We wondered if there was such a thing as a great recipe for homemade biscuits that would not require cutting fat into flour. In effect, could we take the guesswork out of making biscuits to create a foolproof recipe?

We began with a basic recipe calling for 2 cups flour, 2 teaspoons baking powder, 1 tablespoon sugar, and ½ teaspoon salt. Now we had to figure out what to add to this mixture instead of butter or vegetable shortening to make a dough. We decided to try plain yogurt, sour cream, milk, milk combined with melted butter, and whipped heavy cream, an idea borrowed from a scone recipe.

The biscuits made with yogurt and sour cream were a bit sodden in texture, those with the milk and milk/butter combination were tough and lifeless, and the whipped cream biscuit was too light, more confection than biscuit. This last approach also required another step—whipping the cream—which seemed like too much trouble for a simple recipe. So we tried using plain heavy cream, without whipping, and this biscuit was the best of the lot. (Cream biscuits are not our invention. James Beard includes such a recipe in his seminal work *American Cookery* [Little, Brown, 1972]).

Next, we decided to do a blind tasting, pitting the cream biscuits against our favorite buttermilk biscuit recipe, which requires cutting butter into the flour. The result? Both biscuits had their partisans. The cream biscuits were lighter and more tender. They were also richer tasting. The buttermilk biscuits were flakier and had the distinctive tang that many tasters associate with good biscuits. Although neither biscuit was sweet, the buttermilk version seemed more savory.

At this point, we decided that cream biscuits were a worthy (and easier) alternative to traditional buttermilk

biscuits. Still, we were running into a problem with the shape of the biscuits—they spread far too much during baking. We have always followed the conventional advice about not overworking the dough. In our experience, the best biscuits are generally made from dough that is handled lightly. This is certainly true of buttermilk biscuits.

But cream biscuits, being less sturdy than those made with butter, become soft and "melt" during baking. In this case, we thought, a little handling might not be such a bad thing. So we baked up two batches: The first dough we patted out gingerly; the second dough we kneaded for 30 seconds until it was smooth and uniform in appearance. The results were remarkable. The more heavily worked dough produced much higher, fluffier biscuits than the lightly handled dough, which looked short and bedraggled.

Although we find it easy enough to quickly roll out this dough and then cut it into rounds with a biscuit cutter, you can simply shape the dough with your hands or push it into the bottom of an 8-inch cake pan. The dough can then be flipped onto the work surface and cut into wedges.

As for dough thickness, ¾ inch provided a remarkably high rise, more appealing than biscuits that started out ½ inch thick. We also discovered that it was best to add just enough cream to hold the dough together. A wet dough did not hold its shape as well during baking.

Our final ingredient tests included sugar—tasters felt that 1 tablespoon was a bit much, so we dropped it to 2 teaspoons—and baking powder, which we found we could reduce to 1 teaspoon with no decrease in rise. For oven temperature, we tried 375, 400, and 425 degrees, and found the latter best for browning.

WHAT WE LEARNED: Cream is the best choice for turning flour, baking powder, salt, and sugar into light, tender biscuits. Knead the dough slightly to produce higher, fluffier biscuits.

CREAM BISCUITS makes eight 2½-inch biscuits

Bake the biscuits immediately after cutting them; letting them stand for any length of time can decrease the leavening power and thereby prevent the biscuits from rising properly in the oven.

    2   cups (10 ounces) unbleached all-purpose flour
    2   teaspoons sugar
    1   teaspoon baking powder
    ½   teaspoon salt
    1½ cups heavy cream

1. Adjust oven rack to upper-middle position and heat oven to 425 degrees. Line baking sheet with parchment paper.

2. Whisk together flour, sugar, baking powder, and salt in medium bowl. Add 1¼ cups cream and stir with wooden spoon until dough forms, about 30 seconds. Transfer dough from bowl to countertop, leaving all dry, floury bits behind in

bowl. In 1 tablespoon increments, add up to ¼ cup cream to dry bits in bowl, mixing with wooden spoon after each addition, until moistened. Add these moistened bits to rest of dough and knead by hand just until smooth, about 30 seconds.

3. Following illustrations on page 209, cut biscuits into rounds or wedges. Place rounds or wedges on parchment-lined baking sheet and bake until golden brown, about 15 minutes. Serve immediately.

VARIATIONS

CREAM BISCUITS WITH FRESH HERBS
Use the herb of your choice in this variation.

Follow recipe for Cream Biscuits, whisking 2 tablespoons minced fresh herbs into flour along with sugar, baking powder, and salt.

CHEDDAR BISCUITS
Follow recipe for Cream Biscuits, stirring ½ cup (2 ounces) sharp cheddar cheese cut into ¼-inch pieces into flour along with sugar, baking powder, and salt. Increase baking time to 18 minutes.

TASTING LAB: All-Purpose Flour

WE WANTED TO KNOW IF THERE WAS A SINGLE ALL-PURPOSE flour that would be best for those who keep only one kind of flour in the pantry. So we stocked our test kitchen shelves with nine brands of all-purpose flour and started a bake-off that eventually stretched over some six months. We ended up preparing two kinds of cookies, pie pastry, biscuits, cake, muffins, and bread with each brand of flour, often making several batches of each item.

When milling all-purpose flour, a flour company must make a number of choices that will influence the way its product performs in recipes. For starters, there is the essence of the flour, the wheat itself. All-purpose flour is typically made from hard red winter wheat, soft red winter wheat, or a combination of the two. Of the flours we used in the taste tests, five were made from hard winter wheat, one was made from soft wheat, and three were a mix of soft and hard.

Perhaps the primary difference between these types of wheat—and, consequently, the flours made from them—is the variation in protein content. Hard winter wheat is about 10 to 13 percent protein, soft wheat about 8 to 10 percent. Mixtures of the two wheats are somewhere in between. You can actually feel this difference with your fingers; the hard wheat flours tend to have a subtle granular feel, while soft wheat flours feel fine but starchy, much like cornstarch.

High-protein flours are generally recommended for yeasted products and other baked goods that require a lot of structural support. The reason is that the higher the protein level in a flour, the greater the potential for the formation of gluten. The sheets that gluten forms in dough are elastic enough to move with the gas released by yeast yet sturdy enough to prevent that gas from escaping, so the dough doesn't deflate. Lower-protein flours, on the other hand, are recommended for chemically leavened baked goods. This is because baking powder and baking soda are quick leaveners. They lack the endurance of yeast, which can force the naturally resistant gluten sheets to expand. Gluten can overpower quick leaveners, causing the final baked product to fall flat.

A second important difference in flours is whether they are bleached or not. Technically, every all-purpose flour is bleached. Carotenoid pigments in wheat lend a faint yellowish tint to freshly milled flour. But in a matter of about 12 weeks, these pigments oxidize, undergoing the same chemical process that turns a sliced apple brown. In this case, yellowish flour changes to a whiter hue (though not stark white). Early in this century, as the natural bleaching process came to be understood, scientists identified methods to chemically expedite and intensify it. Typically, all-purpose flours are bleached with either benzoyl peroxide or chlorine gas. The latter not only bleaches the flour but also alters the flour proteins, making them less inclined to form strong gluten. Today consumers prefer chemically bleached flour

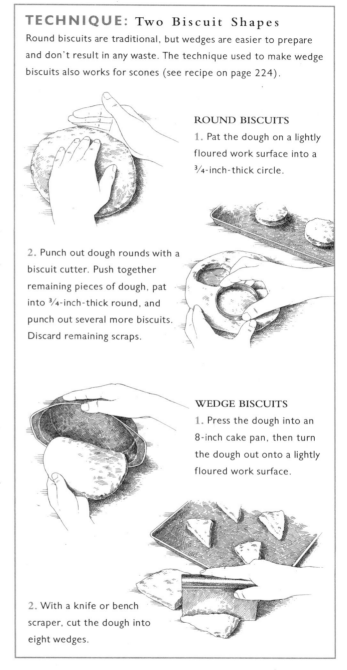

TECHNIQUE: Two Biscuit Shapes

Round biscuits are traditional, but wedges are easier to prepare and don't result in any waste. The technique used to make wedge biscuits also works for scones (see recipe on page 224).

ROUND BISCUITS

1. Pat the dough on a lightly floured work surface into a $3/4$-inch-thick circle.

2. Punch out dough rounds with a biscuit cutter. Push together remaining pieces of dough, pat into $3/4$-inch-thick round, and punch out several more biscuits. Discard remaining scraps.

WEDGE BISCUITS

1. Press the dough into an 8-inch cake pan, then turn the dough out onto a lightly floured work surface.

2. With a knife or bench scraper, cut the dough into eight wedges.

over unbleached because they associate the whiter color with higher quality. In our tests, some of the baked goods made with bleached flour were such a pure white that they actually looked startlingly unnatural and "commercial" versus homemade.

Of all the product taste tests we have run, these flour tastings were undoubtedly the most difficult. The differences in flavor between the various versions of the selected recipes were usually extremely subtle. For example, tasting nine different plain muffins in which the only ingredient difference was the brand of flour required shrewd discrimination on the tasters' part. The most obvious differences were often in appearance.

That is not to say, however, that the tests were inconclusive. As difficult as it was for tasters to pick up differences, they were remarkably consistent in their observations. The performance of each of the flours tested, however, was not so consistent. All of the flours baked up well enough in most of the recipes. And some baked up better than that—at times. Failure also occurred, sometimes without apparent reason.

As an overall category, the four bleached flours in our tests in fact did not perform as well as the unbleached flours and were regularly criticized for tasting flat or carrying "off" flavors, often described as metallic. These characteristics, however, were more difficult to detect in recipes that contained a high proportion of ingredients other than flour. Coincidentally, our cake tests and chocolate chip cookie tests (both sugary recipes) were the two tests in which off flavors carried by the bleached flour went undetected or were considered faint.

Despite the variations and subtleties, however, the good news is that we did end up with two flours we can recommend wholeheartedly. Both King Arthur and Pillsbury unbleached flours regularly made for highly recommended baked goods, producing a more consistent range of preferred products than the other seven flours in the taste tests. If you are going to have only one flour in the house, our advice is to choose one of these two.

No matter the type or brand, we measure all flour by the dip-and-sweep method. Dip a metal or plastic dry measure into

a bag of flour so that the cup is overflowing with flour. Then use a knife or icing spatula to level off the flour, sweeping the excess back into the bag. Short of weighing flour (which is what professional bakers do), this measuring method is your best guarantee of using the right amount of flour. Spooning the flour into the measuring cup aerates it, and you might end up with as much as 25 percent less flour by weight.

EQUIPMENT CORNER: Digital Scales

EVERY SERIOUS COOK NEEDS AN ACCURATE SCALE FOR weighing fruits, vegetables, and meats. When making bread, a scale is even more critical. Professional bakers know that measuring flour by volume can be problematic. A cup of flour can weigh between 4 and 6 ounces, depending on the type of flour, the humidity, whether or not the flour has been sifted, and the way the flour has been put into the cup. Weight is a much more accurate way to measure flour.

There are two basic types of kitchen scales. Mechanical scales operate on a spring and lever system. When an item is placed on the scale, internal springs are compressed. The springs are attached to levers, which move a needle on the scale's display (a ruler with lines and numbers printed on a piece of paper and glued to the scale). The more the springs are compressed, the farther the needle moves along the ruler.

Electronic, or digital, scales have two plates that are suspended at a fixed distance. The bottom plate is stationary, the top plate is not. When food is placed on the platform attached to the top plate, the distance between the plates changes slightly. The movement of the top plate (no more than one thousandth of an inch) causes a change in the flow of electricity through the scale's circuitry. This change is translated into a weight and expressed in numbers displayed on the face of the scale.

We tested 10 electronic scales and 9 mechanical scales. As a group, the electronic scales were vastly preferred. Their digital displays are much easier to read than the measures on most mechanical scales, where the lines on the ruler are so

closely spaced it's impossible to nail down the precise weight within half an ounce. Also, many mechanical scales could weigh items only within a limited range—usually between 1 ounce and 5 pounds. What's the point of owning a scale that can't weigh a large chicken or roast? Most electronic scales can handle items that weigh as much as 10 pounds and as little as ¼ ounce. Among the electronic scales we tested, we found that several features make the difference between a good electronic scale and a great one.

Readability is a must. The displayed numbers should be large. Also, the displayed numbers should be steeply angled and as far from the weighing platform as possible. If the display is too close to the platform, the numbers can hide beneath the rim of a dinner plate or cake pan.

An automatic shut-off feature will save battery life, but this feature can be annoying, especially if the shut-off cycle kicks in at under two minutes. A scale that shuts off automatically after five minutes or more is easier to use.

A large weighing platform (that detaches for easy cleaning) is another plus. Last, we preferred electronic scales that display weight increments in decimals rather than fractions. The former are more accurate and easier to work with when scaling a recipe up or down.

BEST SCALES
Despite the high price tag and minor quirks, the Soehnle Cyber Electronic (right) was the runaway winner in our testing. It has a detachable glass measuring platform that is especially easy to clean. The Salter Electronic Aquatronic (left) is half the price, but food can become trapped between the weighing platform and base.

GREENS

WHAT WE WANTED: Southern-style greens that are tender but not limp. The cooking method should preserve their great color and flavor.

Many cooks think that all leafy greens can be treated alike, even though some are delicate enough for salads while others seem as tough as shoe leather. After cleaning, stemming, and cooking more than 100 pounds of leafy greens, we found that they fell into two categories, each of which should be handled quite differently.

Spinach, beet greens, and Swiss chard are tender and rich in moisture. They require no additional liquid during cooking. They taste of the earth and minerals but are still rather delicate. Kale as well as mustard, turnip, and collard greens are tougher and require the addition of some liquid as they cook. Their flavor is much more assertive, even peppery in some cases, and can be overwhelming.

We tested boiling, steaming, and sautéing tender greens. Boiling produced the most brilliantly colored greens, but they were also very mushy and bland. The water cooked out all of their flavor and texture. While steamed greens were less mushy, the generally unsatisfactory results of steaming showed us these tender greens did not need any liquid at all. Damp greens that were tossed in a hot oil (which could be flavored with aromatics and spices) wilted in just two or three minutes in a covered pan. Once wilted, we found it best to remove the lid so the liquid in the pan would evaporate.

This method has the advantage of flavoring the greens as they cook. Our basic recipe cooks greens in olive oil flavored with garlic, but the choices are endless. Use Asian sesame oil and add ginger along with the garlic. Or use vegetable oil and cook ginger, garlic, chiles, and curry powder before adding the damp greens.

Tougher greens don't have enough moisture to be wilted in a hot pan; they scorch before they wilt. Steaming these greens produces a better texture but does nothing to tame their bitter flavor. Tough greens benefit from cooking in some water, which washes away some of their harsh notes.

We tested boiling 2 pounds of greens in an abundant quantity of salted water and what might be called shallow-blanching in just 2 quarts of salted water. We found that cooking the greens in lots of water diluted their flavor too much. Shallow blanching removed enough bitterness to make these assertive greens palatable, but not so much as to rob them of their character. Blanched greens should be drained and then briefly cooked with seasonings.

Our preferred method is to heat some olive oil, garlic, and hot red pepper flakes, add the blanched and drained greens, and then stir to coat the greens with seasonings. Tough greens have a tendency to dry out—even after blanching—so we found it best to add a little chicken stock to the pan and cook the greens, covered, just until well seasoned. To change seasonings, use a different oil or add other ingredients—such as diced ham, olives, peppers, or ginger—to the oil before tossing the blanched greens into the pan.

WHAT WE LEARNED: Leafy greens can be divided into two categories—tender and tough—and each must be cooked differently. Tender greens like spinach should be wilted in a hot pan with seasonings. Tough greens like collards should be blanched in a minimum of water, drained, then sautéed with seasonings.

SAUTÉED TENDER GREENS serves 4

To stem spinach and beet greens, simply pinch off the leaves where they meet the stems. A thick stalks runs through each Swiss chard leaf, so it must be handled differently; see top illustration at right. A large, deep Dutch oven or even a soup kettle is best for this recipe.

> 3 tablespoons extra-virgin olive oil
> 2 medium cloves garlic, minced
> 2 pounds damp tender greens, such as spinach, beet greens, or Swiss chard, stemmed, washed in several changes of cold water, and coarsely chopped
> Salt and ground black pepper
> Lemon wedges (optional)

1. Heat oil and garlic in Dutch oven or other deep pot and cook until garlic sizzles and turns golden, about 1 minute. Add wet greens, cover, and cook over medium-high heat, stirring occasionally, until greens completely wilt, about 2 to 3 minutes.

2. Uncover and season with salt and pepper to taste. Cook over high heat until liquid evaporates, 2 to 3 minutes. Serve immediately, with lemon wedges if desired.

VARIATION

SAUTÉED TENDER GREENS WITH RAISINS AND ALMONDS

This Italian recipe works surprisingly well with our roast ham. If you prefer, replace the almonds with an equal amount of toasted pine nuts.

Follow recipe for Sautéed Tender Greens, adding ¼ teaspoon hot red pepper flakes with garlic, ⅓ cup golden raisins with spinach, ½ teaspoon minced lemon zest with salt and pepper, and 3 tablespoons toasted slivered almonds just before serving.

TECHNIQUE: Preparing Leafy Greens

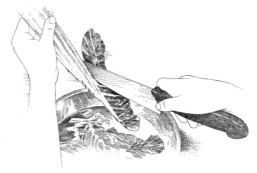

A. To prepare Swiss chard, kale, collards, and mustard greens, hold each leaf at the base of the stem over a bowl filled with water and use a sharp knife to slash the leafy portion from either side of the thick stem.

B1. Turnip greens are most easily stemmed by grasping the leaf between your thumb and index finger at the base of the stem and stripping it off by hand.

B2. When using this method with turnip greens, the very tip of the stem will break off along with the leaves. The tip is tender enough to cook along with them.

QUICK-COOKED TOUGH GREENS serves 4

See the box on page 213 for tips on stemming kale, collards, mustard greens, and turnip greens. Shallow-blanched greens should be shocked in cold water to stop the cooking process, drained, and then braised. Shocked and drained greens can be held for up to an hour before being braised.

          Salt
    2   pounds assertive greens, such as kale, collards,
         mustard, or turnip, stemmed, washed in several
         changes of cold water, and coarsely chopped
    2   large cloves garlic, sliced thin
    ¼   teaspoon hot red pepper flakes
    3   tablespoons extra-virgin olive oil
    ⅓–½ cup homemade chicken stock or canned
         low-sodium chicken broth
         Lemon wedges (optional)

1. Bring 2 quarts water to boil in soup kettle or other large pot. Add 1½ teaspoons salt and greens and stir until wilted. Cover and cook until greens are just tender, about 7 minutes. Drain in colander. Rinse kettle with cold water to cool, then refill with cold water. Pour greens into cold water to stop cooking process. Gather handful of greens, lift out of water, and squeeze until only droplets fall from them. Repeat with remaining greens.

2. Heat garlic, red pepper flakes, and oil in large sauté pan over medium heat until garlic starts to sizzle, about 1 minute. Add greens and stir to coat with oil. Add ⅓ cup stock, cover, and cook over medium-high heat, adding more stock if necessary, until greens are tender and juicy and most of stock has been absorbed, about 5 minutes. Adjust seasonings, adding salt and red pepper flakes to taste. Serve immediately, with lemon wedges if desired.

VARIATIONS

QUICK-COOKED TOUGH GREENS WITH PROSCIUTTO

Follow recipe for Quick-Cooked Tough Greens, adding 1 ounce thin-sliced prosciutto that has been cut into thin strips along with garlic and red pepper flakes. Proceed as directed, stirring in ¼ teaspoon grated lemon zest just before serving.

QUICK-COOKED TOUGH GREENS WITH RED BELL PEPPER

Follow recipe for Quick-Cooked Tough Greens through step 1. Sauté ½ thinly sliced red bell pepper in oil until softened, about 4 minutes. Add garlic and red pepper flakes and proceed as directed.

QUICK-COOKED TOUGH GREENS WITH BLACK OLIVES AND LEMON

Follow recipe for Quick-Cooked Tough Greens, adding ⅓ cup pitted and chopped black olives, such as kalamatas, after garlic starts to sizzle. Add greens and proceed as directed, stirring in ¼ teaspoon grated lemon zest just before serving.

QUICK-COOKED TOUGH GREENS WITH BACON AND ONION

Follow recipe for Quick-Cooked Tough Greens through step 1. Fry 2 bacon slices, cut crosswise into thin strips, in large sauté pan over medium heat until crisp, 4 to 5 minutes. Remove bacon with slotted spoon and set aside on small plate. If necessary, add vegetable oil to bacon drippings to yield 2 tablespoons of fat. Add 1 small onion, minced, and sauté until softened, about 4 minutes. Add 2 minced garlic cloves and cook until fragrant, about 1 minute. Add greens and proceed as directed, sprinkling bacon bits and 2 teaspoons cider vinegar over greens just before serving.

A light cream and sugar glaze applied before baking gives scones an attractive sheen and burst of crunchy sweetness.

MUFFINS & scones

CHAPTER 17

Muffins and scones are both quick breads, leavened chemically with baking powder and/or baking soda rather than yeast. Few baking projects deliver such satisfying rewards in so little time. You can enjoy homemade blueberry muffins or scones in less than an hour, including baking and cooling time.

Just because these muffin and scone recipes are fast, it doesn't mean that they are foolproof. When quick breads go wrong, they really go wrong. If not handled properly, quick breads can turn out dry and tough. There's a reason why the English refer to some scones as rock cakes.

We think the ideal muffin is tender and delicate, like a butter cake. Too often, though, muffins are gargantuan and tough. Scones can suffer similar indignities. They should be tender and buttery, not coarse and craggy.

To solve these problems, we turned the test kitchen into the neighborhood bakeshop. The smells of freshly baked blueberry muffins and cream scones filled the air from morning until nightfall. Our final recipes are simple but memorable.

BLUEBERRY MUFFINS

WHAT WE WANTED: Rich, moist, and dainty muffins, not the big, bland, coarse muffins so popular today.

The Oxford Companion to Food defines American muffins as "small, squat, round cakes," yet today's deli muffins are, by comparison, big and buxom, inflated by chemical leavening and tattooed with everything from chocolate chips to sunflower seeds. We wanted a blueberry muffin with a daintier stature, a moist, delicate little cake that would support the blueberries both physically, and, if we may say so, spiritually (in terms of flavor).

Despite the easy promise of a gingham-lined basket of warm, cuddly blueberry muffins, much can go wrong from kitchen to table. We made a half-dozen recipes, producing muffins that ranged from rough and tough to dense, sweet, and heavy to the typical lackluster coffee shop cake with too few blueberries and too little flavor. It was clear that blueberry muffins came in no one style, flavor, or size, so we asked tasters to state which basic style of muffin they fancied: round tea cake or craggy biscuit. Of the 15 tasters, all but one said tea cake.

Since minor fluctuations in ingredients occasioned seismic differences in the resulting muffins, we thought it best to hold fast to a recipe whose proportions landed in between the two extremes in the original tests. That meant we would be working with 1 stick of butter, 1 cup sugar, 2 cups flour, and ½ cup milk. It was not a perfect recipe but would be a serviceable springboard for future testing.

The two principal methods available to the muffin baker are mixing and creaming. The former is a one-two-three-done courtship in which dry ingredients go in one bowl, liquid in another, and then join up under a light touch. The second method, called creaming, is standard procedure for butter cakes. Everyone knows the drill: You beat butter with sugar until light and fluffy, add eggs one at a time, and then stir in dry ingredients and milk or cream alternately.

But creaming is a nuisance when you want to whip up muffins for breakfast. It's a nuisance to soften butter and haul out a mixer. In side-by-side tests using the control recipe above, we got a firsthand taste of both methods. Had we been merely licking batter off our fingers, there would have been no contest. The creamed version was like a cake batter you could suck through a straw. But the two baked muffins were nearly identical. Though the mixed muffin was slightly squatter than its creamed companion, its texture was not inferior. We were pretty sure this was a technique we could work with—or around.

For flour we remained true to unbleached all-purpose. Cake flour produced a batter that was too light to hold the blueberries aloft. Bleached flour lacked the flavor spectrum of unbleached. We set off next in pursuit of the perfect amount of butter to turn out a moister, richer muffin, more like the tea cake our tasters had preferred. Increasing the butter in the control recipe simply weighed down the crumb without making the muffins any more moist. We also increased the liquid (we tested both milk and buttermilk) and added extra egg yolks. Neither approach brought improvement. When we substituted yogurt for milk, the muffins had the springiness of an old camp mattress.

Knowing that sour cream is often used in quick breads such as muffins, we decided to give it a try. At the same time, we wondered if the egg white protein from two eggs might be too much of the wrong type of liquid—adding structure rather than tenderness. Our new recipe, then, called for 1 egg, 1 cup sour cream, no milk, and only half a stick of butter. It was a great success—the muffin was tender and rich, and the sour cream played up to the blueberries' flavor. An additional ¼ cup sour cream made even nicer muffins.

Through additional testing, we discovered that this rather heavy batter required a full tablespoon of baking powder to rise and shine, but tasters noted no off chemical flavor. (When too much chemical leavener is used, the baked good

often suffers from a bitter, soapy flavor.) Next, we refined the mixing method. Hoping to get more lift into the picture, we whisked the egg and sugar together by hand until the sugar began to dissolve, whisked in the melted butter, then the sour cream, and poured them into the dry ingredients. This method of mixing promised to deliver more air—and lift—to the egg, sugar, and butter. We folded everything together using the gentlest strokes possible. (We found that these muffins, like most others, become tough when overmixed.) This modified technique produced lovely muffins with a nice rise and beautifully domed crowns.

Until now, the major player in this muffin had been not only off-stage but out of season as well. Our winter testing left us with a choice between pricey fresh blueberries the size of marbles and tiny frozen wild berries. The flavor and sweetness of the frozen berries gave them a big edge over the

puckery, flavorless fresh berries. In addition, the tiny wild berries distributed themselves in the batter nicely, like well-mannered guests, whereas the cultivated berries took the muffin by storm, leaving huge pockets of sour fruit pulp. So impressed were we by the superiority of the wild berries that we resolved to offer them top billing in the recipe. (You shouldn't have to be vacationing in Maine to make a decent blueberry muffin.) We came across one last trick. Frozen blueberries tend to be bleeders—and gummy when tossed with flour—so we discovered that they must remain completely frozen until stirred into the batter. The maximum amount of berries our batter could support was 1½ cups.

These were perfect workaday muffins, but we wanted to give them a chance to play dress-up, to be more like little cakes. With that in mind we considered a couple of options. A big fan of pebbly streusel topping dusted with confectioners' sugar, we picked up the recipe from our Dutch apple pie topping and pared it down to meet the demands of a dozen muffins. The streusel weighed heavily on the muffins and diminished their lift. Even after raising the oven temperature to 375 degrees (up from 350 degrees) and increasing baking time by five minutes, this topping was too heavy and too dry.

Our next topping idea came from Marion Cunningham's *Breakfast Book* (Knopf, 1987) in which she rolls whole baked muffins in melted butter and then dries them in cinnamon-sugar. The concept was a winning one. The melted butter seeped into the muffin's crown, the sugar stuck, and the muffin was transformed into a tender sugar-tufted pillow.

We also made a simple syrup glaze with lemon juice. Brushed on the muffin tops it made a nice adhesive for the granulated sugar (which we mixed with either finely grated lemon zest or fresh ginger). Finally, muffins to take to the ball.

WHAT WE LEARNED: You don't need to cream the butter and sugar together. Simply mix the dry ingredients in one bowl, the wet in another, and then combine. Sour cream makes muffins rich and tender, while frozen wild blueberries taste great and are just the right size for muffins.

BLUEBERRY MUFFINS makes 12 muffins

When making the batter, be sure to whisk vigorously in step 2, then fold carefully in step 3. There should not be large pockets of flour in the finished batter, but small occasional sprays may remain.

2	cups (10 ounces) unbleached all-purpose flour
1	tablespoon baking powder
½	teaspoon salt
1	large egg
1	cup (7 ounces) sugar
4	tablespoons unsalted butter, melted and cooled slightly
1¼	cups (10 ounces) sour cream
1½	cups frozen blueberries, preferably wild

1. Adjust oven rack to middle position and heat oven to 350 degrees. Spray standard muffin tin with nonstick vegetable cooking spray.

2. Whisk flour, baking powder, and salt in medium bowl until combined. Whisk egg in second medium bowl until well-combined and light-colored, about 20 seconds. Add sugar and whisk vigorously until thick and homogenous, about 30 seconds; add melted butter in 2 or 3 additions, whisking to combine after each addition. Add sour cream in 2 additions, whisking just to combine.

3. Add frozen berries to dry ingredients and gently toss just to combine. Add sour cream mixture and fold with rubber spatula until batter comes together and berries are evenly distributed, 25 to 30 seconds. (Small spots of flour may remain and batter will be thick. Do not overmix.)

4. Use ice cream scoop or large spoon to drop batter into greased muffin tin. Bake until light golden brown and toothpick or skewer inserted into center of muffin comes out clean, 25 to 30 minutes, rotating pan from front to back halfway through baking time. Invert muffins onto wire rack,

TECHNIQUE: Portioning Batter

Use an ice cream scoop to portion batter into a muffin tin.

stand muffins upright, and cool 5 minutes. Serve as is or use one of the toppings below.

VARIATIONS

CINNAMON SUGAR–DIPPED BLUEBERRY MUFFINS

While muffins are cooling, mix ½ cup sugar and ½ teaspoon ground cinnamon in small bowl and melt 4 tablespoons butter in small saucepan. After baked muffins have cooled 5 minutes, and working one at a time, dip top of each muffin in melted butter and then cinnamon sugar. Set muffins upright on wire rack; serve.

GINGER- OR LEMON-GLAZED BLUEBERRY MUFFINS

While muffins are baking, mix 1 teaspoon grated fresh ginger or grated lemon zest and ½ cup sugar in small bowl. Bring ¼ cup lemon juice and ¼ cup sugar to simmer in small saucepan over medium heat; simmer until mixture is thick and syrupy and reduced to about 4 tablespoons. After baked muffins have cooled 5 minutes, brush tops with glaze, then, working one at a time, dip tops of muffins in lemon sugar or ginger sugar. Set muffins upright on wire rack; serve.

EQUIPMENT CORNER: Muffin Tins

THE MAJORITY OF MUFFIN TINS ON THE MARKET ARE MADE of coated aluminum and are lightweight. We purchased two tins of this type as well as two heavy-gauge "professional" aluminum tins and one "air-cushioned" aluminum tin. Three had a nonstick coating.

We baked up two different varieties of muffins to test the two things that really matter—browning and sticking. We wanted the muffins to brown uniformly and to be easily plucked from the tin. Corn muffins were ideal for the browning test, blueberry for the sticking test—no one wants a sweet, sticky berry left in the tin rather than the muffin.

Browning ended up being the deciding factor in these tests. Sticking was not an issue as long as the tins were sprayed with cooking oil. The best tins browned the muffins evenly, the worst browned them on the top but left them pallid and underbaked on the bottom. As we had observed in other bakeware tests, darker coated metals, which absorb heat, do the best job of browning baked goods. The air-cushioned tin produced pale muffins that were also small (the cushioning made for a smaller cup capacity, about ⅓ cup rather than the standard ½ cup).

We found the heavier-gauged aluminum tins to have no advantage—they are much more expensive than other tins, weigh twice as much, and do not produce superior muffins. Their heft may make them durable, but unless you bake commercially, the lightweight models will last a lifetime. The $5 Ekco Baker's Secret tin took top honors, besting tins that cost five times as much.

TASTING LAB: Butter

BUTTER IS A KEY INGREDIENT IN MUFFINS AND SCONES, and there's no reason you can't slather more butter over both when they come warm from the oven. For this purpose (and so many others), we wondered if the brand of butter makes a difference. To answer this question, we embarked on a two-month odyssey, testing eight brands of butter in six different applications. We tasted the butters plain (both at room temperature and melted), in pie crust, in yellow cake, in buttercream frosting, and in sautéed turkey cutlets.

All butter must consist of at least 80 percent milk fat, according to U.S. Department of Agriculture standards. Most commercial butters do not exceed this. European butters and Hotel Bar's Plugrá are exceptions, with anywhere from 82 to 88 percent milk fat. All butters contain about 2 percent milk solids, and the remainder is water.

The results of our extensive testing were somewhat surprising. Although the two high-fat butters in the tasting (Plugrá and Celles Sur Belle, a French brand sold in many gourmet stores) performed well in most tests, they were not runaway winners. In fact, most tasters felt that all the cakes, pie crusts, and sautéed turkey cutlets tasted pretty much the same, no matter which brand of butter was used. Even tasted plain the results were fairly close.

One test did reveal some discernible differences. In a rich buttercream frosting made with softened butter, confectioners' sugar, and a little milk, the Plugrá was head and shoulders above the others for both a pleasant, delicate butter flavor and an airy texture. The other high-fat butter, Celles Sur Belle, scored well but was not judged to have as light a texture as the Plugrá. In this one instance, the butter is such an important ingredient and the recipe is so simple that a higher-fat butter created a noticeable difference in both flavor and texture.

Overall, however, we recommend that you pay more attention to the condition in which you buy the butter and the conditions under which you store it than to the particular brand. Throughout the testing, we ran across sticks of butter that were rancid or stale-tasting. We attributed these problems to improper shipping or poor storage at the market, not the manufacturer. We recommend that you purchase butter from a store that has a high turnover of products.

Butter can also spoil in your refrigerator, turning rancid from the oxidation of fatty acids. Exposure to air or light is particularly damaging, which explains why Land O'Lakes takes the precaution of wrapping its unsalted butter in foil. We find that the best way to store butter is sealed in an airtight plastic bag in your freezer, pulling out sticks as you need them. Butter will keep in the freezer for several months and in the refrigerator for no more than two to three weeks.

The fat in butter is vulnerable not only to oxidation but also to picking up odors. While butter is particularly susceptible at warmer temperatures, it can take on odors even when chilled or frozen. For this reason, we advise against storing butter in your refrigerator's butter compartment, which tends to be warmer because it's inside the door. To find out how much of a difference this made, we stored one stick of butter in its original wrapper in the butter compartment and one in the center of the refrigerator. After one week, the butter in the compartment had begun to pick up off flavors, while the one stored in the center still tasted fresh.

One final note about butter. We use unsalted butter in our test kitchen. We like its sweet, delicate flavor and prefer to add our own salt to recipes. We find that the quality of salted butter is often inferior and that each manufacturer adds a different amount of salt, which makes recipe writing difficult. While you can certainly get away with using salted butter in some savory recipes (as long as you adjust the total amount of salt in the recipe), we strongly recommend using unsalted butter when baking.

TASTING LAB: Store-Bought Muffins

1. STICKY SURFACE   2. MASHED BERRIES   3. ARTIFICIAL BERRIES   4. COARSE TEXURE   5. FLAT TOP

A lot can go wrong with blueberry muffins. Some problematic muffins we encountered in our testing, from left to right: (1) Cottony grocery-store muffins often have sticky, clammy tops. (2) Muffins made with mashed berries taste fine but look all wrong. (3) A quick packaged mix with artificial berries baked up into little hockey pucks. (4) This deli muffin is dry and coarse, with mushy, marble-sized blueberries. (5) If the muffin cups are overfilled with batter, the baked muffins will have flat tops.

SCONES

WHAT WE WANTED: Light, tender scones with a buttery flavor and gentle sweetness.

Scones, the quintessential tea cake of the British Isles, are delicate, fluffy biscuits, which may come as a surprise to Americans—the clunky mounds of oven-baked sweetened dough called rock cakes by the English are often called scones in our restaurants and coffee shops. Unlike rock cakes, in which dough is dropped from a spoon onto a baking sheet, traditional scones are quickly rolled or patted out and cut into rounds or wedges.

We started our testing by focusing on the flour. We made a composite recipe with bread flour, with all-purpose flour, and with cake flour. The differences in outcome were astonishing. The scones made with bread flour were heavy and tough. The scones made with all-purpose flour were lighter and much more flavorful. Cake flour produced scones that were doughy in the center, with a raw taste and poor texture. Subsequent tests revealed that a low-protein all-purpose flour, such as Gold Medal or Pillsbury, is better than a high-protein flour, such as King Arthur. (Lower-protein flours produce more tender baked goods.)

After trying scones made with butter and with lard, we decided we preferred the rich flavor of butter. (If we made scones commercially we might reconsider because day-old scones made with lard hold up better. The preservative effects of different fats, along with lower cost, may be why store-bought scones are often made with margarine or other hydrogenated fats.) We found that 5 tablespoons butter (a rather modest amount) to 2 cups flour was just right. More butter and the scones almost melted in the oven. Less butter and they baked up dry and tough.

The choice of liquid can also profoundly affect the flavor of a scone. We tested various liquids and found that cream made the best scones—tender and light. Scones made with milk were bland and dry. Buttermilk gave the scones plenty of flavor, but they were too flaky and biscuit-like. Scones made with cream were more moist and flavorful than any others.

We tried adding an egg and found that it made the scones cakey, more American-style than British. Because many tasters liked the scones made with egg and because egg helps the scones hold onto moisture and remain fresher longer, we decided to use one in a variation called Cakey Scones.

In traditional recipes, one to two tablespoons of sugar is enough to sweeten an entire batch of scones. American scones tend to be far sweeter than the British versions, which are usually sweetened with toppings such as jam. Americans seem to eat their scones like muffins, without anything more than a smear of butter, so the sweetness is baked in. We prefer the British approach but decided to increase the sugar slightly to 3 tablespoons.

Finally, scones are often glazed to enhance their appearance and add sweetness. We tried brushing the dough with a beaten egg as well as with heavy cream just before baking. Scones brushed with egg can become too dark in the oven. We preferred the more delicate look of scones brushed with cream and then dusted with a little granulated sugar.

Scones can be mixed by hand or with a food processor. (The processor is used to cut fat into flour; minimal hand mixing is required afterward.) We found the food processor to be more reliable than our hands, which would sometimes overheat the butter and cause it to soften. Once the dough comes together, we prefer to pat it into a cake pan, gently turn it out onto a floured surface, and then cut the dough into eight wedges. We found this method to be easier and more reliable than using a rolling pin.

WHAT WE LEARNED: All-purpose flour is a better choice than cake flour, cream adds richness and moisture, and butter is a must, but you don't need as much as you might think. For a texture that's more cakey than biscuit-like, add an egg.

CREAM SCONES makes 8

The easiest and most reliable approach to mixing the butter into the dry ingredients is to use a food processor fitted with a steel blade. Resist the urge to eat the scones hot out of the oven. Letting them cool for at least 10 minutes firms them up and improves their texture.

    2   cups (10 ounces) unbleached all-purpose flour,
        preferably a low-protein brand such as
        Gold Medal or Pillsbury
    1   tablespoon baking powder
    3   tablespoons sugar
    ½   teaspoon salt
    5   tablespoons chilled unsalted butter, cut into
        ¼-inch cubes
    ½   cup currants
    1   cup heavy cream

1. Adjust oven rack to middle position and heat oven to 425 degrees.

2. Place flour, baking powder, sugar, and salt in large bowl or workbowl of food processor fitted with steel blade. Whisk together or pulse six times.

3. *If making by hand,* use two knives, a pastry blender, or your fingertips and quickly cut in butter until mixture resembles coarse meal, with a few slightly larger butter lumps. Stir in currants. *If using food processor,* remove cover and distribute butter evenly over dry ingredients. Cover and pulse 12 times, each pulse lasting 1 second. Add currants and pulse one more time. Transfer dough to large bowl.

4. Stir in heavy cream with rubber spatula or fork until dough begins to form, about 30 seconds.

5. Transfer dough and all dry, floury bits to countertop and knead dough by hand just until it comes together into a rough, slightly sticky ball, 5 to 10 seconds. Following illustrations for Wedge Biscuits on page 209, cut scones into 8 wedges. Place wedges on ungreased baking sheet. (Baking sheet can be wrapped in plastic and refrigerated for up to 2 hours.)

6. Bake until scone tops are light brown, 12 to 15 minutes. Cool on wire rack for at least 10 minutes. Serve warm or at room temperature.

VARIATIONS
GLAZED SCONES
A light cream and sugar glaze gives scones an attractive sheen and sweeter flavor. If baking scones immediately after making the dough, brush the dough just before cutting it into wedges.

Follow recipe for Cream Scones, brushing tops of scones with 1 tablespoon heavy cream and then sprinkling with 1 tablespoon sugar just before baking them.

CAKEY SCONES
An egg changes the texture and color of the scones and helps them stay fresher longer, up to 2 days in an airtight container.

Follow recipe for Cream Scones, reducing butter to 4 tablespoons and cream to ¾ cup. Add 1 large egg, lightly beaten, to dough along with cream.

OATMEAL-RAISIN SCONES
Mix this dough in the food processor; the metal blade breaks down the coarse oats and incorporates them into the dough.

Follow recipe for Cream Scones, making dough in food processor and substituting 1 cup rolled oats for ½ cup all-purpose flour. Increase sugar to 4 tablespoons and butter to 6 tablespoons. Replace currants with ¾ cup raisins.

GINGER SCONES
Follow recipe for Cream Scones, substituting ½ cup chopped crystallized ginger for currants.

Breakfast Strata with Spinach and Gruyère page 262

225

Short Ribs Braised in Red Wine with Bacon, Parsnips, and Pearl Onions page 191

226

Cream Biscuits **page 208**

Garlic Mashed Potatoes **page 195**

Roast Fresh Ham **page 204**

Lemon-Glazed Blueberry Muffins **page 220**

Raspberry Squares **page 270**

Classic Apple Pie page 303

Kiwi, Raspberry, and Blueberry Tart **page 284**

233

Chocolate Cream Pie page 290

234

Free-Form Apple Tartlets page 307

235

Lattice-Top Fresh Peach Pie **page 313**

Rhubarb Fool page 333

237

Panna Cotta **page 328** with Raspberry Coulis **page 329**

Bittersweet Chocolate Roulade page 341

BACON, EGGS, & home fries

CHAPTER 18

Bacon, eggs, and potatoes are the classic components of an all-American breakfast. When the bacon is crisp, the omelet tender, and the home fries perfectly browned, this combination can be divine. But as anyone who eats in diners knows, this meal can fall far short of this ideal.

Every diner in America serves home fries, but the potatoes are rarely memorable. Home fries seem to fall into two categories—burnt and dry versus soft and mushy. Is it possible to brown the exterior of home fries while getting the interior tender and moist?

Bacon should be easy to cook—just heat until browned—but why is it so often brittle in some spots, raw in others? Is the microwave the solution to this problem, or does it make matters worse? We cooked up pounds and pounds of bacon to figure out a foolproof method.

A cheese omelet is a simple yet special way to enjoy eggs. But for a dish that requires nothing more than eggs, cheese, butter, salt, and pepper, lots can go wrong. The cheese sometimes leaks out of the omelet or, worse still, doesn't melt. The eggs can overcook and become tough. This dish requires perfect execution—but how to go about it?

IN THIS CHAPTER

Bridget is ready for Chris to roll a cheese omelet onto her plate. (She returns the favor on page 247.)

HOME FRIES

WHAT WE WANTED: Cubes of potatoes that would be deep golden brown and crisp on the outside and tender on the inside.

When we began trying to uncover the secret of the ultimate home fries, we went right to the source—to diners. But soon we learned that the problems with this dish are often the same, no matter where they are cooked and consumed. Frequently, the potatoes are not crisp, they are greasy, and the flavorings are either too bland or too spicy.

Our first step was to define home fries—individual pieces of potato cooked in fat in a frying pan on top of the stove and mixed with caramelized onions. We also knew what they should look and taste like: They should have a deep golden brown crust and a tender interior with a full potato flavor. The potatoes should not be greasy but instead feel crisp and moist in your mouth.

Although there are dozens of varieties, potatoes can be divided into three major categories based on their relative starch content. Experience has taught us that high-starch potatoes (like russets) make the best baked potatoes and French fries, while low-starch potatoes (all red-skinned and new potatoes) are the top choice for boiling, making salads, and roasting. Medium-starch potatoes (like all-purpose and Yukon Gold) can be roasted, baked, or mashed. Because the cooking method and the type of potato used are so intimately interconnected, we decided it made sense to try each cooking method with all three types of potatoes.

We knew the potatoes would end up in a skillet with fat, but would it be necessary to precook them, as our research suggested? We began testing with the simplest approach: dice them raw and cook them in a hot skillet with fat. But in test after test, no matter how small we cut them, it proved challenging to cook raw potatoes all the way through and obtain a crisp brown crust at the same time. Low temperatures helped cook the inside, but the outside didn't crisp. High temperatures crisped the outside, but the potatoes had to be taken off the heat so early to prevent scorching that the insides were left raw. We decided to precook the potatoes before trying them in a skillet.

Because a common approach to home fries is to use leftover baked potatoes, we baked some of each type, stored them in the refrigerator overnight, then diced them and put them in a skillet with fat. These tests were disappointing. None of the resulting home fries had a great potato flavor. They all tasted like leftovers, and their texture was somewhat gummy. The exterior of the red potatoes was not crisp, although they looked very good, and the starchier russet potatoes fell apart.

Next we tried starting with freshly boiled potatoes. Potatoes that were boiled until tender broke down in the skillet, and the inside was overcooked by the time the exterior was crisp. So we tried dicing and then braising the potatoes, figuring we could cook them through in a covered pan with some water and fat, remove the cover, let the water evaporate, and then crisp up the potatoes in the remaining fat. Although this sounded like a good idea, the potatoes stuck horribly to the skillet.

Finally, we considered a technique we found in Lydie Marshall's book *Passion for Potatoes* (HarperPerennial, 1992). Marshall instructs the cook to cover diced raw potatoes with water, bring the water to a boil, then immediately drain the potatoes well and sauté them. This treatment allows the potatoes to cook briefly without absorbing too much water, which is what makes them susceptible to overcooking and breaking down.

We tested this technique with russets, Red Bliss potatoes, and Yukon Golds. Eureka! It worked better with all three varieties of potato than any of the other methods we had tried. The Yukon Golds, though, were the clear favorite. Each individual piece of potato had a crisp exterior, and the

inner flesh was tender, moist, and rich in potato flavor. The appearance of each was superior as well, the golden yellow color of the flesh complementing the crispy brown exterior. The russets were drier and not as full flavored but were preferred over the Red Bliss by all tasters. These potatoes were somewhat mushy and tasted disappointingly bland.

We decided to test another medium-starch potato. All-purpose potatoes also browned well and were tender and moist on the inside, but they lacked the rich buttery potato flavor and yellow color of the Yukon Golds, which remained the favorite.

Having discovered the ideal cooking method and the preferred potato variety, we moved on to the best way to cut the potatoes. We found sliced potatoes much harder to cook than diced ones. A pound of sliced potatoes stacks up three or four layers deep in a large skillet. The result is uneven cooking, with some slices burning and others remaining undercooked. Countless tests had convinced us that one of the keys to success

in cooking home fries is to cook the potatoes in a single layer. When a pound of potatoes is diced, one cut side of each potato piece can have contact with the skillet at all times. We tested dices of various size and found the ½-inch cube to be ideal: easy to turn and to eat, characterized by that pleasing combination of crispy outside and soft fleshy inside.

Deciding whether or not to peel the potatoes was easy. All tasters preferred the texture and flavor contributed by the skin. Leaving it on also saves time and effort.

Thus far we had determined that letting the potatoes sit undisturbed in hot fat to brown each side was critical to a crisp exterior. We found it best to let the potatoes brown undisturbed for four to five minutes before the first turn, then to turn them a total of three or four times. Three tablespoons turned out to be the ideal amount of fat for 1 pound of potatoes. When sampling potatoes cooked in different frying mediums, we found that a combination of butter and oil offered the best of both worlds, providing a buttery flavor with a decreased risk of burning (butter burns more easily than vegetable oils). Refined corn and peanut oils, with their nutty overtones, were our first choice.

Soft, sweet, and moist, onions are the perfect counterpoint to crispy potatoes, but we had to determine the best way to include them. Tests showed the easiest and most efficient way also produced the best results: Dice the onions and cook them before cooking the potatoes. More flavor can be added with help from parsley, red or green bell peppers (sautéed with the onion), or cayenne pepper, as you wish. Whatever your choice, these are going to be home fries worth staying home for.

WHAT WE LEARNED: Yukon Golds are the best-looking, best-tasting potatoes for home fries. To keep them from turning mushy when cooked, precook briefly in water, then fry. When frying, use butter for flavor and oil to lower the risk of burning.

DINER-STYLE HOME FRIES serves 2 to 3

If you need to double this recipe, cook two batches of home fries separately. While making the second batch, keep the first batch hot and crisp by spreading the fries on a baking sheet placed in a 300-degree oven. The paprika adds a warm, deep color, but it can be omitted. An alternative is to toss in 1 tablespoon minced parsley just before serving the potatoes.

2½	tablespoons corn or peanut oil
1	medium onion, chopped small
1	pound (2 medium) Yukon Gold or all-purpose potatoes, scrubbed and cut into ½-inch cubes
1¼	teaspoon salt
1	tablespoon unsalted butter
1	teaspoon paprika
	Ground black pepper

1. Heat 1 tablespoon oil in 12-inch heavy-bottomed skillet over medium-high heat until hot but not smoking. Add onion and sauté, stirring frequently, until browned, 8 to 10 minutes. Transfer onion to small bowl and set aside.

2. Meanwhile, place diced potatoes in large saucepan, cover with ½ inch water, add 1 teaspoon salt, and place over high heat. As soon as water begins to boil, about 6 minutes, drain potatoes thoroughly in colander.

3. Heat butter and remaining 1½ tablespoons oil in now-empty skillet over medium-high heat until butter foams. Add potatoes and shake skillet to evenly distribute potatoes in single layer; make sure that one side of each piece is touching surface of skillet. Cook without stirring until one side of potatoes is golden brown on bottom, about 4 to 5 minutes, then carefully turn potatoes with wooden or heat-proof plastic spatula. Spread potatoes in single layer in skillet again and repeat process until potatoes are tender and browned on most sides, turning three or four times, 10 to 15 minutes longer. Add onions, paprika, remaining ¼ teaspoon salt, and pepper to taste; stir to blend and serve immediately.

EQUIPMENT CORNER: Colanders

A COLANDER IS ESSENTIALLY A PERFORATED BOWL designed to allow liquid to drain through the holes. It has many uses: draining potatoes, pasta, and more. In our initial survey of models, we were not surprised to find colanders made from a range of materials: plastic, enameled steel, stainless steel, anodized aluminum, and wire mesh (which is like a screen). What did surprise us was the range of prices. Who would have thought that you could drop almost $115 on a simple colander, especially in light of the price tag on the least expensive contestant, just $3.99? This made the idea of a test even more tantalizing.

As is our fashion in the test kitchen, we put the colanders through a battery of tests to obtain an objective assessment of their performance. We drained pounds and pounds of cooked spaghetti, orzo, and frozen baby peas in each one. Early in testing, we splashed scalding water and hot pasta out of a tiny 3-quart model by pouring it too fast from the cooking pot, so we eliminated that size from the running. The 5- and 7-quart models (10 altogether) performed on par, so we included both in our tests.

Most colanders on the market come with one of two types of bases, either a circular metal ring attached to the bottom, on which the bowl sits pedestal-style, or individual feet soldered to the bottom of the bowl. No matter which

BEST COLANDER
The Endurance Colander/Strainer has a meshlike perforated bowl that traps even the smallest bits of food.

type it is, the base should be unfailingly stable, to prevent spills. Our research and reading on colanders consistently noted the superiority of the ring over the feet, claiming that a colander on feet is less stable because it touches the ground in only three or four spots. That sounded like a reasonable theory to us until we tested the two models in the group with feet.

These colanders (the Endurance Stainless Steel Footed Colander and the Norpro Expanding Over-the-Sink Colander with Stand) were perfectly stable. During none of the tests did either one tip and spill its contents. (The Norpro can also be suspended between the sides of a sink by extending two metal arms. On our test kitchen sinks, this feature worked just fine, but on some sink designs this colander may be less stable.) In fact, the Endurance remained upright even when we accidentally bumped it with a heavy stockpot. Similarly, and as we expected, the eight colanders with ring bases also enjoyed total stability.

We also expected that the size, placement, and pattern of the drainage holes would be key for quick, efficient draining. Seven of our 10 colanders had the look we expected, that of a metal or plastic bowl with perforations arranged in straight lines, starbursts, or circles; the remaining three had more unusual designs. True to its name, the Endurance Colander/Strainer was a hybrid with a metal bowl that was

so thoroughly perforated it almost looked like wire mesh. Two other colanders, the Harold Imports and the Norpro expandable colander, were made from wire mesh, like a strainer. These three colanders had more holes than their more traditional counterparts, and each one performed very well, draining quickly and completely, with no pooling of water and no food—even the wily orzo—slipping through the holes. In truth, though, all of the other colanders also met—or came darn close to meeting—these standards. The traditional colanders with larger holes did allow some orzo to slip through (anywhere from just a few pieces for the Rösle to almost three-quarters of a cup for the Silverstone), but only the Silverstone allowed so much orzo through that it merited a downgrade in the ratings.

When all was said and drained, every colander in the group got the job done, be it the $4 Hoan plastic model or the gleaming $115 Rösle stainless steel model. To make a recommendation, then, we have to be a bit more subjective than usual. So here it is: Based on this testing and our gut feeling, the colander we'd most like to bring home is the Endurance Colander/Strainer. It's reasonably priced at $25, it's solid and comfortable to wield, it drains like a pro and keeps all its contents in check, and many editors here considered it to be an unusually handsome specimen of a colander. When it comes to this basic kitchen utensil, extra money is not well spent.

BACON

WHAT WE WANTED: Crisp, evenly cooked bacon with a minimum of mess and hassle.

Many home cooks now use the microwave to cook bacon, while others still fry bacon in a skillet. In restaurants, many chefs "fry" bacon in the oven. We decided to try each of these methods to find out which worked best.

For each cooking technique, we varied temperature, timing, and material, cooking both a typical store-bought bacon and a thick-cut mail-order bacon. The finished strips were compared in terms of flavor, texture, and appearance, while the techniques were compared for consistency, safety, and ease.

While the microwave would seem to have the apparent advantage of ease—stick the pieces in and forget about them—it turned out that this was not the case. Strips were still raw at 90 seconds; at two minutes they were medium-well-done in most spots, but still uneven; but by two minutes and 30 seconds the strips were hard and flat and definitely overcooked. The finished product didn't warrant the investment of time it would take to figure out the perfect number of seconds. Microwaved bacon is not crisp, it is an unappetizing pink/gray in color even when well-done, and it lacks flavor.

The skillet made for a significantly better product. The bacon flavors were much more pronounced than in the nuked version, the finished color of the meat was a more appealing brick red, and the meat had a pleasing crispness. There were, however, a number of drawbacks to pan-frying. In addition to the functional problems of grease splatter and the number of 11-inch strips you can fit into a 12-inch round pan, there were problems of consistency and convenience. Because all of the heat comes from below the meat, the strips brown on one side before the other. Moreover, even when using a cast-iron pan, as we did, heat is not distributed perfectly evenly across the bottom of the pan. This means that to get consistently cooked strips of bacon you have to turn them over and rotate them in the pan. In addition, when more strips are added to an already-hot pan, they tend to wrinkle up, making for raw or burnt spots in the finished product.

The best results from stovetop cooking came when we lowered the heat from medium to medium-low, just hot enough to sizzle. The lower temperature allowed the strips to render their grease more slowly, with a lot less curling and spitting out of the pan. Of course, this added to cooking time, and it did not alleviate the need for vigilance.

Oven-frying seemed to combine the advantages of microwaving and pan-frying while eliminating most of the disadvantages. We tried cooking three strips in a preheated 400-degree oven on a 9 by 12-inch rimmed baking sheet that would contain the grease. Bacon was medium-well-done after 9 to 10 minutes and crispy after 11 to 12 minutes. The texture was more like a seared piece of meat than a brittle cracker, the color was that nice brick red, and all of the flavors were just as bright and clear as when pan-fried. Oven-frying also provided a greater margin of error when it came to timing than either of the other methods, and, surprisingly, it was just about as easy as microwaving, adding only the steps of preheating the oven and draining the cooked bacon on paper towels. Finally, the oven-fried strips of bacon were more consistently cooked throughout, showing no raw spots and requiring no turning.

Our last test was to try 12 strips of bacon—a pretty full tray—in a preheated oven. This test was also quite successful. The pieces cooked consistently, the only difference being between those in the back and those in the front of the oven; we corrected for this by rotating the tray once from front to back during cooking. That was about the limit of our contact with the hot grease.

WHAT WE LEARNED: For crisp, evenly cooked bacon that requires almost no attention, the oven is definitely the way to go.

OVEN-FRIED BACON   serves 4 to 6

Use a large, rimmed baking sheet that is shallow enough to promote browning, yet tall enough (at least ¾ inch in height) to contain the rendered bacon fat. If cooking more than one tray of bacon, exchange their oven positions once about halfway through the cooking process.

12   slices bacon, thin- or thick-cut

Adjust oven rack to middle position and heat oven to 400 degrees. Arrange bacon slices in baking sheet or other shallow baking pan. Roast until fat begins to render, 5 to 6 minutes; rotate pan front to back. Continue roasting until bacon is crisp and brown, 5 to 6 minutes longer for thin-sliced bacon, 8 to 10 minutes for thick-cut. Transfer with tongs to paper towel–lined plate, drain, and serve.

TASTING LAB: Orange Juice

CAN ANYTHING RIVAL THE JUICE YOU SQUEEZE AT HOME? To find out, we gathered 34 tasters to evaluate 10 brands of supermarket orange juice as well as juice we squeezed in the test kitchen and juice fresh-squeezed at the supermarket.

Our top choice had been squeezed the day before at a local supermarket, closely followed by the juice we squeezed ourselves. Cartons of chilled not-from-concentrate juices took third and seventh places, with three brands of frozen concentrate squeezed in the middle. Chilled juices made from concentrate landed at the bottom of the rankings.

How could juice squeezed the day before at a supermarket beat out juice squeezed minutes before the tasting? And how could frozen concentrate beat out more expensive chilled juices from concentrate?

The produce manager at the store where we bought fresh-squeezed juice told us he blends oranges to produce good-tasting juice. This can be a real advantage, especially when compared with juice squeezed at home from one kind of orange. Any loss in freshness can be offset by the more complex and balanced flavor of a blended fresh juice, as was the case in our tasting.

Although no one was surprised that the two fresh juices took top honors, the strong showing of the frozen concentrates was a shock. It seems that frozen concentrate doesn't deserve its dowdy, old-fashioned reputation.

Why does juice made at home from frozen concentrate taste better than prepackaged chilled juice made from concentrate? Heat is the biggest enemy of orange juice. Frozen concentrates and chilled juices not made from concentrate are both pasteurized once at around 195 degrees to eliminate microorganisms and neutralize enzymes that will shorten shelf life. Chilled juices made from concentrate are pasteurized twice, once when the concentrate is made and again when the juice is reconstituted and packaged. This accounts for the lack of fresh-squeezed flavor in chilled juices made from concentrate.

CHEESE OMELET

WHAT WE WANTED: A foolproof method for cooking a cheese omelet with a tender, supple mouthfeel, a creamy interior filled with completely melted cheese, and no leaks.

Cheese omelets are fraught with problems. First and foremost is the issue of how to achieve perfect texture. Just a few seconds too long in the pan can turn an omelet from light, soft, and creamy to dark, tough, and rubbery. But you can't skimp too much on cooking time, either, because the cheese must melt completely before the omelet leaves the pan. And, speaking of cheese, we wanted to know if there was a way to make sure that none of that delicious filling would creep out of its egg casing during cooking.

Some initial tests convinced us about some basics. A good-quality, nonstick skillet with gently sloped sides is the superior implement for the production of a great omelet. We found that beating the eggs thoroughly ensures uniform texture for the exterior and interior of the omelet, a quality that is particularly important for filled omelets. We also concluded that the texture of an omelet is improved by stirring the eggs once they are in the pan; eggs cooked without stirring produced an uneven, loose omelet. Further testing confirmed that heavy cream, half-and-half, milk, and water all diffused the delicate flavor of the eggs and should not be added. Finally, we agreed that butter added rich flavor.

Now that we had the basics in hand, we set out to refine our technique. We began cooking three-egg cheddar omelets for anyone who came within range of the stove. Tasters liked best the omelets filled with 3 tablespoons of cheese. But with this large amount of cheese, we found that our trusty 8-inch skillet was no longer big enough. When we opted for a 10-inch skillet, the eggs spread out to a thinner shell that was much easier to wrap around the cheese.

We also discovered that merely folding or rolling the eggs around the cheese was insufficient to contain it. The cheese inevitably found a way out. The perfect method turned out to be the classic French style, in which a pan is tilted and jerked to shape the omelet.

Even after making several omelets with this method, we noticed that they were all a little too well-done and brown. We played around with the idea of reducing the heat after the eggs set up, but we found it impractical to have to readjust the heat, especially on an electric stove. Eventually, we realized that every stove has one universal temperature setting: no heat. We started the omelet with the same technique that we had been using, but this time we turned the flame off completely, hoping that the residual heat in the pan would be sufficient to finish cooking the omelet.

Oddly enough, even with the flame off, the omelet colored a little too much. Next we tried taking the pan off the heat completely. This time the omelet was perfect. As it turns out, once the cheese has been added, the pan retains enough residual heat to continue cooking the omelet. This new method produced perfectly colored, blond omelets, no matter the stove, no matter the cook.

The on-burner, off-burner technique had one drawback. The cheese, which had melted perfectly until this point, now melted only partially. We hoped this could be remedied with a finer grating of cheese. We threw the box grater back in the drawer and pulled out the fine grater we often use for Parmesan. This time the cheese melted throughout.

It was now time to see which cheeses worked best in the omelet. Only the harder cheeses (Pecorino Romano, Asiago, Parmesan) failed to melt completely within the small window of time open to them. Many other cheeses worked well. The only rule of thumb is to use a cheese that can be grated.

WHAT WE LEARNED: Use a nonstick 10-inch pan, tilt and jerk the pan to enclose the cheese, and then finish cooking the omelet off heat to prevent toughening.

CHEESE OMELET serves 1

Making perfect omelets takes some practice, so don't be disappointed if your first effort fails to meet your expectations. For those times when a plain cheese omelet just won't do, we developed a few more substantial variations. Limit the amount of filling to a maximum of ¼ cup—anything more and the omelet will burst open. Just about any ingredient must be sautéed beforehand; the less-than-a-minute cooking time of the eggs is not sufficient to properly cook the filling. Be sure to prepare the filling before you begin making the omelet.

3	large eggs
	Salt and ground black pepper
½	tablespoon unsalted butter, plus melted butter for brushing on finished omelet
3	tablespoons very finely grated Gruyère, cheddar, Monterey Jack, or other cheese of your choice
1	recipe filling, optional (recipes follow)

1. Beat eggs and salt and pepper to taste with fork in small bowl until thoroughly combined.

2. Heat butter in 10-inch nonstick skillet over medium-high heat; when foaming subsides and butter just begins to color, pour in eggs. Cook until edges begin to set, 2 to 3 seconds, then, with rubber spatula, stir in circular motion until slightly thickened, about 10 seconds. Use spatula to pull cooked edges in toward center, then tilt pan to one side so that uncooked egg runs to edge of pan. Repeat until omelet is just set but still moist on surface, about 20 to 25 seconds. Sprinkle cheese and filling, if using, down center of omelet, perpendicular to handle of skillet.

3. Remove skillet from burner. Use rubber spatula to fold lower third (nearest you) of omelet to center; press gently with spatula to secure seams, maintaining fold.

4. Run spatula between outer edge of omelet and pan to loosen. Jerk pan sharply toward you a few times to slide omelet up far side of pan. Jerk pan again so that 2 inches of unfolded edge folds over itself, or use spatula to fold edge over. Invert omelet onto plate. Tidy edges with spatula, brush with melted butter, and serve.

SAUTÉED MUSHROOM FILLING WITH THYME makes about ½ cup, enough to fill 2 omelets

This filling is particularly good when paired with Gruyère.

Heat 1 tablespoon butter in medium skillet over medium heat until foaming; add 1 small shallot, minced (about 1 tablespoon), and cook until softened and just beginning to color, about 2 minutes. Add 2 medium white mushrooms (about 2 ounces), cleaned and sliced ¼ inch thick. Cook, stirring occasionally, until softened and lightly browned, about 3 minutes. Off heat, stir in 1 teaspoon fresh minced thyme leaves and salt and pepper to taste; transfer mixture to small bowl and set aside until ready to use.

SAUTÉED RED BELL PEPPER FILLING WITH MUSHROOM AND ONION makes about ½ cup, enough to fill 2 omelets

Monterey Jack is our choice of cheese for this filling.

Heat 1 tablespoon butter in medium skillet over medium heat until foaming; add ½ small onion, chopped fine, and cook, stirring occasionally, until softened but not browned, about 2 minutes. Add 1 medium white mushroom (about 1 ounce), cleaned and sliced ¼ inch thick. Cook, stirring occasionally, until softened and beginning to brown, about 2 minutes. Add ¼ red bell pepper (about 2 ounces), seeds discarded, cut into ½-inch dice; cook, stirring occasionally, until softened, about 2 minutes. Off heat, stir in 1 teaspoon minced fresh parsley leaves and salt and pepper to taste; transfer mixture to small bowl and set aside until ready to use.

After tasting nine brands of
maple syrup on as many waffles,
it's time to clean up.

FRENCH TOAST, waffles, & breakfast strata

CHAPTER 19

Most people we know are passionate about breakfast, especially weekend breakfasts, when there's time for something other than a bowl of cold cereal or a slice of dry toast and juice. Because we get to eat a real breakfast so infrequently, we have high expectations when it comes to these classic dishes.

Soggy, overly eggy French toast simply won't do. Neither will rubbery, bland waffles. If you are going to spend the time making French toast and waffles, they better be good.

In addition to the right recipes, you need to think about equipment. Waffles require a good waffle iron, but they all look pretty much the same—how do you pick the best model? Some chefs swear by griddles for preparing French toast; can a skillet work just as well? We've tested these items and also rated the number one breakfast condiment—maple syrup. With the right tools and ingredients on hand, you can make a great breakfast, no matter how bleary-eyed you might be.

Sometimes it's nice to take a break from tradition. A breakfast strata—a savory bread pudding made with stale bread, cheese, eggs, and milk—is a good change of pace. All the ingredients are familiar, but the presentation and concept are fresh. Best of all, a strata is best assembled a day in advance, so you can sleep in on Sunday morning, pop the casserole dish in the oven when you wake up, and have a great breakfast on the table by the time you've read the morning paper.

IN THIS CHAPTER

THE RECIPES

French Toast for Challah or Sandwich Bread
French Toast for Firm European-Style Bread

Buttermilk Waffles
Almost-as-Good-as Buttermilk Waffles

Breakfast Strata with Spinach, Shallots, and Gruyère
Breakfast Strata with Sausage, Mushrooms, and Monterey Jack
Breakfast Strata with Potatoes, Rosemary, and Fontina

EQUIPMENT CORNER

Griddles
Refrigerators
Waffle Irons

SCIENCE DESK

Why Commercial Baking Powder Doesn't Work in Waffles

TASTING LAB

Maple Syrup

FRENCH TOAST

WHAT WE WANTED: French toast that's crisp on the outside and custardy on the inside. The toast shouldn't be too eggy, either.

French toast (or *pain perdu*, "lost bread") started out as a simple way to use up old bread by dipping it in a beaten egg and frying it. Many recipes today deviate little from this basic technique, calling for a couple of eggs and a touch of milk. What they produce, however, is a toast that tastes mostly of fried egg and that, depending on the amount of liquid, is either overly soggy or still dry in the middle.

We wanted something quite different: bread that was crisp and buttery on the outside, soft and custardlike inside. We wanted to taste a balance of flavors rather than just egg. We wanted our French toast to be sweet enough to eat with only a sprinkling of confectioners' sugar, but not so sweet that we couldn't top it with syrup or macerated fruit if we chose to.

We started testing with a simple formula: 2 eggs beaten with ½ cup milk to soak four slices of ¾-inch-thick, day-old French bread. From this starting point, we wanted to settle first on which bread works best for French toast, but that proved to be the hardest part of the testing. At first, it seemed simple. One-inch-thick slices of any sort of bread were too thick; they either soaked up too much liquid and didn't cook through, or they stayed dry in the middle with shorter soaking. So we stuck with ¾-inch slices and tried different kinds of bread: baguettes, supermarket breads, challah, brioche, and a dense white bread.

At the end of these tests, we thought we had the answer. Challah was clearly best, adding a lot of flavor and richness, staying generally crisp outside and somewhat moist inside—not perfect, but likely to improve with changes in the liquid component. Baguette slices and slices of a high-quality Italian bread, so long as they weren't more than a day old, came in second. Hard-to-find brioche was only acceptable.

Brioche can vary widely in quality, and the open-textured version we had failed to take up the liquid evenly. Dense white bread simply tasted like fried bread, so it rated near the bottom. Presliced sandwich bread was acceptable in a pinch, although just barely. Worst, though, was the supermarket bakery version of French or Italian bread. Spongy and flabby, this bread simply fell apart when we took it out of the liquid. For the moment, the bread issue seemed resolved. So, using challah for testing, we moved on to the liquids.

Because we didn't want our French toast to be too eggy, we first tried dropping one egg from the test recipe. That decision showed an immediate improvement, yielding a finished product that was crispier outside but still soft inside. To be sure that fewer eggs made for a better result, we tried going the opposite way, using 3 eggs to ½ cup milk. That confirmed it: More egg seemed to create a barrier on the outside of the bread, causing the interior to stay dry while the outside tasted like fried egg.

The next logical step seemed to be to increase the milk, given that a higher proportion of milk to egg had worked so far. A jump to 1 cup milk made the bread too wet inside, but it was better than ½ cup. Three-quarters cup

milk proved to be ideal, as the toast stayed custardlike inside and fairly crisp outside.

When we tried half-and-half instead, we could not discern enough difference in taste to warrant the additional grams of fat. Cream was certainly good, but after we added other flavorings to the basic recipe, we returned to milk, as the cream became too rich. A test with buttermilk, which we generally love, was awful, with a sharp, almost metallic edge.

Throughout our tests with egg and dairy, our basic recipe had tasted flat. We were looking forward to the final tests, when we would add other ingredients. We first tried salt, which gave the recipe a big boost: just ¼ teaspoon and the toast finally had some flavor. We added sugar next, which also made a great difference. At this point, 1 tablespoon seemed like a good amount for toast that would be covered with syrup; after making the recipe adjustments described below, though, we found that 2 tablespoons proved best. Finally, we added vanilla. Few recipes call for it, but 2 teaspoons really pulled things together, balancing the flavors.

At this point, we were ready to develop some variations on our basic recipe. We tried cinnamon, almond extract, and various liqueurs in place of the vanilla. The cinnamon and almond were nice alternatives, but the liqueurs were wholly unsuccessful.

After all this, we had a French toast that was better than any we could remember, yet still not ideal. It was fairly crisp, but not exactly what we were after: an almost deep-fried crispness. We knew the sugar helped, but there had to be something else. More butter in the skillet (until now we'd been using 1½ tablespoons for 4 pieces of bread) only made the challah greasier, and a heat level higher than medium to medium-high simply burned the toast. When one editor mentioned a French toast version she'd once had in which the bread was dipped in pancake batter, plus a recipe that called for a pinch of flour, it got us thinking about what flour could do. Ultimately, what it did was solve the puzzle.

At first we liked 1 tablespoon flour to help get the exterior extracrisp and not greasy, but in later tests we noticed that this made the toast somewhat soggy inside; yet when we went up to 2 tablespoons, the bread became tough. So we started trying more flour—but with butter added to keep the bread from toughening. After a few more tests, we finally had fabulous French toast: A batter with ⅓ cup flour balanced by 2 tablespoons melted butter gets the outside of the challah evenly crisped and brown and lets just enough moisture through to the interior to keep it custardlike but not heavy.

A few other tests answered some final questions. We tried cooking in all kinds of skillets and ended up liking cast iron best, with a regular (not nonstick) skillet a close second. Using medium heat with 1 tablespoon butter worked well with these skillets; nonstick skillets made the bread too greasy, even with less butter and other heat settings.

Unfortunately, our perfect French toast recipe worked wonders with challah but failed with chewy French and Italian breads. While we strongly recommend using challah if you can, we know it's less likely to be the day-old bread people have on hand. So we worked out a separate recipe for French and Italian breads, but we recommend it with a caveat: If you're using soft supermarket-style French bread or sliced white sandwich bread, go with the challah recipe.

With a chewier, drier French or Italian loaf, however, the high amount of flour in the batter used for challah prevented needed moisture from soaking into the bread. Also, the exterior had a harder time crisping because the rougher surface of this somewhat open-textured bread didn't make good contact with the pan. To get the interior moist, we tried dropping some of the flour; to get the exterior crisped, we again tried a two-egg recipe. Neither trick worked. In the end, more tests showed that the recipe needed even more milk for a custardlike interior and just 1 tablespoon of flour to aid in crisping; with this little flour, the batter needed no butter.

WHAT WE LEARNED: Different breads require different kinds of custard. Challah makes the best French toast, but crusty French or Italian bread can be used as well as sandwich bread in a pinch. Use plenty of milk to keep the French toast from tasting too eggy; add flour to crisp the exterior of the toast and melted butter to keep the interior tender.

FRENCH TOAST FOR CHALLAH OR SANDWICH BREAD
makes 4 or 5 slices from challah or 6 to 8 slices from sandwich bread

Though thick-sliced challah is best for French toast, you can substitute high-quality, presliced sandwich bread. Flipping challah is easiest with tongs, but a spatula works best with sandwich bread. To speed the cooking of large quantities of French toast, heat two or more skillets to brown a few batches at once. To vary the flavor of the batter, try adding ¾ teaspoon ground cinnamon or ½ teaspoon ground nutmeg with the dry ingredients, or try substituting almond extract for the vanilla extract.

    1   large egg
    2   tablespoons unsalted butter, melted,
        plus extra for frying
    ¾   cup milk
    2   teaspoons vanilla extract
    2   tablespoons sugar
    ⅓   cup all-purpose flour
    ¼   teaspoon salt
    4–5 slices day-old challah, cut ¾ inch thick,
        or 6 to 8 slices day-old sandwich
        bread

1. Heat 10- to 12-inch skillet (preferably cast iron) over medium heat for 5 minutes. Meanwhile, beat egg lightly in shallow pan or pie plate; whisk in butter, then milk and vanilla, and finally sugar, flour, and salt, continuing to whisk until smooth. Soak bread without oversaturating, about 40 seconds per side for challah or 30 seconds per side for sandwich bread. Pick up bread and allow excess batter to drip off; repeat with remaining slices.

2. Swirl 1 tablespoon butter in hot skillet. Transfer prepared bread to skillet; cook until golden brown, about 1 minute 45 seconds on first side and 1 minute on second side. Serve immediately. Continue, adding 1 tablespoon butter to skillet for each new batch.

FRENCH TOAST FOR FIRM EUROPEAN-STYLE BREAD
makes 4 or 8 slices, depending on the loaf

This recipe has less flour, allowing the batter to penetrate more easily into drier, chewier French or Italian loaves.

    1   large egg
    1   cup milk
    2   teaspoons vanilla extract
    2   tablespoons sugar
    1   tablespoon all-purpose flour
    ¼   teaspoon salt
    4–8 slices firm, day-old European-style bread, such
        as French or Italian, ¾ inch thick
        Unsalted butter to grease skillet (about
        1 tablespoon per batch)

1. Heat 10- to 12-inch skillet (preferably cast iron) over medium heat for 5 minutes. Meanwhile, beat egg lightly in shallow pan or pie plate; whisk in milk and vanilla, and then sugar, flour, and salt, continuing to whisk until smooth. Soak bread without oversaturating, about 30 seconds per side. Pick up bread and allow excess batter to drip off; repeat with remaining slices.

2. Swirl 1 tablespoon butter in hot skillet. Transfer prepared bread to skillet; cook until golden brown, about 2 minutes on first side and 1 minute and 15 seconds on the second. Serve immediately. Continue, adding 1 tablespoon butter to skillet for each new batch.

EQUIPMENT CORNER: Griddles

YOU JUST CAN'T MAKE A LOT OF FRENCH TOAST AT THE same time in a skillet, so we decided to test griddles, which have a much larger surface area, to see what they could do.

First we checked out four nonstick electric griddles. We preheated each to 400 degrees, gave it a coating of butter, and added as many batter-dipped bread slices as would comfortably fit. All four electric griddles accommodated between seven and nine slices of challah French toast, versus only two in the cast-iron skillet, but none was able to produce the crustiness we were after. Some browned a little more evenly than others, but even the best of them had cool spots around the edges or corners, perhaps because a single heating coil runs beneath the cooking surface.

We next tested a stove-top cast-iron griddle that spans two burners. We heated it up over medium heat, coated the surface with butter, and placed six slices of bread on top to cook. As we expected, the slices that rested on the center surface of the griddle, with no burner underneath, failed to brown at all. Hence, we were able to successfully make only four slices of French toast. These four slices, however, did have the crispy crust that we were looking for.

After all this testing, we concluded that our hands-down preference for making French toast was still the cast-iron skillet, even if it means making slices continuously as people eat them.

EQUIPMENT CORNER: Refrigerators

ALTHOUGH WE DON'T OFTEN THINK ABOUT IT, EVERY refrigerator has hot and cold spots. Together they create a complex food storage matrix inside a basic three-shelf refrigerator. You can make the temperature flux in your refrigerator work to your advantage by learning where these hot and cold spots are located.

We spoke with several refrigeration experts about hot and cold spots, and the information we gathered was consistent. To verify this data in the real world, we hooked up a test kitchen refrigerator to a piece of equipment called a chart scan data recorder. The recorder was connected to a laptop computer as well as several temperature monitors placed in strategic locations on the shelves and drawers inside the refrigerator. The refrigerator was then closed and left undisturbed for 24 hours while the interior temperatures were monitored and recorded.

Keeping in mind that a refrigerator goes through many cooling cycles throughout a 24-hour period (that is, at times the temperature may be well above or below 34 degrees Fahrenheit, the optimal temperature for a home refrigerator), our results provided some interesting information. For example, the butter compartment was not the warmest spot in the fridge, as we had expected, although it wasn't very cold either. Instead, the middle shelf on the door and front portion of the bottom cabinet shelf registered the highest readings—all the way up to 43 degrees. Not a place where you would want to store your milk or eggs, both of which should be kept below 40 degrees.

The meat compartment remained the coolest area of the refrigerator (on average, 33 degrees), making it perfect for storing what it is supposed to store: meat. Other cool spots included the back of the top, middle, and bottom shelves, as well as the bottom compartment on the refrigerator drawer. The crisper drawer was moderate-to-cool, making it an ideal place to keep vegetables, which should stay well above the 32-degree mark.

WAFFLES

WHAT WE WANTED: A waffle with a crisp, well-browned exterior and a moist, fluffy interior. It should be like a rich, just-cooked soufflé encased in a flavorful crust.

After testing more than 15 recipes, we realized that our ideal waffle requires a thick batter, so the outside can become crisp while the inside remains custardy. We also learned that a good waffle must be quickly cooked; slow cooking evens out the cooking rate, causing the center to overcook by the time the exterior is crisp and brown.

Many waffle batters are too thin, usually because the proportion of milk to flour—at 1 cup each—is too high. Such thin batter results in disappointing, gummy-textured waffles with dry, unappealing interiors. We found that ⅞ cup buttermilk, or ¾ cup regular milk, to 1 cup flour is a far better proportion.

Most recipes omit buttermilk entirely or, at best, list it as an option. Yet we found that buttermilk is absolutely crucial. Why? Because buttermilk, when teamed up with baking soda, creates a much thicker batter than the alternative, regular milk paired with baking powder. We eventually found a way to make good waffles with regular milk (reduce the amount of liquid and use homemade baking powder for a thicker batter), but buttermilk waffles will always taste better.

Although many recipes for buttermilk waffles call for baking powder, it's not necessary. All that's required is baking soda, which reacts with the acid in the buttermilk to give the batter lift. Baking powder is essentially baking soda plus cream of tartar, an acidic ingredient. Baking powder is useful when the batter itself contains no other source of acid. We eliminated the baking powder from our working recipe and found not only that it wasn't necessary but that it wasn't all that helpful; these waffles cooked up crispier. Out of curiosity, we also tried to make a waffle with buttermilk and baking powder, eliminating the baking soda. The waffle was inedible. (See the Science Desk on page 258 for more information on how baking powder and soda work.)

Some waffle recipes call for separating the egg and then whipping the white and folding it into the mixed batter. We made waffles this way and found that folding in beaten egg whites improves things. The batter is glossier, and the waffle is fluffier inside. If you cut through a cooked waffle made with beaten egg whites, you can actually see pockets of air trapped inside. The same examination of a whole-egg waffle revealed a flatter, more consistent texture.

Look at a number of waffle recipes and you'll see a wide range of recommendations as to how to combine ingredients. But most have this in common: They add all of the liquid ingredients at once. This practice necessitates overmixing and usually results in clumps of unmoistened flour. When we used a whisk to combine the ingredients until they were smooth, the batter was thin and the waffle tough.

The objective is to moisten the flour thoroughly, not to create a smooth batter, and for this there is no question that a gentle hand is crucial. This is the technique that worked best for us: Pour the liquid ingredients into the dry ingredients very slowly, mixing gently with a rubber spatula. When most of the liquid has been added, the batter becomes thicker; switch to a folding motion, similar to that used in folding egg whites, to finally combine and moisten the batter. Then continue folding as you add the beaten egg white.

When you bake waffles, remember that darker waffles are better than lighter ones. The browning reaction promotes the development of flavor. Waffles should be cooked until medium-brown, not lightly tanned. Toasty brown waffles will also stay crispier longer than manila-colored waffles, which are likely to become soggy by the time they get to the table.

WHAT WE LEARNED: More flour than liquid creates a thick batter that makes waffles crisp on the outside and moist on the inside. Buttermilk provides the best flavor, and whipping the egg white makes waffles lighter.

BUTTERMILK WAFFLES makes 3 to 4, depending on size of waffle iron

The secret to great waffles is a thick batter, so don't expect a pourable batter. The optional dash of cornmeal adds a pleasant crunch to the finished waffle. This recipe can be doubled or tripled. Make toaster waffles out of leftover batter—undercook the waffles a bit, cool them on a wire rack, wrap them in plastic wrap, and freeze. Pop them in the toaster for a quick breakfast.

- 1 cup (5 ounces) unbleached all-purpose flour
- 1 tablespoon cornmeal (optional)
- ½ teaspoon salt
- ¼ teaspoon baking soda
- 1 large egg, separated
- ⅞ cup buttermilk
- 2 tablespoons unsalted butter, melted and cooled

1. Heat waffle iron. Whisk dry ingredients together in medium bowl. Whisk yolk with buttermilk and butter.

2. Beat egg white until it just holds a 2-inch peak.

3. Add liquid ingredients to dry ingredients in thin, steady stream while mixing gently with rubber spatula. (Do not add liquid faster than you can incorporate it into batter.) Toward end of mixing, use folding motion to incorporate ingredients. Gently fold egg white into batter.

4. Spread appropriate amount of batter onto waffle iron. Following manufacturer's instructions, cook waffle until golden brown, 2 to 5 minutes. Serve immediately. (In a pinch, you can keep waffles warm on wire rack in 200-degree oven for up to 5 minutes.)

VARIATION
ALMOST-AS-GOOD-AS BUTTERMILK WAFFLES makes 3 or 4

If you're out of buttermilk, try this variation with milk. By making your own baking powder (using baking soda and cream of tartar; see the Science Desk on page 258) and by cutting back on the quantity of milk, you can make a thick, quite respectable batter. The result is a waffle with a crisp crust and moist interior.

Follow recipe for Buttermilk Waffles, adding ½ teaspoon cream of tartar to dry ingredients and substituting scant ¾ cup milk for buttermilk.

EQUIPMENT CORNER: Waffle Irons

NO MATTER HOW FOOLPROOF THE RECIPE, ALL WAFFLES will be rubbery and flaccid if cooked in the wrong waffle iron. To find out which waffle irons work the best, we gathered six traditional (not Belgian) waffle makers, with prices ranging from $20 to $50. We narrowed our selection to include only round models, as they account for 60 percent of waffle iron sales.

The differences in brands were dramatic. The top-rated models turned out crisp, well-browned waffles in just three minutes. The worst models produced rubbery or hard waffles that took nearly twice as long to cook.

What makes the difference? The critical issue is how hot the waffle iron can get. We tested each waffle maker with an infrared thermometer, measuring the temperature of each quadrant and then averaging the results for each machine. The models producing the rubbery waffles had an average temperature of 330 degrees, while the highly rated models averaged 380 degrees. That difference is enough to sear and crisp the exterior without drying out the interior. The weaker models didn't have enough heat to set up the contrasting textures—crisp on the outside, creamy in the middle—that we wanted.

All models tested had lights indicating when the iron was ready to use, but many of these lights were inconveniently placed and difficult to see. Only a few models also had a "done" light, indicating when the waffles were fully cooked. This feature effectively eliminated all guesswork—

simply set the degree of doneness, and voilà, a perfectly browned, crisp waffle.

Our favorite waffle irons were the Farberware Millennium Deluxe ($30) and the Cuisinart Classic Round ($50). The Villaware Perfect Waffler ($40) also received high marks, but testers soon wearied of the piercing chirp this model emitted when the waffles were done.

SCIENCE DESK: Why Commercial Baking Powder Doesn't Work in Waffles

BAKING POWDER IS MADE FROM TWO MAJOR ELEMENTS: an acid (such as cream of tartar) and baking soda. A batter made with regular milk, for example, instead of with an acidic ingredient such as yogurt or buttermilk, will not rise without the help of the acid in baking powder. Baking powder is used in place of baking soda when there is no natural acidity in the batter.

When baking soda comes in contact with a moist, acidic environment, carbon dioxide gas is produced, which in turn provides "rise." This chemical reaction is quite pronounced in a buttermilk batter—buttermilk contains lactic acid, which reacts strongly with the soda, generating a thick, spongy batter in seconds.

The reaction between regular milk and baking powder isn't as strong, so the batter remains thin. This is partially because most baking powder is "double acting"—that is, it produces a rise once at room temperature, when added to the batter, and once in the oven, when the temperature climbs above 120 degrees. Baking powder is designed to create gas slowly, so that a cake, for example, will have plenty of time to rise in the oven before the bubbles dissipate and the cake sets.

In our tests, it was clear that most of the rise with baking powder occurs at oven temperature. Since waffles are cooked so quickly, baking powder is not ideally suited to this type of batter; the amount of "room-temperature" acid it can provide is insufficient. With waffles you want a lot of room-temperature reaction, and therefore it's best, when using regular milk instead of buttermilk, to make your own recipe for baking powder, using cream of tartar (which works at room temperature) and baking soda.

TASTING LAB: Maple Syrup

WHAT ARE WAFFLES OR FRENCH TOAST (OR PANCAKES FOR that matter) without maple syrup? We wondered how the consumer should buy maple syrup. By grade? By source (is Vermont syrup really better than the rest)? We also wondered if any of the pancake syrups—those supermarkets staples made with a tiny percentage of maple syrup—were demonstratively better than their peers.

In general, a maple syrup's grade is determined by the period during which it was made (the sugaring season lasts from February to early April). Technically, the grades of maple syrup are measured by the amount of light that can pass through the syrup. Straight from the tree, maple sap is clear, consisting of about 98 percent water and 2 percent sugar. To make maple syrup, the water has to be boiled off to a concentration of 66 percent sugar. (This means boiling off about 39 gallons of water to get one gallon of syrup.)

Early in the season, maple syrups tend to be near-transparent because the sugar molecules in the boiled-down sap are able to reflect much light. As temperatures warm outside, wild yeasts in the sap begin feeding on and breaking down the sugar. As a result, light can be absorbed. So as the season progresses, the syrup darkens.

This breakdown of sugar also affects flavor. If maple sap is concentrated without boiling (by freeze-drying, for example), the syrup will taste sweet but otherwise have little flavor. The flavor we perceive as "maple" is actually the result of chemical reactions that occur when the sap is boiled. One of the two primary flavor notes is derived from the compounds that form when sugar molecules break down. The process is similar to caramelization. This may explain why the darker syrups produced later in the season have more of the caramel notes distinct to maple syrup. The second flavor

note is vanilla, which is produced from compounds in the sap that the tree uses to make wood.

While vanilla and caramel are essential maple flavor elements, the full flavor of maple is far more complex. One producer's syrup can vary from a neighbor's because of differences in the soil, the tree chemistry, or the method of heating the sap.

The season's earliest sap flow produces Grade A light, or "Fancy," as it is called in Vermont. Honey gold and near-transparent, it has a pronounced sweetness and a delicate vanilla flavor. Grade A light can be the most expensive syrup and is not typically found in supermarkets. While it takes no more energy to produce than the other grades, its higher

price was established more than 100 years ago, when "sugaring" was about just that—turning maple syrup into sugar. The lighter syrup made a finer sugar that could be sold at a higher cost, which simply never changed. Today Grade A light syrups are primarily used to make maple sugar candies.

The season's second syrup is Grade A medium amber. This has a warmer caramel color with a medium-strength flavor. It is generally touted as the syrup for pancakes. Right on the heels of medium amber is Grade A dark amber, which is slightly deeper in color and has a more pronounced flavor.

After the ambers falls Grade B, the darkest and typically least expensive of the syrups on the market. It is traditionally considered cooking grade because of its strength of flavor. Only Vermont makes Grade B syrup for consumer table use. Other states make a similar syrup but sell it only in bulk to the food industry because it is deemed too strong and too dark. Some natural foods stores carry it in bulk.

Last, there is a Grade C, characterized by strong, almost molasses-like flavor. It is sold only to the food industry.

Of the nine samples in our tasting, tasters decided that if they had the choice, they would reach for the Vermont "B" syrup to drizzle on their pancakes. Most tasters were won over by the depth of flavor and the dark rum color of the syrup. Many wrote comments such as "tastes real." And, unlike many of the syrups, which lost their distinction when poured on a waffle, this one's bold characteristics held up.

The close runner-up in our tasting was a Grade A dark amber. Overall, tasters preferred the dark amber syrups to the medium ambers, which failed to spark tasters' interest, apparently because they were not bold enough. Not surprisingly, then, tasters flat-out rejected the one "Fancy" grade syrup we included in the tasting. None of our results indicated syrup made from one region or state is superior to another, and industry experts agree that it is difficult, if not impossible, to determine by taste where a syrup is made.

Because pancake syrups far outsell real maple syrups, we decided to do an additional tasting of the three top-selling national pancake syrups. The high scorer was Aunt Jemima, which is made of high fructose corn syrup.

BREAKFAST STRATA

WHAT WE WANTED: A hearty breakfast casserole with bread, eggs, milk, and cheese—basically a savory bread pudding—that is puffed and golden.

What's quicker than quiche, sturdier than soufflé, and combines the best qualities of both? The answer is strata, a layered casserole that, in its most basic form, comprises bread, eggs, cheese, and milk or cream. Layered among them are flavorful fillings that provide both substance and character, and the result is essentially a golden brown, puffed, hearty, savory bread pudding. Strata is easy to prepare, can be made ahead, and feeds a crowd for breakfast or brunch.

But strata is not without its issues. First, it is easy to go overboard with too much of a good thing. Many of the stratas we sampled in the test kitchen to kick off the recipe development process were simply too rich for breakfast, with a belly-busting overabundance of custard. Strata is breakfast food, so it should fill you up without making you feel sick or lazy for the rest of the day. The bread should neither call attention to itself nor get lost among the other ingredients. And then there are the fillings. In our experience, strata often suffers from largesse, with recipes adding as many fillings as they can possibly squeeze in. This everything-but-the-kitchen-sink approach leads to wet, sagging, overwrought stratas, like one we sampled early on that included mustard, garlic, nutmeg, marinated artichoke hearts, raw green peppers, cherry tomatoes, ham, Parmesan, fontina, and goat cheese. Such overindulgence not only sends unlucky diners scrambling for Maalox but also turns a simple, workhorse dish into a parody of itself. A good strata should have a restrained filling with a couple of components chosen to accent the bread, custard, and cheese.

In essence, then, we wanted to scale strata back, keeping it just rich enough and choosing fillings that would add to the picture without stealing the show. We also wanted a cohesive casserole rather than a bunch of stray ingredients baked together in a pan. All the principal aspects of the dish—custard, bread, and fillings, and how and when they were assembled and cooked—were open to inspection.

Bread is the foundation of strata. Though sliced white sandwich bread was the type specified in most recipes, we also saw calls for Italian, French, sourdough, multigrain, rye, pumpernickel, challah, focaccia, and even hamburger and hot dog buns. We tried them all, and tasters preferred supermarket Italian and French breads for their strong crumb and neutral flavor. Since tasters had no objection to the crust, we left it in place. Also, while many recipes specify cubes of bread, we preferred slices because they added to the layered effect of the casserole. The slices were best at about ½-inch thick, as thicker slices remained too chewy and really thin ones just melted away. We also learned that the texture of stale bread (or fresh bread dried briefly in the oven) was preferable to that of fresh and that we appreciated the richness and flavor added by a little butter on the slices.

The tender custard that binds the bread was our other major target. In a battery of custard tests, tasters' preferences were divided between mixtures with equal parts dairy and egg and those with twice as much dairy as egg. The solution was to meet in the middle, adding just a little extra dairy to the 50/50 mixture. Along the way, we also tested different dairy products. Recipes commonly call for low-fat or whole milk or half-and-half and sometimes even heavy cream (usually in combination with another dairy liquid). We tried each one of these alone and in every conceivable combination, and most tasters preferred half-and-half on its own. The last adjustment we made to the custard was its overall quantity, which for many tasters was too little, making for a dry strata. Increasing the ratio of custard to bread made the strata more moist and cohesive.

Though our basic strata was very good, it's the flavorings and fillings that catapult it to glory. As a basic flavoring, sautéed shallots won over onions and garlic. We had a surprise in store when we tested another flavoring common to strata recipes, namely, white wine. It showed promise, lightening the flavor of the whole dish. But it also imparted a boozy flavor that was out of place. We corrected this problem by reducing the wine to cook off the alcohol and concentrate the flavor. This eliminated the alcoholic overtones, and the reduced wine brightened the flavor of the whole dish considerably.

One last observation we can offer about the most basic seasonings, salt and pepper: A heavy hand is best. Strata required a generous dose of each, and seasoning both custard and filling individually and liberally was the most effective way to bring all the flavors into focus.

Even with the right basic ingredients in the right proportions, test after test proved that high-moisture fillings such as sausage and raw vegetables ruined the strata's texture. Their moisture leached into the casserole, leaving it wet enough to literally slosh and ooze when cut. To correct this problem, we took to sautéing all filling ingredients until they looked dry in the pan. This step saved the day by evaporating moisture that would otherwise end up in the strata. Whatever your filling choice, this critical step will make the difference between a moist, tender dish and one that's more like a sopping-wet sponge mop.

One of strata's charms is that it can—in fact, most recipes claim it should—be assembled well ahead of time. We tested stratas that had been assembled and rested overnight for four hours, for one hour, and one that had not been rested at all. Only the fresh-made strata, which was noticeably less cohesive than the rested versions, failed to make the cut. Otherwise, there wasn't much difference between them in texture. So you can give it the rest that fits your schedule best, anywhere from one hour to overnight.

A test kitchen colleague suggested weighing down the assembled strata during its rest, and this step had a dramatic effect. Without exception, the weighted stratas had a perfectly even, custardy texture throughout. In stratas rested without the weight, we were apt to encounter a bite of bread that had not been fully penetrated with custard.

In the oven, we found that a wide, shallow baking dish allowed the strata to bake much more evenly than the deep soufflé dish recommended in many recipes. Lowering the baking temperature from the widely recommended 350 degrees to 325 was another tactic we adopted to even out the cooking.

Cooking the strata until the top was crisp and golden brown was a common recommendation, but we found that this usually overcooked the interior, leaving it too firm, even a bit rubbery. Instead, we found it best to remove the strata from the oven when the top was just beginning to brown and the center was barely puffed and still slightly loose when the pan was jiggled gently. Though we wondered if the strata was cooked through, with just a five-minute rest it not only cooled enough to eat without burning our throats on the way down, but the center finished cooking from residual heat, reaching the perfectly set, supple texture we prized.

WHAT WE LEARNED: Use stale Italian or French bread, make the custard with half-and-half and eggs, and sauté all filling ingredients to remove excess water. For a cohesive texture, assemble the strata in advance and weight the top while it rests before baking.

BREAKFAST STRATA WITH SPINACH AND GRUYÈRE
Makes one 8 by 8-inch strata, serving 6

To weigh down the assembled strata, use two 1-pound boxes of brown or powdered sugar, laid side by side over the plastic-covered surface. To double this recipe or those that follow, use a 9 by 13-inch baking dish greased with only 1½ tablespoons butter and increase baking times as suggested in each recipe.

8–10 (½-inch thick) slices supermarket French or Italian bread (6–7 ounces)
5 tablespoons unsalted butter, softened
4 medium shallots, minced (about ½ cup)
1 (10-ounce) package frozen chopped spinach, thawed and squeezed dry
Salt and ground black pepper
½ cup medium-dry white wine, such as Sauvignon Blanc
6 ounces Gruyère cheese, grated (about 1½ cups)
6 large eggs
1¾ cups half-and-half

1. Adjust oven rack to middle position and heat oven to 225 degrees. Arrange bread in single layer on large baking sheet and bake until dry and crisp, about 40 minutes, turning slices over halfway through drying time. (Alternatively, leave slices out overnight to dry.) When cooled, butter slices on one side with 2 tablespoons butter; set aside.

2. Heat 2 tablespoons butter in medium nonstick skillet over medium heat. Sauté shallots until fragrant and translucent, about 3 minutes; add spinach and salt and pepper to taste and cook, stirring occasionally, until combined, about 2 minutes. Transfer to medium bowl; set aside. Add wine to skillet, increase heat to medium-high, and simmer until reduced to ¼ cup, 2 to 3 minutes; set aside.

3. Butter 8-inch square baking dish with remaining 1 tablespoon butter; arrange half of buttered bread slices, buttered-side up, in single layer in dish. Sprinkle half of spinach mixture, then ½ cup grated cheese evenly over bread slices. Arrange remaining bread slices in single layer over cheese; sprinkle remaining spinach mixture and another ½ cup cheese evenly over bread. Whisk eggs in medium bowl until combined; whisk in reduced wine, half-and-half, 1 teaspoon salt, and pepper to taste. Pour egg mixture evenly over bread layers; cover surface flush with plastic wrap, weigh down (see note), and refrigerate at least 1 hour or up to overnight.

4. Remove dish from refrigerator and let stand at room temperature 20 minutes. Meanwhile, adjust oven rack to middle position and heat oven to 325 degrees. Uncover strata and sprinkle remaining ½ cup cheese evenly over surface; bake until both edges and center are puffed and edges have pulled away slightly from sides of dish, 50 to 55 minutes (or about 60 minutes for doubled recipe). Cool on wire rack 5 minutes; serve.

VARIATIONS

BREAKFAST STRATA WITH SAUSAGE, MUSHROOMS, AND MONTEREY JACK

8–10 (½-inch thick) slices supermarket French or Italian bread (6–7 ounces)
3 tablespoons unsalted butter, softened
8 ounces bulk breakfast sausage, crumbled
3 medium shallots, minced (about ⅓ cup)
8 ounces white button mushrooms, cleaned and quartered
Salt and ground black pepper
½ cup medium-dry white wine, such as Sauvignon Blanc
6 ounces Monterey Jack cheese, grated (about 1½ cups)
6 large eggs
1¾ cups half-and-half
2 tablespoons minced fresh parsley leaves

Follow recipe for Breakfast Strata with Spinach and Gruyère through step 1. Fry sausage in medium nonstick skillet over medium heat, breaking sausage apart with wooden spoon, until it loses raw color and begins to brown, about 4 minutes; add shallots and cook, stirring frequently, until softened and translucent, about 1 minute longer. Add mushrooms to skillet, and cook until mushrooms no longer release liquid, about 6 minutes; transfer to medium bowl and season to taste with salt and pepper. Reduce wine as directed in step 2; continue with recipe from step 3, adding parsley to egg mixture along with salt and pepper and substituting sausage mixture for spinach. (For doubled recipe, increase baking time to about 1 hour 20 minutes.)

BREAKFAST STRATA WITH POTATOES, ROSEMARY, AND FONTINA

8–10	(½-inch thick) slices supermarket French or Italian bread (6–7 ounces)
5	tablespoons unsalted butter, softened
	Salt and ground black pepper
12	ounces new potatoes (about 2 medium), cut into ½-inch cubes
3	medium shallots, minced (about ⅓ cup)
2	medium cloves garlic, minced or pressed through garlic press
1½	teaspoons minced fresh rosemary leaves
½	cup medium-dry white wine, such as Sauvignon Blanc
6	ounces fontina cheese, grated (about 1½ cups)
6	large eggs
1¾	cups half-and-half
2	tablespoons minced fresh parsley leaves

Follow recipe for Breakfast Strata with Spinach and Gruyère through step 1. Bring 1 quart water to boil in medium saucepan over medium-high heat; add 1 teaspoon salt and boil potatoes until just tender when pierced with tip of paring knife, about 4 minutes; drain potatoes. Heat 2 tablespoons butter in medium nonstick skillet over medium heat and cook potatoes until just beginning to brown, about 10 minutes. Add

shallots and cook, stirring frequently, until softened and translucent, about 1 minute longer; add garlic and rosemary and cook until fragrant, about 2 minutes longer. Transfer mixture to medium bowl; season to taste with salt and pepper and set aside. Reduce wine as directed in step 2; continue with recipe from step 3, adding parsley to egg mixture along with salt and pepper and substituting potato mixture for spinach. (For doubled recipe, increase baking time to about 1 hour 10 minutes.)

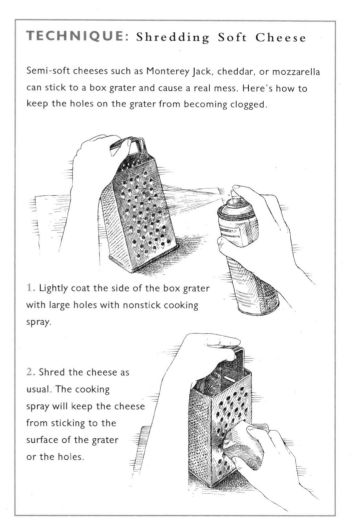

TECHNIQUE: Shredding Soft Cheese

Semi-soft cheeses such as Monterey Jack, cheddar, or mozzarella can stick to a box grater and cause a real mess. Here's how to keep the holes on the grater from becoming clogged.

1. Lightly coat the side of the box grater with large holes with nonstick cooking spray.

2. Shred the cheese as usual. The cooking spray will keep the cheese from sticking to the surface of the grater or the holes.

Lining a baking pan with foil makes removal of baked raspberry squares a breeze—just lift out the entire block and slide it onto a cutting board.

BAR cookies

Everyone loves bar cookies—especially the cook, because there's no need to form individual balls of dough. But baking dough in a pan, rather than in balls on a cookie sheet, can cause problems.

Many cooks wait until the tester poked into the center of a pan of brownies comes out dry before removing them from the oven. That's a big mistake. Dusty, dry brownies have almost no chocolate flavor and need a lot of milk to go down easily. We like our brownies fudgy and chewy, with a big hit of chocolate. After making 50 batches, we finally hit upon the right recipe.

Few cookies are more comforting than a raspberry crumble bar with oats and nuts. But this is one of those desserts that usually sounds better than it tastes. After making plenty of dull bars, the test kitchen discovered the secret to this homey dessert: give part of the dough a headstart in the oven and then add the preserves and topping. This way the bottom crust bakes up crisp, not soggy, and offers a great contrast to the filling and streusel topping.

BROWNIES

WHAT WE WANTED: Brownies with a moist, velvety texture, a hint of chew, and deep chocolate flavor.

Americans are passionate about brownies. Some are passionate about eating them, about a brownie's rich, chocolatey decadence. Others are passionate about a recipe, scrawled on a stained index card bequeathed to them by their mother, guaranteeing everyone they meet that this family heirloom produces the best brownie of all.

We've sampled good brownies, but rarely have we ever encountered the brownie to beat all others. And yet somehow we know exactly how the perfect brownie ought to taste and look. Those light cakey versions are not for us. We imagine a moist, dark, luscious interior with a firm, smooth, velvety texture that your teeth glide through easily, meeting just a little resistance in chewing. Our perfect brownie must pack an intense chocolate punch and have deep, resonant chocolate flavor, but it must fall just short of overwhelming the palate. It must not be so sweet as to make your teeth ache, and it must certainly have a thin, shiny, papery crust and edges that crisp during baking, offering a contrast with the brownie's moist center.

Our baking sense told us that the taste and texture of the brownie we sought lay in a delicate balance of the five ingredients basic to all brownie recipes: chocolate, flour, sugar, butter, and eggs. After gathering a number of recipes that promised to deliver a fudgy brownie, we made a select six that confirmed our expectations. The varying proportions of these five ingredients produced batches of brownies that were soft and pasty; dry and cakey; or chewy, like a Tootsie Roll. Chocolate flavor was divergent, too, ranging from intense but one-dimensional jolts to weak, muted passings on the palate. Our next step was to cobble together a composite recipe that would incorporate the best traits of these six recipes. It would serve as the foundation for all of our testing.

The two essential qualities we were looking for in these brownies were a chewy, fudgy texture and a rich chocolate flavor. We went to work on flavor first. After making the six initial test recipes, we knew that unsweetened chocolate was a good source of assertive chocolate flavor. Semisweet and bittersweet chocolates don't have as much chocolate punch because of the large amount of sugar they contain. But this is also why they are smoother and milder. One of our favorite recipes from the initial test yielded a brownie with exceptional chocolate flavor. This recipe combined unsweetened and bittersweet chocolates, so to the composite recipe we tried adding varying amounts of the two chocolates. (Semisweet and bittersweet chocolates are not identical but can be exchanged for one another in many recipes; we'll refer to semisweet from here on because it's what we used when testing the recipes.)

Too much unsweetened chocolate and the brownies were sour and acrid, too much semisweet chocolate and they were one-dimensional and boring. We found that 5 ounces of semisweet and 2 ounces of unsweetened created just the right flavor balance. Next we thought to add some cocoa powder, which typically adds flavor but no harshness.

We were pleased with this combination. The unsweetened chocolate laid a solid, intense chocolate foundation, the semisweet provided a mellow, even, sweet flavor, and the cocoa smoothed any rough edges and added depth and complexity. We tried both Dutch-processed cocoa and natural cocoa and found them to work equally well.

We then fiddled with the type and quantity of sugar needed to sweeten the brownies, given the amount and types of chocolate and cocoa they contained. In addition to white sugar, we tried brown sugar to see if it might add flavor, but it didn't. We also tried a bit of corn syrup, thinking it might add moistness and chew, but it only made the brownies wet and gummy and the crust dull. Satisfied that white sugar was the best sweetener for the job, we tested varying amounts. We knew we didn't want overly sweet brownies. Too little sugar, though, left the brownies with a chocolate flavor that was dull, muted, and flat, much like mashed potatoes without salt. Just the right degree of sweetness was provided by 1¼ cups sugar.

Satisfied with the flavor of the brownies, we moved on to refining the texture, starting with flour. Our composite recipe contained ¾ cup flour, but wanting to exhaust all reasonable quantities, we baked brownies with as little as ¼ cup and up to 1¼ cups, increasing the quantity in ¼ cup increments. The batch with the least amount of flour was like goopy, sticky, chocolate-flavored Spackle, so pasty it cemented your mouth shut. The one with 1¼ cups flour had good chew, but it verged on dry, and the chocolate flavor was light and muted. One cup was perfect. The chocolate flavor remained deep and rich, and the texture was fudgy, smooth, and dense, the moist crumb putting up a gentle resistance when chewed.

Butter was up next. Melting butter, rather than creaming it with sugar and eggs, makes for a dense, fudgy texture. Creaming produces an aerated batter, which bakes into lighter, cakier brownies. Had we questioned this baker's axiom after the initial test, in which all of the six recipes employ the melted butter technique, any doubts would have been dispelled. But now the question of how much butter remained.

Semisweet chocolate contains more fat than unsweetened chocolate, yet many recipes that call exclusively for one type of chocolate frequently call for the same amount of butter (some 16 tablespoons) per cup of flour. As it stood, our working recipe used semisweet and unsweetened chocolate, cocoa, 1 cup flour, and 10 tablespoons butter. The texture of the brownies this recipe produced was moist and dense, albeit a bit sodden and pasty. Improvement came with less butter. Minus 2 tablespoons, the brownies shed their soggy, sodden quality but still remained moist and velvety.

With butter and flour set, we went to work on eggs. We tried as few as two and as many as six. Two eggs left the brownies dry and gritty and compromised the chocolate flavor. With four or more eggs, the brownies baked into cakey rubber erasers with an unattractive, high-domed, dull matte crust. Three was the magic number—the brownies were moist and smooth, with great flavor and delicate chew.

We finalized the recipe by making adjustments to vanilla and salt and then began to examine other factors that might have an impact on the brownies. First we tried baking in a water bath, a technique used for delicate custards, reasoning that gentle heat might somehow improve texture. Not so. We got a grainy, sticky, puddinglike brownie.

We experimented with midrange oven temperatures. Three-hundred-fifty degrees did the job and did it relatively quickly, in about 35 minutes (many brownies bake for nearly an hour). As is the case with most other brownies, if baked too long, these brownies run the risk of drying out; they must be pulled from the oven when a toothpick inserted into the center comes out with some sticky crumbs clinging to it.

After making more than 50 batches, we really appreciated an aspect of brownies quite beside their rich flavor and texture—with only a couple of bowls, a whisk, and a spatula, the batter can be mixed and in the oven in 10 minutes.

WHAT WE LEARNED: **Use three kinds of chocolate— unsweetened, semisweet, and cocoa powder—for the most complex, richest flavor. Don't go overboard with the butter, and use three eggs for good chew.**

CHEWY, FUDGY TRIPLE-CHOCOLATE BROWNIES
makes sixty-four 1-inch brownies

Either Dutch-processed or natural cocoa works well in this recipe. These brownies are very rich, so we prefer to cut them into small squares for serving.

5	ounces semisweet or bittersweet chocolate, chopped
2	ounces unsweetened chocolate, chopped
8	tablespoons (1 stick) unsalted butter, cut into quarters
3	tablespoons cocoa powder
3	large eggs
1¼	cups (8.75 ounces) sugar
2	teaspoons vanilla extract
½	teaspoon salt
1	cup (5 ounces) unbleached all-purpose flour

1. Adjust oven rack to lower-middle position and heat oven to 350 degrees. Spray 8-inch-square baking pan with non-stick cooking spray. Fold two 16-inch pieces of foil lengthwise to measure 7 inches wide. Fit one sheet in bottom of greased pan, pushing it into corners and up sides of pan (overhang will help in removal of baked brownies). Fit second sheet in pan in same manner, perpendicular to first sheet. Spray foil with nonstick cooking spray.

2. In medium heatproof bowl set over pan of almost-simmering water, melt chocolates and butter, stirring occasionally until mixture is smooth. Whisk in cocoa until smooth. Set aside to cool slightly.

3. Whisk together eggs, sugar, vanilla, and salt in medium bowl until combined, about 15 seconds. Whisk warm chocolate mixture into egg mixture; then stir in flour with wooden spoon until just combined. Pour mixture into prepared pan, spread into corners, and level surface with rubber spatula; bake until slightly puffed and toothpick inserted in center comes out with small amount of sticky

crumbs clinging to it, 35 to 40 minutes. Cool on wire rack to room temperature, about 2 hours, then remove brownies from pan using foil handles. Cut into 1-inch squares and serve. (Do not cut brownies until ready to serve; brownies can be wrapped in plastic and refrigerated up to 5 days.)

VARIATION

TRIPLE-CHOCOLATE ESPRESSO BROWNIES
Follow recipe for Chewy, Fudgy Triple-Chocolate Brownies, whisking in 1½ tablespoons instant espresso or coffee powder along with cocoa in step 2.

SCIENCE DESK:
Chocolate Flavor Diffusion

ONE OF THE MORE INTERESTING IDEAS WE HEARD ABOUT the dos and don'ts of working with chocolate desserts was proposed to us by famed New York chef Jean-Georges Vongerichten, who stated that the less one cooks chocolate, the better it tastes. We decided to check this out with Tom Lehmann, director of bakery assistance at the American Institute of Baking. He agreed.

Chocolate, Lehmann explained, is a very delicate substance, full of highly sensitive, volatile compounds that give chocolate much of its flavor. When chocolate is heated, the liquids in it turn to steam and carry away these volatile compounds. That's what makes the kitchen smell so good when brownies are in the oven. The bad news is that these volatile compounds are no longer in the brownies—which is where you really want them to be. Exposure to heat, therefore, has no benefits; it simply makes chocolate more bitter and less complex tasting.

So, what are the lessons to be learned about baking with chocolate? First, underbaking is always better than overbaking. Dry chocolate desserts will have much less flavor and tend to be bitter. Second, use as much fat as possible. Fat increases the retention of volatile compounds. That's why low-fat chocolate desserts usually taste like sugar but not chocolate.

RASPBERRY SQUARES

WHAT WE WANTED: A buttery, tender, golden brown crust and crumb topping with just the right amount of sweet/tart raspberry preserves in the middle.

Raspberry squares are one of the best, and easiest, bar cookies to prepare. With raspberry squares, the filling is ready-made (it comes straight from a jar of raspberry preserves). And these homey bars have textural interest created by the layering of filling on crust.

A short pastry (such as that used in raspberry squares) has a tender, almost sandy crumb that it gets by way of the right combination of flour, fat, sugar, and salt—with an emphasis on the fat and the flour. In a short pastry (think of shortbread), a generous amount of fat is required to coat the particles of flour, the purpose of this coating being to restrict the flour's access to liquid. Flour contains proteins that when combined with water form gluten—a substance that is desirable in bread, where you want chew, but not in a raspberry square, where you want tenderness.

In the many recipes for all manner of "short" bar cookies we looked at, the amount of butter ranged from ½ cup to 1 cup for about 2½ cups of flour. We found that a whole cup of butter made the raspberry squares greasy, whereas ½ cup left them on the dry side; ¾ cup butter was just right.

The sugar in many of the recipes also ranged from ½ cup to 1 cup, with some calling for white sugar, some for brown, some for a mix of the two. Here, too, we went for the midway, deciding on equal amounts of white and light brown sugar, which made for a deeper flavor than white alone, and on a total of ⅔ cup, which was sweet enough to be pleasing but not cloying.

We were attracted by the idea of adding some oats or nuts, which would make a more subtle contribution to flavor while also adding some textural interest. The oats, with their bulk and absorbency, would have to displace some of the flour. After trying various proportions we found

that we liked the combination of 1¼ cups oats to 1½ cups flour. We played around with the nuts and found ourselves preferring a pairing of sweet almonds with nutty pecans (although either also works on its own).

We were now pretty pleased with our crust except for one nagging problem: It was rather pale, not golden brown. We wanted that golden brown color not only for appearance' sake but for flavor; we knew that a deeply colored crust would have a more developed, nutty flavor.

The procedure we had been following to prepare the squares for baking was recommended in a number of recipes. It involved lining the bottom of the pan with most of the dough, spreading the preserves on top, and then covering the preserves with the rest of the dough. One or two recipes had recommended baking the bottom crust alone first to brown it and firm it up, but we had rejected this option as being a bit fussy. Now we tried this procedure and were happy to learn that it effectively colored—and flavored—the crust.

WHAT WE LEARNED: For a flavorful, golden brown bottom crust, prebake it before layering with raspberry preserves and top crust. Add oats and nuts to the crust for textural interest and complementary flavors.

RASPBERRY SQUARES makes 25 squares

Lining the pan with foil makes removal of the squares for cutting very easy (just lift out the entire block and place it on a cutting board to cut). For a nice presentation, trim ¼ inch off the outer rim of the uncut baked block. The outside edges of all cut squares will then be neat.

1½	cups (7.5 ounces) unbleached all-purpose flour
1¼	cups quick-cooking oats
⅓	cup (2.3 ounces) granulated sugar
⅓	cup packed light brown sugar
¼	teaspoon baking soda
¼	teaspoon salt
½	cup finely chopped pecans or almonds, or a combination
12	tablespoons (1½ sticks) unsalted butter, cut into 12 pieces and softened but still cool
1	cup raspberry preserves

1. Adjust oven rack to lower-middle position and heat oven to 350 degrees. Spray 9-inch-square baking pan with non-stick cooking spray. Fold two 16-inch pieces of foil lengthwise to measure 8 inches wide. Fit one sheet in bottom of greased pan, pushing it into corners and up sides of pan (overhang will help in removal of baked squares). Fit second sheet in pan in same manner, perpendicular to first sheet. Spray foil with nonstick cooking spray.

2. In bowl of standing mixer, mix flour, oats, sugars, baking soda, salt, and nuts at low speed until combined, about 30 seconds. With mixer running at low speed, add butter pieces; continue to beat until mixture is well-blended and resembles wet sand, about 2 minutes.

3. Transfer ⅔ of mixture to prepared pan and use hands to press crumbs evenly into bottom. Bake until starting to brown, about 20 minutes. Using rubber spatula, spread preserves evenly over hot bottom crust; sprinkle remaining oat/nut mixture evenly over preserves. Bake until preserves bubble around edges and top is golden brown, about 30 minutes, rotating pan from front to back halfway through baking time. Cool on wire rack to room temperature, about 1½ hours, then remove from pan using foil handles. Cut into 1¼- to 1½-inch squares and serve.

TASTING LAB: Raspberry Preserves

JELLY, JAM, PRESERVES, FRUIT SPREAD—WHAT'S THE difference, and is any one of these products better than the other for baking or spreading on toast? We put eight leading brands to a taste test to find out. But before we give you the results, some definitions are in order.

A jelly is a clear, bright mixture made from fruit juice, sugar, and often pectin or acid. No less than 45 pounds of fruit must be used for each 55 pounds of sugar.

A jam is a thick mixture of fruit and sugar that is cooked until the pieces of fruit are very soft and almost formless. It is also made with 45 pounds of fruit combined with 55 pounds of sugar. Preserves are almost identical to jams, but preserves may contain large chunks of fruit or whole fruit.

Fruit spreads, which have become common grocery store stock over the last 10 years, do not fall under the labeling standards applied to jellies and jams—hence the generic name, fruit spreads. These products are usually made with concentrated grape and/or pear juice or low-calorie sweeteners, which replace all or part of the sugar.

TECHNIQUE:
Packing Brown Sugar

When a recipe calls for some quantity of packed brown sugar, fill the correct dry measure with the sugar and use the next smallest cup to pack it.

Although tasters preferred preserves and jams to jellies (they liked bits of fruit), they were most concerned with flavor. Too many brands were overly sweet—so sweet it was hard to taste the raspberries. The top two brands were Trappist Jam and Smucker's Preserves. Interestingly, both of these products are made with corn syrup, yet tasters felt these brands had the strongest raspberry flavor.

Tasters were not wild about fruit spreads. Although fruit spreads are less sweet than traditional jams and jellies, tasters felt that the concentrated fruit juices obscured the flavor of the raspberries. The result was a generic "fruit roll-up flavor."

EQUIPMENT CORNER: Coffee Makers

IN THE TEST KITCHEN WE LOVE A GOOD CUP OF COFFEE to wash down brownies or raspberry squares. But what's the best means of brewing it? To find out, we assembled a group of appliances representing the major methods used to brew coffee: a percolator, an expensive automatic-drip machine with thermos, an inexpensive automatic-drip machine with burner plate, a manual plastic drip cone that fits over a glass carafe, a flip pot (also known as a Napoletana), a plunger pot (also called a French press), and a vacuum coffee maker. We rated each set-up based on the temperature, flavor, and body of the coffee it produced, as well as on ease of use.

We quickly dismissed several methods based on the poor quality of the coffee or the hassle involved in getting the device to work. A flip pot can brew only one or two cups of coffee at a time, takes 20 minutes to work, seems excessively dangerous (you must flip the burning hot metal pot), and makes gritty, slightly burnt coffee.

A plunger pot is easier to use, but tasters felt that too much sediment passed through the mesh filter that separates the spent grounds from the coffee, even when coarsely ground beans were used.

The percolator performed as expected. It worked quickly and delivered very hot coffee, but tasters complained about weak flavor. That's because the water doesn't spend much time in contact with the coffee—it's too busy being recycled through the inner tubing in this device.

Our two automatic-drip machines were easy to use, but the coffee tasted bitter, especially when we tried to make a full pot. According to experts we spoke with, the water and grounds should stay in contact for four to six minutes. Beyond the six-minute mark, the grounds start to release bitter compounds that will harm the flavor of the coffee. We found that automatic drip machines can turn out two or three cups of coffee within the proper time frame but that it often takes 10 minutes to yield six cups.

The model tested with the burner had an added problem—coffee that was so-so right after brewing quickly developed a horrible burnt flavor. The drip machine with the thermos did not have this problem.

Two brewing methods stand out as superior, at least in terms of quality. Coffee brewed in a vacuum pot has much to offer—properly hot temperature, a rich flavor that captures the nuances in expensive beans without any bitterness, and a full body without sediment. The real problem here is convenience. This showy device relies on a vacuum created between two glass bowls. Although not hard to use, the glass bowls are wobbly and liable to break. As an intriguing finale to an occasional meal, this conversation piece makes sense, but not every day at six in the morning.

Our favorite coffee brewing method is the manual drip. The convenience factor is second only to an automatic drip. Grind and measure the coffee into the filter-lined cone, then add water just off a boil in batches. You can't leave the kitchen, but the coffee tastes great without the bitterness associated with an automatic drip machine. That's because the plastic cones on manual drip models are larger than the cones inside automatic drip machines, so the water runs through the grounds more quickly.

If you let the coffee drip into an insulated thermos (prewarmed by rinsing it with hot tap water) rather than a glass carafe, the coffee will stay hot and fresh-tasting for hours. Best of all, you can pick up a plastic cone for $5 and a thermos for $25.

Brushing a fruit tart with hot jelly can move the berries and disrupt a perfect design. To glaze a tart and keep the design intact, use a pastry brush to dab, drizzle, and flick the hot jelly onto the fruit.

TWO FRENCH tarts

Just as pies are a true expression of fine American cooking, tarts represent the very best in French pastry. The crust should be tender, buttery, and crumbly—almost like a good butter cookie. The fillings are usually rich and creamy, so a little goes a long way.

A lemon tart, filled with nothing more than lemon curd, is perhaps the simplest French tart for the home cook to prepare. When made right, this tart is light, refreshing, and altogether delicious. But when things go wrong—as they often do—the filling can be thick, eggy, harsh, or gluey.

Glistening in the windows and glass cases of pâtisseries, fresh fruit tarts are things of beauty. But these fruit tarts are tarts indeed. They draw you in with their beguiling looks—but venture beneath the surface and you are quickly disappointed with their substance. Most often, the pastry cream filling is an institutional pudding with either a goopy, overstarched texture or a stiff, rubbery demeanor. Even when the pastry cream filling is well made, it typically infuses the crust with a different malaise: If the tart has been sitting pretty long enough (and you can bet it has), the crust has gotten soggy. Or, in the worst case, juices have begun to seep out of the fruit to form a sticky puddle in which the tart wallows.

These simple, elegant tarts demand the finest ingredients. They are also best made at home, where care can be taken in their preparation and timing can be controlled. Our tarts will put even the finest pâtisseries to shame.

IN THIS CHAPTER

THE RECIPES
Sweet Tart Pastry (Pâte Sucrée)

Lemon Tart

Fresh Fruit Tart with Pastry Cream

EQUIPMENT CORNER
Rolling Pins
Tart Pans

SCIENCE DESK
Eggs and Acid

TASTING LAB
Lemon Zest, Oils, and Extracts

SWEET TART PASTRY

WHAT WE WANTED: Tart dough can be finicky and hard to roll out. We wanted to produce a crisp, flavorful pastry dough using the fastest and most foolproof method available.

Over the years we have come to value the virtues of a traditional pie dough as much as those of its European cousin, pâte sucrée (literally, "sugar dough"). But many American pie bakers have yet to discover the virtues of sweet pastry dough. What is it, and how does it differ from regular pie dough? Does it deserve a place at our table? The answer is, emphatically, yes.

While a regular pie dough is tender and flaky, a sweet tart dough is tender and crisp. Fine-textured, buttery rich, and crumbly, it is often described as cookielike. In fact, cookies are actually descendants of sweet pastry dough—a dough deemed so delicious by the French that it was considered worth eating on its own. There are also differences in the dough's relationship to the filling. Rather than encasing a deep hearty filling, a tart shell shares the stage with its filling. Traditional tart fillings—caramel, marzipan, pastry cream, or even jam, often adorned with glazed fresh fruits or nuts—would seem excessive if housed in a deeper pie. But these intense flavors and textures are perfect in thin layers balanced by a crisp, thin pastry.

We have eaten our share of thick, tough, and flavorless tart doughs. Many American recipes for these doughs call for too little butter or sugar, thus compromising texture, but more often poor technique is to blame.

Though you can make sweet pastry as you would cookie dough, by creaming the butter and sugar together, then adding flour and finally egg, we found this technique too time-consuming. Like pie pastries, most sweet pastry recipes direct the cook to cut butter into flour by hand or food processor and then add liquid. Knowing cold butter and minimal handling to be critical to the success of this method, we headed straight for the food processor. Pulsing very cold butter with dry ingredients to obtain a fine, pebbly consistency took all of 15 seconds.

The addition of liquid was a trickier matter. We were reluctant to use a food processor, feeling it gave us less control. But the alternative, tossing the pebbly dough onto a countertop and fluffing the liquid in by hand, followed by a *fraisage* (flattening the dough in short strokes with the heel of the hand to incorporate ingredients) seemed tiresome and unnecessary. Though the manual method for adding liquid produced a marginally more delicate, tender dough, we found that in fact the difference was barely discernible— and only in side-by-side comparisons. Addition of liquid ingredients with the food processor took about 25 seconds. Armed with this quick, no-fuss technique, we wanted to tweak the major players in the dough to tease out the most tender, tastiest pastry imaginable.

The first ingredients to come under scrutiny were the butter and sugar. The higher the proportion of butter in a pâte sucrée, the more delicate its crumb. We experimented with the amount and found 10 tablespoons (5 ounces) to be the maximum allowable for ease of handling. More butter simply made the dough too soft and did not improve its flavor or texture. As for the sugar, the traditional half cup did not seem overly sweet, and any less than that produced a dough lacking in flavor and tenderness. Most recipes recommend the use of superfine sugar (thought to be important for dissolving in a dough with so little liquid), but because few people (if any) have it in their pantry, we tried confectioners' sugar, an ingredient most people have on hand. We found that ¾ cup confectioners' sugar gave us a crisper dough than the one made with granulated sugar.

Next up for examination were the liquid ingredients. Though most recipes call for a whole egg, some call for a combination of egg yolk and cream. (As in any cookie dough, the egg lends structure to a dough that would otherwise be completely crumbly.) Testing these side by side, we discovered that the yolk and cream combination (1 yolk and 2 tablespoons of cream) created a lovely crust with a degree of flakiness, a quality we value over the slightly firmer dough produced when using a whole egg alone.

The last major player to be manipulated was the flour. Perfectly happy with our tests using all-purpose, we nevertheless performed a couple of tests using half all-purpose and half pastry flour, as well as half all-purpose and half cake flour. Our reasoning was this: Low-protein flours, such as pastry and cake flours (equal in protein percentage at about 8 percent, compared with all-purpose at about 11 percent) tend to retard gluten development, thus yielding a more tender dough. We were surprised to learn that in composition pastry and cake flours are identical; cake flour is simply bleached. (Bleaching improves the rise of high-sugar batters, like those used in cakes; pastry flour is used in pie doughs, where rise isn't so important.) To be honest, we liked the dough made with half pastry flour. It was a bit more tender and delicate than that made entirely with all-purpose and no more difficult to work with. But the improvement was not impressive enough to cause us to recommend the pastry flour, particularly since it's often not that easy to find. The dough made with half cake flour had a pleasing texture as well, but a less-pleasing flavor; bleaching can impart a slightly metallic taste to flour.

In the end, the proportions we were using made too much dough for a 9-inch tart pan. While many recipes calling for 1½ cups flour declared a yield of dough for one 9- or 11-inch tart, we scaled our proportions back to fit the pan.

Sweet pastry dough typically requires at least an hour of refrigerated resting time for the liquid ingredients to hydrate the dough fully and make it more manageable. In fact, a two-hour rest was even better. The butter gives the dough a nice plasticity if the dough is cold enough and makes rolling relatively easy. We knew it would be a challenge to roll out the dough directly on the counter. Best results were obtained with minimal flouring and by rolling the dough out between double layers of wide parchment paper or plastic wrap without letting it become warm. Though many recipes suggest

that a sweet pastry dough can simply be pressed into a pan, our tests did not support this recommendation. The patchwork technique made the crucial "even thickness" all but unattainable, and the imperfectly fused pieces did not have the same structural integrity as a correctly fitted, single sheath of dough. The patched crust tended to crumble along the fault lines as it was unmolded or cut.

A half hour in the freezer "set" the dough nicely to prepare it for "blind baking" (baking the shell without any filling). A baking sheet placed directly beneath the tart shell (to conduct heat evenly to the crust bottom) browned the tart beautifully. Because of the crust's delicate nature, the metal weights used to blind-bake the tart are best left in place until the crust's edges are distinctly brown, about 30 minutes, at which point the weights can be removed and the top side of the crust allowed to brown.

WHAT WE LEARNED: Make the dough in the food processor and roll it out between sheets of parchment or plastic to prevent excess flouring or sticking. Use confectioners' sugar for extra crispness and a combination of egg yolk and heavy cream for extra flakiness.

SWEET TART PASTRY (PÂTE SUCRÉE) makes one 9- to 9½-inch tart shell

makes 20 tartlets

If the dough becomes soft and sticky while rolling, rechill it until it becomes easier to work with. Better to rechill than to add too much flour, which will damage the delicate, crisp texture of the dough. We find a tapered French rolling pin to be the most precise instrument for rolling tart pastry. Bake the tart shell in a 9- to 9½-inch tart pan with a removable bottom and fluted sides about 1 to 1⅛ inches high.

- 1 large egg yolk
- 1 tablespoon heavy cream
- ½ teaspoon vanilla extract
- 1¼ cups (6.25 ounces) unbleached all-purpose flour
- ⅔ cup (3 ounces) confectioners' sugar
- ¼ teaspoon salt
- 8 tablespoons (1 stick) very cold unsalted butter, cut into ½-inch cubes

1. Whisk together yolk, cream, and vanilla in small bowl; set aside. Pulse to combine flour, sugar, and salt in bowl of food processor fitted with steel blade. Scatter butter pieces over flour mixture; pulse to cut butter into flour until mixture resembles coarse meal, about fifteen 1-second pulses. With machine running, add egg mixture and process until dough just comes together, about 25 seconds. Turn dough onto sheet of plastic wrap and press into 6-inch disk. Wrap in plastic and refrigerate at least 1 hour or up to 48 hours.

2. Remove dough from refrigerator (if refrigerated longer than 1 hour, let stand at room temperature until malleable). Unwrap and roll out between lightly floured large sheets of ~~parchment paper~~ or plastic wrap to 13-inch round. (If dough is soft and sticky, slip onto baking sheet and refrigerate until workable, 20 to 30 minutes.) Transfer dough to tart pan by rolling dough loosely around rolling pin and unrolling over 9- to 9½-inch tart pan with removable bottom. Working around circumference of pan, ease dough into pan corners by gently lifting dough with one hand

use plastic + sticks less

while pressing dough into corners with other hand. Press dough into fluted sides of pan. (If some edges are too thin, reinforce sides by folding excess dough back on itself.) Run rolling pin over top of tart pan to remove excess dough. Set dough-lined tart pan on large plate and freeze 30 minutes. (The dough-lined tart pan can be sealed in a gallon-sized zipper-lock plastic bag and frozen up to 1 month.)

3. Meanwhile, adjust oven rack to middle position and heat oven to 375 degrees. Set dough-lined tart pan on baking sheet, press 12-inch square of foil inside frozen tart shell and over edge, and fill with metal or ceramic pie weights. Bake for 30 minutes, rotating halfway through baking time. Remove from oven and carefully remove foil and weights by gathering edges of foil and pulling up and out. Continue to bake until deep golden brown, 5 to 8 minutes longer. Set baking sheet with tart shell on wire rack.

EQUIPMENT CORNER: Rolling Pins

WE PURCHASED TWO WOODEN PINS WITHOUT HANDLES— one with tapered ends, and one that was straight. Three other wooden pins had standard dowel-type handles with ball bearings and represented three different sizes: The largest weighed in at 3½ pounds and was 15 inches long, another was a quite small 1½ pounds and 10½ inches long, and the last was in between these two, at 2½ pounds and 11½ inches long. We purchased three novelty pins—one marble, one nonstick coated aluminum, and one wooden model with ergonomic comfort grips. The grips on this last model were made of molded plastic and had the feel of a steering wheel, with thumbs on top and wrists straight. Prices ranged from $6.99 to $35.99.

We decided to test the pins on three kinds of dough: a standard pie dough, a delicate sugar cookie dough, and a resilient yeasted coffee cake dough. We were particularly interested in the versatility of these pins—whether they could perform equally well in all tasks. No one wants more than one pin in the kitchen. For all three doughs, we were looking for a fast, easy roll—one that allowed us to feel the dough and did not require application of too much pressure.

Almost immediately a favorite and a least favorite became evident. The tapered wood pin without handles ($6.99) took first place. Testers could easily turn and pivot the tapered pin and apply pressure as needed across the dough. In addition, this pin measured 20 inches long, making it suitable for any task. Many of the other wooden pins were too short (some just 10 or 11 inches in length) and could not be used to roll out large pieces of dough.

The marble pin ($8.99) was a bit heavy over delicate sugar cookie dough, but this pin could be refrigerated before handling buttery doughs, which was a plus. It landed in second place. The ergonomic pin ($35.99) landed near the bottom of the ratings, as did the nonstick model ($9.99), which was much too light and most definitely not stickfree.

EQUIPMENT CORNER: Tart Pans

TART PANS WITH REMOVABLE BOTTOMS ARE AVAILABLE IN three types of finishes. The traditional tinned steel tart pan is silver and reflective. Then there is the nonstick version coated with a brown finish inside and out. The third type, a black steel tart pan (also sometimes called blue steel), is quite difficult to find, at least in this country.

A tinned steel pan is what we used throughout recipe development of the fruit tart—without incident. So we wondered what a nonstick tart pan—at 2½ times the cost— could possibly improve upon. The answer is nothing, really. Tart pastry is brimming with butter and is not likely to stick to flypaper, so a nonstick tart pan is superfluous. And despite its darker finish, it browned the pastry at the same rate as the tinned steel pan.

The black steel pan was another matter. Colored to absorb heat and encourage browning, it did just that, actually taking the pastry a bit past even our preference for very deeply browned. This pan would be fine for baking a filled tart (the filling slows down the baking), but for unfilled pastry—like the lemon tart and fruit tart in this chapter—it was a bit impetuous. If you own one and are using it to prebake tart pastry, try lowering your oven temperature by about 25 degrees.

BEST TART PAN

Unlike a black steel pan, a tinned steel pan won't cause over-browning. And because tart dough has so much butter, we found there's no point spending extra money for a nonstick finish.

LEMON TART

WHAT WE WANTED: A lemon tart with a silken texture, the perfect balance of tart and sweet, and a taste that isn't too "eggy."

With its minimal interplay of ingredients and straightforward style, the lemon tart achieves a near-transcendent simplicity of form and content. Light, refreshing, and beautiful, when it's good, it is very, very good—but when it's bad, you wish you'd ordered the check instead. Despite its apparent simplicity, there is much that can go wrong with a lemon tart. It can slip over the edge of sweet into cloying; its tartness can grab at your throat; it can be gluey or eggy or, even worse, metallic-tasting. Its crust can be too hard, too soft, too thick, or too sweet. If by chance you bring more than one of these flaws to bear on a single tart, the results are horrific.

There is more than one way to fill a tart, of course. We considered briefly but dismissed the notion of an unbaked lemon filling—a lemon pastry cream or a lemon charlotte. In each case, the filling (the former containing milk and thickened with eggs and flour, the latter containing cream and thickened with eggs and gelatin) is spooned into a baked tart shell and chilled. Not only did we find the flavor of these fillings too muted and their texture too billowy, but we realized that we wanted a proper lemon tart, one in which the filling is baked with the shell. That meant only one thing: lemon curd, and a thin, bracing layer of it at that.

Originally an old English recipe that was to be eaten like a jam and called lemon cheese, lemon curd is a stirred fruit custard made of eggs, lemon juice, sugar, and, usually, butter. Cooked over low heat and stirred continuously, the mixture thickens by means of protein coagulation. The dessert owes its bright flavor not to lemon juice but to oils released by finely grated peel, the equivalent of a lemon twist in a vodka martini. Butter further refines a lemon curd's flavor and texture. The result is a spoonable custard that can be spread on scones or used as a base for desserts. When baked, its color deepens and it "sets up," remaining supple and creamy yet firm enough to be sliceable. It is intense, heady stuff, nicely modulated—if you must—by a cloud of whipped cream.

Several variables warranted exploration. Most straightforward was the ratio of sugar to lemon juice. We wanted just enough sugar to offset the acid. More complex was the proportion of eggs. Egg yolks contain both cholesterol and lecithin, which act as emulsifiers and create a satiny texture. Whole eggs contain albumin as well, the protein in the egg white that is responsible for "setting" a custard. What, we wondered, would produce the best texture—whole eggs, the egg yolks alone, a combination of egg yolks and whole eggs, or maybe even whole eggs plus egg whites? Temperature is the critical factor in coaxing a custard to thicken without curdling, and the slower the journey, the more forgiving the process. Cook the eggs too quickly and you won't know when to pull back. The heat within will have gathered force and taken the curd to the breaking point even if you've pulled the pan off the stove. Chemical reactions, too, accelerate at higher temperatures. Then what, exactly, is the correct temperature for cooking this stirred custard? Would a double boiler be necessary to produce a fine curd, or could we simply proceed with care (and proper equipment) over direct heat? As for the butter, should it be added at the outset of cooking or stirred in at the end?

We began by following the usual test kitchen protocol of preparing a number of classic recipes. For an 8- or 9-inch tart we estimated that we would need about 3 cups of filling. The traditional lemon curds all contained between 1 and 1½ cups sugar, but the amount of lemon juice varied widely, between ½ and 1½ cups. There was also quite a bit of play between whole eggs and yolks, with the average falling between 8 and 10 eggs total. Though the recipes were divided on the matter of using direct heat versus a double

still-liquid curd proved superior to whisking the butter in after stovetop cooking. Though the latter curd looked glossy and beautiful before it was baked, the butter aerated the filling, causing it to rise in the oven and overrun the shell's borders.

Holding the proportions of the above ingredients constant, we made a number of lemon curds testing various combinations of whole eggs and yolks. Somewhat surprisingly, the curds that tasted great in a spoon were not always the ones that tasted best baked. The curd made with whole eggs alone had a light texture in the spoon and a gorgeous sheen, but it had a muted color and a texture most tasters described as "mayonnaise-like" when baked. The curd made with whole eggs and whites had a smooth, translucent surface but firmed up too much, while the curd made with an equal ratio of whole eggs to yolks was faulted for being cloyingly rich. In the end, most tasters preferred a curd made principally with yolks and only a couple of whole eggs for structure. Creamy and dense with a vibrant color, it did not become gelatinous when baked, as did those curds made with all whole eggs, but it did set up enough to slice. Its flavor also lingered and teased. This made sense, because fats carry flavors and hold them on the palate. Egg yolks are high in fat.

But the most interesting discovery was still to come. Remembering a lemon mousse we had made, we wanted to see what a softening splash of cream might do to the curd. Adding cream before cooking the curd on the stovetop gave it a cheesy flavor. But 3 tablespoons of cold, raw cream stirred in just before baking proved a winning touch. It cooled the just-cooked curd, blunted its acidity, and lightened its final baked texture to a celestial creaminess. If you don't get around to baking a crust, buy some fresh berries and grab a spoon.

WHAT WE LEARNED: For the creamiest texture and most vibrant color, make lemon curd with mostly egg yolks and add two whole eggs for structure. Cook butter with lemon, sugar, and eggs, then stir a little chilled cream into the finished curd for superb creaminess.

boiler, most were quite cavalier about cooking time, with visual descriptions of the desired final texture ranging from "thick" to "very thick" to "like whipped cream." Only two mentioned cooking temperatures: 160 and 180 degrees, a rather wide range when dealing with eggs. Some recipes added butter at the beginning of the cooking time; others preferred to whisk it in later.

During these early experiments, certain proportions emerged easily. The balance of sweetness and tartness we sought came in at roughly 2 parts sugar to 1 part lemon juice. Four full tablespoons of finely grated lemon zest (strained out after cooking, along with any hardened bits of egg whites) packed enough lemon punch without having to linger in the final custard, where it would become bitter or usurp the silky texture. A pinch of salt brightened the flavor. Four tablespoons of butter were perfect, smoothing taste and refining texture. Adding cold butter chunks to the

LEMON TART serves 8 to 10

Once the lemon curd ingredients have been combined, cook the curd immediately; otherwise it will have a grainy finished texture. To prevent the curd from acquiring a metallic taste, make absolutely sure that all utensils coming into contact with it—bowls, whisk, saucepan, and strainer—are made of nonreactive stainless steel or glass. Since the tart pan has a removable bottom, it is more easily maneuvered when set on a cookie sheet. If your prebaked tart shell has already cooled, place it in the oven just before you start the curd and heat it until warm, about 5 minutes. Serve the tart with lightly whipped cream (see page 294), which is the perfect accompaniment to the rich, intensely lemon filling.

make 20 tartlets

1   fully baked tart shell, 9 to 9½ inches (see page 276), warm
7   large egg yolks, plus 2 large eggs
1   cup plus 2 tablespoons (7.9 ounces) sugar
⅔   cup juice from 4 to 5 medium lemons, plus ¼ cup finely grated zest
     Pinch salt
4   tablespoons unsalted butter, cut into 4 pieces
3   tablespoons heavy cream

1. Adjust oven rack to upper-middle position and heat oven to 375 degrees. Place tart pan with shell on cookie sheet.

2. In medium nonreactive bowl, whisk together yolks and whole eggs until combined, about 5 seconds. Add sugar and whisk until just combined, about 5 seconds. Add lemon juice, zest, and salt; whisk until combined, about 5 seconds. Transfer mixture to medium nonreactive saucepan, add butter pieces, and cook over medium-low heat, stirring constantly with wooden spoon, until curd thickens to thin saucelike consistency and registers 170 degrees on an instant-read thermometer, about 5 minutes. Immediately pour curd through single-mesh stainless steel strainer set over clean nonreactive bowl. Stir in heavy cream; pour curd into warm tart shell immediately.

3. Bake until filling is shiny and opaque and the center 3 inches jiggle slightly when shaken, 10 to 15 minutes. Cool on wire rack to room temperature, about 45 minutes. Remove outer metal ring, slide thin metal spatula between bottom crust and tart pan bottom to release, then slip tart onto cardboard round or serving plate. Cut into wedges and serve.

SCIENCE DESK: Eggs and Acid

WHEN WE BEGAN TESTING LEMON TART RECIPES, WE wondered how such a high proportion of eggs in the presence of a relatively small amount of liquid could produce the creamy, silken texture of lemon curd, while the same proportion of eggs and cream, for example, would simply scramble.

We suspected that it had something to do with acid content. So we did a little experiment. We placed one egg in each of three separate pans over medium heat and added 2 tablespoons rice vinegar to one pan, 2 tablespoons lemon juice to the second pan, and the same amount of water to the third pan. The egg stirred with vinegar cooked quickly and remained pale yellow and very creamy. The egg stirred with lemon juice turned a more lemony yellow, took longer to cook, and, though it also remained creamy, formed a more solid gel than the egg cooked with vinegar. The egg stirred with water took almost twice as long to cook as the first egg and contained distinctly coagulated bits of bright yellow egg—just like scrambled eggs.

Egg proteins are tangled bundles of amino acids. Each bundle carries a similar electrical charge, which causes them to repel each other. Applying heat causes the bundles to unravel, at which point they are inclined to pull together and form a clump. In the process of clumping, the amino acid molecules squeeze out any liquid that comes between them. This is known as curdling.

Introducing an acid to the egg proteins can increase their electrical charges. Consequently, when the proteins are heated and unwind they are even more strongly repelled from one another and are inclined to interact more with the liquid. The effect is to create a layer of liquid between the ribbons of protein, like a sandwich. This creates what we know as a gel, the effect that we pleasantly experienced with our lemon curd ("curd" is a misnomer in this case). The vinegar created a similar but different effect because different acids have different degrees of ability to change the charge on the proteins. Thus the lemon juice, while encouraging an egg to cook and form a solid, keeps the solid moist and creamy.

TASTING LAB:
Lemon Zest, Oils, and Extracts

WHEN MAKING A LEMON TART OR ANY DESSERT WITH lemon, is there an acceptable substitute for lemon zest? There are lemon oils and lemon extracts on the market, but can they pinch-hit for the real thing? To find out, we tested grated zest, two lemon oils, and two lemon extracts (one natural, one imitation) in four different applications—lemon soufflé, lemon curd, lemon pound cake, and lemon butter-cream frosting.

Tasters had no trouble picking out the desserts made with real lemon zest. Zest provided a wider range of lemon flavor, from bitter to sweet, which made desserts more complex tasting and more interesting. With zest, the front of the tongue immediately picks up the sharp bite of lemon, which then mellows in the back of the mouth.

In general, tasters found that the extracts were the worst choices, producing dull desserts. The extracts also gave delicate desserts, such as lemon curd and lemon soufflé, a harsh alcoholic flavor. Imitation extract was particularly alcoholic and devoid of lemon flavor.

Oils produced good lemon flavor, but it was monochromatic. The oils lacked the highs and lows of zest. Of the two oils tested, Boyajian Pure Lemon Oil was the hands-down favorite. This oil is pressed from fresh lemons and boasts lemon flavors without any mysterious undertones.

FRESH FRUIT TART WITH PASTRY CREAM

WHAT WE WANTED: Our own pâtisserie creation that, unlike most bakery tarts, tastes as good as it looks.

The perfect fresh fruit tart has components working in concert to produce complementary textures and flavors. Its crust is buttery and sweet, crisp and sugar-cookie-like, not flaky like a pie pastry. The pastry cream filling is creamy and lithe, just sweet enough to counter the tartness of fresh fruits and just firm enough to support their weight. A finish of jellied glaze makes the fruits sparkle and keeps them from drying out. With each forkful, you experience the buttery crumbling of crust, the chill of cool, rich, silky pastry cream, and the juicy explosion of lusty ripe fruit.

The pastry for a fresh fruit tart is called pâte sucrée, or sweet pastry (see page 276). The tart shell is baked empty (aka prebaked, blind-baked, or baked *au blanc*) until it reaches a deep golden hue. It is then cooled completely, filled with pastry cream, topped with fruit, glazed, et voilà.

Pastry cream is cooked in a saucepan on the stovetop like a homemade pudding. Making it is not necessarily difficult, but making it just right, we knew, would mean finding the perfect balance of ingredients—milk (or cream), eggs, sugar, and starch (usually either cornstarch or flour). We gathered and then prepared a number of recipes for pastry cream and even included a couple of atypical fruit tart fillings—whipped cream and crème anglaise (stirred custard), both stabilized with gelatin. These anomalies were quickly and unanimously rejected by tasters for being uninteresting and Jell-O-like, respectively. We also included basic pastry creams stabilized with gelatin and lightened with egg whites or whipped cream (both often called crème chiboust in the French pastry vernacular), but these more labor-intensive preparations turned out not to be worth the effort. It was evident from this tasting that a simple, basic pastry cream was the one to pursue.

With the information gleaned from this first round, we were able to formulate a working recipe from which we could test components systematically. We sought to determine which was preferable: milk, half-and-half, or heavy cream. Milk was lean on flavor, and cream was superfluous in its fat. Half-and-half was the dairy of choice; the pastry cream made with it was silky in texture and agreeably, not overly, rich. To fill a 9- to 9½-inch tart shell, we needed 2 cups, sweetened with only ½ cup of sugar.

Egg yolks—and sometimes whole eggs—help thicken and enrich pastry cream. A whole egg pastry cream was too light and flimsy. An all-yolk cream was richer, fuller flavored, and altogether more serious. Three yolks were too few to do the job, four (a very common proportion of yolks to dairy) were fine, but with five yolks the pastry cream was sensational—it was like smooth, edible silk, with a remarkable glossy translucency much like that of mayonnaise.

Thickener was up next. We made four batches of pastry cream, using 3 or 4 tablespoons of cornstarch or flour in each one. Four tablespoons of either starch made gummy, chewy, gluey messes of the pastry creams. Three tablespoons was the correct amount; any less would have resulted in soup. In equal amounts, cornstarch and flour were extremely close in flavor and texture, but cornstarch inched out in front with a slightly lighter, more ethereal texture and a cleaner and purer flavor; flour had a trace of graininess and gumminess. That a cornstarch pastry cream is marginally easier to cook than one made with flour was a bonus. Once a cornstarch cream reaches a boil, it is done. A pastry cream with flour must remain on the heat for a few minutes to allow the raw flour flavor to cook off and the cream to reach maximum viscosity.

Most pastry cream recipes finish with a whisking of butter into the just-made cream. As fine-grained sandpaper removes the smallest burrs and gives wood a velveteen finish, butter, we found, rounds out the flavor of pastry cream and endows it with a smooth, silken texture. We found that a relatively generous amount of butter (4 tablespoons) also helped the chilled cream behave better when it came time to slice; it resisted sliding and slipping much more than it had without the extra butter. When the tart was well chilled, the pastry cream held its own.

As for timing, we found it best to prepare the pastry cream before beginning the pastry shell. In fact, it can be made a day or two in advance. This gives the cream adequate time to chill, and we did find a fruit tart with filling that is cool on the tongue much more thrilling to eat. And since it is best to fill the pastry fairly close to serving time lest it become soggy, the cream must be cold when it goes into the shell and is topped with fruit.

Small, soft, self-contained fruits—in other words, berries—are ideal atop fresh fruit tarts. Raspberries, blackberries, and blueberries require no paring and no slicing. That means no breaking of fruit skin to release juices that can ruin a tart. Strawberries are certainly acceptable. They do need to be hulled, and sliced strawberries can make an attractive display if arranged, glazed, and served swiftly. While fruits like mangoes and papayas, with their juicy, soft, creamy textures, might seem inviting, they aren't good candidates for a tart because they quickly send their juices flowing. What's more, their irregular and awkward shapes can be difficult to slice and arrange attractively. Kiwis, however, work well and are gorgeous complements to the berry reds and blues. But use kiwis sparingly, as they, too, can water things down. We do not wash berries that are destined to grace a fruit tart. They need to be utterly dry and completely bruise- and blemish-free. Any excess water can cause the tart to weep, which ultimately results in a soggy bottom.

In the test kitchen, the tarts that met with the most flattery were the simple ones that showed restraint, not the overdesigned ones with lots of fanfare. If you are not inclined to create your own design, follow one of those suggested on page 285. If you are so inclined, bear in mind that one goal is to arrange the fruit in a tight design so that very little to none of the ivory-toned pastry cream peeks out of the spaces between the fruit. Also, the nicest designs are those in which the tallest points are at the center of the tart, with a gradual and graceful descent to the edges.

The finishing touch on a fruit tart is the glaze. For tarts that are covered only with berries of red and blue hues, garnet-colored red currant jelly is perfect. For tarts covered with kiwi and other fair-colored fruits (for instance, golden raspberries), apricot jam is the norm because of its neutral tones, but we took to using apple jelly because it eliminated the need to strain out chunks of fruit and then reheat.

Fresh fruit tarts are often displayed with a shellacked armor of glaze painted on the fruit. After glazing dozens of tarts, we can vouch that sticky brush bristles can ensnare and dislodge bits of fruit, wrecking a design. Instead, we adopted a technique of dabbing/drizzling/flicking the glaze on the tart with a pastry brush. The result is not a smooth, even coat but something more dazzling—a sheath of droplets that catch light and glisten like dewdrops. The caveat is that the glaze must have the correct consistency. Too thin and the glaze will run off the fruit and pool in valleys; too thick and it falls from the brush in heavy globules. We found it helpful to bring the jelly to a boil, stirring it occasionally to ensure that it melts entirely, then use it straight off the stove.

WHAT WE LEARNED: **Make a basic pastry cream thickened with egg yolks and cornstarch. Add butter to the finished cream for flavor and improved consistency. Chill the pastry cream before spreading it in a cooled tart shell, top with whole berries, and then drizzle and dab with hot jelly glaze.**

Crust –
2 cube butter, melted
½ c powdered sugar
2 c flour
Press into tart pans
Bake 350° 12–15 min or til browned.

FRESH FRUIT TART WITH PASTRY CREAM

serves 8 to 10

Remove the chalazae with your fingers (see right). The pastry cream can be made a day or two in advance, but do not fill the prebaked tart shell until just before serving. Once filled, the tart should be topped with fruit, glazed, and served within half an hour or so.

pastry cream

2 cups half-and-half
½ cup (3.5 ounces) sugar
Pinch salt
5 large egg yolks, chalazae removed (see box, above right)
3 tablespoons cornstarch
4 tablespoons cold unsalted butter, cut into 4 pieces
1½ teaspoons vanilla extract

1 fully baked tart shell, 9 to 9½ inches (see page 276), cooled to room temperature

fruit and glaze

Fruit, unwashed (see Three Fruit Tart Designs on page 285)
½ cup red currant or apple jelly (see Three Fruit Tart Designs on page 285)

1. FOR THE PASTRY CREAM: Heat half-and-half, 6 tablespoons sugar, and salt in medium heavy-bottomed saucepan over medium heat until simmering, stirring occasionally to dissolve sugar.

2. Meanwhile, whisk egg yolks in medium bowl until thoroughly combined. Whisk in remaining 2 tablespoons sugar and whisk until sugar has begun to dissolve and mixture is creamy, about 15 seconds. Whisk in cornstarch until combined and mixture is pale yellow and thick, about 30 seconds.

TECHNIQUE: Removing the Chalazae

The cordlike strands of egg white protein attached to the yolk, called the chalazae, will harden when cooked. Removing them when separating the yolks and whites precludes the need to strain the pastry cream after cooking.

3. When half-and-half mixture reaches full simmer, gradually whisk simmering half-and-half into yolk mixture to temper. Return mixture to saucepan, scraping bowl with rubber spatula; return to simmer over medium heat, whisking constantly, until 3 or 4 bubbles burst on surface and mixture is thickened and glossy, about 30 seconds. Off heat, whisk in butter and vanilla. Transfer mixture to medium bowl, press plastic wrap directly on surface, and refrigerate until cold and set, at least 3 hours or up to 2 days.

4. TO ASSEMBLE AND GLAZE THE TART: Spread cold pastry cream over bottom of tart shell, using offset spatula or large spoon. (Can press plastic wrap directly on surface of pastry cream and refrigerate up to 30 minutes.) Arrange fruit on top of pastry cream, following a design on page 285.

5. Bring jelly to boil in small saucepan over medium-high heat, stirring occasionally to smooth out lumps. When boiling and completely melted, apply by dabbing and flicking onto fruit with pastry brush; add 1 teaspoon water and return jelly to boil if it becomes too thick to drizzle. (Tart can be refrigerated, uncovered, up to 30 minutes.) Remove outer metal ring of tart pan, slide thin metal spatula between bottom of crust and tart pan bottom to release, then slip tart onto cardboard round or serving platter; serve.

THREE FRUIT TART DESIGNS

KIWI, RASPBERRY, AND BLUEBERRY TART:

Peel 2 large kiwis, halve lengthwise, and cut into half-moon slices about ⅜ inch thick. Arrange them cut-side down in an overlapping circle propped up against the inside edge of the pastry. Sort two ½ pints raspberries by height, and arrange them in three tight rings just inside the kiwi, using the tallest berries to form the inner ring. Mound ½ pint blueberries in the center. Use apple jelly to glaze this tart.

STRAWBERRY TART:

Brush dirt from 3 quarts ripe strawberries of medium, uniform size; slice off the tops. Sort the berries by height and place the tallest strawberry in the center of the tart. Arrange the nicest and most evenly shaped berries in tight rings around the center, placing them in order of descending height to the edge of the pastry. Quarter the remaining berries lengthwise and use them to fill gaps between the whole berries (see tips below). Use red currant jelly to glaze this tart.

MIXED BERRY TART:

Sort ½ pint blueberries, ½ pint blackberries, and two ½ pints raspberries, discarding any blemished fruit. Place all berries in a large plastic bag, then very gently shake the bag to combine them. Empty the berries on top of the tart, distributing them in an even layer. Then, using your fingers, adjust the berries as necessary so that they cover the entire surface and the colors are evenly distributed. Use red currant jelly to glaze this tart.

TECHNIQUE: Tips for Perfect Tarts

FOR KIWI, RASPBERRY, AND BLUEBERRY TART: To peel kiwi, cut off the ends, then slip a wide, shallow spoon between skin and flesh. Rotate the kiwi while pushing the spoon into the fruit, freeing it from the skin.

FOR STRAWBERRY TART: To fill gaps between the whole berries, begin at the center of the tart and place berries cut in quarters between them, pointed side up and skin-side out, leaning the quartered berries toward the center.

FOR MIXED BERRY TART: Place the berries in a large plastic bag. Hold the bag closed with one hand, and use the other to gently jostle the berries about to combine them.

DINER pies

CHAPTER 22

Those cream-topped pies in the revolving case at the diner always look better than they taste. Given what is required of these pies (they must look great for days on end), it's no surprise that these institutional creations are generally made with too much thickener and too few quality ingredients. But when prepared at home, where they can be enjoyed the day they are made, these pies can be a revelation.

Chocolate cream pie has almost universal appeal. Who doesn't like chocolate pastry cream and whipped cream delivered in a chocolate cookie crust? The key is to create a filling that is soft and creamy yet stiff enough to be cut cleanly. It's not as easy as it sounds. Use too much starch and the filling is thick and stodgy. Don't add enough egg yolks or starch and the filling literally runs all over the plate.

Key lime pie presents similar issues. This American classic begins with sweetened condensed milk. Many recipes don't require baking, but when made this way we found the filling to be loose and slurpy. After suffering through a dozen failed pies, we discovered that 15 minutes in the oven transforms the filling, making it sliceable and more flavorful.

Julia shows Chris how whisking lime zest with egg yolks tints the yolks a lovely shade of green and dispenses with the need for food coloring when making Key lime pie.

CHOCOLATE CREAM PIE

WHAT WE WANTED: A filling of voluptuous creaminess that would also be sliceworthy, with a well-balanced chocolate flavor somewhere between milkshake and melted candy bar.

Despite its grand flourishes and snowcapped peaks, a chocolate cream pie is essentially pastry cream whose substance has been given form. Comprising very basic ingredients—milk or cream, eggs, sugar, flour or cornstarch, butter, vanilla, and chocolate—it is cooked on the stovetop in a matter of minutes, chilled in a baked pie shell for a couple of hours, then topped with whipped cream. This pie, while looking superb, can be gluey or gummy, too sweet, even acrid.

A pastry cream, while in essence a quick, simple production, will form tapioca-like lumps of varying diameter in the presence of sloppiness or inattention. Sequencing is pretty standard: While the milk or cream is brought to a boil with most of the sugar, a small portion of the sugar is held back, combined with the starch, and mixed thoroughly with the yolks. This yolk mixture is then tempered, or warmed with a fraction of the simmering milk or cream, allowing the starch molecules to expand gently. The warmed emulsion is reintroduced to the simmering milk or cream, and the whole is brought rapidly to a boil under constant stirring or whisking. Despite the fact that it contains eggs, a pastry cream can and must boil if the starch molecules are to expand and thicken.

We began by assessing a classic pastry cream recipe—4 egg yolks, ½ cup sugar, 3 tablespoons cornstarch, 2 cups milk, 1 teaspoon vanilla extract, and 2 tablespoons butter—realizing that the proportions might require substantial modification for a chocolate filling. We wanted first to settle on the ingredient base and ran some comparative tests, most of which left us true to our original candidates. Egg yolks, for example, produced a cream of unsurpassed texture and flavor, far superior to one made with whole eggs. Cornstarch tasted lighter and cleaner than flour. Cold butter stirred into the finished cream effected tremendous improvements in texture and flavor, making the pastry cream supple and lush. One ingredient was to change. Half-and-half provided enhanced mouthfeel and textural support for the chocolate; it was markedly better than milk or cream.

Through multiple trials and tweakings we developed a basic recipe that contained all of the ingredients mentioned above, along with more half-and-half to increase overall volume. It also called for higher proportions of egg yolks (6) and butter (6 tablespoons) than a standard pastry cream. Testing had convinced us that the texture of a chocolate cream filling benefits immeasurably when fats are used as thickeners and basic starch is minimized. Butter, egg yolks, and half-and-half render a silky texture and provide most of the requisite thickening with greater finesse than cornstarch.

We had three chocolate options: semisweet (or bittersweet, which is quite similar), unsweetened, or a mixture of the two. Tasters felt that fillings made exclusively with semisweet or bittersweet chocolate lacked depth of flavor, while those made with unsweetened chocolate alone hit a sour note. Without exception, tasters wanted the filling to land on the dark, intense bittersweet side and the cream topping to be sweet and pure.

The roundest, most upfront chocolate flavor, with lingering intensity at the finish, came in the form of 6 ounces semisweet and 1 ounce unsweetened chocolate. The apparently negligible amount of unsweetened chocolate contributed hugely to the flavor. Unsweetened chocolate, which does not undergo the kneading, grinding, and smoothing process known as conching, retains all of its strong and sometimes bitter flavors that translate well in small amounts.

This was not the only advantage of using a small amount of unsweetened chocolate. Because it further thickened the cream (see the Science Desk on page 291), we were able to reduce the cornstarch from 3 tablespoons to 2.

Next we moved on to compare fancy imported chocolates with domestic grocery store brands. The first test, pitting the widely available Baker's unsweetened chocolate against several unsweetened chocolates with European pedigrees, confirmed our fears that the supermarket stuff would be no match for its European competition. (Of the imported chocolates, all tasters preferred Callebaut.) Even at 1 ounce, the Baker's chocolate contributed an "off" flavor and rubberiness of texture that everyone noticed. But the next round of testing brought unexpected good news: Hershey's Special Dark chocolate was a consistent winner in the semisweet category, beating out not only a premium American semisweet entry but also its European competitors—and you can buy it in a drugstore! Hershey's unsweetened chocolate, while not as refined in flavor and texture as Callebaut unsweetened, placed a respectable second to Callebaut and was miles ahead of Baker's.

Because the filling is three standing inches of pure chocolate, a texture less than faultlessly smooth will deliver an experience less than ethereal. Temperature, timing, and technique are important.

On occasions when we didn't combine the eggs adequately with the sugar and starch (which meant mixing almost until the yolks ribboned) or when we left the emulsion to sit around awaiting the simmering half-and-half, the sugar began to break down the yolks and made the finished texture of the cream grainy. For the pastry cream to attain a flawless texture, the half-and-half in the pan was best left at a simmer—rather than pulled off the stove—while the yolks were tempered. This way the introduction of the warmed yolks barely registered on the half-and-half, which quickly came up to a boil and was finished.

As for the crust, tasters swooned over a crumb crust made with chocolate cookie crumbs to the exclusion of all others. While easier to make than rolled pastry dough and arguably better suited to chilled pudding fillings, crumb crusts are not altogether seamless enterprises. Sandy and insubstantial at one extreme, tough and intractable at the other, they can be a serving nightmare. While no one expects a slice of cream pie to hold up like a slab of marble, it isn't expected to collapse on a bed of grit or lacerate a cornea with airborne shrapnel, either. It's got to slice.

The standard cookie used to make a chocolate crumb crust is Nabisco Famous Chocolate Wafers, but we didn't care for the flavor of these crusts unbaked and found them somewhat tough (if sliceable) baked. After trying without much success to soften the crust with a percentage of fresh white bread crumbs, we made a leap of faith to Oreo cookies pulverized straight up with their filling. We hoped that the creaminess of the centers would lend flavor and softness to the finished crust. The Oreo flavor came through loud and clear, and the creamy centers, along with a bit of butter, prevented the baked crumbs from becoming tough. No additional sugar or even salt was required.

Why did Oreos work so well? Oreo centers are sweetened hydrogenated shortening, like the Crisco icing on an inexpensive wedding cake. Hydrogenation refers to a process in which hydrogen gas is forced under pressure into the molecules of a vegetable oil, expanding, or "saturating," them into a semisolid state. Harold McGee, in *On Food and Cooking* (Scribner, 1984), terms this "a modern oil that is conveniently pre-creamed"—in other words, whipped. It is this quality in an Oreo filling that gives Oreo crumb crusts their edge over crusts made with plain chocolate cookies and melted butter. The fat in a hydrogenated shortening encases millions of air pockets. When the fat melts during baking, the air pockets remain, creating small empty spaces between the crumbs, thereby making the crust register as light and agreeably crisp—not hard—to the teeth.

Ten minutes in a 350 degree-oven set the crust nicely; higher temperatures burned the cocoa. The crisp salty-sweet chocolate crumbs gave the rich filling voice and definition. Cloaked with whipped cream, this piece moves as one.

WHAT WE LEARNED: **Use a combination of bittersweet and unsweetened chocolate for best flavor and texture, and grind Oreos for a crust that's light, crisp, and sliceable.**

CHOCOLATE CREAM PIE serves 8 to 10

For the best chocolate flavor and texture, we recommend either Callebaut semisweet and unsweetened chocolates or Hershey's Special Dark and Hershey's unsweetened chocolates. Do not combine the yolks and sugar in advance of making the filling—the sugar will begin to break down the yolks, and the finished cream will be pitted.

chocolate cookie crumb crust

16   Oreo cookies (with filling), broken into rough pieces, about 2½ cups

2   tablespoons unsalted butter, melted and cooled

chocolate cream filling

2½   cups half-and-half
     Pinch salt

⅓   cup (2.3 ounces) sugar

2   tablespoons cornstarch

6   large egg yolks, room temperature, chalazae removed (see photo on page 284)

6   tablespoons cold unsalted butter, cut into 6 pieces

6   ounces semisweet or bittersweet chocolate, finely chopped

1   ounce unsweetened chocolate, finely chopped

1   teaspoon vanilla extract

3   cups Whipped Cream (page 294), whipped to soft peaks

1. FOR THE CRUST: Adjust oven rack to middle position and heat oven to 350 degrees. In bowl of food processor fitted with steel blade, process cookies with fifteen 1-second pulses, then let machine run until crumbs are uniformly fine, about 15 seconds. (Alternatively, place cookies in large zipper-lock plastic bag and crush with rolling pin.) Transfer crumbs to medium bowl, drizzle with butter, and use fingers to combine until butter is evenly distributed.

2. Pour crumbs into 9-inch Pyrex pie plate. Press crumbs evenly onto bottom and up sides of pie plate. Once crumbs are in place, line pan flush with large square of plastic wrap, and use spoon to smooth crumbs into curves and sides of pan. Refrigerate lined pie plate 20 minutes to firm crumbs, then bake until crumbs are fragrant and set, about 10 minutes. Cool on wire rack while preparing filling.

3. FOR THE FILLING: Bring half-and-half, salt, and about 3 tablespoons sugar to simmer in medium saucepan over medium-high heat, stirring occasionally with wooden spoon to dissolve sugar. Stir together remaining sugar and

cornstarch in small bowl. Whisk yolks thoroughly in medium bowl until slightly thickened, about 30 seconds. Sprinkle cornstarch mixture over yolks and whisk, scraping down sides of bowl, if necessary, until mixture is glossy and sugar has begun to dissolve, about 1 minute. When half-and-half reaches full simmer, drizzle about ½ cup hot half-and-half over yolks, whisking constantly to temper; then whisk egg yolk mixture into simmering half-and-half (mixture should thicken in about 30 seconds). Return to simmer, whisking constantly, until 3 or 4 bubbles burst on surface and mixture is thickened and glossy, about 15 seconds longer.

4. Off heat, whisk in butter until incorporated; add chocolates and whisk until melted, scraping pan bottom with rubber spatula to fully incorporate. Stir in vanilla, then immediately pour filling into baked and cooled crust. Press plastic wrap directly on surface of filling and refrigerate pie until filling is cold and firm, about 3 hours.

5. Just before serving, spread or pipe whipped cream over chilled pie filling. Cut pie into wedges and serve.

SCIENCE DESK: Chocolate as Thickener

EVERYONE KNOWS THAT BITTERSWEET AND UNSWEETENED chocolates have different flavors and levels of sweetness. But their dissimilarities do not end there. As we developed our chocolate cream pie recipe, we discovered that ounce-for-ounce, unsweetened chocolate has more thickening power. We were aware of chocolate's starchy properties (cocoa solids are rich in starches), but we were not prepared for the dramatic differences in texture revealed in side-by-side pie fillings made with each type. Though both fillings had roughly the same amount of cocoa solids by volume, the unsweetened chocolate filling was significantly stiffer and had a viscous, gummy quality. Its counterpart made only with bittersweet chocolate had a smooth and creamy texture.

While many cookbook substitutions fail to take into account the higher starch concentration of unsweetened chocolate, cooks should be mindful of its thickening power. Comparable amounts of bittersweet or semisweet chocolate and unsweetened chocolate plus sugar will not produce identical results. While a direct swap might work well enough in fudgy brownies, it could wreak havoc on a delicate custard or airy cake.

So why did we decide to include unsweetened chocolate in our filling if it can produce such unappealing results? The chocolate's intensity is essential to the filling's character. By using just a single ounce of unsweetened chocolate in our recipe, we were able to attain the perfect balance of nuanced chocolate flavor and pleasing, velvety texture. What's more, as mentioned in our story on developing the recipe for the pie (page 288), the thickening power of even this small amount of unsweetened chocolate helped us keep a cap on the cornstarch, which can detract from a custard's silky texture when added in copious amounts.

EQUIPMENT CORNER: Whisks

THERE IS A BOUNTY OF WHISKS ON THE MARKET—FLAT round, balloon, and coiled. We wanted to see if the average cook needed more than one whisk and, if so, which ones.

We purchased 15 whisks representative of the flat, round, balloon, and coiled varieties. Some models were made of nonstick plastic. Others were silicone-coated. One even had a small round wire cage containing a ceramic ball. The whisks ranged in size from 8 to 12 inches and in price from $5.95 to $21.95. We tested their performance in three classic tasks: making a béchamel sauce (a classic sauce made from butter, flour, and milk), beating egg whites, and whipping cream. All three jobs require constant movement from the whisk.

For the béchamel, we wanted a whisk that would work well in a smaller saucepan, that would keep the roux from burning, and that would emulsify the butter and flour into the milk without lumps. For egg whites and cream, we wanted a whisk that would create a tight foam with minimum effort and forearm cramping. We were also looking for whisks that created the least mess—no splashes of hot milk or dollops of cream and egg white.

Early into the testing, we discovered that, indeed, different whisks are better for different tasks—but only two different whisks are worth owning. A balloon whisk is perfect for air incorporation but too large for sauces and emulsification. Conversely, a flat whisk is ideal for sauces and emulsification but not very good at air incorporation.

The winning whisk for the béchamel was a flat silicone-coated model from Williams-Sonoma ($9). It was both quiet and effective, with the tines conforming to the pan sides perfectly. The least effective flat whisk was the Calphalon flat plastic nonstick whisk. It was cumbersome and had too few tines that were also too large.

Although intrigued by the concept, we were not impressed overall by the unusual coiled models. One had a very uncomfortable handle and required pressure to flatten the coiled head, while the other had a very short handle set at an awkward angle.

The winning balloon whisk was a standard, larger (12-inch) model. It was comfortable in the hand and was large enough to incorporate air quickly and efficiently. Our two least favorite models were the Calphalon nonstick plastic, which was large and messy, and the Williams-Sonoma with the caged ceramic ball, which flung bits of cream out of the bowl and onto our aprons and counters.

WHIPPED CREAM

WHAT WE WANTED: **Perfectly whipped and lightly sweetened cream that could be spooned over a pie, cobbler, or pudding.**

Whipped cream often makes the difference between a good dessert and a great one. But if you are going to the trouble to whip cream, it better be good. You certainly don't want overwhipped cream that's curdled and lumpy. Likewise, achingly sweet cream, or cream marred by the presence of gritty granules of sugar, is not acceptable. For our testing, we wanted to examine the ingredients (the type of cream, the type of sugar) and the best whipping technique.

Ultrapasteurized heavy cream is the standard choice in most dairy cases, although you may occasionally see pasteurized heavy cream or organic heavy cream, which is usually pasteurized rather than ultrapasteurized. We whipped several cartons of each cream and found that pasteurized organic heavy cream was the favorite in the test kitchen. It delivers the sweetest cream flavor, and although it pours the thinnest, it whips up to double its volume.

Regular pasteurized heavy cream is thicker and has a richer mouthfeel, owing no doubt to additives intended to bulk up the texture. However, it was not as sweet and did not whip quite as well as the organic cream.

The ultrapasteurized heavy cream made the worst whipped cream in our testing. While it is the thickest by far out of the container, its volume increased by just 50 percent when whipped. Several experts explained that the high temperatures required for ultrapasteurization destroy some of the proteins and enzymes that promote whipping. The higher heat (which prolongs shelf life) also leaves the cream with a slightly cooked taste. We found that pasteurized cream, which is subject to less heat but has a shorter shelf life, delivers better flavor and volume every time and is worth seeking out. A supermarket or natural foods store that carries organic milk will probably sell organic cream, and we think this is your best bet. If you must use ultrapasteurized cream, the whipping time should be increased by 10 to 20 seconds, and you certainly should not expect the cream to double in volume.

Many sources suggest sweetening cream with confectioners' sugar to ensure that the sugar dissolves. In our tests, regular granulated sugar dissolved just fine as long as it was added before beating, not after. When making a highly sweetened whipped cream topping (with more than 3 tablespoons sugar per cup of heavy cream), it is best to use fine confectioners' sugar to prevent the possibility of grittiness. But we find that cream whipped with this much sugar is unbearably sweet for most uses.

Vanilla extract is a common addition to whipped cream, adding complexity and rounding out the flavors. We found that ½ teaspoon of extract is the right amount for 1½ cups cream.

With our ingredients set, we turned our attention to technique. Most sources indicate that chilled cream will beat more easily and to greater heights than warm cream. We found this to be the case. In fact, for maximum volume we recommend chilling the bowl and beaters as well.

Most recipes for whipping cream are quite vague about mixing speed. We obtained the best results when we started the cream and sugar on low speed, raised the speed to medium, and then finished at high speed. The whole process should take about 1½ minutes. We found that gradually increasing the speed of the mixer allows the cream to hold more air. Cream whipped at high speed from the outset was less stable and not as voluminous.

WHAT WE LEARNED: **For best flavor and volume, use pasteurized rather than ultrapasteurized cream. Granulated sugar, when used in moderate amounts, will dissolve just fine if added before whipping. Finally, whip slowly at first, increasing the speed as you go, to obtain soft, billowy peaks.**

WHIPPED CREAM   makes about 3 cups

When you think the cream is almost properly whipped, you may want to switch from an electric mixer to a whisk for greater control. Cream can go from properly whipped to overwhipped in a matter of seconds. If cream becomes granular and curdled-looking, you've beaten it too long and must start over with a new batch of cream. This recipe can be halved if needed.

1½   cups heavy cream, chilled, preferably
        pasteurized or pasteurized organic
1½   tablespoons granulated sugar
½   teaspoon vanilla extract

1. Chill deep bowl and beaters of electric mixer in freezer for at least 20 minutes. (If freezer is too crowded to fit bowl, place beaters in bowl, fill bowl with ice water, and chill on counter. When bowl and beaters are well chilled, dump out water and dry thoroughly.)

2. Add cream, sugar, and vanilla to chilled bowl. Beat on low speed until small bubbles form, about 30 seconds. Increase speed to medium and continue beating until beaters leave a trail, about 30 seconds. Increase speed to high and continue beating until cream is smooth, thick, and nearly doubled in volume, about 20 seconds for soft peaks or about 30 seconds for stiff peaks (see illustrations at right). If necessary, finish beating with whisk to adjust consistency. Serve immediately or spoon into fine sieve or strainer set over measuring cup and refrigerate for up to 8 hours.

SCIENCE DESK:
Temperature and Whipped Cream

WHY DO SO MANY WHIPPED CREAM RECIPES, INCLUDING ours, call for chilled cream as well as chilled beaters and bowl? Whipped cream is a foam stabilized by fat. The foam is nothing more than air bubbles beaten into the cream by the beaters. When things work right, the fat globules are dispersed evenly among the air bubbles and they stick together, thus supporting the foam.

However, the fat globules must be at the right temperature if they are to stick together. If they are too warm, they won't stick together and the foam collapses. When the cream is cold, the fat globules are stickier.

Keep it cold and cream should whip perfectly. But don't overwhip the cream. If you whip too long, the cream can curdle and separate. That's because prolonged beating has warmed the cream. If the cream gets too warm, the fat globules start to separate and your whipped cream curdles.

TECHNIQUE: Whipping Cream to Soft or Stiff Peaks

SOFT PEAKS
Cream whipped to soft peaks will droop slightly from the ends of the beaters or whisk.

STIFF PEAKS
Cream whipped to stiff peaks will cling tightly to the ends of the beaters or whisk and will hold its shape.

KEY LIME PIE

WHAT WE WANTED: A filling with real lime flavor that would be creamy but firm enough to slice easily.

The standard recipe for Key lime pie is incredibly short and simple: beat 4 egg yolks, add a 14-ounce can of sweetened condensed milk, and then stir in ½ cup lime juice and a tablespoon of grated lime zest. Pour it all into a graham cracker crust and chill it until firm, about two hours. Top the pie with sweetened whipped cream and serve.

It would be lovely if this recipe worked, but we found that it doesn't, at least not to our total satisfaction. Although the filling does set firm enough to yield clean-cut slices, it has a loose, "slurpy" consistency. We tried to fix the consistency by beating the yolks until thick, as some recipes direct, but this did not help. Nor did it help to dribble in the lime juice rather than adding it all at once, as other recipes suggest. We also made the filling with only two yolks and with no yolks at all (such "eggless" versions of the recipe do exist), but this yielded even thinner fillings.

Still, the time spent mixing Key lime pie fillings in various ways was not a total loss. While in the heat of experimenting, we inadvertently threw the lime zest into a bowl in which we had already placed the egg yolks. When we whisked up the yolks, they turned green, and the whole filling ended up tinted a lovely shade of pale lime. What a great way to dispense with food coloring.

Having found the mix-and-chill method wanting, we decided to try baking the pie, as some recipes suggest. We used the same ingredients as we had before and simply baked the pie until the filling stiffened slightly, about 15 minutes in a moderate oven. The difference between the baked pie (which was really a custard) and the unbaked pie (which had merely been a clabber) was remarkable. (See the Science Desk on page 297 for more information on how Key lime pie thickens.) The baked filling was thick, creamy, and unctuous, reminiscent of cream pie. It also tasted more pungent and complex than the raw fillings had, perhaps because the heat of the oven released the flavorful oils in the lime zest.

Up until this point, we had been working with regular supermarket limes (called Persian limes), but we wondered if Key limes would make a better pie. True Key limes, or *Citrus aurantifolia,* have not been a significant commercial crop in this country since storms destroyed the Florida groves early in this century. However, a few growers have recently begun to revive the crop, and Key limes occasionally show up in supermarkets.

We'd love to say that Key lime juice made all the difference in the world, but it didn't. We found that it tasted pretty much the same as the juice of supermarket limes. Key limes are also a nuisance to zest and squeeze. They are thin-skinned, full of seeds, and generally little bigger than walnuts. Whereas you need only three or four Persian limes to make a Key lime pie, you need up to a dozen Key limes. So despite the name of the pie, we actually find the juice of Persian limes preferable as an ingredient.

WHAT WE LEARNED: Whisk the lime zest and yolks together to release oils from the zest and give the filling a lovely green color. Don't just pour the filling into the pie shell and serve. Baking makes the filling reminiscent of cream pie—thick, creamy, and unctuous. The heat of the oven releases the flavorful oils in the lime zest and makes the filling taste better, too.

KEY LIME PIE serves 8 to 10

Despite this pie's name, we found that tasters could not tell the difference between pies made with regular supermarket limes (called Persian limes) and true Key limes. Since Persian limes are easier to find and juice, we recommend them.

lime filling

4	teaspoons grated zest plus ½ cup strained juice from 3 or 4 limes
4	large egg yolks
1	(14-ounce) can sweetened condensed milk

graham cracker crust

11	full-size graham crackers, processed to fine crumbs (1¼ cups)
3	tablespoons granulated sugar
5	tablespoons unsalted butter, melted
1½	cups Whipped Cream (page 294), made without vanilla and whipped to stiff peaks
½	lime, sliced paper thin and dipped in sugar (optional)

1. FOR THE FILLING: Whisk zest and yolks in medium bowl until tinted light green, about 2 minutes. Beat in milk, then juice; set aside at room temperature to thicken.

2. FOR THE CRUST: Adjust oven rack to center position and heat oven to 325 degrees. Mix crumbs and sugar in medium bowl. Add butter; stir with fork until well blended. Scrape mixture into 9-inch pie pan. Press crumbs evenly onto bottom and up sides of pie plate. Once crumbs are in place, line pan flush with large square of plastic wrap, and use spoon to smooth crumbs into curves and sides of pan. Refrigerate lined pie plate 20 minutes to firm crumbs. Bake until lightly browned and fragrant, about 15 minutes. Transfer pan to wire rack; cool to room temperature, about 20 minutes.

3. Pour lime filling into crust; bake until center is set yet wiggly when jiggled, 15 to 17 minutes. Return pie to wire rack; cool to room temperature. Refrigerate until well chilled, at least 3 hours. (Can be covered with lightly oiled or oil-sprayed plastic wrap laid directly on filling and refrigerated up to 1 day.)

4. Decoratively pipe whipped cream over filling or spread evenly with rubber spatula. Garnish with optional sugared lime slices and serve.

SCIENCE DESK: How Key Lime Pie Thickens

THE EXTRAORDINARILY HIGH ACID CONTENT OF LIMES and the unique properties of sweetened condensed milk are responsible for the fact that lime pie filling will thicken without cooking.

The acid in the lime juice does its work by causing the proteins in both the egg yolks and the condensed milk to coil up and bond together. This effect is similar to that of heat. The same process can be observed in the Latin American dish ceviche, in which raw fish is "cooked" simply by being pickled in lime juice.

But this process does not work well with just any kind of milk; it requires both the sweetness and the thickness of sweetened condensed milk. This canned product is made by boiling the moisture out of fresh milk and then adding sugar. Because the milk has been evaporated, or condensed, it is thick enough to stiffen into a sliceable filling when "cooked" by the lime juice. The sugar, meanwhile, plays the crucial role of separating, or "greasing," the protein strands so that they do not bond too tightly. If they did, the result would be a grainy or curdled filling rather than a smooth and creamy one. Of course, a liquidy, curdly filling is exactly what would result if fresh milk were used instead of canned. Fresh milk lacks the crucial added sugar and is also much thinner.

We also discovered that cream is not a viable substitute for sweetened condensed milk. It does not curdle the way milk does because its fat, like the sugar in condensed milk, buffers the effects of the lime juice. Cream is roughly 50 percent liquid, however, and thus it will only thicken, not stiffen, when clabbered.

Apple pies ready for their 15 minutes of fame before the cameras.

APPLE pies

Making good pie crust can be a simple procedure, but almost everyone who has tried can tell horror stories of crusts that turned out hard, soggy, flavorless, oversalted, underbaked, crumbly, or unworkable. Advice is easy to come by: One expert says that butter is the secret to perfect crust; others swear by vegetable shortening, lard, even canola oil. Some omit salt, some omit sugar, some insist that working the dough by hand is essential, some use cake flour or pastry flour in addition to all-purpose flour, some freeze the dough, some do away with the rolling pin . . . and so on.

To test these propositions, we made hundreds of doughs, with all types of ingredients, and in all types of devices. The resulting recipe, American Pie Dough, is the culmination of years of kitchen work and testing.

Of course, you need to fill pie dough with something. We've chosen apples (a similar dough can be used to make peach pie; see the recipe on page 313) and present two versions—the classic pie with a double crust as well as a more rustic free-form tart that bakes on a cookie sheet, not in a pie plate.

AMERICAN PIE DOUGH

WHAT WE WANTED: A great-tasting, flaky dough that is easy to roll out and handle.

Simple as it can be, pie crust—essentially a combination of flour, water, and fat—raises numerous questions: What are the ideal proportions of the main ingredients? What else should be added for character? What methods should be used to combine these ingredients?

The most controversial ingredient in pastry is fat. We've found that all-butter crusts have good taste, but they are not as flaky and fine-textured as those made with shortening. All-shortening crusts have great texture but lack flavor; oil-based crusts are flat and entirely unappealing; and those made with lard are heavy and strongly flavored. After experimenting with a variety of combinations, we ultimately settled on a proportion of 3 parts butter to 2 parts shortening as optimal for both flavor and texture.

Vegetable shortenings such as Crisco are made from vegetable oil that has been hydrogenated, a process in which hydrogen gas is pumped into the molecules of a vegetable oil to incorporate air and to raise its melting point above room temperature. Crisco is about 10 percent gas and does a good job of lightening and tenderizing. (The way the butter is incorporated into the flour also contributes to flakiness. See the Science Desk on page 304 for details.)

Pie crusts are usually made with all-purpose flour. No matter what we've tried—substituting cornstarch for part of the all-purpose flour (a cookie-baking trick that increases tenderness), adding ¼ teaspoon baking powder to increase rise and flakiness, and mixing cake flour or pastry flour with the all-purpose flour (again, to increase tenderness)—we always come back to plain old all-purpose flour. We also tackled the proportions of salt and sugar, which were much easier to resolve. After testing amounts ranging from ¼ teaspoon to as much as 2 tablespoons, we settled on 1 teaspoon salt and 2 tablespoons sugar for a double-crust pie, amounts that enhance the flavor of the dough without shouting out their presence.

We experimented with buttermilk, milk, and cider vinegar. No liquid additions improved our basic recipe, so we recommend that you stick with ice water.

Pie dough can be made by hand, but we've found that the food processor is faster and easier and does the best job of cutting the fat into the flour. Proper mixing is important. If you undermix, the crust will shrink when baked and became hard and crackly. If you overprocess, you'll get a crumbly, cookie-like dough. The shortening should be pulsed with the flour until the mixture is sandy; butter is then pulsed in until the mixture looks like coarse crumbs, with butter bits no larger than the size of a pea.

Once the flour and fat have been combined, ice water is mixed in. We've come to favor a rubber spatula and a folding motion to mix in the water, which exposes all of the dough to moisture without overworking it, something that can happen if the dough is left in the food processor and the water is pulsed in. Using a spatula to incorporate water makes it possible to minimize the amount of water used (less water means a more tender dough) and reduces the likelihood of overworking the dough. Still, we've also learned that it doesn't pay to be too stingy with the water. If there isn't enough, the dough will be crumbly and hard to roll.

Finally, we found that pie dough need not be difficult to roll out if you remember two basic guidelines: Make sure the dough is well chilled before rolling, and add a minimum of flour to the work surface. Flour added during rolling will cause the dough to toughen. If the dough seems too soft to roll, it's best to refrigerate it rather than adding more flour.

WHAT WE LEARNED: Use a mixture of butter for flavor and shortening for flakiness. Cut the fat into the flour in the food processor, but turn the dough into a bowl and incorporate the water with a spatula.

AMERICAN PIE DOUGH for one double-crust 9-inch pie

2½   cups (12.5 ounces) unbleached all-purpose flour
1   teaspoon salt
2   tablespoons sugar
8   tablespoons all-vegetable shortening, chilled
12   tablespoons unsalted butter, chilled, cut into
    ¼-inch pieces
6–8   tablespoons ice water

1. Pulse flour, salt, and sugar in food processor fitted with steel blade until combined. Add shortening and process until mixture has texture of coarse sand, about 10 seconds. Scatter butter pieces over flour mixture; cut butter into flour until mixture is pale yellow and resembles coarse crumbs, with butter bits no larger than small peas, about ten 1-second pulses. Turn mixture into medium bowl.

2. Sprinkle 6 tablespoons ice water over mixture. With blade of rubber spatula, use folding motion to mix. Press down on dough with broad side of spatula until dough sticks together, adding up to 2 tablespoons more ice water if it will not come together. Divide dough into two balls and flatten each into 4-inch-wide disk. Wrap each in plastic and refrigerate at least 1 hour or up to 2 days before rolling.

VARIATIONS
AMERICAN PIE DOUGH FOR LATTICE-TOP PIE

This crust has a firmer texture than the basic recipe, making it easier to work with when creating a lattice top for peach pie (see page 313).

Follow recipe for American Pie Dough, increasing flour to 3 cups (15 ounces), reducing shortening to 7 tablespoons, reducing butter to 10 tablespoons, and increasing ice water to 10 tablespoons. Divide dough into two pieces, one slightly larger than the other. (If possible, weigh pieces. They should register 16 ounces and 14 ounces.) Flatten larger piece into a rough 5-inch square and smaller piece into a 4-inch disk; wrap separately in plastic and chill as directed.

AMERICAN PIE DOUGH FOR FREE-FORM TART

For a rustic free-form tart, we don't mind if the pastry isn't as flaky, so we use butter alone, with no shortening. This dough is also a bit sweeter than our standard recipe.

Follow recipe for American Pie Dough, reducing flour to 1¼ cups (6.25 ounces) and salt to ½ teaspoon. Omit shortening, reduce butter to 10 tablespoons, and reduce ice water to 3 to 4 tablespoons. Do not divide dough. Flatten into single disk; wrap and chill as directed.

EQUIPMENT CORNER: Pie Plates

WE TESTED THREE TYPES OF PIE PLATE—GLASS, CERAMIC, and metal—and found that a Pyrex glass pie plate did the best job of browning the crust, both when filled and baked blind (the bottom crust baked alone, filled with pie weights to hold its shape). Several metal pie plates also browned quite well, but the glass pie plate has a number of advantages.

Because you can see through a Pyrex plate, it's easy to judge just how brown the bottom crust has become during baking. With a metal pie plate, it's easy to pull the pie out of the oven too soon, when the bottom crust is still quite pale. A second feature we like about the traditional Pyrex plate is the wide rim, which makes the plate easier to take in and out of the oven and also supports fluted edges better than thin rims. Finally, you can store a pie filled with acidic fruit and not worry about metal giving the fruit an off flavor.

Pyrex pie plates do heat up more quickly than metal, so pies may be done a bit sooner than you think, especially if you are following a recipe that was tested in a metal plate. All the times in our recipes are based on baking in a glass pie plate; if baking in metal you may need to add two to three minutes for empty crusts and five minutes for filled pies.

APPLE PIE

WHAT WE WANTED: A classic pie that really tastes like apples, with a modicum of juice and a tender crust.

Cooks who slather the apples in their pies with butter, cinnamon, and sugar do themselves and the apples a disservice; we set out to make a pie in which the apples shine through. We started by examining the choice of apples for the filling. We tested the nine best-selling apples, figuring that we wanted a recipe that would work with apples commonly available in supermarkets throughout the year.

We determined that Granny Smith and McIntosh both have excellent qualities; the former is tart with good texture, and the latter has excellent flavor. But each also has its drawbacks. A pie made with Grannies alone was too sour and a bit dull in flavor, while an all-McIntosh pie was too soft, more like applesauce in a crust than apple pie. A pie made with both varieties, however, was outstanding. The Grannies hold up well during cooking, and the Macs add flavor. The mushy texture of the Macs becomes a virtue in this setting, providing a nice base for the harder Grannies and soaking up some of the juice.

We also tested a dozen not-so-common apple varieties, the kinds you may see in local markets during the fall, especially if you live near apple orchards. We found that Macoun, Royal Gala, Empire, Winesap, Rhode Island Greening, and Cortland apples all make excellent pies. Unlike Granny Smiths, these well-balanced apples work well on their own without thickeners or the addition of McIntosh.

We have always used butter in our pies. In fact, we used to use up to 6 tablespoons in a deep-dish pie, cutting this back to a more modest 2 tablespoons over the years. But when we taste-tested pies with and without butter, the leaner pies won hands down. Butter simply dulls the fresh taste of apples, so now we do without it altogether. Lemon juice, however, is absolutely crucial to a good apple pie, heightening the flavor of the apples rather than dulling or masking it. In the end, we settled on 1 tablespoon of lemon juice and 1 teaspoon of zest.

To our thinking, many recipes call for too much thickener (usually flour), and the result is a lifeless filling. A bit of tart, thin juice gives the pie a breath of the orchard, whereas a thick, syrupy texture is dull. In the end, we prefer to thicken the filling for our apple pie very lightly, with just 2 tablespoons flour.

Many cookbooks claim that letting apples sit in a bowl with the sugar, lemon juice, and spices, otherwise known as macerating, is key in developing flavors and juice. We found, however, that this simply caused the apples to dry out, making them rubbery and unpleasant. In addition, the apples themselves lose flavor, having exuded all of their fruitiness into the juice. So macerating, a common step in apple pie making, was clearly out.

In many apple pies, the top crust sets up quickly, leaving an air space between it and the apples, which reduce in volume as they cook. With our crust recipe, however, this is not an issue. Sufficient shortening is cut into the flour so that the crust sinks down onto the apples as they cook. We did notice, however, that this high ratio of shortening produces a very flaky crust, one that is not easily cut into perfect slices. In addition, because there is still a fair amount of juice, which we find essential for good flavor, the filling may spread slightly once the pie is cut into individual slices.

WHAT WE LEARNED: If relying on supermarket apples, use a blend of Granny Smiths for tartness and firmness and McIntosh for flavor and thickening ability. Butter dulls the flavor of the apples (the crust has plenty, anyway), while lemon juice brightens their flavor. Use just a whisper of flour to thicken the filling.

CLASSIC APPLE PIE serves 8

When all of the apples have been sliced, you should have a total of about 8 cups. The pie is best eaten when cooled to room temperature, or even the next day.

1	recipe American Pie Dough (page 301)
1½	pounds Granny Smith apples (about 3 medium)
2	pounds McIntosh apples (about 4 large)
1	tablespoon juice and 1 teaspoon zest from 1 lemon
¾	cup (5.25 ounces) plus 1 tablespoon sugar
2	tablespoons all-purpose flour
¼	teaspoon salt
¼	teaspoon ground nutmeg
¼	teaspoon ground cinnamon
⅛	teaspoon ground allspice
1	egg white, beaten lightly

1. Adjust oven rack to lowest position and heat rimmed baking sheet and oven to 500 degrees. Remove one piece of dough from refrigerator (if refrigerated longer than 1 hour, let stand at room temperature until malleable).

2. Roll dough on lightly floured work surface or between two large sheets of plastic wrap to 12-inch disk. Transfer dough to pie plate by rolling dough around rolling pin and unrolling over 9½-inch pie plate or by folding dough in quarters, then placing dough point in center of pie plate and unfolding. Working around circumference of pie plate, ease dough into pan corners by gently lifting dough edges with one hand while pressing around pan bottom with other hand. Leave dough that overhangs lip of pie plate in place; refrigerate dough-lined pie plate.

3. Peel, core, and cut apples in half, and in half again width-wise; cut quarters into ¼-inch slices and toss with lemon juice and zest. In a medium bowl, mix ¾ cup sugar, flour, salt, and spices. Toss dry ingredients with apples. Turn fruit mixture, including juices, into chilled pie shell and mound slightly in center.

4. Roll out second piece of dough to 12-inch disk and place over filling. Trim top and bottom edges to ½ inch beyond pan lip. Tuck this rim of dough underneath itself so that folded edge is flush with pan lip. Flute edging or press with fork tines to seal. Cut four slits on dough top. If pie dough is very soft, place in freezer for 10 minutes. Brush egg white onto top of crust and sprinkle evenly with remaining 1 tablespoon sugar.

5. Place pie on baking sheet and lower oven temperature to 425 degrees. Bake until top crust is golden, about 25 minutes. Rotate pie and reduce oven temperature to 375 degrees; continue baking until juices bubble and crust is deep golden brown, 30 to 35 minutes longer.

6. Transfer pie to wire rack; cool to room temperature, at least 4 hours.

APPLE PIE WITH CRYSTALLIZED GINGER

Follow recipe for Classic Apple Pie, adding 3 tablespoons chopped crystallized ginger to apple mixture.

APPLE PIE WITH DRIED FRUIT

Macerate 1 cup raisins, dried sweet cherries, or dried cranberries in lemon juice plus 1 tablespoon applejack, brandy, or cognac. Follow recipe for Classic Apple Pie, adding macerated dried fruit and liquid to apple mixture.

APPLE PIE WITH FRESH CRANBERRIES

Follow recipe for Classic Apple Pie, increasing sugar to 1 cup (7 ounces) and adding 1 cup fresh or frozen cranberries to apple mixture.

SCIENCE DESK:
What Makes Pastry Flaky?

WHY IS IT THAT SOME COOKS PRODUCE PIE CRUSTS THAT are consistently tender and flaky, while others repeatedly deliver tough, cookie-like crusts? Part of the answer has to do with butter, and the degree to which it is incorporated in the dough. While shortening makes a big contribution to the flakiness, our pie crust also benefits from relatively large pieces of butter. As the butter melts during baking, evaporation produces steam. The steam creates pockets in the dough, which help to make it flaky.

When a dough is overprocessed and the butter is dispersed too evenly, it coats the flour and prevents it from absorbing liquid; the same thing happens when a dough is made with oil. The result is a crumbly dough rather than a flaky one. Underprocessing, however, will create a tough dough, because the fat has failed to coat the flour enough.

EQUIPMENT CORNER: Paring Knives

AS WE SLICED OUR WAY THROUGH MORE THAN 100 pounds of apples en route to developing these apple pie recipes, the easiest way to peel, core, and slice apples became a hotly debated subject. We began to wonder about all those kitchen gadgets designed to help with some or all phases of apple preparation. Glancing through some catalogs, we came across apple corers, corer/slicers, and a fancy crank-operated gizmo that peels, cores, and slices in a single motion. In addition, we found small paring knives with special curved blades, called bird's beak knives, specifically designed for peeling round fruits. We decided to give them all a try.

Most corers have a diameter between ¾ inch and ⅞ inch (ours was ¾ inch), which is too small to consistently remove all of the seeds and the seed cavity. We had the same

Brae-
burn

Golden
Del.

Pink
Lady

Fu

problem with the corer/slicers, plus the slices were thicker than we wanted. Crank-operated apple-paring machines were something of an improvement, but they didn't wow us. This tool works best with very hard, fresh fruit. Some of our Macs were less than perfectly firm, and the peeling blade slid right over the skin, failing to do its job. When the peeling blade did work well on a firm Granny Smith, it showered us with apple juice as it peeled.

We then went back to the tried-and-true method, using a paring knife. We tested the straight-edged paring knife against the curved blade of the bird's beak model, but none of the testers found the bird's beak to be significantly easier to use or more effective.

But which paring knife is best? Prices range from a modest $5 plus change to a grand $50, which invites the obvious question for a home cook: Is the most expensive knife really 10 times better than the cheapest model? To find, out we put seven all-purpose paring knives through a series of kitchen tests, including peeling and slicing shallots, peeling and slicing apples and turnips, coring tomatoes, peeling and mincing fresh ginger, and slicing lemons and limes.

The way the knives were made (by forging or stamping) wasn't much of a factor in our ratings of paring knives. By definition, a paring knife is used for light tasks where weight and balance are not terribly important (it doesn't take huge effort to peel an apple). The way the handle felt in testers' hands was much more important. Most testers preferred medium-sized, ergonomically designed plastic handles. Slim wooden handles were harder to grasp. Testers also preferred paring knives with flexible blades, which make it easier to work in tight spots. Peeling turnips or sectioning oranges is much easier done with a flexible than a stiff blade. Stiffer blades are slightly better at mincing and slicing, but these are secondary tasks for paring knives. Among the knives tested, expensive forged knives from Wüsthof and Henckels performed well, as did an inexpensive stamped knife made by Forschner.

FREE-FORM APPLE TART

WHAT WE WANTED: Something simpler than apple pie, with a tender, sturdy crust, moist filling, and rich apple flavor.

A free-form apple tart (called a crostata in Italy or a galette in France) is made in the shape of a flat disk. The dough is rolled out into a circle, the filling is piled in the center, and the dough is then gathered up along the edges to form a border around the filling. Because a free-form tart has only a single crust that does not have to be fitted into a pie plate, it's easier to make a tart than a pie. Even so, a number of things can go wrong.

Because a tart has no top crust to seal in moisture, the apple filling can dry out during baking. Another consideration is the type of dough used to form the tart. It must be sturdy enough to contain the filling while also providing a complementary texture and flavor.

We started with the filling. Obviously, the variety of apple used would be key. And the method used to prepare the apples would affect their taste and texture. Should they be sliced thick or thin when placed in the tart? Should they be precooked or raw?

To answer these questions, we gathered some of the most commonly available apple varieties: Granny Smith, Gala, McIntosh, Braeburn, Fuji, and Red and Golden Delicious. We tested each type in a tart. In every case but one the apples cooked up tough, dry, and leathery. The exception was the McIntosh, which baked to the other extreme; they were so moist that they turned to mush.

Of the varieties tested, we found that Granny Smiths, Galas, and McIntosh had the most distinct flavor after being baked. It looked like the solution that had worked in our Classic Apple Pie recipe (to combine Grannies with Macs) would here, too. We tested Macs with both Granny Smiths and Galas and, sure enough, tasters preferred the Granny-Mac combo. The apple filling had good apple flavor and a decent texture, but it was still a bit dry.

Next we attempted to cook the apples before placing them in the tart, hoping this would make the filling more moist. We sautéed the apples, reduced their cooking juices, and added the liquid to the tart. This was not a success. The apples turned mushy, and the pure apple flavor we had wanted to preserve was lost during precooking.

We returned to our original method—layering raw apple slices into the tart—but this time sliced them thinner and increased the oven temperature. These thinner slices were more moist, but still not perfect. A colleague suggested that we sprinkle the apples with sugar as they cooked. This turned out to be a great idea; the sugar prevented the apples from drying out in the oven and the filling was moist but not runny. When sugar is sprinkled on top of fruit during baking, it combines with some of the moisture the fruit has released and forms a syrup. This syrup doesn't give up water easily and thus keeps the filling moist.

With the filling done, we focused on the crust. Our basic pie dough had been working fine, but we wondered if we might make some improvements. Several test cooks felt that an all-butter crust would be appropriate because flakiness is not such an issue here. We made two tarts, one with an all-butter crust, the other with a butter-and-shortening crust. Tasters appreciated the richer flavor of the all-butter crust. Everyone agreed that the dough could be a tad sweeter.

Our free-form tart was perfect, but several test cooks wanted individual tartlets. With a few minor modifications, we were able to produce six tartlets with minimal extra effort. Since tartlets are so much easier to serve than a single tart (no cutting or messy slices), we made them the master recipe. The single tart is offered as a variation.

WHAT WE LEARNED: Use a combination of Granny Smith and McIntosh apples for best flavor and texture. Slice the apples thin, don't bother precooking them, but do sugar the apples during baking to keep them moist.

FREE-FORM APPLE TARTLETS   serves 6

When all of the apples have been sliced, you should have a total of about 6 cups. Use a rimmed baking sheet to catch any juices released during baking. Serve the warm tartlets with a scoop of ice cream or lightly sweetened whipped cream (see page 294).

  1 recipe American Pie Dough for Free-Form Tart
     (page 301)
1¼ pounds Granny Smith apples (about 3 small)
1¼ pounds McIntosh apples (about 3 medium)
  2 tablespoons juice from 1 lemon
  ¼ cup (1.75 ounces) plus 2 tablespoons sugar
  ¼ teaspoon ground cinnamon
  2 large egg whites, beaten lightly

1. Remove dough from refrigerator (if refrigerated longer than 1 hour, let stand at room temperature until malleable). Cut dough into 6 equal pieces and flatten into 3-inch disks. Working one at a time, roll out disks between two sheets of lightly floured parchment paper into circles about 6 inches in diameter. Peel off top sheets of parchment and discard; trim bottom sheets of parchment to rectangles about 2 inches larger than dough. Stack rectangles with parchment on plate; cover plate with plastic wrap and refrigerate while preparing fruit.

2. Peel, core, and cut apples into ¼-inch-thick slices and toss with lemon juice, ¼ cup sugar, and cinnamon in large bowl.

3. Remove dough from refrigerator and arrange parchment-lined dough rounds in single layer on work surface. Following illustrations 1 and 2 on page 308, arrange about 1 cup apple slices, thick edges out, in circular mound on each dough round, leaving 1-inch border of dough. Fold dough border up and over filling, pleating dough to fit snugly around apples. With cupped hands, gently press dough toward filling, reinforcing shape and compacting apples (see illustration 3 on page 308). Using parchment lining for support, slide 3 tartlets onto each of 2 rimmed baking sheets. Chill formed tartlets on pans for 30 minutes.

4. Adjust one oven rack to highest position and other rack to lowest position; heat oven to 400 degrees. Slide pans with tartlets into oven and bake until pale golden brown, about 15 minutes. Brush crusts with beaten egg whites and sprinkle apples with remaining 2 tablespoons sugar. Return pans with tartlets to oven, switching positions, and bake until crusts are deep golden brown and apples are tender, about 15 minutes. Remove pans from oven and cool tartlets on pans for 5 minutes. Using wide metal spatula, remove tartlets from parchment and transfer to cooling rack. Serve tartlets warm.

FREE-FORM APPLE TART

This one tart, with its large mound of apples, must bake longer and at a lower temperature than individual tartlets. This tart is formed in the same way as the individual tartlets (see illustrations at right), but on a larger scale.

1. Remove dough from refrigerator (if refrigerated longer than 1 hour, let stand at room temperature until malleable). Roll dough between two large sheets of lightly floured parchment paper to 15-inch disk. Peel off top sheet and, using parchment lining for support, slide dough onto rimmed baking sheet; cover with plastic wrap and refrigerate while preparing fruit.

2. Peel, core, and cut apples into ¼-inch-thick slices and toss with lemon juice, ¼ cup sugar, and cinnamon in large bowl.

3. Remove dough from refrigerator and arrange apple slices, thick edges out, in circular mound, leaving 3-inch border of dough. Fold dough border up and over filling, pleating dough to fit snugly around apples. With cupped hands, gently press dough toward filling, reinforcing shape and compacting apples. Chill formed tart on pan for 30 minutes.

4. Adjust oven rack to lower-middle position and heat oven to 375 degrees. Slide pan with tart into oven and bake until pale golden brown, about 30 minutes. Brush crust with beaten egg whites and sprinkle apples with remaining 2 tablespoons sugar. Return pan with tart to oven and bake until crust is deep golden brown and apples are tender, about 30 minutes. Remove pan from oven and cool tart on pan for 10 minutes. Loosen parchment where it may have stuck to pan, then, using parchment lining, slide tart onto cooling rack. Place a large, round plate on top of tart, invert tart, peel off parchment, and re-invert tart onto serving platter. Serve tart warm.

TECHNIQUE: Making Tartlets

1. Arrange apple slices in an even circle over the dough, leaving free a 1-inch perimeter of dough for a pleated edge.

2. Fill in the center with additional slices, lending support to the circular wall of apples.

3. Fold the outer lip of the dough snugly inward over the apples and cup with your hands to compress and shape.

PEACH PIE &
cherry cobbler

Nothing quite says summer like a slice of peach pie or a bowl of cherry cobbler. Add a scoop of vanilla ice cream and you've got two of the best desserts imaginable.

But peach pie and cherry cobbler can disappoint. Who hasn't made a peach pie with runny, watery filling and soggy, pale crust? Cherry cobbler can be even trickier. At least with peaches, you know that any fruit that smells and tastes good will make a decent pie. But with cherries, the home cook has no such luck. Sweet Bing cherries become insipid when baked. Sour cherries are a must. But where do you get sour cherries? The season seems to last about three weeks in many parts of the country. Is there an acceptable jarred or canned alternative to fresh fruit?

To answer these questions, we made cherry cobblers in the dead of winter. We talked to experts who had traveled behind the Iron Curtain in the 1980s searching for new cherry cultivars. We also made enough lattice tops for peach pies to cover a garden shed. We're happy to report that our efforts paid off handsomely.

Peach pie so good it
flies out of the plate.

PEACH PIE

WHAT WE WANTED: A filling that would be juicy but not soupy, a well-browned bottom crust, and an easy-to-make lattice top.

Our occasional disappointment with peach pies in the past has taught us to wait for peach season and then buy only intoxicatingly fragrant fruit, peaches ripe enough when squeezed to make you swoon. But even ripe peaches vary in juiciness from season to season and from peach to peach, making it difficult to know just how much thickener or sweetener a pie will need. Because fresh peaches are so welcome, we are inclined to forgive them if the pie they make is soupy or overly sweet or has a bottom crust that didn't bake properly.

But we wanted to remove the guesswork from this anthem to summer. We wanted to create a filling that was juicy but not swimming in liquid, its flavors neither muscled out by spices nor overwhelmed by thickeners. The crust would be buttery, flaky, and well browned on the bottom with a handsome, peekaboo lattice on the top.

Our standard recipe for pie dough is ultrarich, made with butter for flavor and shortening for flakiness (see American Pie Dough on page 301). But when we used this recipe for our first tests with peaches and a lattice-weave top crust, we were confronted with melting lattice strips. We realized that the crust on this particular pie would demand certain adjustments. We needed a sturdier dough, which meant less fat and more flour.

Our second challenge was to find a thickener that would leave the fruit's color and flavor uncompromised. Our favorite thickener for juicy fruit pies is tapioca. But past experience has taught us that tapioca works only in double-crust pies. Sure enough, when we used tapioca in our peach pie, undissolved beads of tapioca could be seen through the pie's open latticework design. We felt we could lessen the problem by pulverizing the tapioca, but that seemed like an unnecessary bother for a simple pie.

Past tests demonstrated that flour and cornstarch made their presence too obvious. Then we found an old recipe that suggested potato starch. We conducted side-by-side tests with flour, cornstarch, pulverized Minute tapioca, and potato starch. Flour and cornstarch fared no better than expected. The ground tapioca performed admirably, having no lumps. But the potato starch scored big. Its clarity outshone flour but was less cosmetically glossy than cornstarch; its thickening qualities rivaled tapioca, but there was no need for pulverizing.

Next we turned our attention to the peaches themselves. After attempting to shave a ripe peach with a vegetable peeler, we resorted to traditional blanching and found that two full minutes in boiling water were necessary to humble even the ripest of peaches. A quick dip in an ice bath stabilized the temperature of the fruit and got the peels moving.

Experimenting with different sugars, we were surprised to discover that both light and dark brown sugar bullied the peaches, while white sugar complemented them. As in most fruit pies, lemon juice brightened the flavor of the peaches. It also kept the peach slices from browning before they went into the pan. A whisper of ground cinnamon and nutmeg and a dash of salt added a note of complexity.

Trying different oven rack levels and temperatures to satisfy the browning requirements of both the top and bottom crust brought us back to our apple pie recipe (page 303), which recommends a low rack, initial high heat (425 degrees), and moderately high heat (375 degrees) to finish. We found that a glass pie dish and preheated sheet pan gave us a pleasantly firm and browned bottom crust. A quick pre-baking spritz of the lattice top with water and a sprinkle of sugar brought this pie home.

WHAT WE LEARNED: Reduce the fat in the dough for a well-structured lattice top. Use potato starch to thicken the peach filling, and season the filling gently.

LATTICE-TOP FRESH PEACH PIE serves 8

If your peaches are larger than tennis balls, you will probably need 5 or 6; if they're smaller, you will need 7 or 8. Cling and freestone peaches look identical; try to buy freestones, because the flesh will fall away from the pits easily. Use the higher amount of potato starch if the peaches are very juicy, less if they are not terribly juicy. If you don't have or can't find potato starch, substitute an equal amount of pulverized Minute tapioca ground for about 1 minute in a food processor or spice grinder. Serve the pie with vanilla ice cream or whipped cream (page 294).

1   recipe American Pie Dough for Lattice-Top Pie (page 301)
6–7 ripe, medium-sized peaches (about 7 cups when sliced)
1   tablespoon juice from 1 lemon
1   cup (7 ounces) plus 1 tablespoon sugar
    Pinch ground cinnamon
    Pinch ground nutmeg
    Pinch salt
3–5 tablespoons potato starch (see note)

1. Remove dough from refrigerator (if refrigerated longer than 1 hour, let stand at room temperature until malleable). Roll larger dough piece to 11 by 15-inch rectangle, about ⅛ inch thick; transfer dough rectangle to baking sheet lined with parchment paper. With pizza wheel, fluted pastry wheel, or paring knife, trim to even out long sides of rectangle, then cut rectangle lengthwise into eight strips, 1¼ inches wide by 15 inches long. Freeze strips on cookie sheet until firm, about 30 minutes.

2. Roll smaller dough piece on lightly floured work surface or between two large sheets of plastic wrap to 12-inch disk. Transfer dough to pie plate by rolling dough around rolling pin and unrolling over 9-inch pie plate or by folding dough in quarters, then placing dough point in center of pie plate

and unfolding. Working around circumference of pie plate, ease dough into pan corners by gently lifting dough edges with one hand while pressing around pan bottom with other hand. Leave dough that overhangs lip of pie plate in place; refrigerate dough-lined pie plate.

3. Remove dough strips from freezer; if too stiff to be workable, let stand at room temperature until malleable and softened slightly but still very cold. Following illustrations 1 through 3 on page 314, form lattice top and place in freezer until firm, about 15 minutes.

4. Meanwhile, adjust oven rack to lowest position, place rimmed baking sheet on rack, and heat oven to 500 degrees. Bring 3 quarts water to boil in large saucepan and fill large bowl with 2 quarts cold water and 2 trays ice cubes. With paring knife, score small X at base of each peach. Lower peaches into boiling water with slotted skimmer or spoon. Cover and blanch until their skins loosen, about 2 minutes. Use slotted skimmer to transfer peaches to ice water and let stand to stop cooking, about 1 minute. Cool peaches, then, starting from scored X, peel each peach, halve and pit it, and cut into ⅜-inch slices.

5. Toss peach slices, lemon juice, 1 cup sugar, cinnamon, nutmeg, salt, and potato starch in medium bowl.

6. Turn peach mixture into dough-lined pie plate. Remove lattice from freezer and place on top of filled pie. Trim lattice strips and crimp pie edges (see illustration 4 on page 314). Lightly brush or spray lattice top with 1 tablespoon water and sprinkle with remaining 1 tablespoon sugar.

7. Lower oven temperature to 425 degrees. Place pie on baking sheet and bake until crust is set and begins to brown, 25 to 30 minutes. Rotate pie and reduce oven temperature to 375 degrees; continue baking until crust is deep golden brown and juices bubble, 25 to 30 minutes longer. Cool pie on wire rack for at least 2 hours before serving.

SCIENCE DESK: How Starches Work

IN ITS NATURAL STATE, STARCH EXISTS IN THE FORM OF essentially insoluble granules. These granules only begin to absorb water with the introduction of energy in the form of heat. As the water seeps into the granules, they swell and begin to bump into one another, so that the mixture thickens. As the mixture is heated further (past 150 degrees), the starch granules begin to leak two kinds of starch molecules—amylose and amylopectin—into the liquid. These molecules, particularly the long amylose chains, form a web that traps the swollen granules, thickening the liquid even further. Amylopectin has a more limited thickening power.

When making cherry cobbler, which has a lot of juice, you want to use a starch high in amylose, such as cornstarch, that will thicken the abundant cherry juices and wine. Peaches, which give off a lot less juice than cherries, don't need such a strong starch. Here a starch higher in amylopectin, such as potato starch, is the better bet. Potato starch thickens the peach juices lightly. High-amylose cornstarch overthickens peach juices, making them gummy.

TECHNIQUE: Making a Lattice Top

1. Lay out 4 strips of dough on parchment paper. Fold the first and third strips back, then place a long strip of dough slightly to the right of the center, as shown.

2. Unfold the first and third strips over the perpendicular strips and fold the second and fourth strips back. Add a second perpendicular strip of dough. Now unfold the second and fourth strips.

3. Repeat this process with two more perpendicular strips (you will have a total of eight strips, four running in each direction). Freeze the lattice until firm, about 15 minutes.

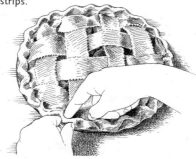

4. Place the lattice on top of the filled pie. Trim off the excess lattice ends, fold the rim of the shell up over the lattice strips, and crimp.

CHERRY COBBLER

WHAT WE WANTED: Real cherry flavor paired with a tender, feather-light, deeply browned biscuit topping.

No more than a fleet of tender biscuits on a sea of sweet fruit, good cobblers hold their own against fancy fruit desserts. But unlike fancy fruit desserts, cobblers come together in a couple of quick steps and can be dished up hot, ready to hit the dance floor with a scoop of vanilla ice cream. Picking fresh sour cherries one summer in Vermont and cooking them up into a compote for crêpes acquainted us with their virtues. Sour cherries have sufficient acidity to cook up well and become truly expressive with a touch of sugar and some heat. (Sweet eating cherries, like Bings, lose their flavor when cooked.) Until then, the only sour, or baking, cherries we had known of were the canned variety. And however plump and lacquered their depiction on the label, those that slid from under a lattice were so pale, so limp and exhausted, that their flavor barely registered. But we knew sour cherries would feel at home in a cobbler—if we could find some good ones.

Though sour cherries are grown in relatively large quantities in Michigan, here in the Northeast our grocery shelves are bereft of sour cherry products, save the crayon-red canned gravy with lumps called "pie filling." So we were grateful to find two different kinds of jarred sour cherries at our local Trader Joe's during the off season (all 11 months of it). In addition, the Cherry Marketing Institute of Michigan provided us with variously processed sour cherries—frozen, canned, and dried. Since it would be months before we could try making cobbler with fresh cherries, we began our tests with processed.

Early tests in which we prepared quick fruit fillings elicited unenthusiastic comments from tasters. While frozen Michigan sour cherries maintained their color well, flavor was left largely to the imagination. Both canned and jarred sour cherries from Michigan were flaccid and developed an anemic pallor when cooked. Adding a handful of dried cherries did little to heighten their impact. Only Trader Joe's jarred Morello cherries drew a crowd. Deep ruby red, plump, meaty, and tart, they delivered bracing flavor and a great chew right out of the jar.

This experience prompted us to do a little research. Sour cherries, we learned, are classified in two groups, amarelles and griottes. The former have lighter flesh—tan on the inside—and clear juices; the latter are dark—even black—with deep red juice. The best known examples of each group are Montmorency (an amarelle) and Morello (a griotte). Most tart cherries grown in the United States are Montmorency. Those from Eastern Europe are Morello. We decided to base our recipe on jarred Morellos.

A cobbler should be juicy, but not swimming in juice, and it should taste like the fruit whose name it bears. Jarred and canned cherries come awash in juices, which we would use to produce the sauce. Since jarred and canned cherries have already been processed, they are already cooked. The less heat they're exposed to thereafter, the better. Straining off the juice, we dumped the drained contents of four 24-ounce jars of Morellos into a 9 by 13-inch baking dish, then thickened and sweetened 3 cups of the juice. The resulting flavor was a bit flat. We replaced 1 cup of the cherry juice with red wine and added a cinnamon stick, a pinch of salt, and a whiff of almond extract. Much better. Red wine and sour cherries have a natural affinity; the cinnamon stick added a fragrant woody depth; and, as with all fruits, salt performed its usual minor miracle. The almond extract brought the entire flavor experience up a couple of notches. For thickener we resolved to go with cornstarch. It could be mixed in with the sugar and brought directly to a simmer with the reserved cherry juices, then poured over the waiting cherries and baked. Lightly thickened fruit is best; a cobbler shouldn't be thick enough to spread on toast.

We also had some requirements for the cobbles. We

wanted them feather-light but deeply browned and crisp. This said a number of things to us. The first was no eggs. Eggs would make our biscuits too heavy and substantial. (After working for years with the test kitchen's scone recipe, a light and tender English biscuit that uses no eggs, we felt supported in that expectation.) The second thing it said was buttermilk. Buttermilk biscuits are famously light and tender. We baked several biscuit variations to confirm these notions, settling on all-purpose flour, a moderate amount of butter, small amounts of baking powder and soda, a touch of sugar (plus more on top for crunch), a wave of buttermilk, and a nice hot oven. Dispensing with rolling altogether, we simply dropped the biscuits onto the fruit. The biscuits had a buttery lightness, a mild tang, and a crunchy, sugary top.

Not quite satisfied with their pale bellies touching the fruit, we undertook to bake the biscuits for 15 minutes on a baking sheet while the filling was coming together on the stove. We then wedded them to the fruit for only 10 minutes in the oven. By then the fruit (already hot from the cooked sauce) was bubbling around the biscuits, which were deeply browned on top and baked through underneath. Heaven in about a half-hour.

Jarred Morellos made a fine cobbler. But we wanted more, and, finally, summer came. Searching for fresh cherries, we made an exciting discovery: Morello cherries had made their way to the United States.

In 1984, well before unrestricted travel and commerce in Eastern Bloc countries became commonplace, Dr. Amy Iezzoni, professor of horticulture at Michigan State University, traveled extensively throughout Hungary to locate a vigorous sour cherry cultivar she could bring home to Michigan. Having spent years hybridizing local sour cherry seedlings, Hungarian breeders were prepared to release new cultivars with improved characteristics.

Iezzoni returned home with a dazzling Morello cultivar, which she named Balaton (after a lake in its native environs). She enlisted it in her breeding program, currently the only sour cherry breeding program in the United States. Under her care, the Balaton has thrived in its new climate.

Unlike the fragile and perishable Montmorency (a 400-year-old cultivar that has not been subject to cross-breeding to make it more vigorous), Balaton cherries are robust enough once harvested to endure shipping well. They are not only larger and plumper than Montmorency cherries, but their dark juices are also beautiful and mysterious.

With this knowledge and some fresh cherries, we got to work in the test kitchen. To test available varieties, we used both Morellos and the more delicate Montmorency cherries.

And how were the fresh cobblers? Both varieties of fresh cherries graced the recipe, yielding cobblers with plump, gorgeous, deeply flavorful fruit. The Montmorency cherries bore a candy apple red and a flavor resonant with almond accents; the fresh Morellos were transcendent, with a smooth richness and complex flavor notes. If you can get your hands on fresh sour cherries during their brief season in July, buy them and start baking. And take heart. When the brief sour-cherry season is over, jarred Morello cherries will create a cobbler that is almost as wonderful.

WHAT WE LEARNED: Jarred Morello cherries are the best year-round choice for a cobbler. Spike the cherry juices with red wine and cinnamon and thicken with cornstarch. For really crisp biscuits, bake them separately for 15 minutes, then slide the biscuits over the warm cherry filling and bake just 10 minutes longer.

SOUR CHERRY COBBLER serves 12

Use the smaller amount of sugar in the filling if you prefer your fruit desserts on the tart side and the larger amount if you like them sweet. Serve with vanilla ice cream or lightly sweetened whipped cream (page 294).

biscuit topping

- 2 cups (10 ounces) unbleached all-purpose flour
- 6 tablespoons (2.6 ounces) sugar plus additional 2 tablespoons for sprinkling
- ½ teaspoon baking powder
- ½ teaspoon baking soda
- ½ teaspoon salt
- 6 tablespoons cold unsalted butter, cut into ½-inch cubes
- 1 cup buttermilk

cherry filling

- 4 (24-ounce) jars Morello cherries, drained (about 8 cups drained cherries), 2 cups juice reserved
- ¾–1 cup (5.25 to 7 ounces) sugar
- 3 tablespoons plus 1 teaspoon cornstarch
  Pinch salt
- 1 cup dry red wine
- 1 (3-inch) stick cinnamon
- ¼ teaspoon almond extract

1. Adjust rack to middle position and heat oven to 425 degrees. Line baking sheet with parchment paper.

2. In workbowl of food processor fitted with steel blade, pulse flour, 6 tablespoons sugar, baking powder, baking soda, and salt to combine. Scatter butter pieces over and process until mixture resembles coarse meal, about fifteen 1-second pulses. Transfer to medium bowl; add buttermilk and toss with rubber spatula to combine. Using a 1½- to 1¾-inch spring-loaded ice cream scoop, scoop 12 biscuits onto baking sheet, spacing them 1½ to 2 inches apart. Sprinkle biscuits evenly with 2 tablespoons sugar and bake until

lightly browned on tops and bottoms, about 15 minutes. (Do not turn off oven.)

3. Meanwhile, spread drained cherries in even layer in 9 by 13-inch glass baking dish. Stir sugar, cornstarch, and salt together in medium nonreactive saucepan. Whisk in reserved cherry juice and wine, and add cinnamon stick; set saucepan over medium-high heat, and cook, whisking frequently, until mixture simmers and thickens, about 5 minutes. Discard cinnamon stick, stir in almond extract, and pour hot liquid over cherries in baking dish.

4. Arrange hot biscuits in 3 rows of 4 over warm filling. Bake cobbler until filling is bubbling and biscuits are deep golden brown, about 10 minutes. Cool on wire rack 10 minutes; serve.

VARIATION

FRESH SOUR CHERRY COBBLER

Morello or Montmorency cherries can be used in this cobbler made with fresh sour cherries. Do not use sweet Bing cherries. If the cherries do not release enough juice after macerating for 30 minutes, cranberry juice makes up the difference.

cherry filling

- 1¼ cups (8.75 ounces) sugar
- 3 tablespoons plus 1 teaspoon cornstarch
  Pinch salt
- 4 pounds fresh sour cherries, pitted (about 8 cups), juices reserved
- 1 cup dry red wine
  Cranberry juice (if needed)
- 1 (3-inch) cinnamon stick
- ¼ teaspoon almond extract

- 1 recipe biscuit topping (see left)

1. Stir together sugar, cornstarch, and salt in large bowl; add cherries and toss well to combine. Pour wine over cherries;

let stand 30 minutes. Drain cherries in colander set over medium bowl. Combine drained and reserved juices (from pitting cherries); you should have 3 cups. If not, add enough cranberry juice to equal 3 cups.

2. While cherries macerate, prepare and bake biscuit topping.

3. Spread drained cherries in even layer in 9 by 13-inch glass baking dish. Bring liquid and cinnamon stick to simmer in medium nonreactive saucepan over medium-high heat, whisking frequently, until mixture thickens, about 5 minutes. Discard cinnamon stick, stir in almond extract, and pour hot liquid over cherries in baking dish.

4. Arrange hot biscuits in 3 rows of 4 over warm filling. Bake cobbler until filling is bubbling and biscuits are deep golden brown, about 10 minutes. Cool on wire rack 10 minutes; serve.

TASTING LAB: Vanilla Ice Cream

IS THERE A BETTER WAY TO CROWN A BOWL OF WARM cherry cobbler than with a scoop of vanilla ice cream? With so many brands on the market, we wondered which would serve our cobbler best. To find out, we gathered 20 tasters to sample eight leading national brands of vanilla ice cream, made in what's known as the French, or custard, style, with egg yolks.

Many ice cream manufacturers add stabilizers—most often carrageenan gum or guar gum—to prevent "heat shock," an industry term for the degradation in texture caused by the partial melting and refreezing that takes place when ice cream is subjected to extreme temperature changes during transit to the supermarket or when an ice cream case goes through its self-defrosting cycle. Gum additives stabilize ice cream by trapping water in the frozen mass and slowing down the growth of ice crystals during melting and refreezing.

We thought that the presence of stabilizers might affect the test results. To our surprise, this was not the case. The top two brands in our tasting, Edy's Dreamery and Double Rainbow, use stabilizers.

We also expected the nature of the ice creams' vanilla flavor—artificial or real—to affect the outcome of the test. Again we were a bit surprised with the results. Blue Bell was the only brand in the tasting that contained artificial vanilla flavor, and it rated smack-dab in the middle, thus negating any link between natural flavor and superior flavor. In fact, tasters took greater issue with several brands made with real vanilla extract—including Häagen-Dazs, Ben & Jerry's, and Edy's Grand—for tasting "artificial" and "boozy." To help explain this odd result, we contacted Bruce Tharp, an independent ice cream consultant based in Wayne, Pennsylvania. He explained that the perceived artificial and alcohol flavors are often caused by the quantity of vanilla extract added to the ice cream. That is, the more extract, the more likely one is to taste the alcohol. Although it's impossible to confirm this theory (manufacturers won't release their recipes to the public), it was clear that the absence of stabilizers and use of natural flavorings were not reliable indicators of quality.

Next up was the issue of butterfat, which contributes to smooth texture, rich flavor, and structure. By law, an ice cream can't be called an ice cream unless its prefrozen mix contains a minimum of 10 percent butterfat. Of the ice creams we tasted, butterfat content ranged from 10 to 16 percent and, in general, the higher the butterfat content, the higher the ice cream rated. Our two top-rated ice creams had butterfat contents of 14.5 percent (Edy's Dreamery) and 15 percent (Double Rainbow). The two lowest rated brands had butterfat contents of 10 to 12 percent and 13 percent.

All commercial ice cream makers also add air to the mix. Oddly enough, this helps to provide structure by dividing and distributing air cells evenly throughout the frozen mass. Without it, the ice cream would look more like an ice cube. The air that is thus incorporated into ice cream is called overrun.

While the top two ice creams had low overruns of 21

and 26 percent, our third favorite had a whopping overrun of 93.5 percent. Furthermore, the two last-place ice creams had very different overruns—26 percent and 100 percent, with 100 percent being the legal limit. Our conclusion? In general, low overrun is preferable, although butterfat content is a better measure of quality. (We also noted that some tasters preferred the fluffier high-overrun ice creams—it is, to some degree, a matter of personal preference.)

The last component we researched was emulsifiers, such as mono- and diglycerides, which are used to control the behavior of fat in ice cream by keeping it from separating out of the ice cream mass. These emulsifiers give an ice cream rigidity and strength, so even if it doesn't have much butterfat or added gums, the ice cream will maintain its round, scooped shape for a prolonged period of time. The only ice cream in our tasting with emulsifiers was also the least favored sample: Edy's Grand. So, according to our taste test, it seems that emulsifiers are not desirable.

The winner of our tasting, as mentioned above, was Edy's Dreamery, with Double Rainbow coming in second and Breyer's third. The real news, however, was the poor showing of the two best-known premium brands, Häagen-Dazs and Ben & Jerry's, which rated fourth and seventh, respectively, out of the eight brands sampled.

EQUIPMENT CORNER: Ice Cream Scoops

WE GATHERED 10 READILY AVAILABLE SCOOPS AND DIPPED OUR WAY THROUGH 20 PINTS OF VANILLA TO FIND THE BEST. We tested three basic types of scoops: classic, mechanical-release (or spring-loaded), and spade-shaped. Testers were unanimous in assigning first place—in both its own category and overall—to the Zeroll Classic Ice Cream Scoop ($22). Its thick handle was comfortable for large and small hands, and its nonstick coating and self-defrosting liquid (which responds to heat from the user's hand) contributed to perfect release, leaving only traces of melted cream inside the scoop.

Although we frequently use a mechanical-release scoop to measure out even portions of cookie and muffin batters, we found these scoops less than ideal for ice cream. They are designed for right-handed users only, and their thin, straight-edged handles were distinctly uncomfortable when considerable pressure was applied. If you need to work your way through multiple gallon-sized containers of ice cream, a spade might be for you. Our preferred model is the Zeroll Nonstick Ice Cream Spade ($19.60).

CLASSIC

These scoops sport a thick handle and curved bowl. They can be used by lefties and righties with equal comfort.

MECHANICAL-RELEASE

These scoops operate with a spring-loaded, squeezable handle (or thumb trigger) that connects to a curved steel lever inside the scoop.

SPADE-SHAPED

With their flat, paddle-type heads, spades are useful when you need to scoop a lot of ice cream for an ice cream cake, but they are too big to fit into pint containers.

CHILLED SUMMER
puddings
CHAPTER 25

For most American cooks, pudding is something you make on the stovetop and thicken with cornstarch. Think chocolate pudding or butterscotch. When you replace the cornstarch with eggs and bake the dessert in the oven, you have something French, a custard such as pot de crème or crème brûlée. Whether made on the stove or in the oven, these desserts are rich and probably best suited to the cooler months.

But puddings don't have to be thickened with eggs or cornstarch. There are lighter options—made with or accompanied by fruit—that are perfect for summer eating.

Summer pudding is an English classic, a sort of trifle without the custard and whipped cream. Stale bread and superripe berries are layered together to create a stunning, refreshing ode to summer.

Panna cotta is the Italian "pudding" of the moment. Unlike crème brûlée or crème caramel, this cream-based, custard-like recipe doesn't contain eggs. Gelatin is the thickener in this bright white, wobbly pudding. Without any eggs, the focus remains on the dairy and vanilla. Raspberry sauce dresses up panna cotta and adds a bracing contrast in color and flavor.

"Fools" have a long history in Britain. Nothing more than cooked fruit and whipped cream, this chilled summer dessert is as simple as it is elegant. With its cool, creamy texture, fool is the perfect way to end a summer meal.

In the busy test kitchen, there's always an extra pair of hands to steady a strainer.

SUMMER PUDDING

WHAT WE WANTED: Sweet-tart berries melded with sliced bread to form a cohesive pudding.

Summer pudding doesn't fit the rich, creamy, silky pudding archetype. In this classic English dessert, ripe, fragrant, lightly sweetened berries are gently cooked to coax out their juices, which are used to soak and soften slices of bread to make them meld with the fruit. This mélange of berries and bread is usually weighted down with heavy cans, then chilled overnight until it is cohesive enough to be unmolded.

We have always been intrigued by this "pudding," drawn in by its rustic, unaffected appeal. Unfortunately, many summer puddings are sweet, and the bread often seems to stand apart from the fruit, as if it were just a casing. We wanted sweet-tart berries and bread that melded right with them.

In a typical summer pudding, berries fill a bowl or mold of some sort that has been neatly lined with crustless bread. Some recipes say to line the bowl with full slices, laying them flat against the bottom and sides of the bowl. Others have you cutting the slices down into triangles and rectangles and arranging them such that when unmolded they form an attractive pattern. Well, trimming the crusts is easy, but trimming the bread to fit the bowl, then lining the bowl with the trimmed pieces, is a bit fussy. After making a couple of puddings, we quickly grew tired of this technique; it seemed to undermine the simplicity of the dessert.

We came across a couple of recipes that called for layering the bread right in with the berries instead of using it to line the bowl. Not only is this bread-on-the-inside method easier, but a summer pudding made in this fashion looks spectacular—the berries on the outside are brilliant jewels. Meanwhile, the layers of bread on the inside almost melt into the fruit.

Our next adjustment to this recipe was to lose the bowl as a mold. We switched instead to a loaf pan. Its rectangular shape requires less trimming of bread slices, and, once unmolded, the pudding better retains its shape. Besides, this version was simply more beautiful than a round one made in a bowl. When we tried making individual summer puddings in ramekins, we found them to be hardly more labor-intensive in assembly than a single large serving. Sure, you have to cut out rounds of bread to fit the ramekins, but a cookie cutter makes easy work of it, and individual servings transform this humble dessert into an elegant one. The individual puddings are also easily served. You simply unmold them into bowls; there's no slicing or scooping involved.

With the form set, we moved on to the ingredients. For 4 pints of berries we were using, ¾ cup sugar was a good amount of sweetener. Lemon juice, we found, perked up the berry flavors and rounded them out. We then sought alternatives to cooking the fruit in an attempt to preserve its freshness. We mashed first some and then all of the berries

with sugar. We tried cooking only a portion of the fruit with sugar. We macerated the berries with sugar. None of these methods worked. These puddings, even after being weighted and chilled overnight, had an unwelcome crunchy, raw quality. The berries need a gentle cooking to make their texture more yielding, more puddinglike, if you will. But don't worry—five minutes is all it takes, not even long enough to heat up the kitchen.

So far, we had been using a mix of strawberries, raspberries, blueberries, and blackberries and were pleased with the variety of flavors, textures, and colors. Strawberries made up the bulk, contributing the most substance and sweetness. Raspberries easily break down with the gentle cooking, providing much juice along with their distinct flavor. Blackberries and blueberries are more resistant; they retain their shape and unique textures. And their deep color is a beautiful addition, like sapphires in a pool of rubies.

The next obvious ingredient to investigate was the bread. We tried six different kinds as well as pound cake (for which we were secretly rooting). Hearty, coarse-textured sandwich bread and a rustic French loaf were too tough and tasted fermented and yeasty. Soft, pillowy sandwich bread became soggy and lifeless when soaked with juice. The pound cake, imbibed with berry juice, turned into wet sand and had the textural appeal of sawdust. A good-quality white sandwich bread with a medium texture, somewhere between Wonder bread and Pepperidge Farm, was good, but there were two very clear winners: challah and potato bread. Their even, tight-crumbed, tender texture and light sweetness were a perfect match for the berries. Challah, available in the bakery section of most grocery stores, is usually sold in unsliced braided loaves and therefore makes for irregular slices. We decided to sidestep this complication and go with potato bread, which tastes every bit as good as challah in this recipe but comes in convenient bagged and sliced loaves.

Most summer pudding recipes call for stale bread. And for good reason. Fresh bread, we found, when soaked with those berry juices, turns to mush. You might not think this would be so noticeable with the bread layered between all those berries, but every single taster remarked that the pudding made with fresh bread was soggy and gummy. On the other hand, stale bread absorbs some of the juices and melds with the berries while maintaining some structural integrity. We tried different degrees of staleness. A day-old loaf was still too fresh, but bread left out long enough to become completely dry easily cracked and crumbled under the cookie cutter or bread knife. We found that simply leaving slices out overnight until they were dry to the touch but still somewhat pliable resulted in bread that was easy to cut and also tasted good in the pudding.

We encountered a few recipes with instructions to butter the bread. Since pound cake doesn't work in a summer pudding, we thought that this might be a nice way of adding a subtle richness. Wrong. The coating of butter prevented the juices from thoroughly permeating the bread and also dulled the vibrant flavor of the berries.

Probably the oddest thing about summer pudding is the fact that it is weighted as it chills. What, we wondered, does this do for the texture? And how long does the pudding need to chill? We made several and chilled them with and without weights for 4, 8, 24, and 30 hours. The puddings chilled for 4 hours tasted of underripe fruit. The bread was barely soaked through, and the berries barely clung together. At 8 hours the pudding was at its peak: The berries tasted fresh and held together, while the bread melted right into them. Twenty-four hours and the pudding was still good, though a hairsbreadth duller in color and flavor. After 30 hours the pudding was well past its prime and began to smell and taste fermented.

No matter how long they chilled, the summer puddings without weights were loose. They didn't hold together after unmolding, the fruit was less cohesive, and the puddings less pleasurable to eat.

WHAT WE LEARNED: Cook the berries lightly to release their juices, layer the berries with slices of stale potato, challah, or white bread, then weight the pudding to create the proper texture.

INDIVIDUAL SUMMER BERRY PUDDINGS

serves 6

Stale the bread for this recipe by leaving it out overnight; it should be dry to the touch but not brittle. Otherwise, put the slices on a rack in a single layer into a 200-degree oven for 50 to 60 minutes, turning them once halfway through. For this recipe, you will need six 6-ounce ramekins and a round cookie cutter of slightly smaller diameter than the ramekins. If you don't have the right size cutter, use a paring knife and the bottom of a ramekin (most ramekins taper toward the bottom) as a guide for trimming the rounds. Challah is the second choice for bread but will probably need to be cut into slices about ½ inch thick. If both potato bread and challah are unavailable, use a good-quality white sandwich bread with a dense, soft texture. Summer pudding can be made up to 24 hours before serving, but any longer and the berries begin to lose their freshness. Lightly sweetened whipped cream (page 294) is the perfect accompaniment to summer pudding.

> 2   pints strawberries, rinsed, hulled, and sliced
> 1   pint raspberries
> ½   pint blueberries
> ½   pint blackberries
> ¾   cup (5.25 ounces) sugar
> 2   tablespoons juice from 1 lemon
> 12 slices stale potato bread, challah, or other
>   good-quality white bread (see note)
>   Nonstick vegetable cooking spray

1. Heat strawberries, raspberries, blueberries, blackberries, and sugar in large nonreactive saucepan over medium heat, stirring occasionally, until berries begin to release their juice and sugar has dissolved, about 5 minutes. Off heat, stir in lemon juice; let cool to room temperature.

2. While berries are cooling, use cookie cutter to cut out 12 bread rounds that are slightly smaller in diameter than ramekins (see illustration 1 for individual summer puddings on page 325).

3. Spray six 6-ounce ramekins with vegetable cooking spray and place on rimmed baking sheet. Following illustrations 2 through 6 for individual summer puddings on page 325, assemble, cover, and weight summer puddings and refrigerate for at least 8 and up to 24 hours.

4. Remove weights, cookie sheet, and plastic wrap. Run paring knife around perimeter of each ramekin, unmold into individual bowls, and serve immediately.

VARIATION

LARGE SUMMER BERRY PUDDING   serves 6 to 8

To ensure that this larger pudding unmolds in one piece, use a greased loaf pan lined with plastic wrap. Because there is no need to cut out rounds for this version, you will need only about 8 bread slices, depending on their size.

Follow recipe for Individual Summer Berry Puddings through step 1. While berries are cooling, remove crusts from bread slices and trim so slices will fit in single layer in 9 by 5-inch loaf pan (see illustration 1 for large summer pudding on page 325). (You will need about 2½ slices per layer and a total of three layers.) Coat loaf pan with vegetable cooking spray and line with plastic wrap. Make sure wrap lays flat against surface of pan, leaving no air space. Place loaf pan on rimmed cookie sheet, and use slotted spoon to place about 2 cups of fruit into bottom of pan (see illustration 2 for large summer pudding on page 325). Lightly soak enough bread slices for one layer in fruit juices and place on top of fruit. Repeat with two more layers of fruit and bread (see illustration 3 for large summer pudding on page 325). Top with remaining juices, cover loosely with second sheet of plastic wrap, and weight with second cookie sheet and several heavy cans. To unmold, remove outer plastic wrap and invert onto serving platter. Lift off loaf pan, remove plastic wrap lining, slice, and serve.

TECHNIQUE: Assembling Summer Berry Puddings

FOR INDIVIDUAL SUMMER PUDDINGS:

1. For individual puddings, cut out rounds of bread with a cookie cutter.

2. With a slotted spoon, place about ¼ cup of fruit into the bottoms of greased 6-ounce ramekins that have been placed on a cookie sheet.

3. Lightly soak a round of bread in the juices and place on top of the fruit in the ramekin.

4. Divide the remaining fruit among the ramekins (about ½ cup more per ramekin).

5. Lightly soak a round of bread and place on top of fruit; it should sit above the lip of the ramekin. Pour any juices over the bread, and cover loosely with plastic wrap.

6. Place a second cookie sheet on top, then weight the sheet with several heavy cans.

FOR LARGE SUMMER PUDDING:

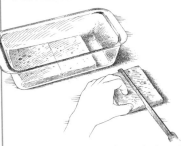  

1. Remove the crusts from the bread slices and trim the slices to fit in a single layer in the loaf pan.

2. Line the greased loaf pan with plastic wrap. Place about 2 cups of fruit into the bottom.

3. Lightly soak one layer of bread slices and place on top of fruit. Repeat 2 more times. Top with juices, cover with wrap, and weight with another loaf pan. Unmold and serve.

PANNA COTTA

WHAT WE WANTED: A delicate cream pudding that would be sturdy enough to unmold from ramekins yet delicate enough to quiver at the touch of a spoon. The flavor should scream cream (lightly sweetened) and vanilla.

Panna cotta seems to have entered the world on tiptoe—or on wing. It is included in neither Waverley Lewis Root's book *The Food of Italy* (Vintage, 1971) nor in Marcella Hazan's *Classic Italian Cook Book* (Knopf, 1973). In fact, no one seems to know much about it. Yet from virtual anonymity 25 years ago, panna cotta has achieved star status in restaurants around the country, becoming the popular successor to tiramisu.

Though its name is lyrical, the literal translation of panna cotta—"cooked cream"—does nothing to suggest its ethereal qualities. In fact, panna cotta is not cooked at all. Neither is it complicated with eggs, as is a custard. Instead, sugar and gelatin are melted in cream and milk, and the whole is then turned into individual ramekins and chilled. It is a virginal dessert, a jellied alabaster cream. It forms a richly neutral backdrop for everything it touches: strawberry coulis, fresh raspberries, light caramel, chocolate sauce.

That, we should say, describes the ideal panna cotta. There are others.

Panna cotta is about nothing if not texture. The cream must be robust enough to unmold but delicate enough to shiver on the plate. Our mission, therefore, was to find correct proportions for four simple ingredients and the most effective way to deal with the gelatin.

We began by preparing five recipes from well-known Italian cookbooks. Each of them used like ingredients in varying proportions and dealt with the ingredients similarly. Two called for powdered sugar (favored in Italian confections). A couple simmered the cream; others merely warmed it. One recipe whipped half the cream and folded it into the base. Procedurally, the recipes were extremely straightforward.

Upon tasting the different recipes, it was clear they fell into two groups. Those with higher proportions of milk were slippery and translucent, their flavor elusive and flat. Those with more cream had a rich mouthfeel and a creamier, more rounded flavor. What united these recipes most noticeably, however, was a toothsomeness, a slight rubbery chew. It was the result of too much gelatin.

It would be practical, we decided, to design the recipe around a single packet of gelatin. Given this amount, we knew we would need to establish the volume of liquid required to set up the cream. But before that we had to determine the best proportion of cream to milk, critical in terms of mouthfeel. Preliminary tastings put us on the side of a 3:1 ratio of cream to milk.

Over the next week we made dozens of panna cotti in the test kitchen. We were surprised to find textural inconsistency between batches that should have been identical. Some were flabby, others stalwart. Serendipity saved the day when we realized that the amount of gelatin included in a packet is not consistent but in fact varies widely from one packet to another. Using a gram scale, we weighed more than 50 individual gelatin packets and found weight discrepancies as great as 20 percent. In fact, in two separate packages of four we found eight different weights. As soon as we began measuring gelatin by the teaspoonful, things began looking up.

In addition to proportions, there was chilling time to consider. Preparation and chilling times should be brief and the dessert quick to the table. Our first priority, therefore, was to create the best dessert to emerge within the shortest chilling time, a panna cotta that would be firm, say, in the space of a few hours. By increasing the amount of gelatin in increments of ⅛ teaspoon, from 2 to 3 teaspoons, we found that 2¾ teaspoons produced a firm enough, yet still fragile, finished texture after four hours.

Yet we wanted the option of an overnight version as

well. Knowing that gelatin grows more tenacious over time—transforming what was a lilting mousse one evening into a bouncing sponge the next—we figured there must also be a statute of limitations on its grip. At what point would the gelatin stop advancing? Research indicated maximum rigidity was reached after about 18 hours. (See the Science Desk on page 330.) At this point we recorded the textural changes occasioned by incremental decreases in gelatin and discovered that an implausibly small decrease (⅛ teaspoon) put the overnight version on par with the texture of the four-hour version.

With flexible time options in place, we moved on to technique. Because gelatin's response is hastened by cold temperatures, it seemed reasonable to keep most of the liquid cold. Why heat all the milk and cream when we only needed hot liquid to melt the gelatin and sugar? We gave the milk this assignment, pouring it into a saucepan, sprinkling the gelatin over it, then giving the gelatin five minutes to swell and absorb liquid. Knowing that gelatin sustains damage at high temperatures, we heated the milk only enough to melt the gelatin—a couple of minutes, stirring constantly—then added the sugar off heat to dissolve. The gelatin did not melt perfectly, and we thought we might have to increase the milk's temperature. Instead, we doubled the softening time to 10 minutes, and the problem was solved.

To do its job of firming the liquid to a gel, melted gelatin must be mixed with other recipe ingredients while its molecules have enough heat energy to move through the mixture. By combining ingredients hastily in the past, we had often precipitated gelatin seizures, causing the melted gelatin to harden into chewy strings, which ruined the texture of the dessert rather than enhancing it. So we stirred the cold cream slowly into the milk to temper it.

In cooking school, several test cooks in the kitchen had learned to stir gelatin-based desserts over an ice bath—allowing the gelatin to thicken somewhat under gentle agitation—before refrigerating them to set. Besides supporting nuts, fruit, or vanilla bean throughout, this process was said to produce a finer finished texture. Hoping to avoid

this step in a recipe that was otherwise so easy, we presented tasters with side-by-side creams, one stirred first over ice, one simply refrigerated. They unanimously preferred the texture of the panna cotta chilled over ice, describing it as "lighter, creamier, and smoother." Given the results, the extra 10 minutes required did not seem unreasonable.

Now it was fine-tuning time. First place for flavor accents went to vanilla, particularly in the company of fruit sauces. We preferred whole bean to extract and Tahitian to Madagascar (see the Tasting Lab on page 329).

This is a gorgeous anytime, anywhere dessert, proving that you don't have to be flocked, layered, filigreed, or studded—you don't even have to be chocolate—to win.

WHAT WE LEARNED: Panna cotta requires more cream than milk for proper texture and richness. Soak the gelatin in cold milk, heat it briefly, and then cool it down with the cream and a quick trip to an ice bath. Measure gelatin by the teaspoon, not the packet, for accurate results. Use less gelatin if you plan on letting the panna cotta set up overnight in the refrigerator.

PANNA COTTA serves 8

Serve panna cotta very cold with strawberry or raspberry sauce or lightly sweetened berries. Though traditionally unmolded, panna cotta may be chilled and served in wine glasses and sauced on top. If you would like to make the panna cotta a day ahead, decrease the gelatin to 2⅝ teaspoons (2½ teaspoons plus ⅛ teaspoon), and chill the filled wine glasses or ramekins for 18 to 24 hours. For more information about how gelatin works, see the Science Desk on page 330.

1	cup whole milk
2¾	teaspoons gelatin
3	cups heavy cream
1	piece vanilla bean, 2 inches long, slit lengthwise with paring knife (or substitute 2 teaspoons extract)
6	tablespoons (2.6 ounces) sugar
	Pinch salt
	Raspberry or Strawberry Coulis (recipes follow)

1. Pour milk into medium saucepan; sprinkle surface evenly with gelatin and let stand 10 minutes to hydrate gelatin. Meanwhile, turn contents of two ice cube trays (about 32 cubes) into large bowl; add 4 cups cold water. Measure cream into large measuring cup or pitcher. With paring knife, scrape vanilla seeds into cream; place pod in cream along with seeds and set mixture aside. Set eight 4-ounce ramekins on baking sheet.

2. Heat milk and gelatin mixture over high heat, stirring constantly, until gelatin is dissolved and mixture registers 135 degrees on instant-read thermometer, about 1½ minutes. Off heat, add sugar and salt; stir until dissolved, about 1 minute.

3. Stirring constantly, slowly pour cream with vanilla into saucepan containing milk, then transfer mixture to medium bowl and set bowl over ice water bath. Stir frequently until thickened to the consistency of eggnog and mixture registers 50 degrees on an instant-read thermometer, about 10 minutes. Strain mixture into large measuring cup or pitcher, then distribute evenly among ramekins. Cover baking sheet with plastic wrap, making sure that plastic does not mar surface of cream; refrigerate until just set (mixture should wobble when shaken gently), 4 hours.

4. To serve, spoon some raspberry or strawberry coulis onto each individual serving plate. Pour 1 cup boiling water into small, wide-mouthed bowl, dip ramekin filled with panna cotta into water, count to three, and lift ramekin out of water. With moistened finger, press lightly on periphery of panna cotta to loosen edges. Dip ramekin back into hot water for another three-count. Invert ramekin over your palm and loosen panna cotta by cupping your fingers between panna cotta and edges of ramekin. Gently lower panna cotta onto small serving plate with coulis. Repeat process with remaining ramekins of panna cotta. Serve immediately.

TECHNIQUE:
Making Raspberry Coulis

Pour the cooked berries into a fine-mesh strainer and use the back of a large spoon or a rubber spatula to push the puree through the strainer and into a bowl. Discard the seeds.

RASPBERRY COULIS makes about 1½ cups

24   ounces frozen raspberries (6 cups)
⅓   cup (2.3 ounces) sugar
¼   teaspoon lemon juice
     Pinch salt

1. Place frozen raspberries in 4-quart nonreactive saucepan. Cover, turn heat to medium-high, and bring to simmer, stirring occasionally, for 10 to 12 minutes. Add sugar and raise heat to high. Boil for 2 minutes.

2. Strain berries through fine-mesh strainer into bowl, using rubber spatula to push berries through strainer; discard seeds. Stir in lemon juice and salt. Cover and refrigerate until chilled, at least 2 hours and up to 3 days.

VARIATION
STRAWBERRY COULIS
Follow recipe for Raspberry Coulis, replacing raspberries with equal amount of frozen strawberries and increasing sugar to ½ cup (3.5 ounces). Increase simmering time in step 1 to 12 to 14 minutes.

TASTING LAB:
Vanilla Beans and Extracts

ALMOST TWO-THIRDS OF THE WORLD'S SUPPLY OF VANILLA beans comes from Madagascar, an island off the eastern coast of Africa. Significant amounts of vanilla beans are also grown in Mexico and Tahiti. Tahitian beans are a hybrid that originated spontaneously on several islands in the South Pacific. Beans grown everywhere else in the world, including Mexico and Madagascar, are from the same species.

Although vanilla beans are convenient to use in custards (the pods are split lengthwise, the seeds scraped into the liquid, and the pods usually added to infuse more flavor), extracts make the most sense for baking jobs, including cakes and cookies. (You could make vanilla sugar by nestling a split bean in some sugar, but this process takes about a week.)

When shopping for extracts, you have two basic choices—pure extract and imitation. Pure vanilla extract is made by steeping chopped vanilla beans in an alcohol and water solution. Imitation vanilla extract is made from vanillin, a product extracted from conifer wood pulp.

When developing our panna cotta recipe, we tried several kinds of beans and extracts. Tasters preferred the flowery flavor of the Tahitian vanilla beans to other vanilla beans. Most experts believe that Tahitian vanilla beans have a more intoxicating aroma, which we found really shines in an eggless custard. That said, tasters preferred panna cotta made with any kind of vanilla bean to those made with extract, so feel free to use other beans. We should note that the presence of black specks is a visual clue that may have influenced tasters when comparing panna cotti made with beans to those made with extracts. In the photo on the opposite page, Chris wears a sleeping mask to prevent him from picking out the samples made with vanilla beans.

If using extract, we wondered if the brand matters, or if you can tell the difference between real and imitation extract. We made panna cotti with nine extracts (seven real, two imitation) and gathered eighteen tasters. We also followed a standard tasting protocol in the vanilla business and mixed each extract with milk at a ratio of 1 part extract to 8 parts milk. Although you would never use so much extract in a real application, this high concentration makes it easier to detect specific characteristics in extracts.

The results of this tasting were so shocking that we repeated it, only to come up with similarly surprising findings. Tasters couldn't tell the difference between real and imitation vanilla. In fact, in the panna cotta tasting, the imitation extracts took first and third place, with Nielsen-Massey and Penzeys leading the pack among real extracts. In the milk tasting, the imitation extracts took the top two spots, followed by real extracts from Nielsen-Massey and Penzeys. Further tests in shortbread confirmed these results. Although we are loath to recommend an imitation product, it seems that most people don't mind imitation extract and, in fact, many tasters actually like its strong flavor.

SCIENCE DESK: How Gelatin Works

GELATIN IS A FLAVORLESS, NEARLY COLORLESS SUBSTANCE derived from the collagen in animals' connective tissue and bones, extracted commercially, and dehydrated. Most culinary uses for gelatin rely on a two-step process—soaking and then dissolving. Gelatin is usually soaked in some cool or cold liquid so it can swell and expand. It is then dissolved in a hot liquid and finally chilled to set.

This dual process results from the fact that when unsoaked gelatin is added directly to hot liquid, the outside edges of each granule expand instantly and form a gel coating, preventing the inside from becoming hydrated. The center of each gelatin particle then remains hard and undissolved. The resulting gelatin mixture doesn't set properly and is full of hard, granular bits.

In contrast, soaking gelatin in cold or cool liquid allows the particles to expand slowly so that they can tie up the maximum amount of liquid (up to three times their weight). Maximum rigidity in gelatin is reached after 18 hours. After that time, desserts will begin to soften again.

RHUBARB FOOL

WHAT WE WANTED: A dessert in which the tartness of the rhubarb was tamed but its true flavor and bright red color were preserved.

Fool is a quick, everyday dessert that just so happens to have a quaint and quirky British name. When we decided to try our hand at this simple dessert—essentially cooked fruit with sweetened whipped cream folded in—we sided with tradition and used rhubarb as the cooked fruit foundation. Although fool is in itself no culinary feat, working with rhubarb can prove tricky. First, its sourness can be overpowering. Second, if boiled, or cooked too hard and fast, it breaks down into a watery, porridge-like mass. Finally, its vivacious red color leaches out easily, leaving the rhubarb a drab gray. We knew that before we could finalize a fool, we would have to tame the rhubarb.

To begin our testing we tried baking the rhubarb, stewing it for a long time, sautéing it in butter, and simmering it for a short time. Baking and sautéing turned the rhubarb pulpy, chalky, and bland, while stewing produced a watery cream-of-rhubarb soup. And in each case the rhubarb lost its attractive red color, presenting instead hues that varied from gray-lavender in the baked version to pale, watery yellow in the stewed. The simmered batch, on the other hand, had a nice pinkish red color, a sweet/tart flavor, and a thick, toothsome texture.

The simmered rhubarb was not ideal, though; it was still too tart for most tasters. Looking further, we found an interesting precooking approach that purported to subdue its acidity: soaking 6-inch pieces in cold water for 20 minutes prior to cutting and simmering. When we gave this trick a try, we were surprised to find the rhubarb much less acidic, with a flavor that was more round and full. But this approach had one drawback: the color had dulled to a pale mauve.

To figure out what happened, we called Barry Swanson, a confirmed rhubarb enthusiast who is a professor of food science at Washington State University in Pullman. Swanson explained that a water-soluble pigment called anthocyanin is responsible for rhubarb's somewhat chalky, tannic mouthfeel as well as its bright pinkish red color. When we presoaked the rhubarb, a portion of the anthocyanin escaped from the rhubarb's cut ends into the water, muting the color as well as the harsh bite.

Swanson also explained that anthocyanin is sensitive to the acidity of its environment. When the pH is high (low acidity), the color shifts to the bluish gray range; when the pH is low (high acidity), the color is red. Thinking about this, we wondered what would happen if we reintroduced an acid with no bitter or tannic qualities, such as the citric acid in orange juice, while the rhubarb simmered. This test was successful. The juice added just enough acidity to restore the rhubarb red without having any ill effects on flavor. Fifty pounds later, we had finally figured out how to cook rhubarb.

We now turned our attention from the rhubarb to the whipped cream and the assembly of the fool. We tried whipping the cream to various degrees of stiffness, and everyone in the test kitchen concurred that a soft-to-medium peak was just right. It gave the fool just enough body without making it sliceable and stiff.

Fool-making tradition dictates that the cream be folded into the fruit, but this gave the dessert a somewhat dull, monochromatic texture and flavor. Arranging the fruit and cream in layers produced a more interesting result. The natural tanginess of the rhubarb played off the sweetness of the cream, and the alternating texture of fruit and cream made for a pleasing contrast.

WHAT WE LEARNED: To remove some of its bitterness, soak rhubarb in cold water for 20 minutes. To keep the color bright, simmer with orange juice. For best presentation and flavor, arrange the rhubarb and whipped cream in layers rather than folding the two elements together.

RHUBARB FOOL serves 8

For more information about buying and whipping heavy cream, see page 293. For a fancier presentation, use a pastry bag to pipe the whipped cream into individual glasses. To make one large fool, double the recipe and layer rhubarb and whipped cream in a 12-cup glass bowl.

2¼ pounds rhubarb, trimmed of ends and cut into 6-inch lengths
⅓ cup juice from 1 large orange
1 cup plus 2 tablespoons (7.9 ounces) sugar
Pinch salt
2 cups heavy cream, chilled, preferably pasteurized or pasteurized organic

1. Soak rhubarb in 1 gallon cold water for 20 minutes. Drain, pat dry with paper towels, and cut rhubarb crosswise into slices ½-inch thick.

2. Bring orange juice, ¾ cup sugar, and salt to boil in medium nonreactive saucepan over medium-high heat. Add rhubarb and return to boil, then reduce heat to medium-low and simmer, stirring only 2 or 3 times (frequent stirring causes rhubarb to become mushy), until rhubarb begins to break down and is tender, 7 to 10 minutes. Transfer rhubarb to nonreactive bowl, cool to room temperature, then cover with plastic and refrigerate until cold, at least 1 hour or up to 24.

3. Beat cream and remaining 6 tablespoons sugar in chilled bowl of standing mixer on low speed until small bubbles form, about 45 seconds. Increase speed to medium; continue beating until beaters leave trail, about 45 seconds longer. Increase speed to high; continue beating until cream is smooth, thick, and nearly doubled in volume and forms soft peaks, about 30 seconds.

4. To assemble fool, spoon about ¼ cup rhubarb into each of eight 8-ounce glasses, then spoon in layer of about ¼ cup whipped cream. Repeat, ending with dollop of cream;

serve. (Can be covered with plastic wrap and refrigerated up to 6 hours.)

VARIATIONS

STRAWBERRY-RHUBARB FOOL
Clean and hull 2 pints strawberries; quarter each berry. Follow recipe for Rhubarb Fool, substituting strawberries for 1¼ pounds rhubarb.

BLUEBERRY-RHUBARB FOOL WITH FRESH GINGER
Follow recipe for Rhubarb Fool, reducing rhubarb to 1½ pounds, adding 1 teaspoon grated fresh ginger to orange juice along with sugar and salt, and gently stirring 1 pint blueberries into rhubarb after it has simmered 2 minutes.

CHOCOLATE desserts

There's a reason why chocolates are a favorite gift on Valentine's Day. What better way to say you really care? Making a great chocolate dessert, such as a soufflé or roulade, says you really, really care.

Of course, a showy dessert that falls flat (which can happen, literally, to a soufflé) also says a lot about the cook (or recipe writer)—not much of which is probably very nice.

But never fear—the test kitchen has figured out how to make a chocolate soufflé that's nearly foolproof. You can even make the batter days in advance, spoon it into individual ramekins, freeze the batter, and then bake off the ramekins as needed. A great after-dinner soufflé without beating an egg white or melting chocolate in front of guests or loved ones—it's a minor culinary miracle.

A chocolate sponge roll cake, filled with coffee-flavored cream and covered with dark, rich chocolate ganache, is a festive way to celebrate almost any holiday. But a sponge cake that won't roll or a frosting that's gritty won't put anyone in a holiday mood. Our test cooks have figured out how to make a showy chocolate dessert with minimum fuss and maximum flavor.

IN THIS CHAPTER

THE RECIPES
Chocolate Soufflé
Individual Make-Ahead Chocolate Soufflés

Bittersweet Chocolate Roulade
Espresso-Mascarpone Cream
Dark Chocolate Ganache

EQUIPMENT CORNER
Fine-Mesh Strainers

SCIENCE DESK
How to Beat Egg Whites

TASTING LAB
Bittersweet Chocolate

Jack won't give Chris any hints as he weighs the pros and cons of four bittersweet chocolates and tries to pick out the brand that won the group tasting.

CHOCOLATE SOUFFLÉ

WHAT WE WANTED: A soufflé with big chocolate flavor, a dramatic rise above the rim, a crusty but airy outer layer, and a rich, loose center that was not completely set.

A great soufflé must convey a true mouthful of flavor, bursting with the deep, rich taste of the main ingredient. In a chocolate soufflé, the chocolate high notes should be powerful.

A primary consideration when trying to create such a soufflé is what to use as the "base," the mixture that gives substance and flavor to the soufflé as opposed to the airiness and "lift" provided by the whipped egg whites. The base can be a béchamel (a classic French sauce made with equal amounts of butter and flour, whisked with milk over heat), pastry cream (egg yolks beaten with sugar and then heated with milk), or a bouillie (flour cooked with milk or water until thickened). After trying several versions of each of these options, we found that we consistently preferred the béchamel base. It provided the soufflé with decent chocolate flavor and a puffed yet substantial texture. By contrast, the versions made with pastry cream and bouillie were too dense and puddinglike.

After a week of refining a recipe using a béchamel base, we thought the soufflé was good but that the chocolate was muted by the milk used in the béchamel. We removed the milk and flour from our recipe (which meant, essentially, no more béchamel), separated a total of six eggs and whipped the whites separately, more than doubled the amount of chocolate, and reduced the amount of butter. This approach resulted in a base of egg yolks beaten with sugar until thick, giving the soufflé plenty of volume. The result was fantastic—the most intense chocolate dessert we had ever tasted.

Our chocolate soufflé now had the intense flavor we had been looking for, but we still weren't completely happy with the texture because the outer layer was a bit cakey.

After several more experiments, though, we discovered that adding two egg whites resolved the problem, giving the soufflé more lift and a better texture.

For most recipes, a 25-degree variance in oven temperature is not crucial, so we were surprised to discover the dramatic impact it had on our soufflé. Our initial oven temperature was 400 degrees, but to be sure this temperature was optimum, we tested both 375 and 425 degrees. The higher oven temperature resulted in an overcooked exterior and an undercooked interior, while the lower temperature did not brown the exterior enough to provide as much flavor and also produced a texture that was too even, given that we were looking for a loose center at the point at which the exterior was nicely cooked. We decided to stick with 400 degrees.

A water bath was a truly awful idea. When we tested it, the outer crust of the soufflé turned out wet, with a gelatin-like appearance, and the soufflé did not rise well.

One factor we found to be of surprising importance was the baking dish. We tried using a standard casserole dish for one of the tests, and the soufflé rose right out of the dish onto the floor of the oven! The problem was that the dish did not have the perfectly straight sides of a soufflé dish. It pays to make sure that you are using a real soufflé dish.

We also tested the theory that a chilled soufflé dish improves the rise and discovered that it did cause our chocolate soufflé to rise higher. During the course of all this testing, we also found that a chocolate soufflé will give you three indications of doneness: when you can smell the chocolate, when it stops rising, and when only the very center of the top jiggles when gently shaken.

WHAT WE LEARNED: Don't block chocolate flavor by using milk or flour in the soufflé base. Just beat the yolks and sugar together and then fold in the melted chocolate and butter and, finally, the beaten egg whites.

CHOCOLATE SOUFFLÉ serves 6 to 8

See the Tasting Lab on page 343 for recommendations about specific brands of chocolate.

5	tablespoons unsalted butter (1 tablespoon softened, 4 tablespoons cut into ½-inch chunks)
1	tablespoon plus ⅓ cup (2.3 ounces) sugar
8	ounces bittersweet or semisweet chocolate, chopped fine
6	large egg yolks
½	teaspoon vanilla extract
⅛	teaspoon salt
8	large egg whites
⅛	teaspoon cream of tartar

1. Adjust oven rack to lowest position and heat oven to 400 degrees. Grease 1½-quart soufflé dish with 1 tablespoon softened butter, coating all interior surfaces. Coat bottom and sides evenly with 1 tablespoon sugar; refrigerate until ready to use.

2. Bring 2 inches water to simmer in small saucepan over medium heat. Combine chocolate and remaining 4 tablespoons butter in small heatproof bowl and cover tightly with plastic wrap. Set bowl over pan, reduce heat to medium-low, and heat until butter is almost completely melted and chocolate pieces are glossy, have lost definition, and are fully melted around edges, about 15 minutes. (Do not stir or let water boil under chocolate.) Remove bowl from pan, unwrap, and stir until smooth and glossy; set aside.

3. In bowl of standing mixer fitted with whisk attachment, beat yolks, 3 tablespoons sugar, vanilla, and salt on high speed until smooth, thick, and pale yellow, 8 to 10 minutes. Transfer mixture to medium bowl; wash mixer bowl and whisk attachment and dry with paper towels. (If you have 2 mixer bowls, leave yolk mixture in mixer bowl; wash and dry whisk attachment, and use second bowl in step 4.)

4. In clean mixer bowl with clean whisk attachment, beat whites, 1 teaspoon sugar, and cream of tartar at medium speed until combined, about 10 seconds. Increase speed to medium-high and beat until frothy and no longer translucent, 1½ to 2 minutes. With mixer running, add 1 tablespoon sugar; continue beating until soft peaks form, about 30 seconds. With mixer still running, add remaining 2 tablespoons sugar and beat to combine, about 10 seconds. Do not overbeat (if whites look dry and granular, they are overbeaten). While whites are beating, stir chocolate into yolks.

5. With rubber spatula, stir one quarter of beaten whites into chocolate mixture. Fold in remaining whites until no streaks remain (see illustrations on page 338). Gently pour mixture into prepared dish; to help soufflé rise properly, run index finger through mixture, following circumference of dish about ½ inch from edge. Bake until exterior is set, center jiggles slightly when shaken, and soufflé has risen 1½ to 2 inches above rim of dish, 20 to 25 minutes. Serve immediately.

VARIATION

INDIVIDUAL MAKE-AHEAD CHOCOLATE SOUFFLÉS serves 6

We had heard of recipes for soufflés that are prepared ahead of time, then refrigerated or frozen, and baked at the last minute. We tried both refrigerating and freezing the batter in individual ramekins. When we baked them, the refrigerated soufflés were a disaster (they hardly rose at all and were very wet inside), but the frozen version worked extremely well.

Follow recipe for Chocolate Soufflé, greasing each of six 1-cup ramekins with about ½ teaspoon softened butter and sprinkling bottom and sides of each with 1 teaspoon sugar. After folding whites into chocolate mixture, divide mixture between ramekins, set ramekins on baking sheet, cover baking sheet with plastic wrap, and freeze at least 3 hours or up to 4 days. Uncover and bake (do not defrost before baking) until exterior is set and soufflés have risen ½ to ¾ inch above rims of ramekins, 18 to 20 minutes. Serve immediately.

TECHNIQUE: Folding Beaten Egg Whites

Numerous recipes, everything from cakes to soufflés, call for beaten egg whites, which are usually folded into the batter just before it is baked. If you beat the eggs in too vigorously, the cake or soufflé may not rise. If you don't incorporate the eggs properly, you may be left with eggy patches in your baked goods. Here's the best way to fold beaten egg whites into a batter. Start by vigorously stirring a portion of the beaten whites (most recipes will call for a quarter or third of the whites) into the batter. This lightens the texture of the batter so the rest of the whites can be folded in more gently.

1. After stirring in a portion of the whites (see text above), scrape the remaining whites into the bowl. Starting at the top of the bowl, use a rubber spatula to cut through the middle of the whites.

2. Turn the edge of the spatula toward you so it moves up the sides of the bowl.

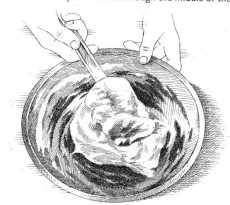

3. Continue this motion, going full circle, until the spatula is back at the center of the bowl again.

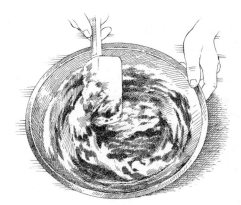

4. Follow this procedure four more times, turning the bowl a quarter turn each time. Finally, use the spatula to scrape around the entire circumference of the bowl.

SCIENCE DESK:
How to Beat Egg Whites

EGG WHITES ARE 88 PERCENT WATER AND 11 PERCENT protein; the remaining 1 percent consists of minerals and carbohydrates. When egg whites are beaten, they produce a foam. Beating an egg white relaxes its tightly wound protein molecules, which begin to unfold and stretch. With continued beating, the stretched proteins begin to overlap and bond together, creating a long, elastic surface. This is the soft-peak phase—the air bubbles are large and the foam is unstable because the proteins have not unwound and bonded to form a stable supporting structure.

With continued beating, the proteins further bond and envelop the air bubbles, trapping and separating them. This creates smaller bubbles and a more stable foam. Continuing to beat the foam after this point will cause it to become too rigid, and the liquid will be squeezed out of the whites.

When baked, these three types of foam will produce dramatically different results. Heat causes air inside the bubbles to expand, which in turns causes the entire structure to rise. The volume of stable, trapped air bubbles in the foam is what determines the success or failure of the rise. The none-too-stable foam that results from underwhipped whites will quickly deflate when combined with flour (for a cake) or a soufflé base, and the resulting baked good will be much shorter. A mixture made with overwhipped whites will suffer a similar fate when baked. The liquid squeezed out of the whites during overbeating signifies a corresponding loss of stable air pockets. In this case, a cake will appear to be fluffy and risen at first, but the overall structure will not be supported by the burst air pockets, and the structure will collapse. This is what happens when a soufflé falls.

There are other measures that can be taken to ensure a perfectly risen soufflé or cake. Adding sugar to the egg whites delays water evaporation by attracting moisture. The protein structure has more time to set up and thus can be beat longer without harmful consequences. Sugar also separates protein molecules, slowing the bonding process and guarding against overbeating. Cream of tartar, an acid, also slows down the bonding process. Acids donate hydrogen ions that interfere with the normal bonding patterns of proteins. The proteins remain more elastic, and the air cells encounter less resistance as they expand under the influence of the heat, resulting in a higher rise.

The conclusion: Smaller air bubbles that are formed slowly make the most stable foam. Beating the egg whites with sugar and cream of tartar results in a foam that is more stable and moist and will therefore rise better in the oven.

EQUIPMENT CORNER:
Fine-Mesh Strainers

A FINE-MESH STRAINER IS COVERED WITH THE SAME MATERIAL used in window screens. This mesh will trap all solid material or break up lumps in dry ingredients such as cocoa powder.

We put five fine-mesh strainers through a series of tests. We poured pureed pea soup through the strainers to test their ability to remove large solid bits. We pushed a raspberry puree through them to see how they would withstand scraping and moderate pressure. Finally, we passed pastry cream through the strainers to test their ability to catch small particles. (All fine-mesh strainers can sift dry ingredients like cocoa and flour, so we did not run this test.)

Based on these tests, we think it's imperative to buy a stainless steel strainer (aluminum can discolor acidic foods) with some heft. You don't want the strainer to buckle under moderate pressure, as several did in our tests. The finer the mesh, the better. Several strainers let solids pass through, which is unacceptable. Other strainers had handles that were uncomfortable, another no-no in our book.

Testers preferred the Williams-Sonoma Piazza 18cm Strainer ($26), which yielded perfectly smooth soup, raspberry puree, and pastry cream. The Küchenprofi 22cm Classic Strainer ($29.99) was the second choice in the test kitchen.

BITTERSWEET CHOCOLATE ROULADE

WHAT WE WANTED: A cake that would be easy to roll yet still moist, tender, and full of chocolate flavor.

A chocolate sponge cake roll—or roulade—begins life as a thin sponge cake baked quickly on a rimmed baking sheet, unmolded, and rolled up around a creamy filling. A rich frosting or glaze is often added to complement the cake and soft filling.

A sponge cake by definition contains little or no butter, and its (usually) separated eggs are whipped with sugar before the dry ingredients are folded in. Structurally speaking, a sponge cake sheet must be thin, even, and "rollable." Given the demands of its form, this cake cannot be fudgy, buttery, or rich. But it must pack serious chocolate flavor, remain moist, tender, and fine-pored, and refrain from being overly sweet.

To begin, we made five chocolate roulade recipes. Several things were immediately evident: Chemical leaveners were superfluous; cakes with more sugar failed to set the filling off to its advantage; and a rich, dark color was key to the cake's overall appeal. Only one of the cakes we baked used chocolate rather than cocoa, and that cake possessed by far the best flavor. Where every last cake fell from grace was in textural terms. We nibbled sheets of thick chocolate felt and soggy chocolate omelets. We wanted a texture that ventured to neither of these extremes.

Having chosen chocolate as the chief flavoring agent, we needed to determine which kind to use. We rejected unsweetened chocolate as too heavy-handed for this light, airy cake. Anything less than six ounces of semi- or bittersweet chocolate rendered a flavor too mild. One-third cup sugar tasted good with both semi- and bittersweet. We also added 2 tablespoons of butter to the melting chocolate. Though not enough to weigh down the cake, this small amount contributed to flavor and tenderness.

Because eggs are usually the sole liquid ingredient in a sponge cake—crucial for lightness of texture and ease of rolling—their number is key. Too few and our cake was not supple. Too many and we got either a wet chocolate sponge (if there was no flour in the recipe) or dry chocolate matting (if the proportion of eggs was too high). Six eggs provided the support necessary to blend the ingredients, the lift required to rise the cake, and the flexibility needed to roll it.

Still, even with chocolate contributing some structure, the fragile egg-and-sugar foam needed more support. We tested ¼ cup flour against the same amount of cocoa and ended up giving them equal partnership. The flour offered structural support, which kept the cake from becoming too moist after it was filled; the cocoa added a chocolatey undercurrent, which dramatically improved the overall flavor of the cake. Because the flavor of cocoa becomes more intense when it is mixed with water, we added 2 tablespoons of water to the recipe. The water helped to deepen the chocolate flavor and made the batter glossy and beautiful.

Recipes offer several techniques for coaxing sheet cakes into their customary cylindrical shape. Our cake responded best when cooled briefly in the pan on a cooling rack and then unmolded onto a kitchen towel rubbed with cocoa to prevent sticking. The cake, still quite warm, was then rolled up, towel and all. Allowed thus to cool briefly, the roll could be unrolled, retain its rolled memory, then be filled and re-rolled.

The roulade was now delectable, with a yielding, melting texture and intense chocolate flavor. It needed a rich but adaptable filling. Not wanting to crack open the cupboards and make a big mess, we decided to use a modified tiramisu filling made with lightly sweetened mascarpone and some ground espresso. A glossy layer of dark chocolate ganache put the final flavor layer in place and made the cake beautiful to gaze upon.

WHAT WE LEARNED: Use bittersweet chocolate and cocoa powder for real chocolate flavor. Butter adds some tenderness to sponge cake, while flour provides some structure.

BITTERSWEET CHOCOLATE ROULADE

serves 8 to 10

We suggest that you make the filling and ganache first, then make the cake while the ganache is setting up. Or, if you prefer, the cake can be baked, filled, and rolled—but not iced—then wrapped in plastic and refrigerated for up to 24 hours. The roulade is best served at room temperature.

6	ounces bittersweet or semisweet chocolate, chopped fine
2	tablespoons cold unsalted butter, cut into two pieces
2	tablespoons cold water
¼	cup Dutch-processed cocoa, sifted, plus 1 tablespoon for unmolding
¼	cup (1.25 ounces) unbleached all-purpose flour, plus more for baking sheet
⅛	teaspoon salt
6	large eggs, separated
⅓	cup (2.3 ounces) sugar
1	teaspoon vanilla extract
⅛	teaspoon cream of tartar
1	recipe Espresso-Mascarpone Cream (recipe follows)
1	recipe Dark Chocolate Ganache (recipe follows)

1. Adjust oven rack to upper-middle position and heat oven to 400 degrees. Spray 12 by 17½-inch rimmed baking sheet with nonstick cooking spray, cover pan bottom with parchment paper, and spray parchment with nonstick cooking spray; dust surface with flour and tap out excess.

2. Bring 2 inches water to simmer in small saucepan over medium heat. Combine chocolate, butter, and water in small heatproof bowl and cover tightly with plastic wrap. Set bowl over pan, reduce heat to medium-low, and heat until butter is almost completely melted and chocolate pieces are glossy, have lost definition, and are fully melted around edges, about 15 minutes. (Do not stir or let water boil under chocolate.) Remove bowl from pan, unwrap, and stir until smooth and glossy. While chocolate is melting, sift ¼ cup cocoa, flour, and salt together into small bowl and set aside.

3. In bowl of standing mixer fitted with whisk attachment, beat yolks at medium-high speed until just combined, about 15 seconds. With mixer running, add half of sugar. Continue to beat, scraping down sides of bowl as necessary until yolks are pale yellow and mixture falls in thick ribbon when whisk is lifted, about 8 minutes. Add vanilla and beat to combine, scraping down bowl once, about 30 seconds. Turn mixture into medium bowl; wash mixer bowl and whisk attachment and dry with paper towels. (If you have 2 mixer bowls, leave yolk mixture in mixer bowl; wash and dry whisk attachment, and use second bowl in step 4.)

4. In clean bowl with clean whisk attachment, beat whites and cream of tartar at medium speed until foamy, about

30 seconds. With mixer running, add about 1 teaspoon sugar; continue beating until soft peaks form, about 40 seconds. Gradually add remaining sugar and beat until whites are glossy and supple and hold stiff peaks when whisk is lifted, about 1 minute longer. Do not overbeat (if whites look dry and granular, they are overbeaten). While whites are beating, stir chocolate mixture into yolks. With rubber spatula, stir one quarter of whites into chocolate mixture to lighten it. Fold in remaining whites until almost no streaks remain (see illustrations on page 338). Sprinkle dry ingredients over top and fold in quickly but gently.

5. Pour batter into prepared pan; using an offset icing spatula and working quickly, even surface and smooth batter into pan corners. Bake until center of cake springs back when touched with finger, 8 to 10 minutes, rotating pan halfway through baking. Cool in pan on wire rack for 5 minutes.

6. While cake is cooling, lay clean kitchen towel over work surface and sift remaining tablespoon cocoa over towel; with hands, rub cocoa into towel. Run paring knife around perimeter of baking sheet to loosen cake. Invert cake onto towel and peel off parchment.

7. Roll cake, towel and all, into jelly roll shape. Cool for 15 minutes, then unroll cake and towel. Using offset spatula, immediately spread filling evenly over surface of cake, almost to edges. Roll up cake gently but snugly around filling. Set large sheet of parchment paper on overturned rimmed baking sheet and set cake seam-side down on top. Trim both ends on diagonal. Spread ganache over roulade with small icing spatula. Use fork to make wood-grain striations on surface of ganache before icing has set. Refrigerate baking sheet with cake, uncovered, to slightly set icing, about 20 minutes.

8. Carefully slide 2 wide metal spatulas under cake and transfer cake to serving platter. Cut into slices and serve.

ESPRESSO-MASCARPONE CREAM   makes about 2½ cups, enough to fill baked cake

Mascarpone is a fresh Italian cheese that is supple and spreadable. Its flavor is unique—mildly sweet and refreshing. It is sold in small containers in some supermarkets as well as most gourmet stores, cheese shops, and Italian markets.

½	cup heavy cream
4	teaspoons whole espresso beans, finely ground (about 2 tablespoons ground)
6	tablespoons (1.5 ounces) confectioners' sugar
16½	ounces mascarpone cheese (generous 2 cups)

1. Bring cream to simmer in small saucepan over high heat. Off heat, stir in espresso and powdered sugar; cool slightly.

2. With spatula, beat mascarpone in medium bowl until softened. Gently whisk in cooled cream mixture until combined. Cover with plastic wrap and refrigerate until ready to use.

DARK CHOCOLATE GANACHE

makes about 1½ cups, enough to cover filled roulade

Rose Levy Beranbaum, author of *The Cake Bible* (William Morrow, 1988), acquainted us with the technique of making ganache in a food processor, a method that beats all others for ease and consistency. If your kitchen is cool and the ganache becomes too stiff to spread, set the bowl over a saucepan of simmering water, then stir briefly until smooth and icing-like. We especially like Hershey's Special Dark for this recipe.

¾	cup heavy cream
2	tablespoons unsalted butter
6	ounces high-quality bittersweet or semisweet chocolate, chopped
1	tablespoon cognac

Microwave cream and butter in measuring cup on high until bubbling, about 1½ minutes. (Alternatively, bring to simmer in small saucepan over medium-high heat.) Place

chocolate in bowl of food processor fitted with steel blade. With machine running, gradually add hot cream and cognac through feed tube and process until smooth and thickened, about 3 minutes. Transfer ganache to medium bowl and let stand at room temperature 1 hour, until spreadable (ganache should have consistency of soft icing).

TASTING LAB: Bittersweet Chocolate

ACCORDING TO THE U.S. FOOD AND DRUG ADMIN-istration, there is no distinction between bittersweet and semisweet chocolate. Most chocolate manufacturers, how-ever, follow the European tradition and produce bittersweet with a higher percentage of cocoa solids (resulting in a lower percentage of sugar) than semisweet. Therefore, bittersweet chocolate has a savory edge and a more intense flavor than sweeter and mellower semisweet chocolate. We generally prefer bittersweet chocolate in desserts, although good-quality semisweet chocolate can be used with good results.

To find out how various bittersweet chocolates per-form in the kitchen, we sampled a mix of 10 American and European brands in a chocolate sauce as well as in our chocolate roulade. We found a strong correlation between results from these two tests.

Callebaut, a famed Belgian brand, took top honors. Lindt Excellence, a Swiss brand, also scored well, landing in fourth place. Several American chocolates also performed surprisingly well. The real shocker was the second-place fin-ish of Hershey's Special Dark, a chocolate sold in many drug stores and supermarkets. Merckens Yucatan Dark, a hard-to-find American brand used by professionals, took third place, and Ghirardelli, a widely available brand from California, came in fifth.

Not all American brands did well, though. Baker's, the leading brand in supermarkets, finished last. Tasters com-plained about off flavors and gritty texture. Several brands with strong followings in the trade also showed poorly. Valrhona and Scharffenberger finished near the bottom of the pack, in part because these chocolates contain very little sugar and tasters found them too potent.

The top four chocolates, both European and Ameri-can, all have a fairly clean, predictable flavor and smooth texture. No funky flavors, nothing too roasted, too potent, or too complex.

INDEX

Creamy Mushroom Soup, *97*
    best ingredients/techniques, 9–10
    sautéed wild mushrooms for, 10–11
Creamy Pea Soup
    basic recipe, 7
    best ingredients/techniques, 6
    buttered croutons for, 7
Crisp-Skin High-Roast Butterflied Turkey
    basic recipe, 166–68
    best ingredients/techniques, 164–65
    Sausage Dressing, 166
Crisp Thin-Crust Pizza, *100*
    basic recipe, 44
    with Arugula, 45
    with Tapenade, 45
Crispy Fried Chicken
    basic recipe, 88
    best ingredients/techniques, 86–87
Croutons, buttered, 7
Crusts, pie
    chocolate cookie crumb, 290
    graham cracker, 296
Currants
    and Pine Nuts, Rice Pilaf with, 151
    Tuna Salad with Apples and, 51
Curry
    Curried Coleslaw with Apples and
        Raisins, 96
    Curried Tuna Salad with Apples and
        Currants, 51
    Sweet, Marinade with Buttermilk, 144
Cutting boards, 93

D

Dark Chocolate Ganache, 342–43
Dates, and Parsley, Indian-Spiced Rice Pilaf
    with, 151
Deep-Dish Pizza
    basic recipe, 39–40
    best ingredients/techniques, 38
    for 10-inch pans, 40
    Fresh Tomato Topping with Mozzarella
        and Basil, 40, *99*
Deviled Breaded Chicken Cutlets, 120
Digital scales, 211
Diner pies. *See* Pies, diner
Diner-Style Home Fries, 244
Dough. *See also* Pastry
    for American pie, 300–301
    for apple tartlets, 301
    for French tarts, 274–76, 301

Dough *(cont.)*
    for pizza
        deep-dish, 38
        flours for, 43
        storing, 46
        techniques for making, 45
        thin-crust, 42–43
Dressings, for turkey, 164–65
    boxed stuffing, 171
    cornbread recipe, 169
    Sausage, 166
Dressings, salad
    approaches to applying, 20
    citrus juices in, 22
    vinaigrettes, 20–21
    vinegars for, 21–22
Dry-toasting garlic, 33
Dutch ovens, 192–93

E

Eggplant, for baba
    ghanoush, 146–48
Egg(s)
    in brownies, 267
    Cheese Omelet, 248–49
    effects of acidity on, 280
    whites
        beating, 339
        folding techniques, 338
        removing chalazae from, 284
    in spaghetti alla carbonara, 17
Equipment
    blenders, 8
    can openers, 52
    coffee makers, 271
    colanders, 244–45
    corkscrews, 81
    cutting boards, 93
    Dutch ovens, 192–93
    food mills, 197
    graters, box, 46–47
    griddles, 254–55
    grill tongs, 148
    grills, gas, 138–39
    ice cream scoops, 319
    knives, for bread, 33–34
    knives, paring, 304
    muffin tins, 221
    pans, for pan-searing steaks, 76
    pans, roasting, 181
    pans, for tarts, 277

Equipment *(cont.)*
    peelers, vegetable, 184–85
    pepper mills, 116–17
    pie plates, 301
    pots, for frying chicken, 90
    presses, for garlic, 67–68
    presses, for hamburger, 131
    refrigerators, 254–55
    rolling pins, 277
    salad spinners, 22–23
    saucepans, 173
    scales, digital, 211
    strainers, 339
    waffle irons, 257–58
    whisks, 292
    zesters, 161
Espresso-Mascarpone Cream, for
    roulade, 341–42
Extra-virgin olive oil, 15–16
Extracts, lemon, 281

F

Fajitas
    best ingredients/techniques, 156
    classic recipe, 156–57
Fat, in hamburgers, 126–27
Fennel, Grilled, 137
Figs, Gorgonzola Cheese Filling with
    Walnuts and, 123
Fillings
    for cheese omelets
        Sautéed Mushroom with
            Thyme, 249
        Sautéed Red Bell Pepper with
            Mushroom and Onion, 249
    for chicken cutlets
        Broiled Asparagus and Smoked
            Mozzarella Cheese, 123
        Gorgonzola Cheese, with Walnuts and
            Figs, 123
        Ham and Cheddar Cheese, 122
        Roasted Mushrooms and Provolone
            Cheese, with Rosemary, 123
Fish. *See* Monkfish
Flank steak
    in fajitas, 156
    sandwiches
        best ingredients/techniques, 55
        with arugula, 56
Flour
    all-purpose, 208–11

Flour *(cont.)*
  in French toast batter, 253
  for pizza dough, 43
  taste test, 208–11
Fond, in pan sauces, 117
Fontina cheese, Breakfast Strata with
    Potatoes, Rosemary, and, 263
Food mills, 197
Food processors, grinding meat
    in, 127
Fools
  Blueberry-Rhubarb, with Fresh
      Ginger, 333
  Rhubarb, 333
  Strawberry-Rhubarb, 333
Fra diavolo
  defined, 64
  Monkfish, with Linguine, 66
  Scallops, with Linguine, 66
  Shrimp, with Linguine, 65–66
Free-Form Apple Tartlets, *235*
  best ingredients/techniques, 306–8
  dough for, 301
French Fries, *107*
  basic recipe, 83
  best ingredients/techniques, 82
French tarts, pastry for, 274–76
French Toast
  best ingredients/techniques, 252–53
  Challah or Sandwich Bread, 254
  Firm European-Style Bread, 254
Fresh Fruit Tart with Pastry Cream
  basic recipe, 284
  best ingredients/
      techniques, 282–83
Fresh Pineapple Margaritas, 159–60
Fresh Raspberry Margaritas, 160
Fresh Roast Ham, choosing/cooking
    techniques, 202–3
Fresh Sour Cherry Cobbler, 317–18
Fresh Tomato Topping with Mozzarella and
    Basil, 40
Fruit(s). *See also specific fruits*
  dried, in apple pie, 304
  for fresh fruit tarts, 284–85
  in coleslaw, 96
  in tuna salad, 51
Frying
  crispy fried chicken, 87
  French fries, 82
  oils for, 90
  pots for, 90

G

Garam Masala, Garlic and Cilantro Marinade
    with, 144
Garlic
  basting oil, for grilled vegetables, 138
  blanching, 15
  butter, 135
  controlling flavor of, 34, 68
  in chicken cutlet recipes, 120
  in grilled shrimp recipes, 72–73
  in mashed potatoes, 195–96
  in pesto, 14
  in shrimp scampi, 63
  in spaghetti alla carbonara, 18
  marinades using, 144
  mincing technique, 67–68
  presses, 67–68
  -Soy Mayonnaise, 56–57
  toasting, 32, 33
  with hamburgers, 129
Garlic Bread
  American, 33
  best ingredients/techniques, 31–32
  Chipotle, 33
  Herb, 33
  Parmesan and Asiago Cheese, 33
Garlic Mashed Potatoes, 195–96, *228*
Gas grilling
  grills, choosing, 138–39
  hamburgers, 128
  shish kebab, 143–44
  shrimp, 72
Gelatin, how it works, 330
Ginger
  Blueberry-Rhubarb Fool with, 333
  Crystallized, Apple Pie with, 304
  Fresh, Cranberry Sauce with Pears and, 173
  -Glazed Blueberry Muffins, 219
  -Orange Glaze, Roasted Carrots with, 199
  Scones, 224
  Spicy Pineapple-, Glaze, 205
  Warm-Spiced Parsley Marinade with, 144
Glazed Scones, 224
Glazes
  for carrots, 199
  for fresh fruit tarts, 284–85
  for ham, 205–06
Golden Cornbread, 169
Gorgonzola Cheese Filling with Walnuts and
    Figs, 123
Graters, box, 46–47
Gravy, Turkey, 169–70

Green Beans
  cooking methods, 184–85
  with Sautéed Shallots and Vermouth, 187
  with Toasted Hazelnuts and Brown
      Butter, *110*, 187
Green-Topped Roasted Carrots, 199
Greens
  best ingredients/techniques, 212–13
  Quick-Cooked Tough, 214
  Sautéed Tender, 213
Griddles, 254–55
Grill tongs, 148
Grilled Cheese Sandwiches, 53–54
Grilled Cheeseburgers, 129
Grilled Fresh Mozzarella Sandwiches with
    Black Olive Paste and Roasted Red
    Peppers, 54, *102*
Grilled Hamburgers, *106*
  best cuts/techniques for, 126
  charcoal grilling, 128
  Cheeseburgers, 129
  gas grilling, 128–29
  with Cognac, Mustard, and
      Chives, 129
  with Garlic, Chipotles, and
      Scallions, 129
  with Porcini Mushrooms and
      Thyme, 129
Grilled Hot Dogs, 132–33
Grilled Shrimp
  with Lemon, Garlic, and
      Oregano Paste, 73
  with Spicy Garlic Paste, 72
Grilled Vegetables
  basting oils for, 138
  best ingredients/techniques, 134
  corn, 135
  eggplant, 147
  endive, 136
  fennel, 137
  Portobello mushrooms, 137–38
  radicchio, 136
Grilling techniques/tools
  grill tongs, 148
  judging temperature of fire, 132–33
  oiling the grilling rack, 129
Gruyère cheese, Breakfast Strata with
    Spinach, Shallots, and, 262
Guacamole
  best ingredients/techniques, 154
  Chunky, 154–55
  with Bacon, Scallions, and Tomato, 155

H

Ham
  and Cheddar Cheese Filling, for
    cutlets, 122
  carving techniques, 205
  cuts for, 202
  fresh, roast,
    basic recipe, 204
    best cuts/cooking techniques, 202–3
    Coca-Cola Ham, 204–5
    glazes for, 205–6
  Prosciutto, with greens, 214
Hamburger presses, 131
Hamburgers, grilled
  best ingredients/techniques, 126
  charcoal grilling, 128
  gas grilling, 128–29
  with Cognac, Mustard, and Chives, 129
  with Garlic, Chipotles, and Scallions, 129
  with Porcini Mushrooms and Thyme, 129
Hanger steak, 157
Hazelnuts, Toasted, and Brown Butter, Green
  Beans with, 187
Herb(s). *See also specific herbs and spices*
  bruising leaves of, 16
  butter, 135
  Garlic Bread, 33
  -Poached Shrimp, 62, 104
Home Fries
  best ingredients/techniques, 242–43
  Diner-Style, 244
Horseradish
  in shrimp cocktail sauce, 61
  Tuna Salad with Lime and, 51
Hot dogs
  grilling, 132–33
  taste test, 132–33

I

Ice cream
  scoops, 319
  vanilla, taste test, 318–19
Indian Spices. *See* Spices, Indian
Individual Make-Ahead Chocolate
  Soufflés, 337
Individual Summer Berry Puddings, 324

J

Jalapeño, Coca-Cola Glaze with Lime
  and, 206

K

Ketchup, taste test, 132
Key Lime Pie
  basic recipe, 296–97
  best ingredients/techniques, 295
Kiwi, Raspberry, and Blueberry Tart, *233*, 285
Knives
  bread knives, 33–34
  paring knives, 304–5

L

Lamb, for shish kebab, 142
Large Summer Berry Pudding, 324
Lattice-Top Fresh Peach Pie, *236*
  best ingredients/techniques, 312
  pie dough, 301
  recipe, 313
Leafy Green Salad, 22. *See also* Greens
Leafy Salad with Vinaigrette, 20
Lemon juice, in baba ghanoush, 146
Lemon(s)
  -Glazed Blueberry Muffins, 220, *230*
  in basting oil for grilled vegetables, 138
  in grilled shrimp recipe, 73
  in mashed potato recipe, 196
  in porter-braised short ribs recipe, 192
  marinade using, 144
  Tart
    basic recipe, 280
    best ingredients/techniques, 278–79
  zests, oils, extracts of, 281
Lime juice
  in guacamole, 154
  in Key lime pie, 295
Lime(s)
  Filling, 296
  in ham glaze recipe, 206
  in tuna salad recipe, 51
Linguine
  Monkfish Fra Diavolo with, 66
  Scallops Fra Diavolo with, 66
  Shrimp Fra Diavolo with, 65–66
Lumpy Mashed Potatoes, 196

M

Maillard reaction, 117
Maple syrup
  Roasted Maple Carrots with Browned
    Butter, 199
  taste test, 258–59

Margaritas
  basic recipe, 159
  best ingredients/techniques, 159
  Fresh Pineapple, 159–60
  Fresh Raspberry, 161
Marinades
  for shish kebab, 142, 144
  how they work, 144
Marsala, Chicken, 114–15
Mascarpone Cream, Espresso-, sauce, for
  chocolate roulade, 342
Mashed Potatoes
  basic recipe, 195
  best ingredients/techniques, 194–95
  Garlic, 195–96
  Lumpy, 196
  with Parmesan and Lemon, 196
  with Root Vegetables, 196
Mayonnaise
  emulsion, scientific explanation for, 57
  for coleslaw, 96
  for flank steak sandwiches, 55
  Garlic-Soy, 56–57
  Quick Food Processor, 56
Meat, resting, 158
Meatballs and spaghetti
  basic recipe, 27–28
  best ingredients/techniques, 26
  Chicken, 28
Mediterranean Vinaigrette, 21
Middle Eastern barbecue
  Baba Ghanoush, 146–48
  Rice Pilaf, 149–51
  Shish Kebab, 142–44
Mint, Rosemary- Marinade, 144
Mixed Berry Tart, 285
Mixed Herb Vinaigrette, 21
Monkfish Fra Diavolo with Linguine, 66
Monterey Jack, Breakfast Strata with
  Sausage, Mushrooms, and, 262–63
Mozzarella cheese, 41
  in grilled cheese sandwiches, 54
  Smoked, and Broiled Asparagus Filling, 123
Muffin tins, 221
Muffins
  Blueberry, 218–20
  store-bought, 222
Mushroom(s)
  and Onion, Sautéed Red Bell Pepper
    Filling with, 249
  Filling with Thyme, Sautéed, 249
  in breakfast strata recipe, 262

Potatoes
  browning of, reason for, 184–85
  French Fries, 107
    basic recipe, 82–83
    Home Fries, 242–44
    in breakfast strata, 263
    Mashed, 194–96
    Pommes Anna, 182–84
    starch in, 197
    storing, 83
    with roasted carrots and
      shallots, 199
Prime Rib
  basic recipe, 178
  best ingredients/techniques, 176–77
  taste test, 178
  tying and carving, 178
Prosciutto, Quick-Cooked Tough Greens
  with, 214
Provolone Cheese, Filling with Rosemary,
  Roasted Mushrooms and, 123
Prunes, Brandy, and Lemon Essence, Porter-
  Braised Short Ribs with, 192
Puddings, chilled
  Panna Cotta, 326–30
  Rhubarb Fool, 332–33
  Summer Berry Puddings, 322–24

Q
Quick-Cooked Tough Greens, 214
  with Bacon and Onion, 214
  with Prosciutto, 214
  with Red Bell Pepper, 214
Quick Tomato Sauce for Pizza, 45

R
Radicchio, Grilled, 136
Raisin(s)
  and Almonds, Sautéed Tender Greens
    with, 213
  Curried Coleslaw with Apples
    and, 96
  Scones, Oatmeal-, 224
Raspberry(ies)
  Coulis, 329
  fresh, margarita using, 161
  preserves, taste test, 270–71
  Squares, 231
    basic recipe, 270
    best ingredients/techniques, 269

Red bell pepper
  omelet filling, 249
  tough greens with, 214
Red Onion, Flank Steak and Arugula
  Sandwiches with, 56
Red wine
  for cooking, selecting, 79–80
  in spaghetti alla carbonara, 18
  in steak sauces, 78
  Sauce, 79
  Short Ribs Braised in, 191–92
Red wine vinegar, 21
Refrigerators, 255
Resting meat, 158
Rhubarb Fool, 237
  basic recipe, 333
  best ingredients/techniques, 332
  Blueberry-, with Fresh Ginger, 333
  Strawberry-, 333
Rice
  cooking techniques, 149–50
  Pilaf
    basic recipe, 151
    best ingredients/techniques, 149
    Indian-Spiced, with Dates and
      Parsley, 151
    with Currants and Pine Nuts, 151
  types of, 149
Rice vinegar, 22
Roast Fresh Ham, 229
  basic recipe, 204
  Coca-Cola Ham, 204–5
  glazes for, 205–6
Roasted Carrots
  basic recipe, 199
  best ingredients/techniques, 198
  Green-Topped, 199
  Maple, with Brown Butter, 199
  with Ginger-Orange Glaze, 199
  with Potatoes, and Shallots, 199
Roasted Mushrooms and Provolone Cheese
  Filling with Rosemary, 122
Roasting
  fresh ham, 203
  prime rib, 177
  turkey, 168–69
Roasting pans, 181
Rolling pins, 277
Root Vegetables, Mashed Potatoes with, 196
Rosemary
  and Fontina, Breakfast Strata with
    Potatoes, 263

Rosemary (cont.)
  Mint Marinade with Garlic and Lemon, 143
  Roasted Mushroom and Provolone
    Cheese Filling with, 123
Rubs, for shish kebab, 142

S
Salad spinners, 22–23
Salads, 13
  best ingredients/techniques, 20
  coleslaws, 94–96
  Leafy Green, 22
  Tuna, 50–51
Salt, effects of, on vegetables, 96
Sandwiches, 48
  Flank Steak, 55–57
  Grilled Cheese, 54
  Tuna Salad, 50–51
Saucepans, 173
Sauce(s)
  carbonara, 12–13, 19
  cocktail, for shrimp, 60–61, 62
  cranberry, 173
  for pan-seared steaks, 78–79
  pan, fond in, 117
  pesto, 14
  raspberry coulis, 329
  strawberry coulis, 329
  tomato, for pasta, 25–26, 27, 30
  tomato, for pizza, 45
Sausage
  in breakfast strata, 262–63
  dressing, for turkey, 166
Sautéed Tender Greens, 213
  with Raisins and Almonds, 213
Sautéed Wild Mushrooms, 10–11
Sautéing techniques, 114, 149–50
Scales, digital, 211
Scallions
  Bacon, and Tomato, Guacamole with, 155
  Garlic and Chipotles, Grilled
    Hamburgers with, 129
Scallops Fra Diavolo with Linguine, 66
Scampi, Shrimp, 65
Scones, Cream
  basic recipe, 224
  best ingredients/techniques, 223
  Cakey, 224
  Ginger, 224
  Glazed, 224
  Oatmeal-Raisin, 224

ALSO BY THE EDITORS OF COOK'S ILLUSTRATED

The Best Recipe
The Best Recipe: American Classics
The Best Recipe: Grilling & Barbecue
The Best Recipe: Italian Classics
The Best Recipe: Soups & Stews

The America's Test Kitchen Cookbook

365 Quick Tips

The Complete Book of Pasta and Noodles
The Cook's Illustrated Complete Book of Poultry

How to Barbecue and Roast on the Grill
How to Cook Chicken Breasts
How to Cook Chinese Favorites
How to Cook Garden Vegetables
How to Cook Holiday Roasts and Birds
How to Cook Potatoes
How to Cook Shrimp and Other Shellfish
How to Grill
How to Make a Pie
How to Make an American Layer Cake
How to Make Cookie Jar Favorites
How to Make Holiday Desserts
How to Make Ice Cream
How to Make Muffins, Biscuits, and Scones
How to Make Pasta Sauces
How to Make Pizza
How to Make Pot Pies and Casseroles
How to Make Quick Appetizers
How to Make Salad
How to Make Sauces
How to Make Simple Fruit Desserts
How to Make Soup
How to Make Stew
How to Sauté
How to Stir-Fry

http://www.cooksillustrated.com

HERE IN AMERICA'S TEST KITCHEN

HERE IN
AMERICA'S TEST KITCHEN

BY THE EDITORS OF
COOK'S ILLUSTRATED

ILLUSTRATIONS
John Burgoyne

PHOTOGRAPHY
Keller + Keller
Bill Miles
Elisabeth O'Donnell
Carl Tremblay
Daniel Van Ackere

BOSTON COMMON PRESS   BROOKLINE, MASSACHUSETTS

Boston Common Press
17 Station Street
Brookline, Massachusetts 02445

ISBN 0-936184-59-0
Library of Congress Cataloging-in-Publication Data
The Editors of Cook's Illustrated

Here in America's Test Kitchen: All-New Recipes, Quick Tips, Equipment Ratings, Food Tastings, and Science
Experiments from the Hit Public Television Show.
1st edition

ISBN 0-936184-59-0 (hardback): $29.95
1. Cooking. 1. Title
2002

Manufactured in the United States of America

Distributed by Boston Common Press, 17 Station Street, Brookline, MA 02445

Designed by Amy Klee
Edited by Jack Bishop

CONTENTS

PREFACE

TELEVISION IS A POWERFUL AND CURIOUS MEDIUM. IT has the ability to make the ordinary extraordinary by lending a larger-than-life patina to what might, in real life, be considered quite ordinary. But I have seen a comforting trend in television lately. "Reality-based" shows are doing well, "how-to" shows with real experts rather than celebrities are popular, and ordinary citizens are popping up on television talk shows as experts. Their only claim to fame is that they know something about the topic at hand.

Of course, this is the essence of country life. One's expertise is at a premium rather than one's reputation. One of my Vermont neighbors, Ken, is not movie star—when he removes his cap, his forehead is as white as a trout's belly and his hair is a riot of straggly bits—but he knows a lot about stone walls. He built a 200-foot stone wall for us in 10 days, hauling the stone from up in the woods in his broken-down pickup. Each stone was perfectly placed, nestled into the curves of its immediate neighbors as if they were sleeping puppies. There is art to his craft, and he knows stone better than most people know their own children. Ken is an expert, but he doesn't brag about himself. He just shows up for work.

At America's Test Kitchen, we are not movie stars, either. The lights and cameras can't disguise the fact that we are just ordinary cooks, like you, our viewers. We just happen to have a lot of time on our hands to investigate what makes a recipe work. Each week, we invite you along for the ride as we try to solve the riddle of the perfect chicken Milanese or the best Texas chili (if there is a "best" chili recipe). America's Test Kitchen is indeed a real place, not a TV set, where the sinks really work and where our staff of cooks test and taste food every working day of the year. Simply put, we show up for work with a keen appetite for investigating recipes. That makes us, I suppose, a "reality-based" TV show, too. We try to show the good and the bad, the successes and the failures. We like to film our disasters rather than hide them because we have learned more from our mistakes than our successes.

Thanks for watching the show and for buying this book. We hope that we know as much about cooking as Ken does about stone walls. At the least, we are happy to share with you what we do know and perhaps we can learn something about cooking together as we test and retest in search of our idea of the "best" recipe.

Christopher Kimball
Founder and editor, *Cook's Illustrated* magazine
Boston, Massachusetts, 2002

ACKNOWLEDGMENTS

THIS BOOK BEGAN WITH THE RECIPES, EQUIPMENT ratings, food tastings, and science experiments conducted by the editors, writers, and cooks in America's Test Kitchen. Editor Jack Bishop shaped this information into a manuscript, and art director Amy Klee and graphic designer Nina Madjid gave these words form. John Burgoyne drew all of the illustrations and Amy Keller, Joe Keller, Elisabeth O'Donnell, Carl Tremblay, and Daniel Van Ackere took the photographs that fill the pages in this book. The photograph on the front cover was taken by Bill Miles.

India Koopman copyedited the manuscript, and Rebecca Hays and Jessica Quirk guided the book through the production process. The following individuals on the editorial, production, circulation, customer service, and office staffs also worked on the book: Ron Bilodeau, Barbara Bourassa, Rich Cassidy, Sharyn Chabot, Mary Connelly, Cathy Dorsey, Ruth Duncan, Jim McCormack, Jennifer McCreary, Amy Monaghan, Nicole Morris, Henrietta Murray, Sumantha Selvakumar, and Mandy Shito.

Without the work of the marketing, publicity, and sales staffs, readers would not find our books. Special thanks to Deborah Broide, Steven Browall, Shekinah Cohn, Connie Forbes, Julie Gardner, Jason Geller, Larisa Greiner, Robert Lee, David Mack, Steven Sussman, Jacqui Valerio, and Jonathan Venier, all of whom contributed to our marketing and distribution efforts.

HERE IN AMERICA'S TEST KITCHEN

AMERICA'S TEST KITCHEN IS A 4,000-SQUARE-FOOT kitchen located in Brookline, Massachusetts, just outside Boston. It is a working kitchen that serves as the home for *Cook's Illustrated* magazine. Founded in 1980, *Cook's Illustrated* (formerly *Cook's Magazine*) is dedicated to finding the best methods for preparing favorite dishes. Every week our cooks test hundreds of recipes to find out which techniques work and which ones don't. Should you melt or cream butter when making chocolate cookies? What's the best way to peel and mince garlic? Which cheese is the best choice for macaroni and cheese? These are typical questions that we try to answer every day. How do we answer them? We answer all questions by performing comparison tests. We will make macaroni and cheese with a dozen kinds of cheese and then taste each one to figure out which cheese (or cheeses) are right for the recipe.

During the year, hundreds of pieces of equipment pass through America's Test Kitchen as we evaluate the basic tools most cooks need at home. Is that $120 German chef's knife better than a $30 knockoff? Which oven thermometers are most accurate and most stable? What's the best scrubber for removing scorched food from pots and pans? As with our recipe tests, we learn by doing. To find out which chef's knife is the sharpest and most comfortable, four editors and test cooks spent several weeks slicing tomatoes and bacon, chopping butternut squash and onions, mincing parsley and ginger, and butchering whole chickens. We went through cases of food before proclaiming one knife the winner. (It turns out that one of the cheap knives we tested is better than many of the expensive knives costing four times as much.)

We put popular food items through the same process. Can canned beef broth or bouillon cubes rival the flavor of homemade stock? Which tortilla chips make the best nachos? Is sea salt better than table salt? What about kosher salt? Can tasters tell the difference between pure vanilla extract and imitation products made from wood pulp? To answer these questions, we conduct dozens of blind taste tests every month. For instance,

we tasted nine brands of salt in five different ways—in plain water, in chicken stock, in pasta cooking water, in biscuits, and sprinkled on beef tenderloin. In most cases, we found that regular table salt (costing just 36 cents per pound) was just as good as fancy sea salts (costing up to 100 times as much).

In addition to figuring out which cooking techniques, pieces of equipment, and ingredients are best, we want to know why they are the best. The science of food is an important element in every test we perform. Why is pie dough made with butter and shortening flakier than pie dough made with just butter? What makes rice sticky? How come evaporated milk makes a smoother sauce for macaroni and cheese than heavy cream? We talk to scientists, develop theories, and run tests to understand why certain techniques and ingredients succeed or fail in a particular recipe. We also rely on a food laboratory to test products. We learn just how much fat is in each brand of chocolate tested or how much bacteria is left in sponges that have been disinfected by various methods.

The Television Show

OUR TELEVISION SHOW BRINGS YOU THE VERY BEST FROM an entire year's work in America's Test Kitchen. We turn our favorite recipes, our most interesting equipment ratings, our most surprising food tastings, and our most unusual science experiments into lively, informative television segments. Christopher Kimball, the founder and editor of *Cook's Illustrated* magazine, is the host of the show and chief skeptic. He wants to know why, what, how, when, and where. He gets those answers from the test cooks and editors that appear on camera.

Julia Collin, Bridget Lancaster, and Matthew Card demonstrate recipes, explaining key points in our testing and development process. They show Chris (and the audience) which techniques and ingredients worked and which ones flopped. Julia, Bridget, and Matt demonstrate the right way to slice onions, sear steaks, bread chicken cutlets, drain pasta, grate cheese, and more. As you watch them cook, you'll learn the

Clockwise from upper left: Adam Ried, Julia Collin, Bridget Lancaster, Matt Card, Dawn Yanagihara, John "Doc" Willoughby, Erin McMurrer, Meg Suzuki, Jack Bishop, and Chris Kimball.

secrets to extra-crisp twice-baked potatoes, chewy molasses cookies, and smoky barbecued baby back ribs.

Adam Ried, our equipment expert, demonstrates the results of extensive kitchen tests. He shows Chris and the audience the pepper mills that received good ratings from our testers and those that failed miserably. Adam teaches us what to look for when shopping for steak knives, rice cookers, non-stick skillets, gas grills, and more. We learn that steak knives with straight (rather than serrated) edges are the best choice and that gas grills with lava rocks are prone to flare-ups and should be avoided. Kitchen equipment can be expensive and often involves a long-term commitment. With Adam's help, you will become a more informed shopper and will avoid those gadgets and tools that sound great but don't deliver.

Jack Bishop focuses on the ingredients that home cooks use every day. Is there even one decent brand of store-bought pie crust? Which brand of pasta tastes best and cooks up firm and chewy every time? What's the difference between mild, robust, and blackstrap molasses? To answer these questions, we assemble several dozen tasters in the test kitchen and have them rate the molasses, the pasta, and the pie crusts. Jack presents highlights of these tastings to Chris, who tastes the products for himself before the cameras. Can Chris pick out the losers and the winners? Just as important, Jack explains what makes one product better than another.

John "Doc" Willoughby is our science buff. He wants to know why something works and helps illustrate complex scientific principles with down-to-earth (and sometimes downright silly) demonstrations. Why does braising make smothered pork chops so tender? Why does buttermilk give quick breads such a good texture? With the help of some dolls, puppets, balloons, water pistols, toy fans, and more, Doc explains the science behind our recipes.

Behind the Scenes

AMERICA'S TEST KITCHEN IS MORE THAN JUST THE EDITORS and cooks you see on air. Recipes, food tastings, equipment tests, and science experiments result from the combined efforts of dozens of editors, cooks, researchers, and writers.

During filming, executive chefs Erin McMurrer and Dawn Yanagihara ran the "back kitchen," where all of the food that appeared on camera originated. Along with the on-air crew, Erin and Dawn also planned and organized the 26 television episodes shot in June 2002. Rebecca Hays and India Koopman helped develop science and equipment segments, and Julia Collin organized all of the tastings for the television show.

Every day chefs Matthew Card and Meg Suzuki were in the kitchen from early in the morning to late at night helping Erin and Dawn cook all of the food needed on set. Chefs Keith Dresser, Nancy Jordan, Kate Neave, Rajeev Samantrai, Merrill Stubbs, and Nina West and assistants Judy Davis, Pring Ram, and Shelley Rashotsky also worked long hours peeling potatoes, making pies, and baking cookies. Shannon Blaisdell and Rebecca Hays helped coordinate the efforts of the kitchen with the television set, readying props, equipment, and food, and Rebecca also made countless shopping trips to pick up ingredients.

Jim McCormack, vice president for operations and technology, and Rich Cassidy, our systems administrator, supervised the process that turned our test kitchen into a television studio. They made sure all of the wiring, computers, and ovens were ready to go.

The staff of A La Carte Communications turned our recipes, tastings, equipment tests, and science experiments into a lively television show. Special thanks to executive producer Geof Drummond; director/editor Herb Sevush; director of photography Dean Gaskill; coordinating producer Kimberly Nolan; production manager Rena Maliszewski; audio engineer Gilles Moran; technical engineer Eliat Goldman; script supervisor/makeup specialist Brenda Coffey; cameramen Tommy Hamilton, Steve Hussar, Michael McEachern, and Mark Rast; jib cameraman Mark Britt; production assistants Leland Drummond and Yale Miller; and grip/gaffers Aaron Frutman, Jack McPhee, and Patrick Ruth.

We hope this book captures the fun that takes place every day in America's Test Kitchen. When we come to work each morning, we never know quite what to expect. The day might begin with tasting 5 New York cheesecakes that were made the day before and have been chilling overnight. Next we might be testing kitchen torches on ramekins of crème brûlée. By lunch, four test recipes of chili might be ready for sampling, and the afternoon might include a tasting of store-bought barbecue sauces.

Although the food changes (almost hourly), our mission remains the same. We want to make your job in the kitchen easier and the food you make better. We hope our television show and this book will do just that. Contact us at www.americastestkitchen.com if you have comments or questions about the show or the book. Visit www.cooksillustrated.com for information about *Cook's Illustrated* magazine.

HERE IN AMERICA'S TEST KITCHEN

We taste-tested five brands of store-bought guacamole and found that none compare with the real thing, made with fresh avocados.

PARTY foods

CHAPTER 1

Nachos, Buffalo wings, and sangría are too down-market, too much like junk food, to merit much attention from the "serious" food press. But let's face it—who doesn't like a plate of good nachos or Buffalo wings? The key is to use good ingredients and proper techniques to make this honest party food taste good.

With nachos, the solution turns out to be relatively simple. Rather than relying on processed cheese, jarred salsa, and packaged guacamole, choose fresh, wholesome ingredients. Follow the test kitchen's lead and you can turn out a plate of nachos good enough for company.

Buffalo wings also suffer from subpar ingredients—bottled blue cheese dressing and poor-quality hot sauces—as well as from poor—or nonexistent—technique on the part of the cook. More often than not, Buffalo wings are flabby and greasy, not perfectly crisp, as they should be.

Finally, sangría is not a serious drink—all you do is add sugar to wine, right? But there's a world of difference between a candy-sweet sangría made with 7UP and the real thing. We'll show you why.

NACHOS

WHAT WE WANTED : To free nachos from the suffo-cating grasp of packaged ingredients and make them taste good again.

Nachos are a simple, culinary pleasure many of us crave: crisp, warm tortilla chips mingling with melted cheese under a colorful banner of spicy salsa, luxurious guacamole, and a dollop of sour cream. Yet as elementary and popular as nachos are, finding a good plate of them can be hard. The worst examples appear at the snack counters of airports and large discount marts, where trays of chips that taste like cardboard are squirted with a few pumps of unnaturally fluid "cheese," doused with watery jarred salsa, and (if you're lucky) served with a miniscule portion of ready-made guacamole. But it doesn't have to be this way.

After sampling some local nacho fare and trying out a few recipes, we homed in on some key issues. First, the chips must be crisp and hot, not lukewarm, soggy, or charred. Second, there must be no shortage of cheese; a chip with-out cheese is just not a nacho. Third, there is no such thing as minimalist nachos. Good nachos require not only a hearty helping of cheese but also ample amounts of garnishes, such as salsa, guacamole, sour cream, jalapeños, and scallions. Finally, although it may seem blindingly obvious, we noted that fresh, quality ingredients make good nachos, while processed ingredients make airport nachos. With these insights in mind, we were ready to create a good plate of nachos, and tasters were already jockeying for position at the kitchen counter.

Finding that 8 ounces of chips made enough nachos for four to six people and fit easily into a 13 by 9-inch baking dish, we made batches with increasing amounts of shredded cheese until tasters cried uncle. Four cups was just right; lesser amounts left some chips neglected, and more just about drowned the chips. To ensure an even distribution, it

was necessary to toss the cheese with the chips before cook-ing. But the act of tossing, we quickly discovered, was brutal on the delicate chips, and some of the cheese was lost to the bottom of the baking dish. Instead, we tried building the nachos in layers—two layers of chips topped with cheese—which ensured even distribution. Not surprisingly, these first few batches tasted far better than any nachos we had eaten elsewhere. The simple pairing of good-quality chips (see the Tasting Lab on page 8) with a generous amount of evenly distributed cheese had already made a huge difference.

Next we held a cheese tasting. Although most recipes call for cheddar or Monterey Jack, we wondered how tasters would react to other types of cheese, such as American, Havarti, Gouda, Muenster, or any of the jalapeño-studded varieties, such as pepper cheddar, pepper Jack, and pepper Havarti. Cheddar turned out to be tasters' overall favorite, with a potent and legitimate flavor, although Gouda was surprisingly good and garnered second place. To our great surprise, Monterey Jack was disappointingly bland and taste-less, while American and the peppered varieties of cheddar, Monterey Jack, and Havarti all tasted commercial and over-processed. The other oddball contestants, Muenster and reg-ular Havarti, had decent if unremarkable flavors but were quick to turn rubbery as they cooled. We tried using pre-shredded cheddar to save time but found the flavor dull and the texture dry. We got much better results by shredding a block of cheese in a food processor fitted with the shredding disk, which was easy enough and took little time. A greased box grater (see the illustrations on page 6) is another good way to accomplish this task quickly and easily.

We had been baking the nachos in a 350-degree oven for 20 minutes to melt the cheese and heat the chips through but wanted to experiment with speedier methods. The broiler caused the top layer of chips to burn before the inner layers of cheese had time to melt. Hot ovens set between 425 and 450 degrees produced chips with charred edges, but a 400-degree oven managed to both melt the cheese and warm the chips through to a lightly toasted crisp in a mere 10 minutes. Not only was this a time saver, but the nachos tasted more fresh and less dried out than those baked for a longer period of time in a cooler oven.

Chips and cheese may be the nacho plate's workhorses, but without salsa, guacamole, and sour cream, nachos look naked. And not just any old salsa or guacamole will do—they have to be fresh and lively tasting. Although salsa and gua-camole are now conveniently sold in jars and tubs in the supermarket, most of these products are just about inedible (see the Tasting Labs on pages 10 and 7). Luckily, both can also be made at home in a few minutes, and the results are more than worth the effort. When and where they are placed on the chips and cheese are also crucial to success. As for when, they must be added after the chips emerge from the oven to provide contrast in temperature, texture, and flavor. As for where, while many recipes tell the cook to spread each topping evenly over each chip, this instruction is both silly and time-consuming. We found that it's easier to simply dump a few scoops of salsa and guacamole on a small por-tion of the chips, off to the side, so that most of the chips remain unencumbered and easy to pick up.

Tasters liked the spicy addition of thinly sliced jalapeños, preferring them fresh rather than canned. They tasted best when sprinkled into the layers along with the cheese, which, when melted, helped the peppers adhere to the chips. Fresh, sliced scallions and wedges of lime—both added when the nachos emerge from the oven—were also welcome additions. The issue of spicy, ground beef and refried beans—common additions to a nacho plate—pro-voked some controversy in the test kitchen. The result? We decided to use these ingredients in variations, as they quickly transform nachos into an indulgent, artery-clogging meal.

WHAT WE LEARNED: Layer shredded cheddar cheese and chips to ensure even coverage, use a hot oven rather than the broiler to melt the cheese, and add sliced, fresh jalapeños for some heat.

CHEESY NACHOS WITH GUACAMOLE AND SALSA serves 4 to 6
See our Tasting Labs on tortilla chips (page 8) and cheddar cheese (page 160) to see which brands we recommend.

8	ounces tortilla chips
16	ounces cheddar cheese, shredded (4 cups)
2	large jalapeño chiles (¾ ounce each), sliced thin (about ¼ cup)
2	scallions, sliced thin
1	recipe Fresh Guacamole (recipe follows)
½	cup (4 ounces) sour cream
1	recipe One-Minute Salsa (recipe follows)
1	lime, cut into 6 wedges

Adjust oven rack to middle position and heat oven to 400 degrees. Spread half of chips in even layer in 13 by 9-inch baking dish; sprinkle evenly with 2 cups cheese and half of jalapeño slices. Repeat with remaining chips, cheese, and jalapeños. Bake until cheese is melted, 7 to 10 minutes. Remove nachos from oven and sprinkle with scallions. Along edge of baking dish, drop scoops of guacamole, sour cream, and salsa. Serve immediately, passing lime wedges separately.

VARIATIONS

CHEESY NACHOS WITH REFRIED BEANS
Follow recipe for Cheesy Nachos with Guacamole and Salsa, dropping ¾ cup (about 6 ounces) refried beans in small spoonfuls on each chip layer before sprinkling with cheese.

CHEESY NACHOS WITH SPICY BEEF
A quickly made ground beef mixture turns nachos into a meal.

2	teaspoons corn or vegetable oil
1	small onion, chopped fine
1	large garlic clove, minced or pressed through garlic press (about 1½ teaspoons)
1	tablespoon chili powder

¼ teaspoon dried oregano
½ teaspoon ground cumin
½ teaspoon ground coriander
¼ teaspoon cayenne
⅛ teaspoon salt
½ pound 90 percent lean (or leaner) ground beef

1. Heat oil in medium skillet over medium heat until shimmering, but not smoking. Add onion and cook, stirring occasionally, until softened, about 4 minutes. Add garlic, spices, and salt; cook, stirring constantly, until fragrant and combined with onion, about 1 minute. Add ground beef and cook, breaking up meat with wooden spoon and scraping pan bottom to prevent scorching, until beef is no longer pink, about 5 minutes.

2. Follow recipe for Cheesy Nachos with Guacamole and Salsa, sprinkling half of beef mixture on each chip layer before sprinkling with cheese.

FRESH GUACAMOLE makes about 1 ½ cups
See the illustrations on page 7 for tips on dicing an avocado.

2 small, ripe avocados (preferably Hass)
1 tablespoon minced red onion
1 small garlic clove, minced or pressed through
   garlic press (about ½ teaspoon)
½ small jalapeño chile, stemmed, seeded, and
   minced (about 1½ teaspoons)
2 tablespoons fresh minced cilantro leaves
   Salt
1 tablespoon juice from 1 lime

1. Halve 1 avocado, remove pit, and scoop flesh into medium bowl. Using fork, mash lightly with onion, garlic, jalapeño, cilantro, and ⅛ teaspoon salt until just combined.

2. Halve and pit remaining avocado. Using a dinner knife, carefully make ½-inch crosshatch incisions in flesh, cutting

down to but not through skin. Using a soup spoon, gently scoop flesh from skin; transfer to bowl with mashed avocado mixture. Sprinkle lime juice over and mix lightly with fork until combined but still chunky. Adjust seasoning with salt, if necessary, and serve. (Can be covered with plastic wrap pressed directly onto surface of mixture, and refrigerated for up to 1 day. Return guacamole to room temperature, removing plastic wrap just before serving.)

TECHNIQUE: Shredding Soft Cheeses

Soft cheeses such as cheddar, Monterey Jack, and mozzarella can stick to a box grater and cause a real mess. Here's how to keep the holes on the grater from becoming clogged.

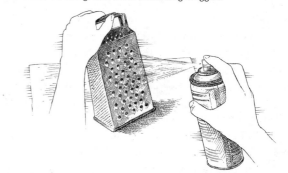

1. Lightly coat the side of the box grater with large holes with nonstick cooking spray.

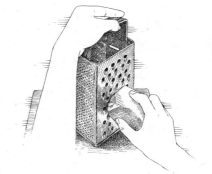

2. Shred the cheese as usual. The cooking spray will keep the cheese from sticking to the grater.

ONE-MINUTE SALSA makes about I cup

This quick salsa can be made with either fresh or canned tomatoes. If you like, replace the jalapeño with ½ chipotle chile in adobo sauce, minced.

½ small jalapeño chile, stemmed and seeded (about 1½ teaspoons)
¼ small red onion, peeled and root end removed
1 small garlic clove, minced or pressed through garlic press (about ½ teaspoon)
2 tablespoons fresh cilantro leaves
¼ teaspoon salt
  Pinch ground black pepper
2 teaspoons juice from 1 lime
2 small ripe tomatoes (about ¾ pound), each cored and cut into eighths, or one (14½-ounce) can diced tomatoes, drained

Pulse all ingredients except tomatoes in food processor until minced, about five 1-second pulses, scraping down sides of bowl as necessary. Add tomatoes and pulse until roughly chopped, about two 1-second pulses.

TASTING LAB: Store-Bought Guacamole

AT THE HEART OF ANY GOOD GUACAMOLE IS A RIPE, HASS avocado. These small, rough-skinned gems soften when left on the counter for a few days. But it can be hard to find fully ripened avocados for a spur-of-the-moment guacamole. Wondering if any of the ready-made tubs of guacamole at the supermarket would be an acceptable substitute, we tasted five brands to compare them with our own recipe.

At first glance, some of these guacamoles looked pretty good. But after sampling just a bite or two, tasters gagged, sealing the fate of these pretenders. The best of the lot, AvoClassic Guacamole, came out of a sealed plastic pouch and garnered comments such as "could be worse," and "not bad with some doctoring." The next best representative was Goya's Guacamole Dip, which had a "thin and mealy" texture and tasted "like nothing." Voicing increasingly negative reactions, tasters found the Trader Joe's and Calavo brands to be harsh and acidic, with flavors that "burned the back of the throat." Ranked at the very bottom was La Mexicana Guacamole, which drew comments such as "What is in this?" By comparison, our freshly made guacamole tasted almost angelic, with a pure, honest avocado flavor. So if you think the mood might strike, buy some avocados a few days ahead.

TECHNIQUE: Dicing an Avocado

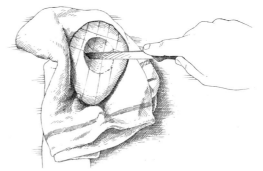

1. Use a dish towel to hold the avocado steady. Make ½-inch crosshatch incisions in the flesh of each avocado half with a dinner knife, cutting down to but not through the skin.

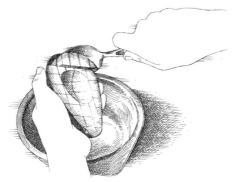

2. Separate the diced flesh from the skin using a soup spoon inserted between the skin and flesh, gently scooping out the avocado cubes.

TASTING LAB: Tortilla Chips

FOR OUR TASTING OF TORTILLA CHIPS, WE DECIDED TO keep things simple: We stuck to chips made from white or yellow corn in the basic triangular shape. In addition, all of the chips we tasted were salted and "full fat." We tasted the chips solo, with salsa (testing each chip for its "scoopability"), and in nachos (testing the chips for durability and texture after blanketing them with cheese and toppings).

Most tortilla chips are made from just three basic ingredients—corn, oil, and salt—and processed in similar fashion (explained below), yet our tasters found a wide range of textures and flavors in the 10 brands we sampled. How, we wondered, could such simple ingredients and a consistent manufacturing process yield such different results?

To understand what gave the chips we tasted such different flavors and textures, we began by examining the manufacturing process and the primary ingredient, corn. Tortilla chips begin with masa, or corn dough. Resembling cookie dough in texture, masa can be made from a number of different corn products, including corn flour, which has the texture of fine sand; stone-ground corn flour, which has a rougher, grittier texture; and stone-ground corn (made from softened whole corn kernels), which is very rough, like pebbly sand. Water is added to the corn product and the dough is mixed. The masa gets flattened into a strip and goes through a contraption that looks something like a giant rolling pin (sometimes called a sheeter) that cuts the dough into triangles. The triangles are baked for less than a minute at up to 800 degrees, which dries out the dough so that it doesn't absorb too much oil when it gets fried. After baking, the dough triangle looks, feels, and tastes like a corn tortilla. Next the chips get cooled on a multilevel conveyor belt. This prevents puffing during the next phase, frying. The baked and cooled chips are flash-fried in 350-degree oil for only 1 minute; then the chips get cooled again in a cooling tunnel, salted, and bagged.

Based on our tasting results, we concluded that a masa made with stone-ground whole corn kernels will result in a grittier, heartier chip than one made from a silky corn flour masa. Many manufacturers make a big deal out of their chips being made from stone-ground masa. A stone-ground corn chip, they say, has more texture, is stronger, and absorbs less oil. While that all sounds good on paper, in reality we found that tasters preferred finer and more fragile chips made with corn flour, like second-place Miguel's, described as "delicate," or third-place Newman's Own, called "crisp." (Frito-Lay, which manufactures our top-rated Doritos chips, would not comment on the ingredients in its masa. However, given the delicate texture of Doritos, it seems likely that corn flour is used here, too.) In contrast, two of the roughest, heartiest stone-ground chips, Nana's Cocina and Kettle Foods, ended up at the bottom of the scorecard. Their textures were described as "stale" and like "cardboard," respectively.

Another argument that enthusiasts of stone-ground corn flour make against the use of fine-ground corn flour is that it acts like a sponge, absorbing more oil. But in our tasting we didn't find that to be true. Both Miguel's and Newman's use fine flours, and neither was greasy. Yet the Nana's Cocina chips, which are made from whole corn kernels ground in lava stones, were called "slick" and "oily." In addition, despite differences in the texture of the masa and the chips, all of the chips we sampled contain similar amounts of fat, from 5.5 to 7 grams per 1-ounce serving.

Finally, we come to the flavor of the masa itself. We thought there might be a continental divide between those who preferred white or yellow corn tortilla chips, but we found that we liked both types. Our first-, third-, and fourth-place chips are all yellow corn varieties, while our second-, fifth-, and sixth-place picks are made with white corn. In general, we found white corn chips to be more subtly corn flavored, whereas yellow corn chips tasted "toasty" and "nutty."

In addition to the masa, salt has a big impact on tortilla chip flavor. Here the results of our tasting were quite clear. More salt makes a tastier chip. Among the top five brands, four have sodium levels between 110 and 120 milligrams

Rating Tortilla Chips

WE TASTED 10 BRANDS OF TORTILLA CHIPS, PLAIN, WITH SALSA, AND IN NACHOS. TASTERS JUDGED THE CHIPS FOR FLAVOR, texture, durability, and size. Chips are listed in order of preference. All brands are sold in supermarkets, and all are available nationally except for Doritos, which is distributed only in the West.

HIGHLY RECOMMENDED
1. Doritos Toasted Corn Tortilla Chips
$3.29 for 13.5 ounces

Tasters loved the "fresh," "toasted corn" flavor and "crisp," "perfect" texture.

HIGHLY RECOMMENDED
2. Miguel's Stowe Away White Corn Tortilla Chips
$2.95 for 7 ounces

These "thick" chips retained a "delicate crispness." Flavor was subtle, with tasters calling it "toasted" and "authentic."

HIGHLY RECOMMENDED
3. Newman's Own Organics Yellow Corn Tortilla Chips
$2.29 for 8 ounces

Chips tasted "home-fried" and "corny." These were the thinnest chips tested; packages had a higher-than-average number of broken chips.

HIGHLY RECOMMENDED
4. Bearitos Stoneground Organic Yellow Corn Tortilla Chips
$2.79 for 16 ounces

Many tasters believed these chips had the "best corn flavor" but complained that the chips were "too hard" and "broke apart" when eaten.

RECOMMENDED
5. Santitas White Corn Tortilla Chips
$1.99 for 18 ounces

This "durable" but "crisp" chip stood up to nachos and salsa. Some tasters commented that these chips "could use more corn flavor."

RECOMMENDED
6. Cape Cod White Corn Tortilla Chips
$1.99 for 9 ounces

Tasters liked the "crisp," "thick" texture but called the flavor "bland," "unremarkable," and reminiscent of "church communion."

RECOMMENDED
7. Tostitos Restaurant-Style White Corn Tortilla Chips
$2.29 for 13.5 ounces

"This is your basic Sunday football chip," said one taster. Others said they were "too flimsy" in flavor and texture and didn't "hold up to heavy dipping."

NOT RECOMMENDED
8. Nana's Cocina Traditional Stoneground Yellow Corn Tortilla Chips
$2.69 for 16 ounces

Chips had a "fatty" mouthfeel that was "slick and oily." Tasters also found these chips to be overly "thin" and somewhat "stale."

NOT RECOMMENDED
9. Old Dutch Original Restaurant-Style Tortilla Chips
$3.19 for 15 ounces

These "thin" chips were deemed "too large" and "fell apart easily" when dunked in salsa. Several tasters picked up on an unwelcome "smoky," "popcorn" flavor.

NOT RECOMMENDED
10. Kettle Foods Five Grain Organic Yellow Corn Tortilla Chips
$1.99 for 8 ounces

Tasters described these chips made with five sprouted grains as being "strangely sweet," with a "stale," "old cornmeal" flavor.

per ounce. The sodium level in the five lowest-ranked brands ranges from 40 to 90 milligrams per ounce.

Now that we understood more about the inner workings of masa and the effect of salt levels on flavor, we moved on to the oil. We thought that the success of our second favorite brand, Miguel's, might be due in part to the corn/oil combination. Miguel's pairs canola oil with its white corn masa chip. Because canola is a neutral-flavored oil, using it with the subtle-flavored masa works well, as the flavor of the oil doesn't overwhelm that of the chip. ·

But then we came to Cape Cod chips, which were something of an anomaly. Like Miguel's, they are made with white corn masa and fried in canola oil. So why were Miguel's chips described as having a "toasted," "authentic" flavor, whereas Cape Cod chips were deemed "bland" and "unremarkable?" The most obvious difference right off the bat was in the packaging. Miguel's tortilla chips are packaged in a "metallized" bag, meaning that the bag's surface has been lined with a very thin film of aluminum.

Craig Mooney, vice-president of sales for Miguel's, says that the metal lining helps to ward off oxidation of the oil by blocking light. "Light can oxidize the product and cause it to go bad," he explained; the foil-lined bag "also creates a moisture barrier to help the chips stay crunchy." In fact, we observed that all of our top three chips, Doritos, Miguel's, and Newman's Own, are packed in metallized bags. Could oxidation be a reason for the lack of flavor in Cape Cod and the "off" flavors in some of the other brands we tasted?

According to Theron Downes, a packaging professor with Michigan State University, "there are piles of evidence" that a metallized bag improves the shelf life of fried foods. In fact, Dr. Downes even refuses to purchase peanuts, a high-fat and light-susceptible food, packaged in clear bags because the oil in the peanuts goes rancid from oxidation within a couple of weeks.

In the end, the results of our tasting were unexpected. Doritos won over smaller, boutique brands like Nana's Cocina and Kettle Foods. Although many boutique brands make a big deal about the organically raised, stone-ground corn they use, it seems that the secret to a great tortilla chip isn't all that complicated. Just use fine corn flour (not coarse stone-ground), add plenty of salt, and then pack the chips in a foil-lined bag to keep the oil from oxidizing.

TASTING LAB: Jarred Salsa

THERE ARE SO MANY JARRED SALSAS ON THE MARKET today that for the preliminary round of our tasting we sampled dozens of brands. We included the brands that dominate the category (Old El Paso, Tostitos, and Ortega), along with some smaller "gourmet" brands. We also included four refrigerated salsas. Unlike jarred salsas, these products, which are sold in plastic tubs, have a shelf life of a month or two. (Jarred salsas keep for a year or more unopened.) Manufacturers add preservatives to keep refrigerated salsas from becoming moldy, but there is little they can do to prevent the mushy texture and slimy mouthfeel. The refrigerated salsas we tasted ranged from possibly edible after many margaritas to inedible under any circumstances. We decided to omit this category from our final tasting.

Supermarket brands of jarred salsa come in three different styles: mild, medium, and hot. Mild salsas are generally quite bland (some would say insipid), and hot salsas can be so hot that they are hard to taste, especially one after another. We decided to test only medium salsas for our final tasting.

Of the 12 jarred salsas we ultimately sampled for our final round of tests, we could not recommend even one—not even in a pinch. All 12 were watery and sweet, with mushy vegetables and overprocessed flavors. None came close to the full, fresh flavors of our homemade salsa. Our advice is to make your own salsa, even if you have to use canned tomatoes.

BUFFALO WINGS

WHAT WE WANTED: Juicy meat with a crisp coating and a spicy, slightly sweet, and vinegary sauce.

First conceived of at the Anchor Bar in Buffalo, New York in the 1960s, Buffalo wings are now found throughout the country at any bar or Super Bowl party worth its salt. The odd combination of chicken wings slathered with hot sauce and dunked in blue cheese dressing may seem like a drunken concoction best forgotten about the next morning, but it is actually a harmonious union. The sauce's bright heat is tamed by the soothing, creamy dip. Under the right circumstances, even bad wings (and we have had our share of flabby, tough wings in greasy sauce) are pretty good. But we wanted to come up with a recipe for really good wings.

For Buffalo wings, the raw chicken wing itself is almost always cut in two segments, the relatively meatless wingtip removed. The wings come packaged as whole wings or as pre-cut segments affectionately referred to as drumettes. We found that pre-cut wings were often poorly cut and unevenly sized, so we chose to buy whole wings and butcher them ourselves, which was easy and economical.

While the wings were easy to butcher, cooking them proved a little trickier because of their high fat content. At the Anchor Bar, Buffalo wings are deep-fried, which renders the fat and leaves the skin crisp and golden. But deep-frying can be a daunting project in a home kitchen. We hoped that oven-roasting might be a viable alternative. We placed the wings on a rack resting on a rimmed baking sheet so that the chicken would not be sitting in fat. At 300 degrees, the wings cooked for an hour and were wan and dry. At 375 degrees, the chicken was still a little flabby after 45 minutes of cooking, and the meat was dry.

We decided to switch gears and try the stovetop. Sautéing the wings did little for their flavor or texture. And they were still greasy because the fat was not rendered. Pan-frying, or cooking the chicken partially submerged in fat, yielded much better results, but turning the chicken midway through cooking prompted hot fat to spatter about. We decided that if we were going to pan-fry, we might as well try deep-frying. Maybe there was something to tradition after all. We found that if we used a deep Dutch oven and kept the oil at a constant 360 degrees, spattering oil was minimal and cleanup easy.

We tossed the wings with salt, pepper, and cayenne and then fried them for about 12 minutes, or until golden. While these wings were juicy and crisp, most tasters wanted an even crispier exterior. We did not want to resort to a batter, so we tried dredging the wings, testing one batch dredged in flour and another in cornstarch. The cornstarch provided a thin and brittle coating, not unlike tempura, that was the tasters' favorite. We found that thoroughly drying the chicken with paper towels prior to tossing with the cornstarch and seasonings ensured crisp skin and no gumminess.

With the wings fried and placed in the oven to keep warm, we were ready to tackle the sauce. Most recipes we found agreed that authentic Buffalo wing sauce, as made at the Anchor Bar, is nothing but Frank's Louisiana Hot Sauce and butter or margarine, blended in a 2-to-1 ratio. Most recipes also suggest intensifying the sauce's heat with a bit of Tabasco or other hot pepper sauce because on its own, Frank's is not quite spicy enough. While we liked this simple sauce, most tasters wanted something a little more dynamic. We included brown sugar to round out the flavors. A little cider vinegar balanced out the sugar and added a pleasing sharpness.

WHAT WE LEARNED: Coat the wings with cornstarch for a supercrisp exterior and deep-fry (rather than roasting, sautéing, or pan-frying) the wings for the best texture. Then deepen the flavor of the traditional hot sauce by adding brown sugar and cider vinegar.

TECHNIQUE: Cutting Up Chicken Wings

1. Cut into the skin between the larger sections of the wing until you hit the joint.

2. Bend back the two sections to pop and break the joint.

3. Cut through the skin and flesh to completely separate the two meaty portions.

4. Hack off the wingtip and discard.

BUFFALO WINGS serves 6 to 8 as an appetizer

Frank's Louisiana Hot Sauce is not terribly spicy. We like to combine it with a more potent hot sauce, such as Tabasco, to bring up the heat. You will need to double the recipe for blue cheese dressing on page 62.

sauce

- 4 tablespoons unsalted butter
- ½ cup Frank's Louisiana Hot Sauce
- 2 tablespoons Tabasco or other hot sauce, plus more to taste
- 1 tablespoon dark brown sugar
- 2 teaspoons cider vinegar

wings

- 1–2 quarts peanut oil, for frying
- 1 teaspoon cayenne
- 1 teaspoon ground black pepper
- 1 teaspoon salt
- 3 tablespoons cornstarch
- 18 chicken wings (about 3 pounds), wingtips removed and remaining wings separated into 2 parts at joint (see illustrations above)

vegetables and dressing

- 4 medium stalks celery, cut into thin sticks
- 2 medium carrots, peeled and cut into thin sticks
- 1½ cups Rich and Creamy Blue Cheese Dressing (see page 62)

1. FOR THE SAUCE: Melt butter in small saucepan over low heat. Whisk in hot sauces, brown sugar, and vinegar until combined. Remove from heat and set aside.

2. FOR THE WINGS: Preheat oven to 200 degrees. Line baking sheet with paper towels. Heat 2½ inches of oil in large Dutch oven over medium–high heat to 360 degrees. While oil heats, mix together cayenne, black pepper, salt, and cornstarch in small bowl. Dry chicken with paper towels and place pieces in large mixing bowl. Sprinkle spice mixture over wings and toss with rubber spatula until evenly coated. Fry half of chicken wings until golden and crisp, 10 to 12 minutes. With slotted spoon, transfer fried chicken wings to baking sheet. Keep first batch of chicken warm in oven while frying remaining wings.

3. TO SERVE: Pour sauce mixture into large bowl, add chicken wings, and toss until wings are uniformly coated. Serve immediately with carrot and celery sticks and blue cheese dressing on the side.

EQUIPMENT CORNER: Kitchen Tongs

SOMETIMES THE MORE THOUGHT YOU GIVE SOMETHING the better, but sometimes good enough is best left alone. The latter seems to be the case with tongs. We found that the simplest design—your basic, lightweight, agile-yet-sturdy restaurant tongs—easily bested all of the new "improved" tongs we tested. Testers dismissed tricky self-locking mechanisms, curved handles, nylon pincers, tight springs, or excess heft.

Oversized tweezers, for example, are not a good substitute for tongs, and the heft you value in a saucepan or stockpot is not a good quality when it comes to tongs. Heavy tongs (one pair weighed 10 ounces, with our top-rated models weighing half that) became tiresome to use, as did tongs with too much tension built into their springs. Tongs that respond to a light touch are the easiest and most comfortable to use as well as the most effective. We also liked tongs with the widest span between the pincers (6 inches or more was ideal) since they could hold big items, such as a roast.

To test the effectiveness of the tongs (and the one pair of tweezers), we used them to pick up slim asparagus spears, to retrieve irregularly shaped corn on the cob from boiling water, to sauté slippery scallops, to pan-fry breaded chicken cutlets, to move ramekins filled with water and chocolate mousse from one spot to another, and to turn a 3-pound pot roast. One pair of lightweight restaurant-style stainless steel tongs passed every test, and another, similar pair came very close.

TECHNIQUE: Disposing of Oil Neatly

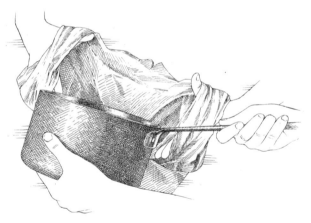

Deep-fried foods, such as Buffalo wings, are a real treat, but cleaning up after frying is not. Disposing of the spent oil neatly and safely is a particular challenge. Here's how we do it. We make a quadruple- or quintuple-layered bag using four or five leftover plastic grocery bags. With someone holding the layered bags open over a sink or in an outdoor area, we carefully pour the cooled frying oil from the pot into the innermost bag. We tie the bag handles shut and dispose of the oil in the garbage.

Rating Kitchen Tongs

WE TESTED NINE PAIRS OF TONGS, EACH AROUND 12 INCHES LONG. WE RAN EACH PAIR THROUGH SEVEN KITCHEN tests to assess ease of use as well as its ability to grasp slippery items, small items, and large items. The tongs are listed in order of preference. See www.cooksillustrated.com for up-to-date prices and mail-order sources for top-rated products.

HIGHLY RECOMMENDED

1. Edlund Locking 12-Inch Tongs

$9.95

These stainless steel tongs turned in a perfect score, excelling in each and every test. They're light, agile, and easy to use.

HIGHLY RECOMMENDED

2. Oxo Good Grips Locking 12-Inch Tongs

$9.99

These stainless steel tongs with rubber handles earned a perfect score in all tests but one—grasping a filled ramekin. Because most cooks are unlikely to use tongs for this purpose, we gave these tongs high marks anyway.

RECOMMENDED

3. Vollrath Stainless Steel Utility Tong

$3.20

These tongs are quite similar to the highly rated Edlund tongs, except they don't open quite as far—just 4 inches from tip to tip versus 6 inches for the Edlund tongs. As a result, it's difficult to grasp large items, such as a roast, with these tongs.

RECOMMENDED WITH RESERVATIONS

4. Chantal Locking Kitchen Tongs, Model KT-TG12

$14.99

These tongs got the job done in each of our tests but not without a fair amount of effort on the part of the cook. The tension built into these stainless steel tongs is too high.

RECOMMENDED WITH RESERVATIONS

5. Amco Stainless Steel and Nylon Locking Tongs

$10.99

These tongs were quite good at grasping solid foods such as corn on the cob, but their thick nylon tips ran into trouble when handling slippery foods.

NOT RECOMMENDED

6. Oneida Self-Locking Tongs

$7.99

These stainless steel tongs were unable to grasp a large pot roast because they did not open far enough. They also had too much built-in tension and a self-locking mechanism that sometimes came into play when you didn't expect it.

NOT RECOMMENDED

7. Calphalon Nylon Tongs

$8.00

These plastic tongs couldn't hold slippery foods. The narrow 2-inch span made it impossible to pick up large items.

NOT RECOMMENDED

8. All-Clad 12-Inch Locking Tongs

$20.00

These sturdy stainless steel tongs are built to last a lifetime, but their heft and the high degree of built-in tension made them somewhat challenging to use.

NOT RECOMMENDED

9. Endurance Sauté Tweezer

$6.99

These oversized stainless steel "tweezers" did a good job of picking up asparagus stalks, but they failed other tests.

SANGRÍA

WHAT WE WANTED: Many people mistake sangría for an unruly collection of fruit awash in a sea of overly sweetened red wine. But we were after a robust, sweet-tart punch, with the operative flavors of wine and citrus balanced against a simple, fruity background.

angría may be a party drink consumed without much thought, but there's no reason why it can't be better than the sweet concoctions served in most punch bowls. Working to find the right ingredient proportions for a standard 750-milliliter bottle of wine, we started by testing the other building blocks of sangría: orange and lemon slices, juice, sugar, and orange-flavored liqueur.

After tinkering with various proportions of cut-up fruit, we settled on a ratio of two oranges to one lemon. We tried limes, too, but found them too bitter. We did note that two sliced oranges and one sliced lemon in the pitcher made it difficult to pour the sangría, so we opted to squeeze the juice from one of the oranges. We also tried peeling the fruit, on the theory that the zest and pith might be contributing some bitterness, but without them, the sangría tasted too winey and a bit flat. Last, we tried mashing the fruit and the sugar together gently in the pitcher before adding the liquids. This improved the sangría by releasing some juice from the fruit and oils from the zest.

We wondered whether the type of sugar was important, since granulated, superfine, and a simple syrup of sugar dissolved in water all appeared in recipes. The flavor difference turned out to be infinitesimal, as did any difference in the mouthfeel of the drink, as each one dissolved completely. What did matter was the amount of sugar—¼ cup gave the punch a pleasant, but not cloying, sweetness.

The orange liqueur that is part of all sangría recipes also provides some sweetness and fruitiness. We tried expensive brands such as Cointreau, Curaçao, and Grand Marnier, as well as the more pedestrian Triple Sec, which was the

surprise prize winner for its bold, sweet flavor. One-quarter cup of Triple Sec was just right; less, or none, made for a bland and one-dimensional sangría.

With the basic formula down, we turned to the choice of wine. Across the board, bartenders, wine merchants, and Spanish restaurateurs all advised us to keep it cheap. They argued that the addition of sugar and fruit would throw off the balance of the wine, so why spend a lot on something

carefully crafted and pricey? Our testing so far had been done with a discount liquor store's house-label Merlot, a medium-bodied wine that cost a whopping $4.49 a bottle. Other wines we had tried included Beaujolais-Villages, which tasters thought too fruity and light; Zinfandel, which tasted bright and acidic; jug Burgundy, which was somewhat richer and rounder; and Rioja, which tasters found a bit flat and dull. We tried a more expensive Merlot (priced at $16.99), but only 1 taster out of 5 preferred the sangría made from it. Our advice, then, is to use cheap wine whose character you know and can live with. Fruity, pleasant Merlot is a good choice.

Many of the recipes we consulted moved well beyond the basic ingredients. Some had long lists of fruits, including apples, grapes, peaches, kiwis, cherries, and berries; others called for nonalcoholic filler ingredients, such as mineral or sparkling water, ginger ale, cold tea, lemonade, pineapple juice, or cranberry juice. One by one, we sampled, and rejected, each of these. Consistently, we all preferred the straightforward flavor of citrus to the floating-fruit-salad approach, and everyone agreed that fillers, even in small amounts, diluted the wine, demoting it to a mere background flavor. Our reactions to more potent additions, including gin, sweet vermouth, port, and the traditional brandy, were similar. Even amounts as small as a tablespoon moved sangría away from our ideal of a light, refreshing, quaffable summer drink.

A number of recipes suggested preparing the sangría ahead of time and letting it rest in the refrigerator before serving. When all was said and done, we came to consider the resting time essential. After tasting an eight-hour-old sangría, a freshly made batch seemed harsh and edgy. Rest assured, though, if you can't stand the anticipation, two hours of refrigeration serves the purpose adequately.

WHAT WE LEARNED: **The best sangría is based on cheap wine and uses oranges and lemons as the only fruit. Let the flavors of the sangría blend in the refrigerator for at least two hours and preferably longer.**

SANGRÍA serves 4

The longer sangría sits before drinking, the more smooth and mellow it will taste. A full day is best, but if that's impossible, give it an absolute minimum of two hours to sit. Use large, heavy, juicy oranges and lemons for the best flavor. Doubling or tripling the recipe is fine, but you'll have to switch to a large punch bowl in place of the pitcher. We tried several inexpensive wines, and tasters thought most of them performed well in this recipe. A fruity Merlot is an especially good choice.

2   large juice oranges, washed; one orange sliced; remaining orange juiced
1   large lemon, washed and sliced
¼   cup sugar
¼   cup Triple Sec
1   (750-milliliter) bottle inexpensive, fruity, medium-bodied red wine, chilled (see note)

1. Add sliced orange, lemon, and sugar to large pitcher; mash gently with wooden spoon until fruit releases some juice but is not totally crushed and sugar dissolves, about 1 minute. Stir in orange juice, Triple Sec, and wine; refrigerate for at least 2 hours and up to 8 hours.

2. Before serving, add 6 to 8 ice cubes and stir briskly to distribute settled fruit and pulp; serve immediately.

Matt and Dawn prepare the ingredients for soup making.

HEARTY soups

Everyone likes hearty soups, especially when the weather turns cold. And the notion of a meal in a bowl is certainly appealing. However, many cooks think more is better when it comes to hearty soups. Stick-to-your-ribs can be an appealing goal for stews, but too often we've found that hearty soups are heavy, starchy, gluey, or just downright tired.

Ham and split pea soup is not a light endeavor. That said, the texture should not be pasty. The peas should melt to form a creamy base for bits of ham and flavorful vegetables, such as onions and carrots. Of course, every spoonful should capture the smoky, sweet essence of ham. We set out to capture this flavor without using a huge bone from a roasted holiday ham.

When it comes to potato-leek soup, potatoes come first in name only. The sweet leek flavor should dominate here. The potatoes are a neutral foil for the leeks and provide the soup with body and heft. Of course, potatoes that fall apart and release their starch can turn this soup into a thick porridge reminiscent of cafeteria food. The trick is to cook the potatoes until tender without letting them dissolve into a starchy mess.

HAM AND SPLIT PEA SOUP

WHAT WE WANTED: Old-fashioned ham flavor from a readily available cut that would also provide enough meat for the soup. The texture must be creamy and thick but not heavy or gluey. Bits of aromatic vegetables (especially onions and carrots) should punctuate the soup.

Old-fashioned recipes for ham and split pea soup start with the bone from a large roast ham that has been nearly picked clean. The bone and some split peas are thrown into a pot with some water and cooked until the meat falls off the bone. By that time, the fat has discreetly melted into the liquid, and the peas have become creamy enough to thicken the soup.

We love split pea soup made this way, but times have changed. Except for the occasional holiday, most cooks rarely buy a bone-in ham, opting more often for the thin-sliced deli stuff. We wondered if we could duplicate this wonderful soup without buying a huge ham.

To test our belief that a ham stock is crucial to split pea soup, we made several pork stocks and pork-enhanced canned chicken broths. In addition to making stock the old-fashioned way from a meaty ham bone, we made stock from smoked pork necks, pork hocks (fresh and smoked), and smoked ham shanks. We also made cheater's stocks: kielbasa simmered in canned chicken broth, kielbasa simmered in water, bacon simmered in chicken broth, and bacon simmered in water.

The stocks based on hocks—fresh as well as smoked—were more greasy than flavorful. In addition, the hocks gave up very little meat, making it necessary to purchase an additional portion of ham to fortify the soup. Ham shanks, which include the hock, made a pleasant but lightweight stock that was a tad greasy and salty—both fixable problems had the stock been more stellar. Pork necks, which are not widely available, made a fairly flavorful but salty stock. All four cheater's stocks failed. Both the kielbasa- and bacon-enhanced chicken broths tasted strongly of overly processed meat, while the water-based versions tasted weak.

Not surprisingly, the stock made from the bone of a big ham was the winner. It was meaty and full-flavored, rich but not greasy, nicely seasoned without being overly salty, and smoky without tasting artificial. Unlike any of the other broths, this one sported bits of meat. And not just good meat—great meat. The tender pieces of ham that fell away from the bone during cooking were not just a nice byproduct of stock making. They were the glory of our split pea soup. But was there a way around buying half a ham (with an average weight of about 8 pounds) just to make a pot of soup?

After checking out the ham and smoked pork cases at several different stores, we discovered the picnic from the pork shoulder. Unlike what we generally refer to as ham, which comes from the back legs of the animal, the picnic comes from the shoulders and front legs. Smaller than a ham, the half-picnic weighs only 4½ pounds. After making a couple more pots of soup, we found that the picnic pork shoulder—with its bones, fat, rind, and meat—made outstanding stock, and, after two hours of simmering, the meat was meltingly tender yet still potently flavorful.

Because we did not need the entire picnic half for our pot of soup, we pulled off and roasted two of its meatier muscles and used the remaining meat, bone, fat, and rind to make the soup. At around 99 cents per pound, a picnic shoulder is usually cheaper than a ham and often cheaper than pork hocks, shanks, or neck bones as well. Here, we thought, was the modern solution. Rather than buy a ham for eating (and eating and eating) with a leftover bone for soup, purchase a picnic for soup, and roast the remaining couple of pounds for eating.

There are several ways to make ham and split pea soup. You can throw all of the ingredients—ham bone, peas, and diced vegetables—into a pot and simmer until everything is tender. Or you can sauté the vegetables, then add the remaining ingredients and cook the soup until the ham and peas are tender. Alternatively, you can cook the ham bone and peas (or give the ham bone a little bit of a head start) until ham and peas are tender and then add raw, sautéed, or caramelized vegetables to the pot, continuing to cook until the vegetables are tender and the flavors have blended.

Although we had hoped to keep the soup a straightforward, one-pot operation, we found out pretty quickly that dumping everything in at the same time resulted in gloppy, overcooked peas and tired mushy vegetables by the time the ham was tender. For textural contrast in this smooth, creamy soup, we ultimately preferred fully—though not overly—cooked vegetables.

Our best soups were those in which the vegetables spent enough time in the pot for their flavors to blend but not so long that they had lost all of their individual taste. Of the soups with vegetables added toward the end of cooking, we preferred the one with the caramelized vegetables. The sweeter vegetables gave this otherwise straightforward meat-and-starch soup a richness and depth of flavor that made the extra step and pan worth the trouble.

Many pea soup recipes call for an acidic ingredient—vinegar, lemon juice, fortified wines such as sherry or Madeira, Worcestershire sauce, or sour cream—to bring balance to an otherwise rich, heavy soup. After tasting all of the above, we found ourselves drawn to balsamic vinegar. Unlike any of the other ingredients, balsamic vinegar contributed a mildly sweet, mildly acidic flavor that complemented the soup perfectly.

WHAT WE LEARNED: Ham stock is essential for this soup, and you can get it with a picnic shoulder, a cut that adds great flavor and provides plenty of meat. For the best flavored and textured aromatic vegetables, sauté them in a separate pan. Finish the soup with a splash of mildly sweet balsamic vinegar.

HAM AND SPLIT PEA SOUP serves 6

Use an entire small 2 1/2-pound smoked picnic portion ham if you can find one. Otherwise, buy a half-picnic ham and remove some meat (see illustrations on page 22), which you can roast and use in sandwiches, salads, or omelets.

1	piece (about 2½ pounds) smoked, bone-in picnic ham
4	bay leaves
1	pound (2½ cups) split peas, rinsed and picked through
1	teaspoon dried thyme
2	tablespoons extra-virgin olive oil
2	medium onions, chopped medium
2	medium carrots, chopped medium

TECHNIQUE: Drip-Free Ladling

Here's how we keep drips and spills to a minimum when ladling soups or stews. Before lifting the filled ladle up and out of the pot, dip the bottom back into the pot, so the liquid comes about halfway up the ladle. The tension on the surface of the soup grabs any drips and pulls them back into the pot.

<table>
<tr><td>2</td><td>medium stalks celery, chopped medium</td></tr>
<tr><td>1</td><td>tablespoon unsalted butter</td></tr>
<tr><td>2</td><td>medium garlic cloves, minced (about 2 teaspoons)</td></tr>
<tr><td></td><td>Pinch sugar</td></tr>
<tr><td>3</td><td>small red potatoes, scrubbed and cut into ½-inch dice (about ¾ cup)</td></tr>
<tr><td></td><td>Ground black pepper</td></tr>
<tr><td></td><td>Minced red onion (optional)</td></tr>
<tr><td></td><td>Balsamic vinegar</td></tr>
</table>

1. Place ham, bay leaves, and 3 quarts water in large stockpot or Dutch oven. Cover and bring to a boil over medium-high heat. Reduce heat to low and simmer until meat is tender and pulls away from bone, 2 to 2½ hours. Remove ham meat and bone from pot and set aside.

2. Add split peas and thyme to stock. Bring back to boil, reduce heat, and simmer, uncovered, until peas are tender but not dissolved, about 45 minutes. Meanwhile, when ham is cool enough to handle, shred meat into bite-sized pieces and set aside. Discard rind and bone.

3. While split peas are simmering, heat oil in large skillet over high heat until shimmering. Add onions, carrots, and celery and sauté, stirring frequently, until most of liquid evaporates and vegetables begin to brown, 5 to 6 minutes. Reduce heat to medium-low and add butter, garlic, and sugar. Cook vegetables, stirring frequently, until deeply browned, 30 to 35 minutes; set aside.

4. Add sautéed vegetables, potatoes, and shredded ham to pot with split peas. Simmer until potatoes are tender and peas dissolve and thicken soup to consistency of light cream, about 20 minutes more. Season with pepper to taste. (The soup can be refrigerated in an airtight container for 2 days. Warm soup over low heat until hot.) Ladle soup into bowls, sprinkle with red onion, if using, and serve, passing balsamic vinegar separately.

HAM AND SPLIT PEA SOUP WITH CARAWAY

Toast 1½ teaspoons caraway seeds in small skillet over medium-high heat, stirring frequently, until fragrant and browned, about 4 minutes. Follow recipe for Ham and Split Pea Soup, substituting toasted caraway seeds for dried thyme.

TECHNIQUE:
Handling a Half-Picnic Ham

A half-picnic ham is readily available in supermarkets but contains too much meat for a pot of soup. Our solution is to pull off several meaty sections of the ham and roast the meat for sandwiches, salads, and egg dishes.

1. With your fingers, loosen the large comma-shaped muscles on top of the picnic half.

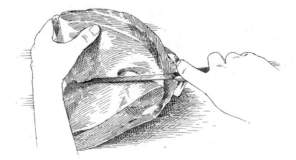

2. Use a knife to cut the membrane separating the comma-shaped muscles from the rest of the roast. The remaining meat and bone can be used to make soup.

RUSTIC POTATO-LEEK SOUP

WHAT WE WANTED: A chunky soup with bits of tender but not mushy potatoes and plenty of leek flavor.

We have always liked the classic creamy soup that French cooks make from potatoes and leeks. But sometimes this recipe seems a little too refined. At times we want these two ingredients at their most basic. So we decided to part company with the creamy French classic and take on the challenge of a more chunky, peasant-style French soup.

Ironically, the two ingredients that should make this soup great (potatoes and leeks) can also be its downfall. The potatoes should actually play only a supporting role; the leeks, gritty and time-consuming to clean though they are, are the real star of this soup. Cooking time is also crucial. Undercook the soup and the flavors will not meld; cook it too long and you will have a mixture of broken-down bits with little flavor or bite.

We tested the potatoes first. (See the Tasting Lab on page 25 for more information on the types of potatoes.) Quickly eliminating high-starch, low-moisture baking potatoes, which broke down immediately, we duly rejected the flavorful, medium-starch Yukon Gold as well. These potatoes broke down, too—just not as quickly. We settled on waxy, low-starch Red Bliss potatoes, which held their texture and did not become waterlogged during cooking. Then we reduced the proportion of potatoes altogether, giving the leeks the leading role.

Next we wanted to pump up the flavor of the soup. We decided to use not only the white part of the leek but also the light green part (the very dark green part is tough and should be discarded), and we left the chopped pieces large enough to create textural interest. A whopping 4 pounds of leeks used this way provided nonstop flavor. Water wasn't dynamic enough, so we used chicken stock instead.

But our real breakthrough came in the province of

technique. We knew that potatoes and leeks would need different simmering times. Stewing the leeks in some butter over a low flame to coax out as much flavor as possible, we added the potatoes later, with the chicken stock, then simmered them until almost tender. At that point we removed the pot from the heat, allowing the potatoes to finish cooking in the hot stock so they would not overcook and become mushy. The result: a soup with perfectly cooked potatoes, sweet and tender leeks, and an outspoken leek flavor. Because the potatoes were not cooked long enough to release their starch and thicken the broth, we added a little flour to cook with the leeks, giving the broth just the right amount of body to pull everything together.

WHAT WE LEARNED: For real leek flavor, use a lot of leeks and sweat them in a covered pot with butter. Don't overcook the potatoes or they will make the soup gluey. This is best accomplished by letting the potatoes finish cooking in the soup off heat.

RUSTIC POTATO-LEEK SOUP serves 6 to 8

This soup is hearty enough to serve as a main course, perhaps accompanied by crusty bread and preceded or followed by salad. Leeks differ. If yours have large desirable white and light green sections, use 4 pounds of leeks; if they're short on these parts, go with 5 pounds.

4–5	pounds leeks (see note)
6	tablespoons unsalted butter
1	tablespoon all-purpose flour
5¼	cups homemade chicken stock or canned low-sodium chicken broth
1	bay leaf
1¾	pounds red potatoes (about 5 medium), peeled and cut into ¾-inch dice
	Salt and ground black pepper

1. Cut off roots and tough dark green portion of leeks, leaving white portion and about 3 inches of light green portion. Clean leeks following illustrations at right. Slice leeks in half lengthwise and chop into 1-inch pieces. (You should have about 11 cups.)

2. Heat butter in large stockpot or Dutch oven over medium-low heat until foaming. Stir in leeks, increase heat to medium, cover, and cook, stirring occasionally, until leeks are tender but not mushy, 15 to 20 minutes; do not brown the leeks. Sprinkle flour over leeks and stir to coat evenly. Cook until flour dissolves, about 2 minutes.

3. Increase heat to high; whisking constantly, gradually add stock. Add bay leaf and potatoes, cover, and bring to a boil. Reduce heat to medium-low and simmer, covered, until potatoes are almost tender, 5 to 7 minutes. Remove pot from heat and let stand, covered, until potatoes are tender and flavors meld, 10 to 15 minutes. Discard bay leaf and season with salt and pepper to taste. (Soup can be refrigerated in airtight container for a day or two. Warm over low heat until hot; do not boil.) Serve immediately.

TECHNIQUE:
Two Ways to Clean Leeks

Leeks are often quite dirty and gritty, so they require thorough cleaning. There are two ways to do this. Both methods require that you first cut the dark green portion into quarters lengthwise, leaving the root end intact.

1. Hold the leek under running water and shuffle the cut layers like a deck of cards.

2. An alternative is to slosh the cut end of the leek up and down in a bowl of water.

RUSTIC POTATO-LEEK SOUP WITH KIELBASA

Eight ounces of cooked ham, cut into 1/2-inch dice, can be substituted for the sausage, if desired. Whichever you choose, season the soup with care, since both ham and kielbasa are fully seasoned.

Follow recipe for Rustic Potato-Leek Soup, stirring in 8 ounces kielbasa sausage, cut into ½-inch slices, just before removing pot from heat in step 3. Proceed as directed.

RUSTIC POTATO-LEEK SOUP WITH WHITE BEANS

Follow recipe for Rustic Potato-Leek Soup, reducing potatoes to 2 medium (about ¾ pound). Just before removing pot from heat in step 3, stir in 1 cup hot water and 1 cup canned cannellini beans that have been drained and rinsed well. Proceed as directed.

TASTING LAB: Potatoes

ALTHOUGH ALL VEGETABLES VARY IN SIZE AND FRESHNESS, most markets carry only a single variety. Broccoli is broccoli, carrots are carrots. Even when there are several varieties (as with heirloom tomatoes), most can be used interchangeably in recipes. Yes, one tomato might look a bit different or be a bit sweeter than another, but they all will taste fine in salads.

With potatoes, this is not the case. Make French fries with Red Bliss potatoes and the fries will be greasy and heavy. Use russets in salad or corn chowder and they will fall apart in a soggy mess.

The fact that dozens of potato varieties are grown in this country makes the question of which potato is best for a specific recipe even more confusing. At any time you may see as many as five or six kinds of potatoes in your supermarket. Go to a farmers' market and you may see a dozen varieties. Some potatoes are sold by varietal name (such as Red Bliss or Yukon Gold), others by generic name (all-purpose, baking, etc.).

To make sense of this confusion, it is helpful to group potatoes into three major categories based on their ratio of solids (mostly starch) to water. The categories are high-starch/low-moisture potatoes, medium-starch potatoes, and low-starch/high-moisture potatoes.

High-starch/low-moisture potatoes, such as russets or Idahos, generally lose their shape when simmered in soups or stews. Because they have so little moisture, they tend to soak up liquid as they cook and eventually implode. In some cases, such as when you want the potatoes to thicken a soup, this can be desirable. Medium-starch potatoes, such as Yukon Golds and Yellow Finns, do a better job of holding their shape but share many traits in common with high-starch potatoes. Low-starch/high-moisture potatoes hold their shape better than other potatoes when simmered. This category includes all red-skinned potatoes, such as Red Bliss and Red Creamer, as well as freshly dug potatoes, which are often labeled "new" potatoes. Low-starch potatoes should be selected when potatoes are to hold their shape, as in Rustic Potato-Leek Soup.

Rating Vegetable Peelers

WE TESTED 10 PEELERS ON SIX DIFFERENT FRUITS AND VEGETABLES. WE WANTED THIN STRIPS OF PEEL WITH LITTLE FLESH from apples, carrots, potatoes, and lemon, which we considered a single category. In a second category were tough-skinned butternut squash and celery root, from which we wanted thicker, fleshier strips of peel. In a third category, maneuverability, we assessed each peeler's performance on items with curves, crevices, and rough skin. We also evaluated handle-grip comfort, hand strain, sharpness of the blade, and the downward pressure required to peel. Peelers are listed in order of preference. See www.cooksillustrated.com for up-to-date prices and mail-order sources for top-rated products.

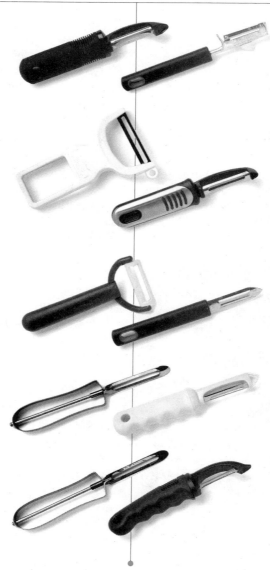

RECOMMENDED

1. Oxo Good Grips Peeler

$6.00

Sharp blade, comfortable grip, great on curves, but bulky in small hands. The best overall peeler.

RECOMMENDED

2. Kuhn Rikon Peeler

$3.25

Takes off very wide, thick strips of peel, so it's especially good on butternut squash and celery root. We keep one around just for these tasks.

NOT RECOMMENDED

3. Kyocera P-1 Ceramic Yoke Peeler

$14.95

Some of the same strengths as the Kuhn Rikon peeler, but blade travel is less smooth and price is much higher.

NOT RECOMMENDED

4. Ekco Deluxe Peeler

$2.49

Familiar, cheap, and adequate for easy peeling, but almost useless on tough jobs like squash. Has stainless steel blade.

NOT RECOMMENDED

5. Ekco Peeler

$1.29

Same as Deluxe version but with carbon steel blade that is not appreciably sharper than stainless steel, and it rusts.

NOT RECOMMENDED

6. Henckels Swivel Peeler

$11.00

An expensive peeler that hugs curves but glides right over the skin on flat surfaces of squash and rough skin of celery root.

NOT RECOMMENDED

7. Farberware Stainless Soft Grip Euro Peeler

$5.99

Blade does not feel sharp, and it slides right over curved surfaces. Bulky in all but large hands.

NOT RECOMMENDED

8. Henckels Vegetable Peeler

$8.00

Exceptionally sturdy, but it feels like you're using a paring knife. Not for thin or delicate skins. Blade angle feels awkward.

NOT RECOMMENDED

9. Farberware Euro Peeler

$3.99

To get decent leverage with the blade, you must really choke up on the handle, which strains the hand. Blade is not particularly sharp.

NOT RECOMMENDED

10. Revereware Comfort Grip Permasharp Peeler

$4.99

The grip feels bulky even in large hands. The blade is recessed so far into the frame that often the blade can't reach the food.

EQUIPMENT CORNER: Vegetable Peelers

YOU MIGHT IMAGINE THAT ALL VEGETABLE PEELERS ARE pretty much the same. Not so. In our research, we turned up 25 peelers, many with quite novel features. The major differences were the fixture of the blade, either stationary or swiveling; the material of the blade, carbon stainless steel, stainless steel, or ceramic; and the orientation of the blade to the handle, either straight in line with the body or perpendicular to it. The last arrangement, with the blade perpendicular to the handle, is called a harp, or Y, peeler because the frame looks like the body of a harp or the letter Y. This type of peeler, which is popular in Europe, works with a pulling motion rather than the shucking motion of most American peelers.

For our tests we narrowed the number of peelers to 10 and then recruited several cooks to peel carrots, potatoes, lemons, butternut squash, and celery root. In most cases, testers preferred the Oxo Good Grips peeler with a sharp stainless steel blade that swivels. Peelers with stationary blades are fine for peeling carrots, but they have trouble hugging the curves on potatoes. As for blade material, we found peelers made from stainless steel, carbon steel, and ceramic that were both sharp and dull. We concluded that sharpness is a factor of quality control during the manufacturing process and not blade material.

The Y-shaped peelers tested well, although they removed more flesh along with the skin on potatoes, lemons, and carrots and therefore did not rate as well as the Oxo Good Grips. The one case where this liability turned into an asset was with butternut squash, where these Y-shaped peelers took off the skin as well as the greenish-tinged flesh right below the skin in one pass. With the Oxo Good Grips, it was necessary to go over the peeled flesh once the skin had been removed. Among Y-shaped peelers, testers preferred the Kuhn Rikon. Because both the Oxo Good Grips and Kuhn Rikon peelers can be had for less than $10, we recommend that you purchase both.

TASTING LAB: Salt

THE FOOD PRESS HAS EXALTED EXOTIC SEA SALTS. WE wondered if a pinch here or a smidgen there is really worth as much as $36 per pound. Will your biscuits or steak taste better if you spend more money on salt?

And what about choosing an everyday salt for adding to pasta water or chicken stock? More home cooks are following the lead of chefs and keeping kosher salt (rather than table salt) next to the stove. Chefs have spread the word that these oversized grains of salt have a pure, clean flavor and that it's much easier to pick up the large crystals with your fingers. While the argument about crystal size is persuasive, we wondered if kosher salt really does taste better than table salt.

Salt is either mined from ancient seas that dried up millions of years ago or obtained by evaporating seawater. In their pure form, sodium chloride, salts from both sources taste the same. What distinguishes one salt from another in color and flavor are the type and amount of minerals (such as magnesium, calcium, and potassium) and/or clays attached to the crystals of sodium chloride. The size and texture of the crystals—whether big flakes, irregularly shaped large grains, or regularly shaped small grains—are largely determined by the way the salt is processed.

Sea salt is obtained from seawater held in large, shallow ponds or large pans. As the water evaporates, coarse crystals of salt fall to the bottom. The crystals are collected by raking. The white fleur de sel, or "flower of the salt," is harvested from salt that forms on the surface of the pans as a thin film and is quickly skimmed. It is extremely expensive. (The brand we tested costs $36 per pound.)

Table salt is usually obtained by pumping water into an underground salt deposit to dissolve the salt, pumping the brine to the surface, settling impurities, and vacuum-evaporating the clear brine. Rapid vacuum evaporation yields the tiny, regularly shaped grains that fit through the holes in a salt shaker. Some table salt is taken from the sea and then processed by vacuum evaporation to yield small crystals.

Kosher salt can be mined or taken from the sea. Processing is designed to produce coarse, irregular crystals that will cling to meat during koshering, in which the salt is applied to draw blood out of just-butchered meats.

Unlike kosher salt and sea salt, most table salts contain additives. Iodized table salt contains potassium iodide, which protects against thyroid disease. Dextrose may be added to help stabilize the iodine, and calcium silicate or one of several other drying agents are often added to prevent caking. Many experts claim these additives can impart an off flavor.

To make sense of all these claims, we tasted two kinds of table salt (one iodized, one not), two brands of kosher salt, and five widely available sea salts. The price per pound ranged from 36 cents to $36. Tests were divided into three categories: salt used at the table (we sprinkled each sample on roast beef), salt used in baking (we used a plain biscuit recipe), and salt dissolved in liquids (we tested each salt in spring water, chicken stock, and pasta cooking water).

Of the five tests run, we uncovered the most profound differences in our beef tenderloin test. Tasters loved the crunch of the large sea salt flakes or crystals when sprinkled over slices of roast tenderloin. Here, Maldon Sea Salt was the clear winner, followed by Fleur de Sel de Camargue and Light Grey Celtic Sea Salt.

Why did the sea salts win this test? According to Dr. Gary Beauchamp, director of the Monell Chemical Senses Center in Philadelphia and a leading expert on the science of taste and smell, flat crystals or crystals with holes cause a taste sensation different from that of regularly shaped small crystals. And, based on our test results, it's clear that large crystals provided a more pleasing sensory stimulation than fine table salt. In fact, tasters really objected to fine salts sprinkled on the beef, calling them "harsh" and "sharp." Tasters did like kosher salt on meat, but not as much as sea salt, which has larger crystals.

Does this mean that our tasters were reacting to the additives in table salt that the chefs had warned us about? It's possible, but given the results in our other tests, we are not convinced. In fact, the one fine sea salt in our tasting (La Baleine) finished next-to-last in this test, and it does not contain any additives. It's hard to sprinkle fine sea or table salt evenly over meat, and we think tasters may have been hitting pockets with a lot of salt and reacting negatively.

In the biscuit tests, Morton table salt was the winner, and most of the sea salts landed at the bottom of the ratings. The explanation here is simple. Small salt crystals are more evenly distributed in baked goods than large crystals, and tasters didn't like getting a big hit of crunchy salt as they nibbled on biscuits.

In the spring water, chicken stock, and pasta cooking water, tasters felt that all nine salts tasted pretty much the same. Why didn't the fancy sea salts beat the pants off plain table salt in these tests? The main reason is dilution. Yes, sea salts sampled right from the box (or sprinkled on meat at the table) did taste better than table salt. And while crystal size did undoubtedly affect flavor perception in the tenderloin test, we suspect that our tasters were also responding favorably to some of the trace minerals in these salts. But mineral content is so low in sea salt (by weight, less than 1 percent in all brands tested) that any effect these minerals might have on flavor was lost when a teaspoon of salt was stirred into a big pot of chicken stock or pasta cooking water.

One final (and very important) point. Our results should not be taken to mean that all salts behave in the same way in the kitchen. For example, salts with a fine texture may seem saltier than coarse salts because of the way the crystals pack down in a teaspoon when measured. For instance, a teaspoon of coarse Maldon Sea Salt contains just half as much salt as a teaspoon of fine table salt.

What, then, can we conclude from the results of these tests? For one, expensive sea salts are best saved for the table, where their delicate flavor and great crunch can be appreciated. Don't waste $36-a-pound sea salt by sprinkling it into a simmering stew. If you like to keep coarse salt in a ramekin next to the stove, choose a kosher salt, which costs just pennies per pound. If you measure salt by the teaspoon when cooking, you might as well use table salt, which is also the best choice for baking.

Rating Salts

NINE SALTS WERE PUT THROUGH A BATTERY OF TESTS. WE FOUND THAT FLAVOR DIFFERENCES WERE SUBTLE. TEXTURE was a consideration in only the biscuit and tenderloin tests. Salts are listed in order of preference based on all tests, but the difference between the first- and last-place brands was small. See www.cooksillustrated.com for up-to-date prices and mail-order sources for sea salts.

RECOMMENDED

1. Maldon Sea Salt, Maldon, England

$6.95 for 8.5 ounces ($13.08 per pound)

These light, airy, crunchy flakes resemble pyramids and are a perfect match with meat. Available in gourmet stores and by mail.

RECOMMENDED

2. Fleur de Sel de Camargue, Provence, France

$9.95 for 4.4 ounces ($36.18 per pound)

The "great crunch" of this hand-harvested salt propelled it to second place in the tenderloin test. "Gritty" in biscuits. Available in gourmet stores and by mail.

RECOMMENDED

3. Morton Kosher Salt, United States

$1.69 for 48 ounces ($0.56 per pound)

This "straightforward" salt finished third in the biscuit test. Tasters liked the crunch of these medium-sized grains on the tenderloin. Available in supermarkets.

RECOMMENDED

4. Diamond Crystal Kosher Salt, United States

$1.99 for 48 ounces ($0.66 per pound)

Tasters enjoyed this salt on the tenderloin. The biscuits were mild and buttery, though one taster detected "pockets of salt." Available in supermarkets.

RECOMMENDED

5. Light Grey Celtic Sea Salt, Brittany, France

$7.75 for 24 ounces ($5.17 per pound)

This hand-harvested salt has a unique grayish hue because of its high mineral content. Coarse "pebbles" were too large in the biscuits but better suited to tenderloin. Available in gourmet stores and by mail.

RECOMMENDED

6. La Baleine Sea Salt Fine Crystals, Provence, France

$4.89 for 26.5 ounces ($2.95 per pound)

This finely ground sea salt comes from the Mediterranean and was judged to have a clean, sweet, mild flavor, but tasters thought powdery grains were "inappropriate for garnishing roasts." Available in supermarkets.

RECOMMENDED

7. Morton Iodized Table Salt, United States

$0.59 for 26 ounces ($0.36 per pound)

This salt won first place in the biscuit test, but tasters disliked the way these small grains "dissolved into nothingness" on the meat. Available in supermarkets.

RECOMMENDED

8. Esprit du Sel de Île de Ré, Brittany, France

$9.00 for 8.8 ounces ($16.36 per pound)

Tasters thought the irregularly coarse grains were just right for tenderloin but resulted in an unappealing, crunchy texture in biscuits. Available in gourmet stores and by mail.

RECOMMENDED

9. Morton Non-Iodized Table Salt, United States

$0.59 for 26 ounces ($0.36 per pound)

This salt was described as "sharp and characterless" when sprinkled on tenderloin. However, these small grains were thought to be perfect for biscuits. Available in supermarkets.

DRESSING UP vegetables

CHAPTER 3

You can't serve steamed broccoli every night. No matter how well executed, it's just too boring. Every cook needs foolproof recipes for dressing up everyday vegetables. Frozen vegetables (such as tired twice-baked potatoes and army-green stuffed bell peppers) are not the answer. You might as well stick with steamed broccoli. Our goal was simple. Rescue two favorite fancy vegetable dishes—twice-baked potatoes and stuffed bell peppers—from the clutches of cafeterias, bad steakhouses, and frozen food manufacturers.

A good twice-baked potato is a study in contrasts. The crisp potato shell nestles a creamy, smooth filling that is rich but not overwhelming. Although this vegetable side dish looks a lot more impressive than your average baked potato, it should not require much more work.

Stuffed bell peppers certainly sound like a good idea. But how many times have you bitten into a pepper that is crunchy or, worse still, slimy and soft? And the rice filling is often soggy, bland, or made sickly sweet with too much ketchup. How can something so classic go so wrong? We knew that the test kitchen could revive these dishes and still keep them simple and straightforward.

Garlic gets sliced, slivered, and minced in preparation for testing vegetable recipes.

TWICE-BAKED POTATOES

WHAT WE WANTED: Twice-baked potatoes are at the apex of American potato cookery. Although they are not difficult to make, the process can be time-consuming. We wanted to perfect the process—from baking the potatoes and readying the shells to preparing the filling and baking when filled.

This simple dish—essentially baked russet potatoes from which the flesh has been removed, mashed with dairy ingredients and seasonings, mounded back in the shells, and baked again—offers a good range of both texture and flavor in a single morsel. When done well, the skin is chewy and substantial without being tough, with just a hint of crispness to play off the smooth, creamy filling. In terms of flavor, cheese and other dairy ingredients make the filling rich and tangy, a contrast with the mild, slightly nutty potato shell.

Because twice-baked potatoes are put in the oven twice, we found it best to bake them for just an hour, rather than the usual 75 minutes we allocate for plain baked potatoes. Oiling the skins before baking promotes crispness, not something you necessarily want in plain baked potatoes but a trait we came to love in creamy twice-baked potatoes.

Our favorite baked potato recipe underscores the importance of opening the potatoes right after baking to release as much steam as possible. For twice-baked potatoes, it's advisable to wait a few minutes for the potatoes to cool before slicing them apart and emptying out the flesh.

Once we had emptied the potato halves of their flesh, we noticed they got a little flabby sitting on the counter waiting to be stuffed. Because the oven was still on and waiting for the return of the stuffed halves, we decided to put the skins back in while we prepared the filling. This worked beautifully, making the shells extra crisp.

Pleased with our chewy, slightly crunchy skins, we now had to develop a smooth, lush, flavorful filling that would hold up its end of the bargain. (Lumpy, sodden, and dull-tasting would not do.) Twice-baked potatoes are usually filled with a mixture of well-mashed potato, shredded cheese, and other dairy ingredients, including one or more of the usual suspects: butter, sour cream, cream cheese, yogurt, ricotta, cottage cheese, milk, cream, and buttermilk. Various herbs and spices also often show up, as do diced meats and sautéed vegetables.

To get an idea of how we wanted to flavor our filling, we prepared 10 different recipes with various ingredient combinations. In a rare display of accord, all tasters agreed on a few general observations. First, everyone preferred tangy dairy products, such as sour cream, yogurt, and buttermilk, to sweet ones, such as milk, cream, and ricotta. Second, the use of only one dairy ingredient produced a rather dull, one-dimensional filling. A second ingredient added depth of flavor and complexity. Third, nobody favored too fatty a mouthfeel, a preference that left the addition of large amounts of butter (some recipes use up to a full stick for four potatoes) and cream cheese out of the running. Dozens of further tests helped us refine our filling to a rich, but not killer, combination of sharp cheddar, sour cream, buttermilk, and just 2 tablespoons of butter.

With the filling mixed and mounded back into the shells, our last tests centered on the final baking. We wanted to do more than just heat the filling through; we were intent of forming an attractive brown crust on it as well. Broiling turned out to be the easiest and most effective method. After about 10 minutes, the potatoes emerged browned, crusted, and ready for the table.

WHAT WE LEARNED: Oil the potatoes before baking for a crisp skin, and bake the hollowed-out shells to prevent sogginess. Use a combination of sour cream, buttermilk, and just 2 tablespoons of butter for a tangy filling that's rich but not heavy. Broil the filled potato shells to create a crisp crust on top.

TWICE-BAKED POTATOES serves 6 to 8

To vary the flavor a bit, try substituting other types of cheese, such as Gruyère, fontina, or feta, for the cheddar. Yukon Gold potatoes, though slightly more moist than our ideal, gave our twice-baked potatoes a buttery flavor and mouthfeel that everyone liked, so we recommend them as a substitute for the russets.

4   medium russet potatoes (7 to 8 ounces each), scrubbed, dried, and rubbed lightly with vegetable oil
4   ounces sharp cheddar cheese, shredded (about 1 cup)
½   cup sour cream
½   cup buttermilk
2   tablespoons unsalted butter, softened
3   medium scallions, sliced thin
½   teaspoon salt
      Ground black pepper

1. Adjust oven rack to upper-middle position and heat oven to 400 degrees. Bake potatoes on foil-lined baking sheet until skin is crisp and deep brown and skewer easily pierces flesh, about 1 hour. Setting baking sheet aside, transfer potatoes to wire rack and let cool slightly, about 10 minutes.

2. Using oven mitt or folded kitchen towel to handle hot potatoes, cut each potato in half so that long, blunt sides rest on work surface (see photograph at right). Using small spoon, scoop flesh from each half into medium bowl, leaving ⅛ to ¼ inch thickness of flesh in each shell. Arrange shells on lined baking sheet and return to oven until dry and slightly crisp, about 10 minutes. Meanwhile, mash potato flesh with fork until smooth. Stir in remaining ingredients, including pepper to taste, until well combined.

3. Remove shells from oven and increase oven setting to broil. Holding shells steady on pan with oven mitt or towel-protected hand, spoon mixture into crisped shells, mounding it slightly at center, and return potatoes to oven. Broil

until spotty brown and crisp on top, 10 to 15 minutes. Allow to cool for 10 minutes. Serve warm.

VARIATIONS

TWICE-BAKED POTATOES WITH PEPPERJACK CHEESE AND BACON

Fry 8 strips (about 8 ounces) bacon, cut crosswise into ¼-inch pieces, in medium skillet over medium heat until crisp, 5 to 7 minutes. With slotted spoon, transfer bacon to paper towel–lined plate to drain; set aside. Follow recipe for Twice-Baked Potatoes, substituting pepperjack cheese for cheddar and stirring reserved bacon into filling mixture.

TWICE-BAKED POTATOES WITH CHIPOTLE CHILE AND ONION

For a slightly smoky aftertaste with just a hint of heat, limit the chipotle to 1 tablespoon; for a little heat, increase the chipotle to 1½ tablespoons.

Heat 2 tablespoons butter in medium skillet over medium heat; add 1 medium onion, chopped fine, and sauté until

GETTING IT RIGHT:
Halving Baked Potatoes

This way

NOT this way

Most potatoes have two relatively flat, blunt sides and two curved sides. Halve the baked potatoes lengthwise so the blunt sides are down once the shells are stuffed, making the potatoes much more stable in the pan during final baking.

taking care not to brown garlic or ginger. Off heat, stir in 1 cup thawed frozen peas; set aside. Follow recipe for Twice-Baked Potatoes, omitting cheese and butter and stirring spiced peas into filling mixture.

TWICE-BAKED POTATOES WITH SMOKED SALMON AND CHIVES

This variation makes a fine brunch dish.

Follow recipe for Twice-Baked Potatoes, omitting cheese and scallions and stirring 4 ounces smoked salmon, cut into ½-inch pieces, and 3 tablespoons minced fresh chives into filling mixture. Sprinkle finished potatoes with additional chopped chives as a garnish just before serving.

TASTING LAB: Black Pepper

AS THE LONG-REIGNING KING OF SPICES, ONCE EQUAL IN value to gold, black pepper has become a kitchen table constant. The hard, dry, blackish kernels we know as peppercorns are derived from long, thin spikes of ripe green berries that grow on a vine reaching up to 100 feet long. Once picked, the berries are typically spread out on concrete slabs or straw mats, where they are left to dry in the sun for a number of days, changing from taut green balls to dark, wrinkled, dense kernels.

Not to be confused with chile pepper (Capsicum annuum), black pepper (Piper nigrum) grows in warm, moist climates all over the world, typically within about 15 degrees of the equator. Although most of us tend to think that one jar of black pepper is the same as another, several varieties exist. The most readily available include Vietnamese pepper, Lampong (from the island of Sumatra), and Malabar and Tellicherry (both from India). Among spice experts, each has gained a reputation for its particular attributes.

Neither a supermarket brand nor sometimes even a gourmet store brand is likely to specify from what part of the world its pepper was sourced. The product is advertised

soft, 3 to 4 minutes. Follow recipe for Twice-Baked Potatoes, omitting butter and adding 1 to 1½ tablespoons minced canned chipotle chiles in adobo sauce, reserved sautéed onion, and 2 tablespoons chopped fresh cilantro leaves to filling mixture.

TWICE-BAKED POTATOES WITH MONTEREY JACK AND PESTO

Follow recipe for Twice-Baked Potatoes, substituting Monterey Jack cheese for cheddar, reducing buttermilk to ¼ cup, omitting butter, and adding ¼ cup prepared pesto to filling mixture.

TWICE-BAKED POTATOES WITH INDIAN SPICES AND PEAS

Heat 2 tablespoons butter in medium skillet over medium heat. Add 1 medium onion, chopped fine, and sauté until soft, 3 to 4 minutes. Add 1 teaspoon finely grated fresh ginger, 3 medium minced garlic cloves (about 1 tablespoon), 1 teaspoon each ground cumin and ground coriander, and ¼ teaspoon each ground cinnamon, ground turmeric, and ground cloves; cook until fragrant, about 30 seconds more,

Rating Black Peppers

WE EVALUATED 10 BRANDS OF BLACK PEPPERCORNS OR GROUND BLACK PEPPER. WHOLE PEPPERCORNS WERE CRACKED within a half hour before tasting. The peppers are listed in order of preference. All of those in the recommended category received relatively close score results. See www.cooksillustrated.com for up-to-date prices and mail-order sources for top-rated products.

RECOMMENDED

1. McCormick/Schilling Whole Black Peppercorns (sold in glass jar)

$4.19 for 1.87 ounces

This pepper imparted a robust, piney aroma with orange notes. This line consists of either Malabar or Lampong pepper. Available in supermarkets. Sold on the West Coast under the Schilling label.

RECOMMENDED

2. Kalustyan's Vietnam Whole Black Pepper Corn

$4.99 for 4 ounces

This sample tasted mild and was noticeably smoky, with a "very distinct woody flavor." Not fiery, but heat "catches up to you." Available by mail.

RECOMMENDED

3. Kalustyan's Lampong Whole Black Pepper Corn

$4.99 for 4 ounces

This Indonesia pepper delivered a pungent aroma described as "penetrating" and "fruity." Its flavor was not as pungent as its aroma. Available by mail.

RECOMMENDED

4. Penzeys Malabar Black Peppercorns

$2.99 for 2.5 ounces

This Indian pepper had a rich fragrance with elements of fresh pine and lemon. Its flavor was "woodsy" and "biting," with "lots of heat." Available by mail.

RECOMMENDED

5. Penzeys Tellicherry Black Peppercorns

$2.99 for 4 ounces

This Indian pepper is left to mature on the vine to develop more flavor. The sample we tasted was "quite pungent," with "intense heat at the end." Available by mail.

RECOMMENDED

6. McCormick/Schilling Whole Black Peppercorns (sold in plastic bottle)

$2.29 for 2.37 ounces

Considered the least premium peppercorn in the McCormick/Schilling line, this pepper nonetheless held up reasonably well. Its flavor was musty as well as biting and pungent. Available in supermarkets.

NOT RECOMMENDED

7. McCormick/Schilling Pure Ground Black Pepper (sold in tin)

$1.89 for 2 ounces

Of all the ground pepper samples, this familiar tin can carried the most flavor but was still deemed bland. Available in supermarkets.

NOT RECOMMENDED

8. Spice Islands Whole Black Pepper

$3.89 for 2.4 ounces

Penetratingly hot and very "bitter" and "dusty." Available in supermarkets.

NOT RECOMMENDED

9. Spice Islands Fine Grind Black Pepper

$4.68 for 2.3 ounces

This pepper was described as "weak," having "no complexity" and only a light, latent heat. Available in supermarkets.

NOT RECOMMENDED

10. McCormick/Schilling Ground Black Pepper (sold in glass jar)

$4.39 for 1.62 ounces

This pricey ground pepper had "no interesting flavor characteristics to speak of," one taster asserted. Available in supermarkets.

simply as "black pepper," leaving the consumer with the choice of whole or ground.

For a spice that we use just about every day, and with a wide variety of foods, it's hard not to wonder if we have taken pepper too much for granted and are missing out on a greater taste experience. Perhaps we should be seeking out black pepper from a particular region of a particular country. Or, at the other end of the spectrum, perhaps all this fuss over grinding fresh whole peppercorns is nonsense, not really providing any improved flavor. We decided to hold a blind tasting to sort it all out.

We included in our tasting the two preeminent national supermarket brands as well as the above-mentioned varieties, which were ordered from specialty spice and gourmet stores. We skipped some varieties of black pepper, such as Brazilian and Ponape, because they proved too difficult to find on the retail level. Even some of those we did include in the tasting can be hard to track down. We also left out white pepper, which comes from the same plant as black pepper but is harvested when the berries are further ripened; they are then soaked, rubbed to remove their shells, and dried. Also excluded from our tasting were green peppercorns, which are unripe pepper berries, and pink peppercorns, which are not true peppercorns at all but come from a tree.

All of the peppers were offered plain but with the option of being tasted on plain white rice. Overall, our tasting confirmed that freshly ground pepper is far superior to pepper purchased already ground. The latter carried minimal aroma and tended to taste sharp and dull, lacking in complexity. Those whole peppercorns that were fresh ground just before the tasting contained bold as well as subtle flavors and aromas that were both lively and complex.

As for differences between the varieties of whole peppercorns that were tasted fresh-ground, we found them to be distinct yet subtle. All were appreciated for their particular characteristics (see the chart on page 35), receiving high scores within a close range of one another. Based on these results, we concluded that what is important is not so much which variety of pepper you buy but how you buy it.

Why did we find the most noticeable differences in pepper to be between fresh ground whole pepper and commercially ground pepper? When a peppercorn is cracked, the volatile chemical components that give pepper its bold aroma as well as its subtle characteristics immediately begin to disperse. These more subtle flavors often include pine and citrus. So with time (and cracking), what remains is the predominant nonvolatile compound in black pepper, piperine. Piperine is the source of black pepper's renowned pungency and is what gives it its characteristic hot, sharp, and stinging qualities. It is also said to stimulate saliva and gastric juices, creating the sensation of hunger.

Knowing this, one of the easiest ways for a home cook to improve his or her cooking is simply by buying whole peppercorns and grinding them fresh with each meal. That way, instead of merely experiencing the sharp sensation that ground pepper has to offer, you will unleash a spectrum of flavors from earthy to exotic.

There are a couple of tips for buying pepper. As with any spice, purchase it from a reputable source that has high product turnover, so that you know you are buying a fresh product. The appearance of the peppercorns can also be an indicator of quality. Peppercorns that were not dried quickly enough take on a white tint to their dark color (not to be confused with white peppercorns) and will not be as flavorful. Quality black pepper should have a dark, shiny appearance and not be sitting in a lot of dust.

STUFFED PEPPERS

WHAT WE WANTED: Tender peppers with enough structure to hold a well-seasoned filling.

Mention stuffed peppers to most people and they think of a U.S. Army green shell crammed with leftovers from the school cafeteria. Although the classic 1950s sweet pepper filled with aromatic rice and beef and topped with ketchup may sound mediocre, this recipe can be delicious if prepared properly.

To get going, we tried a few classic recipes. Although these trial runs produced nothing as bad as what we remembered from the school cafeteria, they were far from perfect. First off, the peppers themselves varied greatly in degree of doneness. Some were so thoroughly cooked that they slumped onto their sides, unable to support their stuffed weight. On the other end of the spectrum, barely cooked peppers added an unfriendly crunch and bitter flavor to the mix. To be a success, the peppers themselves would have to yield a tender bite yet retain enough structure to stand up proudly on the plate.

None of the fillings hit home, either. An all-rice version was uninteresting, while another stuffed with all meat was leaden and greasy. One recipe called for small amounts of so many varied ingredients that it made us think its creator just wanted to clean out her refrigerator. We came away from this first round of tests wanting a simple yet gratifying filling, neither humdrum nor packed with odd ingredients.

To start, we needed a solid pepper venue with minimal crunch. So we steamed, microwaved, roasted, and blanched a round of peppers and lined them up for everyone in the test kitchen to examine. The steamed and microwaved examples were bland in both color and flavor. We tried roasting in an uncovered dish filled with a little water, an uncovered dish with no water, and a covered dish. Each procedure produced a bitter, subpar pepper. We knew that if we allowed the peppers to roast a little longer, their sugars would

eventually caramelize and the peppers would turn sweet. But at that point their texture would also have disintegrated into that of an Italian sandwich ingredient. Tasters unanimously preferred the vibrant color, sturdiness, and overall sweeter flavor of the blanched peppers; the hot water actually seemed to have washed away some of their bitterness.

Usually, a freshly blanched vegetable is plunged immediately into an ice cold water bath in a process known as shocking. The point is to halt the cooking process at just the right moment while stabilizing the vegetable's brightened color. We find water baths to be a real pain, especially in a kitchen where counter space is prime property. Although the shocked peppers had a slightly brighter hue than those that had been blanched but not shocked, they took much longer to heat through in the oven. So we abandoned shocking and instead fussed with blanching times, being careful to remove the peppers a little early and then allow the residual heat to finish their cooking. We found that a three-minute dip in boiling water followed by a cooling period on the countertop yielded the perfect balance of structure and chew.

Even with a pepper that's cooked to perfection, everyone knows that in this dish the stuffing is the star of the show. The options for stuffing ingredients are many, including couscous, polenta, and a number of interesting and unusual grains. But we landed on rice. A universal pantry ingredient, it is a classic in American recipes for stuffed peppers.

Because we wanted these stuffed peppers to work as a quick midweek meal, our goal was to keep the rice-based filling simple and satisfying, with a streamlined ingredient list and preparation method. Tasters did not care much for sausage, heavy seasonings, or a mix of too many ingredients. To our surprise, they were big fans of the classic 1950s version of a pepper stuffed with rice and ground beef. Sautéed onions and garlic rounded out the flavors, while tomatoes added a fresh note and some color. Bound together with a little cheese and topped with ketchup, this retro pepper is a model of simplicity, but it can be easily updated by using different spices and seasonings. We found that Middle Eastern and Italian flavors are especially well suited to this dish.

Now we had a pepper, and we had a filling. All we had to do was figure out the best way to get them together. The first trick is to use the boiling water from the blanched peppers to cook the rice. While the peppers cool and the rice cooks, the onions, garlic, and beef can be sautéed quickly. Then filling and peppers can be assembled and heated through in the oven. The result? Stuffed peppers that take only 45 minutes from start to finish—and that are also truly worth eating.

WHAT WE LEARNED: **Blanch the peppers to improve their flavor, color, and texture before stuffing them. Cook the rice in the hot blanching water to save time. Flavor a classic rice-and-beef filling with tomatoes, cheddar cheese, onion, and garlic for a basic stuffed pepper, or get more adventurous with either Italian or Middle Eastern flavors.**

CLASSIC STUFFED BELL PEPPERS
serves 4 as a light main dish or side dish

When shopping for bell peppers to stuff, it's best to choose those with broad bases that will allow the peppers to stand up on their own. (See the Tasting Lab on page 40 for more guidelines on selecting peppers for this recipe.) It's easier to fill the peppers after they have been placed in the baking dish because the sides of the dish will hold the peppers steady.

	Salt
4	medium red, yellow, or orange bell peppers (about 6 ounces each), ½ inch trimmed off tops, cores and seeds discarded
½	cup long-grain white rice
1½	tablespoons olive oil
1	medium onion, chopped fine (about 1 cup)
12	ounces ground beef, preferably ground chuck
3	medium garlic cloves, minced (about 1 tablespoon)
1	(14½-ounce) can diced tomatoes, drained, ¼ cup juice reserved
5	ounces Monterey Jack cheese, shredded (1¼ cups)
2	tablespoons chopped fresh parsley leaves
	Ground black pepper
¼	cup ketchup

1. Bring 4 quarts water to a boil in large stockpot or Dutch oven over high heat. Add 1 tablespoon salt and bell peppers. Cook until peppers just begin to soften, about 3 minutes. Using slotted spoon, remove peppers from pot, drain off excess water, and place peppers cut-sides up on paper towels. Return water to a boil; add rice and boil until tender, about 13 minutes. Drain rice and transfer it to large bowl; set aside.

2. Adjust oven rack to middle position and heat oven to 350 degrees.

3. Meanwhile, heat oil in 12-inch heavy-bottomed skillet over medium-high heat until shimmering. Add onion and cook, stirring occasionally, until softened and beginning to brown, about 5 minutes. Add ground beef and cook, breaking beef into small pieces with spoon, until no longer pink, about 4 minutes. Stir in garlic and cook until fragrant, about 30 seconds. Transfer mixture to bowl with rice; stir in tomatoes, 1 cup cheese, parsley, and salt and pepper to taste.

4. Stir together ketchup and reserved tomato juice in small bowl.

5. Place peppers cut-sides up in 9-inch square baking dish. Using soup spoon, divide filling evenly among peppers. Spoon 2 tablespoons ketchup mixture over each filled pepper and sprinkle each with 1 tablespoon of remaining cheese. Bake until cheese is browned and filling is heated through, 25 to 30 minutes. Serve immediately.

STUFFED BELL PEPPERS WITH SPICED LAMB, CURRANTS, AND FETA CHEESE

Middle Eastern flavors—ground lamb, warm spices, currants, and feta cheese—are used in this variation.

	Salt
4	medium red, yellow, or orange bell peppers (about 6 ounces each), ½ inch trimmed off tops, cores and seeds discarded
½	cup long-grain white rice
1½	tablespoons olive oil
1	medium onion, chopped fine (about 1 cup)
12	ounces ground lamb
1	tablespoon ground cumin
1	teaspoon ground cardamom
½	teaspoon ground cinnamon
½	teaspoon hot red pepper flakes
3	medium garlic cloves, minced (about 1 tablespoon)
1	(1-inch) piece fresh ginger, minced (about 1 tablespoon)
¼	cup currants
1	(14½-ounce) can diced tomatoes, drained
6	ounces feta cheese, crumbled (1 cup)
2	tablespoons chopped fresh cilantro leaves
	Ground black pepper
⅓	cup roughly chopped salted, toasted cashews

1. Follow recipe for Classic Stuffed Bell Peppers through step 2.

2. Meanwhile, heat oil in 12-inch heavy-bottomed skillet over medium-high heat until shimmering. Add onion and cook, stirring occasionally, until softened and beginning to brown, about 5 minutes. Add ground lamb, cumin, cardamom, cinnamon, and red pepper flakes; cook, breaking lamb into small pieces with spoon, until no longer pink, about 4 minutes. Stir in garlic, ginger, and currants; cook until fragrant, about 30 seconds. Transfer mixture to bowl with rice; stir in tomatoes, cheese, cilantro, and salt and pepper to taste.

3. Continue with recipe for Classic Stuffed Bell Peppers from step 5, substituting chopped cashews for ketchup mixture and cheese topping.

STUFFED BELL PEPPERS WITH CHICKEN, SMOKED MOZZARELLA, AND BASIL
Ground chicken is a neutral background for the Italian flavors in this variation.

	Salt
4	medium red, yellow, or orange bell peppers (about 6 ounces each), ½ inch trimmed off tops, cores and seeds discarded
½	cup long-grain white rice
1½	tablespoons olive oil
1	medium onion, chopped fine (about 1 cup)
12	ounces ground chicken
3	medium garlic cloves, minced (about 1 tablespoon)
1	(14½-ounce) can diced tomatoes, drained
4	ounces smoked mozzarella, shredded (1 cup)
2	tablespoons chopped fresh basil leaves Ground black pepper
⅓	cup fresh bread crumbs

1. Follow recipe for Classic Stuffed Bell Peppers through step 2.

2. Meanwhile, heat oil in 12-inch heavy-bottomed skillet over medium-high heat until shimmering. Add onion and cook, stirring occasionally, until softened and beginning to brown, about 5 minutes. Add chicken and cook, breaking it into small pieces with spoon, until chicken becomes opaque, about 4 minutes. Stir in garlic and cook until fragrant, about

30 seconds. Transfer mixture to bowl with rice; stir in tomatoes, cheese, basil, and salt and pepper to taste.

3. Continue with recipe for Classic Stuffed Bell Peppers from step 5, substituting bread crumbs for ketchup mixture and cheese topping.

TASTING LAB: Bell Peppers

BELL PEPPERS SPANNING THE COLORS OF THE RAINBOW are now commonly found sitting side by side in the grocery store, no matter what the season. Wondering if these cheerfully colored peppers had different flavors or were simply cultivated for eye appeal, we conducted a blind tasting. After masking our colleagues' eyes with scarves, we lined them up to taste both raw and blanched examples of red, yellow, orange, green, and purple peppers fresh from the market.

No one guessed all of the colors correctly, but the differences in taste were dramatic. The favorite colors turned out to be red and orange. Without exhibiting much of a pungent pepper flavor, they were both pleasantly sweet. The yellow pepper, with its mildly sweet and slightly tannic flavor, was also well liked. The green pepper, the most easily recognized, was universally disliked for its unripe bitterness. The absolute worst entry, however, was the thin-skinned purple pepper. Its slimy texture when blanched and its singularly unpleasing flavor elicited comments such as "What we imagine a shoe tastes like" and "Did we just eat a slug?"

As it turned out, these comments weren't far off the mark. As a bell pepper ripens, it turns from green to yellow, orange, or red, depending on the variety. These bright peppers are sweeter simply because they are ripe, whereas the bitter green pepper is unripe. Purple peppers, too, are harvested when immature and would turn an uncommonly dark green if allowed to ripen fully. So unless you're fond of the tannic bitterness of the common green and the purple varieties, we suggest sticking with yellow, orange, or red.

TECHNIQUE: Keeping Stuffed Peppers Upright

Here are four neat ways to keep stuffed peppers from spilling their contents as they bake.

A. Instead of cooking peppers in the baking pan called for in most recipes, put them in a tube pan. The snug fit makes the peppers sit right up.

B. Place the peppers in the cups of a muffin tin.

C. Place each stuffed pepper in an individual ovenproof custard cup. This is a great system when you want to cook only a couple of peppers instead of a whole batch.

D. Reserve the tops of the peppers, which you have cut off to open the peppers for stuffing, and insert them between the stuffed peppers in the pan for added stability.

Rating Pepper Mills

WE RATED 12 PEPPER MILLS, EACH ONE AS CLOSE AS POSSIBLE TO 8 INCHES IN HEIGHT. WE EVALUATED THEM ACCORDING to grind quality, grind speed, ease of filling, and ease of use. The mills are listed in order of preference. See www.cooksillustrated.com for up-to-date prices and mail-order sources for top-rated products.

RECOMMENDED
1. Unicorn Magnum Plus Restaurant Use Peppermill
$45.00
Huge capacity, awesome speed, very easy to adjust the grind, and dazzlingly effective.

RECOMMENDED
2. East Hampton Industries (EHI) Peppermate Pepper Mill, Model 623
$40.00
Detachable cup captures pepper to make measuring easy. Huge opening makes this mill easiest to fill. Among the fastest grinders.

RECOMMENDED
3. Oxo Good Grips Grind It Pepper Mill, Model 41202
$19.99
Difficult to determine grind setting, but lightning-fast speed.

RECOMMENDED
4. Zyliss Large Pepper Mill
$27.50
Largest capacity, easy filling, and exemplary grind quality helps forgive its slower, but still acceptable, grind speed.

RECOMMENDED WITH RESERVATIONS
5. Oxo Good Grips Pepper Mill, Model 32180
$14.99
Excellent grind quality, but adjusting the grind can be a challenge. Comes with a coaster/base to catch spills.

RECOMMENDED WITH RESERVATIONS
6. Chef Specialties Windsor 8-Inch Pepper Mill
$22.99
Traditional design with good grind quality.

RECOMMENDED WITH RESERVATIONS
7. Peugeot Menton 20 cm Pepper Mill
$26.98
All grind adjustments seem to be on the fine side. Not great at producing coarse pepper.

RECOMMENDED WITH RESERVATIONS
8. Trudeau Iceberg Adjustable Pepper Mill, Model 071-7005
$16.98
Smallest capacity, but grind adjustment system uses lever and is well designed. Head with flat sides provides surer grip than round heads.

NOT RECOMMENDED
9. William Bounds Shake 'n Twist Salt and Pepper Grinder
$27.99
Fine grind is OK, but coarse and medium are uneven. Especially poor output.

NOT RECOMMENDED
10. Mr. Dudley Saturn Battery-Operated Peppermill, Model 6003W
$21.99
Gimmicky mill couldn't be easier to use, but how can you leave out something as basic as a grind adjustment? Medium grind only.

NOT RECOMMENDED
11. Zassenhaus Pepper Mill, Model 4
$34.95
Exceptionally difficult to crank. Finial has tiny spring that pops out the moment finial is unscrewed.

NOT RECOMMENDED
12. Chef 'n "The Pepper Ball," Model APG-66CBK
$14.99
Looks more comfortable to use than it actually is. Caused hand fatigue and has no settings between fine and coarse.

EQUIPMENT CORNER: Pepper Mills

PEPPER MILLS COME IN A VAST RANGE OF STYLES AND materials, but what really matters to us and other serious home cooks is performance. Is the fine-ground pepper truly fine? Is the medium grind really medium, or are there coarse particles mixed in? And how about output? Will you have to turn and turn and turn until your arm needs a brace to produce a teaspoon of ground pepper?

In this test we sought out top performers that would make great kitchen partners; appearance was pretty much beside the point. We rounded up 12 mills, each close to 8 inches high. Prices ranged from $14.99 to $45.

Most pepper mills work by similar means. Peppercorns are loaded into a central chamber, through which runs a metal shaft. Near the bottom of the mill, the shaft is connected to a grinding mechanism that consists of a rotating, grooved "male" head that fits into a stationary, grooved "female" ring. Near the top of the male piece, the large grooves crack the peppercorns and then feed the smaller pieces downward to be ground between the finer grooves, or teeth, of the male and female components.

The industry experts we queried explained that the specifics of the grinding mechanism are key to grind quality. Sharper teeth combined with a very tight tolerance between the pieces yield a better grind, which to us means finer fine-ground pepper. Unfortunately, none of these details are evident upon inspecting a pepper mill in a kitchen store.

In addition to having an excellent grind quality, Unicorn Magnum Plus managed an awesome output. In one minute of grinding, the Magnum produced an incredible average of 7.3 grams, or about 3½ teaspoons, of fine-ground pepper. By comparison, honors for the next highest average output went to the Oxo Grind It, at 5.1 grams, while about half the pack hovered around the two-grams-or-less mark (which, at roughly one teaspoon in volume, is perfectly acceptable).

Grind quality and speed are only half the battle—especially if most of your peppercorns land on the floor when you try to fill the mill. So we appreciated mills with wide, unobstructed filler doors that could accommodate the tip of a wide funnel or, better yet, the lip of a bag or jar so that we could dispense with the funnel altogether. The EHI Peppermate took high honors in this category, with a lid that snaps off to create a gaping 3-inch opening, followed by the Zyliss with a 2-inch opening and the Oxo Grind It with a wide-open 1⅜-inch mouth. With its sliding collar door, the Unicorn Magnum Plus was also easy to fill. Along the same lines, the more peppercorns a mill can hold, the less often it has to be filled. The Zyliss held a full cup, and the Unicorn Magnum Plus trailed behind by just 1 tablespoon.

The ease of adjusting the grind was another factor we considered. Changing the grind from fine to coarse involves changing the tolerances of, or distances between, the male and female grinding components. The more space between them, the larger the pepper particles and the coarser the grind. Traditionally, a knob at the top of the mill called the finial is used to adjust the grind. This was our least favorite design for two reasons. First, the finial must be screwed down very tight for a fine grind, which not only requires significant finger strength but also makes the head (or the crank) of the mill more difficult to turn. Second, the finial usually has to be removed entirely to fill the mill, which means you have to readjust the grind with each filling. We preferred mills like the Unicorn Magnum Plus, which use a screw or dial at the base of the grinding mechanism.

More than half of the mills tested did their jobs well, but the Unicorn Magnum Plus was the superstar. Its grind quality is exemplary, its output astounding, and its capacity huge. If that weren't enough, it's also easy to fill and comfortable to use. At $45, however, this mill was one of the two most expensive in the test (the second-place EHI Peppermate was $40). If your budget is a bit more restricted, we recommend both the Oxo Grind It ($19.99) and the Zyliss Large Pepper Mill ($27.50).

Straining the custard for crème brûlée removes the spent vanilla beans as well as any clumps of coagulated egg.

BISTRO *basics*

Bistro classics, such as steak au poivre and crème brûlée, offer a taste of real French cooking without pretension and exhaustive preparation. Both dishes have short ingredient lists and are easily accomplished at home.

That said, there are plenty of bad versions of both dishes floating around. We've followed recipes that yielded overly peppery steaks that were nearly inedible. Often, some of the peppercorns fell off the steaks and burned in the pan, making the brandy-based sauce inedible as well. Talk about a waste of good meat.

Crème brûlée suffers from three main problems. First, too many chefs have tampered with its classic flavors (egg yolks, cream, and vanilla) to produce odd flavor pairings such as raspberry mocha crème brûlée. But even if you don't fiddle with the ingredients, it can be hard to get the texture just right. All too often the custard doesn't set up properly and sloshes around in the ramekin. At the opposite end of the spectrum, the custard can be too firm and rubbery. Finally, the burnt sugar topping, the hallmark of crème brûlée, can be hard to achieve. You don't want to set the sugar on fire, but a pale, thin, grainy crust won't do either.

The test kitchen has taken the guesswork out of these bistro favorites and made them foolproof in the American kitchen.

STEAK AU POIVRE

WHAT WE WANTED: Steak au poivre is often nothing more than uninspired skillet steak. We were after the real thing—a perfectly cooked steak with a well-seared crust of pungent, cracked peppercorns married to a silky sauce.

There's nothing complicated about steak au poivre. When well-executed, the slightly sweet, smooth sauce has more than a hint of shallot and brandy, the steak is well-browned on the outside and cherry-red on the interior, and the crust of cracked peppercorns provides a pungent, slow burn.

That's the good news. A third-rate steak au poivre has peppercorns that fall off the steak only to reveal under-browned meat. What's more, the peppercorn coat prevents the steak from forming drippings in the skillet that are the foundation of a rich sauce, and few home cooks have beef or veal stock on hand to give the sauce the backbone it needs. Because most steak au poivre recipes make no attempt to solve these problems, the home cook is left aghast at the end result: wan, tasteless steaks covered by an insipid sauce.

Our first few tests were useful only in determining the best cut of steak for au poivre. Filets were tender but too mild-flavored. Rib-eyes, always a favorite in the test kitchen, have abundant fat pockets and pronounced veins of gristle that separate two differently textured muscles. A peppercorn crust obscures these imperfections, requiring scrutiny and maneuvering on the part of the diner to eat around these parts. Strip steaks, however, have external lines of gristle that are easily trimmed before cooking, and their neat, tight, even grain makes them particularly suited to steak au poivre.

We quickly determined peppercorn type. Among black, white, and a four-peppercorn blend of green, pink, black, and white, plain old black was the favorite in the test kitchen. Tasters extolled it for its sharp bite, rich and intense flavor, and elusive smokiness.

The steaks we cooked early on were crusted with a scant teaspoon of peppercorns on each side. Loose pepper fell off the steaks and scorched pitifully in the skillet. The pepper that did stick shielded the surface of the steaks, preventing browning and thereby the formation of a fond (the sticky browned bits left in a pan after sautéing) on which to build the sauce. In addition, most tasters thought we were far too liberal in our peppercorn allotment—the heat was vicious and incendiary. Our first thought was to cut back on the peppercorns, but then a light bulb went on. What if the steaks were coated on only one side? The unpeppered side would brown nicely, producing more fond for the sauce, and there would be no peppercorns on that side to singe.

Typically, steaks cook over intensely high heat. But for this new approach, we placed the skillet over medium heat until it was hot, and, after laying the steaks in the skillet—unpeppered-side down—turned up the heat to medium-high. This technique gave the steaks six minutes to brown on the first side and form a fond. Then the steaks were flipped onto their peppered side and given only three to five minutes (depending on desired doneness) to complete their cooking, this time without scorching the pepper.

All steak au poivre sauces contain beef or veal stock and brandy. Most contain cream, though some get their richness from butter only. The stock was the first problem. Most home cooks have only canned chicken and beef broth on hand, and the latter has long been considered either artificial tasting or weakly flavored in the test kitchen (see the Tasting Lab on page 139 for more information). Using chicken broth alone, we cooked down the liquid to concentrate its flavor, but the sauce still lacked meatiness and depth. We tried to doctor it with dried porcini mushrooms, but the mushroom flavor was too distinct. We tried commercial veal demi-glace (superconcentrated veal stock), but the tomato paste-laden demi-glace looked and tasted unnatural. Finally, we tried low-sodium beef broth straight from the can and reduced it. This sauce was beefier, more substantial, and deeper in color—but it was plagued by the tinny flavor characteristic of canned beef broth.

On the verge of giving up, we finally hit upon a solution. We reduced almost equal amounts of chicken and beef broths with sautéed shallots to about one-quarter of their original volume. Finally—a terrific, full-flavored sauce. But the long simmering time threw a wrench in the works. A typical pan sauce for steak is made by deglazing the skillet in which the steaks were cooked. This usually takes no longer than a few minutes and can be accomplished while the steaks repose. The sauce took well over 10 minutes, much longer than you'd want the meat to rest. The solution was straightforward: Reduce the broth mixture before cooking the steaks, then use the resulting liquid to deglaze the skillet.

Introducing brandy to the sauce was no trivial matter. We tried reducing it with the broth mixture to concentrate its flavor. This worked, but because we were also concentrating the sugar in the brandy, the resulting sauce tasted as sweet as butterscotch pudding, with no spirited bite. If we held off adding the brandy until much later in the sauce-making process, it tasted hot and raw. The time to add it was when the reduced broth mixture went into the skillet to deglaze it; the mixture simmers for about five minutes, just long enough for the brandy to reduce a bit, shake its alcoholic harshness, and meld with the broth.

Cream made the sauce luxurious and gave its texture substance. Only ¼ cup was needed, and, when added at the same time as the brandy, the cream had a chance to cook down and lend body to the sauce. To finish, butter whisked in at the end brought silkiness, a bit of raw brandy gave nice bite and fresh brandy flavor, and a teaspoon of lemon juice or champagne vinegar brightened things up.

WHAT WE LEARNED: Coat just one side of the steaks with peppercorns and then cook the steaks on the uncoated side as long as possible to promote browning and prevent scorching of the peppercorns. Make the sauce with a mixture of canned beef broth and canned chicken broth that has first been reduced, and then add brandy, cream, and butter.

STEAK AU POIVRE WITH BRANDIED CREAM SAUCE serves 4

To save time, crush the peppercorns and trim the steaks while the broth mixture simmers. Many pepper mills do not have a sufficiently coarse setting. In that case, crush peppercorns with a sauté pan or rolling pin (see illustrations on page 48). See the Tasting Lab on page 35 for information about peppercorns and see the Equipment Corner on page 42 for information about pepper mills, including models capable of producing crushed peppercorns.

sauce

4 tablespoons unsalted butter
1 medium shallot, minced (about 3 tablespoons)
1 cup canned low-sodium beef broth
¾ cup canned low-sodium chicken broth
¼ cup heavy cream
¼ cup plus 1 tablespoon brandy
1 teaspoon juice from 1 lemon or 1 teaspoon champagne vinegar
Salt

TECHNIQUE: Adhering the Pepper

Pressing the steaks with a cake pan or flat pot lid once they have been placed in the hot skillet promotes browning and ensures that the peppercorns adhere.

steaks

    4   **strip steaks (8 to 10 ounces each), ¾ to 1 inch thick, trimmed of exterior gristle**
          Salt
    1   **tablespoon black peppercorns, crushed**

1. Heat 1 tablespoon butter in 12-inch heavy-bottomed skillet over medium heat; when foaming subsides, add shallot and cook, stirring occasionally, until softened, about 2 minutes. Add beef and chicken broths, increase heat to high, and boil until reduced to about ½ cup, about 8 minutes. Set reduced broth mixture aside. Rinse and wipe out skillet.

2. Meanwhile, sprinkle both sides of steaks with salt; rub one side of each steak with 1 teaspoon crushed peppercorns, and, using fingers, press peppercorns into steaks.

3. Place now-empty skillet over medium heat until hot, about 4 minutes. Lay steaks unpeppered-side down in hot skillet, increase heat to medium–high, firmly press down on steaks with bottom of cake pan (see illustration on page 47), and cook steaks without moving them until well-browned, about 6 minutes. Using tongs, flip steaks, firmly press down on steaks with bottom of cake pan, and cook on peppered side, about 3 minutes for rare, about 4 minutes for medium-rare, or about 5 minutes for medium. Transfer steaks to large plate and tent loosely with foil to keep warm.

4. Pour reduced broth, cream, and ¼ cup brandy into now-empty skillet; increase heat to high and bring to boil, scraping pan bottom with wooden spoon to loosen browned bits. Simmer until deep golden brown and thick enough to heavily coat back of metal tablespoon or soup spoon, about 5 minutes. Off heat, whisk in remaining 3 tablespoons butter, remaining 1 tablespoon brandy, lemon juice or vinegar, and any accumulated meat juices. Adjust seasonings with salt.

5. Set steaks on individual dinner plates, spoon portion of sauce over steaks, and serve immediately.

TECHNIQUE: Crushing Peppercorns

If your pepper mill can't produce coarsely crushed peppercorns, you have two alternatives.

A. Use the back of a heavy pan and a rocking motion to grind peppercorns.

B. Spread the peppercorns in an even layer in a zipper-lock plastic bag and whack them with a rolling pin or meat pounder.

GETTING IT RIGHT:
Properly Ground Peppercorns

For steak au poivre, grind or crush whole peppercorns (left) to a very coarse texture (right). If your pepper mill cannot handle this task, see the alternate methods above. In any case, do not use finely ground pepper in this recipe.

CRÈME BRÛLÉE

WHAT WE WANTED: A proper crème brûlée should have a crackle-crisp bittersweet sugar crust over a chilly custard of balanced egginess, creaminess, and sweetness. Its light, silken, supple texture goes down easily, belying the dessert's richness; it's a masterful work of temperature, taste, and texture.

Beneath either a paltry sugar crust or one that requires a pickax, a majority of crème brûlées suffer from a trio of problems: The custard is tepid, not cold; the custard is leaden, not ethereal; and the flavors are sullen. We set out to fix these problems and create the perfect crème brûlée.

Crème brûlée is not complicated—it requires only six ingredients—and it can be made well in advance of serving. Despite this charming simplicity, however, it presents quite a few opportunities for things to go awry. A search of many recipes revealed standard ingredients, but ratios of eggs to cream varied, as did oven temperatures, so the devil was going to be in the details.

First we sought to settle the issue of eggs. Firmer custard, like that in crème caramel, is made with whole eggs, which help the custard to achieve a clean-cutting quality. Crème brûlée is richer and softer—with a pudding-like, spoon-clinging texture—in part because of the exclusive use of yolks. With 4 cups of heavy cream as the dairy for the moment, we went to work. The custard refused to set at all with as few as six yolks; with eight (a common number for the amount of cream) it was better, but still rather slurpy. With 12, however, a surprisingly large number of yolks, we struck gold. The custard had a lovely lilting texture, an elegant mouthfeel, a glossy, luminescent look, and the richest flavor.

We ventured to make crème brûlées with different kinds of cream. Half-and-half (with a fat content of about 10 percent) was far too lean, and the custard was watery and lightweight. With whipping cream (about 30 percent fat),

the custard was improved but still a bit loose. Heavy cream (about 36 percent fat) was the ticket. The custard was thick but not overbearing, luxurious but not death-defying.

We tested various sugar quantities, from ½ cup to ¾ cup. Two-thirds cup was the winner; with more sugar the crème brûlée was too saccharine, and with less the simple egg and cream flavors tasted muted and dull. We also found that a pinch of salt heightened flavors and that vanilla bean was superior to extract.

With proportions in place, we attempted to find the best cooking technique for the custard. Custard made with icebox-cold eggs and cream can go into the oven, but nearly all recipes instruct the cook to scald the cream before gradually whisking it into the yolks. When compared, a started-cold custard and scalded-cream custard displayed startling differences. The former had a silkier, smoother texture. Some research on custards told me that eggs respond favorably to cooking at a slow, gentle pace. If heated quickly, they set only just shortly before they enter the overcooked zone, leaving a very narrow window between just right and overdone. If heated gently, however, they begin to thicken the custard at a lower temperature and continue to do so gradually until it, too, eventually overcooks. In other words, the scalded-cream method is more likely to produce custard with an overcooked—hence, inferior—texture.

The downside to starting with cold ingredients is that unless the cream is heated, it is impossible to extract flavor from a vanilla bean. Also, if the cream is heated, the sugar can go into the pot for easy dissolution. Otherwise, the sugar must be vigorously beaten with the yolks to encourage it to dissolve. When we did this, the resulting custard was very frothy and baked up with a dry, soap-foam-like surface. Scalding cream and sugar, steeping with vanilla, then refrigerating until cold seemed an overwrought process, so we tested a hybrid technique. We heated only half the cream with the sugar and the vanilla bean. After a 15-minute off-heat steep to extract flavor from the vanilla bean, we added the remaining still cold cream to bring the temperature down before whisking it into the yolks. This hybrid technique created a custard with a fineness equal to the one started cold—and it baked in less time, too.

Next we investigated oven temperatures. At 325 degrees, the custards puffed and browned on the surface. Too hot. At 300 degrees, they fared beautifully. As for the water bath (or bain marie, which prevents the periphery of a custard from overcooking while the center saunters to the finish line), we used a large baking dish that held the ramekins comfortably. (The ramekins must not touch and should be at least ½ inch away from the sides of the dish.) We lined the bottom with a kitchen towel to protect the floors of the ramekins from the heat of the dish and to stabilize them.

The golden rule of custards is that they must not be overcooked lest they lose their smooth, silken texture and become grainy and curdled. Judging doneness by gently shaking the custards or by slipping a paring knife into them were not reliable techniques. An instant-read thermometer tells you exactly when the custards must come out of the oven: between 170 and 175 degrees. If you do not have a thermometer, look at the center of the custard. It should be barely set—shaky but not sloshy. The custard will continue to cook from residual heat once out of the oven. A deep chill then helps to solidify things. If your oven has a history of uneven heating, the custards may finish at different rates, so it is advisable to check each one separately rather than take out the whole lot at once.

For the crackly caramel crust we tried brown sugar, regular granulated sugar, and turbinado and Demerara sugars (the latter two are coarse light brown sugars). Because brown sugar is moist and lumpy, recipes often recommend drying it in a low oven and crushing it to break up lumps. We found that it just isn't worth the effort. Turbinado and Demerara sugars were superior to granulated only because their coarseness makes them easy to distribute evenly over the custards.

There are a few approaches to caramelizing the sugar. The broiler is almost guaranteed to fail; the heat is uneven

and inadequate. A salamander—a long-handled iron plate that is heated and held just above the sugar—is hardly practical because they are hard to come by. A torch accomplishes the task efficiently. A hardware-store propane torch is the tool of choice, but a small butane kitchen torch, available in cookware stores, can do the job, just at a more leisurely pace (see the Equipment Corner on page 53).

While being "brûléed," the custard is unavoidably warmed a bit. In standard round ramekins, usually only the upper third of the custard is affected. But in shallow dishes (our favorite for their higher ratio of crust to custard), the custard can be completely warmed through. In our opinion, a warm custard can ruin an otherwise perfect crème brûlée. To remedy this problem, we refrigerated the finished crème brûlées, and the crust maintained its crackly texture for up to 45 minutes. Beneath the shattering sugar crust lay an interplay of creamy, cold, sweet, bitter, smooth, and crackly . . . perfect crème brûlée.

WHAT WE LEARNED : Lots of yolks, turbinado sugar, an instant-read thermometer, and a final chill are the keys to perfect crème brûlée.

CLASSIC CRÈME BRÛLÉE Serves 8

Separate the eggs and whisk the yolks after the cream has finished steeping; if left to sit, the surface of the yolks will dry and form a film. A vanilla bean gives custard the deepest flavor, but 2 teaspoons of extract, whisked into the yolks in step 4, can be used instead. The best way to judge doneness is with a digital instant-read thermometer. The custards, especially if baked in shallow fluted dishes, will not be deep enough to provide an accurate reading with a dial-face thermometer. For the caramelized sugar crust, we recommend turbinado or Demerara sugar. Regular granulated sugar will work, too, but use only 1 scant teaspoon on each ramekin or 1 teaspoon on each shallow fluted dish. It's important to use ramekins that measure 4 to 5 ounces. To check the size of your ramekins, fill one to the rim with a measured amount of water.

- 4 cups chilled heavy cream
- ⅔ cup (4⅔ ounces) granulated sugar
  Pinch salt
- 1 vanilla bean, halved lengthwise
- 12 large egg yolks
- 8–12 teaspoons turbinado or Demerara sugar (see note)

1. Adjust oven rack to lower-middle position and heat oven to 300 degrees.

2. Combine 2 cups cream, sugar, and salt in medium saucepan; with paring knife, scrape seeds from vanilla bean into pan, submerge pod in cream, and bring mixture to boil over medium heat, stirring occasionally to ensure that sugar dissolves. Take pan off heat and let steep 15 minutes to infuse flavors.

3. Meanwhile, place kitchen towel in bottom of large baking dish or roasting pan and arrange eight 4- or 5-ounce ramekins (or shallow fluted dishes) on towel. Bring kettle or large saucepan of water to boil over high heat.

4. After bean has steeped, stir in remaining 2 cups cream to cool down mixture. Whisk yolks in large bowl until broken up and combined. Whisk about 1 cup cream mixture into yolks until loosened and combined; repeat with another 1 cup cream. Add remaining cream and whisk until evenly colored and thoroughly combined. Strain through fine-mesh strainer into 2-quart measuring cup or pitcher (or clean medium bowl); discard solids in strainer. Pour or ladle mixture into ramekins, dividing it evenly among them.

5. Carefully place baking dish with ramekins on oven rack; pour boiling water into dish, taking care not to splash water into ramekins, until water reaches two-thirds height of ramekins. Bake until centers of custards are just barely set and are no longer sloshy and digital instant-read thermometer inserted in centers registers 170 to 175 degrees, 30 to 35 minutes (25 to 30 minutes for shallow fluted dishes). Begin checking temperature about 5 minutes before recommended time.

6. Transfer ramekins to wire rack; cool to room temperature, about 2 hours. Set ramekins on rimmed baking sheet,

TECHNIQUE: Extra Grip for Tongs

We recommend the use of tongs to remove ramekins of custard from a water bath. Cooks who worry about the ramekins slipping in the tongs can try this tip. Slip rubber bands around each of the two tong pincers, and the sticky rubber provides a surer grip.

cover tightly with plastic wrap, and refrigerate until cold, at least 4 hours or up to 4 days.

7. Uncover ramekins; if condensation has collected on custards, blot moisture with paper towel. Sprinkle each with about 1 teaspoon turbinado sugar (1½ teaspoons for shallow fluted dishes); tilt and tap ramekin for even coverage. Ignite torch and caramelize sugar. Refrigerate ramekins, uncovered, to re-chill, 30 to 45 minutes (but no longer); serve.

VARIATIONS

ESPRESSO CRÈME BRÛLÉE

Place ¼ cup espresso beans in zipper-lock bag and crush lightly with rolling pin or meat pounder until coarsely cracked. Follow recipe for Classic Crème Brûlée, substituting cracked espresso beans for vanilla bean and whisking 1 teaspoon vanilla extract into yolks in step 4 before adding cream.

TEA-INFUSED CRÈME BRÛLÉE

Knot together the strings of 10 bags Irish Breakfast tea. Follow recipe for Classic Crème Brûlée, substituting tea bags for vanilla bean; after steeping, squeeze bags with tongs or press into mesh strainer to extract all liquid. Whisk 1 teaspoon vanilla extract into yolks in step 4 before adding cream.

TECHNIQUE:
Improved Cushion for Water Bath

Many recipes for individual baked custard, including crème brûlée, recommend lining the bottom of the water bath pan with a kitchen towel to both insulate and cushion the ramekins. Of course, this leaves you with a sopping wet towel at the end of cooking. We've found that a nonstick baking mat (called a Silpat) can be used if you happen to own this handy kitchen item.

SCIENCE DESK:
How Egg Yolks Thicken Custard

CUSTARDS LIKE CRÈME BRÛLÉE DEPEND ON THE THICKENING power of egg yolks. How do the yolks do it? A raw egg yolk is filled with tightly curled protein molecules, many of which contain sulfur atoms that are interspersed along their lengths. If given a chance to get together, these sulfur atoms can bond to one another, tying the protein molecules into clumps. That's what thickens a custard.

As long as the sulfur atoms are trapped within tightly wound protein molecules, however, they can't connect. When egg yolks are heated, the proteins unravel (in a process called denaturing) and the sulfur atoms are able to link up, in the process creating a tangled network of protein molecules that can hold water—in other words, a thickened custard.

But you can overdo it. If the protein molecules are heated too much, they straighten out completely, and so many sulfur atoms cross-link that the protein network tightens into tough clumps of curd, squeezing out some of the water. The result is a custard that has curdled or "weeps." That's why proper cooking creates a custard that is smooth and thick, while overcooking creates a custard that is tough and wet.

EQUIPMENT CORNER: Torches

A TORCH IS THE BEST WAY TO CARAMELIZE THE SUGAR ON your crème brûlée. We tested a hardware-store propane torch ($27) against four petite kitchen torches (prices ranged from $30 to $40) fueled by butane.

The propane torch, with its powerful flame, caramelized the sugar quickly and easily, but, admittedly, it's not for the faint-hearted. Although easy to wield, a propane torch puts out a lot of heat and works in just seconds, so you must work very carefully. (In contrast, the kitchen torches took about 1½ minutes to brûlée each custard.) If you opt for a propane torch, make sure to buy a model with a built-in trigger that does not need to be held in place for the torch to remain lit. The most widely available brand, Bernzomatic, worked well in our kitchen tests.

Among the four butane-powered kitchen torches we tested, only one is worth owning. The Bernzomatic Torch ST1100TS ($29.95) has a plastic flame adjuster that is clearly marked and stayed cool enough to handle without burning our fingers. This torch was also the easiest to operate.

The remaining models had flaws. The safety lock on the RSVP Culinary Butane Torch ($29.95) was difficult to engage and the air intake port became red-hot with use. The metal flame-width adjuster on the Bonjour Torch ($29.95) must be held in place during use, but it became very hot to the touch. Finally, although the Messermeister Chefflame Culinary Torch ($39.95) generated the most powerful flame of the kitchen torches tested, testers needed to use both hands to switch it on and found its large size awkward.

BEST TORCHES

With its powerful flame, the Bernzomatic propane torch (left) will brûlée a custard in seconds. If you don't want to use such a powerful torch, the Bernzomatic kitchen torch (right) is the best butane option. Just make sure to purchase a can of butane along with it—otherwise you'll have more luck "brûléeing" with a book of matches. See www.cooksillustrated.com for an up-to-date price and mail-order source for the kitchen torch. Most hardware stores stock the Bernzomatic propane torch.

STEAKHOUSE *dinner*

CHAPTER 5

What's America's favorite restaurant meal? Salad and filet mignon served steakhouse style is a top contender for the title. Crisp lettuce covered with a pungent, creamy dressing (we like blue cheese) starts things off. The main event is a thick, tender piece of filet mignon, perfectly cooked, so the center is rare and the exterior is well browned and crusted. The steak is napped with a thick, luxurious brown sauce, and every bite is worth the high price you are paying.

Of course, this vision is often a fantasy and the real thing closer to a nightmare. The lettuce is limp, the dressing gluey or watery, the steak overcooked or not properly browned, and the sauce characterless. When the check comes, it seems like all you're paying for is heartburn.

The logical solution is to make this meal at home. Although there are plenty of places where you can take a wrong turn, the test kitchen has worked out the kinks in these recipes, so you can rest assured that your money (and time) will be well spent.

IN THIS CHAPTER

THE RECIPES
Pan-Seared Filet Mignon
Bacon-Wrapped Filet Mignon
Madeira Pan Sauce with Mustard and Anchovies
Argentinian-Style Fresh Parsley and Garlic Sauce (Chimichurri)

Rich and Creamy Blue Cheese Dressing
Leafy Salad with Blue Cheese Dressing

EQUIPMENT CORNER
Steak Knives

TASTING LAB
Blue Cheese

We tested eight batches of dressing, each made with a different kind of blue cheese, before choosing our favorite.

FILET MIGNON

WHAT WE WANTED: A well-crusted steak that's perfectly cooked (to our way of thinking, rare or medium-rare) and served with a quick but luscious pan sauce.

When it comes to steak, Americans prize tenderness above all—and filet mignon is the most tender steak there is. It is also expensive, and both factors may drive its perennial popularity as a grand, splashy, celebratory restaurant meal. You've probably noticed that in a restaurant, filet mignon (also known as tenderloin steak or simply as filet) is usually served rare, with a deeply seared crust, and adorned with a rich, luxurious pan sauce or flavored butter.

Well, there is no reason to limit the fun to restaurants. Filets are available in any supermarket with a meat case, and they are not difficult to cook. We wanted to replicate the best restaurant filets at home, which meant developing a deeply browned, rich crust on both sides of each steak without overcooking the interior or scorching the drippings in the pan, which would go on to serve as the basis for a luscious sauce. To that end, we investigated the finer points of both the steaks themselves and the cooking process.

Filets are thick (usually 1¼ to 2 inches), boneless steaks cut from the slender, supertender, ultralean tenderloin muscle. We shopped for filets at six local supermarkets and were not satisfied with the butchering job from a single one. The steaks were usually cut unevenly, with one end noticeably thicker than the other (see Getting It Right on page 58). Beyond that, different steaks in the same package were different sizes and weights. This was far from ideal for expensive, premium steaks. Consistency of size and thickness was important for even cooking within each steak, as well as from steak to steak, in the pan. With that in mind, we purchased a small, roughly 2-pound section of the tenderloin, called a tenderloin roast, and cut our own steaks from it. The process was easy, taking less than two minutes, and our

hand-cut filets were uniform. Tenderloin roasts were available wherever we shopped, so if you can get them, too, we recommend this practice. Alternatively, ask the butcher to cut the steaks for you.

To determine the optimal thickness for filets, we cooked steaks cut 1 and 2 inches thick and at ¼-inch intervals in between. Tasters preferred the 1½-inch cut, which made for a generous (but not over-the-top) portion.

Grilling is a good option for filets, but because we also wanted to make a pan sauce, we decided to cook our filets in a pan. The recipes we looked at suggested a couple of alternatives, including broiling, high-roasting (oven-roasting at high heat), and pan-searing (stovetop cooking over high heat), all of which we tried. Pan-searing was our approach of choice because it developed the deep brown, caramelized crust critical to the flavor of both the meat and the sauce. Right off the bat we confirmed our suspicion that filets are best cooked rare to medium-rare. In our opinion, cooking them to medium begins to compromise their tenderness, which is, after all, their raison d'être.

Our next tests involved searing well-dried filets in a dry pan and in a pan filmed with oil. (Drying the steaks thoroughly with paper towels aids development of a crust.) Not surprisingly for such lean meat, the oil was necessary to produce a deep, dark, satisfying crust, and we found that rubbing the oil right into the steaks reduced the spattering a little.

In our tests of different heat levels, we found that a crust formed over a consistently high flame was better developed than one formed over a medium-high flame. But this approach also created a problem. Over such high heat, the fond (the browned bits left in the pan after the steaks were cooked) was often scorched by the time the meat reached medium-rare, giving the sauce a bitter flavor. We tried a couple of things to remedy the problem.

First, we switched from the 12-inch skillet we'd been using (for four steaks) to a smaller, 10-inch model. The decreased surface area between the steaks helped protect the fond. (A heavy-bottomed or cast-iron skillet is essential here; the All-Clad 10-inch skillets we use in the test kitchen weigh about 2½ pounds. Smaller or lighter pans, we found, overheat too easily.) Second, we revisited the high-roasting method, combining it with our searing method by finishing the seared steaks on a preheated rimmed baking sheet in a hot oven. This approach offered the double advantage of protecting the fond from the direct heat of the oven and giving us a head start on the pan sauce while the steaks finished cooking.

Throughout testing, the oven time needed to achieve a given degree of doneness varied continually, as did our thermometer readings. While internal temperature guidelines for varying stages of doneness certainly do exist, it can be difficult to achieve an accurate reading in such a small piece of meat. The reading can be way off depending on where the thermometer probe hits, and it's surprisingly easy to miss dead center when you're working fast and juggling tongs and a hot steak in one hand and a thermometer in the other. In some cases we had readings as low as 117 degrees and as high as 140 degrees in the same steak. It all depended on the position of the thermometer probe.

What's a cook to do? Just make a small nick in the steak with the tip of a paring knife and look inside. Be sure to remove the steaks from the heat just before they are done to your liking. They will continue to cook a little off the heat, which should give them a perfect finish. This method never failed to produce steaks cooked just the way we like them.

WHAT WE LEARNED: **Sear on the stovetop and finish in the oven. To keep the drippings from burning, choose a pan just large enough to hold four filets (10 inches is just right). Finally, because an instant-read thermometer doesn't work all that well in such small steaks, nick the exterior and take a peak inside to see if the steak is done.**

PAN-SEARED FILET MIGNON serves 4

See Getting It Right on page 58 for information on buying filets or cutting your own from a tenderloin roast. Determining when the meat is cooked to your liking is key to a good steak, so pay close attention to the visual cues in step 3. If you choose to serve the steaks with one of the sauces that follow, have all the sauce ingredients ready before searing the steaks. Begin the sauce while the steaks are in the oven. To cook six steaks instead of four, switch to a 12-inch pan and use 6 teaspoons of olive oil.

4 center-cut filets mignon, 1½ inches thick,
    7 to 8 ounces each, dried thoroughly with
    paper towels
4 teaspoons olive oil
    Salt and ground black pepper

1. Adjust oven rack to lower-middle position, place rimmed baking sheet on oven rack, and heat oven to 450 degrees. When oven reaches 450 degrees, heat 10-inch heavy-bottomed skillet (not nonstick) over high heat on stovetop until very hot.

2. Meanwhile, rub each side of steaks with ½ teaspoon oil and sprinkle generously with salt and pepper. Place steaks in skillet and cook, without moving steaks, until well-browned and a nice crust has formed, about 3 minutes. Turn steaks with tongs and cook until well-browned and a nice crust has formed on second side, about 3 minutes longer. Remove pan from heat, and use tongs to transfer steaks to hot baking sheet in oven.

3. Roast 2 to 4 minutes for very rare (center of steaks will appear cherry red and feel very soft and loose when cut with tip of paring knife), 4 to 6 minutes for rare (centers will appear red and soft), 6 to 8 minutes for medium-rare (centers will appear pink and feel firm but juicy), or 8 to 10 minutes for medium (centers will appear light pink and feel firm and compact). (After transferring steaks to oven, proceed with pan sauce.) Transfer steaks to large plate; loosely tent with foil or cover with bowl (see illustration on page 60), and let rest about 5 minutes before serving.

VARIATION

BACON-WRAPPED FILET MIGNON

Wrap 1 slice bacon around circumference of each filet, overlapping ends and securing to meat with toothpick. Follow recipe for Pan-Seared Filet Mignon, holding the filets two or three at a time on their sides briefly with tongs in skillet to crisp bacon slightly before transferring filets to oven.

MADEIRA PAN SAUCE WITH MUSTARD AND ANCHOVIES makes ⅔ cup, enough for 4 steaks

This sauce was inspired by one served in a Paris bistro, where the menu includes steak frites and nothing else. If you do not have Madeira on hand, sherry makes a fine substitute.

    1   medium shallot, minced (about 3 tablespoons)
    1   cup Madeira
    2   anchovy fillets, minced to paste (about 1
        teaspoon)
    1   tablespoon minced fresh parsley leaves
    1   tablespoon minced fresh thyme leaves
    1   tablespoon Dijon mustard
    1   tablespoon juice from 1 lemon
    3   tablespoons unsalted butter, softened
        Salt and ground black pepper

After transferring steaks to oven, set skillet over medium-low heat; add shallot and cook, stirring constantly, until softened, about 1 minute. Add Madeira; increase heat to high, and scrape pan bottom with wooden spoon to loosen browned bits. Simmer until liquid is reduced to about ⅓ cup, 6 to 8 minutes. (If steaks are not yet out of oven, set skillet off heat and wait for steaks to come out of oven and rest

GETTING IT RIGHT:
Buying the Best Filets

It is not uncommon to find supermarket-butchered filets mignon that are thick at one end and thin at the other, like the steak on the right, which promotes uneven cooking. Well-cut filets, like the one on the left, are even from edge to edge. If your butcher can't (or won't) do this for you, buy a 2-pound piece of center-cut filet mignon (called the Châteaubriand) and use a sharp boning knife to cut decent steaks at home.

WELL-BUTCHERED   POORLY BUTCHERED
FILET   FILET

for 2 minutes before proceeding.) Add accumulated juices from baking sheet and reduce liquid 1 minute longer. Off heat, whisk in anchovies, parsley, thyme, mustard, lemon juice, and butter until butter has melted and sauce is slightly thickened. Season with salt and pepper to taste, spoon sauce over steaks, and serve immediately.

ARGENTINIAN-STYLE FRESH PARSLEY AND GARLIC SAUCE (CHIMICHURRI)
makes I generous cup

Like a loose, fresh salsa in consistency, this mixture is a common accompaniment to sautéed, roasted, and grilled meats in South America. For best results, use flat-leaf parsley.

    1   cup (packed) fresh parsley leaves
    5   medium garlic cloves, peeled
    ½   cup extra-virgin olive oil
    ¼   cup red wine vinegar
    2   tablespoons water

¼   cup finely minced red onion
1   teaspoon salt
¼   teaspoon red pepper flakes

Process parsley and garlic in workbowl of food processor fitted with steel blade, stopping as necessary to scrape down

sides of bowl with rubber spatula, until garlic and parsley are chopped fine (20 one-second pulses); transfer to medium bowl. Whisk in remaining ingredients until thoroughly blended. Spoon about 2 tablespoons over each steak and serve. (Sauce tastes best when used fresh but can be refrigerated, with plastic wrap pressed directly on surface, up to 3 days.)

TECHNIQUE:
Best Tent for Roasts and Steaks

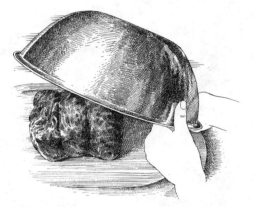

Roasts and steaks need to rest for several minutes before being carved or served to allow the juices to distribute themselves throughout the meat. Most recipes instruct the cook to cover the meat with foil while it rests to retain heat. An overturned bowl is easier to use and does a better job of retaining heat.

EQUIPMENT CORNER: Steak Knives

IF YOU'VE EVER SHOPPED FOR STEAK KNIVES, YOU MIGHT have noticed that sets of four can range in price from as little as $40 to as much as $150. We wondered if price really makes a difference when it comes to the performance of these knives, so we bought five sets of knives and cooked up some steaks to find out.

Our favorites were pricey. A set of four Henckels Four Star Steak Knives or Wüsthof-Trident Classic Steak Knives fetches between $140 and $150. Manufactured in the same manner as the other kitchen knives in their high-quality lines, these knives justly demand a high price. Fresh from their boxes, they had razor-sharp blades that sliced effortlessly through crusts and glided through meat, and their handles made them comfortable to use (Henckels got top

honors here). But if you are lax in the upkeep of your knives, beware—these knives require regular honing and sharpening to be kept in tip-top shape.

Right behind these big shots were Chicago Cutlery Steak Knives, Walnut Tradition. At $40 for a set of four, it's easy to overlook their slightly less comfortable handles and somewhat flimsier feel and rank them right in with the best. These knives were also sharp, and the gently curved angle of the blades made for simple and smooth slicing. And they look like they belong in a butcher shop—or in the fist of a serious steak eater. Don't forget to steel these knives as well to keep them sharp.

Our least favorite knife sets contained knives with serrated blades. Henckels Gourmet Steak Knives, $40 for a set of four, and Dexter Russell Steakhouse Steak Knives, $30 for a set of four, required a good deal of sawing to cut through a steak and produced rather ragged pieces (not that your taste buds care). The cheaper set of Henckels steak knives felt insubstantial in their construction, whereas the Dexter Russell knives were of mammoth proportions. Neither requires steeling for upkeep.

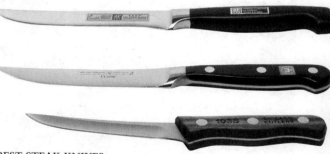

BEST STEAK KNIVES

The Henckels Four Star Steak Knives (top) were the top choice of testers, followed closely by the Wüsthof-Trident Classic Steak Knives (middle). At a fraction of the cost, the Chicago Cutlery Steak Knives, Walnut Tradition (bottom), are a great value with good (if not great) performance in our kitchen tests. See www.cooksillustrated.com for up-to-date prices and mail-order sources for these products.

BLUE CHEESE DRESSING

WHAT WE WANTED : **A dressing that boasts a complex mix of tart, sweet, and creamy.**

Pretty good blue cheese dressing, like that served in many steakhouses, is creamy and tangy, with a hint of sweetness and a few crumbles of blue cheese. It isn't as good as it could be because it isn't cheesy enough. But even at that, it is miles better than bottled blue cheese dressings from the grocery store. To us, those bottled brews are virtually inedible. Harsh, mayonnaise-like concoctions, they are either as sweet as candy or painfully vinegary and sour. In both cases, the result is a one-dimensional dressing completely lacking in that necessary blue cheese punch. We decided it was time to do a little research and development in the test kitchen.

We began by scouring cookbooks for blue cheese dressing recipes. They were all similar: no revelations, just a mixture of blue cheese with a creamy component, such as mayonnaise or sour cream or a combination of the two, thinned with either heavy cream or buttermilk or sometimes bulked up with cottage cheese.

We gathered our recipes and tried them one by one. In the initial tasting, a common complaint was that there wasn't enough blue cheese flavor. We found that the secret to the proper flavor and texture lay in the creamy components. Cottage cheese was the one entirely unwelcome ingredient. It watered down the dressing, and its flabby and bland curds did nothing for the flavor. After much tasting, we concluded that three creamy ingredients were necessary: mayonnaise to give the dressing body, sour cream to supply tang, and buttermilk to both thin out the dressing and support the role of the sour cream. Our challenge was to find the right balance of the three to achieve both good flavor and the right consistency. We tinkered around, and whereas some recipes called for as much as 1/2 cup of mayonnaise to 1/2 cup of crumbled blue cheese, we found only 2 tablespoons of

mayonnaise to be necessary. That amount, taken in combination with 3 tablespoons of sour cream and 3 tablespoons of buttermilk, gave our dressing a pleasant, creamy tang and enough fluidity to gently coat sturdy, leafy greens.

Realizing that buttermilk isn't often at hand in most households, we tried cream in place of it, but the flavor of the dressing fell flat under the weight of the cream. Milk is a better substitute, though it makes a somewhat lighter dressing.

At this point our dressing was good but just a bit dull. We added a smidgen of sugar for sweetness and white wine vinegar for a little zing. That was it. The dressing now had high and low notes that titillated the taste buds, was jam-packed with blue-cheesy flavor, and was delicious not just when eaten on a salad but on a chicken wing or even with a spoon.

Our next step was to investigate different kinds of blue cheese. We were surprised to find that a cheese that made a good dressing didn't necessarily make for good eating. A dressing made with an inexpensive domestic blue cheese—not a $17-per-pound French Roquefort—was our final choice. In general, we found that any rich, creamy blue cheese makes a good dressing. Really pungent cheeses, such as Spanish Cabrales, should be avoided (see the Tasting Lab on page 62 for details).

Finally, we had to decide on a mixing method. Some of the recipes we researched called for making the dressing in a blender or food processor, but we wanted to make our dressing in the simplest way possible with the fewest number of dirty dishes. We took to mashing the crumbled blue cheese and buttermilk together with a fork to break up the cheese a bit. This was an easy means of getting the texture we liked—creamy, with a few small crumbles of cheese, just enough to give the dressing some tooth.

WHAT WE LEARNED : **Use a mild blue cheese and combine it with buttermilk, sour cream, and mayonnaise for a dressing that is pleasantly tart and has plenty of body.**

RICH AND CREAMY BLUE CHEESE DRESSING makes about 3/4 cup

In a pinch, whole milk can be used in place of buttermilk. The dressing will be a bit lighter and milder in flavor, but will still taste good. Remember that aggressive seasoning with salt and pepper is necessary because the dressing will be dispersed over greens.

> 2½ ounces blue cheese, crumbled (about ½ cup)
> 3 tablespoons buttermilk
> 3 tablespoons sour cream
> 2 tablespoons mayonnaise
> 2 teaspoons white wine vinegar
> ¼ teaspoon sugar
> ⅛ teaspoon garlic powder
> Salt and ground black pepper

Mash blue cheese and buttermilk in small bowl with fork until mixture resembles cottage cheese with small curds. Stir in remaining ingredients. Taste and adjust seasoning with salt and pepper. (Dressing can be refrigerated in airtight container for up to 2 weeks.)

LEAFY SALAD WITH BLUE CHEESE DRESSING serves 4

We dressed a variety of different salad greens and found that delicate ones, such as mesclun and butter lettuce, became soggy under the weight of this dressing. Sturdy romaine and curly leaf lettuce were our two favorites.

> 10 cups loosely packed greens, such as Romaine or curly leaf lettuce
> ¾ cup Rich and Creamy Blue Cheese Dressing (recipe at left)

1. Wash and thoroughly dry greens. (Greens can be stored rolled in paper towels and refrigerated in salad spinner for 2 days or zipper-lock plastic bag for 1 week.)

2. Place greens in large bowl. If greens are too large to eat easily, tear them into manageable pieces with your hands. Pour dressing over greens and toss to coat evenly. Serve immediately.

TASTING LAB: Blue Cheese

USING OUR RECIPE, WE PREPARED EIGHT BATCHES OF blue cheese dressing, each containing a different blue cheese, and had our editorial staff engage in a blind taste test. While many tasters preferred the stronger cheeses when eaten alone, most preferred blue cheese dressing made with the milder, less pungent cheeses of the bunch.

Stella brand blue cheese (which is readily available in supermarkets) came out as our tasters' overall favorite for dressing because of its "nicely balanced flavor" and "nice

Rating Blue Cheeses

WE SAMPLED EIGHT BLUE CHEESES ON THEIR OWN AND IN A DRESSING POURED OVER GREENS. EATEN PLAIN, EACH cheese had its fans, but tasters agreed that the milder cheeses were better in the dressing. Cheeses are listed in order of preference based on the dressing test. Some of these cheeses are available in supermarkets, and all are sold in gourmet stores or cheese shops.

HIGHLY RECOMMENDED
1. Stella Blue, Wisconsin
$6.29 per pound

This supermarket brand was extremely crumbly and almost feta-like in texture. The simple flavor and "wet" texture that caused it to flounder as a table cheese made it an excellent addition to our dressing.

HIGHLY RECOMMENDED
2. Danish Blue, Denmark
$11.95 per pound

Danish Blue is straightforward and cheddar-like. It has a strong salty and tangy presence, is slightly crumbly in texture, and is spotted with silvery blue pockets.

RECOMMENDED
3. Maytag Blue, Iowa
$12.99 per pound

Creamy, fresh, and smooth, with a tangy bite of blue cheese flavor, Maytag Blue was very popular among our tasters. This fairly dense cheese is ivory-white in color (the palest of all), with minimal green-blue pockets of mold.

RECOMMENDED
4. Gorgonzola Naturale, Italy
$10.95 per pound

Gorgonzola Naturale was by far the creamiest and softest of all the cheeses included in the tasting. Described as "sweet" and "smooth," this cheese is fairly mild, with a distinguishing "musty" odor. Look for the Gorgonzola labeled Marca d'Oro, which means it is made with the highest quality milk. Be sure to eat it quickly, as it has a shelf life of only about two weeks.

RECOMMENDED
5. Blue Stilton, England
$13.95 per pound

Blue Stilton can be identified by its reddish-gold rind and butter-colored interior speckled with blue-green veins. It is a fairly firm cheese—sliceable, yet crumbly in texture—with a well-balanced, salty flavor that is buttery, nutty, and sweet.

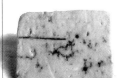

RECOMMENDED
6. Bleu d'Auvergne, France
$9.95 per pound

This very approachable blue cheese was by described by one taster as "mellow" and "refreshing for blue cheese." It is rich, salty, slightly bitter, sweet, and buttery. A great cheese for about half the price of Roquefort.

RECOMMENDED
7. Roquefort, France
$16.95 per pound

This ivory-colored sheep's milk cheese is pocked throughout with dark green-blue mold, and it is very pungent. With a texture so creamy and buttery that it is almost spreadable, it tastes salty, sweet, and a bit tangy.

RECOMMENDED WITH RESERVATIONS
8. Cabrales, Spain
$14.99 per pound

Crumbly, chalky, and complex in flavor, delivering a spicy, peppery kick and a long finish. Deeper in color than the other cheeses we tasted, it is yellow-brown with a cast of gray and streaked with fine lines of gray-green mold. Good eating for those who like a very strong blue cheese flavor but overpowering in dressing.

sweetness." Danish Blue (also sold in many supermarkets) came in second; one taster described it as "bright," with a "good creamy and chunky balance." While pricier blue cheeses such as Stilton and Gorgonzola also did well, the lower-priced versions scored higher, making them the logical choice for our dressing. Stronger, more intense cheeses, such as Cabrales, did not fare well in our dressing taste tests.

TECHNIQUE: Storing Greens

Once greens have been washed and dried in a salad spinner, they can be stored until needed. Greens should be perfectly dry before being stored, so place them on paper towels to blot any remaining moisture. At this point, you have two storage options.

A. You can line the empty salad spinner with paper towels and then layer in the greens, covering each layer with additional towels. In this manner, the greens will keep in the refrigerator for about 2 days.

B. For longer storage (up to 1 week, if the greens are really fresh), loosely roll the greens in paper towels and then place the rolled greens inside a large zipper-lock plastic bag.

Cheesy Nachos with Guacamole and Salsa **page 5**

Rustic Potato-Leek Soup **page 24**

Kung Pao Shrimp **page 92**

Fried Rice with Shrimp, Pork, and Shiitakes **page 83**

Green Bean Casserole **page 229**

Pasta with Garlic and Oil **page 125**

70

Stuffed Bell Peppers with Spiced Lamb, Currants, and Feta Cheese **page 39**

Scalloped Potatoes **page 219**

Charcoal-Grilled Pork Chops **page 169**

Barbecued Baby Back Ribs **page 181**

74

Creamy Dill Cucumber Salad **page 199**

Pan-Seared Filet Mignon **page 57**

Stovetop Macaroni and Cheese **page 159**

Smothered Pork Chops **page 176**

78

Simple Lasagna with Hearty Tomato-Meat Sauce **page 130**

Great fried rice starts with chilled rice that is then piled high with ingredients that have been cooked in batches in a nonstick skillet rather than a wok.

CHINESE takeout

Few things are as seductive (and ultimately as disappointing) as Chinese takeout. The expectations are high—spicy, bold food ready in minutes. The reality is low—greasy, goopy food with way too much soy sauce and not nearly enough flavor.

The problem, of course, is not with the dishes themselves but with how they are prepared. Just as the best hamburger is made at home (not at McDonald's), we find that Chinese favorites taste better when made at home.

We've taken two classics—fried rice and kung pao shrimp—and made them better (a lot better) than just about any takeout version you've had before. We've kept the realities of American cooking in mind and relied on readily available ingredients as well as equipment you already have in your kitchen. Along the way, we hope you'll learn some easily mastered new techniques. So throw out those takeout menus and discover real Chinese cooking, the way it is meant to taste.

IN THIS CHAPTER

THE RECIPES
Fried Rice with Shrimp, Pork, and Shiitake Mushrooms
Fried Rice with Peas and Bean Sprouts
Thai-Style Curried Chicken Fried Rice

Basic White Rice

Kung Pao Shrimp

EQUIPMENT CORNER
Rice Cookers

SCIENCE DESK
What Makes Rice Sticky?

TASTING LAB
Long-Grain Rice
Chile Products

FRIED RICE

WHAT WE WANTED: Not the heavy, greasy, or soggy renditions we've eaten as takeout. To start, we wanted fried rice with firm, separate grains, and we wanted a finished dish so clean and light that we could distinguish its many different flavors in every bite.

Leftovers are an incredible boon to the busy cook—as long as you know what to do with them. Some are obvious, like using up that turkey or ham in sandwiches. Some are a bit more obtuse, like turning leftover mashed potatoes into potato pancakes. But when faced with the question of what to do with leftover rice, we say, "Fry it."

A sample from your local suburban Chinese restaurant, though, might give you pause. There the norm is often a heavy dish doused with so much soy sauce that you can hardly tell the mushrooms from the chicken. But this is no more representative of the virtues of this dish than a fast-food burger is of a great home-grilled version. We wanted a dish with both firm, distinct grains of rice and light, distinctive flavors. We also knew that the success of the dish would depend on the answers to four questions: what to add, how much to add, when to add it, and when to leave it alone.

Fried rice was created as a way to put leftover rice to good, tasty use. Unlike Chinese restaurants, however, most American cooks are unlikely to have leftover rice on hand, so we decided to experiment with making the dish from freshly cooked, still warm rice. It was a disaster. The grains gelled together in large clumps, and the whole dish was very wet. Rice freshly cooked and then allowed to cool to room temperature fared little better, still turning out wet and unappealing fried rice. What produced by far the best fried rice was rice that had been cooked and then chilled in the refrigerator overnight. The grains were more separate and evenly coated with oil, and the overall dish much drier.

But we wanted to see if we could avoid overnight refrigeration. We tried spreading the cooked rice on a sheet pan to cool it down to room temperature rapidly, then placed the pan in the refrigerator to chill completely. The resulting fried rice was drier and the clumps of rice much smaller than in versions prepared with fresh-cooked rice, making this method an option for cooks who want to make fried rice as quickly as possible from freshly cooked rice. But leftover rice is still the best option, as we found when we tried refrigerating cooked rice for different amounts of time. While rice kept in the refrigerator for four hours was acceptable, a whole night in the refrigerator produced the driest, most separate grains and therefore the best fried rice.

We tested various types of rice, including extra-long, long, medium, and short grain. All are suitable for fried rice after an overnight stay in the refrigerator. But don't try making fried rice with store-bought rice that has been precooked, parboiled, or converted. These processed rices become soggy and wet, and the grains quickly begin to break down and disintegrate during frying.

Despite the preference of many Chinese-American restaurants for large quantities of soy sauce in their fried rice, a quick look through many Chinese cookbooks revealed salt as the preferred seasoning. When tested, this rice tasted very clean and light, but tasters longed for a more substantial flavor. We went back to the soy sauce, but the large amount (nearly six tablespoons) needed to fully season the dish caused the rice to turn soggy and ugly. We wanted to find a seasoning with enough flavor intensity to be used sparingly.

The answer was oyster sauce. More appropriately referred to as oyster-flavored sauce, this condiment is a highly concentrated combination of soy sauce, brine, and oyster extracts. It is very thick, salty, and potent. Fried rice made with this sauce was well seasoned but not soggy.

In the process of all this testing, we also figured out how best to add the usual egg and vegetables to the rice. To get the eggs to the right texture, we scrambled them lightly, then removed them from the pan, reserving them to be added back to the pan at the end of cooking for a quick warm-up. Similarly, we found that moisture from vegetables such as peas, mushrooms, green beans, and asparagus caused the rice to clump when added to the pan along with it. Sautéing the vegetables alone in oil first allows sufficient moisture to cook off, producing a drier dish with better-flavored vegetables. More tender vegetables, such as sprouts and scallions, along with herbs, hold their texture and flavor better if added at the end of the cooking process.

The odd thing about fried rice is that it's not truly fried. When food is fried, it is cooked in a large amount of fat, usually enough to cover the food (think of fried chicken). What we call fried rice is actually pan-fried or sautéed, which means it is cooked over relatively high heat in a much smaller amount of fat (in this case, oil). We needed to figure out exactly how much oil would be necessary, and we knew that the pan we used would determine the amount. Because we wanted to make a large quantity of fried rice we limited our testing to large (12-inch) skillets—nonstick and regular—and a 14-inch wok.

The wok held plenty of rice, but the sloped sides and small 6-inch bottom allowed only a small portion of the rice to cook at one time. The wok also required a great deal of oil. The rice on the bottom continually absorbed what was added. The flat surface of the skillet provided a larger cooking surface, and the rice sautéed more quickly and evenly. Choosing between regular and nonstick was easy. The regular skillet required much more oil to keep the rice from sticking, making the dish greasy. We preferred the nonstick skillet for the lighter rice it produced.

Even using a nonstick pan, we found that a moderate amount of oil was required to keep the rice grains separate. Too little oil caused the rice grains to clump together during sautéing.

WHAT WE LEARNED: **For fried rice that is light and flavorful rather than sodden and greasy, cook the ingredients in batches in a large nonstick skillet rather than a wok. Start with chilled rice, and use oyster sauce to season the dish.**

FRIED RICE WITH SHRIMP, PORK, AND SHIITAKES makes about 8 cups, serving 4 to 6

This classic combination can be served as a main course. See the Basic White Rice recipe on page 85 for tips on preparing and cooling rice.

½ ounce (5 to 6 medium) dried shiitake mushrooms
¼ cup oyster-flavored sauce
1 tablespoon soy sauce
3½ tablespoons peanut or vegetable oil
2 large eggs, beaten lightly
8 ounces small shrimp, peeled and deveined
1 cup frozen peas, preferably baby peas, thawed
8 ounces sliced smoked ham, cut into ½-inch pieces
2 medium garlic cloves, minced (about 2 teaspoons)
5 cups cold cooked white rice, large clumps broken up with fingers
1 cup bean sprouts
5 medium scallions, white and green parts, sliced thin (about ½ cup)

1. Cover dried shiitakes with 1 cup hot tap water in small microwave-safe bowl; cover with plastic wrap, cut several steam vents with paring knife, and microwave on high power for 30 seconds. Let stand until mushrooms soften, about 5 minutes. Lift mushrooms from liquid with fork, trim stems, and slice into ¼-inch strips; set mushrooms aside.

2. Combine oyster-flavored sauce and soy sauce in small bowl; set aside.

3. Heat 12-inch nonstick skillet over medium heat until hot. Add 1½ teaspoons oil and swirl to coat pan bottom. Add eggs and cook without stirring, until they just begin to set, about 20 seconds, then scramble and break into small pieces with wooden spoon; continue to cook, stirring constantly, until eggs are cooked through but not browned, about 1 minute longer. Transfer eggs to small bowl and set aside.

4. Return skillet to medium heat and heat until hot; add 1½ teaspoons oil and swirl to coat pan bottom. Add shrimp and cook, stirring constantly, until opaque and just cooked through, about 30 seconds. Transfer to bowl with eggs and set aside.

5. Return skillet to burner, increase heat to high, and heat skillet until hot; add remaining 2½ tablespoons oil and swirl to coat pan bottom. Add peas, mushrooms, and ham; cook, stirring constantly, for 1 minute. Stir in garlic and cook until fragrant, about 30 seconds. Add rice and oyster sauce mixture; cook, stirring constantly and breaking up rice clumps, until mixture is heated through, about 3 minutes. Add eggs, shrimp, bean sprouts, and scallions; cook, stirring constantly, until heated through, about 1 minute. Serve immediately.

FRIED RICE WITH PEAS AND BEAN
SPROUTS makes about 8 cups, serving 4 to 6
This lighter variation is best served as a side dish or for lunch. See the Basic White Rice recipe on page 85 for tips on preparing and cooling rice.

¼	cup oyster-flavored sauce
1	tablespoon soy sauce
3	tablespoons peanut or vegetable oil
2	large eggs, beaten lightly
1	cup frozen peas, preferably baby peas, thawed
2	medium garlic cloves, minced (about 2 teaspoons)
6	cups cold cooked white rice, large clumps broken up with fingers
1	cup bean sprouts
5	medium scallions, white and green parts, sliced thin (about ½ cup)

1. Combine oyster sauce and soy sauce in small bowl; set aside.

2. Heat 12-inch nonstick skillet over medium heat until hot; add 1½ teaspoons oil and swirl to coat pan bottom. Add eggs and cook without stirring, until they just begin to set, about 20 seconds, then scramble and break into small pieces with wooden spoon; continue to cook, stirring constantly, until eggs are cooked through but not browned, about 1 minute longer. Transfer eggs to small bowl and set aside.

3. Return skillet to burner, increase heat to high, and heat skillet until hot. Add remaining 2½ tablespoons oil and swirl to coat pan bottom. Add peas and cook, stirring constantly, 30 seconds; stir in garlic and cook until fragrant, about 30 seconds. Add rice and oyster-flavored sauce mixture; cook, stirring constantly and breaking up rice clumps, until mixture is heated through, about 3 minutes. Add eggs, bean sprouts, and scallions; cook, stirring constantly, until heated through, about 1 minute. Serve immediately.

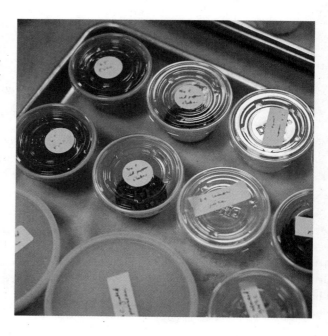

THAI-STYLE CURRIED CHICKEN FRIED RICE makes about 8 cups, serving 4 to 6

Curry powder, fish sauce, fresh chiles, and cilantro flavor this more exotic version of fried rice. See the Basic White Rice recipe at right for tips on preparing and cooling rice.

1	tablespoon dark brown sugar
3	tablespoons fish sauce
1	tablespoon soy sauce
2	small (about 8 ounces) boneless skinless chicken breasts, cut into 1-inch chunks
½	teaspoon salt
3½	tablespoons peanut or vegetable oil
2	large eggs, beaten lightly
1	teaspoon plus 1 tablespoon curry powder
1	large onion, sliced thin
2	medium garlic cloves, minced (2 teaspoons)
5	Thai green or 3 jalapeño chiles, seeded and minced (about 2 tablespoons)
6	cups cold cooked white rice, large clumps broken up with fingers
5	medium scallions, white and green parts, sliced thin (about ½ cup)
2	tablespoons minced fresh cilantro leaves
	Lime wedges for serving

1. Dissolve sugar in fish and soy sauces in small bowl; set aside. Season chicken with ½ teaspoon salt; set aside.

2. Heat 12-inch nonstick skillet over medium heat until hot. Add 1½ teaspoons oil and swirl to coat pan bottom. Add eggs and cook without stirring, until they just begin to set, about 20 seconds, then scramble and break into small pieces with wooden spoon; continue to cook, stirring constantly, until eggs are cooked through but not browned, about 1 minute longer. Transfer eggs to small bowl and set aside.

3. Return skillet to burner, increase heat to high, and heat skillet until hot; add 1½ teaspoons oil and swirl to coat pan bottom. Add 1 teaspoon curry powder and cook until fragrant, about 30 seconds; add chicken and cook, stirring constantly, until cooked through, about 2 minutes. Transfer to bowl with eggs and set aside.

4. Return skillet to high heat and heat until hot; add remaining 2½ tablespoons oil and swirl to coat pan bottom. Add onion and remaining 1 tablespoon curry powder and cook, stirring constantly, until onion is softened, about 3 minutes. Stir in garlic and chiles; cook until fragrant, about 30 seconds. Add rice and fish sauce mixture; cook, stirring constantly and breaking up rice clumps, until mixture is heated through, about 3 minutes. Add eggs, chicken, scallions, and cilantro; cook, stirring constantly, until heated through, about 1 minute. Serve immediately with lime wedges.

BASIC WHITE RICE makes about 6 cups

Serve this rice as is or chill the cooked rice as directed and use it for any fried rice recipe. Toasting the rice in a little oil makes the grains especially fluffy and separate.

2	teaspoons vegetable oil
1	cup long-grain white rice (not converted)
1½	cups water
½	teaspoon salt

1. Heat oil in medium saucepan over medium heat. Add rice and cook, stirring constantly, until transparent, 2 to 3 minutes. Add water and salt. Bring to boil, swirling pot to blend ingredients. Reduce heat to low, cover tightly, and cook until liquid is absorbed, about 15 minutes.

2. Turn off heat; let rice stand on burner, still covered, to finish cooking, about 15 minutes longer. Fluff with fork and serve immediately, or, for use in fried rice, spread cooked rice in even layer on parchment-lined baking sheet, cool to room temperature, about 30 minutes, then refrigerate, uncovered, until completely dry and grains are easily separated, at least 4 hours and up to 24 hours.

very sticky. This is why short-grain rice is perfect for sushi.

Long-grain rice, which is what we use for fried rice, has more amylose than amylopectin. Although the straight, bar-shaped amylose molecules are not as sticky as the amylopectin molecules, they are sticky enough to become tangled and cause individual grains of rice to clump when cooked. As a result, freshly cooked long-grain rice is still too sticky for use in fried rice.

When cooked long-grain rice is cooled, however, the grains go through a process called retrogradation. During this process, the amylose molecules realign within each single grain of rice. As this happens, you end up with separate grains, which is exactly what you want for fried rice.

TASTING LAB: Long-Grain Rice

ESSENTIALLY, WHITE RICE IS BROWN RICE MADE CONVENIENT. Developed thousands of years ago, the technique of stripping the germ and bran layers from brown rice to get white rice saves 30 minutes in cooking time. In today's busy world, that can make a big difference. Yet rice manufacturers have made cooking long-grain white rice even more of a snap with five-minute instant varieties and boil-in-bag options. We could not help but wonder whether so much convenience could still taste good. We decided to find out with a blind taste test.

To avoid comparing apples and oranges, we limited the candidates in our tasting to nationally distributed brands or major regional brands of plain, nonaromatic, long-grain white rice products. This gave us a lineup of eight products, including standard, instant, converted, and boil-in-bag.

To understand the differences in these products, it helps to know what they have in common. To begin with, all the rices in our tasting were long-grain, which means that each kernel is four to five times longer than it is wide when uncooked. Long-grain white rice is characteristically "fluffy" and is the least sticky of the white rices. In part, this is because it contains a high percentage of

SCIENCE DESK: What Makes Rice Sticky?

HOT, FRESHLY COOKED RICE MAKES STICKY, GLUEY FRIED rice, but cold rice fries up light and separate, making much better fried rice. Why? The answer has to do with the starches contained in rice.

Rice contains two types of starch: amylose and amylopectin. When you boil rice, these starches absorb water and swell up, which is why the grains of rice expand. Short-grain rice contains more amylopectin than amylose. Amylopectin molecules are branched, and when they expand the molecules clump together and make the rice

Rating Long-Grain Rices

WE TASTED EIGHT PLAIN, NONAROMATIC, LONG-GRAIN WHITE RICE PRODUCTS. WE PREPARED ALL RICES ACCORDING TO the package directions but omitted salt and butter or oil. Tasters rated the rices on flavor and texture. Rices are listed in order of preference. All brands are available in supermarkets.

RECOMMENDED

1. Uncle Ben's Boil-in-Bag Rice

$1.99 for 15.8 ounces

Startlingly simple if you are not averse to the plastic-pouch concept. Strong on looks but not as great on flavor; one taster best described it as "neutral." Notably moist but not watery, with only minor stickiness.

RECOMMENDED

2. Canilla Extra Long Grain Enriched Rice

$1.49 for 48 ounces

Tasters characterized the grains as stubby (yet slender). The flavor was nutty, somewhat buttery, and, in general, "good." The texture was firm, light, fluffy, and tender.

RECOMMENDED

3. Carolina/Mahatma Extra Long Grain Enriched Rice

$1.59 for 32 ounces

This rice was somewhere between clingy and separate. The grains were a bit pasty and dry, and there was some fraying at the tips, which one taster described as a "natural food appearance." Offsetting these characteristics were its pleasantly "al dente texture" and "clean flavor." This rice is also sold under the Mahatma label.

RECOMMENDED

4. Kraft Minute Brand Boil-in-Bag White Rice

$1.99 for 14 ounces

This rice was described as moist and fluffy but a little bit on the mushy side. Tasters' description of its flavor ranged from "mild," "sort of wheaty," and slightly buttery and nutty to "innocuous" and "boring." The grains were distinctly stubby.

RECOMMENDED

5. Uncle Ben's Converted Original Enriched Parboiled Long Grain Rice

$2.99 for 32 ounces

This rice was lauded for having a lot of flavor character and great potential for pilaf. The grains were very moist, firm, plump, separate, and "not chalky or mushy." The color was slightly off, which is typical of converted rices.

NOT RECOMMENDED

6. Success Enriched Precooked Natural Long Grain Rice

$3.99 for 32 ounces

This boil-in-bag variety was just a little too much of nothing. One taster described it as having "a weird, hollow flavor." Another described it as "flat." This rice was extremely light and fluffy, with very separate but dry grains.

NOT RECOMMENDED

7. Kraft Minute Brand Instant Enriched Long Grain White Rice

$3.49 for 28 ounces

The simplicity of this quick-cooking rice could not make up for its "complete lack of any rice flavor." This soggy, mushy, clumpy "Sno-Kone" white rice "tastes more like boiled rice water," said tasters. A chemical or metallic aftertaste was also criticized. The grains disintegrated in your mouth.

NOT RECOMMENDED

8. Uncle Ben's Enriched Long Grain Instant Rice

$1.99 for 14 ounces

"The strongest tasting rice I've ever eaten," commented one taster, Another described its flavor as "metallic" and "artificial." The rice was also mushy.

amylose, the less sticky of the two starches in rice, the other being amylopectin (see the Science Desk on page 86 for more information).

All of the rices were also milled using the standard process in which the hull is removed and the grains are then rubbed together by machine to remove the bran and germ. (Rice with bran and germ left intact is brown rice.) These two processes create standard white rice. Converted and instant rice are subjected to more processing.

The additional processing for converted rice is done before milling. The unmilled rice is soaked in hot water, then steamed and dried in the husk. This technique is far from modern, dating back about 1,500 years in India, where rice was put in large pots of water, soaked, steamed, and laid out in the sun to dry. Still practiced today in rural parts of India, this method makes it easier to remove the hull. For modern cooks the primary advantage of this processing is that the rice remains firmer and more separate when it's cooked. Some of the starch in the outer portion of the kernel becomes gelatinized when it's steamed in the husk. The rice kernel then dries harder than it is in its original state, and nutrients are retained as they seep from the bran into the kernel. The harder starch makes it more difficult for water to penetrate, so it takes about five minutes more time for converted rice to cook. The result is not only firmer, more separate rice but rice with a tan-yellow tint and a stronger flavor than standard rice.

On the opposite end of the spectrum is instant rice. To make it, milled rice is fully precooked and then dried very fast. This creates cracks or channels that facilitate the movement of water into the kernel as it cooks on the stove. You can see the cracks if you look closely at kernels of instant rice, which tend to be light and porous, like miniature puffed rice. This process makes cooking rice as effortless as making instant soup—stir into boiling water, cover, and let rest off heat for five minutes.

The compromise between the firm, separate kernels of converted rice and the convenience of instant rice seems to be boil-in-bag products. These modern innovations are made by precooking converted rice. In other words, these rices are parboiled prior to hulling, then precooked and dried after hulling and the removal of the bran and germ. The idea is that the parboiling will create rice grains with a firmer texture resistant to breaking down and turning mushy, so that even though they are also precooked they will remain firm and separate during their final 10 minutes of cooking.

When it came to tasting, our panel surprised us. As we expected, standard rices—that had not been subjected to any special processing to make them cook faster or end up with grains that were unusually separate—did well, finishing in second and third place. The surprise was the first-place finish of Uncle Ben's Boil-in-Bag, along with the fourth-place showing of Kraft's Boil-in-Bag. In both cases, the idea behind the dual processing of these rices really paid off. Tasters found the grains of Uncle Ben's, in particular, to be firm, perfectly unbroken, and nicely moist.

The converted rice garnered decent remarks but finished in the middle of the pack. As for instant rices, our tasters found these products unpalatably mushy, and they noted that the individual kernels tended to fall apart and fray. We also detected off flavors.

So if you aren't opposed to preparing your rice in a plastic pouch, a boil-in-bag rice might be the best option when you're looking for convenience. The trade-off, however, is that you get less rice for your dollar and you cannot cook these rices along with other seasonings or ingredients. Standard long-grain white rice takes a total of only 30 to 35 minutes to prepare (including resting time) and requires minimal attention. It also cooks up dry and fluffy, meaning that you can use it in fried rice, something we don't recommend you try with boil-in-a-bag rice, which tends to be moister and softer when cooked.

EQUIPMENT CORNER: RICE COOKERS

WITHOUT A DOUBT, THE EASIEST, MOST RELIABLE METHOD for preparing rice is the rice cooker. Besides turning out good rice (it's fluffy, separate, and still has a nice bite), rice cookers are easy to clean, especially models with a nonstick surface on the cooking pot. (When buying a rice cooker, we consider a nonstick finish a must.)

A rice cooker consists of a large chamber with an electric heating element on the bottom. A cooking pot slips into the holding chamber and is covered with a lid. The heating element brings the rice and water to a boil and maintains a constant temperature. When the temperature inside the cooking chamber rises above 212 degrees—a sign that there is no more steam and all the water has been absorbed—the rice cooker automatically shuts off. Most models actually switch to a "keep warm" mode, which holds rice for several hours without damage.

You can spend $20 for a bare-bones rice cooker or up to $180 for a high-tech fuzzy logic model with a small "electronic brain." We rounded up five rice cookers to see if more money bought a better machine. To put these rice cookers through their paces, we cooked 3 cups of long-grain rice, 3 cups of short-grain rice, and 1 cup of short-grain rice according to the manufacturers' specifications in each cooker. We kept the rice warm for three hours using the warming function, and we assessed cleanup.

We were looking for evenly cooked rice that was neither mushy nor overly firm. Burning on the bottom was considered unacceptable. The good news is that all three Japanese rice cookers passed this test. The Japanese invented rice cookers back in the 1950s and have clearly perfected this technology. The bad news is that the cheaper knock-offs from American companies did not perform as well.

Rice cooked in the Toastmaster Rice Cooker TR-5 ($19.99) was scorched every time. Rice did not burn in the Farberware Nutristeam Rice Cooker/Food Warmer FRA500 ($29.99), but it did come out dry and a bit hard, especially if the warming function was engaged.

Among the three Japanese models tested, we found minor differences in performance, but testers felt that it was best to recommend the least expensive model in this group, the National Rice Cooker/Steamer SR-W10NA, which costs just $37.99. Although some browning occurred on the bottom of the rice (especially if the warming function was used), this did not mar the texture or flavor of the rice. The Sanyo Electric Rice Cooker/Warmer ECJ-5104PF ($89.99) also produced a light brown layer of rice on the bottom.

Only the Zojirushi Neuro Fuzzy Rice Cooker and Warmer NS-JCC10 ($179.99) yielded pot after pot of rice without any browning of the bottom layer, even after several hours on the warming cycle. The dizzying array of options on this cooker include variable settings for "regular," "softer," and "harder" rice; settings for brown rice and rice porridge; and a special extended warming function that kicks in after eight hours. Although this ultrafancy model performed beautifully in tests, we are hard pressed to recommend spending so much money on a rice cooker, especially when the cheaper options perform basic tasks nearly as well.

BEST RICE COOKER

The National Rice Cooker/Steamer has a nonstick pan, an automatic warming feature, and a removable power cord for easy storage. This model turned out batch after batch of good rice and costs far less than high-end models with more bells and whistles. See www.cooksillustrated.com for an up-to-date price and mail-order source for this top-rated product.

KUNG PAO SHRIMP

WHAT WE WANTED: Tired of the sweet, gloppy restaurant renditions of this Sichuan classic, we wanted to take a few Asian pantry staples and just 30 minutes to make a spicy, sweet, salty, savory kung pao that would put most restaurant versions to shame.

This classic Sichuan stir-fry of shrimp, peanuts, and chiles in a rich brown sauce is a Chinese restaurant standard, yet the kung pao we sampled in a half dozen well-reputed spots around Boston was shocking. The first one was abysmal, with tough, tiny little shrimp drenched in a quart of pale, greasy, bland sauce, and things just got worse from there.

This sorry collection of kung pao renditions served as a not-so-subtle hint that we'd be better off making this dish at home. Like most stir-fries, kung pao cooks quickly, so it is well suited for a weeknight meal. Moreover, we thought that by carefully examining the key issues—those being the type and preparation of both the shrimp and the nuts along with the composition and texture of the sauce—we could come up with something much better than what we'd encountered in most restaurants.

Most Chinese stir-fries go heavy on the vegetables, but kung pao dishes are different. The quantity of vegetables is limited, with the emphasis instead on the shrimp and the nuts. The restaurant versions we tried often included green pepper, and some added bamboo shoots, carrots, celery, scallions, and zucchini. Tasters worked their way through these choices and more and settled on a modest amount of red pepper for sweetness and scallion for freshness, bite, and color. Kung pao needs nothing else from the vegetable kingdom.

Taking a step up the food chain, we looked at the shrimp next. Most restaurants use medium to small shrimp, which makes the dish seem skimpy and cheap. We felt that larger shrimp made a more satisfying kung pao, and large

shrimp were easier to peel, too. After checking out jumbo, extra-large, large, and medium (labels that are less helpful than the numbers assigned to shrimp to indicate size, such as 21/25, meaning that 21 to 25 shrimp make 1 pound), tasters selected extra-large (21/25 count) for their combination of succulence and generous appearance.

The best way to prepare the shrimp was a matter of some debate. Traditionally, they are "velveted"—coated with egg white, cornstarch, and seasonings—and then fried in a generous quantity of oil. The idea here is to create a softly crisp coating that will help the sauce adhere. Though velveting does have its supporters, we were not among them, for two reasons. First, the egg coating tended to cook up in unattractive clumps, which would later float about in the dish, and second, the two to three cups of oil required to deep-fry seemed both cumbersome and wasteful. Dealing with all that oil, from measuring it out to disposing of it later, edged the dish out of the realm of simple weeknight cooking. It would be much better, we felt, to quickly stir-fry the shrimp in a film of oil and to thicken the sauce slightly to help it coat the shrimp.

The nuts help define kung pao. In most of the restaurant dishes we tried, the flavor of the nuts was underdeveloped, so they acted more as a garnish than a key element. We wanted to better integrate the nuts into the dish and to deepen their flavor. One move accomplished both goals. Whereas most recipes add the nuts near the end of the cooking time, we stir-fried them right along with the shrimp at the beginning. This way, they toasted briefly in the pan, intensifying in flavor, which they then contributed to the sauce. Most kung pao recipes rely on either peanuts or cashews, and we appreciated the former for their savory flavor and crisp texture. By comparison, cashews seemed both sweet and a little soft.

The test kitchen has conducted extensive investigations into stir-frying technique, so we knew that a wide, heavy skillet, preheated until the oil smokes, is a better mate with the flat American stovetop burner than a deeply curved wok. With all that heat, though, it would be easy to overcook, and therefore toughen, the shrimp and to burn the aromatic garlic and ginger that are part of the sauce. With a little care, both problems are easy to avoid. First, we learned not to cook shrimp all the way through at first because they will finish cooking in the sauce later; an initial stay in the pan of just under two minutes was ideal. With regard to the garlic and ginger, most stir-fry recipes add them near the beginning. We prefer to add them near the end of cooking to prevent burning and preserve their fresh flavors.

When it came to the sauce, we pictured it deep brown, syrupy in texture, and glistening, with balanced elements of sweet, savory, salty, garlicky, and hot. We tried both chicken broth and water as a base and preferred the broth for the savory underpinning it provided. For a bit of sweetness we added sugar in amounts from 1 tablespoon down to 1 teaspoon, but even a mere teaspoon was overkill. Instead, we chose to add the classic trio of hoisin sauce, oyster-flavored sauce, and sesame oil, all available in the supermarket and all good sources of color, flavor depth, and subtle sweetness. An ample supply of garlic—three cloves—gave the sauce authority, and ginger and rice vinegar added brightness. We liked Chinese black rice vinegar (called Chinkiang vinegar) even better because it was more complex—smoky, salty, plum-like, and slightly sweet—but it is hard to come by in the supermarket. Cornstarch is the thickener of choice for Asian sauces, and 1½ teaspoons reliably gelled the sauce to a soft, glazey, shrimp-coating consistency.

Eager to see if we could streamline the recipe by omitting an ingredient (or maybe two?), we systematically retested all of the sauce components. Alas, tasters agreed that each one brought a distinct flavor dimension to the party; without any one of them, the sauce suffered a bit, inching its way back toward the dreaded restaurant

kung pao we were determined to outdo.

Spicy chile heat may be kung pao's true calling card. (For details about the multitude of heat sources we tried, see the Tasting Lab on page 93.) Tasters unanimously chose whole dried chiles, which are traditional for this dish. We did alter the technique with which they are generally used, however, by stir-frying them with the shrimp and peanuts at the beginning of cooking. This extra bit of pan time toasted the chiles, deepening their flavor noticeably.

Now the next time the yen for kung pao hits, we'll leave the sweet, pasty, insipid stuff in the takeout box where it belongs. With fresh shrimp, a few Asian pantry ingredients, 20 minutes of prep time, and five minutes at the stove, we can rival the best that Chinatown has to offer.

WHAT WE LEARNED: Use extra-large shrimp, keep the amount of vegetables in check, add the chiles and nuts early so they toast and develop more flavor, and use a trio of Asian ingredients—hoisin sauce, oyster-flavored sauce, and sesame oil—to create a rich brown sauce.

KUNG PAO SHRIMP serves 4

We like the appearance of whole dried chiles as well as the toasty flavor they develop in the pan, but crushed red pepper flakes are a fine substitute. Feel free to increase the number of chiles to suit your taste. You can also substitute plain rice vinegar for the black rice vinegar (available in Asian markets), but we prefer the latter for its fruity, salty complexity. If you prefer roasted unsalted cashews over peanuts, substitute an equal amount. Unless you have a taste for the incendiary, do not eat the whole chiles in the finished dish. Serve kung pao shrimp with Basic White Rice (page 85). See page 93 for tips on deveining shrimp.

- 1 pound extra-large shrimp (21 to 25 count), peeled and deveined
- 1 tablespoon dry sherry or rice wine
- 2 teaspoons soy sauce
- 3 medium garlic cloves, minced (about 1 tablespoon)
- 1 piece (½-inch) fresh ginger, peeled and minced (about 2 teaspoons)
- 3 tablespoons peanut or vegetable oil
- ½ cup roasted unsalted peanuts

- 6 small whole dried red chiles (each about 1¾ to 2 inches long), 3 chiles roughly crumbled, or 1 teaspoon hot red pepper flakes
- ¾ cup canned low-sodium chicken broth
- 2 teaspoons black rice vinegar or plain rice vinegar
- 2 teaspoons Asian sesame oil
- 1 tablespoon oyster-flavored sauce
- 1 tablespoon hoisin sauce
- 1½ teaspoons cornstarch
- 1 medium red bell pepper, cut into ½-inch dice (about 1 cup)
- 3 medium scallions, white and green parts, sliced thin (about ¼ cup)

1. Toss shrimp with sherry and soy sauce in medium bowl; marinate for 10 minutes. Mix garlic, ginger, and 1 tablespoon oil in small bowl; set aside. Combine peanuts and chiles in small bowl; set aside. Mix chicken broth, vinegar, sesame oil, oyster-flavored sauce, hoisin sauce, and cornstarch in small bowl or measuring cup; set aside.

2. Heat 1 tablespoon oil in 12-inch skillet over high heat until just beginning to smoke. Add shrimp and cook, stirring

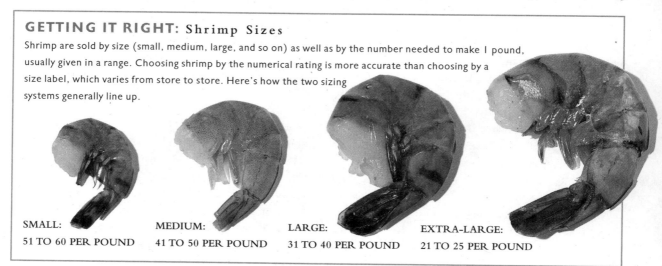

GETTING IT RIGHT: Shrimp Sizes

Shrimp are sold by size (small, medium, large, and so on) as well as by the number needed to make 1 pound, usually given in a range. Choosing shrimp by the numerical rating is more accurate than choosing by a size label, which varies from store to store. Here's how the two sizing systems generally line up.

SMALL: 51 TO 60 PER POUND

MEDIUM: 41 TO 50 PER POUND

LARGE: 31 TO 40 PER POUND

EXTRA-LARGE: 21 TO 25 PER POUND

about once every 10 seconds, until barely opaque, 30 to 40 seconds; add peanuts and chiles, stir into shrimp, and continue cooking until shrimp are almost completely opaque and peanuts have darkened slightly, 30 to 40 seconds longer. Transfer shrimp, peanuts, and chiles to bowl; set aside. Return skillet to burner and reheat briefly, 15 to 30 seconds. Add remaining 1 tablespoon oil, swirl to coat pan, and add red bell pepper; cook, stirring occasionally, until slightly softened, about 45 seconds. Clear center of pan, add garlic-ginger mixture, mash into pan with spoon or spatula and cook until fragrant, 10 to 15 seconds; stir into pepper until combined. Stir broth mixture to recombine, then add to skillet along with reserved shrimp, peanuts, and chiles; cook, stirring and scraping up browned bits on bottom of pan, until sauce has thickened to syrupy consistency, about 45 seconds. Stir in scallions; transfer to serving plate and serve immediately.

TECHNIQUE: Deveining Shrimp

Once the shell has been removed, you should remove the black vein that runs along the curved outer side of the shrimp.

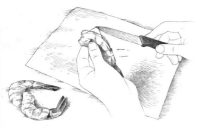

1. Slice along the back of the shrimp with a paring knife to expose the vein, then use the tip of the knife to lift it out.

2. The vein may stick to the knife. Instead of struggling to remove it with your fingers, just wipe the blade against a paper towel. The vein will stick to the towel, which can be discarded once all of the shrimp have been deveined.

TASTING LAB: Chile Products

WITHOUT SPICY CHILE HEAT, IT'S NOT KUNG PAO. THE recipes we consulted, however, offered little agreement about the best source of that heat. We hit the supermarket down the street and picked up the most oft-repeated contenders, including several types of whole dried chiles (the traditional choice), crushed red pepper flakes, fresh chiles, chili oil, and two popular and widely available Asian chili sauces, Sambal and Sriracha. We returned to the test kitchen and conducted a side-by-side kung pao tasting.

The exact formula for Sambal, a chunky chili-garlic paste, varies from maker to maker. Ours was seasoned with salt, sugar, and rice vinegar. Smoother Sriracha is a popular Thai chili sauce, and ours was seasoned with salt, sugar, garlic, and fish extract. Both Sambal and Sriracha are common table condiments, but tasters gave them thumbs-down in the kung pao because they lacked depth and tended to taste too salty. Chili oil was also passed by because the one we used, actually a chili-flavored sesame oil, was judged too mild, and it made the sauce a bit greasy. The fresh chiles—jalapeños, to be exact—provided sharp heat, but the tasters did not appreciate the distinct green, vegetal notes. Crushed red pepper flakes provided a bright, direct heat that was utterly acceptable, but the tasters' favorite by a long shot were the whole dried chiles. They infused the kung pao with a round, even spiciness that gave the dish a deep, toasty, almost smoky dimension as well.

This finding, of course, begged the question of whether one particular type of dried chile would be best, since there are many varieties. With our sights set on relatively small chiles (large chiles simply looked wrong in the dish), we returned to the market and gathered six varieties, including an unnamed Asian specimen from the bulk bin, Japones, Arbol, Guajillo, Costeño, and Cascabel. Tasters strained to detect distinctions between them in the kung pao. We concluded that any small whole dried red chile will do quite nicely.

Stacks of pans ready for sautéing cutlets
or pan-roasting pieces of chicken.

CHICKEN in a flash

While others might live by the mantra, "You can never be too rich or too thin," in the test kitchen our slogan goes something like this: "You can never have too many quick chicken dishes." Readers of the magazine and viewers of the television show tell us that chicken is their favorite weeknight entrée. As such, we are always looking for new dishes and new techniques to keep chicken fresh and interesting.

Italian cooking is always a good source of inspiration for simple but interesting recipes, and chicken is no exception. Chicken Milanese (pan-fried cutlets coated with bread crumbs and Parmesan) is a workhorse in our kitchen. Of course, if the coating fails to brown or falls off altogether, this dish isn't much good. Chicken piccata (with its bracing lemon and caper sauce) is another standby, but the sauce can be bland and pasty.

Another source of quick chicken recipes is restaurant cooking. We were intrigued by the notion of pan-roasting chicken parts—that is, starting them on the stovetop but finishing the cooking in the oven. Our goal was to make this chef's technique work at home.

CHICKEN MILANESE

WHAT WE WANTED: Juicy chicken cutlets covered with a crisp, evenly browned coating of bread crumbs and Parmesan. The coating must not peel away, as often happens, but remain firmly attached to the chicken.

Tender boneless chicken breast, pan-fried with a cloak of mild-flavored crumbs, has universal appeal. In Italy, grated Parmesan is added to the coating, and the dish is called chicken Milanese. Though simple, this dish can fall prey to a host of problems. The chicken itself may be rubbery and tasteless, and the coating—called a bound breading and arguably the best part of the dish— often ends up unevenly cooked, greasy, pale, or burnt.

For a breaded chicken cutlet to be great, the chicken itself must hold up its end of the bargain. Because the test kitchen is fiercely devoted to the benefits of brining poultry, we wondered what effect soaking the cutlets in a mixture of salt, sugar, and water would have. The brined cutlets were a hit, exceptionally juicy and seasoned all the way to the center. Brining takes just 30 minutes, during which time you can pull together other components of the recipe. It's not often that so little work yields such big benefits. (For cutlet recipes with a sauce, such as the piccata on page 104, the sauce adds moisture, and there's no need to brine the chicken.)

Throughout the first series of tests, we noticed that the thin tip of the cutlet and the opposite end, which was much more plump, cooked at different rates. This problem was a cinch to fix; all we had to do was pound the chicken breasts gently to an even ½ inch with a meat pounder (see the Equipment Corner on page 102). To promote even cooking, we also found it best to remove the floppy tenderloin from the underside of each cutlet before pounding.

The ideal breading should taste mild and comforting but not dull and certainly not greasy. To explore the possibilities, we pan-fried cutlets coated with fine, fresh bread crumbs (made from fresh sliced white sandwich bread ground fine in the food processor) and dry bread crumbs. The dry bread crumbs had an unmistakably stale flavor. The fresh bread crumbs swept the taste test, with their mild, subtly sweet flavor and light, crisp texture. We went on to test crumbs made from different kinds of white bread, including premium sliced sandwich bread, Italian, French, and country-style. The sandwich bread was the sweetest and appealed most to tasters in this recipe. That said, fresh crumbs made from all of these breads were good.

During the crumb testing, we made several important observations about the breading process. First, we learned that the cutlets must be thoroughly dried after brining. We also learned that we could not dispense with the coating of flour that went onto the chicken before the egg wash and crumbs. If the cutlets were even slightly moist, or if we skipped the flour coat, the breading would peel off the finished cutlets in sheets. In addition, we found it essential to press the crumbs onto the cutlets to ensure an even, thorough cover. Finally, we discovered that it was best to let the breaded cutlets rest for about five minutes before frying them; this step, too, helped to bind the breading to the meat.

Last, we explored the details of pan-frying. In any breaded preparation, the oil in the pan should reach one-third to one-half of the way up the food for thorough browning. Which fat should be used for sautéing the cutlets? Cutlets sautéed in olive oil were markedly better than those sautéed in vegetable oil.

WHAT WE LEARNED: For a crisp coating that won't fall off, dry the cutlets thoroughly and then flour them before dipping in egg wash and coating with fresh bread crumbs. Let the breaded cutlets rest for at least five minutes before frying them. Finally, use plenty of olive oil to pan-fry the cutlets.

CHICKEN MILANESE serves 4

Brining makes the cutlets juicier and more flavorful and is recommended. However, if you can find kosher cutlets (which have been soaked in saltwater during processing), skip this step and save yourself some time. When covering the cutlets with the bread crumb and cheese mixture, use your hands to pat a thorough, even coating onto the chicken to make sure the crumbs adhere. See the illustrations on page 98 for more tips on breading cutlets. The chicken is cooked in batches of two because the crust is noticeably more crisp if the pan is not overcrowded. Grind fresh or stale sandwich bread in a food processor to make homemade crumbs.

    4   boneless, skinless chicken breasts (5 to 6 ounces
         each), tenderloins removed and reserved for
         another use, fat trimmed (see illustration at
         right)
    ½   cup kosher salt or ¼ cup table salt
    ½   cup sugar
         Ground black pepper
    1¼   cups homemade bread crumbs
    ¼   cup finely grated Parmesan cheese
    ¾   cup unbleached all-purpose flour
    2   large eggs
    1   tablespoon plus ¾ cup olive oil
         Lemon wedges for serving

1. Use meat pounder, rubber mallet, or rolling pin to pound chicken breasts to even ½-inch thickness. Dissolve salt and sugar in 1 quart cold water in gallon-sized zipper-lock plastic bag. Add cutlets and seal bag, pressing out as much air as possible. Refrigerate until cutlets are fully seasoned, 30 minutes. Line baking sheet with triple layer of paper towels.

2. Remove cutlets and lay them in single layer on baking sheet. Cover with another triple layer of paper towels and press firmly to absorb moisture. Allow cutlets to dry for 10 minutes. Carefully peel paper towels off cutlets; sprinkle cutlets with pepper to taste and set them aside.

3. Adjust oven rack to lower-middle position, set large heat-proof plate on rack, and heat oven to 200 degrees. Combine bread crumbs and Parmesan cheese in shallow dish or pie plate. Spread flour in second shallow dish. Beat eggs with 1 tablespoon oil in third shallow dish.

4. Working with one at a time, dredge cutlets thoroughly in flour, shaking off excess. Using tongs, dip both sides of cutlets in egg mixture, taking care to coat them thoroughly and allowing excess to drip back into dish to ensure very thin coating. Dip both sides of cutlets in bread crumb mixture, pressing crumbs with your fingers to form an even, cohesive coat. Place breaded cutlets in single layer on wire rack set over baking sheet and allow coating to dry for about 5 minutes.

5. Meanwhile, heat 6 tablespoons of remaining oil in heavy-bottomed 10-inch nonstick skillet over medium-high heat until shimmering but not smoking, about 2 minutes. Lay two cutlets gently in skillet and cook until deep golden

---

TECHNIQUE: Trimming Cutlets

Most cutlets have a little yellow or white fat still attached to the breast meat. Lay each cutlet tenderloin-side down and smooth the top with your fingers. Any fat will slide to the edge of the cutlet, where it can be trimmed with a knife.

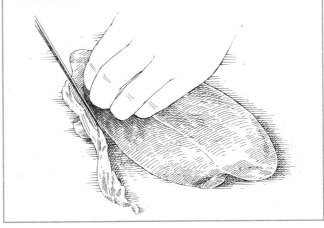

brown and crisp on first side, gently pressing down on cutlets with wide metal spatula to help ensure even browning, about 2½ minutes. Using tongs, flip cutlets, reduce heat to medium, and continue to cook until meat feels firm when pressed gently and second side is deep golden brown and crisp, 2½ to 3 minutes. Line warmed plate with double layer of paper towels and set cutlets on top; return plate to oven.

6. Discard oil in skillet and wipe skillet clean using tongs and large wad paper towels. Repeat step 5, using remaining 6 tablespoons oil and now-clean skillet to cook remaining cutlets. Serve immediately along with first batch and lemon wedges.

VARIATION

BREADED CHICKEN CUTLETS WITH GARLIC AND OREGANO

Follow recipe for Chicken Milanese, increasing bread crumbs to 1½ cups and omitting Parmesan cheese. Beat 3 tablespoons very finely minced fresh oregano leaves and 8 medium garlic cloves, minced to puree or pressed through garlic press (just under 3 tablespoons), into egg mixture in step 3.

EQUIPMENT CORNER: Inexpensive Nonstick Skillets

ALTHOUGH MOST HOME COOKS WOULD LIKE TO HAVE A battery of weighty, expensive, professional-grade pots and pans at their disposal, most of what gets used at home is a lot cheaper. Does lower-cost cookware necessarily mean a big performance trade-off? We examined that question recently by conducting a full set of cooking tests on eight inexpensive nonstick skillets, all purchased at hardware or discount stores for no more than $50 apiece.

Statistics reported by the Cookware Manufacturers Association indicate that 90 percent of all the aluminum cookware sold in the United States in 2001 was nonstick. The reasons to use nonstick are clear: Little or no fat is required to lubricate the food (and thereby prevent sticking), and cleanup is easy. Nonstick is terrific for extremely delicate, quick-cooking foods. Flaky white fish come to mind, as do certain egg dishes, like omelets and eggs sunny-side up, the integrity of which would be

---

TECHNIQUE: Breading Cutlets

1. Dredge the cutlets thoroughly in flour, shaking off the excess.

2. Using tongs, dip both sides of the cutlets in the egg mixture, taking care to coat them thoroughly and allowing the excess to drip back into the dish to ensure a very thin coating. Tongs keep the breading from coating your fingers.

3. Dip both sides of the cutlets in the bread crumbs, pressing the crumbs with your fingers to form an even, cohesive coat.

destroyed were they to stick to the pan.

Those concerned with limiting their fat intake view the reduction of cooking fat as another significant benefit. This makes sense if you want a simply sautéed fish fillet or chicken cutlet garnished with a wedge of lemon or lime. It may mean trouble, however, if you prefer to garnish your food with a pan sauce. Pan sauces rely on fond, the tiny caramelized bits of food that stick to the pan as its contents cook. When liquid is added to the pan (in a process called deglazing), the bits of food dissolve to form the flavorful backbone of the sauce.

Because nonstick coatings prevent sticking, they also, in our experience, inhibit fond development. To test this notion, we sautéed chicken cutlets in each pan and then deglazed the fond left behind with 1 cup of water, which we then boiled hard for one minute. We were looking for rich, dark brown liquid shaded deeply by the dissolved fond. What we got, in each and every case, more closely resembled dirty bathwater. Not a single sample was dark enough to use in a sauce.

The chicken cutlet tests point to another drawback of nonstick cookware. Not only was the fond light, so was the chicken. The savory, caramelized crust that forms on the exterior of a piece of food as it sautés is the very reason to cook that way in the first place—the crust tastes great. None of the nonstick pans in our tests formed a crust on the lean chicken cutlets that would make us proud (or hungry). Nonstick pans are fine, however, when pan-frying in a significant amount of oil, as in our breaded chicken cutlet recipe on page 97. In fact, we like nonstick pans for this task because they are easier to clean than pans with conventional surfaces.

Here in the test kitchen we choose nonstick when we want to cook lightly, keep flavors fresh, or ensure easy cleanup. If browning or fond are important to the dish, we reach for a traditional pan.

The material used for nonstick coating—polytetrafluoroethylene, or PTFE—was developed by chemists at Dupont in the late 1930s. Trademarked originally as Teflon, the formula has evolved over the years, and now several companies in addition to Dupont sell PTFE to cookware manufacturers (many of which use individualized, proprietary, multicoat application processes to bond the coating to their pans). It is our understanding, however, that the majority of nonstick coatings today are made from the same basic substance.

The nonstick, nonreactive magic of PTFE is due, in large part, to one of the two types of atoms it contains—namely, fluorine. Every PTFE molecule contains two carbon atoms and four fluorine atoms. In the atomic world, fluorine is very highly resistant to bonding with other substances. That's why PTFE is so slippery.

And slippery it was. Every pan in our group received a good score in release ability and cleaning tests, the raisons d'être for nonstick. We tested both traits in a purposefully

TECHNIQUE:
Protecting Nonstick Surfaces

If you stack your cookware (as we do), you run the risk of scratching the nonstick surface. Some cooks slip each pan into a large zipper-lock bag before stacking it, while others place plastic lids (from sour cream, coffee, or yogurt containers) between pans to keep them from scratching each other. Our favorite way to protect nonstick cookware is to slide a doubled piece of paper towel between each pan as you stack them.

abusive manner by burning oatmeal into the pans over high heat for 45 minutes. That kind of treatment would trash a traditional pan, but the scorched cereal slid out of our nonstick pans with no fuss, and the pans practically wiped clean.

Most manufacturers recommend using plastic, rubber, coated, or wooden utensils to avoid scratching the nonstick coating (and all caution against using any sharp utensil such as a knife, fork, or beater). Makers of only three of our pans, the Farberware, Innova, and Bialetti, actually sanction the use of metal utensils.

In their new, off-the-shelf condition, all of our pans turned in a reasonable-to-good performance with foods best suited to nonstick cooking: eggs and fish. In fact, every pan but the Revere produced evenly cooked omelets and released them with ease. The omelet made in the Farberware pan was especially impressive. The Farberware also did a nice job searing salmon fillets to an even, crusty, medium

brown. (Salmon is much higher in fat than skinless chicken cutlets and so browns more easily, even in a nonstick pan.) Overall, however, our tests indicate that any of these pans could easily handle such light-duty tasks as cooking eggs. Low cost does not mean a big trade-off here.

Sauté speed is also an important measure of a pan's performance. We tested this by sautéing 1½ cups of hand-chopped onions over medium heat for 10 minutes in the hope of ending up with pale gold onions that bore no trace of burning. And you know what? For the most part, we did. The Wearever, T-Fal, Innova, and Revere pans, which were all on the light side in terms of weight, turned out the darkest onions, but they were still well within an acceptable color range. Onions sautéed in the Farberware, Meyer, Calphalon, and Bialetti were a shade lighter, indicating a slightly slower sauté speed. The Farberware onions, however, took top honors based on how evenly all the pieces colored.

TECHNIQUE: Cleaning Up Spilled Oil

Anyone who has ever dropped a glass bottle of oil on the floor knows how hard it can be to clean up. Here's how to clean an oil-slicked floor and avoid cuts from broken glass shards.

1. Sprinkle a thick layer of flour over the spilled oil and wait a few minutes for the flour to absorb the oil.

2. With a paper towel, or brush if there's any glass, move the flour around until it absorbs all the oil, and sweep it up with a dustpan and broom.

3. Spray the area with window cleaner and wipe away the last traces of oil and flour.

Rating Inexpensive Nonstick Skillets

WE SAUTÉED CHICKEN CUTLETS, SEARED SALMON FILLETS, AND MADE OMELETS IN EIGHT LARGE NONSTICK SKILLETS. WE tested sauté speed by cooking onions in oil over medium heat for 10 minutes. Pans were also evaluated for cleanup and release ability and are listed in ascending order of price within each category. See www.cooksillustrated.com for up-to-date prices and mail-order sources for top-rated products.

RECOMMENDED
1. Farberware Millennium 18/10 Stainless Steel 12" Nonstick Skillet
$29.99
Heaviest pan of the bunch, with the most solid construction. Fantastic omelets, golden brown fish, and evenly sautéed onions. Only with chicken did this pan falter—and not much at that.

RECOMMENDED WITH RESERVATIONS
2. T-Fal Ultrabase Royale Gala 12¼" Sauté Pan
$22.99
Great job on omelets and salmon, but only decent job on chicken and onions. Cool, comfortable, ergonomic handle.

RECOMMENDED WITH RESERVATIONS
3. Wearever Concentric Air Collection Super Slick Nonstick 12" Sauté Pan
$29.99
Comfortable handle came loose during testing. Sauté speed was a slightly slow medium. A little extra effort necessary to clean shiny rim thoroughly.

RECOMMENDED WITH RESERVATIONS
4. Innova Classicor Stainless Steel Excalibur 12" Nonstick Frypan
$39.99
Decent performance but didn't brown foods as evenly as top pans did, and channel around rim made it difficult to remove omelets neatly.

NOT RECOMMENDED
5. Revere Polished Nonstick Open Skillet-12"
$19.99
High sides make omelets a bit tricky. Browning on fish and chicken was unimpressive, and the handle loosened during testing. Our least favorite pan.

NOT RECOMMENDED
6. Bialetti Casa Italia Hi-Base 11"
$19.99
Slow sauté speed means food does not brown well. Handle loosened slightly during testing. Textured pan bottom was of no particular advantage.

NOT RECOMMENDED
7. Meyer Commercial Weight II 12" Nonstick Sauté Pan
$27.99
Solid and heavy, but produces sub-par browning when sautéing. Extra-thick, shiny rim requires extra elbow grease to clean.

NOT RECOMMENDED
8. Simply Calphalon Nonstick 12" Omelette Pan
$49.99
Most expensive pan in the group did not sauté to impress. Neither chicken nor onions browned sufficiently; fish was more successful.

That does not bode well for their future.

Of the pans we tested, the $30 Farberware Millennium offered the best combination of good nonstick performance (in suitable applications), pleasing heft at almost 3½ pounds, and solid construction. It even beat out the priciest pan in the test, the Calphalon.

EQUIPMENT CORNER: Meat Pounders

WHEN DEVELOPING OUR RECIPE FOR CHICKEN MILANESE, we tried several pounding gadgets—makeshift as well as purchased—and found that the best chicken breast pounders were relatively lightweight, with large flat surfaces. A disk-style pounder with a handle in the center was our favorite. As long as we pounded lightly, its relatively large, round surface quickly and efficiently transformed breasts into cutlets. If you don't have this kind of pounder, we suggest pounding gently with what you have on hand, which is likely heavier than our disk-style pounder. A rubber mallet or rolling pin would be our second choice, but the bottom of a small saucepan will work in a pinch.

BEST MEAT POUNDER
We tested several styles of meat pounder and found that a disk-style pounder with a handle in the center is the easiest on delicate chicken cutlets. It is our top choice.

Of course, construction quality is a concern with any piece of cookware, but especially with inexpensive models. Will the thing hold up, or will you have to replace it in six months? Based on our experience, you may well sacrifice a measure of construction quality with a budget pan. Pans with handles that were welded or riveted on to the pan body, including the Farberware, Innova, Meyer, and Calphalon, all felt solid and permanent. But the heat-resistant plastic (called phenolic) handles on the T-Fal, Revere, Bialetti, and Wearever pans were not riveted in place, and all three of them came loose during testing.

CHICKEN PICCATA

WHAT WE WANTED: A classic chicken piccata with perfectly cooked cutlets and a lemony sauce punctuated with plenty of capers.

C hicken piccata—sautéed cutlets with a lemon-caper sauce—is a restaurant classic that translates easily to the home kitchen. We imagined that pic-cata would be easy to perfect—and it was, after we realized that most recipes miss the point. To begin with, many cook-book authors add extraneous ingredients and thereby ruin the pure simplicity of the dish. The other major problem is blandness. Many recipes contain just a tablespoon of lemon juice and a teaspoon of capers, neither of which provides much flavor. Our goals were simple: to cook the chicken properly and to make a streamlined sauce that really tasted of lemons and capers.

Many piccata recipes call for flouring or breading the cutlets. As in past tests conducted, we found that floured cut-lets browned better and were less likely to stick to the pan. Tasters did not like breaded cutlets—what's the point of developing a crisp crust only to douse it with sauce? We also tried dipping the cutlets in milk as well as beaten eggs before flouring them. Although the crust was a bit thicker when cooked, tasters felt that there was little advantage to this extra step.

With our chicken tests completed, we turned our attention to the sauce. We wanted a strong lemon flavor that wasn't harsh or overly acidic. We also wanted a sauce that was thick enough to nap the sautéed cutlets. We knew we wanted to deglaze the empty skillet used to cook the chicken with some liquid to loosen the flavorful browned bits on the pan bottom, then reduce the liquid and thicken it.

Most of the recipes we uncovered in our research called for 1 or 2 tablespoons of lemon juice. All of our tasters agreed that these sauces weren't lemony enough. We found that ¼ cup delivered a nice lemon punch. Recipes that

instructed the cook to deglaze the hot pan with lemon juice and then simmer the sauce for several minutes tasted flat. Adding the lemon juice toward the end of the cooking time helped to keep it fresh-tasting.

Our caper testing led us to a similar conclusion. You need to use a lot of capers—2 tablespoons is just right—and they should be added when the sauce is nearly done so they retain their structural integrity. (For more information on capers, see the Tasting Lab on page 105.)

We next focused on the liquid for deglazing the pan. Chicken broth and white wine were the most obvious can-didates. The wine seemed like a good idea, but it con-tributed more acid to the sauce, which it did not need.

Broth proved a more neutral base for the lemon juice and capers.

Before deglazing the pan, we sautéed some aromatics in the pan drippings. We tested shallots, onions, scallions, and garlic separately. All were fine, although tasters preferred the shallots and garlic (one or the other). Just make sure to watch the pan carefully so that the aromatics don't burn. Add the broth to the pan as soon as the garlic or shallots start to color.

At this point, our sauce was quite good, but we wondered if there was another way to add lemon flavor. In our research, we uncovered several recipes that called for lemon slices. We halved a lemon, then cut it into very thin half-circles. We tried adding the lemon slices with the lemon juice, but the slices were too crunchy and numerous. For the next test, we used just half a lemon and added the slices with the broth. They simmered for five minutes and softened considerably. The longer simmering time also allowed oils from the peel to flavor the sauce. We tried replacing the sliced lemons with grated zest but found the sliced lemons more appealing and less work.

The last remaining issue for testing was thickening the sauce. Some recipes called for a roux (stirring flour into fat before adding the liquid), while others added either softened butter or softened butter mixed with flour once the sauce was cooked. A roux made the sauce too thick. Thickening the sauce at the end seemed more practical. The butter-flour paste gave the sauce a floury taste that dulled the flavors of lemon and capers. Plain butter proved best. Parsley, added with the butter, gave the sauce some color.

WHAT WE LEARNED: **Flour the chicken cutlets (they will brown better), but don't bother breading them (the sauce will just make the coating soggy). For fresh lemon flavor, use both juice and sliced lemons in the sauce. To keep the acidity under control, use chicken broth but not white wine. Finally, adding flour to the sauce to thicken it makes it too heavy; but butter gives the sauce some body without overthickening and is the right choice.**

CHICKEN PICCATA serves 4

Because this sauce is so light, we find that each person should be served 1 1/2 small cutlets. Serve the cutlets and sauce on a single platter and let each person help himself. For tips on juicing lemons, see page 283.

　2　large lemons
　6　boneless, skinless chicken breasts (5 to 6 ounces each), tenderloins removed and reserved for another use, fat trimmed (see illustration on page 97)
　　　Salt and ground black pepper
　1/2　cup unbleached all-purpose flour
　4　tablespoons vegetable oil
　1　small shallot, minced (about 2 tablespoons), or 1 medium clove garlic, minced or pressed through garlic press (about 1 teaspoon)
　1　cup canned low-sodium chicken broth
　2　tablespoons drained small capers
　3　tablespoons cold unsalted butter
　2　tablespoons minced fresh parsley leaves

1. Adjust oven rack to lower-middle position, set large heat-proof plate on rack, and heat oven to 200 degrees.

2. Halve one lemon pole to pole. Trim ends from one half and cut it crosswise into slices 1/8 to 1/4 inch thick; set aside. Juice remaining half and whole lemon to obtain 1/4 cup juice; reserve.

3. Use meat pounder, rubber mallet, or rolling pin to pound chicken breasts to even 1/2-inch thickness. Sprinkle both sides of cutlets generously with salt and pepper. Measure flour into shallow baking dish or pie plate. Working with one cutlet at a time, coat with flour and shake to remove excess.

4. Heat 2 tablespoons oil in heavy-bottomed 12-inch skillet over medium-high heat until shimmering. Lay three chicken cutlets in skillet. Sauté cutlets until lightly browned on first side, 2 to 2½ minutes. Turn cutlets and cook until second side is lightly browned, 2 to 2½ minutes longer. Remove pan from heat and transfer cutlets to plate in oven. Add remaining 2 tablespoons oil to now-empty skillet and heat until shimmering. Add remaining chicken cutlets and repeat.

5. Add shallot or garlic to now-empty skillet and return skillet to medium heat. Sauté until fragrant, about 30 seconds for shallot or 10 seconds for garlic. Add stock and lemon slices, increase heat to high, and scrape pan bottom with wooden spoon or spatula to loosen browned bits. Simmer until liquid reduces to about ⅓ cup, about 4 minutes. Add lemon juice and capers and simmer until sauce reduces again to ⅓ cup, about 1 minute. Remove pan from heat and swirl in butter until butter melts and thickens sauce. Stir in parsley and season with salt and pepper to taste. Spoon sauce over chicken and serve immediately.

VARIATIONS

PEPPERY CHICKEN PICCATA

Follow recipe for Chicken Piccata, adding ½ teaspoon coarsely ground black peppercorns along with lemon juice and capers.

CHICKEN PICCATA WITH BLACK OLIVES

Follow recipe for Chicken Piccata, adding ¼ cup pitted and chopped black olives along with lemon juice and capers.

TASTING LAB: Capers

MANY PEOPLE ASSOCIATE CAPERS WITH ANCHOVIES AND assume that they come from the sea. Others assume that they must be related to peas or beans because of their shape. Capers are actually pickles made from the unopened flower buds of the caper shrub, which grows in the Mediterranean region. These briny morsels are used in countless Italian, Spanish, and Greek recipes.

Capers can be preserved in two ways. More often, the flower buds are soaked in saltwater, then packed in brine or a mixture of brine and vinegar. This is how capers are sold in most supermarkets. The other option is to cure them with salt. This kind of caper costs more and is available only in specialty markets.

In addition to differences in preservation technique, capers vary in size. The smallest capers—no larger than small peas—are called nonpareils. There are several more grades, the largest being the size of small olives and called gruesas. If you drink martinis, you may also have seen caperberries. These oval berries form if the flower buds are allowed to open and set fruit. Caperberries are pickled in brine, just like capers.

To make sense of these variables, we purchased six brands of capers and held a small tasting. We tasted small and large capers packed in brine and vinegar as well as one brand of salted capers. For cooking, tasters agreed that small capers are best because they can be used as is; larger capers are too potent to eat whole and should be chopped. Besides adding an extra step, chopped capers disintegrate when added to sauces.

The taste differences from brand to brand were subtle, although most tasters felt that the brand packed in wine vinegar was the least harsh and therefore the most flavorful. (Labels on the other bottles just said "vinegar.")

Capers packed in salt were unbearably salty straight from the bottle. Rinsing didn't do much to lessen their sting. Soaking in cool water for at least 20 minutes (preferably an hour) washed out enough of the salt to reveal the flavor of the capers. Without the salt (and because there's no vinegar), we picked up hints of herbs (especially oregano) and mustard that we never tasted in the brined capers. These salted capers were delicious, but once we used them in piccata, their subtle traits faded behind the flavors of the other ingredients.

Many sources suggest rinsing brined capers, too. We think you can skip this step. Drain the capers well and taste one. If they seem very salty or vinegary, you can rinse them. In most cases, this step won't be necessary.

PAN-ROASTED CHICKEN

WHAT WE WANTED: Superbly crisp skin on perfectly roasted chicken—all with just 20 minutes of cooking time.

To make a good basic roast chicken, some planning is required, and even then it can be a challenge to cook. For a moist, well-seasoned bird, you brine it; for the crispiest skin, you air-dry it; to coordinate the doneness of the thigh and breast, you flip the bird as it roasts. An hour or so later, the roast chicken emerges from the oven along with some drippings that, if not burnt, can be turned into a gravy or sauce before you dismantle the bird for serving.

In an effort to make roast chicken easier, we decided to investigate a technique found in several recent restaurant cookbooks: pan-roasting. This technique is used to cook cuts of meat, poultry, and fish that for reasons of size or thickness cannot be cooked exclusively on the stovetop without scorching the exterior. For pan-roasted chicken, the chicken is cut up (a slight variation, or cheat, if you must, on the roast chicken concept), browned on both sides on the stovetop, and then slid, skillet and all, into a hot oven to complete cooking. Pan-roasting means no iconic roast chicken to bring to the table, but we were hoping that it would deliver superior skin, shorter preparation time, and a rich, savory pan sauce to boot. The question was whether this technique was as simple and reliable as promised.

We began by cutting a 3½- to 4-pounder into eight pieces, two each of drumsticks and thighs and four breast pieces. This arrangement meant that each serving could consist of a portion of both white and dark meat. The wings we discarded because they are the least favorite sections to eat and the 12-inch skillet was already full without them.

Brining (soaking in a solution of salt and sometimes sugar) has become customary in our test kitchen. Tasting pan-roasted chickens side-by-side, we preferred brined birds for their moistness (which can act as a cushion against the effects of overcooking, if it happens) and for the agreeable

saltiness that permeated the meat. However, we were forced to modify our all-purpose brine recipe, ousting the sugar because it led to uneven browning and burnt drippings. Because we were using a cut-up chicken, brining was expedited—just 30 minutes did the trick. (You can eliminate this step if you purchase a Kosher chicken. They are salted during processing, which has the same net effect as brining.) Air-drying, which we have found necessary to produce ultracrisp skin on roasted poultry, was not necessary. The hot skillet was crisping the skin quite well without adding hours to this weeknight recipe.

The next step was browning. A hot ovenproof skillet was key for achieving deep browning. Medium-high heat was optimal for even, controlled browning. High heat was a tad furious and sometimes resulted in burnt pan drippings (called fond). The chicken could be browned in a skillet without any oil (it had sufficient fat that rendered as it cooked and prevented sticking), but the browning was spotty and not ideal. However, even a mere tablespoon of oil was too much; when the excess fat was poured off before sauce making, the drippings woefully went with it. A teaspoon of oil, the barest coating on the skillet's surface, did the job well.

We browned the chicken parts on both sides before sliding them into the oven to roast. The burning question now was: When the chicken pieces go in the oven, should they be skin-side up or skin-side down? Compared side-by-side, skin-side up chicken was brown but mottled and crisped in some spots, soft in others. Skin-side down chicken was superior. The contact between the chicken skin and the hot metal of the pan clearly fostered a crackling crisp, darker, russet-toned skin. Both cast-iron and heavy-duty heat-conductive skillets performed well.

Suggested oven temperatures ranged from 375 all the way to 500 degrees. Four hundred fifty degrees was the winner; 500 sometimes singed the drippings, and lower temperatures simply took longer to cook the chicken through. The lowest rack setting was best as it seemed better suited to maintaining even heat.

Pan-roasted chicken recipes recommend removing the breast pieces before the leg pieces because the breast is done when it reaches 160 degrees and the leg 175 degrees (the identical problem that plagues whole roasted poultry). However, the digital thermometer told us that the breast pieces—despite being cut into quarters—and the leg pieces were finishing at about the same time. It appeared that the thickness of the breast pieces made them cook more slowly than the flat, thin thigh pieces and slim drumsticks.

Once the chicken was removed from the skillet, the fond (browned bits in the pan bottom) was crusty and plentiful, so we needed only a handful of ingredients to turn it into a sauce, keeping the flavors honest and simple. Using a potholder and utmost caution because the skillet handle was burning hot, we discarded most of the fat, sautéed minced shallots, and, in a step called deglazing, poured in chicken broth and white wine (vermouth, for more interesting flavor), scraping the skillet to loosen the fond. A couple sprigs of thyme added a herbaceous note. The liquid simmered to about half its original volume as the chicken reposed. With the flavors of the sauce concentrated and its consistency slightly thickened, we added juices that the resting chicken released and whisked in knobs of butter along with seasonings. A quick return to the skillet brought the chicken back up to serving temperature (skin-side up, of course, to keep the skin crisp).

Judging from the enthusiasm with which a plateful of pan-roasted chicken (and sauce) met, it was clear that this roast chicken was receiving high marks. Crisp-skinned roast chicken with an impressive sauce is possible on a weeknight.

WHAT WE LEARNED: **Brown the chicken parts in the barest film of oil on top of the stove, then put the chicken (still in the pan) into the oven, skin-side down, and roast until cooked through, about 10 minutes. As the chicken rests on a plate, add chicken broth and vermouth to turn the pan drippings into a flavorful sauce.**

PAN-ROASTED CHICKEN WITH SHALLOT AND VERMOUTH SAUCE serves 4

Brining the chicken is optional but highly recommended. If you opt not to brine, use a kosher chicken if one is available (kosher chickens are salted during processing and have the moistness and flavor of brined chickens). This recipe requires a 12-inch ovenproof skillet. The skillet handle will be blisteringly hot after being in the oven, so be sure to use a potholder or oven mitt to remove the skillet from the oven and when handling the skillet as you make the sauce. Dry white wine can be substituted for the vermouth.

chicken

1½ cups kosher salt or ¾ cup table salt
1 chicken (3½ to 4 pounds), cut into 8 pieces (4 breast pieces, 2 thighs, and 2 drumsticks, wings discarded) and trimmed of excess fat
   Ground black pepper
1 teaspoon vegetable oil

shallot and vermouth sauce

1 large shallot, minced (about 4 tablespoons)
¾ cup canned low-sodium chicken broth
½ cup dry vermouth
2 sprigs fresh thyme
3 tablespoons cold unsalted butter, cut into 3 pieces
   Salt and ground black pepper

1. Dissolve salt in 2½ quarts cold tap water in large container or bowl; submerge chicken pieces in brine and refrigerate until fully seasoned, about 30 minutes. Rinse chicken pieces under running water and pat dry with paper towels. Season chicken with pepper.

2. Adjust oven rack to lowest position and heat oven to 450 degrees.

3. Heat oil in heavy-bottomed 12-inch ovenproof skillet

and let rest while making sauce. (If not making sauce, let chicken rest 5 minutes before serving.)

4. Still using potholder or oven mitt, pour off most of fat from skillet, add shallots, then set skillet over medium-high heat; cook, stirring frequently, until shallots are softened, about 1½ minutes. Add chicken broth, vermouth, and thyme; increase heat to high and simmer rapidly, scraping skillet bottom with wooden spoon to loosen browned bits. Simmer until slightly thickened and reduced to about ⅔ cup, about 6 minutes. Pour accumulated chicken juices into skillet, discard thyme, and whisk in butter one piece at a time. Season sauce to taste with salt and pepper. Return chicken pieces skin-side up to skillet; simmer to heat through, about 1 minute. Serve immediately.

VARIATIONS

PAN-ROASTED CHICKEN WITH SHERRY-ROSEMARY SAUCE

Follow recipe for Pan-Roasted Chicken with Shallot and Vermouth Sauce, substituting dry sherry for vermouth and 2 sprigs fresh rosemary for thyme.

PAN-ROASTED CHICKEN WITH COGNAC-MUSTARD SAUCE

Follow recipe for Pan-Roasted Chicken with Shallot and Vermouth Sauce, substituting ¼ cup each white wine and Cognac or brandy for vermouth and 1 tablespoon Dijon mustard for an equal amount of butter.

SCIENCE DESK: Is the Pan Hot Yet?

MOST HOME COOKS DO NOT PROPERLY PREHEAT THEIR skillets, which results in a lack of both crust and flavor development. This may be due in part to the advice of high-quality cookware manufacturers, who often suggest preheating a pan with a film of oil over low heat for only one to two minutes. Overheating, they warn, can cause

over medium-high heat until beginning to smoke, about 3 minutes; swirl skillet to coat evenly with oil. Brown chicken pieces skin-side down until deep golden, about 5 minutes; turn chicken pieces, and brown until golden on second side, about 4 minutes longer. Turn chicken skin-side down and place skillet in oven. Roast until juices run clear when chicken is cut with paring knife, or thickest part of breast registers about 160 degrees on instant-read thermometer and thickest part of thighs and drumsticks registers about 175 degrees, about 10 minutes longer. Using potholder or oven mitt to protect hands from hot skillet handle, remove skillet from oven. Transfer chicken skin-side up to platter, discoloration. We followed their recommendations and were appalled at the sorry state of the food: pale, crustless, and with feeble browning. In our opinion, richly browned foods are worth risking discoloration, which, by the way, is easily removed with a little elbow grease.

How do you know when your skillet is properly pre-heated? We began with the common cookbook advice of sprinkling water in the preheated pan. If the droplets immediately bead up and dance on the skillet's surface, the pan is hot enough. Not exactly. Beading and dancing occur even when the skillet is too cool. We held outstretched palms a few inches above the surface of the skillet, but this proved to be a very inaccurate measure. We put bread crumbs, bread slices, sugar, popcorn kernels, rice, salt, ice cubes, and measured amounts of water into cold skillets, turned on the heat, and waited for some sort of sign. Bread crumbs and slices charred and smoked much too soon. Sugar melted, began to caramelize, and made a mess. Popcorn and rice browned unevenly and erratically after a few minutes, before the skillet was hot enough. Salt was lame. It showed no visible changes, even after the skillet was hotter than we cared for. Heated until every trace of water evaporated, ice cubes and measured amounts of water showed some promise, but given that boiling points vary with elevation, we thought the method a bit unreliable.

It was oil—smoking oil, to be exact—that held the answer. Measured into a cold skillet and heated for a few minutes, oil gives off wisps of smoke that serve as a visual alarm that the skillet is hot and ready. We tested our theory with beef steaks, chicken (skin-on), fish fillets, and steaks. In each case, oil that had just begun to smoke was a good indicator that the skillet was hot enough to produce well-crusted, good-tasting, and good-looking food without overcooking.

That said, not every kind of oil is suitable for high-heat browning and searing. Unrefined oils, such as extra-virgin olive oil, should not be used because their smoke points are low. Refined oils like vegetable, canola, corn, and peanut (be careful of the unrefined peanut oil carried in some grocery stores) work well because their smoke points are high (above

400 degrees). A word to the wise: Using just-smoking oil as a heat indicator is good only for browning and searing in very little oil, no more than a couple tablespoons. Smoking oil is simply too hot for pan-frying and deep-frying.

A few final words on browning and searing in a white-hot skillet. To minimize splattering and maximize browning, wick away excess moisture on the surface of the food with paper towels. For more serious splatter containment, use a splatter screen. And be prepared to turn on your exhaust fan or crack open a window. The light smoke that will waft from the skillet will dissipate more quickly with some ventilation.

Our favorite graters are modeled after a wood rasp, and they quickly turn a hunk of Parmesan into a fluffy mountain of cheese.

PASTA classics

CHAPTER 8

Even cooks who don't know much about Italian cooking have probably heard of puttanesca and Bolognese. These two classic Italian pasta sauces appear in countless menus and nearly every Italian cookbook. Many gourmet markets sell their own "homemade" renditions.

But as with most ethnic dishes that obtain a certain level of popularity, these Italian sauces have been bastardized. Puttanesca should be a lively, fresh-tasting tomato sauce with garlic, anchovies, capers, and hot red pepper flakes. All too often the sauce is thick and gloppy, and the ingredients have dissolved into a stew-like mess.

Bolognese, the classic meat sauce from the city of Bologna in central Italy, is subjected to even worse treatment. Real Bolognese is all about the meat, with tomatoes, dairy, and wine adding supporting flavor but definitely kept in the background. Many American versions of this sauce are nearly all tomato with tiny flecks of meat.

The test kitchen has restored these classics to their full glory. Neither recipe is complicated, but the difference between the real thing and the offering at your local Italian restaurant might surprise you.

PASTA WITH PUTTANESCA SAUCE

WHAT WE WANTED: A balanced, lively tomato sauce in which each ingredient—the garlic, anchovies, olives, and capers—remains distinct.

Said to have been created by Neapolitan ladies of the night, puttanesca is a pasta sauce with attitude. Most home cooks buy this lusty sauce by the jar or know it as restaurant fare: a slow-cooked tomato sauce with garlic, hot red pepper flakes, anchovies, capers, and black olives tossed with spaghetti. But those of us who have once sampled the real thing are often disappointed with these efforts. Chock-full of high-impact ingredients, puttanesca is often overpowered by one flavor; it is too fishy, too garlicky, too briny, or just plain salty and acidic. It can also be unduly heavy and stew-like or dull and monochromatic. We were searching for a simple, satisfying sauce with aggressive but well-balanced flavors.

We started our testing by tossing all of the ingredients—minced garlic, minced olives, whole capers, minced anchovies, and hot red pepper flakes—into a base of canned tomatoes and simmering the lot for 25 minutes. The result was a dull sauce with undeveloped flavors. Our first revision began with sautéing the garlic in olive oil to deepen the garlic flavor. We soon found out that the garlic should not be allowed to brown; when it did, the sauce quickly became bitter. To rectify the problem, we mixed a bit of water with the garlic before it went into the pan. The water slowed the cooking, making the garlic less likely to brown and burn.

Deciding how to prepare and cook the olives was the next task. After several tests, we decided to toss coarsely chopped olives into the sauce at the very last minute, allowing the residual heat of the tomatoes to warm them. This preserved their flavor, their texture, and their independence. As for which olives worked best, we started with Neapolitan gaeta olives—small, black, earthy, and herbaceous. For good measure, we also tested alfonso, kalamata, and canned black

olives in place of the gaetas. Tasters unanimously rejected the "insipid," "springy" canned olives but liked both the alfonso and kalamata olives for their "soft," "melting" qualities.

Capers were the least of our worries. Of all the ingredients, they were the most resilient, well able to retain their shape, texture, and flavor. Rinsing them thoroughly and adding them at the end of cooking along with the olives proved best.

Up to this point, the anchovies in the sauce, added along with the tomatoes to simmer, tasted flat and salty and gave the sauce a funky, fishy taste. We tried mashing whole fillets into the oil with a fork and found the process tedious and ineffective; stray chunks were left behind and inevitably ended up offending anchovy-sensitive tasters. What worked best was mincing the anchovies to a fine paste and then

adding them to the oil in the pan with the garlic. In two or three minutes, the anchovies melted into the oil on their own (no fork necessary), and their characteristically full, rich flavor blossomed.

Blooming an ingredient in oil is a technique often used to develop flavor. Because it worked so well with the garlic and anchovies, we decided to try it with the hot red pepper flakes instead of simmering them with the tomatoes, as we had in the original test. As they cooked with the garlic and anchovies, their flavor permeated the oil.

As for the tomatoes, we tested crushed tomatoes, canned whole tomatoes (chopped by hand), canned diced tomatoes, and fresh. The canned diced tomatoes were the winner. They had a sweet flavor and clung nicely to the pasta. But we still weren't sure whether we should use the diced tomatoes along with their juices or not. Testing the two options head to head made the choice easy. When cooked with tomatoes and their juices, the sauce took 25 minutes to cook down to the right consistency; when cooked with the diced tomatoes alone, it reached the optimum consistency in a mere eight minutes. Tasters were also unanimously in favor of the lightly cooked sauce, finding its flavor fresh and "less stewed" as well as "sweet." They also liked the "meaty texture" and firm bite of the tomatoes in this version of the sauce.

One last discovery improved the sauce still further. In the test kitchen, we are in the habit of reserving a little pasta cooking water to toss with the finished pasta to keep the sauce from drying out. On a whim, we decided to substitute some of the drained tomato juice for the water, which gave the sauce a brighter, livelier flavor.

WHAT WE LEARNED: For a sauce with the best tomato flavor and a slightly clingy consistency, use canned diced tomatoes, and hold the cooking time to a minimum to keep the flavor fresh. Cook the garlic, anchovies, and hot red pepper flakes before adding the tomatoes so their flavors bloom. Add the olives and capers when the sauce is done to keep them intact.

SPAGHETTI PUTTANESCA serves 4

The pasta and sauce cook in just about the same amount of time. If you like the fruitiness of extra-virgin olive oil, toss I tablespoon into the sauced pasta before serving.

3	medium cloves garlic, minced to paste or pressed through garlic press (about 1 tablespoon)
	Salt
1	pound spaghetti
2	tablespoons olive oil
1	teaspoon hot red pepper flakes
4	teaspoons minced anchovies (about 8 fillets)
1	(28-ounce) can diced tomatoes, drained, ½ cup juice reserved
3	tablespoons capers, rinsed
½	cup black olives (such as gaeta, alfonso, or kalamata), pitted and chopped coarse
¼	cup minced fresh parsley leaves

1. Bring 4 quarts water to rolling boil in large pot. Meanwhile, mix garlic with 1 tablespoon water in small bowl; set aside. When water is boiling, add 1 tablespoon salt and pasta; stir to separate noodles. Immediately heat oil,

GETTING IT RIGHT: Chopping Olives

Minced olives (left) produced a muddy sauce and purple spaghetti. Coarsely chopped olives (right) won't color the pasta and taste better.

garlic mixture, hot red pepper flakes, and anchovies in large sauté pan or skillet over medium heat. Cook, stirring frequently, until garlic is fragrant but not browned, 2 to 3 minutes. Stir in tomatoes and simmer until slightly thickened, about 8 minutes.

2. Cook pasta until al dente. Drain, then return pasta to pot. Add ¼ cup reserved tomato juice and toss to combine.

3. Stir capers, olives, and parsley into sauce. Pour sauce over pasta and toss to combine, adding more tomato juice to moisten if necessary. Adjust seasonings with salt to taste and serve immediately.

TASTING LAB: Anchovies

TO SOME, ANCHOVIES ARE THOSE "STINKY LITTLE FISH" that adorn (or despoil) the top of a pizza. But to us, those little fish are a pantry mainstay, contributing flavor to many sauces, salads, and sautés. But are all anchovies the same? A glance at the supermarket aisle revealed there were plenty of choices, and we set out to find the best one.

All preserved anchovies—small silver-skinned fish usually caught in warm Mediterranean waters—have been cured in salt, but they come to the market in two forms, packed in olive oil (we've all seen those flat, little tins), and packed in salt. Of the two kinds, the salt-packed variety are the least processed, having only their heads and some entrails removed, leaving the filleting and rinsing to the home cook. Oil-packed anchovies have been filleted at the factory and are ready-to-use. We purchased four brands of oil-packed anchovies along with one brand of salt-packed. Also included in the tasting was an anchovy paste sold in a tube.

We tasted the anchovies in our Caesar salad dressing and straight up and found ourselves liking best an expensive oil-packed brand from Spain. Tasters commented on the good flavor and firm texture of Ortiz oil-packed anchovies, which cost about $6 for a 3-ounce jar. The salt-packed anchovies were a very close second, but they can be hard to find. The remaining brands of oil-packed anchovies did not fare as well, and tasters hated the anchovy paste. Although food snobs may insist that salt-packed anchovies are the only way to go, our tasters found that the right oil-packed anchovies can be just as good.

BEST ANCHOVIES
Ortiz oil-packed anchovies from Spain won our tasting of six leading brands. Tasters liked the salty and pleasantly fishy flavor as well as the firm, "meaty" texture of this expensive brand. See www.cooksillustrated.com for up-to-date prices and mail-order sources.

TASTING LAB: Dried Pasta

IN THE NOT-SO-DISTANT PAST, AMERICAN PASTA HAD A poor reputation, and rightly so. It cooked up gummy and starchy, and experts usually touted the superiority of Italian brands. We wondered if this was still the case. To find out, we tasted eight leading brands of spaghetti—four American and four Italian. Each brand was cooked in salted water until we judged the pasta to be al dente, then drained and served unadorned so we could really taste the pasta.

The results of the tasting—which was done in two rounds, one with our usual staff of test cooks and editors and another with a panel of Italian cookbook authors and chefs—were shocking. In both cases, American brands took two of the three top spots, while two Italian brands landed

Rating Dried Pastas

WE TASTED EIGHT LEADING BRANDS OF SPAGHETTI STRAIGHT FROM THE POT, UNSEASONED, UNSAUCED, AND AL DENTE. Tasters evaluated the pastas on both flavor and texture. All brands are available in supermarkets or gourmet stores.

HIGHLY RECOMMENDED

1. Ronzoni Spaghetti **$.99 for 16 ounces**

Won tasters over with its firm "rockin'" texture and its "nutty," "buttery," "classic" flavor. "Tastes most like pure pasta," said one taster.

RECOMMENDED

2. DeCecco Spaghetti **$1.79 for 16 ounces**

"Chewy" came to mind for more than a couple of tasters when sampling this pasta. Some tasters detected a distinctive wheat flavor, though others found it a bit "bland."

RECOMMENDED

3. Mueller's Spaghetti **$.89 for 16 ounces**

Several tasters remarked on this pasta's "clean" and "wheaty" flavor. Most agreed that its texture was firm, but some found it "a little rubbery."

RECOMMENDED

4. Barilla Spaghetti **$.99 for 16 ounces**

Several tasters complained about the lack of chew in this pasta, calling it "soft" and "yielding." A few complained about bland flavor, but others noted a "wheaty" and "toasted" flavor.

NOT RECOMMENDED

5. Rienzi Spaghetti **$.75 for 16 ounces**

While a few tasters picked up on a favorable egg flavor, most characterized this pasta as "bland." "Gummy" was another word that kept popping up.

NOT RECOMMENDED

6. 365 Brand Whole Foods Market Spaghetti **$.79 for 16 ounces**

Tasters faulted this pasta for having too much flavor, with complaints such as "strong egg flavor," "smoky flavor," and "a little bitter—like burnt toast." Some described its texture as thick and firm, but others found it grainy and rubbery.

NOT RECOMMENDED

7. Martelli Spaghetti **$3.00 for 17.5 ounces**

This pasta was repeatedly called "bland," and a few tasters noted an artificial flavor. The texture didn't win many fans either, with tasters labeling it "mealy," "gritty," "starchy," and "mushy."

NOT RECOMMENDED

8. Delverde Spaghetti **$.79 for 16 ounces**

Several tasters described this pasta as having a "raw" and "artificial" flavor. Comments on texture ranged from "not cooked" to "spongy" and "gummy."

at the bottom. It seems that American companies have mastered the art of making pasta.

American-made Ronzoni was the top finisher, with tasters praising its "nutty, buttery" flavor and superb texture. Mueller's, another American brand, took third place.

DeCecco was the highest-scoring Italian brand, finishing second in the tasting. It cooked up "very al dente" (with a good bite) and was almost chewy. Other Italian brands did not fare quite so well. Martelli, an artisanal pasta that costs three times as much as the winner, finished in next-to-last place, with comments like "gritty" and "mushy" predominating on tasters' score sheets. Another Italian brand, Delverde, sank to the bottom of the ratings.

Our conclusion: Save your money and don't bother with most imported pasta—American brands are just fine. If you want to serve Italian pasta in your home, stick with DeCecco.

EQUIPMENT CORNER: Sauté Pans

WITH SOME KITCHEN EQUIPMENT, THE DIFFERENCE between pricey and inexpensive models just isn't that big a deal—either will get the job done. But sauté pans are another story, primarily because of the nature of sautéing. When you sauté, you cook food quickly, with minimal fat, in a very hot pan. As it cooks, the food develops a nice, dark, flavorful crust, which is the glory of sautéing.

But there is a thin line between crusty and burnt—and it's a line that you definitely don't want to cross. To sauté successfully, you need a pan that distributes heat evenly, without hot spots that can cause food to scorch or burn outright. Additional factors to consider include browning performance, ovenworthiness (can the pan be used in the oven?), heft (does it feel substantial without being too heavy?), and construction (does it feel solid, with the handles attached firmly?). A number of pans on the market claim to fit the bill, but, at well over $100, many of them are also quite expensive. We opened our wallet and chose eight popular models in the 3-quart size, then headed off to the test kitchen for a two-week sauté-a-thon.

The popularity of nonstick pans compelled us to consider several in our tests. By and large, the nonstick pans performed on a par with the other pans in our tests. Yet for all of their virtues, the nonsticks had, in our opinion at least, what amounted to a serious flaw: They resist the development of a fond, the sticky, brown, caramelized film and bits that form on the pan bottom as the food cooks. When released from the pan bottom with the addition of liquid, which is then boiled to dissolve those bits (in a process called deglazing), the fond provides the savory underpinnings of sauces, stews, and braises. Fond develops because the drippings from the food stick to the pan—no sticking, no fond. As a result, when we used nonstick pans to make the sauce for a braised chicken dish, the sauce looked light and tasted weak. We advise you to stick with a traditional cooking surface.

Differences in the pans' sautéing and browning performance were not as significant as we had imagined they would be. All of the pans in our price range were thick enough to allow good conduction with no significant hot spots that could cause food to burn. Beyond that, each metal has a thermoconductivity coefficient; this refers to the amount of heat it can transfer over a centimeter of length in one second. Honors for best conductivity go to copper, at 0.94, and pure aluminum, at 0.53. At the other end of the spectrum is cast iron, which has a thermoconductivity coefficient of 0.12. This is the reason our enamel-covered cast-iron Le Creuset pan was so slow to heat, especially when compared with the copper Mauviel.

To our surprise, though, we discovered that the superconductivity of copper was not for us, especially in light of its high price. In our view, pans that sauté reliably at a medium pace—meaning that they hedge the threat of burning by heating neither too hot nor too fast—are preferred. In our tests, the copper did its work a bit too fast. It cooled quickly when we turned the flame down, but we would just as soon avoid the need to adjust the heat in the first place.

While variations in the sautéing and browning performance of the pans turned out to be relatively undramatic,

Rating Sauté Pans

WE EVALUATED EIGHT SAUTÉ PANS, EACH SOLD INDIVIDUALLY, WITH A CAPACITY OF 3 QUARTS (OR AS CLOSE to it as we could find in that manufacturer's line), and rated them according to a battery of kitchen tests. The pans are listed in order of preference. See www.cooksillustrated.com for up-to-date prices and mail-order sources for top-rated products.

RECOMMENDED

1. All-Clad Stainless Steel Covered 3 Quart Sauté Pan, Model 5403

$165.00

A winner in design and performance—the best overall pan tested. Promoted beautiful crust when browning burgers, turkey cutlets, or chicken. Developed impressive fond; very spacious.

RECOMMENDED

2. All-Clad Stainless Steel Nonstick Covered 3 Quart Sauté Pan, Model 5403-NS

$174.00

Same subpar fond as on all nonstick pans, but otherwise as good as the top-rated All-Clad, and it cleaned up more easily.

RECOMMENDED WITH RESERVATIONS

3. Calphalon Commercial Hard-Anodized 3 Quart Sauté Pan

$137.00

Nice job at browning, but it sautéed and simmered a tad slow. Flat lid rested on food in chicken braise, thereby limiting capacity and compromising seal.

RECOMMENDED WITH RESERVATIONS

4. KitchenAid Stainless Steel 3 Quart Covered Sauté Pan

$180.00

Watch the heat if using this pan—it browned and sautéed rather quickly. We adjusted the heat to avoid burning pan drippings. Slightly smaller diameter means a snug fit for many foods.

RECOMMENDED WITH RESERVATIONS

5. Look Classic Cookware 3.2 Quart Covered Sauté Pan, Model #128

$87.00

Extra spacious (easily holds cut-up chicken for braising) and cleans up nicely. Sauté speed was not perfectly consistent, so keep an eye on the heat.

RECOMMENDED WITH RESERVATIONS

6. Analon Anodized Nonstick 3 Quart Sauté Pan

$80.00

Sauté speed was a tad slow; better at browning turkey cutlets than burgers. Phenolic (plastic) handle stayed cool.

NOT RECOMMENDED

7. Mauviel Cuprinox 3 Quart Covered Sauté Pan

$235.00

Browned well but a little faster than we thought was ideal. Sauté speed was a bit fast, too. This pan is also heavy, and its brass handle gets blazing hot.

NOT RECOMMENDED

8. Le Creuset 10-Inch Deep Covered Sauté Pan

$119.00

Sautés and browns on the slow side, but heat really builds so that burnt drippings become a real possibility. Extremely heavy (more than 10 pounds) and hard to lift.

certain aspects of pan design made a much bigger difference to us than we had anticipated. For example, each pan was rated at or very close to 3 quarts, but the pan diameters varied by more than an inch, from about 10 inches for the KitchenAid, Analon, and Mauviel to about 11 inches for the Look and All-Clad pans. A little larger diameter was a big advantage for the cook. For instance, the 11-inch All-Clad accommodated the chicken in our braised chicken test more comfortably than the smaller KitchenAid, Analon, and Mauviel, which were snug. This meant it was easier to slide tongs or a spatula into the All-Clad to move the chicken pieces without accidentally gouging or damaging them or splashing the sauce. It also meant more favorable conditions for sautéing turkey cutlets, which are wide and flat and need space around them to brown properly.

Handles were another important difference. If we're removing a dish from the oven, we always remember to don oven mitts, but we are not always so careful before grabbing the handle of a hot pan on the stove. If that handle is hot, we're in for a rude surprise. Hot handles turned out to be a problem with only two of the pans, the Le Creuset and the Mauviel copper. The stainless-steel handles of the All-Clad and KitchenAid pans and the cast-steel handle of the

Calphalon stayed cool (though the KitchenAid tended to heat near the base), as did the phenolic (heat-resistant plastic) handles of the Look and Analon pans. Incidentally, the handles on all of the pans were ovenworthy, though up to only 350 degrees for the Analon and 500 degrees for the Look because of the phenolic material. All of the pans except for the Look and Mauviel have a helper handle, usually consisting of a small loop opposite the long handle so that the cook can use two hands to lift the pan when desired. We find the helper handle especially useful when we're hoisting full pans in and out of the oven.

What, at the conclusion of testing, do we recommend? Though none of these pans come cheap, the notoriously expensive copper (and our pan was not even the most expensive copper on the market) was not worth the extra money for the kind of cooking we do. Likewise, we did not like the Le Creuset pan, which was too slow to heat up and heavy to carry. For our money, the All-Clad pan, with a traditional cooking surface, provided the best combination of great design, ample proportions, and reliable performance. The Calphalon, KitchenAid, Analon, and Look pans all performed well, too, and some cost a few dollars less, but each had a design flaw that caused it to fall behind the All-Clad.

SCIENCE DESK: What Makes Some Pasta So Sticky?

IN REPEATED TESTS, WE'VE FOUND THAT YOU MUST COOK pasta in abundant water (4 quarts for 1 pound of pasta) to keep the strands from sticking together. When cooked in less water, the strands stick together, but why?

As the pasta cooks, various starches dissolve into the water. If there's plenty of water in the pot, the starches don't cause a problem. If there's not much water in the pot, however, the starches find each other—and the pasta—and form a sticky, starchy tangle. Keeping the water at a strong boil—the bubbles in the water move the pasta around—also helps to keep the dissolved starches and pasta from sticking together.

PASTA WITH BOLOGNESE SAUCE

WHAT WE WANTED: A complex sauce for pasta, with a good balance of flavors. The meat should be first and foremost, but sweet, salty, and acidic flavors should be present in the background.

Scores of delicious meat-based sauces are made in Italy and elsewhere, but slow-simmering Bolognese (it comes from the city of Bologna, hence the name) is perhaps the best. Unlike meat sauces in which tomatoes dominate (think jars of spaghetti sauce with flecks of meat in a sea of tomato puree), Bolognese sauce is about the meat, with the tomatoes in a supporting role. Bolognese also differs from many tomato-based meat sauces in that it contains dairy—butter, milk, and/or cream. The dairy gives the meat an especially sweet, appealing flavor.

Bolognese sauce is not hard to prepare (the hands-on work is less than 30 minutes), but it does require hours of slow simmering. The result must be worth the time. All Bolognese recipes can be broken down into three steps. First, vegetables are sautéed in fat. Ground meat is then browned in the pan. The final step is the addition of liquids and slow simmering over very low heat.

After an initial round of testing in which we made five styles of Bolognese, we had a recipe we liked pretty well. We preferred using only onions, carrots, and celery as the vegetables, and we liked them sautéed in butter rather than oil. We also discovered that a combination of ground beef, veal, and pork made this sauce especially complex and rich-tasting. The veal adds finesse and delicacy to the sauce, while the pork makes it sweet. Settling on the liquid element of the recipe proved more difficult.

The secret to a great Bolognese sauce is the sequential reduction of various liquids over the sautéed meat and vegetables. The idea is to build flavor and tenderize the meat, which toughens during the browning phase. Many recipes insist on a particular order for adding these liquids. The most common liquid choices we uncovered in our research were milk, cream, stock, wine (both red and white), and tomatoes (fresh, canned whole, crushed, or paste). We ended up testing numerous combinations to find the perfect balance.

Liquids are treated in two ways. In the earlier part of the cooking process, liquids are added to the pan and simmered briskly until fully evaporated, the point being to impart flavor rather than to cook the meat and vegetables. Wine is always treated this way; if the wine is not evaporated, the sauce will be too alcoholic. Milk and cream are often but not always treated this way. Later, either stock and/or tomatoes are added in greater quantity and allowed to cook off very slowly. These liquids add flavor, to be sure, but they also serve as the cooking medium for the sauce during the slow simmering phase.

We tested pouring wine over the browned meat first, followed by milk. We also tried them in the opposite order—milk, then wine. We found that the meat cooked in milk first was softer and sweeter. As the bits of meat cook, they develop a hard crust that makes it more difficult for them to absorb liquid. Adding the milk first, when the meat is just barely cooked, works better. The milk penetrates more easily, tenderizing the meat and making it especially sweet. We tried using cream instead of milk but felt that the sauce was too rich. Some recipes add a bit of cream at the end of cooking to finish the sauce, but we found even this addition overpowering. Milk provides just enough dairy flavor to complement the meat flavor. Wine, then, became the second liquid. While we liked both white and red, white wine was a bit more delicate and is our choice for the basic recipe.

Then we moved on to the final element in most recipes, the cooking liquid. We did not like any of the recipes we tested with stock. As for tomato paste, we felt that it had little to offer; with none of the bright acidity of canned whole tomatoes and no fresh tomato flavor, it produced a dull sauce.

We tried tomatoes three more ways—fresh, canned diced, and canned crushed. Fresh tomatoes did nothing for the sauce and were a lot of work, as we found it necessary to peel them. (If not peeled, the skins would separate during the long cooking process and mar the texture of the sauce.) Crushed tomatoes were fine, but they did not taste as good as the canned whole tomatoes that we chopped. Diced tomatoes have an additional benefit—the packing juice. Because Bolognese sauce simmers for quite a while, it's nice to have all that juice to keep the pot from scorching.

Our recipe was finally taking shape, with all the ingredients in place. But we still wanted to know if it was necessary to cook Bolognese sauce over low heat and, if so, how long the sauce must simmer. When we tried to hurry the process by cooking over medium heat to evaporate the tomato juice more quickly, the meat became too firm and the flavors failed to meld. Low simmering over the lowest possible heat—a few bubbles may rise to the surface of the sauce one at a time, but it should not be simmering all over—is the only method that allows enough time for flavor to develop and for the meat to become tender.

As for the timing, we found that the sauce was too soupy after two hours on low heat, and the meat was still pretty firm. At three hours, the meat was much softer, with a melt-in-the-mouth consistency. The sauce was dense and smooth at this point. We tried simmering the sauce for four hours but found no benefit. In fact, some batches cooked this long overreduced and scorched a bit.

WHAT WE LEARNED: **For the most tender texture, cook the meat just until it loses its pink color and don't let it brown. For the best flavor, keep the vegetables to a minimum, add the milk before the wine, and use diced canned tomatoes. Finally, there are no shortcuts to great Bolognese—the sauce must simmer at the lowest possible heat for about three hours.**

FETTUCCINE WITH BOLOGNESE SAUCE
serves 4

Don't drain the pasta of its cooking water too meticulously when using this sauce; a little water left clinging to the noodles will help distribute the very thick sauce evenly over the noodles, as will the addition of 2 tablespoons of butter along with the sauce. If doubling this recipe, increase the simmering times for the milk and the wine to 30 minutes each, and increase the simmering time once the tomatoes are added to 4 hours.

    5   tablespoons unsalted butter
    2   tablespoons minced onion
    2   tablespoons minced carrot
    2   tablespoons minced celery
    ¾   pound meatloaf mix or ¼ pound each ground
        beef chuck, ground veal, and ground pork
        Salt
    1   cup whole milk
    1   cup dry white wine
    1   (28-ounce) can diced tomatoes with their juice
    1   pound fresh or dried fettuccine
        Freshly grated Parmesan cheese

1. Heat 3 tablespoons butter in large, heavy-bottomed Dutch oven over medium heat. Add onion, carrot, and celery and sauté until softened but not browned, about 6 minutes. Add ground meat and ½ teaspoon salt; crumble meat into tiny pieces with edge of wooden spoon. Cook, continuing to crumble meat, just until it loses its raw color but has not yet browned, about 3 minutes.

2. Add milk and bring to a simmer; continue to simmer until milk evaporates and only clear fat remains, 10 to 15 minutes. Add wine and bring to a simmer; continue to simmer until wine evaporates, 10 to 15 minutes longer. Add tomatoes and their juice and bring to a simmer. Reduce heat to low so that sauce continues to simmer just barely, with occasional bubble or two at surface, until liquid has evaporated, about 3 hours (if lowest burner setting is too high to allow very low simmer, use flame tamer—see right). Adjust seasonings with salt to taste. Keep sauce warm. (The sauce can be refrigerated in an airtight container for several days or frozen for several months. Warm over low heat before serving.)

3. Bring 4 quarts water to rolling boil in large pot. Add 1 tablespoon salt and pasta. Cook until al dente. Drain pasta, leaving some water dripping from noodles. Toss with sauce and remaining 2 tablespoons butter. Distribute among individual bowls and serve immediately, passing Parmesan cheese separately.

VARIATIONS

FETTUCCINE WITH BEEF BOLOGNESE SAUCE

There is something very appealing about the simplicity of an all-beef sauce. While it may lack some of the finesse and sweetness of the master recipe, its pure beef flavor is uniquely satisfying.

Follow recipe for Fettuccine with Bolognese Sauce, substituting ¾ pound ground beef chuck for meatloaf mix.

FETTUCCINE WITH BEEF, PANCETTA, AND RED WINE BOLOGNESE SAUCE

All ground beef (rather than meatloaf mix) works best with the pancetta in this sauce. If you can't find pancetta, use prosciutto, but don't use American bacon, which is smoked and will overwhelm the beef. We found that red wine stands up to the more robust flavors in this sauce better than white wine.

Follow recipe for Fettuccine with Bolognese Sauce, adding 2 ounces minced pancetta to butter along with vegetables, substituting ¾ pound ground beef chuck for meatloaf mix, and substituting an equal amount of red wine for white wine.

TECHNIQUE: Improvised Flame Tamer

A flame tamer (or heat diffuser) is a metal disk that can be fitted over an electric or a gas burner to reduce the heat output. This device is especially useful when trying to keep a pot at the barest simmer. If you don't own a flame tamer (it costs less than $10 and is stocked at most kitchenware stores), you can improvise with tools you have on hand, as shown below. Another option (which might work on some gas stoves) is to stack two burner grates on top of each other.

A. A foil ring elevates the pot slightly above the flame or electric coil, allowing you to keep a pot of Bolognese sauce at the merest simmer. To make one, take a long sheet of heavy-duty aluminum foil and shape it into a 1-inch-thick ring that will fit on your burner. Make sure that the ring is of an even thickness so that a pot will rest flat on it.

B. A cast-iron skillet can absorb some of the heat from the burner and protect another pot from direct heat. Place the Dutch oven with the sauce inside a cast-iron skillet set on the burner.

PASTA quick and easy

Every cook needs quick pasta recipes in his or her repertoire. Pasta with garlic and oil is perhaps the most famous quick pasta dish. It starts with ingredients on hand—garlic, good olive oil, hot red pepper flakes—and turns them into something special, something uncommonly good. Of course, details make or break such a simple recipe. If the garlic is burned or the pasta sticks together, this dish is ruined. We've examined every aspect of this recipe in the test kitchen and finally perfected it.

Almost no one thinks of lasagna as quick or easy. Most recipes require a day's worth of labor. Although the results usually justify the effort, we wondered if there was another way. Starting with no-boil noodles (a convenience product that has become widely available in the past decade), we set out to make a great meat lasagna that could be in the oven in just 40 minutes. The surprise was that we succeeded and surpassed our expectations of just how good a "quick" lasagna could be.

Garlic ready for its starring role in
pasta with garlic and olive oil.

PASTA WITH GARLIC AND OIL

WHAT WE WANTED: A flawless version of this quick classic, with bright, deep garlic flavor and no trace of bitterness or harshness.

Pasta with garlic and oil, or *aglio e olio* in Italian, looks guileless. It reads: "tangle of spaghetti flecked with parsley." But its subtext shouts garlic in every register, in every pitch. Twirled hot on a fork, this is among the most satisfying (and simple) dishes on earth. It has the texture of innocence and a tyrant's bite.

At first, we wondered why anyone would need a recipe for this dish. You take spaghetti or capellini, perfume it straight from its bath with high-quality olive oil and as much fresh garlic as decency allows, add a dusting of hot red pepper flakes, a little fistful of parsley, and there it is, pasta aglio e olio. And yet, and yet. Who hasn't ordered it in a restaurant to find its fresh scent tormented by burnt garlic or its noodles gripped in a starchy skein dripping with oil? Clearly, there was much to learn.

Diving into Italian cookbooks, we found general agreement on ingredients: all those mentioned above, along with a splash of hot pasta cooking water to keep the components in motion. Beyond the basics were regional variations that included a selection of fresh herbs, savory accents such as capers and anchovies, and bread crumbs. We first pursued the perfect garlic flavor, working down the list of possibilities from whole crushed cloves to grated raw garlic and using a pound of pasta for each test. We didn't care for sautéed whole or slivered garlic, whether ultimately removed from the dish or left in. In fact, no one cared for browned garlic at all—it was acrid and one-dimensional. Raw minced or grated garlic alone was zingy and metallic. We needed a third way.

We knew of a technique associated with Mexican cookery in which a large amount of minced garlic is sautéed slowly until it turns golden and mellow, thus producing a

garlic flavor far more complex than does a simple sauté. We tried this with a full head of garlic (about ¼ cup minced) and were delighted to discover that the garlic, given low heat and constant stirring, became sticky and straw-colored, with a flavor that was butter-nutty and rich, adding a pronounced depth to the dish. But alone, this slow-sautéed garlic lacked brightness. We decided to combine the forces of cooked and raw by reserving a tablespoon of raw garlic, then stirring it into the fully cooked, candied garlic off the heat to release its perfume and spicy sharpness. The effect of this one-two garlic punch was outstanding, causing waves of flavor to resonate within the dish.

While conducting garlic experiments, it became obvious that other ingredient ratios—for example, the amount of oil—had to be established contiguously. Too much oil removed the silky mouthfeel we wanted for the pasta, but too little left the garlic mute. The amount of oil necessary varied with the diameter of the pasta as well—thicker strands, such as spaghetti, required more oil, even when the total weight of each batch of pasta was the same. In fact, the diameter of the pasta strands altered the behavior of the recipe to such a degree that we decided to work with just one type of pasta—spaghetti, which, unlike some thinner pastas, is available in every grocery store.

Olive oil contributes much of the freshness and verve to this dish; extra-virgin is a must. We settled on 6 tablespoons: 3 to sauté the garlic, 3 tossed into the pasta at the end for flavor.

Parmesan cheese is not conventional in this dish, but, heathens that we are, we liked the nutty depth of flavor it added. Resist, by all means, an urge to pour the contents of a little green cylinder on this dish—it will be forever ruined. A very modest sprinkle of coarsely grated Parmigiano-Reggiano, on the other hand, improves it. (Be sure to do your grating on the larger holes of a box grater; this will discourage the cheese from getting into a sticking contest with the pasta.)

We liked parsley for its freshness but didn't want it slipping around on the noodles like mower clippings; 3 tablespoons did the trick. Gentle seasoning improvements were effected with a touch of lemon juice and sea salt flakes—the bright citrus notes and wee crunch made a big difference.

Finally, sequence and timing matter greatly with this dish. Perhaps to a larger degree than other pastas, pasta aglio e olio suffers from being dumped into cold serving bowls or waiting around for diners to make their way to the table. The most familiar pasta tool, a set of tongs, cannot be recommended for tossing; bits of garlic get stuck in its craw, right where you don't want them. We recommend that you toss the hot strands with a heatproof spatula and use tongs only to transfer the pasta to bowls.

WHAT WE LEARNED: **Cook most of the garlic over low heat until sticky and straw-colored for a mellow flavor, but add some raw garlic at the end for a complementary bite. A splash of lemon juice and a sprinkle of Parmesan may not be traditional, but they add finesse to this simple recipe.**

PASTA WITH GARLIC AND OIL serves 4 to 6

For a twist on pasta with garlic and oil, try sprinkling toasted fresh bread crumbs over individual bowls, but prepare them before proceeding with the pasta recipe. We like the crunch of Maldon sea salt flakes (see the Tasting Lab on page 27) for this dish, but ordinary table salt is fine as well. Given the large amount of garlic in this recipe, you may want to mince it in a food processor. A garlic press or chef's knife are other options.

Salt (see note)
1 pound spaghetti
6 tablespoons extra-virgin olive oil
¼ cup minced garlic (about 30 small, 20 medium, 10 large, or 5 extra-large cloves) from 1 or 2 heads
¾ teaspoon hot red pepper flakes
3 tablespoons chopped fresh parsley leaves
2 teaspoons juice from 1 lemon
½ cup coarsely grated Parmesan cheese (optional)

TECHNIQUE:
Reserving Pasta Water to Thin a Sauce

In that last flurry of activity before saucing the pasta, it's easy to forget to save a bit of the pasta cooking water. To make sure you always have some pasta cooking water when you need it, set up the colander in the sink and place a measuring cup inside the colander. The cup will nudge your memory to scoop out some cooking water before draining the pasta.

1. Adjust oven rack to lower-middle position, set large heat-proof serving bowl on rack, and heat oven to 200 degrees. Bring 4 quarts water to rolling boil in large pot. Add 1 tablespoon salt and pasta to boiling water, stir to separate noodles, and cook until al dente; reserve ⅓ cup pasta cooking water and drain pasta.

2. While water is heating, combine 3 tablespoons oil, 3 tablespoons garlic, and ½ teaspoon salt in heavy-bottomed nonstick 10-inch skillet. Cook over low heat, stirring constantly, until garlic foams and is sticky and straw-colored, 10 to 12 minutes. Off heat, add remaining tablespoon raw garlic along with hot red pepper flakes, parsley, lemon juice, and 2 tablespoons pasta cooking water and stir well to keep garlic from clumping.

3. Transfer drained pasta to warm serving bowl; add remaining 3 tablespoons olive oil and remaining reserved pasta

TECHNIQUE:
Combating Odoriferous Ingredients

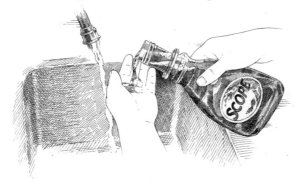

After working with pungent ingredients such as garlic, onions, or fish, many cooks use a little lemon juice to wash away any lingering odors from their hands. But sometimes the smell is stronger than the citrus. When that's the case, try washing your hands with a couple of tablespoons of mouthwash. Any inexpensive brand is fine.

cooking water and toss to coat. Add garlic mixture and ¾ teaspoon salt; toss well to combine. Serve immediately, sprinkling individual bowls with portion of Parmesan cheese, if desired.

EQUIPMENT CORNER:
Pasta Paraphernalia

NOWADAYS, COOKWARE STORES AND CATALOGS CONTAIN a mind-boggling array of pots, utensils, and gadgets for cooking pasta. They fall into two basic categories—tools intended to make it easier to drain pasta and tools intended to make it easier to handle cooked pasta. We tested a wide variety; here are our results.

Pot with Perforated Insert: We have to confess that we don't understand the growing popularity of these pasta pots. We tried both the 8-quart Multi Pot, which goes for about $45, and the All-Clad 7-quart Pasta Pentola, which sells for a steep $269. To get 4 quarts of water (the amount we recommended for cooking 1 pound of pasta) into the Multi-Pot insert, you must fill the pan with 6 quarts of water. If you do that, we found, the pot is prone to boiling over. The All-Clad insert is an inch smaller in diameter than the 8½-inch-diameter pot and sits 6 inches below the pot edge. It has a deceptive 2½-inch lip that sits above the pot edge, making it look as if it has a much greater capacity. In fact, as it turns out, the insert to this expensive 7-quart pot has a capacity of just 3 quarts; add any more and the water begins to boil over.
Mesh Inserts: The inexpensive mesh inserts sold in cookware stores proved much too small to be useful. They also tend to bob out of the water, which creates a suction at the bottom of the pan. When the suction releases, gurgles of boiling water are hurled from the pan.
Pasta Pronto: This pan takes a different approach to the issue of straining pasta. It has a perforated strainer lid with handles that swivel to hold the lid in place. It seems clever, but the handles do not actually lock the lid in place—your

grip does. Once you tilt the pan to strain, the grip can become awkward. We lost our grip once, and the sink was not so clean that we dared try to salvage the fallen noodles.

Strainer Plate: Just as it is to the Pasta Pronto pan, the risk of losing your noodles is inherent to the strainer plate, a crescent-shaped perforated stainless-steel plate meant to fit around the pot edge for straining. We found that it fits comfortably only with pans of certain sizes—and, again, sureness of grip was essential.

Pasta Rakes: The tines on the wooden versions of these rakes, designed to retrieve pasta, tend to fall out over time. The tines on the stainless-steel variety are welded in. But why spend $24 on a single-purpose utensil when a $5 pair of tongs works just fine?

Pasta Tongs: Again, why pay $14 for a pasta-particular utensil when an inexpensive pair of all-purpose tongs will toss and serve just as well? In addition, the handle on this utensil is too short for fetching noodles out of hot cooking water. (See page 13 for information on basic kitchen tongs.)

Pasta Forks: This is the only pasta-specific tool that we found useful. It effectively combs through long, sticky strands of noodles to separate them. The wood variety tends to be clunky and is prone to splitting with use, but both the plastic and stainless-steel versions work fine.

BEST PASTA TOOL
We tried a variety of devices for cooking, straining, and stirring pasta. Only one, a plastic pasta fork, is worth owning. Avoid wood forks, which we found tend to crack over time.

STREAMLINED LASAGNA

WHAT WE WANTED: Traditional lasagna takes the better part of a day to make. We wanted a really good meat lasagna that could be on the table in just 90 minutes.

Most families have homemade lasagna once, maybe twice a year, on holidays (especially if you are Italian) or birthdays. Lasagna is not enjoyed more frequently because it takes the better part of a day to boil the noodles, slow-cook the sauce, prepare and layer the ingredients, and then finally bake it off. Although this traditional method does produce a superior dish, we were interested in an Americanized version, one that could be made in two hours or less from start to finish. We would have to sacrifice some of the rich flavors of a traditional recipe, but we were hoping to produce a lasagna good enough for a family gathering. A bland, watery casserole just wouldn't do.

We knew from the start that to expedite the lasagna-making process we would have to use no-boil lasagna noodles (see the Tasting Lab on page 131). For those unfamiliar with or wary of them, relax. After a few initial tests, we discovered that the secret of no-boil noodles is to leave your tomato sauce a little on the watery side. The noodles can then absorb liquid without drying out the dish overall. With all this in mind, we got to work on the other components of the lasagna.

Italian cooks build the sauce from the meaty browned bits left in the pan from the meatballs and Italian sausages they cook and later layer into the lasagna. By combining top-quality tomato products with a four-hour simmer, they make a rich, thick, and complex-tasting sauce. We were after the same depth of flavor, but, as time was of the essence, meatballs and a slow simmer were out of the question. We began by concentrating on different kinds of ground meat.

Working with a base of sautéed aromatics (onions and garlic), an all-beef sauce turned out to be one-dimensional and dull. Adding ground pork was an improvement and certainly more interesting. Although the combination of beef and sweet Italian sausage (removed from its casing and browned with the beef) was even better, tasters were still left wanting. Finally, we turned to meatloaf mix, a combination of equal parts ground beef, pork, and veal sold in one package at most supermarkets. The flavor of the sauce this trio produced was robust and sweet. The texture wasn't right, though; it was still too loose and taco-like. We wanted something richer, creamier, and more cohesive, so our thoughts turned to Bolognese (see page 119), the classic three-hour meat sauce enriched with dairy. Borrowing the notion of combining meat and dairy, we reduced a quarter cup of cream with the meat before adding the tomatoes. The ground meat soaked up the sweet cream, and the final product was rich and decadent. Even better, at this point we had been at the stove for only 12 minutes.

Because no-boil noodles rely primarily on the liquid in the sauce to rehydrate and soften, we had to get the moisture content just right. If the sauce was too thick, the noodles would be dry and crunchy; too loose and they would turn flaccid, limp, and lifeless. We started building the sauce with two 28-ounce cans of pureed tomatoes, but tasters found this sauce too heavy for the lasagna, overwhelming the other flavors. Two 28-ounce cans of diced tomatoes yielded too thin a sauce. We settled on one 28-ounce can of each. The combination of pureed and diced tomatoes yielded a luxurious sauce, with soft but substantial chunks of tomatoes. We added the tomatoes to the meat mixture, warmed it through (no reduction necessary), and in just 15 minutes on the stove the meat sauce was rich, creamy, ultra-meaty, and ready to go.

Most Americans like their lasagna to be cheesy. It was a given that we would sprinkle each layer with mozzarella cheese—the classic lasagna cheese—and, after a test of whole versus part-skim, we found that whole milk mozzarella

was the best for the job. It had a more intense flavor than its part-skim counterpart and nicer melting qualities, which are crucial to this dish. We also tested shredded, bagged mozzarella, but because it has a very low moisture content, it melted oddly and was somewhat dry, not to mention unappetizing. Shredding a 1-pound block of whole milk mozzarella on a box grater or in the food processor is the ticket.

Ricotta was the next cheese up for scrutiny. As it turned out, it made little difference whether we used whole milk or part-skim ricotta. They were characteristically creamy and rich, and tasters gave them both a thumbs-up.

For added sharpness, we tested the ricotta mixture with Parmesan and Pecorino Romano cheeses. Tasters unanimously rejected the Pecorino for giving the lasagna a "sheepy" and "gamey" flavor. Grated Parmesan added a nice little kick to the mild, milky ricotta. An egg helped to thicken and bind this mixture, and some chopped basil added

flavor and freshness. Tucked neatly between the layers of lasagna, this ricotta mixture was just what we were after.

With all of the components of the lasagna decided, it was time to concentrate on the layering procedure. Smearing the entire bottom of a 13 by 9-inch glass dish with some of the sauce was the starting point. Next came the first layer of no-boil noodles, which we topped with ricotta, then mozzarella, and, finally, more meat sauce. We built two more layers using this same process. For the fourth and final layer, we covered the pasta with the remaining meat sauce and remaining mozzarella and then sprinkled the top with grated Parmesan.

In our tests, we found that covering the lasagna with foil from the outset of baking prevented the loss of moisture and helped soften the noodles properly. Removing the foil for the last 25 minutes of baking ensured that the top layer of cheese turned golden brown. An oven temperature of 375 degrees proved ideal. By the time the top was browned, the noodles had softened.

We found that lasagna made with no-boil noodles takes a little longer in the oven than conventional lasagna. The real time savings is in the preparation. Start to finish, the meat and tomato lasagna took about an hour and a half to make: 40 minutes prep time, 40 minutes in the oven, and 10 minutes to rest. Measuring the final product against an authentic Italian lasagna may not be entirely fair, but having the time to make it on a weeknight, or whenever the craving strikes, is satisfying beyond compare.

WHAT WE LEARNED: Meatloaf mix (a combination of ground beef, veal, and pork) adds complexity to a quick meat sauce, while cream adds richness. No-boil noodles work fine as long as you don't reduce the sauce too much (the noodles need some liquid to soften) and you cover the baking dish during its first 15 minutes in the oven (to build up some steam).

SIMPLE LASAGNA WITH HEARTY TOMATO-MEAT SAUCE serves 6 to 8

If you can't find meatloaf mixture for the sauce, or if you choose not to eat veal, substitute 1/2 pound ground beef and 1/2 pound sweet Italian sausage, casings removed, for the meatloaf mixture. The assembled, unbaked lasagna, if wrapped tightly in plastic wrap and then in foil, will keep in the freezer for up to 2 months. To bake, defrost it in the refrigerator for a day or two and bake as directed, extending the baking time by about 5 minutes.

tomato-meat sauce

- 1 tablespoon olive oil
- 1 medium onion, chopped fine (about 1 cup)
- 6 medium garlic cloves, minced or pressed through garlic press (about 2 tablespoons)
- 1 pound meatloaf mix or 1/3 pound each ground beef chuck, ground veal, and ground pork (see note)
- 1/2 teaspoon salt
- 1/2 teaspoon ground black pepper
- 1/4 cup heavy cream
- 1 (28-ounce) can pureed tomatoes
- 1 (28-ounce) can diced tomatoes, drained

ricotta, mozzarella, and pasta layers

- 15 ounces whole milk or part-skim ricotta cheese (1¾ cups)
- 2½ ounces grated Parmesan cheese (1¼ cups)
- 1/2 cup chopped fresh basil leaves
- 1 large egg, lightly beaten
- 1/2 teaspoon salt
- 1/2 teaspoon ground black pepper
- 12 no-boil lasagna noodles from one 8- or 9-ounce package (for brand preferences, see the Tasting Lab on page 131)
- 16 ounces whole-milk mozzarella cheese, shredded (4 cups)

1. Adjust oven rack to middle position and heat oven to 375 degrees.

2. Heat oil in large Dutch oven over medium heat until shimmering, about 2 minutes; add onions and cook, stirring occasionally, until softened but not browned, about 2 minutes. Add garlic and cook until fragrant, about 2 minutes. Increase heat to medium-high and add ground meats, salt, and pepper; cook, breaking meat into small pieces with wooden spoon, until meat loses its raw color but has not browned, about 4 minutes. Add cream and simmer, stirring occasionally, until liquid evaporates and only fat remains, about 4 minutes. Add pureed and drained diced tomatoes and bring to simmer; reduce heat to low and simmer slowly until flavors are blended, about 3 minutes; set sauce aside. (Sauce can be cooled, covered, and refrigerated for 2 days; reheat before assembling lasagna.)

3. Mix ricotta, 1 cup Parmesan, basil, egg, salt, and pepper in medium bowl with fork until creamy; set aside.

4. Smear entire bottom of 13 by 9-inch baking dish with 1/4 cup meat sauce (avoiding large chunks of meat). Place 3 noodles in baking dish to create first layer. Drop 3 tablespoons ricotta mixture down center of each noodle and level domed mounds by pressing with back side of measuring spoon. Sprinkle layer evenly with 1 cup shredded mozzarella cheese. Spoon 1½ cups meat sauce evenly over cheese. Repeat layering of noodles, ricotta, mozzarella, and sauce two more times. Place 3 remaining noodles on top of sauce, spread remaining sauce over noodles, sprinkle with remaining 1 cup mozzarella, then with remaining 1/4 cup Parmesan. Lightly spray a large sheet of foil with nonstick cooking spray and cover lasagna.

5. Bake 15 minutes, then remove foil. Return lasagna to oven and continue to bake until cheese is spotty brown and sauce is bubbling, about 25 minutes longer. Cool lasagna about 10 minutes; cut into pieces and serve.

TASTING LAB: No-Boil Lasagna Noodles

OVER THE PAST FEW YEARS, NO-BOIL (ALSO CALLED OVEN-ready) lasagna noodles have become a permanent fixture on supermarket shelves. Much like instant rice, no-boil noodles are precooked at the factory. The extruded noodles are run through a water bath and then dehydrated mechanically. During baking, the moisture from the sauce softens, or rehydrates, the noodles, especially when the pan is covered as the lasagna bakes. Most no-boil noodles are rippled, and the accordion-like pleats relax as the pasta rehydrates in the oven, allowing the noodles to elongate.

No-boil lasagna noodles come in two shapes. The most common is a rectangle measuring 7 inches long and 3½ inches wide. Three such noodles make a single layer in a conventional 13 by 9-inch lasagna pan when they swell in the oven. In local markets, we found three brands of this type of no-boil lasagna noodle: Ronzoni (made by New World Pasta, which sells the same product under the American Beauty, Skinner, and San Giorgio labels in certain parts of the country), Pasta DeFino (made in the United States), and Barilla (imported from Italy). Italian noodles made by Delverde came in 7-inch squares. We made lasagnas with each of the four noodles to see how they would compare.

Ronzoni and DeFino are both thin and rippled, and although tasters preferred the Ronzoni for their flavor and the DeFino for their sturdiness, both brands worked well. Barilla noodles tasted great but their texture was subpar. Two squares of Delverde noodles butted very closely together fit into a 13 by 9-inch pan, but, when baked, the noodles expanded and the edges jumped out of the pan and became unpleasantly dry and tough. The only way to avoid this is to soak these noodles in hot water until tender. You then can cut them with scissors to fit the measurements of the pan. These noodles were no timesaver.

In the end, we rejected the Italian noodles in favor of the two American brands tested. At least when it comes to convenience, American pasta companies are the leaders.

Rating No-Boil Lasagna Noodles

WE TESTED FOUR BRANDS OF NO-BOIL NOODLES IN our lasagna recipe. Tasters evaluated the noodles for flavor and texture. All brands are available in supermarkets.

RECOMMENDED
1. Ronzoni Oven Ready Lasagne
$.99 for 8 ounces
With its "lightly eggy" and "wheaty" flavor, and "tender," "perfectly al dente" texture, Ronzoni was the tasters' favorite.

RECOMMENDED
2. Pasta DeFino No Boil Lasagna
$2.29 for 8 ounces
These "fairly thick" noodles were praised for their "firm," "toothsome" texture and "mild" flavor.

RECOMMENDED WITH RESERVATIONS
3. Barilla Oven-Ready No-Boil Lasagna
$1.59 for 9 ounces
These flat noodles were the most "like fresh pasta" in the bunch. However, they were "a little too thin" and "slightly limp."

NOT RECOMMENDED
4. Delverde Instant No-Boil Lasagna
$4.59 for 17.5 ounces
These noodles were "unevenly cooked" with "hard, dry edges" and a "tender interior." They did have a "good, clean" flavor.

France's greatest beef stew starts with basic ingredients such as mushrooms, thyme, and butter.

BEEF burgundy

If the Louvre were just a museum, then boeuf à la bourguignonne might be just beef stew. Both are French and utterly extraordinary, but only one can be enjoyed at home.

We liken beef Burgundy more to a fabulous prime steak napped with a rich red wine reduction sauce than to a mundane beef stew. The beef in beef Burgundy is cut into satisfyingly large chunks that become utterly tender. The braising liquid, brimming with voluptuous wine and infused with aromatic vegetables, garlic, and herbs, is finessed into a sauce of burgundy velvet studded with mushrooms and pearl onions. Beef Burgundy is earthy, big, robust, warm, and welcoming in a brooding sort of way.

At least that's what it is at its best. We have had versions that fell far short of this, with tough meat or a dull sauce with no flavor complexity. We wanted to find a way to bring this classic dish to its full potential in a home kitchen.

BEEF BURGUNDY

WHAT WE WANTED: A stew with satisfyingly large chunks of tender meat. A velvety sauce brimming with the flavor of good Burgundy wine and studded with caramelized mushrooms and pearl onions.

Recipes for beef Burgundy are very much alike. Aromatic vegetables (onions, garlic, and carrots), red wine, stock, herbs, mushrooms, and pearl onions are all requisite ingredients; their combinations and proportions and the variations in preparation and technique are where the recipes diverge.

We started by completing four recipes, and from these four we deduced a couple of things. First, marinating the beef in the red wine and herbs that will later go into the braise—a common recommendation in recipes—does not improve the flavor of the cooked meat. Second, the braising liquid requires straining to rid it of bits of aromatic vegetables and herbs so that it may become flawlessly smooth. We found that bundling in cheesecloth all the goods that must eventually come out of the pot made their extraction possible in one easy step. When wrapped in cheesecloth, however, the aromatic vegetables cannot first be sautéed—a customary step, the omission of which we feared would adversely affect the flavors of the braise. Remarkably, it did not. But perhaps this is why it took such generous amounts of chopped onions, carrots, and garlic as well as parsley, thyme, peppercorns, and bay leaves to create a balanced mélange of flavors.

The cut of beef best suited to the long braise of beef Burgundy is a chuck roast. It's the cut that almost every recipe calls for and the one we prefer in regular beef stew because of its rich, meaty flavor. Because the beef in a beef Burgundy is cut into chunks larger than those in a beef stew—a good 1½ to 2 inches—we found it necessary to take extra care to trim off as much fat and silver skin as possible; larger pieces of beef also mean larger,

more detectable bites of these undesirables.

Each and every beef Burgundy begins with either salt pork or bacon cut into lardons, or small strips, and fried to a crisp; the fat that results is used to brown the beef chunks. The crisped pork is added to the pot to simmer alongside the beef so that it can relinquish its flavors to the braise, providing a subtle, sweet underpinning and lending the sauce roundness and depth. We tried both bacon and salt pork and favored the cleaner, purer, more honest flavor of salt pork. Moreover, the thicker, more toothsome strips of salt pork had better texture than the thin, lifeless pieces of bacon. Salt pork can be a challenge to find in grocery stores, so we reasoned that just as blanching salt pork removes excess salt that would otherwise crystallize on the surface during frying, blanching thick-cut bacon ought to calm the smoke and sugar and make it appropriate for beef Burgundy. This worked well. The thick-cut bacon had more textural appeal than regular bacon and was an acceptable substitute for salt pork.

As for the stock that goes into the braise, most recipes call for beef, preferably homemade. Because making beef stock is so time-consuming, we wanted to try canned broth. Based on our tasting, we knew that canned beef broth does not make an acceptable substitute homemade beef stock (see the Tasting Lab on page 138 for details). Therefore, in all subsequent tests, we used what we have found to be the next best option—canned chicken broth—with excellent results. Still, beef Burgundy necessitates a good amount of liquid for braising, and too much chicken broth tasted too chickeny. Water was a fine filler, especially since the braising liquid is later reduced to create the sauce. We then tried something a bit unorthodox to boost flavor. Just a small amount of dried porcini mushrooms wrapped into the cheesecloth package brought the meatiness and savory quality that homemade beef stock would conceivably have added. A modicum of tomato paste added color and sprightliness.

Wine was the next issue. Beef Burgundy does not exist

without a healthy dose of it. We concluded after several batches that anything less than a whole bottle left the sauce lacking and unremarkable. After numerous experiments, we had determined that a Burgundy, or at least a decent Pinot Noir, is indeed the wine of choice (see the Tasting Lab on page 140 for more details). Though most recipes indicate that all of the wine should be added at the outset, one recipe, as well as one wine expert, recommended saving just a bit of the wine to add at the very end, just before serving. This late embellishment of raw wine vastly improved the sauce, brightening its flavor and giving it resonance.

Midway through testing, we decided we needed an alternative to browning the meat in a Dutch oven, where it would eventually be braised. Browning in batches took too long, and the drippings, or fond, that are essential flavor providers frequently burned. Evidently, the small cooking surface of even a large Dutch oven was a liability. We took to browning the beef in two batches in a heavy, large 12-inch skillet. To keep the fond from going to waste, we deglazed the pan with a bit of water and poured it directly

into the braising pot, where it would eventually marry with the broth and wine.

Next we went to work to find the best means of adding flour to thicken the braising liquid that must blossom into a velvety sauce. Tossing the beef in flour before browning interfered with the color the beef could attain and ultimately affected its flavor. We found it preferable to make a roux in the skillet and add broth and water to it, then have it join the beef, wine, and vegetable and herb bouquet in the braising pot. This afforded us the opportunity to cook the roux until it achieved a light brown color, which made a favorable impact on the flavor of the dish.

With everything assembled in the Dutch oven, into the oven it went, where the constant, all-encompassing heat produced an even simmer that required little attention. This was the time to prepare the mushrooms and pearl onions, both of which would later join the sauce. Peeling fresh pearl onions is a nuisance, but opening a bag isn't. We embraced peeled frozen pearl onions; contrary to expectations, when browned, the frozen onions are not inferior in flavor or texture to fresh, as they are when boiled. A brisk simmer in a skillet with some water, butter, and sugar, and then a quick sauté with the mushrooms, created glazed beauties that were ready to grace the sauce. The final flourish was a swish of brandy that added richness and warmth to an already magnificent boeuf à la bourguignonne.

WHAT WE LEARNED: Start with a chuck roast cut into large chunks. Don't marinate the meat in wine but do brown it in a large skillet, using the rendered fat from salt pork to cook the meat. Make a roux (with butter and flour) to thicken the sauce, and wrap the aromatic vegetables in cheesecloth so they can be easily removed before building the sauce from the braising liquid. Finally, braise the meat in a combination of canned chicken broth and good red wine but save a little wine to add just before serving.

BEEF BURGUNDY serves 6

If you cannot find salt pork, thick-cut bacon can be substituted. Cut it crosswise into 1/4-inch pieces and treat it just as you would the salt pork, but note that you will have no rind to include in the vegetable and herb bouquet. Boiled potatoes are the traditional accompaniment, but mashed potatoes or buttered noodles are nice as well.

beef braise

6	ounces salt pork, trimmed of rind (see illustration on page 141), rind reserved, and salt pork cut into 1/4 inch by 1/4 inch by 1-inch pieces
10	sprigs fresh parsley, torn into quarters
6	sprigs fresh thyme
2	medium onions, chopped coarse
2	medium carrots, chopped coarse
1	medium head garlic, cloves separated and crushed but unpeeled
2	bay leaves, crumbled
1/2	teaspoon black peppercorns
1/2	ounce dried porcini mushrooms, rinsed (optional)
4–4 1/4	pounds beef chuck roast, trimmed and cut into 2-inch chunks (see illustrations on page 137) Salt and ground black pepper
4	tablespoons unsalted butter, cut into 4 pieces
1/3	cup all-purpose flour
1 3/4	cups canned low-sodium chicken broth
1	bottle (750 ml) wine, red Burgundy or Pinot Noir
1	teaspoon tomato paste

onion and mushroom garnish

36	frozen pearl onions (about 7 ounces)
1	tablespoon unsalted butter
1	tablespoon sugar
1/2	teaspoon salt
10	ounces white button mushrooms, whole if small, halved if medium, quartered if large
2	tablespoons brandy
3	tablespoons minced fresh parsley leaves

1. Bring salt pork, reserved salt pork rind, and 3 cups water to a boil in medium saucepan over high heat. Boil 2 minutes, then drain well.

2. Cut two 22-inch lengths of cheesecloth. Following illustrations on page 138, wrap parsley, thyme, onions, carrots, garlic, bay leaves, peppercorns, porcini mushrooms, and blanched salt pork rind in cheesecloth and set in large oven-proof Dutch oven. Adjust oven rack to lower-middle position and heat oven to 300 degrees.

3. Set 12-inch skillet with salt pork over medium heat; sauté until lightly brown and crisp, about 12 minutes. With slotted spoon, transfer salt pork to Dutch oven. Pour off all but 2 teaspoons fat and reserve. Dry beef thoroughly on paper towels, then season it generously with salt and pepper. Increase heat to high and brown half of beef in single layer, turning once or twice, until deep brown, about 7 minutes; transfer browned beef to Dutch oven. Pour 1/2 cup water into skillet and scrape pan with wooden spoon to loosen browned bits. When pan bottom is clean, pour liquid into Dutch oven.

4. Return skillet to high heat and add 2 teaspoons reserved pork fat; swirl to coat pan bottom. When fat begins to smoke, brown remaining beef in single layer, turning once or twice, until deep brown, about 7 minutes; transfer browned beef to Dutch oven. Pour 1/2 cup water into skillet and scrape pan with wooden spoon to loosen browned bits. When pan bottom is clean, pour liquid into Dutch oven.

5. Set now-empty skillet over medium heat and add butter. When foaming subsides, whisk in flour until evenly moistened and pasty. Cook, whisking constantly, until mixture has toasty aroma and resembles light-colored peanut butter, about 5 minutes. Gradually whisk in chicken broth and 1 1/2 cups water. Increase heat to medium-high and bring to a simmer, stirring frequently, until thickened. Pour mixture into Dutch oven. Add 3 cups wine, tomato paste, and salt and pepper to taste to Dutch oven and stir to combine. Set Dutch oven over high heat and bring to a boil. Cover and place pot in oven. Cook until meat is tender, 2½ to 3 hours.

6. Remove Dutch oven from oven and, using tongs, transfer vegetable and herb bouquet to mesh strainer set over pot. Press liquid back into pot and discard bouquet. With slotted spoon, transfer beef to medium bowl; set aside. Allow braising liquid to settle about 15 minutes, then, with wide shallow spoon, skim fat off surface and discard.

7. Bring liquid in Dutch oven to boil over medium-high heat. Simmer briskly, stirring occasionally to ensure that bottom is not burning, until sauce is reduced to about 3 cups and thickened to consistency of heavy cream, 15 to 25 minutes.

8. While sauce is reducing, bring pearl onions, butter, sugar, ¼ teaspoon salt, and ½ cup water to a boil in medium skillet over high heat. Cover, reduce heat to medium-low, and simmer, shaking pan occasionally, until onions are tender, about 5 minutes. Uncover, increase heat to high, and simmer until all liquid evaporates, about 3 minutes. Add mushrooms and remaining ¼ teaspoon salt. Cook, stirring occasionally, until liquid released by mushrooms evaporates and vegetables are browned and glazed, about 5 minutes. Transfer vegetables to large plate and set aside. Add ¼ cup water to skillet and stir with wooden spoon to loosen browned bits. When pan bottom and sides are clean, add liquid to reducing sauce.

9. When sauce has reduced to about 3 cups and thickened to consistency of heavy cream, reduce heat to medium-low. Stir beef, mushrooms, and onions (and any accumulated juices), remaining wine from bottle, and brandy into Dutch oven. Cover pot and cook until just heated through, 5 to 8 minutes. Adjust seasonings with salt and pepper and serve, sprinkling individual servings with minced parsley.

TECHNIQUE: Cutting Stew Meat

Packages of stew meat usually contain misshapen pieces of various sizes, often from undesirable parts of the cow. To get stew meat pieces that are cut from the right part of the animal and regularly shaped, we suggest buying a boneless roast and cutting the meat yourself. This way you also ensure that all the pieces are the same size and will cook at the same rate.

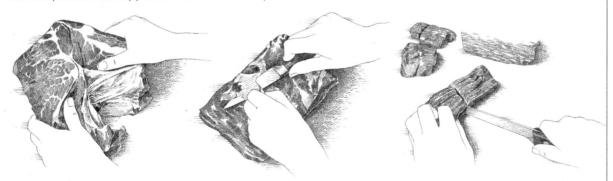

1. Pull apart the roast at its major seams (delineated by lines of fat and silver skin). Use a knife as necessary.

2. With a paring knife, trim off excess fat and silver skin.

3. Cut the meat into 2-inch chunks for beef burgundy or 1-inch cubes for chili.

DO-AHEAD BEEF BURGUNDY

The braise can be made a day or two ahead, and the sauce, along with the onion and mushroom garnish, can be completed the day you intend to serve.

TECHNIQUE:
Making the Vegetable and Herb Bouquet

If you don't have cheesecloth, you can use a cloth stuffing bag, which is readily available in most supermarkets.

1. Cut two 22-inch lengths of cheesecloth and unfold each piece once lengthwise so that each forms a 2-ply, 22 by 8-inch piece. Lay the cheesecloth in a medium bowl, placing sheets perpendicular to each other. Place the designated ingredients in the cheesecloth-lined bowl.

2. Gather the edges of the cheesecloth securely and fasten with kitchen twine. Trim excess cheesecloth with scissors if necessary.

1. Follow recipe for Beef Burgundy through step 5. Using tongs, transfer vegetable and herb bouquet to mesh strainer set over Dutch oven. Press liquid back into pot and discard bouquet. Let beef cool to room temperature in braising liquid in Dutch oven. The braise can be kept covered in the refrigerator for 1 to 2 days.

2. To complete the dish, use slotted spoon to skim congealed fat off top and discard. Set pot over medium-high heat and bring to a simmer. With slotted spoon, transfer beef to medium bowl and set aside. Simmer sauce briskly, stirring occasionally to ensure that bottom is not burning, until reduced to about 3 cups and thickened to consistency of heavy cream.

3. Continue with recipe from step 8.

TASTING LAB: Beef Broth

BEEF BROTH IS A TRADITIONAL EUROPEAN AND AMERICAN staple, a key ingredient in many classic sauces as well as the basis for popular beef soups. Over the past few years, however, sales of beef broth have lagged. The most recent statistics for annual sales show that canned chicken broth outsells canned beef broth by 4 cans to 1.

When we tasted commercial beef broths, the reason for their slack sales became obvious: Most beef broths simply do not deliver full-bodied, beefy flavor. There might be subtle beef suggestions, but after tasting nearly all of the selected broths—bouillon-based, canned, gourmet, and organic—there remained one nagging question: "Where's the beef?"

As things stand, U.S. regulations for beef broth do not require much beef. A commercial beef broth need contain only 1 part protein to 135 parts moisture, according to the U.S. Department of Agriculture's standards. That translates to less than about an ounce of meat (or about one-quarter of a hamburger) to 1 gallon of water. To contain costs, most commercial producers stay very close to that limit. Generally, manufactured beef broth derives its flavor from

Rating Beef Broths

WE TASTED 10 BRANDS OF BEEF BROTH SOLD IN SUPERMARKETS. WE ALSO INCLUDED OUR HOMEMADE BEEF BROTH, which was picked out by every single taster as the best choice by far. Broths are listed in order of preference, although differences between "not recommended" products were more about how awful one was relative to another rather than any positive attributes.

RECOMMENDED IN A PINCH
1. Superior Touch Better Than Bouillon Beef Base
$4.00 for 8-ounce jar, which makes 10 quarts
This product actually includes beef and concentrated beef stock at the top of its ingredient list. More beef flavor than other choices, but can't compare with homemade. Many tasters complained about too much salt.

NOT RECOMMENDED
2. Herb Ox Beef Bouillon Cubes
$2.29 for 25 cubes, which makes about 6 quarts
"Tastes like it was produced in a lab, not a kitchen." Better than other bouillon products but still deemed "watery." One taster quipped, "Almost no beef flavor—a cow walked by the pot?"

NOT RECOMMENDED
3. Health Valley Beef Flavored Broth
$1.29 for 14.25 ounces
Lower in salt than other canned broths and "less offensive."

NOT RECOMMENDED
4. Campbell's Beef Broth
$1.25 for 10.5 ounces
Dark, coffee-like appearance and extreme saltiness. Its acidic (and salty) flavor was repeatedly compared with soy sauce.

NOT RECOMMENDED
5. Wyler's Bouillon Granules
$1.69 for 2¹/₂-ounce jar, which makes 4¹/₂ quarts
More like vegetable broth than beef broth. "Beef is elusive."

NOT RECOMMENDED
6. Knorr Beef Bouillon
$1.49 for 12 cubes, which makes 6 quarts
"Where's the beef?" asked one taster. Perhaps lingering somewhere behind the salt? Broth made from these bouillon cubes was very salty and greasy. Tasters complained of "commercial" and "industrial" flavors.

NOT RECOMMENDED
7. Bovril Concentrated Beef Flavored Liquid Bouillon
$3.69 for 4.2-ounce jar, which makes 6 quarts
Rich-colored broth "looks better than it tastes." Like too many other products we sampled, tasters rejected this one for its "blah flavor."

NOT RECOMMENDED
8. Swanson's Beef Broth
$.89 for 14.5 ounces
"Tastes extremely fake," wrote one taster. The consensus was that this broth was too greasy as well. The artificial taste of this major brand was a big turn-off.

NOT RECOMMENDED
9. College Inn Beef Broth
$.99 for 14.5 ounces
"Off" flavors were described by some tasters as being similar to "burnt plastic" or "metallic." Several tasters called this broth "horrific."

NOT RECOMMENDED
10. Walnut Acres Beef Broth
$2.99 for 15.5 ounces
This organic broth was the greasiest one tested. No beef flavor. As one taster said, "I thought it could not get any worse."

bare beef bones and a boost of various additives. A glance at the label on the side of any canned broth or boxed bouillon cubes will confirm this.

We wanted to talk to the manufacturers of beef broths to verify our impressions of the way they make their products, but calls to broth giants Hormel Foods and Campbell Soup Company were dead ends. Both declined to answer questions about the way they make their beef broths. But beef bones plus additives would certainly explain why none of the 10 commercial broths we tasted came even close to the full-bodied, beefy flavor of our homemade stock—made with 6 pounds of meat and bones in 2 quarts of water. Nearly all of the commercial broths were thin and flavorless except for their "off" or artificial flavors.

What seems to distinguish most supermarket broths from homemade, gourmet, or natural foods store broths is a riddling of flavor additives. Monosodium glutamate (MSG) can be found in nearly all supermarket beef broths (see the Science Desk on page 141). Disodium guanylate and disodium isonate, which are both yeast-based, hydrolyzed soy protein, are also typically added to commercial broths. Yeast extracts find their way into most of these broths as well. All approved by the U.S. Food and Drug Administration (FDA), these additives are intended to "enhance" flavor. As one FDA spokesperson explained, "You've got something that's kind of 'blah,' so to give it a little more taste they add these things."

Salt—and lots of it—also adds to the flavor of these broths. Most beef broth products contain about 35 percent of the daily allowance for sodium per serving. Salt is also added to help extract the needed protein from the bones.

The preferred product in our commercial broth tasting was a jarred beef base, Superior Touch Better Than Bouillon, but even this "winner" had an unflattering score of 4.6 on a scale of 0 to 10. Herb Ox Beef Bouillon Cubes lagged not too far behind but weren't good enough to recommend, even in a pinch. Even if you can get your hands on one of the "top finishers," however, we don't recommend their use in a recipe where the flavor of beef broth predominates, as it does in beef soup or stew.

TASTING LAB:
Does It Have to Be Burgundy?

BEEF BURGUNDY IS RIGHTFULLY MADE WITH TRUE Burgundy wine. This means a red wine made from the Pinot Noir grape grown in the French province of Burgundy. Characteristically, these wines are medium-bodied but also deep, rich, and complex, with earthy tones and a reticent fruitiness. They are also expensive. Throughout our testing, we emptied a $12 bottle of Burgundy—the least expensive we could find—into each batch of beef Burgundy. Quite frankly, it was making outstanding beef Burgundies.

Nonetheless, we wanted to try more costly, higher-quality Burgundies and found that they bettered the dish—a $30 bottle gave a stellar, rousing performance. We thought it worth exploring other wines, but, wanting to remain faithful to the spirit of the dish, we limited ourselves to Pinot Noirs made on the West Coast of the United States, which are slightly less expensive than Burgundies. We made beef Burgundies with domestic Pinot Noirs at three different price points, and even the least expensive wine—a $9 bottle—was perfectly acceptable, although its flavors were simpler and less intriguing than those of its Burgundian counterpart.

Both the Burgundies and the Pinot Noirs exhibited the same pattern—that is, as the price of the wine increased, so did the depth, complexity, and roundness of the sauce. We can advise with some confidence to set your price, then seek out a wine—either Burgundy or Pinot Noir—that matches it. But if your allegiance is to a true Burgundy, be warned that they can be difficult to find because production is relatively limited. We also caution you to beware of several very inexpensive mass-produced wines from California of questionable constitutions that are sold as "Burgundy." They are usually made from a blend of grape varieties, and whether or not they actually contain so much as a drop of Pinot Noir is a mystery. We made a beef burgundy with one of these wines, and it resulted in a fleeting, one-dimensional, fruity, sweet sauce.

SCIENCE DESK: The Benefits of MSG

BECAUSE MOST OF THE COMMERCIAL BEEF BROTHS IN our tasting (see the Tasting Lab on page 138) use monosodium glutamate (MSG) as a flavor enhancer, we decided to find out just how this product affects flavor. To provide the most dramatic illustration, we cooked up a batch of classic French beef stock, a practically flavorless liquid made with bones (without meat) and vegetables. We then tasted it plain and with ½ teaspoon of MSG per quart.

The difference was more distinct than we had expected. The plain stock was characterized by excessive vegetable and sweet flavors, while beef flavors were indiscernible. In contrast, the stock with MSG had, as one taster described, "higher flavor notes" that included beefy and more savory flavors and a subdued sweetness. What's more, it tasted nothing like the lowest-rated commercial broths we had sampled.

Just how that half-teaspoon of MSG can make such a difference is something scientists cannot fully explain, says food science professor F. Jack Francis of the University of Massachusetts at Amherst. MSG, like many other flavor enhancers, does not change the flavor of the substance to which it is added. Instead, it is believed to enhance the response of a person's taste buds, especially to meats and proteins, says Francis. Exactly how this happens scientists have yet to learn. Some describe it not only as a taste enhancer but also as a stimulator of a fifth taste perception in addition to sweet, sour, salty, and bitter. The Japanese call this taste perception umami, and it is best described as meaty or mushroom-like.

Popular as MSG is with commercial broth makers, it has not been especially popular with the American public. In the 1980s, people began to associate it with "Chinese restaurant syndrome," which has been reported to include symptoms such as headache, digestive upset, and chest pain. Even though numerous studies have failed to turn up an association between such symptoms and MSG, the reputation has stuck. It has been speculated that a type of bacteria quick to grow on cooked rice left at room temperature and able to cause food poisoning is the real source of trouble for those diners with "Chinese restaurant syndrome."

Nowadays most Chinese restaurants tout "No MSG" on their menus. Yet many people do not realize that it's still lurking in their hot-and-sour soup as well as many other non-Chinese dishes. That's because MSG is the salt form of glutamate, a naturally occurring substance found in such foods as peanut butter, rice, flour, and mushrooms.

TECHNIQUE:
Trimming Rind from Salt Pork

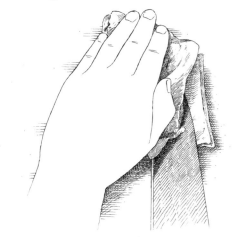

Salt pork is usually sold with the rind attached, and you must remove the tough rind before slicing or chopping it. Steady the salt pork with one hand, and with the other hand slide the blade of a sharp chef's knife between the rind and the fat, using a wide sawing motion to cut away the rind in one piece. Save the rind—it is added to the cheesecloth bundle with the vegetables and herbs.

EQUIPMENT CORNER:
Oven Thermometers

HAVE YOU EVER BAKED A CAKE OR PIE THAT WAS ONLY half-done after the suggested cooking time? We have, and often the reason was a poorly calibrated oven. The accuracy of your oven can spell the difference between disaster and culinary triumph. Just how bad is this problem? To find out, we tested 16 different ovens in the homes of friends and colleagues, setting each oven to 350 degrees. We then measured the temperature inside each oven and found that the actual temperatures ranged from 300 to 390 degrees. In fact, only two of 16 ovens tested registered within 10 degrees of the 350-degree mark.

Even the ovens here in our test kitchen often stray from reliability in between service calls from the professionals who recalibrate them. Recently, for example, we found that the ovens in our double wall-oven unit differed from each other by 30 degrees when set to the same temperature. That's why we often use an oven thermometer to tell us what's really going on. In fact, we consider the oven thermometer such an important tool that we rounded up eight popular models to test. With our ovens freshly calibrated and a computerized, supersensitive thermometer (the ChartScan Portable Data Recorder) in hand to accurately monitor oven temperatures, we set out to assess the various models based on readability, accuracy, and stability.

Cooking in an oven is not as straightforward a process as you might think. In fact, three different dynamics of heat transfer are simultaneously in play. Radiation is the heat energy (generated by the heating element) carried through the air inside the oven cavity. Convection is the movement of the hot air itself; think of the fan inside a convection oven. Last is conduction, which is the transfer of energy from one hot surface to another; think of a piece of meat browning while in contact with the surface of a hot pan. Of these three dynamics, radiation from the heating element is responsible for the lion's share of browning that occurs when you bake or roast in the oven.

Conversations with David Anderson, senior product manager at Whirlpool, revealed that the average oven designed for home use does not simply heat up to the temperature set on the dial and then stay there. Anderson noted that an oven's heating elements are either on at full power or off—with no middle ground. To maintain the desired temperature, the heating elements cycle within a manufacturer-determined tolerance, heating up and cooling down to temperatures just above and below the desired temperature. The precise temperature tolerances and timing of the cycles vary from manufacturer to manufacturer. For instance, Anderson said that Whirlpool uses one-minute intervals, so the elements will be on for one minute, then off for the next, then on again, and so forth as necessary. This cycling process is regulated by an internal temperature sensor located in the oven cavity.

We wanted to put this information to the test, so we hooked up our ChartScan Portable Data Recorder to an electric oven in the test kitchen and programmed it to record the temperature once every 10 seconds for 1½ hours. We placed 15 temperature sensors, called thermocouples, at different locations up and down and side to side in the oven cavity and set the dial to 350 degrees. At the dead-center location in the oven, we found the temperature cycled within a range of roughly 25 degrees, from a low of about 335 degrees to a high of about 361 degrees. We analyzed a gas oven in the same manner and found the temperature spread to be somewhat narrower, between 343 and 359 degrees.

A careful look at the numbers generated by our ChartScan tests also confirmed the common assertion that the heat within an oven cavity is not consistent; that, in effect, there are hot and cold spots. Though we might have expected otherwise, we found that the bottom of our electric test oven tended to run hotter than the top, usually by 5 to 15 degrees. We also found that the rear of our oven ran hotter than the front by roughly 5 to 10 degrees. There was

Rating Oven Thermometers

WE RATED EIGHT OVEN THERMOMETERS AND EVALUATED THEM ACCORDING TO READABILITY, ACCURACY (IF THE temperature was off by more than 8 degrees the thermometer was downgraded slightly; if the temperature was off by more than 17 degrees the thermometer was downgraded more seriously), and temperature increments (10-degree increments proved more precise than 25-degree increments). Tests were performed in the same freshly calibrated electric oven in the test kitchen. The thermometers are listed in order of preference. See www.cooksillustrated.com for up-to-date prices and mail-order sources for top-rated products.

HIGHLY RECOMMENDED
1. Taylor Classic Oven Guide Thermometer, Model 5921
$12.99

Temperature readings were spot on, and this Taylor passed our knock-over test with flying colors. The most stable thermometer of the group, in part because of its 4-inch length.

RECOMMENDED
2. Component Design Magnet Mounted Oven Thermometer, Model MOT1
$7.99

The magnet mounted on the back of the dial is a boon to stability. That, and the uncluttered dial graphics, earned the Component Design a second-place rating.

RECOMMENDED WITH RESERVATIONS
3. Cooper Oven Thermometer, Model 24HP
$7.95

The bold numbers on its compact face provide average readability. Not as stable as the top models.

RECOMMENDED WITH RESERVATIONS
4. Pyrex Accessories Oven Thermometer, #16416
$4.99

Excellent readability owing to its large, uncluttered, stark white dial face with clear, simple graphics. No Celsius scale and seems a bit flimsy.

RECOMMENDED WITH RESERVATIONS
5. Hoan Stainless Steel Oven Thermometer, Style No. 43460
$6.99

Bold numbers with red markers every 50 degrees make this thermometer easy to read despite its small dial face. No Celsius scale. Falls through oven rack easily.

RECOMMENDED WITH RESERVATIONS
6. Taylor Serviceman's Folding Oven Test Thermometer, Model 5903
$31.50

Arrived with neither instructions nor a hook, so we could not hang it from the rack. Very easy to read, and it's stable if you place it diagonally on the oven rack. No Celsius scale. The only thermometer tested that uses mercury.

RECOMMENDED WITH RESERVATIONS
7. Taylor Classic Oven Dial Thermometer, Model 5931
$5.99

Bold-face numbers help readability, but the poor design of the hanger hinders readability because it causes the dial face to tilt downward. No Celsius scale.

NOT RECOMMENDED
8. Polder Oven Thermometer
$7.95

Get out your reading glasses—you'll need them to decipher the crowded dial face. Two complete scales for Fahrenheit and Celsius are the culprits.

also a stunning difference from right to left in our oven, with the right side sometimes running up to 50 degrees hotter than the left!

The uneven heat is the reason why many cookbook authors suggest rotating pans in the oven when you bake. We ran a simple test of baking sugar cookies to confirm this advice. Sure enough, the cookies were browned a little less evenly from one side of the pan to the other when we failed to turn the cookie sheet partway through the baking time (see page 271 for details).

Curious as to whether there was any truth to the common kitchen wisdom that electric ovens heat more evenly than gas ovens, we repeated the ChartScan tests on a gas range in the test kitchen. The temperatures recorded in our tests bore out some validity in this axiom. For instance, the temperature differential between the bottom and top of the cavity was closer to 50 degrees, where it had been just 5 to 15 degrees in the electric oven.

An oven thermometer will give you a fighting chance in the guessing game of temperatures inside your oven. Widely available in stores from the local supermarket right up to fancy kitchenware emporia, we wondered if price—which ranged from a low of about $5 for the Pyrex model to a high of almost $32 for a mercury-based Taylor model—really mattered.

As awareness of mercury's toxic properties has increased, the mercury-based thermometers that were once common have become rare. In fact, the Taylor Serviceman's Folding Oven Test Thermometer was the only mercury-based model in our group of eight. In another Taylor model, the Classic Oven Guide Thermometer, blue-dyed alcohol took the place of mercury, but all of the other models were based on a bimetal coil. Engineers from Taylor Environmental Instruments explained that the bimetal coil, mounted inside the thermometer and attached at one end to the pointer on the dial, is made from two types of metal, bonded together, which have different rates of expansion and contraction when subjected to changes in temperature. When the temperature increases or decreases, the coil changes length, which causes the pointer on the dial face to rotate to indicate the temperature.

According to our tests at moderate to high oven temperatures, most of the thermometers were pretty accurate, but only one model, the Taylor Classic Oven Guide Thermometer, was spot-on at all the temperatures we tested. On the other hand, only three models—the Taylor Serviceman's Folding Oven Test Thermometer (with the mercury), the Taylor Classic Oven Dial Thermometer, and the Polder—produced readings that were more than 17 degrees off, which was the limit of our tolerance (see chart on page 143 for details).

During the testing, we also noted that two models in particular, the Cooper and the Polder, could be difficult to read owing to small dial faces that are overstuffed with graphics. When you shop, look for an uncluttered thermometer face with bold numbers for good readability. A large dial face (of 2 inches or more) is also preferred.

The last issue that affects everyday use is stability. All of the thermometers we tested can either sit on the oven shelf or hang from it. Either way, unfortunately, it is easy to knock over the thermometer while maneuvering a pan in or out of the oven. Even more irritating is when the thermometer falls through the wires of the rack to the bottom of the cavity. Both instances occasion a clumsy retrieval process with a hand shod in a bulky oven mitt. Two of the thermometers, the Taylor Classic Oven Guide, with its extrawide, 4-inch base, and the Component Design, with its built-in magnet, minimized such antics; they were exceptionally stable in our knock-over tests. At the same time, the Taylor Oven Guide and the Component Design are each only 2 inches tall, so it was easy to maneuver pans up and over without disturbing them.

All in all, most of the thermometers performed acceptably, but one, the moderately priced Taylor Classic Oven Guide, shone especially bright in every test. Though it is not the least expensive of the contestants, its readability, stability, and accuracy represent a good value as far as we're concerned.

Chris tries to spray Doc with water
after a heated demonstration on
the appeal of chiles.

TEXAS *chili*

CHAPTER II

A strictly Texan chili, known as chili con carne, depends on either pureed or powdered ancho chiles, uses beef, excludes tomato, onion, and beans, and features a high proportion of meat to chiles. We wanted a chili that would be hearty, heavy on the meat, and spicy but not overwhelmingly hot. In other words, we wanted the real thing. We wanted a creamy consistency somewhere between soup and stew. The flavors would be balanced so that no single spice or seasoning competed with the chile or beef.

We traveled to chili country, cooked with various experts in their kitchens, and tried out dozens of recipes in the test kitchen. In the end, we think our chili is good enough to compete in any chili cook-off, even in Texas.

CHILI CON CARNE

WHAT WE WANTED: The real deal, with big chunks of meat, plenty of chile flavor but not searing heat, and a smooth, rich sauce that could be ladled over rice or soaked up with cornbread.

Because chiles are the heart of chili con carne, we decided to begin our research by learning about the different types. After considerable testing and tasting, we settled on a combination of ancho and New Mexico for the dried chiles (see the Tasting Lab on page 151 for more information), with a few jalapeños added for their fresh flavor and bite. Chilis made with toasted and ground whole dried chiles tasted noticeably fuller and warmer than those made with chili powder. The two main toasting methods are oven and skillet, and after trying both, we went to the oven simply because it required less attention and effort than skillet toasting. The chiles will puff in the oven, become fragrant, and dry out sufficiently after five to six minutes. One caveat, though: Overtoasted chiles can take on a distinctly bitter flavor, so don't let them go too long.

With the chiles chosen and toasted, the next big question was how best to prepare them. The two options here are to rehydrate the toasted chiles in liquid and process them into a puree or to grind them into a powder. It didn't take long for us to select grinding as the preferred method. It was easier, faster, and much less messy than making the puree, which tasters felt produced a chili that was too rich, more like a Mexican enchilada sauce than a bowl of chili.

This felt like the right time to determine the best ratio of chile to meat. Many of the recipes we looked at in our research suggested that a tablespoon of ground chile per pound of meat was sufficient, but we found these chilis to be bland and watery. Three tablespoons per pound of meat, on the other hand, produced chili with too much punch and richness. Two tablespoons per pound was the way to go.

There was little agreement in the recipes we had col-lected as to when the chile powder should be added. After running several tests, we found that sautéing the spices, including the chiles, is key to unlocking their flavor. We also discovered that blending the chile powder with water to make a paste keeps it from scorching in the pot; this step is advised.

Since chuck is our favorite meat for stewing, we knew it would work best in chili. Still, there were some aspects of the meat question that had to be settled. Should the chuck be standard hamburger grind, coarser chili grind, hand-cut into tiny cubes, or a combination? The chili made from cubes of beef was far more appealing than those made from either type of ground beef; they both had a grainy, extruded texture. Most of the recipes we looked at specified that the meat should be cut into ¼-inch cubes. However, we found that larger 1-inch chunks gave the chili a satisfying chew. In addition, cutting a chuck roast into larger chunks was much, much faster and easier than breaking it down into a fussy, ¼-inch dice.

Next we set out to determine the best type, or types, of liquid for the chili. The main contenders were water, chicken stock, beef stock, beer, black coffee, and red wine. We tried each one on its own, as well as in any combination we felt made sense. The surprise result was that we liked plain water best because it allowed the flavor of the chiles to come through in full force. Both stocks, whether on their own, combined in equal parts with each other, or with water, muddied the chile flavors. All of the other liquids, used either alone or mixed with an equal part of chicken stock or water, competed with the chile flavor.

Another basic factor to determine was the garlic. Tasters agreed that three cloves were too few and eight were too many, so we settled on five. We found many recipes that called for powdered garlic rather than fresh. Out of obligation, we tested powdered versus fresh garlic and found fresh to be far superior.

Though common in modern recipes, Texas chili lore leaves tomatoes and onions out of the original formula. These two ingredients may break with tradition, but we found both to be essential. The acidity of the tomato and the sweetness of the onion, both used in small amounts, add interest and dimension to the chili. The batches we tested without them were decidedly dull. We tested various amounts and types of tomato products and determined that more than one cup pushed the flavor of the chili toward that of spaghetti sauce. Products with a smooth consistency, such as canned crushed tomatoes or plain tomato sauce, helped create the smooth sauce we wanted.

We found that bacon gave the chili a subtly sweet, smoky essence that is most welcome. Other "secret" ingredients fell by the wayside. Coke imparted a sourish, off taste. Brown sugar cut the heat of the chiles too much. An ounce of unsweetened chocolate gave the chili a rounder,

deeper flavor, and 2 tablespoons of peanut butter made the sauce creamier and earthy tasting. Much as we liked both peanut butter and chocolate, however, we decided they were not essential.

Chili is generally thickened to tighten the sauce and make it smoother. Flour, roux (a paste of flour and melted butter), cornstarch, and masa harina (a flour ground from corn treated with lime, or calcium oxide) are the most common options. Dredging the meat in flour before browning and adding a roux along with the liquid were both effective, but these approaches made it more difficult to finesse the consistency of the finished product because both were introduced early in the cooking process. Roux added at the end of the cooking left a faint taste of raw flour. We did prefer thickening at the end of cooking, though, because we could control the consistency by adding thickener gradually until the chili reached the right consistency. We like chili thick enough to coat the back of a wooden spoon, like the custard base of homemade ice cream.

Our first choice for thickening was masa harina, added at the end of cooking. Masa both thickened the chili and gave it a slightly sweet, earthy corn flavor. If masa harina is not available in your grocery store and you'd rather not mail-order it, use a cornstarch and water slurry. It brings no flavor to the chili, but it is predictable, easy to use, and gives the gravy a silky consistency and attractive sheen.

One last note. Time and time again, tasters observed that chili, like many stews, always improved after an overnight rest because the flavors blended and mellowed. If you can, cook your chili a day ahead. The result will be worth the wait.

WHAT WE LEARNED: **Make your own chili powder by toasting and grinding two kinds of dried chiles. Cut a chuck roast into 1-inch cubes for a hearty texture, and add bacon for a subtle smokiness. Stock, beer, and wine compete with the chili flavor, so use water. Just before serving, thicken the chili with masa harina for a silky consistency and a hint of corn flavor.**

CHILI CON CARNE serves 6

To ensure the best chile flavor, we recommend toasting whole dried chiles and grinding them in a minichopper or spice-dedicated coffee grinder, all of which takes only 10 (very well-spent) minutes. Select dried chiles that are moist and pliant, like dried fruit.

To toast and grind dried chiles: Place chiles on baking sheet in 350-degree oven until fragrant and puffed, about 6 minutes. Cool, stem, and seed, tearing pods into pieces. Place pieces of the pods in a spice grinder and process until powdery, 30 to 45 seconds.

For hotter chili, boost the heat with a pinch of cayenne, a dash of hot pepper sauce, or crumbled pequin chiles near the end of cooking.

Serve the chili with any of the following side dishes: warm pinto or kidney beans, corn bread or chips, corn tortillas or tamales, rice, biscuits, or just plain crackers. Top with any of the following garnishes: chopped fresh cilantro leaves, minced white onion, diced avocado, shredded cheddar or Jack cheese, or sour cream.

3   tablespoons ancho chili powder, or 3 medium pods (about ½ ounce), toasted and ground (see note)

3   tablespoons New Mexico chili powder, or 3 medium pods (about ¾ ounce), toasted and ground (see note)

2   tablespoons cumin seeds, toasted in dry skillet over medium heat until fragrant, about 4 minutes, and ground

2   teaspoons dried oregano, preferably Mexican

4   pounds beef chuck roast, trimmed of excess fat and cut into 1-inch cubes (see illustrations on page 137)
    Salt

7–8 slices bacon (about 8 ounces), cut into ¼-inch pieces

1   medium onion, minced

5   medium garlic cloves, minced (about 5 teaspoons)

4–5 small jalapeño chile peppers, stemmed, seeded, and minced

1   cup canned crushed tomatoes or plain tomato sauce

2   tablespoons lime juice

5   tablespoons masa harina or 3 tablespoons cornstarch
    Ground black pepper

1. Mix chili powders, cumin, and oregano in small bowl and stir in ½ cup water to form thick paste; set aside. Toss beef cubes with 2 teaspoons salt in large bowl; set aside.

2. Fry bacon in large Dutch oven over medium-low heat until fat renders and bacon crisps, about 10 minutes. Remove bacon with slotted spoon to paper towel–lined plate; pour all but 2 teaspoons fat from pot into small bowl; set aside. Increase heat to medium–high; sauté meat in four batches until well-browned on all sides, about 5 minutes per batch, adding 2 teaspoons bacon fat to pot each time as necessary. Set browned meat aside in large bowl.

3. Reduce heat to medium and add 3 tablespoons bacon fat to now-empty pan. Add onion and sauté until softened, 5 to 6 minutes. Add garlic and jalapeños and sauté until fragrant, about 1 minute. Add chili powder mixture and sauté until fragrant, 2 to 3 minutes. Add reserved bacon and browned beef, crushed tomatoes or tomato sauce, lime juice, and 7 cups water. Bring to simmer. Continue to cook at steady simmer (lowering heat as necessary) until meat is tender and juices are dark, rich, and starting to thicken, about 2 hours.

4. Mix masa harina with ⅔ cup water (or cornstarch with 3 tablespoons water) in small bowl to form smooth paste. Increase heat to medium, stir in paste, and simmer until thickened, 5 to 10 minutes. Adjust seasonings generously with salt and ground black pepper to taste. Serve immediately or, for best flavor, cool slightly, cover, and refrigerate overnight or for up to 5 days. Reheat before serving.

SMOKY CHIPOTLE CHILI CON CARNE

Grill-smoking the meat in combination with chipotle chiles gives this chili a distinct, but not overwhelming, smoky flavor. Make sure you start with a chuck roast that is at least 3 inches thick. The grilling is meant to flavor the meat by searing the surface and smoking it lightly, not to cook it.

1. TO SMOKE THE MEAT: Mince 4 medium garlic cloves with 2 teaspoons salt on cutting board to form smooth puree. Rub intact chuck roast with puree, and sprinkle evenly with 2 to 3 tablespoons New Mexico chili powder; cover and set aside. Meanwhile, build hot fire in grill. When you can hold your hand 5 inches above grill surface for no more than 3 seconds, spread hot coals to area about size of roast. Open bottom grill vents, scatter 1 cup soaked mesquite or hickory wood chips over hot coals, and set grill rack in place. Place meat over hot coals and grill-roast, opening lid vents three-quarters of way and covering so that vents are over roast. Sear meat until all sides are dark and richly colored, about 12 minutes per side. Remove roast to bowl; when cool to touch, trim and cut into 1-inch cubes, reserving juices.

2. TO MAKE THE CHILI: Follow recipe for Chili Con Carne, omitting the browning of beef cubes and substituting 5 minced canned chipotle peppers in adobo sauce for jalapeños. Add grilled meat and juices with cooked bacon.

TASTING LAB: Dried Chiles

FOR THE MOST PART, CHILI CON CARNE IS BASED ON FAIRLY mild dried chiles. The most common of these are dark, mahogany red, wrinkly skinned ancho chiles, which have a deep, sweet, raisiny flavor; New Mexico Reds, which have a smooth, shiny, brick-red skin and a crisp, slightly acidic, earthy flavor; California chiles, which are very similar to New Mexico Reds in appearance but have a slightly milder flavor; and long, shiny, smooth, dark brown pasilla chiles. Pasillas, which are a little hotter than the other three varieties, have grapey, herby flavor notes, and, depending on the region of the country, are often packaged and sold as either ancho or mulato chiles.

We sampled each of these types, as well as a selection of preblended commercial powders, alone and in various combinations in batches of chili. Though the chilis made with individual chiles tasted much more pure and fresh than any of the premixed powders, they nonetheless seemed one-dimensional on their own. When all was said and done, the two-chile combination we favored was equal parts ancho, for its earthy, fruity sweetness and the stunning deep red color it imparted to the chili, and New Mexico, for its lighter flavor and crisp acidity.

Chile heat was another factor to consider. Hotter dried chiles that appear regularly in chili include guajillo, de árbol, pequin, japonés, and cayenne. Though we did not want to develop a fiery, overly hot chili, we did want a subtle bite to give the dish some oomph. We found that minced jalapeños, added with the garlic to the chili pot, supplied some heat and a fresh vegetal flavor.

TASTING LAB: Chili Powder

ALTHOUGH WE PREFER TO MAKE OUR OWN CHILI POWDER for chili con carne, we know that many cooks will use commercial chili powder. Chili powder is a curious product, often misunderstood. For one thing, the kind you find in the supermarket on the A-to-Z shelf of single herbs and spices is not itself a single spice, made only from powdered dried chiles. While there is no established formula for making chili powder, it typically consists of about 80 percent chile pepper blended with garlic powder, oregano, ground cumin seed, sometimes salt, and occasionally monosodium glutamate. Some blends even include traces of clove, allspice, anise, and coriander. Although a number of powders made solely from chiles can now be found in ethnic and specialty

Rating Chili Powders

WE TASTED NINE BRANDS OF CHILI POWDER IN A BARE-BONES RECIPE CONSISTING OF ONION, GROUND BEEF, crushed tomatoes, salt, and chili powder. The chili powders were rated for their aroma, depth of flavor, freshness, and spiciness. The products are listed in order of preference. See www.cooksillustrated.com for up-to-date prices and mail-order sources for top-rated products.

HIGHLY RECOMMENDED

1. Spice Islands Chili Powder
$2.77 for 2.4 ounces

This well-known supermarket brand was the clear winner. "It's got a big flavor that stands out compared to the others." Some tasters noted a smoky character likened to chocolate and molasses. Available in supermarkets, primarily on the West Coast.

RECOMMENDED

2. The El Paso Chile Company's Chili Spices and Fixin's
$2.95 for 2.5 ounces

Tasters liked this sample for its decent depth of flavor, freshness, and "pizazz." It was described as "deep yet sweet and complex," "smoky," and "earthy." This blend was deep red in color and contained no salt. Available by mail.

RECOMMENDED

3. Pendery's Top Hat Chile Blend
$4.73 for 2.56 ounces

This blend had many fans, who cheered it on for its warmth, depth of flavor, and "definite character." One taster put it simply: "Very nice punch. Makes me sweat." Contains MSG. Available by mail.

RECOMMENDED WITH RESERVATIONS

4. McCormick/Schilling Chili Powder (sold in glass bottle)
$4.49 for 2.12 ounces

Tasters' comments on this chili powder were brief owing to the overwhelming consensus that there just was not much flavor to discuss. "Uninteresting, but not offensive." Available in supermarkets. Sold under the Schilling label on the West Coast.

RECOMMENDED WITH RESERVATIONS

5. McCormick/Schilling Chili Powder (sold in plastic bottle)
$2.99 for 2.5 ounces

This chili powder was recommended by one taster as "good for people who don't like very spicy food." For many other tasters, this meant "bland" and "boring." Available in supermarkets.

NOT RECOMMENDED

6. Tone's Mild Chili Powder
$1.08 for .65 ounces

This product was deemed the spiciest but for all the wrong reasons, or, actually, just one reason—an excess of oregano. Available in Midwest supermarkets.

NOT RECOMMENDED

7. Gebhardt Chili Powder
$4.00 for 3 ounces

This brand, which can be hard to find outside of Texas, is extremely popular among chili cook-off competitors. Our tasters were not as enamored. It was remarkably bland but did give the chili a "nice, bright red color." Available in Texas supermarkets and by mail.

NOT RECOMMENDED

8. Pendery's Original Chile Blend
$4.14 for 2.24 ounces

This blend was noticeably sweet, with an assertive cumin flavor. Available by mail.

NOT RECOMMENDED

9. Durkee Chili Powder
$1.99 for .87 ounces

This chili powder offered "nothing exciting and nothing off-putting." In sum: "Needs oomph." Available in supermarkets.

markets, we stuck to blends because they are what most Americans cook with.

Another curious thing about chili powder is that it is usually not the source of the fiery heat for which much chili con carne is so beloved. Fresh chiles or additional dried chiles are typically added to drive up the heat.

Before we held our tasting, we spoke to a number of chili experts—chefs, cookbook authors, manufacturers, and other aficionados—to gain a better understanding of the flavor profile we might be seeking from the ideal chili powder. We learned that the key to a successful chili powder is a careful blending of the chiles, spices, and seasonings. No one component is meant to stand out boldly. In other words, a successful chili powder should contribute a complexity of flavors that can be hard to pinpoint and that work on different levels. Our idea of success was also an "independent" chili powder, capable of making a bowl of chili tasty with little or no help from other spices and seasonings. In other words, while we appreciated the idea of complexity of flavor, we also wanted some bravado.

For the most part, the results reinforced this estimation of an ideal chili powder. Those chili powders that delivered the most depth and assertiveness of flavor, otherwise described as "oomph," were the most highly rated. Unfortunately, only a few products were up to the task. Most were too subtle, leaving tasters wanting more spice and heat. A few tasters preferred the milder samples simply because they do not care for strong-flavored chili.

First and foremost, "Fresh is flavor," said Park Kerr, founder of the El Paso Chili Co., whose chili powder took second place in the tasting. Because, like most spices, chili powder contains volatile flavor components, it is important to purchase it from a source that has steady turnover. A busy supermarket or specialty spice store is probably where you'll find the freshest product.

Our panel of experts also emphasized that good chili powder depends less on the type of chile or chiles used in the blend than on their quality. Manufacturers of the three top-ranked products in the tasting credited their product's success to careful selection of quality chiles. Pat Haggerty, president of Pendery's, likened chili powder to sausage making: the ingredients can be carefully selected or they can be mixed in with "scraps." Unfortunately, none of the manufacturers we contacted were willing to give us more information about the types of chiles they use in their powder or about how the chiles are treated, since they consider this proprietary information.

There is really no great secret, however, as to the general kind of chiles used to make chili powders. The most common are large pod-type red chiles, such as New Mexico, California, and pasilla chiles. On the heat level scale, these are at the dead bottom. (Most of the chiles used in chili powder average about 1,000 to 2,000 Scoville units, the standard measure for chile pepper heat. To compare, jalapeño chiles, which are not typically used in commercial chili powders, are rated at an average of 10,000 Scoville units.)

Most chili powder manufacturers buy the chiles for their chili powders dried and roasted to their specifications. Some manufacturers will have the chile seeds included in the grind, which is said to contribute a more nutty flavor. Others, such as Pendery's, insist that the seeds be removed, claiming that they dilute the chile flavor and act as mere filler. The ground chiles are then blended with spices according to a specific formula and technique the manufacturer develops.

A third aspect of quality concerned salt content. Most of the less expensive chili powders in the tasting contained twice as much sodium as the more expensive brands. While this didn't seem to make them taste salty, the potency of their flavor was decidedly less assertive.

Finally, serious chili cooks rate a chili powder for its ability to contribute to the famed rich, bright color of a "bowl of red." This may explain why Gebhardt, which is a startlingly bright red, is a popular choice with chili cook-off competitors nationwide. While we found it lacking in flavor, this very lack may appeal to cooks who want to use it as a base on which to begin building a unique flavor profile. Ironically, the top-scoring product, by Spice Islands, had a much deeper color, more like a rich rust. According to

Donna Tainter, director of quality control and research and development for Spice Islands, the rich color is attributed not so much to the blend of spices but to a caramelization process that occurs as the chiles and spices are blended. This not only deepens the color but imparts a distinct, complex flavor that won over tasters.

EQUIPMENT CORNER: Pot Scrubbers

AT THE END OF EVERY MEAL COMES THE CHORE NO COOK likes: cleaning the pots and pans. Even perfectly cooked food often leaves behind a trail of pots with caked-on grease and grime. And if you've burned something, the job is that much more difficult.

There are a number of pot scrubbers on the market—everything from traditional steel wool pads to scouring pads made of copper wires—and all are designed to handle heavy-duty cleanup jobs. We rounded up eight types of scrubber and put them to work.

We tested each one by cleaning stainless steel pots and pans that had been used to cook rice, ground beef, jam, oatmeal, and a white sauce. In each case, we overcooked the food so that some stuck to the bottom of the pan. We used a small amount of liquid soap with each scrubber. We also tested durability by using the same scrubber to clean four pots with burned rice on the bottom. After the oatmeal test, we measured the ease with which food could be removed from the scrubbers themselves.

In the end, tasters liked the scouring pads with copper wires. They handled the dirtiest pans and were extremely durable. Regular-old steel wool pads were fine for finishing up pans, but they are not the best choice for pots with burned, stuck-on food. (We put S.O.S pads through the complete battery of kitchen tests, but other steel wool pads with soap, including Brillo, showed similar strengths and weaknesses in tests.) We also like Dobie pads, sponges covered with soft nylon. These pads were good for easy-to-moderate jobs and were especially easy on testers' hands.

SCIENCE DESK: Why Do We Eat Chiles?

CHILES ARE MYSTERIOUS IN MANY WAYS. WHY DO WE SAY they are "hot" when they are not hot in temperature? Why do people in hot climates tend to eat more chiles than people in cold climates? And, perhaps oddest of all, why do people enjoy eating something that causes pain?

There are several interesting theories about this last question. A psychologist named Paul Rozin came up with a theory years ago that still makes sense to us. He says that eating chiles is an example of what he calls "benign masochism." What's that?

Riding a rollercoaster is an example of benign masochism. As the rollercoaster goes up and down, your heart pounds faster and you have an adrenaline rush. Although it can feel dangerous, you know the ride will end safely. That's also what happens when you eat chiles—your body reacts to the physical sensation of danger, including the release of those chemicals called endorphins that give you a sense of well-being once you realize the danger has passed. So you get the thrill that follows the experience of danger without experiencing real danger. Other people have called chile eating "mouth surfing" for the same reason.

And why do you suppose people in hot climates eat more chiles? Two reasons. One, that's where chiles are grown. Two, eating chiles produces sweat, and when sweat evaporates you feel cooler, which is a good thing in hot tropical weather.

Rating Pot Scrubbers

WE TESTED EIGHT WIDELY AVAILABLE POT SCRUBBERS, CLEANING PANS WITH BURNT RICE, GROUND BEEF, JAM, oatmeal, and white sauce. The scrubbers are listed in order of preference and top-rated brands are sold in supermarkets.

RECOMMENDED

1. Chore Boy Copper Scouring Pads **$1.59 for 2 pads**

The king of scouring pads—very tough on sticky, tough jobs, cleans up pretty well, and has good durability. The copper wires are very abrasive and are good for stubborn messes that nothing else will remove.

RECOMMENDED

2. S.O.S Steel Wool Soap Pads **$1.89 for 10 pads**

After repeated uses, these pads began to fall apart. But given that 10 pads come in each box, we consider these pads disposable after 2 or 3 uses. Perfect for "finishing" pans once most of the big mess has been removed.

RECOMMENDED

3. Scotch-Brite Dobie Cleaning Pad **$1.19 for 1 pad**

This pad—a conventional sponge covered with nylon mesh—was good for easy-to-moderate cleaning jobs. Comfortable nylon won't irritate hands. Easy to clean and durable.

RECOMMENDED WITH RESERVATIONS

4. S.O.S. Heavy Duty Extra Thick Scrubber Sponge **$.99 for 1 sponge**

This conventional sponge comes with a coarse scrubber pad attached to one side. The sponge provided a comfortable grip and is great for finishing the job once the heavy scrubbing is complete. However, the scrubber only performed adequately. Good if you don't have lots of tough cleaning jobs and don't want a separate scrubber.

RECOMMENDED WITH RESERVATIONS

5. Lifetime Hoan Corp. Nylon Scrubber Set **$1.49 for 3 scrubbers**

These round nylon scrubbers were easy to grab and fit nicely into the corners of pots. They didn't show any wear and tear after repeated use, but performance was a notch below top choices.

RECOMMENDED WITH RESERVATIONS

6. Scotch-Brite Heavy Duty Scour Pads **$.79 for 2 pads**

These thin, coarse green pads look like artificial turf and worked best if folded in half—the flat design doesn't provide anything to hold onto. These pads lost their "oomph" over time and are difficult to clean thoroughly.

NOT RECOMMENDED

7. S.O.S. Clean Rinse Scrubber Sponge **$.89 for 1 sponge**

This conventional sponge with soft, plastic bristles on one side didn't remove much food from pans. Barely passable only for the lightest of jobs.

NOT RECOMMENDED

8. Williams-Sonoma Brass Brush **$3.50 for 1 brush**

This brush has a long wooden handle and coarse brass bristles. Unfortunately, we couldn't get the brush into pan corners. Our hands didn't get wet, but the pans didn't get clean, either. Available at Williams-Sonoma stores.

AMERICAN casseroles

Americans love casseroles. We serve them at potluck dinners, church suppers, and family meals. The challenge when making a good casserole is keeping the ingredients as fresh-tasting as possible. Too many casseroles are overcooked and dull, reminiscent of the worst cafeteria food.

Macaroni and cheese and turkey Tetrazzini are two classic casseroles, but they are rarely as good as they can be. Macaroni and cheese from a box is horrid. Frozen versions aren't much better. The real thing boasts a cream sauce loaded with real cheese flavor. The sauce should be smooth (no lumps) and easy to make. Recipes for turkey Tetrazzini often start with canned cream of mushroom soup and bake so long that the noodles turn to mush. We knew we could do better—much better—in the test kitchen.

Turkey Tetrazzini starts with spaghetti cooked on top of the stove.

MACARONI AND CHEESE

WHAT WE WANTED: A rich, creamy casserole with plenty of cheese flavor, properly cooked noodles, and a flawlessly smooth sauce.

There are two distinct styles of macaroni and cheese. In the more common béchamel-based style, macaroni is blanketed with a cheese-flavored white sauce, usually topped with crumbs, and baked. In the less common custard-based style, a mixture of eggs and milk is poured over layers of grated cheese and noodles. As the dish bakes, the eggs, milk, and cheese set into a custard. This macaroni and cheese is also topped with bread crumbs and baked.

Even though macaroni and cheese can be a wonderful, satisfying dish, many of the recipes we tested were tired, leaden, and uninspired. Others attempted to perk up the dish with canned green chiles, scallions, or olives. And, of course, there were attempts to lighten it. No one seemed to really love the dish enough to give it the care it deserves.

Then we ran across a recipe in John Thorne's *Simple Cooking* (Penguin, 1989). "As it happens," he begins, "I'm very fond of macaroni and cheese, and keep a special spot in my heart for cooks who genuinely love it: they are not that many." After reading his four-page essay, we suspected that his recipe for macaroni and cheese would be the real thing, the others mere shadows.

Making the dish confirmed suspicions. Thorne's macaroni and cheese was the best. His recipe starts with macaroni cooked just shy of al dente. The hot, drained macaroni is then tossed with butter in a heatproof pan or bowl. Evaporated milk, hot red pepper sauce, dry mustard, eggs, and a large quantity of cheese are stirred into the noodles. The combination is baked for 20 minutes, with the addition of more cheese and milk and a thorough stir every 5 minutes. Frequent stirrings allow the eggs to thicken without setting, which results in an incredibly silky sauce. During cooking, the sauce settles into the tubular openings of the pasta, offering a burst of cheese with each bite.

Out of curiosity, we baked the two styles of macaroni and cheese defined earlier: one with a cheese-flavored béchamel sauce, the other thickened with eggs, milk, and cheese. The béchamel-based version was grainy and tasted exactly as Thorne predicted: not like macaroni and cheese but like "macaroni with cheese sauce." In terms of texture, Thorne's macaroni and cheese was smooth silk, while the béchamel dish was thick velvet. The custard-based macaroni and cheese, really a baked version of Thorne's recipe, held more promise, and we thought we might offer it as an alternative to his stirred version. A side-by-side tasting proved the two dishes to be very different, however. The stirred version had a luxuriously silky cheese sauce, while the baked egg, milk, and cheese formed an unappealingly dry custard that set around the noodles.

With the competition ruled out, we moved forward to study Thorne's recipe a little more closely. We wondered if the dish really required evaporated milk or if this was a carryover from the late 1930s, when the recipe was first published in *The Home Comfort Cook Book* (Wrought Iron Range Company, 1937). Wouldn't regular milk or half-and-half work equally well and taste better? What cheeses besides sharp cheddar would taste good?

After testing the recipe with whole and low-fat milks and half-and-half, we realized that evaporated milk was indeed an important ingredient. All the macaroni and cheese dishes made with fresh dairy curdled a bit, resulting in a chalky, grainy texture. The dish made with evaporated milk remained flawlessly smooth. We learned that the evaporation and sterilization process used to produce evaporated milk stabilizes the milk; this in turn stabilizes the macaroni and cheese. (See the Science Desk on page 162 for details on how this works.)

As for the cheese, we tried several sharp and extra-sharp cheddars and preferred the former. Because the recipe calls for such a large quantity, a slightly milder cheese is preferable. Further testing confirmed this point. Macaroni and cheese made with Gruyère was so strong we couldn't even eat it. To our surprise, highly processed cheeses like American performed quite well. Similar to the case of the evaporated milk, the processing stabilizes the cheese and makes for a more creamy dish. For flavor, use cheddar; for texture, buy American. We also found the dish did not suffer when prepared with only 12 ounces of cheese as opposed to the pound called for in the original recipe.

Our one final problem to solve concerned the temperature of the macaroni and cheese when served. We found that at the end of the 20 minutes of baking recommended by Thorne, the dish was hot but hardly piping. By the time tasters had consumed their portions, the cheese sauce had cooled and set a bit. This problem, we learned, could not be remedied by leaving the dish in the oven much longer than the suggested 20 minutes. To do so meant running the risk of curdling the eggs, and the dish would develop a subtle grainy texture.

We wondered if we could cook the macaroni and cheese on top of the stove instead of in the oven. We found that by using a heavy-bottomed pot and cooking over low heat, it was possible to make the macaroni and cheese on top of the stove in less than five minutes. Not only was this method quicker, it kept the macaroni and cheese piping hot. If you like macaroni and cheese baked in a casserole dish, simply put the finished macaroni and cheese in a dish, cover with crumbs, and broil to toast the crumbs.

WHAT WE LEARNED: Don't use a flour-thickened béchamel or baked custard for this dish. For the best texture and flavor, make macaroni and cheese on the stovetop (not in the oven) and use evaporated milk in the sauce. For some crunch, sprinkle with toasted buttered bread crumbs just before serving.

STOVETOP MACARONI AND CHEESE

serves 4 as a main course or 6 to 8 as a side dish

If you're in a hurry or prefer to sprinkle the dish with crumbled crackers (saltines aren't bad), you can skip the bread crumb step. To make fresh bread crumbs, trim crusts from about 5 slices of good-quality white bread (we like Pepperidge Farm Toasting White) and grind them in the food processor until evenly fine-textured, 20 to 30 seconds.

toasted bread crumbs

- 2 tablespoons unsalted butter
- 1 cup fresh bread crumbs (see note)
  Pinch salt

creamy macaroni and cheese

- 2 large eggs
- 1 (12-ounce) can evaporated milk
- 1/4 teaspoon hot red pepper sauce
- 2 teaspoons salt
- 1/4 teaspoon ground black pepper
- 1 teaspoon dry mustard, dissolved in 1 teaspoon water
- 1/2 pound elbow macaroni
- 4 tablespoons unsalted butter
- 12 ounces sharp cheddar, American, or Monterey Jack cheese, grated (about 3 cups)

1. FOR THE BREAD CRUMBS: Heat butter in large skillet over medium heat until foam subsides. Add bread crumbs; cook, tossing to coat with butter, until crumbs just begin to color, about 10 minutes. Season to taste with salt; set aside.

2. FOR THE MACARONI AND CHEESE: Mix eggs, 1 cup evaporated milk, pepper sauce, 1/2 teaspoon salt, pepper, and mustard mixture in small bowl; set aside.

3. Meanwhile, bring 2 quarts water to a boil in large heavy-bottomed saucepan or Dutch oven. Add remaining 1½ teaspoons salt and macaroni; cook until almost tender but still a little firm to the bite. Drain and return to pan over low heat. Add butter; toss to melt.

4. Pour egg mixture over buttered noodles along with three-quarters of cheese; stir until thoroughly combined and the cheese starts to melt. Gradually add remaining milk and cheese, stirring constantly, until mixture is hot and creamy, about 5 minutes. Serve immediately, topped with toasted bread crumbs.

VARIATION
"BAKED" MACARONI AND CHEESE
This dish is for those who prefer their macaroni and cheese served out of a baking dish. Smooth and creamy like the stovetop version, this version is broiled just long enough to brown the crumb topping.

Follow recipe for Stovetop Macaroni and Cheese, pouring cooked macaroni and cheese into 9-inch-square gratin dish (or another heatproof baking dish of similar dimensions). Spread crumbs evenly over top. Broil until crumbs turn deep brown, 1 to 2 minutes. Let stand to set a bit, about 5 minutes, and serve immediately.

TASTING LAB: Cheddar Cheese

A GREAT FARMHOUSE CHEDDAR CHEESE IS HARD, FINE-textured, and flaky, with a sharp, tangy edge that's a little sweet, nutty, slightly bitter, and herbaceous. These various flavors come together to create a well-balanced, complex, and rewarding taste experience. The bad news is that farmhouse cheddars are expensive ($11 to $19 per pound) and often hard to find. Because supermarket cheddars are so easy to find and afford, we were interested in exploring their merits. We organized a blind tasting of eight common brands to find out which ones were best fresh out of the package and which fared best in a grilled cheese sandwich.

Before conducting the tasting, we were keen to find out what sort of cheese qualifies as cheddar. Unlike other great cheeses, such as Parmigiano-Reggiano and Stilton, cheddar is not name-protected. Anyone can make cheddar cheese anywhere and in any way. Although the U.S. government has set standards for the final product (the cheese must have no less than 50 percent milk fat solids and no more than 39 percent moisture), the means by which manufacturers produce cheddar are ungoverned. This is why there is so much variation in flavor and why even within the "sharp" category we found some cheeses as mild as mozzarella and others as robust as Parmesan.

The traditional method for making cheddar cheese is called cheddaring. During cheddaring, the curd (made by adding acid-producing cultures and clotting agents to unpasteurized whole milk) is cut into slabs, then stacked, cut, pressed, and stacked again. Along the way a large amount of liquid, called whey, is extracted from the curd base. The remaining compacted curd is what gives farmhouse cheddars their hard and fine-grained characteristics.

The quicker, safer, more cost-effective way to make cheddar, which is employed by most manufacturers to meet the ever-increasing demand of the mass market for cheese, is called the stirred-curd method. Instead of being stacked and weighted, as in the cheddaring process, the curd is

Rating Cheddar Cheeses

WE TASTED EIGHT CHEDDAR CHEESES AVAILABLE IN SUPERMARKETS AND NATURAL FOODS STORES. WE LIMITED THE TASTING to "sharp" cheddars, which are aged from 60 days up to one year. Cheeses were tasted cubed and in grilled cheese sandwiches. Cheeses are listed in order of preference based on their combined scores when sampled raw and in sandwiches.

RECOMMENDED

1. Cabot Sharp Vermont Cheddar Cheese **$2.99 for 8 ounces; aged 5 to 8 months**

This cheese won both the grilled cheese and the raw tastings. Tasters liked its approachable flavor, described as "sharp," "clean," and "tangy." In a grilled cheese sandwich, it was "buttery" and "mellow" without being even the slightest bit greasy.

RECOMMENDED

2. Tillamook Sharp Cheddar Cheese **$6.99 for 1 pound; aged 9 months**

As the only cheese in the tasting that is annatto-colored (it's orange rather than white), raw Tillamook cheddar stood out not only for its color but for its "tangy" and "piquant" characteristics. Tasters liked this cheese less in the grilled cheese sandwich, where it was criticized for "sweet" and "sour" flavors.

RECOMMENDED

3. Cracker Barrel Sharp White Cheddar Cheese **$3.29 for 10 ounces; aged 2 months**

Called "flavorful and easy," Cracker Barrel won tasters over with its "mellow," "clean" flavor. In the grilled cheese sandwich, it was described as "good and generic," with a "smooth" and "cohesive" texture.

RECOMMENDED

4. Grafton Village Cheese Company Premium Vermont Cheddar Cheese **$3.89 for 8 ounces; aged 1 year**

Grafton uses unpasteurized milk and traditional cheddar-making methods. The crumbly texture and pungent flavor earned top scores among many tasters. Some, however, found it too "pungent."

RECOMMENDED WITH RESERVATIONS

5. Horizon Organic Cheddar Cheese **$3.99 for 8 ounces; aged 6 to 9 months**

Many tasters commented that Horizon Organic cheddar "didn't taste like cheddar"—that it was too potent. While some liked its strength, others called it "stinky" and "barnyardy." Most tasters found the cheese too "runny" when melted.

RECOMMENDED WITH RESERVATIONS

6. Land O Lakes Sharp Cheddar Cheese **$1.99 for 8 ounces; aged 6 to 12 months**

"This cheese is like the kind on a supermarket deli platter," commented one taster, with other tasters agreeing, calling it "bland," "boring," and "rubbery" when eaten out of hand. In the grilled cheese sandwich, some called it "dull," but others liked the "classic grilled cheese" flavor. Called Lake to Lake Cheddar Cheese on the West Coast.

NOT RECOMMENDED

7. Organic Valley Organic Raw Milk Sharp Cheddar **$10.59 for 1 pound; aged 10 months**

Described as "buttermilky" and "sour," this unpasteurized cheddar didn't find many fans. Its texture was described as "rubbery" and "gummy" when raw and "greasy" and "oozy" when melted.

NOT RECOMMENDED

8. Heluva Good Sharp Cheddar Cheese **$2.19 for 8 ounces; aged 2 to 9 months**

"Tastes like mozzarella," said one taster, while another called it "completely one-dimensional." Most found it "tasteless" and "rubbery" both when eaten raw and when melted in a grilled cheese sandwich.

stirred and then pressed against the sides of a large vat to remove the whey. This shortcut changes the texture of the curd slightly, producing a softer, more pliable cheese. Is stirred-curd cheese still technically a cheddar cheese even though it's not cheddared? According to federal standards, it is—as long as it meets the composition requirements for milk fat solids and moisture.

Grafton Village (number four in the tasting) is one of the only companies in the tasting that still hand-cheddars its cheese. This was evident to our tasters, who overwhelmingly described Grafton's cheddar as "flaky" and "crumbly," just like a farmhouse cheddar. Brands made with the stirred-curd method were universally described as even-textured and smooth. To our surprise, tasters did not automatically mark down brands with a smooth texture. In fact, Cabot, Tillamook, and Cracker Barrel, all made using the stirred-curd method, rated higher than Grafton Village's hand-cheddared cheese.

One of the great surprises of our tasting was the success of Cracker Barrel, which, at a mere $3.29 for 10 ounces, outpolled Organic Valley cheddar, which sells for $10.59 per pound and is made with raw milk. Part of the reason for Organic Valley's low rating was its performance in a grilled cheese sandwich. When melted, Organic Valley cheddar became greasy as the fat separated from the milk solids in the cheese. Melted Cracker Barrel, on the other hand, was described by tasters as both "smooth" and "cohesive."

We also had to confront the proclivities of our palates. Because most of us were raised on lower-quality supermarket cheddars, we aren't used to "barnyard" flavors, such as those found in the Horizon Organic and Organic Valley brands. At first, we thought that our rejection of these flavors was merely a lack of sophistication, but this notion was quickly set aside when we tasted authentic farmhouse cheddars that were full-flavored but also sweet, nutty, and herbaceous. All four of the farmhouse cheddars we tasted outpolled Cabot, our top choice among supermarket cheddars. Our favorite farmhouse cheddar comes from England and is produced by a company called Keen's. This cheese is tangy, nutty, and rich. Expect to pay about $18 per pound for this fine cheese.

SCIENCE DESK:
Why Doesn't Evaporated Milk Curdle?

ALL OF THE MACARONI AND CHEESE RECIPES WE TESTED with fresh milk curdled a bit, resulting in a chalky, grainy texture. The one made with evaporated milk remained silky smooth. Why?

Evaporated milk begins as fresh whole milk. In processing, about 60 percent of the water in the milk is removed as the milk is boiled in a vacuum, creating a thickened liquid. This thickened milk is then canned and sterilized. The result is shelf-stable evaporated milk

The process by which the milk is initially heated is called fore-warming. This gentle, controlled heating of the milk helps to condition the proteins to make them more resistant to curdling. The main proteins in question here are large molecules called casein. When exposed to heat, casein molecules tend to clump; these are the chalky bits we saw in the sauce of the macaroni and cheese made with fresh milk. During fore-warming, the big casein molecules are surrounded by smaller molecules of whey protein, and the whey proteins get in the way of the clumping of the casein molecules.

Also interfering with the clumping of the casein molecules are additives in the evaporated milk. Salts, in the form of disodium phosphate and/or sodium citrate, are added to improve the ability of the proteins in the mix to retain water (the release of water is another symptom of curdling). A gum called carrageenan may also be added to prevent fat separation in storage.

How does evaporated milk differ from condensed milk? Evaporated and condensed milk are both made in the same way at the start: by heating milk in a vacuum so that 60 percent or more of the water evaporates. The resulting thick liquid is then either given a high-temperature treatment to sterilize it, making evaporated milk, or heavily sweetened to preserve it, making condensed milk. Both evaporated and condensed milk have about twice the concentration of fat and protein as regular whole milk.

TURKEY TETRAZZINI

WHAT WE WANTED: Turkey Tetrazzini can be an interesting blend of toasted bread crumbs, silky sauce, and a modicum of turkey meat, all bound together by one of our favorite foods: spaghetti. Or it can taste like stale cafeteria food. We wanted the former, not the latter.

The downside of most casseroles—in which the fusion of individual tastes and textures diminishes them—is especially true about turkey Tetrazzini. This dish is often stodgy and heavy, but we wondered if a basic noodle casserole could be reengineered so that this eminently practical American dish could be made worthy of a well-laid table.

A bit of culinary sleuthing solved the most pressing problem: the fact that the ingredients are double-cooked. (Most casserole recipes are two-step affairs: Cook the ingredients, mix them together, and then bake them in a casserole.) In *American Cookery* (Little, Brown & Co., 1972), James Beard suggests using a shallow baking dish rather than a deep casserole. Paired with a very hot (450-degree) oven, this reduces the baking time to a mere 15 minutes, a fraction of the time suggested by most cookbooks. Tasted against casseroles made with longer baking times in slower ovens, those made with this quick method won, hands down; their fresher-tasting vegetables set them leagues apart from the overcooked dullness of cafeteria cuisine.

Next we adjusted the sauce. The traditional choice is béchamel, a sauce in which milk is added to a roux, a paste made from flour and hot fat. We decided to use a velouté, a sauce based on chicken stock rather than dairy. This brightened up both the texture and the flavor, since dairy tends to dampen other flavors. We also played around with the amount of sauce, trying larger and smaller quantities, and found that more sauce overran the taste of the other ingredients. In this case, less was more. It still needed a burst of flavor, however, so we spruced it up with a shot of sherry

and a little lemon juice and nutmeg; a bit of Parmesan cheese provided tang and bite; and a full 2 teaspoons of fresh thyme also helped freshen the flavor.

Most recipes do not toast the bread crumbs before baking. Doing so does add an extra step (in a pinch, you can skip the toasting), but it also adds to the flavor and texture of the dish; it's worth the minimal effort required. Tossing the toasted bread crumbs with a bit of grated Parmesan also helps to boost the flavor.

WHAT WE LEARNED: Pass up the traditional milk-based béchamel sauce and use instead a chicken broth–based velouté sauce, which brightens the flavor of the dish and makes it less heavy. Bake the casserole only briefly in a shallow gratin dish in a hot oven to keep the pasta and vegetables from overcooking.

TURKEY TETRAZZINI serves 8

Tetrazzini is also great when made with leftover chicken. Using a shallow baking dish without a cover and a very hot oven benefits both texture and flavor. Don't skimp on the salt and pepper; this dish needs aggressive seasoning. To make fresh bread crumbs, trim crusts from about 8 slices of good-quality white bread (we like Pepperidge Farm Toasting White) and grind them in the food processor until evenly fine-textured, 20 to 30 seconds.

bread crumb topping

1½ cups fresh bread crumbs (see note)
    Pinch salt
4   tablespoons unsalted butter, melted
¼   cup grated Parmesan cheese

filling

8   tablespoons unsalted butter, plus extra for baking dish
8   ounces white button mushrooms, cleaned and sliced thin (about 3 cups)
2   medium onions, chopped fine (about 1½ cups)
    Salt and ground black pepper
¾   pound spaghetti or other long-strand pasta, strands snapped in half
6   tablespoons unbleached all-purpose flour
3   cups canned low-sodium chicken broth
4   tablespoons dry sherry
¾   cup grated Parmesan cheese
¼   teaspoon grated nutmeg
1   tablespoon juice from 1 lemon
2   teaspoons minced fresh thyme leaves
2   cups frozen peas
4   cups leftover cooked boneless turkey or chicken meat, cut into ¼-inch pieces

1. FOR THE TOPPING: Adjust oven rack to middle position and heat oven to 350 degrees. Mix bread crumbs, salt, and butter in small baking dish; bake until golden brown and crisp, 15 to 20 minutes. Cool to room temperature and mix with ¼ cup Parmesan in small bowl. Set aside.

TECHNIQUE: Breaking Long Pasta Strands Neatly

Though we don't usually recommend breaking strand pasta that we plan to sauce and eat, broken spaghetti or linguine is used in some casseroles, such as turkey Tetrazzini. Here's a neat way to break the spaghetti in half without causing short strands to fly every which way in the kitchen.

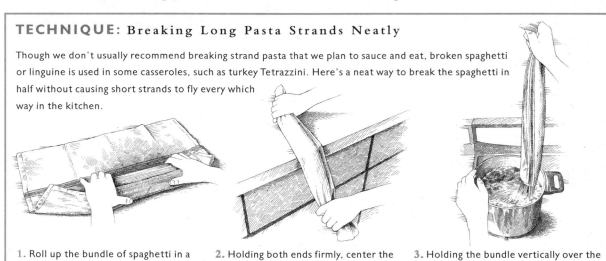

1. Roll up the bundle of spaghetti in a kitchen towel that overlaps the pasta by 3 or 4 inches at both ends.

2. Holding both ends firmly, center the rolled bundle over the edge of a counter. Push down with both hands to break the pasta in the middle of the bundle.

3. Holding the bundle vertically over the pot of boiling water, release the bottom of the towel so that the pasta slides neatly into the pot.

2. FOR THE FILLING: Increase oven temperature to 450 degrees. Heat 2 tablespoons butter in large skillet over medium heat until foaming subsides; add mushrooms and onions and sauté, stirring frequently, until liquid from mushrooms evaporates, 12 to 15 minutes. Season with salt and pepper to taste; transfer to medium bowl and set aside. Clean skillet.

3. Meanwhile, bring 4 quarts water to a boil in large pot. Add 1 tablespoon salt and pasta and cook until al dente. Reserve ¼ cup cooking water, drain spaghetti, and return to pot with reserved liquid.

4. Melt remaining 6 tablespoons butter in cleaned skillet over medium heat. When foam subsides, whisk in flour and cook, whisking constantly, until flour turns golden, 1 to 2 minutes. Whisking constantly, gradually add chicken stock. Turn heat to medium-high and simmer until mixture thickens, 3 to 4 minutes. Off heat, whisk in sherry, Parmesan, nutmeg, lemon juice, thyme, and ½ teaspoon salt. Add sauce, sautéed vegetables, peas, and turkey to spaghetti and mix well; adjust seasonings to taste.

5. Turn mixture into buttered 9 by 13-inch gratin dish (or other shallow, ovenproof baking dish of similar size), sprinkle evenly with reserved bread crumbs, and bake until bread crumbs brown and mixture is bubbly, 13 to 15 minutes. Serve immediately.

EQUIPMENT CORNER: Gratin Dishes

WE FOUND THAT A WIDE, SHALLOW DISH IS THE KEY TO good turkey Tetrazzini. A gratin dish (gratin means crust and usually refers to a cheese or bread crumb topping that browns in a hot oven) maximizes the surface area while giving the heat easy access to the crumbs on top. A tour of any kitchen store, however, doesn't limit the possibilities for dishes that fit this bill. We found eight possible options, priced from $7 to $160, including several specifically labeled "gratin dishes" as well as those sold as "casserole dishes" or "oval dishes." We tested these eight dishes to see what differences, if any, we could find.

First and foremost, you must match the surface area of the dish with the recipe. We found that a dish that is too small caused the crumbs to pack on top of one another, creating a layer beneath the surface that never browned. On the other hand, a dish that is too large caused the crumbs to scatter too far apart so that no cohesive layer could form. A dish that is perfect for one recipe might not work in another, so pay attention to sizes in recipes.

We also found the depth of the dish to be important. The 4-inch-high sides of the Corning Ware 4-quart oval roaster ($21.99) cast a shadow over the contents that prevented the edges from browning. Most dishes have shallower sides (we found 2 inches to be ideal) that promote browning.

Another factor is material. Le Creuset's 14-inch oval dish is made of enameled cast-iron, which heats up very slowly. The gratins and casseroles made in this dish were still cool by the time the crust was toasted. We found that lighter, faster-heating materials, such as glass, porcelain, and stainless steel, are better choices for a gratin dish.

Which dish should you buy? We produced hot, nicely browned gratins in several dishes—the Pyrex 2-quart casserole dish ($7), the Emile Henry 13-inch oval dish ($35), the Apilco #14 oval au gratin dish ($68), and the All Clad Stainless oval au gratin dish ($160). All these dishes have shallow sides, between 1¾ and 2 inches high. More money might buy better looks, but it doesn't buy better performance.

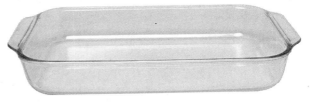

BEST GRATIN DISH
We found that a Pyrex casserole dish, available in any hardware store or kitchen shop, performs well and costs a fraction of the price of other options.

Unlike a fork, tongs won't puncture pork chops and let the juices run out. Tongs are our first choice for turning all meats as they cook.

PORK CHOPS *two ways*

CHAPTER 13

We love a juicy, flavorful pork chop. Too bad most pork chops are dry and bland. The pork industry has reduced the fat in pigs by 50 percent since the 1950s. Yes, pork is now the "other white meat," nearly as lean as chicken. But along with all that fat went flavor and juiciness.

Because modern pork is so lean, the home cook has to use new cooking methods to get good results. Well-done pork chops will be tough as shoe leather and won't taste much better. When grilling, this means cooking the chops until they are just a touch rosy in the center. Brining—soaking foods in a solution of water, salt, and sometimes sugar—is another option we wanted to consider.

On the stovetop, we like old-fashioned smothered pork chops in a rich onion gravy. This recipe suffers from twin problems—the pork is tough (not tender, as it should be) and the gravy often starts with canned soup and tastes artificial and pasty. We knew we could do better.

GRILLED PORK CHOPS

WHAT WE WANTED: Thick-cut pork chops that are seared and crispy outside and juicy and perfectly cooked inside.

Burgers and chicken are predictable grilling fare, but throw a thick, juicy pork chop on the fire and you have something exceptional, at least in theory. The reality of many a grilled pork chop is a burnt exterior, raw interior, tough meat, nary a hint of flavor—the list goes on. We were looking for perfection: a plump, Rubenesque chop with a seared crust reminiscent of chiaroscuro and an interior that would be juicy and flavorful all the way to the bone. We wanted a chop that looked and tasted so good that it transcended the far reaches of backyard grilling and became art.

Thick pork chops usually come from the loin of the pig, which runs from the shoulder to the hip (see Getting It Right on page 170). To determine which cut would be best, we conducted a blind taste test with four different chops, starting with the blade chop, which is from the shoulder end, or front, of the loin. Because the shoulder region of the loin has the most fat and is riddled with connective tissue, tasters found the blade chops to be full of flavor but also tough and chewy. At the hip end of the loin are the sirloin chops. These were dry, somewhat tasteless, and a bit tough. Moving on to the center of the loin, we tested the center-cut chop and the rib chop. Although both were tender and flavorful, tasters preferred the rib chops, which were juicy and well marbled with fat.

Although rib chops are flavorful on their own, we wanted to see if we could boost their flavor by using a spice rub, marinade, or brine. We tested two types of rub: dry and wet. The wet rubs, made with spices and a liquid, gave the chops good flavor but also caused their exterior to turn syrupy. Tasters preferred the dry rubs, which combine potent dried spices with sugar to create big flavor and a crisp crust.

Next we tried marinating the chops in an acidic oil mixture flavored with herbs and garlic. While the marinade succeeded in flavoring the exterior of the chops, it did little for the interior. Moreover, the meat took on a slimy texture that prohibited formation of a good crust.

Finally, we tried brining, a method we often turn to here at America's Test Kitchen, in which lean cuts of meat (usually pork or poultry) are soaked in a solution of water and salt and sometimes sugar. (Brining yields moist, well-seasoned meat and poultry that are hard to overcook, an important factor when grilling.) The brined chops were well seasoned throughout, not just on the surface. They were also extremely juicy—each bite was full of moist, seasoned pork flavor, complemented by the warm crunch of the spice rub.

It was now time to grill. As a preliminary test, we pitted hardwood charcoal against the more traditional charcoal briquettes. After grilling a few chops over each, we found we preferred the hardwood for its intensely hot fire and slightly smoky flavor. As for the fire itself, we always begin testing with a single-level fire—that is, a fire of even and generally high heat made by spreading coals evenly across the grill. We threw the chops over the fire and watched as they browned to a beautiful bronze within minutes. But when we pulled the chops off the grill and cut into one, it was rare at the bone. Moderating the temperature of the fire only drew out the cooking time and sacrificed the deep, caramelized crust we had achieved over high heat.

Moving next to a two-level fire, which is achieved by banking more hot coals on one side of the grill than on the other, we tried a multitude of temperature combinations, each time starting the chops over high heat to develop a nicely browned crust. Moving the chops from high to medium, high to low, and high to no heat were all tested, but none of these combinations produced a thoroughly cooked interior in a reasonable amount of time. Throwing the grill lid back on after the initial sear cooked the chops all the way through—a breakthrough to be sure—but the flavor of the meat was adversely affected. (The inside of most charcoal grill covers is coated with a charcoal residue that readily imparts bitter, spent flavors to foods.) Seizing on the notion of covering the chops for part of the cooking time, we turned to a handy disposable aluminum roasting pan to solve the problem. We threw the pan over the chops after searing them over high heat and moving them to the cooler part of the grill. This time we had a crisp crust, juicy meat, and no off flavors.

In our eagerness to serve these perfect chops, we cut into them right off the grill and watched as the juices ran out onto the plate. We allowed the next round of chops to sit covered under the foil pan for five minutes. When we cut into the chops this time, only a little of the juice was expelled. We were surprised, however, to find that these chops were slightly tougher than the chops that did not rest. We took the internal temperature and found that it was now nearly 165 degrees—overcooked in our book. (At 145 degrees, pork is cooked, safe to eat, and still juicy. Temperatures above 150 degrees yield dry, tough meat.) We cooked one more batch of chops and this time took them off the grill earlier, once they had reached an internal temperature of 135 degrees, and let them sit under the foil pan for a good five minutes. Thanks to the residual heat left in the bone, the temperature shot up an average of 10 to 15 degrees, bringing the meat into that desirable range of 145 to 150. Magic. Or perhaps this was art.

WHAT WE LEARNED: Buy bone-in rib chops, brine them to promote juiciness, sear them quickly, and then allow the interior of the chop to finish cooking over a cooler part of the grill and under a disposable aluminum pan. Pull the chops from the grill when they reach an internal temperature of 135 degrees, cover them with a foil pan, and let the chops rest until the temperature rises 10 to 15 degrees higher and the juices are redistributed in the meat.

CHARCOAL-GRILLED PORK CHOPS serves 4

Rib loin chops are our top choice for their big flavor and juiciness. Spice rubs add a lot of flavor for very little effort, but the chops can also be seasoned with pepper alone just before grilling. You will need a large disposable aluminum roasting pan to cover the chops and help them finish cooking through to the bone.

¾ cup kosher salt or 6 tablespoons table salt
6 tablespoons sugar
4 bone-in pork loin rib chops or center-cut loin chops, each 1½ inches thick (about 3 pounds total)
1 recipe spice rub (recipes follow) or ground black pepper

1. Dissolve salt and sugar in 3 quarts cold water in 2-gallon zipper-lock plastic bag. Add chops and seal bag, pressing out as much air as possible. (Alternatively, divide brine and chops evenly between two 1-gallon zipper-lock bags.) Refrigerate, turning bag once, until fully seasoned, about 1 hour. Remove chops from brine and dry thoroughly with paper towels. Coat chops with spice rub or season generously with pepper.

2. Ignite large chimney starter filled with hardwood charcoal (about 6 quarts) and burn until covered with thin coating of light gray ash. Build two-level fire by stacking most of coals on one side of grill and arranging remaining coals in single layer on other side. Set cooking grate in place, cover grill with lid, and let grate heat up, about 5 minutes. Use wire brush to scrape cooking grate clean.

3. Cook chops, uncovered, over hotter part of grill until browned on each side, 2½ to 3 minutes per side. Move chops to cooler part of grill and cover with disposable

aluminum roasting pan. Continue grilling, turning once, until instant-read thermometer inserted through side of chop and away from bone registers 135 degrees, 7 to 9 minutes longer. Transfer chops to platter; cover with foil pan, and let rest 5 minutes. Internal temperature should rise to 145 degrees. Serve immediately.

VARIATION

GAS-GRILLED PORK CHOPS

Because gas grill lids don't build up a residue that can impart an off flavor to foods (as charcoal grills do), they can be used to concentrate heat to cook the pork chops through; there's no need for a disposable roasting pan.

Follow step 1 of recipe for Charcoal-Grilled Pork Chops. Light grill and turn all burners to high; cover and heat grill 15 minutes. Use wire brush to scrape cooking grate clean. Turn off all but one burner. Place chops over hotter part of grill, cover, and cook until browned on each side, 3 to 4 minutes per side. Move chops to cooler side of grill. Cover and continue cooking, turning once, until instant-read thermometer inserted through side of chop and away from bone registers 135 degrees, 7 to 9 minutes longer. Transfer chops to platter, tent loosely with foil, and let rest 5 minutes. Internal temperature should rise to 145 degrees. Serve immediately.

BASIC SPICE RUB FOR PORK CHOPS

makes ¼ cup, enough for 4 chops

1 tablespoon ground cumin
1 tablespoon chili powder
1 tablespoon curry powder
1 teaspoon ground black pepper
2 teaspoons brown sugar

Combine all ingredients in small bowl.

GETTING IT RIGHT: Shopping for Chops

Pork chops come from the loin of the pig. A whole pork loin weighs 14 to 17 pounds and can be cut into blade chops, rib chops, center-cut chops, and sirloin chops. The loin muscle runs the entire length of the backbone. Starting midway back, the tenderloin muscle runs along the opposite side of the backbone. Center-cut and sirloin chops contain both kinds of muscle. We found that the tenderloin cooks more quickly than the loin and can dry out. This is one reason why we prefer rib chops, which contain only loin meat. Following are tasters' impressions after sampling four different chops cut from the loin. Rib chops were tasters' top choice, followed by center-cut chops.

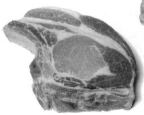

BLADE CHOP
Fattiest, toughest, juiciest, most flavor

RIB CHOP
Some fat, relatively tender, juicy, great flavor

CENTER-CUT CHOP
Little fat, relatively tender, less juicy, good flavor

SIRLOIN CHOP
Tough, quite dry, little flavor

INDIAN SPICE RUB FOR PORK CHOPS

makes scant ¼ cup, enough for 4 chops

- 1 tablespoon fennel seeds
- 1 tablespoon ground cumin
- 1 teaspoon ground coriander
- 1 teaspoon ground cardamom
- 1 teaspoon dry mustard
- ½ teaspoon ground cinnamon
- ¼ teaspoon ground cloves
- 2 teaspoons brown sugar

Grind fennel seeds to powder in spice grinder. Mix with remaining ingredients in small bowl.

EQUIPMENT CORNER: Gas Grills

GAS GRILLS NOW ACCOUNT FOR 6 OUT OF EVERY 10 GRILLS SOLD IN this country. The reasons for their increasing popularity are clear: The fire is easy to light and control. We tested six grills from the leading manufacturers and came to the following conclusions.

In general, we found that you get what you pay for. Inexpensive gas grills, priced at $200 or less, are generally inferior. If you are willing to spend more money (about $350), you can buy a gas grill that works extremely well, with results that can compete with the charcoal grill.

Several features and design elements separate a good gas grill from a poor one. A built-in thermometer that registers real numbers (not just low, medium, and hot) is essential. A gauge that tells you how much gas is left in the tank is also a plus. As you might expect, a large grill offers the cook more possibilities. Unless the cooking surface has an area of at least 400 square inches, you will be able to cook only one slab of ribs at a time. In addition to size, the number of burners is critical. It's not possible to cook by indirect heat on a grill with only one burner because the burner is usually positioned in the center of the grill and the "cool" parts of the grill are too small to accommodate most foods. Indirect

cooking requires a grill with at least two burners. With one burner on and one burner off, at least half of the grill will be cool enough for slow cooking.

We found that most gas grills are plenty hot. A bigger problem is that gas grills are often unable to sustain temperatures low enough for barbecuing. Many of the cheaper grills we tested were unable to barbecue a brisket without burning the exterior before the meat was tender. A good grill will maintain a temperature of 250 degrees when the lid is down and just one burner is lit and turned to low.

Perhaps the most shocking conclusion we came to during our testing of gas grills concerned flare-ups. We found that lava rocks soak up dripping fat and will catch fire as

TECHNIQUE:
Checking the Fuel Level in a Tank

There's nothing worse than running out of fuel halfway through grilling. If your grill doesn't have a gas gauge, use this technique to estimate how much gas is left in the tank.

1. Bring a cup or so of water to a boil in a small saucepan or glass measuring cup (if using the microwave). Pour the water over the side of the tank.

2. Feel the metal with your hand. Where the water has succeeded in warming the tank, it is empty; where the tank remains cool to the touch, there is still propane inside.

soon as there is some sort of flare-up. Several times we moved flaming chicken parts to the cool side of the grill (without a lit burner), and they still flamed from below for several minutes. It wasn't the chicken that was on fire, it was the lava rocks, which had caught fire even though the burner underneath them was cool.

Lava rocks are not the sole reason for flare-ups. Poor design that traps grease on the bottom of the grill doesn't help either. We consider a drainage system mandatory. The bottom of the cooking chamber should be sloped so that fat runs through an opening in the center and into a drip pan below.

Our favorites among the grills tested, Weber grills, do not have lava rocks. Bars, made from steel coated with porcelain-enamel and shaped like an upside-down V, channel fat down into the bottom of the grill and eventually into a drip pan attached to the underside of the cooking chamber. We find this drainage system to be far superior to other options. For all of these reasons, our favorite grills are the Weber Genesis Silver series, which comes in three different models.

BEST GAS GRILL

We tested grills from leading manufacturers and preferred the Weber Genesis Silver series. The Silver C (seen here) costs $500 and boasts three main grilling burners plus a side burner for heating sauces, beans, or other side dishes. The Silver B ($450) is the same grill minus the side burner. The Silver A ($350) has just two grilling burners. See www.cooksillustrated.com for up-to-date prices and mail-order sources for top-rated products.

GETTING IT RIGHT: Anatomy of a Gas Grill

When shopping for a gas grill, make sure the model you choose has a temperature gauge that registers real numbers, not just low, medium, and high. A fuel gauge, which lets you know when the tank is running low, is another helpful feature.

A warming rack can be useful, but you may want to remove it before grilling for full access to the cooking surface. Weber grills, our top choices, have flavorizer bars—we prefer them to lava rocks—which help direct fat down into the drip pan. To avoid flare-ups, make sure to buy a grill with a good system for draining fat.

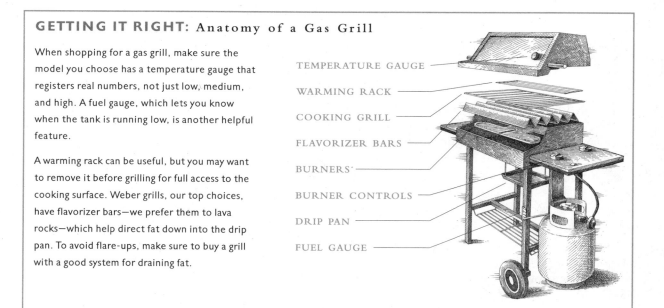

TEMPERATURE GAUGE

WARMING RACK

COOKING GRILL

FLAVORIZER BARS

BURNERS

BURNER CONTROLS

DRIP PAN

FUEL GAUGE

SCIENCE DESK:
Why Are Bone-In Chops Better?

WE KNEW FROM PAST EXPERIENCE THAT BONE-IN CHOPS taste better than boneless chops, but we wanted to test this notion more systemically. To find out how boneless chops would fare on the grill, we removed the bones from several rib chops, grilled them, and compared them with their bone-in counterparts in a blind taste test. (We took the meat off the grilled bone-in chops and then sliced the meat from both chops so as not to tip off tasters.) The results were clear. Every taster preferred the meat that had been cooked on the bone. It was much more juicy and had more pork flavor than the meat cooked without the bone. We contacted several food scientists, who offered a few explanations.

First, because bone is a poor conductor of heat, the meat located next to the bone doesn't cook as quickly as the rest. Although this factor doesn't alter the cooking time

TECHNIQUE:
Protecting Gas Grill Controls

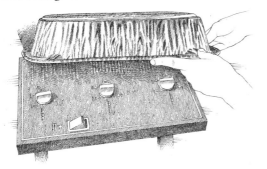

The ignition and burner control knobs on some gas grills can be persnickety if they get wet or dirty from exposure to the elements, especially if the grill is kept outdoors in the snow during the winter. If you don't own a grill cover, try inverting a disposable aluminum roasting pan over the control panel and tape it in place on either end with duct or electrical tape.

significantly, having a section of the pork chop cook at a slightly slower rate contributes to a juicier end product.

The bone also insulates the muscle closest to it, protecting it from exposure to the air. In a boneless chop, a larger area of muscle is exposed, so more of the flavorful juices evaporate during grilling.

Finally, fat is a crucial source of flavor, and, as it melts during cooking, it also increases the perceived juiciness. In certain cuts, especially ribs and chops, deposits of fat are located next to the bone. When the bone is removed, some fat is removed as well. With less fat, the boneless chops cook up with less pork flavor and seem drier.

TASTING LAB: Enhanced Pork

TODAY'S PORK IS 50 PERCENT LEANER THAN ITS COUNTER-part in the 1950s, and less fat means less flavor and moisture. The industry has addressed this issue by introducing a product called enhanced pork, meat injected with a solution of water, salt, and sodium phosphate. The idea is to both season the pork and keep it from drying out. (The sodium phosphate increases the pH of the meat, which improves its water-retention abilities.) We wondered if we could skip brining and save time by using enhanced pork.

In a side-by-side test, we compared enhanced and unenhanced pork chops as well as brined versions of both. The enhanced pork was salty and had a somewhat artificial flavor. When brined, these chops were extremely salty and inedible. The unenhanced pork that was not brined was dry and bland. The unenhanced pork that had been brined was juicy and well seasoned—it was the clear winner.

As far as we are concerned, the benefits of brining pork are clear. First, you control the salt and avoid any artificial aftertaste. Second, brining guarantees moist meat (as long as you don't overcook pork).

During our research, we found a few supermarkets that carried only enhanced pork. If you must buy enhanced pork, skip the brining step in our grilled pork chop recipe.

SMOTHERED PORK CHOPS

WHAT WE WANTED: Tender, flavorful chops complemented by a heady onion gravy with a satiny, just-thick-enough texture.

Smothered pork chops, a homey dish of chops braised in deeply flavored onion gravy, are folksy, not fancy; denim, not worsted wool. Despite a straightforward cooking process—brown the chops, remove them from the pan, brown the onions, return the chops and cover them with the onions and gravy (hence the term smothered), and braise until tender—initial recipe tests produced bland, dry pork, and near-tasteless gravies with woeful consistencies ranging from pasty to processed to gelatinous to watery.

Poor texture and shallow flavor robs smothered pork chops of their savory-sweet glory. To get it right, we knew we'd have to identify the best chop and the best way to cook it. And the gravy was no less important.

Some of our research recipes specified sirloin chops, which are cut from the rear end of the loin. Our tasters found this cut a little dry and often unavailable. Blade chops, cut from the far front end of the loin, were juicier but suffered the same spotty availability. Of the two remaining types of chops, center-cut loin and rib, we found the latter to be the juiciest and most flavorful because it had a bit more fat (see Getting It Right on page 170).

We tried rib chops as thick as 1½ inches and as thin as ½ inch and were shocked when tasters unanimously chose the thin ½-inch chops. Thick chops overwhelmed the gravy, which we felt should share equal billing with the meat. Thin chops also picked up more onion flavor during cooking. We also tried boneless chops, but they turned out dry so we decided to stick with bone-in for optimum juiciness.

Also in the service of juiciness and thorough seasoning, we indulged our passion for brining by soaking the chops in a simple salt-sugar-water solution before cooking them. It turned out that brining was ill-suited to this dish for two reasons. First, these chops cook in a moist environment provided by the gravy, so why spend time instilling extra moisture to protect them from the harsh, dry heat of grilling, searing, or roasting? Second, no matter how we adjusted the salinity of the brine, the salt-infused meat caused the gravy to become intolerably salty.

Last we tackled the question of cooking time. Although we prefer to slightly undercook pork to ensure tenderness, this is one application where further cooking was necessary because we wanted to infuse the meat with the flavor of the gravy and onions. After their initial browning, the chops registered a rosy 140 degrees on an instant-read thermometer. They were cooked through and tender, but since they had yet to be smothered, they had none of the onion flavor we demanded. Fifteen minutes of braising in the gravy boosted the flavor but toughened the chops, which now registered almost 200 degrees. At that temperature, the meat fibers have contracted and expelled moisture, but the fat and connective tissue between the fibers, called collagen, have not had a chance to melt fully and turn into gelatin. It is this gelatin that makes braised meats especially rich and tender. Another 15 minutes of braising time solved the problem. At this point, the chops registered 210 degrees, and the extra time allowed the fat and collagen to melt completely, so the meat was tender and succulent as well as oniony from the gravy.

It was important that the gravy build on the flavor of the browned pork chops. The canned, condensed soup called for in some recipes produced gravies that tasted processed and glue-like. Water produced a weak, thin gravy, but chicken stock improved the picture, adding much-needed flavor.

For liquid to morph into gravy, it must be thickened. Cornstarch is an easy solution, but it resulted in a gelatinous, translucent sauce that looked and felt wrong. Next we tried adding flour in three different ways. Flouring the chops before browning turned their exteriors gummy and left the

gravy with a chalky mouthfeel. Flouring the onions left the gravy tasting of raw flour. Last, we called upon a roux, a mixture of flour and fat (in this case, vegetable oil) cooked together. This occasioned the need for an extra pan that we'd hoped to avoid, but the results were fantastic. The roux was easy to make, it thickened the sauce reliably without adding the taste of raw flour, and it gave the gravy both a smooth finish and another layer of flavor that was slightly nutty.

The roux was good, but we tried to improve it with two oft-used refinements. First, we fried a couple of slices of bacon and substituted the rendered fat for the vegetable oil in the roux. What a hit! The sweet/salty/smoky bacon flavor underscored and deepened all of the other flavors in the dish. Beyond that, we followed in the footsteps of many a gravymaster who has eked out even more flavor from the roux by browning it for five minutes to the shade of peanut butter. Cooking the flour this way unlocks a rich, toasty flavor that builds as the shade deepens. Both techniques are widespread and justly popular, as they turned out to be huge flavor builders.

The onions play a title role in the gravy. We tried them minced, chopped, and sliced both thick and thin. Thin-sliced onions cooked to a melting texture that was our favorite. We tried different quantities of onions, from one to four, for four pork chops and found that two was best. We tried simply softening the onions until they were translucent versus cooking them for a few more minutes until their edges browned, a winning technique that accentuated their natural sweetness. Perhaps the most important onion test was trying different types, including standard-issue supermarket yellow onions, red onions, and sweet Vidalia onions. The yellow onions triumphed for their "deep brown hue" and "balanced flavor." By comparison, tasters found the red onions to be harsh tasting and ugly and the Vidalias to be "bland" and "wan" looking.

The onions cook in the same pan used to brown the chops. We wanted to make sure that the onions released enough moisture to dissolve (or deglaze) the flavorful, sticky, brown bits (called fond) left in the pan by the chops, so we salted them lightly. The heat and salt worked together to jumpstart the breakdown of the onions' cell walls, which set their juices flowing. We also added 2 tablespoons of water to the pan for insurance.

Our last flavor tweak was an unusual one for us—we eliminated the salt we'd be using to season the chops themselves. Tasters agreed that the salt added to the onions, along with the naturally salty bacon and chicken stock and the garlic, thyme, and bay used to build extra flavor in the gravy, seasoned the dish adequately. These chops were hearty, deeply flavored, and comforting.

WHAT WE LEARNED: For a nice balance with the gravy and to allow for the best absorption of the gravy's flavors, use thin, not thick, rib chops. Brown them well to build the flavor for the gravy, make a nut-brown, bacon-flavored roux to further build flavor, and add thinly sliced yellow onions that will give up their moisture easily. For tender chops, combine the sauce and browned chops and braise for a full 30 minutes.

SMOTHERED PORK CHOPS serves 4

Use low-sodium chicken broth in this recipe; regular chicken broth can result in an overseasoned sauce. Serve smothered chops with a starch to soak up the rich gravy. Simple egg noodles was the test kitchen favorite, but rice or mashed potatoes also taste great.

    3   ounces bacon (about 3 slices), cut into ¼-inch
        pieces
    2   tablespoons all-purpose flour
 1¾   cups canned low-sodium chicken broth
        Vegetable oil
    4   bone-in pork loin rib chops, ½ to ¾ inch thick
        Ground black pepper
    2   medium yellow onions, halved pole to pole and
        sliced thin (about 3½ cups)
        Salt
    2   tablespoons water
    2   medium garlic cloves, pressed through garlic
        press or minced (about 2 teaspoons)
    1   teaspoon minced fresh thyme leaves
    2   bay leaves
    1   tablespoon minced fresh parsley leaves

1. Fry bacon in small saucepan over medium heat, stirring occasionally, until lightly browned and fat is rendered, 8 to 10 minutes. Using slotted spoon, transfer bacon to paper towel–lined plate, leaving fat in saucepan (you should have 2 tablespoons bacon fat; if not, supplement with vegetable oil). Reduce heat to medium-low and gradually whisk flour into fat until smooth. Cook, whisking frequently, until mixture is light brown, about the color of peanut butter, about 5 minutes. Whisk in chicken broth in slow, steady stream; increase heat to medium-high and bring to boil, stirring occasionally; cover and set aside off heat.

2. Heat 1 tablespoon oil in 12-inch skillet over high heat until smoking. Meanwhile, dry pork chops with paper towels and sprinkle with ½ teaspoon pepper. Brown chops in single layer until deep golden on first side, about 3 minutes. Flip chops and cook until browned on second side, about 3 minutes longer. Transfer chops to large plate and set aside.

3. Reduce heat to medium and add 1 tablespoon oil, onions, ¼ teaspoon salt, and water to now-empty skillet. Using wooden spoon, scrape up browned bits on pan bottom; cook, stirring frequently, until onions are softened and browned around edges, about 5 minutes. Stir in garlic and thyme and cook until fragrant, about 30 seconds longer. Return chops to skillet in single layer, covering chops with onions. Pour in warm sauce and any juices collected from pork; add bay leaves. Cover, reduce heat to low, and simmer until pork is tender and paring knife inserted into chops meets very little resistance, about 30 minutes.

4. Transfer chops to warmed serving platter and tent with foil. Increase heat to medium-high and simmer sauce rapidly, stirring frequently, until thickened to gravy-like consistency, about 5 minutes. Discard bay leaves, stir in parsley, and adjust seasonings with salt and pepper. Cover chops with sauce, sprinkle with reserved bacon, and serve immediately.

VARIATIONS

SMOTHERED PORK CHOPS WITH CIDER AND APPLES

Follow recipe for Smothered Pork Chops, substituting apple cider for chicken broth and 1 large or 2 small Granny Smith apples, peeled, cored, and cut into ⅓-inch wedges, for one of the onions, and increasing salt added to onion and apple to ½ teaspoon.

SMOTHERED PORK CHOPS WITH SPICY COLLARD GREENS

Follow recipe for Smothered Pork Chops, increasing oil in step 3 to 2 tablespoons, omitting one onion, and increasing garlic to 4 cloves. Just before returning browned chops to pan in step 3, add 4 cups thinly sliced collard greens and ½ teaspoon crushed red pepper flakes.

SCIENCE DESK: How Braising Works

WHEN YOU GRILL PORK CHOPS YOU WANT TO TAKE THEM off the grill when they are still rosy at the center and the internal temperature registers just 135 degrees. Let the chops stay on the grill any longer (say, until they reach an internal temperature of 160 degrees) and they will be tough and dry. When you braise pork chops, as in the smothered pork chop recipe, you cook them through to an internal temperature of 210 degrees. So how come smothered pork chops are tender but overcooked grilled pork chops are tough and dry?

When you cook pork chops, the bonds between the protein and water rupture. At the same time, the bonds between individual protein molecules become stronger and tighter. In fact, these bonds become so tight that they drive out water from the meat. Eventually, the pork chops become tough and dry.

However, once the internal temperature of the meat reaches about 150 degrees, a second process begins. Pork chops contain a fair amount of collagen, a connective tissue that will begin to melt and become gelatin-like as the temperature climbs. The melted collagen makes the pork chops seem tender and moist. Because collagen won't completely melt until the internal temperature reaches 200 degrees, you must really cook the pork to make full use of this phenomenon.

So braised pork chops cooked to a high internal temperature will seem more moist and more tender than braised chops cooked to a lower internal temperature. That's the magic of collagen.

GETTING IT RIGHT: Develop Flavor in Every Step

Brown is good when it comes to flavor. Cooking each component fully contributes greater flavor to the finished dish.

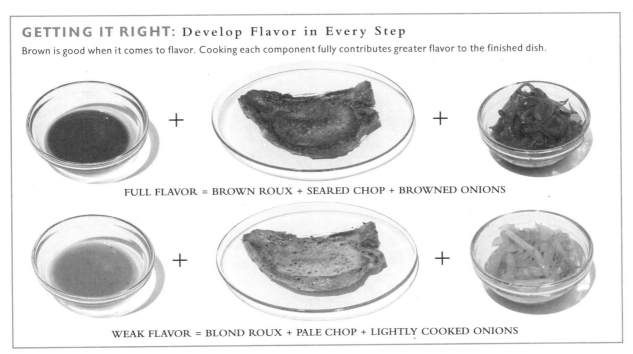

FULL FLAVOR = BROWN ROUX + SEARED CHOP + BROWNED ONIONS

WEAK FLAVOR = BLOND ROUX + PALE CHOP + LIGHTLY COOKED ONIONS

All-American potato salad adds hard-boiled eggs and minced sweet pickles to perfectly cooked potatoes.

BACKYARD bbq

CHAPTER 14

IN THIS CHAPTER

THE RECIPES

Barbecued Baby Back Ribs on a
    Charcoal Grill
Barbecued Baby Back Ribs on a
    Gas Grill

American Potato Salad with
    Hard-Boiled Eggs and Sweet
    Pickles
Foolproof Hard-Boiled Eggs

EQUIPMENT CORNER

Wood Chunks and Chips

TASTING LAB

Barbecue Sauces

On a hot summer's day, life doesn't get much better than a big, juicy, smoky slab of spicy, mouth-watering ribs. But more often than not, baby back ribs cooked at home come out tasting like dry shoe leather on a bone. Given the expense (two slabs, enough to feed four people, run about $24) and time commitment (many recipes require half a day), bad ribs are a true culinary disaster. Our goal was to produce flavorful, juicy, tender ribs that would be well worth the time, money, and effort.

Potato salad is the natural accompaniment to ribs, and an American version, with mayonnaise, hard-boiled eggs, and sweet pickles, is classic. Potato salad is easy to prepare, but most recipes fail on one of two counts: The potatoes are watery, sloppy-looking, or mushy, or the dressing is dull and heavy. We wanted to fix both problems and create a salad worthy of the finest ribs.

BARBECUED BABY BACK RIBS

WHAT WE WANTED: Ribs barbecued at home can be flavorless and dry. We wanted lots of smoky flavor and moist, tender meat.

Great baby back ribs start at the meat counter. We quickly learned that you have to shop carefully. Unfortunately, labeling of pork ribs can be confusing. Some slabs are labeled "baby back ribs," while other, seemingly identical ribs are labeled "loin back ribs." After a bit of detective work, we learned that the only difference is weight. Both types of ribs are taken from the upper portion of a young hog's rib cage near the backbone (see the illustration on page 181) and should have 11 to 13 bones. A slab (or rack) of loin back ribs generally comes from a larger pig and weighs more than 1¾ pounds; a slab of ribs weighing less is referred to as baby back ribs. (That being said, most restaurants don't follow this rule, using the term baby back no matter what they've got because it sounds better.) During testing, we came to prefer loin back ribs because they are meatier.

There is one other shopping issue to consider. Beware of racks with bare bone peeking through the meat (along the center of the bones). This means that the butcher took off more meat than necessary, robbing you and your guests of full, meaty portions. Once you've purchased the ribs, there remains the question of whether the skin-like membrane located on the "bone side" of the ribs should be left on during cooking. One theory holds that it prevents smoke and spice from penetrating the meat, while some rib experts say that removing it robs the ribs of flavor and moisture. We found that the skin did not interfere with flavor; in fact, it helped to form a spicy, crispy crust.

It was time to start cooking. Our first step was to research the range of grilling times and techniques called for in other recipes. Most recommend a total cooking time of 1½ to 3 hours. Some use a very hot grill, while others use a moderate grill. We tested all of these recipes and found the resulting ribs to be extremely tough. High-heat cooking was particularly troublesome, as it quickly dried out the meat. Ribs cooked over moderate heat for three hours were better, but they were still too tough.

We realized that the only way to go was the classic "low and slow" method. We built a two-level fire, in which only half of the grill is covered with charcoal, thinking it would be best to smoke the ribs indirectly—on the coal-less side of the grill—to prevent overcooking. (Two full racks of ribs fit on one side of a 22-inch grill.) To add flavor, we placed soaked wood chunks on the bed of coals and then put the cooking grate in place and laid down the spice-rubbed ribs. Finally, we put the grill cover in place, with the vent holes over the ribs to help draw heat and smoke past the meat.

We found that maintaining a temperature between 275

and 300 degrees for four hours produced ribs that were tasty and tender, with meat that fell off the bone. Decent ribs could be had in less time, but they weren't as tender as those cooked for a full four hours. It's easy to tell when the ribs are ready—the meat pulls away from the bone when the ribs are gently twisted.

The problem was that the dry heat of the grill produced ribs that were not as moist as we would have liked. Our next test, then, was to cook the ribs halfway in an oven, using steam, and to finish them on the grill. These ribs were more moist, but now flavor was the problem; these ribs lacked the intense smokiness of ribs cooked entirely on the grill. Hoping to find another way to add moisture, we simmered the ribs in water for two hours. This robbed them of valuable pork flavor.

It then occurred to us that brining the ribs prior to cooking them might be the solution. We used our standard brining formula, which when applied to two 2-pound racks of ribs amounted to a two-hour immersion in 4 quarts of cold water mixed with 2 cups of kosher salt and 2 cups of sugar. This method produced, well, two very highly seasoned racks of ribs. Why? Ribs pack much more bone per pound than other cuts of meat, and all of the meat is right there on the exterior, so the brine doesn't have very far to go. We figured that a 2-pound rack of ribs must soak up the brine much more quickly than an equal-sized roast. We cut back the salt, sugar, and brining time by half, and the results were better, but the meat was still too sweet. We cut back the sugar by half once more, and this time the meat was both moist and perfectly seasoned.

These ribs were so good they didn't even need barbecue sauce, although you certainly could add some if you like. A quick rub with an easy-to-mix spice blend before going on the grill gave them just the right warm and savory touch.

WHAT WE LEARNED: **Choose meaty ribs (racks as close to 2 pounds as possible), brine them to add moisture, rub the exterior with spices, and then barbecue over a low fire for four hours for an intense smoky flavor.**

BARBECUED BABY BACK RIBS ON A CHARCOAL GRILL serves 4

For a potent spice flavor, brine and dry the ribs as directed, then coat them with the spice rub, wrap tightly in plastic, and refrigerate overnight before grilling. You will need two wood chunks, each about the size of a lemon, for this recipe.

brine

1   cup kosher salt or ½ cup table salt
½   cup sugar
2   racks (about 2 pounds each) baby back or loin back ribs

spice rub

1   tablespoon plus ½ teaspoon sweet paprika
1½   teaspoons chili powder
1¾   teaspoons ground cumin
1½   teaspoons dark brown sugar
1½   teaspoons kosher salt or ¾ teaspoon table salt
¾   teaspoon dried oregano

GETTING IT RIGHT:
Locating Baby Back Ribs

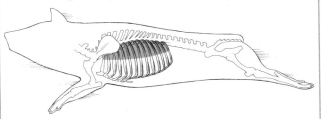

Baby back ribs (also referred to as loin back ribs) are cut from the section of the rib cage closest to the backbone (shaded in the drawing above). Lean center-cut roasts and chops come from the same part of the pig, which explains why baby back ribs can be expensive. Spareribs are cut closer to the belly of the pig, which is also where bacon comes from. Spareribs are larger and much fattier than baby back ribs.

¾   teaspoon ground black pepper
1   teaspoon ground white pepper
½   teaspoon cayenne pepper

1. TO BRINE RIBS: Dissolve salt and sugar in 4 quarts cold water in stockpot or large plastic container. Submerge ribs in brine and refrigerate 1 hour until fully seasoned. Remove ribs from brine and thoroughly pat dry with paper towels.

2. While ribs are brining, cover two 3-inch wood chunks with water in medium bowl; soak wood chunks for 1 hour, then drain and set aside. Combine spice rub ingredients in small bowl. When ribs are out of brine and dried, rub each side of racks with 1 tablespoon spice rub; refrigerate racks 30 minutes.

3. TO BARBECUE RIBS: Open bottom vents on grill. Ignite large chimney starter filled three-quarters with charcoal briquettes (about 4½ quarts, or 65 briquettes) and burn until covered with thin coating of light gray ash. Empty coals into one side of grill, piling them up in mound two or three briquettes high. Place wood chunks on top of charcoal. Put cooking grate in place and cover grill with lid. Let grate heat for 5 minutes, then scrape clean with wire brush.

4. Arrange ribs on cool side of grill parallel to fire; cover, positioning lid so vents are opposite wood chunks to draw smoke through grill (grill temperature should register about 350 degrees on grill thermometer, but will soon start dropping). Cook for 2 hours, until grill temperature drops to about 250 degrees, flipping rib racks, switching their position so that rack that was nearest fire is on outside, and turning racks 180 degrees every 30 minutes; add 10 fresh briquettes to pile of coals. Continue to cook (grill temperature should register 275 to 300 degrees on grill thermometer), flipping, switching, and rotating ribs every 30 minutes, until meat easily pulls away from bone, 1½ to 2 hours longer. Transfer ribs to cutting board, then cut between bones to separate ribs; serve.

BARBECUED BABY BACK RIBS ON A GAS GRILL

If you're using a gas grill, leaving one burner on and the other(s) off mimics the indirect heat method on a charcoal grill. Use wood chips instead of wood chunks and a disposable aluminum pan to hold them.

Follow recipe for Barbecued Baby Back Ribs on a Charcoal Grill through step 2, making following changes: Cover 2 cups wood chips with water and soak 30 minutes, then drain. Place soaked wood chips in small disposable aluminum pan; set pan on burner that will remain on. Turn all burners to high, close lid, and heat grill until chips smoke heavily, about 20 minutes. (If chips ignite, extinguish flames with water from squirt bottle.) Scrape grill grate clean with wire brush; turn off burner(s) without wood chips. Arrange ribs on cool side of grill and cover (grill temperature should

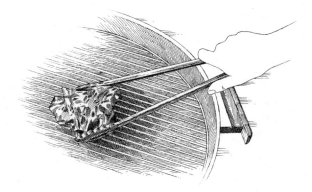

TECHNIQUE:
Brushless Grill Rack Cleaning

Food that is being grilled is much less likely to stick to a clean grate. We recommend cleaning the hot grate with a wire brush designed specifically for that purpose. However, if you find yourself without a brush, you can improvise with a pair of tongs and a crumpled wad of aluminum foil.

register about 275 degrees on grill thermometer). Cook for 4 hours, until meat easily pulls away from bone, flipping rib racks, switching their position so that rack that was nearest fire is on outside, and turning racks 180 degrees every 30 minutes. Transfer ribs to cutting board, then cut between bones to separate ribs; serve.

EQUIPMENT CORNER:
Wood Chunks and Chips

WHEN CHOOSING YOUR SMOKING WOOD, CHOICES probably seem limited, as most hardware stores sell only the two most popular types: hickory and mesquite. But many grilling enthusiasts swear by harder-to-find, more exotic woods. We wondered whether it was worth the bother (and expense) to find these woods. We also wondered about the differences between "chips" and "chunks."

It turns out that both wood chips and wood chunks have a place in the world of barbecue. Chunks, because of

their larger size, burn considerably longer. More smoke means more flavor, so chunks are our choice for a charcoal grill. We soak the chunks in water for an hour to promote smoking and avoid flaming, and then nestle them into the bed of burning coals.

Unfortunately, when placed on the bottom of a gas grill, wood chunks do not get hot enough to smoke. On a gas grill, you must use wood chips, which should be soaked in water for a minimum of 30 minutes (so they smoke rather than ignite) and then placed in a disposable aluminum pan (to shield them from the lit burner).

With the basics covered, our search for rare wood began. We found a wide selection on Web sites that specialize in barbecuing. We chose nine different types and tested them for flavor differences while barbecuing baby back ribs. The ribs had been brined for 1 hour and were coated with spice rub. We wanted to see how each type of wood smoke would stand up to these big flavors.

We must admit, before testing these woods for differences in flavor, we doubted that we would find much. Isn't wood just

---

TECHNIQUE: Emptying Ashes from a Charcoal Grill

No matter how you do it, emptying a kettle grill of cool ashes is a messy procedure. Here's a neat way to fashion a grill scoop out of a plastic 1-quart or 1/2-gallon milk jug with a handle.

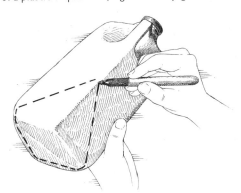

1. Cut off a bottom corner of the jug to form a scoop.

2. The plastic conforms to the curve of the grill bottom, which lets you collect a lot of ashes with a single sweep.

wood? One by one, we were proved wrong. Here are the nine woods we tested with comments about their flavor.

Apple and cherry woods produced slightly sweet and fruity smoke. Peach produced a slightly sweet and very woodsy smoke. Maple, a traditional choice with ham, produced a mellow, sweet smoke, which nicely balanced the spiciness of the ribs. Oak had a very perceptible but not unpleasant acidic note. Hickory produced a strong, pungent, hearty smoke that really stood up to the bold flavors of the spice rub. Pecan, the Southern cousin to hickory, is a bit more mellow but similar to hickory. Alder is the traditional choice with salmon (see page 191), and it has a mild, woodsy flavor. Mesquite is great for grilling because it burns very hot and lends a tangy smoke flavor to food over a short period of time. During the long, slow heat of barbecuing, however, we found the tanginess turned to bitterness. In the end, tasters enjoyed ribs cooked over all of the woods tested, with the exception of mesquite.

BEST WOOD
Wood chunks (left) burn more slowly than wood chips (right) and are our first choice for barbecuing in a charcoal grill. Wood chunks won't work in a gas grill, so use chips and soak them so they smoke rather than ignite.

TASTING LAB: Barbecue Sauce

DESPITE THE BEST OF INTENTIONS, THERE'S NOT ALWAYS time to make barbecue sauce. It's no surprise that many cooks turn to bottled sauces.

We wondered if some brands of bottled barbecue sauce were much better than others. Are the "gourmet" brands worth the extra money, or will a supermarket brand suffice?

We tasted 10 samples to find out. We limited the tasting to tomato-based sauces because they are far and away the most popular and represent what most Americans picture when they think "barbecue sauce."

In general, tasters were not overly impressed with these bottled sauces. Most were much too sweet and had an overly thick, gummy texture. The ingredients responsible were high-fructose corn syrup and food starch. We did find one sauce that everyone agreed was quite good and another three sauces worth considering. Three of these four sauces were more expensive "gourmet," organic offerings, so, at least when it comes to barbecue sauce, more money does buy a better product.

Our favorite sauce is Mad Dog, a boutique brand from Boston. Although the ingredient list is mercifully short (many other sauces have long lists of hard-to-pronounce ingredients), tasters thought this sauce was more complex and balanced than the rest of the pack. It also contained less sugar than most brands and no corn syrup, an ingredient found in all but three of the sauces tested.

Bull's Eye, Sweet Baby Ray's, and Muir Glen received decent scores and mixed comments. Like most supermarket offerings, Bull's Eye is very sweet and has a thick, glossy consistency, but it also delivers a decent hit of smoke, something missing from other mass-market sauces. Tasters liked the strong molasses flavor in the Sweet Baby Ray's and Muir Glen sauces, although neither was an overwhelming favorite. The rest of the sauces were so bad that tasters felt they harmed rather than improved the flavor of plain broiled chicken. With one exception then, this tasting did not uncover products we could get excited about.

As with homemade barbecue sauce, bottled sauces are finishing sauces, not basting sauces. They all contain sweeteners and tomatoes, which will cause foods to burn within minutes after application. Food destined for the grill should not be marinated in barbecue sauce. The food will burn and taste awful. Just brush a little sauce on during the last two or three minutes of the cooking time, and then brush again just before serving.

Rating Barbecue Sauces

WE TASTED 10 BRANDS OF BARBECUE SAUCE, INCLUDING SUPERMARKET BRANDS AS WELL AS SOME "BOUTIQUE" SAUCES sold in upscale markets, dipping broiled chicken in the sauces to evaluate them for flavor and texture. Sauces are listed in order of preference. See www.cooksillustrated.com for up-to-date prices and mail-order sources for top-rated products.

RECOMMENDED

1. Mad Dog Original BBQ Sauce
$5.99 for 19 ounces

The only brand tested without sugar or corn syrup. Molasses delivers modest sweetness. Tasters found this sauce to be "spicy right up front," with smoky, "roasted tomato" flavor.

RECOMMENDED WITH RESERVATIONS

2. Bull's Eye Sweet Hickory Smoke BBQ Sauce
$1.99 for 18 ounces

This "sweet" sauce contains both high-fructose corn syrup (listed first on the label) and molasses (listed fourth). Several tasted complained that "smoke overpowered other flavors," but everyone liked its "glossy" consistency.

RECOMMENDED WITH RESERVATIONS

3. Sweet Baby Ray's Barbecue Sauce
$1.99 for 18 ounces

The first two ingredients are high fructose corn syrup and corn syrup. Not surprisingly, tasters picked up a "strong" corn syrup flavor, but they liked the spice flavors.

RECOMMENDED WITH RESERVATIONS

4. Muir Glen Organic Grill Chef Original Barbecue Sauce
$2.99 for 17 ounces

This sauce is "strong on vinegar and tomato," with a "heavy smoke flavor."

NOT RECOMMENDED

5. Lea and Perrins Original Barbecue Sauce
$2.39 for 18 ounces

Strong, "sweet" tomato flavor could use more "heat" and spices.

NOT RECOMMENDED

6. Gates Original Classic Bar-B-Q Sauce
$5.99 for 18 ounces

"Heavy on the cumin and vinegar" was the verdict about this "thin, loose" sauce.

NOT RECOMMENDED

7. KC Masterpiece Original Barbecue Sauce
$2.29 for 18 ounces

"Big liquid smoke aftertaste," wrote one taster about this smoky-sweet sauce. Others found the sauce is so thick it seemed "more like pudding."

NOT RECOMMENDED

8. Kraft "Slow-Simmered" Original Barbecue Sauce
$1.99 for 18 ounces

This sauce was the only one tested to list vinegar first on the ingredient list. As might be expected, tasters complained about the "sour" flavor.

NOT RECOMMENDED

9. Stubbs Mild Bar-B-Q Sauce
$3.69 for 18 ounces

Tasters did not like the strong hits of vinegar and mustard in this peppery sauce. The "thin, watery" consistency didn't win many fans either.

NOT RECOMMENDED

10. Hunts BBQ Original Recipe Barbecue Sauce
$1.99 for 18 ounces

"Way too sugary" was the overall consensus about this "almost too thick" sauce. Several tasters picked up an "odd maple-cinnamon flavor."

AMERICAN POTATO SALAD

WHAT WE WANTED: A mayonnaise-based potato salad that looks good (no falling-apart, sloppy spuds) and tastes even better.

We decided to focus on a mayonnaise-based salad with hard-boiled eggs, pickles, and celery, the classic accompaniment to any summer picnic or backyard barbecue. We first wanted to know what type of potato to use and how to cook it. Recipe writers seemed split down the middle between starchy potatoes (like russets) and waxy potatoes (like Red Bliss), with starchy praised for being more absorbent and waxy admired for their sturdiness. When making potato salad, we have always just boiled potatoes with the skin on, but steaming, microwaving, roasting, and baking were all options worth trying.

Next, should the potatoes be peeled? If so, when? Some recipes called for cooking potatoes with the skin on, then peeling and seasoning them immediately, working on the assumption that hot potatoes absorb more flavor than cold ones. We wondered if the extra step of seasoning the cooked potatoes with vinegar, salt, and pepper first made any difference. Could we instead just toss all of the ingredients together at the same time?

After boiling, steaming, baking/roasting, and microwaving four different varieties of potatoes—Red Bliss, russets, all-purpose, and Yukon Golds—we found Red Bliss to be the potato of choice and boiling to be the cooking method of choice. Higher-starch potatoes—all-purpose and Yukon Golds as well as russets—are not sturdy enough for salad. They fall apart when cut, making for a sloppy-looking salad.

Next we wanted to see if we could boost flavor at the cooking stage by boiling the potatoes in chicken broth or in water heavily seasoned with bay leaves and garlic cloves. The chicken broth might just as well have been water—there wasn't a hint of evidence that the potatoes had been cooked in broth. The bay leaves and garlic smelled wonderful as the potatoes cooked, but the potatoes were still bland.

The fact that nothing seemed to penetrate the potatoes got us wondering: Does the potato skin act as a barrier? We performed an experiment by cooking two batches of unpeeled potatoes, the first in heavily salted water and the second in unsalted water. We rinsed them quickly under cold running water and tasted. Sure enough, both batches of potatoes tasted exactly the same. We tried boiling peeled potatoes, but they were waterlogged compared with their unpeeled counterparts.

We found the paper-thin skin of the boiled red potato not unpleasant to taste and certainly pleasant to look at in what is often a monochromatic salad. Although this saved the peeling step, we found the skin tended to rip when cutting the potato. Because the skin was particularly susceptible to ripping when the potatoes were very hot, we solved the problem in two ways. First, we cut the potatoes with a serrated knife, which minimized ripping, and second, we let them cool before cutting them.

To find out if the now-cool potatoes would have the capacity to absorb seasoning, we made two salads, letting one cool completely before dressing with vinegar, salt and pepper, and mayonnaise and letting the other cool just till warm and preseasoning with vinegar and salt and pepper well before adding the mayonnaise. (We found the potatoes could still be cut cleanly as long as they were warm but not hot.) The results were clear. The salad made with potatoes seasoned when still warm was zesty and delicious. The other salad was bland in comparison.

WHAT WE LEARNED: For great potato salad, boil unpeeled, low-starch, red-skinned potatoes in unsalted water, cool them slightly, and then cut the potatoes with a serrated knife to minimize tearing of the skin. While the potatoes are still warm, drizzle them with vinegar and season with salt and pepper. When cool, add the mayonnaise and other seasonings.

AMERICAN POTATO SALAD WITH HARD-BOILED EGGS AND SWEET PICKLES serves 4 to 6

Use sweet pickles, not relish, for the best results.

2 pounds red potatoes (about 6 medium or 18 small), scrubbed
¼ cup red wine vinegar
  Salt and ground black pepper
3 hard-boiled eggs (recipe follows), peeled and cut into ½-inch dice
1 medium stalk celery, minced (about ½ cup)
2 tablespoons minced red onion
¼ cup sweet pickles, minced
½ cup mayonnaise
2 teaspoons Dijon mustard
2 tablespoons minced fresh parsley leaves

1. Cover potatoes with 1 inch of water in stockpot or Dutch oven. Bring to simmer over medium-high heat. Reduce heat to medium and simmer, stirring once or twice to ensure even cooking, until potatoes are tender (a thin-bladed paring knife or metal cake tester can be slipped into and out of center of potatoes with no resistance), 25 to 30 minutes for medium potatoes or 15 to 20 minutes for new potatoes.

2. Drain; cool potatoes slightly and peel if you like. Cut potatoes into ¾-inch cubes (use serrated knife if they have skins) while still warm, rinsing knife occasionally in warm water to remove starch.

3. Place warm potato cubes in large bowl. Add vinegar, ½ teaspoon salt, and ¼ teaspoon pepper and toss gently. Cover bowl with plastic wrap and refrigerate until cool, about 20 minutes.

4. When potatoes are cool, toss with remaining ingredients and season with salt and pepper to taste. Serve immediately or cover and refrigerate for up to 1 day.

FOOLPROOF HARD-BOILED EGGS makes 3

You can double or triple this recipe as long as you use a pot large enough to hold the eggs in a single layer, covered by an inch of water.

3 large eggs

1. Place eggs in medium saucepan, cover with 1 inch of water, and bring to a boil over high heat. Remove pan from heat, cover, and let sit for 10 minutes. Meanwhile, fill medium bowl with 1 quart water and 1 tray ice cubes (or equivalent).

2. Transfer eggs to ice bath with slotted spoon and let sit 5 minutes. Tap each egg all over against countertop to crack shell, then roll egg gently back and forth several times. Begin peeling from air-pocket (wider) end. The shell should come off in spiral strips attached to thin membrane. Hard-boiled eggs can be refrigerated for several days.

TECHNIQUE:
Identifying Hard-Boiled Eggs in the Refrigerator

It can be hard to tell which eggs in your refrigerator are raw and which are hard-boiled. To keep them straight, purchase white eggs, and when cooking them add a little balsamic vinegar to the cooking water. This dark brown vinegar will tint the eggshells so you can tell the hard-boiled eggs apart from bright white raw eggs.

BARBECUED salmon

Salmon is America's favorite fish for grilling, but that doesn't mean that it's easy to get it right. Most people who have grilled salmon have had the experience of cooking it to perfection only to lose half of the pieces to the grill. Just as bad are pale salmon steaks with little color or grilled flavor.

We were intrigued with the notion of barbecuing a whole side of salmon. Our goal was to have this large piece of fish spend enough time over the coals to pick up some real wood flavor. Of course, keeping the salmon from drying out would be a big challenge, as would perfecting a method for getting the fish on and off the grill in one piece.

To accompany the salmon, we wanted something more interesting than the raw cucumber garnish that often attends sides of poached salmon at weddings and other fancy parties. For a summer barbecue, we thought a bright cucumber salad would add cool, tart, and creamy flavors to complement the smoky-flavored salmon.

A dozen charcoal
and gas grills were
used to prepare food
for the cameras.

BARBECUED SALMON

WHAT WE WANTED: Smoked salmon flavor achieved on the grill with a whole side of salmon. The texture would be firm but not overly dry, and the fish would be complemented by a strong hit of smoke and wood.

Is it possible to make smoked salmon at home without a smoker? We thought it was worth a try and started off by attempting to make a covered grill act like a cold smoker, which cooks foods at a range of 75 to 110 degrees. We used very few coals, adding them as we went along, often putting out the fire when we added wet wood chunks. The results were disappointing; the salmon was lacking in flavor, and the texture was a bit wet.

Patience is supposed to be a virtue, but in this case impatience turned out to be the key to success. We simply got tired of messing with the process of cold smoking. In fact, at this point we realized that cold smoking, which is used by commercial smokers to make smoked salmon, is simply not practical for home cooks. It takes a very long time, requires both skill and patience, and, because of the low cooking temperatures involved, can be disastrous if health precautions are not followed carefully. We decided to use more briquettes in the initial fire. This eliminated the need to add more coals during the smoking process, and the larger fire was less likely to go out when we added wet wood chunks. This time the results were gratifying. The hotter fire cooked the fish more thoroughly, giving it a more pleasing and flaky texture.

We continued to refine this method over many months of trial and error. Eventually, we perfected a procedure that yields a salmon that has many of the attributes of good smoked salmon but that is crustier and a whole lot easier to make. In fact, the technique is similar to traditional barbecue. The difference between barbecued salmon and cold-smoked salmon is largely one of texture: the cold-smoked salmon is more silky, like lox, whereas barbecued salmon

will actually flake.

But the drawback of this method—and the reason why salmon is usually cold-smoked—is that it dries out the fish. We figured that brining in a saltwater solution might help the fish hold onto moisture as it cooked and experimented with various brining times, eventually settling on three to four hours for a fillet weighing 2½ to 3 pounds. Any longer and the flavor of the brine was too intense; any shorter and it didn't produce the desired results as far as texture was concerned. This brined, barbecued salmon definitely had the moist texture we had been longing for, but we were still looking for more flavor to complement its smokiness.

To improve the flavor we added some sugar to the brine. We also experimented with various salt/sugar/water ratios, with different brining times (from two to 24 hours), and with all manner of smoking woods. We eventually settled on the recipe below, which calls for three hours of brining in a solution of 1 cup each of sugar and salt to 7 cups of water and which favors alder wood chunks for the distinctive flavor they give the fish. The salmon this recipe produces has a moist but flaky texture and is just smoky enough, with the natural flavors of the salmon getting a boost from the brining process.

Barbecued salmon can be served warm off the grill as well as chilled, and it works as both a traditional hors d'oeuvre and, somewhat surprisingly, an entrée. For hors d'oeuvres, it is absolutely delicious as is or accompanied with Melba toast (or any other flat bread or cracker), finely chopped white onion, capers, and lemon wedges. If you serve the salmon as an entrée, wedges of lemon will suffice, or you might try one of our sauce recipes.

WHAT WE LEARNED: To protect the fish against the drying effects of the grill, brine it before cooking it. Don't try to cold-smoke salmon at home—use a bit more heat and barbecue it.

BARBECUED SALMON ON A CHARCOAL
GRILL serves 4 to 6 as a main course

The grill rack must be hot and thoroughly clean before you place the salmon on it; otherwise the fish might stick. Use foil or the back of a large rimmed baking sheet to get the fish onto the grill. Alder wood is our first choice for this recipe, but hickory works fine, too (see the Equipment Corner on page 183 for more information about the flavors imparted by various types of wood). You will need two wood chunks, each about the size of a lemon, for this recipe.

 1   cup kosher salt or ½ cup table salt
 1   cup sugar
 1   skin-on salmon fillet (about 2½ pounds), pin
     bones removed (see illustration at right)
 2   tablespoons vegetable oil
 1½ teaspoons sweet paprika
 1   teaspoon ground white pepper

1. Dissolve salt and sugar in 7 cups cold water in gallon-sized zipper-lock plastic bag. Add salmon, seal bag, and refrigerate until fish is fully brined, about 3 hours.

2. Meanwhile, cover two 3-inch wood chunks with water in medium bowl; soak for 1 hour, then drain and set aside.

3. Remove salmon from brine and blot completely dry with paper towels. Place fillet, skin-side down, on 30-inch sheet of heavy-duty foil. Rub both sides of fillet, especially skin side, with oil. Dust flesh side of fillet with paprika and pepper.

4. Meanwhile, open bottom vents on grill. Ignite large chimney starter filled halfway with charcoal briquettes (about 3 quarts, or 45 coals), and burn until covered with thin coating of light gray ash. Empty coals into one side of grill, piling them up in mound two or three briquettes high. Place wood chunks on top of charcoal. Put cooking grate in place, open grill lid vents completely, and cover. Let grate heat for 5 minutes and scrape clean with wire brush.

5. Slide salmon off foil and onto grill rack opposite fire so that long side of fillet is perpendicular to grill rods. Cover, positioning lid so that vents are opposite wood chunks to draw smoke through grill. Barbecue until cooked through and heavily flavored with smoke, 1½ hours. (Temperature will drop from about 350 degrees at start of cooking to about 250 degrees by time salmon is done.)

6. Following illustration 1 on page 192, use two spatulas to remove salmon from grill. Serve either hot or at room temperature, cutting through flesh but not skin to divide salmon into individual portions and sliding spatula between flesh and skin to remove individual pieces, leaving skin behind (see illustrations 2 and 3 on page 192). Serve as is or with one of the sauces that follow.

TECHNIQUE:
Removing Pin Bones from Salmon

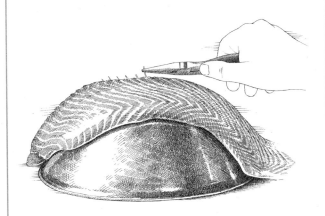

Locating and removing the pinbones from a side of salmon can be tricky. Running your fingers along the flesh is one way to locate them, but we like to drape the salmon over an inverted mixing bowl. The curvature of the bowl forces the pinbones to stick up and out, so they are easier to spot, grasp with needle-nose pliers or tweezers, and remove.

TECHNIQUE: Key Steps for Barbecued Salmon

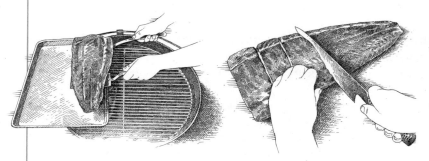

1. Use two spatulas to transfer the cooked fish from the grill to a jelly roll pan or cutting board.

2. Cut through the pink flesh, but not the skin, to divide into individual portions.

3. Slide a spatula between the fillet and the skin to remove individual pieces, leaving the skin behind.

VARIATIONS

BARBECUED SALMON ON A GAS GRILL

If you're using a gas grill, leaving one burner on and turning the other(s) off mimics the indirect heat method on a charcoal grill. Use wood chips instead of wood chunks and a disposable aluminum pan to hold them. Keep a close eye on the grill thermometer to make sure that the temperature remains around 275 degrees.

Follow recipe for Barbecued Salmon on a Charcoal Grill through step 3, making following changes: Cover 2 cups wood chips with water and soak 30 minutes, then drain. Place soaked wood chips in small disposable aluminum pan; set pan on burner that will remain on. Turn all burners to high, close lid, and heat grill until chips smoke heavily, about 20 minutes. (If chips ignite, extinguish flames with water from squirt bottle.) Scrape grill grate clean with wire brush; turn off burner(s) without wood chips. Slide salmon onto grill as directed in step 5 and proceed with recipe.

HORSERADISH CREAM SAUCE makes about 1 cup

Horseradish and crème fraîche are natural partners to the smoky salmon.

- 1 cup crème fraîche or sour cream
- 2 tablespoons prepared horseradish
- 2 tablespoons minced fresh chives
  Pinch salt

Combine all ingredients in small bowl. (Sauce can be refrigerated in airtight container overnight.)

MUSTARD-DILL SAUCE makes about 1 cup

Use Dijon, honey, or grainy mustard, as desired. Depending on your choice of mustard, this sauce can be fairly hot.

- 1 cup mustard
- ¼ cup minced fresh dill

Combine all ingredients in small bowl. (Sauce can be refrigerated in airtight container overnight.)

TASTING LAB: Paprika

THE BRILLIANT RED POWDER WE CALL PAPRIKA COMES from the dried pods (fruit) of the plant species *Capsicum annuum L.*, the clan of peppers that ranges from sweet bells to the very hottest chiles. Several varieties of Capsicum annuum L. are used to produce paprika; there is no one specific "paprika pepper." Pods differ in shape and size and vary in degree of potency. Some are round; others are elongated. Some show no pungency; others are fairly hot.

The best paprika is thought to come from Hungary and Spain, with the Hungarian noted for its flavor and the Spanish for its color. In the United States, California and Texas are the main producers. Most European paprika pods are set out to dry naturally in the sun, a process that takes up to 25 days. Domestically grown paprika pods are oven-dried in all of about 30 hours.

Rating Paprika

WE TESTED SIX BRANDS OF PAPRIKA, USING EACH IN CHICKEN PAPRIKASH (A HUNGARIAN STEW MADE WITH A LOT OF paprika). We also tasted each paprika sprinkled over plain white rice. Tasters judged samples on flavor as well as color. Paprikas are listed in order of preference. See www.cooksillustrated.com for up-to-date prices and mail-order sources for top-rated products.

RECOMMENDED

1. Penzeys Hungary Sweet Paprika
$3.39 for 2.4 ounces
The overall favorite, this paprika was hailed for its "roasty," "bold," and "balanced" flavor. The spice did not overpower other ingredients, but it had plenty of depth. Available by mail order.

RECOMMENDED

2. Pendery's Spanish Paprika
$3.25 for 2.72 ounces
This "deeply colored" paprika earned a strong second place in the tasting. It had an "earthy" quality and very rich flavor (though not as rich as our winner), with fruity notes. Available by mail order.

RECOMMENDED

3. McCormick/Schilling Paprika
$3.19 for 2.12 ounces
This California paprika was touted for its "lush," "big red pepper" flavor. Available in supermarkets; sold on the West Coast under the Schilling label.

NOT RECOMMENDED

4. Szeged Hungarian Hot Paprika
$3.49 for 5 ounces
This paprika was deemed intense and slightly bitter. Tasters felt it overwhelmed other flavors in the paprikash. Available in supermarkets.

NOT RECOMMENDED

5. Whole Foods Organic Paprika
$4.79 for 1.68 ounces
This California paprika was judged to be bland and uninteresting. Available in Whole Foods supermarkets.

NOT RECOMMENDED

6. Igo Basque Piment d'Espelette
$12.50 for 1 ounce
This Spanish paprika was so hot that it was hard to detect any flavor; tasters liked this incendiary and extremely expensive paprika the least. Available by mail order.

Paprika can be hot, sweet, or somewhere in between. The differences in pungency, color, and flavor relate to the proportion of *mesocarp* (fruit wall), *placenta* (the white veins), and seeds that are ground together. Sweet paprika is made mostly from peppers' mesocarp, while hot paprika is a product of the placenta and seeds. The latter are ground to yield a spicy powder with an orange-brown color and, some spice experts say, poor flavor. It is almost as pungent as common chile powders and cayenne pepper.

The problem with all of this information is that except for allowing you to choose intelligently between sweet and hot paprika, it does you little practical good at the supermarket when you're trying to figure out which brand of paprika to buy. We came up with six choices: McCormick's (from California), Whole Foods Organic (also California), Penzeys Hungarian Sweet, Szeged Hungarian Hot, Pendery's Spanish Sweet, and Igo Basque Piment d'Espelette (also from Spain).

To test these paprikas, we sprinkled them over plain white rice and used them in a chicken paprikash recipe that called for 3 tablespoons of paprika. (We thought the smoke and fish flavors of the barbecued salmon would make a difficult background against which to taste this delicate spice.)

Penzeys Hungarian Sweet emerged as the overall favorite. The spice did not overpower the stew, but it had plenty of depth. Pendery's Spanish Sweet was the runner-up. It had an "earthy" quality and very rich flavor (though not as rich as our winner), with fruity notes. Although we expected the European brands to do well, we were surprised by the strong third place finish of McCormick's, the leading supermarket brand made with California paprika.

The other three paprikas received less favorable comments. Szeged Hungarian Hot was deemed intense and slightly bitter, the Whole Foods paprika was judged bland and uninteresting, and the Igo Basque Piment d'Espelette was thought to be searingly hot.

Our conclusion? Hungarian sweet paprika in the best choice, but other sweet paprikas (from Spain or California) can deliver good results. Don't use hot paprika.

EQUIPMENT CORNER: Charcoal Grills

FLICKING A SWITCH TO LIGHT A GAS GRILL MAY BE convenient, but for many die-hard grillers nothing beats cooking over a live charcoal fire. The pleasure is utterly visceral—the glowing, red-hot coals, the smoke, the intense sizzle, the interplay of food and flame, and the aroma of searing meat. And, of course, there is the flavor. Charcoal-fueled fires infuse food with characteristic notes of wood and smoke that no gas fire can match.

Yet deciding which charcoal grill to buy is not so straightforward. They come in different shapes and sizes, with different features, and at vastly different prices. We chose six grills from five manufacturers that ran the gamut—from round to rectangular, bare-bones to fully featured, smaller to larger, and less than $50 to more than 10 times that in cost—and pressed them into service in the alley behind the test kitchen for evaluation. A few weeks of grilling steaks, hamburgers, bone-in chicken breasts, and ribs led us to some interesting observations and a couple of decent choices, but not, alas, to a grill that is perfect in all respects.

Grilling a mountain of food over several weeks revealed very little difference in cooking performance among our grills. Each developed fires hot enough to sear the food, which is what charcoal grilling is all about. Each also offered vents to control airflow and thereby the intensity of the fire, but we were not able to detect any advantages or disadvantages based on the number or position of the vents. It was possible, however, to identify two important design factors: the size of the grill and the depth of the grill cover.

A large surface area for grilling is essential if you cook for large groups and is useful even if you don't because it affords the opportunity to grill some extra food alongside tonight's dinner. For instance, we rarely grill a meal without covering every available inch of grill space with vegetables to have on hand for tomorrow's antipasto or pizza or pasta salad. It is also easier to build a two-level fire (hot on one side and cooler on the other) in a large grill. In short, size

Rating Charcoal Grills

WE TESTED SIX GRILLS BY PRESSING THEM INTO DAILY SERVICE IN THE ALLEY OUTSIDE THE TEST KITCHEN. WE JUDGED the grills on size (we preferred larger grills with lids tall enough to accommodate a turkey), attached tables (the bigger, the better), and adjustability of the charcoal or cooking grate. See www.cooksillustrated.com for up-to-date prices and mail-order sources for top-rated products.

BEST BUY

1. New Braunfels Santa Fe, Model 01308725

$99.00

A large, user-friendly grill with better features (built-in thermometer, lower storage shelf) than structural integrity. Huge cooking surface, two wide side tables, and a door into the charcoal area are all great features. We did, however, have to revisit this grill with a wrench to keep it tight and solid.

RECOMMENDED WITH RESERVATIONS

2. Weber Performer

$399.00

The Luxo-version of the classic kettle grill has many nice touches, including a thermometer with real numbers, a large table, hinged cooking rack, lid holder, ash catcher, and overall solid construction. Gas ignition is useful but utterly nonessential. With so many thoughtful features, why didn't Weber make the charcoal or cooking racks adjustable?

RECOMMENDED WITH RESERVATIONS

3. Sunbeam 22-inch Square Portable Charcoal Grill

$49.96

A very nice grill but for three major flaws: relatively small cooking area, a cooking grate that slides around whenever you move the food on it, and a flimsy overall feel.

RECOMMENDED WITH RESERVATIONS

4. The Cajun Grill PG200

$519.00

So heavy and solid it feels like it could weather a cyclone or two intact. Best charcoal rack adjustment system we encountered, yet the rack itself is too narrow to provide even heat over 100 percent of the cooking surface. No way to add charcoal to a fire without removing the cooking rack. Very few features for the money.

RECOMMENDED WITH RESERVATIONS

5. Weber One-Touch Silver

$99.00

Solid and competent but so bare-bones. The only frill here is the grill rack with handles. The archetypal kettle grill could stand to offer more features for the money.

RECOMMENDED WITH RESERVATIONS

6. Thermos 22½-inch Kettle Grill

$59.99

Thoughtfully featured and fine to grill on, but too small. Because most home cooks have just one charcoal grill, we'd skip this model, which is too shallow to accommodate large cuts for grill-roasting.

does matter. In our group, the New Braunfels Santa Fe was the size champ, with 468 square inches of grilling space.

We generally don't use the cover when grilling over high heat, but it is necessary when grill-roasting large cuts, such as a turkey or prime rib, over lower heat. To trap heat and contain any flavorful smoke generated from wood chunks, the grill cover must fit comfortably over the food and form a tight seal with the grill bottom. We recommend 12 to 14-pound turkeys for grill-roasting (see recipe on page 204), and only the covers on the New Braunfels and Sunbeam grills closed over a 14-pounder (set on a V-rack to promote even cooking). All of the grills in the group except for the Thermos swallowed the 12-pounder.

In some respects, charcoal grills are a little like cars. Any new car will get you from point A to point B, but extra features like traction control or anti-lock brakes make the car easier to drive, and goodies like a sunroof or heated seats help you enjoy the ride more. Likewise, all charcoal grills will cook your food, but there are several features that make the process easier and more enjoyable.

Though we never would have guessed it, the presence of an attached table made a huge difference. After years of precariously balancing trays and platters on deck railings and chair arms, having a secure, accessible place to put dishes and utensils was a welcome relief. The New Braunfels grill doubled the pleasure with two large tables, one on each end of the grill. Score another point for New Braunfels. Among our group, only the Weber One-Touch Silver and the Thermos lacked tables of any kind.

If you plan to barbecue or grill-roast (both methods entail long cooking over a relatively low fire), some means of easily adding charcoal to the fire is useful. Once again, the New Braunfels offered the perfect solution—a small door to the charcoal tray, which made it a breeze to tend the fire and add fuel. The Webers offered a different solution—cooking grates that are either hinged or open at the ends so you can slip charcoal through. If you have to add fuel to any of the other grills, you must endure the hassle of removing the food and the cooking grate to get to the fire.

Another thoughtful feature is some means of adjusting the height of either the charcoal rack or the cooking grate. If given no respite from a hot fire, many foods, such as thick steaks, pork chops, or chicken breasts, will burn on the outside before cooking through on the inside. So they must be finished over a cooler fire. This is easy to accomplish if you can adjust the charcoal tray down away from the cooking grate, as is the case with the New Braunfels, the Cajun, and the Thermos. On the Sunbeam, the charcoal tray is fixed but you can adjust the height of the cooking grate, so the effect is the same. Still, the ability to adjust either the charcoal or cooking grate is not essential. On the Webers, which do not offer such adjustability, you can build a two-level fire that is hot on one side and cool on the other to achieve the same effect. This simply takes a little extra knowledge on the part of the griller. It is easier, though, if you can change the level of the fire with the shift of a lever or the turn of a dial.

Some additional features we encountered were nice but non-essential. Notable among them were the gas ignition on the Weber Performer, which did its job well but added expense and weight. A chimney starter is so easy to use that we could happily forego the gas ignition. Likewise storage racks and bins. On the other hand, an ash catcher, which is simply a container attached to the bottom of the grill to trap ashes—makes life easier when it comes time to clean out the grill. When you barbecue or grill-roast, a built-in thermometer is handy, though if it isn't there you can either use an oven thermometer on the grill rack or put a grill thermometer through lid vents instead.

In the end, value, which we define as the balance of size, features, and price, determined our recommendations. This formula makes the New Braunfels look pretty good, with its impressive size and host of features, all for a modest $99. But it was not perfect. The charcoal tray adjustment system was limited to three positions and it struck us as flimsy, especially compared with the solid, well-designed, seven-position system on the Cajun Grill. Also, the New Braunfels grill did not impress us with awesome structural integrity.

We had to tighten its nuts and bolts several times through-out the testing.

Though the Weber Performer did not offer an adjust-ment system for moving the charcoal and we viewed its gas ignition system as superfluous, it was solid and extremely well outfitted. The caveat here is price—nearly $400, or four times that of the New Braunfels. (Weber does offer a similar model, the One-Touch Platinum, that comes with an ash catcher and a large attached table, but without the gas ignition system or the thermometer, for about $249. This grill strikes us as a better value than the Performer because it has all of the Performer's important features but none of the bells and whistles that add mightily to the price tag.)

In the end, we'd say the general guideline is to buy the largest, best-outfitted grill your budget will allow. And, silly as it may sound, whatever you do, make sure there is a table attached.

EQUIPMENT CORNER: Charcoal

WOULD YOU EVER HAVE GUESSED THAT HENRY FORD WAS to thank for your charcoal-grilled steak tonight? That's right. Ford pioneered the charcoal briquette industry as a way to profit from the scrap wood generated by manufac-turing all those Model T's in the 1920s.

Generally speaking, charcoal is the carbonized remains of wood that has been burned in the absence of oxygen. Without oxygen, resins and moisture in the wood evaporate, leaving behind lightweight, easily lit, combustible charcoal.

Three types of charcoal dominate the market. They are hardwood charcoal (also called charwood, lump charwood, or lump hardwood), which, like the wood used to make it, consists of irregularly shaped pieces and is additive-free; square, pillow-shaped briquettes made from scrap wood and sawdust that is burned and then compacted along with chemicals and other binders that help them both ignite and burn evenly; and a Kingsford product called Match Light, which consists of briquettes that have been permeated with lighter fluid and thereby promise to ignite with the touch of a lit match. (Match Light did live up to its name, quickly producing a spectacular 3-foot column of flame on the windy day we conducted our tests.)

We were anxious to test the common assertion that hardwood charcoal burns hotter and faster than briquettes, so we hooked up a sophisticated, high-range temperature sensor to the cooking grate above fires made from each of the three types of charcoal. We recorded temperatures after five minutes, 15 minutes, and 25 minutes to gauge the drop-off in heat. Sure enough, the hardwood fire was the hottest initially at just above 700 degrees, compared with 660 degrees for the briquettes and 550 degrees for the Match Light; the hardwood also dropped off the most dramati-cally—by almost 450 degrees—after 25 minutes.

We were also curious to see if we could detect flavor differences in foods grilled with the three types of charcoal, so we sampled steak (because it's hearty) and zucchini (because it's delicate). Though the hardwood charcoal fire formed the thickest, most deeply brown crust on the steaks, tasters did not detect any significant flavor differences in the three steaks. It was another story, however, with the zuc-chini. The zucchini grilled over hardwood charcoal colored the fastest and tasted the smokiest. The briquette-grilled zucchini had the lightest grilled flavor (but no off flavors), and the Match Light–grilled sample demonstrated a faint but odd bitterness.

So where does this leave us? We'd just as soon avoid any off flavors in delicate foods, so we'll pass on the Match Light charcoal. For grill-roasting over a longer time period at a lower temperature, such as our barbecued salmon recipe, we'd opt for briquettes because they burn a little cooler and a lot longer than hardwood charcoal. But for straight-ahead grilling applications, especially when there's meat on the menu that cries out for a deep sear, we'll take hardwood. Grilling is all about high heat, and we'll take every extra degree that we can get.

CUCUMBER SALAD

WHAT WE WANTED: More often than not, by the time you eat a cucumber salad, the cucumbers have gone soft and watery, losing their appealing texture and diluting the dressing to near tastelessness. This made the primary goal of our testing simple: Maximize the crunch.

Water is the enemy when making cucumber salad. The standing recommendation for ridding watery vegetables such as cucumbers, zucchini, and eggplant of unwanted moisture is to salt them. The salt creates a higher concentration of ions (tiny, charged particles) at the surface of the vegetable than exists deep within its cells. To equalize the concentration levels, the water within the cells is drawn out through permeable cell walls. In the case of cucumbers, this leaves them wilted, yet very crunchy. Of course, some culinary questions remain: How much salt should be used? Should the cucumber slices be weighted, or pressed, to squeeze out the liquid? How long should they drain?

To find out if pressing salted cucumbers really squeezes out more liquid, we trimmed and seeded six cucumbers to 8 ounces each, sliced them on the bias, and tossed each batch with a teaspoon of salt in its own colander set over a bowl. Three of them had zipper-lock freezer bags filled with 1 quart of water placed on top of them; no additional weight was added to the other three. Then we left them all to drain, measuring the liquid each had released after 30 minutes and after 1, 2, 3, and 12 hours. At each time point, the weighted cucumbers had released about 1 tablespoon more liquid than the unweighted cucumbers; 3 versus 2 after 30 minutes, 4 versus 3 after 1 hour, and so on. Interestingly, the weighted cukes gave off no more liquid after 12 hours than they had after 3 (7 tablespoons at both points). So weighting the cucumbers is worthwhile, but forget about draining the cucumbers overnight; it's not necessary.

At the one-hour mark, we could not detect an appreciable difference in flavor or texture between weighted and unweighted cukes. But we wanted to see how they would perform in salads with different types of dressings. We mixed one batch each of the weighted and unweighted cucumbers with three types of sauce—creamy, oil-based, and water-based—and allowed each to sit at room temperature for one hour. This is where the true value of better-drained cucumbers became obvious; every single taster preferred the salads made with pressed cucumbers for their superior crunch and less diluted dressings.

As for the amount of salt, some cooks recommend simply using the quantity you would normally use to season the cucumbers, while others say you should use more, up to 2 tablespoons per cucumber, and then rinse off the excess before further use. We tried a few cucumbers, prepared exactly as those described above except with 2 tablespoons of salt. The cucumbers with 2 tablespoons did give up about one more tablespoon of liquid within the first hour than those drained with one teaspoon had, but they also required rinsing and blotting dry with paper towels. And despite this extra hassle, they still tasted much too salty in the salads. We advise forgoing the extra salt.

WHAT WE LEARNED: Salt and weight seeded and sliced cucumbers to draw off excess moisture, then rinse, pat dry, and toss the cucumbers with vinaigrette or a creamy dressing made with sour cream or yogurt.

SESAME LEMON CUCUMBER SALAD serves 4

Mild rice vinegar works well in this Asian-inspired dressing.

- ¼ cup rice vinegar
- 1 tablespoon juice from 1 small lemon
- 2 tablespoons Asian sesame oil
- 2 teaspoons sugar
- ⅛ teaspoon hot red pepper flakes, or to taste
- 1 tablespoon sesame seeds, toasted
- 3 medium cucumbers (about 1½ pounds), sliced, salted, and drained (see illustrations, below)

Whisk all ingredients except cucumbers in bowl. Add cucumbers; toss to coat. Serve chilled or at room temperature.

YOGURT MINT CUCUMBER SALAD serves 4

Known as raita, this creamy salad traditionally serves as a cooling contrast with curry dishes.

- 1 cup plain low-fat yogurt
- 2 tablespoons extra-virgin olive oil
- ¼ cup minced fresh mint leaves
- 2 small garlic cloves, minced (about 2 teaspoons)
  Salt and ground black pepper

- 3 medium cucumbers (about 1½ pounds), sliced, salted, and drained (see illustrations, below)

Whisk yogurt, oil, mint, garlic, and salt and pepper to taste in medium bowl. Add cucumbers; toss to coat. Serve chilled, adjusting seasonings if necessary.

CREAMY DILL CUCUMBER SALAD serves 4

Salting and draining the onion along with the cucumbers in this recipe removes the sharp sting of raw onion.

- 1 cup sour cream
- 3 tablespoons cider vinegar
- 1 teaspoon sugar
- ¼ cup minced fresh dill
  Salt and ground black pepper
- 3 medium cucumbers (about 1½ pounds), sliced, salted, and drained (see illustrations, below)
- ½ medium red onion, sliced very thin, salted and drained with cucumbers

Whisk sour cream, vinegar, sugar, dill, and salt and pepper to taste in medium bowl. Add cucumbers and onion; toss to coat. Serve chilled, adjusting seasonings if necessary.

TECHNIQUE: Slicing and Salting Cucumbers

1. Peel and halve each cucumber lengthwise. Use a small spoon to remove the seeds and surrounding liquid from each cucumber half.

2. Lay the cucumber halves flat-side down on a work surface and slice them on the diagonal into ¼-inch-thick pieces.

3. Toss the cucumbers and 1 tablespoon salt in a colander set in a bowl. Weight with a gallon-size plastic bag filled with water. Drain for 1 to 3 hours. Rinse well and pat dry.

Cooking turkey on a grill produces extra-crisp skin, moist meat, and a great smoky flavor.

THANKSGIVING
from the grill

CHAPTER 16

Most cooks don't like to experiment when it comes to holiday foods. In many homes, the Thanksgiving menu is sacrosanct. That said, most cooks would agree that there's plenty of room for improvement. The turkey rarely comes out with both crisp skin and moist meat. It seems that one goal must always be sacrificed to achieve the other. And even if things do go well, the turkey hogs the oven all day, making it difficult to prepare all of the other holiday dishes—the casseroles, the pies—that need to be baked. We wanted to figure out how to use the grill to cook the bird. We hoped to free up oven space and turn out a better-tasting bird.

Sweet potatoes and cranberry sauce are must-haves in most homes at Thanksgiving, but we don't like the overly sweet, marshmallow-topped sweet potato casserole and the stiff cranberry jelly from a can that have become traditional. We wanted to focus on flavor and make the sweet potatoes and cranberry sauce something special while keeping their preparation as simple as possible.

GRILL-ROASTED TURKEY

WHAT WE WANTED: A smoky-tasting turkey with super-crisp skin and juicy, tender meat.

We can still remember the first time we cooked a whole turkey in a covered grill. We lit the charcoal, banked the coals to one side, added some wood chips, and placed a small turkey over the cool part of the grill. Two hours later, we had the best-looking and best-tasting turkey ever—the crispiest skin imaginable coupled with moist meat that had been perfumed with smoke.

Unfortunately, we can also remember the second time we tried this feat. We must have built the fire a little too hot; when we checked the bird after the first hour, the skin had burned. We nonetheless continued grilling, and, before serving, removed the charred skin from the blackened bird. We also served some juicy mango salsa to camouflage the dryness of the overcooked breast.

We have continued to grill-roast turkeys over the years not only because the bird sometimes turns out to be fantastic but also because using the grill for the turkey frees up the oven for all of the other components of a holiday meal. But the results have been consistently inconsistent.

Part of the problem is the inherent unpredictability of grill-roasting over charcoal. Sometimes the fire can be too hot, other times it can be too cool. If the day is particularly windy, the fire will cool down faster than on a hot, sultry night. Because you are cooking with the cover down to conserve fuel (frequent peeking will cause the fire to die down and is a no-no), it's hard to know what's happening inside the grill.

We decided to get serious and figure out what the variables are when grill-roasting a turkey and then devise a method for controlling these variables. Our goal was simple: We wanted a bird with crisp, browned skin, moist meat, and a good smoky flavor—every time.

Because gas grilling involves fewer variables than charcoal grilling, we decided to start with gas. We quickly learned that a small turkey (fewer than 14 pounds) works best when grill-roasting. Even on a really large gas grill, we found that the skin on a large bird burns by the time the meat comes up to temperature. For the same reason, you can't cook a stuffed turkey on the grill. A stuffed bird takes longer to cook through, and this added time almost guarantees that the skin will blacken.

Following the lead of previous turkey recipes developed in the test kitchen, we also confirmed that brining the turkey is a must for a tender, juicy bird. Grilling is even more punishing on delicate breast meat than oven roasting. The bird's proximity to the heat source, coupled with all that smoke (which tends to dehydrate foods), puts brining in the position of making a real difference in the quality of the white meat. If you can't be bothered with brining, buy a kosher bird (the bird is soaked in saltwater during processing, which has an effect similar to brining) or season a regular bird liberally with salt just before grilling and be prepared to serve the white meat with plenty of cranberry sauce.

Next we turned to the question of trussing. Our test kitchen generally ties the legs of the turkey together to keep them from splaying open as they roast. When we tried this, we noticed that the inner thigh cooked more slowly than the rest of the bird. Trussed birds needed an extra 10 to 15 minutes on the grill to get the shielded portion of the thigh up to the correct internal temperature. While this may not sound like much extra time, it translated into overcooked breast meat. Even worse, the skin burned. When we abandoned any trussing or tying of the legs, the temperature in the thighs and breasts was equalized and the skin was extremely crisp and dark brown, but not black.

Our next set of experiments centered on turning the bird. As with oven roasting, we found it best to start the bird breast-side down. After an hour, we flipped the bird breast-side up for the remainder of the cooking time. We noticed that the side (wing and leg) closest to the fire was cooking faster than the other side of the bird. To eliminate this problem, we found it necessary to rotate the bird twice—once when it is turned breast-side up, and once when the cooking is almost completed. Each time, we turned the bird so that the opposite wing and leg faced the heat source.

We next focused on whether to cook the bird right on the grill grate or on a rack. We found that the turkey placed in a nonadjustable V-rack cooked more evenly and with less scorching of the skin than the bird placed right on the grate. But a rack with a sturdy metal base is essential. If the V-rack rests on just two little legs, those legs can fall between the grill grates and the turkey can topple over.

Our last area of investigation on the gas grill concerned temperature. Clearly, we needed to grill-roast the bird over indirect heat, with one burner lit and the other burner(s) turned off. Our question was how to keep the heat on the lit burner. We tested this recipe on three grills—two models with two burners and one model with three burners. We found it best to leave the lit burner turned to high in each case. At lower settings, there was not enough heat to cook the bird properly. The temperature gauges on the three grills we worked with ranged from 300 to 350 degrees during the entire cooking time. Total cooking time for a 12- to 14-pound bird varied from 2 to 2½ hours. (Count on the longer time if the weather is cool or windy.)

Turkey cooked on a gas grill is delicious. The recipe is foolproof, and the skin becomes especially crisp and richly colored. But getting smoke flavor into a gas-grilled bird is not so easy. While adding wood chips before lighting the grill helped some, the resulting smoke flavor was mild. A mildly smoked bird may be fine for some meals, but we think that if you are going to bother with grilling, you might as well get the added benefit of a stronger smoke flavor. The problem with gas grills is that there's no way to add chips once the fire is going. We concluded that removing the turkey, trying to lift off the hot, heavy cooking grate, and then placing more chips over the lit burner was much too dangerous.

Charcoal is another matter. We quickly realized that because we had to add fuel to the fire at the halfway point anyway, we could add more wood at the same time. We came to this conclusion after producing yet another blackened bird. We foolishly thought we could build a really big fire on one side of the grill, put the turkey on the cool side, throw on the cover, and come back two hours later. While it's possible to get the meat up to temperature with this method, the intense initial heat (upward of 425 degrees) causes the skin to burn.

We found it far better to build a moderate fire, bank the coals to one side of the grill, and cook the turkey breast-side down for one hour, just as we had on the gas grill. After an hour, the temperature inside the grill dropped from a high of 350 to 375 degrees to somewhere around 275 degrees. At this point, the grill needed more fuel to finish cooking the turkey. Because we were removing the cooking grate anyway, we decided to add more wood along with a dozen unlit briquettes. (Unlike the very heavy gas grate, you can lift a charcoal grate with heavy-duty tongs. You can also simply toss wood into a pile of charcoal; for gas, you must position the foil tray over the burner, an impossible task when the grill is hot.)

At about this point we began experimenting with chunks of wood versus wood chips. We found that chunks, although not suitable for use with a gas grill, were far superior (they gave off a lot more smoke) and easy to use with a charcoal grill.

So would we cook our next turkey over gas or charcoal? Gas is certainly more convenient and more reliable if the weather is especially cold or windy. However, the extra smoky flavor that only charcoal and wood chunks can deliver makes the kettle grill our first choice for grill-roasting a turkey.

WHAT WE LEARNED: **Brine the bird to keep it moist, and don't bother trussing the turkey; it only serves to slow down the cooking of the dark meat. Grill-roast the turkey over a moderate fire. Use a V-rack to improve air circulation, and turn the bird twice for evenly bronzed skin.**

GRILL-ROASTED TURKEY ON A CHARCOAL GRILL serves 10 to 12

Charcoal gives you the opportunity to add wood twice—at the outset of grilling and when the bird is turned breast-side up at the 1-hour mark—for a stronger smoke flavor. You will need six wood chunks, each about the size of a lemon, for this recipe. (For more information about wood chunks, see the Equipment Corner on page 183.) Hardwood charcoal burns faster and hotter than briquettes, so be sure to use briquettes when grill-roasting turkey. The total cooking time is 2 to 2¹/₂ hours, depending on the size of the bird, the ambient conditions (the bird will require more time on a cool, windy day), and the intensity of the fire. Check the internal temperature in the thigh when rotating the bird at the 1-hour-and-45-minute mark. If the thigh is nearly up to temperature (the final temperature should be 175 to 180 degrees), check the temperature again after about 15 minutes. If the thigh is still well below temperature (145 degrees or cooler), don't bother checking the bird again for at least another 30 minutes.

TECHNIQUE: Protecting the Wings

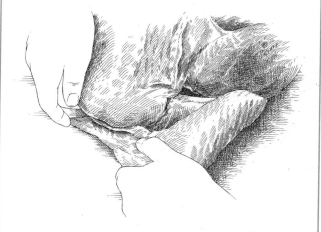

Tucking the wings under the bird will prevent them from burning on the grill.

2 cups kosher or 1 cup table salt
1 turkey (12 to 14 pounds), giblets and tail removed, rinsed thoroughly, and wings tucked (see illustration at left)
  Nonstick vegetable cooking spray
2 tablespoons unsalted butter, melted

1. Dissolve salt in 2 gallons of water in large (at least 16-quart) stockpot or clean bucket. Add turkey and refrigerate or set in very cool spot (between 32 and 40 degrees), 12 hours or overnight. (For information about brining outside of the refrigerator, see page 205.)

2. Toward end of brining time, cover six 3-inch wood chunks with water in medium bowl; soak wood chunks for 1 hour, then drain and set aside.

3. Keep bottom vents on grill completely open. Ignite large chimney starter filled three-quarters with charcoal briquettes (about 4½ quarts or 45 coals) and burn until covered with thin coating of light gray ash.

4. Meanwhile, spray V-rack with nonstick cooking spray. Remove turkey from brine and rinse inside and out under cool running water to remove all traces of salt. Pat turkey dry with paper towels; brush both sides with melted butter. Set turkey, breast-side down, in V-rack.

5. Empty coals into one side of grill, piling them up in mound two or three briquettes high. Place 3 wood chunks on top of charcoal. Put cooking grate in place and put V-rack with turkey over cool part of grill. Open grill lid vents halfway and cover, turning lid so that vents are opposite wood chunks to draw smoke through grill. Cover and grill-roast for 1 hour.

6. Remove lid from grill. Using thick potholders, transfer V-rack with turkey to rimmed baking sheet or roasting pan. Remove cooking grate and place 12 new briquettes and 3

remaining wood chunks on top of coals; replace grate. With wad of paper towels in each hand, flip turkey breast-side up in rack. Return V-rack with turkey to cool part of grill so that leg and wing that were facing coals are now facing away. Cover and grill-roast for 45 minutes.

7. Using thick potholders, carefully turn V-rack with turkey (the breast remains up) so that leg and wing that were facing coals are now facing away from coals. Insert instant-read thermometer into each thigh to check temperature and gauge how much longer turkey must cook (see note).

8. Cover and continue grill-roasting until thermometer inserted into thigh registers 175 to 180 degrees, 15 to 45 minutes more.

9. Remove turkey from grill, cover loosely with foil, and let rest 20 to 30 minutes. Carve and serve.

VARIATION

GRILL-ROASTED TURKEY ON A GAS GRILL

If you're using a gas grill, leaving one burner on and turning the other(s) off mimics the indirect heat method on a charcoal grill. Use wood chips instead of wood chunks and a disposable aluminum pan to hold them. The total cooking time is 2 to 2 1/2 hours, depending on the size of the bird, the ambient conditions (the bird will require more time on a cool, windy day), and the intensity of the fire. Check the internal temperature in the thigh when rotating the bird at the 1-hour-and-45-minute mark. If the thigh is nearly up to temperature (the final temperature should be 175 to 180 degrees), check the temperature again after about 15 minutes. If the thigh is still well below temperature (145 degrees or cooler), don't bother checking the bird again for at least another 30 minutes.

Follow recipe for Grill-Roasted Turkey on a Charcoal Grill through step 4, making following changes: Cover 3 cups wood chips with water and soak 30 minutes, then drain. Place soaked wood chips in small disposable aluminum pan; set pan on burner that will remain on. Turn all burners to high, close lid, and heat grill until chips smoke heavily, about 20 minutes. (If chips ignite, extinguish flames with water from squirt bottle.) Turn off burner(s) without wood chips. Place turkey over cool part of grill and proceed as directed.

TECHNIQUE:
Brining Outside of the Refrigerator

If refrigerator space is at a premium, you may want to brine the bird in a cool spot. Line a 16-quart stockpot, a large bucket, or a cooler with a turkey-sized oven bag. Make the brine and add 4 or 5 frozen gel packs along with the turkey. Tie the bag shut, cover the pot or bucket or close the cooler, and brine as directed, adding more gel packs if necessary.

MASHED SWEET POTATOES

WHAT WE WANTED: A mash with true, earthy, not overly sweet flavor and a flawlessly smooth, creamy texture.

For the holidays, mashed sweet potatoes are often overdressed in a Willie Wonka–style casserole topped with marshmallows and whipped cream. But this candied concoction doesn't hold a candle to an honest, sweet potato mash in terms of flavor. With a deep, natural sweetness that doesn't require much assistance, we knew that the humble sweet potato would taste far better if prepared using a minimum of ingredients.

Still, mashed sweet potatoes have their own set of problems. Nailing a fork-friendly puree every time is like cooking roulette. Mashed sweet potatoes often turn out overly thick and gluey or, to the other extreme, sloppy and loose. We also found that most recipes overload the puree with pumpkin pie seasonings that obscure the potatoes' natural flavor. We wanted to develop a recipe that would bring the deep, earthy sweet potato flavor to the forefront and that would produce a silky puree with enough body to hold its shape while sitting on a fork. Focusing first on the cooking method, we figured we could then test the remaining ingredients, from butter to heavy cream, and finally fiddle with the seasonings.

To determine the best method, we tested a variety of techniques: baking unpeeled potatoes, boiling the potatoes whole and unpeeled, boiling peeled and diced pieces, steaming peeled and diced pieces, and microwaving the potatoes whole and unpeeled. Adding a little butter and salt to the potatoes after they were mashed, we found huge differences in texture, flavor, and ease of preparation. The baked potatoes produced a mash with a deep flavor and bright color, but they took more than an hour to bake through, and handling them right out of the oven was a precarious endeavor. We also found that sweet potatoes range drastically in size, altering their baking times by nearly 30 minutes.

Boiling whole sweet potatoes in their skins turned out a wet puree with a mild flavor. Using a fork to monitor the potatoes as they cooked created holes that seemed to let flavor seep out and excess water in.

Steaming and boiling pieces of peeled potato produced the worst examples, offering zero flavor and loose, applesauce-like texture. The microwave, although fast and easy, was also a disappointment. The rate of cooking was difficult to control, and the difference between an undercooked and overdone potato was about 30 seconds. Over-microwaving the potatoes, even slightly, produced a pasty mouthfeel and an odd plastic flavor. By all accounts, this first round of testing bombed. Yet it did spark an idea.

Focusing on the sorry results, we learned a few things about cooking sweet potatoes. First, their deep, hearty flavor is surprisingly fleeting and easily washed out. Second, the tough and dense flesh reacts much like winter squash when it's cooked, turning wet and sloppy. We also found it safer to peel the sweet potatoes when they were raw and cold rather than cooked and hot. Taking all of this into account, we wondered if braising the sweet potatoes might work. If cut into uniform pieces and cooked over low heat in a covered pan, it seemed plausible that the sweet potatoes would release their own moisture slowly and braise themselves.

Beginning with a little bit of water to get the process going, we found the sweet potatoes were tender in about 40 minutes. We then simply removed the lid and mashed them right in the pot. To our delight, they were full of flavor because they had cooked, essentially, in their own liquid. We tried various pots and heat levels and found that a medium-sized pot (holding two to three layers of potatoes) cooked over low heat worked best. Higher heat levels cooked the potatoes unevenly and in some cases burned them. We also noted that the potatoes cooked quickly when sliced thin rather than cut into chunks. Out of curiosity we tried shredding the potatoes before adding them to the pot, but, as we had expected, the shreds simply oxidized and discolored before they were fully cooked, turning out puree with a pale color and stale flavor.

Up to this point, we had been adding only butter to the puree. We wondered what the typical additions of cream, milk, or half-and-half would do. Making four batches side by side, we tasted mashes made with only butter, with butter and milk, with butter and half-and-half, and with butter and heavy cream. Tasters found the butter-only batch boring, while milk turned the puree bland and watery. The batch with half-and-half came in second, with a heartier flavor and fuller body, but the heavy cream stole the show. Two pounds of potatoes tasted best when blended with 4 tablespoons of unsalted butter reinforced by 2 tablespoons heavy cream. Although this may seem like a miniscule amount of cream, more simply ran over the sweet potato's delicate flavor.

We found that ½ teaspoon of salt was plenty for 2 pounds of potatoes and noted that a bit of sugar did wonders to bolster the flavor. We tried honey, light and dark brown sugar, and molasses but liked the clean, indistinguishable flavor of white sugar for the master recipe. Other common sweet potato seasonings, such as nutmeg, vanilla, allspice, and cinnamon, were simply distracting.

As we had made this recipe many times now, a glaring oversight became obvious. Why didn't we replace the small amount of water used to cook the potatoes with the butter and heavy cream? Curious how the recipe would react without the water, we were gratified when this streamlined technique produced a puree that stood up on a fork with a luxurious texture that was neither loose nor gluey. And having eliminated the water from the mixture, the sweet potato flavor was now more intense than ever. This final twist not only simplified the recipe but also brought the flavor to a higher level.

WHAT WE LEARNED: Peel the sweet potatoes and slice them thin, then braise in a covered pot with a touch of heavy cream and butter. Don't bother with the typical pumpkin pie seasonings, but do try intriguing complementary flavors from around the world.

MASHED SWEET POTATOES serves 4

Cutting the sweet potatoes into slices of even thickness is important so that they cook at the same rate. A potato masher (see the Equipment Corner on page 209) will yield slightly lumpy sweet potatoes; a food mill will make a perfectly smooth puree. The potatoes are best served immediately, but they can be covered tightly with plastic wrap and kept relatively hot for 30 minutes. This recipe can be doubled and prepared in a Dutch oven; the cooking time will need to be doubled as well.

4   tablespoons unsalted butter, cut into 4 pieces
2   tablespoons heavy cream
½   teaspoon salt
1   teaspoon sugar
2   pounds sweet potatoes (about 2 large or 3 medium-small potatoes), peeled, quartered lengthwise, and cut crosswise into ¼-inch-thick slices
    Pinch ground black pepper

1. Combine butter, cream, salt, sugar, and sweet potatoes in 3- to 4-quart saucepan; cook, covered, over low heat, stirring occasionally, until potatoes fall apart when poked with fork, 35 to 45 minutes.

2. Off heat, mash sweet potatoes in saucepan with potato masher, or transfer mixture to hopper of food mill and process into warmed serving bowl. Stir in pepper; serve immediately.

VARIATIONS

INDIAN-SPICED MASHED SWEET POTATOES WITH RAISINS AND CASHEWS

Follow recipe for Mashed Sweet Potatoes, substituting dark brown sugar for granulated sugar and adding ¾ teaspoon garam masala to saucepan along with sweet potatoes. Stir ¼ cup golden raisins and ¼ cup roasted unsalted cashews, chopped coarse, into mashed sweet potatoes along with black pepper.

GARLIC-SCENTED MASHED SWEET POTATOES WITH COCONUT MILK AND CILANTRO

Thai flavors provided the inspiration for this variation. Shake the can of coconut milk thoroughly before opening it to combine the coconut cream that rises to the top with the liquid beneath.

Follow recipe for Mashed Sweet Potatoes, substituting ½ cup coconut milk for butter and cream and adding ¼ teaspoon hot red pepper flakes and 1 small garlic clove, minced, to saucepan along with sweet potatoes. Stir in 1 tablespoon minced fresh cilantro along with black pepper.

MAPLE-ORANGE MASHED SWEET POTATOES

Follow recipe for Mashed Sweet Potatoes, stirring in 2 tablespoons maple syrup and ½ teaspoon grated orange zest along with black pepper.

TASTING LAB: Sweet Potatoes

IT'S AN AGE-OLD CULINARY QUESTION: WHAT'S THE difference between a yam and a sweet potato? The answer: it depends on where you live. In American markets, a "yam" is actually a mislabeled sweet potato. If you can get a glimpse of the box they're shipped in, you'll see the words "sweet potato" printed somewhere, as mandated by the U.S. Department of Agriculture. In other parts of the world, the word "yam" refers to a true yam, which is of no relation to the sweet potato. Sold under the label of *ñame* (ny-AH-may) or *igname* here in the United States, a true yam has hairy, off-white or brown skin and white, light yellow, or pink flesh. This tuber is usually sold in log-shaped chunks that weigh several pounds each. Unlike a sweet potato, a true yam is very bland, with an ultra-starchy texture.

So now you know the difference between a sweet potato and a yam. But did you know there are numerous varieties of sweet potatoes available and that they range in

MASHED SWEET POTATOES WITH AFRICAN FLAVORS

Toast ½ teaspoon ground coriander and ⅛ teaspoon cayenne in medium saucepan over medium heat until fragrant, about 30 seconds. Follow recipe for Mashed Sweet Potatoes, cooking butter, cream, salt, sugar, and sweet potatoes in saucepan with toasted spices. Stir in 1 tablespoon chunky peanut butter and 1 tablespoon minced fresh cilantro along with black pepper.

color from pale white to shocking purple? Having developed our recipe for mashed sweet potatoes with the conventional orange-fleshed variety found at our local grocery store, we wondered what difference, if any, these other varieties would make.

Mashing seven varieties of sweet potato side by side, we found the resulting differences in flavor and texture astounding. Of the orange varieties, Beauregard (usually sold as conventional sweet potatoes) was favored for its "standard sweet potato flavor" and perfect texture, while Jewel (sold as a "yam") was "moderately sweet" with a wetter mash, and Red Garnet (sold as a "yam") was downright "savory" and "loose."

In the non-orange category, the white-fleshed Japanese Sweet was "unbelievable," with a "buttery," "chestnut" flavor unlike anything we had ever tasted. By comparison, the similar but less potent flavor of the White Sweet was considered "nice" and "creamy," but the flavor was "fleeting." Ranking at the bottom were the off-white Batata, with its mild flavor and "Play-Doh-like" texture, along with the purple Okinawa, which produced a "dry," nutty-flavored mash with an intense violet hue that was "a bit scary to look at."

EQUIPMENT CORNER: Potato Mashers

THERE ARE TWO CLASSIC STYLES OF POTATO MASHER—wire-looped mashers with a zigzag presser and disk mashers with a perforated round or oval plate. Modern mashers, as it turns out, are simply variations on these two original designs. We tested a total of eight mashers to find those with the most comfortable grip and the most effective mashing mechanism.

When we wrapped up our mash-fest, we concluded that the wire-looped mashers were second-rate, because the space between the loops made it hard to achieve a good, fast mash. Most of the potato pieces escaped between the loops unscathed. Several disk mashers were flimsy and bent under the weight of a few strong mashes. Likewise, steer clear of flat-handled varieties, as they were uncomfortable to grip.

One disk masher, the Exeter ($9.99), is worth mentioning, however, since it is spring-loaded and uses a double-tiered set of wire loops for mashing. It took some muscle to use this masher, but it was the fastest masher tested, turning a pot of boiled potatoes into a smooth puree with just 20 strokes.

In general, the disk mashers outperformed the wire-looped models, and the Profiplus ($15.99) was our favorite. With its small holes, this oval-based masher turned out soft and silky spuds with a reasonable 40 thrusts. Its rounded edges snuggled right into the curves of the saucepan, enhancing its efficacy, and its round handle was easy to grip. The runner-up, the Oxo Good Grips Smooth Masher ($9.99), has an oval metal base and rectangular perforations. The larger perforations allowed a bit more potato through, so it took 50 mashes to do the trick, but the squat device with a cushiony handle was very easy to use. We did not like the all-plastic Oxo Good Grips masher—it has an awkward grip and an ineffective mash—so shop carefully if buying this brand. In any case, avoid disk mashers with perforations larger than ¼ inch.

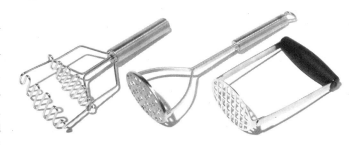

BEST POTATO MASHERS
The disk-style Profiplus Masher (middle) is our favorite because it yielded silky spuds with little effort. The Oxo Good Grips Smooth Masher (right) was the runner-up in our testing. This disk masher was comfortable to use but a bit slower than our top choice. The spring-loaded Exeter Masher (left) was very fast but a bit awkward to use. That said, it was the best wire loop masher tested. See www.cooksillustrated.com for up-to-date prices and mail-order sources for these top-rated products.

CRANBERRY SAUCE

WHAT WE WANTED: A well-balanced sauce—neither too sweet nor too tart—with a soft gel-like texture and some whole berries.

Although cranberry jelly, molded in the shape of the can and sliced into neat disks, is one of the test kitchen's guilty pleasures, it's usually not our first choice for the holiday table. There, a soft, tart-sweet sauce with plenty of whole berries reigns. The best cranberry sauce has a clean, pure cranberry flavor, with enough sweetness to temper the assertively tart fruit but not so much that the sauce is cloying or candylike. The texture should be that of a soft gel, neither too liquidy nor too stiff, cushioning some softened but still intact berries.

Because simple cranberry sauce has only three ingredients—cranberries, sweetener, and liquid—the variables to test were straightforward. Though many of the recipes we researched called for 1 pound of cranberries, we wanted to base ours on 12 ounces of berries simply because all of the bags in stores are that size; we couldn't see the point of opening a second bag to use only a third of it.

Most cranberry sauce recipes use granulated sugar as a sweetener, but we also tried other possibilities, including brown sugar, honey, maple syrup, and corn syrup. Granulated sugar was the tasters' favorite because it balanced the tartness of the berries with a direct sweetness, without adding a strong flavor profile of its own. The corn syrup tasted flat and bland, while the flavors of the maple syrup, brown sugar, and honey were too pronounced, compromising that of the berries. The amount of sugar called for in the recipes we turned up during our research ranged from $3/8$ cup to $1\frac{1}{2}$ cups for 12 ounces of berries. In our tests, tasters unanimously favored 1 cup of sugar.

The liquids used to make the sauce ran a wide gamut. We tried batches made with apple juice and cider, white and dark grape juice, orange juice, pineapple juice, cranberry juice cocktail, 7UP, red wine, white wine, port, and champagne. Except for the port and champagne, tasters agreed that none of these liquids—even the orange juice, which is traditional—offered a significant flavor advantage over plain water. In testing different amounts of water, we found that $3/4$ cup provided the ideal sauce-to-berry ratio once the sauce had reached serving temperature.

Tests of the various cooking times revealed that less is more. About five minutes over medium heat was all it took to achieve a supple, just-firm-enough set in the cooled sauce. Cranberries are high in pectin, a naturally occurring carbohydrate in many fruits. In the presence of sugar and acid (cranberries contain both), the large pectin molecules bond to produce the characteristic jelled consistency. Since pectin molecules are released as the cells of the fruit break down during cooking, the longer the fruit cooks, the more pectin is released (and the more liquid is evaporated), and the stiffer the finished gel becomes. Cooking the sauce for 10 minutes, for instance, resulted in a gel you could slice with a knife. We also tested using a skillet instead of a saucepan and high heat rather than medium heat. We could see no advantage either way and decided to leave well enough alone.

The last round of tests focused on seasoning. Many recipes call simply for cranberries, water, and sugar, while others specify additions such as lemon juice, almond or vanilla extract, and salt. Lemon juice was much too tart, and both extracts left tasters cold, but we were amazed by the dramatic improvement a little salt could make. Just $1/4$ teaspoon of salt revealed heretofore unknown sweetness in the cranberries and heightened the flavor of the sauce overall, letting loose a full range of high and low flavor notes.

WHAT WE LEARNED: Keep it simple—just water, granulated sugar, and cranberries make the best sauce. Keep it short—simmering for more than five minutes results in a stiff, sliceable gel. And don't forget the salt.

BASIC CRANBERRY SAUCE makes 2¼ cups

The cooking time in this recipe is intended for fresh berries. If you've got frozen cranberries, do not defrost them before use; just pick through them and add about 2 minutes to the simmering time.

¾	cup water
1	cup sugar
¼	teaspoon salt
1	(12-ounce) bag cranberries, picked through

Bring water, sugar, and salt to a boil in medium nonreactive saucepan over high heat, stirring occasionally to dissolve sugar. Stir in cranberries; return to a boil. Reduce heat to medium; simmer until saucy, slightly thickened, and about two-thirds of berries have popped open, about 5 minutes. Transfer to nonreactive bowl, cool to room temperature, and serve. (Can be covered and refrigerated up to 7 days; let stand at room temperature 30 minutes before serving.)

VARIATIONS

CRANBERRY-ORANGE SAUCE

Orange juice adds little flavor, but we found that zest and liqueur pack the orange kick we were looking for in this sauce.

Follow recipe for Basic Cranberry Sauce, heating 1 tablespoon grated orange zest with sugar mixture. Off heat, stir in 2 tablespoons orange liqueur (such as Triple Sec or Grand Marnier).

CRANBERRY SAUCE WITH PEARS AND FRESH GINGER

Peel, core, and cut 2 medium-sized firm, ripe pears into ½-inch chunks; set aside. Follow recipe for Basic Cranberry Sauce, heating 1 tablespoon grated fresh ginger and ¼ teaspoon ground cinnamon with sugar mixture and stirring pears into liquid along with cranberries.

CRANBERRY SAUCE WITH CHAMPAGNE AND CURRANTS

Follow recipe for Basic Cranberry Sauce, substituting champagne for water and adding 3 tablespoons dried currants to liquid along with the cranberries.

A no-cook parsley sauce enlivens our
roast beef tenderloin.

HOLIDAY dinner

CHAPTER 17

America is a land of meat and potato eaters. While the phrase meat and potatoes may seem mundane (it sounds like we are talking about Tuesday-night supper), there's no reason why meat and potatoes can't be special enough for a holiday dinner, especially when the meat is beef tenderloin and the potatoes are scalloped.

Beef tenderloin costs a small fortune, but it is one of the quickest and easiest large cuts to serve to a crowd. The key is to get good color development on the exterior without overcooking the interior. A pale roast won't do, and neither will one that's gray inside.

Betty Crocker may have put scalloped potatoes in a box and thus made them easy enough for everyday cooking, but we think scalloped potatoes should be done right—from scratch—and served with special meals. That said, no one wants to spend hours slicing and layering potatoes into a gratin dish. We were determined to figure out a way to make this dish great while keeping the workload manageable. A thick, gluey sauce (the kind boxed versions yield) wouldn't do, either. We wanted the real thing—creamy, smooth, rich, and cheesy.

IN THIS CHAPTER

THE RECIPES

Roast Beef Tenderloin
Parsley Sauce with Cornichons and Capers

Scalloped Potatoes
Scalloped Potatoes with Wild Mushrooms

EQUIPMENT CORNER

Boning Knives

SCIENCE DESK

What Happens to Meat as It Rests?

ROAST BEEF TENDERLOIN

WHAT WE WANTED: Perfectly cooked meat with a rosy interior and a well-crusted, browned exterior.

For large holiday parties, few cuts can top beef tenderloin. The tenderloin, which comes from the short loin, starts out very tender and can be cooked at a high oven temperature. This elegant roast thus cooks quickly, and its rich, buttery slices are always fork-tender.

Despite its many virtues, however, beef tenderloin is not without its liabilities. Price, of course, is the biggest. Even at a local warehouse-style supermarket, the going rate for a whole beef tenderloin is $7.99 per pound—making for an average sticker price of about $50.

There is good reason for the tenderloin's hefty price. Because it sits up under the spine of the cow, it gets no exercise at all and is therefore the most tender piece of meat. It is one of the two muscles in the ultra-premium steaks known as the porterhouse and the T-bone, so when it is removed from the cow as a whole muscle, it is going to sell for an ultra-premium price. We confirmed this by heading to the supermarket and the local butcher and purchasing $550 worth of beef tenderloin—which bought us just 11 roasts.

A whole beef tenderloin can be purchased "unpeeled," with an incredibly thick layer of exterior fat left attached, but it's usually sold "peeled," or stripped of its fat. Because of our many bad experiences with today's overly lean pork and beef, we purchased six of the 11 roasts unpeeled, determined to leave on as much fat as possible. However, after a quick examination of the unpeeled roasts, we realized that the excessively thick layer of surface fat had to go. Not only would such a large quantity of rendering fat smoke up the kitchen, it would also prohibit a delicious crust from forming on the meat. We dutifully peeled the thick layer of fat from the six tenderloins, but even after removing the sheaths of fat, there were still large pockets of fat on the interior as well as significant surface fat.

Does it make sense to buy an unpeeled roast and trim it yourself? We think not. We paid $6.99 per pound at the butcher for our unpeeled tenderloins, each weighing about 8 pounds. After cleaning them up, the peeled tenderloins weighed about 5 pounds, with a whopping 3 pounds of waste. We purchased peeled tenderloins of similar quality from another source for only $7.99 per pound. Clearly, the unpeeled tenderloins were more expensive with no benefits. And although we don't like tenderloins that have been picked clean, right down to the meat, we recommend buying peeled roasts, with their patches of scattered fat, and letting them be.

The tenderloin's sleek, boneless form makes for quick roasting, but its torpedo-like shape—thick and chunky at one end, gradually tapering at the other end—naturally roasts unevenly. For those looking for a range of doneness, this is not a problem, but for cooks who want a more evenly cooked roast, something must be done.

Folding the tip end of the roast under and tying it bulks up the tenderloin center to almost the same thickness as the more substantial butt end. This ensures that the tenderloin cooks more evenly. (Even so, the tip end is always a little more well-done than the butt.) Tying the roast at approximately 1½-inch intervals further guarantees a more uniformly shaped roast and consequently more even slices of beef. Snipping the silver skin (the translucent sheath that encases certain cuts of beef) at several points also prevents the meat from bowing during cooking. This occurs when the silver skin shrinks more than the meat to which it is attached.

Over the years, we've come to like slow-roasting for large roasts. The lower the heat, we've found, the more evenly the roast cooks. To develop a rich brown crust on these low-roasted larger cuts, we pan-sear them up front or increase the oven temperature for the last few minutes of roasting—or we may do both.

But a beef tenderloin is a different proposition. Though

relatively large, its long, thin shape would seem to dictate a relatively quick cooking time. To determine the ideal roasting temperature, we started at the two extremes, roasting one tenderloin at 200 degrees, the other at 500. As expected, the roast cooked at 500 degrees not only created a very smoky kitchen from the rendering fat, it was also overcooked at each end and around the perimeter. However, the high oven heat had formed a thick, flavorful crust. A good crust is crucial to this rich yet mild-tasting roast, whose flavor is sometimes barely recognizable as beef. Despite the even, rosy pink interior of the beef cooked at 200 degrees, this roast lacked the all-important crust. Neither oven temperature was ideal, so we kept roasting.

Because the higher roasting temperature provided the rich flavor this roast desperately needs, we decided to roast it at as high a temperature as possible. A 450-degree oven still gave us smoke and uneven cooking, so we moved down to 425 degrees. For comparison, we roasted another tenderloin at 200 degrees, this time increasing the oven temperature to 425 degrees at the end of cooking to develop a crust. Both roasts emerged from the oven looking beautiful, and their meat looked and tasted almost identical. Because the tenderloin roasted at 425 degrees was done in just 45 minutes (compared with the slow-roasted tenderloin, which took just about twice as long), we chose the high-heat method.

Although all roasts should rest 15 to 20 minutes after cooking, we found that beef tenderloin improves dramatically if left uncarved even longer. If cut too soon, its slices are soft and flabby. A slightly longer rest—we settled on 30 minutes—allows the meat to firm up into a texture we found much more appealing. Before carving, we preferred removing the big pockets of excess fat, which become more obvious at warm and room temperatures.

WHAT WE LEARNED: **Buy a peeled tenderloin (it's a better value than an unpeeled roast), tie up the tip end to ensure even cooking, roast in a 425-degree oven to create a flavorful crust, and then let the tenderloin rest for 30 minutes so the juices distribute themselves back into the meat.**

ROAST BEEF TENDERLOIN serves 12 to 16

To give the tenderloin a more pronounced pepper crust, increase the amount of pepper to 6 tablespoons and use a mixture of strong black and white and mild pink and green peppercorns. Be sure to crush the peppercorns with a mortar and pestle or with a heavy-bottomed saucepan or skillet. Do not use a coffee or spice grinder, which will grind the softer green and pink peppercorns to a powder before the harder black and white peppercorns begin to break up. See the illustrations on page 216 for more information on preparing the tenderloin.

1   whole peeled beef tenderloin (5 to 6 pounds), thoroughly patted dry
2   tablespoons olive oil
1   tablespoon kosher salt or 2 teaspoons table salt
2   tablespoons coarse-ground black pepper
    Parsley Sauce with Cornichons and Capers (recipe follows)

1. Remove tenderloin from refrigerator 1 hour before roasting to bring meat up to room temperature. Use sharp knife to carefully nick silver skin on side opposite tip with shallow slashes at 1½-inch intervals. Tuck tip end under and tie roast crosswise, knotting at 1½-inch intervals.

2. Adjust oven rack to upper-middle position and heat oven to 425 degrees. Set meat on sheet of plastic wrap and rub all over with oil. Sprinkle with salt and pepper; then lift plastic wrap up and around meat to press on excess.

3. Transfer prepared tenderloin from wrap to wire rack on shallow roasting pan. Roast until instant-read thermometer inserted into thickest part of roast registers about 125 degrees (meat will range from medium-rare to medium in different areas), about 45 minutes. Let stand for about 30 minutes before carving. (Can be wrapped in plastic, refrigerated up to 2 days, sliced, and served chilled.) Cut meat into ½-inch thick slices. Arrange on serving platter and serve with sauce.

TECHNIQUE:
Preparing a Beef Tenderloin

1. To keep the meat from bowing as it cooks, slide a knife under the silver skin and flick the blade upward to cut through the silver skin at five or six spots along the length of the roast.

2. To ensure that the tenderloin roasts more evenly, fold the thin tip end of the roast under about 6 inches.

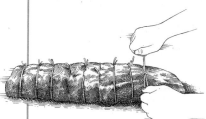

3. For more even cooking and evenly sized slices, use 12-inch lengths of kitchen twine to tie the roast every 1 1/2 inches.

4. Set the meat on a sheet of plastic wrap and rub it all over with oil. Sprinkle with salt and pepper, then lift the plastic wrap up and around the meat to press on excess. This method guarantees even coverage.

PARSLEY SAUCE WITH CORNICHONS AND CAPERS makes about 1 1/4 cups

Prepare this sauce while the roast rests or several hours in advance and keep it covered at room temperature.

- 3/4 cup minced fresh parsley leaves
- 12 cornichons, minced (6 tablespoons), plus 1 teaspoon cornichon juice
- 1/4 cup capers, chopped coarse
- 2 medium scallions, white and light green parts, minced
  Pinch salt
- 1/4 teaspoon ground black pepper
- 1/2 cup extra-virgin olive oil

Mix ingredients together in medium bowl.

SCIENCE DESK:
What Happens to Meat as It Rests?

A FINAL BUT VERY IMPORTANT STEP WHEN COOKING tenderloin (and all red meats) is allowing it to rest before slicing. As the proteins in the meat heat up during cooking they coagulate, which basically means they uncoil and then reconnect, or bond, with each other, in a different configuration. When the proteins coagulate, they squeeze out part of the liquid that was trapped in their coiled structures and in the spaces between the individual molecules. The heat from the cooking source drives these freed liquids toward the center of the meat.

This process of coagulation explains why experienced chefs can tell how done a piece of meat is by pushing on it and judging the amount of resistance: the firmer the meat, the more done it is. But the coagulation process is apparently at least partly reversible, so as you allow the meat to rest and return to a lower temperature after cooking, some of the liquid is reabsorbed by the protein molecules as their capacity to hold moisture increases. As a result, if given a

TECHNIQUE:

Learning to Tie Butcher's Knots

Many cooks have trouble tying roasts properly. If that's the case, practice with a roll of paper towels and strands of butcher's twine. It's a lot neater than practicing on a roast.

chance to rest, the meat will lose less juice when you cut into it, which in turn makes for much juicier meat. In the case of beef tenderloin, the texture of the meat also improves, becoming a bit firmer as it rests.

EQUIPMENT CORNER: Boning Knives

THE SLIM, FLEXIBLE BLADE OF A BONING KNIFE MAY LOOK eccentric, but it is perfectly designed to slide nimbly through joints and between bones. It is an essential tool for such tasks as removing cutlets from a whole chicken breast and can also be used to remove fat and silver skin from a beef tenderloin. The slim blade creates less drag through the meat, and the slices made are neater than those possible with the wider blade on a chef's knife.

Because most home cooks are likely to use a boning knife infrequently, we wondered if a cheaper knife would do. To find out, we tested six leading knives with blades between 5 and 7 inches long and prices between $9 and $71. Both large- and small-handed testers used each knife to butcher a whole chicken and to trim beef ribs of fat and silver skin. Each knife was evaluated for handle comfort, slipperiness (hands become very greasy when butchering),

agility (including flexibility), and sharpness.

The winning Forschner (Victorinox) Fibrox boning knife, priced at $17.90, received high marks for its uniquely designed ergonomic handle as well as its slim, highly maneuverable blade and razor-sharp edge. The plastic handle nestled comfortably into both large and small hands, and it stayed there even when our hands became slick with fat. The blade was the narrowest of the lot, which made it very agile. While all the knives arrived with razor-sharp edges, the Forschner seemed exceptionally keen, gliding effortlessly through tough tendon and thick skin.

The J.A. Henckels Professional S boning knife ($49.99) finished a close second. Its blade was nearly as agile as the Forschner, but the handle was somewhat slippery. The Wüsthof-Trident Grand Prix boning knife ($54) was "fiendishly sharp," but the wide blade was not as agile as the top models and the handle became slippery when coated with chicken fat. The textured metal handle of the Global boning knife ($70.99) received mixed reviews, and testers did not like the boxy handle on the Chicago Cutlery boning knife ($14.99) or the flimsy blade on the Farberware Professional boning knife ($8.99).

BEST BONING KNIFE

The Forschner (Victorinox) Fibrox knife boasts a handle that testers found "easy-to-grip" and a narrow blade that shows "great flexibility around bones." Everyone raved about the "amazing" sharpness of this knife out of the box. For an up-to-date price and mail-order source for this top-rated product, see www.cooksillustrated.com.

SCALLOPED POTATOES

WHAT WE WANTED: Layers of thinly sliced, tender potatoes, creamy sauce, and a nicely browned, cheesy crust.

Thinly sliced potatoes layered with cream and baked until they are bubbling and browned are a classic accompaniment to a holiday ham or roast beef. Although the supermarket shelves are lined with "add water, heat, and serve" versions of scalloped potatoes, making them from scratch doesn't have to take much time, and the differences in flavor and texture are tremendous.

To start, we tested three different techniques for "scalloping" potatoes. First, we boiled the potatoes, combined them with a cream sauce thickened with flour (also known as a béchamel), and then finished them in the oven. This method produced a thick, pasty sauce and hollow-flavored potatoes, not to mention several dirty pots.

For our next test we combined raw, sliced potatoes with an unthickened cream sauce, allowing it to cook through and thicken in the oven. While these potatoes had more flavor and the sauce had a better consistency, the cooking time was more than an hour and half.

Wanting to speed up the process a bit, we tried cooking the potatoes in simmering cream for a few minutes before transferring the potatoes and cream to a casserole dish and finishing the potatoes in the oven. This technique allowed the potatoes to get a good head start on cooking and also encouraged them to release some of their starch, which naturally thickened the cream to the consistency of a good sauce. We did find it necessary to cover the pot to prevent the heavy cream and the starch from reducing and thickening too far in advance. By cooking the potatoes in the cream, covered, for about 15 minutes, we were able to reduce the oven time to a mere 20 minutes, resulting in perfectly cooked potatoes and a smooth, lightly thickened cream sauce.

With the technique set, we moved on to the different types of potatoes, testing Yukon Gold, all-purpose, and russet. Although each variety cooked up differently, none was terrible. Yukon Gold and all-purpose potatoes were both a bit too waxy and buttery when mixed with the rich cream. Russet potatoes turned out a bit more tender, and their earthier flavor was the tasters' favorite.

The thickness of the potato slices also made a noticeable difference in the final texture of the casserole. We found that potatoes cut into $1/8$-inch-thick slices kept their shape but were still flexible enough to form tight layers that stuck together to create a neat casserole. Thicker slices formed a looser, sloppier casserole, while thinner slices melted together and gave the finished dish the texture of mashed potatoes.

Focusing now on the sauce, we noticed that those made with all heavy cream were overbearingly heavy. We tried half-and-half but found that it wasn't rich enough. Even worse, the sauce made with half-and-half curdled in the oven. Half-and-half simply doesn't have enough fat to keep the dairy proteins from coagulating under high heat, which makes the sauce look curdled. In the end, we simply tempered the heavy cream with a little whole milk, which lightened the rich sauce just enough while keeping its texture smooth.

Scalloped potatoes also contain cheese. We found that a sprinkling of cheese formed a golden crust on the top of the dish while still allowing the cream to bubble up around the edges and thicken. Cheddar is the classic choice, but we got nice results with other cheeses with good melting properties, including Parmesan, Monterey Jack, and Gruyère.

WHAT WE LEARNED: Don't use flour to thicken the sauce (it will be pasty) but instead rely on heavy cream lightened with a little whole milk. To cut the cooking time, simmer the potatoes briefly in the cream and then dump the whole mixture into a baking dish. Use russet potatoes for the best texture and flavor, and slice them thin so they form neat layers.

SCALLOPED POTATOES serves 8 to 10

For the fastest and most consistent results, slice the potatoes in a food processor. See the Equipment Corner on page 165 for information about choosing a gratin dish for this recipe.

2   tablespoons unsalted butter
1   small onion, minced
2   medium garlic cloves, minced
     (about 2 teaspoons)
3   cups heavy cream
1   cup whole milk
4   sprigs fresh thyme
2   bay leaves
2   teaspoons salt
½   teaspoon ground black pepper
4   pounds russet potatoes, peeled and cut into
     ⅛-inch-thick slices
1   cup shredded cheddar cheese (about 4 ounces)

1. Heat oven to 350 degrees. Meanwhile, melt butter in large Dutch oven over medium-high heat until foaming subsides, about 1 minute. Add onion and sauté until it turns soft and begins to brown, about 4 minutes. Add garlic and sauté until fragrant, about 30 seconds. Add cream, milk, thyme, bay leaves, salt, pepper, and potatoes and bring to simmer. Cover, adjusting heat as necessary to maintain light simmer, and cook until potatoes are almost tender (paring knife can be slipped into and out of center of potato slice with some resistance), about 15 minutes.

2. Remove and discard thyme sprigs and bay leaves. Transfer potato mixture to 3-quart gratin dish and sprinkle with cheese. Bake until cream has thickened and is bubbling around sides and top is golden brown, about 20 minutes. Cool for 5 minutes before serving.

VARIATION

SCALLOPED POTATOES WITH WILD MUSHROOMS

Cover ½ ounce dried porcini mushroom pieces with ½ cup hot tap water in small microwave-safe bowl; cover with plastic wrap, cut several steam vents with paring knife, and microwave on high power for 30 seconds. Let stand until mushrooms soften, about 5 minutes. Lift mushrooms from liquid with fork and mince, using chef's knife (you should have about 2 tablespoons). Pour soaking liquid through strainer lined with paper towel and reserve. Follow recipe for Scalloped Potatoes, adding 3½ ounces fresh shiitake mushrooms, sliced ¼ inch thick, and 5 ounces fresh cremini mushrooms, sliced ¼ inch thick, to foaming butter along with onion and cook until mushrooms release their moisture, about 2 minutes. Add minced, rehydrated porcini along with their liquid and cook until all mushrooms are tender and liquid has reduced to about 2 tablespoons, about 3 minutes. Add garlic and proceed as directed, replacing cheddar with Gruyère or Parmesan.

HAM dinner

Ham with green bean casserole makes for a classic American dinner. But a well-stocked supermarket offers many different kinds of ham to choose from, and green bean casserole can be pretty sorry stuff. We wanted to figure out how to make the most of both.

We started by testing all of the major types of hams (as well as brands) available in supermarkets and found that we liked best the spiral-sliced ham with natural juices. It is neither overly pumped up with water nor packed into a cylindrical loaf shape. And for the test kitchen staff, who had to carve all of the hams before the tasting, it was hands-down the most convenient of the bone-in hams.

The green bean casserole of the 1950s was a 1-2-3 recipe consisting of frozen green beans, canned soup, and canned fried onions. It was a testament to convenience at the expense of good taste. We thought we'd be willing to trade some of that convenience for a casserole that tasted really good, starting with fresh green beans instead of frozen and our own simple sauce.

IN THIS CHAPTER

THE RECIPES
Spiral-Sliced Ham
Dried Cherry and Stout Sauce
  with Brown Sugar and Allspice
Mustard Sauce with Vermouth
  and Thyme

Green Bean Casserole

EQUIPMENT CORNER
Timer/Thermometers

TASTING LAB
Spiral-Sliced Hams

Good green bean casserole begins with fresh beans that are cooked in salted boiling water, shocked in a bowl of ice water, and then drained.

SPIRAL-SLICED HAM

WHAT WE WANTED: The ideal ham is neither dry nor mushy. It should have a nice chew and be accompanied by a complex sauce that's not too sweet. Finally, the ham should be as easy to carve as possible.

We've always been fond of ham. We love its toothy, meaty chew and its unique flavor combination of sweet, salt, and smoke. Despite this devotion to ham, we have to admit that the versions appearing on most holiday tables are far from ideal. Very often they are dry as dust or mushy as a wet paper towel. We decided to find the best possible way to prepare a precooked supermarket ham so that it could live up to its full potential.

Hams vary in terms of the amount of water added during the curing process. A ham that has no added water is labeled just plain "ham." While some manufacturers still make these hams, they are very hard to find in supermarkets. "Ham with natural juices" (as the label would state) has 7 to 8 percent water added; "ham-water added" has 12 to 15 percent water added; and "ham and water product" contains more than 15 percent added water. The more water a ham contains, the less expensive it is per pound. They also vary in terms of bone. They may be boneless, semiboneless, or completely bone-in.

The results of our tasting were pretty predictable: More bone and less water seemed to make for the tastiest hams. Boneless and semiboneless hams had "compressed" textures that we did not like, and the hams with the most water added had the most dilute flavor. Bone-in, spiral-sliced hams with natural juices were the favorite in our tasting. They were neither overly pumped up with water nor packed into a cylindrical loaf shape. They were also the favorite of the test kitchen staff in terms of convenience. After having to carve many of the hams in the testing, we were quite happy to meet up with a ham that had been carved for us. Spiral-sliced hams were hams were

hands-down the most convenient of the bone-in choices.

"Cooking" (really, only heating) these fully cooked hams is a no-brainer, which is why, we'll bet, that these hams are so popular around the holidays. The problem is that heating instructions for spiral-sliced hams differ from package to package. To add to the confusion, there are discrepancies in recommended final internal temperatures. Such imprecision wouldn't be such an issue if these hams didn't readily dry out and turn to jerky when improperly heated.

One factor that had to be decided at the outset was the internal temperature to which the ham should be heated. Spiral-sliced hams are fully cooked, and so long as the sell-by date hasn't come and gone, the ham can be served straight out of the package. While most cooks would still elect to heat the ham before serving, there is no consensus as to what temperature it should reach before being brought to the table. The label of one package said 120 degrees. The National Pork Producers Council said 140 degrees. Two manufacturers didn't include a temperature in their heating directions, so we called to inquire and were told 150 degrees by one and 155 degrees by the other. This discrepancy is unfortunate, because heating the ham to the proper internal temperature is critical to helping it retain its juices.

When we heated a ham to 140 degrees it lost a large amount of liquid and was dry. Heating to 130 degrees was an improvement, but we found that taking the ham to only 100 degrees was better yet. The outer inch of the ham registered at about 145 degrees, and residual heat caused the internal temperature to continue rising as the ham rested, covered, after coming out of the oven. After 40 minutes it peaked at 115 to 120 degrees, which had been our original goal. Though this may sound like a low temperature, the ham was warm to the touch and, most important, had remained moist and juicy. And, after all, we are dealing with a precooked cut of meat here.

Having settled on the final temperature, we needed to

figure out exactly how to get there. Our first task was to determine the proper oven temperature. We quickly found that a high (400 degrees) or even a moderate (325 degrees) oven was no good. Though the hams were covered with foil for protection, when subjected to these temperatures they lost an astounding amount of liquid (up to 2 cups); the meat was dry and leathery and the slices torqued and splayed.

We then began experimenting with low oven temperatures. These worked much better, but the cooking time now became an issue. At the low end of the scale, an average 9-pound ham heated in a 225-degree oven was both juicy and moist and held its shape, but it took a grueling 3 ¼ hours to heat up. In a 250-degree oven, the ham was just as good, but it heated in 2¾ hours, shaving 30 minutes off the cooking time.

Although easy, this was still a long process, so we sought means to speed it up. We tried different combinations of high and low temperatures, but they were either detrimental to the moistness of the ham or did nothing to speed its heating.

Someone in the test kitchen then suggested a plastic oven bag instead of the foil cover. Quite to our astonishment, this simple, flimsy looking accouterment trimmed off a few minutes of cooking time per pound. While this may sound insignificant, it can translate into a 20- to 30-minute differential when cooking a piece of meat the size of a ham. How did it work? We posited that the oven bag, wrapped tightly around the ham, eliminated the air space—an insulation of sorts—formed between the foil and the ham, thereby giving the ham direct exposure to heat and speeding its heating. Another step that speeds the heating process is letting the ham stand at room temperature for 90 minutes before putting it in the oven. This, too, takes off a couple of minutes per pound. By using an oven bag and letting the ham stand at room temperature, we had whittled the heating time down to about 2 hours, with a 40-minute rest out of the oven. Protracted though this process may seem, it's great in that it frees the oven for other last-minute cooking tasks.

With the cooking method in place, we now had two more points to consider: making the sauce and carving the ham. We wanted to come up with something better than the gooey glaze that comes in a packet with many hams. And we wanted to see which of the two cuts of spiral-sliced ham available—the shank or the sirloin—would be easier to carve.

Most spiral-sliced hams come with an enclosed packet of glaze. We tossed them all aside because we have found that glazes, whether prepackaged or homemade, do little to enhance this kind of ham. Instead, they tend to sit on the surface like a layer of gooey candy. Although this may appeal to children, we much prefer to make an interesting, flavorful sauce to accompany the ham. The sauce, since it doesn't use any pan drippings, can be made ahead and reheated. It dresses up the ham, making it look and taste more elegant, and it also adds moisture to carved ham slices, which tend to dry out somewhat as they sit uncovered on a serving platter, waiting for guests to reach for seconds.

We also discovered that the shank end of the ham is substantially easier to carve than the sirloin, or butt, end because of the bone configuration. The packages aren't labeled as such, but the shank can be identified by the tapered, more pointed end opposite the cut side. The sirloin, on the other hand, has a very blunt, rounded end. If you can't find a shank half, however, don't despair; both halves taste equally good. Your knife will just encounter a few more bumps and curves while carving the sirloin half.

WHAT WE LEARNED: Bake the ham in a 250-degree oven to a low internal temperature to preserve juiciness. Remember that ham is a fully cooked product and that the goal is only to reheat it. To make carving easier, buy a shank-end ham. For grown-up flavor, serve the sauce on the side rather than coating the ham with a sticky glaze.

SPIRAL-SLICED HAM serves 20 to 30

You can put the ham in the oven cold, bypassing the 90-minute standing time. If you do, add a couple of minutes per pound to the heating time. If using an oven bag, cut slits in the bag so it does not burst. Allow about 3 to 4 servings per pound for a bone-in ham. We recommend buying a shank portion because the bone configuration makes it easier to carve; look for the half ham with a tapered, pointed end (see Getting It Right at right).

1   spiral-sliced half ham (7 to 10 pounds), preferably shank end

1. Unwrap ham and remove and discard plastic disk covering bone. Place ham in plastic oven bag, pull tightly for a close fit, tie bag shut, and trim excess plastic (see illustration on page 226). Set ham cut-side down in 13 by 9-inch baking dish and cut four slits in top of bag with paring knife. Alternatively, place unwrapped ham cut-side down in baking dish and cover tightly with foil. Let stand at room temperature 90 minutes.

2. Meanwhile, adjust oven rack to lowest position and heat oven to 250 degrees. Bake until center of ham registers about 100 degrees on instant-read thermometer, 1½ to 2½ hours (about 14 minutes per pound if using plastic oven bag, about 17 minutes per pound if using foil), depending on size of ham.

3. Remove ham from oven and let rest in baking dish in oven bag or with foil cover until internal temperature registers 115 to 120 degrees on instant-read thermometer, 30 to 40 minutes. Cut open oven bag or remove foil, place ham on carving board, and slice according to illustrations on page 225. Serve immediately with one of following sauces, if desired.

GETTING IT RIGHT: Choosing A Ham

SHANK END

BUTT END

For easy carving, look for a shank-end ham (left), which has a tapered, pointed end opposite the cut side. The sirloin, or butt, end (right) has a rounded, blunt end.

DRIED CHERRY AND STOUT SAUCE WITH BROWN SUGAR AND ALLSPICE makes about 4 cups

Stout is a strong, dark beer made from toasted barley. Here it makes a rich, full-bodied sauce with subtle smoky notes and a characteristically bitter finish.

1   cup canned low-sodium chicken broth
2   tablespoons cornstarch
2   tablespoons unsalted butter
3   medium shallots, minced (about 9 tablespoons)
⅛   teaspoon ground allspice
4   cups stout
⅓   cup packed brown sugar
1   cup dried tart cherries (about 5 ounces)
1½   tablespoons balsamic vinegar
     Salt and ground black pepper

1. Whisk together chicken broth and cornstarch in small bowl; set aside. Heat butter in 12-inch skillet over medium heat until foaming; add shallots and sauté until softened, about 3 minutes. Stir in allspice; cook until fragrant, about 30 seconds. Add stout, brown sugar, and dried cherries; increase heat to medium-high, bring to a simmer, and cook until slightly syrupy, about 10 minutes.

2. Whisk broth and cornstarch mixture to recombine, then gradually whisk into simmering liquid; return to simmer to thicken sauce, stirring occasionally. Off heat, stir in balsamic vinegar; season to taste with salt and pepper. (The sauce can be cooled to room temperature and refrigerated up to 2 days. Reheat in medium saucepan over medium-low heat.) Serve with ham.

MUSTARD SAUCE WITH VERMOUTH AND THYME makes about 3 ½ cups
The Dijon mustard lends a creaminess to this sauce, while the whole-grain mustard adds texture and visual appeal.

- 1½ cups canned low-sodium chicken broth
- 2 tablespoons cornstarch
- 2 tablespoons unsalted butter
- 3 medium shallots, minced (about 9 tablespoons)
- 2 cups dry vermouth
- 1 tablespoon packed brown sugar
- ½ cup Dijon mustard
- ¼ cup whole-grain mustard
- 1 tablespoon chopped fresh thyme leaves
  Salt and ground black pepper

1. Whisk together chicken broth and cornstarch in small bowl; set aside. Heat butter in 12-inch skillet over medium heat until foaming; add shallots and sauté until softened, about 3 minutes. Stir in vermouth and sugar; increase heat to medium-high and simmer until alcohol vapors have cooked off, about 4 minutes.

2. Whisk chicken stock and cornstarch mixture to recombine, then gradually whisk into simmering liquid; return sauce to simmer to thicken, stirring occasionally. Off heat, whisk in mustards and thyme; season to taste with salt and pepper. (Sauce can be cooled to room temperature and refrigerated up to 2 days. Reheat in medium saucepan over medium-low heat.) Serve with ham.

TECHNIQUE: Carving a Spiral-Sliced Ham

1. With the tip of a paring or carving knife, cut around the bone to loosen the attached slices.

2. Using a long carving knife, slice horizontally above the bone and through the spiral-cut slices, toward the back of the ham.

3. Pull the cut portion away from the bone, and cut between the slices to separate them fully.

4. Beginning at the tapered end, slice above the bone to remove the remaining chunk of meat. Flip the ham over and repeat the procedure for the other side.

TECHNIQUE: Trimming the Oven Bag

Use scissors to trim the oven bag, leaving 1 inch above the tie.

TASTING LAB: Spiral-Sliced Hams

SPIRAL-SLICED HAMS OFFER THE BEST COMBINATION OF flavor, texture, and convenience when it comes to slicing, but are all spiral-sliced hams the same? To find out, we rounded up the five most widely available bone-in, spiral-sliced hams. All were heated according to our recipe and served plain (without a sauce or glaze).

We found a wide variety in both flavor and texture. The Cook's Spiral Sliced Hickory Smoked Honey Ham ($2.29 per pound) was the clear winner. Almost all tasters appreciated this ham's clean and meaty flavor, though a few were left wanting stronger sweet, salt, smoke, and spice flavors. Overall, it was declared an "honest ham" that "doesn't seem processed" or "taste like it's pumped full of chemicals."

The Hillshire Farm Spiral Sliced Brown Sugar Cured Ham ($1.79 per pound) also received mostly positive comments. Most tasters noted a pleasant balance of salt and sweet, but others thought the flavor insubstantial and "lacking much assertion." As for the texture, many found it a bit chewy and dry, while a couple of tasters said these qualities made it a "real man's ham."

The other hams in the tasting did not fare as well. Almost every taster remarked on the pock-marked meat of the Hillshire Farm Spiral Sliced Honey Cured Ham ($1.79 per pound). Its appearance, coupled with the rubbery, wet, very "pumped" texture, made this very sweet ham "look and taste like a sponge." Tasters could not get too enthused about the Colonial Spiral Sliced Ham ($2.69), either, finding it spongy and soft. The most expensive ham in the tasting, the Carando Spiral Sliced Hickory Smoked Ham ($3.99 per pound), landed at the bottom of the rankings. Sold under the Farmland label in the Midwest and on the West Coast, this ham elicited comments such as "sour," "acidic," and "musty" from tasters. The meat verged on dry, with a coarse, crumbly, "fall-apart" quality.

EQUIPMENT CORNER:
Timer/Thermometers

A REGULAR TIMER IS FINE FOR REMINDING YOU THAT A certain period of time has elapsed. But it can't tell you precisely when your ham or roast is done. You still need to pull out an instant-read thermometer and check the meat. What if you could combine the timer and thermometer into one handy device? Several companies have done so in making the timer/thermometer, which allows you to use its timing and thermometer functions separately or at the same time. Here's how it works.

Attached to a standard timer-type base is a long wire that ends with a sensor probe that measures temperature. To use this device, you insert the sensor probe into foods before they go into the oven (or on the grill). You place the food in the oven and snake the long wire cord through the oven door opening. The cord attaches to the base unit, which sits on a counter near the oven or attaches to the oven door via a back-mounted magnet. You program the base unit with the desired internal temperature (say 125 degrees for a rare roast beef). Once the sensor probe determines that the meat has reached this temperature, the timer unit will beep. It also provides you with a constant display of the temperature of the food as it rises.

We rounded up six timer/thermometers, ranging in price from $20 to $50, to see which model is the best option for the home cook. We tested each device in beef roasts and set the timer to beep at various temperatures. We doubled-checked these temperatures with a separate thermometer and found that all six models were accurate—they beeped right on cue.

Ease of operation and features, however, revealed some differences. Several models had short wire cords that made them harder to use. Also, the magnet on some timer/thermometers was not strong enough, and we worried that the units would come crashing down onto the floor. A few models were harder to program and read.

In the end, testers agreed that the Polder Cooking Thermometer/Timer ($24.99) was the best choice. It was

the easiest and most intuitive to figure out and use. It also has a long 4-foot cord and the loudest alarm of those tested, making it the best choice to use on the grill. We were intrigued by the Maverick Redi-Check Remote Timer/Oven Thermometer ($49.99), which actually reads the temperature from remote locations using a transmitter in the probe and a receiver in the base unit. However, several minor design flaws (it was less stable than other models and the cord was shorter) and hard-to-follow instructions kept this unusual model from scoring high on our test.

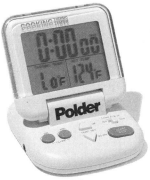

BEST TIMER/THERMOMETER
Among the six models tested, the Polder Cooking Thermometer/ Timer was the most stable and sounded the loudest alarm. It also had the longest cord and was the easiest to use. For an up-to-date price and mail-order source for this top-rated product, visit www.cooksillustrated.com.

GREEN BEAN CASSEROLE

WHAT WE WANTED: We wanted to resurrect this dinosaur and transform it by using fresh instead of prepared ingredients to make it taste better. Much better.

Often referred to as the Classic Green Bean Bake, this casserole was developed by Campbell's in 1955 using frozen green beans, canned cream of mushroom soup, and a topping of canned fried onions. The company touted the recipe as "delicious and easy to make, easy to remember, and leaves room for creativity." We thought we would exercise the creativity clause. We started by making the original recipe and then began to experiment.

The frozen beans recommended in the original recipe were certainly easy to use, but they also had a watery taste and a mushy texture in this dish. Fresh beans not only offered more flavor, but we were able to cook them to the appropriate doneness and leave a little bit of crunch. We tried sautéing and steaming the green beans but ended up liking the bright green color and seasoned flavor obtained when they were blanched in boiling, salted water. (Blanching means to submerge briefly in boiling water.) We found the beans tasted best when blanched in 4 quarts of water heavily seasoned with 2 tablespoons of salt for 4 to 5 minutes. We then plunged the beans into ice water (a process called shocking) to stop them from further cooking. Blanching then shocking allowed us maximum control over the cooking process, which meant that the beans were perfectly cooked every time.

Our next concern was the cream-based mushroom sauce. We did not enjoy the thick, pasty texture and lackluster flavor of condensed soup. What we did want was a smooth, velvety sauce filled with potent mushroom flavor. We began by testing two popular methods for making a cream sauce: reducing the cream to the proper consistency, and thickening the cream with flour and butter (also known as a roux). Sauces made by simply reducing cream were too

heavy and took too much time for our holiday-size casserole, while sauces thickened with flour tasted pasty and lacked depth of flavor. By combining the methods—using a little flour and reducing the sauce a bit—we got a svelte, flavorful sauce that was neither too rich nor too floury. After testing half-and-half and whole milk, we found neither up to sharing the title ring with lush heavy cream. We tried adding cheese but found the extra flavor to be both overpowering and unnecessary.

Up until now, we had been using white button mushrooms but were disappointed with their lack of flavor. By replacing half of the button mushrooms with cremini and using some dried porcini, we were able to give the sauce a full, earthy, and complex mushroom flavor. While we liked the flavor of portobellos, we found that their meaty texture required more cooking than button mushrooms, making them difficult to incorporate into our otherwise streamlined recipe. Onion, garlic, and fresh thyme were great companion flavors for the mushrooms, while chicken broth helped to pull all of the flavors in the sauce together. We also tried adding bacon, white wine, Madeira, and shallots to the sauce, but found their flavors unwelcome and discordant.

With the green beans and mushroom sauce nailed down, all that was left was the fried onion topping. While deep frying our own onions was out of the question because of the time it takes, we found the canned fried onions simply tasted too commercial to use on their own. By mixing the canned, fried onions with some fresh, seasoned bread crumbs we were able to remove the "from the can taste" of the traditional topping.

WHAT WE LEARNED: Use blanched fresh green beans (not frozen beans), build a sauce with fresh mushrooms, onions, and cream (not canned soup), and mix canned fried onions with fresh bread crumbs to temper their commercial flavor.

GREEN BEAN CASSEROLE serves 8 to 10

All the components of this dish can be cooked ahead of time. The assembled casserole needs only 15 minutes in a 375-degree oven to warm through and brown. A gratin dish works nicely with this recipe. See page 165 for information on our favorite.

topping

4	slices sandwich bread with crusts, each slice torn into quarters
2	tablespoons unsalted butter, softened
¼	teaspoon salt
⅛	teaspoon ground black pepper
3	cups canned fried onions (about 6 ounces)

beans

	Salt
2	pounds green beans, ends trimmed, cut on the diagonal into 2-inch pieces
½	ounce dried porcini mushrooms
6	tablespoons unsalted butter
1	medium onion, minced
3	medium garlic cloves, minced (about 1 tablespoon)
12	ounces white button mushrooms, wiped clean, stems trimmed, and sliced ¼ inch thick
12	ounces cremini mushrooms, wiped clean, stems trimmed, and sliced ¼ inch thick
2	tablespoons minced fresh thyme leaves
¼	teaspoon ground black pepper
2	tablespoons all-purpose flour
1	cup canned low-sodium chicken broth
2	cups heavy cream

1. FOR THE TOPPING: Pulse bread, butter, salt, and pepper in workbowl of food processor fitted with metal blade until mixture resembles coarse crumbs, about ten 1-second pulses. Transfer to large bowl and toss with onions; set aside.

2. FOR THE BEANS: Heat oven to 375 degrees. Bring 4 quarts water to boil in large pot. Add 2 tablespoons salt and beans. Cook until bright green and slightly crunchy, 4 to 5 minutes. Drain beans and plunge immediately into large bowl filled with ice water to stop cooking. Spread beans out onto paper towel–lined baking sheet to drain.

3. Meanwhile, cover dried porcini with ½ cup hot tap water in small microwave-safe bowl; cover with plastic wrap, cut several steam vents with paring knife, and microwave on high power for 30 seconds. Let stand until mushrooms soften, about 5 minutes. Lift mushrooms from the liquid with fork and mince using chef's knife (you should have about 2 tablespoons). Pour liquid through paper towel–lined sieve and reserve.

4. Melt butter in large nonstick skillet over medium-high heat until foaming subsides, about 1 minute. Add onion, garlic, button mushrooms, and cremini mushrooms and cook until mushrooms release their moisture, about 2 minutes. Add porcini mushrooms along with their strained soaking liquid, thyme, 1 teaspoon salt, and pepper and cook until all mushrooms are tender and liquid has reduced to 2 tablespoons, about 5 minutes. Add flour and cook for about 1 minute. Stir in chicken broth and reduce heat to medium. Stir in cream and simmer gently until sauce has consistency of dense soup, about 15 minutes.

5. Arrange beans in 3-quart gratin dish. Pour mushroom mixture over beans and mix to coat beans evenly. Sprinkle with bread crumb mixture and bake until top is golden brown and sauce is bubbling around edges, about 15 minutes. Serve immediately.

We found that a tube pan produces a better-looking and better-tasting coffee cake than a Bundt pan.

WEEKEND brunch

CHAPTER 19

Coffee cake has left home, abandoning grandma's kitchen for the shelves of ready-made supermarket pastries. Consisting of little more than a flat, dry, rectangular yellow cake topped with hard, pellet-like crumbs and nary a cinnamon swirl in sight, it is a far cry from the coffee cake of yesteryear—the sour cream coffee cake.

That's not to say that there aren't some bad sour cream coffee cakes out there. They're likely to be too dense and wet, too dry and tough, too sweet or too spicy, or just plain bland. The streusel inside the cake may be damp and pasty, and the streusel topping, if any, sometimes melts into the cake, while other times it remains sandy and granular, a world apart from the cake. We wanted the perfect sour cream coffee cake—a weekend indulgence that would be easy enough to make even when company wasn't coming.

Fruit salad is always simple, and when the fruit is good, so is the salad. But how about a great fruit salad with flavor above and beyond the ordinary? That's what we wanted.

Finally, what's brunch without coffee? We investigated grinders, French roast beans, and decaffeination and dispelled some common coffee myths along the way.

SOUR CREAM COFFEE CAKE

WHAT WE WANTED: There are three kinds of coffee cake: the ersatz convenience-store cake, the low-fat variety, and the real thing, packed with sour cream, butter, and sugar. We set out to explore the secrets of the latter, a classic, rich coffee cake that is worth waking up for.

Whether tall and round, loaf-shaped, cake-shaped, or Bundt-shaped, with streusel on the inside, on the outside, or both, sour cream coffee cake is distinguished by two indisputable facts. One: Hardly anyone makes it anymore (and that is a shame). Two: When it is made, it should be an ultra-moist cake, pleasantly rich and dense from the addition of sour cream.

After a first round of testing five different recipes, we came to a few conclusions. First, this is not a lean cake. Made from large amounts of sour cream, eggs, and butter, this cake is decadent. Second, we wanted to find a method of putting this cake together that was simple enough to tackle even before our first cup of coffee. Third, we love crispy, crunchy, yet melt-in-your-mouth streusel so much that we wanted not one but two layers of it on the inside, as well as a sizable amount on the cake top, and we knew that this would require a careful arrangement of sugar, flour, butter, nuts, and spices.

Cake flour is the norm in many sour cream coffee cake recipes, but this is a heavy cake that needs more structure, so we switched to the sturdier all-purpose flour. Brown sugar, a common coffee cake batter ingredient, had too much flavor, so we opted for the lower-profile granulated white sugar. We decided on four eggs, which produced the traditional buttery-yellow cake color and helped to provide for a tight crumb (we didn't want an open crumb, full of gaping, craggy holes). To give the cake tenderness and a capacity to remain moist for days, we relied on butter and, of course, sour cream. One-and-a-half sticks of butter and 1½ cups of sour cream produced the best flavor as well as a velvety mouthfeel.

Quite a few recipes use both baking powder and baking soda to lighten the cake's heavy load, and, after testing a few cakes, we found we didn't disagree. (The baking soda, which reacts with acids to create lift, is necessary because of the quantity of sour cream used.) These recipes, however, used a mere ½ to 1 teaspoon of each, and we disliked the squat, dense cakes that were coming out of our oven. After increasing the amount of leavening bit by bit, we discovered that a hefty 1 tablespoon of baking powder along with ¾ teaspoon of baking soda would lift the cake to a nearly statuesque height.

For the mixing method, we started by creaming the butter and sugar (whipping them to incorporate air), a common cake-making technique. The resulting cake was pleasingly tall, but it also had a crumb that was airy and cakey instead of tight, as we wanted. We then tried a method used in our basic yellow cake recipe, developed several years ago in the test kitchen. This two-stage method starts out by taking slightly softened butter and some of the sour cream and cutting them right into the dry ingredients, as is done for a pie dough. The liquid ingredients—in this case, eggs and more sour cream—are mixed together and then added to the butter/sour cream/dry ingredient mixture. The batter is then beaten until aerated and pale in color. The result was a cake with a tight crumb and a tender texture, and, best of all, it was quick to put together.

The real joy of great sour cream coffee cake is its elegant streusel swirls and crunchy streusel topping. Starting out with the sugar, we tried using solely brown sugar in the streusel, as many recipes dictate. We ended up preferring the appearance and flavor of a streusel made with a combination of granulated and dark brown sugar. What we did not like was the way this streusel melted and congealed into cement-like shards, so we took a cue from several recipes and added flour to prevent this from happening. Cinnamon, nutmeg, allspice, cloves, and even cocoa make regular appearances in

interior layers of streusel pasty and mealy, we reserved it, along with the nuts, for the topping. We also found that we preferred the texture of streusel topping made by cutting cold butter into the dry ingredients; melted butter produced unsightly knobby chunks of streusel. One benefit of this approach is that it eliminated the need to toast the nuts. The pecans in the streusel topping toasted quite nicely on their own during baking. As far as the interior streusel, we liked it to be sweeter than the topping, so we added another ¼ cup of brown sugar.

Now we had the cake, the streusel filling, and the streusel topping. All we had to do was bake the cake. Easier said than done. Time after time we ended up with cakes that seemed underdone. We tried placing the cake in a very hot 475-degree oven, then immediately lowering the temperature. Unfortunately, this blast of heat was enough to burn the sugary streusel topping. We tried adding the streusel 30 minutes into the baking time, but this meant maneuvering a hot pan out of and into the oven—not the safest approach to baking a coffee cake. Noticing that our pan was nearly full of batter, we tried cutting the amount of batter by about a fourth. When combined with baking the cake on the bottom oven rack at a steady 350 degrees for a full hour, this step produced a cake that was cooked all the way through yet was still pleasingly tall. What's more, the streusel was perfectly browned. We found it best to let the cake cool in the pan for at least 30 minutes before unmolding to keep it from cracking. Best of all, if stored well, this cake actually improves with age.

sour cream coffee cake. In the end, we found cinnamon—and a potent 2 tablespoons of it at that—was the only spice needed to lend warmth to the streusel's flavor. Pecans were favored over walnuts, although we found that almonds work equally well, and both tasted better when toasted.

Our coffee cake was now well on the road to success, but some tasters objected to the use of nuts in the streusel to be used as filling. The answer? We blended the basic streusel ingredients—flour, granulated sugar, and brown sugar—together in the food processor, then removed some of the mixture to a bowl to use as filling. Nuts went into the food processor for the topping. Because butter made the

WHAT WE LEARNED: Use plenty of butter, eggs, and sour cream for a cake that is rich and moist and has a tight crumb. Don't bother with cake flour but do make sure to use plenty of baking powder so this heavy batter rises. Use two layers of streusel and add nuts and butter to the third layer that goes on top.

SOUR CREAM COFFEE CAKE WITH BROWN SUGAR–PECAN STREUSEL serves 12 to 16

A 10-inch tube pan (with a 10-cup capacity) is best for this recipe (see Getting It Right at right for details).

streusel

- ¾ cup (3¾ ounces) unbleached all-purpose flour
- ¾ cup (5¼ ounces) granulated sugar
- ½ cup (3½ ounces) packed dark brown sugar
- 2 tablespoons ground cinnamon
- 2 tablespoons cold unsalted butter, cut into 2 pieces
- 1 cup pecans, chopped

cake

- 12 tablespoons (1½ sticks) unsalted butter, softened but still cool, cut into ½-inch cubes, plus 2 tablespoons softened butter for greasing pan
- 4 large eggs
- 1½ cups sour cream
- 1 tablespoon vanilla extract
- 2¼ cups (11½ ounces) unbleached all-purpose flour
- 1¼ cups (8¾ ounces) granulated sugar
- 1 tablespoon baking powder
- ¾ teaspoon baking soda
- ¾ teaspoon salt

1. FOR THE STREUSEL: In food processor, process flour, granulated sugar, ¼ cup dark brown sugar, and cinnamon until combined, about 15 seconds. Transfer 1¼ cups of flour/sugar mixture to small bowl; stir in remaining ¼ cup brown sugar and set aside to use for streusel filling. Add butter and pecans to flour sugar mixture in food processor; pulse until nuts and butter resemble small pebbly pieces, about ten 1-second pulses. Set aside to use as streusel topping.

2. FOR THE CAKE: Adjust oven rack to lowest position and heat oven to 350 degrees. Grease 10-inch tube pan (with 10-

GETTING IT RIGHT:
Best Coffee Cake Pan

Both Bundt and tube pans (also called angel food cake pans) are standard equipment for coffee cakes. A Bundt pan bakes the cake upside-down, and, when flipped upright, the bottom becomes the top. In our testing, we didn't care for the streusel topping baked in this pan. It never became crunchy, and it was compacted from the weight of the cake batter. The tube pan—in which the streusel sits on top of the cake—won hands down for presentation. We preferred tube pans made from a single piece of metal because they can't leak batter as can sometimes happen with a two-piece pan with a removable bottom. In a pinch you can use a tube pan with a removable bottom. Set this pan on a large sheet of foil, then fold the foil up and around the sides of the pan before filling it with batter.

BUNDT PAN

TUBE PAN

cup capacity) with 2 tablespoons softened butter. Whisk eggs, 1 cup sour cream, and vanilla in medium bowl until combined.

3. Combine flour, sugar, baking powder, baking soda, and salt in bowl of standing mixer; mix on low speed for 30 seconds to blend. Add remaining butter and sour cream; mix on low speed until dry ingredients are moistened and mixture resembles wet sand, with few large butter pieces remaining, about 1½ minutes. Increase to medium speed and beat until batter comes together, about 10 seconds; scrape down sides of bowl with rubber spatula. Lower speed to medium-low and gradually add egg mixture in 3 additions, beating for 20 seconds after each addition and scraping down sides of bowl as necessary. Increase speed to medium-high and beat until batter is light and fluffy, about 1 minute.

4. Using rubber spatula, spread 2 cups batter in bottom of prepared pan, smoothing surface. Sprinkle evenly with ¾ cup streusel filling without butter or nuts. Repeat with another 2 cups batter and remaining ¾ cup streusel filling without butter or nuts. Spread remaining batter over, then sprinkle with streusel topping with butter and nuts.

TECHNIQUE: Chopping Nuts Quickly

To make fast work of chopping nuts, place the nuts on a cutting board and hold two chef's knives parallel to each other in one hand and chop. Use the other hand to guide the knives through the nuts.

---

5. Bake until cake feels firm to touch and long toothpick or skewer inserted into center comes out clean (bits of sugar from streusel may cling to tester), 50 to 60 minutes. Cool cake in pan on wire rack for 30 minutes. Invert cake onto rimmed baking sheet (cake will be streusel-side down); remove tube pan, place wire rack on top of cake, and reinvert cake streusel-side up. Cool to room temperature, about 2 hours. Cut into wedges and serve. (Cake can be wrapped in foil and stored at room temperature up to 5 days.)

VARIATIONS

LEMON-BLUEBERRY SOUR CREAM COFFEE CAKE

We prefer frozen wild blueberries for their size and flavor, but frozen cultivated blueberries will work, too.

Toss 1 cup frozen blueberries with 1 teaspoon grated lemon zest in small bowl. Follow recipe for Sour Cream Coffee Cake with Brown Sugar–Pecan Streusel, sprinkling ½ cup blueberries over bottom and middle layers of cake batter before sprinkling with streusel.

SOUR CREAM COFFEE CAKE WITH CHOCOLATE CHIPS

Follow recipe for Sour Cream Coffee Cake with Brown Sugar–Pecan Streusel, sprinkling ½ cup chocolate chips over bottom layer of cake batter and additional ½ cup chocolate chips over middle layer of cake batter before sprinkling with streusel.

APRICOT-ALMOND SOUR CREAM COFFEE CAKE

Follow recipe for Sour Cream Coffee Cake with Brown Sugar–Pecan Streusel, substituting 1 cup slivered almonds for pecans in streusel topping and ½ teaspoon almond extract for vanilla extract in cake batter. Measure ½ cup apricot jam; spoon jam in six 2-teaspoon mounds over bottom and middle layers of cake batter before sprinkling with streusel.

SCIENCE DESK:
How Does Decaffeination Work?

CAFFEINE IS ONE OF HUNDREDS OF DIFFERENT MOLECULES found in a coffee bean. Because its shape and size are different from other molecules, manufacturers can use one of several techniques to filter out the caffeine molecules. Here's how three of the most common techniques work.

One method relies on a direct chemical solvent. The beans are first soaked or steamed in water to soften them. They are then steeped in a solvent—either methylene chloride, a man-made chemical, or ethyl acetate, a naturally occurring chemical in fruit—for up to 12 hours. During this time the solvent binds with the caffeine molecules. When the solvent is removed, the caffeine goes with it. Unfortunately, some of the flavor molecules are also removed and lost in this process.

Another method relies on an indirect chemical solvent. The beans are soaked in water long enough to remove the caffeine and many flavor compounds. The caffeine-and-flavor-packed water is then drained off and solvent is added to the water. The solvent binds with the caffeine molecules, and the solvent, along with the caffeine, is removed from the water, which now contains just flavor molecules. The beans are then soaked in the caffeine-free, flavor-charged water so they will reabsorb the flavor molecules. Unfortunately, not every molecule gets reabsorbed and some flavor is lost in this process.

A third process relies on a charcoal filter to remove the caffeine molecules from the water in which the beans have been soaked. The charcoal filter traps the caffeine molecules but lets the flavor molecules pass through. The water with the flavor molecules is then poured back over the soaked beans. Unfortunately, the charcoal filters traps some flavor compounds and they are lost in the process.

The moral of the story: No matter how coffee is decaffeinated, some flavor is lost.

TASTING LAB: French Roast Coffee

WHEN YOU ORDER A LARGE COFFEE FROM YOUR LOCAL coffee bar on any particular day, you can't be sure just where the beans came from; it may be one of a dozen different countries. But one thing is likely: The beans have been dark-roasted. They may even be French roast beans. Of course, all coffee beans are roasted before being ground and brewed, but a French roast is dark—very dark—and, thanks to Starbucks and other specialty retailers, it is also very popular. It seemed to us, then, that the obvious question for the consumer was, Which brand of French roast beans is best? We tasted nine supermarket brands to find out.

In the first round of tasting Chock Full o' Nuts squeaked by Starbucks for first-place honors, indicating that price (Starbucks costs more than twice as much as Chock Full o' Nuts) is no guarantee of satisfaction. Because the ratings were so close for all brands, we repeated the tasting. The second time around the results were just as close, but the rankings were different. What this second round of tasting made clear, however, was that some tasters consistently preferred a darker roast and others a lighter roast, a key factor that contributed to the odd results. In other words, tasters were not responding to quality per se, they were simply expressing a preference as to what degree the beans were roasted. Is it possible, then, that all French roasts—no matter the type of bean—are not created equal? To try to settle the matter, we decided to turn to some experts and set out for the Excellent Coffee Company, a coffee roaster in Pawtucket, R.I.

We took our nine brands on the road and this time subjected them to an Agtron reading, which measures the amount of light reflected from particles of ground coffee. The darkest roast measured on the scale an Agtron reading of 15, the lightest a reading of 80. According to common industry standards, a French roast usually falls in the range of 20 to 30. Based on their Agtron readings, only four of the nine coffees we tested were true French roasts. Two qualified as Italian roasts, with readings under 20, and three qualified as Viennese roasts, with readings over 30. So brand does make a difference. The beans in brands advertised as French roast are in fact roasted to very different degrees. Coffee drinkers who favor that charred, heavily roasted flavor should go for Starbucks, which has an Agtron reading of 16.9, but if you like a lighter, more subtle cup of coffee, you might choose Chock Full o' Nuts, which has a reading of 31, or Eight O'Clock, with a reading of 38.1.

But what about French roast itself? Despite its popularity, the confusing taste test results made us wonder if the roasting process somehow camouflaged the quality of the beans, thus making brand recognition difficult. We turned to Kevin Knox of Allegro coffee, one-time Starbucks quality-control man and co-author with Julie Sheldon Huffaker of *Coffee Basics* (John Wiley & Sons, 1996). He summed up

TECHNIQUE:
Keeping the Remote Control Clean

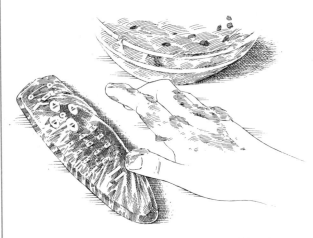

Many cooks enjoy listening to music or watching TV as they cook. Before cooking, wrap the remote control unit in a layer of clear plastic wrap. The buttons remain visible and operable but don't get smeared by sticky hands.

French roast by saying, "It's just burnt coffee."

To understand just what Knox means, it's necessary to know a bit about the coffee-roasting process. Beans can be roasted from light (American) to medium (Full City) to dark (Viennese, French, and Italian, the darkest roast). Although these are imprecise terms, the method is simple enough. Beans are roasted by hot air and then cooled. They can be roasted slowly or quickly, and the cooling method can vary as well, and variations in both factors affect flavor. The reason French roast beans are often considered burnt is that they are roasted until many of their carbohydrates (sugar and cellulose) are converted to carbon (that is, incinerated), causing the beans to lose up to 20 percent of their weight in the process. Thus many experts believe French roasting destroys flavors, rendering the differences between high- and low-quality beans meaningless. Forget about the subtle flavor of honeysuckle in Kenyan beans or the bittersweet chocolate taste of Guatemalan Antigua.

To test this theory, we did a tasting at Excellent Coffee of both high-quality and mediocre beans roasted to both light and dark stages. While expert and staff tasters could tell which bean was which when the beans were lightly roasted, the differences between the high-quality and low-quality beans were harder to detect when the beans were darkly roasted; in fact, some tasters preferred the lower-quality dark roast beans to the higher-quality dark roast beans. Knowing that character flaws and nuances in flavor can be masked by dark roasting, professionals "cup," or taste, coffee brewed from very lightly roasted beans.

We also asked the Excellent Coffee experts to blind-taste French roast Starbucks and Chock Full o' Nuts. The result? They preferred the cheaper Chock Full o' Nuts, a lighter roast that they found "mild and sweet," opposed to the dark roast Starbucks, which they found "smoky and sharply acidic." (The tasters did comment, however, that they could discern a higher-quality bean in the Starbucks coffee than in the Chock Full o' Nuts, although they didn't care for the burnt taste of the roasting.)

So the best question to ask when it comes to supermarket French roast coffees isn't "Which brand is best?" Even though Starbucks uses high-quality beans, its coffee doesn't have much on Folgers or Eight O'Clock when the beans are French roasted. George Howell, founder of the Coffee Connection, goes so far as to say that "taste can wind up having little to do with quality." What is certain is that for dark roast coffees, the roasting process has a bigger impact on flavor than bean quality.

What is the best question to ask when selecting a French roast coffee? Probably, "How do you like your coffee?" As Howell points out, if given French roast, the person who prefers light roast "will feel like he is walking into a dark room. It's all thickness and no clarity." Meanwhile, someone who favors dark roast but is given light roast "feels like he is being attacked by the corrosive rays of the sun." So forget about beans, price, and country of origin and simply choose the brand of French roast best suited to your palate. If you like a really dark roast, go for something like Starbucks (the beans will be almost black in color). If you like a lighter roast, try Chock Full o' Nuts or Eight O'Clock (the beans will be medium brown). Keep in mind that how you drink your coffee may also influence your choice. Black coffee drinkers may prefer a lighter roast, whereas those who add milk and sugar might find the darker roasts more appealing.

EQUIPMENT CORNER: Coffee Grinders

JUST AS CORN ON THE COB TASTES BEST IF IT'S BOILED within minutes of being picked, coffee tastes best if the beans are ground fresh before they are brewed. With a wide variety of countertop coffee grinders on the market, it is no problem for home cooks to grind beans on demand. The greater challenge is deciding which grinder to buy. Most of the reasonably priced grinders, which generally cost around $20, employ propeller-type blades that work like a blender, literally chopping the beans as they spin. But any coffee enthusiast will quickly allege that blade grinders are rife with problems—namely, that they grind unevenly, they

produce too much superfine coffee dust, and the friction from the spinning blades overheats the coffee grounds. We wondered if any of this would really affect the flavor and body of the brewed coffee or if these allegations barely amounted to a hill of beans.

With a self-imposed price cap of $50, a limit that allowed us to include several low-end burr grinders (a fancier type of machine that works like a motorized pepper mill), we bought 10 popular models from seven manufacturers and 30 pounds of coffee beans. Then we let the grounds fly to determine just how good a grinder $50 (or less, in many cases) would buy.

The first issue we addressed was the evenness of the grind. Michael Kramm, president of Capresso, maker of the Capresso Cool Grind included in our tests, explained that blade grinders actually chop the beans with their furiously spinning blades. In a burr grinder, on the other hand, beans are truly ground a few at a time between two grooved disks, one stationary and the other rotating just above it. The grounds are fed out through a chute into a sealed container. According to Kramm, the disks operate at roughly 7,000 to 9,000 revolutions per minute (RPM), while the motors in most blade grinders spin at 14,000 to 20,000 RPM.

Kramm agreed with other coffee authorities that the blade grinders' rough treatment of the beans often results in unevenly ground coffee, with particles ranging from dust to large chunks in the same batch. Our observations corroborated this, although we found we could improve the evenness of the blade grind either by grinding in short, quick bursts, with stops in between to shake the grinder to redistribute the grounds, or by shaking the grinder as it ground, much as you would a martini in a cocktail shaker (see the illustration on page 240).

The burr grinders produced a more even grind, but tasters did not find that more evenly ground coffee translated into improved flavor. Tasters did prefer the rich body of burr-ground coffee, but they also noticed the tendency of this coffee to taste slightly bitter, owing in part, no doubt, to the more fine and even grind, which made for the coffee's

Rating Coffee Grinders

WE RATED 10 COFFEE GRINDERS, NONE PRICED HIGHER THAN $50, AND EVALUATED THEM ACCORDING TO CAPACITY (more was judged to be better), design, ease of cleaning, and the temperature increase of the coffee (heat can destroy flavor, so the lower the increase during grinding, the better). We tested each unit by grinding 2 ounces of coffee beans (about 8 tablespoons) and using those grounds to brew full, 40-ounce pots of coffee in a new automatic drip coffee maker. The grinders are listed in order of preference. See www.cooksillustrated.com for up-to-date prices and mail-order sources for top-rated products.

RECOMMENDED

1. Capresso Cool Grind, Model 501

$19.95

Has a large capacity and a deep cup, the features we value most in a blade grinder. Some large pieces of bean were left after grinding, however.

RECOMMENDED

2. Krups Fast-Touch Coffee Mill, Model 203

$19.99

No cord wrap, but excellent fit between lid and base. Grinds fine, yet does not create an excessive amount of coffee dust.

RECOMMENDED

3. Mr. Coffee Coffee Grinder, Model IDS55

$14.99

Nice deep lid prevents the (unevenly) ground coffee from spilling. No cord wrap.

RECOMMENDED

4. Braun Aromatic Coffee Grinder, Model KSM 2B

$19.99

Tended to grind on the fine side, rarely leaving large chunks of bean. Did create a noticeable quantity of coffee dust, though.

RECOMMENDED

5. Mr. Coffee Burr Mill, Model BM3

$29.99

Grinds thoroughly and pretty evenly, but not completely without dust. No automatic timer, which is fine. We liked the control offered by a simple on/off toggle.

NOT RECOMMENDED

6. Proctor-Silex Fresh Grind Coffee Grinder, Model E160B

$12.99

So small that you have to grind twice to get enough coffee for one 8-cup pot.

NOT RECOMMENDED

7. Cuisinart Coffee Bar Coffee Grinder, Model DCG-20BK

$19.95

Cord stores in an internal chamber, which makes it difficult to use. Shallow lid spills ground coffee, and there was a loose fit between lid and base.

NOT RECOMMENDED

8. Starbucks Barista Blade Grinder

$19.95

Attractive design, but the lid is so small that coffee spills easily. The coffee is ground evenly, except for the few whole beans usually left behind.

NOT RECOMMENDED

9. Braun Coffee Mill, Model KMM 30

$49.99

We didn't care for the automatic timer because the machine's notion of the proper grind time often did not jibe with our own. Does grind evenly.

NOT RECOMMENDED

10. Capresso Burr Grinder, Model 551

$49.99

Creates more coffee dust than we expected. Also, the power switch is too easy to hit by mistake, an error that sends coffee grounds flying.

greater exposure to and prolonged contact with the water in the coffee maker. These combined forces caused what coffee experts call overextraction, which occurs when too much flavor is extracted from the beans. In our tests, we were less likely to encounter this problem if the coffee was ground coarse, more so than even the coarsest setting on the burr grinders could accomplish.

We were surprised to discover that the coffee brewed with blade-ground beans was less likely to turn out bitter. The tasters did note that coffee from blade-ground beans had less body than coffee from burr-ground beans, but we were happy to sacrifice a little body for the reduced risk of brewing bitter coffee. We also learned that we could improve the body of the coffee somewhat by defying the blade grinders' instructions and grinding the beans a little longer, 20 to 25 seconds, rather than the recommended 10 to 15, without overheating the beans or jeopardizing smooth flavor in the coffee.

Overprocessing the beans into superfine coffee dust was another concern. Experts agree that the best grinders produce minimal dust, which can block waterflow through the filter in many coffee makers. None of the grinders we tested, however, produced enough dust to clog the filter.

The temperature of the coffee grounds was another factor we considered. Ideally, the beans should not heat up too much as they are ground because heat causes the flavorful oils to evaporate, resulting in a loss of flavor. Most experts claim that cheap blade grinders overheat the coffee beans. According to the infrared thermometer we used to measure the temperature of the grounds, this isn't true. The burr grinders actually caused a greater increase in temperature, albeit a slight one. Our tasters, however, were not able to correlate a greater increase in temperature with poorer coffee flavor. The temperature increases we measured seemed to make very little difference.

Any appliance that you use first thing in the morning, while you are half-asleep, had better be well designed and user-friendly. The two design factors that came to matter to us most were capacity and, on blade grinders, depth of the cup. Any grinder should have a capacity large enough to grind in a single batch the beans necessary for a full pot of coffee. Likewise, the cup should be deep enough to contain the grounds without spilling as you remove them from the grinder. All of the burr grinders and the Capresso Cool Grind, Krups Fast Touch, Mr. Coffee Coffee Grinder, and Braun Aromatic blade grinders made the cut here. But the blade grinders offered additional advantages. They were easy to clean, often requiring just a careful wipe of the hopper with a damp paper towel to remove coffee dust, and they were inexpensive, hovering around the $15 to $20 mark. Truth be told, we recommend all of the four blade grinders mentioned above.

That said, we do have one caveat for espresso drinkers. Most manufacturers advise against using a blade grinder— any blade grinder—to grind coffee for use in a pump-driven espresso machine. These grinders simply cannot grind the coffee fine enough. We concur. If this limits your choice to a burr grinder, then we'd go for the Mr. Coffee model because it has a simple on/off switch, which we felt worked better than the timers found on the other two burr models.

TECHNIQUE:
Efficient Coffee Grinding

Many inexpensive blade-type grinders grind coffee beans unevenly, producing some powder as well as some larger pieces of bean. Here's how to even out the grind. With your hand over the hopper, lift the whole unit off the counter and shake it gently as it grinds. (The motion is akin to blending a martini in a cocktail shaker.) By moving the beans around, you help the machine grind more evenly.

FRUIT SALAD

WHAT WE WANTED: Good fruit salads shouldn't taste like sugary desserts. We wanted something both light and flavorful, with a clear emphasis on the fruit.

Making a good, fresh fruit salad is not that hard when good fruit is available. Nor is it very hard, we found, to make a truly great fruit salad, complemented by a simple, sweet-tart dressing that enhances the fruit and adds layers of interest and flavor.

That said, most of the recipes we tested failed to deliver on this promise. Fruit salads are traditionally dressed with yogurt or sugar syrup or simply served plain. We felt that yogurt dressings fell short because they mask the colors, shapes, and jewel-like beauty of cut fruit. And the inescapable truth is that no matter what sort of flavoring you add, yogurt dressing always tastes like, well, yogurt. The fruit almost falls by the wayside. Sugar syrup can be insipidly sweet, and plain cut-up fruit can be boring.

So we chose another route, adapting a classic French dressing called *gastrique*. The definition of gastrique varies from cookbook to cookbook, but we agree with the renowned culinary encyclopedia *Larousse Gastronomique*, which says that a gastrique is a reduction of an acidic liquid, usually vinegar, and sugar; it typically accompanies savory dishes made with fruit, such as duck à l'orange. The process of reducing the liquid over high heat couldn't be simpler, and, after some experimentation, we found that 1 cup of acidic liquid reduced with ¼ cup of sugar produced just the right balance of tart and sweet. The mixture complemented all the fresh fruits we wanted to use.

This technique worked beautifully with citrus, wine, and spirits, allowing us to introduce complex flavors beyond the traditional vinegar. We also got great results from infusing the gastriques with additional flavors, such as cinnamon in the brandy mixture for plums and figs or lemon zest and cardamom in the champagne mixture for

nectarines and berries. Our last step was to add some high, bright flavor notes with both lemon juice and zest. With that, we achieved a complex layering of flavors in 16 minutes flat.

WHAT WE LEARNED: A reduction of something acidic (like wine, citrus juice, or vinegar) and sugar is the perfect "sauce" for fruit salad. This reduction complements the fruit and can be flavored with spices, extracts, or citrus zests.

STRAWBERRIES AND GRAPES WITH BALSAMIC AND RED WINE REDUCTION

makes about 6 cups

An inexpensive balsamic vinegar is fine for use in this recipe. Save high-quality vinegar for other preparations in which the vinegar is not cooked.

- ¾ cup balsamic vinegar
- ¼ cup dry red wine
- ¼ cup sugar
- Pinch salt
- 3 whole cloves
- 1 tablespoon grated zest plus 1 tablespoon juice from 1 lemon
- ¼ teaspoon vanilla extract
- 1 quart strawberries, hulled and halved lengthwise (about 4 cups)
- 9 ounces large seedless red or black grapes, each grape halved pole to pole (about 2 cups)

1. Simmer vinegar, wine, sugar, and salt in small, heavy-bottomed nonreactive saucepan over high heat until syrupy and reduced to ¼ cup, about 15 minutes. Off heat, stir in cloves, lemon zest and juice, and vanilla; steep 1 minute to blend flavors, and strain.

2. Combine strawberries and grapes in medium bowl; pour warm dressing over fruit and toss to coat. Serve immediately at room temperature or cover with plastic wrap, refrigerate up to 4 hours, and serve chilled.

NECTARINES, BLUEBERRIES, AND RASPBERRIES WITH CHAMPAGNE-CARDAMOM REDUCTION makes about 6 cups

Dry white wine can be substituted for the champagne.

- 1 cup champagne
- ¼ cup sugar
- Pinch salt

TECHNIQUE: Handling a Mango

Mangoes are notoriously hard to peel, owing to their shape and slippery texture. Here's how we handle this tough kitchen task.

1. Start by removing a thin slice from one end of the mango so that it sits flat on a work surface.

2. Hold the mango cut-side down and remove the skin with a sharp paring knife in thin strips, working from top to bottom.

3. Once the peel has been removed, cut down along the side of the flat pit to remove the flesh from one side of the mango. Do the same thing on the other side of pit.

4. Trim around the pit to remove any remaining flesh. The flesh can now be chopped or sliced as desired.

1 tablespoon grated zest plus 1 tablespoon juice from 1 lemon
5 cardamom pods, crushed
3 medium nectarines (about 18 ounces), cut into ½-inch wedges (about 3 cups)
1 pint blueberries
½ pint raspberries

1. Simmer champagne, sugar, and salt in small, heavy-bottomed nonreactive saucepan over high heat until syrupy, honey-colored, and reduced to ¼ cup, about 15 minutes. Off heat, stir in lemon zest and juice and cardamom; steep 1 minute to blend flavors, and strain.

2. Combine nectarines, blueberries, and raspberries in medium bowl; pour warm dressing over fruit and toss to coat. Serve immediately at room temperature or cover with plastic wrap, refrigerate up to 4 hours, and serve chilled.

HONEYDEW, MANGO, AND BLUEBERRIES WITH LIME-GINGER REDUCTION

makes about 6 cups

Cantaloupe can be used in place of honeydew although the color contrast with the mango won't be as vivid.

1 cup juice plus 1 tablespoon grated zest from 4 limes (zest limes before juicing)
¼ cup sugar
Pinch salt
1 (1-inch) piece fresh ginger, peeled and minced (about 1 tablespoon)
1 tablespoon juice from 1 lemon
½ small honeydew melon, seeds and rind removed, cut into 1-inch pieces (about 2 cups)
1 mango (about 10 ounces), peeled and cut into ½-inch pieces (about 1½ cups)
1 pint blueberries

1. Simmer lime juice, sugar, and salt in small, heavy-bottomed nonreactive saucepan over high heat until syrupy, honey-colored, and reduced to ¼ cup, about 15 minutes. Off heat, stir in lime zest, ginger, and lemon juice; steep 1 minute to blend flavors, and strain.

2. Combine melon, mango, and blueberries in medium bowl; pour warm dressing over fruit and toss to coat. Serve immediately at room temperature or cover with plastic wrap, refrigerate up to 4 hours, and serve chilled.

RED PLUMS AND FIGS WITH BRANDY-CINNAMON REDUCTION makes about 6 cups

Red plums make the best visual contrast with the dark-colored figs.

1 cup brandy
¼ cup sugar
Pinch salt
1 (3-inch) stick cinnamon
1 tablespoon grated zest plus 1 tablespoon juice from 1 lemon
4 red plums (about 1¼ pounds), pitted and cut into ½-inch-thick wedges (about 4 cups)
12 fresh black mission figs (about 12 ounces), quartered lengthwise (about 2 cups)

1. Simmer brandy, sugar, and salt in small, heavy-bottomed nonreactive saucepan over high heat until syrupy, honey-colored, and reduced to ¼ cup, about 15 minutes. Off heat, stir in cinnamon and lemon zest and juice; steep 1 minute to blend flavors, and strain.

2. Combine plums and figs in medium bowl; pour warm dressing over fruit and toss to coat. Serve immediately at room temperature or cover with plastic wrap, refrigerate up to 4 hours, and serve chilled.

QUICK breads

Quick breads are leavened chemically with baking powder and/or baking soda rather than yeast. Most quick breads are easy to prepare and ready to bake in a matter of minutes. The appeal of quick breads, such as cinnamon buns and banana bread, is clear. They are quick, sweet, and . . . did we say, quick? Of course, just because something is quick doesn't mean you want to eat it.

Supermarket cinnamon buns (the kind that come in a tube) are quick, but in a kitchen tasting we found that they all have an odd, artificial flavor and sponge-like texture that no one liked. Real cinnamon buns are a day-long affair that require a yeasted dough. We figured there had to a better way—a fast recipe that relied on baking powder but still delivered the tender, light crumb of the real thing.

Banana bread sounds so thrifty. Unfortunately, many banana breads are dry on the inside and sticky on the outside. Just because this recipe starts with over-the-hill bananas doesn't mean it should taste like leftovers. We knew there had to be a way to make a tender, moist loaf with real banana flavor without becoming spendthrifts.

We prefer metal measuring cups over plastic ones. The metal cups are sturdy enough to withstand constant use in the test kitchen.

CINNAMON BUNS

WHAT WE WANTED: Yeasted cinnamon buns take hours to make, and store-bought buns are dreadful. Could we transform a recipe for baking-powder biscuits into quick, high-rise cinnamon buns?

Cinnamon buns are quick to please: You bite into one, and you're happy. The bun is tender and fluffy, the filling is sweet and spicy, and the glaze is sinful, encouraging even the well-bred to lick the gooey remnants from their fingers. It's a shame, then, that making cinnamon buns at home can try the patience of the most devoted cooks. Most recipes call for yeast, which means they also call for a lot of time and skill as well as a standing mixer (or powerful biceps). The alternative is to make cinnamon buns from a tube or a box, options that produce inferior buns whose flavor lies somewhere between chemicals and cardboard. Our aim was to put cinnamon buns back in the home kitchen in good time, sacrificing neither flavor nor fluffiness for speed. In short, we wanted great buns without the hassle.

We started with a tasting of our favorite yeasted cinnamon buns. With a soft and resilient texture and a bready, open crumb, the texture of these buns was top-notch, and the combination of cinnamon and yeast produced a grown-up flavor. Unfortunately, the start-to-finish time was nearly five hours. Now we knew what texture and flavor we wanted from cinnamon buns. We just wanted it quicker and easier.

Toward this end, the first decision we made was to work from recipes leavened with baking powder rather than yeast. The next step was to determine the best method for incorporating the fat into the other ingredients. First we tried the classic mixing method of cutting cold butter into dry ingredients, as is done for pie dough. This method turned out cinnamon buns that were dense, flaky, and craggy rather than tender, light, and fluffy.

The next mixing method we tried called for combining melted butter with the liquid ingredients in a food processor, then adding the dry ingredients. While we hoped that the food processor would make the mixing process easier, these baked-off buns weren't worth the effort. The dough was very sticky, making it difficult to work with.

The last method we tried was a quick cream biscuit method, in which heavy cream is added to flour, sugar, baking powder, and salt. What makes this dough unique is its complete lack of butter. The dough relies entirely on the heavy cream for tenderness and flavor. Still better, the dough can be mixed in a minute using just one bowl. This process was by far the fastest and easiest, and we wanted to go with it, but a few refinements would be required before it produced really good cinnamon buns.

To make the dough more tender, our first thought was to replace the all-purpose flour with more delicate, lower-protein cake flour. But low-protein cake flour turned the dough into a sticky mess that was hard to roll out.

Our next inclination was to test whole or skim milk in place of heavy cream, but whole milk made the buns too heavy, and skim milk made them tough and bland. We increased the amount of baking powder to achieve lightness but ended up with metallic-tasting buns. We then tested buttermilk, a common ingredient in biscuit doughs, and had some success. (We also added ½ teaspoon of baking soda to balance the acidity of the buttermilk. Baking soda reacts with the acid in buttermilk to produce carbon dioxide gas, which causes lift.) The acid in the buttermilk gave the buns a more complex flavor and tenderized the gluten in the dough, making the interior airy and light.

But now the dough was too lean for our taste (owing to the buttermilk, most of which is made by adding acidic cultures to skim or partially skimmed milk—see the Science Desk on page 249). We arrived at the solution when we added 2 tablespoons of melted butter to the buttermilk. Just as we had hoped, the dough was tender, complex, and rich.

Whereas most recipes instruct bakers to roll out the dough, we found it easier to pat the dough into a rough-shaped rectangle, thus making the recipe even simpler. For the cinnamon-sugar filling we decided on a union of brown sugar, white sugar, cinnamon, cloves, and salt. Before sprinkling the filling on the dough, we brushed it with 2 tablespoons of melted butter to help the filling cling to the dough. Because the cinnamon mixture was loose and dry, however, it was still apt to fall away from the dough when the buns were cut and transferred to the baking pan. The easy solution was to add 1 tablespoon of melted butter to the dry ingredients, which made the mixture the consistency of wet sand, allowing us to press it into the dough easily. This time the filling stayed put.

Next we tackled the rolls' appearance. Instead of rising to the occasion in the oven, they were slouching in their seats. We reviewed the quick cream biscuit recipe to see if we might find the source of the problem there. Sure enough, the recipe stated that if the dough wasn't kneaded before being shaped, it didn't rise nicely in the oven. We made two batches of dough, kneading one and not the other, and were surprised to find that just a quick 30-second knead solved the problem. Contrary to what one might think, the short knead didn't toughen the buns; it just provided the dough with enough strength to take in a big breath and hold it.

To finish the buns, we tried a host of different glazes, all based on a quick confectioners' sugar and water glaze, which is inherently pasty and grainy. After a few trials, we found a way to sufficiently mask the graininess and pasty flavor by combining buttermilk and cream cheese, then sifting the confectioners' sugar over the paste (if the sugar is not sifted, the glaze will be lumpy). This glaze was smooth, thick, and pleasantly tangy, although it does add one more ingredient to the shopping list for the buns: cream cheese.

As for what to bake the buns in, we tried muffin tins, pie plates, cookie sheets, springform pans, glass baking dishes, and cake pans. With its straight sides, round shape, and perfect size, we chose a 9-inch nonstick cake pan. We started baking at 425 degrees and got lucky the first time out. The buns baked in 25 minutes, rose and browned nicely, and were cooked all the way through.

Now the moment of truth had come. It was time for a blind tasting of our quick cinnamon buns head-to-head with our yeasted cinnamon buns. The quick buns got a quick nod of approval, with many tasters even preferring them to the more sophisticated and elegantly flavored yeasted buns. Best of all, these shortcut cinnamon buns can be on the table in an hour—a fact you may very well choose to keep to yourself.

WHAT WE LEARNED: **Whisk buttermilk and melted butter into the dry ingredients to create a light, tender dough with plenty of flavor. Don't bother rolling out the dough—just pat it into a rectangle, cover with the spiced brown sugar filling, roll it up into a log, and cut into individual buns. Cream cheese masks the chalkiness in a quick buttermilk and powdered sugar glaze.**

QUICK CINNAMON BUNS WITH
BUTTERMILK ICING makes 8 buns

Melted butter is used in both the filling and the dough and to grease the pan; melt the total amount (8 tablespoons) at once and measure it out as you need it. The buns are best eaten warm, but they hold up reasonably well for up to 2 hours.

1 tablespoon unsalted butter, melted, for pan

cinnamon-sugar filling

- ¾ cup (5¼ ounces) packed dark brown sugar
- ¼ cup (1¾ ounces) granulated sugar
- 2 teaspoons ground cinnamon
- ⅛ teaspoon ground cloves
- ⅛ teaspoon salt
- 1 tablespoon unsalted butter, melted

biscuit dough

- 2½ cups (12½ ounces) unbleached all-purpose flour, plus additional flour for work surface
- 2 tablespoons granulated sugar
- 1¼ teaspoons baking powder
- ½ teaspoon baking soda
- ½ teaspoon salt
- 1¼ cups buttermilk
- 6 tablespoons unsalted butter, melted

icing

- 2 tablespoons cream cheese, softened
- 2 tablespoons buttermilk
- 1 cup (4 ounces) confectioners' sugar

1. Adjust oven rack to upper-middle position and heat oven to 425 degrees. Pour 1 tablespoon melted butter into 9-inch nonstick cake pan; brush to coat pan. Spray wire cooling rack with nonstick cooking spray; set aside.

2. TO MAKE CINNAMON-SUGAR FILLING: Combine sugars, spices, and salt in small bowl. Add 1 tablespoon melted butter and stir with fork or fingers until mixture resembles wet sand; set filling mixture aside.

3. TO MAKE BISCUIT DOUGH: Whisk flour, sugar, baking powder, baking soda, and salt in large bowl. Whisk buttermilk and 2 tablespoons melted butter in measuring cup or small bowl. Add liquid to dry ingredients and stir with wooden spoon until liquid is absorbed (dough will look very shaggy), about 30 seconds. Transfer dough to lightly floured work surface and knead until just smooth and no longer shaggy.

4. Pat dough with hands into 12 by 9-inch rectangle. Brush dough with 2 tablespoons melted butter. Sprinkle evenly with filling, leaving ½-inch border of plain dough around edges. Press filling firmly into dough. Using bench scraper or metal spatula, loosen dough from work surface. Starting at long side, roll dough, pressing lightly, to form tight log. Pinch seam to seal. Roll log seam-side down and cut evenly into eight pieces. With hand, slightly flatten each piece of dough to seal open edges and keep filling in place. Place one roll in center of prepared nonstick pan, then place remaining seven rolls around perimeter of pan. Brush with 2 tablespoons remaining melted butter.

5. Bake until edges are golden brown, 23 to 25 minutes. Use offset metal spatula to loosen buns from pan. Wearing oven mitt, place large plate over pan and invert buns onto plate. Place greased cooling rack over plate and invert buns onto rack. Cool about 5 minutes before icing.

6. TO MAKE ICING AND FINISH BUNS: While buns are cooling, line rimmed baking sheet with parchment paper (for easy cleanup); set rack with buns over baking sheet. Whisk cream cheese and buttermilk in large nonreactive bowl until thick and smooth (mixture will look like cottage cheese at first). Sift confectioners' sugar over; whisk until smooth glaze forms, about 30 seconds. Spoon glaze evenly over buns; serve immediately.

SCIENCE DESK:
The Magic of Buttermilk

BUTTERMILK IS THE SECRET INGREDIENT IN OUR CINNAMON bun recipe. What gives this dairy product its magical powers? Originally, buttermilk was the liquid left after churning milk to make butter. All the fat went into the butter and the liquid that was leftover—a thin, watery, somewhat sour liquid with occasional little dots of yellow butter floating in it—was called buttermilk because of the little pieces of butter.

This is how buttermilk was made on the farm. Today, buttermilk is something quite different. In fact, modern buttermilk should really be called butterless milk. It is a fermented dairy product, like yogurt or sour cream. Fermentation creates deep, complex flavors in foods. Think of beer, cheese, coffee, and chocolate—all of which are products of fermentation. In the fermentation of skim milk to make buttermilk, citric acid and a buttery tasting compound called diacetyl are produced. Together, the citric acid and diacetyl create a tangy, slightly sour milk with a bit of butter flavor. That's why quick breads made with buttermilk are so tasty.

BANANA BREAD

WHAT WE WANTED: A soft, moist, and tender bread for snacking or toasting, with real banana flavor.

Overripe bananas on the kitchen counter are an excellent excuse to make banana bread. However, many banana breads are flat, gritty, or heavy. Worse, some loaves taste only remotely of bananas. Good banana bread is soft and tender, with plenty of banana flavor and crunchy toasted walnuts. It should be moist and light, something so delicious that you look forward to the bananas on the counter turning soft and mushy.

In our testing, we found it very important to pay close attention to the condition of the bananas. Sweet, older, darkly speckled bananas infused the bread with both moisture and flavor, which meant that the bread, whether still warm or day-old, succeeded with less butter (just 6 tablespoons) than the amount used in most recipes (8 tablespoons).

We also experimented with the way we prepared the bananas for the batter: slightly mashed, mashed well, and pureed. Loaves with slightly mashed bananas left chunks of fruit. We preferred a smoother texture, but pureeing the bananas turned out to be a bad idea, because the batter did not rise as well. Leavener probably escaped before the thin batter developed enough structure to trap gases. Bananas that we mashed well by hand kept the batter thick but lumpfree.

We still wanted more moisture in the bread, so we tried mixing in milk, buttermilk, sour cream, and plain yogurt. Sour cream added richness, but it also made for a heavy texture and an unattractive, pebbly crust. Milk added little flavor and created a slick crust. Buttermilk added a delightful tang, but yogurt let the banana flavor stand out. And because yogurt has more solids than buttermilk, it made for a more solid loaf, which we preferred.

While the yogurt softened the bread's crumb, we still sought a more delicate, open grain. So we decided to experiment with various mixing methods to see how they affected the final texture. We considered the quick bread method (dry ingredients mixed in one bowl, liquids in another, with the two then gently stirred together) and the creaming method (butter and sugar creamed together, dry and wet ingredients then alternately mixed in).

The creaming method created a soft texture (reminiscent of butter cake) and good volume from the whipped sugar and butter. However, its lighter color looked less appetizing next to the golden-brown loaf achieved with the quick bread method. The quick bread method produced a delicate texture, too, and the less consistent crumb looked hearty and delicious. It also rose more than the creamed loaf. All in all, it was a better choice.

Take caution when mixing, though. When we stirred the wet and the dry ingredients into a smooth batter, the loaves turned out small and tough. Flour contains protein, and when protein mixes with water, gluten develops. The more you stir with a spoon, the more the gluten proteins arrange into long, orderly bundles. These bundles create an elastic batter that resists changing shape and cannot rise as well. To minimize gluten development, fold together the wet and dry ingredients gently, just until the dry ingredients are moistened. The batter should still be thick and chunky, but without any streaks of unincorporated flour.

Although we liked the simple flavors of bananas and toasted walnuts for the master recipe, we also found that banana bread works well with more adventurous flavors, including chocolate, macadamia nuts, orange zest, cinnamon, and nutmeg.

WHAT WE LEARNED: Ripe bananas are the key to proper texture and flavor in this bread. Yogurt adds a nice tang to the loaf and keeps the bread moist. Don't bother with creaming the butter and sugar—just melt the butter and fold all of the wet ingredients into the dry ingredients for a delicate but sturdy crumb.

BANANA BREAD makes one 9-inch loaf

For this recipe, use a loaf pan that measures 9 inches long, 5 inches across, and 3 inches deep. See the Equipment Corner on page 252 for more information about buying loaf pans. To toast walnuts, place them in a dry skillet over medium heat and toast, shaking pan occasionally, until they are fragrant.

  2   cups (10 ounces) unbleached all-purpose flour
  ¾   cup (5¼ ounces) sugar
  ¾   teaspoon baking soda
  ½   teaspoon salt
  3   very ripe, soft, darkly speckled large bananas, mashed well (about 1½ cups)
  ¼   cup plain yogurt
  2   large eggs, beaten lightly
  6   tablespoons butter, melted and cooled
  1   teaspoon vanilla extract
  1¼   cups walnuts, toasted and chopped coarse

1. Adjust oven rack to lower-middle position and heat oven to 350 degrees. Grease and flour 9 by 5-inch loaf pan; set aside.

2. Whisk flour, sugar, baking soda, and salt together in large bowl; set aside.

3. Mix mashed bananas, yogurt, eggs, butter, and vanilla with wooden spoon in medium bowl. Lightly fold banana mixture into dry ingredients with rubber spatula until just combined and batter looks thick and chunky. Fold in walnuts. Scrape batter into prepared loaf pan and smooth surface with rubber spatula.

4. Bake until loaf is golden brown and toothpick inserted in center comes out clean, about 55 minutes. Cool in pan for 5 minutes, then transfer to wire rack. Serve warm or at room temperature.

VARIATIONS
BANANA-CHOCOLATE BREAD

Follow recipe for Banana Bread, reducing sugar to 10 tablespoons and mixing 2½ ounces grated bittersweet chocolate (heaping ½ cup) into dry ingredients.

BANANA-COCONUT BREAD WITH MACADAMIA NUTS

Adjust oven rack to middle position and heat oven to 350 degrees. Toast ½ cup flaked, sweetened coconut and 1 cup chopped macadamia nuts on small baking sheet, stirring every 2 minutes, until golden brown, about 6 minutes. Follow recipe for Banana Bread, substituting toasted macadamias and coconut for walnuts.

ORANGE-SPICE BANANA BREAD

Follow recipe for Banana Bread, adding 1 teaspoon ground cinnamon, ¼ teaspoon grated nutmeg, and 2 tablespoons grated orange zest to dry ingredients.

TECHNIQUE: Freezing Bananas

Rather than throwing away one or two overripe bananas, they can be saved until you have enough to make banana bread. Place the overripe bananas in a zipper-lock plastic bag and freeze. As needed, add more bananas to the bag. When you are ready to make bread, thaw the bananas on the counter until softened.

BANANA BREADS FOR UNMOLDING & EATING (SCENE 3)

EQUIPMENT CORNER: Loaf Pans

A GOOD LOAF PAN WILL EVENLY BROWN BANANA BREAD and other quick breads (as well as yeast breads, such as sandwich bread). In addition, the pan should release loaves cleanly and it should be easy to get the pan in and out of the oven, with little chance of sticking an oven mitt into the batter or baked bread.

We tested 10 loaf pans made from a variety of materials, including metal, glass, and stoneware. Some of the pans were nonstick-coated and others were not. Several pans were "professional grade" and quite heavy, others were light. Prices ranged from $3 to $16. We baked two quick breads and one yeasted white bread in each pan and focused on browning, release of the loaf, and ease of handling the pan.

We found that dark-colored metal loaf pans browned breads more evenly than light-colored metal pans. Most of the dark metal pans were lined with a nonstick coating that also made the release of baked breads especially easy. We found that sweet breads, such as banana bread, were especially prone to burning in glass loaf pans. Sticking was also a problem in these pans. Stoneware loaf pans did a decent job of browning, but we had trouble removing loaves from these pans. Pans with handles at either end were easier to work with because they kept us from sticking an oven mitt into the edge of a baked loaf.

In the end, we recommend that you buy a metal loaf pan with a nonstick coating. Although there's no harm in spending more money on heavier pans, one of the cheapest, lightest pans in our testing (Ekco Baker's Secret, $3.99) was the favorite. One final piece of advice: Even with the nonstick coating, we recommend greasing and flouring your loaf pan to ensure easy release.

Rating Loaf Pans

WE TESTED 10 STANDARD-SIZE LOAF PANS BY BAKING AT LEAST THREE LOAVES, ONE EACH OF WHITE SANDWICH BREAD, cornbread, and lemon loaf cake, all baked to the same internal temperature. Pans were greased with nonstick cooking spray. Depth and evenness of browning, loaf release, and design factors such as the presence of handles and the width of the pan (as it affected the loaves' appearance) were equally important criteria. Performance differences between the recommended pans were so minor that we've arranged them in order of price, from cheapest to most expensive. See www.cooksillustrated.com for up-to-date prices and mail-order sources for top-rated products.

RECOMMENDED

1. Ekco Baker's Secret Non-Stick Large Loaf Pan

$3.99

Handles on both ends made this pan easy to move in and out of the oven. Browning was excellent, and release was a breeze, as was cleaning.

RECOMMENDED

2. Chicago Metallic SilverStone Bakeware Medium Loaf Pan

$5.99

Handles made it easy to work with and performance was fine, though the crust on white bread was just a tad light.

RECOMMENDED

3. Kaiser Backform Loaf Pan

$10.99

Exemplary browning, great release, and handles add up to a great pan.

RECOMMENDED

4. Chicago Metallic Professional Loaf Pan

$13.99

Slightly better browning of the white bread than with the less expensive Chicago Metallic SilverStone pan, but has no handles.

RECOMMENDED

5. Calphalon Nonstick Professional Bakeware Medium Loaf Pan

$15.99

Heavy pan with a high-quality feel. Produced beautifully shaped, beautifully browned loaves but for a hefty price.

TASTING LAB: Yogurt

PLAIN YOGURT MAY NOT BE THE WORLD'S SEXIEST FOOD, but there is plenty of mystique surrounding this refrigerator staple, perhaps owing to that ad campaign featuring centenarian Georgians (the Soviet variety) who ate yogurt every day. Once consumed mainly by hippies, yogurt is now a mainstream product, available in countless flavors, including cotton candy and kiwi. We were interested in plain yogurt, which bakers often use to add moistness to quick breads and muffins.

We had three questions at the outset of our research. First, does the inclusion of certain bacteria (the "active cultures" in yogurt) affect flavor? Second, does fat content make a difference in flavor and/or texture? You can buy nonfat, low fat, or whole milk yogurt, and we wanted to taste all three. Third, are the leading supermarket brands just fine, or is it worth seeking out specialty brands, especially those found in natural foods stores?

Yogurt was probably first made by chance when milk was accidentally fermented by wild bacteria. Today, the process is controlled. Milk (whole, low fat, or skim) is pasteurized and usually homogenized. (Some companies leave whole milk unhomogenized to retain a separate cream layer in their yogurt.) Active bacteria cultures are then added to the milk, and the milk is poured directly into cups and kept in a warm environment for several hours. The bacteria convert the milk sugar (called lactose) into lactic acid, causing the proteins in the milk to coagulate and thicken. Lactic acid also gives yogurt its characteristic tang. Finally, the yogurt is cooled and refrigerated.

We rounded up 10 leading brands of yogurt, including four made with whole milk, two with low fat milk, and four with skim milk, and tasted them straight from the container. We quickly determined that the type of bacteria used to culture the milk had no discernible effect on our tasters' ratings. Fat content was more complicated. Yogurts made with low fat milk and whole milk took the top four spots. However, two whole milk yogurts fared poorly. Yes, our

tasters appreciated the richness and flavor contributed by the extra fat, but in the end other considerations took precedence.

In terms of flavor, a happy medium between tart and bland carried the day. Yogurts that were extremely tart landed at the bottom of the rankings.

In terms of texture, our tasters spoke loud and clear. They preferred smooth, creamy yogurts to those that were lumpy, chalky, grainy, watery, or curdlike. In fact, tasters put such a high premium on smoothness that two nonfat brands with decent textures finished a respectable fifth and sixth in our tasting.

Our ideal yogurt is creamy and smooth and has some tang without being sour or acidic. Some milk fat is a plus. While it's easy to pick out the yogurt that meets these criteria on a spoon, what about when baking? Would the higher-fat products make better banana bread?

To find out, we baked loaves with nonfat, low fat and whole milk yogurt. Tasters had a hard time detecting differences, and all of the loaves were enjoyed. The texture of the yogurt didn't matter (watery and smooth yogurt baked up the same), nor did the flavor (the other ingredients in the recipe masked the sourness of even the most sour samples). Given the small amount of yogurt in this recipe, this result is not surprising. We also tried a corn muffin recipe that calls for 1 cup of yogurt and found that the muffins made with whole milk yogurt were both more moist and more tender than muffins made with low fat or nonfat yogurt.

Rating Plain Yogurts

WE PURCHASED 10 BRANDS OF PLAIN YOGURT AVAILABLE AT SUPERMARKETS AND NATURAL FOODS STORES. EACH yogurt was sampled straight from the container, although we did mix the yogurts just prior to the tasting to incorporate any separated liquid or cream. Tasters were asked to evaluate each yogurt on both texture and flavor. The yogurts are listed in order of preference.

HIGHLY RECOMMENDED

1. Colombo Low Fat Plain Yogurt

$2.69 for 32 ounces

Tasters gave this brand a big thumbs up, praising the "clean taste" and "mild tang" of this "creamy," "silky" yogurt.

RECOMMENDED

2. Brown Cow Organic Whole Milk Plain Yogurt

$2.39 for 24 ounces

Tasters liked this "rich," "buttery" yogurt, which was described as "slightly sweet, slightly lemony." A couple of tasters noticed a pleasant "goaty" quality to this "creamy" and "smooth" yogurt.

RECOMMENDED

3. Stonyfield Farm Organic Low Fat Plain Yogurt

$3.39 for 32 ounces

Tasters thought this yogurt was a bit "mild" and some went so far as to call it "bland." However, its "velvety" texture assured high scores.

RECOMMENDED

4. Stonyfield Farm Organic Cream on Top Whole Milk Plain Yogurt

$3.19 for 32 ounces

This yogurt was pretty "sour" and "acidic." Although "smooth," the consistency was thinner than other top brands.

RECOMMENDED WITH RESERVATIONS

5. Dannon Fat Free Plain Yogurt

$2.69 for 32 ounces

Tasters liked the "mildly tangy" flavor of this yogurt. Several panelists detected a "mineral taste." Others detected a "grainy," "chalky" consistency.

RECOMMENDED WITH RESERVATIONS

6. Colombo Fat Free Plain Yogurt

$2.99 for 32 ounces

Several tasters noted an "unpleasant" aftertaste in this "acidic" yogurt. The texture was slightly "gelatinous" but not objectionable.

RECOMMENDED WITH RESERVATIONS

7. Brown Cow Cream Top Whole Milk Plain Yogurt

$2.99 for 32 ounces

Unlike the other Brown Cow product made with whole milk, this one was not a clear winner. Several tasters picked up the same "goat-like" flavor, but the texture was "watery," "mealy," and "lumpy."

NOT RECOMMENDED

8. Stonyfield Farm Nonfat Plain Yogurt

$3.19 for 32 ounces

This "bland" yogurt had a "watery," "lumpy" texture that was a real turn-off for tasters.

NOT RECOMMENDED

9. Brown Cow Nonfat Plain Yogurt

$2.89 for 32 ounces

"Very sour," with a "bitter aftertaste." "Grainy," "lumpy" texture assured a low finish.

NOT RECOMMENDED

10. Erivan Acidophilus Yogurt

$1.99 for 16 ounces

This whole milk yogurt was so sour and acidic that one taster complained that it "hurts the back of the throat." The "lumpy," "watery" texture did not help.

RUSTIC BREAD
at home

Real country bread, the kind made by an artisan and never found at the supermarket, is a thing of beauty. The crust is shatteringly crisp, the crumb is chewy and filled with plenty of holes. The flavor is hearty and rugged. This loaf can be slathered with butter or used to build a sandwich with personality. We wanted to develop a recipe that was every bit as good as the best country loaves baked in a hearth at the finest bakeries but that was still doable for the home cook baking in a home oven. After baking hundreds of loaves, we think you'll agree that our loaf meets this challenge.

A loaf of rustic country bread sliced
and ready for a close-up.

RUSTIC COUNTRY BREAD

WHAT WE WANTED: A large, crusty European-style country loaf with great flavor and chew.

Flour, water, yeast, and salt. That's about as simple as it gets in the kitchen, or so we thought when we set out to develop a reliable home recipe for a crusty, full-textured, European-style country bread. This is the kind of bread that is a main course all by itself; the first bite hits you with a heady burst of crackle and chew, an inspired whiff of yeast, and a hint of sourness.

We expected that a sponge starter (a "sponge" of flour, water, and yeast is left to ferment, then additional flour, water, and other ingredients are added in) would produce more flavor than a quick rise using a greater amount of yeast, and this turned out to be true. In fact, we only used ½ teaspoon of instant yeast (most recipes call for up to a tablespoon) for 6 cups of flour. We also varied the sponge recipe by using equal amounts of whole wheat and white flour for added flavor and texture.

The next element to consider was water. Professional bakers know that a high water content produces more texture and chew. To figure out the percentage of water in a bread recipe (as a percentage of the flour weight), you calculate the weight, in grams, of water in the recipe (each cup of water weighs 237.5 grams) and divide that by the weight of the flour (1 cup of flour weighs 130 grams). After some research, we figured that a water content of 68 percent would be about right. The theory was that the higher percentage of water—most bread recipes run around 60 percent—would improve the chew. We tried this formula and got mediocre results. It was good bread, but without the big-league chew we wanted.

We then visited Iggy's Bakery just outside of Boston. The bread made there has a big chew, a big crust, and big flavor. The chief baker told us we needed to push the water level even higher. He pointed to the plastic vats filled with rising dough—a sticky mass that would just about pour. This was a breakthrough. Our idea of bread dough had been a nonstick satin ball, easy to handle and more solid than liquid. But this stuff puddled and pulled, shimmered and shook. At Iggy's, they use a mixture of three flours—high protein, whole wheat, and rye—for optimum flavor and texture.

Back in the test kitchen, we increased the water percentage to near-dangerous levels. The revised recipe now had 2½ cups of water to 6 cups of flour, which brought the percentage of water to flour up to a whopping 76 percent, a percentage so high it borders on heresy. However, this high percentage was slightly counteracted by the fact that almost 30 percent of the total flour used was whole wheat and rye. We chose these flours for flavor, but they also absorb more water than white flour does.

Professional bakers use giant mixers and special shaping machines that handle moist dough easily. In our test kitchen we use the same equipment that home cooks use, and the bread stuck to our hands, the wooden counter, the mixer bowl, the damp dish towel, and even the heavily floured peel (the shovel-like tool used to get breads in and out of the oven). We tried to knead the dough by hand, but this was almost impossible without adding lots of flour. Still, at the end of the day, the bread was vastly improved. Although a bit sticky, the inside had cavernous air holes and some real chew.

We now turned our attention more closely to the flour. Up until now, we had been using a professional baker's bread flour, which has a very high level of protein (about 14 percent). We decided to try both a regular bread flour and an all-purpose flour to see if protein content would have a noticeable affect on the finished product. The all-purpose flour yielded an extremely wet, unworkable dough; the dough made with regular bread flour was wetter than the high-protein loaf but still workable. Of most interest, however, was the fact that these lower-protein flours produced a chewier, crustier loaf, although we felt that the loaf made with all-purpose flour was a little too tough. After additional testing, it became clear that we had to adjust the recipe to accommodate the lower-protein flours, which can't absorb as much water as higher-protein flour. When we reduced the amount of water used in our regular bread flour dough to 2⅓ cups, the results were even better. Because this flour is sold in supermarkets, we decided to use it in our recipe.

We also wanted to try varying the amount of the other ingredients we were using: salt and honey. Most recipes with 6 cups of flour use 2 teaspoons of salt, and this amount was just right. Honey is often added to boost flavor and promote browning of the crust (sugar promotes browning). When we added 2 tablespoons of honey, the flavor was a bit deeper and the crust turned a rich nut-brown.

Kneading by hand was not our first choice (it can be done, however). We tried using a food processor with a metal blade, which worked fine except that our $250 machine sounded like a lawnmower in a dense patch of weeds; all that was missing was a curl of blue smoke and the smell of burning rubber. The machine simply could not handle 6 cups of quicksand. We tried the recipe in two half-batches, which worked pretty well. We found that leaving the metal blade in the processor between batches is best (you won't get absolutely all of the first batch out of the processor bowl); otherwise your hands will get sticky and dough may ooze out around the center core of the bowl when the second batch is mixed. We recommend that you process for no more than 30 seconds, which is enough time to knead the dough, and we recommend this method only for home cooks with a good heavy-duty processor.

The best solution was a heavy-duty standing mixer with a dough hook. We simply threw in the ingredients, mixed them briefly with a large, stiff rubber spatula, and then turned the machine on at the lowest setting for 15 minutes. We then transferred the dough to an oiled bowl to rise for about 2 hours, or until tripled in volume. Allowing the dough to triple in volume both improves flavor and helps the dough to develop more "muscle," which helps the bread maintain its shape when baked.

Even after 15 minutes of kneading, the dough was difficult to handle. After a few tries with various methods, we came up with the following, which was the least messy. For the first rise, simply use a rubber spatula to transfer the wet dough to the oiled bowl (a plastic tub is fine, too). After letting the bread rise for about 2 hours, use the same spatula to transfer the dough onto a lightly floured surface. Now flour both your hands and the dough (the latter lightly). Press the dough very gently into a round and then fold it into a ball. Note that you should handle the dough as little as possible at this point both because it is still a little sticky (you'll be tempted to add extra flour) and because excessive handling is bad for rustic bread—you want an irregular texture with lots of air holes. This point goes for all bread making: Strong kneading after the first rise will harm the delicate structure of the dough.

The best way to move the dough from here on in is to use a large dough scraper, two metal spatulas, or a thin floured baking sheet. Transfer the dough smooth-side down into a colander or a basket that has been lined with a piece of muslin or linen that has been well floured. The flour should be rubbed into the fabric so the dough will not stick. A banneton is a cloth-lined woven basket designed just for this purpose. You can purchase one or try making your own, as we did. Muslin, which is cheaper than linen, works well and comes in different grades from fine (the most expensive) to coarse (the least expensive). Use the cheaper variety to line your basket, and make sure that it is 100 percent unbleached cotton. A real banneton has the linen or muslin sewn right into the basket, an optional refinement. The basket we used was 4 inches high, 7 inches wide across the bottom, and 12 inches wide across the top. A colander is also a perfectly good option. It works well because it allows for air flow (the dough is more likely to stick to the muslin when sitting in a bowl).

For its second rise the dough needs to be covered directly. We tried a damp dish towel, but it stuck to the dough. It was like unwrapping a piece of saltwater taffy on a hot day. Aluminum foil proved more effective because the dough is less likely to stick to it and it allows the dough to breathe, keeping the dough from rising too much. If the dough rises too much at this point you will end up with a fluffy texture (plastic wrap, for example, will cause too much rising). The foil gives the dough shape and allows you to transfer it easily to the peel when the second rise is completed.

The last major issue was the crust. The key, according to most experts, is steam. Just to test this theory, we baked one loaf with no steam at all, and the crust was thin and unappealing. This bread does need steam, but there are many ways in which to provide it. For convenience' sake, we chose to spray the loaf before putting it in the oven.

We also tested starting oven temperatures. We began testing with 500-degree oven and then immediately turned the heat down to 400 degrees, working under the assumption that the higher temperature would offset the drop in temperature caused by opening the oven door and adding the dough (the dough absorbs a great deal of heat quickly). The resulting crust was thin and disappointing. Next we tried baking the bread at 500 degrees for the first 15 minutes and then reducing the temperature to 400. The crust was scorched. It cooked so fast that the interior had no time to cook properly. The best baking temperature turned out to be a constant 450 degrees.

WHAT WE LEARNED: For good flavor, use very little yeast and let it ferment in a sponge before adding most of the flour and water. Use some rye and whole wheat flours for flavor, and add a lot of water for good chew. Let the dough rise twice (the second time in a muslin-lined basket), and bake until the crust is deeply browned and the internal temperature reaches 210 degrees.

RUSTIC COUNTRY BREAD makes 1 large round loaf

Whole wheat and rye flours contribute to this bread's full flavor, and extra oven time gives the bread its thick crust. Because of its high water content, the bread will be gummy if pulled from the oven too soon. To ensure the bread's doneness, make sure its internal temperature reads 210 degrees by inserting an instant-read thermometer into the bottom of the loaf. Also look at the crust—it should be very dark brown, almost black. Because the dough is so sticky, a heavy-duty standing mixer is best for kneading, but food processor and hand-kneading instructions follow this recipe. Keep in mind that rising times vary depending on kitchen temperature (the times listed below are minimums). You can vary the texture by increasing or decreasing the flour. For bread with a finer crumb and less chewy texture, increase the flour by 1/4 cup increments. For coarser, chewier bread, decrease the flour by the same increments. To develop a crisp crust, you need to bake the bread on tiles or a stone. To vary flavors, add 1 tablespoon minced hearty herbs, such as rosemary or thyme, with the salt, or mix in 1/2 cup chopped toasted walnuts or pecans just before kneading ends.

sponge

- 1/2 teaspoon instant dry yeast (see Tasting Lab on page 262)
- 1 cup water (room temperature)
- 1 cup (5½ ounces) bread flour
- 1 cup (5 ounces) whole wheat flour

dough

- 3½ cups (19¼ ounces) bread flour, plus more as needed to lightly dust work surface, hands, and dough
- ½ cup (2½ ounces) rye flour
- 1⅓ cups water (room temperature), or more as needed
- 2 tablespoons honey
- 2 teaspoons salt

1. FOR THE SPONGE: Stir yeast into water in medium bowl until dissolved. Mix in flours with rubber spatula to create stiff, wet dough. Cover with plastic wrap; let sit at room temperature for at least 5 hours, preferably overnight. (Can be refrigerated up to 24 hours; return to room temperature before continuing with recipe.)

2. FOR THE DOUGH: Mix flours, water, honey, and sponge in bowl of standing mixer with rubber spatula. Knead dough, using dough hook attachment, on lowest speed until dough is smooth, about 15 minutes, adding salt during final 3 minutes. If dough looks dry after salt is added, add water in 1-tablespoon increments every 30 seconds until smooth consistency is reached. Transfer dough to large, lightly oiled container or bowl. Cover with plastic wrap; let rise until tripled in size, at least 2 hours.

3. Turn dough onto lightly floured surface. Dust dough top and hands with flour. Lightly press dough into round by folding edges of dough into middle from top, right, bottom, and left, sequentially, then gathering it loosely together. Transfer dough, smooth-side down, to colander or basket lined with heavily floured muslin or linen. Cover loosely with large sheet of aluminum foil; let dough rise until almost doubled in size, at least 45 minutes.

4. Meanwhile, adjust oven rack to low-center position and arrange baking tiles to form surface that is at least 18 by 12 inches or place large baking stone on rack. Heat oven to 450 degrees.

5. Cover peel or back of large baking sheet with large piece of parchment. Invert dough onto peel and remove muslin. Use scissors or serrated knife to cut three slashes on dough top. With scissors, trim excess parchment around dough. Fill spray bottle with water and spritz dough four or five times.

6. Slide dough, still on parchment, from peel onto tiles or stone; remove peel with quick backward jerk. Bake until

instant-read thermometer inserted in bread bottom registers 210 degrees (see illustration below) and crust is very dark brown, 35 to 40 minutes, turning bread around after 25 minutes if not browning evenly. Turn oven off, open door, and let bread remain in oven 10 minutes longer. Remove, then let cool to room temperature before slicing, about 2 hours. To crisp crust, place cooled bread in 450-degree oven for 10 minutes.

VARIATIONS

RUSTIC COUNTRY BREAD KNEADED IN A FOOD PROCESSOR

Make sponge as directed in recipe for Rustic Country Bread. Mix half of sponge and half of flours and honey in food processor fitted with metal blade. Pulse until roughly

---

TECHNIQUE:
Taking the Temperature of Bread

Professional bread recipes often suggest taking the internal temperature of a loaf to gauge when it's done.

A. For bread that is baked free-form, tip the loaf up with a hand shielded by an oven mitt or potholder and insert the probe through the bottom crust into the center of the loaf.

B. For bread that is baked in a loaf pan, insert the probe from the side, just above the edge of the loaf pan, directing the probe at a downward angle toward the center of the loaf.

blended, 3 to 4 one-second pulses. With machine running, add half of water (⅔ cup) slowly through feed tube; process until dough forms ball. Let sit for 3 minutes, then add half of salt and process to form smooth dough, about 30 seconds longer. Transfer dough to large, lightly oiled container or bowl, leaving metal blade in processor (some dough will remain under blade). Repeat process with remaining half of ingredients. Proceed with recipe as directed.

RUSTIC COUNTRY BREAD KNEADED BY HAND

Make sponge as directed in recipe for Rustic Country Bread. Place sponge and all dough ingredients, except 2 cups of bread flour, in large bowl. Stir mixture with wooden spoon until smooth, about 5 minutes. Work in reserved flour and then turn out onto floured board. Knead by hand for 5 minutes, incorporating no more than additional ¼ cup flour as you work. Dough will be very wet and sticky. Proceed with recipe.

TASTING LAB: Yeast

ALONG WITH FLOUR AND WATER, YEAST IS AN ESSENTIAL ingredient in bread recipes. Several kinds are available to home cooks. All yeast begins as a small, cultured, purified sample that feeds and multiplies continuously in a liquid medium until it reaches the desired volume and stage of development. This liquid yeast is sold by the tankerful to commercial food manufacturers. For bakeries, yeast companies remove some of the moisture from liquid yeast to create a product called "crumbled yeast," which is sold in 50-pound bags. The next processing step extrudes the yeast to make a product that remains fully hydrated yet fine enough to press into the small cakes you see for sale on supermarket shelves and labeled cake yeast, fresh yeast, or compressed yeast. Further processing yields dried, powdered yeast, called active dry yeast. The same process is used to make other dry yeasts, including instant yeast (also called

rapid-rise or quick-rise yeast), although this product starts with different strains of yeast.

We wondered whether the type or brand of yeast made a difference when making bread. To find out, we tested several different brands as well as the three major categories of yeast—cake, active dry, and instant. We prepared three recipes with each yeast—an American sandwich bread (with a small amount of butter, sugar, and milk), a baguette (without sugar or dairy), and a kuchen (with substantial amounts of butter, sugar, and dairy). We placed the doughs made with instant yeast in a warmed oven for just 40 minutes, whereas breads made with the cake and regular active dry yeast took about two hours when left to rise on the counter. We followed the general recommendations regarding the strength of cake yeast and used twice as much cake yeast as dry active or instant yeast.

Although we expected slower-rising active dry and cake yeasts to promote more flavor in the finished loaves, this was not the case. Our tasters actually preferred the breads made with instant yeast. The faster rise, in fact, yielded more flavor and produced a noticeably sweeter bread. One theory is that a rapid rise provides less time for the creation of the acidic byproducts of fermentation, hence a sweeter loaf. It is also true that instant yeast has superior enzyme activity, which converts starches to sugar faster (and so perhaps more completely) than regular-rise varieties.

Even more to the point, though, is the fact that instant yeast is not necessarily an inferior product. Yeast is a plant, and different varieties have quite different qualities, as do different varieties of, say, roses. Instant yeast has been genetically engineered to reproduce the best characteristics of yeasts from around the world. Although genetic engineering often results in loss of flavor, our blind taste tests confirmed that in this case it produced an excellent product.

As for why this yeast works faster, there are two primary reasons. In addition to the more rapid enzyme activity described above, instant yeast also has an open, porous structure, which means that it can absorb liquid instantly. When this yeast was introduced for home use, consumers

had some difficulty with it because they continued to follow their habit of "proofing" the yeast—dissolving it in water to see if it bubbled, which was "proof" that the yeast was alive and could do its work—rather than mixing it directly into the flour, as instructed by the manufacturer. Because of its efficiency, this new yeast dissolved in water rapidly and ran out of food (starch) and died before the rising process was complete. To correct this problem, scientists went back and added more starch to the mix, giving the yeast enough food to survive proofing.

Today, however, most yeast does not need to be dissolved in water before being used in a recipe. For one thing, yeast is now marked with an expiration date for freshness, so there's no need to proof, or test, the yeast as long as the

expiration date hasn't passed. (Note that these expiration dates should be taken seriously. We tried baking a loaf with yeast that was one month past expiration, and the rising times were double those experienced with fresh yeast. The resulting loaf was more dense, with a smaller rise.)

Keep in mind that whether you dissolve yeast directly in liquid or add it to the flour, the temperature of the water or milk used is crucial. Dry yeast will die in ice water or in liquids at 125 degrees or higher.

We rely on instant yeast in our recipes. If you want to use active dry yeast, you can use an equal amount, but note that rising times will be longer. If you want to use cake yeast, you'll need twice as much yeast as recommended in the recipe. Note that cake yeast is highly perishable and must be refrigerated.

EQUIPMENT CORNER:
Dry Measuring Cups

MEASURING CUPS ARE BASIC NECESSITIES IN THE kitchen; without them, even the simplest cookie recipe would be compromised. Kitchen stores offer a wide range of measuring cups, from those with rubber comfort grips on their handles to heavy-gauge aluminum and stainless steel. We wondered if one kind of cup would be easier or more efficient to use than another. To find out, we put eight readily available measuring-cup sets to the test and came up with clear guidelines for your next purchase. Prices ranged from $2.99 to $19.99.

We tested every individual measuring cup by measuring flour and sugar with our favored "dip and sweep" method (dipping the cup into the bin, scooping out a heaping cupful, then leveling the cup with the straight side of a knife or icing spatula). While dipping and sweeping, we paid particular attention to cup construction—our measuring cups need to stand up to hundreds of repeated dips in the flour or sugar bin. Given the uncompromising nature of baking, accuracy was also important, so we weighed each cup of flour to make sure they all maintained the standard weight of 5 ounces of flour per cup.

Across the board, measured weights were remarkably consistent. We found that the precision of the measurements depended more on the consistency of the measuring method than on the construction of the cups themselves.

We did find, however, that a sturdy handle is critical to successful dipping and sweeping. Some plastic handles actually bent when the cup was full. (They seemed likely to snap under extra pressure—say, when measuring shortening.) Other handles were simply too short, forcing the hand to snuggle close to the cup and get covered in flour. More than one set was so heavy-handled that the cups tipped over when sitting on the counter—annoying when cups are empty and a disaster when full. Sturdy, riveted stainless steel handles were highly rated and preferred.

Material played a dual role in the usefulness of a cup, affecting both sturdiness and ease of cleaning. Plastic failed to impress on both counts. It's more likely to melt if you inadvertently place it near a heat source or to warp in a particularly hot dishwasher. Plastic models were also troublesome when it came to cleaning. They are more likely to scratch, creating rough surfaces that cause bits of sugar or flour to stick. Our testers universally preferred heavy-gauge metal. It stood up to heavy dipping and resisted any type of scratch or ding.

If you're looking for a measuring cup that offers ease of use and longevity, choose one with a long, sturdy handle and a heavy, well-constructed base. The cup will make measuring a breeze and give you years of use.

Rating Dry Measuring Cups

WE RATED EIGHT SETS OF MEASURING CUPS BY REPEATING "DIP AND SWEEP" MEASUREMENTS OF FLOUR AND SUGAR hundreds of times. (We dipped the cup into a bin of flour or sugar, scooped up a heaping cupful, then leveled the contents with the straight edge of an icing spatula.) The cups are listed in order of preference. See www.cooksillustrated.com for up-to-date prices and mail-order sources for top-rated products.

RECOMMENDED

1. Amco Stainless Steel Measuring Cups

$12.99

Heavy and sturdy; downgraded only for the handle, which meets the cup below the top, making leveling more difficult.

RECOMMENDED WITH RESERVATIONS

2. Oxo Good Grips Stainless Steel Measuring Cups

$19.99

Sturdy but heavy comfort-grip handles cause the cups to tip over when empty and balance precariously when full. They do not nestle together well and must be wrestled apart.

RECOMMENDED WITH RESERVATIONS

3. Fox Run Stainless Steel Measuring Cups

$6.99

Good set for infrequent use; the metal is thinner than in other models and the handles less securely riveted, imparting a flimsy feel and an occasional tip-over.

NOT RECOMMENDED

4. Oneida 18/8 Stainless Steel Measuring Cups

$19.99

Shiny, sturdy, and an interesting design, but not very functional—downgraded for small handles and measurement marks printed on the bottom of the bowl instead of the sides of the cup or the handles.

NOT RECOMMENDED

5. Oneida Colour Grip Measuring Cups

$7.99

Nice grip, good leveling, and heat-resistant plastic material, but the color-coded handles bent while scooping flour from a bin.

NOT RECOMMENDED

6. Oxo Good Grips Measuring Cups

$4.99

Very light and flimsy feeling, with easily scratched black plastic. The cups tip over when empty and they are not easy to level because the rim edge is too thick.

NOT RECOMMENDED

7. Pyrex Accessories Measuring Cups

$2.99

Very short, awkward handles are hard to grip, especially when scooping flour from a bin. Easily scratched plastic surface is difficult to clean.

NOT RECOMMENDED

8. Pyrex Accessories Professional Clear Measuring Cups

Price: $9.99

Lexan plastic cups tipped over from heavy, long handles. The cups do not nestle together cleanly, but they are easy to level.

No peeking. Jack makes Chris wear a blindfold for the tasting of cookies made with light, dark, and blackstrap molasses.

COOKIE JAR favorites

CHAPTER 22

Cookies are so simple, so basic, so American, so easy. How is it then that most Americans buy bad supermarket cookies? Except for the sweetness of sugar, these cookies are devoid of flavor (close your eyes and you can't tell whether the cookie is made with chocolate or molasses), and the texture is either dry and crumbly or unnaturally gooey and soft. There is a better way, and it's not as difficult as you might think.

The test kitchen has taken two classics—soft, fudgy chocolate cookies and spiced molasses cookies—and made them great again. We've figured out the secrets to superior flavor as well as an irresistible chewy texture. Best of all, these recipes are easy. Yes, they demand some attention to detail—two or three minutes in the oven can make the difference between a chewy cookie and a dry one—but the techniques are so easy that even the novice baker will succeed the first time out.

CHOCOLATE COOKIES

WHAT WE WANTED: A chocolate cookie so fudgy and so flavorful it would be unforgettable.

Obsessions often begin with chance encounters, a wry, fetching smile glanced out of the corner of an eye or perhaps one's first taste of a home-grown tomato. One of our greatest obsessions has been the first transcendent bite of the perfect chocolate cookie, still warm out of the oven. That first bite would reveal a center of hot fudge sauce, and the texture would call to mind chocolate bread pudding with a deep, complex chocolate flavor. This would be the sort of confection that creates intense focus while it is consumed, sights and sounds subordinate to taste, overloading the other senses to the point of dysfunction.

The problem is that we have, for years, been trying to perfect this cookie. We have created large, dense cookies that were rich and decadent, but the chocolate flavor was dull. We have also experimented with thin, crisp cookies (nice but not intense), chewy cookies (good but not showstoppers), and cakelike chocolate cookies, which tend to be dry and uninspiring. The test kitchen also made a half-dozen recipes from various cookbooks and discovered a world of difference in texture, flavor, and appearance, from soft mocha-colored disks to thick mounds of pure fudge. This panoply of outcomes gave us pause, since the ingredient lists seemed to have more in common than the cookies themselves. Figuring out what makes a chocolate cookie tick was going to require weeks of testing and a great deal of detective work.

Our first step was to strip the recipes down to their basics to understand the fundamentals. A chocolate cookie is a mixture of melted chocolate, sugar, eggs, butter, flour, baking soda or powder, and salt. Vanilla, coffee, and nuts are extras.

The key issues were how to handle the butter and eggs.

The butter can be melted or creamed, and the eggs can be beaten or just whisked into the batter. For the first test batch, we melted the butter and whipped the eggs. The results were good, but the cookies were a bit cakey and loose, without any chew. For the next batch we melted the butter and did not beat the eggs. These cookies were a bit dry and cakey. When we started creaming the butter and beating the eggs into it after creaming, we noticed an immediate improvement. However, we finally settled on a modified creaming method with minimal beating to produce moist cookies that were not cakey.

The next issue was one of proportions, that is, the ratio

of flour to butter to eggs to sugar to chocolate. This was going to be crucial to the thickness of the cookie, its texture, and the degree to which the taste of chocolate would dominate. Looking over the recipes we had tested, we saw so many permutations that we felt like the British trying to crack the German secret code in World War II.

To organize the facts, we made a chart of the various ratios of eggs, sugar, chocolate, and butter to flour, with related comments on the taste, texture, and shape of each cookie we had tested. We quickly noted that the ratio of eggs and butter to flour was less important than the ratio of sugar and chocolate to flour. The driest cookie used less than ½ cup of sugar per cup of flour; the richest, wettest cookie used 3 cups. The cookie with the faintest chocolate flavor and a relatively firm, dry texture used only 2 ounces of chocolate per cup of flour, whereas other recipes used up to a pound of chocolate with only ½ cup of flour. After many tests designed to balance sweetness and moisture, we settled on 1 cup of sugar and 8 ounces of chocolate to 1 cup of flour. Finally, we had a moist cookie with good chocolate flavor. Nonetheless, we thought the flavor and texture could be still better, so we moved on to other ingredients.

We started with all white granulated sugar and then tested a mixture of brown sugar and granulated, which seemed to improve the flavor and added just a bit more moisture. We also tried corn syrup, which had little effect. A small amount of vanilla extract and instant coffee powder rounded out the flavors. Throughout the testing, we had been using all-purpose flour. We decided to try cake flour, but the resulting cookies were a bit too delicate. We also varied the quantity of flour throughout the testing process, starting at 3 cups and eventually working our way down to 2 cups. To create a thicker, more stable cookie, we tried replacing some of the butter with vegetable shortening (Crisco), but this created an unattractive, greasy-looking cookie with a pale white sheen. We thought that the choice

of leavener might be important, so we tested baking powder against baking soda and found that the cookies with the powder were slightly thicker.

At this point our cookie was thick and very good, but still not the sort of thing that would reduce the average adult to tears of joy. The flavor was remained a bit dull, and the texture was moist but monochromatic. We wondered if we could solve this problem by varying the type of chocolate. We found that unsweetened chocolate, an ingredient often called for in chocolate cookie recipes, added intensity to the flavor. Unfortunately, we also discovered an aggressive sour note in these cookies, even when the sugar level was adjusted for the bitterness of the chocolate. Semisweet and bittersweet chocolate turned out to be better choices owing to their rounder, less potent flavors. These chocolates undergo more processing than unsweetened, and they also get other flavorings; this no doubt gives them a smoother, richer flavor overall. (For more information on types of chocolate, see the Science Desk on page 271.)

Our hunt was almost over, but now we wondered if a bit of cocoa powder might add more depth of flavor to our cookie. One-half cup of Dutch-processed cocoa was substituted for the same amount of flour, and the chocolate flavor became both smoother and deeper. (We also tried a batch of cookies made only with cocoa powder and no chocolate and they were disappointing, having just a faint chocolate flavor.) At last, we had brought our fantasy to life: a double-chocolate cookie that was both rich and soft, with an intense chocolatey center that would drive anyone to distraction.

WHAT WE LEARNED: For smooth, rich chocolate flavor, use a combination of semisweet chocolate and Dutch-processed cocoa powder. Add enough flour to give the cookies structure; any more flour only makes the cookies drier and cakier.

THICK AND CHEWY DOUBLE-CHOCOLATE COOKIES makes about 3½ dozen cookies

To melt the chocolate in a microwave, heat at 50 percent power for 2 minutes, stir, then continue heating at 50 percent power for 1 more minute. If not completely melted, heat an additional 30 to 45 seconds at 50 percent power. We recommend using a spring-loaded ice cream scoop to scoop the dough. Resist the urge to bake the cookies longer than indicated; they may appear underbaked at first but will firm up as they cool.

2 cups (10 ounces) unbleached all-purpose flour
½ cup Dutch-processed cocoa powder
2 teaspoons baking powder
½ teaspoon salt
16 ounces semisweet chocolate, chopped
4 large eggs
2 teaspoons vanilla extract
2 teaspoons instant coffee or espresso powder
10 tablespoons (1¼ sticks) unsalted butter, softened
1½ cups packed (10½ ounces) light brown sugar
½ cup (3½ ounces) granulated sugar

1. Sift together flour, cocoa, baking powder, and salt in medium bowl; set aside.

2. Melt chocolate in medium heatproof bowl set over pan of almost-simmering water, stirring once or twice, until smooth; remove from heat. Beat eggs and vanilla lightly with fork, sprinkle coffee powder over to dissolve, and set aside.

3. In bowl of standing mixer fitted with paddle attachment, beat butter at medium speed until smooth and creamy, about 5 seconds. Beat in sugars until combined, about 45 seconds; mixture will look granular. Reduce speed to low and gradually beat in egg mixture until incorporated, about 45 seconds. Add chocolate in steady stream and beat until combined, about 40 seconds. Scrape bottom

GETTING IT RIGHT: Size Matters

The balls of raw dough should be about the size of a golf ball. Don't skimp or the cookies won't be moist and fudgy.

and sides of bowl with rubber spatula. With mixer at low speed, add dry ingredients and mix until just combined. Do not overbeat. Cover with plastic wrap and let stand at room temperature until consistency is scoopable and fudgelike, about 30 minutes.

4. Meanwhile, adjust oven racks to upper-middle and lower-middle positions and heat oven to 350 degrees. Line two baking sheets with parchment paper. Leaving about 1½ inches between each ball, scoop dough onto parchment-lined cookie sheets with 1¾-inch ice cream scoop.

5. Bake, reversing position of baking sheets halfway through baking (from top to bottom and front to back), until edges of cookies have just begun to set but centers are still very soft, about 10 minutes. Cool cookies on sheets about 10 minutes, slide parchment with cookies onto wire racks, and cool to room temperature. Cover one baking sheet with new piece of parchment paper. Scoop remaining dough onto parchment-lined sheet, bake, and cool as directed. Remove cooled cookies from parchment with wide metal spatula and serve.

THICK AND CHEWY TRIPLE-CHOCOLATE COOKIES

If you like bursts of warm melted chocolate in your cookies, include chocolate chips in the batter. The addition of chips will slightly increase the yield of the cookies.

Follow recipe for Thick and Chewy Double-Chocolate Cookies, adding 12 ounces (about 2 cups) semisweet chocolate chips to batter after dry ingredients are incorporated in step 3.

SCIENCE DESK: Types of Chocolate

THERE ARE MANY OPTIONS WHEN IT COMES TO CHOCO-late: unsweetened, bittersweet, semisweet, cocoa powder, and chips. The question is, how are they different?

Unsweetened chocolate, often called baking chocolate or chocolate liquor, is made from roasted cocoa beans and contains about 50 percent solids from the beans and 50 percent cocoa butter. Bittersweet and semisweet chocolates (also called dark chocolates) are made from unsweetened chocolate that is ground with sugar and then further refined. Because bittersweet and semisweet chocolates are about 50 percent sugar, they have less chocolate flavor than unsweetened, which has no added sugar. (Although individual brands may vary, bittersweet averages around 46 percent sugar by weight; semisweet is about 57 percent sugar.) The chocolate flavor they do have, however, is less bitter and more complex, features appreciated by many bakers.

Chocolate chips are made from chocolate with relatively little cocoa butter, about 30 percent or even less. (Dark chocolates, by comparison, must have at least 35 percent cocoa butter.) This is because the chips will not hold their shape with more fat. This lower percentage of cocoa butter makes for a less buttery flavor and a grainier texture.

Cocoa powder is made from unsweetened chocolate. Much of the fat is removed by pressing, leaving behind the solids. These leftover solids are then fluffed up and packaged. Dutch-processed cocoa is less acidic than regular cocoa, and many people feel that this results in a stronger, more interesting chocolate flavor.

Another factor that affects the quality of one brand of chocolate over another is the use of additives. Most processed dark chocolates include vanilla, lecithin (which makes chocolate smoother when poured), and other flavorings, often including soy. In addition, some manufacturers roast their beans for a shorter time on the theory that when the chocolate is baked by consumers it will undergo additional processing.

As for which type of semisweet chocolate is best for a chocolate cookie, we tested four major brands head to head:

GETTING IT RIGHT:
The Secret to Evenly Baked Cookies

Does your oven turn out trays of baked cookies that vary in color and texture as in the photo above? Are some cookies burnt around the edges, while others on the same baking sheet are not quite done? Most ovens do this because the temperature varies from back to front, side to side, and top to bottom. The solution is simple. At the halfway mark in the baking time, rotate the cookie sheet so that the back side now faces front. If there are two cookie sheets in the oven, switch their position so that top goes to bottom and bottom goes to top. Follow this regimen and the result will be batch after batch of evenly baked cookies.

Nestlé, Baker's, Ghirardelli, and Callebaut. The Baker's turned out a gritty cookie that received low marks, Nestlé had an off, somewhat fruity taste, and the Ghirardelli had a muted but pure chocolate flavor that was quite pleasant. Callebaut was our favorite, with a big chocolate flavor that was clean, direct, and full of punch.

EQUIPMENT CORNER:
Measuring Spoons

MEASURING SPOONS DON'T USUALLY GET A LOT OF CON-sideration: bought once and done. But have you ever wondered if your set of spoons is accurate? Would an expensive set do a better job? To find out, the test kitchen purchased 10 different sets of measuring spoons, made from both plastic and stainless steel, ranging in price from $1.99 to $14.99.

First we wanted to determine whether the spoons measured accurately. According to the Office of Weights and Measures, a division of the National Institute of Standards and Technology, a true tablespoon of water should weigh precisely 14.742 grams. We filled each of the spoons with water and then weighed the water to see how close the measurement came to the official standard.

We also assessed each set of measuring spoons for durability. Would the spoons break under pressure? Melt? Dent? And we looked at usability, too. Was it easy to level the spoons when measuring dry ingredients? Was it easy to fill the spoons with liquid?

We were prepared for large differences in degree of accuracy but found none. All of the spoons weighed in within a few hundredths of grams of the official standard—not enough to compromise even the most exacting recipe. But technical accuracy does not always beget accurate measurement. If a spoon cannot be leveled easily, for instance, or if it is dented, accuracy is compromised. Usability and durability are therefore the determinants of accuracy when it comes to most measuring spoons.

In terms of usability, testers preferred spoons with

deeper bowls as opposed to those with narrow and elongated or wide and shallow bowls. Shallow bowls allowed more liquid to spill as the result of a slight misstep or unsteady hand. The narrow, elongated bowls made dipping and scooping into anything but a very deep container impossible. Many spoons were difficult to level cleanly. Some had bumps along the rim of the bowl, and others had handles that did not meet the bowl neatly. (To level, we used the back of a dinner knife or icing spatula, sliding along the base of the handle, onto the bowl.)

In terms of durability, all testers preferred stainless steel spoons—plastic models, no matter how thick, felt flimsy and more likely to break, bend, crack, or melt. Heavier stainless steel models were sturdier and therefore less likely to become dented or scratched. In the end, we found a heavy-duty stainless steel set of spoons that fit the bill and cost just $4.

Rating Measuring Spoons

WE TESTED 10 SETS OF MEASURING SPOONS MADE FROM A VARIETY OF MATERIALS. WE ASSESSED DURABILITY AND usability (how easy is it to measure and level dry ingredients? are liquid ingredients more or less likely to spill over the edge?). Spoon sets are listed in order of preference. See www.cooksillustrated.com for up-to-date prices and mail-order sources for top-rated products.

RECOMMENDED

1. Progressive International Stainless Steel Measuring Spoon Set

$3.99

The easiest to level and fill, so they also proved to be the most consistent in terms of accuracy. Sturdy and firm.

RECOMMENDED WITH RESERVATIONS

2. Oneida 18/8 Stainless Steel Measuring Spoon Set

$14.99

Easy to level and extremely sturdy. Spoons could not be linked together, and the measurement label are on the underside of the handles.

RECOMMENDED WITH RESERVATIONS

3. Rowoco Long Handle Measuring Spoons

$5.99

Long handles were useful when reaching into deep or narrow containers. However, the handle curved down before meeting the bowl, which made leveling more difficult.

RECOMMENDED WITH RESERVATIONS

4. Progressive International Stainless Steel Measuring Spoons with Colored Handles

$2.99

The wide, shallow bowls made measuring difficult, as did the handles, which curved down to meet the bowl.

RECOMMENDED WITH RESERVATIONS

5. Oneida Plastic Heat Resistant Colourgrip Measuring Spoons

$5.99

Best of the plastic models because of the spoons' good grip and deep bowls.

RECOMMENDED WITH RESERVATIONS

6. Pyrex Plastic Measuring Spoon Set

$1.99

Firmer plastic than most models, with a 25-year guarantee—second best among the plastic models.

RECOMMENDED WITH RESERVATIONS

7. Good Cook's Collection Stainless Measuring Spoons

$2.49

Our least favorite stainless spoons. A slight misstep and most of the contents were lost from the extra-wide, shallow bowls. Thin steel makes the spoons easy to bend or dent.

RECOMMENDED WITH RESERVATIONS

8. Oxo Good Grips Plastic Measuring Spoon Set

$2.99

These plastic spoons were flimsy and light with bowls that scratched quickly.

NOT RECOMMENDED

9. Pyrex Professional Clear Spice Jar Measuring Spoon Set

$4.99

These clear plastic spoons with extra-long, narrow bowls were unusually difficult to work with. Bumpy, uneven plastic ridge on bowl rims made leveling very difficult.

NOT RECOMMENDED

10. Kitchen Art Adjust-a-Spoon Measuring Spoon

$3.99

This single plastic spoon has a sliding level for each measurement. Dry and wet ingredients became trapped inside the hollow base, and the pushing mechanism was sticky and slow.

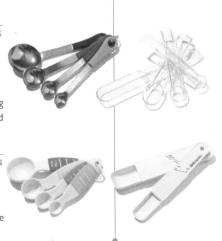

MOLASSES SPICE COOKIES

WHAT WE WANTED: An uncommonly moist, soft, yet chewy, tooth-sinking texture and a warm, tingling spiciness paired with the dark, bittersweet flavor of molasses.

Molasses cookies are the cookie pariahs, the dowdy group in the cookie crowd—permanently out of style and hopelessly old-fashioned. But we've come to appreciate good molasses cookies for their honesty and simplicity. On the outside, their cracks and crinkles give them a humble, charming countenance. Unfortunately, molasses spice cookies are often miserable specimens, no more than flat, tasteless cardboard rounds of gingerbread. They can be dry and cakey without the requisite chew; others are timidly flavored with molasses and are either recklessly or vacantly spiced.

We started by testing a half-dozen different recipes, using a variety of fats, flours, and mixing methods. Although these early experiments yielded vastly different cookies in terms of both flavor and appearance, a few things were clear. The full, rich flavor of butter was in, flat-tasting shortening was out. Flour required no fussing over—unbleached all-purpose flour was perfectly suited to the task. The mixing technique was a standard one: Cream the butter and sugar, add any eggs, then the molasses, and, finally, stir in the dry ingredients.

Molasses is at the core of these cookies. Enough must be used to give them a dark, smoky, bittersweet flavor, but we found that a surfeit of molasses creates a sticky, unworkable dough. For the amount of butter (12 tablespoons) and flour (2¼ cups) we were using, the molasses ceiling was ½ cup. We had been using mild (also called light) molasses up to this point, but in an attempt to boost flavor, we baked batches with dark and blackstrap molasses. Cookies made with dark molasses were filled with bold flavor and rich color, and they garnered much praise. Those made with blackstrap molasses had a few fans, but, for most of us, the wicked brew overtook the spices and embittered the cookies.

Molasses alone cannot supply the cookies with enough sweetness, so either granulated or brown sugar would be required. Dark brown sugar (we chose dark over light for its stronger molasses flavor) yielded cookies that were surprisingly puffy and cakey, and they spread too little on the baking sheet. Granulated sugar yielded cookies that were pale both in color and flavor. A combination of granulated and brown sugars was the ticket. The brown sugar fortified the molasses flavor while the granulated sugar, a spreading agent, allowed the cookies to attain a good, even thickness in the oven without much puff. After some fiddling, we found equal amounts of brown and granulated sugar to be ideal.

Most molasses cookie recipes call for no more than a single egg to bind things together. The white of a whole egg—harmless as it may seem—made the dough sticky. The difference was subtle, but the white also caused the baked cookie to have a slightly cakelike crumb and a firmer, drier feel than we cared for. A lone yolk was all the cookies wanted or needed.

Molasses is a mildly acidic ingredient, so baking soda, an alkali that reacts with the acidity of the molasses to provide lift, is the logical leavener for these cookies. In our testing, cookies with too little baking soda were flat and failed to develop those attractive fault lines. The proper amount of baking soda (1 teaspoon) gave the cookies nice height—a pleasure to sink your teeth into—and a winsome appearance, with large, meandering fissures.

It was time to refine the flavor of the cookies. A teaspoon of vanilla extract complemented generous amounts of sharp, spicy ground ginger and warm, soothing cinnamon. Cloves, rich and fragrant, and allspice, sweet and mysterious, were added, but in more judicious quantities. Nutmeg was pedestrian and had little to offer. Finely and freshly ground black pepper, however, added some intrigue—a soupçon of heat against the deep, bittersweet flavor of the molasses.

To shape the molasses cookies, we rolled generous heaping tablespoons of dough into balls, coating them with granulated sugar, which, after baking, gave the cookies a frosted

sparkle. Out of a 375-degree oven, the cookies were perfect—the edges were slightly crisped and the interiors soft and chewy. We determined that the cookies must be baked one sheet at a time since cookies baked on the lower rack inevitably baked up puffed and smooth rather than craggy and cracked.

Most important, we noted that the cookies must come out of the oven when they appear substantially underdone, otherwise their soft, moist, chewy texture will harden upon cooling. Whisk them out when the edges are hardly set, the centers are still soft and puffy, and the dough looks shiny and raw between the cracks. The cookies finish baking with residual heat, so don't shortchange them of a five-minute repose on the baking sheet before removal to the cooling rack.

While the spicy aroma lingers in the kitchen, bite into a warm, soft, chewy molasses spice cookie. These cookies may be out of style, but they are definitely not out of favor.

WHAT WE LEARNED: Use a blend of molasses, light brown sugar, and granulated sugar for good flavor and proper spreading of the dough in the oven. Use only a single egg yolk to keep the cookies from puffing up as they bake. Finally, bake just one cookie sheet at a time and take the cookies out of the oven when they still look underdone to guarantee a moist, chewy texture.

MOLASSES SPICE COOKIES makes about 22 cookies

For best flavor, make sure that your spices are fresh. Light or mild molasses gives the cookies a milder flavor; for a stronger flavor, use dark molasses. (See the Tasting Lab on page 277 for more information about molasses.) Either way, measure molasses in a liquid measure. If you find that the dough sticks to your palms as you shape the balls, moisten your hands occasionally in a bowl filled with cold tap water and shake off the excess. Bake the cookies one sheet at a time; if baked two at a time, the cookies started on the bottom rack won't develop the attractive cracks. Remove the cookies from the oven when they still look slightly raw and underbaked. If you plan to glaze the cookies (see recipe below), save the parchment paper used to line the cookie sheet during baking.

⅓ cup (about 2½ ounces) granulated sugar, plus ½ cup for dipping
2¼ cups (11¼ ounces) unbleached all-purpose flour
1 teaspoon baking soda
1½ teaspoons ground cinnamon
1½ teaspoons ground ginger
½ teaspoon ground cloves
¼ teaspoon ground allspice
¼ teaspoon finely ground black pepper
¼ teaspoon salt
12 tablespoons (1½ sticks) unsalted butter, softened
⅓ cup packed (2¾ ounces) dark brown sugar
1 large egg yolk
1 teaspoon vanilla extract
½ cup light or dark molasses

1. Adjust oven rack to middle position and heat oven to 375 degrees. Line two baking sheets with parchment paper. Place ½ cup sugar for dipping in 8- or 9-inch cake pan.

2. Whisk flour, baking soda, spices, and salt in medium bowl until thoroughly combined; set aside.

3. In standing mixer fitted with paddle attachment, beat butter with brown sugar and remaining ⅓ cup granulated sugar at medium-high speed until light and fluffy, about 3 minutes. Reduce speed to medium-low and add yolk and vanilla; increase speed to medium and beat until incorporated, about 20 seconds. Reduce speed to medium-low and add molasses; beat until fully incorporated, about 20 seconds, scraping bottom and sides of bowl once with rubber spatula. Reduce speed to lowest setting; add flour mixture and beat until just incorporated, about 30 seconds, scraping down bowl once. Give dough a final stir by hand to ensure that no pockets of flour remain at bottom. Dough will be soft.

4. Using tablespoon measure, scoop heaping tablespoon of dough and roll it between your palms into 1¼- to 1½-inch ball; drop ball into cake pan with sugar and repeat to form about 4 balls. Toss balls in sugar to coat and set on prepared baking sheet, spacing them about 2 inches apart. Repeat with remaining dough.

5. Bake, one sheet at a time and reversing position of baking sheet from front to back halfway through baking, until cookies are browned, still puffy, and edges have begun to set but centers are still soft (cookies will look raw between the cracks and seem underdone), about 11 minutes. Do not overbake.

6. Cool the cookies on baking sheet for 5 minutes, then use wide metal spatula to transfer cookies to wire rack; cool cookies to room temperature and serve.

VARIATIONS

MOLASSES SPICE COOKIES WITH DARK RUM GLAZE

For the glaze, start by adding the smaller amount of rum; if the glaze is too thick to drizzle, whisk in up to an additional ½ tablespoon rum.

Follow recipe for Molasses Spice Cookies. When completely cool, return rack with cookies to cooled parchment-lined baking sheets. Whisk 1 cup confectioners' sugar (about 4 ounces) and 2½ to 3 tablespoons dark rum in medium bowl until smooth. Drizzle glaze over cookies with soup spoon (see illustration below), dipping spoon into glaze as necessary. Transfer cookies to wire rack and allow glaze to dry, 10 to 15 minutes.

MOLASSES SPICE COOKIES WITH ORANGE ESSENCE

The orange zest in the sugar coating causes the sugar to become sticky and take on a light orange hue, giving the baked cookies a unique frosty look.

In workbowl of food processor, process ⅔ cup granulated sugar and 2 teaspoons grated orange zest until pale orange, about 10 seconds; transfer sugar to 8- or 9-inch cake pan and set aside. Follow recipe for Molasses-Spice cookies, adding 1 teaspoon grated orange zest to dough along with molasses and substituting orange sugar for granulated sugar when coating dough balls in step 4.

TECHNIQUE: Glazing Cookies

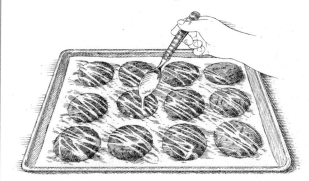

Once the cookies are completely cool, return them to the parchment-lined baking sheets. Dip a spoon into the glaze, then move the spoon over the cookies so that glaze drizzles down onto them.

TASTING LAB: Molasses

MOLASSES, A BYPRODUCT OF THE CANE SUGAR–REFINING process, is the liquid that is drawn off after the cane juice has been boiled and undergone crystallization. The resultant molasses is then subjected to subsequent boilings; with each boiling, the molasses grows increasingly dark, bitter, and potent, as more sugar is extracted from it.

There are three types of molasses. Light molasses comes from the first boiling, dark molasses from the second, and blackstrap from the third. In the past, sulfur dioxide was often added to molasses to clarify it. Although this process made molasses more attractive, it also added an unappealing flavor. Today, most molasses, including all major brands, is unsulfured.

Grocery store shelves are not packed with molasses options. Grandma's is the baseline offering, and Brer Rabbit brand can be found in well-stocked supermarkets nationwide. Blackstrap molasses is commonly available in natural foods stores. We made cookies with five different bottles of molasses. Tasters liked both brands of light and dark molasses but found blackstrap molasses too overpowering in a cookie. The moral of the story: Use either light or dark molasses based on your preference for a mellow or intense molasses flavor.

Rating Molasses

WE TESTED FIVE BRANDS OF MOLASSES IN OUR molasses spice cookies. Tasters evaluated the cookies on both color and flavor. All of the brands, except one, were highly rated and received similar scores. All brands are available in supermarkets and/or natural foods stores.

RECOMMENDED
1. Grandma's Original Molasses
$2.39 for 12 ounces
Cookies made with this light molasses had a warm bronze color. The molasses flavor was solid, decently rich, and "nicely balanced." Good choice for those who like molasses but not its bitterness.

RECOMMENDED
2. Grandma's Robust Molasses
$2.39 for 12 ounces
This dark molasses filled the cookies with both dark color (akin to a chocolate cookie) and deep flavor. They were criticized as "too strong" by one taster but touted as "spicy and rich" by another.

RECOMMENDED
3. Brer Rabbit Mild Flavor Molasses
$3.75 for 12 ounces
Cookies made with this molasses turned a lovely sepia color. The cookies garnered comments such as "complex and nuanced" and "fruity" with a "clean finish."

RECOMMENDED
4. Brer Rabbit Full Flavor Molasses
$3.75 for 12 ounces
These cookies had an even richer sepia color than those made with mild Brer Rabbit. "Straight-up" and "smooth" molasses flavor without even so much as a trace of bitterness.

NOT RECOMMENDED
5. Plantation Blackstrap Molasses
$2.99 for 15 ounces
A couple of tasters admired the potent molasses flavor, but most others remarked that the molasses was so overwhelming that the spices could hardly be tasted. User discretion advised.

LEMON meringue pie

THE RECIPES
Lemon Meringue Pie

EQUIPMENT CORNER
Rolling Pins

TASTING LAB
Store-Bought Pie Crusts

Lemon meringue pie is a three-component recipe: crust, lemon filling, and meringue. Each part of this recipe can be tricky to prepare. Without the weight of a filling to keep it in place, the pie shell can shrink or balloon in the oven as it prebakes. The lemon filling can be too loose, too gluey, too bland, or too puckery. And the meringue topping can exude liquid and break down, ruining the filling and crust underneath.

Our challenge was to take each component of this recipe and perfect it. We started with the crust and developed a method for blind-baking a pie shell that works every time. A secret ingredient helps this crust remain crisp when filled. The filling proved to be rather simple. It requires a careful balance of ingredients to get the right texture and flavor, but the technique is straightforward. The meringue was another story. We tested it nearly 30 times before we hit upon a method that ensures the underside (next to the filling) is fully cooked without causing the top of the meringue to burn.

278 HERE IN AMERICA'S TEST KITCHEN

Real pie weights (made from either metal or ceramic) are heavier than the usual stand-ins (rice or dried beans) and do a better job of preventing empty pie shells from ballooning in the oven.

LEMON MERINGUE PIE

WHAT WE WANTED: The ideal lemon meringue pie has a rich filling that balances the airy meringue without detracting from the flavor of lemon. The lemon filling should be soft but not runny, firm enough to cut but not stiff and gelatinous. The meringue itself should not break down and puddle on the bottom or "weep" on top, not even on rainy days. Finally, the crust must be crisp, not soggy.

Lemon meringue pie begins with a fully baked pie shell. Baking an unfilled pie pastry, called blind baking, can be the ultimate culinary nightmare. Without the weight of a filling, a pastry shell placed in a hot oven can shrink dramatically, fill with air pockets, and puff up like a linoleum floor after a flood. The result? A shrunken, uneven shell that can hold only part of the filling intended for it.

We started with our favorite pie dough recipe and began to investigate the effects of resting the dough (in the refrigerator or the freezer), docking it (pricking the dough before it bakes), and weighting the crust as it bakes to keep it anchored in place. All three tricks are used by professional bakers to prevent common problems encountered when blind-baking a crust.

We found that refrigeration does the best job of preventing shrinkage. Pastry shrinkage is caused by gluten. Simply put, when you mix flour with water, the proteins in the flour react to form elastic strands of gluten. The strands of gluten in the dough get stretched during the rolling process, and if they are not allowed to relax after rolling, the pastry will snap back like a rubber band when baked, resulting in a shrunken, misshapen shell. Resting allows the tension in the taut strands of dough to ease so that they remain stretched and do not shrink back when heated.

This process does not occur, however, if the dough is immediately placed in the freezer to rest after rolling. When frozen, the water in the crust solidifies, freezing the gluten

in place so it is not free to relax. When the dough is baked, the tense, stretched strands of gluten snap back, causing the crust to shrink.

We might have concluded that pie dough should be refrigerated and not frozen if we hadn't noticed that the frozen crusts, although shrunken, were much flakier than the refrigerated crusts. Pastry is made up of layers of dough (protein and starch from the flour combined with water) and fat. Dough and fat have different heat capacities. When you place the pastry in the oven after freezing it (rather than just refrigerating it), the dough heats up and starts to set relatively quickly in comparison with the time it takes for the butter to melt and then vaporize, as butter has a much higher proportion of water than the dough. As a result, by the time the water in the butter starts to turn to steam, the dough is well into its setting phase. The air spaces occupied by the frozen butter, now that it has largely turned to steam, hold their shape because the dough is far along in the baking process. And this makes for a very flaky pie crust.

Dough that has been refrigerated, on the other hand, is not as well set by the time the butter vaporizes. The air pockets disappear as the soft dough sinks into the spaces left by the butter. We came to a simple conclusion: First refrigerate the pie shell to relax the gluten, thus solving the problem of shrinkage during baking, then pop the dough in the freezer to improve flakiness.

This bit of science led us to yet another discovery. It is common knowledge that lard or vegetable shortening such as Crisco produces very flaky doughs. In fact, we use a combination of butter and shortening in our recipe because of the improvement in texture over an all-butter crust (the butter is what gives the crust its flavor). The explanation for this phenomenon is simple. Lard and Crisco don't melt as quickly as butter when heated. Therefore, they retain their shape as the dough sets up, keeping the layers of pastry separate.

While this combination chilling method prevents

are also better heat conductors and promote more thorough browning of the pastry.

We got the most consistent results and even browning by baking the crust in the middle rack at a constant 375 degrees. At higher temperatures the pastry was prone to overbrowning and burned in spots, while lower temperatures caused the edges to brown well before the bottom did. More important than temperature and placement, though, was cooking time.

There are two stages in prebaking. In the first stage, the dough is baked with a lining and weights. This stage usually takes about 25 minutes; the objective is to cook the dough until it sets, at which point it can hold its shape without assistance. When the dough loses its wet look, turns off-white from its original pale yellow, and the edges just start to take on a very light brown color, the dough is set. If you have any doubts, you can carefully (the dough is hot) touch the side of the shell to make sure the crust is firm. If you remove the pie weights too soon, the sides of the dough will slip down, ruining the pie shell. For the second stage, the foil and weights are removed, and the baking continues until the crust is deep golden brown.

We discovered one final trick when baking the pie shell. The lemon filling tends to make even a fully baked, golden brown crust a bit soggy. We discovered that coating the dough with graham cracker crumbs while rolling it out helps counter any ill effects from the filling and the crust remains crisp longer.

With the pie shell baked, we focused next on the filling. The standard ingredients in lemon meringue pie were established some time ago: sugar, water (or sometimes milk), cornstarch (sometimes mixed with flour), egg yolks, lemon juice (and usually zest), and a little butter. To our tastes, the straightforward lemon flavor of the water-based filling is pleasant, but it is also one-dimensional, lacking depth. Milk, however, subdues the lemon flavor. The solution is to rely

shrinkage, ballooning can occur when air pockets form beneath the crust. Typically, bakers dock (or prick) the dough with the tines of a fork before it goes into the oven. However, we found that docking was not necessary as long as the dough is weighted. Because weighting is a must—it not only prevents ballooning but keeps the shell, especially the sides, in place as it bakes—we do not bother to dock pastry dough. Some professional bakers swear by "official" pie weights, while others make do with rice or dried beans. We found that metal or ceramic pie weights do a better job than rice or beans. They are heavier and therefore more effective at preventing the pastry from puffing. Pie weights primarily on water and a lot of egg yolks (we use six rather than the more conventional three), eliminating the milk altogether. This has another benefit: The extra yolks allow you to cut back on cornstarch and still achieve a firm filling.

The meringue is much more tricky. On any given day it can shrink, bead, puddle, deflate, burn, sweat, break down, or turn rubbery. Most cookbooks don't even attempt to deal with the problems of meringue. They follow the standard recipe—granulated sugar and cream of tartar beaten slowly into the egg whites—assuming, apparently, that there is no way around the flaws. After making 30-something lemon meringue pies, we're not sure we blame anyone for skirting the issue. For as easy as it was to figure out the perfect lemon filling, the meringue remains, finally, only a manageable mystery.

The puddling underneath the meringue is from undercooking. Undercooked whites break down and return to their liquid state. The beading on top of the pie is from overcooking. This near-the-surface overcooking of the meringue causes the proteins in the egg white to coagulate, squeezing out moisture, which then surfaces as tears or beads. This double dilemma might seem insurmountable, but we hit upon a solution.

If the filling is piping hot when the meringue is applied, the underside of the meringue will not undercook; if the oven temperature is relatively low, the top of the meringue won't overcook. Baking the pie in a relatively cool oven also produces the best-looking, most evenly browned meringue. To stabilize the meringue further, we like to beat in a tiny bit of cornstarch; if you do this, the meringue will not weep, even on hot, humid days.

WHAT WE LEARNED: Apply graham cracker crumbs to keep the crust crisp. Refrigerate and freeze the pie dough before baking for a crust that won't shrink and is extra flaky. Use water rather than milk in the filling to keep the focus on the lemon juice and zest. Apply the meringue to piping-hot filling and bake the pie in a cool oven for perfectly cooked meringue that won't puddle or weep.

282 HERE IN AMERICA'S TEST KITCHEN

LEMON MERINGUE PIE serves 8

Make the pie shell, let it cool, and then begin work on the filling. As soon as the filling is made, cover it with plastic wrap to keep it hot and then start working on the meringue topping. You want to add hot filling to the pie shell, apply the meringue topping, and then quickly get the pie into the oven.

graham cracker–coated pie shell

- 1¼ cups (6¼ ounces) unbleached all-purpose flour
- ½ teaspoon salt
- 1 tablespoon sugar
- 3 tablespoons all-vegetable shortening, chilled
- 4 tablespoons unsalted butter, chilled, cut into ¼-inch pieces
- 4–5 tablespoons ice water
- ½ cup graham cracker crumbs

lemon filling

- 1 cup (7 ounces) sugar
- ⅛ teaspoon salt
- 1½ cups water
- ½ cup juice from 2 or 3 lemons (see illustrations on page 283)
- 6 large egg yolks
- ¼ cup cornstarch
- 1 tablespoon grated zest from 1 lemon
- 2 tablespoons unsalted butter

meringue topping

- 1 tablespoon cornstarch
- ⅓ cup water
- ¼ teaspoon cream of tartar
- ½ cup (3½ ounces) sugar
- 4 large egg whites
- ½ teaspoon vanilla extract

1. FOR THE PIE SHELL: Pulse flour, salt, and sugar in food processor fitted with steel blade until combined. Add shortening and process until mixture has texture of coarse sand,

about 10 seconds. Scatter butter pieces over flour mixture; cut butter into flour until mixture is pale yellow and resembles coarse crumbs, with butter bits no larger than small peas, about ten 1-second pulses. Turn mixture into medium bowl.

2. Sprinkle 4 tablespoons ice water over mixture. With blade of rubber spatula, use folding motion to mix. Press down on dough with broad side of spatula until dough sticks together, adding up to 1 tablespoon more ice water if it will not come together. Flatten dough into 4-inch disk. Wrap in plastic and refrigerate at least 1 hour, or up to 2 days, before rolling.

3. If dough has been refrigerated longer than 1 hour, let stand at room temperature until malleable. Generously sprinkle work area with 2 tablespoons graham cracker crumbs. Place dough on work surface and scatter more crumbs over dough. Roll dough to 12-inch disk, sprinkling remaining crumbs underneath and on top of dough as it is rolled. Dough should be heavily coated with crumbs. Transfer dough to pie plate by rolling dough around rolling pin and unrolling it over 9-inch pie plate or by folding dough in quarters, then placing dough point in center of pie plate and unfolding. Working around circumference of pie plate, ease dough into pan corners by gently lifting dough edges with one hand while pressing around pan bottom with other hand. Trim dough edges to extend about ½ inch beyond rim of pan. Fold overhang under itself; flute dough or press tines of fork against dough to it flatten it against rim of pie plate. Refrigerate dough-lined pie plate until firm, about 40 minutes, then freeze until very cold, about 20 minutes.

4. Adjust oven rack to lower-middle position and heat oven to 375 degrees. Remove dough-lined pie plate from freezer and press doubled 12-inch piece of heavy-duty foil inside pie shell and fold edges of foil to shield fluted edge; distribute 2 cups ceramic or metal pie weights over foil. Bake, leaving foil and weights in place until dough looks dry and is light in color, 25 to 30 minutes. Carefully remove foil and weights by gathering corners of foil and pulling up and out.

TECHNIQUE: Juicing Lemons

We've found that the following method yields the most juice from lemons (and limes, too). In kitchen tests, room-temperature lemons gave up their juice more easily than chilled lemons. If your lemons are in the refrigerator, microwave them for five to 10 seconds before starting to juice them.

1. Roll the lemon hard on the counter, pressing down firmly with your hand to break membranes inside the fruit.

2. Cut the lemon in half. Use a wooden reamer to extract the juice into a bowl. To catch the seeds, place a mesh strainer over the bowl.

Continue baking until deep golden brown, about 12 minutes more. Transfer pie shell to wire rack.

5. FOR THE FILLING: Bring ¾ cup sugar, salt, water, and lemon juice to simmer over medium-high heat in medium, nonreactive saucepan, stirring occasionally with wooden spoon to ensure sugar dissolves. Meanwhile, whisk yolks, remaining ¼ cup sugar, cornstarch, and lemon zest in medium bowl until thick and combined. Gradually whisk simmering liquid into egg mixture to temper, then return mixture to saucepan and bring to boil over medium heat, stirring constantly; boil until thickened, 1 to 2 minutes. Off heat, whisk in butter. Place plastic wrap directly on surface of filling to keep hot and prevent skin from forming.

6. FOR THE MERINGUE: Mix cornstarch with water in small saucepan; bring to simmer, whisking occasionally at beginning and more frequently as mixture thickens. When mixture starts to simmer and turn translucent, remove from heat. Let cool while beating egg whites.

TECHNIQUE:
Applying Meringue Topping

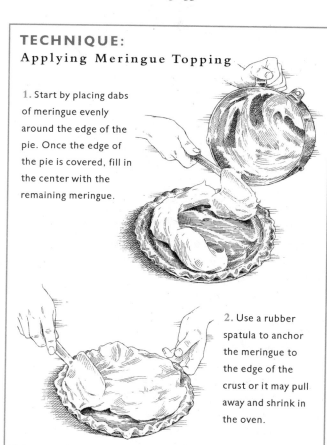

1. Start by placing dabs of meringue evenly around the edge of the pie. Once the edge of the pie is covered, fill in the center with the remaining meringue.

2. Use a rubber spatula to anchor the meringue to the edge of the crust or it may pull away and shrink in the oven.

7. Heat oven to 325 degrees. Mix cream of tartar and sugar together in small bowl. Beat egg whites and vanilla in bowl of standing mixer until frothy. Beat in sugar mixture, 1 tablespoon at a time; until sugar is incorporated and mixture forms soft peaks. Add cornstarch mixture, 1 tablespoon at a time; continue to beat meringue to stiff peaks. Remove plastic from filling and return to very low heat during last minute or so of beating meringue (to ensure filling is hot).

8. Pour filling into pie shell. Using rubber spatula, immediately distribute meringue evenly around edge and then center of pie to keep it from sinking into filling (see illustration 1, at left). Make sure meringue attaches to pie crust to prevent shrinking (see illustration 2, at left). Use spoon to create peaks all over meringue. Bake pie until meringue is golden brown, about 20 minutes. Transfer to wire rack and cool to room temperature. Serve.

EQUIPMENT CORNER: Rolling Pins

A GOOD ROLLING PIN CAN QUALIFY AS A FAMILY heirloom. But if your grandmother's tried-and-true pin has not been passed down to your kitchen and you want to buy one, you have quite an array of choices. Should you buy a pin with a nonstick coating, one that is made of marble, or one with ergonomic handles? Could any one pin really make a difference in your baking? We tested eight models readily found in kitchen and hardware stores and decided on a definite favorite.

We purchased two wooden pins without handles—one with tapered ends, and one that was straight. Three other wooden pins had standard dowel-type handles with ball bearings and represented three different sizes: the largest weighed in at 3½ pounds and was 15 inches long, another was a quite small 1½ pounds and 10½ inches long, and the last was in between these two, at 2½ pounds and 11 ½ inches long. We purchased three novelty pins—one marble, one nonstick-coated aluminum, and one wooden model with

ergonomic comfort grips. The grips on this last model were made of molded plastic and had the feel of a steering wheel, with thumbs placed on top and wrists straight. Prices ranged from $6.99 to $35.99.

We decided to test the pins on three kinds of dough: a standard pie dough, a delicate sugar cookie dough, and a resilient yeasted coffee cake dough. We were particularly interested in the versatility of these pins—whether they could perform equally well in all tasks. No one wants more than one pin in the kitchen. For all three doughs, we were looking for a fast, easy roll—one that allowed us to feel the dough and did not require application of too much pressure.

Almost immediately a favorite and a least favorite became evident. The tapered wood pin without handles took first place. Testers could easily turn and pivot the tapered pin and apply pressure as needed across the dough. In addition, this pin measured 20 inches long, making it suitable for any task. Many of the other wooden pins were too short (some just 10 or 11 inches in length) and could not be used to roll out large pieces of dough.

The marble pin was a bit heavy over delicate sugar cookie dough, but this pin could be refrigerated before handling buttery doughs, which was a plus. It landed in second place. The ergonomic pin landed near the bottom of the ratings, as did the nonstick model, which was much too light and most definitely not stickfree.

TASTING LAB: Store-Bought Pie Crusts

EVERYONE KNOWS THAT HOMEMADE PIE CRUST OFFERS the best combination of buttery flavor and flaky texture. The ingredient list couldn't be shorter—just flour, fat, sugar, salt, and ice water—and making the dough takes just seconds in a food processor. However, few tasks inspire as much fear, even among seasoned cooks, as does rolling out pie pastry. It's no surprise then that many cooks turn to store-bought frozen or refrigerated pie crust. We wondered if any of these products could compete with the real thing made at home.

Rating Rolling Pins

WE SELECTED EIGHT PINS AND USED THEM TO ROLL OUT TENDER SUGAR COOKIE DOUGH, STANDARD PIE DOUGH, AND stiff yeasted coffee cake dough. The rolling pins are listed in order of preference. See www.cooksillustrated.com for up-to-date prices and mail-order sources for top-rated products.

RECOMMENDED

1. Thorpe Solid French Pie Rolling Pin

$6.99

This 20-inch tapered wooden pin was a joy to work with. Testers could easily turn and pivot this pin and apply pressure as they liked all across the dough. This pin is also great for whacking cold, rested doughs to soften them up for rolling.

RECOMMENDED WITH RESERVATIONS

2. Himark Classic White Marble Rolling Pin

$8.99

This marble pin was a little too short (just 10 inches long) and ran a bit heavy over delicate dough (it weighed in at a whopping 4 1/2 pounds), but it was a smooth performer in all other areas. A bonus is that it stays cold after refrigeration for working with particularly buttery doughs.

RECOMMENDED WITH RESERVATIONS

3. Thorpe Hardwood Rolling Pin

$31.99

This standard wood rolling pin with handles had good speed, but we needed to use a bit more pressure than expected, as it is so much larger (3 inches in diameter) and heavier than the other pins tested. It always felt a bit out of control.

RECOMMENDED WITH RESERVATIONS

4. Williams-Sonoma Straight Baker's Pin

$14.00

Some testers (with larger hands) liked this solid, straight wooden pin, but most felt that it was too thick. This pin was awkward to use, and it was hard to get a sense of how the dough was responding.

NOT RECOMMENDED

5. Williams-Sonoma Maple Rolling Pin

$32.99

This pin was shorter than most other wooden models tested and therefore less useful for rolling out medium or large pieces of dough. Testers found it necessary to exert a fair amount of pressure on the handles of this lightweight pin.

NOT RECOMMENDED

6. Foley Rolling Pin

$11.99

This small pin (just 10 1/2 inches long) was not a good performer. It was both too light and too short, which necessitated putting a lot of pressure on the handles. It was good for neither the doughs nor testers' wrists.

NOT RECOMMENDED

7. Comprep Comfort Pin

$35.99

The plastic ergonomic handles on this wooden pin not only looked silly, but they were difficult to work with and offered no benefit whatsoever. If this pin was used by someone with long fingernails, the grip would be both painful and unworkable.

NOT RECOMMENDED

8. Fox Run Non-Stick Rolling Pin

$9.99

All three doughs stuck to this aluminum pin with a nonstick coating. The pin was ineffective at all tasks. Light and flimsy, it could also be dented or easily nicked.

We also wondered (especially given the fact that some cooks will never make their own pie crust) if some of these products are better (or less terrible) than others.

To find out, we purchased five pie crusts, baked them according to package directions, and compared them with our homemade pie shell, which we prebaked according to our recipe. (We omitted the dusting of graham cracker crumbs so as not to confuse matters.)

As expected, tasters had no trouble picking out the homemade pie crust. The texture was flaky and the flavor was buttery and natural. None of the store-bought crusts came close in terms of texture, and only one was deemed to have decent flavor.

The Whole Foods crust was too crumbly, tender, and moist, but tasters commented on the "buttery flavor" of this crust. Just as important, tasters did not complain about odd, chemical flavors, which plagued the other crusts. Not surprisingly, the Whole Foods crust is the only one to have an ingredient list close to that for homemade pie dough—just flour, butter, and water.

The four other store-bought pie crusts were made with either partially hydrogenated vegetable shortening or partially hydrogenated lard. As might be expected, tasters found these crusts to be lacking in flavor. Perhaps because these crusts are made without butter, manufacturers add other ingredients to compensate, including corn syrup and food colorings. Our tasters disliked these crusts, describing them with terms such as "chemical aftertaste," "plastic," "stale," "rancid," and "fake."

None of the store-bought crusts, including our "winner," wowed tasters with their texture. None came close to our flaky ideal. Tasters used terms like "greasy," "brittle," "tough," and "mushy" when describing the texture of the store-bought crusts.

For the best flavor and texture, we recommend making your own pie dough. If that's not an option, look for an all-butter crust at an upscale supermarket or gourmet store. Based on our experience, this crust may not have the best texture, but it probably will taste pretty good.

Rating Store-Bought Pie Crusts

WE PURCHASED FIVE STORE-BOUGHT PIE CRUSTS (four frozen, one refrigerated) and baked them according to the package directions. Tasters were asked to evaluate each crust in terms of both flavor and texture. The crusts are listed in order of preference and are available in supermarkets.

RECOMMENDED IN A PINCH

1. Whole Foods Pie Shells

$3.99 for two 9-inch crusts

Tasters praised the "buttery flavor" in this supermarket brand. Made with just flour, butter, and water, this crust is free of chemical flavors that plagued the rest of the field.

NOT RECOMMENDED

2. Oronoque Orchards Regular Pie Crusts

$2.59 for three 9-inch crusts

This crust made with vegetable shortening was faulted for its "bland," "dull," "starchy" flavor and chemical aftertaste.

NOT RECOMMENDED

3. Pillsbury Pie Crusts

$2.50 for two 9-inch crusts

Unlike the other crusts tested, this one is sold in the refrigerator case. The crust is folded in quarters—you unfold the crust and fit it into your own pie plate. Tasters thought this well-known crust was "sweet," "greasy," and "stale."

NOT RECOMMENDED

4. Pillsbury Pet-Ritz Deep-Dish Pie Crusts

$1.25 for two 9-inch crusts

A few tasters faulted this crust for being "bland;" most were more harsh, complaining about "bad shortening taste."

NOT RECOMMENDED

5. Mrs. Smith's 9" Deep Dish Pie Crusts

$2.50 for three 9-inch crusts

Tasters detected unusual flavors here, which they described as "fake sour taste," "strange aftertaste," and "uncooked sweet flavor."

Mashed Sweet Potatoes **page 207**

Pan-Roasted Chicken **page 107**

American Potato Salad with Hard-Boiled Eggs and Sweet Pickles **page 187**

Basic Cranberry Sauce **page 211**

Grill-Roasted Turkey **page 204**

Red Plums and Figs with Brandy-Cinnamon Reduction **page 243**

Banana Bread **page 251**

Sour Cream Coffee Cake with Brown Sugar–Pecan Streusel **page 234**

Quick Cinnamon Buns with Buttermilk Icing **page 248**

Flourless Chocolate Cake **page 326**

298

Sour Cherry Cobbler **page 311**

Thick and Chewy Double-Chocolate Cookies **page 270**

Lemon Meringue Pie **page 282**

New York–Style Cheesecake with Strawberry Topping **page 332**

Individual Hot Fudge Pudding Cakes **page 321**

We went through crates of strawberries before hitting on the best way to prepare them for shortcake.

SHORTCAKE & cobbler

CHAPTER 24

What could be more all-American than strawberry shortcake? But when the "cake" consists of store-bought spongy rounds with no flavor and the berries are rock-hard specimens trucked in from thousands of miles away, strawberry shortcake can go very wrong. Luckily, it's easy to fix these problems. Start with a homemade shortcake and use only ripe, juicy berries. We'll show you how.

Cherry cobbler can be trickier. At least with strawberries, you know that any fruit that tastes good will make a decent dessert. But with cherries, the home cook has no such luck. Sweet Bing cherries become insipid when baked. Sour cherries are a must. But where do you get sour cherries? The season seems to last only about three weeks in many parts of the country. Is there an acceptable jarred or canned alternative to fresh fruit?

To answer these questions, we made cherry cobblers in the dead of winter. We had crates of frozen berries shipped to the test kitchen. We talked to experts who had traveled behind the Iron Curtain in the 1980s searching for new cherry cultivars. We're happy to report that our efforts paid off.

STRAWBERRY SHORTCAKE

WHAT WE WANTED: A rich, cakey biscuit offset by juicy, sweet berries and mounds of whipped cream.

Shortcakes may seem similar to crisps and cobblers, but there is one important difference—the fruit is not cooked. For a true shortcake, sweetened fruit, usually strawberries, is spread between a split biscuit. A dollop or two of whipped cream is also added. The contrast of the cool fruit, warm and cakey biscuit halves, and chilled whipped cream places this dessert in a category by itself.

Because the fruit is not cooked, frozen fruit is not an option. The fruit must be ripe as well. Half-ripe berries will bake up fine in a pandowdy but will make a second-rate shortcake. Also, because the fruit is not baked, only softer fruits are appropriate. A pear or apple shortcake does not make sense. Strawberries are soft enough and have enough flavor to be used uncooked.

We don't like quartered or sliced strawberries in shortcake—they often slide off the split biscuit—but we don't like the look of a crushed fruit shortcake either. So we found a happy compromise by slicing most of the strawberries and then crushing the remaining portion of the berry mixture to unify the sliced fruit. The thick puree anchors the remaining whole or sliced fruit so that it won't slip off the split biscuit.

The rest of our testing for this recipe revolved mostly around the biscuit. Strawberry shortcake requires something different from the biscuit topping used in our cherry cobbler recipe. There, the fruit is so juicy and sweet that a light, tender biscuit works best. Shortcake, on the other hand, must be substantial enough to withstand splitting and layering with juicy fruit and whipped cream. It should be more dense and cakey. We assumed that a richer biscuit—that is, one made with eggs—would work best.

To make sure, we tried four very different recipes for sweetened biscuits—a baking powder version, with fat cut into flour, baking powder, salt, and sugar and then moistened with milk; a buttermilk biscuit, with buttermilk in place of milk and baking soda substituted for part of the baking powder; a cream biscuit, with heavy cream standing in for the milk and some of the fat; and an egg-enriched cream biscuit, with an egg and half-and-half replacing the milk. After sampling each, we felt that the egg-enriched biscuits had the advantage. The baking powder and buttermilk biscuits weren't rich enough. The cream biscuits were good looking but gummy inside. The egg and half-and-half biscuits were finer-textured and more cakelike.

With our general direction settled, we began to test individual ingredients. Because biscuits should be tender, we assumed that low-protein cake flour would deliver the best results. Defying our predictions, the cake flour biscuit came in last, with a meltingly tender but powdery and dry texture that was too much like shortbread. There was not enough gluten in this flour to support all the fat. Shortcake made with all-purpose flour were tender, moist, and cakey. They were our clear favorites, besting a combination of cake and all-purpose flours as well as the plain cake flour.

We then experimented with liquids, figuring that the egg might be crucial but maybe not the half-and-half, which had won in our initial test. Buttermilk made the biscuits too savory, while heavy cream made them squat and dense. Milk was fine, but the richer flavor of half-and-half made it our first choice.

The food processor is foolproof and is our preferred method for mixing biscuits. For cooks without a food processor, we suggest freezing the butter and then using a box grater to shave the butter into bits before cutting it into the flour.

When testing dough shaping, we made an interesting discovery. Although hand-formed biscuits look attractive, we found they were fairly easy to overwork, since warm hands can cause the dough's surface butter to melt. A biscuit cutter

STRABERRY SHORTCAKE serves 6

STRAWBERRY SHORTCAKE serves 6

Start the recipe by preparing the fruit, then set the fruit aside while preparing the biscuits to allow the juices to become syrupy. We find that pasteurized cream has a better flavor than ultrapasteurized cream. Many organic brands are pasteurized.

fruit

8	cups hulled strawberries
6	tablespoons (2⅔ ounces) sugar

shortcake

2 cups (10 ounces) unbleached all-purpose flour, plus more for work surface and biscuit cutter
5 tablespoons (about 2¼ ounces) sugar
1 tablespoon baking powder
½ teaspoon salt
8 tablespoons unsalted butter, chilled, cut into ½-inch cubes
1 large egg, lightly beaten
½ cup plus 1 tablespoon half-and-half or milk
1 large egg white, lightly beaten

whipped cream

1 cup chilled heavy cream, preferably pasteurized or pasteurized organic
1 tablespoon granulated sugar
1 teaspoon vanilla extract

requires less handling, and dough rounds cut this way develop a natural crack around the circumference during baking, making them easy to split by hand. We also realized we didn't need a rolling pin. Patting the dough to a thickness of ¾ inch on a floured work surface was fast and easy.

After cutting six perfect rounds of dough, we found that the scraps could be pulled together, kneaded, and cut to get one or two more rounds. These shortcakes, however, will be a little tougher and less attractive than those from the first cutting.

WHAT WE LEARNED: Mash some of the berries and slice the rest for a chunky puree that won't slide off the biscuits. Add an egg and half-and-half to make a biscuit rich enough and cakey enough for dessert.

1. FOR THE FRUIT: Place 3 cups hulled berries in large bowl and crush with potato masher. Slice remaining 5 cups berries and stir into crushed berries along with sugar. Set fruit aside to macerate for at least 30 minutes and up to 2 hours.

2. FOR THE SHORTCAKE: Adjust oven rack to lower-middle position and heat oven to 425 degrees. In workbowl of food processor fitted with metal blade, pulse flour, 3 tablespoons sugar, baking powder, and salt to combine. Scatter butter pieces over and process until mixture resembles coarse meal, about fifteen 1-second pulses. Transfer to medium bowl.

3. Mix beaten egg with half-and-half in measuring cup. Pour egg mixture into bowl with flour mixture. Combine with rubber spatula until large clumps form. Turn mixture onto floured work surface and lightly knead until it comes together.

4. Use your fingertips to pat dough into 9 by 6-inch rectangle about ¾ inch thick, being careful not to overwork dough. Flour 2¾-inch biscuit cutter and cut out 6 dough rounds. Place rounds 1 inch apart on small baking sheet, brush tops with egg white, and sprinkle with remaining 2 tablespoons sugar. (Biscuits can be covered and refrigerated for up to 2 hours before baking.)

5. Bake until shortcakes are golden brown, 12 to 14 minutes. Place baking sheet on wire rack and cool cakes until warm, about 10 minutes.

6. FOR THE WHIPPED CREAM: As soon as shortcakes go into oven, place nonreactive, deep bowl and beaters of electric mixer in freezer for 20 minutes. (If freezer is too crowded to accommodate bowl, place beaters in bowl, fill with ice water, and chill on counter. When bowl and beaters are well chilled, dump out ice water and dry thoroughly.)

7. While biscuits are cooling, remove bowl from freezer and add cream, sugar, and vanilla. Beat on low speed until small bubbles form, about 30 seconds. Increase speed to medium and continue beating until beaters leave a trail, about 30 seconds. Increase speed to high and continue beating until cream is smooth, thick, and nearly doubled in volume, about 20 seconds for soft peaks.

8. TO ASSEMBLE: When shortcakes have cooled slightly, split them in half crosswise (see illustration below). Place

each cake bottom on individual serving plate. Spoon portion of fruit and then dollop of whipped cream over each cake bottom. Cap with cake top and serve immediately.

TECHNIQUE: Hulling Strawberries

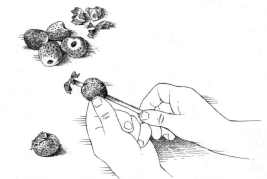

If you don't own a huller, you can improvise with a melon baller or ¼ teaspoon measure. We also use a plastic drinking straw for this job. Just push the straw through the bottom of the berry and up to the leafy stem. The straw will remove the core as well as the leafy top in one motion.

TECHNIQUE: Splitting Shortcake

When the shortcakes have cooled, look for a natural crack around the circumference. Gently insert your fingers into the crack and split the shortcake in half.

CHERRY COBBLER

WHAT WE WANTED: Real cherry flavor paired with a tender, feather-light, deeply browned biscuit topping.

A fleet of tender biscuits on a sea of sweet fruit, good cobblers hold their own against fancy fruit desserts. But unlike fancy fruit desserts, cobblers come together in a couple of quick steps and can be dished up hot, ready to hit the dance floor with a scoop of vanilla ice cream. Sour cherries have sufficient acidity to cook up well and become truly expressive with a touch of sugar and some heat. (Sweet eating cherries, like Bings, lose their flavor when cooked.) Because fresh sour cherries are so hard to find (their season lasts just a few weeks in summer), we tested a half-dozen alternatives (see the Tasting Lab on page 312 for details). Jarred sour cherries (specifically the Morello variety) beat out canned and frozen sour cherries as well as fresh cherries in various forms.

A cobbler should be juicy, but not swimming in juice, and it should taste like the fruit whose name it bears. Jarred cherries come awash in juices, which we would use to produce the sauce. Because jarred cherries have already been processed, they are already cooked: the less heat they're exposed to thereafter, the better. Straining off the juice, we dumped the drained contents of four 24-ounce jars of Morellos into a 13 by 9-inch baking dish, then thickened and sweetened 3 cups of the juice. The resulting flavor was a bit flat. We replaced 1 cup of the cherry juice with red wine and added a cinnamon stick, a pinch of salt, and a whiff of almond extract. Much better. Red wine and sour cherries have a natural affinity; the cinnamon stick added a fragrant woody depth; and, as with all fruits, salt performed its usual minor miracle. The almond extract brought the entire flavor experience up a couple of notches. For thickener we resolved to go with cornstarch, which could be mixed in with the sugar. The cherry juices were then brought to a simmer and poured over the waiting cherries and baked. Lightly thickened fruit is best; a cobbler shouldn't be thick enough to spread on toast.

We also had some requirements for the cobbles. We wanted them feather-light but deeply browned and crisp. This said a number of things to us. The first was: No eggs. Eggs would make our biscuits too heavy and substantial. (After working for years with the test kitchen's scone recipe, a light and tender English biscuit that uses no eggs, we felt supported in that expectation.) The second thing it said was buttermilk. Buttermilk biscuits are famously light and tender. The third precept came by way of a number of Southern recipes, which said a wet dough made a nice light biscuit. We baked several biscuit variations to confirm these notions, settling on all-purpose flour, a moderate amount of butter, small amounts of baking powder and soda, a touch of sugar (plus more on top for crunch), a wave of buttermilk, and a nice hot oven. Dispensing with rolling altogether, we simply dropped the biscuits onto the fruit with an ice cream scoop. The biscuits had a buttery lightness, a mild tang, and a crunchy, sugary top.

Not quite satisfied with their pale bellies touching the fruit, we undertook to bake the biscuits for 15 minutes on a baking sheet while the filling was coming together on the stove. We then wedded them to the fruit for only 10 minutes in the oven. By then the fruit (already hot from the cooked sauce) was bubbling around the biscuits, which were deeply browned on top and baked through underneath. Heaven in about a half-hour.

Jarred Morellos made a fine cobbler. But we were anxious to try fresh, and then summer finally came. Fresh sour cherries, we learned, are classified in two groups, amarelles and griottes. The former have lighter flesh—tan on the inside—and clear juices; the latter are dark—even black—with deep red juice. The best known examples of each group are Montmorency (an amarelle) and Morello (a griotte). Most tart cherries grown in the United States are Montmorency.

Those from Eastern Europe are Morello. However, as we researched this subject, we made an exciting discovery: Morello cherries had made their way to the United States.

In 1984, well before unrestricted travel and commerce in Eastern Bloc countries became commonplace, Dr. Amy Iezzoni, professor of horticulture at Michigan State University, traveled extensively throughout Hungary to locate a vigorous sour cherry cultivar she could bring home to Michigan. Having spent years hybridizing local sour cherry seedlings, Hungarian breeders were prepared to release new cultivars with improved characteristics.

Sure enough, Iezzoni returned home with a dazzling Morello cultivar, which she named Balaton (after a lake in its native environs). She enlisted it in her breeding program, currently the only sour cherry breeding program in the United States. Under her care, the Balaton has thrived in its new climate. Cherry trees prefer long winters, Iezzoni told us, as well as cooler spring and summer temperatures, which favor normal fruit and flower development and lower the incidence of disease. The moderating winds of Lake Michigan reduce the probability that cherry flowers will be killed by an early freeze, much as Europe's continental climate buffers harsh weather.

Unlike the fragile and perishable Montmorency (a 400-year-old cultivar that has not been subject to cross-breeding to make it more vigorous), Balaton cherries are robust enough once harvested to endure shipping well. Not only are they larger and plumper than Montmorency cherries, but their dark juices are beautiful and mysterious.

With this knowledge and some fresh cherries, we got to work in the test kitchen. To test available varieties, we used both Morellos and the more delicate Montmorencies.

And how were the cobblers with fresh cherries? Both varieties of fresh cherries graced the recipe, yielding cobblers with plump, gorgeous, deeply flavorful fruit. The Montmorency cherries bore a candy apple red and a flavor resonant with almond accents; the fresh Morellos were transcendent, with a smooth richness and complex flavor notes. If you can get your hands on fresh sour cherries

during their brief season in July, buy them—quickly—and start baking. And take heart. When the brief sour cherry season is over, jarred Morello cherries will create a cobbler that is almost as wonderful.

WHAT WE LEARNED: Jarred Morello cherries are the best year-round choice for a cobbler. Spike the cherry juices with red wine and cinnamon and thicken them with cornstarch. For really crisp biscuits, bake them separately for 15 minutes, then slide the biscuits over the warm cherry filling and bake just 10 minutes longer.

SOUR CHERRY COBBLER serves 12

Use the smaller amount of sugar in the filling if you prefer your fruit desserts on the tart side and the larger amount if you like them sweet. Serve with vanilla ice cream or lightly sweetened whipped cream.

biscuit topping

2	cups (10 ounces) unbleached all-purpose flour
6	tablespoons (2½ ounces) sugar plus additional 2 tablespoons for sprinkling
½	teaspoon baking powder
½	teaspoon baking soda
½	teaspoon salt
6	tablespoons cold unsalted butter, cut into ½-inch cubes
1	cup buttermilk

cherry filling

4	(24-ounce) jars Morello cherries, drained (about 8 cups drained cherries), 2 cups juice reserved
¾–1	cup (5¼ to 7 ounces) sugar
3	tablespoons plus 1 teaspoon cornstarch
	Pinch salt
1	cup dry red wine
1	(3-inch) stick cinnamon
¼	teaspoon almond extract

1. Adjust oven rack to middle position and heat oven to 425 degrees. Line baking sheet with parchment paper.

2. FOR THE BISCUIT TOPPING: In workbowl of food processor fitted with steel blade, pulse flour, 6 tablespoons sugar, baking powder, baking soda, and salt to combine. Scatter butter pieces over and process until mixture resembles coarse meal, about fifteen 1-second pulses. Transfer to medium bowl; add buttermilk and toss with rubber spatula to combine. Using a 1½- to 1¾-inch spring-loaded ice cream scoop, scoop 12 biscuits onto baking sheet, spacing them 1½ to 2 inches apart. Sprinkle biscuits evenly with 2 tablespoons sugar and bake until lightly browned on tops and bottoms, about 15 minutes. (Do not turn off oven.)

3. FOR THE CHERRY FILLING: Meanwhile, spread drained cherries in even layer in 13 by 9-inch glass baking dish. Stir sugar, cornstarch, and salt together in medium nonreactive saucepan. Whisk in reserved cherry juice and wine, and add cinnamon stick; set saucepan over medium-high heat, and cook, whisking frequently, until mixture simmers and thickens, about 5 minutes. Discard cinnamon stick, stir in almond extract, and pour hot liquid over cherries in baking dish.

4. TO ASSEMBLE: Arrange hot biscuits in 3 rows of 4 over warm filling. Bake cobbler until filling is bubbling and biscuits are deep golden brown, about 10 minutes. Cool on wire rack 10 minutes; serve.

VARIATION

FRESH SOUR CHERRY COBBLER

Morello or Montmorency cherries can be used in this cobbler made with fresh sour cherries. Do not use sweet Bing cherries. If the cherries do not release enough juice after macerating for 30 minutes, cranberry juice makes up the difference.

cherry filling

1¼	cups (8¾ ounces) sugar
3	tablespoons plus 1 teaspoon cornstarch
	Pinch salt
4	pounds fresh sour cherries, pitted (about 8 cups), juices reserved
1	cup dry red wine
	Cranberry juice (if needed)
1	(3-inch) cinnamon stick
¼	teaspoon almond extract
1	recipe Biscuit Topping (see preceding recipe)

1. Stir together sugar, cornstarch, and salt in large bowl; add cherries and toss well to combine. Pour wine over cherries;

let stand 30 minutes. Drain cherries in colander set over medium bowl. Combine drained and reserved juices (from pitting cherries); you should have 3 cups. If not, add enough cranberry juice to equal 3 cups.

2. While cherries macerate, prepare and bake biscuit topping.

3. Spread drained cherries in even layer in 13 by 9-inch glass baking dish. Bring juices and cinnamon stick to simmer in medium nonreactive saucepan over medium-high heat, whisking frequently, until mixture thickens, about 5 minutes. Discard cinnamon stick, stir in almond extract, and pour hot juices over cherries in baking dish.

4. Arrange hot biscuits in 3 rows of 4 over warm filling. Bake cobbler until filling is bubbling and biscuits are deep golden brown, about 10 minutes. Cool on wire rack 10 minutes; serve.

TASTING LAB: Cherries

FRESH SOUR CHERRIES MAY BE THE BEST CHOICE FOR baking, but they are available only for a few weeks during the summer. What's the best option at other times of the year when making cherry cobbler? Should you use fresh sweet cherries? What about processed sour cherries? We rounded up six contenders—fresh sweet cherries, frozen sweet cherries, canned sweet cherries, jarred sour cherries, frozen sour cherries, and canned sour cherries—and made cobbler fillings with each one.

Although most of these cherry products made a cobbler filling that looked good, only one—jarred Morello

---

TECHNIQUE: Pitting Cherries

A cherry pitter (sold in most kitchenware stores) is the best tool for removing pits from fresh sour cherries. If you don't own this gadget, you can improvise as follows. With any of these methods, work over a bowl to catch the cherry juices.

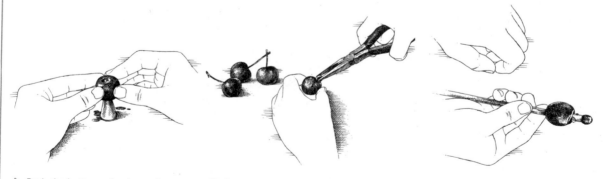

A. Push the bottom of a cherry down onto the pointed, jagged end of a pastry bag tip. The pastry tip will push the pit out the top. Take care not cut your fingers on the points as they pierce the fruit.

B. Pierce the skin at the stem with a pair of needle-nose pliers, spread the pliers just enough to grasp the pit, and pull it straight out.

C. Push a drinking straw through the bottom of the cherry, forcing the pit up and out the top.

Rating Cherry Products

WE TESTED SIX ALTERNATIVES TO FRESH SOUR CHERRIES IN OUR COBBLER FILLING RECIPE. TASTERS EVALUATED THE cooked cherries in terms of flavor, color, and texture. They also rated the "sauce" made by each cherry product when cooked with the other filling ingredients. For varieties without packing liquid, we substituted cranberry juice. Cherries are listed in order of preference. All of these products are widely available in supermarkets, with the exception of our winner, which is available in Trader Joe's markets. See www.cooksillustrated.com for an up-to-date price and mail-order source for jarred Morello cherries.

RECOMMENDED
1. Trader's Joe Dark Morello Cherries in Light Syrup
$2.29 for 24.7 ounces

These jarred sour cherries from Germany are packed in water and sugar. Tasters praised their "true, fruity" flavor and remarked that the cherries were "plump" and "still had some chew." They made a sauce that was "complex," with "winey notes" and "good body."

NOT RECOMMENDED
2. Fresh Bing Cherries
$6.98 per pound

Sweet Bing cherries are the variety you find in supermarkets. They were deemed "mildly fresh" and "sweet." Their texture was "very, very firm," and they seemed "undercooked." The sauce they made was "too sweet" and "thin."

NOT RECOMMENDED
3. Cascadian Farm Frozen Sweet Cherries
$3.79 for 10 ounces

These organic sweet cherries come from Chile and cooked up with a "mushy," "jamlike" texture. Their flavor was "sweet" and "winey." The sauce they made tasted more like other fruits (tasters mentioned plums and blueberries), and it was extremely thick.

NOT RECOMMENDED
4. Comstock Canned Dark Sweet Pitted Cherries
$2.99 for 15 ounces

These sweet cherries are packed in heavy syrup and were judged to be "bland," "flavorless," and "stale." Their texture was described as "limp" and "mushy." The "runny" sauce they made was "sour" and "like cough syrup."

NOT RECOMMENDED
5. Comstock Canned Tart Red Pitted Cherries
$1.99 for 14.5 ounces

These sour cherries are packed in water, which may explain their very poor finish. They were "flat tasting" and "flavorless," with a "strange gummy texture." They made a "watery" sauce that "burned the throat" with its tartness.

NOT RECOMMENDED
6. Friske Orchards Frozen Red Tart Cherries
$7.50 for 24 ounces

The individually quick frozen (IQF) cherries from northern Michigan were a real disappointment. They tasted "sour" and "harsh," and panelists complained about their "spongy," "rubbery" texture. The sauce they made was deemed "dull" and "medicinal."

cherries from Trader Joe's—made a filling that tasted good. We loved their deep ruby red color, tart flavor, and plump and meaty texture. In fact, these cherries delivered bracing flavor and a great chew right out of the jar.

The other sour cherries (canned and frozen) landed at the bottom of the rankings. None of the three sweet cherry products (fresh, frozen, and canned) scored all that well either, although tasters felt that fresh Bing cherries were the best sweet option. In the end, tasters concluded that jarred Morello cherries were the only product worth using—cobblers made with the other cherry products were lackluster and bland.

Why did the jarred sour cherries sweep the tasting while the frozen and canned sour cherries couldn't even beat mediocre sweet cherry products? We have two explanations for these curious findings. First, the jarred sour cherries that we tested were Morellos, an especially flavorful variety. Second, these cherries (unlike the frozen or canned sour cherries) were packed in sugar syrup. The canned sour cherries we tested were packed in water, which seemed to wash away their flavor. The frozen cherries were frozen as is, and this delicate fruit just doesn't freeze all that well. The lightly sweetened packing liquid from the jarred cherries added flavor to the cobbler filling and helped give it a pleasing, slightly thickened texture.

SCIENCE DESK:
Browning and Baking Soda

THE BAKING SODA AND THE BAKING POWDER IN THE biscuits for our cherry cobbler recipe provide leavening. But did you know that the baking soda also serves another function? It enhances browning. In fact, many pastry chefs add a little baking soda to baked goods to promote browning rather than to cause lift.

Browning is an extremely important phenomenon in cooking because browned food tastes better. When carbohydrates and proteins are heated together, the sugar (from the carbohydrates) and the amino acids (from the proteins) combine to form hundreds of new, distinct flavor compounds in a process called the Maillard reaction. These newly formed compounds are what makes browned food taste so much more complex and interesting than food that is not browned. So increasing browning is a good thing.

Why does baking soda increase browning? Because browning occurs best in an alkaline environment. Here's how it works. An amino acid molecule has two ends—one is the amino end and one is the acid end. As you might guess, the acid end is acidic, but (as you might not guess) the amino end is alkaline. It's the alkaline end that has to react with the sugar molecules for browning to occur. In an acidic solution, the alkaline ends are destroyed. In an alkaline environment, the amino ends thrive and are free to react with the sugar to create browning.

The biscuit portion of our cobbler recipe contains buttermilk, which is very acidic. Baking soda, being an alkaline itself, reacts with the buttermilk to create a rise in the dough, but it also creates an alkaline environment, thus permitting the amino ends of the amino acid molecules to react with the sugar and produce browning. A biscuit recipe with buttermilk and baking powder alone may or may not rise (depending on how much you use), but it certainly won't brown very well.

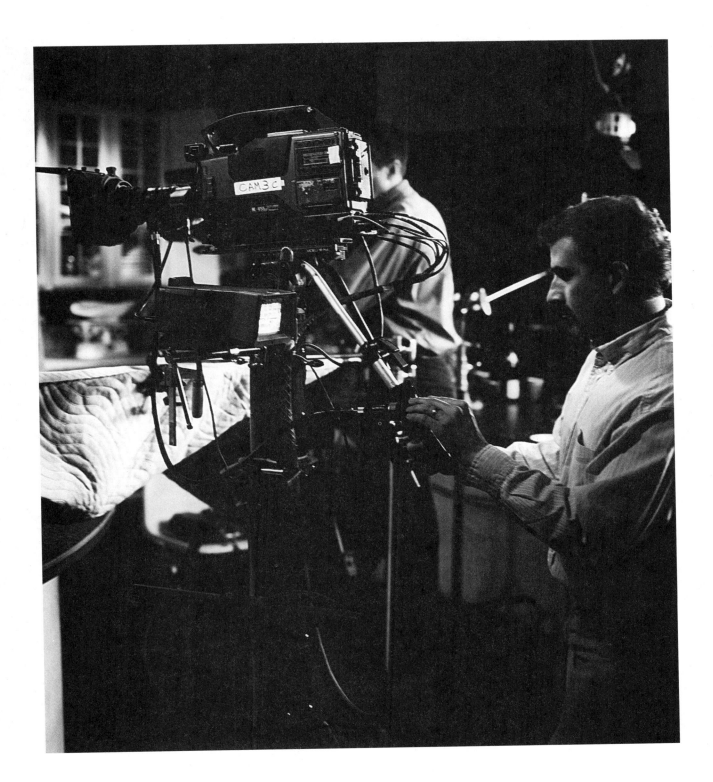

Doc dons his conquistador outfit to help illustrate the dramatic history of chocolate.

TWO CHOCOLATE cakes

Who can resist a chocolate cake? No one in the test kitchen, that's for sure. The words "chocolate cake" can mean different things to different people. It might be a lopsided layer cake that you've spent hours making, baking, and frosting. Or it might be a flavorless sheet cake from the supermarket. We have two requirements for chocolate cake: It has to taste great, and it should be easy to prepare. We also have two recipes—one plain looking, one fancy looking—that meet both of these requirements.

A hot fudge pudding cake is an old-fashioned American cake straight from the pages of community cookbooks. Although this two-layer concoction, with cake and sauce baked together in one pan, will never win any beauty contests, its flavor is pure chocolate and the gooey texture is addictive, especially if served warm with ice cream on top. Unfortunately, many versions of this recipe fail to deliver the right balance of cake to sauce.

A flourless chocolate cake is a thing of beauty. Like a chocolate cheesecake, only with more flavor and a better texture, this mousse-like cake whispers elegance (and chocolate) with every bite. Yes, this recipe requires a springform pan and a water bath, but there are only three ingredients—chocolate, butter, and eggs—so the batter goes together in a flash. Our goal was to figure out the right proportions of these ingredients and the best baking method in order to turn out a cake that was neither too light nor too heavy.

IN THIS CHAPTER

THE RECIPES
Hot Fudge Pudding Cake
Individual Hot Fudge Pudding Cakes

Flourless Chocolate Cake

EQUIPMENT CORNER
Digital Kitchen Scales

SCIENCE DESK
The Allure of Chocolate

TASTING LAB
Vanilla Extract

HOT FUDGE PUDDING CAKE

WHAT WE WANTED: A homey, no-fuss chocolate cake with hot fudge sauce—baked together in one dish.

Hot fudge pudding cake has several aliases: Denver pudding cake, chocolate upside-down cake, brownie pudding cake, or sometimes simply chocolate pudding cake. This 1950s community cookbook recipe may be a bit dated, but it's a boon to the cook looking for a simple baked dessert that requires no creaming or whipping. Hot fudge pudding cake is definitely not a dessert for entertaining; it does not impress with its looks. It's a humble, homely dessert with bumps, lumps, and cracks, an easy one to turn up your nose at. But those who have eaten hot fudge pudding cake know its charms: unpretentious, moist, brownie-like chocolate cake sitting on a pool of a chocolate sauce so thick it's reminiscent of pudding, with both miraculously baked at the same time in the same dish. Served warm with vanilla ice cream, this cake more than makes up for its lack of looks.

In the matter of pudding cakes, there are two distinct styles. The fussier version requires beaten egg whites rather than chemical leaveners for lift and a hot water bath to produce a soufflé-like cake above a custard-like sauce. Then there's the absurdly simple hot fudge pudding cake that resembles a chemically leavened brownie and can be made by a rookie baker equipped with only a few bowls and a whisk. It was the latter style that we were pursuing, so we gathered a few recipes and tried them. All were disappointing. Instead of deep and chocolatey, they tasted dull and mild. Instead of providing enough spoon-coating sauce to accompany the cake, some were dry, with a disproportionate amount of cake, while the others were soupy, with a wet, sticky, underdone cake.

For those who aren't familiar with the magic of pudding cakes, here's how they work. The batter is made in the manner of a brownie batter, but with milk added. After the batter goes in the baking dish, things take an unusual turn. A mixture of sugar and cocoa is sprinkled over the batter, then liquid is poured on top, and the mess goes into the oven. (Depending on the recipe, the cocoa and sugar may first be dissolved in hot water, then poured over.) The step of pouring liquid over the batter is so odd that the cook making a hot fudge pudding cake for the first time quickly becomes skeptical. With baking, however, what looks to be a mistake is transformed into a dessert. The cake rises to the surface, and the liquid that started out on top sinks to the bottom, taking the sugar and cocoa with it, becoming the "hot fudge" part of the dessert.

With a working recipe cobbled together, our first goal was to pump up the chocolate flavor, suspecting that the problem was that most recipes call for cocoa rather than chocolate. In our experience, cocoa alone carries potent—sometimes acrid—chocolate flavor, but it cannot deliver the complexity or richness of chocolate. We tried adding different amounts of bittersweet chocolate to the pudding cake. Two ounces in addition to the ⅓ cup of cocoa was the ideal amount to obtain fuller flavor. More chocolate and the cake was too wicked with chocolate and its texture became sodden.

We also thought to try regular "natural" cocoa versus Dutch-processed cocoa. The former is lighter in color and more acidic than the latter. In a side-by-side tasting, we were stunned by the difference. The "natural" cocoa version tasted sharp and harsh, but the one made with Dutch-processed cocoa (we used Droste, a brand widely available in supermarkets) tasted smooth, round, and full. It was unanimous. Every person who tasted the two cakes vastly preferred the one made with Dutch-processed cocoa. To sweeten the cake and counter the bitterness of even the Dutch-processed cocoa, ⅔ cup of sugar was required. We tried substituting some brown sugar for granulated but found it a nuisance because of the way it clumps (not a problem if the butter and sugar were being creamed

together, but this cake was too easy for that). Besides, the brown sugar added no significant flavor benefit.

The next issue to settle was that of eggs, and there seemed to be two choices: recipes that contained an egg and those that didn't. The eggless cakes were mushy and crumbly. Their crumb lacked structural integrity, and, because they were soft and mushy, there seemed to be little distinction between what was supposed to be cake and what was supposed to be hot fudge. We tried as many as two whole eggs, but our preference was for a pudding cake made with just one yolk. It was brownie-like, with a nice, tooth-sinking crumb. Cakes made with whole eggs were drier and slightly rubbery.

So far, we had been using 1 cup of unbleached all-purpose flour, but the cake layer was a tad too thick. We tried smaller amounts of flour, hoping that the texture wouldn't suffer as a consequence. We ended up preferring the cake with ¾ cup of flour. It tasted more richly of chocolate and had a moist, brownie-like texture. It had a little less height, but this made it a better match for the amount of sauce.

The butter in hot fudge pudding cake is always melted,

never creamed. (This cake requires a heavy-duty leavener, such as baking powder, to force the cake layer up through the sludge that becomes the sauce. Although creaming is one way to provide lift, in this case we found that the contribution made by aerated butter was minimal and not worth the effort.) With only 4 tablespoons of melted butter, the cake tasted lean and dry. With 8, it was leaden and greasy. Six tablespoons was the ideal amount. Like most other cakes, hot fudge pudding cake contains some dairy, usually milk. We tried heavy cream and half-and-half to see if either had desirable effects. Heavy cream made a slick, greasy, fat-laden cake. With half-and-half, the cake was somewhat greasy and a little too rich. Milk was the way to go.

For lift, we relied on baking powder. One recipe called for 2 tablespoons per cup of flour ("chemical warfare" was one taster's term for this mixture). Two teaspoons of baking powder was just fine. To heighten flavor, we added ¼ teaspoon salt and 1 tablespoon vanilla (there was a lot of chocolate flavor to contend with).

As mentioned above, there are two ways to add the ingredients destined to become the fudge sauce. A mixture of cocoa and sugar can be sprinkled on the batter and water then poured over it, creating what looks like a pan-full of river sludge. Alternatively, the cocoa and sugar can first be dissolved in boiling water. We compared two such pudding cakes. The one with the sprinkled cocoa/sugar mixture baked up with crisp edges and a faintly crisp crust that we preferred over the uniformly soft, cakey surface of the other. It was as if some of the sugar, moistened by the water, remained at the surface even after the liquid seeped to the bottom, and then caramelized to form a pleasing crust.

We tried different amounts of cocoa in the sauce-to-be and landed at ⅓ cup, the same amount we put in the cake. A mixture made with all granulated sugar resulted in a toffee-like crust, rather sticky and tough, with one-dimensional sweetness. We preferred a mix of granulated and brown sugar, with the molasses flavor of the latter producing a full, round taste.

The amount of water poured over the cake determines the amount of sauce at the bottom. One and one-half cups—a little more than what most recipes call for—was ideal, yielding an ample amount of sauce with the right consistency. Some hot fudge pudding cake recipes suggest using coffee instead of water. Indeed, we thought the coffee was a nice addition. It didn't interfere with the chocolate flavor but nicely complemented it, cutting through some of the cake's cloying qualities and enriching the flavor. For ease, we took to using 2 teaspoons of instant coffee mixed into the water, but cold, brewed coffee cut with a little water works as well.

We tested different oven temperatures and baking times. While most recipes indicated 350 degrees for about 35 minutes, we preferred 325 degrees for 45 minutes. The lower temperature helped keep the sauce from rapidly bubbling, a phenomenon that can cause spillage if left unchecked. In addition, the slightly longer baking time promoted a nicer crust. We noted that this cake combined lots of pleasing textures: a silky sauce, a moist, cakey crumb, and a thin, brittle crust, especially around the edges.

When attacked with a spoon straight from the oven, the hot fudge pudding cake revealed a thin, blistering-hot sauce and a sodden cake. If allowed to cool for 20 to 30 minutes, the sauce became pudding-like and the cake brownie-like. The warm cake cries out to be served with vanilla or coffee ice cream (whipped cream just isn't serious enough). For serving to guests, we adapted the recipe to bake in individual ramekins so that apologies for the cake's dowdy appearance need not be made so profusely. Leftovers reheat well in the zap of a microwave, but don't count on having any.

WHAT WE LEARNED: For the best flavor and texture, use a combination of Dutch-processed cocoa and melted bittersweet chocolate in the cake layer. For the sauce, sprinkle the cake batter with a mixture of cocoa, brown sugar, and granulated sugar and then cover with coffee.

HOT FUDGE PUDDING CAKE serves 8

If you have cold, brewed coffee on hand, it can be used in place of the instant coffee and water, but to make sure it isn't too strong, use 1 cup of cold coffee mixed with 1/2 cup of water. Serve the cake warm with vanilla or coffee ice cream. Leftovers can be reheated, covered with plastic wrap, in a microwave oven.

    2   teaspoons instant coffee
 1½   cups water
    ⅔   cup (2½ ounces) Dutch-processed cocoa
    ⅓   cup packed (1¾ ounces) brown sugar
    1   cup (7 ounces) granulated sugar
    6   tablespoons unsalted butter
    2   ounces bittersweet or semisweet chocolate,
          chopped
    ¾   cup (3¾ ounces) unbleached all-purpose flour
    2   teaspoons baking powder
    1   tablespoon vanilla extract
    ⅓   cup whole milk
    ¼   teaspoon salt
    1   large egg yolk

1. Adjust oven rack to lower-middle position and heat oven to 325 degrees. Lightly spray 8-inch square glass or ceramic baking dish with nonstick cooking spray (see illustration on page 321). Stir instant coffee into water; set aside to dissolve. Stir together ⅓ cup cocoa, brown sugar, and ⅓ cup granulated sugar in small bowl, breaking up large clumps with fingers; set aside. Melt butter, remaining ⅓ cup cocoa, and chocolate in small bowl set over saucepan of barely simmering water; whisk until smooth and set aside to cool slightly. Whisk flour and baking powder in small bowl to combine; set aside. Whisk remaining ⅔ cup sugar, vanilla, milk, and salt in medium bowl until combined; whisk in yolk. Add chocolate mixture and whisk to combine. Add flour mixture and whisk until batter is evenly moistened.

2. Pour batter into prepared baking dish and spread evenly to sides and corners. Sprinkle cocoa/sugar mixture evenly over batter (cocoa mixture should cover entire surface of batter); pour coffee mixture gently over cocoa mixture. Bake until cake is puffed and bubbling and just beginning to pull away from sides of baking dish, about 45 minutes. (Do not overbake.) Cool cake in dish on wire rack about 25 minutes before serving.

VARIATION

INDIVIDUAL HOT FUDGE PUDDING CAKES

Follow recipe for Hot Fudge Pudding Cake, heating oven to 400 degrees and lightly spraying eight 6- to 8-ounce ramekins with nonstick cooking spray; set ramekins on baking sheet. Divide batter evenly among ramekins (about ¼ cup per ramekin) and level with back of spoon; sprinkle about 2 tablespoons cocoa/sugar mixture over batter in each ramekin. Pour 3 tablespoons coffee mixture over cocoa/sugar mixture in each ramekin. Bake until puffed and bubbling, about 20 minutes. (Do not overbake.) Cool ramekins about 15 minutes before serving (cakes will fall).

TECHNIQUE: No-Mess Spraying

To keep cooking spray from covering your counters with an oily film, try this trick. Open the dishwasher door, place the item to be greased on the door, and spray away. Any excess spray will be cleaned off the door the next time you run the dishwasher.

TASTING LAB: Vanilla Extract

ALMOST TWO-THIRDS OF THE WORLD'S SUPPLY OF VANILLA beans comes from Madagascar, an island off the eastern coast of Africa. Significant amounts of vanilla beans are also grown in Mexico and Tahiti. Tahitian beans are a hybrid that originated spontaneously on several islands in the South Pacific. Beans grown everywhere else in the world, including Mexico and Madagascar, are from the same species.

Although vanilla beans are convenient to use in custards (the pods are split lengthwise, the seeds scraped into the liquid, and the pods usually added to infuse more flavor), extracts make the most sense for baking, including cakes and cookies. (You could make vanilla sugar by nestling a split bean in some sugar, but this process takes about a week.)

When shopping for extracts, you have two basic choices: pure extract and imitation. Pure vanilla extract is made by steeping chopped vanilla beans in an alcohol and water solution. Imitation vanilla extract is made from vanillin, a product extracted from conifer wood pulp that has been chemically rinsed.

We figured that tasters would have no trouble picking out pure vanilla extract from imitation products. We also expected the gourmet brands available in upscale markets and by mail to outpoll supermarket offerings. Well, we sure were wrong.

We tried nine extracts (seven pure, two imitation) in a basic sugar cookie with just flour, butter, and sugar. It turns out that most people, including pastry chefs, can't even tell the difference between a cookie made with vanilla extract and a cookie made with the imitation stuff, let alone the differences between brands of real vanilla. In a cookie (as well as in chocolate cake, or any cake for that matter), the quantities of extract are so small and the other ingredients so flavorful that these differences are hard to detect.

We decided to try our pure and imitation extracts in an eggless custard. We choose a panna cotta recipe that calls for just cream, milk, sugar, and gelatin. We also followed a standard tasting protocol in the vanilla business and mixed each extract with milk at a ratio of 1 part extract to 8 parts milk. Although you would never use so much extract in a real application, this high concentration makes it easier to detect specific characteristics in extracts.

The results of this tasting were so shocking that we repeated it, only to come up with similarly surprising findings. Tasters couldn't tell the difference between real and imitation vanilla. In fact, in the panna cotta tasting, the imitation extracts took first and third place, with two "premium" brands, Nielsen-Massey and Penzeys, leading the pack among real extracts. In the milk tasting, the imitation extracts took the top two spots, followed by real extracts from Nielsen-Massey and Penzeys. Although we are loath to recommend an imitation product, it seems that most people don't mind imitation extract and, in fact, many tasters actually like its flavor. Note that you won't save money by choosing an imitation extract—it costs about the same as pure vanilla extract.

EQUIPMENT CORNER: Digital Scales

IN OUR TEST KITCHEN, WE WEIGH MOST BAKING INGREDIENTS as well as meats, fruits, and vegetables for cooking. An apple pie, for example, would look uninspiring if it were filled with only 2½ pounds of apples instead of 4 pounds, which is why making a recipe that simply calls for "X" number of medium apples without a specific weight can be risky. If you were to choose apples that were smaller than those intended by the recipe writer, you'd end up with a flat pie.

This is why we reviewed 13 kitchen scales some seven years ago. Testers preferred electronic models with digital readouts because they were easier to read and seemed more accurate than the mechanical models with dial displays. The natural question then was, which electronic scale is best? To find out how things look now, we recently scrutinized eight popular models, ranging in price from just over $25 to $125, and discovered a few differences that made some units easier to use than others.

Perhaps the biggest advantage of digital scales over dial-face models is readability. Some digitals, however, are easier to read than others. We found that readability depends equally on the design of the scale and the size of the display. Scales with large displays that were angled steeply and set far away from the weighing platform were the easiest to read because the display was not hidden beneath the rim or in the shadow of the vessel on the platform, be it a dinner plate, cake pan, or mixing bowl. For these reasons, and because its weighing platform was elevated far above the scale base, the Soehnle Cyber was the exemplar in terms of design and readability. The Cuisinart and the Salter were also particularly easy to read.

A few other features made some scales easier to use than others. For instance, the two Soehnles tested had the largest weighing platforms, at roughly 7 inches, which could accommodate a large portion of ground meat or a raw chicken without letting anything spill onto the base. That feat would be much less likely on the Measurement Specialties and Terraillon scales, with their comparatively small 5-inch platforms. For the sake of comparison, the platform on the professional electronic scale in our test kitchen measures a full 11 inches wide.

Large capacity was another feature we valued highly. The Soehnle Cyber, Salter, Cuisinart, and EKS were the best of the lot, all with 11-pound capacities, which meant they could easily weigh a large roast. The Sunbeam and the Terraillon, on the other hand, could handle weights up to only 4½ pounds, and the Measurement Specialties was designed to hold only 2 pounds, so you couldn't even weigh a large chicken on it.

All of the scales but one, the Measurement Specialties, offered a metric conversion feature, and every single scale offered something called a tare feature, which allows you to set the scale back to zero with a container such as a mixing bowl on the platform, thus giving you a reading on the weight of the food alone. All of the scales also had an automatic shut-off feature. While this is certainly a good way to preserve battery life, we found it annoying when the scale shut itself off after a short cycle of less than two minutes, often before we were

Rating Digital Kitchen Scales

WE TESTED EIGHT DIGITAL KITCHEN SCALES AND RATED THEM ACCORDING TO DISPLAY VISIBILITY, CAPACITY (THE HIGHER, the better), platform size (the larger, the better), ease of use, accuracy, and measuring increments. Display visibility was the most important criterion, followed by capacity and the size of the measuring platform. The scales are listed in order of preference. See www.cooksillustrated.com for up-to-date prices and mail-order sources for top-rated products.

HIGHLY RECOMMENDED

1. Soehnle Cyber Electronic Kitchen Scale, Model 8048

$124.95

Detachable glass platform was large and especially easy to clean. Easy-to-read display and high capacity were also pluses.

RECOMMENDED

2. Salter Electronic Aquatronic The Baker's Dream, Model 3007

$59.95

Well liked for its long 5-minute automatic shut-off time, fluid weight feature, and rubber feet, which prevent sliding. On the downside, the ridge between the weighing platform and the base can trap food particles.

RECOMMENDED

3. Cuisinart Precision Electronic Scale, Model SA-110A

$69.95

Good display and long 6-minute automatic shut-off time; rubber feet help prevent sliding. The ridge between the weighing platform and the base can trap food particles.

RECOMMENDED WITH RESERVATIONS

4. Soehnle Magnum Electronic Baking & Domestic Scale, Model 8038 63

$64.95

Good accuracy, generous weighing platform, and decimal weighing increments were pluses, but scale slides around on the countertop and the flat display can be hard to read.

RECOMMENDED WITH RESERVATIONS

5. EKS Electronic Scale

$69.00

Very accurate, but the textured weighing platform is hard to clean. The display starts in metric and must be changed to the U.S. standard every time, which is irritating, as is the short automatic shut-off time.

NOT RECOMMENDED

6. Sunbeam Deluxe Digital Scale, Model 6025

$49.95

Good accuracy, but low capacity (less than 5 pounds) will pose problem for some kitchen tasks. The scale often did not return to zero when the weight was removed.

NOT RECOMMENDED

7. Measurement Specialties Thinner Electronic Food/Diet Scale, Model MS-11

$26.92

Intended for dieting, so display reads out in ounces only, not pounds. Despite 2-pound capacity claim, we found actual capacity to be 10 pounds.

NOT RECOMMENDED

8. Terraillon Electronic Food Scale, Model BE225-T

$44.95

Good accuracy, but low capacity (less than 5 pounds) and a small weighing platform held it back. Also, unimpressive automatic shut-off time, and did not always return to zero when weight was removed.

finished adding ingredients to the bowl. Guilty on this count were the Measurement Specialties, the Terraillon, and the EKS. The Soehnle Cyber, Salter, and Cuisinart scales provided a reliable margin of five or six minutes.

Last, we preferred scales that displayed weight increments in decimals, including both Soehnles, the Sunbeam, and the Measurement Specialties. Decimals were easier to work with when scaling recipes up or down, and they had a minor advantage in terms of accuracy because they measured in increments of one tenth of an ounce, or 0.1, in the lower weight ranges. The scales that displayed fractions—the Salter, Cuisinart, EKS, and Terraillon—measured in increments of one-quarter ounce, or 0.25, in those ranges.

Philosophically, we feel that every scale should be perfectly accurate all of the time. Realistically, we found otherwise. In fact, after extensive testing with calibrated laboratory weights, only one of the scales tested, the EKS, proved to be absolutely accurate every time. Up through 4 pounds, the scale with the largest average inaccuracy, just a hair over 0.25 ounce, was the Cuisinart. The others were off by about 0.2 ounce, or even less. In the higher weight ranges of 8 pounds or more, the margins of inaccuracy increased to just above 0.5 ounce for both Soehnles and to a full ounce for both the Salter and the Cuisinart. We noted with all of the scales that placing them on a very flat, solid surface helped produce a sure reading. If the surface was at all unstable or wobbly, the readings would fluctuate from one increment to the next.

Philosophy aside, all of our scales were accurate enough in the lower weight ranges for most home cooks, particularly when making savory dishes. No one would be able to tell, for instance, if your meatloaf contained 7.75 ounces of ground pork rather than 8 ounces. Even in baking, inaccuracy of 0.25 ounce would be all right in the vast majority of recipes.

For its sleek and thoughtful design, good accuracy, and superior readability, the handsome but expensive Soehnle Cyber was the star of this show. Understandably, though, many cooks may be reluctant to drop $125 on a scale. In that case, both the Salter and the Cuisinart offer optimal readability and 11-pound capacities for about $70 or less.

FLOURLESS CHOCOLATE CAKE

WHAT WE WANTED: A dense, moist, ultra-chocolate cake with a texture somewhere between an airy mousse and a heavy cheesecake.

To our knowledge, flourless chocolate cake is the only dessert that is named for a missing ingredient. Besides this, the word cake stretches the point in describing this very popular dessert; although some recipes replace flour or crumbs with ground nuts, the quintessence of the genre contains only chocolate, butter, and eggs—nothing that could conceivably be called a dry ingredient. The result is more confection than cake, like a dense baked mousse or chocolate cheesecake, with butter replacing cheese.

Although the ingredient choices are limited—chocolate, butter, and eggs, sometimes sugar, and sometimes liquid such as water, coffee, or liqueur—the proportions as well as mixing and baking methods differed considerably in the recipes we researched.

We selected and baked six recipes that represented the array of choices. The results were staggering in their variety. One cake resembled a flourless fudge brownie, one was more like an ultra-dense, creamy custard, and one was a pouffy, fallen soufflé-like affair.

Although nearly all of the desserts were enticing in their own way, we were quickly able to define our criteria for the ultimate flourless chocolate cake. We wanted something dense, moist, and ultra-chocolatey, but with some textural finesse. We wanted a mouthfeel and texture somewhere between a substantial marquise au chocolat—that dense, buttery, and just slightly aerated chocolate mousse with a characteristically dry yet creamy texture—and a heavy New York–style cheesecake, which requires the mouth to work for just a second before the stuff melts and dissolves with sublime flavor. We wanted the flavor and character of good, eating-quality chocolate to reign supreme, with no unnecessary sweetness and not even the slightest grain of sugar on the palate. In short, we wanted an intense, bittersweet "adult" dessert, not a piece of fudge or a brownie or a thick chocolate pudding, and certainly nothing fluffy.

Some recipes used unsweetened chocolate instead of semisweet or bittersweet, but we rejected this idea after tasting just one cake made with unsweetened chocolate. Neither flavor nor texture was smooth or silky enough for us, and there was a slight chalky sensation on the palate. This made perfect sense. Unsweetened chocolate is coarse and needs high heat to blend perfectly with the sugar required to sweeten it. It is most successful in desserts with a cakey or fudgy texture, when perfect smoothness is unnecessary. Hot fudge sauce made with unsweetened chocolate is smooth because it is cooked to a temperature high enough to melt the sugar and change the physical properties of the chocolate. But our flourless chocolate cake is more like chocolate mousse, chocolate truffles, or ganache—ingredients are few, cooked very gently, and the results must be perfectly smooth. Made to be nibbled, semisweet and bittersweet chocolates are incomparably smooth, refined so that chocolate and sugar are intimately married and every particle is smaller than the human palate can detect.

The next decision had to do with the baking temperature and whether or not a water bath was indicated. The original recipe for this now-popular dessert was flawed by hard, crumbly edges—surely caused by baking for a short time at a high temperature without a water bath. We tried a similar recipe baked at a high temperature for a short time but in a water bath. It was creamier by far, but we could taste raw egg. We guessed that, like cheesecake, this dessert required a longer baking time at a lower temperature in a water bath to allow the interior to reach a safe temperature without overcooking the edges. We found that 325 degrees in a water bath produced a successful sample.

The trick in baking this cake, however, was knowing when to stop. Just like cheesecake, our flourless chocolate cake must be taken from the oven when the center still jiggles and looks quite underdone, as it continues to cook after it comes out of the oven. The center of the cake should register 140 degrees on an instant-read thermometer.

Before determining the perfect quantities of butter and eggs for a pound of chocolate, we decided to test textures. We were pretty sure that the ultimate cake would need some form of aeration from beaten eggs to achieve the texture that we wanted. In the first test, we whisked the eggs over gentle heat to warm them (as for a génoise, or very light sponge cake without leavening), and then beat them until about triple in volume and the consistency of soft whipped cream. We then folded the whipped eggs into the warm chocolate and butter in three parts. In the second test, we separated the eggs and whisked the yolks into the warm chocolate and butter and then beat the whites to a meringue before folding them in. In the third test, we simply whisked the eggs, one by one, into the warm chocolate and butter, as though making a custard.

The sample made with eggs simply whisked into the melted chocolate and butter was dense and smooth like a very rich custard or crème brûlée. Our definition of the ultimate flourless chocolate cake ruled this version out. The cake with beaten whole eggs differed from the one with yolks and meringue more than we expected. Surprisingly, the difference in flavor was greater than the difference in texture. Whole beaten eggs produced a dessert with nicely blended flavors, while the cake with separated eggs tasted as if the ingredients had not been completely integrated. Along the way, we realized that we could eliminate the step of warming the eggs before beating them, since cold eggs produce a denser foam with smaller bubbles, which in turn gave the cake a more velvety texture.

WHAT WE LEARNED: **Just three ingredients— whipped whole eggs, a good-quality bittersweet or semisweet chocolate, and butter—will yield a dense, rich texture and true chocolate flavor. Make sure not to overbake this cake or the texture will be ruined.**

FLOURLESS CHOCOLATE CAKE serves 12 to 16

Even though the cake may not look done, pull it from the oven when an instant-read thermometer registers 140 degrees. (Make sure not to let tip of thermometer hit the bottom of the pan.) It will continue to firm up as it cools. If you use a 9-inch springform pan instead of the preferred 8-inch, reduce the baking time to 18 to 20 minutes. We like the pure flavor of chocolate. However, coffee or liqueur (choose something that tastes like nuts, coffee, or oranges) can added if desired. In any case, choose a high-quality chocolate that you enjoy eating out of hand.

- 8 large eggs, cold
- 1 pound bittersweet or semisweet chocolate, chopped
- ½ pound (2 sticks) unsalted butter, cut into ½-inch chunks
- ¼ cup strong coffee or liqueur (optional)
  Confectioners' sugar or cocoa powder for decoration

1. Adjust oven rack to lower-middle position and heat oven to 325 degrees. Line bottom of 8-inch springform pan with parchment and grease pan sides. Cover pan underneath and along sides with sheet of heavy-duty aluminum foil and set wrapped pan in large roasting pan. Bring kettle of water to boil.

2. Beat eggs with handheld mixer at high speed until volume doubles to approximately 1 quart, about 5 minutes. Alternately, beat in bowl of electric mixer fitted with wire whip attachment at medium speed to achieve same result, about 5 minutes.

3. Meanwhile, melt chocolate and butter (adding coffee or liqueur, if using) in large heatproof bowl set over pan of almost simmering water, until smooth and very warm (about 115 degrees on an instant-read thermometer), stirring once or twice. (To use microwave, melt chocolate at 50 percent power for 2 minutes, stir, add butter, and continue heating at 50 percent power, stirring every minute, until chocolate and butter have melted and are smooth, another 2 to 3 minutes total.) Using large rubber spatula, fold ⅓ of egg foam into chocolate mixture until only a few streaks of egg are visible; fold in half of remaining foam, then last of remaining foam, until mixture is totally homogenous.

4. Scrape batter into prepared springform pan and smooth surface with rubber spatula. Set roasting pan on oven rack and pour enough boiling water to come about halfway up side of springform pan. Bake until cake has risen slightly, edges are just beginning to set, thin glazed crust (like a brownie) has formed on surface, and instant-read thermometer inserted halfway through center of cake registers 140 degrees, 22 to 25 minutes. Remove springform pan from water bath and set on wire rack; cool to room temperature. Cover and refrigerate overnight to mellow flavors. (Cake can be covered and refrigerated for up to 4 days).

5. About 30 minutes before serving, remove springform pan sides, invert cake on sheet of waxed paper, peel off parchment pan liner, and turn cake right-side up on serving platter. Sieve light sprinkling of confectioners' sugar or unsweetened cocoa powder over cake to decorate, if desired.

SCIENCE DESK:
The Allure of Chocolate

SINCE THE DAYS OF THE ANCIENT AZTECS, WHO BELIEVED that chocolate conferred sexual prowess on those who consumed it, chocolate has been not just a food but a passion. Many have attempted to deter chocolate fanatics from the object of their obsession, but to little avail. When a sixteenth-century Spanish priest tried to prevent his New World parishioners from drinking chocolate during mass, swords were drawn to protect the coveted drink. The next day the priest was found dead of poisoning.

As it turns out, there may be a scientific reason for our intense desire for chocolate. Researchers have recently discovered that chocolate contains unusually large amounts of phenylethylamine, a stimulant similar to chemicals released by the human body during sex. Other scientists say that the caffeine in chocolate causes the craving. Still other experts attribute chocolate's addictive properties to chemicals called cannabinoids, which are in the same family as certain molecules found in marijuana.

But do these explanations make sense? To get the same amount of caffeine that's in an 8-ounce cup of coffee, you'd have to eat one pound of chocolate. To get any pharmacological effect from the cannabinoids, you'd have to eat 27 pounds of chocolate.

As these numbers suggest, it may be the chocolate itself—in its entirety—that satisfies one's cravings, not any single compound it contains. A recent study supports this theory. In this experiment, one group of people was given white chocolate, which doesn't contain the pharmacologically active components in chocolate, and another group was given capsules with the chemical components in chocolate that some scientists believe are responsible for its addictive power. The white chocolate, without the chemical compounds, did a better job of satisfying cravings than the capsules with the compounds.

So it seems that the flavor and mouthfeel of chocolate is what people crave. But there is a bit of science to mouthfeel—the almost otherworldly silken texture that cocoa butter gives to a bar of chocolate. Unlike other fats, which melt at room temperature, cocoa butter stays firm up to 92 degrees. As a result, chocolate stays solid until you put it into your mouth. The temperature inside the human mouth is a couple of degrees higher than the melting point of cocoa butter, so the chocolate melts very slowly. In fact, it seems to melt into—rather than just in—your mouth. Now, that's a source of passion all by itself.

Cheesecake ingredients come together quickly in a standing mixer.

NEW YORK cheesecake

Cheesecake has taken a tawdry twist these days, sullied by ice cream–style flavors such as Irish coffee, cappuccino crunch, and Key lime. We all know that the only true cheesecake—the one with unimpeachable credentials—is the New York cheesecake. It is a subtle orchestration of different textures made sublime by a rare and welcome exercise in restraint. Rejecting the Ben and Jerry school of everything-but-the-kitchen-sink concoctions, the ideal New York cheesecake is timeless in its adherence to simplicity.

It should be a tall, bronze-skinned, and dense affair. At the core, it should be cool, thick, smooth, satiny, and creamy. Radiating outward, it goes gradually from velvet to suede, then, finally, around the edges, it becomes cake-like and fine-pored. The flavor should be pure and min-imalist, sweet and tangy, and rich to boot.

A New York cheesecake should not taste citrusy or vanilla-laden, nor should it be fluffy, mousse-like, leaden, gummy, chewy, or starchy. It should not be so dry as to make you gag, and it definitely should not bake up with a fault line as large as the San Andreas (we're talking New York, after all).

If we met all these goals, our cheesecake would be good enough to be named after New York.

IN THIS CHAPTER

THE RECIPES
New York–Style Cheesecake
Fresh Strawberry Topping

EQUIPMENT CORNER
Kitchen Timers

SCIENCE DESK
Why Do Cheesecakes Crack?

TASTING LAB
Store-Bought Cheesecakes

NEW YORK–STYLE CHEESECAKE

WHAT WE WANTED: A tall, bronze-skinned, dense cheesecake that would be creamy in the middle and cake-like around the edges. The flavors should be pure and minimalist.

There is no shortage of New York cheesecake recipes in cookbooks or magazines or on the Internet. We began our recipe testing by baking up five promising recipes. One turned out looking and tasting more like a gargantuan round of goat cheese than a cheesecake. The other four were good, but tasters cited each for some sort of infraction—an overabundance of orange zest, a taste of raw flour, a pasty mouthfeel, or a texture too light for New York cheesecake that compromised every one of them. We wanted a cheesecake far simpler and purer in flavor, with a flawless texture. With this lucid vision of New York cheesecake and a fierce appetite, we embarked on a long journey.

Some recipes claim that a pastry crust was the crust of choice for the original New York cheesecake, so we tried one. That effort, though, resulted only in a crust that became soggy beneath the filling. Most recipes forgo the pastry crust for a crumb crust—cookie or cracker crumbs are tasty and more practical options. Every taster considered a mere dusting of crumbs on the bottom of the cheesecake insufficient. We wanted a crust with more presence.

A graham cracker crust—made with 1 cup of crumbs, some sugar, and melted butter, pressed into the bottom of a springform pan, and prebaked until fragrant and browning around the edges—was ideal at a thickness of about ⅜ inch. If served within a day of being baked, it retained its crispness. (When held for a couple of days, the crust softened, but tasters still appreciated its sweet toasty flavor, and the texture was superior to a gummy pastry crust.) Brown sugar and ground cinnamon did not improve the crust. We also tried substituting gingersnaps and then chocolate wafers for the graham crackers. Although the former were overpowering,

the latter worked well, remaining crisp even longer than the graham cracker crumbs. Nonetheless, most tasters preferred graham crackers, so we decided to include the chocolate wafers as an alternative.

A great New York cheesecake should be of great stature. One made with 2 pounds (four bars) of cream cheese was not tall enough. We threw in another half pound, reaching the springform pan's maximum capacity, and the cheesecake stood tall. The amount of sugar was quickly settled at 1½ cups. The cheesecake struck a perfect balance of sweet and tangy.

Cheesecakes require a dairy supplement to the cream cheese, such as heavy cream, sour cream, or sometimes both. We made a cheesecake without additional dairy and quickly discovered why it is necessary. Cream cheese on its own produces a pasty cake, akin to mortar—much like a bar of cream cheese straight out of its wrapper. Additional dairy loosens up the texture of the cream cheese, giving the cake a smoother, more luxurious texture. Although some recipes call for as much as 1½ cups of sour cream per 8 ounces of cream cheese, we found that ⅓ cup sour cream combined with 2½ pounds cream cheese was ideal. (Too much sour cream makes cheesecake taste sour and acidic.) As for heavy cream, another common addition, we found that amounts large enough to improve the texture of the cheesecake also dulled the flavor. So it was cream cheese and sour cream—and, once again, restraint was key.

Eggs help bind the cheesecake, make it cohesive, and give it structure. They also help create a smooth, creamy texture. Whole eggs alone are often called for in softer, airier cheesecakes of non–New York persuasions. Recipes for New York cheesecake, however, agree that a few yolks in addition to whole eggs help to produce the velvety, lush texture of a proper New York cheesecake. After much testing, we settled on 6 whole eggs plus 2 yolks, a combination that produced an agreeable texture: dense but not heavy, firm but not rigid, and perfectly rich.

Starch—usually either flour or cornstarch—helps to thicken cheesecake, but, as evidenced by the half-dozen or so starch-laced cakes we made, even in amounts as small as a tablespoon, a gummy, starchy presence can be detected. Tasters much preferred the meltingly luxurious quality of a completely starch-free cheesecake.

Perfecting the flavor was a weighty issue, but an easy one to work through. Tasters moaned that orange zest made cheesecake that tastes like a Creamsicle, so it was out of there in a New York minute. Next to go was lemon zest because its flavor was distracting. A couple teaspoons of lemon juice, however, perked things up without adding a distinctively lemon flavor. Just a bit of salt (sodium is already part of cream cheese) and a couple of teaspoons of vanilla extract rounded out the flavors. Thankfully, all of the tasters in the kitchen were on the same page. We all appreciated a minimalist cheesecake.

One reason cheesecake is well loved by cooks is that it goes together easily. Even so, we noted that care must be used when mixing the ingredients lest the batter end up with small nodules of unmixed cream cheese that mar the smoothness of the baked cake. Frequent and thorough scraping of the bowl during mixing is key to ensuring that every bit of cream cheese is incorporated. It's also helpful to start with semisoftened cream cheese. It doesn't need to be at room temperature, and it definitely doesn't need to be microwaved. Simply cutting the cream cheese into chunks and letting it stand while preparing the crust and assembling the other ingredients—30 to 45 minutes—makes mixing easier. (When icebox-cold, the cream cheese resists being mixed. It clings to the beaters and bowl in firm, waxy chunks and requires much scraping and beating before it will cooperate.)

There are many ways to bake a cheesecake—in a moderate oven, in a low oven, in a water bath, or in the New York fashion, in which the cake bakes at 500 degrees for

about 10 minutes and then at 200 degrees for about an hour. We tried them all, but the New York method was the only one that yielded the attractive nut-brown surface we were after. This supersimple, no-water-bath (no leaking pans, layers of foil prophylactics, or boiling water), dual-temperature baking method also produced a lovely graded texture—soft and creamy at the center and firm and dry at the periphery.

The New York baking method was not without flaws, however. After an hour at 200 degrees, the very center of the cheesecake—even after chilling—was loose and slurpy, the result of underbaking. Some recipes leave the cheesecake in the still-warm, turned-off, propped-open oven for about 30 minutes to finish setting up. When we tried this, the cheesecake was marginally better but still insufficiently baked.

Next we extended the hour-long oven time to 90 minutes, baking the cheesecake to an internal temperature of about 150 degrees. Once chilled, it was cheesecake perfection. With a cleanly set center rather than a wet and sloppy one, it sliced into neat slabs. And though each slice kept its shape, every bite was satiny on the tongue. Because all ovens bake differently, it's important to guard against overbaking the cheesecake. Taken to internal temperatures of more than 160 degrees, our test cheesecakes were hopelessly cracked (see the Science Desk on page 334 for details). To avoid this problem, use an instant-read thermometer. It is the most reliable means of judging the doneness of the cheesecake.

Cheesecake is also well loved (by the sweet tooth, not the waistline) because it lasts longer in the refrigerator than a dessert should. After a day or two, the crust is a little soggy, but the cake tastes every bit as good. For breakfast, forget the bagel. Go for the cheesecake.

WHAT WE LEARNED: The secret to the perfect New York cheesecake is a character trait that most New Yorkers would never admit to—restraint. Don't add extraneous flavor or use flour, which mars the texture. And don't overbake. Once the center is cleanly set (or reaches 150 degrees on an instant-read thermometer), the cheesecake is done.

NEW YORK–STYLE CHEESECAKE
makes one 9-inch cheesecake, serving 12 to 16

For the crust, chocolate wafers (Nabisco Famous) can be substituted for graham crackers; you will need about 14 wafers. The flavor and texture of the cheesecake is best if the cake is allowed to stand at room temperature for 30 minutes before serving. When cutting the cake, have a pitcher of hot tap water nearby; dipping the blade of the knife into the water and wiping it clean with a kitchen towel after each cut helps make neat slices.

graham cracker crust
1   cup (4 ounces) graham cracker crumbs (8 whole crackers, broken into rough pieces and processed in food processor until uniformly fine)
1   tablespoon sugar
5   tablespoons unsalted butter, melted, plus additional 1 tablespoon melted butter for greasing pan

cheesecake filling
2½   pounds cream cheese, cut into rough 1-inch chunks and left to stand at room temperature for 30 to 45 minutes
⅛   teaspoon salt
1½   cups (10½ ounces) sugar
⅓   cup (2½ ounces) sour cream
2   teaspoons juice from 1 lemon
2   teaspoons vanilla extract
2   large egg yolks plus 6 large whole eggs

1. FOR THE CRUST: Adjust oven rack to lower-middle position and heat oven to 325 degrees. Combine graham cracker crumbs and sugar in medium bowl; add 5 tablespoons melted butter and toss with fork until evenly moistened. Brush bottom and sides of 9-inch springform pan with most of remaining melted butter, making sure to leave enough butter to brush pan in step 3. Empty crumbs into springform pan and press evenly into pan bottom (see

illustration on page 334). Bake until fragrant and beginning to brown around edges, about 13 minutes. Cool on wire rack while making filling.

2. FOR THE CHEESECAKE FILLING: Increase oven temperature to 500 degrees. In standing mixer fitted with paddle attachment, beat cream cheese at medium–low speed to break up and soften slightly, about 1 minute. Scrape beater and bottom and sides of bowl well with rubber spatula; add salt and about half of sugar and beat at medium–low speed until combined, about 1 minute. Scrape bowl; beat in remaining sugar until combined, about 1 minute. Scrape bowl; add sour cream, lemon juice, and vanilla, and beat at low speed until combined, about 1 minute. Scrape bowl; add yolks and beat at medium–low speed until thoroughly combined, about 1 minute. Scrape bowl; add whole eggs two at a time, beating until thoroughly combined, about 1 minute, and scraping bowl between additions.

3. Brush sides of springform pan with remaining melted butter. Set springform pan on rimmed baking sheet (to catch any spills if springform pan leaks). Pour filling into cooled crust and bake 10 minutes; without opening oven door, reduce oven temperature to 200 degrees and continue to bake until instant-read thermometer inserted into center of cheesecake registers about 150 degrees, about 1½ hours. Transfer cake to wire rack and run paring knife between cake and side of springform pan. Cool until barely warm, 2½ to 3 hours. Wrap tightly in plastic wrap and refrigerate until cold, at least 3 hours. (Cake can be refrigerated up to 4 days.)

4. To unmold cheesecake, remove sides of pan. Slide thin metal spatula between crust and pan bottom to loosen, then slide cake onto serving plate. Let cheesecake stand at room temperature about 30 minutes, then cut into wedges and serve.

FRESH STRAWBERRY TOPPING

makes about 1 ½ quarts

The dense, creamy richness of a New York cheesecake makes it the perfect candidate for some kind of fruity foil. A ruby-colored, glazed strawberry topping is the classic fruit accompaniment to New York cheesecake. This topping is best served the same day it is made.

2 pounds strawberries, cleaned, hulled, and cut lengthwise into ⅛ to ¼-inch slices
½ cup (3½ ounces) sugar
   Pinch salt
1 cup (about 11 ounces) strawberry jam
2 tablespoons juice from 1 lemon

1. Toss berries, sugar, and salt in medium bowl; let stand until berries have released juice and sugar has dissolved, about 30 minutes, tossing occasionally to combine.

2. Process jam in food processor until smooth, about 8 seconds; transfer to small saucepan. Bring jam to simmer over medium-high heat; simmer, stirring frequently, until dark

GETTING IT RIGHT:
Preventing a Cracked Cheesecake

Overbaking will cause an unsightly crack to develop, as will cooling the baked cheesecake without first freeing the sides of the cake from the pan.

and no longer frothy, about 3 minutes. Stir in lemon juice; pour warm liquid over strawberries and stir to combine. Let cool, then cover with plastic wrap and refrigerate until cold, at least 2 hours or up to 12 hours. To serve, spoon a portion of topping over each slice of cheesecake.

SCIENCE DESK:
Why Do Cheesecakes Crack?

SOME COOKS USE THE CRACK TO GAUGE WHEN A cheesecake is done. We say if it's cracked, it's overdone, not to mention unsightly. Exactly what happens, you may ask, that causes the cheesecake to form a fault line?

What we learned from two months of baking was that when the internal temperature of a cheesecake rose beyond 160 degrees, it almost always cracked. The best way to prevent cheesecake from cracking is to use an instant-read thermometer to test its doneness. Take it out of the oven when it reaches 150 degrees at the center to avoid overbaking.

That said, there is a second opportunity for the cheesecake to crack, this time outside of the oven. During testing, a perfectly good-looking cake cracked as it sat on the cooling rack. Evidently, the cake shrank during cooling and clung to the sides of the springform pan. If the cake clings tenaciously enough, it splits at its weakest point, the center. To avoid this type of late cracking, free the cheesecake from the sides of the pan with a paring knife as soon as it comes out of the oven.

TASTING LAB: Store-Bought Cheesecakes

COULD IT BE POSSIBLE THAT EVEN GOOD COOKS MIGHT be better off simply defrosting a store-bought frozen cheesecake instead of baking a fresh one at home? We wanted to make sure our efforts (and possibly yours) weren't in vain, so we thawed four commercial cheesecakes and conducted a blind taste test, adding our homemade version

as one of the contenders.

The contestants were Sara Lee Classic New York Style Cheesecake ($6.29 for 32 ounces); The Ultimate New York Cheesecake ($8.99 for 15 ounces), made by David Glass, a gourmet dessert company; Original Cheesecake from The Cheesecake Factory ($16.95 for 38 ounces), a chain of eateries featuring more than 30 flavors of cheesecake; and Trader Joe's New York Style Cheesecake ($3.69 for 18 ounces), sold by the discount natural foods grocery chain.

TECHNIQUE:
Patting the Crust into Place

1. Use bottom of ramekin or drinking glass to press crumbs into bottom of buttered springform pan. Press crumbs as far as possible into edges of pan.

2. Use teaspoon to neatly press crumbs into circumference of pan to create clean edge.

It was a landslide, with our homemade cheesecake winning easily. Tasters prized its "fresh," "tangy" flavor and "crisp" crust with "true graham flavor." To our surprise, Sara Lee earned second place for its "soft," "smooth" texture, though a few tasters remarked that it left a "burning sensation" in the back of their throats. Sara Lee easily beat out more expensive "gourmet" cheesecakes made by David Glass and The Cheesecake Factory. Tasters described the David Glass entry as "artificially vanilla," with an "overly cinnamony crust." The Cheesecake Factory cake was deemed "acidic and sour." Each and every taster put the Trader Joe's cheesecake in last place, uniformly rejecting it as "pasty," "floury," and "absolutely tasteless."

The lesson here is clear: Don't be lured by the ease of store-bought cheesecake. Take the time to make it at home, and you won't be disappointed. If you simply don't have the time to make your own cheesecake, don't waste money on "gourmet" brands. Sara Lee is just fine.

EQUIPMENT CORNER: Kitchen Timers

A KITCHEN TIMER IS ONE OF THOSE PIECES OF EQUIPMENT to which most home cooks don't give much thought. In a professional test kitchen, however, a good timer is essential. We use the same models available to home cooks, but we rely on them dozens of times every day. Each test cook has his or her own timer, and we decided to find out which model is best.

We gathered eight digital kitchen timers, ranging in price from $7 to $30. (We don't see the point of using an old-fashioned dial timer that you turn and set. It's impossible to measure short periods with these timers and hard to tell the difference between six minutes and seven.) Although it seems obvious that a timer will be accurate, we checked all eight digital timers to make sure. As expected, each one kept time accurately.

Because each of the timers were accurate, we focused on other features that would we thought would appeal to the home cook. Among the most important were the ability to count in seconds (good for delicate foods such as eggs); maximum time (we preferred timers that could cover at least 10 hours—enough to tackle an all-day barbecue project or overnight bread rising); more than one built-in timer (for timing several dishes at once); and continued count-up after the alarm sounds (so you know how long a dish has been cooking past the desired time). Important ease-of-use considerations included size and readability of the display (the bigger, the better), and the design of the buttons (large, raised buttons were preferred).

One timer had all these features and more, and it quickly emerged as the winner. As the name suggests, the West Bend Clock/Triple Timer model 40053 ($29.99) has 3 separate timers. It measures in seconds, counts up to 24 hours, and counts up after the alarm sounds. It also includes interrupt, memory, and stopwatch features. The large displays and buttons are exceptionally easy to read and use.

The Pyrex Professional Programmable Timer/Clock Model #17105 and the Polder Triple Kitchen Timer/Clock Model 891, both $19.99, were also well liked but neither was as easy to use as the winning West Bend model. The other five models tested lacked one or more of the above-mentioned features (most did not record seconds) and failed to impress our testers.

BEST KITCHEN TIMER
The West Bend Clock/Triple Timer does it all and was the clear winner in our tests. See www.cooksillustrated.com for up-to-date prices and a mail-order source for this product.

PHOTO CREDITS

Keller + Keller

xii, xiv (lower-middle right, bottom right), 17, 18, 30, 36, 84, 86, 94, 109, 110, 123, 132, 145, 146, 160, 177 (top), 212, 227 (top), 245, 249, 257, 263, 264, 279, 280, 285, 304, 315, 316, 324, 328

Bill Miles

iv

Elisabeth O'Donnell

viii, xiv (top left & right, upper-middle left & right, lower-middle left, bottom left), xv, 2, 13, 16, 25, 39, 41, 44, 50, 52, 55, 59, 64, 102 (left), 118, 127 (top), 154, 157, 166, 178, 189, 200, 205, 211, 219, 221, 230, 252, 254, 266, 272, 277 (left), 286, 314

Carl Tremblay

15, 23, 34, 37, 62, 80, 91, 92, 103, 108, 112, 124, 129, 135, 148, 163, 175, 180, 208, 226, 233, 241, 246, 268, 275, 307, 310, 319, 331

Daniel van Ackere

9, 14, 26, 29, 33, 35, 42, 48, 53, 58, 60, 63, 87, 89, 101, 102 (right), 113, 114, 115, 117, 127 (bottom), 131, 139, 143, 152, 155, 161, 165, 170, 172, 177 (bottom), 184, 185, 193, 195, 209, 217, 224, 227 (bottom), 234, 239, 253, 255, 265, 270, 271, 273, 277 (right), 287, 288, 313, 323, 333, 335

INDEX

Blueberry(ies):
- Honeydew, and Mango with Lime-Ginger Reduction, 243
- Lemon Sour Cream Coffee Cake, 235
- Nectarines, and Raspberries with Champagne-Cardamom Reduction, 242–43

Blue cheese:
- Dressing, 61–62
  - Leafy Salad with, 62
  - Rich and Creamy, 62
- tasting of, 62–64

Bolognese Sauce, Fettuccine with, 119–21
- Beef, 121
- Beef, with Pancetta and Red Wine, 121

Boning knives, rating of, 217
Bouquet, vegetable and herb, 138
Braising, science of, 177
Brandy(ied):
- Cinnamon Reduction, Red Plums and Figs with, 243, *294*
- Cream Sauce, Steak au Poivre with, 47–48

Breading cutlets, 98
Breads, 244–63
- Banana, 250–51, *295*
  - Chocolate, 251
  - Coconut, with Macadamia Nuts, 251
  - Orange-Spice, 251
- Cinnamon Buns, 246–48
  - Quick, with Buttermilk Icing, 248, *297*
- loaf pans for, rating of, 252–53
- quick, 244–51
  - buttermilk in, 249
- Rustic Country, 258–62
  - Kneaded by Hand, 262
  - Kneaded in Food Processor, 261–62
- taking temperature of, 261
- yeast for, tasting of, 262–63
- yogurt in, tasting of, 254–55

Brining, outside of refrigerator, 205
Broth, beef:
- MSG in, 141
- tasting of, 138–40

Browning:
- baking soda and, 314
- flavor development and, 177
- nonstick coatings and, 99, 116
- preheating skillets and, 108–9
- sauté pans and, 116

Brown sugar:
- Dried Cherry and Stout Sauce with Allspice and (for ham), 224–25
- Pecan Streusel, Sour Cream Coffee Cake with, 234–35, *296*

Brunch, 231–43
- Cinnamon Buns, 246–48
  - Quick, with Buttermilk Icing, 248, *297*
- Fruit Salad, 241–43
  - Honeydew, Mango, and Blueberries with Lime-Ginger Reduction, 243
  - Nectarines, Blueberries, and Raspberries with Champagne-Cardamom Reduction, 242–43
  - Red Plums and Figs with Brandy-Cinnamon Reduction, 243, *294*
  - Strawberries and Grapes with Balsamic and Red Wine Reduction, 242
- Potatoes, Twice-Baked, with Smoked Salmon and Chives, 34
- Sour Cream Coffee Cake, 232–35
  - Apricot-Almond, 235
  - with Brown Sugar–Pecan Streusel, 234–35, *296*
  - with Chocolate Chips, 235
  - Lemon-Blueberry, 235

Buffalo Wings, 11–12
- cutting up chicken wings for, 12
- disposing of oil from, 13

Bundt pans, for coffee cakes, 234
Buns, Cinnamon, 246–48
- Quick, with Buttermilk Icing, 248, *297*

Burgundy, Beef, 134–38
- cutting stew meat for, 137
- Do-Ahead, 138
- making vegetable and herb bouquet for, 138
- tasting of wines for, 140

Butcher's knots, tying, 217
Buttermilk:
- baking soda and, 314
- Icing, Quick Cinnamon Buns with, 248, *297*
- science of, 249

C

Caffeine, decaffeination methods and, 236
Cakes:
- Chocolate, Flourless, *298*, 325–27

Cakes: *(cont.)*
- Coffee, Sour Cream, 232–35
  - Apricot-Almond, 235
  - with Brown Sugar–Pecan Streusel, 234–35, *296*
  - with Chocolate Chips, 235
  - Lemon-Blueberry, 235
- Hot Fudge Pudding, 318–21
  - Individual, *303, 321*
- *see also* Cheesecakes

Capers:
- Chicken Piccata, 103–5
  - with Black Olives, 105
  - Peppery, 105
- Parsley Sauce with Cornichons and (for beef tenderloin), 216
- Pasta with Puttanesca Sauce, 112–14
- tasting of, 105

Caraway, Ham and Split Pea Soup with, 22
Cardamom-Champagne Reduction, Nectarines, Blueberries, and Raspberries with, 242–43
Cashews, Indian-Spiced Mashed Sweet Potatoes with Raisins and, 207
Casseroles, 156–65
- Green Bean, *69*, 228–29
- Macaroni and Cheese, 158–60
  - "Baked," 160
  - evaporated vs. fresh milk in, 162
  - Stovetop, 77, 159–60
- Turkey Tetrazzini, 163–65
  - breaking long pasta strands for, 164
  - gratin dishes for, 165

Champagne:
- Cardamom Reduction, Nectarines, Blueberries, and Raspberries with, 242–43
- Cranberry Sauce with Currants and, 211

Charcoal, rating of, 197
Charcoal grills:
- emptying ashes from, 183
- rating of, 194–97

Cheddar cheese:
- Macaroni and Cheese
  - "Baked," 160
  - Stovetop, 77, 159–60
- tasting of, 160–62
- Twice-Baked Potatoes, 33

Cheese(s):
- Blue, Dressing, 61–62
  - Leafy Salad with, 62

Filet Mignon, 56–59
    Argentinian-Style Fresh Parsley and
        Garlic Sauce for (Chimichurri),
        58–59
    Bacon-Wrapped, 58
    Madeira Pan Sauce with Mustard and
        Anchovies for, 58
    Pan-Seared, 57–58, 76
    well- vs. poorly butchered, 58
Fish:
    combating odor of, 126
    see also Anchovies; Salmon
Flame tamers, improvised, 121
Flavor development, brown color and, 177
Flourless Chocolate Cake, 298, 325–27
Fond development, nonstick cookware and,
    99, 116
French:
    Beef Burgundy, 134–38
        Do-Ahead, 138
    Crème Brûlée, 49–52
        Classic, 51–52
        Espresso, 52
        Tea-Infused, 52
    gastrique, 241
    Steak au Poivre, 46–48
        with Brandied Cream Sauce, 47–48
Fried Rice, 82–85
    Basic White Rice for, 85
    Curried Chicken, Thai-Style, 85
    with Peas and Bean Sprouts, 84
    with Shrimp, Pork, and Shiitakes, 68,
        83–84
Fruit Salad, 241–43
    Honeydew, Mango, and Blueberries
        with Lime-Ginger Reduction, 243
    Nectarines, Blueberries, and Raspberries
        with Champagne-Cardamom
        Reduction, 242–43
    Red Plums and Figs with Brandy-
        Cinnamon Reduction, 243, 294
    Strawberries and Grapes with Balsamic
        and Red Wine Reduction, 242
Fudge, Hot, Pudding Cake, 318–21
    Individual, 303, 321

G

Gadgets and utensils:
    box graters, shredding soft cheeses
        with, 6
    flame tamers, improvised, 121

Gadgets and utensils: (cont.)
    knives
        boning, rating of, 217
        steak, rating of, 60
    ladles, drip-free ladling with, 21
    measuring cups, dry, rating of, 264–65
    measuring spoons, rating of, 272–73
    meat pounders, rating of, 102
    pasta paraphernalia, 126–27
    pepper mills, rating of, 42–43
    potato mashers, rating of, 209
    pot scrubbers, rating of, 154–55
    rolling pins, rating of, 284–87
    scales, digital, rating of, 322–24
    thermometers
        oven, rating of, 142–44
        taking temperature of bread with,
            261
    timers, kitchen, rating of, 335
    timer/thermometers, rating of, 227
    tongs
        extra grip for, 51
        kitchen, rating of, 13–14
        pasta, 127
    torches, rating of, 53
    vegetable peelers, rating of, 26–27
Garlic:
    Breaded Chicken Cutlets with Oregano
        and, 98
    combating odor of, 126
    and Parsley Sauce, Argentinian-Style
        (Chimichurri) (for filet mignon),
        58–59
    Pasta with Oil and, 70, 124–26
    Pasta with Puttanesca Sauce, 112–14
    -Scented Mashed Sweet Potatoes with
        Coconut Milk and Cilantro, 208
Gas grills:
    anatomy of, 172
    checking fuel level in tank of, 171
    protecting controls of, 173
    rating of, 171–72
Gastrique, 241
Ginger:
    Fresh, Cranberry Sauce with Pears and,
        211
    Lime Reduction, Honeydew, Mango,
        and Blueberries with, 243
Glazing cookies, 276
Graham cracker:
    –Coated Pie Shell, 282–83
    Crust, 332–33

Grapes and Strawberries with Balsamic and
    Red Wine Reduction, 242
Graters, box, shredding soft cheeses with, 6
Gratin dishes, rating of, 165
Green Bean Casserole, 69, 228–29
Greens:
    Collard, Spicy, Smothered Pork Chops
        with, 176
    Leafy Salad with Blue Cheese Dressing,
        62
    storing, 64
Grilled:
    Baby Back Ribs, Barbecued, 74,
        180–83
        on Charcoal Grill, 181–82
        on Gas Grill, 182–83
        smoking wood for, 183–84
    Pork Chops, 168–71
        Basic Spice Rub for, 170
        on Charcoal Grill, 73, 169–70
        on Gas Grill, 169–70
        Indian Spice Rub for, 170
    Salmon, Barbecued, 190–92
        on Charcoal Grill, 191
        on Gas Grill, 192
        Horseradish Cream Sauce for,
            192
        key steps for, 192
        Mustard-Dill Sauce for, 192
Grilling equipment:
    charcoal, rating of, 197
    charcoal grills
        emptying ashes from, 183
        rating of, 194–97
    gas grills
        anatomy of, 172
        checking fuel level in tank of, 171
        protecting controls of, 173
        rating of, 171–72
    grill racks, brushless cleaning of, 182
    wood chunks and chips, rating of,
        183–84
Grill-Roasted Turkey, 202–5, 293
    on Charcoal Grill, 204–5
    on Gas Grill, 205
    protecting wings of, 204
Guacamole:
    Cheesy Nachos with Salsa and, 5, 65
        with Refried Beans, 5
        with Spicy Beef, 5–6
    Fresh, 6
    store-bought, tasting of, 7

Silpat (nonstick baking mats), cushioning
water baths with, 52
Skillets:
    nonstick
        inexpensive, rating of, 98–102
        protecting surfaces of, 99
    preheating, 108–9
Smoking wood, rating of, 183–84
Smothered Pork Chops, *78,* 174–76
    with Cider and Apples, 176
    with Spicy Collard Greens, 176
Soups:
    drip-free ladling of, 21
    Ham and Split Pea, 20–22
        with Caraway, 22
    hearty, 19–25
    Potato-Leek, Rustic, 23–25, *66*
        with Kielbasa, 25
        with White Beans, 25
Sour Cream Coffee Cake, 232–35
    Apricot-Almond, 235
    with Brown Sugar–Pecan Streusel,
        234–35, *296*
    with Chocolate Chips, 235
    Lemon-Blueberry, 235
Spaghetti:
    breaking long strands of, 164
    with Puttanesca Sauce, 112–14
    Turkey Tetrazzini, 163–65
        gratin dishes for, 165
Spice:
    Molasses Cookies, 274–76
        with Dark Rum Glaze, 276
        glazing, 276
        with Orange Essence, 276
    Orange Banana Bread, 251
Split Pea and Ham Soup, 20–22
    with Caraway, 22
Steak(s):
    Filet Mignon, 56–59
        Argentinian-Style Fresh Parsley and
            Garlic Sauce for (Chimichurri),
            58–59
        Bacon-Wrapped, 58
        Madeira Pan Sauce with Mustard
            and Anchovies for, 58
        Pan-Seared, 57–58, *76*
        well- vs. poorly butchered, 58
    au Poivre, 46–48
        adhering pepper to steaks for, 47
        with Brandied Cream Sauce, 47–48
        crushing peppercorns for, 48

Steak(s): *(cont.)*
    resting before carving, 60
Steak knives, rating of, 60
Stews:
    Beef Burgundy, 134–38
        Do-Ahead, 138
    Chili con Carne, 148–51
        Smoky Chipotle, 151
        tasting of chili powder for, 151–54
        tasting of dried chiles for, 151
    cutting meat for, 137
    drip-free ladling of, 21
Storing:
    bananas, freezing, 251
    greens, 64
Stout and Dried Cherry Sauce with Brown
    Sugar and Allspice (for ham), 224–25
Strawberry(ies):
    and Grapes with Balsamic and Red
        Wine Reduction, 242
    hulling, 308
    Shortcake, 306–8
        splitting shortcake for, 308
    Topping, Fresh, *302, 333–34*
Streusel, Brown Sugar–Pecan, Sour Cream
    Coffee Cake with, 234–35, *296*
Stuffed Bell Peppers, 37–40
    blanching peppers for, 37–38
    with Chicken, Smoked Mozzarella, and
        Basil, 40
    Classic, 38–39
    with Spiced Lamb, Currants, and Feta
        Cheese, 39–40, *71*
Sweet potatoes:
    Mashed, 206–8, *289*
        with African Flavors, 208
        Garlic-Scented, with Coconut Milk
            and Cilantro, 208
        Indian-Spiced, with Raisins and
            Cashews, 207
        Maple-Orange, 208
    tasting of, 208–9
    yams vs., 208

T

Tastings:
    anchovies, 114
    barbecue sauces, 184–85
    beef broth, 138–40
    capers, 105
    cheesecakes, store-bought, 334–35

Tastings: *(cont.)*
    cheeses
        blue, 62–64
        cheddar, 160–62
    cherry products, 312–14
    chile(s)
        dried, 151
        products, 93
    chili powder, 151–54
    coffee, French roast, 236–38
    guacamole, store-bought, 7
    hams, spiral-sliced, 226
    molasses, 277
    paprika, 193–94
    pasta
        dried, 114–16
        lasagna noodles, no-boil, 131
    pepper, black, 34–36
    peppers, bell, 40
    pie crusts, store-bought, 286–88
    pork, enhanced, 173
    potatoes, 25
    rice, long-grain, 86–88
    salsa, jarred, 10
    salt, 27–29
    sweet potatoes, 208–9
    tortilla chips, 8–10
    vanilla extract, 321–22
    wine, for beef Burgundy, 140
    yeast, 262–63
    yogurt, plain, 254–55
Tea-Infused Crème Brûlée, 52
Techniques:
    avocados, dicing, 7
    bananas, freezing, 251
    beef
        roasts and steaks, tent for resting
            before carving, 60
        tenderloin, preparing, 216
    bread, taking temperature of, 261
    butcher's knots, tying, 217
    charcoal grills, emptying ashes from, 183
    cheesecake, preventing cracks in, 333
    cheeses, soft, shredding, 6
    cherries, pitting, 312
    chicken
        cutlets, breading, 98
        cutlets, trimming, 97
        wings, cutting up, 12
    cookies
        baking evenly, 271
        glazing, 276